Twentieth-Century Literary Criticism

Topics Volume

Guide to Gale Literary Criticism Series

For criticism on	You need these Gale series
Authors now living or who died after December 31, 1959	*CONTEMPORARY LITERARY CRITICISM (CLC)*
Authors who died between 1900 and 1959	*TWENTIETH-CENTURY LITERARY CRITICISM (TCLC)*
Authors who died between 1800 and 1899	*NINETEENTH-CENTURY LITERATURE CRITICISM (NCLC)*
Authors who died between 1400 and 1799	*LITERATURE CRITICISM FROM 1400 TO 1800 (LC)* *SHAKESPEAREAN CRITICISM (SC)*
Authors who died before 1400	*CLASSICAL AND MEDIEVAL LITERATURE CRITICISM (CMLC)*
Authors of books for children and young adults	*CHILDREN'S LITERATURE REVIEW (CLR)*
Black writers of the past two hundred years	*BLACK LITERATURE CRITICISM (BLC)*
Short story writers	*SHORT STORY CRITICISM (SSC)*
Poets	*POETRY CRITICISM (PC)*
Dramatists	*DRAMA CRITICISM (DC)*
Major authors from the Renaissance to the present	*WORLD LITERATURE CRITICISM, 1500 TO THE PRESENT (WLC)*

For criticism on visual artists since 1850, see

MODERN ARTS CRITICISM (MAC)

ISSN 0276-8178

Volume 50

Twentieth-Century Literary Criticism

Topics Volume

**Excerpts from Criticism of Various Topics
in Twentieth-Century Literature, including Literary
and Critical Movements, Prominent Themes and
Genres, Anniversary Celebrations, and Surveys
of National Literatures**

Laurie Di Mauro
Editor

**Jennifer Gariepy
Christopher Giroux
Thomas Ligotti
Kyung-Sun Lim**
Associate Editors

 Gale Research Inc. • *DETROIT* • *WASHINGTON, D.C.* • *LONDON*

STAFF

Laurie Di Mauro, *Editor*

Jennifer Gariepy, Christopher Giroux, Thomas Ligotti, Kyung-Sun Lim, *Associate Editors*

Jeffery Chapman, Margaret A. Haerens, Malabika Camellia Purkayastha, Lynn M. Spampinato, *Assistant Editors*

Jeanne A. Gough, *Permissions & Production Manager*
Linda M. Pugliese, *Production Supervisor*
Donna Craft, Paul Lewon, Maureen Puhl, Camille P. Robinson, Sheila Walencewicz, *Editorial Associates*
Elizabeth Anne Valliere, *Editorial Assistant*

Sandra C. Davis, *Permissions Supervisor (Text)*
Maria L. Franklin, Josephine M. Keene, Michele Lonoconus, Shalice Shah, Denise Singleton, Kimberly F. Smilay, *Permissions Associates*
Jennifer A. Arnold, Brandy C. Merritt, *Permissions Assistants*

Margaret A. Chamberlain, *Permissions Supervisor (Pictures)*
Pamela A. Hayes, Keith Reed, *Permissions Associates*
Susan Brohman, Arlene Johnson, Barbara A. Wallace, *Permissions Assistants*

Victoria B. Cariappa, *Research Manager*
Maureen Richards, *Research Supervisor*
Robert S. Lazich, Mary Beth McElmeel, Donna Melnychenko, Tamara C. Nott, *Editorial Associates*
Karen Farrelly, Kelly Hill, Julie Leonard, Stefanie Scarlett, *Editorial Assistants*

Mary Beth Trimper, *Production Director*
Catherine Kemp, *Production Assistant*

Cynthia Baldwin, *Art Director*
Barbara J. Yarrow, *Graphic Services Supervisor*
Nicholas Jakubiak, *Desktop Publisher/Typesetter*
Willie F. Mathis, *Camera Operator*

Library of Congress Catalog Card Number 76-46132
ISBN 0-8103-7975-9
ISSN 0276-8178

Printed in the United States of America
Published simultaneously in the United Kingdom
by Gale Research International Limited
(An affiliated company of Gale Research Inc.)
10 9 8 7 6 5 4 3 2 1

I(T)P™

The trademark **ITP** is used under license.

Contents

Preface ix

Acknowledgments xiii

Australian Literature

Espionage Literature

Madness in Twentieth-Century Literature

Negritude

Occultism in Modern Literature

Preface

S ince its inception more than ten years ago, *Twentieth-Century Literary Criticism* has been purchased and used by nearly 10,000 school, public, and college or university libraries. *TCLC* has covered more than 500 authors, representing 58 nationalities, and over 25,000 titles. No other reference source has surveyed the critical response to twentieth-century authors and literature as thoroughly as *TCLC*. In the words of one reviewer, "there is nothing comparable available." *TCLC* "is a gold mine of information—dates, pseudonyms, biographical information, and criticism from books and periodicals—which many libraries would have difficulty assembling on their own."

Scope of the Series

TCLC is designed to serve as an introduction to authors who died between 1900 and 1960 and to the most significant interpretations of these author's works. The great poets, novelists, short story writers, playwrights, and philosophers of this period are frequently studied in high school and college literature courses. In organizing and excerpting the vast amount of critical material written on these authors, *TCLC* helps students develop valuable insight into literary history, promotes a better understanding of the texts, and sparks ideas for papers and assignments. Each entry in *TCLC* presents a comprehensive survey of an author's career or an individual work of literature and provides the user with a multiplicity of interpretations and assessments. Such variety allows students to pursue their own interests; furthermore, it fosters an awareness that literature is dynamic and responsive to many different opinions.

Every fourth volume of *TCLC* is devoted to literary topics that cannot be covered under the author approach used in the rest of the series. Such topics include literary movements, prominent themes in twentieth-century literature, literary reaction to political and historical events, significant eras in literary history, prominent literary anniversaries, and the literatures of cultures that are often overlooked by English-speaking readers.

TCLC is designed as a companion series to Gale's *Contemporary Literary Criticism,* which reprints commentary on authors now living or who have died since 1960. Because of the different periods under consideration, there is no duplication of material between *CLC* and *TCLC.* For additional information about *CLC* and Gale's other criticism titles, users should consult the Guide to Gale Literary Criticism Series preceding the title page in this volume.

Coverage

Each volume of *TCLC* is carefully compiled to present:

- criticism of authors, or literary topics, representing a variety of genres and nationalities

- both major and lesser-known writers and literary works of the period

- 10-15 authors or 4-6 topics per volume

- individual entries that survey critical response to each author's work or each topic in literary history, including early criticism to reflect initial reactions; later criticism to represent any rise or decline in reputation; and current retrospective analyses.

Organization of This Book

An author entry consists of the following elements: author heading, biographical and critical introduction, list of principal works, excerpts of criticism (each preceded by an annotation and followed by a bibliographic citation), and a bibliography of further reading.

- The **Author Heading** consists of the name under which the author most commonly wrote, followed by birth and death dates. If an author wrote consistently under a pseudonym, the pseudonym will be listed in the author heading and the real name given in parentheses on the first line of the biographical and critical introduction. Also located at the beginning of the introduction to the author entry are any name variations under which an author wrote, including transliterated forms for authors whose languages use nonroman alphabets.

- The **Biographical and Critical Introduction** outlines the author's life and career, as well as the critical issues surrounding his or her work. References to past volumes of *TCLC* are provided at the beginning of the introduction. Additional sources of information in other biographical and critical reference series published by Gale, including *Short Story Criticism, Children's Literature Review, Contemporary Authors, Dictionary of Literary Biography,* and *Something about the Author,* are listed in a box at the end of the entry.

- Most *TCLC* entries include **Portraits** of the author. Many entries also contain reproductions of materials pertinent to an author's career, including manuscript pages, title pages, dust jackets, letters, and drawings, as well as photographs of important people, places, and events in an author's life.

- The **List of Principal Works** is chronological by date of first book publication and identifies the genre of each work. In the case of foreign authors with both foreign-language publications and English translations, the title and date of the first English-language edition are given in brackets. Unless otherwise indicated, dramas are dated by first performance, not first publication.

- Critical excerpts are prefaced by **Annotations** providing the reader with information about both the critic and the criticism that follows. Included are the critic's reputation, individual approach to literary criticism, and particular expertise in an author's works. Also noted are the relative importance of a work of criticism, the scope of the excerpt, and the growth of critical controversy or changes in critical trends regarding an author. In some cases, these annotations cross-reference excerpts by critics who discuss each other's commentary.

- **Criticism** is arranged chronologically in each author entry to provide a perspective on changes in critical evaluation over the years. All titles of works by the author featured in the entry are printed in boldface type to enable the user to easily locate discussion of particular works. Also for purposes of easier identification, the critic's name and the publication date of the essay are given at the beginning of each piece of criticism. Unsigned criticism is preceded by the title of the journal in which it appeared. Some of the excerpts in *TCLC* also contain translated material. Unless otherwise noted, translations in brackets are by the editors; translations in parentheses or continuous with the text are by the critic. Publication information (such as footnotes or page and line references to specific editions of works) have been deleted at the editor's discretion to provide smoother reading of the text.

- A complete **Bibliographic Citation** designed to facilitate location of the original essay or book follows each piece of criticism.

- An annotated list of **Further Reading** appearing at the end of each author entry suggests secondary sources on the author. In some cases it includes essays for which the editors could not obtain reprint rights.

Cumulative Indexes

- Each volume of *TCLC* contains a cumulative **Author Index** listing all authors who have appeared in Gale's Literary Criticism Series, along with cross references to such biographical series as *Contemporary Authors* and *Dictionary of Literary Biography*. For readers' convenience, a complete list of Gale titles included appears on the first page of the author index. Useful for locating authors within the various series, this index is particularly valuable for those authors who are identified by a certain period but who, because of their death dates, are placed in another, or for those authors whose careers span two periods. For example, F. Scott Fitzgerald is found in *TCLC*, yet a writer often associated with him, Ernest Hemingway, is found in *CLC*.

- Each *TCLC* volume includes a cumulative **Nationality Index** which lists all authors who have appeared in *TCLC* volumes, arranged alphabetically under their respective nationalities, as well as Topics volume entries devoted to particular national literatures.

- Each new volume in Gale's Literary Criticism Series includes a cumulative **Topic Index**, which lists all literary topics treated in *NCLC, TCLC, LC 1400-1800*, and the *CLC* yearbook.

- Each new volume of *TCLC*, with the exception of the Topics volumes, contains a **Title Index** listing the titles of all literary works discussed in the volume. In response to numerous suggestions from librarians, Gale has also produced a **Special Paperbound Edition** of the *TCLC* title index. This annual cumulation lists all titles discussed in the series since its inception and is issued with the first volume of *TCLC* published each year. Additional copies of the index are available on request. Librarians and patrons will welcome this separate index; it saves shelf space, is easy to use, and is recyclable upon receipt of the following year's cumulation. Titles discussed in the Topics volume entries are not included *TCLC* cumulative index.

Citing *Twentieth-Century Literary Criticism*

When writing papers, students who quote directly from any volume in Gale's literary Criticism Series may use the following general forms to footnote reprinted criticism. The first example pertains to materials drawn from periodicals, the second to material reprinted from books.

[1]T. S. Eliot, "John Donne," *The Nation and the Athenaeum,* 33 (9 June 1923), 321-32; excerpted and reprinted in *Literature Criticism from 1400 to 1800,* Vol. 10, ed. James E. Person, Jr. (Detroit: Gale Research, 1989), pp. 28-9.

[2]Clara G. Stillman, *Samuel Butler: A Mid-Victorian Modern* (Viking Press, 1932); excerpted and reprinted in *Twentieth-Century Literary Criticism,* Vol. 33, ed. Paula Kepos (Detroit: Gale Research, 1989), pp. 43-5.

Suggestions are Welcome

In response to suggestions, several features have been added to *TCLC* since the series began, including annotations to excerpted criticism, a cumulative index to authors in all Gale literary criticism series, entries devoted to criticism on a single work by a major author, more extensive illustrations, and a title index listing all literary works discussed in the series since its inception.

Readers who wish to suggest authors or topics to appear in future volumes, or who have other suggestions, are cordially invited to write the editors.

Acknowledgments

The editors wish to thank the copyright holders of the excerpted criticism included in this volume, the permissions managers of many book and magazine publishing companies for assisting us in securing reprint rights, and Anthony Bogucki for assistance with copyright research. We are also grateful to the staffs of the Detroit Public Library, the Library of Congress, the University of Detroit Library, Wayne State University Purdy/Kresge Library Complex, and the University of Michigan Libraries for making their resources available to us. Following is a list of the copyright holders who have granted us permission to reprint material in this volume of *TCLC*. Every effort has been made to trace copyright, but if omissions have been made, please let us know.

COPYRIGHTED EXCERPTS IN *TCLC*, VOLUME 50, WERE REPRINTED FROM THE FOLLOWING PERIODICALS:

Africa Report, v. 11, May, 1966. Copyright © 1966 by The African-American Institute. Published by permission of Africa Report.—*Africa Today,* v. 17, First quarter, 1970. © Africa Today Associates. Reprinted by permission of *Africa Today,* Graduate School of International Studies, University of Denver, Denver, CO 80208.—*African Literature Today,* n. 7, 1975. Copyright 1975 by Heinemann Educational Books Ltd. All rights reserved. Reprinted by permission of Heinemann Educational Books Ltd. In the U.S. reprinted by permission of Africana Publishing Corporation, New York, NY.—*The American Scholar,* v. 34, Spring, 1965. Copyright © 1965 by Jacques Barzun. Reprinted by permission of the publisher.—*The Armchair Detective,* v. 19, Winter, 1986. Copyright © 1986 by *The Armchair Detective.* Reprinted by permission of the publisher.—*Australian Literary Studies,* v. 10, October, 1981 for "Australian Short Fiction from 'While the Billy Boils' to 'The Everlasting Secret Family'" by Elizabeth Webby. Reprinted by permission of the author.—*Boston University Journal,* v. XXII, Spring, 1974. Copyright 1974 by The Trustees of Boston University.—*Clues: A Journal of Detective,* v. 9, Spring-Summer, 1988. Copyright 1988 by Pat Browne. Reprinted by permission of the publisher.—*Diogenes,* n. 48, Winter, 1964. Copyright 1964 by Mario Casalini Ltd. Reprinted by permission of the publisher.—*L'Esprit Créateur,* v. X, Fall, 1970. Copyright © 1970 by *L'Esprit Créateur.* Reprinted by permission of the publisher.—*Ethics,* v. 76, July, 1966. © 1966 by The University of Chicago. All rights reserved. Reprinted by permission of the publisher.—*The Journal of Contemporary History,* v. 22, April, 1987. Copyright © 1987 The Institute of Contemporary History. Reprinted by permission of Sage Publications Ltd.—*The Journal of Modern African Studies,* v. 3, December, 1965 for "Négritude or Black Culture Nationalism" by Abiola Irele; v. 3, December, 1965 for "Négritude—Literature and Ideology" by Abiola Idele. © Cambridge University Press. Both reprinted with the permission of Cambridge University Press and the author.—*Journal of Popular Culture,* v. IX, Spring, 1976./ v. 20, Fall, 1986. Copyright © 1976, 1986 by Ray Browne. Both reprinted by permission of the publisher.—*Journal of the New African Literature and the Arts,* ns. 7-8, Spring-Fall, 1969./ v. 7-8, Spring-Fall, 1969 for "Négritude: A Sober Analysis" by Henri Lopes. Reprinted by permission of the author.—*Kansas Quarterly,* v. 10, Fall, 1978 for "Developments in Espionage Fiction" by G. Jay Rausch and Diane K. Rausch. © copyright 1978 by the *Kansas Quarterly.* Reprinted by permission of the publisher and G. Jay Rausch.—*The Massachusetts Review,* v. VI, Winter, 1964-65. © 1965. Reprinted from *The Massachusetts Review,* The Massachusetts Review, Inc. by permission.—*The New African,* London, v. 5, April, 1966. © 1966 IC Publications Limited.—*Optima,* v. 16, March, 1966.—*Pan-African Journal,* v. 5, 1972. Reprinted by permission of the publisher.—*Partisan Review,* v. XIV, Winter, 1947 for "Writers and Madness" by William Barrett. Copyright 1947 by *Partisan Review.* Renewed 1974. Reprinted by permission of the publisher and The Literary Estate of William Barrett.—*PHYLON: The Atlanta University Review of Race and Culture,* v. XXXIV, fourth quarter (December, 1973). Copyright, 1973, by Atlanta University. Reprinted by permission of *PHYLON.*—*Symposium,* v. XXXVI, Spring, 1982 for "Reclaiming the Great Mother: A Feminist Journey to Madness and Back in Search of a Goddess Heritage" by Gloria Feman Orenstein. Copyright © 1982 Helen Dwight Reid Educational Foundation. Reprinted by permission of the author.—*University Review,* v. XXXII, Spring, 1966 for "Neurosis and Poetry: A Myth of Madness?" by E. Hale Chatfield. Copyright 1966 The Curators of the University of Missouri. Reprinted by permission of the publisher and the author.—*Victorian Studies,* v. 24,

Summer, 1981 for "Spies and Gentlemen: The Birth of the British Spy Novel, 1893-1914" by David A. T. Stafford. Reprinted by permission of the Trustees of Indiana University and the author.—*West Africa,* n. 2820, July 2, 1971; n. 2827, August 27, 1971. © West Africa Publishing Company Ltd., 1971. Both reprinted by permission of the publisher.—*World Literature Today,* v. 64, Winter, 1990. Copyright 1990 by the University of Oklahoma Press. Reprinted by permission of the publisher.—*Yale French Studies,* n. 52, 1975. Copyright © *Yale French Studies* 1975. Reprinted by permission of the publisher.

COPYRIGHTED EXCERPTS IN *TCLC,* VOLUME 50, WERE REPRINTED FROM THE FOLLOWING BOOKS:

Baker, A. W. From *Death is a Good Solution: The Convict Experience is Early Australia.* University of Queensland Press, 1984. © A. W. Baker 1984. Reprinted by permission of the publisher.—Barclay, Glen St. John. From *Anatomy of Horror: The Masters of Occult Fiction.* Weidenfeld and Nicolson, 1978. Copyright © 1978 by Glen St. J. Barclay. All rights reserved. Reprinted by permission of the publisher.—Bowman, Frank Paul. From "Occultism and the Language of Poetry," in *The Occult in Language and Literature.* Edited by Hermine Riffaterre. New York Literary Forum, 1980. Copyright © New York Literary Forum 1980. All rights reserved.—Brantlinger, Patrick. From *Rule of Darkness: British Literature and Imperialism, 1880-1914.* Cornell, 1988. Copyright © 1988 by Cornell University. All rights reserved. Used by permission of the publisher, Cornell University Press.—Brench, A. C. From *The Novelists' Inheritance in French Africa: Writers from Senegal to Cameroon.* Oxford University Press, London, 1967. © Oxford University Press 1967. Reprinted by permission of the publisher.—Carroll, Dennis. From *Australian Contemporary Drama 1909-1982: A Critical Introduction.* Lang, 1985. © Peter Lang Publishing, Inc., New York 1985. All rights reserved. Reprinted by permission of the publisher.—Cawelti, John G. and Bruce A. Rosenberg. From "The Appeal of Clandestinity," in *The Spy Story.* By John G. Cawelti and Bruce A. Rosenberg. The University of Chicago, 1987. © 1987 by The University of Chicago. All rights reserved. Reprinted by permission of the publisher.—Craig, Patricia and Mary Cadogan. From *The Lady Investigates: Women Detectives and Spies in Fiction.* St. Martin's Press, 1981. © 1981 by Patricia Craig and Mary Cadogan. Reprinted by permission of the respective authors.—Feder, Lillian. From *Madness in Literature.* Princeton University Press, 1980. Copyright © by Princeton University Press. All rights reserved. Reprinted by permission of the publisher.—Ferrier, Carole. From "Introductory Commentary: Women Writers in Australia," in *Gender, Politics and Fiction: Twentieth Century Australian Women's Novels.* Edited by Carole Ferrier. University of Queensland Press, 1985. Introduction and compilation © Carole Ferrier 1985. Reprinted by permission of the publisher.—Freud, Sigmund. From *Introductory Lectures on Psychoanalysis.* Edited and translated by James Strachey. Norton 1977. Copyright © 1966 by W. W. Norton & Company, Inc. Reprinted by permission of the publisher.—Gerould, Daniel and Jadwiga Kosicka. From "The Drama of the Unseen-Turn-of-the Century Paradigms for Occult Drama," in *The Occult in Language and Literature.* Edited by Hermine Riffaterre. New York Literary Forum, 1980. Copyright © New York Literary Forum 1980. All rights reserved.—Goodwin, Ken. From *A History of Australian Literature.* St. Martin's Press, 1986, Macmillan, Basingstoke, 1986. All rights reserved. Used with permission of St. Martin's Press, Inc. In Canada by Macmillan, London and Basingstoke.—Hadgraft, Cecil. From "Literature," in *The Pattern of Australian Culture.* Edited by A. L. McLeod. Cornell, 1963. © 1963 by Cornell University. Renewed 1991 on behalf of A. L. McLeod by Cornell University Press. Used by permission of the publisher.—Hamilton, K. G. From "A Prefatory Sketch," in *Studies in the Recent Australian Novel.* Edited by K. G. Hamilton. University of Queensland Press, 1979. © University of Queensland Press, St. Lucia, Queensland, 1978. Reprinted by permission of the author.—Heseltine, Harry. From *The Uncertain Self: Essays in Australian Literature and Criticism.* Oxford University Press, Melbourne, 1986. © Harry Heseltine 1986. Reprinted by permission of the publisher.—Jahn, Janheinz. From *A History of Neo-African Literature: Writing in Two Continents.* Translated by Oliver Coburn and Ursula Lehrburger. Faber & Faber Limited, 1968. This translation © 1968 Faber and Faber and Grove Press, New York,. Reprinted by permission of Faber & Faber Ltd.—Kesteloot, Lilyan. From *Black Writers in French: A Literary History of Negritude.* Translated by Ellen Conroy Kennedy. Temple University Press, 1974. English translation © 1974 by Temple University. All rights reserved.—Kiernan, Brian. From "Literature, History, and Literary History: Perspectives on the Nineteenth Century in Australia," in *Bards, Bohemians, and Bookmen: Essays in Australian Literature.* Edited by Leon Cantrell. University of Queensland Press, 1976. © University of

Australian Literature

INTRODUCTION

European settlement of Australia began when the British government transported the first group of English convicts to the continent in 1788. For several decades afterward, literature in Australia took the form of nonfiction accounts by colonists who documented their observations and experiences in their new homeland. By the mid-nineteenth century the colonial period in Australian history was reflected in fiction and poetry by writers born in Australia. During the later nineteenth century, Australian writers began displaying a concern with national identity. This search for self-definition gained focus and articulation with the founding in 1880 of the *Bulletin,* a magazine devoted to the appreciation of literature written by Australians. The *Bulletin* often featured works of fiction based on life in the bush, juxtaposing the harsh, primitive conditions of the Australian outback with the magnificent beauty of the land. During the nineteenth and early twentieth centuries, Australian literature primarily depicted the lives of convicts, immigrant families, or individuals attempting to survive the hardships of frontier life. The attention given by Australian writers to characters whose experience is limited by their struggle for subsistence has prompted many critics to assert that Australian literature is more visceral and less complex than European literature, which, by contrast, was considered more intellectual. The tendency of Australians to judge their own literature unfavorably in comparison with those of other English-speaking countries has been called the "Cultural Cringe." During the 1950s and 1960s poetry, fiction, and drama in Australia underwent a literary renaissance, displaying diversity in content and experimentation with form. Australian writers have been supported by the proliferation of literary magazines and a generous governmental grant program. The emergence of Aboriginal literature in English has added a new dimension to Australian literature, as writers document the efforts of Aboriginal peoples to overcome dispossession and discrimination and to define a new cultural identity in modern Australia.

REPRESENTATIVE WORKS

Boldrewood, Rolf
  Robbery under Arms: A Story of Life and Adventure in the Bush and in the Goldfields of Australia (novel) 1888; revised edition, 1889
Brennan, Christopher
  XVIII Poems (poetry) 1897
  XXI Poems: MDCCCXCIII-MDCCCXCVII; Towards the Source (poetry) 1897

Poems 1913 (poetry) 1914
  A Chant of Doom, and Other Verses (poetry) 1918
Burns, David
  The Bushrangers (drama) 1842
Clarke, Marcus
  His Natural Life (novel) 1874
Davis, Jack
  The First Born (poetry) 1970
  Poems From Aboriginal Australia (poetry) 1978
  The Dreamers (drama) 1982
  Kullark (drama) 1982
Esson, Louis
  Three Short Plays (dramas) 1911
  The Drovers (drama) 1923
  Mother and Son (drama) 1923
  The Bride of Gospel Place (drama) 1926
FitzGerald, Robert D.
  Moonlight Acre (poetry) 1938
  Forty Years' Poems (poetry) 1965
Franklin, Miles
  My Brilliant Career (novel) 1901
  Up the Country [as Brent of Bin Bin] (novel) 1928
  Ten Creeks Run [as Brent of Bin Bin] (novel) 1930
  All that Swagger (novel) 1936
  Laughter, Not for a Cage (criticism) 1956
Furphy, Joseph
  Such Is Life [as Tom Collins] (novel) 1903; abridged edition, 1937
  Rigby's Romance [as Tom Collins] (novel) 1905-06; published in journal *Barrier Truth;* unabridged edition, 1944
  Poems (poetry) 1916
  The Buln-Buln and the Brolga (novel) 1948
Hope, A. D.
  The Wandering Islands (poetry) 1955
  Poems (poetry) 1960
  Collected Poems, 1930-1970 (poetry) 1972
Keneally, Thomas
  The Chant of Jimmie Blacksmith (novel) 1972
  Schindler's List (novel) 1982
Kingsley, Henry
  The Recollections of Geoffry Hamlyn (novel) 1859
Lawler, Ray
  Summer of the Seventeenth Doll (drama) 1954
Lawson, Henry
  Short Stories in Prose and Verse (short stories and poetry) 1894
  While the Billy Boils (short stories) 1896
  On the Track, and Over the Sliprails (short stories) 1900
  Joe Wilson and His Mates (short stories) 1901
  Children of the Bush (short stories and poetry) 1902
  For Australia, and Other Poems (poetry) 1913
Narogin, Mudrooroo

Wild Cat Falling [as Colin Johnson] (novel) 1965
Dr. Wooreddy and His Prescription for Enduring the End of the World (novel) 1983
Paterson, A.B.
  The Man From Snowy River, and Other Verses (poetry) 1895
Richardson, Henry Handel
  Maurice Guest (novel) 1908
  The Fortunes of Richard Mahoney (novel) 1917
  The Way Home; Being the Second Part of the Chronicle of the Fortunes of Richard Mahoney (novel) 1925
  Ultima Thule; Being the Third Part of the Chronicle of the Fortunes of Richard Mahoney (novel) 1929
  The Young Cosima (novel) 1939
Slessor, Kenneth
  Thief of the Moon (poetry) 1924
  One Hundred Poems, 1919-1939 (poetry) 1944
Stewart, Douglas
  Ned Kelly (drama) 1943
  Dosser in Springtime (poetry) 1946
Walker, Kath
  We Are Going (poetry) 1964
Warung, Price (pseudonym of William Astley)
  Tales of the Convict System (short stories) 1892
White, Patrick
  The Aunts' Story (novel) 1948
  The Tree of Man (novel) 1955
  Voss (novel) 1957
  Four Plays (dramas) 1961
  The Burnt Ones (short stories) 1964
  The Vivisector (novel) 1970
  The Eye of the Storm (novel) 1973
Wright, Judith
  The Moving Image (poetry) 1946
  Woman to Man (poetry) 1949

ORIGINS AND DEVELOPMENT

Harry Heseltine

[*In the following essay, Heseltine views the history of Australian literature through representative authors and works.*]

> What do I know? myself alone,
> a gulf of uncreated night,
> wherein no star may e'er be shown
> save I create it in my might.
>   Christopher Brennan *Poems 1913,* No. 42

> On a swing at midnight in the black park. Between poplars which are towers of light for a hidden street lamp and inky she-oaks my arc is maintained. From lighter to darker I go, from dark to light; but only, as ever, to return.
>   Chris Wallace-Crabbe 'The Swing'

The main vantage points from which Australian literary history has been viewed are familiar enough: they have

permitted us to discern in its development thematic patterns, ethical patterns, colonial patterns giving way to nationalist patterns, and so on. One vantage point, however, which has until now attracted very few observers is that which reveals works of literature as shaped out of the interaction between the creating self, whatever audience the artist believes he may address, and whatever materials may be to hand to form the subjects of his art. It is exactly to that interaction that I shall address myself in this essay, in the hope less of furnishing a comprehensive interpretation of the national literature than of providing some suggestive notes from which such an interpretation might be constructed.

For the historian who takes the creating self as the focus of his attention, the crucial fact about the literature of modern Australia is the period of its beginnings—the late eighteenth century. In 1788, when the First Fleet dropped anchor in Sydney Cove, Dr Johnson was barely three years dead, William Blake was already at work on the *Songs of Innocence,* England's American colonies were ten years lost, the French Revolution barely twelve months in the future; Adam Smith had published *The Wealth of Nations* a decade earlier, a decade later Wordsworth and Coleridge would publish the first edition of their *Lyrical Ballads.* An English colony was founded in the remote South Seas, that is to say, at the very moment when the value systems by which English society lived were in a state of radical change, and when literature was caught between competing conventions of style and form. That bare fact made an indelible impression on the subsequent history of virtually every aspect of Australian culture, not least the understanding that the literary artist would hold of his own imagination, his own identity. Thrust as it were into a cultural vacuum, without the support of a sanctioned tradition, his central task became that of authenticating his own uncertain self in an unfamiliar world.

The paradoxes which attended the foundation of Australian literature find their emblem in one of the first significant events in the public culture of the colony: the performance on the night of 4 June 1789 of Farquhar's play, *The Recruiting Officer.* A scant six weeks before the Bastille fell at the assault of a Paris mob, Australian theatre was born, on the occasion of the birthday of George III, with a performance by a convict cast, to an audience of military overseers, of a comedy of manners which mirrored the customs and mores of an England a hundred years gone. Convict satire apart, everything about the event seems in retrospect to have been designed to divert the imaginations of all concerned from the actualities in which they were enmeshed. Diversion, indeed, was the principal function of the Australian theatre for the next one hundred and fifty years.

Although a vigorous theatrical industry had been established by the middle of the nineteenth century, no corresponding body of native play texts appeared. It was as if a society brought into being with no sure sense of the writer's role was unable to produce that branch of serious literature which, most of all, demands a confidence strong enough to create selves quite distinct from the author's own. That there was implanted deep in Australian culture a dreadful uncertainty about the creating self is further suggested by the fact that even as late as 1964 Harry Kippax, a leading critic of our theatre, could lament the stop-go quality of what he called our 'stalled drama'. Addressing himself to signs of a quickened growth after the appearance of Ray Lawler's *Summer of the Seventeenth Doll* in 1954, Kippax [in his 'Australian Drama Since *The Doll*', *Meanjin Quarterly,* 1964] nevertheless detected in some of the best plays of the 1950s and 1960s flaws which argued a persistently unhappy confusion about the playwright's sense of his own role and identity, his relation to the society he portrayed. Two weaknesses he noticed in particular: the first, a 'failure to relate action to dramatic purpose', the second, a 'resort . . . to melodramatic contrivance to express dramatic purpose'.

If Kippax was right in his diagnosis (as I believe he was), then Australian drama was failing at a quite fundamental level, and in a way that suggests a radical weakness in the national culture. In the years since 1964, however, there have been some astonishing changes in our dramatic achievement. The evidence for consistent improvement in both quality and quantity of dramatic writing is laid bare in the pages of the new edition of Leslie Rees's standard text, *A History of Australian Drama*. Volume I, covering the years between 1788 and 1969, occupies 435 pages; Volume II, 'Australian Drama in the 1970s', runs to 270 pages. After nearly two hundred years, Australian drama seems to have caught up (in excellence and consistency of achievement as well as in output) with the other literary forms. While I shall make no further direct examination of this curious phenomenon in our drama, the general problems that it implies will underlie all that I have to say about our poetry and prose.

During the first quarter-century after the settlement of 1788, easily the most accomplished (and seemingly dominant) literary form in the colony was descriptive prose, documentary reportage. Examples of the form are numerous enough and of an excellence which suggests that its failure to assume a permanently central role in our literary tradition can only be a matter of regret. The causes, however, of the initial pre-eminence of documentary prose and of its early decline are not far to seek. Here, on the one hand, was a new country offering new data for assimilation to the European-trained mind and eye. On the other, there were readily available the conventions of Enlightenment prose, perfectly suited to the public purposes of disseminating information to an ignorant, interested and far-removed audience. The reports of First Fleeters like Watkin Tench and David Collins, for instance, manifest a complete assurance about the purpose they were serving and the public they were addressing. Men of the middling kind, steeped in the habits of common-sense rationality, their aim was to convey information without fuss, if possible under aristocratic patronage. They aimed at (and achieved) a formalized syntax and an impersonal tone calculated to suggest a public duty honourably performed.

The first quarter-century, then, of colonial life produced a rich harvest of physical and social notation. Yet as a formal manoeuvre of the creative imagination, its possibilities were soon exhausted—and not simply because, as a

generation of native-born white Australians grew up in New South Wales, the need to send back reports to a public 12,000 miles away was in some measure diminished, nor because Augustan conventions of prose were more and more felt to be stilted, outmoded, false. There was something in the Australian experience itself which soon made the artifice of Augustan reportage utterly inadequate to the needs of the truly creative imagination. When Charles Sturt sailed down Sydney Harbour for the first time in 1827, he registered a response which contained the seeds of one of the central developments of nineteenth-century Australian prose:

> It was with feelings peculiar to the occasion, that I gazed for the first time on the bold cliffs at the entrance of Port Jackson, as our vessel neared them, and speculated on the probable character of the landscape they hid; and I am free to confess, that I did not anticipate anything equal to the scene which presented itself both to my sight and my judgment, as we sailed up the noble and extensive basin we had entered, towards the seat of government. [*Two Expeditions into the Interior of Southern Australia*]

'I . . . speculated on the probable character of the landscape': the enormous adjustments required of the earliest settlers in learning to live with the unfamiliar antipodean world have often been noted, the new responses demanded of the creative imagination perhaps less frequently. Among the most creative responses was clearly the urge to explore. The annals of Australian exploration are full of episodes at once heroic and extreme, sometimes fatal. In almost every instance, however, it seems that creative energy was so fully absorbed in the act of exploration itself as to make speculation on the landscape, aesthetic contemplation, beyond the reach of the explorer's imagination. Edward John Eyre may stand as a case in point. His journey across the southern face of the continent in 1840-41 plainly demanded every resource of body, nerve and spirit that he could muster. A hundred years after the event, Francis Webb could wring from it that extraordinary poem, 'Eyre All Alone'. The best registration that Eyre himself could manage of one of the most extreme moments of his ordeal is couched in a colourless prose style disguising rather than revealing the intensity of the experience he had been through:

> The frightful, the appalling truth now burst upon me, that I was alone in the desert. He who had faithfully served me for many years, who had followed my fortunes in adversity and in prosperity, who had accompanied me in all my wanderings, and whose attachment to me had been his sole inducement to remain with me in this last, and to him alas, fatal journey, was now no more. For an instant, I was almost tempted to wish that it had been my own fate instead of his. The horrors of my situation glared upon me in such startling reality, as for an instant almost to paralyse the mind. [*Journals of Expeditions of Discovery into Central Australia*]

In writing such as this the conventions of eighteenth-century prose reach the dead end of their expressive possibilities. From the 1840s onward, discursive prose, which had promised so bright an achievement, fragmented into a myriad more modest purposes—social commentary, literary criticism, anecdote and memoir. Thenceforward, the best energies of our prose writers would be channelled into fiction. The novelist emerged as the type of imagination most apt to contemplate the land rather than traverse or conquer it. Unwilling or unable to find the aesthetic resources for that searing personal confrontation which Eyre knew in 1841, he could yet slough off the restraints of Augustan artifice and find in narrative a means of transforming insight into art.

Alexander Harris's *The Emigrant Family* (1849) is wholly characteristic of the mid-century Australian novel. In its pages a frankly documentary and informative intention is incorporated into a narrative which permits a minimal concern for fictional characters and (quite as importantly) for the developing variant of the English language through which white Australians were beginning to take hold of their environment. Not only representative of the best qualities of 'guidebook fiction', *The Emigrant Family* also labours under a general aesthetic difficulty of fiction composed out of a new and relatively raw culture. The famous paragraphs in Henry James's life of Hawthorne are probably the best-known enunciation of the view that fiction finds in a new society a sadly thin diet when compared with the dense complexities of older civilizations. Some twenty-three years before James lamented the absence from the American scene of Ascot, the Derby and the rest, Frederick Sinnett in 1856 had deplored a similar lack in the young country below the equator:

> No storied windows, richly dight, cast a dim, religious light over any Australian premises. There are no ruins for that rare old plant, the ivy green, to creep over and make his dainty meal of. No Australian author can hope to extricate his hero or heroine, however pressing the emergency may be, by means of a spring panel and a subterranean passage . . .
>
> ['The Fiction Fields of Australia']

The difficulties of creating fiction in a largely unformed society are real enough, though not perhaps as desperate as they have sometimes been represented. In Australia, the difficulty (however dimly or clearly apprehended) seems to have been answered by two fairly distinct lines of formal development in the novel. One was to enter into the pleasant pastures of romantic action, using the local data without really examining them, forcing them into patterns of narrative and character largely derived from Sir Walter Scott. Two of the best-known of Australia's colonial novels reveal the pattern quite clearly: Henry Kingsley's *The Recollections of Geoffry Hamlyn* (1859) and Rolf Boldrewood's *Robbery Under Arms* (1882-83).

Neither writer was a serious artist, as we understand art today; undisturbed by any profound self-searching, they were able to compose undemanding romantic tales out of whatever colonial experience came their way. Henry Kingsley, the younger brother of the author of *Westward Ho!*, made a comparatively brief visit to Australia but was nevertheless able to make of *Geoffry Hamlyn* 'a novel which probably influenced the writing of Australian fiction more than any other single work of fiction about Aus-

tralia during the nineteenth century', as John Barnes says [in his *Henry Kingsley and Colonial Fiction*]. The level at which that influence operated is, however, fairly indicated by Barnes's further comment that 'Hamlyn's style is characterized by an almost boyish enthusiasm for his characters and the stories he has to tell about them'. The effect of *Geoffry Hamlyn* may have been to direct Australian novelists towards some readily usable structures but it was almost certainly to diminish the creative impulse, the effort to use fiction as a means of bringing the literary artist, the environment he was still learning to look at, and the society he must learn to live with, into some kind of rapport. The same kind of charge can be laid against Rolf Boldrewood. Combining readiness of invention, a superficial fluency and Victorian habits of industry, he constructed a career as a novelist in the course of which he observed Australian manners far more scrupulously and in greater detail than had Kingsley. *Robbery Under Arms,* however, enjoys its reputation among historians of Australian literature by virtue of what was for Boldrewood a most untypical narrative strategy—that of telling the tale in the first person, through the mouth of one of its principal characters. The novel represents the first significant occasion in Australian prose narrative when the Australian language became an integrated, organic element in the very form and substance of fiction.

By and large, however, Boldrewood did little to lift the nineteenth-century Australian novel above its function of providing a romantic gloss on native experience. His solution to the problem of the artist's status and identity was to remove both to the area of technical-commercial skill. That, however, was not the only path open to the Australian novel in the middle and later years of the nineteenth century. Henry Savery's *Quintus Servinton* (1830-31), antedating *The Emigrant Family* by almost twenty years, had indicated another route that it might follow. The fact that Savery's plot is largely displaced autobiography is of less consequence than that it is ferociously melodramatic. Curiously, although the novel has no right to be taken with any real seriousness, it manages to convey the sense that it is a melodrama not of concocted romance but of experiential extremity. Eyre would discover what Australia could impose on those who sought to penetrate her; Savery had already sensed, in an oddly impressive way, the means by which such knowledge might be brought within the ambit of fiction. The mode of Gothic allegory offered Australian fiction one of its most significant early successes in the form of Marcus Clarke's *For the Term of His Natural Life* (1870-72).

Clarke's professed purpose in this novel was to prevent the recurrence of the social injustices wrought by 'the System', and to that end he had undertaken some documentary research. Furthermore, he was by the 1870s building on an already existing corpus of convict literature of a predominantly documentary or protestant kind. Yet his signal achievement in *For the Term of His Natural Life* was to wring from a violent history a symbolic vision of crime and punishment, suffering and redemption. Symbolic allegory was not, however, the only solution available to other writers of Clarke's generation who might wish to make the country's convict beginnings the object of their artists'

MARCUS CLARKE

IN 1866 AT 20

Marcus Clarke (1846-81).

speculation. Price Warung, for instance, forged from convict material not the vivid shapes of allegory but the intensities of irony, protest and disgust. The other feature, of course, which distinguishes Warung's work from Clarke's is that of scale. Where Clarke's concern with the System was concentrated into one massive encounter, Warung's traffic with the convict past was spread over a decade's contributions to the Sydney *Bulletin*. The short story was the ideal vehicle for his bitter snapshots of warders and convicts; it also had for Warung the kind of psychological value it must have for many writers anxious about their stature as artists. For such writers, the short story provides the opportunity of saying something important to themselves without risking the full-scale revelations entailed by the novel. Warung's convict tales, in the savage treatment of their materials, in the terse irony of their tone, betray, it seems to me, an imagination possessed by its subject but unsure of its power to possess.

Orthodox histories identify the short story of the 1890s as the form in which Australian literature first achieved unequivocal excellence with a distinctive national hue. The key figure in such a reading of our literary development is Henry Lawson, whose work is regarded as both the apogee of the colonial imagination in prose and the fountain-

head of mainstream Australian writing for at least half of the twentieth century. From the point of view of cultural diagnostics, however, perhaps the most significant fact about Lawson's career is the profound insecurity on which it was based. Manning Clark's recent study [*In Search of Henry Lawson*] has made the deep divisions of Lawson's life abundantly plain, and it may be that it is precisely those divisions which make Lawson the supreme representative of Australian life in both the nineteenth century and our own. Nothing suggests more acutely the motif of the uncertain self running through our colonial literature than the brief success and long tragedy of Lawson's life, the handful of great stories wherein the conflicting fragments of his sensibility coalesce into a splendid art.

Although the idea of 'mateship' has been so strongly attached to Henry Lawson, the most elaborate version of this socio-ethical code to be found in our nineteenth-century writing grew in the mind of the writer who, of all his generation, was most literally isolated—Joseph Furphy. Sixty years old when his masterpiece *Such is Life* was published in 1903, he had composed it in Shepparton, far removed from the centres of literary polity in Melbourne and Sydney. It was perhaps this very innocence of literary coteries, together with his long experience as bushman and bullocky, that gave Furphy the confidence to attempt the extraordinary comic masterpiece which is *Such is Life,* of which the intricate complexities of plot create an enormous gap between the ultimate purpose of the novel and the stuff of which it was made. By a tremendous effort of the will and imagination Furphy bridged that gap through the very artifice of his plotting, an effort which for once allowed a nineteenth-century novelist almost to escape the tyranny of an uncertain self.

Almost, but not quite. The rock against which all criticism of *Such is Life* founders is the need to distinguish between the author Joseph Furphy and the alleged author Tom Collins. There is in *Such is Life* an aesthetic ambivalence which in the end must be seen as a like ambivalence in the writer's felt situation as artist and individual. Furphy's uncertainty about his audience can be sensed in the false aplomb of the Introduction to *Such is Life;* about his created narrator in the insistent, mocking identification of Tom Collins with Hamlet. If Furphy's original simplicity of motive anywhere survives, it is in the opening sentence of the review of his own novel that he wrote (at A. G. Stephens's behest) for the Sydney *Bulletin:* 'Nowhere is literary material more copious in variety, or more piquant in character, than in legendless Australia'. *Such is Life* is nothing less than an attempt to use the resources of the self as the means of celebrating a nation as yet unstoried, artless, unenhanced.

Such a claim stands good even in the face of that other great fictional compilation of nineteenth-century Australian experience—Henry Handel Richardson's *The Fortunes of Richard Mahony* (1917-1929). Richardson's unique distinction is that, where Furphy celebrated the still-new society, she flayed it open, anatomized it to reveal the tragic bones of colonial experience—individual and social, both. The controlled modulations of style from *Australia Felix* to *Ultima Thule* have often caused the trilogy to be seen as the point through which Australian fiction turned from a nineteenth- to a twentieth-century aesthetic. Just as truly, those same phenomena of language could be regarded as the culminating improvisation on the motif of the unattached, insecure self in our nineteenth-century prose.

For the hundred years after 1788, our poets grappled with basically the same problem as that which tasked the writers of prose: how to realize the demands of the creating self in the kind of cultural vacuum to which they were condemned. The poets' answers were at once more extreme and more tentative than those of the prose writers. Relegating the documentary possibilities of literature to folk song and ballad, the poets for most of the century floundered uneasily in the hiatus between rationalism and Romanticism; unattached to any certain beliefs or reliable aesthetic conventions, they fell back more and more upon the resources of self, without understood means of artistic realization. The range of improvisations attempted by our nineteenth-century poets is resumed in the life and work of three of their number—Charles Harpur, Henry Kendall, Christopher Brennan.

Born in Australia in 1813, Harpur from the outset of his career was certain of only two things: that the new nation needed a tradition of poetry, and that it was his destiny to found it. As a teenager he confided his ambition to the lines entitled 'To the Lyre of Australia':

> Wild Lyre of Australia, in song could I vie
> With the strength of a Burns, of a Byron the fire,
> Oh, then I would raise thee in glory on high,
> As the guardian of beauty, of valour the sire:
> And might I but hope that one song I may waken,
> As a voice in the gale that drives over the glade,
> Should ride, when my country her empire hath taken,
> On the flood of her ages, I'd count me repaid.

There was little else, however, of which Harpur could feel sure. What he might say or what needed to be said, how to reach his Australian audience, how even to go about writing poems—these were matters on which the circumstances of colonial Australia could offer him no serviceable guide. Born to the English language, he perforce looked to the poetic traditions it enshrined—acquired indeed an impressive acquaintance with all of them from the days of Chaucer through to Robert Browning. But born into a penal colony of a metropolis itself caught up in doubt and change, he could find no principle for selecting among all the models he so earnestly assimilated. His writing in consequence exhibits a bewildering array of modes and manners—Augustan prospect poems, formal verse satire, a sonnet sequence, Romantic outpourings (after Wordsworth, Coleridge, Keats), Miltonic epic, Shakespearean pastiche. The very range of Harpur's formal experiments bears pathetic testimony to the difficulties of being a colonial poet. The landscape resisted his best attempts to humanize it into the likeness of a northern world he had never seen; his inner experience remained locked within the prison of inert conventions; the society of which he wrote remained apart from him, untouched by the demand for attention his verse implicitly placed upon it.

Early in his career Harpur confidently instructed his compatriots in their public duties, admonished them on general principles of conduct. Their almost total disregard of his injunctions, however, more desperate even than contumely or contempt, led in his later years to a bitterness towards his countrymen who had failed to form the enlightened audience just as necessary to a poetic tradition as the poets themselves. At the head of the 1863 manuscript of his work he placed the following note:

> I cannot forbear adding to the above Memory, that it is my somewhat unpleasant impression, the future (capable) reader of the Manuscript, will be anything but gratified by the fact, that the Poems which make up the contents of it, should for a period of twenty years, have gone a begging as it were—and in vain about the land of their inspiration . . .

By the end of his career (pursued almost literally to his deathbed) Harpur was reduced to composing an extraordinary verse narrative, 'The Witch of Hebron', of which the sole arbiter would be himself. Harpur's immediate successor, Henry Kendall, in selecting out from the older poet's achievement what he found most congenial, narrowed the possibilities of nineteenth-century Australian poetry. Of a more vivid and volatile temperament than Harpur, though of less intellectual gravity and power, he thrust the tradition initiated by Harpur in the direction of Romantic specialization. No longer seeking to domesticate landscape under the guise of eighteenth-century topography, he made of the mountainous coastal region that he knew the arena of an idealized Romanticism. That Romanticism, which he discovered mainly within his own disturbed personality, never sat quite happily within the confines assigned to it. The result is, even in Kendall's best nature poetry, a certain crudeness of technique and (by implication) a coarseness of sensibility. On other occasions, when landscape does not mediate between Kendall and the inner tensions which constitute the true subject of nearly all his poetry, his work was potentially of greater power and penetration than anything that Harpur wrote. But potential was never fully converted into achievement because, again, Kendall could neither discover nor master a creative apparatus apt to the purposes of an imagination still unattached to cultural tradition or social actuality.

The most dramatic evidence of the massive internal difficulties which marred the work and nearly destroyed the man is to be found in Kendall's complete nervous breakdown at the age of 32—what he afterwards referred to as 'the Shadow of 1872'. We cannot now be sure if that collapse was cause or consequence of Kendall's embracing the poet's vocation; we can say, however, that it is a fit emblem of the disaster which, in one form or another, overtook so many of the individuals who essayed the poet's role in nineteenth-century Australia. Kendall was more fortunate than some, in that in the middle 1870s he contrived a partial reconstruction of his personality; in a manner, however, which represented a retreat from that whole-souled commitment to art which had characterized his earlier years. After 1872 he wrote (or pretended to write) as much for money as for art's sake.

Yet in his later work Kendall did point the way towards

a further advance for Australian poetry—its closer liaison with the stream of popular ballad and song which had flowed so strongly ever since 1788. There is in a piece like 'The Song of Ninian Melville' an infusion of unpretentious, salty colloquialism which promised a healthy antidote to the Swinburnian preciousness of so many of Kendall's lines before 1870. The tendency for the popular and serious streams of Australian versifying to meet and mingle was hastened in the 1890s, most famously in the work of 'Banjo' Paterson and Henry Lawson. Where Paterson brought an aristocratic insouciance to his jaunty treatment of outback tales, Lawson depended on an unabashedly sentimental display of nationalism, social protest or commonplace feeling. Both writers have become enshrined as culture heroes of the 1890s. Neither really succeeded in wedding the language of the tribe to the purposes of high art; neither significantly influenced the subsequent development of Australian poetry.

In that regard, a figure of much greater consequence is Christopher Brennan, author of *Poems 1913*, notoriously the most 'difficult' book of verse to have issued from our nineteenth-century literary culture. Brennan and his book have produced one of the largest 'industries' in Australian literary scholarship, so perhaps little more need be said here other than that his career, which came so close to being that of our first great literary master, was ultimately a failure, and that that failure was probably as much the measure of the shortcomings of a whole culture as of a single individual.

In brief, *Poems 1913* is a *livre composé*—a sequence of 105 interrelated poems composed according to a Mallarméan aesthetic, and constituting the chronicle of an individual's search for identity within the mode of myth. For a decade and more Brennan so dedicated himself to the task of self-discovery through the means of poetry as progressively and woundingly to detach himself from everything which had originally given his life its meaning—faith, family, friends. Even in the middle 1890s (seemingly his most confident years) his only answer to the question 'What do I know?' had been 'myself alone'. By 1908 that solipsistic response had taken on the quiet desperation of the close of the 'Wanderer' sequence:

> I am the wanderer of many years
> who cannot tell if ever he was king
> or if ever kingdoms were . . .
>
> and saying this to myself as a simple thing
> I feel a peace fall in the heart of the winds
> and a clear dusk settle, somewhere, far in me.

The author of *Poems 1913* had come, it seems plain, to the dead end of the first great movement in our poetic history. The creative artist, uneasy in his lack of received conventions and understood materials for the making of poems, had turned inward on himself to find both material and means for his art, and in so doing had been brought finally to nought.

There can be no doubt that *Poems 1913* conveys a sense of things ending. Yet, just as *The Fortunes of Richard Mahony* was the fulcrum for Australian fiction's movement from its colonial to its modern phase, so did Bren-

nan's lines perform the same function for Australian poetry. The continuities between our nineteenth- and our twentieth-century poets are plainly marked in the work of our first great 'modern' poets—Kenneth Slessor and Robert D. FitzGerald, born in 1901 and 1902 respectively. Of the two, Slessor seemed easily the more 'modern' to their contemporaries in the 1920s and 1930s. In spite of his acknowledged debt to Tennyson, Slessor unmistakably displayed the ironic flair, the edgy timing, the paradoxical wit which were to his generation the hallmark of modernism everywhere. From another point of view, however, his work is just as plainly an extension of Brennan's. Where Brennan's imaginative wanderings brought him at last to the bleak solipsism of 'The Wanderer', Slessor moved through his century of poems towards an even more thorough-going nihilism of feeling and belief. 'Five Bells', the great elegy which stands much in the same relation to twentieth-century Australian verse as Robert Lowell's 'The Quaker Graveyard in Nantucket' does to American, is marked by a hopelessness beyond despair:

> I felt the wet push its black thumb-balls in,
> The night you died, I felt your eardrums crack,
> And the short agony, the longer dream,
> The Nothing that was neither long nor short;
> But I was bound, and could not go that way,
> But I was blind, and could not feel your hand.

In lines such as these the substantive thrust of Brennanism reached its dead end. If Slessor's work significantly forecasts later trends in our verse, it may be in its heavy reliance on what Alec King called the physical imagination, 'a sense of objective things vividly present but not deeply imagined in feeling'.

Against Slessor's surrender to darkness FitzGerald has stood firm throughout his career. Often suffering under such labels as 'Romantic optimist', he has steadfastly regarded human life as a quest of the spirit which, in the face of all the odds, can bring to mankind at least a measure of hope and fulfilment. In his earliest work he took over from Brennan, even more obviously than Slessor, the image of the Wanderer, but discovered in it themes and attitudes quite the reverse of those it revealed to his contemporary. Characteristically it is to the future that FitzGerald turns in the closing stanza of his major collection, *Forty Years' Poems:*

> But more than to look back
> we choose this day's concern
> with everything in the track,
> and would give most to learn
> outcomes of all we found
> and what next builds to the stars.
> I regret I shall not be around
> to stand on Mars.

Such Browningesque exhilaration in the face of the universe has not, it must be said, recommended itself to many of FitzGerald's successors. Where Slessor's chief legacy to later Australian poets has perhaps been a mode of sensibility, FitzGerald has demonstrated to them the utility of certain formal structures. The poem which first brought FitzGerald widespread recognition was the sesquicentenary prize-winning piece, 'Essay on Memory' (1937). His successful management of contemplative-discursive verse not only heralded some of his own later master-works but also pointed the way to some of the most distinguished poets of later generations—James McAuley with his 'Letter to John Dryden', for instance, or Bruce Beaver's 'Letters to Live Poets'. A much later work of FitzGerald's, 'The Wind at Your Door' of 1959, is no less significant than 'Essay on Memory' in focusing some of the major formal and modal achievements of twentieth-century Australian poetry. Like 'Essay on Memory', 'The Wind at Your Door' concentrates itself finally to personal meditation, but the meditation grows out of historical narrative rather than discursive argument. And again there can be no doubt that one of the singular features of contemporary Australian poetry has been its engagement with verse narrative. McAuley's 'Captain Quiros', Douglas Stewart's 'Worsley Enchanted', John Couper's 'The Book of Bligh', Francis Webb's 'A Drum for Ben Boyd'—the list speaks for itself. Australian poets, we may say, working out their themes in the arena of their own identities, could arrive at a union of meaning and action long before our dramatists were able to achieve that *sine qua non* of dramatic art.

Slessor and FitzGerald, then, severally and in relation to each other, typify whole tracts of twentieth-century Australian poetry. Even the inevitable coupling of their names seems to betray a recurring pattern. Slessor and FitzGerald, Stewart and Wright, Hope and McAuley, Shapcott and Hall, Murray and Lehmann—there is something here other than cultural accident. The pendulum swing between Slessor and FitzGerald of substance and sensibility, theme and form, optimism and pessimism summarizes what we may describe as the whole trend of Australian poetry since it turned through *Poems 1913* into the twentieth century. That trend may be described something like this: since Brennan was defeated on the very ground of self to which his own imagination and all prior Australian poetry had directed him, our verse writers have not been willing to quit that territory but have sought to avoid its uncertainties by great polarizing swoops between opposing tendencies in form, attitudes, styles.

One of the clearest substantive manifestations of this polar oscillation is in the lines of Chris Wallace-Crabbe which stand as the second epigraph to this essay. Day and night, light and dark, reason and irrationality have been the opposing themes between which our poets have characteristically moved in their efforts to make art out of their experience of this country and their relation to their compatriots. It is possible to view the formal history of modern Australian poetry in the same way—a pendulum-like swinging between extremes of behaviour in order to control (or avoid?) the difficult centre position where so much damage had been worked in colonial times. One of the extremes of Australian verse has thus been the lyric, which (like narrative) has been cultivated in this country with greater single-mindedness than in other English-speaking societies. Many of our twentieth-century poets, indeed, have operated by translating their perceptions into the mode of song, making melodic rapture out of the light and darkness of the world, out of their joys and distress, out of their very observation of the world of things. John Shaw Nielson, Hugh McCrae, Mary Gilmore, Douglas Stewart,

Judith Wright—the line is clear and unmistakable, and (with variations) is projected right down to the present time.

To subdue the uncertain self through the power of song has not, however, been the only manoeuvre attempted by our more recent poets. Substantively, we may say that the work of A. D. Hope and James McAuley makes them poets of sweet reason, of the light. Formally, their distinct achievement has been to wed sweet reason to the lyric mode—to give Australians an Apollonian as well as a Dionysian song. They are artists for whom the imagination comprehends high intelligence as well as irrational energy, for whom a tough reasonableness is an essential concomitant of any lyric grace. Their example has been followed by a line of poets as impressive in its way as that of the Romantic singers. It includes, for instance, Vincent Buckley, Chris Wallace-Crabbe, Evan Jones—and later, and in a curious way, even Rodney Hall and Thomas Shapcott, David Malouf and Geoffrey Lehmann.

The aspiration towards an Apollonian radiance is, I believe, a comparatively late phenomenon in our verse; it appeared, furthermore, as a counter to not only Romantic song but also a darker, more anarchic form of Bacchic energy. The chief theoretical text of that energy is probably Norman Lindsay's *Creative Effort* (1920), its most dogmatic exponent, William Baylebridge. But the willingness to grapple head-on with unreasoning darkness has had no more impressive issue than in the poetry of Francis Webb. Webb's *Collected Poems* of 1969 reveals an imagination that works characteristically in the expressionist mode in order to confront all the least orderly elements of its own identity.

Webb, too, has had his latter-day successors—notably Michael Dransfield and Charles Buckmaster, young men whose wild integrity brought them both to untimely death. In one respect at least, however, neither was able (though both most certainly tried) to match Webb in a vital element of his art—the use of an internalized landscape as a means of bringing the anarchic self under control. And, indeed, some of the most striking successes of our twentieth-century poets (no matter what their intellectual persuasion, their stylistic habit) have been effected when they have referred theme, form, self to the Australian land. I am thinking here less of an organized movement like the Jindyworobaks than of individual poems by FitzGerald and Slessor, Stewart and Wright, Hope, even, and McAuley. Or, if we are to search for a current instance, we need think only of Les Murray. Murray can be wilfully countrified or citified or knowingly cosmopolitan. But when he writes out of the Australian earth, few poets now at work have the power so to stop the mind and heart. His career reassures us that in this generation, as in every generation since Brennan, our poets have been able to make some few poems which exist at the point of balance between those sweeps between light and darkness which characterize our poetic history since 1900.

Not even Murray's verse, however, can surpass the feeling for the *genius loci* which animates the most astonishing starburst of our recent fiction, Xavier Herbert's *Poor Fellow My Country* (1975). This mammoth novel is perhaps the most passionately knowledgeable speculation on the Australian landscape ever to have shaped itself in the mind of a white Australian. At the same time, it is committed to action as a metaphor for the human condition with the kind of absolute conviction which, as H. G. Kippax felt, was lacking in our drama even into the 1960s. *Poor Fellow My Country,* that is to say, in one sense may be thought of as a realization of the urge to an imaginative possession of Australia which Sturt had felt in 1827. Even more than Patrick White's *Voss,* Herbert made this country his by right of vision.

If *Poor Fellow My Country* represents at last the triumph of self through its absorption into the numinous, it is at the same time the culmination of a major structural tradition of Australian fiction which has not always been put to that purpose. Ever since Henry Handel Richardson, our novelists have seemingly felt the need to work out their themes in fictions of quite remarkable length—often in trilogies or even tetralogies. Vance Palmer, Katharine Susannah Prichard, Miles Franklin, Frank Dalby Davison, Eleanor Dark, George Johnston, George Turner, Donald Stuart—the list speaks for itself. In one series after another, our novelists have endeavoured to authenticate their still-uncertain selves by submission to some dominant theme of wide extent—time, national history, socioeconomic fact, cultural aspiration.

Some of these prolonged essays in national definition command respect more for their earnest application than their artistic success. Throughout the first half of the century, however, any apparent community of national purpose could not conceal deep divisions of sensibility and commitment. The most obvious polarization was in matters of style. One characteristic attempt to synthesize a national personality out of local experience was through the cultivation of eloquence—rhetorical or lyrical. Miles Franklin might be thought of as representative of the tendency. More general, however, was the opposite practice of a deliberately low-keyed utterance, a reaching out to the phenomenal world through an antipodean equivalent of Joyce's 'style of scrupulous meanness'. Vance Palmer formulated the aesthetic of a whole generation when in 1942 he endorsed Verlaine's advice to 'take eloquence and wring its neck'. Perhaps, however, the finest practical vindication of that aesthetic is to be found in the short stories of the 1940s—a decade which saw a flowering of the form reminiscent in both quantity and quality of the 1890s. Gavin Casey, Brian James, Peter Cowan, Davison, Palmer himself (to name only a few) achieved in their shorter fiction an assured understatement through which they annexed whole tracts of Australian experience as their own.

The stylistic extremes of eloquence and laconic reticence produced by the 1940s an extraordinary jostle of attitudes and stances; Jindyworobak and Angry Penguin, left-wing nationalist and right-wing Australia Firster competed for supremacy in an atmosphere rendered electric by the fact of war. The variety of directions and postures attempted in those years suggests that an analysis into polar opposites is far too simplistic. So various indeed was the literary achievement of the 1940s that some effort at large-scale synthesis can be seen in retrospect to have been more and

more needful. The need was answered with the return of Patrick White from London after demobilization from the RAF, and the publication of that series of novels which begins with *The Tree of Man* in 1955.

That White's mastery over his self, his situation and his art would be won hard and at some cost was signalled as early as 1948 in the phrase from Henry Miller which appears as part of the epigraph to Part II of *The Aunt's Story* (1948)—'the great fragmentation of maturity'. After a century and a half of European experience in this country, White grasped unhesitatingly what had become the unavoidable theme and the most potent threat to the Australian literary imagination, and converted it into a source of power. The story of Theodora Goodman offers an idea of personal maturity radically at odds with the liberal-humanist dogmas of the previous hundred years.

In the years following *The Aunt's Story* Patrick White, through characters like Voss, Himmelfarb, Hurtle Duffield, continued his radical assault on Australian pieties held too easily or too long. His prose style was no less calculated to unsettle fictional orthodoxies. His attack on 'dreary dun-coloured . . . journalism' is widely known. Less familiar, although occurring in the same essay ('The Prodigal Son'), is White's positive description of what he hoped his language might achieve: 'Writing . . . became a struggle to create completely fresh forms out of the rocks and sticks of words'. An aim at once so austere and so melodramatic, united to the thematic radicalism of White's writing, has undoubtedly thrust Australian fiction towards new kinds of perception. Yet his massive contribution to our literature has not been, as I say, without personal cost, but a cost of a different kind from that paid by earlier Australian writers—Kendall, for instance, Lawson, Brennan, Slessor. White has neither suffered personal disintegration nor fallen into silence. The price he has paid to keep the imagination vigorously alive is shown rather in his work—most of all, perhaps, in that increasingly strained articulation of his vision which (as some commentators believe) marks his writing from, say, *The Vivisector* on.

Whatever the difficulties or the costs, no other writer has come anywhere near to White's capacity to assimilate his Australian experience to his vision and his art. What has been evident, especially in our fiction, in the years since his influence began to be felt has been not only a higher level of professional excellence but a more intense concern for the aesthetic of the novel. Many of the old polarities persist, now expressed in structures of greater complexity than before. The old Dionysian urge, for instance, continues, in the comic mode and located in the industrial world, in the work of Peter Mathers and David Ireland. Thea Astley and Thomas Keneally, sharing memories of a Catholic childhood, continue to explore the polarities in our treatment of love and violence, social satire and spiritual aspiration, the light and dark of all our lives. Where Dal Stivens in a novel like *A Horse of Air* (1970) acclimatizes to Australia Nabokovian subtleties of personality, Frank Hardy has learnt in *But the Dead are Many* (1975) the means of relating the themes of social and personal division in a work which relates him more powerfully and directly to the Lawson that Manning Clark revealed to us than any of the turgid social comment of his first novel, *Power Without Glory* (1950). Neither Stivens nor Hardy has so far been able to synthesize so much of life and of art as Patrick White. Yet they, along with many of our best writers since *The Tree of Man,* have accepted and used what is perhaps White's supreme gift to his fellow Australian writers: the confidence to make of the divided self the subject and support of a complex, sophisticated and penetrating art.

That the accomplishments of Australian literary prose have broadened as well as deepened during the past two decades is attested by the new excellence discovered in autobiography. While Australian autobiography is almost as old as Australian literature, most of the earlier examples of the form either exist in isolation or retain interest chiefly as sociological observation. In the 1950s, however, autobiography as a genre seems to have taken firm enough root in our culture to start producing an abundant and continuing harvest. One of the first important works from this period is Alan Marshall's *I Can Jump Puddles,* of 1955. We need not be mindful of the special appeal of this work (the triumph of a country boy over the tragedy of poliomyelitis) to accord it a secure place among our leading autobiographies. Marshall's particular distinction is to

have convincingly identified the joys and sorrows of the young lad who was himself with the common experiences and emotions of a whole people. Too often in our writing such an identification has remained at the level of dogmatic assertion; in *I Can Jump Puddles* it is a matter of realized fact. Marshall's instinct served him well when he chose as title for his next autobiographical volume *This is the Grass* (1962) a phrase from Walt Whitman, the poet par excellence of the merging of the single, separate person with life *en masse.*

Other recent autobiographies—those for instance of Douglas Stewart, Katharine Susannah Prichard, Martin Boyd, Colin MacInnes—have been more personal than Marshall's, in the sense that the experiences they record are less fused with a whole way of life than those of *I Can Jump Puddles.* Nevertheless, all these autobiographers write with the assurance that Australian life has become dense enough to make an account of growing up worth telling for its own sake, as well as for its representative quality. It is as if the Australian artist no longer feels himself condemned to that thin diet of observation that James imputed to Hawthorne; Australian lives are now rich enough in themselves and in their social connections to make autobiography both possible and worth while.

Portrait of Patrick White (1912-1990) by Brett Whiteley.

None of our recent autobiographers is more persuaded of this fact than Donald Horne. He prefaces *The Education of Young Donald* with a remark which provides the rationale for more autobiographies than his own:

> Technically this is an autobiography, but "autobiography" seems to suggest a sense of self-importance that is so far from what I had in mind that when people first used the word I had the feeling of someone who looks over his shoulder to see what is being talked about . . . since the central character is presented as a social animal, his adolescent revolt shaped and coloured by social circumstance, I would use the word "sociography" rather than "autobiography".

Horne's bold coinage does not, however, quite fit the work of our most distinguished autobiographer, Hal Porter. His three works of autobiography, starting with *The Watcher on the Cast-Iron Balcony* in 1963, brilliantly catch nuances of national tone and attitudes, but they are by no means the deliberate exercises in socio-cultural reconstruction that *The Education of Young Donald* sets out to be. What is more usually perceived as the dominant theme within Porter's idiosyncratic manner (neither flat nor rhetorical but coruscatingly exact in its registration of feeling and sensation) is a sense of deprivation at the impermanence of human attachments. Porter himself, however, reveals what is the deepest motif of his autobiographical writing in a passage from the second volume of the series, *The Paper Chase* (1966):

> The most discomposing paradox in my luggage of new information is that I prefer to live alone because I am too fond of those I love.
>
> One wants to be alone, fundamentally, not to escape others but to escape oneself, the versions of self compelled into existence by others. It is safer for me to be mere wood than to be wood painted to look like wood.

Such an assertion may well affront that code of 'mateship' which the conventional wisdom has been telling us for so long is the special Australian contribution to practical ethics. Nevertheless, and as I have tried to indicate, it can also be construed as a definitive statement of the contemporary situation of the most successful Australian literary artists. In Porter's autobiographical prose, the anxious solipsisms of the past, the aesthetic and cultural indecisions, the fundamental reliance on the physical imagination, have at last modulated into a personal utterance no longer apologetic for the form it takes or the ground on which it stands.

The rise of autobiography during the 1950s and 1960s is (outside drama) the most recent formal manoeuvre of the creative imagination identifiable to Australian literary historians. The patterns assumed by contemporary experiment must for the present remain conjectural. In closing these remarks, however, I must record one of the most widely accepted conjectures about our current writing if only for the sake of bringing a highly selective survey a little closer to the immediate present.

Writing in the *Australian Book Review* of August 1970, Thomas Shapcott asserted the appearance of a new generation of young poets, the 'generation of 1968'. Nurtured by the upheaval in values, lifestyles, beliefs which characterized the decade, these new writers tended to avoid the established channels of literary culture, rejected traditional canons of metrics and prosody, cultivated a style that mixed, in varying proportions, public exhortation, intimate self-revelation, and truncated *aperçus* into social or environmental data. From among their number, at least some poets have emerged with personal staying power and a talent which seems likely to last: Robert Adamson, Richard Tipping, John Tranter are three names selected arbitrarily from among a group whom it is still invidious to 'rank' into any kind of hierarchy. The brief careers of Michael Dransfield and Charles Buckmaster, tragically closed by early death, are all too representative of that quality of personal extremity which has characterized so much of the verse of the past decade.

The notion of a major break with the literary tradition is not, however, restricted to the younger poets. Michael Wilding makes the same sort of claim for the new prose writers in an essay appended to his anthology of *avant-garde* fiction, *The Tabloid Story Pocket Book*. As Shapcott had argued for verse, so Wilding asserts a major hiatus in the development of our prose fiction in the late 1960s. The near side of this watershed has a number of discernible features: a concerted attempt to woo a 'counter-culture' audience, a determined effort to expand the subject matter of fiction (especially into the areas of sexuality and libertarian politics), a conscious rejection of the 'Lawson-nationalist' tradition in favour of narrative freer in both form and attitude. The older traditions of Australian prose (like those of verse) are now felt to be a constraint upon the imaginations of those writers most vitally in touch with contemporary Australia.

As with poetry, so the welter of new prose has produced at least some few authors whose work seems likely to last—(again by arbitrary selection) Wilding himself, Peter Carey, Frank Moorhouse. Moorhouse in particular, working away at what he calls his 'discontinuous narratives', is notable as much for the inventiveness of his fictional forms as for his keenly observant eye. In basing his writing on documentary observation, Moorhouse is, of course, maintaining a function for prose that goes back to its very beginnings in this country. Indeed, in this respect as in many others, Moorhouse's status may be regarded as emblematic of a great deal of new Australian writing. Self-consciously international in outlook, it cannot avoid a native colouration; restlessly searching for new forms of expression, it discovers the main areas defined by the very conditions of settlement two hundred years ago; turning its back on mainstream traditions, it cannot avoid the pressure of the past. By the very act of proclaiming their polar discontinuity with their immediate predecessors, it may be that our newest writers continue one of our major literary traditions, are absorbed into the systolic rhythms of our culture. (pp. 1-21)

Harry Heseltine, "The Uncertain Self: Notes on the Development of Australian Literary Form," in his The Uncertain Self: Essays in Australian Literature and Criticism, *Oxford University Press, Melbourne, 1986, pp. 1-21.*

Faye Zwicky on the nature of Australian literature:

America started as a theocratic state; our lot was dumped. The brutality of our beginning was not conducive to religion. With the start the convicts had here you'd give up on God quickly. I think of it as our having wandered out of the earshot of God. In Western Australia there are no seasons. Only wet and dry. Seldom are there clouds. The sky is an endless, relentless electric blue. The sun will knock a spiritual awareness right out of you. If you have a cloudless blue sky where there is no drama in it, it colors your inner responses. How could you write a *Wuthering Heights?* What contrasts are possible here when there are no contrasts? Who thinks of evil when the sky is blue?

Faye Zwicky, in Australian Voices: Writers on Their Own Work, *1991.*

A. W. Baker

[*In the following essay, Baker examines the origins and development of convict literature in Australia.*]

> My grandfather was a shorter, and my father was a smasher; the one was scragg'd and the other lagg'd.
>
> *The Romany Rye*

The findings of anthropologists continue to push the beginnings of human habitation of the Great South Land further back into the past. The events of these countless generations have been handed down and interpreted in the myths of the Dreamtime. The very timelessness and enigmas of these myths display the accommodation of the Aborigines' spirit to that of their homeland.

The findings of archaeologists indicate a long history of European and Asian contacts with Australia. Wrecks and artefacts pose mysteries that will doubtless be resolved with scientific exactitude.

There is no puzzle about the date of the beginning of European habitation of Australia (though *why* it began may never be resolved). The foundation and early years of Australia have been more extensively documented than those of many other nations. Unlike their Aboriginal compatriots, white Australians lack a dreamtime.

The effect of this lacuna is yet to be determined, though Mircea Eliade's generalization about western societies appears relevant.

> Through culture a desacralized religious universe and a demythicized mythology formed and nourished western civilization—that is, the only civilization that has succeeded in becoming exemplary. There is more here than a triumph over mythos. The victory is that of the *book* over oral tradition, of the document—especially of the written document—over a living experience whose only means of expression were preliterary.

The thousand or so founding fathers (convict or free) of this nation would not have given a fig for Eliade's observations. Theirs was a "land of d—d realities" as Charles Lamb noted. It was a land where the here and now inhibited reflection on the hereafter, on the why or the wherefore.

This was because survival was difficult, and because for many years the majority of European settlers were professional criminals transported as a punishment for their misdeeds. Between 1788 and 1868 some 160,000 persons were thus transported. Known variously as government men, lags, exiles, convicts and felons, they played a part in the foundation of every Australian state, with the exception of South Australia.

The typical convict, we are told,

> was an urban thief, single, aged twenty-five, previously convicted at least once and transported for seven years for larceny. He was well treated according to the standards of the day on the voyage to Australia and when he arrived he was assigned to a settler. He probably had a number of masters and suffered punishment five times, mainly for such offences as being absent without leave or drunk. If he were a rebellious spirit and his master turned nasty, his transportation could become a very severe punishment, which it was meant to be. He might be flogged; but no more than approximately fifteen per cent of prisoners were ever sent to a penal settlement, and most convicts were not flogged. Usually men secured a ticket of leave within three years and this enabled them to work for themselves provided they reported regularly to the police. Upon fair behaviour (not necessarily exemplary behaviour) the prisoner would be granted a conditional pardon before full sentence was completed.

Apart from its valuable insights into the background of the convict, Dr Robson's description is noteworthy for two other reasons.

In the first instance, it is obvious that the description is at variance with the popular conception of the convict's life as it was portrayed in works like Marcus Clarke's *For the Term of His Natural Life:* "However, when all is said, the horrors depicted by Marcus Clarke in *For the Term of His Natural Life* are not in the least typical of Australian conditions. Considerably fewer than ten per cent of the prisoners transported ever saw the inside of a penal settlement and many who did so were there only for brief periods".

Nevertheless, when Marcus Clarke set off for Tasmania to gather material for his book, he informed his publisher that he was going to "write up the convict documents". William Hay, whose bent was far less sensational, believed that this procedure was inevitable for any writer of an Australian historical novel. Most other writers about the convict days also claimed familiarity with the records.

It is clear that those who wrote (and indeed, write) about the convict days tended to portray a reality that did not correspond at all points with historical facts.

It appears reasonable to infer that there is a received mode of writing about the convicts. That is, despite the wealth of documentation, writers and readers have hit upon an interpretative code which is acceptable as an account of our beginnings. According to one's perspective this code may be designated as a myth or fable or legend; one may believe with Mark Twain that it reads like "the most beautiful lies".

Dr Robson's description, cast as it is as an approximation of a biography, is a reminder that most of the early writings about convicts were biographical in form. Individual convict records were tersely biographical and generally speaking, factual. It was when these biographies were published without official sanction or control that they exhibited the perspective, content and tone that have become accepted. These attributes became evident within decades of the date of first settlement.

"It is natural to suppose that, during the early years of its foundation, a dependent colony will draw to a considerable extent upon the literary as well as the general resources of the mother country." The early emergence of a formula to describe the convict's life implies the adoption of an existing model. In fact, when the first convicts came to Australia, and throughout the transportation era, there was in England a long-standing mode of discussing crime and punishment. This tradition was embodied in criminal biographies, which were widely disseminated.

Convicts transported to Australia used this traditional form when they came to write about their experiences. They also tended to use the form orally when they told their stories to observers.

The biographical form was modified to suit Australian conditions, first by the selection of a vocabulary, and second by the adoption of an increasingly stylized formula. This formula, in turn, underwent modifications as experiences in Australia became more diversified.

There was a concomitant oral tradition. Largely anecdotal, this tradition contained stories of celebrated incidents and personalities. The oral tradition was encountered by succeeding waves of transportees in prisons, hulks and convict ships. In Australia, convict tales were rehearsed around camp-fires, in bark huts and drawing-rooms. Towards the end of the nineteenth century these tales became the property of the convict residuum on the one hand and variants of them became the property of pioneering families on the other. Ultimately, parts of both oral traditions found their way into written accounts.

Thus, when works of fiction came to be written, the criminal biography and the oral traditions provided their structure. When writers had recourse to the documents, this structure was reinforced, since the documents were primarily biographies, the stages of which corresponded to those of the traditional English formula.

This formula contained recurrent components: "early life"; "introduction to crime"; "progress in crime"; "capture"; "trial"; "execution" or "transportation". Interwoven with the foregoing were "hardships"; "sufferings" and "reformation". Obviously, the formula provided no precedents for describing life in the antipodes. Moreover, as will be seen, the experiences of convicts transported to America provided minimal guidance.

The modifications of the formula and its amplification to include components describing life in the colonies represented one of the first achievements of Australian literature. In the eighteenth century English literature was rich in resources. It was the nature of the early—and unwilling—colonists that determined that one of the first borrowings would be the treatment of crime and punishment and its usual focus: the criminal biography.

While foreign observers believed that enthusiasm for this kind of account was peculiar to eighteenth-century Englishmen, the English had long displayed an interest in such matters.

With the advent of printing, and the progressive secularization that has characterized the history of English literature since that time, old tales of transgressions against the law, such as those contained in the *Disciplina Clericalis,* were often translated without their edifying codas. Even where sin was described to convert the sinner, there was always the problem that the sin might be more fascinating than conversion. Thus in a collection of stories like *C. Merry Tales* (1526), despite the author's concluding that "By this ye may see . . . ", the reader was led to admire the cleverness of the Welshman who stole the Englishman's cock, rather than to despise theft. The tension between reformatory zeal and the insidious charms of vice is found throughout the literature to be discussed here.

As writers outgrew random collections of tales, they were confronted with the problem of unifying the anecdotes they presented. One method they employed was to allow the reader to witness a procession of rogues, or to take him on a tour of infamous haunts. Such literary devices were adopted by John Skelton in "The Tunnyng of Elynour Rummyng" (1517); by Robert Copland in *Hyeway to the Spytel House* (1535), and *Howleglas* (1510); and by John Awdeley in *Fraternitye of Vacabones* (1565). While these accounts were at times lurid, a more sober note characterized William Baldwin's collection, *A Myrrovre for Magistrates* (1559). This set of poems, written by "dyvers learned men whose many gifts nede fewe praises", contained many of the biographical components that will be dealt with in these pages.

Thomas Dekker claimed to be innovating when he wrote *English Villainies Discovered by Lantern and Candlelight* (1608): "And the honest intelligencer that first opened the den of these monsters was the Bellman of London". Dekker's exposé purported to be a tour of dens of iniquity by Pamersiel, who had been sent from Hell to make fresh converts for the Devil. In rapid succession the reader learned of the depredations of "gull-gropers", cardsharps, horse-stealers, prostitutes, and so on. Pamersiel's visit to a prison was a model for many subsequent accounts.

Meanwhile, denunciations of specific crimes had emerged in pamphlets such as Gilbert Walker's *A Magnificent Detection of the Most Vile and Detestable Use of Diceplay* (1552) and in Robert Greene's *The Third and Last part of Cony-Catching with the New Devised Knavish Art of Fool-Taking, the Like Cozenages and Villainies Never Before Discovered* (1592).

This pamphlet, claiming to be based on notes provided by a justice of the peace, contains anecdotes about rogues.

For example, the reader is told of the cutpurse who has a cutler fashion a knife. The cutler knows the criminal purposes for which the knife is being made, but he cheerfully puts the fee in his purse, which becomes the thief's first prize. In this anecdote there is the exuberance of criminal ingenuity that characterizes many of the English criminal biographies. The same vigour is to be found in James Hardy Vaux's *Memoirs* and James Tucker's *Ralph Rashleigh*. However, it dies out in the Australian biographies, to be replaced by a notable sourness and sullenness.

Throughout the seventeenth century similar accounts of criminal behaviour and prison life were produced. For example, Geoffrey Mynshul (who had been in prison with Dekker) wrote *Certain Characters and Essays of Prison and Prisoners* in 1618.

A more sensational note soon began to creep into the titles of pamphlets: John Reynold's *The Triumphs of God's Revenge Against the Crying and Execrable Sin of Murther in Thirty Severall Tragicall Histories* (1621) went through several editions, being augmented in 1679 by ten stories showing "God's Revenge against the Abominable Sin of Adultery". Titles of similar tenor appeared, including *A true Relation of the Lives and Deaths of the two most famous English Pyrats, Purser and Clynton* (1639) and *The Penitent Murderer* (1657).

The development so far outlined progressed from a survey of crime, to specific crimes, to stories of perpetrators of crimes; that is, biographies. Richard Head's *Meriton Latroon* (1655) is an early example of the biography of a criminal. (pp. 1-7)

In this brief outline it has been possible to do no more than sketch in some of the kinds of literary works inspired by crime and punishment. It was a subject which interested many writers.

Side by side with the collection and surveys that have been noted were the ballads. If we may generalize from the case of William Ainsworth, who had some claim to knowledge of this literature, the ballads do not appear to have been known outside the haunts in which they were sung.

Visits to haunts of crime, denunciations of crime, the production of criminal biography, and the importation of a sensational tone, continued to be popular during the eighteenth century.

A successor to Dekker's *Bellman*, Ned Ward's *The London Spy* (1698-1700) appeared in eighteen monthly parts. In this work Ward took an ironical view of the seamier side of London life, as did Tom Brown in his *Amusements Serious and Comical Calculated for the Meridian of London* (1700) and in his *Cheats of London* (1704).

The eighteenth century also saw a more scientific and dispassionate note introduced into the discussion of crime and punishment: it became important to examine why so much crime existed. At the beginning of the century, Jonathan Swift saw a connection between crime and poverty. He believed that much poverty (and resultant crime) was self-inflicted:

> Perhaps there is not a word more abused than

> that of the poor, or wherein the world is more generally mistaken. Among the number of those who beg in our streets, or are half starved at home, or languish in prison for debt, there is hardly one in a hundred who doth not owe his misfortunes to his own laziness or drunkenness, or worse vices.

Daniel Defoe, however, believed that necessity drove people to crime. This sentiment is to be found throughout his works, but most clearly in the *Review* (1711):

> Men rob for bread, women whore for bread. Necessity is the parent of crime; Ask the worst High-Way Man in the Nation, ask the lewdest strumpet in the town, If they would not willingly leave off the Trade if they could live handsomely without it—And I dare say not one will but acknowledge it.

In his *Enquiry* (1751) Henry Fielding asserted that it is the "lower orders'" love for entertainment that leads to crime. He believed that they should learn to curb their appetites, while "the great" must "answer for the employment of their time to themselves or their spiritual governors". At the end of the century Patrick Colquhoun shared these sentiments, while William Godwin declared that the "criminal is propelled to act by necessary causes and irresistible motives".

There were other, and very important, discussions of crime written by lawyers and philosophers: Beccaria's *Treatise of Crimes and Punishments* was translated into English in 1765; in the same year Blackstone wrote his *Commentaries*. Howard's *State of the Prisons* appeared in 1777; in 1780 Bentham's *Introduction to the Principles of Morals and Legislation* appeared. Romilly completed his *Rights and Duties of Juries* in 1785 and his *Thoughts on Executive Justice* in 1786. Colquhoun's *Police of the Metropolis* was published in 1795, two years after Godwin's *Enquiry Concerning Political Justice*. Interested readers could also have delved into the relevant treatises of Voltaire, Rousseau and Kant. The foregoing works were written for the serious reader. Popular tastes were well catered for in other ways.

To put these "other ways" in perspective it must be remembered that the publications were chiefly biographical and that for the most part they stemmed from public executions. At the scaffold it was usual for the criminal to be accompanied by a clergyman (for example, the ordinary of Newgate). Above the tumult, the ordinary would strive for the soul of the condemned person, while the latter would deliver his "last dying speech and confession".

The custom of making such a speech appears to be of ancient origin. In England, for example, both Henry VIII and Thomas More knew that the latter would be expected to speak at the scaffold. Fearing More's eloquence, Henry ordained that More speak briefly. More complied. While the text has not survived, its general thrust and various aphorisms have been preserved.

To add to their income the ordinaries began the custom of publishing these speeches. The *British Museum Catalogue* records such a speech as early as 1684; however, it was Paul Lorrain (ordinary of Newgate, 1698-1719) who in 1712 began the custom of regularly printing them, copies being available at eight o'clock on the morning following the execution. It is probable that the ordinaries, having to write in such haste, fell back on the model offered by the familiar printed funeral panegyric, with the obvious substitution of the criminal's misdemeanours for the hero's or saint's virtues.

In fact, the ordinary's account became so perfunctory and so little attuned to the sentiments of the crowd that it came to be held in almost universal contempt. In a letter to Pope, for example, Bolingbroke referred disdainfully to "that great Historiographer, Paul Lorrain". Again, in John Gay's *The Beggar's Opera* (1728), Mrs Peachum gives the following directive to Filch: "But now, since you have nothing better to do, even go to your book and learn your catechism: for really, a man makes but an ill figure in the ordinary's paper who cannot give a satisfactory answer to his questions."

Fielding was one of the many who expressed similar sentiments: "The ordinary's account where all the apologies of the lives of the rogues and whores which have been published within these twenty years have been inserted".

The ordinary's account may not have been very efficacious, but it was profitable, and the ordinaries did all they could to maintain proprietorship of it. Nevertheless, last dying speeches were also printed as broadsheets and disseminated widely. In the nineteenth century, as many as 2,500,000 broadsheet copies were made of the last speech of a notorious murderer. The broadsheets were often decorated with crude drawings and embellished with ballads and edifying verses. Ballad singers were among the principal purveyors of these sheets. In their hands the broadsheets became even a greater travesty of their avowed intent, since the ballad singers often worked hand-in-glove with pickpockets, as John Gay pointed out (1716):

> Let not the ballad singer's thrilling strain
> Amid the swarm thy list'ning ear detain
> Guard well they pocket, for these Syrens stand
> To aid the labours of the diving hand:
> Confed'rate in the cheat they draw the throng;
> And cambrick handkerchiefs reward the song.

This complicity is depicted in Rowlandson's engraving, *Last Dying Speech and Confession.*

It is pertinent here to outline some nineteenth-century developments of the broadsheet, as it continued to be a possible element of the "education" of transported convicts.

The heyday of the broadsheet coincided with that of the presses in the Seven Dials, particularly the Catnach Press (founded 1813). Other centres of the trade were Birmingham, Lincoln and Preston. Henry Mayhew was told by one of the Seven Dials writers that:

> Many ballads are written expressly for the Seven Dials press, especially the Newgate and political ones. . . . There are five known authors of the Dials press, and they are street ballad-singers. I am one of them myself. My little knowledge I picked up bit by bit so that I hardly know how I came by it. I certainly knew my letters before I left home, and I got the rest off the dead walls

and out of the ballads and papers I have been selling. I write most of the ballads now for the printers in the Dials. I get a shilling for a "copy of verses written by the wretched culprit the night previous to his execution".

Whatever truth remained in the written word tended to be dissipated by the enthusiastic patter of the vendor:

> Now my friends, here you have, just printed and published, a full, true and pertickler account of the life, trial, character, confession, behaviour, condemnation and hexecution of that unfortunate malefactor. Yes, my customers to which is added a copy of the serene and beautiful verses, pious and immoral, as wot he wrote with his own blood and skewer.

Thus, those who did not witness the execution, and those who could not read, could still be regaled with the salient details of the crime and punishment.

The broadsheets were printed on cheap paper. More durable bound collections of chronicles of crime and punishment were also available. For example, that indefatigable biographer, Captain Alexander Smith, published in 1713 his *History of the Lives and Robberies of the Most Noted Highway-Men, Foot-Pads, House-Breakers, Shop Lifts and Cheats of Both Sexes in and about London and Westminster.* This two-volume compendium was followed by a third volume in 1720. Between the production of these two parts Smith found time to publish (1716) *The School of Venus,* or *Cupid Restor'd to Sight: Being a History of Cuckolds and Cuckold-makers.*

In 1728 the first edition of *The Newgate Calendar* appeared; there was another in 1773, and a third in 1809; there have been at least eight others produced since then. A work of similar scope but of more obvious reformatory purpose had been published as early as 1690. The *Annual Register* first appeared in 1758; ten years later the *Tyburn Chronicle* was printed.

In the nineteenth century this genre continued to be popular. The two volumes of the *Terrific Register* became available in 1825; it was followed by George Borrow's *Celebrated Trials* in the same year, and "Camden Pelham's" *Chronicles of Crime* (1841). In the preface to his six-volume collection, Borrow denounced the *Newgate Calendars* as "chronicles of roguery and vulgar depravity in their various forms, [which] have usually been compiled in language which sympathized and accorded with their subjects". As his work was for "respectable and popular circulation", Borrow excluded cases which involved "details contrary to decency". He mentioned that he drew upon the *Causes Célèbres* and "many curious documents" but that he "adopted no existing model".

"Camden Pelham's" accounts of early crime were " . . . derived from sources of information peculiarly within the reach of the editor while those of a later period are compiled from known authorities as accurate as they are complete".

The bound chronicles noted above were usually biographical in form and reformatory in purpose. Borrow's charge that the *Newgate Calendar* "sympathized" with its subjects was often made by other writers; yet a dispassionate reading of the *Calendars* (and Borrow's own *Chronicles*) reveals little of a provocative tendency.

Between the broadsheets and the chronicles and calendars were the chap-books. These crude publications contained lurid accounts of the crime and punishment of criminals like Judas Iscariot and M. Bamfylde Moore Carew. Other chap-books dealt with *The Horrors of Jealousie or the Fatal Mistake* or *The Unfortunate Family*. These publications contain a bizarre combination of fact, superstition and exhortation to virtue. They are frequently illustrated with woodcuts and often include verses.

Yet another eighteenth-century method of treating crime and punishment was the engraving. Horace Walpole complained in 1750: "You cannot conceive the ridiculous rage there is of going to Newgate, the prints that are published of the malefactors and the memory of their lives set forth with as much panache as Marshal Turenne's".

Henry Fielding, on the other hand, discerned great merit in Hogarth's work: "I almost dare affirm that those two works of his which he calls the Rake's Progress and the Harlot's Progress are calculated more to serve the cause of Virtue and the Preservation of Mankind than all the Folios of Morality that have been written".

Hogarth produced his *Harlot's Progress* (1732) and *The Rake's Progress* (1735) for a wealthy clientèle, but for his series *Industry and Idleness* (1747) he drastically lowered the purchase price so that it "would be within reach of those for whom [it was] chiefly intended". Contrary to his usual practice, he embellished the series with symbolic motifs and descriptive verse.

This outline of eighteenth-century ways of treating crime and punishment has so far dealt with accounts which were supposedly factual. Even without analysis, it will be obvious from some titles cited that there was a good deal of exaggeration, even of fantasy, in some works. In other words, there was a perceptible drift from reportage to fiction.

It is customary to view the early and middle eighteenth century as witnessing the birth of the novel. Whatever may have been the first novel, whoever may have been the father of the genre, the fictional works of the eighteenth century were primarily imitations of biography. The life of a fictitious individual became the force that lent cohesion to his picaresque ramblings.

At the end of the century, James Boswell believed that he had devised the best mode of biography: "I am absolutely certain that my mode of biography, which gives not only a *history* of Johnson's *visible* progress through the world and of his publications, but a *view* of his mind in his letters and conversations, is the most perfect that can be conceived and will be *more* of a life than has ever yet appeared".

Yet, however revolutionary Boswell's strategy may have been, in recording Samuel Johnson's judgments so exactly he helped to perpetuate Johnson's own methods of recording and evaluating the lives of others. In other words, biography was encouraged to remain—as it has been in ha-

giography and in the "pleasant history" of the seventeenth century—a matter of considering a man's acts and sentiments as emanating from discrete faculties and of measuring these acts and sentiments against absolute standards of good and evil.

Howard Miles sums up this outlook and procedure:

> Johnson uses certain plain terms that for him stand adequately for distinct and definable qualities—*openness, confidence, affection, brave, benevolent, honest.* Similarly, the feelings or passions are distinct and nameable. . . . Elsewhere Johnson sees the mind as constituted of various distinct faculties—*genius, judgment, knowledge.*

It is to be expected, therefore, that Johnson would stress the normative aspect of fiction. Having described contemporary fiction as that which "exhibits life in its true state—and influenced by passions and qualities which are readily to be found in conversing with mankind", he proceeded to specify the proper end of fiction:

> In narratives where historical veracity has no place I cannot discover why there should not be exhibited the most perfect idea of virtue, of virtue not angelical nor above probability, for what we cannot we shall never imitate, but the highest and purest that humanity can reach, which exercised in such trials as the various revolutions of things shall bring upon it, may, by conquering some calamities, and enduring others, teach us what we may hope for and what we may perform.

Those of Johnson's contemporaries who strove to create works of fiction based on crime and punishment, indeed many of the other earlier novelists, professed to share his moral concern: if they did not exhort to "the most perfect idea of virtue", at least they displayed the consequences of vice, and presumably, thereby encouraged virtue. Daniel Defoe realized that the "gust and palate of the reader" will determine the degree of edification got from a book: "But as this work (*Moll Flanders*) is chiefly recommended to those who know how to read it and how to make the good uses of it which the story all along recommends to them, so it is to be hoped that such readers will be more pleased with the moral than the fable".

In the same year he prefaced similar sentiments to *Colonel Jacque:* in reading about the Colonel (Defoe maintained) one can perceive " . . . Virtue and the ways of wisdom every where applauded; Vice and all kinds of Wickedness attended with Misery [and] many Kinds of Infelicities".

Some dramatists evinced the same moral purpose. Thus, however ironical his intent, Gay's Beggar declared in *The Beggar's Opera:* "Through the whole of the piece you may observe . . . a similitude of manners in high and low life. Had the play remained as I first intended, it would have carried a most excellent moral. 'Twould have shown that the lower sort of people have their vices in a degree as well as the rich: and that they are punished for them."

Three years later (1731) George Lillo wrote in the Dedication of *The London Merchant:* " . . . the end of tragedy [is] the exciting of passions in order to the correcting such of them as are criminal either in their nature or through their excess".

It will have become obvious that the realities of criminal life were not readily amenable to being viewed with a moral squint. In the underworld there was a solidarity that made nonsense of attempts to describe crime solely in terms of sin and virtue. The tension that this contradiction caused lay at the heart of the criminal biography, finding expression in literature as sanctimoniousness, cynicism, irony or naiveté. In penal administration it bred idealistic schemes doomed to failure, or a pragmatism that most often expressed itself as brutality; cruelty seemed to produce results.

The nature of the underworld and a narrowly reformatory vision merit closer attention.

In his *Fraternitye of Vacabones* Awdeley had described an organized criminal class. The leader of the gangs he portrayed was known as the "upright man" who took the lion's share of booty for himself. The gangs had their argot or cant which served as a bond of solidarity and as a means of concealing the thieves' plans from outsiders. The use of an argot for such a purpose no doubt goes back to the beginnings of civilization; certainly thieves' guilds and argot existed in ancient Greece and Rome. However, Dekker later believed that English thieves' cant was of relatively recent origin: "By none but the soldiers of these tattered bands is it [cant] familiarly or usually spoken yet within less than fourscore years now past not a word of this language was known. The first inventor of it was hanged, yet left he apt scholars behind him who had reduced that into their method which he on his death bed (which was a pair of gallows) could not so absolutely perfect as he desired."

In the lives of Meriton Latroon and Bamfylde Moore Carew and in Vaux's *Memoirs* we find primitive cant dictionaries. . . . [Many] observers noted the use of cant among the Australian convicts.

Dekker provided more information about these gangs: "There is no lusty rogue but hath many sworn brothers and the morts his sworn sisters vow themselves body and soul to the Devil to perform these ten articles . . . " He provides us with the criminals' *curriculum vitae*: "But the Devil is their tutor, Hell their school, thieves' roguery and whoredom the arts they study. Before Doctor Storey they dispute and at the gallows are made graduates of Newgate and other gaols, the hangman's colleges."

Because he showed such promise as a thief, Head's Meriton Latroon was invited to join a society of thieves: "If I would swear to be secret and faithful, and become a Brother of the Society he would not only tell me how all this (afore recited) might be performed, but would likewise introduce me into the place where these jolly blades used to congregate."

Over a century later, Fielding exclaimed: "What indeed may not the public apprehend when they are informed as an unquestionable fact that there are at this time a great gang of rogues, whose number falls little short of a hundred, who are incorporated in a body, have officers and a treasury and have reduced theft and robbery into a regular system".

In *Moll Flanders, Colonel Jacque, Jonathan Wild* and *The Beggar's Opera* we are given further insights into these societies. *Jonathan Wild* (1743) contains an extensive description of one of them. Possibly because Jonathan Wild's career as a receiver offered a glimpse into the workings of the underworld, he was a figure who appealed to the popular imagination. In the year he was executed (1725), he was the subject of eight full-scale biographies.

If it was not Wild, it was some other receiver who was usually depicted as playing a vital part in the workings of a criminal society. Receivers were often pawnbrokers, and Colquhoun complained that: "Any person, even the most notorious rogue or vagabond who can raise ten pounds to pay for a licence, may at present set up trade as a pawnbroker; and it is even said that some have got licences, who have actually been on board the hulks. This class of swindling pawn-brokers are uniformly receivers of stolen goods".

Rightly or wrongly, Colquhoun believed that Jews were prominent among the receivers. His judgment may have been correct; he may have been alarmed at the revival of the widely misunderstood Cabbala or he may have been guilty of what Chesney Kellow was to describe later as "the prejudice of the Victorians".

A number of ironic attempts were made to present a rationale for criminal societies and behaviour. For example, in 1714 Bernard Mandeville claimed that: "If all people were strictly honest, and nobody would meddle or pry into anything but his own, half the smiths of the nation would want employment; and abundance of workmanship is to be seen everywhere both in town and country that would have never been thought of, but to secure us against the attempt of pilferers and robbers".

In a similar vein, John Gay has Mat and Mint say in *The Beggar's Opera*:

> We retrench the superfluities of mankind. The world is avaricious and I hate avarice. A covetous fellow, like a Jackdaw, steals what he was never made to enjoy, for the sake of hiding it. These are the robbers of mankind; for money was made for the free-hearted and generous: and where is the injury of taking from another what he hath not the heart to make use of?

Whatever the real sentiments of the denizens of the thieves' kitchens were we do not know, but it is obvious that these criminals were organized and that they had a secret language. At the heart of these societies lay a tension between loyalty on the one hand and the individual's self-interest on the other. Out of this tension sprang both defiance of legal authority and treacherous capitulation to that authority: some criminals "died game", while others betrayed their companions. A similar solidarity and treachery will be found in accounts about transported thieves and other criminals.

The equation of crime with sin was expressed succinctly by Henry Mayhew as late as 1862: "To thieve, however, is to offend, at once socially, morally, and religiously; for not only does the social but the moral and religious law, one and all, enjoin that we should respect the property of others".

Criminal acts were usually described in terms of "dissipation", "profligacy", "idleness", "irregularity", "riot", "debauchery", and "licentiousness". Thus, when he wanted to demonstrate the virtues of Dr Johnson, Boswell asserted that: "In a man whom religious education has secured from licentious indulgence, the passion of love, when once it has seized upon him, is exceeding strong; being unimpaired by dissipation and totally concentrated in one object".

This frame of reference was to be often employed by observers describing Australian convicts. John Dunmore Lang, for example, believed that "The concentration of an emancipated convict population, as Governor Macquarie's experiment sufficiently proves, will infallibly be a concentration of vice and villainy, profligacy and misery, dissipation and ruin."

We have seen crime attributed to necessity, compulsion and poverty; other observers believed that evil-doing had its basic cause in the depravity of the human heart. "Failure and defects [are] inseparable from humanity", wrote Johnson. Edward Gibbon, who could not be reckoned overly religious, perceived it as one of the historian's tasks "to discover the inevitable mixture of error and corruption which she [religion] contracted in a long residence upon earth among a weak and degenerate race of beings".

William Wilberforce (1759-1833) put the matter more bleakly: "From it [Christianity] we learn that man is an apostate creature, fallen from his high original, degraded in his nature and depraved in his faculties: indisposed to good and disposed to evil; prone to vice, it is natural and easy to him; disinclined to virtue, it is difficult and laborious; that he is tainted with sin, not slightly or superficially, but radically, and to the very core".

If crime had these sinful overtones, then turning away from crime was frequently described in terms of religious reformation. Daniel Defoe defined the scope of reformation with some precision:

> "But hark ye William", says I, "the nature of repentance, as you hinted once to me, included reformation, and we can never reform; how then can we repent?"
>
> "Why can we never reform?" says William.
>
> "Because", says I, "we cannot restore what we have taken away by spoil."

More frequently reformation meant a general sorrow for one's sinfulness. To effect this change of heart in the criminal, authorities looked to the Bible and to the Church. However, the Latitudinarian church of the eighteenth century seemed to have little to offer: "Never was there a time when religion in England was at a lower ebb, or when vice was coarser or more shameless."

While Boswell admired the fervour of Mr Moore at the execution of Gibson and Payne and John Wesley was impressed by Mr Vilette, the ordinaries of Newgate were usually seen as defective tools of the law:

> The ordinary of Newgate came to me and talked a little in his way, but all his divinity ran upon confessing my crime, as he called it (though he knew not what I was in for), making a full discovery, and the like, without which he told me God would never forgive me; and he said so little to the purpose that I had no manner of consolation from him; and then to observe the poor creature preaching confession and repentance to me in the morning and find him drunk with brandy by noon—this had something in it so shocking that I began to nauseate the man and his works too by degrees for the sake of the man; so that I desired him to trouble me no more.

More fervent clergymen may have met with some success, but Johnson probably expressed the general level of the clergy's attainment when he said: " 'Sir, one of our regular clergy will probably not impress their [criminals'] minds sufficiently: they should be attended by a Methodist preacher; or a Popish priest.' "

When subordinates perceive a considerable gap between a professed ideal and what is actually accomplished they are often provoked into hostility or cynicism. These attitudes towards religion were adopted by many of the English and Australian convicts. Satire was employed frequently by eighteenth-century writers and in the disparity between the power of organized crime and the helplessness of the law and religion they found scope for their talents.

Not all writers were satirical, of course. No doubt there were many who believed simply and sincerely that in writing cautionary tales they were fostering the spiritual welfare of their readers. Whether satire or edification were their motives, many writers used the components of the criminal biography to achieve their aim. The first of these components was "birth and parentage".

Gibbon believed that this component occurred so frequently in biography that "it must depend on the influence of some common principle in the minds of men". He may have been right, but a sufficient explanation is to be found—at least for western readers—in hagiography, which no doubt was based originally on the biblical precedents, where the Old Testament begins with the origin of Adam and the New Testament with the genealogy of Christ. So frequently does the Old Testament give the antecedents of its personages that the Church Fathers often commented on Melchisedech, whose forbears are not named. The Roman Breviary and the various lives of the saints perpetuated the biblical custom, and it was natural for writers of secular biography to use this time-honoured model. The addition of details about education may possibly be attributed to Calvinistic and Scottish influences.

Despite "good parents" the criminal embarked on a life of crime. Most biographies record the central character's introduction to crime, which was frequently ascribed to weaknesses of character like idleness or vanity or Pope's "ruling passion strong in death". Sometimes the beginning of a life of crime was seen as the result of swearing, sabbath-breaking or gambling. Often criminals blamed "bad companions" for their fall.

Considerable space was given to describing how the character became increasingly wicked. A progress in vice or virtue had been common in popular thought since the late medieval period, when the metaphors of the ladder to heaven or hell became fused with the concept of the stages of the life of man. Hogarth's *Idle Prentice* series is an excellent illustration of the downward path trodden by the eighteenth-century criminal. It should be noted that progress in crime was most frequently represented by the criminal's increasing addiction to alcohol and whoring, or by his adoption by a gang of thieves; thereafter his moral deterioration was conveyed by the frequency and audacity of his criminal acts.

However celebrated the criminal's career, the genre demanded that he be captured. In numerous biographies the criminal is captured many times, sometimes by fate, or through the more obvious agency of the Bow Street Runners, into whose hands he may have been betrayed by his own folly or the treachery of his accomplices. Considerable stress is frequently placed upon the capture which preceded the criminal's execution or transportation.

John Howard (1726-90) observed that the builders of Old Newgate "seem to have regarded in their plan, nothing but the single article of keeping prisoners in safe custody". He discovered many deficiencies in the English prisons, but the indiscriminate bundling together of prisoners was one of the chief defects criticized by many observers. After the loss of freedom, the prisoner's chief source of torment seems to have been his fellow-prisoners.

Gaols had long been demoralizing places. Dekker, for example, concluded that he could

> call a prison an enchanted castle by reason of the rare transformation therein wrought, for it maketh a wise man lose his wits, a fool to know himself. It turns a rich man into a beggar, and leaves a poor man desperate. He whom neither snows nor alps can vanquish but hath a heart as constant as Hannibal's—him can the misery of a prison deject. And how brave an outside soever his mind carries, open his bosom and you see nothing but wounds. Wouldst thou dive into the secret villanies of man? Lie in prison.

"Hell" was a metaphor frequently used to describe prisons. For example, when Tobias Smollett (1762) depicts Sir Lancelot Greaves in prison, the chapter is entitled "In which our Hero descends into the Mansions of the Damned". "The children of wretchedness" seem to have delighted in confirming each other in perdition: "In some gaols you see (and who can see it without sorrow) boys of twelve or fourteen eagerly listening to the stories told by practised criminals of their adventures, successes, stratagems and escapes".

This perverse educative function had been noted by Pepys in 1667: "He [Sir Richard Ford] says also [it] hath been made appear to them [the court of aldermen] that the keeper of Newgate, at This Day, hath made his house the only nursery of rogues and whores and pickpockets in the world; where they were lived and entertained and the whole society met."

Despite Howard's efforts, the prisons remained schools of crime at the end of the eighteenth century: "Convicts discharged from prison and the hulks after suffering the sentence of the law: [are] too often instructed in all the arts and devices which attach to the most extreme degree of human depravity and in the perfect means of perpetrating crimes and eluding justice."

Well into the nineteenth century prisons still retained the image of the *alma mater* for criminals as they picked their way through the *Newgate Calendar.*

Scarcely less intolerable than the shifts of fellow prisoners were the vagaries of justice when the prisoner was finally brought before the court. Some accounts satirized the greed and corruption of lawyers and witnesses. Great stress was frequently laid upon the ceremonial of pronouncing the death sentence. After the imposition of this sentence prisoners often urged their friends to petition for mercy. If mercy was exercised, the sentence was commuted to transportation. If mercy was refused, the criminal underwent the grim ritual of the final service in the chapel and then faced his execution.

Fielding described Wild's execution as his "apotheosis". Earlier, Swift had ironically advised his footman to

> Mount the Cart with Courage. Fall on your knees. Lift up your eyes: Hold a Book in your Hands although you cannot read a word; Deny the fact at the Gallows; Kiss and forgive the hangman and so Farewell: You shall be buried in Pomp at the charge of the Fraternity: The Surgeon shall not touch a limb of you, and your fame shall continue until a successor of equal renown succeeds in your place.

Despite the riotous behaviour around the gallows and the frequent obduracy of the condemned criminal, Shaftesbury believed that the "mere Vulgar of mankind often stand in need of such a rectifying Object as *the Gallows* before their eyes", and Dr Johnson regretted the abolition of the procession to the scaffold (1783) because "the publick was gratified by a procession; the criminal supported by it". Thirty years earlier, Fielding with a magistrate's eye viewed the matter differently:

> His [the convicted felon's] procession to Tyburn and his last moment there, all are triumphant; attended with the compassion of the meek and tender hearted and with the applause, admiration and envy of all the bold and hardened. His behaviour in his present condition, not the crimes how atrocious soever which brought him to it is the subject of contemplation. And if he hath any degree of decency, his death is spoken of by many with honour, by most with pity and by all with approbation.

The irony of the public execution is nowhere better portrayed than in Hogarth's engraving *The Idle 'Prentice Executed at Tyburn* (1747). We see the ordinary ensconced in a carriage while in the tumbril a dissenting minister labours to move the condemned man; the vast throng is in a holiday mood; the dominant foreground figure is that of the ballad singer hawking the last dying speech.

Some criminals escaped execution only to find themselves sentenced to transportation. Although criminals were banished to the American colonies as early as 1607, large-scale transportation did not begin until 1717. Between then and the cessation of transportation in 1767, some 30,000 English and Scots and about 10,000 Irish criminals were transported. It was the custom for gaolers to hand over convicts to contractors who sold their interest in their "cargo" to American planters for the terms of their prisoners' sentences. This phase of penal history appears to have made little impact on the popular imagination either in America or in England:

> The convict element in the composition of early American society long since dropped out of sight, so much so, indeed that it is difficult now [1889] to find even an allusion to it in the literature of the present century. The explanation is not difficult. The convicts scattered over the immense territory of the plantations were so rapidly absorbed in the general population that all traces of their identity were soon lost in the crowd, a result largely owing to the means of reformation afforded them by free grants of land and assistance in the work of cultivation.

Among the first of the few biographies which include transportation is Richard Head's *Meriton Latroon* (1665–71). In the first section of this biography Latroon's life follows the conventional pattern: he is born of prosperous parents and receives a sound education. Having diligently entered upon his indentures, he is led astray by an evil companion and he begins to drink and whore. His progress in crime leads him to associate with gypsies (from whom he learns thieves' cant) and with a gang of thieves. He is caught and finds prison to be "a temporary Hell", and "a place that will learn a young man more villainy if he be apt to take it in six months than at twenty gaming ordinaries, bowling alleys or bawdy houses and an old man more policy than if he had been a pupil to Machiavel". He is released, and after many other adventures is returned at the end of the first part of the book to Newgate, where he exhorts his reader to avoid such a terrible fate and asks forgiveness if any parts of his story have offended against modesty. In the second part we find him and some companions condemned to transportation. In transit they are captured by Turks and experience adventures in Ceylon, Siam, Mauritius and Bantam. Thus, in this biography, transportation plays only a token part.

Fifty years later (1722) Daniel Defoe treated transportation more fully. Moll Flanders is told that "many a Newgate bird becomes a great man" in America, and she certainly prospers there.

Although he is trepanned and not transported, Defoe's Colonel Jacque finds his lot cast with that of transported convicts. The Colonel mentions numerous convicts who prospered on the termination of their sentences. He himself becomes a compassionate overseer and ultimately a well-to-do planter. During his twenty-year sojourn in America he witnesses numerous scenes and encounters many problems that were to recur in Australia. For instance, as an overseer he must decide his attitude to corporal punishment. He resolves to be humane and he is applauded by his master, who abhors flogging as "a Violence upon Nature in every way [and as] the most disagreeable thing in the world to a generous mind". Other problems considered are the cause of crime, remorse, recidivism and the need for penal reform. These issues were to be faced in Australia, but the texture of Defoe's novel differs from its Australian counterparts because *Colonel Jacque* is a picture of a different society. This difference appears very clearly in the steps that were taken to set up the well-conducted American expirees on their own plantations. In the early days, Australian expirees received land grants, but many of these persons frittered their opportunities away and, generally speaking, they did not enjoy the esteem bestowed upon their American counterparts.

Latroon, Moll Flanders and Colonel Jacque were fictional characters; Bampfylde Moore Carew was an historical personage whose life was first written in 1745 and reworked "a couple of dozen" times thereafter. Of "no ordinary and mean Parentage" he early took an "immoderate Delight in several Sports and Exercises" and associated with bad companions and gypsies. He, too, learned cant from these persons and included a cant "dictionary" in his *Life*. After many adventures he was transported for seven years. He was perplexed "Whether at that Period of Time, Mankind was more profligate than usual; or whether there was a more than ordinary Demand for Men in his Majesty's Colonies".

This ironic tone is maintained throughout his account, which includes a brief sketch of his eleven-week voyage to Maryland and a lengthy description of that settlement. Upon landing and being asked his occupation he replied that he was a "Rat-Catcher, Mumper and Dog-Merchant". His prospective masters were nonplussed by this reply and placed him in custody. He absconded, was caught, flogged and loaded with an iron collar. He absconded a second time, and fell in with Indians whose king, Lillycraft, befriended him. After much imposture he contrived to return to England only to be trepanned: "dragg'd to Slavery by the lawless Hand of Power, without the mandate of sovereign Justice". On his second voyage the convicts were racked by a "violent fever". On arrival Carew again managed to escape. Although this expedient was highly dangerous he incurred the risk because he "thought Death preferable to Slavery".

It will become obvious that some of the components and vocabulary of Carew's story are included in Australian convict narratives. It is impossible to determine the extent to which *The King of the Beggars* influenced them but it is quite probable that at least James Hardy Vaux and James Tucker had read Carew's book. Carew's *Life* also appeared in chap-book form which is likely to have been widely disseminated, and thus known to many of the Australian convicts.

Among other eighteenth-century writers who wrote about transportation, Fielding opposed the principle of commuting sentences to transportation: he believed that it was "the sixth encouragement of felons". His disapproval of transportation in itself was indicated by his inclusion of a spurious period of transportation in the life of Jonathan Wild, who was represented as spending his sentence in a "continued scene of whoring, drinking and removing from one place to the other". Later in the century Bentham, Godwin and Coleridge, also opposed transportation.

In the nineteenth century Macaulay recalled the story of 841 Puritans whom Judge Jeffreys (1648-89) sentenced to transportation to the West Indies. More than one fifth of the convicts were "flung to the sharks"; crowding, illness and scanty provisions on board the transport made the survivors so feeble that they had to be fattened before they could be sold. Macaulay found this story in a manuscript, so that in all probability the account was not widely known before he related it.

In all, there would appear to be little evidence that the first convicts transported to Australia knew much about transportation. It is true that Lord George Gordon (1751-93) transmitted to Pitt and the keepers at Newgate "a petition from the prisoners at Newgate to Lord George Gordon praying him to prevent them from being sent to Botany Bay", but the petition appears to have been a function of Gordon's dementia rather than an expression of the general will of Newgate. Watkin Tench reported that the first convicts felt apprehension at leaving their homeland but he did not say that they feared the horrors of transportation. The accounts of the first convicts were so confused and fragmentary that it is obvious that they had no models to fall back upon when they described their Australian experience. Head, Carew and Defoe may have influenced later writers like Vaux and Tucker, but a sufficient explanation of similarities may be found in experiences and sentiments which convicts transported to America and Australia had in common. (pp. 7-28)

William Godwin had come to maturity by the time the First Fleet set out for Australia in 1787. By that year he had abandoned religious belief; he had also become a republican. (In many ways, his shifts in intellectual position and his varying fortunes make his career similar to that of the more prominent convicts sent to Australia.) In the 1790s he published three books which set out his political theories.

One of these books, *The Adventures of Caleb Williams or Things as They Are,* was a novel, written as "a general review of the modes of domestic and unrecorded despotism by which a man becomes the destroyer of man".

To his usual research in religion and politics Godwin added, as a preparation for this book, the reading of works like "God's Revenge against Murder" and he became "tremendously conversant with the *Newgate Calendar* and the *Lives of the Pirates*". He was therefore familiar with a range of literary treatments of crime and the criminal.

In Godwin's novel, Caleb Williams, of poor and humble stock, receives a sound but rudimentary education before becoming secretary to the wealthy Falkland. A precursor of the Byronic hero, Falkland is led by "the persecution of malignant destiny" to murder a "tyrannical" squire, Tyrrel. Falkland suffers paroxysms of guilt, both for the

murder and for allowing others to be convicted for it. He purges his guilt by admitting it to a sympathetic court. Then he dies.

Falkland has other grounds for remorse: through his imprudent curiosity Williams discovers his master's secret. Falkland falsely accuses him of theft and Williams embarks upon a flight which leads him among a gang of thieves. He is arrested and cast into prison where he suffers from the caprice of gaolers and the villainy of his fellow captives. He is eventually exonerated but remains miserable knowing that he was in some sense responsible for Falkland's exposure and death.

Godwin's debt to the popular tradition is obvious. He was also indebted to the gothic novels for the portrait of Falkland. Like the convicts and officials who had recently settled in Australia, Godwin was heir to centuries of tradition. At the end of the eighteenth century the beaten track can be seen to split into two paths. Godwin took one path. He would be followed by Dickens, Ainsworth, Bulwer Lytton and many others. The convicts and their observers stumbled along the other path. They had no difficulty in describing their journey to the parting of the ways, but for what lay ahead there was no precedent. The mapping of the new path would produce a new literature. (pp. 28-30)

A. W. Baker, "The Background," in his Death Is a Good Solution: The Convict Experience in Early Australia, *University of Queensland Press, 1984, pp. 1-30.*

CHARACTERISTICS OF AUSTRALIAN LITERATURE

Ken Goodwin

[*Goodwin is an Australian educator and critic. In the following essay, he discusses the defining characteristics of Australian literature.*]

Land and language have been the two major rival determinants of written literature in Australia. Two hundred years ago, in 1788, white settlers, bringing with them an alphabetically written language, the concept of a distinction between literature and utilitarian or ephemeral writing, and the technology for producing multiple copies of what needed to be widely disseminated, came to establish a penal colony for Britain. A colony, penal or otherwise, immediately establishes a tension between the introduced culture, with its language, law, education and scale of values, and the indigenous qualities of the land that is settled and its existing inhabitants. A sense of exile may, through the perspective of distance, sharpen appreciation and assessment of the homeland, but it can also be an inhibiting factor in coming to terms with the new circumstances. The initial puzzlement, incomprehension and near-despair of some of the first white colonists in Australia was offset by the enterprise, curiosity, and wonderment of others. Many convicts and free settlers, together with some officers and soldiers, soon realised that this was no temporary exile but a new home, with qualities different from those of the British Isles.

The contrast between gloom and hope runs roughly parallel to the contrast between colonialism and nationalism in the first century or so of settlement. Language, with its often unrecognized cultural biases, tended to pull the settlers back towards British values. The land, with its many phenomena unnamable in the English language, tended to pull them towards a sense of national uniqueness.

British values were, of course, often disguised as universal values, though from at least the last two decades of the nineteenth century a genuine internationalism was advocated by J. F. Archibald and others as an antidote to purely British literary and cultural values. Opposition to British values was often also a disguised form of support for Irish culture and political aspirations. From early in the period of transportation a high proportion of convicts were of Irish origin and they, with Irish settlers and officers, formed the nucleus of a vociferous and influential element in Australian culture. While the present-day population of Australia has fewer than 20 per cent of Irish origin,

the contribution of the Irish to Australian literature has been very substantially greater.

Australia still contains substantial numbers of advocates for cultural colonialism (the 'cultural cringe'), who emphasize commonality with and derivativeness from Britain. They exist alongside vociferous nationalists—advocates, for instance, of republicanism and a new national flag—and those who reject both colonialism and nationalism in favour either of internationalism (that is, emancipation from the pull of both language and land) or of personal withdrawal and self-identification (that is, emancipation from all social pressures, expectations and categories).

These divisions in Australian culture, literature, and criticism bear no close correlation with the purely literary division between the solid descriptiveness of social realism on the one hand and a more ironic, poetic, romantic or comic mode on the other. Social realists tend to be left-wing nationalists, but many left-wing nationalists (such as Xavier Herbert) are far from being social realists, and some would-be social realists, such as Katharine Susannah Prichard, are really romance writers. In any case, the modes of fiction in Australian writing, as in other literatures, became very mixed from the 1960s onwards, and all

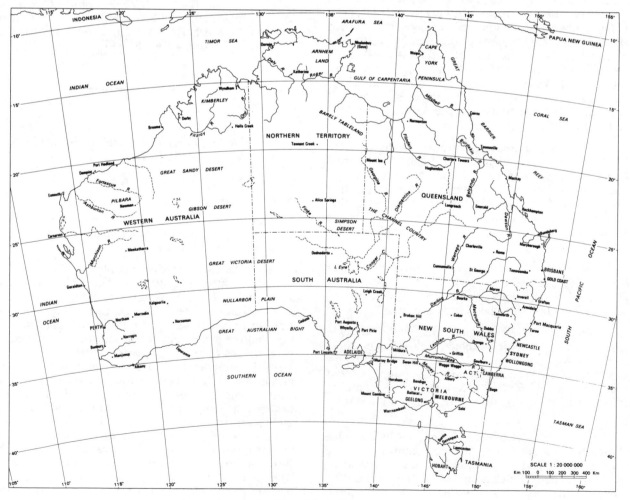

Map of Australia.

one can say now is that pure social realism is a discredited mode.

The same period is also one in which two groups of writers, Aborigines and non-English-speaking migrants, have come to prominence. Both groups have cause to express a sense of alienation from land and from language. Both have lost their homelands and both are required to use an alien tongue.

For at least a hundred years, there has also been another kind of alienation from the land expressed by settlers of British and Irish origin. The early sense of the land's hostility was replaced by a sense of its possibilities for the creation of agricultural, pastoral and mineral wealth, but the success of large ventures of this type enabled substantial numbers of people to become urbanized. As a result, from the latter part of the nineteenth century onwards literature reflects a continuing opposition between the interests of country-dwellers and those of city-dwellers. The expression 'Sydney or the bush' is a product of urban preference for the easier life of a city and contempt for the discomforts and lack of pastimes in the bush. Even today, writers often align themselves in their preference for subjects and values with one side or the other of this choice.

For a variety of reasons and from a variety of cultural backgrounds, writers in Australia have emphasized such themes as the search for identity by a wanderer or explorer, the establishment of a habitation and family line, the quest to recover the past, the sense of being an outcast, and the threat of impending violence. The wanderer or explorer, in the work of such writers as Furphy, Brennan, Herbert, McAuley, White or Stow, is likely to be more engaged on a metaphysical quest than a topographical one, though it is often the strangeness and featurelessness of what he encounters that leads to dissociation from previous accepted standards and even to madness. The exploratory quest to discover what lay at the heart of the continent—a quest not completed until the early twentieth century—provided a natural metaphor for the exploration of the country of the mind.

The urge to settle the country, to tame the frontier, to acquire such tracts of land as the Old Country could not provide and to found a dynasty was both an historical fact and a literary commonplace—as it was in the prairie literature of Canada. One difference between the more popular and romantic treatments of this myth and the treatment by such writers as Henry Handel Richardson, Brian Penton and Patrick White is that the former tend towards triumphant success, the latter towards ironic incapacity by nature or human genetics.

The quest for the past, associated through the operation of memory with the attempt to align chronological and experiential measurements of time or to escape entirely from the dominance of chronological measurement, has been a major feature of Australian literature, especially from the 1930s onwards. Historical novels from at least *His Natural Life* pursue this theme, but so too do poets such as Fitz-Gerald, Wright, Shapcott and Malouf. The search is rarely, however, for a lost Eden, for historically the beginnings of white settlement in Australia were brutal and dismal.

The outcast figure may be a runaway convict, a bushranger, an Aboriginal or a new migrant. *His Natural Life* is the quintessential escaped-convict novel, *Robbery under Arms* probably the best of the bushranger novels. *Capricornia, Poor Fellow my Country, The Chant of Jimmie Blacksmith*, and *A Kindness Cup* are competent treatments of Aborigines by white writers, and the novels of Colin Johnson the best historical works by an Aboriginal writer. The new migrant is represented by treatments both of the 'new chum' in literature of the 1890s and of the non-English-speaking newcomer in the work of many recent ethnic writers.

A sense of oppression, loneliness, alienation, and fear is often symbolized by or is preliminary to violence or the threat of violence. Australian literature, in novels, stories, plays and poems, is a literature of violence in its treatment of judicial punishment, male-female relationships, gang warfare and declared war. Literature about convicts is inevitably full of brutality; what is more surprising is a similar brutality in the work of writers as diverse as Patrick White, Thea Astley, David Ireland, Roger McDonald, Colin Johnson and Archie Weller. Its presence is often associated with a sense of the absence or fragility of culture, a sense that culture is never here and now but always elsewhere or at another time.

Whatever its theme, Australian literature in its characterization and its own literary character is in large measure a literature of persistence, endurance and repetition almost beyond endurance. These are qualities of man's experience against the continent, of course, and they are the qualities often evident in its fictional representation. But they are also qualities of construction and style. Australian authors wear down and wear out their readers by the repetition of horrors, instances of similar incidents, lists of details, or stylistic mannerisms. Bush ballads, with their insistent, inevitable refrains, practise seduction by exhaustion. Marcus Clarke piles sensation on sensation, horror on horror, sorrow on sorrow to produce an effect of weariness of spirit and a sense of the insupportability of life. Joseph Furphy makes his story-telling so heavy-laden with its recondite references that a similar sense of surrender by the reader to the impression willed by the writer occurs. There is a similar unrelenting quality in Henry Handel Richardson and Xavier Herbert. In the modern short story many writers amass detail to nullify resistance by the reader or to reduce the reader to a state of nervous tension, waiting for the repeated pattern to be lifted. Patrick White characterizes his creations with detail after detail, long after the general impression has been gained. Hal Porter amasses stroke after feline stroke. John Bryson creates through repetition a sense of nervous tension, of fearful expectation. Peter Carey sometimes seems merciless in his tolerance of repetition. Frank Moorhouse uses repetition for his characteristic mixture of black humour and nervous strain.

Perhaps this stylistic quality operates as an analogue of the land itself. Whatever the reason though, Australian literature has within it frequently an air of infinitude, timelessness, changelessness, endless space, the still moment out of time, and the endless progress through space. It is, once again, a characteristic found also in the Canadian prairie novel. It is, in fact, a common characteristic of imperial-pioneering literature in various countries. Boundlessness and timelessness can represent either absence of cultural landmarks or a return to the void of Nature or the loss of self-identity or a mystical union with the divine. All of these possibilities are laid out in Australian writing—all can, for instance, be found in the novels of Patrick White and Randolph Stow, as they can in various degrees in the late Romanticism of Harpur, Kendall, Gordon, Clarke, Lawson and Furphy. Such writers often begin from the premise that Australia is a materialistic society, bordering on philistinism, and hence liable to alienate and despise its writers. Novels about writers or other artists who are ill at ease with their environment have been a staple of Australian writing since the 1930s.

Writing in Australia obviously began as a literature metaphorically in chains, the shackles of British expectations of what a colony and its writing should be. New South Wales was a colony founded before the Romantic revival had made an impact in Britain, and it is not surprising that in modes of writing, as in styles of architecture, the new colony clung to eighteenth-century Georgian models long after they had fallen out of fashion in Britain. In time, the Romantic ethos spread from Britain to Australia. Because of its emphasis on the communion of the poet with the surroundings, on spontaneity and on the individual alone in the landscape it was perhaps a more appropriate model for describing a newly discovered kind of nature. At any rate Romanticism and post-Romanticism served as the prevailing modes for poetry and prose until the second half of the twentieth century. *Le néant,* the void, the essential hollowness of existence is a characteristic concern of post-Romantic nineteenth-century Europe. In Australia the bush in its melancholy aspects and the oppressed or fugitive nature of convictism are the commonest symbols of personal solitude and despair. Whatever symbols are used, however, the void is a central concern of such writers as Harpur, Lawson, Brennan, Richardson, Wright, Hope and White as it is of mid-twentieth-century painters such as Russell Drysdale, Sidney Nolan and Arthur Boyd.

Twentieth-century modernism was a late arrival, in visual art and in literature. Despite some flutterings of experimentalism by Slessor and a small number of others in the 1930s and the efforts of the *Angry Penguins* group in the 1940s, most Australian poets wrote in a Romantic style into the 1960s. Then, in a sudden bound that bypassed such modern masters as T. S. Eliot, the mode changed to the American tradition of William Carlos Williams, Black Mountain and the New York poets. At about the same time fiction writers discovered the ludic and ironic modes, and playwrights caught up with Brecht.

Some chauvinistic critics would find such statements contentious. There is some hostility in Australia to the whiggish notion that Australian literature has experienced 'development', partly on ideological grounds about the nature of literary history, partly on xenophobic, especially anglophobic, grounds that development may imply imitation at a temporal distance of some external model. Antipathy to such tendentious statements as 'Australian litera-

ture is a branch of English literature, and however great it may become and whatever characteristics it may develop, it will remain a branch' is understandable. It is understandable too that much structuralist theory, with its emphasis on synchronic pattern, is not easily able to accommodate long periods of history. This account of Australian literary history does not, however, seek to avoid notions of periodicity. Nor does it accept the crasser forms of either the theory that literature is determined by its social origins or the theory that literature is entirely self-referential. It is a study that seeks to be eclectic in its notion of what constitutes a literary work and in its acceptance of the value of both plain and tropological modes. Australian literature in its rich variety is not amenable to critical reductionism. (pp. 1-7)

> *Ken Goodwin, "The Nature of Australian Literature," in his* A History of Australian Literature, *St. Martin's Press, 1986, pp. 1-7.*

T. Inglis Moore

[*In the following excerpt from his study* Social Patterns in Australian Literature, *Moore defines and analyzes the most prominent social traits reflected in Australian literature.*]

This study originated, aptly enough, in "the *Bulletin* pub", the hotel near the *Bulletin* office in George Street, Sydney, whose bar had been the happy rendezvous of Australian writers for decades. There Roderic Quinn, Frank Davison and I were drinking and yarning one day when we were joined by the late Percy Lindsay. Beer in hand, radiating his genial charm, Percy told a story of the days when he, his brother Norman, and other artists were painting in a small settlement outside Melbourne. On Saturday nights they forgathered at the local pub and were good friends with the pubkeeper and his daughter Molly. One night when they were engaged as usual in drinking, singing, and arguing over art, life, and women, Molly came over to them and said, "I'm sorry, boys, but would you mind breaking it down a bit."

They were taken aback at this unusual request, and at their look of surprise she explained, apologetically, "Dad's gone and hanged himself in the woodshed."

"And sure enough," said Percy, "there was the poor bastard hanging from a rafter, dead as a doornail. He had his mouth half open in a funny way, and looked a bit grim. We had quite a job getting him down."

This story struck me as peculiarly Australian in many ways: in its matter-of-fact realism, with a dash of hardness, hinting at the callous; its sombreness, with a touch of the macabre; its stoic lack of emotion or melodrama, shown in the girl's laconic announcement of her father's suicide; the understatement, both emotional and verbal, with the meiosis of the idiomatic "a bit" used by both Molly and Percy; the easy, friendly democratic equality with which she treated the artists in her "I'm sorry, boys"; the kindly, almost "matey" consideration in her apology for disturbing them; and the ironic contrast between the revelling of the artists in the bar and the grimness of their host's body suspended in the woodshed, suggesting the harsh irony familiar to a people living in a land where the bounty of a good season is soon mocked by the death and desolation of the drought. Australian, too, is the conjunction of care-free pleasure and calm endurance, the hedonism of the artists complementing the stoicism of the pubkeeper's daughter.

This story, with its distinctive combination of characteristics, could not have occurred in any other country than Australia. In England, for instance, the daughter of a local innkeeper would not have treated a group of professional men with such egalitarian camaraderie. An American account of the suicide would have been marked by over-statement rather than under-statement. In any European country Dad could not have hanged himself in the woodshed without arousing emotion and drama.

Listening to Percy Lindsay's story, I was immediately reminded of certain tales and sketches of Henry Lawson that embodied the same qualities—"The Union Buries its Dead", "The Bush Undertaker", "In a Dry Season", and "The Drover's Wife". Afterwards I looked them up, and was impressed by their strong and unmistakable rendering of basic Australian ideas and sentiments. So I began a general search into our literature to see how far, as a body of national writing, it expressed distinctive ways of life and thought and feeling, working inductively to discover what the literature itself revealed to an objective analysis.

[*Social Patterns in Australian Literature*] then, is the result of that search. It is a sociological study, although its primary source material is Australian creative and critical writing, reinforced by some relevant historical work. It has a double concern, first with *what* the social patterns are, and then with *why* they developed as they did. The exploration of their origins goes beyond the literature to draw on biology, geography, and history in presenting an ecological synthesis.

In the first concern the literature is taken as a social mirror reflecting those traits of sentiment and outlook distinguishing a particular society which are best called *social patterns*. These are associated as a complex in which a common home in a country, common blood, a common language and literature, a common system of government, education and religion, all serve to unite the members of a society, make it a community, and give it a collective spirit that differentiates it from other societies. Although various societies have similar social patterns, each has a special combination of them which is distinctive.

Since societies are organized in a national framework, it is said that national literatures reflect national characteristics. In his ingenious and often penetrating study, *Englishmen, Frenchmen, Spaniards,* Salvador de Madariaga contends that

> However hasty these sketches of national types may be, they have the merit of establishing beyond doubt the great fact which many a dogmatic internationalist would have us forget. There *is* such a thing as national character. Opinions may differ as to the influences which create or alter it. Race, climate, economic conditions, may enter for a greater or a lesser part in its inception

and development. But the fact is there and stares us in the face. History, geography, religion, language, even the common will are not enough to define a nation. A nation is a fact of psychology. It is that which is *natural* or *native* in it which gives its force to the word *nation*. A nation is a character.

Even granting that there is such a thing as "national character", the fact remains that the word "national" today carries many confusing connotations, whilst the term "national characteristics" often implies unscientific assumptions of racial psychology and inherited group qualities. If a nation is a fact, sometimes an elusive and ambiguous one, a race is frequently only an ancillary myth employed for political ends. A society, however, is a concrete fact which is clear and definite. The term "social", moreover, is wider than "national", whilst it retains a more objective character, free of the restrictive sentiments and confusing prejudices evoked by "national". Historically it is more precise here, since Australia developed a distinctive society with its own *mores* long before it evolved into the further stage of nationhood. Where "national characteristics" may be suspect, therefore, "social patterns" can be used objectively and with historical aptness.

At the same time, most, if not all, of the social patterns discussed have become accepted over the years by Australians generally, so that they have finally developed into national traditions. Indeed, I might well have used the term "national traditions" correctly in a broad sense, and it was tempting to adopt such a popular usage. The temptation was resisted, however, for the sake of exactness, since a tradition connotes a general conscious acceptance of it by society, whereas several of the patterns have not yet gained this explicit recognition, even if they are recognized unconsciously and implicitly.

Moreover, the term "social patterns" is more suitable to a consideration of the social element in literature and its relation to the other two elements contained in literature as a work of art, the personal and the universal. In this triad of art the personal element is the one most easily apparent in every literary work, which is *sui generis,* an individuation as a specific utterance of the writer's personality, unique as embodying the flesh, blood, and mind of its creator. It is determined by his special beliefs—a complex which has never occurred before in exactly the same shape and will never happen again. None of us can ever escape from the irrevocable fate of always being ourselves. We are all bound to the Promethean rock of our ego by unbreakable chains. All writing, even the most imaginative, is ultimately autobiographical, spun with thread drawn, like a spider's web, from the body of the writer's perceptions and thoughts, dreams and desires and memories.

Every great work also contains a universal element that goes beyond person, time and place. It is shaped into a form that expresses the thoughts and feelings common to mankind and recognizable as such. Without abdicating personality, it also transcends it to reach the plane of the universal. The writer can then proclaim with Walt Whitman: "I pass death with the dying and birth with the new-wash'd babe, and am not contain'd between my hat and boots." With such a passing into the universal the poet can sound his "barbaric yawp", not merely to himself or a shocked, unbelieving America, but "over the roofs of the world". He creates, in Shelley's phrasing of the poet's task, "Forms more real than living man, Nurslings of Immortality". Whether a writer has created such forms is determined by the judgement of time and men.

This power of endurance, bred of a happy marriage between artistic form and significant content, is the specific literary quality in any writing. It is more important, of course, than any personal or social element since it alone connotes survival, whether in a limited degree within a national literature or in full-blown universality as a work of world literature.

Here, for the special purpose of this study, our concern is concentrated on the third element in literature, the social one. Whatever his personal or universal character, every writer is also a part of his society, his country, and his century. As Sir Leslie Stephen pointed out in his *English Literature and Society in the Eighteenth Century:*

> Every writer may be regarded in various aspects. He is, of course, an individual, and the critic may endeavour to give a psychological analysis of him. . . . But every man is also an organ of the society in which he has been brought up. The material upon which he works is the whole complex of conceptions, religious, imaginative, and ethical, which forms his mental atmosphere. Fully to appreciate any great writer, therefore, it is necessary to distinguish between the characteristics due to the individual with certain idiosyncrasies and the characteristics due to his special modification by the existing stage of social and intellectual development.

Thus Dante and Shakespeare were social writers who reflected their times: "The *Divina Commedia* also reveals in the completest way the essential spirit of the Middle Ages", whilst "If any man ever initiated and gave full utterance to the characteristic ideas of his contemporaries it was Shakespeare, and nobody ever accepted more thoroughly the forms of art which they worked out". Indeed, it is impossible to imagine Shakespeare writing characteristically as a Frenchman, a contemporary of Pope, or a mid-Victorian. Despite his universality he is nothing if not an Englishman and an Elizabethan.

The social element is naturally marked in literature since of all the arts it contains the greatest conceptual content. It is more concrete than such arts as painting, sculpture and music, which contain more of the abstract and approach closer to pure form, a point illustrated by the masterly discussion of the abstract and concrete elements in music by Albert Schweitzer in his illuminating *J. S. Bach.* A sonata or a statue may contain little but the pure formal beauty of sound or shape, but a novel or short story, drama or epic, even a lyrical poem, has a content which naturally tends to hold some social significance as it describes humanity or nature, tells a story, fashions a character, depicts human action, or voices feelings and ideas.

Literature, although it exists primarily for its own sake, is also a function of its society. It fulfils the purpose of acting, as defined by Hamlet to the players: "to hold, as 'twere, the mirror up to nature; to show virtue her own feature, scorn her own image, and the very age and body of the time his form and pressure". Hence literature becomes, in Taine's phrase, "a transcript of contemporary manners, a manifestation of a certain kind of mind". This manifestation may be made in two different ways: through the content of the work, with its scene, action, and characters, or through the writer, expressing his personal outlook and sympathies.

Similarly, the social element with its patterns may be expressed either implicitly or explicitly. It is usually implicit in the attitude of the writer to his subject, and even nonsocial poets like Neilson and McCrae express it unconsciously in this way. On the whole, however, the social patterns find a conscious articulation in Australian writing, just as they do with the majority of modern writers in England, Europe, and America—with Shaw, Wells, and Joyce, T. S. Eliot and Greene; with Toller, Thomas Mann, Sartre, and Pirandello; with Hemingway, Steinbeck, and Faulkner. In contemporary American writing the strength of the social element has been well described in an article in *The Times Literary Supplement* [16 August 1957] on the "American Way":

> It is the commitment of every American writer to express and explore something of the American identity, the American way of life, of that elusive state of mind which makes an American an American, which makes all Americans, whatever clothes they wear, or jobs they hold, equal, which is symbolized not by a queen, not even by a President, but by an abstract flag, the Stars and Stripes.

Australian writers, especially the novelists and short story writers, are similarly committed to exploration of their own world and its way of life, creating a *littérature engagée.*

In any literature this social element is generally mingled with the personal one without any contradiction, since the writer is a social being as well as an individual. Part of his personality, at least, is determined by his environment, including the cultural matrix in which he is embedded. Thus the great majority of Australian writers express some of the prevailing social patterns. The strongest representations of the national traditions come from such writers of fiction as Henry Lawson, Joseph Furphy, and Katharine Susannah Prichard, and such poets as O'Dowd, Mary Gilmore, and Judith Wright, who are especially social and national in outlook. In their case the personal and social elements are closely identified with each other.

At the same time the social element, like the personal and universal elements, varies considerably in character and degree with each writer. It is negligible in a few writers who live in their own imaginative worlds and seem to owe little to the world around them. This occurs with poets rather than novelists and dramatists. Walter de la Mare offers a fit example in modern English writing, Christopher Brennan in Australian literature. Only a few poems of Brennan's deal with the local scene or contain such images drawn from his native background as "My days of azure have forgotten me". His true skies, however, were not Australian but European, in which shone his guiding lights of French symbolism and German romanticism. His poetry, as he himself said, might as well have been written in China as in his own country. He was never happily at home here, remaining, as Hugh McCrae put it inimitably, "a star in exile, unconstellated at the south". Yet even he expressed, as we shall see, some Australian qualities.

So, too, in fiction Henry Handel Richardson drew upon European naturalism for her outlook and technique. As an expatriate she wavered in her attitude towards her homeland: she stated in one letter that she had always considered herself a good Australian; in another she wrote, "Hartley Grattan is beginning to think that I am not a good enough Australian. God forbid that I ever should be!" Yet she confessed in *Myself when Young* that she was strongly influenced by the Australian environment of her youth, she drew her themes largely from her experiences within it, and she became the most powerful exponent of the realistic spirit common to most Australian novelists. Richardson fits into our scope, therefore, whilst writers like Brennan find a relatively small place in a study of social patterns in Australian literature for the same reason that Professor Parrington gives scant consideration in his *Main Currents in American Thought* to Edgar Allan Poe, who stood apart from such currents.

Any disregard of non-social writers here does not, of course, reflect in any way upon their artistic merit, since the social and universal elements are distinct. There is no necessary correlation between them. The folk ballads and Henry Lawson, for example, are both rich in social significance, but the ballads lack literary form whilst Lawson is an original artist in the short story. Brennan is a fine poet who has little Australian content, but his compeers in Neilson, FitzGerald, Slessor, and Judith Wright are deeply concerned with their Australian earth and society. Usually the Australianity of a writer and his literary quality are commingled and unified; sometimes they bear no relation to each other.

Indeed, the distinction between the social and universal elements, or, to use the more common phrasing, between national and literary values, is a clear and elementary one which should not need discussion. Yet the failure to make this fundamental distinction has caused considerable confusion in Australian literary criticism. On the one hand the two elements have often been fallaciously equated, on the other they have been opposed in a false contradiction.

The confusion is common amongst nationalist critics who tend to assume that if a work is strongly Australian in subject and outlook it is *ipso facto* a good one; if it is not Australian it is bad. The more national a work is, the better it is. A nationalist inflation was displayed in the worship of Gordon by his devotees, the idolizing of Lawson as a poet by his old mates, and Miles Franklin's claim that Furphy is superior to Henry James, Proust, and Joyce.

The bias of an ardent nationalism produced in turn an equally unbalanced reaction from critics who tended, in their eagerness to affirm literary standards, to go to the other extreme and fall into the fallacy of assuming that if a work was wholeheartedly Australian it must be bad.

They assumed, implicitly as a rule, that to be universal a writer should be un-Australian or even anti-Australian.

In both of these cases an irrelevant non-literary criterion—the presence or the absence of national values—was used to make judgements on literature. In particular the anti-nationalist bias has had a curious, anachronistic revival since the last world war. The flogging of the dead nationalist horse has persisted long after the writers themselves, both in prose and in poetry, have passed beyond nationalism to a natural, mature acceptance of the world they live in.

A rootless cosmopolitanism, furthermore, is as shallow as the sentimental nationalism of the past. Nor should this be confused with a true universality, which arises out of the particular. The anti-nationalist of today shudders at the mention of an unabashed gumtree, that crude Australian object of the bush which comes between the wind and his sophisticated, urban nobility. Then Judith Wright disposes of this attitude convincingly by her "Gum-trees Stripping", a beautiful lyric that combines a universality of concept with concrete, imaginative particulars:

> Wisdom can see the red, the rose,
> the stained and sculptured curve of grey,
> the charcoal scars of fire, and see
> around that living tower of tree
> the hermit tatters of old bark
> split down and strip to end the season;
> and can be quiet and not look
> for reasons past the edge of reason.

Thus Judith Wright shows that the despised tree can call forth, no less than a classical myth, lyrical power and depth of vision, with "this fountain slowed in air" turned into a universal symbol of the "silent rituals" of seasonal earth. The fault, dear Brutus, is not in our gum-trees, but in ourselves if we are underlings unable to create high poetry out of them, or, indeed, to create enduring literature out of the Australian world we live in. Shaw Neilson, who joins Judith Wright as one of the two finest Australian lyrists, can similarly make a subtle, intangible magic out of a common orange-tree or transmute a mushroom into autumnal enchantment. In fact, the best of Australian writing in poetry and prose alike, with only a few exceptions, strikes its roots deep into its own earth and its own people.

This leads to the fundamental point that the social and universal elements, the national and the literary, are not in themselves opposed or contradictory. They may be dissociated, but in general they join harmoniously in the work of literature. The great writers are usually both national and international. Louis Esson, whose ideal was the building up in Australia of an indigenous theatre expressing the national spirit, has drawn attention to the sound comments of a leading French author on this precise point:

> The position of the writer in relationship to his country and to humanity in general has been stated clearly and justly by André Gide. In an address given in Paris to an international group of writers, Gide declared that no one was more specifically Spanish than Cervantes, more English than Shakespeare, more Russian than

Gogol, more French than Rabelais or Voltaire, and at the same time more universal and more profoundly human, his contention being that it is precisely in literature that this triumph of the general in the particular and of the human in the individual is most fully realised. [*Australian Writers Speak,* a series of talks arranged by the Fellowship of Australian Writers for the Australian Broadcasting Commission (Sydney, 1942)]

It might be added that in Australian literature no one is more specifically Australian than Lawson, and at the same time "more universal and more profoundly human". Thus Mitchell is both swaggie and sardonic Hamlet of the bush. Joe Wilson, the struggling selector, is also the lover and the father. Australian to the core, he is also Everyman.

Esson also drives home his point where he says sensibly:

> The Australian writer asks no more than is taken for granted by the writers of every other country.
>
> No one would accuse Balzac, Dickens, or Tolstoy of being local or provincial, lacking in universal appeal, because their subject comprised characters and themes typical of their own country and period. As Havelock Ellis once put it, "the paradox of literature is that only the writer who is first truly national can later become international."

The great majority of Australian writers are certainly "truly national", since here the literature, like the society it mirrors, developed a distinctive character of its own. Again, the national or social element is especially strong in Australian literature for several reasons. To begin with, it is stronger than in some other literatures simply because Australian writing, being younger than they are, is more concerned with exploring its environment. Older literatures, having already made this exploration and arrived at definitions of their societies as geographical and national entities, have often passed on to more universal concerns, such as metaphysical issues and the intimate processes of the mind. Australian literature is still highly localized, particularly in its fiction; over-busied with description of its external surroundings. Whilst this local exploring places limits on fiction's literary value, since it conduces at times to a superficial concentration on externals and results in reportage instead of creative imagination, it produces, on the other hand, a richness of social content.

A strong social consciousness, moreover, has always been a characteristic of Australian writing. This finds expression not only in an exploration of its environment but also in two other forms: the depiction of social groups rather than of individuals, and a criticism of society which springs from the characteristically Australian demands for democratic equality and social justice.

The social group has always been particularly stressed in Australian writing. From the beginning, when Kingsley, Clarke, and Boldrewood concentrated on such social themes as the life of the pastoralists, the convict system, and bushranging, the novelists have been concerned with depicting communities and occupational groups. Their approach has been communal, not individual, whether it

was Furphy rendering the Riverina world of teamsters and squatters, the host of historical novelists tracing the fortunes of the pioneers, the social realists giving critical accounts of contemporary society, or the reformers attacking the social problem of the aborigines. A representative novelist like Katharine Prichard describes such groups as timber-workers, pioneers, squatters and aborigines in the north-west, opal miners and gold miners. Another, like Kylie Tennant, ranges from the country town, bagmen on the dole, and city slum-dwellers to coastal villagers, juvenile delinquents, and travelling bee-keepers. The result of this dominant trend is that fiction has often lacked the depth and universality of individual character, but shown abundance of social description and criticism. Some novelists such as Prichard, Vance Palmer, and M. Barnard Eldershaw combine character and environment, but relatively few novelists—with exceptions like Richardson, Eleanor Dark, and Christina Stead—concentrated on the psychology of the individual until the last two decades, which has been marked by the psychological novels of such writers as White, Stow, Astley, Harrower, and Keneally.

So, too, the lively social conscience which flourishes in the Australian society appears in its writing as an important aspect of the pattern of radicalism. This radical strain has produced a wealth of social criticism from the folk ballads through the poems, novels, and short stories of the nationalist period down to the contemporary fiction of social realists and the verse of the left-wing poets.

The poetry, however, has been more universal in character and less highly localized than the fiction, since it is predominantly lyrical and so concerned with the emotions common to all mankind. Love and hate, anger and grief transcend all national frontiers. The poets, moreover, have often been preoccupied with universal concepts and metaphysical questions such as the nature of the universe, the meaning of life, and the problem of time. A tradition of philosophical poets has been established, running from Brennan and O'Dowd to Wilmot and Baylebridge, FitzGerald, Mary Gilmore and Judith Wright. Just as the poets have produced more universal thinking than have the novelists until the coming of Patrick White, so they have become more advanced in completing their assimilation to the environment. This advance has enabled them to use their country as a natural background, not to keep it in the foreground as the novelists tend to do, but to pass on to wider fields of thought and feeling. The advance in assimilation has been aptly phrased by "a distinguished Australian poet and critic" in an article in a *Current Affairs Bulletin*: "The best Australian poetry today gives the impression of poets who start *from* the local scene as something given, rather than the impression the older poetry gave of poets who aimed *at* the local scene as something to be domesticated in literature. ["Standards in Australian Literature", anonymous article (by A. D. Hope) in *Current Affairs Bulletin,* 26 November 1956]

On the other hand, there has also been a strong social strain amongst the poets, occurring even in such lyrists as McCrae and Neilson. The bulk of the lyrical poetry has been descriptive, limning the country and the feelings it has inspired. In contemporary poetry there has been a development of other forms than the lyric, such as satire, drama, and the narrative. These forms naturally contain more of the social element than the pure or descriptive lyric. Thus Paul Grano, A. D. Hope, James McAuley and Bruce Dawe offer satirical comments on the national society. Douglas Stewart deals with history in his drama *Shipwreck* and with a national tradition in his *Ned Kelly*. Stewart, FitzGerald, Slessor, Francis Webb, and Judith Wright have given tales and pictures of the explores, adventurers, and pioneers, creating a new significance out of the nation's past. They are myth-makers building up from history and legend viable concepts of the Australian heritage. They are fulfilling the ideal of the Jindyworobak movement of the 1930s in creating new "environmental values", although they stand apart from the Jindyworobak poets, who voiced their fervent nationalism in a cult of the aborigine and a mystique of the soil.

The social approach of many contemporary poets only follows, however, a social tradition in poetry going back to the folk ballads. Whatever their crudeness of literary form, the old bush songs and ballads gave a clear and often forceful articulation to the people's ideas and feelings, offering a wealth of social history and repository of Australian social patterns. This tradition was continued by the *Bulletin* literary balladists of the nineties, so that Lawson and Paterson, Dyson, Ogilvie and a host of other bush balladists gave graphic accounts of bush life and formulated as a permanent, seminal tradition of Australian literature and society the indigenous social patterns which had gradually evolved, decades before, in the pastoral age. This formulation was particularly effective as a social force because the balladists spoke the language of the people and expressed popular sentiments so that they found their audience not in a few literary readers but in a whole nation. A further formulation, more conscious, more intellectual, and more purposive, was provided by poets who were also thinkers and social reformers—Bernard O'Dowd, Frank Wilmot as "Furnley Maurice", and Mary Gilmore.

This development of the social tradition moves in the dimension of time. Each age will have its own spirit, its *Zeitgeist,* mirrored in its literature. Hence there are, in a very real sense, as many literatures as times. If, for example, we try to generalize about the social patterns of English literature, do we mean Elizabethan, Restoration, Augustan, Romantic Revival, Victorian or modern literature? The writing of each period varies sharply in character, just as each succeeding form of society differs in economic structure, social classification, intellectual currents, religious and ethical beliefs, and prevailing temper. French literature, for instance, shows marked variations in the ages of Corneille and Racine, Mallarmé and Baudelaire, Camus and Anouilh. Is there, indeed, any common factor in the spirit of the times reflected in American literature by Longfellow and Lowell, Mark Twain and Whitman, John Dos Passos and Tennessee Williams? What of the operation of the *Zeitgeist* in Australian literature?

The spirit of the age manifests itself, in fact, in Australian as in all other literatures. Times have changed, the society has evolved, and the writing expresses the changes. It is a far cry from Barron Field to Kenneth Slessor, from *Quintus Servinton* to *Riders in the Chariot.* Each writer reflects, in general, the climate of his own day. Kendall, writing in the sixties and seventies, was as much a product of a society that was only starting to move away from the old colonial complex as Paterson was of the nationalist period, or as Judith Wright is of the atomic age. Thus Kendall, "a singer of the dawn", as he called himself, invoked the Muse of Australia with an image of sunlight, "A lyrebird lit on a shimmering space", whilst Judith Wright, preoccupied with the darkness of war-threatened times, takes a blind man as her symbol. A. G. Stephens wrote in 1900 in a spirit impossible in 1850 or 1950, since his exuberant nationalism could not have been socially developed at the earlier period, whilst his optimistic utopianism could hardly have been preserved undimmed if he had experienced two world wars.

On the whole, however, Australian literature has had too short a life to cover, like the literatures of the older nations, a great variety of ages and societies. It includes, broadly, three main periods: the colonial, nationalist, and modern. The colonial period runs from the beginnings of settlement to 1880, when the *Bulletin* was founded to usher in and dominate the nationalist period. The latter may be taken to conclude in 1918, after the first world war had broken down the Australian dream of a self-contained community developing in isolation from the rest of the world, and taken Australia willy-nilly into the modern age with all its problems and complexities. The war itself, of course, intensified national sentiment and created the Anzac tradition, but in literature the nationalist fervour of the nineties, which had been cooling down during the first decade of the twentieth century, was replaced by internationalist movements and a drift into individual writing.

The writing during the colonial period came mainly from English, Scottish, and Irish immigrants who preserved quite naturally their old outlook when describing the new environment. It has been a common error to condemn this writing as the nostalgic literature of exiles. In fact, the note of yearning for the homeland is only struck occasionally, and in fiction such novelists as Charles Rowcroft, Catherine Spence, Henry Kingsley, and Marcus Clarke were interested in the strange, difficult, or exciting life of this antipodean land, its problems and possibilities, the adventures of the immigrants and the horrors of the convict system. Although Gordon, the only migrant poet of significance, wrote largely on oversea themes, he also identified himself sufficiently with the country and its people in his galloping balladry of action for Marcus Clarke to say with justice that the reader of Gordon's poems would "find in them something very like the beginnings of a national school of Australian poetry."

The native-born writers were also "colonial" in that they followed English models. But also, even the earliest of the poets, such as the nationalist Wentworth and the pensive Charles Tompson, cherished pride in their homeland and love of its beauties. Australian sentiment became a passion with Charles Harpur and Henry Kendall. Indeed, Kendall, who signed himself on occasion as "N.A.P."—Native Australian Poet—earned his title.

Rolf Boldrewood also made the country more familiar in *Robbery Under Arms,* with its national scene, character, and idiom. He stands out as the first genuine *Australian* novelist just as Kendall was the first truly Australian poet. These two are transitional figures coming at the close of the colonial period and opening the way to the succeeding stage of nationalist writing. They begin to embody more fully the social patterns of the people which had only been expressed in part and occasionally by earlier literary writers, although the popular ballads and old bush songs had been a rich repository of them.

This embodiment became complete in the writing of the nationalist period. By the 1890s the native-born, who had been a rebellious minority in earlier decades, were emerging as an assured majority of the adult population in the Australian colonies, a majority which kept increasing. This change in the composition of the Australian people was accompanied by a corresponding change in the literature from a colonial to a national character. The nationalist sentiment which had been accumulating slowly during the nineteenth century now swelled to full volume and flooded into national utterance. In the *Bulletin* and other popular magazines writers who came from the people wrote of the people and for them. Where Kendall had found a few hundreds of cultivated readers, Lawson and Paterson were read by thousands all over Australia, and were recited in city and shearing shed and by the campfires of a continent. Steele Rudd created bush characters who became living portraits in the national mind. Furphy and O'Dowd, more intellectual and less popular, formulated the nationalist values, with their revolt against colonialism, their ardent democratic spirit, republican sentiment and socialist faith, radical criticisms of the present society, and utopian dreams for its future.

Some of the ideas and sentiments expressed in the nationalist period, such as republican tenets, were peculiar to the time, but in general, as will be seen more fully later, this period crystallized and made explicit the pioneering patterns evolved during the first half of the nineteenth century. These were now acclaimed as the national *ethos,* since the writers made writing in Australia fully Australian in theme and spirit and language. In doing so they fixed a humanist, democratic, radical, and realistic mould for Australian literature.

During the modern period after 1914 this mould endured, even if it became chipped, battered, and changed in some ways as a result of the different nature of the modern age. The nationalist sentiment itself weakened after the establishment of the Commonwealth, blazed forth most strongly during the first world war, then was dimmed in the disillusionment of the 1920s, only to find a fresh renaissance during the thirties and forties. After 1918 there was a slight break with the past as literary trends swung towards either individual writing, apart from the people, like that of Henry Handel Richardson and Baylebridge, or to international attitudes, such as that of the *Vision* group led by Jack Lindsay. Where the nineties were centripetal, the twenties were centrifugal. The unity of the nationalist period, with the *Bulletin* as a central integrating influence, dissolved into separate, unrelated efforts. Simplicity was replaced by complexity. Literature lost its popular character, its close touch with the people.

The thirties and forties, however, linked up again with the nineties. The times, indeed, exerted a sobering and maturing influence. The youthful ebullience had gone. The national feeling in literature moved more quietly, but it ran deeply. It ran, for instance, in a strong stream of historical novels and pioneering sagas. These two decades were marked especially by the growth of the novel, and such novelists as Katharine Susannah Prichard, Vance Palmer, Miles Franklin, M. Barnard Eldershaw, Frank Dalby Davison, Leonard Mann, Xavier Herbert, and Kylie Tennant continued the basic traditions of the nationalist period. The old note of radical criticism, with its implication of an idealist faith, was strengthened by the economic depression of the thirties, and the contemporary school of "social realists" in fiction has sought to widen the appeal of its Leftism by claiming kinship with the radical nationalism of the nineties as well as by finding historical continuity with such earlier events as the Eureka Stockade.

The short story, developing fresh vigour in the forties, showed the same trends as the novel. From the thirties and the appearance of Ion L. Idriess's *Lasseter's Last Ride* (1931) a spate of travel writers made descriptive prose a popular medium for fresh discoveries of the Australian scene, even if none of the later writers had the interpretative penetration shown earlier in Dr C. E. W. Bean's brilliant travel books *On the Wool Track* (1910) and *The Dreadnought of the Darling* (1911). Although the lack of an indigenous theatre and lack of support from either commercial entrepreneurs or public stifled efforts, like those of the Pioneer Players, to found a national drama, Australian plays have slowly fought their way to acceptance. Early playwrights such as Esson, Palmer, Tomholt, and Dann were followed by Douglas Stewart and Locke-Elliott. Lawler's success with *Summer of the Seventeenth Doll* marked a temporary break-through of local drama. With the partial exception of Tomholt, all these playwrights had given dramatic shape to the social patterns of a common national tradition. With Lawler's *The Piccadilly Bushman* and the plays of Beynon and Seymour came, however, a more critical questioning of aspects of this tradition, together with an extension of theme and outlook. A further expansion of the drama was given by Patrick White's plays in their expressionist revolt against the current realism and their introduction of symbolism and satire.

In fiction, too, White's three later novels—*The Tree of Man* (1955), *Voss* (1957) and *Riders in the Chariot* (1961)—came as a revolutionary phenomenon. They went far beyond the work of the social realists to new dimensions of imaginative depth, psychological insight, and spiritual issues. White's influence has already been exerted on younger novelists, notably Randolph Stow. Like the fiction, the poetry has experienced a new movement in the post-war period and expansion into fresh modes. A. D. Hope has proved, like White in fiction, a brilliant and significant revolutionary figure. He has led the way to an intellectualist approach, a neo-classical style, the symbolist use of classical myth, and witty, mordant satire. His influence is seen in the work of McAuley and Buckley, who have also written a religious poetry hitherto alien to the literary tradition. All these modernist developments have cut across the traditional social and literary patterns, making the post-war writing richer and more complex than that of previous periods.

On the other hand, the growth of enthusiastic interest in the old bush songs and folk ballads from the fifties onwards offers a striking example of the way in which the sentiment of today, in search of a national heritage, has gone back to the past and the patterns shaped in pioneering times.

Despite the complexity of the modern period, therefore, and the growth of conflicting movements, there remains a broad continuity of the literary tradition. This continuity, although challenged, is still stronger than the instances of revolutionary change. The persistence of the dominant traditions means that Australian literature can be viewed validly as one consistent, developing body of writing. Changes wrought by the *Zeitgeist* are subordinate, so far, to the general unity. The social patterns can still be caught and described effectively.

Before defining them, however, some preliminary qualifications must be made, some warnings issued. It must be recognized at the outset that a society and its literature by no means form a perfect equation. The literary looking-glass has its limitations as well as its powers of significant reflection of prevailing patterns. The glass distorts as well as reflects. On the one hand, it contains personal elements belonging to the writer which are not characteristic of the society at large, such as the spiritual hunger of a Brennan or Patrick White, the fantasy of McCrae, or the old-world elegance of Ethel Anderson. On the other hand, it does not contain some patterns typical of the community. Sport, for instance, is a dominant interest of the Australian people, but its expression in literature is negligible. Religion, too, has played an important part in the community life but has been largely disregarded by writers until its recent emergence in the novels of White and the poetry of McAuley, Buckley and Francis Webb. Religious poems had been written earlier by Ada Cambridge, William Gay, and Bishop Gilbert White, but these had been exceptional.

Whilst some social elements have been thus neglected, others have been exaggerated in relation to their actual role in the society. Most Australians today, for example, accept the general *status quo* of society even when they desire specific changes for their own economic or social benefit, whereas Australian writers, like writers in most other countries, naturally question the existing order more critically. They tend to be more radical than the majority of their comfortable fellow citizens. Thus radicalism, which has been a feature of Australian society in the past, today appears more strongly in literature than in ordinary life. So, too, there is a deeper stress on utopianism, since writers usually cherish ideals, including those for the future of their country, more deeply than the average Australian concerned with his material present, his work, family, and sport. He does not enter fully into the passionate idealism

of such patriots as Lawson, Furphy, and O'Dowd, Miles Franklin or Katharine Prichard. Our myths and ideals are far larger in our literature than in our life.

Indeed, one of the most striking facts to emerge from an objective study of the social patterns in the literature is the occasional disparity between these and the contemporary reality. This is due mainly, of course, to the fact that the prevailing patterns pictured came from a pioneering past which was vastly different in many respects from the industrialized, urban, atomic present. Other differences arise from a particular emphasis made by the writers. They have largely concentrated, for example, on the working class as a subject. The large middle class of business and professional groups has received comparatively little representation in literature. Again, through their selection of themes the writers have also exercised a further kind of literary gerrymandering by largely disfranchising the citics as against the country. Ever since the earliest days the population has been concentrated in the coastal cities, and today Australia is the most highly urbanized country in the world. Yet its literature has always been predominantly rural. It is a phenomenal case of the literary tail wagging the demographic dog.

A few of the earlier novelists, such as Catherine Helen Spence, Caroline Leakey, and Mrs Campbell Praed, wrote of the cities. Then the country took over, with only a trickle of urban fiction until after the second world war when the trickle swelled into a vigorous stream with such contributaries as Patrick White, Judah Waten, Elizabeth Harrower, Thea Astley, and Thomas Keneally. Fiction is now coming to close grips with the contemporary city realities, just as it is turning away from the reporting of the external world by social realism to a more imaginative, more creative, probing of the inner world of the mind.

The new impulses of the last two decades in both prose and poetry have compelled comment on the disparity often occurring between the traditional literary picture and the contemporary actuality. It may be argued, with some truth, that our literature in general presents many scenes, characters, and ideas of the past that have been transformed into myths, legends, and dreams remote from the present.

Yet the social patterns discussed here are still powerful as national traditions, operating as forces conditioning our contemporary ways of thought, feeling, and behaviour. As such they are not mythical or legendary but factual, current realities to be reckoned with. Furthermore, their representation in our literature is also an undeniable fact; and when I set out here that fact of representation, with all the weight of the evidence, I am dealing with entities, not as mythical as the Jack of Spades, but as real as yesterday's strike and today's drought in the wheat belt.

As I worked through our literature a number of social patterns became patent, but it seemed to me that ten of these emerged as major ones of national significance. They may be described in different phrases or placed in varying orders, of course, but I shall discuss the following as the major patterns.

1. *The Spell of the Bush,* that has been dominant in Aus-

tralian society and literature alike as the primary force, since the social patterns as a whole were born of the land itself and bred in the bush. This dominance runs throughout our writing, from the old bush songs down to *The Tree of Man* and *Voss*. The bush has been the matrix of our sentiments and ideals, symbol of a distinctive national character, and a religious mystique invoking salvation for the spirit. It still holds the people's imagination.

2. *The Clash of Cultures* as the established colonialism, based on the imported British way of life, was challenged by the growing indigenous ethos, creating a long-drawn-out conflict between their contrasting values, until the two cultures became integrated finally in an independent Australian culture, even if in a few cases the old struggle between colonialism and nationalism is still not entirely resolved. In general the organism was forced to adapt itself to the environment by means of a new culture: the people who came to change and subdue the land were themselves changed by it in the end, and compelled to submit to its demands.

3. *Realism,* the outlook inevitably developed amongst the pioneer pragmatists by a hard land which brooked no romantic emotion or false illusion but demanded acceptance of reality for survival, so that the writers in turn grew realists and developed a creed of integrity to the truth of life. This realism achieves honesty and power, but often falls into reportage of externals, uses observation rather than the creative imagination, and misses the wonder and mystery of life.

4. *Sombreness,* discussed under the title of "The Cry of the Crow". Its main causes were the unpredictable onslaught of drought, flood, and fire, the struggle with an arid and recalcitrant land, the loneliness of a harsh bush life, and the tragic death of explorers. Like the realism with which it is interlinked, it also had the convict system as an historical determinant. In the literature the social realists became professional specialists in sombreness as they concentrated on the ills of society.

5. *The Keynote of Irony,* hard and realistic, sardonic and sansculottist, which is dominant in Australian humour, more significant, more distinctive, and also more subtle than such other forms of humour as broad farce, tall stories, trickster tales, satire, and comedy of character. Arising, like the sombreness, out of the land's vicissitudes, it has been used as a self-protective device to stave the sombreness off, a kind of philosophic whistling to keep one's courage up in facing disaster. Lawson employs it in masterly suggestiveness, sometimes drily, sometimes bitterly. It is acidly incisive in Lennie Lower, satirical in Kylie Tennant, and savage in Xavier Herbert. Upon it Furphy bases the whole intricate, ingenious design of *Such is Life* and his concept of Tom Collins.

6. *The Creed of Mateship,* the loyalty of man to man in a special relationship, born of the land as a practical necessity for bushmen living in a vast, lonely, and often dangerous environment, and hence, like irony, a defensive mechanism against the land; strengthened by the lack of women and religion in the outback; widening into a national convention in alliance with the democratic pattern; strongest amongst bushmen, workers in hazardous occupations, and the men of the fighting services in wartime; varying from a superficial friendliness to a religious depth of self-sacrifice.

7. *Radical Democracy,* the combination of the two patterns of radicalism and democratic belief, so closely interwoven that they are best treated as two aspects of the one embracing social pattern emphasizing equality and its consequent demand for social justice. Ecologically this was drawn mainly from the organism, not the environment, from the kind of people rather than the type of place, with a background of historical factors such as the French Revolution, English liberalism, Scottish independence, the rebel Irish, the emancipists, and the struggle for the land. Ultimately, however, the pattern only operated effectively because the workers enjoyed independence on account of the strong demand for their labour, which in turn resulted from the smallness of the population and the largeness of the land with all its undeveloped resources.

8. *The Great Australian Dream,* a utopian vision which was, like the creed of mateship, a form of idealism that complemented the common realism. The greatness of the land and its potentialities were joined with such forces as nationalism and socialism to stimulate the dream of a paradise on Australian earth, an Eden of prosperity, freedom, equality, and justice. Australia was to be a Commonwealth devoted to serving the common weal. This social pattern arose early and its expression has persisted through all the periods of the literature.

9. *Earth-vigour,* a physical vitality grown into a national tradition of sporting prowess, generated by the environment of a temperate climate and favorable living conditions, and developed by a pioneering life on the land. So, too, whatever the shortcomings of the literature in artistic form, it is marked by vigour. Despite the strain of sombreness, there is a positive affirmation of life, of courage and endurance, of human endeavour and the individual will, an affirmation expressed powerfully in FitzGerald's poem "Essay on Memory" and Douglas Stewart's verse play *The Fire on the Snow*. In poetry this earth-vigour is also symbolized by a celebration of Pan, the earth-god, patron of shepherds and herdsmen.

10. *Humanism,* the faith in the human spirit, with man as the measure of values, is . . . closely allied with the pagan earth-vigour . . . . Whereas the Christian religions have played a significant part in the history of Australian society, it is a striking fact that the Australian literature, from the old bush songs and the balladists, through the socialists like Lawson, Furphy, and O'Dowd, down to the more modern writers like the poets McCrae and Neilson and novelists of social realism, has shown itself as either completely indifferent to religion or highly critical of it. In general the writers, like the society, turn, not to God, but to man; not to Heaven but to a utopia for men on earth. The writing is nothing if not humanist in its outlook and sympathies, hedonistic in its enjoyment of life, and stoic in its facing of adversity.

Since the last world war this humanism has been challenged by a new strain of religious feeling voiced by Patrick White and some Roman Catholic poets. The humanist tradition, however, still remains in the ascendant. Few writers would wish to follow White's Voss into a journey towards God and humility, but most would have a fellow feeling for Brennan when, facing misery, he found a humanist salvation in the friendly sky and wind, his own manhood, and man's "note of living will":

> I said, this misery must end:
> shall I, that am a man and know
> that sky and wind are yet my friend,
> sit huddled under any blow?
> so speaking left the dismal room
> and stept into the mother-night
> all fill'd with sacred quickening gloom
> where the few stars burn'd low and bright,
> and darkling on my darkling hill
> heard thro' the beaches' sullen boom
> heroic note of living will
> rung trumpet-clear against the fight;
> so stood and heard, and rais'd my eyes
> erect, that they might drink of space,
> and took the night upon my face.

(pp. 2-22)

T. Inglis Moore, "The Social Element in Literature," in his Social Patterns in Australian Literature, *University of California Press, 1971, pp. 1-22.*

HISTORICAL AND CRITICAL PERSPECTIVES

Brian Kiernan

[*Kiernan is an Australian critic and educator whose works reflect his interest in Australian and American literature of the nineteenth century. In the following essay, he examines nineteenth-century perspectives on Australian literature.*]

To trace the growth of letters in the community, from the earliest period of our history to the present time, and to show in what manner that growth had been influenced by the productions of the Mother Country . . . would amount to a literary history of the country, and it was hoped that such a history would serve more than one useful service. It would enable the reader to form an exact idea of the progress, extent and prospects of literary enterprise among us, more readily than could be done by means of any general statement; it would constitute a bibliographical account that might be practically useful, not only to those who are interested in our literature, but also to those who may hereafter be engaged in historical enquiries; it would serve to throw some light, from a new point of view, on our social history; and lastly, it would preserve the memory, and give some notion of the achievement, of men whose name could scarcely be expected to survive their generation.

So wrote G. B. Barton, Reader in English at the University of Sydney, in the introduction to his *Literature in New South Wales* (1866). This and his critical anthology *The Poets and Prose Writers of New South Wales* (also 1866) were the first books on Australian literature. Although Barton recorded much valuable bibliographical information, he did not provide any systematic review along the lines he suggests in the above passage; however, his ideal of what literary history ought to provide comprehends the intentions of many who were to follow him with their accounts of the "growth of letters" in this country.

Barton's intention of enabling the reader to form an opinion of the "progress" of literature in this country reminds us that he was writing in the mid-Victorian period—and three years after the first appearance of Taine's *History of English Literature*. "Progress" in accordance with the universal laws of evolution was assumed by most nineteenth century (and perhaps later) commentators on Australian literature. As a new society, a new race, evolved in response to the new environment, so would a new literature, which (ambiguously) would be an agent in and a product of this evolution. And "prospects" had a particular poignancy for the scholar turning his attention to the literature of his own colony; what he surveyed could be only the first fruits plucked from a vine that had scarce taken root in this thin soil; it would be a later age that reaped the harvest. Later literary historians have traced the extent of the Mother Country's influence on local writing, and of Europe's and America's. Bibliographies have been compiled, and the memories of men whose names could scarcely be expected to survive their generation have been preserved. Here, I want to consider the success with which Barton's other, and elusive, aim—that of throwing some light "from a new point of view" on our social history—has been fulfilled.

Broadly, one can imagine a literary "history" that has no awareness of social history at all. The various "Histories of English Literature" written for schools and civil service examinations in England last century approach this extreme, being chronological listings of authors and descriptions of their works, located in time by reference to ruling monarchs or wars. Then there is the "social history" of literature itself: literary movements, literary influences, even the lives of writers do not always correspond with the periods postulated on economic or other grounds. But at the point that even the most historical of literary historians moves beyond texts and chronology to considerations of conditions of authorship, the writer's expression of social values, or other relationships between the writer, his work, and his society, he is encountering history and, consciously or otherwise, offering an interpretation of the past and of the nature of these cultural relationships. At the opposite extreme from the literary chronicle would be a work—such as Taine's—highly aware of literature as a social institution. In Australia, although there were no attempts to provide inclusive literary histories between Barton's books and H. M. Green's *Outline of Australian Literature* in 1930, many of the problems, assumptions, and issues of Australian literary history had emerged by then.

The first of these problems was that of defining the field—

what is *Australian* literature? ("What is Australian *literature?*" and the issue of whether the historian should confine himself to an Arnoldian notion of literature or adopt an anthropological approach to literary culture did not, for obvious reasons, preoccupy early historians like Barton or Walker.) Although we most usually think of the concept of a national literature emerging in the eighties and nineties of last century, it is a concept that was present almost from the beginning of the century in literary expectations—expectations because these all but preceded the literature. Romantic literary theory in England and on the Continent had seen literature as the history of the national mind and as the expression of the genius of the individual race. The peculiar problems of a country sharing the language and cultural inheritance of the English but encountering and mastering a different environment, and developing a new culture, had been experienced in America. There the issue of a national literature—the issue, simply of whether a writer's obligations were to be American or a writer first of all—remained contentious at least until the Civil War; and the contention was not diminished by English observers such as Sidney Smith enquiring in the *Edinburgh* in 1820: "Who in the four quarters of the globe reads an American book?" William Ellery Channing, who felt that it were "better to have no literature than form ourselves unresistingly on a foreign one" addressed the issue in 1830 in his lecture "The Importance and Means of a National Literature". In this he defined literature as "the expression of a nation's mind" and claimed that "literature is plainly among the powerful methods of exalting the character of a nation, of forming a better race of men".

Such exalted views of literature's function were quite orthodox on both sides of the Atlantic—and soon after on the other side of the Pacific. For as George Nadel documents in *Australia's Colonial Culture,* these were also the principles of those who took upon themselves the education and moral improvement of the Australian colonies. Literature and culture were virtually co-extensive terms, and the propagation of literature was expected to alleviate the depressingly materialistic tone of the Australian colonies, restore a lost sense of community, and morally elevate the masses. Nadel shows how, from the 1830s onwards, literary culture was related to nationalism: "In whatever fashion the argument was disseminated the basic point seemed to be that sheep and acres did not give a country nationality, but that literature did: indeed there could be no patriotism without literature" and he quotes the essay "Literature—Its Advancement and Results" from the first issue of the *Australian Era* (1850). The author of the essay saw Australia "as standing on the brink of nationality . . . Literature created nationality, because nationality presupposed national thought and a national intelligence, themselves the product of literature".

The connection between literature and nationality came early—we might say it was imported before much imaginative writing had appeared in Australia. One of the first (of many, as it turned out) to proclaim the emergence of a national literature was William Walker in his lecture "Australian Literature" delivered at the Windsor School of Arts in 1864. His historical survey, he felt, showed that Australia had a "a literature of her own of a progressive

and promising character", and one, his title implied, that transcended colonial borders and jealousies. So impressed was Walker with the progress already made that he felt another lecture would be necessary to do full justice to the poetry, and that there was every probability that Australia would produce writers worthy to be placed alongside Bacon, Shakespeare, Byron, and Scott. Such optimism reminds one of Melville in America earlier—"Believe me, my friends, men not very inferior to Shakespeare are being born this day on the banks of the Ohio"—and the American parallel was one that occurred naturally to critics as Australia enjoyed its own debate over a national literature in the last quarter of the nineteenth century. While "universalists" agonized over whether one could meaningfully speak of American literature (if a work were good enough it surely belonged to English literature?), the "nationalists" were inspired with confidence, as were the republicans in politics, by the American precedent. The confident national literature they saw as emerging with Hawthorne, Longfellow, Bret Harte, and others seemed an important indication of the most likely course of Australia's own literary maturation. The invariable analogies between literary and biological or organic growth (mothers and daughters, trees and branches, with America always at a later stage of development) fitted the general belief in the inevitability of evolutionary progress and must have seemed, subconsciously, to guarantee eventual social and literary maturation. The American parallel provided the historical model which was to be employed by later historians of Australian literature. After a colonial period in which immigrant writers discovered a strange new land, native-born writers would emerge to express their acceptance of this land and society as their own; eventually, after a period of nationalistic selfconsciousness, a mature, assured, unselfconsciously national literature would be established. Consistently, from about 1870 onwards (and well into this century) Australian critics were proclaiming the beginning of this second stage, the emergence of distinctively Australian writers; just as in this century they have proclaimed the achievement of the final stage, the coming of age.

Although, for obvious reasons, there were no full-scale literary histories written in the nineteenth century, critical discussions in books and periodicals presupposed views of the development of Australia and literature's relationship to this. Australia had done well for a pioneering country with a small population which, of necessity, had to get on with more immediate matters than pursuing culture; on the other hand, Australia was too materialistic (a view that Barton questioned) and its prosperous class that could afford time and money for culture was too philistine, too nouveau-riche to offer the traditional patronage of the European aristocracy and haute-bourgeoisie. Whichever way the argument ran, this sense of literature as an index of cultural attainment and social history was common to a number of books that appeared around the turn of the century. These were not literary histories in the sense that they pretended to any systematic inclusiveness, but their assumptions concerning the relationships between literature and the society in which it was produced, like those in many other studies of particular writers or partial views of Australian writing in the periodicals, contributed to an awareness of literature as part of our general or cultural history. Indeed, the most frequent assumptions, issues, and phrases, of later literary history can be found in these books which appeared within a brief space of time at the end of last century: Patchett Martin's *The Beginnings of Australian Literature* (1898), a pamphlet originally delivered in London as a lecture by a former editor of the *Melbourne Review;* Desmond Byrne's *Australian Writers* (1896), a collection of biographical and critical discussions of Clarke, Kingsley, Cambridge, Gordon, Boldrewood, Praed and "Tasma" introduced by a general discussion; and Turner and Sutherland's *The Development of Australian Literature* (1898), the only one to be published in Australia with primarily an Australian audience in mind.

Turner's introductory "General Sketch of Australian Literature", (which is then followed by Sutherland's biographies of Clarke, Gordon, and Kendall) expresses the conventional literary historical assumptions about the relationship between the size of the population, the country's stage of development, and its literature. Turner, writing at a time when the population was four million, says that the growth of a large population sharing local experience "must inevitably bring strength and maturity to a national literature". The present stage in cultural development Turner sees as restricted by the necessity for culture to take a second place in a pioneering community and the lack of national feeling. Until leisure is possible and a national spirit is developed ("as it will be unless the tradition of our race suffers decay") we must be content "with the productions of local literature, essentially English in its characteristics, but moulded by climatic and scenic surroundings into a form that gives it sufficient distinctiveness to justify the term 'Australian'."

Scepticism towards this attitude that linked the "development" of Australian literature with the expansion of society, and its corollary that what literature had been produced was admirable for a society at such an early stage of its development, was also expressed. Professor T. G. Tucker, an editor of the *Australasian Critic,* constantly attacked this attitude, as also did Byrne in his introduction to *Australian Writers.* Taking up the parallel with America which had been used so often to prophesy the inevitable emergence of an Australian literature, Byrne inverts it to question its assumptions (Benjamin Franklin, he points out, appeared considerably before America achieved nationhood) and to shatter any complacency about Australian cultural life. Australians, he says, take no pride in creative intellectual work; despite Government provision of education and cultural establishments public taste has not improved; clubs and societies devoted to literature are elitist; the lack of support for local periodicals and books, because of public preference for what is approved by the English public, has meant that it is impossible to live by writing in Australia. These facts, Byrne suggests: "may not be found to explain why there is yet no sign of the coming of an Antipodean Franklin or Irving, or Hawthorne or Emerson; but they will help to show why the literature of the country grows so unevenly, why it is chiefly of the objective order and leaves large tracks of the lives of the people untouched."

In later literary historical accounts, the years in which these views of the relationships between society and culture in Australia were being advanced were also the years when a national feeling (and a politically unified nation) was emerging, and finding expression, particularly in the *Bulletin.* Byrne, writing in England, seemed unaware of the *Bulletin* writers; the others however were not, though their contemporary view was not that of later generations. Turner's conservatism made him critical of Lawson's radicalism and wary of exaggerating the place of the *Bulletin* writers; Patchett Martin was more warmly disposed towards them as indicating the commencement of an Australian school of writing; Francis Adams employed by the *Bulletin* in the late eighties was contemptuous of local poetry and prose. It would be interesting to establish when the view of the *Bulletin*'s central role in the development of a national literature—a view shared by many of its writers and, presumably, readers also—became a historical view. Nettie Palmer's *Modern Australian Literature* (1924) would seem to have been very influential here. As its title suggests, it is concerned with the first quarter of the twentieth century, and its necessarily summary treatment of the previous century became orthodox in many later accounts. Nettie Palmer was among the first to take a historical view of the decades before and after Federation and to draw a sharp division between the "colonial" literature which presented Australia through the eyes of expatriate Englishmen (or "bias-bleared spectacles" as A. G. Stephens had expressed it characteristically in 1901) and the "Australian" literature that had emerged with the new nation. Of course writers involved in the conscious movement to establish a national literature—Stephens, Lawson, Vance Palmer—felt that the *Bulletin* schools had achieved those long anticipated characteristics by which the national literature would be recognized: a lack of self-consciousness in the use of Australian experience and the assumption of a local rather than an English audience. As Jose wrote in his *History of Australasia* in 1909: "during the last twenty years there has sprung up a school of young Australians who tell of their own life in their own natural way, and describe their own country as men who love it; so that through them a stranger can get at the heart of the people, not merely at the ideas about the people formed by interested outsiders." *Modern Australian Literature* endorsed such contemporary views as historically accurate. The long-awaited nationhood and national literature had been achieved. For the literary historian the task was to reveal what was essentially Australian in the literature, and the elusive relationships between the land, the people, and the literature that for a long time it had been presupposed would emerge.

Although literary historical issues had been discussed for the best part of a century, it was not until 1930 that the first attempt to provide a comprehensive account of imaginative writing appeared with H. M. Green's *Outline of Australian Literature.* It was presented, in its introduction, as preliminary to "a short history of Australian literature" in which an attempt would be made "to relate the literature of each period to its social, political and other conditions". As we now know, it was to be another thirty years before that work, which attempted the higher literary historical aim of exploring the relationships between literature and society, appeared. The earlier *Outline,* however, is conceptually unadventurous. It is a "pure" literary history, and a history of "pure" literature, which makes only passing references to historical events and developments and is concerned only with "high" literary culture. The interpretative framework remains vague and general, and its opening sentence retains the favourite metaphor and the guarded stance of the "colonial" critic: "Australian literature is a branch of English literature, and however great it may become and whatever characteristics it may develop, it will remain a branch." For Green, as for so many of the nineteenth century critics, "the literature of a country is obviously an expression of the characteristic qualities of its life", and he lists the characteristics he discerns:

> Most apparent are the qualities, positive and negative, which one would expect to find in the literary work of any young and comparatively undeveloped country, such as vigour and freshness, crudity and lack of architecture and craftsmanship generally; these last, however, no longer mark the best Australian work. But there is also apparent at times a richness, an almost tropical warmth and colouring which may be noticed particularly in the verse of Hugh McCrae and Dorothea Mackellar. More widely spread are certain other qualities which are only in part literary, since their presence in any work which involves representation of character will be derived from the characters represented as well as from the temperament and experience of the writer and their result upon his literary method and point of view. These qualities are an independence of spirit, a kind of humorous disillusion, a careless willingness to take a risk, a slightly sardonic good nature and a certain underlying hardness of texture.

The first two sets of characteristics are conventionally evolutionist and synthesize much nineteenth century discussion which emphasized the difficulties encountered by a pioneering society, and speculated that climatic and other environmental factors would mould the people and their culture. The third set relates to national character and its expression through literature, and although he does not develop these here it is these characteristics and their relationship to historical experience and social institutions, including literature, that were to become so important in later accounts, including Green's own.

In the same year as the *Outline* another book appeared which was to affect views of Australian social history, culture, and literary history for generations to come—W. K. Hancock's *Australia.* Like Tocqueville, who "tried to explain to cultivated Europeans the characteristics of democracy in a 'new' country", Hancock tried to explain to cultivated Europeans the paradoxes of Australian life. His success can be gauged from the fact that *Australia* has assumed something of the same classic status for historians and commentators on society here as *Democracy in America* has in that country. Although not a history, being as much concerned with what could be considered separately as politics, economics, culture, or sociology (for each of which areas it contributed concepts), it

was the first study to seek "dominant themes" in Australian life that would relate the past to the present. It provided an interpretative framework that related the social, economic, and cultural in bold hypotheses which many later scholars have examined. For example, the statement that "Australian nationalism took definite form in the class struggle between the landless majority and the land monopolizing squatters", although it synthesizes attitudes that had been expressed many times at various stages in the past, confers a historical validation upon them, and anticipates the major theme of Australian historians in later decades. Hancock's influence on historians and social commentators has been discussed and criticized by R. W. Connell (in *Quadrant,* vol. 12, no. 2, 1968): here I want only to draw attention to its similar influence on the concept of history found in the work of literary critics. Again as an example of the bold generalization that anticipates or stimulated later writers we could take his statement that "Recurrent in Australian poetry is a note of renunciation, sometimes regretful, sometimes defiant . . . and a note of expectation, of waiting upon the future for an Australia which has not been known to the past . . . " which accords with Judith Wright's later study of the preoccupations with exile and utopia in Australian poetry.

Hancock sees literature as part of the total cultural development he traces and analyzes, and sees it as expressing "the prevailing ideology of Australian democracy": "in Lawson and Collins, and almost every other writer of the *Bulletin* school, Australian nationalism expressed itself as a repudiation of English conventions and standards, as a vindication of equality and democracy and an assertion of the supreme worth of the average man." Hancock is synthesizing the nationalism and egalitarian democracy that were expressed (however more complexly) by these writers. But he is also defining in social and political terms what was "characteristic" of Australian literature and providing the literary historian with the link between literature and society in terms of the values expressed in the literature of the nationalist period. These were not the links perceived, or so explicitly formulated, by literary historians (for example, Nettie Palmer or H. M. Green) up to this time. However, the tradition Hancock postulated was to be elaborated by historians and critics from then on. It provided the opportunity to interpret the development of literature in terms of social history and to use literature to illustrate the formation of an egalitarian national culture and character. By the time H. M. Green's full history appeared this had become an orthodoxy—though already an orthodoxy under attack—which provided in numerous summaries a stereotyped view of literature developing in accordance with national consciousness. It is also an orthodoxy that clearly affects Green's consideration of the relationship of "the literature of each period to its social, political and other conditions".

The *History of Australian Literature* (1961) opens with much more confidence in its subject as an entity than does the *Outline* with its branch-of-the-tree image: "It is scarcely necessary to argue nowadays that the literature of Australia is worth discussing on its own account, and not merely as part of the great literature in English, of which it is an outgrowth. This great literature is like a banyantree, whose branches bend down, and, striking the ground, take root and grow up as independent individuals." And the *History* reflects the growth of interest in, and reinterpretation of, the nineteenth century that had developed since 1930. Green in his concluding section mentions key contributors to this greater awareness of the past, as much historical and broadly cultural as specifically literary: Russel Ward, A. A. Phillips, Cecil Hadgraft, whose own history of Australian literature had appeared in 1960, Vincent Buckley, and others. A. A. Phillips in *Meanjin* (in essays later collected in *The Australian Tradition*) and other contributors to that journal including Manning Clark had elaborated the connections between literature and society Hancock had discerned. Vance Palmer, whose first essay on an Australian national literature had appeared in 1905, and Russel Ward had both explored the social historical bases of the "legend" that linked the past to the present in a national consciousness. And in the criticism of Buckley and others a reaction against the democratic nationalist interpretation of literature and social history had emerged, so that Green in introducing his discussion of the period "Self-Conscious Nationalism" could observe "a tendency nowadays to underrate the achievement of the third Period of Australian literature".

In the *History* Green's sympathies are on the side of those who had expounded an Australian social and literary tradition. He confesses, in a footnote, of having made the mistake in his *Outline* of "concentrating too much upon literature in its more aesthetic aspect". This "aesthetic" writing in earlier periods was thin and nostalgic in comparison with the "rough spun" indigenous material: "beyond the world of books . . . material was accumulating that was to form the basis of important elements in the literature to be . . . yarns and anecdotes . . . old bush songs . . . sketches . . . recollections, diaries, memoirs. . . " Following Russel Ward and other historians, Green perceives in the popular culture of the earlier nineteenth century the bases of an Australian tradition. In dealing with the nineties, his analysis seems to owe more to Hancock and his influence than to what had already been written in the *Outline*: "In Australia, the spirit of the nineties and early nineteen-hundreds was a spirit . . . which took the form in literary as well as in the social and political worlds, of a fervent democratic nationalism: it was based upon a broad social consciousness, a feeling of mutual relationship, that found its most characteristic expression in Lawson's doctrine of mateship". Here, the characteristics of a distinctive Australian literature are defined in social and political terms, although the vaguer perceptions of the pre-Hancock *Outline* are retained also—"a kind of warmth and glow which seems to be a reflection of heat and light and the colour-effects of the landscape". After his period of "Self-Conscious Nationalism", Green abandons the attempt to relate social and literary developments closely. His promise to discuss national types and characteristics at the end is not fulfilled; perhaps because, as the introduction to the "Modern Period" suggests, the democratic idealism of those earlier decades had become dissipated in cosmopolitanism and superficiality.

The *History of Australian Literature* most fully achieves the aims Barton had suggested nearly a century before. The mass of information it assembles on the press, the social groupings of writers, and the economics of authorship make it an important contribution to social and cultural history as well as a more narrowly literary study. So comprehensive, in fact, is Green that the broad interpretation he offers on social and literary relationships in the nineties is qualified by his recognition that there were many periodicals other than the *Bulletin,* writers like Brennan, Baylebridge, and Richardson as well as Lawson, Furphy, and Paterson, and the influences of the Celtic twilight as well as democratic nationalism on a host of minor writers. In these ways, the *History* avoids the stereotyped account of the development of a national literature that had been advanced by wedding Hancock's social analysis to literary history. Now that the major role for the literary historian was no longer to provide the basic biographical and bibliographical information (as had been necessary in 1930), critical interpretations of the stereotypes appeared. Cecil Hadgraft's *Australian Literature* was published the year before Green's *History*. It concentrates on "pure" literature and the methodological problems of establishing "periods" that will reconcile the temper of a particular time with the literary works of distinction produced within it. Thus on his first period, Hadgraft writes: "The name Colonial Period has been suggested for these seventy years. If poetry alone is considered then the name is pertinent. But to apply it to a period that includes Clarke's masterpiece seems almost defamatory. It is worth noting, however, that the literature of the period does not much express Australian ideals." For his second period 1880–1930 Hadgraft postulates two "subperiods", 1880–1914 and 1900–1930, to account for the diversity of writing, some consciously nationalistic, some unconcerned with issues of nationality, and for the stubborn refusal of facts to fit the stereotypes neatly: "the nineties, often thought of as prolific in valuable and representative works are really rather thin. Only two volumes of Lawson's tales and one of his verse and only one volume of Paterson's verse, for instance, appeared before 1900."

A similar awareness that the courses of literary and social history did not always run parallel had already been expressed by G. A. Wilkes, in an essay on the decade that is the focus of literary historical interpretation—the 1890s:

> Was there a literary period "the nineties" in Australia? The stages of Australian literary history have still to be determined. The present tendency is to fix them in accordance with existing political or economic divisions, so that a new age is dated from the gold-rushes of 1851, for instance, another from the nineties or the attainment of Federation in 1901, and another from the Great War of 1914–18. This is to determine periods of literary development by reference to non-literary criteria, and the boundaries that result are often fallacious.

Wilkes sees the literature of the period having been distorted by the emphasis placed on democratic and nationalistic writing, which was not the only kind of writing, was not necessarily the best—and was certainly not the best because it was democratic. He combines a historian's responsibility to take account of all relevant evidence with a critic's attention to the interpretation of texts (for example, what Furphy was concerned with) and their artistic quality (the best of Lawson's work would not include his political verse). "The Eighteen Nineties" is the only critically conscious discussion of the hybrid nature of literary history by an Australian critic, and the same awareness of conceptual and methodological problems is found in Wilkes's later *Australian Literature: A Conspectus,* (1969). Like Hadgraft's *Australian Literature* this admirably fulfils the literary historian's traditional role of providing a guide for the nonspecialist, while establishing an interpretative framework that is critical of received and stereotyped formulations. By implication, the opening sentence which sees the continual interaction of two cultural strands—European and indigenous—as operating throughout the course of Australian literature, dismisses as irrelevant the riddle "What is *Australian* literature" with which most previous historians had felt compelled to begin. There is no attempt at an explanation of literary developments in social terms, and wariness of such explanations is suggested by the observation on Neilson and Mc-Crae that they remind us how "literature at any period may escape parochialism through the artist with the vitality and perception to create his own imaginative world".

As well as these comprehensive literary histories there have been other studies which suggest that the earlier nineteenth century was not as discontinuous with the nineties and the twentieth century as earlier accounts had assumed. Historical studies such as George Nadel's *Australia's Colonial Culture* (1957), Michael Roe's *The Quest for Authority in Eastern Australia* (1965), Henry Mayer's *Marx and Engels in Australia* (1964), and Manning Clark's *History of Australia* (1962) made it clear that Australia had a more complex and vital culture than the stereotype of generations awaiting the coming of the *Bulletin* allowed. It was, of course, a "literary" culture in the fullest sense of that word, and most of its literature assumes most interest for us today in relation to that culture and its issues. Judith Wright in her *Preoccupations in Australian Poetry* (1965), which searches for correspondences between literary attitudes towards Australia and the historical social reality, also questions assumptions of cultural discontinuity. The dual vision she traces as a recurrent theme of poets throughout the nineteenth century and later sees Australia as a land of exile and a utopia simultaneously in each period, rather than each aspect representing a different stage of development.

Other reinterpretations of a deliberately provocative kind have appeared more recently. Humphrey McQueen's *A New Britannia* (1970) although not a literary study (despite its title) impinges on literary history because of his attack on Russel Ward's *The Australian Legend* (1958), the democratic egalitarianism of the social and literary tradition postulated by critics and historians in the forties and fifties, and his iconoclastic assault on its most "representative" literary figure, Henry Lawson. Since the appearance of the third volume of Manning Clark's *History* (1973) it would seem any point in McQueen's diatribe against Australian society as capitalist, racist and militaristic that is relevant to Australian culture in the first half

of the nineteenth century has found more substantial and responsible expression in Clark's analysis of the conflicts in this period and the ensuing dominance of bourgeois values of Australian society. Coral Lansbury's *Arcady in Australia* (1970) argues that recurrent images of Australia in literature before the "nationalist" period were formed in fact in England and represented expectations there that the colonial writer observed. The facts Coral Lansbury adduces have been questioned; her argument is partial, but it has the virtue of suggesting the complexity of social forces that enter into the forming of literary images and conventions. The image of idyllic possibilities of life in the Australian landscape is a persistent one that her study stimulatingly draws attention to—even though the stimulus might be to disagreement and qualification. Barry Argyle's *The Australian Novel: 1830–1930* (1972) is also partial, reckless in its procedures, and desperate to assert a continuity in Australian literature and society of the violence and cruelty established in the convict era; but like the others it is most interesting in manifesting a concern to revalue the past, to discover continuities with the nineteenth century, and to depart from received stereotypes (though each of these writers seems equally anxious to establish his own).

The attitudes of historians, literary or otherwise, towards culture in nineteenth century Australia have acquired a history of their own by now. The closing decades of the century especially provide a focal point for any general account of Australian culture, so that, today, we cannot look back directly to the nineteenth century itself without being conscious of the interpretations and evaluations of it that have been offered in the seventy years that intervene between its close and our own vantage point in time. The "colonial" period probably seems more interesting now that it has in earlier decades this century. Its literature may not be granted any intrinsically higher value than it has been accorded previously, but when the different later perspectives are taken into account, the period raises interesting issues for cultural history. These issues concern the social ramifications of literature and culture generally, and here most later commentators have much in common with nineteenth century critics, who were similarly concerned with relating social and cultural development and with suggesting formative and causal connections. The basic assumptions here, and the forms of the arguments advanced, have not changed essentially over more than a century, and these are valuably rehearsed in Geoffrey Serle's *From Deserts the Prophets Come* (1973), the first book to provide a comprehensive cultural history of Australia.

One of the many virtues of Serle's outline is that, like Desmond Byrne's earlier analysis, it brings into the open assumptions which prefer to shelter shyly behind a hedge of organicist analogies. "Culture is a highly perishable growth which, transplanted, cannot bloom as before", Serle himself writes, and quotes from James's *Hawthorne,* the now classic statement about the thinness of the soil in which the American novelist found himself planted. The analogy, implicit in our uses of the word "culture", between man's cultivation of the natural world and his "cultivation" of what he has created himself begs many questions. Talk of "transplanting", of tending slips or seedlings in the new soil in the expectation of a later harvest, follow naturally—such tropes come as second nature to literary men. But what sort of growth is being presupposed—qualitative or quantitative—and is there any essential relationship between the two? What ensures this growth—are "natural" processes involved, is time essential? Or is this a pseudo-explanation that disguises only a confidence that what has happened elsewhere will happen here, eventually? What is the "soil"—the people, all the people, or culturally conscious groups and individuals? James's emphasis on the need for "an accumulation of history and custom . . . a complexity of manners and types, to form a fund of suggestion for a novelist" has been very influential in later discussions of the relationship of the individual talent to a social tradition. It tells us a lot about the position James felt himself to be in, but he was clearly wrong about the writer in mid-nineteenth century America: not only was there Hawthorne, there were Emerson, Melville, Whitman, Poe, and others producing one of the most vital periods in any national literature in that century. These writers did not go unobserved in Australia, by Harpur, by Kendall, by many critics. As Frederick Sinnett intimated in 1856, the Australian writer, deprived of such properties of romance as ivied ruins or even a house with seven gables, could better concentrate on the serious concerns of fiction.

The need for Australia to grow in scale and diversity and to move towards nationhood Serle also lists as important factors in the "theory of cultural growth" he advances. Again, nineteenth century critics (for example, the historian Turner in 1898) had nominated these as essential for the eventual development of a national literature; but are these "essential factors", do they contribute to an explanation of how culture "grows", or do they provide a description of the social conditions against which it grew in America or Australia? If, as did the majority of Australian critics in the nineteenth century, we assume a natural evolution or growth at work, how do we explain the relative lack of "progress" in the 1920s in Australia? Was the federationist and nationalist idealism which has been seen as the stimulus behind the literature of the preceding decades in advance of actual social conditions, and did this become apparent in the twenties? Are the arts really active agents in social change, or are they, like seeds waiting for the right season, soil, and water, passively dependent on fertile social conditions? Serle himself sees not only "growth" but "maturity" as important, and argues that the delayed development in literature and painting in the twenties is related to the delayed development of national independence and to the continuation of cultural isolation. This is a succinct, accurate expression of one's "sense" of the period but how is "maturity" (as distinguished from "growth", which is thereby assigned a more quantitative or descriptive role) determined: is *For the Term of His Natural Life,* by all accounts the finest novel of the "colonial" period, necessarily a lesser achievement than the novels (all of them, or the best of them) that were produced at a more "mature" stage of our cultural development?

A general pattern of links connecting literature and soci-

ety in a causal way remains as elusive as ever. At one level there are the abstractions of "society", "culture", and "literature", at another level the particular works of individual writers (in dealing with these the critic and biographer can also contribute to our historical understanding, by bringing these abstractions to life in the case of his chosen subject). Too much insistence on social and economic conditions, publishing outlets and markets, political ideology and established conventions can lead to a deterministic sense that the "age" has produced the literature; at the other extreme too great an insistence on the autonomy of imaginative literature can ignore the involvement, direct or indirect, of writers with their society. In confronting this dilemma and attempting to find a point of balance, Australian literary historians have thrown, in Barton's words, "some light, from a new point of view, on our social history". They have contributed to our awareness of the culture of the past and raised issues of its interpretation from a later vantage point in time and its relevance to the present. These are not issues that can be disposed of finally, because they reconstitute themselves for each generation. Beyond recording biographical and bibliographical facts, what the literary historian can do most successfully is register his understanding—and to some extent this will be the understanding of his time—of the past. What the nineteenth century or earlier twentieth century critics had to say about individual writers and works is most interesting today as a record of their understanding of and attitudes towards the past. In this way literary historians themselves have some claim on posterity: for later generations the best of them will become part of what they have described, part of literary history. (pp. 1-18)

> *Brian Kiernan, "Literature, History, and Literary History: Perspectives on the Nineteenth*

Thomas Keneally on Australia's self-perception:

Commercial considerations are thought to be the lowest of artistic considerations in Australia; the state is supposed to look after these considerations by giving the writer grants, and I am delighted that the state does do that. But yes, I did start out looking beyond Australia, but even before there was a commercial reason. In Australia we were raised to believe that there was another world out there where Europeans really lived. I was about to begin my first year of primary school when A. D. Hope wrote his famous poem "Australia" in which he said we were "second-hand Europeans pullulating timidly on the edge of alien shores." That was a common perception which pervaded society in Australia when I was a kid. Australians have had a passion for travel, a need to get out and compare, whether it be Memphis or Minsk, to try to understand that new place. Before people know who they are, the passion for self-definition is a driving force. We are desperate to know who we are, to put ourselves in a world context and to understand ourselves in that context.

Thomas Keneally, in Australian Voices: Writers on their own work, *1991.*

Century in Australia," in Bards, Bohemians, and Bookmen: Essays in Australian Literature, *edited by Leon Cantrell, University of Queensland Press, 1976, pp. 1-18.*

Arthur Phillips

[*Phillips is an Australian educator and critic. In the following essay, he identifies an Australian critical bias against domestic cultural products and explores the effect of this "Cultural Cringe" on perceptions of national identity.*]

The Australian Broadcasting Commission has a Sunday programme, designed to cajole a mild Sabbatarian bestirment of the wits, called 'Incognito'. Paired musical performances are broadcast, one by an Australian, one by an overseas executant, but with the names and nationalities withheld until the end of the programme. The listener is supposed to guess which is the Australian and which the alien performer. The idea is that quite often he guesses wrong or gives it up because, strange to say, the local lad proves to be no worse than the foreigner. This unexpected discovery is intended to inspire a nice glow of patriotic satisfaction.

I am not jeering at the A.B.C. for its quaint idea. The programme's designer has rightly diagnosed a disease of the Australian mind and is applying a sensible curative treatment. The dismaying circumstance is that such a treatment should be necessary, or even possible; that in any nation, there should be an assumption that the domestic cultural product will be worse than the imported article.

The devil of it is that the assumption will often be correct. The numbers are against us, and an inevitable quantitative inferiority easily looks like a qualitative weakness, under the most favourable circumstances—and our circumstances are not favourable. We cannot shelter from invidious comparisons behind the barrier of a separate language; we have no long-established or interestingly different cultural tradition to give security and distinction to its interpreters; and the centrifugal pull of the great cultural metropolises works against us. Above our writers—and other artists—looms the intimidating mass of Anglo-Saxon culture. Such a situation almost inevitably produces the characteristic Australian Cultural Cringe—appearing either as the Cringe Direct, or as the Cringe Inverted, in the attitude of the Blatant Blatherskite, the God's-Own-Country and I'm-a-better-man-than-you-are Australian Bore.

The Cringe mainly appears in an inability to escape needless comparisons. The Australian reader, more or less consciously, hedges and hesitates, asking himself 'Yes, but what would a cultivated Englishman think of this?' No writer can communicate confidently to a reader with the 'Yes, but' habit; and this particular demand is curiously crippling to critical judgment. Confronted by Furphy, we grow uncertain. We fail to recognise the extraordinarily original structure of his novel because we are wondering whether perhaps an Englishman might not find it too complex and self-conscious. No one worries about the structural deficiencies of *Moby Dick.* We do not fully savour the meaty individualism of Furphy's style because we are wondering whether perhaps his egotistic verbosity is not too Australianly crude; but we accept the egotistic verbosity of Borrow as part of his quality.

But the dangers of the comparative approach go deeper than this. The Australian writer normally frames his communication for the Australian reader. He assumes certain mutual preknowledge, a responsiveness to certain symbols, even the ability to hear the cadence of a phrase in the right way. Once the reader's mind begins to be nagged by the thought of how an Englishman might feel about this, he loses the fine edge of his Australian responsiveness. It is absurd to feel apologetic towards *Such Is Life,* or *Coonardoo* or *Melbourne Odes* because they would not seem quite right to an English reader; it is part of their distinctive virtue that no Englishman can fully understand them.

I once read a criticism which began from the question 'What would a French classicist think of *Macbeth?*' The analysis was discerningly conducted and had a certain paradoxical interest; but it could not escape an effect of comic irrelevance.

A second effect of the Cringe has been the estrangement of the Australian Intellectual. Australian life, let us agree, has an atmosphere of often dismaying crudity. I do not know if our cultural crust is proportionately any thinner than that of other Anglo-Saxon communities; but to the intellectual it seems thinner because, in a small community, there is not enough of it to provide for the individual a protective insulation. Hence, even more than most intellectuals, he feels a sense of exposure. This is made much worse by the intrusion of that deadly habit of English comparisons. There is a certain type of Australian intellectual who is forever sidling up to the cultivated Englishman, insinuating: '*I,* of course, am not like these other crude Australians; *I* understand how you must feel about them; *I* should be spiritually more at home in Oxford or Bloomsbury.'

It is not the critical attitude of the intellectual that is harmful; that could be a healthy, even creative, influence, if the criticism were felt to come from within, if the critic had a sense of identification with his subject, if his irritation came from a sense of shared shame rather than a disdainful separation. It is his refusal to participate, the arch of his indifferent eye-brows, which exerts the chilling and stultifying influence.

Thinking of this type of Australian Intellectual, I am a little uneasy about my phrase 'Cultural Cringe'; it is so much the kind of missile which he delights to toss at the Australian mob. I hope I have made it clear that my use of the phrase is not essentially unsympathetic, and that I regard the denaturalised Intellectual as the Cringe's unhappiest victim. If any of the breed use my phrase for his own contemptuous purposes, my curse be upon him. May crudely-Dinkum Aussies spit in his beer, and gremlins split his ever to be preciously agglutinated infinitives.

The Australian writer is affected by the Cringe because it mists the responsiveness of his audience, and because its influence on the intellectual deprives the writer of a sympathetically critical atmosphere. Nor can he entirely escape its direct impact. There is a significant phrase in

Henry Handel Richardson's *Myself When Young*. When she found herself stuck in a passage of *Richard Mahony* which would not come right, she remarked to her husband, 'How did I ever dare to write *Maurice Guest*—a poor little colonial like me?' Our sympathies go out to her—pathetic victim of the Cringe. For observe that the Henry Handel Richardson who had written *Maurice Guest* was not the raw girl encompassed by the limitations of the Kilmore Post Office and a Philistine mother. She had already behind her the years in Munich and a day-to-day communion with a husband steeped in the European literary tradition. Her cultural experience was probably richer than that of such contemporary novelists as Wells or Bennett. It was primarily the simple damnation of being an Australian which made her feel limited. Justified, you may think, by the tone of Australian life, with its isolation and excessively material emphasis? Examine the evidence fairly and closely, and I think you will agree that Henry Handel Richardson's Australian background was a shade richer in cultural influence than the dingy shop-cum stuffy Housekeeper's Room-cum sordid Grammar School which incubated Wells, or than the Five Towns of the eighteen-eighties.

By both temperament and circumstance, Henry Handel Richardson was peculiarly susceptible to the influence of the Cringe; but no Australian writer, unless he is dangerously insensitive, can wholly escape it; he may fight it down or disguise it with a veneer of truculence, but it must weaken his confidence and nag at his integrity.

It is not so much our limitations of size, youth and isolation which create the problem as the derivativeness of our culture; and it takes more difficult forms than the Cringe. The writer is particularly affected by our colonial situation because of the nature of his medium. The painter is in some measure bound by the traditional evolution of his art, the musician must consider the particular combinations of sound which the contemporary civilised ear can accept; but ultimately paint is always paint, a piano everywhere a piano. Language has no such ultimate physical existence; it is in its essence merely what generations of usage have made it. The three symbols m-a-n create the image of a male human being only because venerable English tradition has so decreed. The Australian writer cannot cease to be English even if he wants to. The nightingale does not sing under Australian skies; but he still sings in the literate Australian mind. It may thus become the symbol which runs naturally to the tip of the writer's pen; but he dare not use it because it has no organic relation with the Australian life he is interpreting.

The Jindyworobaks are entirely reasonable when they protest against the alien symbolisms used by O'Dowd, Brennan or McCrae; but the difficulty is not simply solved. A Jindyworobak writer uses the image 'galah-breasted dawn'. The picture is both fresh and accurate, and has a sense of immediacy because it comes direct from the writer's environment; and yet somehow it doesn't quite come off. The trouble is that we—unhappy Cringers—are too aware of the processes in its creation. We can feel the writer thinking: 'No, I mustn't use one of the images which English language tradition is insinuating into my mind; I

must have something Australian: ah, yes—' What the phrase has gained in immediacy, it has lost in spontaneity. You have some measure of the complexity of the problem of a colonial culture when you reflect that the last sentence I have written is not so nonsensical as it sounds.

I should not, of course, suggest that the Australian image can never be spontaneously achieved; one need not go beyond Stewart's *Ned Kelly* to disprove such an assumption. On the other hand, the distracting influence of the English tradition is not restricted to merely linguistic difficulties. It confronts the least cringing Australian writer at half-a-dozen points.

What is the cure for our disease? There is no short-cut to the gradual processes of national growth—which are already beginning to have their effect. The most important development of the last twenty years in Australian writing has been the progress made in the art of being unself-consciously ourselves. If I have thought this article worth writing, it is because I believe that progress will quicken when we articulately recognise two facts: that the Cringe is a worse enemy to our cultural development than our isolation, and that the opposite of the Cringe is not the Strut, but a relaxed erectness of carriage. (pp. 299-302)

Arthur Phillips, "The Cultural Cringe," in Meanjin, *Vol. IX, No. 4, December, 1950, pp. 299-302.*

POETRY

Andrew Taylor

[*Taylor is an Australian educator and writer, notable for his several volumes of poetry. In the following essay, he explores the development and definition of Australian poetry.*]

It is not so long ago that mention of a book on Australian poetry would have been greeted by a certain kind of academic with the comment "I didn't know there was any Australian poetry, much less a book on it". The implication was not, of course, that no poetry had been written in Australia, but that no poetry written here was good enough or interesting enough to warrant a book on it. Manifestly foolish as such a comment would be today, it serves nonetheless to raise the whole problematic of Australian poetry—just what is it and, equally important, how do we know what it is?

Things are very different today from thirty, or even twenty, years ago. The notion that there is some unitary tradition of English literature with its capital still in London has been replaced by the acceptance of a multiplicity of traditions. Even the image of literature in English as some kind of tree—the great trunk, consisting of Chaucer, Shakespeare, Milton, and so on, branching at various historical moments into American, Australian, Canadian, etc., literature—seems a little antiquatedly colonialist.

Rather, the English language—and perhaps one should say languages—is or are seen as seed, scattered in different places and at different times, and over differing races, cultures, and social classes or groups; thus it germinates into a variety of literatures which include not only the "high" but also the popular which almost always coexist with it. Thus we no longer feel guilty when we study—or teach—Brennan instead of Wordsworth, Slessor instead of Eliot. Brennan and Slessor have their places within a field designated Australian literature (sub-section Australian poetry), a field which to a considerable extent provides the frame within which they can be read as Australian poets. Yet at the same time the field itself is also to a large part constituted by their presence within it.

How this field is accounted for (if for the present we can set aside the ideology of the value judgments that determine which texts constitute it, are permitted entry) varies somewhat from critic to critic. But by and large the format of the Pelican volume, *The Literature of Australia,* edited by Geoffrey Dutton, exemplifies a procedure which explicitly or otherwise still underlies the practice of many Australian critics. A social, political and historical matrix (the "history of Australia") is invoked, in relation to which a number of writers judged to be important are considered in such a way that the "development" of Australian writing from convict days to the present is shown to have taken place. Although none of the contributors to *The Literature of Australia* can ultimately account for a writer's output totally in terms of them (and in fact none of them actually tries to do so), the motivating assumption of this model is that literature grows out of, or is produced by, society and history. Most studies of Australian writing have stressed this "commonsense" priority of society and history to literature; John Docker's concern [in his *In a Critical Condition*] with the two-way formative processes of cultural history is only a more recent sophistication of an approach which has long distinguished commentators on Australian literature from the erstwhile New Critical or Leavisite practice of some of their academic colleagues, who tended to isolate literature from any political-historical matrix. But this re-insertion of Australian literature into history has rarely taken into account the sophistications of contemporary Marxist criticism, in particular the fact that history as we know it is not an empirical "given", but our reading of our past. Without dwelling on this point in any detail at the moment, I would argue that history is available to us only as a text, as yet another text among a multiplicity of texts. As Fredric Jameson writes in a recent and sophisticated account [in his *The Political Unconscious*] of this notion:

> What Althusser's own insistence on history as an absent cause makes clear, but what is missing from the formula as it is canonically worded, is that he does not at all draw the fashionable conclusion that because history is not a text, the "referent" does not exist. We would therefore propose the following revised formulation: that history is not a text, not a narrative, master or otherwise, but that, as an absent cause, it is inaccessible to us except in textual form, and that our approach to it and to the Real itself necessarily

passes through its prior textualization, its narrativization in the political unconscious.

Thus how we read history—which means, simply, what history is for us at any given moment—depends in some measure on how we have learned to read it by means of our practice with it and other texts.

For example, Patrick White's *Voss,* although loosely based on the historical story of Leichhardt, is not itself history in any verifiable sense; yet it has become a powerful influence on the way many Australians of the present see their country's past and, therefore, on the way they inhabit its present. Similarly, the various "cultural" readings of the Anzac story (from Alan Seymour's *The One Day of The Year,* for example, to Peter Weir's film *Gallipoli*) provide influential interpretations of that event to today's Australians, almost none of whom actually participated in it. No Australian historian with any claim to a knowledge of his field can plausibly be untouched by these cultural readings of the past, any more than he can be by similar readings of the present. Therefore I want to suggest that to treat history as prior to, and thus in some way productive of, literature involves a hierarchical ordering of the duality "history/literature" in which history is the privileged term, an ordering which could be readily subverted so as to indicate that literature contributes to and thus helps to generate our (reading of) history.

A less debatable matter is the general consensus that Australian culture has developed under the progressively weakened dominance of its parent culture—the English—in a process endemic to all colonial cultures. This process of maturation is conveniently outlined by Elaine Showalter in her book on women's literature, *A Literature of Their Own:*

> In looking at literary subcultures, such as black, Jewish, Canadian, Anglo-Indian, or even American, we can see that they all go through three major phases. First, there is a prolonged phase of *imitation* of the prevailing modes of the dominant tradition, and *internalization* of its standards of art and its views on social roles. Second, there is a phase of *protest* against these standards and values, and *advocacy* of minority rights and values, including a demand for autonomy. Finally, there is a phase of *self-discovery,* a turning inward freed from some of the dependency of opposition, a search for identity.

Given the peculiar beginnings of white settlement in Australia as a convict colony, one can perceive elements of the second phase of this development right from the start. Nonetheless this model is as apt for Australia, in its general outlines, as it is for any of the cultures Showalter mentions. Beginning as a process of submission yet imitation, then giving way to a rebellion leading finally through self-discovery to independence, it is clearly akin to the development of a child through adolescence to adulthood. In many respects it resembles Harold Bloom's Oedipal or Promethean model of the development of a "strong" poet [in his "Coleridge: The Anxiety of Influence" in *Literary Criticism: Idea and Act,* W. K. Wimsatt, ed.], particularly when we bear in mind that any culture which successfully wins its independence from the powers of influence has become, in Bloom's sense, a "strong" culture.

The gist of Bloom's rather complex argument is that any poet (and for the purposes of this discussion we could substitute the word culture for poet) who becomes "strong" does so not by neglecting his or her precursors but as a result of an obsession with a parental figure whose work he or she must wrestle with and ultimately rewrite, wrench askew, in order that it might be made right, got right. As Bloom writes:

> The meaning of a strong poem is another strong poem, a precursor's poem which is being misinterpreted, revised, corrected, evaded, twisted askew, made to suffer an inclination or bias which is the property of the later and not the earlier poet. Poetic influence, in this sense, is actually poetic misprision, a poet's taking or doing amiss of a parent poem. . . .

In order to gain a place for himself, the younger must displace the older; the success of the younger is won "at the expense of his forebears as much as his contemporaries". One could translate this into Oedipal terms by saying that the young culture or "strong" poet must in some sense deform or destroy his father in order to take possession of his father's wife, who in this case is the muse, his own true mother. Obviously the terms of this model could be changed from he to she without damaging its structure.

Although in the long run it is nothing more than a trope, such a model seems to be of considerable use, particularly when deployed simultaneously on an individual and on a national level. It provides an account, for example, of the failure of Christopher Brennan ever to displace Milton, the dominating father figure, from the centre of his poetic world and to create a space at Milton's expense within which he could mature as a strong poet. In this respect Brennan was manifestly less a "strong" poet than Milton himself, who was prepared to grapple with no less a father figure than the Protestant god himself in order "to justify the ways of God to men". Brennan's tactic, on the contrary, was to evade, rather than seek out, confrontation. Writing in the last decade of the nineteenth century when Australia, as a federated nation, was not yet in existence, Brennan was further disadvantaged by writing within a poetic culture which had barely embarked on adolescent rebellion against parental authority. Whether any poet could have achieved Brennan's ambition at that moment of Australia's cultural development is problematic, though one must not ignore the achievement of his contemporaries in other fields, notably in fiction and painting. One could hazard the hypothesis that in prose that necessary rebellion was already further advanced, as could be easily enough demonstrated by the nationalism apparent within it. Consequently Lawson's and Furphy's aim would have been less to emulate British precursors than to subvert them and render them unfit for their role as dominating father. Certainly some such operation seems to be going on in Furphy's satire and parody. Their ultimate aim was thus to write Australian literature; whereas Brennan's was still to win himself a place within English or, more grandly still, within European literature.

This trope or model of cultural development also offers a way of discussing the tensions within a culture at any particular time as new writers develop by testing their strength against their precursors. And it enables us to read Australian poetry in relation to English precursors and contemporaries, and Australian poetry of one period of development in relation to Australian poetry of another. But it also entails certain problems. When it is applied to a young culture (as distinct from an individual writer) in the process of its development toward maturity, it could be seen as serving to support or underwrite the notion of poetry as a "corpus", even a kind of "body politic", united at any historical moment in some adversary relationship with parental tyranny. It would be a naive critic indeed who would claim that all Australian poetry of, for example, the last decade of the nineteenth century was unified and coherent in its position vis-à-vis English poetry. Nonetheless the common habit of characterising poetry in terms of decades ("the poetry of the nineties", for example) indicates a deep-rooted tendency to classify in terms of likeness and to minimize disparities and differences. It seems more congenial to characterize a body of poetry in terms of similarity rather than in terms of its internal differences: the corpus of Australian poetry thus consists less of a diversity of parts, each adapted for specific ends, than of what fits together, what shares common characteristics. This stress on what is common underlies many attempts to define the corpus. Definition is—by definition—the establishing of limits, the erection and policing of boundaries around a common ground. Within these limits we have Australian poetry. Beyond them we have something else.

To define the corpus is, psychologically, an attempt to eliminate diversity, to establish inner coherence by excluding what is discordant, disruptive, other. (To continue the Oedipal comparison, it is an attempt to rid Thebes of all that would corrupt and subvert its purity: ostensibly the Sphinx but, as we should know, really Oedipus himself.) The corpus of Australian poetry thus consists of those poets and those poems sharing a family likeness, those which are akin. This does not mean, of course, that they are all absolutely alike, and critics and anthologists—those organizers of family reunions—pride themselves on the diversity of the family members they manage to assemble in one place. Still, they all must have some kinship; and it is when one asks of what, precisely, this kinship consists, that difficulties arise. Few critics or anthologists today would insist on some more or less explicit quality of "Australianness" in the way that Douglas Sladen did in his *A Century of Australian Song,* published in 1888. Still, writers as diverse as Les A. Murray and John Tranter have firmly held ideas about what direction they wish to see Australian poetry going and thus what, properly speaking, is or is not part of that family.

Murray wishes to eradicate or discourage certain qualities he considers alien to some kind of genuine Australianness which he sees exemplified in rural or small town life and threatened by urban sophistication, excessive intellection and the seductions of mere faddishness. Deeply distrustful of the academy, he champions [in his *The Peasant Mandarin*] a "fundamentally democratic style" which is "the central and best tendency of Australian poetry, an enlightened, inclusive, civil mode of writing which belongs ultimately to the middle style". Criticizing John Tranter's poetry for being "mannered, controlled, discussing feeling rather than evoking it and disciplined out of any simplicity or largesse", he claims that "the memory and aspiration of community . . . have kept the best Australian poetry humane in a time when it has often seemed more natural to accept the apparent drift of things and become wholly elitist". His wide-ranging choice of poems in *The New Oxford Book of Australian Verse,* with its generous selection of Aboriginal material, exemplifies this position.

Tranter, on the other hand, wishes to lop off developments which he sees as antiquated, enfeebled and incapable of vigorous new growth, and to graft onto the old stock a cosmopolitan awareness of new possibilities: to arrange a good marriage for Australian poetry, in other words. Combating Murray's endorsement of a national tradition, he promotes a poetry involved in the developments of international modernism [in *The New Australian Poetry*]:

> The poets of the Generation of '68 have left the duties of priest, psychotherapist and moral administrator to those who feel they are best trained to enact them. They have instead devoted their energies to that field of human action where their skills and talents arm them with a unique authority, where meaning embodies itself as speech, and words emerge as that most ancient yet most contemporary voyage of discovery, literature.

Despite his explicitly cosmopolitan and anti-conservative stance, Tranter, just as much as Murray, is attempting an ideologically based purification of the family of Australian poetry, in that the spouse he chooses for it is seen as eminently capable of producing offspring whose vigour will unequivocally proclaim them as the true heirs to, and rightful possessors of, this country's poetic inheritance. It should not surprise us that the definitions of Australian poetry underlying both Murray's and Tranter's procedures result not from simple exclusion of the unfamilial, but from expulsion of members of the family deemed unworthy of their place within it. Only by rejecting, excluding Australian poetry, it seems, can Australian poetry be defined.

Another way of attempting to define the corpus or family of Australian poetry—and it is, of course, inextricably intertangled with what Murray and Tranter are doing too—involves some more or less defined criteria of literary quality, that is, goodness or badness. And here we enter onto hazardous ground indeed. The fact that judgments of literary quality have a very large—and largely unconscious—ideological dimension is something that critics, reviewers, anthologists, and even writers in Australia are still reluctant to come to terms with. The concealment of ideology as common sense, or as sensibility, is still so widely practised that it is rarely recognized for what it is. Critics praise what is moving, profound, powerful, invigorating, vital, and so forth—without adding the essential qualifications, "for whom" and "why for whom". Therefore it was heartening to read, at the end of her introduction to *The Oxford History of Australian Literature,* Leonie Kramer's

declaration that "We have tried to take a clear view of the very large body of literature before us, and to expose the critical assumptions upon which our judgments rest".

It is consequently disappointing when we turn to Vivian Smith's section on poetry in *The Oxford History* to find that nowhere within its one hundred and fifty-five pages is this exposure actually made. When he claims, early in his essay, that "somewhere between the pressures of inherited forms which need to be individually mastered and not simply imitated, and the burdens of a culture in perpetual difficulties, individual work of considerable value and impressiveness has been created" he does not go on to give an explicit account of how value is constituted. One suspects that value here has something to do with being impressive, but there is no real attempt at a careful theoretical analysis of who is being impressed, particularly in relation to subjectively held social or other values that are not explicitly acknowledged. Similarly the whole problematic of "inherited forms"—suggesting the interlocking questions of a writer's relation with previous writing and a young culture's relation to an older one which I have touched on earlier—receives little rigorous attention. One would also welcome some analysis of what is meant by "a culture in perpetual difficulties". If one were to find food for thought in Fredric Jameson's provocative thesis that "a given style [is] a projected solution, on the aesthetic or imaginary level, to a genuinely contradictory situation in the concrete world of everyday social life", then those "perpetual difficulties"—whatever they might be—might be read as culturally productive rather than as "burdens" to be sloughed off.

When one turns to actual critical analysis in Smith's essay, one finds that evaluation is performed by means of an impressionistic and frequently metaphorical language which leaves untouched the deeper questions of value formation. Several examples, taken almost at random, can illustrate this. Discussing James McAuley, he writes:

> If many of the later lyrics are slight the best are by no means superficial, and in the finest like "At Rushy Lagoon" and "In Northern Tasmania" the valedictory mood—the sense of a fading life—comes together with the sense of a vanishing way of life to achieve a poignant music.

One cannot take issue with his thematic analysis, although one should remind oneself that the words "slight" and "superficial" when applied to poetry—as they so often are—are actually metaphors. But it is the reference to "poignant music" which is of interest here. Music is devoid of semantic significance: it is less answerable to its listeners' demands for signification than poetry is, since the apparent offer of "meaning" is one of the things we habitually ask of poetry. (In fact in the poem that Smith is discussing McAuley makes his meaning quite clear: "A way of life is in decline, / And only those who lived it know / What it is time overwhelms . . . ") The implication of the image Smith uses to praise McAuley is that his finest late poetry gains in quality as it leaves semantic signification behind, in so far as it becomes something other than poetry. What we have here, concealed behind an impressionistic evaluative characterization of the poem's quality, is an apparently unconscious endorsement of Pater's dictum that poetry aspires to the condition of music.

Elsewhere, in his discussion of David Campbell, Smith praises him in these terms:

> It is the strength of Campbell's art (as of the lyric in general) to affirm the paradoxical resistance of the small and frail in front of the great and overwhelming, in a poem that avoids both sentimentality and preciosity; to demonstrate how a sustaining truth may be perceived through the apparently insignificant.

The resident values of a conservative liberal humanism are closer to the surface here, more explicit. Campbell's poetry is good because of the values it thematizes: a championing of the underdog, a mistrust of the big, a dislike of both sentimentality and the precious, a belief in sustaining truth. But Smith then goes on to discuss Campbell's later poems in this way:

> His poems have become smoother and rounder but more deliberately random. He no longer writes with the plucked staccato tension of *Speak with The Sun,* but his poems have retained one quality throughout: the capacity for looking at the commonplaces of nature and life with a fresh eye. His imagery is always clear and alertly observed in the manner of folk songs.

Implicit in the description of the poems becoming "smoother and rounder" is the image of water-worn stones, water-worn stones which look, incidentally, "with a fresh eye". Again, as with the McAuley passage, the poems are praised in terms of what they are not, in terms this time of passivity, inertness, non-signification. The reference to folk songs is also interesting. Contrary to what is claimed, "the manner of folk songs" is not one of clear and alert observation—"a fresh eye"—but of clear and alert reference to social and cultural codes immediately retrievable. Folk song's stock of tropes is small when compared with that of "high" literature, and they function by familiarity and convention, unlike the tendency of "high" literature towards originality and unfamiliarity. If such tropes appear vivid to middle-class university educated people such as Vivian Smith and myself—readers rather than singers—it is because they are not so familiar to us as they are to habitual singers and listeners of folk songs. Transposed into a different social context, they acquire the unfamiliarity and hence the vividness that we praise in "high" literature. Implicit in Smith's remarks, therefore, is a failure to take account of the complex social and conventional operations at work in any reading of literature, and the role they play in any kind of evaluation.

I have written at some length on these three passages, not because Smith is a particularly flagrant example but because he is so representative of commentators on Australian poetry who, eschewing a rigidly historical approach, attempt a definition of the field of Australian poetry in terms of literary values. Literary values, literary standards, are themselves conventional and ideological, and are not absolute. Yet rarely are the ideological bases for their value judgments made explicit. Ideology, in general, masquerades as common sense, good taste, a firm knowledge of literature and an appreciation of what it means to be an Australian, or some such apparently self-explanatory quality. Needless to say, the picture of Australian poetry which emerges is nonetheless intimately related to the ideologies so disguised, and not to any chimerical absolute sense of literary worth.

James McAuley employed another metaphor in attempting a definition of Australian poetry when he titled his book *A Map of Australian Verse.* But for all its implicit claim to a technical impartiality, a scientific disinterestedness, mapmaking is not an innocent activity. A map is a deployment of conventional signs which are simultaneously passive (their signification assigned to them by society and history) and active (they signify certain things by excluding the signification of others). Any map, whether it be of Australian verse or of Australia itself, is thus interpretation, a reading of the field, in which certain features are omitted in order that other features become visible. The signs themselves are not passively obedient to the cartographer's will. They help to determine not only what form his expression will take but also what he will find to map in the first place. In addition, this cartographic reading is itself subject to further factors not originating within it, and not the product of what is read either, as "pure" or "innocent" response. As Jonathan Culler states in *The Pursuit of Signs,* "Meaning is not an individual creation but the result of applying to the text operations and conventions which constitute the institution of literature". These "operations and conventions" which make reading "an interpersonal activity" originate neither in McAuley nor anyone else, nor in the text itself, but in society and history (history which is accessible to us only as a text). They constitute themselves within us as ideology, or as the pathways along which ideology advances itself. To an extent that "commonsense" or sensibility critics would consider preposterous, they actually determine what will be seen as poetry, what will be read as poetry at any moment, and how that poetry will be read. In this way it is they that draw the map, determining what can appear on it and what cannot. McAuley's "map", therefore, is really a reading of a map already drawn, in that the conventions and signs determining his interpretation of Australian poetry are always—and always already—in place.

By way of concluding this part of my discussion, I would just observe that it is one of the paradoxes of literary studies that while we claim that one of literature's greatest qualities is its ability to unsettle and disturb, the urge to relate, integrate and even unify—the urge to privilege the familiar and the familial, that which works on us in ways which we can understand because it does not subvert what our understanding is grounded in—still activates most studies of literature. This integrative activity, I want to stress, consists simultaneously and necessarily of its opposite: of a divisive, exclusive drawing of limits. The irreducible, and largely unexamined, ideological subjectivity, (what Jameson calls "the political unconscious"), determining the drawing of these limits in no way prevents them from being drawn. In fact, it may be organic with the wish to locate the other as outside the self, rather than as radically within it, constitutive of it.

Thus when the locus of poetic discourse is actually claimed to be the other itelf, this is an ideological act which not only challenges orthodox versions of the corpus of Australian poetry, but also reveals their ideological formation. This is the effect of anthologies such as *Off the Record* and *The Penguin Book of Australian Women Poets.* Both books can be seen as specific interventions aimed at changing common perceptions of Australian poetry. Although questions of poetic quality are addressed by the editors, neither anthology is concerned primarily with them. Instead, they aim to make heard voices which common preconceptions of Australian poetry have rendered inaudible. *Off the Record* paradoxically is a collection of poems which are in most cases not primarily intended for printed presentation, but meant to be presented orally—performance poetry. The irony of this is not lost, of course, on its editor who, in a lengthy introduction, claims that print-oriented poetry in Australia is the product and the property of the middle class establishment and the academic support system which controls its production and distribution. Performance poetry, on the other hand, is not so much the voice of another class as the voice of those who challenge this perceived hegemony: "Poetry was losing its high-art nose, its meaningful pause and its class-diseased larynx . . . It was now in the hands of chemists, carpenters, teachers, housewives, journalists, architects and factory hands." *The Penguin Book of Australian Women Poets* is, like similar anthologies elsewhere, an attempt to rescue the voices of women from the obscurity to which a patriarchal critical apparatus would condemn them. It challenges the assumptions of value-formation which have served to privilege male poets over female, or to favour that poetry by women which best consorts with male-defined conceptions of female gender. These two anthologies claim to speak from "outside" a perceived social establishment or received discourse, and in doing so they draw attention to the ideological bases—and hence limits—of what until recently was regarded as a largely aesthetic practice. Their essentially partisan nature is thus a challenge to any unitary conception of Australian poetry which earlier practices may have fostered.

In a way that is in no sense exhaustive, I have attempted to suggest several of the problems that emerge when critical discourse attempts to engage with the notion of Australian poetry in some sense conceived as a whole: as a body of work emerging from a colonial situation and akin to a child developing towards maturity and independence from parental authority; as a family held together by kinship and defining itself in terms of its difference from what is "outside" while being still, as families are apt to be, fraught with internal differences and incompatibilities; as a terrain and as a reading of a terrain. For the last part of this discussion I want to turn to those two words "Australian poetry" which are responsible for, and constantly vex, the critics' and the anthologists' nightmare: whom to include, whom to exclude. The mention of anthologists here is deliberate because the anthology, like the critical study, is a signifier, both in its production and in its consumption. And it works, like all other signifiers, by exclusion. An anthologist's reading of Australian poetry is, inevitably and simultaneously, a writing of it: a writing out of it by means of a writing off of (parts of) it. I have already touched on the way this reading is effected by putting into play certain operations and conventions which are to a greater or lesser extent as unconscious as those we both activate and conform to while driving a car; and I have pointed to the fact that these are ideological, often unconsciously so. So the further question remains: just what is it that the critic and the anthologist are reading/writing?

The obvious answer to this question is, of course, Australian poetry. But at this point we must tackle the question of what this phrase means. Take the second term, poetry, first. M. H. Abrams's invaluable handbook, *A Glossary of Literary Terms,* does not list it, and wisely so. For despite the fact that enormous attention has been paid to the structures and language of literature in recent years, no fully satisfying definition of poetry has emerged. Nor can it. What will be acknowledged as poetry is what the conventions of reading operative within a reader in a given place and time permit him or her to read as poetry. Although this may sound tautological, it is not meaningless. To start with, it indicates that whatever it is that constitutes poetry is not to be sought in formal structures which can typologically exclude unwanted intruders, in the way that A. D. Hope, as one amongst many, once attempted. Nor can it be located in "the words on the page", where English departments in Australia were—and largely still are—wont to look for it. Rather, it is to be found in what happens to those words when they go off the page, when they are read. This formulation also indicates that how the words will be read is not a matter of simple, innocent response, but depends on the activity of numerous codes available to and operating through the reader and which ultimately must be ascribed to society and history. The meaning of a poem therefore is not something "contained" within it, manifestly inherent in its words, to be apprehended by a "judicious" or "sensitive" reading (the "content" of a literary "form"); rather, meaning is what happens in the encounter of a text with a reader, when the text of, for example, a poem is inscribed within the ambit of that complex web of texts, textual activities, which is the reader, by means of the act of reading. For as Roland Barthes says, "this 'I' which approaches the text is already itself a plurality of other texts, of codes which are infinite or, more precisely, lost (whose origin is lost)".

A simple illustration will serve to show how not only poetic meaning is generated by reading, but also how what is poetry is determined extrinsically rather than intrinsically. When the Ern Malley poems were first devised by James McAuley and Harold Stewart in 1944, they were intentionally conceived by their authors as not poetry. The "poems" deliberately failed to satisfy their expectations of intelligibility, formal clarity and a certain coherence or "logic" of imagery. Devised specifically to frustrate these expectations, their purpose presumably was to demonstrate that the editors of *Angry Penguins* and its readers either failed to hold these laudable expectations or held them at such a low level of importance that even pastiche satisfied them. However it seems that one convention operative (largely unconsciously) in any act of reading poetry is an expectation of unity or coherence. Without that expectation and the resultant willingness to search for coherence and even to construct it when it is not immediately manifest, our reading of poetry would fall apart at the first metaphor. In the case of the Ern Malley poems, the editors of *Angry Penguins* clearly placed less importance on manifest coherence in the text, and more importance on the readers' activity of searching for it, struggling to find it within the poems' (deliberate) attempts to frustrate them. What has happened, since 1944, is that readers now expect to have to work harder in making coherence of the poems they read than McAuley and Stewart then felt they should. The result is that we can now read the Ern Malley poems as poetry. They have become poems, even if not major or particularly good ones, because their incoherences no long exclude them from the space our reading habits allocate to poetry.

If a definition of poetry can be approached only circuitously, by assigning it a place within the reading process and simultaneously assigning to the reading process certain cultural (in the widest as well as the narrower sense) and historical determinants, which themselves result from an individual's reading of culture and history, how do we fare when we approach that other term of our problematic phrase, "Australian poetry"?

At perhaps the simplest level, do we mean poetry written by Australians? If so, then we would have to exclude all poetry written in Australia by holders of British, New Zealand, Canadian or American passports, not to mention those residents from countries whose language is other than English and who have not taken out Australian citizenship. If and when such writers acquired Australian citizenship, would only their subsequent poetry be Australian or could their earlier poetry (involved, possibly, with the problems of a new resident in Australia) be admitted along with the poet? Clearly there is something wrong with this method of determining the Australianness of poetry according to the passport of its author. Could we then say that any poetry written within Australia is Australian? But Australia as a nation has existed only since 1901, so we would have to exclude all poetry written before then. We could counter this one by claiming all poetry written within the land-mass of what is now Australia, and in doing so manage to recover the Aboriginal poetry as well. But we would have to exclude all poems written by Australians abroad, for example A. D. Hope's "A Letter from Rome" which was not only written, as it tells us, in Italy, but is about Italy too. And we would have to include all poems written here by visitors, irrespective of whether these were in English or any other language spoken here, and of whether they were ever published, let alone read, here. Even if we were to relax the guidelines a little, and say that Australian poetry is all poetry written by people normally resident in Australia, we still have problems. What, for example, does "normally" mean? Ninety-five per cent, seventy per cent of one's time? Where would this place Peter Porter, or Randolph Stow? Or J. R. Rowland who, as a diplomat, normally spends much of his time overseas and yet who, also as a diplomat, represents, even signifies, Australia in that obscure grammar which is diplomacy?

Since all these attempts at determining by way of prove-

nance what the word "Australian" in this context means, it may be necessary to look within the poetry itself. In terms of content, A. D. Hope's "Australia" is clearly Australian. Just as clearly, the same poet's "Imperial Adam", "The Double Looking Glass" and "In Memoriam: Gertrude Kolmar", all poems which "Australian poetry" would be poorer without, are not. Could it then be a matter of linguistic or stylistic characteristics that we need to be looking for? But Bruce Dawe's colloquialism and air of chat is in these respects far closer to the American Frank O'Hara than he is to Christopher Brennan who, in turn, is closer to the periodic noncolloquiality of Milton than to any recognizable version of Australian linguistic practice. Could it be, in fact, that neither Dawe nor Brennan writes Australian poetry? What we can be sure of, to cut this vexing matter short, is that any attempt at defining Australian poetry in terms of qualities inherent in the poetry will, as with our attempts at defining it in terms of provenance, external qualities, inevitably fail. If the phrase "Australian poetry" has any meaning at all, it is, like what it signifies, conventional, approximate, and subject always to revision.

Because, in one sense, we all know what Australian poetry is. It is that body of poetry, expressing certain themes in certain formal ways, and in certain linguistic modalities (although to be accurate, for "certain" we must also read "uncertain") which, as a result of our reading, our education and even our conversation, we have come habitually to associate with the country and the nation we call Australia. If we wish to be a little more precise, we would have to say that Australian poetry is that poetry selected from this field at its widest extent by critics, reviewers, teachers, readers, and the poets themselves, to signify, to stand for (by means of substitution) the field itself. And, as we have seen, this signification is done by a process of exclusion, frequently based on unconscious ideologies. Only by excluding Australian poetry can Australian poetry be signified. Only in terms of what it is not can Australian poetry actually *be*.

So it seems that the apparently innocuous and self-explanatory term "Australian poetry" is not only hard but actually impossible ultimately to pin down. Australian poetry reveals itself both as a kind of individual developing to maturity, to freedom from a parental culture, and also as a family within which this Oedipal revolt and others are already and always occurring; it is both a terrain and the map of the terrain; it is both something which defies definition and its definition which substitutes itself for it as both signifier and signified. It is, by excluding itself as much as by excluding what is extrinsic to it (what is written in another country and in another language, for example). Australian poetry is, always and inextricably, in terms of what it is not; it is always being overtaken and supplanted by its own definitions, and always being excluded in order that it be manifest. Furthermore, while it is in one sense deeply and inescapably historical, its historicity is constituted by our immediate and contemporary acts of reading.

It should not be surprising, therefore, that a book on Australian poetry, any discourse which attempts to engage meaningfully with whatever that phrase means, is necessarily problematic. Any book on Australian poetry is both a reading of it and a signification of it; it is both an inscription and an exclusion; finally, and perhaps foremost, it is both personal and inescapably cultural and historical. (pp. 7-21)

Andrew Taylor, "A Book on Australian Poetry," in his Reading Australian Poetry, *University of Queensland Press, 1987, pp. 7-21.*

Cecil Hadgraft

[*Hadgraft is an Australian educator and critic. In the following excerpt, he surveys the leading figures in Australian poetry.*]

The earliest Australian literature was already old. This was a necessary consequence of history. Poetry began in Australia as an imitation, rather belated, of typically eighteenth-century forms and themes. It remained imitative for nearly a century.

A sprinkling of verses appeared in the official newspaper, the *Sydney Gazette,* soon after its establishment in 1803. The first thin trickle of verse came from Michael Massey Robinson (1747-1826), a convicted blackmailer, pardoned after arrival, who from 1810 to 1821 wrote odes celebrating public occasions. The convict was followed by a judge, Barron Field (1786-1846), friend of Charles Lamb, who produced the colony's first volume of verse in 1819. Field's verse was as poor as his law, and today only the professed student recalls more than the following two lines of it:

> Kangaroo, Kangaroo!
> Thou spirit of Australia.

Field found Australia sometimes comic, but always distasteful. Others found it repellent. There was no reason why they should love it—they had not wanted to go there. The native-born was likely to have a different opinion. Such was William Charles Wentworth (1792-1872), the first and still among the greatest of Australian statesmen. After his matriculation at Cambridge, he wrote *Australasia,* which took second place to Winthrop Mackworth Praed's entry in competition for the Chancellor's Medal in 1823. Wentworth writes in couplets, in diction worn faceless by a century of use, but with an affection for his distant homeland which, with the help of the anthologists, has kept him remembered as a poet. He looks forward to colonial and national glories: should Britannia, bow'd by luxury, yield its pride of place,

> May this—thy last-born infant—then arise,
> To glad thy heart, and greet thy parent eyes,
> And Australasia float, with flag unfurl'd,
> A new Britannia in another world!

But all this was, in a way, occasional verse, written by a man with something more important to do. The next two were men who wanted rather badly to be honored by their country for their poetic devotion to it. Both were derivative, both tended to see the Australian scene through the spectacles of their reading in English poetry; but both had something in them of the poet dedicated to a calling.

Charles Harpur (1813-1868), whose life was a punctuated catalogue of misfortunes, had read his Milton, his neoclassics, his Wordsworth—but to more than some purpose. His blank verse, too reminiscent of his great master, falls away into sandy wastes; his descriptions are redolent of Augustan phrasing. His best work is found in his narratives, where he can capture, for instance, the excitement and tension of an escape from hostile aborigines. His historical place is as the first Australian poet with some bulk of work; and in one poem he greenly suggests what at the end of the century was to appear as the bush ballad. This short verse-tale of Harpur's, "Ned Connor," with its flavor of "The Rime of the Ancient Mariner," has a bush setting, some movement, and a gathering speed, but its formality is rather far from the colloquial roughness of the bush ballad.

Harpur's admirer, Henry Kendall (1839–1882), weaker in character and as unfortunate, but luckier in his friends, reveals a greater variety. Like Harpur he is full of echoes, and his poetry recalls Tennyson, Arnold, Byron, and Swinburne in varying degrees. This tendency to repeat others—and himself—is one of his two obvious failings; the other is his addiction to the "poetical" word, his belief that *splendid, sublime, stately,* and other such vaguely connotative words will produce the adequate response. Kendall is best read in a selection; for instance, Tom Inglis Moore's *Selected Poems of Henry Kendall,* which contains an Introduction that, though perhaps too kindly, is likely to remain the standard estimate. The variety in his verse stretches from lyric to satire (this last a little unexpected in its trenchancy), with elegy, narrative, description, and humor along the way. Despite his faults of vagueness and bathos, Kendall remains among the sweetest of our singers, pensive and nostalgic, finding often in the voice and hue of creek and mountain the echoes and reflections of his own inner melancholy:

> I think I hear the echo still
> Of long forgotten tones,
> When evening winds are on the hill,
> And sunset fires the cones.

The last poet of any concern in this period offers considerable contrast to Harpur and Kendall. They were both born in Australia, knew and loved its coastal areas, and tried with what powers they had to render its softness or its ruggedness, its music or its silence. Adam Lindsay Gordon (1833–1870) arrived in Australia at the age of twenty and remained English to his death. A myopic roughrider, he wrote little description. Careless in verse as in life, he told of risks taken, dangers overcome, the excitement of the chase. His chief importance is that a few of his narratives set the fashion which the *Bulletin* later fostered into the bush ballads. He has been the subject of one of the queerest incidents in our literature. A few misguided enthusiasts, hero-worshiping Gordon, finally stormed Westminster Abbey, so that in Poets' Corner there now stands a bust of Gordon inscribed "Poet of Australia," an odd memorial to one who was never of Australia and—so some may think—was barely a poet.

The poetry of this period, then, leans heavily on that of England. Consequently, when it describes the new and sometimes bizarre land, it lacks ways to capture the essential quality. It will, for instance, use words like *dell,* where the associations now seem to us grotesquely inappropriate. In a way, wherever they were born, the poets of this period are like English poets put down in Australia. (pp. 42-4)

The poets of the period from 1880 to 1914 may be loosely gathered into three groups: the "public" poets, commemorating or reprehending and often looking hopefully to the future; a smaller group that it is a little misleading but very tempting to call "aesthetes"; and the largest group, the bush balladists, themselves of more than one type.

The most notable of the "public" poets was James Brunton Stephens (1835–1902), a cultured Scot, metrically deft, who wrote some of the best comic verse and a narrative, "Convict Once," that has been both overpraised and undervalued. He also wrote a few poems exhorting his new fellow countrymen, which cover a quarter of a century and begin with hope and aspiration:

> So flows beneath our good and ill
> A viewless stream of Common Will,
> A gathering force, a present might,
> That from its silent depths of gloom
> At Wisdom's voice shall leap to light,
> And hide our barren feuds in bloom,
> Till, all our sundering lines with love o'ergrown,
> Our bounds shall be the girdling seas alone.

Stephens later urges the separate states to forget their jealousies and to federate as a dominion. In a third poem he offers a hymn of triumph as though the dominion had already come into being. He lived to see his hopes realized, dedicating his "Fulfilment" to Queen Victoria. But the note of warning, something of a favorite tune with public poets of the time, is sounded also; the future of the Federation lies in his readers' hands:

> But not so ends the task to build
> Into the fabric of the world
> The substance of our hope fulfilled.

George Essex Evans (1863–1909) was the most vocally hortative of the group. Like Stephens he shows variety—humor, narrative, public verse. Inferior to the elder man in skill, he equals his force with a coarser vigor and writes of figures and incidents of the time. Although he is in the main not deluded by visions of the future, he still echoes the slightly overblown sentiments of nationalism and patriotism:

> This is the last of all the lands
> Where Freedom's fray-torn banner stands,
> Not wrested yet from freemen's hands.

Perhaps his very lack of sensibility makes him the more representative of such contemporary attitudes.

Not one of these "public" poets was born in Australia. But they appear to have had some sense of obligation before reaching the new land, and on arrival they found causes and movements to engage their dutiful enthusiasm. The resultant verse may inspire, but it is unlikely to be inspired. It is Australian in a political or national manner, and it has native idealism; but it hardly represents in an everyday fashion what comes home to men's business and bosoms.

Of the small group who seem to stand aside from the Australian scene, the best known is Victor Daley (1858–1905), an Irishman who reached Australia at the age of twenty. The conventional idea of Daley as a Bohemian—a facile writer of an idealized past, of nostalgia and lost love, all in a diction of the type prevalent in England in the nineties—is now sixty years old and seems certain to prevail. The attempt made, in a volume collected years after his death—*Creeve Roe* (1947)—to show him as essentially a democratic singer lashing abuses, has proved futile. It is ironic that in one poem, "Corregio Jones," he reprehends Australian painters for their neglect of native subjects and their fondness for the past—in short, for doing with paint what he was doing with words. Today Daley reads like a diluted Dowson.

The other member of the group—if indeed it can be called a group as it had no overt aim—is Roderic Quinn (1867–1949), more robust but more unequal than Daley. His "Currency Lass" still is remembered as catching, with some rhythmic dexterity, a sort of macabre, ballad-like quality. Both Daley and Quinn show a greater formal competence in verse than any earlier poet except Brunton Stephens. In the period they blossom like thin-rooted exotics.

Their robust opposites are the bush balladists. These are not to be confused with the writers of the old bush songs. Most bush songs, and probably the best, were composed before 1860, the end of the gold-rush days. The authors are, in general, unknown. (Douglas Stewart and Nancy Keesing's collection, *Old Bush Songs and Rhymes of Colonial Times* (1957), which contains over two hundred and covers a period almost up to yesterday, lists about three-quarters as anonymous.) The words, as often as not, are modified versions of songs already known, and the tunes had existed previously. The themes, sometimes treated humorously, sometimes nostalgically, sometimes seriously, range from convictism to bushranging to the hard life in the outback. Sociologically, they provide treasure for the student; from the literary point of view they are rather poor stuff. But they capture something of the early outlook and to that extent are folk poetry. But they are not, despite assertions to the contrary, "the stones upon which all the later edifice rests." Indeed, had they never existed at all, it is difficult to see that our literature from the eighties on would have been at all different.

The bush ballads are another matter. They are mostly narratives by known authors; they were read and often enough recited. Their forerunners were occasional: Harpur wrote an approximation to a bush ballad, Kendall a couple, and Gordon three in language a little formalized and romanticized, but John Farrell was perhaps the earliest who may justly be called a balladist. The spate began about the middle 1880's. Most of the seeds lay in Gordon's efforts, but it is doubtful if we should have had the harvest but for a weekly periodical, the *Bulletin.*

The foundation of this paper was the most important single happening in Australian literary history in the last century. The *Bulletin* was founded in 1880 by J. F. Archibald and J. Haynes. After a period of indecisive aims, Archibald—in some ways hardly a literary man, but in most ways a highly gifted editor—laid down the principles it was to follow for over a generation. It was to break with the past and the memories of convictism and officialdom and to assert the principle of nationalism; in doing all this it accepted and paid for contributions from its very numerous readers. It was democratic, brash, vitally alive, and enormously influential. It is not too much to say that the bush ballad and the Australian short story were its children.

To its staff Archibald, in 1894, added A. G. Stephens (1865–1933), the most potent critic, if not the best, that this country has had. The few volumes of criticism Stephens has left are no indication of his importance; for most of his work was in his reviews on "The Red Page" of the *Bulletin,* in the letters he wrote to writers, and the influence he exerted on them. He knew practically all the literary men of the period, and however perverse he may occasionally have been, he encouraged and fostered talent when it came his way; Shaw Neilson, for instance, owed him much, and Joseph Furphy's work would almost certainly not have appeared when it did—perhaps only by lucky accident ever—but for his insistence.

In the pages of the *Bulletin* the bush ballad found a home. The prime example of a balladist is A. B. ("Banjo") Paterson (1864–1941). By far the most popular poet ever to have written in Australia, he produced what may be considered the typical bush ballad—a rousing, swinging narrative of events and men of the outback. Though he began writing in the nineties, he looks back to the eighties or earlier and rather heroicizes his figures. These range through most of the types: the station owner, shearer, horseman, swagman, trooper, and so forth. The picture of the country is idealized to correspond with man and incident, and when drought and flood intrude, they magnify this virile and adventurous saga. Paterson's best poem is "The Man from Snowy River," and it remains the bush ballad par excellence. His "Waltzing Matilda" has become the unofficial Australian national anthem.

A contrast appears in the poems of Henry Lawson (1867–1922), the greatest writer of the Australian short story, but not a typical balladist. If Paterson paints rather too rosy a picture, Lawson redresses the balance with his descriptions—he wrote few narratives—of outback disaster and depression. The poems of the two men reflect both their lives and their temperaments—Paterson in fairly easy circumstances and apt to see the outback he knew so well as brighter than it was; Lawson always struggling and embittered, viewing (at least in verse) the outback, which he knew less well than Paterson, in darker shades.

The rather bookish, romantic balladist appears in W. H. Ogilvie (1869–1963), who writes like Scott transferred to Australia, in diction that often appears alien to the rough reality he describes. Edward Dyson (1865–1931) deals with the life and fellowship of the prospector. E. J. Brady (1869–1952), a balladist by concession, is one of the few Australian poets of the sea. Barcroft Boake (1866–1892) survives by virtue of one poem, "Where the Dead Men Lie," a grim and somber threnody.

These varied writers of the ballad were a few among scores. In their fashion, the balladists were (though it may seem odd to say so) conventional. Rough diction, rough galloping meter, rough but kindly men, sardonic humor, and wry acceptance—these were parts of a stock in trade. Readers devoured it all with perhaps a half-conscious awareness that things and men of the outback were really not quite like that. Implicitly it was assumed that in the outback was to be found the true spirit of Australia.

The bush ballad bloomed in Paterson. As years passed, the tradition became a little worn at the edges. After the First World War a newly written bush ballad seemed artificial, an imitation of past fashion. No ballad, early or late, could aspire to be considered great literature, but the type served, and still does, as the expression of a former Australian ethos or even an ideal. (pp. 47-52)

The poets of the Federation period mark a new era quite distinctly. They were, with all their faults, much more mature in outlook and technique than their predecessors and dwindling contemporaries; and, with the exception of Bernard O'Dowd and to a lesser degree Mary Gilmore, they had little of the nationalistic note of the "public" poets or the Australian note of the balladists.

Seven of these poets call for discussion. One of them lived till recently, Mary Gilmore (1865–1962), who was created a Dame of the Order of the British Empire in 1936. Her gifts retained their freshness, and her last volume, *Fourteen Men* (1954), bears witness to the flowering tenderness and pity which in most of her work is instinctive. She is the poet of love, if that word is given a wide meaning—love of woman for child, of wife for husband, of observer for bird and flower, of a human being for the past to which we are all in debt. The objects of her regard are neglected things—the hunted and forgotten aboriginal tribes, the lonely shepherd, even the convict bowed under his task or straining against bonds and blows. She is, then, rather like a national conscience.

Her most delicate and successful effects are with sounds. She can capture the susurration of wings (swans, for instance, appear frequently in her verse), the clang and hoot of flocks of birds, even the void of silence. It is tempting to label her verse as a woman's verse: it has the reactions thought characteristic, it is pitiful and loving, it is patient and suffering, and it trusts in resurgence. These qualities reflect her sympathies and beliefs; for long, especially since the turn of the century, she played a part in the growing labor movement. She still lives as a memory of an age more radiant than our own in its hope for human betterment.

One of these poets has obvious affiliations with former Australian writers: the note of adjuration, heard earlier in Brunton Stephens and Essex Evans, reaches orchestral volume in the poems of Bernard O'Dowd (1866–1953). Born into the Roman Catholic faith, he came under the scientific and socialistic influences of the eighties and nineties; and his intellectual doubts caused him to abandon, with hesitation and reluctance and yet with finality, many beliefs of his youth. Soundly educated, he read closely and widely; he was an admirer of Walt Whitman and corresponded with him; he sharpened his considerable intelligence on the problems of legal drafting; and he used poetry rather as an instrument for exhortation than as the record of experience.

His influence and reputation, once considerable, have decreased, perhaps unduly; his aspiration has a forcefulness that puts him rather by himself. Probably, indeed, this clangor and sense of hortative mission are the very things that have, apart from some modern critical hostility, worked most against him. His reserves of verbal felicity or imaginative insight were never considerable, and so he remains more as a voice heard in one's childhood than as a living force. Even his learning, like his aims, is obtrusive, sowing his verse with recondite allusions and images that stand like grotesque granitic boulders in the field he plowed.

Writing after the federation of the states, he looks forward with mingled hope and doubt to the future of the Commonwealth:

> Last sea-thing dredged by sailor Time from
> Space,
> Are you . . .
> A new demesne for Mammon to infest?
> Or lurks millennial Eden 'neath your face?

These lines from "Australia," his best-known sonnet, suggest his particular quality: an intellectual and national enthusiasm that can occasionally glow into incandescence.

The greatest poet of the seven, indeed by consent of most critics the greatest poet the continent has produced, is Christopher Brennan (1870–1932). He was primarily a scholar—an honors graduate of the University of Sydney, a postgraduate student in Germany (where his chief interest lay in the French symbolists), and eventually an associate professor of German and comparative literature at his old university. His learning was regarded by his contemporaries and by many later as extraordinary in its scope. As a figure he riveted attention and was the subject of legendary tales—great in bulk, aquiline of nose, blackmaned, largely smoking and drinking, volubly talking. A modern critic may wonder if something of this effect has colored the verdict on his poetry, which at the hands of some admirers has been elevated into comparison with that of the greatest in this century.

His verse was collected in 1960. Formerly it was accessible only in anthologies and in the volumes, hard to find except in the larger libraries, that he published at irregular intervals. For some critics this anthologizing has worked in Brennan's favor: he is so uneven, it has been asserted, that his stature is enhanced because we read only his best. Others believe that Brennan must be read as a whole since his poetry forms a massive structure that, however defective in parts, has few equals in its architectonic effect.

Something may be said in favor of both views. But whatever the conclusion, it is undoubtedly true that there are obvious contrasts in Brennan. He is certainly massive in effect; at the same time he is the victim of a phraseology that seems old-fashioned and often pretentious or even strident. He is far more profound and powerful, and at the same time more subtle, than his Australian contemporaries, while (perhaps in consequence) he almost always lacks that appearance of spontaneity which delights and transports in such poets as McCrae and Neilson.

Brennan's life after his return to Australia in 1894 became progressively less contented, and he ended his days, after dismissal from the university, in sporadic dissipation. The philosophy adumbrated in his most important volume, *Poems* (1913), bears some relation to his life until that point. It has been analyzed with sympathetic insight by G. A. Wilkes as a search for a lost Eden. In his expression of this, Brennan traces the vain valuation of love, the despair of the soul's night, the skeptical appraisal of the philosophic (and therefore human) analysis of reality, and the resignation in accepting the universal process of becoming.

These spiritual and emotional experiences are couched in terms not easy of access. Brennan's knowledge of psychology (he is astonishingly modern in outlook), his reading in myth, legend, and literature, and his capacity for symbolic suggestion gave him a verbal armory that he used with great lavishness. The result has been a great deal of puzzled and even resentful explanation, and even Wilkes's authoritative explication has not met with complete acceptance. Some of Brennan's poems, then, are still open to dispute. The surface effect may be strikingly empathetic (as in "Lightning"), or subtly evocative and delicately nostalgic (as in "Sweet Silence After Bells"), or filled with a kinesthetic and tactile imagery (as in "Fire in the Heavens"), and a first reading may give a first agreement. But the significance that is almost certainly symbolized, the place that it occupies, and the part it plays in Brennan's deployment of ideas are not so readily apprehended.

As a technician he is full of sins and redemptions. He is capable of prosaic lines, but more often of mouthed declamations and outmoded, hollow stridencies; phrases such as "antient amplitude" and "mailed miscreant unchaste," for instance, are no uncommon apparitions. But he can also give us—what is not always the lucky or fashioned fate of scholarly poets—the phrase or word where etymological overtones enrich enormously the texture of implication. In

> Those metal quiring hymns
> shaped ether so succinct

the last word gains from our—and Brennan's—awareness of its derivation.

As an Australian poet, he hardly reflects the country he lived in. There are a few passages where knowledge from outside the poems allows us to identify a spot, but the local relevance has little importance in evaluation; it would not affect our reading in the least if his poetry had been written in Timbuktu. Brennan is, then, a poet in the European tradition. He is far distant from Australian preoccupations with the outback or with nationalistic aspirations. He is not clear; he has no narrative, except that of ratiocinative processes; he describes no significant physical actions. He is, in short, the poet of impassioned speculation.

This puts him much aside from his Australian period and surroundings. We have to wait until R. D. FitzGerald before we encounter a poet who bears any relation to him in tendency, however different in outlook. In the years, then, from the first settlement to the sesquicentenary, he is on his own. Over a century had elapsed before Australian poetry reached an adult development. Brennan's *Poems* is the first Australian volume of verse that any critic would venture to appraise as a significant part of the corpus of poetry written in English.

Given the background and upbringing of the next of these seven, few would have dared to predict poetry as the result. John Shaw Neilson (1872–1942) had a hard youth, a meager education, and in thirty years had gone through some two hundred jobs, all of them manual labor. His eyesight grew continually weaker; at last he could hardly see to write and often dictated his verse to an unlettered and wondering companion. Out of that unpromising soil blossomed some of the most delicate poems in Australian literature. All poetry appears in a measure miraculous, but Neilson's by contrast with his scanty opportunities seems even more astonishing. It is, for instance, apparently quite simple; and this we might expect. But the surface simplicity is no mere artlessness: it appears to be a spontaneous *cri de coeur,* but it is very often, as we know from records and manuscript readings, the result of careful revision. A. G. Stephens of the *Bulletin* encouraged Neilson and even suggested alternative versions of lines—which Neilson did not always accept. Again, as the surface technique conceals an art that is really not simple or naïve, so the surface meaning, ostensibly pellucid, has undertones and suggestions that are very rich in their implications. Even his descriptive passages, where he catches the essential quality that makes a thing—bird or beast or fruit— unique, are careful pieces of complex art:

> Across the stream, slowly and with much
> shrinking
> Softly a full-eyed wallaby descends.

The danger that attends such verse as Neilson's is a collapse into bathos. It cannot be denied that Neilson is occasionally a victim. Then the simplicity can dissolve into mawkishness and the childlike becomes the childish. The charm that sufficed before—sinew and strength absent— now cloys like diluted honey. At his most successful, however, as in "Love's Coming," Neilson is an unpredictably magical poet:

> Without hail or tempest,
> Blue sword or flame,
> Love came so lightly
> I knew not that he came.

The poem for which he is known everywhere in Australia is "The Orange Tree," a capturing of elusive mood—the child's developing from attention to listening to identification, the man's coarser sensibility providing a contrast. Slighter than Wordsworth's "Immortality" ode, it is thematically reminiscent of it and suggests by imagery what Wordsworth describes by comparison or philosophic disquisition:

> Listen! the young girl said. There calls
> No voice, no music beats on me;
> But it is almost sound: it falls
> This evening on the Orange Tree.

In a comment on the poem Neilson later wrote, "There was . . . something which I tried to drag in, some enchantment or other." In most of his poems he attempted the same task, and with varying success. In this poem, to which no excerpt does justice, he superlatively succeeded.

In contrast with the others, Hugh McCrae (1876–1958) has an air of not belonging to this world of today. Son of a poet, he was a magnificent figure of a man, and to his extreme age preserved his vikinglike look. Rebellious against constraint, whether of domestic or commercial ties, he avoided the company of other than personal friends.

His poetry, often classified as belonging to the school of Vitalism, corresponds. He turns to the stories and legends of the past, to history or myth. Through his pages centaurs and satyrs strut, nymphs and dryads gambol, hunters gallop in the chase. His favorite bird is the eagle. This suggests an air of vivid unreality, and it is true that McCrae seemed to regard the world of facts and figures as something outside his concern; but this is merely a statement of his themes, not an evaluation.

Through his verse there runs an intense love of life and its overt activity. When he looks below the vibrant surface he uses nature as a reflection of his moods, and these are mostly optimistic. The archer in the path, in one such poem, aims his arrow; the poet momentarily hesitates and then springs to the attack; the arrow whistles harmlessly overhead, and the threatening visitant vanishes. Fear, in other words, is our own creation, and action will dissipate it. Even when death and tragedy enter his pages, the extraordinary and the bizarre offset any effect of despair.

He is mostly a very positive poet. An air of joyousness fills his work. Much of this results from his mastery of empathetic and kinesthetic imagery. Few of his lines are so well known as the conclusion of his "Ambuscade," where the stallions, warned of the approach of centaurs, gallop to the rescue of the mares:

> A roar of hooves, a lightning view of eyes
> Redder than fire, of long straight whistling
> manes,
> Stiff crests, and tails drawn out against the skies,
> Of angry nostrils, webbed with leaping veins,
> The stallions come!

Easily wise after the event, we may yet think of McCrae as fitting into his period. Too competent and too paganly robust to have appeared earlier than the nineties, he would be an oddity after the Second World War. In the Australian twenties, with their reaction against nationalism in art and with their Dionysian cult, he occupied a prominent position. He is among the most individual of our poets, the lusty exponent of a *joie de vivre,* never preaching, expressing no social program or national ethos, little concerned with any morality, but responding to the urgency of physical demand.

Personal and social tensions strain in Frank Wilmot (1881–1942), who adopted the name Furnley Maurice in 1905 to get his verse into the *Bulletin* past the presumedly biased eye of A. G. Stephens. He was diffident and often noncommittal, but in booklets and periodicals he published over four hundred poems. He held fairly firm liberal or socialist views, but his verses on social questions generally stop short at comment rather than push on to advocacy of action. He knew the experimental work of Pound and Eliot, but his own techniques remained traditional until the early 1930's.

He wrote too much for what he had to say, probably because of a reluctance to revise, so that themes seem to recur. The early poems depend largely on the stock response to obvious attacks on a reader's sympathies and reliance on "poetical" adjectives like *eternal.* He had, in short, the courage of a man—but not that of an original poet. In 1916, in the middle of a war that called out the extremest feelings, he published "To God: From the Weary [later changed to Warring] Nations," where, for once, his courage finds adequate expression:

> God, let us forget
> That we accused of barbarous intent
> The foe that lies in death magnificent.
> How can we hate forever, having proved
> All men are bright and brave and somewhere
>   loved?

But his ambivalence, perplexing and distressing to his friends, produced another poem, in which war is lauded as an inevitable instrument of justice.

Maurice's reputation depends today on his *Melbourne Odes* (1934), a collection of urban poems where tension in theme appears, reflecting in part the unresolved conflicts of the poet. The city is built on trade and on huckstering, but into the sky rise the towers the traders have built; into the agricultural show, dusty and tawdry and yet evocative, pour the products of the areas outside the city; and as the folk go homeward,

> Drenched with the colour of unexperienced
>   days,

they are brought back to industrial realities. It is in these poems, with their more direct vision and their more realistic diction, that Maurice both consciously and unconsciously exhibits the results of his study of modern poets such as Eliot. Maurice led no movement, answered no problems, showed no way. He suddenly found his way, and he had his prayer answered—that God would let him do his best things last.

Derivative yet independent, dubiously nationalistic yet different from patriots like O'Dowd, there remains the enigmatic poet William Baylebridge (1883–1942) who was born Blocksidge, under which name he wrote some of his early poems. Baylebridge is in one way like Maurice: he developed from an apprentice to a much more competent craftsman. But whereas Maurice turned to models late in his career and then rather suddenly became a poet, Baylebridge worked on models from the start. The imitations he produced gave little promise of future success. That is the weakness of literary prophecy; for Baylebridge was indefatigable, and some measure of achievement was his reward. Even his sonnets, so obviously Shakespearian, can often be effective in their phrasing.

Throughout his life Baylebridge presented a puzzling fa-

çade to the world of readers. He had means to indulge his tastes, he published his volumes in private and often limited editions, and these often contained revised versions of earlier work. His bibliography—some volumes, for instance, announced but apparently never printed—and his text still remain problems.

The puzzle is seen also in his later work and the social and national philosophy it seems to have been intended to embody. He has been labeled a Nietzschean, a perfervid nationalist, a would-be Nazi or Fascist. Analyses of the last volume, *This Vital Flesh* (1939), a sumptuous limited edition, are in consequence often contradictory. Sometimes the verses are terse, gnomic utterances, sometimes ultra-Miltonically magniloquent, sometimes caustic and vitriolic. Much of his prose is as mannered as his verse. He stands aside from the prevailingly democratic tendencies of many of the writers of the nineties and the earlier portion of this century; and this, together with his other traits, distinguishes him as one of our most idiosyncratic poets. (pp. 57-65)

Both quantity and quality of writing have been considerable in recent years. The number of competent poets has never been so great. The editors of *The Penguin Book of Australian Verse* (1958) chose poems from fifty-nine poets of this century, of whom about a dozen are no longer living. The list was not long enough to suit reviewers; some twenty additional names of living poets were reproachfully or indignantly placarded as inexcusable omissions. In simple arithmetic, this suggests that there are nearly seventy good poets at present writing in this continent of ten million people.

There are, of course, more than seventy—if "good" means having claims to inclusion in a Penguin twentieth-century anthology. But both editors and critics were right. There is a hard core of names, on four of whom all critics would agree—Judith Wright, R. D. FitzGerald, A. D. Hope, and Kenneth Slessor. But after that any choice is going to be invidious.

Here, for instance, are two defensible groups to fill out the round dozen: (1) Douglas Stewart, Nancy Keesing, Vincent Buckley, John Manifold, Francis Webb, John Thompson, David Campbell, David Rowbotham; (2) James McAuley, John Blight, Harold Stewart, Roland Robinson, Geoffrey Dutton, Rosemary Dobson, Ray Mathew, Randolph Stow. A third group, easy to compile, would contain names that many critics would prefer to some of those chosen. Such being the difficulties of anthologists, the writer of a sketch of our literature must simply be content to add to the agreed four a few representatives that his taste imposes, and then resign himself to the inevitable accusation of critical insensitivity.

To classify the poets of the period satisfactorily seems impossible. Groupings may be made, but they serve merely as devices of convenience; there have been "schools," if the term is loosely used, and some poets today hold similar views on the purpose and techniques of their art; but there is surprising diversity of individual performance.

So far as experimentation is concerned, Australian poets since the thirties have been of three kinds—those who

Cover of Outrider *(1962), a collection of poems by Randolph Stow.*

have espoused allusiveness and even opaqueness and some devices of "modernistic" poets; those who have rejected and indeed attacked such experiments; and those who have remained traditional or orthodoxly individual.

Of those rejecting the more extreme experiments, the most influential is A. D. Hope (b. 1907), professor of English at Canberra and certainly the most technically accomplished poet now living in Australia. His work presents him as a double Janus figure. One face of one figure is set determinedly toward clarity: among other things a reader recalls an annihilating attack on the opacities of Max Harris, a caustic review of a novel by Patrick White, and a parody on Hopkins, which takes that poet to task for his idiosyncratic handling of English. The other face is not so readable and has caused some of his verse to be charged with obscurity. The surface effect is for the most part clear enough; but it often symbolizes a more significant yet elusive reality.

One face of the second figure is set, if not with determination perhaps with a sort of compulsion, toward sexual imagery. This aspect has awakened much fascination in youthful readers. Some of these poems, for instance "Imperial Adam," are elaborated, sumptuous, and even luscious:

The pawpaw drooped its golden breasts above
Less generous than the honey of the flesh;
The innocent sunlight showed the place of love;
The dew on its dark hairs winked crisp and
fresh.

Some poems—one hesitates to call them love poems, for suggestions of fulfillment are so sparse—deal with physical relations. Here many readers feel a note of frustration or incompleteness. Such poems seem deprived of any woman. There are, indeed, two persons present, but both are the poet; he is the participant and at the same time the watcher—an autovoyeur who never applauds. The other face is that of the moralist. Hope is the finest satirist the literature has yet seen. Fastidious, impatient, suffering no fool or rogue gladly, he finds the contemporary scene an inevitable target for his barbs. His "Australia" affords a representative quotation:

And her five cities, like five teeming sores,
Each drains her: a vast parasite robber-state
Where second-hand Europeans pullulate
Timidly on the edge of alien shores.

His prolific verbal dexterity of phrase and rhyme appears as patent in these satires as in his more serious poems, and sometimes it is so rich that it even seems to take away from the satiric effect. The poet enjoys hating—it is almost an emotional indulgence—and the reader participates in the orgy.

Hope's great competence makes him a master of the prodigious squib, a superlatively adroit affirmer of the negative. If one may ungraciously complain after the satisfaction he affords, it would be to lament that he has not given us more of such verse as "Meditation on a Bone." This is a poem stripped bare as the bone he writes on, instinct with a bitter and unusual poignancy that is glimpsed on the sudden lifting of the mask that some suspect this poet always wears.

Influenced by Hope—at any rate a holder of some of the same critical tenets—James McAuley (b. 1917) has written mainly two forms of poetry, the satiric and the religious. Some of his satire has been influenced by his religion (he is a Roman Catholic convert) and is molded in the spirit that Dryden gave many of his attacks. The force of McAuley's satire is considerable, and the beliefs whose validity he assumes drive his pen in deep. Oddly enough in a writer who, like Hope, is impatient of much modern experimentation in poetry, his own poems yield examples of the enigmatic and the esoteric. Here, unlike Hope, he presents difficulty not by general, but by particular implication: it is a matter of the unusual and allusive word and phrase.

His bright, hard, and yet sensitive and penetrating diction suffers a change in his second book, *A Vision of Ceremony* (1956). This contains most of his religious verse, and the theme has influenced his style. Sincerity of belief demands, so McAuley maintains, a treatment that should concern itself with naked truths rather than with personal doubts:

Scorn then to darken and contract
The landscape of the heart
By individual, arbitrary

And self-expressive art.

A reader, thinking of Donne and Hopkins, may wonder.

But the style has gone further. Augustan verse, admirably used by McAuley for satire, can even in his modern hands result in some odd mistimings when turned to other purposes. These lines from "Palm" are an extreme example:

> But mostly, stilled to trance, O palm,
> Your paradisal plumage rears
> Its fountain, and amidst the calm
> A milky flowering spathe appears;
>
> Which an ascending youth incises
> Deftly with a bamboo knife,
> Whence a fermenting fluid rises
> Like joy within the common life.

Great religious verse has possessed on the one hand an Edenlike simplicity (which McAuley has not), on the other a tortured and complex force (which McAuley has renounced). The application of a critical credo has limited the religious verse of this poet, an effect the very opposite of that desired.

McAuley's kinship to the eighteenth century and his distrust of certain "modern" trends took a startling form in 1943. He collaborated with his friend Harold Stewart in composing some bogus verse, ostensibly esoteric and experimental, with the ambiguous title *The Darkening Ecliptic*. This was sent to Max Harris, a member of the avant-garde. Harris and many others swallowed the bait; the verse was printed, and the presumed author, "Ern Malley," was acclaimed as "a poet of tremendous power." When the trick was revealed, the victims were gleefully pilloried by the newspapers. Three not necessarily exclusive reactions to the jape were, and still are, current: that it was all a brilliant hoax, the bubble of solemnity was pricked, and nobody was much the worse; that some of the bogus verse was really respectable poetry, the authors not being able to control the mental associations that made their own writings good poetry; that it was all rather a pity, since the laughter resulting tended to cover not only the objects of the trick, but also any experimental poets. Whatever view one holds, the affair remains the most successful literary hoax in our history.

The second of the two "Ern Malley" hoaxers, Harold Stewart (b. 1916), is also a craftsman of considerable polish and virtuosity. His first volume, *Phoenix Wings* (1948), passed with little notice, but it displays his unusual control over aural imagery. In his second volume, *Orpheus* (1956), Stewart tells the myth of the descent and return. Two changes have occurred. The theme is no longer a love story or a nature myth, but a psychological comment on the subconscious springs of poetical activity. It is interesting to recall this when reviewing Stewart's part in the "Ern Malley" affair. The second change is a wit transformation. Stewart uses a five-lined stanza of tetrameters, with a varied rhyme arrangement; and the language is a modernized Augustan:

> With cloven hoof and pointed ear
> Capricious urges leap and leer.

Dexterously neat, brilliantly sophisticated, with a flavor

of Prior or Gay, Stewart is an unusual figure in Australian literature.

The nationalistic tendencies in poetry, together with the idiom of expression, have oddly fluctuated. Last century English poetry and the memories of English poetry and the English scene came between poets and the Australia they saw. The bush ballads went to the opposite extreme: language and theme were pressed into the service of a convention, vigorous, national, and yet in its extremes a little bogus. The other poets addressed themselves to exhortation. The early years of the new century produced only one poet of note who resembled these—O'Dowd. The rest were poets first, Australian poets second, if at all.

But the ballads were still being written and have continued to make belated appearances until this period; the last ones of Ogilvie, for instance, were published in 1937. A deliberated doctrinaire reaction against nationalism in verse showed itself in the twenties. The vehicle was *Vision,* a short-lived quarterly. The moving spirits were Norman Lindsay and his son Jack, and poets like Kenneth Slessor and Hugh McCrae contributed vitality to the Vitalism that has been used by some critics as a label for the group. The setting tended to move back to a poetically pagan era, and here the decorative genius of Norman Lindsay provided illustration. In *Vision* appeared (though more playfully than in other pictures) his satyrs and his bronzed men, arrogantly male, strenuously clasping the characteristic Lindsay women, slit-eyed, long-chinned, mildly afflicted with goiter and elephantiasis. The general air of riotous life should have stimulated everybody. But *Vision* was too extreme, or too precious, or even too good for its period, and only four issues came out.

One poet who outgrew this niche of the twenties is Kenneth Slessor (b. 1901). The poems he contributed to the vociferous *Vision* were often like McCrae's—vital, but to us now occasionally old-fashioned:

> Good roaring pistol-boys, brave lads of gold,
> Good roistering easy maids, blown cock-a-hoop
> On floods of tavern-steam, I greet you! Drunk
> With wild Canary, drowned in wines of old.

His limited output is contained in *One Hundred Poems* (1944; 1957 with omissions and additions). In spite of the small number, the poems range variedly. There are, for instance, the early dealings with historical or legendary scenes. In a very few, a sardonic eye dwells on Australian settings—here, "Country Towns":

> At the School of Arts, a broadsheet lies
> Sprayed with the sarcasm of flies.

But this note is rare with Slessor—the visible world is for him a constant stimulant, food for the senses to enjoy. Even soiled clothing is an experience in a sort of sensuousness, in "William Street":

> Ghosts' trousers, like the dangle of hung men,
> In pawnshop-windows, bumping knee by knee.

And it awakens the unexpected response:

> You find this ugly, I find it lovely.

His most notable poems, such as "Five Visions of Captain

Cook," have dealt with the sea—those who early voyaged on it:

> So, too, Cook made choice,
> Over the brink, into the devil's mouth,
> With four months' food, and sailors wild with dreams
> Of English beer, the smoking barns of home;

those who, like the old salt in "Captain Dobbin," left it:

> But the sea is really closer to him than this,
> Closer to him than a dead, lovely woman,
> For he keeps bits of it . . .
> What you might call a lock of the sea's hair;

those who died in it:

> I felt the wet push its black thumb-balls in,
> The night you died, I felt your eardrums crack,
> And the short agony, the longer dream;

and the poet himself, who saw a bubble on its surface as the fragile mirror of a world momentarily free of time and time's destructive power:

> Leaning against the golden undertow,
> Backward, I saw the birds begin to climb
> With bodies hailstone-clear, and shadows flow,
> Fixed in a sweet meniscus, out of Time.

These frequent extracts from Slessor are not an expediency to escape the task of comment. They serve to stress his quotability. In his small body of work the level of craftsmanship is very high, and almost any page affords examples of his capacity at or near its best. He is a poet drunk on things. So it is surprising and disappointing to find that he has decided to stop at certain points. He stopped writing some years ago, at the verge of the "modernistic" techniques, and only one or two brief poems have appeared since. There are, it is true, some passages in his work, as in "Five Bells," where the meaning does not readily yield itself to inspection, but on the whole he is brilliantly and illuminatingly and sensuously lucid.

Slessor's professed concern is with sheer verbal virtuosity. He is an admirer of Tennyson, and his own lines contain words upon which the lines seem to pivot. What Chesterton said of Tennyson—that in a Tennysonian line such a word is like the keystone of an arch, which would fall into ruin without it—is not quite so true of Slessor, who tends to spread his risks. Nevertheless, lines of much this tenor can be found:

> The lighted beach, the sharp and china sand,

and

> Crow-countries graped with dung,

and

> Between the sob and clubbing of the gunfire.

One may call his credo ostensible, for it holds a suggestion of limitation, of deprecation. Admirably adapted to quotation as they are, his verses are not a scattering of "gems," but (especially the later ones) a coherent body of artistry shot through with a reserved pity and a sardonic regret for our mortality—and his own.

In all these poets the note of reflection necessarily is heard, but philosophical poetry as such has made only occasional appearances. An early major example was the work of Brennan. The only modern to be compared with him in that sphere is R. D. FitzGerald (b. 1902), whose poetical career has stood normal expectation on its head: instead of beginning with narrative and moving sedately with age to poetry of reflection, he began, after some short poems, with philosophical verse and later turned to narrative. But there is no real dislocation; the narratives provide particular examples of the philosophical themes.

The best and most famous of his philosophical poems is his "Essay on Memory," one section of his *Moonlight Acre* (1938). A long poem in couplets, which in FitzGerald's hands are sometimes hardly noted as couplets, it is an eloquent and strangely vivid dissertation upon causality. The memory that he writes of is symbolized by the rain:

> Rain in my ears: impatiently there raps
> at a sealed door the fury of chill drops.

The room is the self. To it the past is often only a blur of sound. In the succession of verbally created independent moments, held in the mind because the mind can conceive or verbalize them, there is the sequence of the past. But the sequence is not one of individual unrelated instants: they are linked in a chain that is unbreakable, though we may not recognize this. Memory for FitzGerald, then, is not our transient recollection, but a sort of infinite memory, the relation of all to the past that has created each present; it is in effect necessity, ineluctable cause and effect. We ourselves perceive only the surface of the process and cannot predict—indeed, we often enough misinterpret the past. Any trust we have in our future must be manifested in our choice of action:

> then, launched above that steep,
> venture shall cant bold wings and with their sweep
> splinter such clogging silence as they met
> in older abyss where time slept stirless yet.

This considerable and complex poem has taken its place in our poetry. It is surprising in at least one technical device: FitzGerald is dealing with an essentially abstract theme, and he has chosen the most material of imagery to express it—imagery that concerns touch, muscular tensions, forces that are to be felt. This is found unexpectedly and brilliantly adequate, for as even the short extracts given suggest, the sense of plastic influence is inherent in them as in the conception the poet is molding, or by which he is molded.

FitzGerald's turning from this conceptual poetry to poetry of action is susceptible of two possible explanations: that he had exhausted his philosophical stores and was obliged to resort to narrative; or that, having stated his thesis, he proceeded to illustration. Those who value his poetry will choose the second explanation. In *Heemskerck Shoals* (1949), the rumination of Tasman, the Dutch explorer, the approach is tentative. In *Between Two Tides* (1952), it is more direct. A story of the South Seas, of island conflict, it is a study in particular choices. Told in a series of enveloped narratives—stories within stories—it is prefaced and concluded by reflection. The action is vivid, but it is often shown to be nugatory or sterile. Fitz-Gerald's latest poem, *The Wind at Your Door* (1959), looks back to an incident in colonial history, the flogging of a convict. All concerned were partly guilty, partly innocent. And to all of them we in the present are bound and indebted:

> That wind blows to your door down all these
>   years.
> Have you not known it when some breath you
>   drew
> Tasted of blood?

This body of work by FitzGerald can, then, be regarded as a more coherent sequence than may at first appear: an author's credo, followed by the exemplifications and qualifications with which he has chosen to illuminate it. In subtlety, if not profundity of thought, his poetry can bear comparison with Brennan's.

One poet who may serve as the all-rounder, spreading his talent over a wide field of writing, is Douglas Stewart (b. 1913), editor, reviewer, critic, anthologist, short-story writer, poet, dramatist. In verse he has moved from lyric to description. His prentice pieces, as so often with young poets, have a touch of the portentous; although poetry is a serious business, he demonstrates this too obviously. In his second phase he is seriously playful, as though he felt he could relax after learning. And like a disclaimer, many of the poems are put into the mouths of his subjects—bunyip, cricket, lizard, an old fossicker, magpie, and the rest. Descriptive poems are found in *The Birdsville Track* (1955), the best sequence of desert pictures we have. Here the dead bullocks:

> Cleaned by the wind, by hot sun dried,
> With folded legs and heads turned back
> Just as they lived, just as they died,
> Hollow and gaunt and bony-eyed
> They stare along the Birdsville Track.

In his last poem, "Rutherford," he reveals an unexpected gift for reflection.

In lyric, Australian poetry has naturally enough been most prolific. Of the poets listed at the beginning of this section, all but one or two are essentially writers of this kind, all varying widely in theme and form, and ranging in age from about thirty to fifty. At the moment only a few (Thomas Shapcott and David Malouf, for example) are in their twenties still.

Among the living lyrists the finest, indeed the finest of all Australian lyrists, is Judith Wright (b. 1915). Her first volume, *The Moving Image* (1946), was hailed with surprised delight as poetry of almost unbounded promise, full of fresh imagery and delicate response of a kind not offered before. Here were aspects of Australia reinterpreted, seen as if for the first time by an eye unjaded, unjaundiced, pristinely tender. Not every reader has believed the promise wholly fulfilled; but her later volumes are still the work of a poet of distinction.

Her poetry began as the inner reaction to externals and has moved in the direction of an inner reaction to internals. The freshness of the first volume never wholly vanishes, but the stress has come to dwell rather more in reflection. This change has been due partly perhaps to an increasing deafness, partly to the impact of war on a nature to whom life and love have so intense a significance that the mounting threat of nuclear destruction acts like a blight on the human spirit. This particularly applies to a poet for whom at first, as for Gautier, the visible world existed. The later change, to an identification or empathetic absorption of the self with all that is, may be adaptation as well as natural development.

A great deal of her verse concerns the need for fulfillment, and it finds an answer in different ways. Her poems of pregnancy and motherhood are answers of a woman. Her "Woman to Man," which gives the title to her second volume (1949), is the most perfect work of this kind in all our poetry—the blossoming of the expectant woman:

> The eyeless labourer in the night,
> the selfless, shapeless seed I hold,
> builds for its resurrection day—
> silent and swift and deep from sight
> foresees the unimagined light—

and in the last stanza an efflorescent and startling change to the particular transfigures poem, poet, and reader alike:

> This is the maker and the made;
> this is the question and reply;
> the blind head butting at the dark,
> the blaze of light along the blade.
> Oh hold me, for I am afraid.

In "Twins" she suddenly sees beneath appearance the significance of identity, an answer to the individual loneliness:

> How sweet is the double gesture, the
>   mirror-answer . . .
> and moving in its web of time and harm
> the unloved heart asks, "Where is my reply,
> my kin, my answer? I am driven and alone."

One frustration of fulfillment—the sense of separation, or separation itself—is our own doing; and only we ourselves can give us our self-knowledge. This is another answer. These are not proffered as solutions to the ills of our society, but implied as individual poetic reactions. As she has continued to write, the poet has tended to look toward the quietness—or even the quietude—and acceptance that age, with life's experience behind it, can confer on us.

This may suggest that Judith Wright's poetry is troubled and torn by the conflicts that life and the threat of extinction awaken. It is true that the threat hangs over some later poems, and a reader may feel wonder that a sensitive personality should not have been drained dry by it. But, on the whole, her verse is full of hope. Pictures of drought, of dearth, of physical and spiritual malaise appear, but they are counterbalanced by rebirth. Even change which brings decay, though resented humanly, is accepted poetically as a necessity. This is part of her paradox. In her verse appears the tension of contradictions and opposites: love of the union which yet demands disparates for its very existence; the perfection of calm, but the necessity of human activity even if only in the art that mirrors it; loss of the self in that nothing which completes the self.

She has contrived often enough her perfections. It is, then, a measure of her truth that nevertheless she almost despairs of art. That art is one of the few permanent realities—the conceptual and its expression—this she does not deny: art is "thought's crystal residue." But she dwells in her later verse more and more on the difficulty of snaring reality in the meshes of language:

> Word and word are chosen and met.
> Flower, come in.
> But before the trap is set,
> the prey is gone.

Judith Wright's readers will not be deterred by such disclaimers. She has grown in her own fashion and developed her own language, and the Australian flavor has tinged unobtrusively her reaction to the Australian scene.

It is possible that we have been rather impatient of our poets in their slow development to this compromise or balance. When Burns writes

> Bye attour, my gutcher has
> A heich house an' a laich ane,
> A' forbye my bonie sel,
> The toss o' Ecclefechan!

we may not be much enlightened, but we do not overly object. When A. B. Paterson writes

> The tarboy, the cook and the slushy, the sweeper
>   that swept the board,
> The picker-up, and the penner, with the rest of
>   the shearing horde,

some tend to feel that he is dragging in the Australian background and idiom.

One aspect of this problem—the assimilation of the Australian background and its conveyance in an adequate form—though rather a side issue, has awakened dispute. This is the work of the Jindyworobaks (or, more briefly, Jindies). Their founder, Rex Ingamells, in his manifesto, *Conditional Culture* (1938), made two points. The first was the danger for the Australian poet in using words with inappropriate associations; if *castle* were part of a comparison, then an aura of age, battlements, chivalry, and so forth immediately became felt and could discolor the Australian atmosphere. The second was that we should be in greater cultural debt to aboriginal lore. These original inhabitants of Australia are, in the view of the Jindies, the only people with direct and living connection with the soil. The essential spirit of the Australian landscape can therefore be found in their art. Even through their language will seep this spirit. And so we find in some Jindyworobak poetry lines like these:

> Far in moorawathimeering,
> safe from wallan darenderong.

This is admittedly an extreme example, but it offers a warning: it is as dangerous to borrow from the aborigines as it was from the Romantics. Australian poets have to fend for themselves. (pp. 73-86)

> Cecil Hadgraft, "Literature," in The Pattern of Australian Culture, *edited by A. L. McLeod, Cornell, 1963, pp. 42-101.*

Manning Clark on the nature of Australian Literature:

Our literature continues to reflect the striking thing in our history—the speed of material development. It is this which eases out the refinement of manner, and makes the style of many of our writers rugged, often lacking in polish. It also helps to explain why the man interested in the 'deeper' problems of life and death still turns, in many instances, to European writers for instruction. The content of *The Brothers Karamazov* is, of course, intelligible to an Australian reader—but so far life here has been too crammed with worldly problems for our writers to produce such a work. And it is probably this ready accessibility of European literature which explains the odd attitude we take to Australian writing—the pleasure of recognition, of having our own way of life made articulate, and yet the expectation of something more. Perhaps that is the price we have to pay for belonging to an older civilisation, while living in a young and vigorous society.

Manning Clark, in Meanjin, *1949.*

FICTION

K. G. Hamilton

[*In the following excerpt, Hamilton discusses the development of the Australian novel.*]

If one were asked to name a holy trinity of Australian novels published before 1930, then the answer would certainly be Marcus Clarke's *His Natural Life* (1874), Joseph Furphy's *Such Is Life* (1903), and Henry Handel Richardson's trilogy, *The Fortunes of Richard Mahony* (1917, 1925, and 1929). These at least would have to be saved from the everlasting bonfire.

Different as they are, these three novels have something in common—something, moreover, which is the basis of their lasting importance. Clarke shows us conditions and events battering a man who can do little more than resist with a stubborn integrity; Furphy's characters both change circumstances and are changed by them; Richardson's Mahony becomes the reader's chief concern, not merely because he is the chief character but because the complexity of his temperament preoccupies the reader. With Clarke and Furphy the background is important: without the peculiarly local settings, the Tasmanian convict system and the Riverina, *His Natural Life* and *Such Is Life* could not exist. With Richardson, despite the pictures of the diggings, of Melbourne life, of small country towns, the background is less important. But equally for all three, even with different settings, the essential theme would still be available. This is significant, for man is more important than things—or rather man in his relationship to things is more important, at least to man, than things themselves—and it is because of their realization of this that these three works have lived, lasting evidence of the early maturity of the Australian novel.

No similar trinity is to be found in the years between 1930 and the end of World War II; for a comparable figure the literature had to wait until Patrick White's later novels offered their rich choices. This period lacks peaks; but its significance is considerable. It has at least sixteen novelists whose names would demand mention in even a cursory sketch of our fiction. Six of these had published before 1930—Miles Franklin, Henry Handel Richardson, Katharine Susannah Prichard, Vance Palmer, Martin Boyd, and M. Barnard Eldershaw. And, except for Richardson, they were to write some of their best novels in this period. (Even William Gosse Hay, first appearing in 1901, issued an expiratory effort in 1937). Ten others who first published novels in this period are, in order of appearance, Frank Dalby Davison, Eleanor Dark, Leonard Mann, Helen Simpson, Brian Penton, Christina Stead, Kylie Tennant, Kenneth (Seaforth) Mackenzie, Xavier Herbert, and Patrick White. An impressive group of writers; indeed, from our position in the seventies we may question whether a comparable group of first novels in the fifteen years to, say, 1985, is likely to emerge. They are not the first to bring the Australian novel to prominence, but they consolidate its position—and, with the work of White, add the distinction of international recognition.

Leaving aside the few significant names and, at the opposite end of the scale, a spate of urban novels by three distinctly minor writers—Ada Cambridge, Jessie Couvreur, and Rosa Praed—the novelists of the period from 1830 to 1930 looked mostly at the oddities of their environment, present or past—flora and fauna, aboriginality, convictism, bushranging, pioneering, pastoral life. They described the externals they saw or the externals they remembered or read about. They looked very little at their own lives. The trend of the fifteen years after 1930 is different. Only three of the ten new novelists, for instance, wrote historical novels—Dark, Simpson, and Penton—an indication of maturity, one may think; for proliferation of historical fiction in a period suggests uncertainty in the consciousness of national identity. The accounts of externals, too, are different. The last century tended to deal with such things because they were new and surprising; this period portrays them because they are familiar. Nor are they introduced for their own sake: they serve a functional purpose in the fictional structure. What had been true of the Australian novel only at its highest levels becomes more nearly its general rule.

These novelists then differ from all but the best who preceded them. They differ also from one another. Even contentious, if defensible, potted comments serve to underline their variety—the empathetic sympathy of Davison, the earlier tortuosity and later panoramic sweep of Dark, the psychological stresses of Mann, the deceptive ease of Simpson's lucid and even brilliant style, the implacable brutalities of Penton, the inexhaustible cumulative detail of Stead, the ironic humorous sympathy and political awareness of Tennant, the richly multitudinous farrago of Herbert, the delicate probings of Mackenzie, the complex symbolism and intricate nuances of White. But along with such differences they have a common interest in people, in the individual human being; and even more in the web of social relationships that enmesh them. They are social novelists, and for this reason they seem to belong to a "modern" period. Some passages from Ada Cambridge may have a tart subtlety in analysis of character and motive that is not bettered by these novelists of the thirties; but the patina of older customs—dress, manners, speech, and outlook—is so thick in Cambridge that the gap between even her later work and that of these writers twenty or thirty years afterwards seems unbridgeable. Nobody wrote or would wish to write in her fashion a generation after her. However, it should be said that this aspect of "modernism" entails a difference in theme, and more particularly of a choice of stress within that theme; it does not entail at this time any noticeable modernity in structure or stylistic methods. Apart from Stead and White, these novelists seem unaware of what happened in English fiction in the 1920s.

The extent to which they depict the Australian world and life of their time varies from member to member of the group. But there are two omissions that may seem either unexpected or remarkable or both. The reasons for the omissions are hypothetical. The writers may have felt constrained by their interest in the individual human personality, an interest felt by all. Some, or perhaps most, of them may have felt or recognized there were some themes lying beyond their normal provenance or perhaps capacity. Or that the themes may have required, so to speak, a period for emotional assimilation before any use could be made of them in fiction. These two themes were, of course, the Great Depression and World War II, which in their world-wide impact spared no nation. Except for Tennant, and Barnard Eldershaw's later *Tomorrow and Tomorrow* (1947), any of the group using the Depression uses it almost incidentally: it is there, it affects certain characters, but the stress is not on the economic and humanly disastrous consequences or the nationally traumatic changes in outlook. Even Tennant, with political sympathies strongly felt, uses it mostly as a sort of backdrop, a varied landscape through which her vivid oddities find their way. In scope and vision and intensity there is nothing to compare, for instance, with John Steinbeck's *The Grapes of Wrath* (1939). As for World War II, the only novel from the group to deal directly with it was written outside this period—Mackenzie's *Dead Men Rising* (1951)—and the setting lay in Australia in a camp for Japanese prisoners of war. It is interesting that the omissions are rectified (if that is the right word) in the poetry and short stories of the period. And, in any case, the position may only be made to seem apparent by a perhaps arbitrary choice of significant writers. There *were* novels on the theme of the war—by, for example, Lawson Glassop, Russell Braddon, and T. A. G. Hungerford. (pp. 1-4)

The second half of the forties produced very few new novelists—most of the relatively small number of novels published in these years immediately after the war were by well-established, older novelists. Of the new novelists only Robert Close (*Love Me Sailor*, 1945), Morris West (*Moon in My Pocket* by "Julian Morris", 1945), Jon Cleary (*You Can't See Round Corners*, 1947), and Frank Hardy (*Power*

Without Glory, 1950) are worth mentioning and still worth reading. None could be regarded as extending the frontiers of the Australian novel, though they all attracted popular attention: Morris West made the international best-seller lists; Hardy and Cleary subsequently saw their books produced on Australian television; Close and Hardy earned court appearances for their work.

These years saw the arts before the Bench and before the delighted public gaze as the butt of some characteristic anti-intellectual contempt on several occasions. In 1944 the "Ern Malley" hoax (and its attendant obscenity trial) and the legal squabble over William Dobell's right to the Archibald Prize each, according to some commentators, put the cause of their moderately progressive movements back years. In 1948 Sumner Locke-Elliott's play *Rusty Bugles* was banned by the New South Wales chief secretary for its "indecent language"; for a similar offence in *Love Me Sailor,* Robert Close was imprisoned in Victoria. In 1951 Frank Hardy had to defend his *Power Without Glory* against a charge of libel.

In addition to this sort of internal nervousness there were other international signs that the recently won peace was a precarious one. There were the beginnings of atomic bomb tests, the Berlin blockade, the establishment of a rocket range in Australia (at Woomera), the McCarthy committee in the United States, and the outbreak of war in Korea. Within Australia other developments were beginning which shaped society for the next quarter of a century. Between 1945 and 1949 the new immigration campaign (based on a nervous "populate or perish" thesis) brought half a million immigrants to Australia; the national economy flourished; the spread of suburbia (to accommodate the products of the post-war baby boom) began in earnest, and in 1948 the first Holden car was produced. In 1949 the Labor Party departed from the federal government for the next twenty-three years. (pp. 6-7)

But, for years which at first glance appear to have been lean ones for the Australian novel, the actual achievement was remarkably solid. Most importantly there were major novels by three of the best modern Australian writers. Christina Stead, nearing the end of her most prolific years, produced *For Love Alone* (1944), *Letty Fox, Her Luck* (1946), and *A Little Tea, A Little Chat* (1948). While the latter two works contain little to extend her reputation, *For Love Alone* is undoubtedly one of her greatest novels—alongside *The Man Who Loved Children* (1940). It also links various elements in Australian literature, with its fine realistic social observation, its socio-economic awareness, its psychological insight, and its mythic extensions. Indeed the underlying myth, that of Odysseus, or the wanderer/voyager figure, is one that appears in the other two major novels of the period, Martin Boyd's *Lucinda Brayford* (1946) and Patrick White's *The Aunt's Story* (1948). It is also remarkable that all three novels are concerned with heroines who leave Australia and who, though concerned with their relationship to their birthplace, do not (at least within the narrative) return to it. Of these three novelists, White and Stead had published their first novel about ten years earlier and Boyd about twenty years earli-

er, but with these books of the mid-forties they undeniably "arrived" as major forces in Australian fiction.

Most of the other notable novelists who published in these years had more or less secure reputations: many indeed, in terms of interests, style, technique, and reputation, look back to a previous era. The two important trilogies that were begun in this period each has this quality. They were Katharine Susannah Prichard's "Goldfields" trilogy, *The Roaring Nineties* (1946), *Golden Miles* (1948), and *Winged Seeds* (1950); and Vance Palmer's "Donovan" trilogy, *Golconda* (1948), *Seedtime* (1957), and *The Big Fellow* (1959). Each, too, is political but in strikingly different ways: with Prichard, politics informs and directs the point of view; for Palmer it is the subject-matter, the fascinatingly related personal and political fortunes of the union organizer who becomes state premier.

Other survivors of the twenties and earlier included Miles Franklin and also Norman Lindsay, who completed, with *Halfway to Anywhere* (1947), the boisterous Ballarat boyhood trilogy begun with *Redheap* (1930) and *Saturdee* (1933). Indeed, the interest shown in the trilogy by novelists writing in this period is remarkable. In addition to those begun by Palmer and Prichard and concluded by Lindsay, there appeared also the middle volume of Eleanor Dark's historical trilogy, *The Timeless Land* (1941), *Storm of Time* (1948), and *No Barrier* (1953). Hal Porter and George Johnston, both of whom later produced autobiographical trilogies, published their first books in the 1940s. Of these two writers, Johnston was the more prolific, but his early works are of a stature and genre distinctly different from those for which he is well known, and of the several books appearing by 1950 only *High Valley* (1949), written in collaboration with his wife, Charmian Clift, is of much interest. The much more productive collaboration between Marjorie Barnard and Flora Eldershaw came to an end in 1947 with the last M. Barnard Eldershaw novel, *Tomorrow and Tomorrow,* a view, among other things, of the history of Sydney in the 1930s as seen by a young man writing in the closing years of the century. The previous year also witnessed the appearance (the book was written about forty years earlier) of the last novel to which Miles Franklin affixed her own name, *My Career Goes Bung.* Like so many authors of the period, these two notables are best remembered for their work in the historical novel genre such as *A House is Built* (1929), *All That Swagger* (1936) and the "Brent of Bin Bin" novels.

The 1950s began as a lean period for Australian fiction—and for Australian literature generally. Indeed, the decade was half over before the tide turned, although when it did the change was dramatic. Our major novelists were either not publishing (as in the case of Patrick White) or were working totally outside the Australian cultural and publishing context (as in the case of Christina Stead, whose *People with the Dogs* appeared in New York in 1952). Even Boyd, with two novels during the period to his credit—*The Cardboard Crown* (1952) and *A Difficult Young Man* (1955)—was outside the mainstream of what was happening in Australian fiction. His return to this country, with the intention of staying, had been short-lived, and he returned permanently to Europe in 1951. Both *The Card-*

board *Crown* and *A Difficult Young Man* are concerned with the rival claims and tensions of the old world and the new, and form the first two volumes of what has become known as the "Langton" series, a tetralogy not completed till 1962. For all of their at times infuriating preciousness, these novels speak deeply of such things as cultural heritage and spiritual harmony. They enjoyed considerable popularity in the south of England, but their readership and impact in Australia were not large. Indeed, Boyd's themes and style were curiously old-fashioned, even at the time he was writing. *A Difficult Young Man* ends in 1911, leaving one with the impression that Boyd preferred writing of a bygone age, with its assurance and ease, because the contemporary world was too terrible to contemplate. Certainly the contemporary world, and some of the most unpleasant aspects of it, was frequently the subject of novels by other Australian writers of the time. Frank Hardy's *Power Without Glory* (1950), with its exposé of the roughness and toughness of the political machine, stands at the head of a line of novels about the exploitation of the working class and the importance of political commitment.

Indeed, the relationship between what was happening in Australian politics (and world politics, for that matter) and what was happening in the Australian novel and in Australian literature generally is of vital, if unclear, importance during the 1951-55 period. The victory of Menzies in 1949, at the height of the cold war, polarized political opinion in Australia. The attempts to outlaw the Communist Party, the participation in the Korean War, the Petrov "conspiracy", were brilliant electoral ploys which left the Labour Party and the socialist opposition generally disunited and dispirited, though aware that they were participants in a major struggle. There were a number of literary manifestations of this political polarization. The Australasian Book Society, founded in 1952, was designed to publish democratic literature, especially novels and stories, in a co-operative, self-help way. It had close links with the left of the Labour Party and with the Communist Party, and published novels by Judah Waten, *The Unbending* (1954), Eric Lambert, Ralph de Boissiere, and F. B. Vickers. At the same time the Realist Writers group in Melbourne (Frank Hardy was a prominent and revered member) produced their journal, *The Realist Writer* (1952-54), which was hard-line in both politics and literature. One of the editors, Stephen Murray-Smith, broke from the journal's Moscow orientation in 1954 to found *Overland* ("Temper, democratic; bias, offensively Australian"), and the right-wing Congress for Cultural Freedom responded in 1956 with *Quadrant.*

A more subtle manifestation of the politicization of Australian literature during this time comes from a consideration of the themes of a representative range of novels. Dymphna Cusack and Florence James's *Come in Spinner* (1951) was the forerunner of a number of novels about the corrupting influence of American soldiers in Sydney during the war. Gambling, drinking, prostitution are its recurrent concerns, as they are in Xavier Herbert's *Soldiers' Women,* not published till 1961 though written during this time. In *Southern Steel* (1953) Cusack writes of Newcastle during the war, of the American soldiers, and of the Sweetapple family, split between working for the war ef-

fort through the corporation that owns the steelworks and through the Communist Party, with its plans to nationalize all industry. Such political themes, using the novel as a part of political strategy, are perhaps the major hallmark of Australian fiction during this time. And though one does not object to ideology in fiction (it is present in all novels), the Australian social realists of the early fifties tended to allow ideology to swamp their art or, to put it a less kind way, attempted to cover up the paucity of their art with a veneer of ideology. Waten's *The Unbending,* one of the best of the Australasian Book Society novels, is concerned with a Jewish migrant family in Australia at the time of World War I. They are forced to take a stand on such issues as conscription and the radical role of the IWW (International Workers of the World) as well as come to terms with an entrenched community, suspicious of foreigners and Jews. Several elements in the book (for instance, the relationship between Hannah and her husband, the migrant couple) suggest material for another novel, for Waten is not completely successful in welding his "documentary" work to his character studies. Indeed, the former is often more interesting than the latter, suggesting perhaps that had the social realists stuck to their basic purpose of expressing the aims of the working class, they could have produced works of more even quality. As it is, Waten's picture of Australian class and racial prejudices veers off in the direction of D. H. Lawrence's concept of family politics and ends, like so many Lawrence novels, on a not very convincing note of hope.

Dal Stivens was never closely associated with the left-wing school of Australian novelists, but his *Jimmy Brockett* (1951), perhaps partly inspired by *Power Without Glory* (though it has American antecedents as well), fits well into their ideological framework. It is a mildly humorous study of a Sydney commercial and political boss in the 1920s, ruthlessly bent on building his empire of wealth and power. Two other novelists from the period are worth mentioning, for they lie somewhat outside this general picture. Kenneth Mackenzie had published two novels in the late thirties, before *Dead Men Rising* (1951) and *The Refuge* (1954). *Dead Men Rising* is a fictionalized account of the break-out from the Cowra prisoner-of-war camp by the Japanese in 1944. It suffers principally from centring its concerns on the guards, who are much less energetic and impassioned than the prisoners themselves. Among Australian novelists only Hal Porter, in some stories, and in *The Actors* (1968) or *The Paper Chase* (1966), has been able to write convincingly of Japanese ways. *The Refuge* is a more successful work, a variant on the emigrant theme, in which a refugee from European totalitarianism meets an Australian counterpart in the person of her lover, a Sydney journalist. Mackenzie's novels (he also published several volumes of verse) give the impression of talent which is never fulfilled. He does continue the trend towards realism, however, though his accounts of city life lack the ideological coherence and patterning of the socialist writers. Perhaps the potential of his art combined with their ideology could have produced the major novel the period lacks.

Tom Ronan's novels *Vision Splendid* (1954) and *Moleskin Midas* (1956) stand out as two of the few novels from the earlier fifties (apart from *The Tree of Man* and the first appearance of several Miles Franklin works written years before) which are concerned with life outside of the cities or towns. *Vision,* which won first prize in the Commonwealth Jubilee literary competition in 1951, traces the fortunes of Charles Toppingham in the Northern Territory during the twenties and thirties. No doubt partly inspired by *Capricornia* (it is interesting that both the sesquicentenary prize of 1938 and the jubilee prize of 1951 should go to novels about life in the Northern Territory), it is a racy, adventurous account of cattle musters, droughts, and drinking sprees and may have been at least partly concerned with "putting down" Herbert's account of racial and class inequality in the Territory. Ronan's "vision splendid" is largely one of blue skies and unlimited potential for those prepared to do a full day's work.

The five years 1950-54 were not a major period for local fiction in terms of the novels actually published. It was, however, a time of intense literary activity, and it is not altogether surprising that the next five years should have been a watershed in the recent development of Australian literature, as it was also in Australian history. The factors that produced this watershed in politics, culture, and literature were in each case international, national, and personal. This was a period in which international recognition came to Australia in many apparently unrelated fields, and Australia, as if attempting to prove the now-famous theory of the "cultural cringe"—a term coined at the time by A. A. Phillips in an essay in *Meanjin* (4/1950)—responded with the customary mixture of assertiveness and uncertainty. In politics the Australian prime minister, R.G. Menzies, had appeared as a statesman on the world stage in the Suez crisis, and the image of Australia as a world diplomatic power was briefly offered to an unsuspecting world. In the same year (1956) world attention was focused even more directly on Australia with the staging of the first Olympic Games to be held outside of Europe and North America. National fervour was aroused by the sight of Australian sportsmen winning the heats (though less frequently the finals) of a large number of events. Nevertheless, feature articles on Australia and its way of life appeared in most countries at this time. Coinciding with these events was the almost simultaneous awakening of interest in Patrick White and Sidney Nolan in London and the consequent attention paid to other Australian novelists, dramatists, and painters in the years that followed.

Within Australia the optimism, material growth, and political complacency and conservatism culminated in another Menzies victory in the election of 1958, which was based on the slogan "Australia Unlimited". This slogan was also the theme of numerous newspaper and magazine documentaries of this period and in subsequent years. This was now the "Lucky Country" that Donald Horne was to write about a few years later (1964). Another phenomenon, whose effect on the Australian novel has been debated often, was introduced (in Sydney) at the end of 1955—television. It is also arguable that other non-literary events of the early fifties had consequences for the Australian novel in this period. The unsuccessful referendum to have communism made illegal, the Petrov "spy" case, and the

Labor Party "split" all had the result of discrediting the Left and the social-realist writers associated with it, or of inhibiting them, or of simply causing them to be too busy reorganizing in these years to have much time to write. For one reason or another, the late fifties saw the end of the social-realist hegemony over Australian fiction. As in politics (with Menzies) and painting (with Nolan) so in literature the personal achievement of Patrick White was the pre-eminent symbol of a new order. Many reviewers in fact commented on the significance of the almost simultaneous release in Australia of White's *Voss* and Vance Palmer's *Seedtime* (1957). It would be hard to imagine a more apposite pair of novels to highlight the watershed. The death of Vance Palmer in 1959 represented in many ways the end of an era for which he had been a leading spokesman, practitioner, and critic. (pp. 8-15)

While there were a number of exciting new writers in this period, some of the most notable achievements were often by authors returning to publishing after a period of apparent inactivity. Xavier Herbert's *Seven Emus* (1959) came twenty-one years after *Capricornia;* White's two remarkable novels *The Tree of Man* (1955) and *Voss* (1957) were preceded by seven years of silence; Hal Porter's poems *The Hexagon* (1956) and his novel *A Handful of Pennies* (1958) were his first books for fourteen years. In poetry there were new volumes, after long pauses, from James McAuley and David Campbell.

There were nevertheless a number of new novelists of considerable promise and some achievement. The most important of these was Randolph Stow, whose *A Haunted Land* (1956), *The Bystander* (1957), and *To the Islands* (1958) demonstrated a great talent for the subtle combination of literary extravagance, psychological intensity, and a symbolic use of landscape surpassed only by the much older and more experienced White. The relationship of character and landscape, exploited by Stow with great ingenuity in each of these novels, culminates in the final words of Heriot in the third of them, "My soul is a strange country" and clearly puts Stow in the "country of the mind" school. This phrase of course derives from *Voss,* which, with *The Tree of Man,* shows White at his best in exploring the utmost of man's relationship, not to individual or to social man, but to himself and the universe through his peculiar experience of the Australian environment. Herbert's *Seven Emus,* concerned with Aboriginal traditions and the white man's ignorance and disrespect of them, might have been a more germane cousin of these novels by White and Stow had it not been distracted by its unsuccessful syntactical experimentation. As it is, it remains an interesting pointer to the way in which Herbert was to develop his particular version of this theme of "the country of the mind" much later in *Poor Fellow My Country.*

Most of the other new novelists of this period were conscious literary craftsmen. The most important, or at least the most promising, of them were three writers who each, like White and Stow, were already employing a style of considerable virtuosity in the interests of exploring individual minds of more than average sensitivity caught in social environments and personal relationships of more than average oppressiveness. They were Elizabeth Harrower (*Down in the City,* 1957); Christopher Koch (*The Boys in the Island,* 1958; revised edition, 1974), and Thea Astley (*Girl with a Monkey,* 1958). None has unequivocally fulfilled all of that early promise, though Astley has published, at fairly regular intervals, six more novels of increasing assurance. Koch's book, a fine study of the passage from adolescence to maturity which rates comparison with Australia's two other major contributions to this twentieth-century genre, Kenneth Mackenzie's *The Young Desire It* (1937) and Christina Stead's *For Love Alone,* was followed by only one more novel, the less successful *Across the Sea Wall* (1965). Harrower's subsequent output, *The Long Prospect* (1958) and *The Catherine Wheel* (1960), struggled with the problem that was increasingly Patrick White's also: the relationship between the sensitive outsider and the splenetically observed insiders. *The Catherine Wheel,* with its London setting, solves this problem in a most successful manner, but the lesson is not so effectively applied in her fourth (and last?) novel, *The Watch Tower* (1966).

There were two other quite different directions discernible in the Australian novel in the late 1950s. On the one hand there was the rise of the best-selling novels of John O'Grady ("Nino Culotta"), Morris West, and Nevil Shute. O'Grady's *They're a Weird Mob* (1957) obviously appealed to a popular taste eager for self-indulgent manifestations of the national character, a taste which had been satisfied less complacently in the vernacular drama already discussed, and which was one of the subjects of Ward's *Australian Legend* of the following year. At the same time, despite the apparent slackening of social-realist energy, there were still notable books from Kylie Tennant, Miles Franklin, Vance Palmer, Frank Hardy, and Ron Tullipan. Apart from the last of these, whose *Follow the Sun* was a first novel, the others all have a retrospective interest. The best of Tennant's novels in this period, *The Honey Flow* (1956), has the same blend of the picaresque, the sentimental, the sardonic, and an apologetic feminism as her Depression novels. In terms of her œuvre and in terms of the Australian novel it is not an advance but a repeat. Much the same can be said for the final novels of both Palmer, whose *The Big Fellow* (1959) was the last of a trilogy begun in 1948, and Franklin, whose *Gentleman at Gyang Gyang* (1956) was written nearly forty years earlier. Hardy's *Four-Legged Lottery* (1958) has the social indignation at a public evil which characterized *Power Without Glory* but not its rhetorical control or structural focus.

Throughout the fifties and the early sixties a rise in interest in Aboriginal themes and characters was discernible. There are, for example, such collections of legends as Alan Marshall's *People of Dreamtime;* Roland Robinson's *Legend and Dreaming,* and Rex Ingamell's *Aranda Boy,* all published in 1952. Among other novels in this group are D'Arcy Niland's *The Shiralee* (1955), Gavin Casey's *Snowball* (1958), Donald Stuart's *Yandy* (1959), Kylie Tennant's *Speak You So Gently* (1959), Nene Gare's *The Fringe Dwellers* (1961), Nan Chauncy's *Tangara* (1960), dealing with the Aborigines of Tasmania, and Leonard Mann's *Venus Half-Caste* (1963). These may perhaps be seen as leading up to Colin Johnson's *Wild Cat Falling* (1965). The only novel by a writer of Aboriginal blood, this treats the problems of a displaced part-Aboriginal youth in Perth. It was a work of more promise than achievement, but because of its subject, seen from inside, it occupies an important place.

Patrick White's *Riders in the Chariot* and Xavier Herbert's *Soldiers' Women,* both appearing in 1961, were not only notable achievements by two of the most distinguished novelists but also signalled new directions for them and for the Australian novel. White had earlier shown his talent for satirical social observation in his counterpointing of the spiritual searches and transcendence of his leading characters against the clogging forces of social conformity, but in *Riders* he focused his social satire on contemporary Australian suburbia, wielding the lash too bitterly and heavily for some readers. In his later works he continued to attack suburbia but was to show some sympathy with its victims. Herbert's *Soldiers' Women* showed him turning from the outback (the far north) setting of *Capricornia* to Sydney and combining a savage social observation with an inquiry into man's chances of rising above the animal level. Love, as against spiritual transcendence in White, is Herbert's means of testing man's capacities and failures.

Both novelists in their different ways showed a spirited attempt to revive and transfigure social realism, by going beyond social documentation both thematically and technically. Both *Riders* and *Soldiers' Women* are highly patterned novels. The patterning shows itself in a complex structure of imagery and symbol through which (as well as through action) man's social life is explored and measured, and which lifts the novels above literal realism though they keep a grip on social detail. It could be argued that both novels are too highly patterned—perhaps in the case of White as a reaction away from the limitations of realism—but they were important in extending the range of the Australian novel. Both represented a claim for the spiritual capacities of man as a main concern of the novel and at the same time a claim of poetic language and artistic pattern as necessary for any deeply revealing picture of social life. White had already been influential in this direction through *The Aunt's Story, The Tree of Man,* and *Voss,* but the greater concentration on suburbia was new and was an interest that White was to develop and refine. *Soldiers' Women* was not favourably received on first publication, but though it may not have been an influence it was crucial in Herbert's own development towards the enormously ambitious *Poor Fellow My Country.*

Appearing in the same year (1961) as *Riders in the Chariot* and *Soldiers' Women* is another important novel, Hal Porter's *The Tilted Cross.* A poetic evocation of Australia's past and a re-interpretation of its life and myths, it is comparable to *Voss* (though without its metaphysical ambitions) and looks forward to Keneally's first main novel, *Bring Larks and Heroes*—like it, set in the convict era.

The other notable novels of the period 1961-65 fit within the two broad (and not always separable) categories of social realism and the exploration of the spiritual life, of which *The Fortunes of Richard Mahony* (1930) represented for many years a lone peak (though it also exemplified a combination of the two streams). Thea Astley brings to her social observation a sensitive style and deflating wit as well as a sympathetic understanding of the emotionally vulnerable, as in the young adolescent of *The Slow Natives* (1956). David Martin's *The Young Wife* (1962) is probably the best novel about European (non-British) migrants in Australia; he writes of them with realistic and psychological power, revealing their emotional turmoil and not simply their practical problems. Judah Waten in *Time of Conflict* (1961) treats the economically underprivileged during the Depression years with a similar fidelity to social experience but including the political element in the form of a character who turns to communism. The novels of Martin and Waten are set in Melbourne. Martin's *The Hero of Too* (1965) is a witty satire on Australian myth (focusing on the noble bushranger) and looks forward to similar comic deflations by Peter Mathers and Barry Oakley. George Turner in his Treelake series, *A Stranger and Afraid* (1961), *The Cupboard Under the Stairs* (1962), *Waste of Shame* (1965), and *The Lame Dog Man* (1967), deals with the pressures of social life on the individual in country towns and is today a neglected novelist.

The year 1963 saw the appearance of two notable autobiographies, Hal Porter's *The Watcher on the Cast-Iron Balcony* and Xavier Herbert's *Disturbing Element*. Up to this time autobiography was a form almost totally neglected by Australian novelists. Both autobiographies evoke the past in their attempts at self understanding, but in Porter the past becomes almost a subject in itself (as in many of his short stories); also, Porter was more interested in autobiography as a literary form (as shown also in his later continuations, *The Paper Chase*, 1966, and *The Extra*, 1975) than Herbert, who concentrated more on vividness of event than on loving, subtle evocation. The main influence of these works (and of Donald Horne's *The Education of Young Donald*, 1967) is perhaps to be seen in a crop of autobiographical novels of the early 1970s by younger writers. Some also appeared in the 1960s, either by way of influence or because the time was ripe in their personal development or the development of Australian fiction. Stow's latest novel *The Merry-Go-Round in the Sea* (1965), draws on his early life in Geraldton, on country stations, and in Perth and turns away from the interior, mystical explorations of *To the Islands* and *Tourmaline* (1963) to concentrate on the experiences of childhood and adolescence, though Stow's poetic talent shows no lessening. Of Keneally's two early novels preparatory to the final establishing of his reputation, *The Fear* (1965) is a gripping, if uneven novel of the experiences of a young boy; and the earlier *The Place at Whitton* (1964), a gothic thriller of memorable episodes, draws autobiographically on at least the scenes of Keneally's years in a seminary. George Johnston's *My Brother Jack* (1964) skilfully evokes through recollections of childhood and family life a vivid picture of Melbourne during World War I and after. In Johnston's two later works which complete a trilogy, *Clean Straw for Nothing* (1969) and *A Cartload of Clay* (1971), the autobiographical element and the personal search were to dominate the social picture (which was widened to include expatriate life). With Johnston we see the main and perhaps the only direct influence in the

1960s of Porter's first volume of accomplished autobiography. (pp. 16-22)

Although it produced no individual giants, the second half of the 1960s was an important time for the Australian novel. It was a time of comings and goings; three long careers were terminated and a number of new novelists appeared. It was a time of promise: the novel as a genre was buoyant (despite television), the society was becoming more self-conscious, and this was manifest in the novel by a new streak of satire. Finally, in the emergence of Thomas Keneally, Australia found its most important novelist to appear since the prematurely silent Randolph Stow.

Of the established writers, few if any produced their best work in these years. After turning for a time in the early 1960s to the drama, Patrick White returned to the novel to continue his exploration of mystical value, in apparently nondescript lives in *The Solid Mandala* (1966) and in an extraordinary life in *The Vivisector* (1970), but neither of these has all the sweep and command of his previous four novels. Christina Stead broke a long silence with *Cotter's England* (1966), but again this does not develop the power that one finds in her novels of two decades earlier, such as *For Love Alone* and *The Man Who Loved Children*. The long career of Martin Boyd came to an end with *The Tea Time of Love* (1969), one of a number of recent novels—albeit if in this instance somewhat tongue in cheek—which explore the exotic romanticism of Europe, thus reversing a dominant trait of the nineteenth century novel which explored the exotic romanticism of Australia. Shirley Hazzard, another expatriate novelist, similarly writes anti-sentimentally, yet with sensitivity, of love in post-war Italy in *The Evening of the Holiday* (1966)—all her novels are set either in Italy or America. It is interesting that two of the fictional autobiographies appearing at this time imply that geographical distancing is necessary for perspective. These are George Johnston's *Clean Straw for Nothing* and David Martin's *Where a Man Belongs* (1969). Another important fictional autobiography (which does not, however, exploit geographical dislocation in this way) is Hal Porter's *The Paper Chase* (1966).

Apart from Boyd's, two other notable careers came to an end in the late sixties. Katharine Susannah Prichard's *Subtle Flame* (1967) was her final novel, more than fifty years after she published *The Pioneers*. Frank Dalby Davison's swansong was *The White Thorntree* (1968), a book that demonstrated that it is possible to write interminable sagas about urban Australian life as well as about parched bucolic dynasties.

Thomas Keneally is the one novelist whose stature increases significantly through work published in these years. His first two novels had been quickly and casually written, but in *Bring Larks and Heroes* (1967) he cultivated the method of imaginatively filling out a historical situation with the ironical, almost sardonic, exploration of human vulnerability that has forged his most powerful fiction since then. Subsequent novels, *Three Cheers for the Paraclete* (1968), and *The Survivor* (1969) were slighter, and although there was an interesting fable *A Dutiful Daughter* (1970), it was not until he resumed the historical formula in the seventies that he again produced his best work.

Another feature of the half-decade is a general interest in the novel, evidenced in part by the influx of writers better known in other genres. While writers often publish in a number of different modes, one notices a preference for the novel form by dramatists like Alan Seymour with his novel-of-the-play *The One Day of the Year* (1967) and *The Coming Self-Destruction of the USA* (1969); or David Ireland with his *The Chantic Bird* (1968); or Barry Oakley with *Wild Ass of a Man* (1967); or the short-story writer Peter Cowan with *Seed* (1966); and the all-rounder Geoffrey Dutton with *Andy* (1968) and *Tamara* (1970). Of these at least Ireland has continued to find the form viable. (pp. 22-4)

Despite some flurries of political consciousness in literary circles, the political novel has never been particularly important in Australia; however, an increase in self-consciousness in the society of the sixties is reflected in the fiction by the end of the decade. With the withdrawal of Menzies from politics, the founding in 1964 of a national newspaper, *The Australian,* and conscription for the Vietnam war, not to mention a succession of prime ministers who were either drowned or sacked or who sacked themselves, Australian public affairs took on an interest which they had not previously commanded. This awareness, which is manifested in a rash of socio-cultural analyses such as Horne's *The Lucky Country* and his text of *Southern Exposure* (1967), George Johnston's text of *The Australians* (1966), Humphrey McQueen's *A New Britannia* (1970), or Ronald Conway's *The Great Australian Stupor* (1971), also appears in fictional analyses of various aspects of Australianness. The late sixties and seventies saw the publication of Davison's massive Kinsey report on Sydney's northern suburbs, of Keneally's and Mather's probings of the underlying violence in an allegedly phlegmatic and laconic national character, and of the upturning of the conventional society of Melbourne by the outrageous anti-heroes of Oakley's *Let's Hear it for Prendergast* (1970), of Mather's *Trap* (1966), and of David Williamson's play, *The Coming of Stork* (1970).

This strand of satire, which may owe something to the success of Barry Humphries' stage and cartoon characters of the early sixties, is pronounced through the decade. It includes some works already mentioned—David Martin's spoof on the not-so-virile bushranger in *The Hero of Too,* Donald Horne's attack on bureaucracy in *The Permit,* and Peter Mather's on racism in *Trap.* It is a strand that is picked up and broadened in the drama of David Williamson, Fred Hibberd, and Alexander Buzo in the seventies, as well as in such novels as David Ireland's *The Unknown Industrial Prisoner* (1971), Henry Williams's *My Love Has a Black Speed Stripe* (1973), and Mathers's *The Wort Papers* (1972); and it is one characterized, particularly in the novels of Ireland and Mathers, by a comic experimentation which reflects society's disconnections by its departure from any linear plot development in favour of a largely disconnected narrative line.

The strength of the novel in the seventies has also been demonstrated in part by the continued interest of writers already established in other forms. Michael Wilding, making his mark in short stories, Sumner Locke Elliott, long known as a playwright, and well-known young poets David Malouf and Rodney Hall, all turned out novels. Wilding's *Living Together* (1974) is genuinely light entertainment, but his recent *Short Story Embassy* (1975) and *Scenic Drive* (1976) combine comedy with a serious concern for the stylistic and structural problems confronting the contemporary novelist; Locke-Elliott's *The Man Who Got Away* (1973) and *Going* (1975) demonstrated the dramatist's Coward-like ease with dialogue; Malouf's *Johnno* (1975) and Hall's *A Place Among People* (1975) revealed their sensibilities within the ampler, often nostalgic, content. Among other poets turning to fiction are Robert Adamson and Bruce Hanford, whose *Zimmer's Essay* (1973) gives a picture of prison life from the inside. On the other hand, Hal Porter returned to the short story in *Fredo Fuss Love Life* (1973). Something of a crop of novels about growing up in Australia sprang up in the early 1970s—Lauri Clancy's *A Collapsible Man* (1975) and Gerald Murname's *Tamarisk Row* (1973) both have Catholic boyhood autobiographical backgrounds; and there are also such novels by Desmond O'Grady and D. R. Burns. Among a group of novels with a specifically Queensland background are Malouf's *Johnno,* already mentioned and set in Brisbane of the war years, Ronald McKie's *The Mango Tree* (1974), and Thea Astley's *A Kindness Cup* (1974), a mythic novel about a small Queensland town and one of a projected series. Rather similar, apart from its setting in Macedon, Victoria, is Geoff Wyatt's *Tidal Forest* (1973). Suzanne Holly Jones, whose *Harry's Child* (1964) caused her to be regarded as something of a child prodigy, at last appeared again with *Crying in the Garden* (1973).

David Ireland, already noted for his experimentation, continued to display versatility and has indeed been prolific— *The Unknown Industrial Prisoner, The Flesheaters* (1972), *Burn* (1974), and *The Glass Canoe* (1976) are all concerned with exploring aspects of society (especially its dispossessed and impoverished classes) which other recent novelists have tended to ignore. In doing this, Ireland has maintained his interest in experimentation with form, and he must now be regarded as one of the major and most lively innovators in our fiction. Frank Moorhouse's *The Americans, Baby* (1972) and *The Electrical Experience* (1974) are also vigorously experimental.

Some of those writers who had long proved their standing in prose fiction have continued to produce. Thomas Keneally, after *The Chant of Jimmie Blacksmith,* gave us *Blood Red, Sister Rose* in 1974, *Gossip from the Forest* in 1975, and *A Season in Purgatory* in 1976. Patrick White produced in 1973 *The Eye of the Storm,* which some believe to be the most ambitious and successful of his many major contributions to world literature, as well as *The Cockatoos* (1974), a collection of novellas, and *A Fringe of Leaves* (1976). Thea Astley's *A Kindness Cup* has already been mentioned, and she also published *The Acolyte* (1972), possibly her best work to date. Christina Stead, once more living in Australia, came up with *The Little Hotel,* a rather slight work published in 1974 though apparently written as early as 1948, and then in 1976, with

Miss Herbert: The Suburban Wife, a "depressingly good" study of complacent self-deception. Frank Hardy's *But the Dead Are Many* (1975) was a more elaborate, more literary, and more carefully distanced statement of his abiding political concerns. Then Xavier Herbert re-emerged in the same year with his mightiest undertaking, *Poor Fellow My Country,* breaking all records for length, provoking attention for comprehensiveness as much as for Australianness, challenging reader, reviewer, and scholar to assess the extent of its riches. (pp. 24-7)

> K. G. Hamilton, "A Prefatory Sketch," in Studies in the Recent Australian Novel, edited by K. G. Hamilton, University of Queensland Press, 1979, pp. 1-28.

Carole Ferrier

[*In the following excerpt, Ferrier examines the works of notable female Australian novelists.*]

A large proportion of the novels published in Australia this century have been by women. But the response of critics to them has been limited and deficient. The work of Barnard Eldershaw and Nettie Palmer in discussing novels by their female contemporaries was not developed and extended seriously until the 1970s, with a very few exceptions, including Miles Franklin's *Laughter, Not for a Cage,* H. M. Green's *History of Australian Literature,* and Miller and Macartney's essentially bibliographical *Australian Literature.* Some valuable critical commentary on the work of women writers and its surrounding conditions of production can be found in the letters they exchanged about their own and others' work, but these are still for the most part unpublished.

At the beginning of the twentieth century there were, very broadly speaking, two alternative traditions within the framework of which writers could operate. Either they could draw on the tradition of "European", often "psychological", novels (as did Henry Handel Richardson, with *Maurice Guest*) or they could use the chronicles of bush and pioneer life (as did Prichard, with *The Pioneers*). Later, Franklin's *All that Swagger* and much of Tennant's work continued the "temper democratic, bias offensively Australian" strand of this latter tradition, while, more recently, writers such as Elizabeth Harrower have found the former tradition more congenial. Works such as Franklin's *My Brilliant Career* or Barbara Baynton's *Bush Studies* and *Human Toll* made an attempt partly to fuse the psychological and "pioneer picaresque" traditions to ironic effect—while attempting also to add the "emotional" dimension denigrated by Henry Lawson: "I hadn't read three pages when I saw what you will no doubt see at once—that the story had been written by a girl. . . . I don't know about the girlishly emotional parts of the book—I leave that to girl readers to judge."

Clearly, being influenced by one of the two traditions did not necessarily preclude the use of the other (though G. A. Wilkes, Leonie Kramer, and others see them as counterposed, and Barnard Eldershaw [in *Essays in Australian Fiction*] commented upon "a reorientation of the mind that almost amounts to dislocation" in reading

Prichard after Richardson). In many cases, however, deep contradictions were exposed: a writer such as Eve Langley in the 1940s can be seen to be poised uncomfortably between what is presented as the literary, (her character Steve's lyrical flights of fancy on classical themes) and an attempt to convey a sense of Australian landscape with the romance that is perceived in Gippsland and with which Steve endows the figure of her lover, Macca. Many readers responded ambivalently to *The Pea-Pickers;* Prichard commented to Miles Franklin: "I like the imagery and use of words in the early stages . . . but like you got fed up with the young women. Too posey and egocentric. . . . There's an audacity and original attack though, which ought to lead somewhere in another book." A temporary escape into the transfiguring imagination is not an option for Sybylla Melvyn, heroine of Franklin's first novel, *My Brilliant Career,* published at the turn of the century. Franklin comments [in *Laughter, Not For A Cage*]: "The girl's story was conceived and tossed off on impulse in a matter of weeks, spontaneously out of inexperience and consuming longings and discontents and half humorously . . . to show how impossible the Australian scene was for novel-making."

Franklin herself wanted the word *Brilliant* in the title to be followed by a question mark, but the title reads ironically even without one to most readers now: no "brilliant career" was possible at the turn of the century for women in the position of Sybylla Melvyn, or of Ursula in Barbara Baynton's *Human Toll. My Brilliant Career* could have been expected to strike a deep chord with many women writers: Prichard wrote in 1930 to Franklin about how the book had affected her: "It made a very vivid engraving on my mind at about the time I had just left school and I am sure matured my mind in the direction of reality and truth at that moment as nothing else did."

Prichard's own novels, however, could be read as devaluing women's artistic aspirations. In the presentation of such characters as Sophie in *The Black Opal,* Elodie in *Intimate Strangers,* and Violet in the goldfields trilogy—all singers or musicians whose "careers" fail to be brilliant—can be read a refusal to endorse artistic expression as a valid central preoccupation of a woman's life. Take Sophie's pleasure in her life on the Ridge after her failed singing career in New York:

> Sophie had a sense of hunger satisfied in the life she was leading . . . her soul was satisfied by breathing the pure, calm air of the Ridge, and by feeling her life was going on the way the lives of other women on the Ridge were going. She expected her life would go on like this, days and years fall behind unnoticed; that she and Potch would work together, have children, be splendid friends always, live out their simple days in the simple, sturdy fashion of the Ridge folk.

Her continuing aspirations for more than this are expressed in her relationship with Arthur Henty. However, in the class context, Prichard can be read as seeing artistic production as petty bourgeois, as peripheral to the building of the pioneer society and the Australian "nation". On the other hand, as Kay Iseman has demonstrated [in her "Katharine Susannah Prichard: Of an End a New Beginning", in *Arena*], she can be read as endorsing the force of instinctive "natural", often "anti-social" passion that should, in Lawrencean terms, be given full rein and which often overwhelms other desires or ambitions. Nevertheless, she was herself an ambitious artist who saw literary production as important. It is instructive to compare several of the women artists depicted in novels from the earlier part of this century in terms of their representation of artistic production by women who were, themselves, in the situation of being artists. Relevant novels include Barnard Eldershaw's *The Glasshouse,* Richardson's *Maurice Guest,* Devanny's *Out of Such Fires,* Prichard's *The Black Opal,* and Eleanor Dark's *The Little Company.*

Sophie in *The Black Opal* and Louise Dufrayer in *Maurice Guest* are both singers in training; both find their aspirations come into conflict with their relationship with a man, though both novels have ostensibly "happy" resolutions: Louise finally marries the fellow musician who earlier abandoned her, and Sophie returns to the mining settlement from which she had originally fled to become a singer in New York and marries a son of the soil, Potch. The structure of metaphor running through *The Black Opal* identifies Sophie with the priceless black opal which she drops and smashes into a thousand fragments—glittering but not solid, and Potch with the opal-bearing rock, the basis of the Ridge settlement. Both women sacrifice their artistic careers and acquiesce in the dominant ideology's endorsement of the primacy of an alliance with a man.

The overt ideological message that could be read in both Richardson and Prichard is that, for women, a central commitment to art is undesirable or impossible. (Yet both writers in their correspondence present themselves as serious artists.) In Barnard Eldershaw's *The Glasshouse* too, the central character, Stirling Armstrong, sees the importance of her writing as minimal compared with her sudden passion for the Norwegian captain of the ship on which she is returning to Australia:

> This was not a pain her mind could juggle with. She could only stand still under it, trembling a little, as a ship has paused and shivered in the teeth of the gale. She turned over the sheets of manuscript she had written on board and debated whether she would throw them into the sea. Their small comprehensions, their little flickering malice, meant nothing now.

It is suggested here that putting down words on paper ultimately has little value compared with the pursuit of a sexual connexion with a man; female characters who value their own creative ability, in text after text, either succumb to a Lawrencean male or fail to get one—and this is the most interesting thing that happens in the novel. In Jean Devanny's *Out of Such Fires,* Helena Savine goes as a "general" to a remote sheep station, much as Devanny herself did soon after arriving in Sydney in the Depression years; she is presented as maintaining an elevated detachment from her surroundings at first but eventually succumbs to the aforementioned overpowering sexual attraction and, unlike Barnard Eldershaw's heroine, marries the object of her attachment.

The Little Company is probably the most interesting of these novels dealing with female artists in that it is also self-reflexive. A male writer is given more attention than the two women writers in the book, but the focus on a group of writers gives Dark an opportunity to comment on the process of literary production and the different situations of male and female writers. Marty and her brother Gilbert both write quite differently:

> She wrote as naturally and easily as she talked and, while he recognised that her candidly topical matter, her carelessly colloquial manner might not rank as "literature" in the more austere sense of the word, he had recognised its value in a world where most people only read if they could keep on running at the same time.

Gilbert, by contrast, has a writer's block; his novels so far have been directed towards "the reader, who while priding himself on his intellectualism, still did not wish to be intellectually disturbed" and who was likely to find in them "an approach and an interpretation which—though it could not be accused of escapism—was gratifyingly rooted in established values". His attempts to develop away from this is also expressed in his move away from his wife, Phyllis, and towards the writer Elsa Kay.

Phyllis tries to read the economics texts Gilbert has begun to study but finds that society's construction of her as female inhibits this:

> She struggled through the first dozen pages of a score of books; their closely printed page peppered with statistics, with the polysyllabic words and obscure phrases of economic jargon, failed utterly to hold an attention which wandered helplessly to the pleasanter intricacies of a knitting pattern, the contents of the larder, or the material for Virginia's new frock.

Phyllis, predictably, does not find the writing of Elsa Kay, the other female writer in the novel, appealing but, rather, "hard and sarcastic". Elsa marries a conventional man eventually, and Gilbert begins to plan his new novel taking over an idea of Elsa's, sure that it would not be recognizable as the same material even if Elsa did eventually write her novel on this theme also. It is interesting that Elsa is seen earlier typing for Gilbert—even though this was only a letter to the newspaper. However, Dark makes these feminist points within a wider political context which connects the oppression of women to other aspects of the social structure.

None of these novels approaches a central focus on the development and consciousness of the female artist that would allow us to discuss them as *Künstlerromane. My Brilliant Career,* its sequel *My Career Goes Bung,* and Eve Langley's lyrical *White Topee* are, however, closer to this latter category. In *The Pea-Pickers,* the difficulty of combining artistic expression with "the procession of perambulators" required of a wife and mother is brought out; the argument is taken further in *White Topee* with an extended argument on how the artist can thrive on unsatisfied love:

> Ah, but I was lonely; the great Australian loneliness, that old disease of mine, swept over me, making my blood slow and painful along my

veins. I was lonely and I was unloved. And worse, far ahead into the future my soul struggled and saw no end of it, no end for ever to my thirst for love. Because, you see, I really didn't want to be loved. Not at all. What I really wanted was to be a man, and free for ever to write and think and dream. I had the utmost contempt for love, and a very real fear of it—"the beastly second best". I would rather have wandered the earth and written for ever than bothered about love.

Franklin goes into this question also much earlier with the character of Sybylla (who remains one of the most intransigent characters in women's fiction) and took up it again later in the figure of Ignez Milford in *Cockatoos,* one of her Brent of Bin Bin novels.

To return to the juxtaposed traditions that were available for use, Baynton and Richardson provide an interesting comparison in these terms. Baynton has been read as writing from a standpoint of what Showalter would categorize as a "feminine" sensibility and as shrinking from male brutality depicted as an aspect of pioneer life. A striking incident in *Human Toll* is a man's jumping, after a sexual encounter, out of the window right onto a baby lamb a few days old, smashing its body with his foot before wandering off to fall onto his bed in a drunken stupor with blood-spattered socks. Earlier, male friends talking at the bush dance have likened him to "the bull on Keen's mustard", and Baynton can be read as presenting a society in which men are vicious animals to which, in their unseeing and often drunken brutality, children, lambs, and the like are vulnerable—as are women. Another animal affinity favoured by several of these women writers is that of women with horses; Prichard's and Franklin's pervasive deployment of this metaphor has been examined by Judy Turner [in her thesis "For the Term of Her Natural Life"].

The approaches of Richardson and of Velia Ercole to either living and surviving in Australia or hankering for a (largely mythical) more liberating environment in Europe provide another interesting comparison. Franklin's Australian ire was aroused by Ercole's abandonment of her country, and in 1933 she begged Richardson to return to Australia. The heroes of Ercole's *No Escape* and Richardson's trilogy, Italian and English male doctors respectively, both long to return to what they see as the centre of culture and life—Europe—and consume much of their lives in longing for this. They differ interestingly from many of Prichard's characters who articulate a glorification of Australia as, in this passage from *The Pioneers* (written in England), a place of escape and liberation from aspects of the old world: " 'They may talk about your birthstain by and by, Dan,' she said, 'but that will not trouble you, because it was not this country that made the stain. This country has been the redeemer and blotted out all those old stains.' "

While it is, of course, methodologically doubtful to equate the views of any particular character with an overall authorial ideology, and while this latter is rarely mediated unproblematically in any literary text, there is more in *The Pioneers* than conversation to evoke sympathy with this view of Australia. In all three works, a sense of nationality is central: in Richardson and Ercole it is an alienated nationality that longs to be "at home" somewhere else. In *No Escape,* an Italian doctor, Leo Gherardi, and his wife, Teresa, pine for their Italian home town of Bologna. After Teresa's suicide, produced mainly by her awareness of Leo's gradual assimilation into the small provincial town in which they have settled, Leo finds a new, Mary Mahony-like wife in Olwen, who belongs to Banton, and marriage with whom expresses his acceptance by, and of, that place. Leo, unlike Richard Mahony, who spends his days driven mad by the contradictions of his personality and his aspirations, accepts a straitened but useful life within the small-town community. The real striving and desperation from which there is "no escape" is Teresa's; as a woman, her only escape would be to return to Bologna and abandon her husband—she is not in Richard's situation of knowing that his faithful spouse would follow him wherever he went.

The habit of expatriation for Australian women writers is a question that goes beyond mere geographical location—though many of these writers did not draw out its full implications in their writing. Ercole became Mrs Waterson Gregory and moved to Britain; according to Miles Franklin in *Laughter, Not for a Cage,* unable to write of any country except Australia, she wrote of Australia and then transposed the locations. Christina Stead also transposed geographic location in setting her partly autobiographical *The Man Who Loved Children* in the United States. Baynton lived in London after 1904, though she made frequent visits to Australia. Richardson left Australia for Leipzig to study music when she was in her twenties and made only one brief trip back to Australia in 1912, mainly to gather material for the writing of her father's life in fictional form in *The Fortunes of Richard Mahony.* Franklin left in 1905 and, except for two brief visits, stayed overseas until 1933, writing her "Brent" novels, set in Australia, while away. Christina Stead was to follow a similar pattern of expatriation to that of Richardson, except that she moved around a great deal more. She went to London in 1928, where she wrote her first novel, *Seven Poor Men of Sydney,* dealing with the Sydney Left milieu, and lived in various parts of Europe and America, only returning to live in Australia a few years before her death in 1983. An editor of Richardson's letters to Nettie Palmer comments: "Altogether, the letters show us a remarkable woman who spent her life as a stranger in and out of her country."

Moving about from one country to another and the nature of publishing at this period made it difficult for these writers to build a (national) reputation. Jean Devanny, for example, wrote a number of novels set in New Zealand and then in Australia, almost all of which were published in Britain. These writers, and their (often female) allies, had to work hard as their own publicists. Palmer, for example, tried to make Richardson's novels better known in Australia by a series of articles and then a book. Writing in 1927 in "The Novel in Australia", she commented: "All H. H. Richardson's works, even those whose setting is wholly Australian, are better known in Europe than here, and are discussed at length in German and Scandinavian literary encyclopaedias and reviews. In America, too, they have received great attention."

During the earlier part of the century, many women writers maintained close and supportive relationships with one another, often despite political differences which emerged clearly, for example, in the various writers' groups in the 1930s and 1940s, discussed in detail by Drusilla Modjeska [in her *Exiles at Home*]. Marjorie Barnard, indeed, wrote to Nettie Palmer in 1949: "The only literary club of any value was that of your friends and correspondents." These relationships were not uncritical, as some published and many more unpublished comments show. Franklin's comments in *Laughter, Not for a Cage* on many other fellow women writers are sharp. As seems to be the case with some of Devanny's comments about Prichard, literary rivalry interacts with a feeling that other women were better able to develop their talent because of an apparently less demanding or difficult personal life. Franklin wrote of Richardson:

> Self-centredness, in which she had been grounded by her mother's and her sister's lives subserving hers, and invincible self-confidence, fostered by her self-effacing husband, at length harvested some grain from a dark, costive talent. Self-engrossed, with such a belief in her own eminence that she could be condescending about other writers whose works may yet be considered as valuable as hers, it would seem that neither thought nor time was frittered in mere companionship or joy of living with any who did not feed this grim ego by offering incense.

Several of these writers were very conscious of their situation as women compared with that of those male writers who had a supportive family environment. Although Stead and Richardson were able to gain a "room of their own", and Dark and Prichard among those with children had *some* privacy to work, their situation was less favourable than that of many male writers. Franklin compares her own position with that of a particular contemporary male writer whom she sees as having "a woman to hang on his every breath and not a chore or care in the world [but who, however,] has found his work so sapping that he is away somewhere under doctor's orders. I wish he would follow in my tracks for a day, the exercise might harden him as well as frustrate him."

Most of these women writers had problems at various stages in reconciling prescribed female roles with literary production. Jean Devanny encountered many difficulties in literary, political, and personal spheres. Marjorie Barnard conducted a love affair every Monday night for eight years till 1942. In a letter to Devanny, she wrote, "I know well enough that it is ridiculous to let a purely personal pain darken the sun, there are bigger issues in the world and I have got the better of it. . . . You're wise enough to know [ ] wasn't to blame, and that anyhow men can't be judged on these things." In another letter written in 1947, she commented to Devanny on how personal relations could affect one's whole life: "It's odd isn't it how when one key brick is knocked out the whole apparently substantial structure collapses? You found that too."

Even the apparently invulnerable Richardson was left shattered by the death of her husband:

> The whole thing fell on me so unexpectedly, and I was stunned for the time being by the shock of it. Now I am beginning to come alive again, and to grasp what has happened to me.
>
> He was by far my most intimate friend, and had been at my side ever since I began to take my first uncertain steps as a writer. His sympathy and encouragement were unfailing, and all through those years of silence and neglect I wrote for him alone. Now the bottom seems to have fallen out of my world.

The fact that caring for relatives and domestic chores was perceived in general as a female responsibility posed other difficulties for women writers. The usual conditions of women's lives militated against writing; this is brought out, for example, in Eleanor Dark's picture of Marty snowed under with household chores in *The Little Company*:

> A day of dusting, preparing vegetables, carrying groceries from the shops, cooking, sewing on buttons for Pete, washing dishes. A day of dragging her mind away from Sally Dodd [her heroine] who clamoured incessantly for attention, and bullying it into concentration upon the clock and the routine of domestic duty. Sentences, whole paragraphs, had formed themselves in that rebellious mind, only to slide away unrecorded, and now forgotten; the tiredness born of conflict between what she wanted to do and what she must do, made her feel old.

Miles Franklin commented in 1932: "The trouble with Australia is that we are fast becoming a nation of charwomen. I'm too busy doing chores, myself, to write any more."

Eleanor Dark wrote to Jean Devanny: "I'm trying to work all the time, but other things are demanding these days and domestic help a thing of the past, so I don't make much headway." Though domestic help was not a thing of the past for Marjorie Barnard at this period, her attempts to exploit it met difficulties: "We have been trying for five months to get rid of a woman who was originally engaged as a domestic help but won't do any work and is full of venom." Prichard and Franklin compared notes in October 1940 on their home situations, Prichard commenting:

> Sometimes, I'm sure I work harder than anybody in the world. And at so many different kinds of jobs—keeping house for my beautiful son who is grown-up now, cooking, sweeping, washing, mending, etc., organisational work and lectures and, somewhere in between, I've got to find time to write and earn my living. All this, most of the time, with head and heart too weary for words and the terrible pressure of financial anxieties never growing less.

and Franklin replying: "I housekeep for two men—brother and orphan nephew. I have no more strength now for writing—and the financial anxiety, as you say, never grows less—it will catch us all presently."

Their health and energy faltered under these complex demands. Dark found her family situation gave her difficulties in finishing *Storm of Time:*

> Eric was working on his book all last year too, so with both of them in the throes of getting born, plus the usual practice and domestic routine, plus Mike at home and sitting for the Leaving, it seemed a more than usually exhausting year, and I felt a pretty limp and useless bit of humanity at the end of it. So the Monster was finished under difficulties, and its completion sort of mixed up in my mind with other sad things that I still feel a sort of shrinking from it, and am glad to be told by an honest person like yourself that it wasn't all wasted effort.

Similarly, Barnard in a letter in 1945 referred to her feelings of "compound exhaustion". Franklin wrote to Dymphna Cusack in 1940: "I don't like to hear of your frequent indispositions. I think it results from mental disharmony." Devanny refused a conventional family role, but a multiplicity of other pressures contributed to the crumbling of her health. Richardson suffered from sciatica: "And it's no new thing for me to be ill," she wrote to Nettie Palmer, "a good quarter of my life has been spent on bed or sofa."

Apart from problems with the roles traditionally prescribed by their gender, particularly in relation to housework and the expectations of men and children in family relationships, committed activists like Devanny and Prichard had an added problem, also experienced by some men, of combining political work with making time to write and even with justifying this latter activity. In Devanny's *Roll Back the Night,* another novelist, Eleanor, asks her friend Helen whether in fact those committed to politics should give up writing; but Helen rejects this: " 'No, no!' she says. 'You are participating in the actual struggles of the people by writing . . . Marx was a writer . . . A writer must be on one side of the people's struggles or the other'."

Within the Communist Party, writing was often not perceived as significant compared with routine Party work. Devanny reports a conversation with a keen young comrade as follows: "A promising young speaker to whom I had lent *Cindie* returned the book, after weeks, unread. 'I didn't get time to open it', he said, and added: 'why don't you get down to some important work, Comrade Devanny?' 'Such as?' 'Well, we need speakers and paper sellers, you know.' " In another context she was abused by an older comrade: " 'The trouble with Comrade Devanny is that she thinks she can teach us something. Because she has scribbled a lot of rubbishy books she thinks she knows something about cultural work that we don't.' " Some of Devanny's friends outside the Party saw her writing as hampered by her Party membership. Miles Franklin expressed to others her anger at Devanny's treatment by the Communist Party during the period of her "expulsion".

Devanny and Prichard both spent the 1930s and early 1940s speaking and agitating around Australia, still attempting at the same time to write books and bring up children. They also aimed at work experience—or, at least, personal observation—of the different occupations and ways of life dealt with in their novels, even if it was

often only practicable to engage in this for short periods. Dorothy Hewett followed in this tradition when she made her (admittedly short) experience of work in the Sydney spinning mills the subject of her only published novel, *Bobbin Up* (1959). In this they partly freed themselves from the sometimes class-bound attitudes articulated in writers like Barnard or Franklin, as expressed, for example, in Sybylla Melvyn's view of what it would be to become "poor Mary Ann": "I could be a cook or a housemaid and slave all day under some nagging woman and be a social outcast." Devanny in *Out of Such Fires,* based on seven weeks that she spent as a cook on a remote sheep station in 1929, places her central female character, Helena, in this situation; however, she has a greater strength and sense of personal worth than Sybylla. Helena is described as gathering material for a book from the start and is more detached from the personal and social pressures of her situation than Sybylla could be.

The political commitment of Devanny and Prichard led them to adopt a form of socialist realist writing. Both attempted trilogies of working-class life, Prichard's dealing with the goldfields and Devanny's with the canefields of north Queensland. Devanny's earlier *Sugar Heaven* focuses centrally upon the way the wives of canecutters are drawn into support of the strike and out of their privatized situation within the family. This concern was associated with the practical work she was doing in organizing women in the Women's Progress Clubs in the 1930s as part of the Popular Front strategy.

Kylie Tennant and Dymphna Cusack show much less political certainty while still in many ways writing within a similar tradition which they perceived as essentially Australian. Tennant is one of the more "feminist" of the later generation in that in her writing the notion of the impossibility of men and women living comfortably together, especially in the countryside, is frequently articulated. Mallee Herrick in *The Honey Flow* comments:

> I quite agreed with all the people, including Hilda, who had warned me that it was not possible to be friends with men. The mistake I had been making all my life is that I always thought you could. I like friends. I like being friends with men, but only a fool will go trying to do the impossible. No, men and women should live in separate worlds with the doors locked between them. Centuries of training are needed before men and women can be civilized to the stage where they can be friends.

There is a tension in most of Tennant's work between rural and urban life, with Tennant inclining strongly towards the rural despite her problematic relationship to the ideal of "mateship". In her own earlier life, Tennant had lived the Australian pioneer picaresque lifestyle she delineates.

The work of these writers and others provides key material for considering the situation of women in Australia before the second wave of the women's movement which brought in its wake some changes on the ideological and publishing fronts at least. In the earlier part of the century, many of the women writers had confessed themselves beaten. Jean Devanny wrote in 1945: "That's where I failed. Dissipation of energies. And now that I realise it and am prepared to do the job it seems to be too late. . . . I had always the will and desire to rise above one long series throughout my life of crushing trials and blows but never the ability to do more than rise above them." Miles Franklin wrote to Dymphna Cusack: "You flatteringly ask how I reconciled the claims of job, personal and literary life. Well, I *didn't*. I have never written except rough fragments which are merely a sample of all that was once dammed-up in me, and which is now atrophying."

Nevertheless, Franklin was an inspirational figure for other writers. Nene Gare wrote to Cusack: "What I want and would value is a scrap of writing in Miles's own hand expressing a viewpoint . . . I shall be able to look at it and feel some of that indomitable spirit seeping into me. What she could do, I can attempt to do, and by this I do not mean writing necessarily." (pp. 7-15)

> *Carole Ferrier, "Introductory Commentary: Women Writers in Australia," in* Gender, Politics and Fiction: Twentieth Century Australian Women's Novels, *edited by Carole Ferrier, University of Queensland Press, 1985, pp. 1-21.*

Fay Zwicky on Australian national identity:

People are trying to define something because it has never really been spoken. Don't forget we're still an appendage of Britain. We still have a Governor-General approved by Britain. It's all very well to talk about freedom and independence, but America has it, and Australia hasn't. That's something that has always rankled in the national mind. To an American it looks funny to be clamoring about our identity, but it's still an issue when you're not independent, you're still not a republic. And then again you realize that, stuck out here, in the middle of nowhere, we are still identity-less in the sense that we're not sure how close we should be to Asia, which is our neighbor, or how we should relate to European powers. That's where the trouble really lies in Australia, in not knowing where we belong. This landmass that's stuck right out in the middle of nowhere. In my view, Australia has every reason in looking to Asia. It's a much more viable interest. On the other hand, I can see equally our cultural roots with Europe. We're stuck in this dilemma. You find writers trying to use an Asian setting. I'm thinking of Christopher Koch and Robert Drewe. They drop their characters down in Asia. It's clear they're feeling some need to link Australian experience with what is geographically closer.

Fay Zwicky, in Australian Voices: Writers on Their Own Work, *1991.*

Elizabeth Webby

[In the following essay, Webby provides a thematic and historical overview of short fiction in Australia.]

As every writer on or of short fiction knows, beginnings and endings are vital. The boundaries of this critical out-line of twentieth-century Australian short fiction were easily arrived at: Henry Lawson's first major collection and Frank Moorhouse's most recent one. How to deal with the middle was more of a problem. It would have been easy, if tedious, to make a chronological survey of developments in the Australian short story between 1896 and 1980. Instead, I have attempted to look at these developments from two perspectives, seeing them as part of the process of a relatively new literary genre as well as of that of a new national literature.

Earlier views of 'Australian short fiction' seem to have stressed the first adjective at the expense of the rest of the term. Writers have been valued for their Australianness rather than their individuality; as reflectors of reality rather than as inventors of fictions. This one-eyed concentration on content rather than form has produced, among other things, a critical monster, the Lawson-Furphy tradition. In terms of style and structure, the two writers could hardly be less alike. When its component writers are examined in these terms, the so-called Lawson tradition of the Australian short story also begins to look distinctly mythical.

Mythical or not, this tradition has exerted a powerful influence on conceptions of Australian short fiction, one which has disguised similarities as well as differences. If, however, one's criterion is form rather than content, there are some surprising resemblances between Lawson's short fiction and that of contemporary Australian writers. In terms of content, the contrast between the boiling billy of 1896 and the secret family of 1980 is an extreme one, pointing to the move away from the bush and other distinctively Australian subjects and locales, to the seemingly more sophisticated, international approach of the contemporary writers. Indeed, one of the latter, Michael Wilding, in his afterword to *The Tabloid Story Pocket Book* (1978), sees recent Australian short fiction very much in terms of a reaction against the Lawson tradition of the Australian short story. As he is careful to point out, this involved a rejection not of Lawson's own work but of the tradition expounded by nationalist critics like Vance and Nettie Palmer. Here are two examples, separated in time by thirty years, but equally favouring life over art, reality over fiction. In *Modern Australian Literature, 1900-1923* (1924), Nettie Palmer stated that:

> Lawson seems to have led the way to the real short story in Australia . . . Lawson had too deep a respect for the life he described to falsify it for the sake of mechanical effects, and it can be seen now that his early 'Drover's Wife', although not his best story, was a definite standard of truth, and opened the eyes of other writers to what was really poignant and dramatic in the life around them.

Writing on Lawson in *The Legend of the Nineties* (1954), Vance Palmer claimed:

> in his stories, he founded a tradition of democratic writing that has affected the work of nearly all who have come after him. The feature of it is a natural acceptance of human equality, a tendency to look at life through the eyes of the swagman as well as the squatter, and to take for

granted the values people act upon in life rather than those they might be persuaded to accept as novel-readers.

The Palmers' determination to dismiss all pre-Lawsonian Australian fiction as colonial blinded them to some of the continuities between his work and that of his predecessors. Perhaps it would be fairer to say that they didn't bother to look since they were convinced that Lawson took all from life and nothing from books. To be fairer still, they would have had to look not so much in books, though Boldrewood's *Robbery Under Arms* is an obvious one, as in newspapers and magazines. If they had, they would have discovered that, like Lawson, many earlier Australian authors wrote pieces which were not stories in the sense of having a connected plot. The nineteenth-century term for them was sketches, to denote their predominantly descriptive nature, and much of the short fiction written about Australia before Lawson was of this type. Descriptions of walks around Sydney, scenes in the outback, character sketches of drovers and bullock drivers abound in the early magazines and newspapers. There were plenty of heavily-plotted stories too but their authors usually preferred to set them in the more romantic environs of the old world. Many of Lawson's earlier pieces were character or travel sketches: 'Mitchell: A Character Sketch', 'Hungerford', 'In a Wet Season' and 'In a Dry Season'. Even such classic pieces of Lawsonia as 'The Drover's Wife' and 'The Union Buries Its Dead' have such a minimal amount of plot that they could just as easily be termed sketches as stories. Most of the early reviewers did in fact do just that, writing, for example, of Lawson's 'sketches, which for the most part are too slight to be designated stories'.

So when Michael Wilding speaks of *Tabloid Story* being set up at the end of the sixties to oppose the dominance in Australian short fiction (at least that which got published) of 'formula bush tales', 'beginning, middle and end' stories and the 'well rounded tale' it is obvious that other influences besides Lawson had been at work in producing the standard Australian story. These influences were, as I shall argue later, as much international as national.

Wilding dates the beginning of reaction against 'formula' stories to 1968-69. An 'International Symposium on the Short Story', published in the *Kenyon Review* in these same two years, included two contributions from Australia, by Henrietta Drake-Brockman and Elizabeth Harrower, besides a piece by Christina Stead, representing England. Stead's was the most fascinating, if least relevant to my argument, revealing much about herself and her approach to fiction, though nothing about the current state of the short story in England. Stead is, of course, one of the writers who have suffered most from the previous nationalist bias in Australian criticism. Her novels are at last starting to be studied but her remarkable early collection *The Salzburg Tales* (1934) remains largely unread. A survey of fourteen anthologies of Australian short fiction published since 1951 revealed that Stead appears in only two. The vitality and stylistic and formal variety of Stead's stories would, I think, be quite a revelation to younger Australian writers who would be staggered to discover her anticipation of the current fabulist mode. The opening sentence of her *Kenyon Review* piece is worth quoting as

a demonstration of Stead's own inclusive approach to short fiction and also the usefulness of that term as a substitute for short story:

> I love *Ocean of Story*, the name of an Indian Treasury of story; that is the way I think of the short story and what is part of it, the sketch, anecdote, jokes cunning, philosophical, and biting, legends and fragments.

The official Australian representatives in the *Kenyon Review* Symposium provide two contrasting accounts of the state of short fiction in Australia in the late sixties. Henrietta Drake-Brockman is very much of the nationalist school, as one sees from her opening sentence, or pronouncement: 'The art of the short story is indigenous to Australia'. She proceeds to justify this by tracing the development of Australian short fiction from Aboriginal legends via tales around the camp fire to 'the genius of Henry Lawson and the skills of other Australian writers of the '90s' who:

> established what is now a generally accepted criterion by which earlier fiction is seen to be 'colonial'—with a British-oriented bias obscuring the quality and reality of actual Australian experience . . .

All the nationalist assumptions are evident here— rejection of overseas influence, insistence on realism, closeness to life and, most importantly, 'Australianness'. Lawson is the presiding genius, accompanied by other (characteristically unnamed) writers of the nineties. Equally characteristically, Lawson is valued not for his skill as a writer but for 'his personal philosophy of good mateship and elevation of egalitarian principles which helped to build, and remains integrated with, the national ethos'.

Mrs Drake-Brockman goes on to outline the expansion of interest in short fiction that took place in Britain and America during the twenties and thirties and eventually found its way to Australia. Although she does not say so directly, her description of the writers who came to prominence during this period—Katharine Susannah Prichard, Vance Palmer, Frank Dalby Davison and Cecil Mann—as 'now polished, craft-conscious, more involved with psychological exploration' implies that these were qualities not found in the work of Lawson and the nineties school. A further implication is that they were the product of overseas influences, as indeed they were though it would have been sacrilegious for a nationalist to have admitted it.

The first of her examples, Katharine Susannah Prichard, was less reticent, telling us in the Foreword to her selected stories, *Happiness* (1967) that:

> Guy de Maupassant's 'Contes Normands' gave me the short story technique which, more or less unconsciously, has influenced my telling of incidents and happenings in the country districts, and on the goldfields and in the cities of Australia.

'Happiness' itself, however, shows her using a more modern technique, presenting all the events through the eyes

Cover of Happiness *(1967), a collection of short stories by Katherine Susannah Prichard.*

of an old Aboriginal woman. This dramatic method allows the contrast between black and white perceptions and values to be made much more subtly and effectively than in Prichard's later stories on similar themes which are technically closer to Maupassant. 'Happiness' comes from Prichard's first collection, *Kiss on the Lips* (1932), the source of all her regularly anthologised and most praised stories. As well as 'Happiness' and that stark dramatisation of aboriginal life 'The Cooboo', it contains an intriguing stylistic experiment, 'The Curse', and an equally intriguing feminist piece 'The Cow'. In the latter story Prichard explicitly rejects the equation of human and animal she had humorously employed in 'The Grey Horse'. This equation, though not found in Lawson's work, is also seen in a number of stories by Prichard's contemporaries, for example, Vance Palmer's 'The Little Duck' and 'The Trap' and Frank Dalby Davison's 'Return of the Hunter'. Prichard's two later collections, *Potch and Colour* (1944) and *N'goola* (1959), unfortunately lack the stylistic and thematic variety of her first one, partly it would seem because of a deliberate attempt to match Lawsonian content with a Maupassant technique.

In many of Vance Palmer's stories, too, one sees a similar blend of such content and overseas-influenced forms and styles. In 1968 John Barnes [in his 'Lawson and the Short Story in Australia' in *Westerly*] drew attention to the influence of Chekhov on Palmer's stories, also suggesting that the so-called Lawson tradition of the Australian short story should, more correctly, be labelled the *Bulletin* tradition. The 1962 reprint of Palmer's first collection of short fiction, *The World of Men* (1915), shows that Palmer, like Katherine Mansfield, also owed a good deal to A. R. Orage, editor of the English magazine, *The New Age*. Orage, Palmer wrote, gave him 'a chance to do different work—sketches based on what he called my "unique personal experiences"'. Palmer's best stories are, indeed, those which derive from a personal rather than a deliberately Australian, or Lawsonian, vision. These are the stories which explore, sometimes seriously, sometimes comically, the world of childhood and adolescence—'The Foal', 'Josie', 'Mathieson's Wife'—an area which Lawson could never approach without the props of sentimentality and melodrama. Amusingly enough, 'Josie' and 'Mathieson's Wife' were the two Palmer stories chosen by Douglas Stewart for *Short Stories of Australia: The Lawson Tradition* (1967).

Like Prichard's and Palmer's, the stories of many Australian writers of the forties and fifties can be called Lawsonian only in terms of their use of bush characters and locales. In terms of form and style, they also depart markedly from Lawson's, following such overseas developments as social realism, dramatic realism or the stylistic simplification of Sherwood Anderson and Hemingway. 'How much are you influenced by other writers?' was one of the questions put to the seventeen Australian and New Zealand writers included in *Speaking of Writing* (ed. R. D. Walshe, 1975). Only the New Zealander, Frank Sargeson, acknowledged Lawson as an influence, along with Mark Twain and Sherwood Anderson. Marjorie Barnard and Dal Stivens denied any conscious influences; Alan Marshall mentioned Gorky and Conrad; Judah Waten, Joyce, Sherwood Anderson and Chekhov. Sargeson is, I think, the only major short fiction writer to have been influenced by Lawson in any positive way. Indeed, some of Sargeson's stories, such as 'That Summer', seem much more 'Lawsonian' in their apparent casualness, use of local idiom, espousal of mateship and egalitarian principles, than anything Lawson himself wrote.

In considering why Lawson should have had a much more positive influence on New Zealand short fiction than on Australian it is helpful to turn to Frank O'Connor's *The Lonely Voice: A Study of the Short Story* (1963). O'Connor suggests that:

> We can see in the short story an attitude of mind that is attracted by submerged population groups, whatever these may be at any given time—tramps, artists, lonely idealists, dreamers and spoiled priests.

When Lawson commenced writing, the bushman and bushwoman were a submerged population group in Australian literature. Adam Lindsay Gordon had written 'The Sick Stockrider' and Kendall and Marcus Clarke some poems and stories about bush characters but none of them had done enough to securely establish working class characters in Australian literature in the way that Bret Harte's stories had in American. This was left to Lawson and the *Bulletin* school. When Frank Sargeson began writing in the thirties working class characters were still a submerged population group in New Zealand literature but tended to dominate Australian. Hence the most effective stories of the Australian writers in the supposed Lawson tradition are those in which the writers have discovered submerged population groups of their own. Prichard's aborigines, Palmer's and Alan Marshall's children, Gavin Casey's miners, John Morrison's waterside workers, Judah Waten's immigrants. Writers who, like Brian James, stuck to the bush now seem largely of historical interest. Marjorie Barnard, though definitely not of the Lawson school in either style or content, also found some submerged population groups of her own, women and city-dwellers. The title story of her only collection, *The Persimmon Tree* (1944), is the standard anthology piece but, as D. R. Burns has pointed out [in *The Directions of Australian Fiction 1920–1974*], she has much else to offer. A reprinting of *The Persimmon Tree* is definitely called for. Two others who began publishing at much the same time as Barnard, Peter Cowan and Dal Stivens, have persisted with short fiction. Their work, unlike that of many of their contemporaries, displays a willingness to experiment with the formal and stylistic possibilities of the genre.

A great awareness of the formal and stylistic possibilities of short fiction is, of course, also the hallmark of Hal Porter's work. Porter was obviously not influenced by Lawson, who is (it would seem deliberately) left out of Porter's anthology *It Could Be You* (1973), though it includes Rudd and Dyson. Equally Porter does not seem to have influenced any of the younger writers. Michael Wilding, in discussing their rejection of the Lawson tradition, makes no mention of Porter's earlier similar problems in finding a publication outlet for stories that were not in the Lawson mode. In his Introduction to *The Penguin Book of Australian Short Stories* (1976), Harry Heseltine makes a valiant effort to fit Porter into a tradition of Australian short fiction. But the criteria he uses—Porter's fidelity to 'the experienced quality of his total environment', 'his making the authentication of that experience (to himself and to others) the prime responsibility of his language'— are so broad as to be applicable not just to Australian short fiction but to fiction in general. As with all good writers it is the individual quality of Porter's experience and language which singles him out. The same is true of Patrick White whose best short fiction resembles Porter's only in the very general terms of Heseltine's definition and in their common rejection of the Lawson tradition. In some of their weaker stories—such as White's 'Willy Wagtails by Moonlight' and Porter's 'Vulgar's the Word'—there is more similarity, resulting I think from a common influence, the satire of Australian suburbia initiated by Barry Humphries in the mid-fifties. Michael Wilding rightly sees this trend, apparent in much Australian short fiction of the sixties, as just the flip side of the earlier tradition, with celebration of the bush and male mateship transposed into denigration of the suburbs and female bitchiness. Or, as Wilding very nicely puts it, 'from the plain account of the

harsh environment to the harsh account of the plain environment'.

Neither of these two faces of Australian short fiction of the sixties seems to have proved particularly appealing to the new writers who began to become known then. Randolph Stow, Thomas Keneally, Thea Astley all concentrated on the novel rather than short fiction. Another of them, Elizabeth Harrower, was in 1969 pretty pessimistic about the current state of the short story in Australia. In her piece for the *Kenyon Review* Symposium Harrower wrote:

> Without canvassing the continent, it seems safe enough to say that there is not one full-time short story writer in Australia, nor one who supports himself even marginally on the proceeds of short story writing.

In a reference to Beatrice Davis's *Short Stories of Australia: The Moderns* (1967), she noted that the youngest of these modern writers was born in 1931: 'Reviews made much of the omission of the talented young, but refrained from mentioning names for the very good reason that none could be thought of '.

Where were the talented young in the late sixties? Some were publishing in the girlie magazines which were then the only outlet for their radical and usually sexually-oriented short fiction. A girlie magazine publisher brought out Frank Moorhouse's first collection, *Futility and Other Animals,* in 1969. In the years since then the short fiction scene in Australia has changed markedly from the one described by Elizabeth Harrower. A number of new writers have achieved reputations solely or almost solely on the basis of their short fiction. Helped by the greatly increased government support for the arts which the seventies brought, writing short fiction has also become a more economic proposition.

One of the major differences between this resurgence of interest in short fiction in Australia and the first flowering of the eighteen-nineties was that contemporary writers had to establish their own publication medium. Lawson found in the *Bulletin* a magazine eager to publish short fiction of the type he was writing. Moorhouse, Wilding and Carmel Kelly began producing their own magazine, *Tabloid Story,* in 1972 following the decline in the soft-porn girlie magazines with the freeing of censorship restrictions. Wilding later went on to found his own publishing firm, Wild and Woolley. The other main force in the publishing of new Australian short fiction has been the University of Queensland Press, the source of Wilding's earlier volumes, Peter Carey's *The Fat Man in History* (1974) and *War Crimes* (1979), Murray Bail's *Contemporary Portraits* (1975), Barry Oakley's *Walking through Tigerland* (1977), Gerard Lee's *Pieces for a Glass Piano* (1978), Trevor Shearston's *Something in the Blood* (1979) and John Emery's *Summer Ends Now* (1980). The traditional publisher of Australian short fiction, Angus and Robertson, was, until its recent publication of Glenda Adams's *The Hottest Night of the Century* (1979), associated only with Frank Moorhouse, whom they took up from his second collection, *The Americans, Baby* (1972). In 1977, however, they did put the imprimatur on the arrival of the new writers by issuing the first anthology of their work, *The Most*

Beautiful Lies, containing stories by Moorhouse, Wilding, Carey, Bail and Morris Lurie.

Once the new writing became respectable, it had to be christened. The usual label has been the Balmain school—after the Sydney inner-suburb where Wilding, Moorhouse, Carey and many other young writers lived. But, just as the *Bulletin* school label tends to gloss over the enormous differences in the stories produced by, say, Lawson, Barbara Baynton, Edward Dyson and Steele Rudd, so the Balmain label is misleading. In his Introduction to *The Most Beautiful Lies* Brian Kiernan rejects the idea of a school of contemporary short fiction though he does allow the new writers certain tendencies in common

> . . . a tendency for their stories to present themselves self-consciously as 'fictions', to be less mimetic, less concerned with character and social situation and more with style and form as part of the stories' 'content'; and a tendency to employ less realistic forms, such as the fable and science-fiction tale.

And these tendencies, as Michael Wilding noted in *The Tabloid Story Pocket Book,* were influenced not by earlier Australian writers but by ones from the U. S. A., Latin America and Europe.

How then, is it possible to argue that Lawson and contemporary Australian short fiction writers have anything in common? Beneath the obvious differences in locale, idiom and subject matter there are, I think, several striking similarities. Like the contemporary writers, if perhaps never as self-consciously, Lawson broke away from the standard Australian short story of his time. His innovations in style and form have long been recognised, most notably by Arthur Phillips in 'The Craftmanship of Lawson', first published in *Meanjin* in 1948. But while Lawson's rejection of nineteenth-century literary rhetoric and such clumsy conventions as the framed story-within-a-story gave his work an immediacy and authenticity lacking in most earlier Australian fiction, he was never a realist in the Zolaesque sense of that term. He never attempted to totally remove his personality from his work, he was always conscious of his audience. Even in one of his most objective stories, 'The Drover's Wife', one finds direct addresses to the reader and personal asides:

> You might walk for twenty miles along this track without being able to fix a point in your mind, unless you are a bushman. This is because of the everlasting, maddening sameness of the stunted trees—that monotony which makes a man long to break away and travel as far as trains can go, and sail as far as ships can sail— and further.

For much of the nineteenth century realism was more a matter of content than of style or form. A writer was called realistic if he dealt seriously and sympathetically with such submerged population groups as workers or prostitutes, if he wrote on contemporary rather than historical subjects, if he used local rather than exotic settings. It did not matter if his plots were loaded with coincidences and contrivances, if his tone was melodramatic or sentimental, if his style was highly idiosyncratic. Hence the hailing of Bret Harte as a realist. Gradually, as the nineteenth century moved on to the twentieth, realism came to mean a method of writing which aimed to be objective and impersonal, which avoided anything which looked made-up, which pretended that it was not the product of a writer but of life itself. The influence of this type of realism can be seen in the work of many twentieth-century Australian writers, particularly those in the so-called Lawson tradition. It was the dominant note of Australian short fiction in the first half of the century, a note which Hal Porter, Patrick White and the contemporary short fiction writers all in turn rejected.

A short-hand indication of the different attitudes to short fiction during the years 1896-1980 may be gained from the titles of collections which were not just named after one of their component stories. Lawson's *While the Billy Boils,* for example, indicates a lot more than a bush locale: the shortness and apparent casualness of most of its contents and, in particular, awareness of the relationship between story-teller and audience. In contrast, Vance Palmer's titles, such as *The World of Men* and *Sea and Spinifex* focus squarely on locale, though there is a certain loosening up in *Let the Birds Fly,* title of his last and best collection. Hal Porter's *A Bachelor's Children* clearly indicates his sense of his stories as personal products rather than 'slices of life', while Patrick White's *The Burnt Ones* lets us know that his main concerns will be thematic and symbolic. Frank Moorhouse's *The Americans, Baby* is a direct address to the reader; his *Tales of Mystery and Romance* a deliberate rejection of realism.

Their rejection of objective realism and their conscious recognition of the reader have, I think, brought the new writers closer to Lawson than was possible for Australian short fiction writers trapped in the realist mode of the first half of this century. Another similarity is the contemporary writers' fondness for a type of first person narrative which directs considerable irony at the narrator himself. Lawson's Joe Wilson and the self-conscious narrator of the 'Imogene Continued' section of Moorhouse's *The Everlasting Secret Family* move in completely different worlds yet Lawson's description of Joe's 'natural sentimental selfishness, good-nature, "softness" or weakness' could be applied to both. The mode of the *Joe Wilson* stories is very close to the confessional mode favoured in much contemporary short fiction. Structurally, too, this series anticipates the discontinuous narrative used by Moorhouse and others.

This essay is not, however, an attempt to make out a case for a new Lawson tradition of the Australian short story. Rather, it is an attempt to point out that the most successful writers in this genre have been those who consciously saw themselves as writers of fictions, those who aimed to create art from rather than simply reflect life. Tom Paulin has recently suggested that 'Stylistic self-consciousness and a playful awareness of "established literary models" are essential to the short story'. As Brian Kiernan has argued [in his 'Ways of Seeing: Henry Lawson's "Going Blind" ', in the *Times Literary Supplement*], these qualities are to be found in Lawson's best stories. They are equally apparent in the work of Hal Porter and Frank

Moorhouse, the other two major short fiction writers Australia has so far produced. It is impossible to slot these three into any tradition of Australian short fiction. The tradition they belong to is that of short fiction itself, which transcends national boundaries. (pp. 147-56)

> Elizabeth Webby, "Australian Short Fiction from 'While the Billy Boils' to 'The Everlasting Secret Family'," in Australian Literary Studies, Vol. 10, No. 2, October, 1981, pp. 147-56.

DRAMA

Dennis Carroll

[Carroll is an Australian-born American educator and critic whose works reflect his interest in Australian, Finnish, and Hawaiian theater. In the following excerpt, he presents a thematic and historical overview of Australian drama.]

The birth of modern Australian drama arguably began with the first one act plays of Louis Esson (1879-1943), the first playwright to weld the emergent conventions of modern European drama to palpably Australian material. The coming of age of that drama is complete with the work of the present generation of Australian playwrights, who include Stephen Sewell and Louis Nowra. This generation has proved itself capable of imaginatively using most of the stylistic conventions employed elsewhere in the West, and they have the confidence and the need to apply them both to Australian and to international material.

Forms of art and literature have developed within a nation which at first was geographically isolated from its European roots as much as its separate units of settlement were isolated from each other—and these geographical circumstances have made their mark on the coming of age of Australian drama. The country is 7,682,300 km in size, as large as the continental US excluding Alaska, and it is an island continent comparatively isolated in the South Pacific from any near neighbors. Each of the separate state capitals of Sydney (N. S. W.), Melbourne (Victoria), Adelaide (South Australia), Brisbane (Queensland), Hobart (Tasmania) and Perth (Western Australia) was the nucleus of a separate British colony established for different reasons, some for the purposes of convict settlement, and the isolation of the towns was compounded by the difficulty of access between them, which was real and daunting even as late as the 1940's. And the center of the country is a "dead heart," a desert rich in minerals and awesome natural beauty but harsh in its challenges to man. A major motif of nineteenth century Australian history is that of the exploration of, endurance in, and conquest of inhospitable landscape—a motif that is also seminal in early literature and drama. But it is arguable that the geographic isolation of the colonies and their comparatively late Federation in 1901 did not cause marked regional differences within the country. The two largest cities, Sydney and Melbourne, have always been rivals, and there have been studies of the differences of culture and outlook between them. But this is hardly as great as between New York and Los Angeles, for example. And neither are there notable regional differences of speech in Australia.

The coming of age has also been affected by both sociological and artistic circumstances. A nineteenth century "Australianist" ethos became tarnished and eroded in the years following Federation in 1901. Certain playwrights' preoccupations in theme and subject matter failed to sit easily with social and cultural change. And the development of a mature drama has been delayed by the retarded development of the theatre. The basically commercial character of the Australian professional theatre since Federation prevented the development of less commercial forms of it which could have nurtured Australian modern drama. (pp. 1-2)

Many of the themes and preoccupations that tend to recur in Australian literature and drama are centered on what social historians and literary critics have called the "democratic tradition" or the "Australianist legend." The male-oriented traditions and values the legend celebrates have failed to gyve with the increasing social complexities of modern Australia. Though variants of Russel Ward's exposition of this legend have appeared in recent years and aspects of it have been vigorously challenged, it is worth summarizing Ward's exposition briefly here for the thematic insights it gives into some of our major modern plays.

Ward traces the legend's genesis to the support system of convicts transported to Australia in the late 18th and early 19th centuries. These were men and women who developed a fierce loyalty to other criminals, and were inherently opposed to the triple pillars of conventional colonial authority: police, military, and church. Their bonding, and the attitudes behind it, disproportionately influenced the free immigrants. Their attitude also influenced the so-called "currency children," those born of marriages between convicts, or convicts and free settlers. Security of employment, good wages and a sense of freedom drew many immigrants and ex-convicts to opened-up hinterlands—the "outback"—and so the values of the emerging nationalist legend were associated with the outback rather than the cities, and these were picked up by the next big population influx, the diggers who flocked to the goldfields following the first discoveries in 1851. Out of the goldfields society emerged the first Republican challenge to the crown in Australian history—the Eureka Stockade episode of 1854, where diggers defied the licensing inspections of the colonial government and briefly flew the Southern Cross over the Union Jack. After the goldrush period, the less successful diggers became shearers, fencers, jackeroos and others who provided the solidarity behind the strikes of the 1890's, the beginnings of the Trade Union movement, and the birth of the Labor Party. Nascent Republican defiance was transformed into a national feeling which culminated in Federation.

The Australian legend derives largely from two articles of faith: that the authentic lives lived by real men can best be lived in the outback, not the cities; and that the "mateship" or brotherhood of working men is an especially hallowed relationship.

The first of these highlighted man's paradoxical relationship to the Australian landscape. The look and feel of the Australian outback differs a great deal from that of the American West. It has little of the majestic beauty and variety of parts of California and the Pacific Northwest. It has a sameness, often a parched hardness, which spells gloomy endurance rather than bracing challenge. The early drama, especially, reflects this. In some of it, we find the attitude that the outback will reveal its secrets to man, even nurture him, if he develops the skills and life rhythms in harmony with it. But very often, too, the outback mesmerizes man and brings about his defeat.

The second article of faith involves the still unique Australian institution of mateship. This of course embraced individualized forms of male friendship, friendships often made more intense in the outback through the absence of regular sexual relationships, for at first men vastly outnumbered women there. But it was also a collectivist bonding to enable men to survive the rigors of the outback, and it soon developed important institutional definition in terms of vested interests it ranged itself against: the big country landowners, the colonial aristocracy and middle class, the developing British-derived urban life of the cities, foreign countries and foreign races and, last but not least, women with marriage in mind. In the twentieth century, especially after 1945, it became a very problematic and equivocal institution.

But the individual's relationship to the "mateship group" has never been clearly defined in the legend and has always been riddled with paradoxes. The man of the legend was ideally working class, a rural rather than an urban type, dextrous at manual skills and sport, laconic, inarticulately loyal, undomesticated, capable of surviving in a hostile landscape and hence heroic—but also egalitarian, and hence capable of pledging his loyalty to the group. The legacy of this Australianist tension between the heroism of individual action, admired because heroic but sometimes suspect because accomplished alone, and mateship with its outgoing acquiescence often on the verge of conformity, produces a leitmotif which is in its intensity and frequency unique to modern Australian drama. And it has profoundly affected the presentation of character in Australian drama as well, for such tension inhibits full self-expression, encouraging D. H. Lawrence's famous "withheld self ", and it leaves in limbo how much, and how far, an individual may achieve beyond and outside the checks and balances of mateship. And allied to and sometimes overlapping with the motif of the tension between individualism and group consensus is another—that of the outsider and his relationship to group or social norms.

The main forces in the life of the new nation which eroded the legend's articles of faith were overseas influences and pressures on the country, the change in Australian society from a rural to an urban based majority, and the impact of immigration.

The pressure of overseas influence in Australia, and the positive and negative aspects of it, imparted many paradoxes to the legend, especially to the relationship of mateship to the "vested interests" represented by such influence. The three-tiered new Federal government of the new nation owed formal allegiance to Great Britain, and Britain was of course the most dominant overseas power in Australian affairs from 1901 until World War II. Stepped-up American influence dates from the Battle of the Coral Sea in 1942, when American military power saved Australia from Japanese invasion and American military personnel visited Australian capital cities in large numbers. Two treaties—the ANZUS Treaty of 1951 and the SEATO Manila Pact of 1954—ensured that Australia was to be associated with, and protected by, the United States in the event of armed attack by any militant power. In the postwar period, developments in the media made American customs and popular culture more pervasive in Australia than the British had ever been. In the economic sphere, large scale investments by American firms made it possible for Australian businesses and industries to benefit a great deal from American technical, marketing and research methods; but at the same time a fear developed that the control of many Australian businesses was being taken out of Australian hands. Australia's involvement in the Vietnam war alongside the United States unleashed a strong, compensatory period of aggressive nationalism in reaction to what some felt was coercion by a superpower. The influence of powerful overseas neighbors on Australian foreign policy and domestic life has no doubt largely been responsible for the lack of security in national identity behind the cycles of xenophobic nationalism and "internationalism," defiance of and then deference to overseas influences, "cultural cringe" and assertive protestation of self-sufficient judgement, the flaunting and damning of the most idiosyncratic articles of the Australianist legend, which have marked the development of the Australian cultural life.

But more pertinent to the status of the living relevance of the Australianist legend has been the increasing urbanization of Australian life, and the alien cultural influences introduced by immigration. The two matters are related. Increased urbanization was apparent even in the 1920's, and by 1940, 47.5 per cent of the Australian population lived in the capital cities. And most of the new immigrants came to the cities where government agencies were most equipped to handle them, thus increasing the urbanization in Australian life. Australia's immigrants until World War II were mostly Anglo Saxon—with a significant minority of Irish Catholics. Assisted passage migration started at the beginning of the 1920's. But since the war, the population of the country has almost doubled; it now stands at 14,615,000, and of these, one fifth were born overseas. Moreover, most of the immigrants were not Anglo Saxon. Swelling the influx from Southern Europe, Greece, Italy and Great Britain were additional waves from Hungary (after 1956), Czechoslovakia (after 1968), Lebanon (after 1976) and most recently from South East Asia (after 1979). Immigration eroded the Anglo-Saxon notions of national and cultural identity, Australianist legend included. Longtime residents had to open themselves up to a new and complex cultural pluralism—which included a new awareness of the dispossessed aboriginals, now numbering only 1.2 per cent of the total population.

These twentieth century developments have made the question of what is a modern national identity and the question of what is truly "Australian" very problematic. In Australian modern drama, the most powerful and arresting of the early plays are connected with Australianism and the Australianist legend as promulgated in the nineteenth century. Early plays involving more urban and international material seem to lack assurance and any individuality, and have not survived in the national repertoire except as curiosities. On the other hand, some recent Australian plays have international settings clearly observed through a distinctively Australian sensibility. Australian drama has developed a "pluralism" in subject matter which surely reflects greater acceptance of a cultural pluralism in Australian society—but at the same time even very recent drama shows preoccupations which result from the heritage of Australianism.

While the Australian commercial professional theatre has always flourished essentially by importing overseas hits, the non-commercial professional theatre did not develop until the 1950's. The first theatre dedicated to the production of Australian plays, Esson's and Palmer's Pioneer Players, really only functioned for three seasons. Sydney's Community Playhouse, founded by Carrie Tennant in 1930, fared little better. Both were amateur theatres. Various Repertory Theatres founded from 1904 onwards and "little theatres" founded during the 1930's occasionally included an Australian play on their bills, but their major stress was on imported plays and again they were not professional theatres. The flash in the pan success and commercial tour of Sumner Locke-Elliott's *Rusty Bugles* in 1948, did not appreciably change things. Then in the 1950's came three crucial events: the foundation of the Australian Elizabethan Theatre Trust in 1954, the foundation of the Melbourne Union Theatre Repertory Company, first of the non-commercial regional theatres which were fully professional, two years earlier, and the success and overseas tour of a play nurtured by both these bodies—Ray Lawler's *Summer of the Seventeenth Doll* (1955). But promise for the heady development of Australian modern drama did not become consistent achievement until the advent of government funding in the late 1960's with the founding of the Australian Council for the Arts (later the Australia Council). This speeded up the establishment of several major state regional professional companies and gave additional solidity to those already established. It also consolidated the successful establishment of several ebullient alternative theatre companies in the capitals, notably the Nimrod Theatre in Sydney and the Australian Performing Group and La Mama in Melbourne. Federal and state government funding also made possible the revival of the Australian film industry and developments in New Wave Australian film. Thus the maturity of Australian drama catalysed rapidly from the late 1960's.

A major reason for the late development of Australian drama lies in the power of the Australian commercial theatre organizations, founded in the nineteenth century, and their disinterest in modern Australian plays.

The Australian theatre had been born at a very early period of settlement, but it developed in a big way in the decade following the gold rushes (1851-61), when the entire population of the Australian colonies doubled. Touring reached new heights of exuberance, and the theatre became a hugely profitable enterprise in which "stars," mostly past their zenith elsewhere, came, conquered, and were pelted with nuggets from gold diggers' windfalls. The cautious resident commercial companies ensconced in the separate colonies were gradually out-maneuvred by several actor-managers who built up commercial theatre empires through imported touring companies performing melodramas and operettas, with sometimes some Shakespeare or novelties thrown in. Increasingly, these tours bypassed the country towns and concentrated on takings in the burgeoning state capitals. The cartels were later to justify their light-minded repertoire on the grounds of financial necessity; these state capitals were sometimes thousands of miles apart, and touring costs of casts, sets and costumes were exorbitant. The two most important of the commercial cartels were J. C. Williamson's and the Tivoli, the latter managed at first by Harry Rickards. They were to dominate the Australian professional theatre for over fifty years.

In general, the nineteenth century commercial theatre in Australia was far more encouraging to the Australian play than its twentieth century counterpart. From the 1830's on, several Australian melodramas, "closet dramas," operas and burlettas were written, as well as some nascent realist plays modelled on those of Tom Robertson. Many were set in distant places and distant times, but some dealt with the Australian locale, and even emergent Australian themes and characters. From a theatrical point of view, the most important were the melodramas presented by the managements of Alfred Dampier, George Darrell, and later, Bland Holt and William Anderson. According to Leslie Rees [in his *The Making of Australian Drama*], the themes clustered around convictism, the search for gold, and, perhaps most significantly, bushranging. They also sometimes evidenced crude versions of the outsider-versus-group theme. Very early on appeared the figure of the English "new chum" migrant, a superior, sometimes effete character who in the end is reconciled to, and accepted by, the group of crude but sincere Australians.

Though the melodramas continued to be popular on stage long after they appeared in the medium of silent films, an ultimately longer lasting nineteenth century tradition also manifested itself. This was vaudeville and music hall, later fruitful in the drama of the 1960's. Far more than J. C. Williamson, Harry Rickards gave support to Australian-written vaudeville material, and took care to see that a fair percentage of Australian artists performed it. This did a great deal towards establishing an Australian type of humor in the Tivoli bills, a living tradition which continued until it degenerated into camp nostalgia in the 1950's. A third company was even more important in contributing to the same tradition: Bert Bailey's, with his adaptations of the outback stories of "Steele Rudd" from

1912 to the 1930's. The most famous such production was *On Our Selection,* first performed in 1912. The Rudd/Bailey characters of Dad and Dave were Australian archetypes who "regarded life in the bush as a pantomime and the distant city as a terrifying wilderness," and they gave strong stage embodiment to many of the premises of the Australianist legend. Both the melodramas and the vaudevillian comedies disguised their obsolescence in the early days of the new century by borrowing Belasco-like from the "verisimilitude" of realism by the creation of spectacular and representational stage effects: sunsets, floods, bushfires, and even gumleaves and marsupials in theatre lobbies.

Meanwhile, the first Australian modern plays were slow to come, and there are several possible reasons. Plays staged in the nineteenth century theatre, especially in Australia, pleased throngs of working class people in both matter and manner—but the emergent European modern drama of the 1880's generally did not. Some of the early naturalistic plays dealt with working people circumscribed by their environments, but the audiences which flocked to the novelties of the naturalist theatres were mostly educated and middle class. The spirit of the emergent contemporary drama, embodied in the theory of Emile Zola and the practice of Ibsen with his modified "well made" play structure, were firmly founded in scientism and middle class faith in tangible materialism. And all of this was antithetical to the blowsy romanticism of the nineteenth century popular theatre. The basically urban and middle class orientation of the first modern plays made for some particularly difficult problems of adaptation to Australian myths and realities of the time—especially the Australianist legend, with its working class and outback orientation.

The birthdate of Australian contemporary drama can fairly be fixed in the year 1909, when an art critic, William Moore, presented the first of four Australian Drama Nights to decorous, well-dressed middle class audiences at Melbourne's Oddfellows Hall. They included plays by two important early dramatists: Louis Esson and Katharine Susannah Prichard. Earlier, signs of a forthcoming Australian modern drama had been allied with emergent European realism. One of the cartels had presented Ibsen's *A Doll's House* with imported star Janet Achurch as early as 1890, to drunken incomprehension from the gallery. Leon Brodzky, a friend and critic of Louis Esson's, put out a fiery call for an opportunity to stage, or at least read aloud, the plays of the new drama, and castigated their neglect by the commercial managements. In 1904, he founded the Australian Theatre Society, which had as its object the production of "important" plays of the time and new Australian plays which "seemed to be of sufficient merit," but the scheme collapsed when Brodzky immigrated to the United States. In 1896, the Adelaide Repertory Theatre was founded by Bryceson Traherne, a music teacher, and this prefigured the more important founding of East Coast Repertories in Melbourne (1911) and Sydney (1920), both by Gregan MacMahon. These Repertory Theatres were funded by audiences of middle class subscribers and were usually thus able to hire large, well equipped theatres for matinees, and even a profes-sional actor or two, to present congenial new plays by playwrights such as the early Shaw, Pinero or Wilde. Such plays were sometimes called "theatre of ideas" plays or discussion plays, for they often dealt with educated characters talking out, if not living through, pertinent new issues. The Repertories provided the first venue for the staging of such plays, as well as Australian imitations of them by Arthur Adams, Marguerite Dale, E. H. C. Oliphant and others. In 1912, the Melbourne Repertory Society staged perhaps the only such play by an Australian which has stood the test of time, Louis Esson's *The Time is Not Yet Ripe* (1912).

There are possibly two reasons why the "theatre of ideas" play did not prove a springboard for the first genuine development of modern Australian drama. In the century's first two decades, Australian urban middle class life does not seem to have spawned a dialogue idiom that was sufficiently different from British idiom to have a uniquely local flavor. It had perhaps not even happened by the 1920's, as it had on Broadway for example, with the middle class comedies of Maxwell Anderson, Philip Barry and S. N. Behrman. The first Australian "theatre of ideas" plays are not distinguishable, apart from in their stated settings, from inferior British plays of the same kind.

The other reason was that the most gifted of Australia's pioneer modern playwrights turned their back on the "theatre of ideas" in favor of a different manifestation of emergent contemporary drama, that of the Irish folk play as exemplified in the plays of Synge and Lady Gregory. It seemed to Esson and Palmer that the poetic, rural, working class emphasis of the Irish theatre was deeply consonant with Australian life and the Australianist legend. Though this development proved problematic for Australian drama, it did ensure that the Irish Australian plays, because of their outback settings and outback (or urban) working class idioms, have some distinctive local flavor. The Irish influence led in 1921 to Esson and Palmer's foundation of the Pioneer Players—the first theatre formed for the exclusive purpose of presenting new Australian plays. (pp. 2-9)

> *Dennis Carroll, in a preface to his* Australian Contemporary Drama 1909-1982: A Critical Introduction, *Peter Lang, 1985, pp. 1-12.*

Alan L. McLeod

[McLeod is an Australian educator, poet, and critic. In the following essay, he discusses the late development of Australian dramatic literature.]

Although the beginnings of an identifiably Australian drama can be discerned in plays written during the 1930's, it was not until about 1960 that plays of lasting or literary merit were frequently printed or performed. For convenience, Ray Lawler's *Summer of the Seventeenth Doll* (pr. 1955) is often regarded as the precursor of modern Australian drama, yet in 1956, A. D. Hope, in a *Current Affairs Bulletin* article, "Standards in Australian Literature," published by the University of Sydney, noted that "there is not much to say about Australian drama," and Cecil Hadgraft, in *Australian Literature: A Critical Ac-*

count of 1955 (1960), a highly regarded conspectus, wholly omitted any consideration of plays.

The late flowering of Australian drama is not readily explained: Though the national population has always been small, it has consistently been urban and relatively literate and affluent, sustaining almost all the other forms of culture, both popular and high, with the exception of the ballet. Paradoxically, both at home and abroad Australians have been keen theatergoers, and until the advent of television Australians were among the world's most frequent moviegoers, yet few local writers produced film scripts.

In June, 1789, only eighteen months after the arrival of the First Fleet, George Farquhar's *The Recruiting Officer* (pr. 1706) was performed in Sydney by a cast of convicts as a King's Birthday entertainment for an audience of sixty that included the colonial governor. Thereafter, musical entertainments as well as civil and religious spectacles and stage plays were commonplace; that is, theater became an integral part of the regional culture, and, taking into account the educational background of some of the convicts, one might have expected original dramatic materials making use of the novel local milieu. Convicts, soldiers, settlers, and Aborigines isolated in a generally inhospitable and inaccessible environment would seem to have offered ample scope for plays on themes of expatriation, penitence, ambition, fortitude, and rivalry set in unusual, if not exotic, locales, but a deference to established, successful models, a reluctance to experiment, and minimal leisure combined to keep local drama imitative, derivative, and repetitious in structure, theme, and characters. These traits are to be found in the other genres also; it was some time before recognizably Australian characters, speech, and subjects were widely incorporated into Australian literature.

Literary reputations in Australia were traditionally based on achievement in poetry or fiction, while the dominance of comedy and musical comedy in commercial theaters (a reflection of British theater offerings) eliminated the stimulus to attempt serious plays and tragedies, which were relegated to little theaters—located in suburbs or in the insalubrious sections of the capital cities, in the main. A publishing industry that could rarely justify poetry, short stories, and novels commercially was understandably reluctant to print plays. The almost total absence of professional theater personnel militated against successful staging of plays by Australian authors.

Although most of these impediments have been removed and there are indications that the drama—for stage, broadcast, film, and literary study—has attained the artistic level of Australian poetry and prose fiction, there is still no playwright of the international stature of South African Athol Fugard; there are, however, many of commendable achievements.

The first play written in Australia was *The Bushrangers* (pr. 1829), a typical nineteenth century melodrama set in Tasmania in 1825 and dealing with contemporary subject matter and characters. Its author was a Scots settler and editor of *The South Briton: Or, Tasmanian Literary Journal,* David Burn. In all, Burn wrote eight plays, some in prose, some in verse, that attempted most of the forms—melodrama, farce, blank-verse tragedy, and historical drama. They became the first plays published in Australia (1842). Curiously, the two plays set in Australia were never staged there.

The Bushrangers was produced in Edinburgh in 1829. In its episodic structure, satire of officialdom, social criticism, and juxtaposition of government and highwayman moralities it is reminiscent of John Gay's *The Beggar's Opera* (pr. 1728). Like Gay's ballad opera, *The Bushrangers* had its imitators: two of identical title were written by Henry Melville (pr. 1834) and Charles Harpur (wr. 1835), while a plethora of others utilized contemporary social antagonisms and issues as subjects. Some, such as Edward Geoghegan's *The Currency Lass* (pr. 1849), were original; others, such as Garnet Walch and Alfred Dampier's *Robbery Under Arms* (pr. 1891) and Thomas Somers and Dampier's *His Natural Life* (pr. 1886), were adaptations of successful Australian novels.

Throughout the nineteenth century, however, local playwrights tended to imitate the current London stage fare with melodramas, farces, and pantomimes or tableaux that made only minimal concessions to the location. When American plays were introduced, they, too, were imitated. J. C. Williamson and Maggie Williamson's *Struck Oil* (pr. 1874) had its replications in Francis R. C. Hopkins' *All for Gold* (pr. 1877), Dampier's *The Miner's Right* (pr. 1891), and his and Kenneth MacKay's *To the West* (pr. 1896). Some imaginative dramatists attempted to fuse British, American, and Australian elements, so that Euston Leigh and Cyril Clare's *The Duchess of Coolgardie* (pr. 1896), set in the Western Australian goldfields, could have an Aborigine's lines written in an approximation of South Carolinian Gullah dialect and an implausible cast and improbable plot. Yet the play was successful: It was performed in Drury Lane Theatre, printed in London, and imitated by George Darrell's *The King of Coolgardie* (pr. 1897).

The increasing nationalism at the close of the century became a feature of all forms of Australian culture. With federation in 1901, chauvinism became less strident yet no less apparent: Australia's participation in the Boer War, World War I, and the Versailles Peace Treaty sustained the sense of national identity. In the drama, William Moore (who organized a writers' theater) and Louis Esson (who had met William Butler Yeats and been advised by him to write "Australian plays") accepted responsibility for the encouragement of an Australian drama.

Esson's *Three Short Plays* (pb. 1911), which included *The Woman Tamer, Dead Timber,* and *The Sacred Place,* helped establish the one-act play as a national norm and influenced the choice of theme and characters. (The one-act play became the dramatic equivalent of the short story in Australian fiction; Esson's role was thus similar to that of Henry Lawson.) Esson redirected the play from the melodrama of his forerunners to social realism, represented both city and country issues, and included the attitudes, problems, and antipathies of the several social classes. Accordingly, some critics have noted the influence of Henrik Ibsen and George Bernard Shaw rather than of Yeats and

John Millington Synge or Lady Augusta Gregory. In *The Woman Tamer,* Esson explores interrelationships in a slum household; in *Dead Timber,* he reveals the monotonous struggle for existence and for love in the Outback; *The Sacred Place* suggests that slum life has its own morality and that this is justified. Impressive as these plays are, they have not been as popular as *The Drovers* (pr. 1923), in which an injured drover is of necessity abandoned by his mates and cared for by an Aborigine whose eerie wails accompany the drover's death and enhance the pathos. In this play, the influence of Synge's *Riders to the Sea* (pb. 1903) seems obvious. Later plays, such as *Mother and Son* (pr. 1923), which reexamines the loneliness of bush life and the disconcerting effects of an inhospitable environment, and *The Bride of Gospel Place* (pr. 1926), a study of city violence, demonstrated that Esson was adept in the full-length dramatic form. His place in Australian drama is secure, though his plays are infrequently staged; his satiric, sardonic, yet sympathetic approach is largely representative of the national ethos, and his themes and subjects are at once historical and regional, continuing and universal.

Compared with Esson's plays, those of two of his contemporaries are inferior, yet they have earned a niche in Australian dramatic literature. Vance Palmer's *Hail Tomorrow* (pb. 1947), about the 1891 shearers' strike, uses characters and issues dear to the Australian heart, yet the play suffers from an inadequate comprehension of dramatic conventions. Like John Steinbeck, Palmer was a fine fiction writer but was unable to work with ease and conviction in drama. Sydney Tomholt's *Bleak Dawn* (pb. 1936) is a praiseworthy study of the divorced working-class woman living in a male-oriented society.

The role of women in Australia, which has increasingly become the focus of sociological studies, has been explored with understanding and feeling by several competent dramatists, among them Katharine Susannah Prichard, Betty Roland, and Dymphna Cusack. Prichard, author of twenty-four published novels, also wrote seventeen plays, eleven of which were produced in Australian little theaters. Only one, *Brumby Innes,* which won a drama contest run by *The Triad* magazine in 1927, was published (1940); it remained unproduced until 1972, possibly because it had been expanded into the very successful novel *Coonardoo* (1929). Set in the Outback, *Brumby Innes* is a mature investigation of black-white and male-female interrelationships, which, it suggests, follow a course from affection and accommodation to sensuality, dominance, and brutal imperiousness. *Brumby Innes,* in its analysis of alienation, self-doubt, domination, and denigration, perhaps reflects the influence of Eugene O'Neill.

Roland's *The Touch of Silk* (pr. 1928) has continued to hold a unique position in Australian drama: It was published by a university press and continues to enjoy readership and discussion, unlike Roland's later, more propagandist plays, the best known of which is probably *Are You Ready, Comrade?* (pr. 1938). *The Touch of Silk* is a study of the difficulties of a sensitive young French woman, Jeanne, to adapt to the cultureless and unaesthetic Outback, with its materialism, crudities, and primitive possessiveness, predicated on the unequal roles and status of men and women and resulting in the very denial of love. After Jeanne buys lingerie from a traveling salesman and goes to a dance with him, she pretends that she has had an affair: The illusion is a necessary balance for a loveless life in an unbeautiful and isolated environment.

Cusack's full-length plays *Red Sun at Morning* (pb. 1942) and *Morning Sacrifice* (pb. 1943) deserve greater recognition than they have gained. The first has as subject matter the flight of a mistress from an overbearing military officer, and so treats a continuing Australian phenomenon, the pervasive authoritarianism in society, while also examining interpersonal relationships outside marriage. The play's historical setting (1812), however, and the improbability of the means of escape militate against its success. *Morning Sacrifice* has a wider appeal. It is set in a girls' school, where the students are conditioned "to accept all, question nothing and grow into nice, well-behaved yes-girls": The indictment of the national educational-social outlook is forceful, the examination of teacher-supervisor roles is perspicacious, and individual weaknesses and ambitions are carefully scrutinized. The simulated sincerity, the frustrations, jealousies, and ambitions of the teachers, become paradigmatic of society; the badinage and ripostes suggest the depth of animosity that underlies surface compatibility. The minuscule society of the school tragedy is a metaphor for life itself.

During the 1940's, other dramatists developed their art. Max Afford wrote and adapted plays for radio: His *Lady in Danger* (pr. 1944), a well-constructed, popular comedy-thriller, has retained its enthusiasts, though it is subliterary. Sumner Locke-Elliott, author of *Interval* (pr. 1942), a sophisticated piece set in London that demonstrated his mastery of dramaturgy, achieved fame with *Rusty Bugles* (pr. 1948), "a play of inaction" as one critic termed it, which has no principal characters, includes the coarse language characteristic of soldiers stationed in an isolated ordnance camp, and engages its characters in antiwar discussions. After the success of *Rusty Bugles,* the playwright moved to New York, where he regularly wrote and adapted plays for Studio One, Sunday Night Playhouse, and other broadcast series. He adapted his first novel, *Careful, He Might Hear You,* into a successful film in 1984.

The radio dramas and verse plays of New Zealand-born Douglas Stewart gave indications that he was properly to be compared with Louis MacNeice and Christopher Isherwood as a major dramatist in these forms, but the virtual eclipse of radio drama after World War II, the growth of theater-going, and the demise of verse drama have combined to deflect attention from Stewart's very remarkable plays. In an environment where even standard English was a rarity, Stewart's language (with its finely turned phrases and impeccable nuances of diction) clearly created an impression, but where the predisposition of the public was for musical comedy, operetta, and the domestic comedy, his expressed interest in the creation of national myths from legendary individuals established barriers to the realization of his goals. It is therefore noteworthy that he continued his course and gained wide popularity.

Stewart's principal dramas are *Ned Kelly* (pr. 1942), written in both stage and radio versions, a study of the legendary bushranger and archetypal antihero; *The Fire on the Snow* (pr. 1941), a moving radio play treating the unsuccessful polar expedition of Robert Falcon Scott in 1912; and *Shipwreck* (pr. 1947), another historical play, which treats the 1629 massacre of a majority of the passengers of the *Batavia* while the captain, Pelsart, was in search of help. In each of these plays, Stewart reexamines the popular concept of the dreamer, the visionary, the leader, with his illusions of invincibility, showing also the relationship between national legends and cultural archetypes.

Considerable attention has been given in histories of Australian literature to Lawler's *Summer of the Seventeenth Doll,* which was staged in London and New York to critical acclaim. There is a consensus that this overseas recognition resulted in a resurgence of playwriting in Australia. Certainly it provided a helpful fillip, but it should be remembered that the themes of alienation, physical isolation, mateship, and country-city and man-woman interrelationships had long been the very substance of the national drama. Yet *Summer of the Seventeenth Doll* did add dimensions to established materials: It explored with understanding the inevitable disillusionments of middle life, the disintegration of friendships, and the decreasing importance of hollow ritual and token remembrances. Lawler's subsequent play, *The Piccadilly Bushman* (pr. 1959), examined the reactions to and of a returning expatriate (a common Australian experience, treated most memorably by Henry Handel Richardson in *The Fortunes of Richard Mahony,* one of the classic Australian novels, in 1917).

Richard Beynon's *The Shifting Heart* (pr. 1957) is yet another treatment of the perennial Australian confrontation with nonnatives, whether they be Aborigines or Europeans. Better than most of its genre, it shows the depth and suggests the causes of this xenophobia, exclusiveness, and even small-mindedness that is finally disappearing. Alan Seymour's *The One Day of the Year* (pr. 1961) used the artificial camaraderie of Anzac Day (the national veterans' holiday) to deflate myths, to explore the concept of mateship, and to show the irrelevance of some myths when seen across the generation gap. This play was a timely reassessment of subjects of national importance.

After 1960, Australian dramatists attempted most of the modern techniques of the theater and wrote in other than realist terms. The influences of Absurdism, Expressionism, and Symbolism could be noted. Bertolt Brecht and Friedrich Dürrenmatt became as influential as Shaw and Ibsen, Arthur Miller and Tennessee Williams, Eugène Ionesco and Samuel Beckett. As a consequence, a narrowly nationalistic and dominantly realist drama became cosmopolitan in the widest sense. The transformation was aided by the establishment of drama schools and professional theaters, extended university education, overseas travel, and the influx of blind adherence to outdated and overused dramatic modes. Among the important new playwrights to develop were David Williamson, Alexander Buzo, Jack Hibberd, Ric Throssell, Dorothy Hewett, and Patrick White.

With four plays produced between 1961 and 1964, White—best known as a novelist—established himself as a dramatist of some stature. *The Ham Funeral* (pr. 1961), which is informed by Ibsen's theory that illusion is essential for equanimity, shows that there is poetry in even circumscribed, dreary lives. *The Season at Sarsaparilla* (pr. 1962), a patently Expressionist play subtitled *A Charade of Suburbia,* is a devastating comedy of conformism. The main characters lead lives not quite of quiet desperation but lives where "there's practically no end to the variations of monotony." *A Cheery Soul* (pr. 1963)—based on one of White's own short stories—explores the artificiality of a voluble, self-satisfied suburban do-gooder, while *Night on Bald Mountain* (pr. 1964), a darker play, subsumes all the themes and essential character-types of the author's earlier work to stress the sterility of the proud, the detached, and the intellectual. Toward the end of the play, Professor Sword says, "You and I are here on the edge of the world, and might so easily slip over, into this merciless morning light . . . along with the illusions of importance and grandeur that we had." The theme of the play is summed up in Sword's later aphorism, "Failure is sometimes the beginnings of success."

David Williamson's *Don's Party* (pr. 1971) and *The Removalists* (pr. 1971), Jack Hibberd's *A Stretch of the Imagination* (pr. 1972) and *A Toast to Melba* (pr. 1976), and the several plays of the prolific Alexander Buzo are among the more inventive, substantial, and likely to survive as both literature and theatre. Buzo's *Norm and Ahmed* (pr. 1968) is one of the most affecting treatments of xenophobia; *The Front Room Boys* (pr. 1969) lays bare the sterile life of the office worker confined to the routines of the large corporation. In both, there is the sure touch of the playwright who has an ear for the speech and interests of the common man and the analytic methodology of the sociologist.

Screenplays for films which have been shown throughout the world—films such as *Gallipoli* (1980) and *Breaker Morant* (1980) no less than adaptations of such literary classics as *My Brilliant Career* (1979) and *The Chant of Jimmy Blacksmith* (1978)—are further indication of the vitality of Australian drama. Only television drama remains to be brought up to international standards. (pp. 2430-36)

Alan L. McLeod, "Australian Drama," in Critical Survey of Drama: English Language Series, Vol. 6, *edited by Frank N. Magill, Salem Press, 1985, pp. 2430-36.*

ABORIGINAL LITERATURE

Mudrooroo Narogin

[Narogin is an Aboriginal educator and author whose novels Wild Cat Falling *(1965) and* Dr. Wooreddy's Prescription for Enduring the Ending of the World *(1983) treat racial themes. In the following essay, Narogin analyzes Aboriginal writing within a historical perspective.]*

I am seeking the truth of my countries
where the ancestors lived in the past.
I am far away from my country
and my family's living in a different way.
In my memories I hear the song of my
    tribes . . .

Aboriginal literature begins as a cry from the heart directed at the whiteman. It is a cry for justice and for a better deal, a cry for understanding and an asking to be understood. In some ways it is different from other national literatures which are directed towards a national readership and only after that to other nations. Black writers, such as Kevin Gilbert and Oodgeroo Noonuccal have a White Australian readership firmly in mind when they write and it is their aim to get across to as many people as possible the Aboriginal predicament in Australia. A predicament which has resulted in many Aborigines becoming strangers in their own land, so alienated that sometimes they seem to have lost the will to survive. Invasion, occupation and dispossession have resulted in the coming into being of a people without visible means of support, a *lumpenproletariat* objectified in these lines from my *Song Circle of Jacky:*

> The shuffling drunk the street derides,
> God staggers by in drunken rage.

Both white and black writers have written of the predicament and this has resulted in a strong literature which is evergrowing. But it may be said that over the last decades conditions have improved and with this improvement Aboriginal literature has begun to turn towards cultural and self-introspection. Guilt and blame are not enough for the continuation of a literature, and so histories from an Aboriginal viewpoint are being constructed. Life stories (often in collaboration), novels, short stories and poems are devoting their words to the Aboriginal existential being in what is now said to be a multicultural Australia.

These topics are not new, though they are becoming of increasing concern to Aboriginal writers. From the strong beginnings of Aboriginal literature in the sixties and seventies, Kevin Gilbert, a major writer of the fringe states in *Living Black,* that the existential predicament of the modern Aborigine resides in 'a rape of the soul'. In his works, he consciously analyses the decay of Aboriginal society which has occurred and is occurring all across Australia, seeing it as the result of a historical process rather than as a reality to be endured as Archie Weller appears to do in some of his stories, such as 'Pension Day' in his book *Going Home.*

These two writers are critical of the degradation often found within Aboriginal communities. They do not romanticise this culture of poverty in which drunkenness plays too great a part, in which pensioners are robbed of their pensions by youngsters, in which cruel revenge is taken, in which parents gamble the day away while their children stumble around brain-damaged from sniffing petrol. The coarseness of life is painful to witness—in fact it may seem that entire communities are deliberately attempting to wipe themselves out; but Aboriginal writers refuse to see this as an inherent trait, or as a social Darwinism based on an evolution which stresses that only the

strong shall survive and that when a people is confronted by a different race equipped with strange and terrifying things, then everything is lost and that people unable to adapt become extinct.

Aboriginal writers developing away from the urge to establish a connection between the races of Australia have turned their attention towards understanding the dilemma of their people and their communities. It would be easy to blame the watjela or gubba for all the ills of Aboriginal communities, but they refuse to take this negative trail though they are fully cognisant of what happens to a people which has suffered a rape of the soul with continuing effects to the present.

Perhaps this picture written is too white and it would be if Aboriginal writers only concentrated on the evils which bedevil Aboriginal society, but they also write of the bright things, the human warmth, the spontaneity and humour with which life and its problems are faced. Still . . . the existential condition of Aborigines and their historicity must be taken into account. Aboriginal literature does not exist in an aesthetic vacuum, but within the context of Aboriginal affairs. It must be seen holistically within a cultural, historical and social context. To try and approach Aboriginal writers and their literature as things existing apart from their communities would be a falsity. Not only this, but contemporary Aboriginal communities are the end result of 200 years of white history, and this past must never be forgotten.

Aboriginal writers may be labelled 'committed' writers. They all are deeply concerned with the problems of their communities even to the extent that community is stressed at the expense of the individual. In writing about these problems, they become aware of similar problems facing minorities in Australia and other countries of the world and give their support to those communities fighting for a place under the sun, free from the domination of national majorities. Still, they acknowledge that their primary goals are to understand their own communities, the basis of their literature, and from there to create a literature which will not only be of use to the community, but will help to spread a knowledge about the Aborigines of Australia and their unique culture. These are their aims. Aims often shared by some white academic and creative writers.

To have an understanding of this literature coming from the different communities—the Nangas, Nyoongahs, Djamadjis, Murris, Kooris, Yolngus and the other regional groups making up the unity of people placed under the white term, *Aboriginal*—there first must be a general schema of history which may be fleshed out from the works of the writers and storytellers.

I will divide Aboriginal history into a number of periods and it is these periods which not only go towards forming the style of the writers of the fringe, but also supply the contents of their works

THE DIVISIONS OF ABORIGINAL HISTORY

1. *From the Beginning to 1788:*
   The Dreaming; Prehistory; Before The Coming of the Europeans.

2. *The Time of the Invasion(s):*
For the first time, the Aboriginal peoples of Australia are confronted with another people who come not to visit, but to conquer. Around the areas of conquest they go down under the onslaught. Aboriginal culture is placed under threat, and begins to change and adapt new ways of communication.

3. *The Utter Conquering of the Aboriginal Peoples:*
A typical oppressive colonial-type regime is established in Australia. Many of the old ways of communication are destroyed, or drastically changed.

4. *The Colonial Period:*
At first there is outright oppression which gives way to paternalism, then a policy of assimilation. The remnants of the peoples are to be forced into the mainstream of European civilisation. Opposed to this are a number of Europeans such as anthropologists who seek ways of preserving Aboriginal cultures.

5. *The Period of Self-Determination:*
This dates from the time of the Whitlam Government in the late 1960s and is still continuing, though with a strong tincture of assimilation. It is a time when the Aboriginal communities are penetrating official Australian history and life as a people with definite aims and objectives. It is the time of the rise of an identifiable Aboriginal literature, distinct from collections of myths, and with a certain ideology of *Aboriginality.*

Aboriginal being and history until now, the last period, has been dominated by *Anglo-Celts. The Time of the Dreaming,* is called *prehistory* and a whole theoretical structure has been erected with little recourse to the Aboriginal communities. As with possibly all conservative communities, the past was the basis for all explanation of the present and future. This way of placing time and things in a continuum is called *mythology* by Europeans and is contrasted with the scientific way of thinking which seeks to explain the past from the present. Scientists and scholars prefer to work backwards from what is now to what was and tend to ignore any accounts found in the mythology of the Aboriginal communities, though this mythology is the *oral records* of the communities. Different scholars argue different things from the evidence they collect and often their accounts and theories seem more fantastic than the myths they seek to replace. Their investigations wander over and under the land. They measure and chart data from which they postulate things about the Aboriginal people: whether they are one or many, whether they have remained in the Stone Age or not.

Theories are fashioned and discarded like European fashions, and as there is a history of fashion so there is a history of theories. This is called anthropology. A genealogy of much speculation is the origin of the Aboriginal people. We have been said at different points of the genealogy to have been here from the beginning; to once have been part of the ancient population of Gondwanaland; to have floated here, either deliberately, or accidentally after walking across Indonesia when the seas froze during the last Ice Age and the islands became a single landmass except for one wide stretch of water. This last theory at the moment is the one generally accepted. It is popular because it has political implications. The Aboriginal peoples may be seen as the first immigrants and *thus* just like the other peoples in Australia though it is admitted that we arrived on the continent some tens of thousands of years before anyone else. This means politically that we were the original possessors of Australia. This genealogy of theory may be contrasted with Aboriginal history as contained in the oral records. There it is stated that some peoples have been here from the very beginning of humanity. Later arrivers, such as the Wawilak sisters and their brothers, landed to find the *country inhabited.*

It must be admitted that the beginnings of Aboriginal occupation of Australia are lost in the mists of time. It is difficult, if not impossible, to place a definite date on when human beings arrived. Often, forty or fifty thousand years is stated, but these dates have been arrived at by dating archeological sites such as Keilor and Lake Mungo in Eastern Australia. Scientifically, all that they say is that at that time people camped, or buried their dead there.

Few if any peoples can date their origins with any certainty. Mythology only tells of the events happening when they were created, or when they arrived at a certain country. If dates are given, they often are found to have been added long afterwards. In Australia, many myths dealing with the origins of the different Aboriginal communities have either been lost, or incorrectly recorded. This means that much of the oral literature of the Aboriginal people is no longer available for examination and that it is impossible to deconstruct records dealing with each and every community. Some extant accounts describe events which happened thousands of years ago. These may provide dates when people were in a certain area. Thus there is an account which describes the eruption of volcanoes around Mount Gambier in South Australia which happened some six thousand years ago.

Oral literature is important in that it describes Aboriginal life in Australia before the invasion, though I must modify this to say that the formal oral literature as preserved in religious cults may be considered to have suffered less change and thus is more reliable for reconstituting pre-invasion Aboriginal lifestyles. This oral literature often detailing the early wanderings of the creative ancestors, or ancestral beings, in lines of long songs has received some study. A theory has it that the routes of these beings are early migratory trails along which the different communities travelled to spread all over the continent; but this is uncertain. The portions which are still treasured show that Australia was never a trackless wilderness. If all these records had been collected, a detailed road map might have been constructed. As it is, the surviving fragments are important to Aborigines and others as a classical literature. In future it may serve as an aesthetic basis for the written literature. They are as important to the Aborigines as the *Iliad* is to Europeans.

The Time of the Dreaming, the time of the great epics, lasted for thousands of years. The first British settlement at

Port Jackson marks an end of this period, and the beginning of a steady decline of Aboriginal culture and literature. Remains of that traditional culture and literature may be found scattered throughout various books of ethnology and in the minds of numbers of men and women. Some scholars, for example the anthropologist T. G. H. Strehlow in his *Songs of Central Australia* (1971), collected, translated and explained parts of this literature.

There are collections of stories and legends which preserve examples of pre-invasion literature, though often these are heavily Europeanised. The uniqueness of Aboriginal communication and the aesthetic use of language is lost in the translation. It is only recently that scholars are beginning to be concerned with *narrative discourse,* the way in which the story is told and structured, but in many areas it is too late to collect authentic structures of Aboriginal narrative discourse in the original language. The languages have been replaced with an English of varying degrees of standardisation.

The Time of the Invasion(s) began when Europeans visited the shores of Australia. Dutch, French and British established initial aggressive relations which were not propitious for the future. William Dampier the first Englishman to land on the western coast of the continent met Aboriginal resistance which drove him back to his ship. In his journal, he made a number of assertions which for the next centuries, with a short interlude for the concept of the noble savage, were to be held by most European invaders. In his words, the people differed but little from brutes.

It may be said that such statements are neither made lightly, nor innocently. Colonisation had to be justified by a Christian people which prided itself on a superior morality and culture. One way of doing this was by seeing a people in possession of a wanted land as being uncivilised, savages or even animals. British colonial expansion was not a blind immoral course of action, but a deliberate policy with an ever shifting ideology of justification behind it. Thus the British sailing to establish a settlement at Port Jackson rehearsed their ideology. They speculated on the place of the Aborigines in creation and arrived at a consensus that they occupied the bottom-most rung on the ladder of humanity, along with the various primitive peoples of Africa and the Americas. This, in their opinion, was justification for the invasion of lands already inhabited.

The different Aboriginal communities also had their own ideology when meeting with Europeans. There are oral accounts of Aboriginal people meeting Europeans for the first time, and some writers have put down accounts of when they first saw Europeans. One of these, the Walmajarri writer, Peter Skipper, in his book, *The Pushman* (n.d.) has given a short account of when he came in from the desert and of how he reacted to the Gadiya and their strange animals and objects. An overriding emotion was fear, but there was an ideological framework into which Europeans could be incorporated. The pale skinned strangers were accepted as ghosts of the deceased returning. Modern Aboriginal writers in English, using oral and written sources, have reconstructed accounts of the initial contact.

At Port Jackson, after the first contact the Aborigines appear to have avoided the English invaders, perhaps in the hopes that they would return to their ships and sail away. But the settlement was permanent and an active Aboriginal resistance under Pemulwuy began. Smallpox arrived with the invaders. It became an epidemic and effectively ended Aboriginal resistance. Koori writers, such as Bobby Merritt, in his play, *The Cake Man* (1978) have portrayed the effects of the invasion. Eric Willmot in his historical novel, *Pemulwuy, the Rainbow Warrior* (1987) has detailed Aboriginal resistance around Port Jackson. Other writers, including Jack Davis, James Miller and myself have dealt with this period in plays, histories and novels.

Throughout Australia, as the weakened and demoralised tribes went down or fell back before the guns of the colonists, a more compassionate invader came to soothe the pillows of a dying race. These were the Christian missionaries who although they saw Aboriginal culture as intrinsically pagan and thus evil, did bring with them a policy of education which in effect helped to foster the first Aboriginal writings in English. One of the first Aboriginal writers, David Uniapon, was the product of a mission school. Some missionaries, for example the Germans C. G. Teichelmann and C. W. Schurmann in South Australia even used the native language, but eventually English became the language of instruction. The missionaries laboured to soften the coarse pioneering spirit of the first settlers, who often considered the Aborigines vermin to be destroyed. They accepted the Aborigines as human beings and educated them and eventually Christianised them so that today there is a strong current of Christianity running through much of Aboriginal writing.

As soon as Aboriginal resistance was crushed, there began a period of complete colonial subjugation. The peoples were herded into mission or government stations. Those outside on the vast cattle runs and farms which had been carved from their homelands were exploited for their labour value. In fact punitive laws were passed to prevent them from leaving these stations. They in effect became slaves, working for rations of tobacco, sugar and tea. While the men worked in the fields, the women worked as domestics in the homesteads of masters who weren't averse to the soft feel of 'black velvet'. Aborigines were outside the white law, or incarcerated under special Aboriginal laws which prevented them from any assertion of rights. In fact they were declared 'wards of the state' and had no rights. Any resistance was put down by the police, or settlers. The result of this oppression is what is often accepted as the public face of the Aborigine: shiftless, dirty drunken natives fighting and carrying on without hope for a future of grace and dignity.

There was slight mixing between the two races except during the course of work and for sexual intercourse between whitemen and black women. This led to the rise of a *mestizo* class, the coloured or half-caste, people of colour who served as intermediaries between the two races. They might even find a place in the white township and be allowed to drink in the hotel. But the separation of races was instituted from the beginning of the invasion and has continued to this day. These times have been described in works by Aboriginal writers and white writers. The biography of Jack Davis is one example.

Separation and domination continues in many rural areas of Australia to this day and has resulted in the deaths of Aboriginal people. Jack Davis' play, *Barungin (Smell the Wind)* (1989) is about Aboriginal deaths at the hands of police. The death of one young man, John Pat—allegedly kicked to death by the police in the streets of Roebourne, Western Australia in 1983—has led to any number of poems. Aboriginal literature suffered a loss when the promising poet, Robert Walker, was brutally killed in Fremantle Prison, Western Australia in 1984.

In Australia a policy of separation, and economic conditions, forced many Aborigines into living on the fringes of white towns. This has been the subject of a play, *Coodah* (1986), by Richard Walley. A gap is shown to exist between white and black and this is bridged by the *mestizo,* the do-gooder and the missionary, though these latter intermediaries were constantly under attack for seeking to educate the native. A. O. Neville, the Commissioner of Native Affairs in Western Australia, and a character in two of Jack Davis' plays, *Kullark* and *No Sugar,* was no friend of the missionary or of education for the Aborigines. He described the Nyoongah people thus:

> A nameless, unclassified outcast race, increasing in numbers but decreasing in vitality and stamina, and largely unemployable . . . They have very little in the way of education, but some of them have just enough to enable them to become defiant and unrestrained.

Richard Walley in *Coodah* and Jack Davis in his realist drama, *No Sugar,* depicts these days under this commissioner, and the conditions and rules under which the Nyoongah people had to live. Robert Bropho in his work, *Fringedweller* (1980) describes the conditions on the so-called native reserves and the problems faced in the search for decent living standards. These authors do not accept the explanation that Aborigines are not used to proper houses, and must do with sub-standard housing, tin sheds for which they must appear grateful. Instead they demand adequate shelter, a sense of human dignity and fair play towards their community.

The existential being of the Aborigine in Australia has been seen by some white writers to be akin to that of a child, but it is Aboriginal writers who seek to explain this result as stemming from a paternalist attitude which forced the Aborigine into the attitude of a child asking for help from a benign white person. Under the gaze of 'the other', the Aborigine became as a child. Unable to help himself, he sat waiting for the kind adult to offer succour, and this was often forthcoming. But for all his assumed being of child, he was not a child, but an adult, and his act of continuing bad faith led him into a self-hatred. An adult gazed into a mirror and saw not the face of a child smiling back, but the scowling face of an adult. This instead of leading to action, often led only to confusion and a passivity which was strengthened through alcohol. Drunk and stumbling bleary-eyed through life, he indeed could pretend to be a child. This state of abjection is portrayed in the play, *The Cake Man* by the character Sweet William living a childlike existence on a reserve.

In *Because a Whiteman'll Never Do It* (1973), Kevin Gilbert shows how wounding such paternalism is. Because Aborigines are treated as children, children of nature, not quite human, but quite charming on occasion and able to perform simple tasks, disease, crime and poverty may be put down to their childlike nature. Thus they need to be looked after on the missions; the paternal station owner may take care of the rest using them as slave labour, while the fringe dwellers, the half-castes unable to help themselves, must be bred into the European population and assume adult status as the child blood is diluted.

This attitude of *paternalism* lasted officially until 1937 when representatives of all the state governments came together to discuss the Aboriginal problem. The problem was what to do with them. Victoria had almost solved the problem by genocide; New South Wales reported much the same success with only a miserable remnant living on reserves or mission stations and a growing body of people of Aboriginal descent living in extreme poverty on the fringes of country towns; Western Australia and Queensland still had large populations of Aborigines living cowed in missions and stations kept under control by stringent laws; while the Northern Territory had a huge problem in that the Aboriginal population still outnumbered the white and if steps weren't taken they might eventually take over the state.

Different states formulated different policies to deal with the problem. Western Australia declared that it was going to merge the native race into its white community. Queensland decided that it was going to keep the Aboriginal population under paternal care and control on special reserves. This was until recently their policy though, like an angry father, the authorities could expel troublesome children from their homes, or even place them in special centres of detention such as Palm Island. The Northern Territory's policy was to keep the majority of the Aboriginal population firmly under control in missions, except for those *coloureds* who might be bred into the European population.

It was declared outright that the reason behind this policy was fear: fear of a people of Aboriginal descent eventually breeding into an underprivileged, angry militant majority. A result of this policy has been the separation of so-called coloureds from Blacks. In Western Australia the policy of assimilation was used as a tool of separation. A split developed between the assimilated and the unassimilated which is still seen today. Most Aboriginal writers writing in English are a direct result of such divide and control policies. Assimilation did give them a limited education, though it must be admitted that the incarceration of the most militant Aborigines in the prisons also helped the rise of Aboriginal writing in English. Prison for many Aborigines has been their college. But the experience has often led to a literature of anger and frustration rather than to a literature of Aboriginality based on traditional forms.

The Aboriginal writers who arose in the sixties were the products of assimilation revolting against assimilation.

Assimilation was seen as the policy of division, of seeking to alienate individual Aborigines from their communities and pushing them into European society. These individuals, it was hoped, would be completely estranged from their families and become like Europeans. Children were forcibly removed from their parents and placed in institutions. These became the only homes these people ever knew and it is a sadness of the policy that today some Aboriginal people knowing no other childhood look back with fondness on these institutions. In Western Australia numbers of Aborigines became completely institutionalised, and made the trip down the Canning River on which most of these institutions were located to the port of Fremantle and the prison there. They could exist nowhere else but in an institution and the outer world was a frightening place to be deadened by grog until the inevitable happened and they found themselves safely inside again.

The policy of assimilation attempted to submerge a dark minority, the remnants of the victims of a brutal colonisation, in Anglo-Celtic life and culture without questioning the right to do so. A first step was to make all Aborigines wards of the state without any rights of citizenship. They were trainee citizens who had to earn their right to be white. But in tandem with assimilation went a racism which effectively broke the policy. Even when granted citizenship rights, Aborigines still found themselves discriminated against, still found that they were not accepted by the white majority. They were caught in a no-man's-land between Black and White. To the Whites they were considered black and to the Blacks they were considered quislings or 'Jackies'. It was from these contradictions that there arose the struggles for dignity in the mid-sixties when a benign government came to power, and when there were enough Aborigines formally or informally trained to lead the struggle. Aboriginal writers such as Oodgeroo Noonuccal and Kevin Gilbert were at the forefront of the struggle, and have been there ever since.

At this time the political struggles for justice, land rights and self-management were developed. The struggle still continues and it is difficult to see any result or lasting achievement coming from it. In fact with increased education and job opportunities there is an impetus towards a merging into the majority culture, identified here as Anglo-Celtic. Thus the stage of active struggle for an independent identity may be passing. Assimilation, although discredited, still operates through government education and employment policies. New writers such as Sally Morgan and Glenyse Ward do not see themselves as part of an active ongoing movement, but as individuals either searching for their roots or seeking equal opportunity in a multicultural Australia. It might even be said that Aboriginal affairs is entering a stage of post-activism in that any separate goals are being replaced for those of equal opportunity in the wider Australian community.

This was clearly seen in 1988 when two hundred years of white rule was celebrated. Some Aboriginal writers saw the year as an opportunity to forge links between the Aboriginal minority and the white majority. The poster for the Aboriginal day celebrations (NAIDOC) bore the slogan 'Come and Share Our Culture'. Any separatist sentiments were downplayed and there was a return to a call for understanding such as we find in the poems of Oodgeroo Noonuccal dating from the first rise of Aboriginal literature in the early sixties. Thus there might seem to be a movement away from a literature being used as a weapon to raise the consciousness of Aboriginal people and to articulate their concerns.

Activist literature has moved to a literature of understanding. A literature not committed to educating individuals as to their place in Aboriginal society, but one committed to explaining Aboriginal individuals to a predominantly white readership. It is significant that in 1988 creative writing was replaced in importance by the life story. A form of literature akin to biography and autobiography, but having its roots in the methods of the American anthropologist Oscar Lewis. This is a heavily edited literature often written and revised in conjunction with a European. Its message is one of understanding and tolerance, which may be a good thing in regard to an Aboriginal place in a multicultural Australia, but it is a literature dealing only with the past. It is not concerned with the future aims and aspirations of the Aboriginal people. The closing words of Glenyse Ward's, *Wandering Girl* (1988) reveals the accommodation found in this literature:

> We will be making sure that our
> Kids will be given every opportunity
> In their lives to get a good education,
> So that they can take their places
> In today's society as Lawyers or Doctors,
> Or etc.—and be equal in the one human,
> Race!

(pp. 1-15)

> *Mudrooroo Narogin, "Introducing the Fringe," in his* Writing from the Fringe: A Study of Modern Aboriginal Literature, *Hyland House, 1990, pp. 1-15.*

Emmanuel S. Nelson

[*In the following essay, Nelson analyzes the struggle for identity in Aboriginal literature.*]

> *But everyone must be born somewhere and everyone is born in a context: this context is his inheritance. If he were a Muslim, or a Jew, or an Irish, Spanish, Greek or Italian Catholic, if he were a Hindu or a Haitian or a Brazilian, an Indian or African chief, his life may be simpler in some ways and more complex in others; more closed in another. An inheritance is given: in struggling with this given, one discovers oneself in it—and one could not have been found in any other place!—and, with this discovery, and not before, the possibility of freedom begins.*
> James Baldwin [in his *Just above My Head*]

As the black American writer James Baldwin points out, our coming to terms with our inheritance—which is what we involuntarily carry from our cultural past—is vital for forging an authentic sense of personal and collective identity. However, for postcolonial peoples everywhere this struggle with their inheritance has special pain, since their inheritance involves a colonial past that holds memories of defeat, subjugation, and indignity. Nevertheless, their

Fay Zwicky on the weakness of Australian literature:

I think it goes back to our beginnings, that the diffidence, the uncertainty, the tenuous connection that European Australians have had with this land has inhibited us to a degree. Either writers become overly strident in their proclamation of a national identity or they withdraw and look inside and turn to more quietistic cultures for a confirmation of identity. It has to do with time. We have been here two hundred years, which is a very short time in terms of grow-- ing a national identity. . . . It is the feeling of displacing someone. Fundamentally, I think Australians are very tenuously based in this country, even though they cling, and rightly so, to their Western traditions. At the same time, one is conscious all the while that there are the aboriginal traditions that have been displaced in order to keep a dominance. The conflict is there all the time. Where is the great upsurge of a literary consciousness which is complex enough to tell us that we are presumptuous and to say that this presumptuousness and self-destruction is at the root of the national heart? There are upsurges of activism in this country, but no one is transmitting this in literature. Writers are not telling us this. They are telling us how wonderful this country is, sometimes with irony, I know. But generally if this sort of truth comes out in literature at all, it comes out in a way that I feel preached at. I don't see the tragic vision coming out as it did with the great American writers. This is what I feel we are missing, particularly in fiction. We need a writer with a prophetic vision.

Fay Zwicky, in Australian Voices: Writers on Their Own Work, *1991.*

confrontation with their complex past is indispensable, for to "see oneself as part of an historical process, as entrusted by the past with a legacy for the future" is to have identity. It is precisely this vital and fundamental nexus between establishing a meaningful connection with the past and achieving a healing sense of self that prompts the postcolonial writer to engage in constant dialogue with history.

Inevitably, then, the postcolonial writer runs into intellectual conflict with European-generated, imperialist historical discourses. He is faced with the need to reappropriate his past from colonialist historical narratives; he has to salvage his past from distortions and denigrations; and he must reinvent his history so that he can define his past in a way that is meaningful to him. His dialogue with those colonialist versions of history therefore assumes a subversive character. Chinua Achebe's novel *Things Fall Apart* is perhaps the most celebrated imaginative attempt to create an oppositional version of history through fiction, but similar texts appear in a variety of postcolonial literary traditions.

Although this preoccupation with versions of history is discernible in many postcolonial literatures, it manifests itself with special urgency in Australian Aboriginal writing. This urgency, I think, stems from the particularly tragic and complicated nature of the Aboriginal encounter with colonialism: indigenous Australians have not only

been colonized but have been permanently rendered a mistreated and marginalized minority group on a continent which was once theirs. They constitute less than 2 percent of Australia's population of about sixteen million, so the possibilities of any radical political action or even any sustained cultural resistance are minimal. Furthermore, the Aboriginal culture remains deeply traumatized by the profound postcontact dislocations of the last two hundred years. It is necessary, then, to confront, examine, understand, accept, and affirm that past—though that past might represent defeat, dispossession, and discontinuity. Such a meaningful connection with the past is essential for racial self-retrieval, for forging a valid and liberating sense of personal and cultural wholeness. It is indispensable for healing the cultural fracture caused by the catastrophic impact of colonial intrusion; it is a prerequisite for cultural reclamation, for continued resistance.

The black writer who is intent on constructing an oppositional version of history from an Aboriginal perspective faces a formidable corpus of white-authored historical and quasi-historical discourses that distort or dismiss the Aboriginal role in the story of Australia. Here are a few quotations from a variety of white texts that represent the vast body of writing that has shaped white Australian perceptions of the Aborigines during the last two hundred years. William Dempier, an English sailor who recorded in 1688 the first European impressions of the Aborigines, declared that the indigenous Australians "are the miserablest people in the World. . . . Setting aside their human shape, they differ but little from Brutes". In 1843 Father Raymond Vaccari, a Passionist missionary, wrote in his memoirs: "Among the evil dispositions of the Aborigines, I may mention an extreme sloth and laziness in everything, a habit of fickleness and double-dealing, so much so that they stop at nothing in the pursuit of revenge. They are deceitful and cunning and they are prone to lying. They are given to extreme gluttony and, if possible, will sleep both day and night".

Henry Parkes, the editor of *The Empire*—a Sydney-based newspaper that was considered quite progressive by prevailing standards—complained in an editorial published on 30 January 1851 of the Aborigine's "mental imbecility" and "remarkable inferiority". In 1882 Sir W. M. Snowden concluded that Aborigines were "less manlike than a grinning, chattering monkey". Alfred Giles, a pious Christian missionary, declared in 1887 that the Aborigines have "no moral laws" and that "their songs, rituals, and ceremonies are utterly revolting and fiendish". In 1899 Richard Simon, a historian, asserted, "The Aborigines are nothing but nomadic huntsmen, and this very circumstance is the reason for their low intelligence level and scantily developed artistic sense. . . . They are entirely devoid of imagination".

These observations cannot be dismissed or excused merely as products of intellectually and culturally limited nineteenth-century European minds, for these beliefs still enjoy considerable respectability in modern Australia. Knut Dahl, a Norwegian naturalist, recorded in 1924 that several characteristics of the Aborigines are "reminiscent of monkeys". Frederick McCartney, an influential Australian historian and literary critic, wondered in a 1967 article titled "Literature and the Aborigines" whether the indigenes were capable of any "heights of feeling" and declared that any Aboriginal philosopher is "on a lower mental level than that of any ordinary thoughtful man amongst ourselves". Although McCartney's absurd observation says more about his own mental level than about anybody else's, it is still quite disturbing that this comment was made as recently as 1967 by a man widely respected in Australian intellectual circles.

Even more insidious and politically more dangerous than McCartney's blatant racism are the more subtle strategies of writing Aborigines completely out of history. P. R. Stephenson, a contemporary Australian historian, wrote recently: "Australia is a whole continent, unique in its natural features, and unique in the fact of its continual uniformity of race and language. We are the only continent on earth inhabited by one race, under one government, speaking one language and sharing one culture". That a leading Australian academic can so easily and cheerfully forget the presence of tens of thousands of black Australians, is, to say the least, shocking. We can only speculate whether this peculiar forgetfulness just signals a disastrous failure of scholarship or a curiously racist brand of amnesia. That the European attitude toward Aborigines has not yet changed significantly is illustrated with distressing clarity by Auberon Waugh, Evelyn's journalist son. While visiting Sydney to report on the Australian bicentennial celebration in 1988, he wrote of the Aborigines, "They had no form of civil society at all, beyond whatever social organization may be observed in a swarm of locusts." He proceeded to conclude that their art "must be judged the merest piffle by civilized standards".

Texts similar to the ones quoted above have, historically, served as repositories of racist ideologies; they have functioned as instruments of preservation as well as of transmission of those ideologies. Tools of imperial domination, such texts have assured an easy victory for the Europeans in their cultural and political conflicts with the indigenes: the Aboriginal culture, with its exclusive reliance on oral-performance forms, was until recently unable to counter these white-authored texts and the ideologies embedded in them. Aboriginal orality was helpless in the face of European literacy. The very absence of any Aboriginal challenge simply granted further validity to the racist assumptions of the European-generated discourses. As Kateryna Arthur argues, the unequal conflict between Aboriginal and European Australians has indeed been "to a large extent, the struggle between literacy and orality".

However, the ongoing transformation of Aboriginal culture from an oral to an increasingly written base—from tribal culture to print culture—has radically redefined the terms of Australian racial politics. The cultural representatives of contemporary black Australia, its writers and artists, no longer have to rely only on oral forms of cultural expression to counter the European textual onslaught; they can now appropriate and press into service the very tools from their enemy's arsenal: written texts and the English language itself. If European texts had functioned as instruments of cultural destruction for the blacks, the Ab-

original texts can now serve as means of cultural regeneration. Those tools that were used to distort Aboriginal history can now be deployed to redeem the Aboriginal past and to construct revisionist versions of history, and many black Australian writers have articulated the need for such revisions. For example, Kevin Gilbert—an influential poet, dramatist, and political strategist—has eloquently argued for the need to "remove the distortions and lies from history". Jack Davis, an Aboriginal playwright of international stature, asserts that "history is more important, more inseparable [for Aborigines] than is the case for white writers. . . . [For whites] history is in safe hands, white hands. . . . Aboriginal people have been excluded from the pages of white history" [in *Aboriginal Writing Today,* edited by Jack Davis and Bob Hodge].

Attempts by black Australian writers to redeem their past fall into four general categories: recording Aboriginal legends and myths in order to ensure their survival; writing revisionist historical narratives; producing autobiographical texts and collating testimonies of Aboriginal survivors; and subverting white historical discourses through imaginative literature. Ironically, however, each effort to regain the past entails compromises, even losses. The academic concept of History itself, for example, is a European one; it is fundamentally at odds with the Aboriginal notion of Dreaming, of mythic timelessness. Therefore, for an Aboriginal writer to adopt a Western view of history—of history as a linear course of events—is in itself a compromise. To write in English is to court further dangers; if language *is* culture, the act of an Aboriginal artist appropriating the imperial language becomes what a critic has aptly called "a form of cultural transvestism" [in Kateryna Arthur's "Fiction and Rewriting of History" in *Westerly*]. If language is a complex system of signs, one might ask if those signs themselves (in a European language, such as English) carry built-in ideological values that endorse semiotic structures favoring the European world view. However, given the existing power relationship between blacks and whites in contemporary Australia, it seems the battle can be fought only in European terms, largely with European tools. Initial compromise, then, is a necessity; any gain therefore becomes a victory of sorts. The first among the four categories of writing used to retrieve Aboriginal history—recording and/or translating Aboriginal myths and legends—involves the most severe loss. Imaginative writing, particularly Aboriginal drama, appears to be the most effective means of achieving the objective.

Numerous traditionally oral Aboriginal legends and stories now exist in print. Some are in Aboriginal texts with English translations; some exist only in the translated form. Although recorded and translated works do provide non-Aboriginal and detribalized readers a glimpse of the richness and complexity of the traditional Aboriginal world view, they also pose two major problems: the consequences of translation (from oral to written form, from Aboriginal languages to English); and popularization, a feature unique to technology-oriented cultures. Writing removes oral texts from the immediate context of community to a larger field of anonymity; it eliminates the room for improvisation that is a regular feature of oral performance; it violates the ritual framework of the legends and stories; and often, when taken out of their functional tribal contexts, the stories may sound merely quaint or even absurd. Translations such as Obed Regett's *Stories of Obed Regett* (1980), even if they are by Aboriginal authors, pose a hidden problem: white editorial intervention. There can also be conscious distortion of the original material by Aboriginal writers, as is the case in David Unaipon's *Native Legends* (1929?), wherein the author deliberately alters the stories to make them more appealing to Western audiences. Sometimes the translations are done by detribalized, urban Aborigines (e.g., Kath Walker's *Stradbroke Dreamtime* and Dick Roughsey's *Giant Devil Dingo*), whose sensibilities are at least partially Anglicized and who are, to some extent, disconnected from tribal life. The authenticity of such translations is also suspect.

Attempting revisionist historical narratives is a more direct way of countering colonialist versions of history. Only a few such works exist, however. Clearly the most substantial and powerful among these is Kevin Gilbert's *Because a White Man'll Never Do It* (1973). A thoroughly scholarly work of Aboriginal history by an Aboriginal writer remains unavailable, yet Gilbert's work, along with those of other Aboriginal revisionist historians such as Len Watson and Neville Perkins, seems to have succeeded in forcing contemporary white Australian historians to modify their versions of history by integrating more fully the Aboriginal presence into their discourses. The highly acclaimed history of colonial Australia by Robert Hughes, *The Fatal Shore* (1986), is an example of a recent white Australian historical narrative that makes considerable effort to reinscribe the Aboriginal presence and participation into the collective historical consciousness of white Australians.

Much more numerous than revisionist historical discourses are autobiographies and recorded oral testimonies. Such texts serve as moral statements by bearing witness to the truths of individual lives. Moreover, their documentary nature and ethnographic realism also enable them to serve as versions of oppositional history, for autobiographies are not only recorded recollections but are also "modes of interrogating history." An autobiography is an individual attempt to establish a "validating relationship with a collective past" and therefore can be a valuable "fragment of collective history". An aggregation of those individual stories can indeed offer us a glimpse of the larger patterns of social, economic, and political forces that shape history.

Aboriginal autobiographical works such as Dick Roughsey's *Moon and Rainbow* (1971), Robert Bropho's *Fringe Dweller* (1980), Sally Morgan's *My Place* (1987), and Glenyse Ward's *Wandering Girl* (1988) take us on a journey through the Other Australia. They probe the brutal underside of the Antipodean nation/continent in poignantly human terms and reveal what white Australia is anxious to conceal about its past and reluctant to disclose about its present. Even more significantly, such texts help perserve many folkloric Aboriginal beliefs and related cultural practices. Thus these texts function on many levels: as personal recollective narrative acts, as historical correc-

tives, and as repositories of traditional lore and folk wisdom.

It is in the area of imaginative writing, however, that black writers in Australia have made the most sustained and clearly the most successful efforts to salvage their past. Colin Johnson's *Long Live Sandawara* (1979) is an attempt to explore the interconnectedness of the Aboriginal past and the present, to find in past moments of heroism a viable basis for contemporary activism. The novel centers on Sandawara, a nineteenth-century Aboriginal hero who spearheaded a highly successful resistance movement against the white invasion of western Australia. Johnson seeks in those heroic moments in Sandawara's life the very essence of the Aboriginal spirit. Though Aboriginal history is littered with defeats and dispossessions, Johnson finds in the life of Sandawara an occasion for celebration. Here literature triumphs over history. By affirming those moments in the Aboriginal past by "freezing" them in art, Johnson is able to transcend imaginatively that past which signifies pain and thus liberates himself from it.

On a larger scale, Johnson's most recent novel, *Doctor Wooreddy's Prescription for Enduring the Ending of the World,* offers a vigorous challenge to imperialist versions of Australian history by narrating the fatal encounter between Tasmanian Aborigines and European invaders—an encounter that Robert Hughes's book *The Fatal Encounter* characterizes as the only "systematic genocide" in British colonial history—from an uncompromisingly Aboriginal point of view. Johnson's revisionist stance, coupled with his talent for effective characterization and brilliant humor, makes *Doctor Wooreddy* one of the most memorable and successful works in recent Australian history.

Doctor Wooreddy is set in early nineteenth-century Tasmania; through the life of its titular protagonist Johnson re-creates the white occupation of Tasmania and the systematic extermination of the indigenous population. The Aborigines face attack from many directions; they are uprooted and dislocated by senseless government statutes; they are subjected to the grotesquely aggressive evangelical zeal of Robinson, a Christian missionary; and they face periodic physical violence from the European settlers and convicts. The Aboriginal population dwindles rapidly, and with the death of Doctor Wooreddy, the last surviving male member of the tribe, the liquidation of all full-blooded Aborigines is complete.

What is remarkable about the novel's re-creation of the historical genocide is its Aboriginal point of view, which entails many sharp reversals. The European settlers, for example, are not presented as glorious pioneers but as aggressive savages. The missionary is not viewed as a harbinger of civilization but as an obscene agent of colonialism. Proselytism is perceived as a tool of imperial aggression: the missionary, in his overzealous imposition of a foreign metaphysical system on the indigenous people, destabilizes their cultural fabric, distorts their world view, and undermines their identity and self-image. Even the humanity of the Europeans is challenged; the Aborigines in the novels consider themselves human and view the whites as *num* or ghosts. The physical and verbal "oddities" of the whites are a source of mirth for the blacks, and the Aborigines are even convinced that the whites have cannibalistic tendencies.

Johnson's fictionalized revisionist historical narrative thus effectively challenges the imperialistic ideologies that inform white versions of history. It redeems the Aboriginal past from distortion and dismissal. It rehumanizes the Aborigines, validates their culture, and celebrates their dignity. It legitimizes the Aboriginal past and thus attempts to reshape the white Australian historical awareness. Above all, it offers its Aboriginal audience a tangible, definable, and authentic past with which to identify.

Contemporary Aboriginal theater offers an even more powerful forum to reinvent Australian history by defamiliarizing white versions of it. The stage provides space for re-creation of ancient rituals; it allows room for fuller expression of the orality of traditional Aboriginal culture; and the visual attributes of dramatic production vastly enhance the overall emotional impact on the audience. Sensing the political value of the stage, Aboriginal playwrights such as Jack Davis, Robert Merritt, and Bob Maza have made effective use of the theater. Reconstructions of the precolonial Aboriginal past and examinations of the post-contact cultural trauma continue to be the dominant themes of Aboriginal drama. Davis's *Kullark* (1982), *The Dreamers* (1988), and *No Sugar* (1988), Merritt's *Cake Man* (1978), and Maza's play *The Keepers* (1988) are dramatically and politically powerful attempts to re-create Aboriginal history and to validate the vital relevance of ancient Aboriginality in contemporary constructions of black Australian identity.

The most powerful among the Aboriginal historical plays is Davis's *Kullark,* a carefully researched work in which many of the characters are based on and named after historical personalities. The action of the play focuses on the Yorlahs, a contemporary Aboriginal family living in a small town near Perth, but chronologically the play moves back and forth, first to a farm in the 1820s, then to an Aboriginal reservation in the 1930s, and finally to western Australia in 1945. The predicament of the Yorlahs, in a general sense, is representative of the plight of tens of thousands of impoverished urban Aboriginal families who live on the fringes of affluent white Australia. As the action moves back and forth between the past and the present, Davis develops the play's central theme: that it is in their past that the contemporary Aborigines must seek their symbolic anchors and spiritual centers. It is through an understanding of their racial history, Davis argues, that they can forge a sense of coherence which is necessary to counter the contemporary conditions of disorder and dislocation.

When the dramatic action of *Kullark* (an Aboriginal word that means "home") first moves from the present to the 1820s, the focus is on the initial black-white confrontation. In particular, the action centers on Yagan, an Aboriginal leader who organizes numerous attacks on white settlements, destroying lives and property. He survives many reprisals until he is duped into a setup and shot to death; he is decapitated, his skull smoked and sent to England for public display. When the action moves to the 1930s, the

focus is on the forced removal of the Aborigines, now a defeated people, to missions and reserves under the new legislations of the Australian government. When the scene moves to the midforties, the ironic focus is on the plight of Aboriginal soldiers returning home to their outcaste status in their own country after fighting the Japanese. The play thus re-creates some of the most disgraceful moments in white Australian history, which are also some of the most painful moments in the Aboriginal past. Nevertheless, the play is also a celebration, a celebration of Aboriginal survival in the face of monumental obstacles. The spirit of militant resistance that Yagan demonstrates in the first part of the play prevails to the end, and the work concludes with an Aboriginal anthem of unyielding resistance.

Kullark, then, seeks catharsis through confrontation with history. It is an attempt to understand the current trauma of Aboriginal culture in the larger context of postinvasion history. Since colonialism is a historical disaster with ongoing consequences, Davis suggests, the regeneration of the Aboriginal self is possible only through a spiritual reconnection with and healing affirmation of the past.

The recent four-part, made-for-television historical drama *Women of the Sun* (1988) by Hyllus Maris and Sonia Borg shows that Aboriginal theater can now electronically enter the living rooms of Australia. Thus, within a few decades, Aboriginal writers' attempts to regenerate their cultural selves by reclaiming their past has moved from a tribal context through the print medium to electronic transmission. The vibrancy of black writing in contemporary Australia suggests that the battle lines of racial politics are being redrawn; the struggle is now being taken to a new level. Once the Aboriginal culture was helpless in the face of European textual abuse, but now black texts, with their oppositional historical perspectives, are not only reappropriating the Aboriginal but reshaping the white past as well by decentering white historical fictions. Losses there have been along the way, but the victories too have been substantial. (pp. 30-4)

> *Emmanuel S. Nelson, "Literature Against History: An Approach to Australian Aboriginal Writing," in* World Literature Today, *Vol. 64, No. 1, Winter, 1990, pp. 30-4.*

FURTHER READING

Anthologies

Friederich, Werner P. *Australia in Western Imaginative Prose Writings: An Anthology and a History of Literature.* Chapel Hill: University of North Carolina Press, 1967, 279 p.
    Contains anthology of Australian fiction, historical information, and bibliography of Australian fiction from 1600 to 1960.

Hadgraft, Cecil, and Wilson, Richard, eds. *A Century of Australian Short Stories.* London: Heinemann, 1963, 336 p.

Includes most of the well-known Australian short stories from the late nineteenth and twentieth centuries.

Murray, Les A., ed. *The New Oxford Book of Australian Verse.* Melbourne: Oxford University Press, 1986, 399 p.
Contains a wide range of Australian poetry, including Aboriginal poetry translated into English.

Secondary Sources

Andrews, Barry G., and Wilde, William H. *Australian Literature to 1900: A Guide to Information Sources.* Detroit: Gale Research Co., 1980, 472 p.
Annotated guide to Australian literature from 1788 to 1900, organized by general bibliography, individual authors, and selected nonfiction prose.

Arthur, Kateryna Olijnk. "Recasting History: Australian Bicentennial Writing." *The Journal of Narrative Technique* 21, No. 1 (Winter 1991): 52-61.
Asserts that the fiction written during 1988 and 1989 challenges the Australian sense of national identity and inspires the enterprise of historical reconstruction.

Baker, A. W. *Death Is a Good Solution: The Convict Experience in Early Australia.* St. Lucia: University of Queensland Press, 1984, 223 p.
Chronicles convict literature in Australia from settlement to the end of transportation. Baker includes a bibliography of convict literature.

Bayliss, John F. "Slave and Convict Narratives: A Discussion of American and Australian Writing." *The Journal of Commonwealth Literature,* No. 8 (December 1969): 147-49.
Proposes that "in many ways the Australian convict was a slave like his Negro American counterpart."

Bennett, Bruce. "Australian Experiments in Short Fiction." *World Literature Written in English* 15, No. 2 (November 1976): 359-66.
Survey of experimental writers, particularly Murray Bail, Peter Carey, Frank Moorhouse, and Michael Wilding.

———, ed. *The Literature of Western Australia.* Nedlands: University of Western Australia Press, 1979, 304 p.
Essays published to commemorate the sesquicentenary of Western Australia.

Berndt, Catherine, and Berndt, Ronald. "Aboriginal Australia: Literature in an Oral Tradition." *Review of National Literatures* 11 (1982): 39-63.
Describes the history and significance of the oral tradition in Aboriginal culture and literature.

Brissenden, Alan, ed. *Aspects of Australian Fiction.* Nedlands: University of Western Australia Press, 1990, 205 p.
Collection of essays on representative figures and themes in Australian fiction.

Buckley, Vincent. "National and International." *Southerly* 38, No. 2 (1978): 145-56.
Explores the decolonialization of Australian poetry since the end of the Second World War, and encourages a new, nationalist voice for the future.

Burns, D. R. "Australian Fiction since 1960." *World Literature Written in English* 11, No. 2 (November 1972): 53-63.
Argues that the Australian novel "exhibits the sort of powers and vents the sort of enthusiasm which one might associate with late adolescence."

Cantrell, Leon, ed. *Bards, Bohemians, and Bookmen: Essays in Australian Literature.* St. Lucia: University of Queensland Press, 1976, 350 p.
Collection of essays on Australian literature and literary criticism.

Capone, Giovanna, ed. "European Perspectives: Contemporary Essays on Australian Literature." Special edition of *Australian Literary Studies* 15, No. 2 (1991).
Collection devoted to studies of Australian literature by overseas critics.

Clark, Manning. "Tradition in Australian Literature." *Meanjin* 8, No. 1 (Autumn 1949): 16-22.
Maintains that the national literature reflects a unique mix of influences including Australia's convict origins, an influx of immigrant laborers, and harsh climactic and geographical conditions.

Craig, Alexander, ed. Introduction to *Twelve Poets: 1950-1970,* pp. 1-19. Milton, Queensland: Jacaranda Press, 1971.
Surveys twelve contemporary poets and provides a brief critical history.

Daniel, Helen. "The Picaresque Mode in Contemporary Australian Fiction." *Southerly* 38, No. 3 (1978): 282-93.
Examines the re-emergence of the picaresque form to depict the modern search for identity in a diverse and chaotic world.

Drake-Brockman, Henrietta. "Australia." *The Kenyon Review* XXX, No. 4 (1968): 478-85.
Overview of the development of the Australian short story from Aboriginal myth to contemporary writing.

During, Simon. "Mourning after Criticism." *Meanjin* 46, No. 3 (1987): 301-10.
Evaluates the state of contemporary Australian literary criticism.

Dutton, Geoffrey, ed. *The Literature of Australia.* Rev. ed. Ringwood: Penguin Aust., 1976, 612 p.
Contains sections on fiction, poetry, and drama as well as individual authors. Dutton also includes a selected bibliography.

Elliott, Brian. *The Landscape of Australian Poetry.* Melbourne: F.W. Cheshire, 1967, 346 p.
Examines the theme of topography in Australian poetry from settlement to 1950.

Ferrier, Carole, ed. *Gender, Politics, and Fiction: Twentieth-Century Australian Women's Novels.* St. Lucia: University of Queensland Press, 1985, 262 p.
Views Australian women writers and their work within a feminist context. Ferrier includes a bibliography of Australian women's novels and feminist literary criticism.

Goodwin, Ken. *A History of Australian Literature.* New York: St. Martin's Press, 1986, 322 p.
Traces development of Australian literature from colonial beginnings to mid-1980s.

Gostand, Reba. "The Comic Mask in Contemporary Australian Drama." *Southerly* 40, No. 2 (1980): 127-43.
Describes "the violent and grotesque comedy currently

predominant in Australian drama . . . as a cry for help against the pressures of a nightmare world."

Green, H. M. *A History of Australian Literature: Pure and Applied.* 2 vols. Sydney: Angus & Robertson, 1961, 1469 p.
Considered the definitive history of Australian literature up to 1950.

Gronowski, Irene. "Modern Australian Drama: An Outsider's View." *Quadrant* V, No. 2 (Autumn 1961): 67-74.
Maintains that Australian drama "lives in the present and the future; it has no past, no history and tradition to stand on."

Hadgraft, Cecil. *Australian Literature: A Critical Account.* London: Heinemann, 1960, 302 p.
Explores poetry, fiction, and literary criticism in Australia from settlement (1788) to 1955.

Hamilton, K. G. *Studies in the Recent Australian Novel.* Queensland: University of Queensland Press, 1978, 257 p.
Collection of essays that examine aspects of Australian novels.

Hanger, Eunice. "Australian Drama Now." *Modern Drama* VIII, No. 1 (May 1965): 73-81.
Assesses the development of contemporary drama in Australia. According to Hanger: "The curious development in Australian drama at present is that its true vitality and its greatest fertility are not to be found in the writers who have been professionally produced and published but in what may be called the underground."

Healy, J. J. *Literature and the Aborigine in Australia 1770-1975.* New York: St. Martin's Press, 1978, 305 p.
Discusses the Aborigine as represented in white Australian literature, and includes criticism on recent Aboriginal writers.

Heseltine, Harry. *The Uncertain Self: Essays in Australian Literature and Criticism.* Melbourne: Oxford University Press, 1986, 222 p.
Includes essays on literary historiography, literary autobiography, and contemporary writers.

Hope, A. D. "The Literary Pattern in Australia." *University of Toronto Quarterly* XXVI, No. 1 (October 1956): 122-32.
Thematic and historical overview of Australian literature.

Hutton, Geoffrey. "Playwrights in Search of a Direction." *Overland,* No. 67 (1977): 17-21.
Asks "when will the great Australian play appear, sharply observed without being brittle, topical without being trendy, truthful without being turgid?"

Jacobson, Howard. "Measuring up the Age and Place." *Times Literary Supplement,* No. 4,417 (27 November 1987): 1307-09.
Discusses Australian fiction, and the shift away from whimsy and minimalism toward boldness.

Jones, Dorothy. "Mapping and Mythmaking: Women Writers and the Australian Legend." *Ariel* 17, No. 4 (October 1986): 63-86.
Concludes that women writers in Australia have succeeded in "establishing their own mythic tradition."

————. "Evoking the Past in Contemporary Australian Poetry." In *The Writer's Sense of the Past: Essays on Southeast Asian and Australasian Literature,* edited by Kirpal Singh, pp. 198-211. Kent Ridge, Singapore: Singapore University Press, 1987.
Discusses ways in which contemporary Australian poets have utilized personal recollections to explore such subjects as national origin and the effects of climate and geography.

Jones, Joseph, and Jones, Johanna. *Australian Fiction.* Boston: Twayne Publishers, 1983, 177 p.
Survey of Australian fiction, including discussions on convict life, expatriation, Aboriginal life, and counter-culture writings. A selected bibliography includes science fiction titles.

Kiernan, Brian. *Criticism.* Australian Writers and Their Work, edited by Grahame Johnston. Melbourne: Oxford University Press, 1974, 52 p.
Traces the development of literary criticism in Australia.

Kramer, Leonie. "Literary Criticism in Australia." *Overland,* No. 26 (April 1963): 25-7.
Maintains that Australian literary criticism "cannot fulfil its proper function if it rests on a narrow basis of nationalistic fervor or provincial self-consciousness. . . . "

————, ed. *The Oxford History of Australian Literature.* Melbourne: Oxford University Press, 1981, 509 p.
Provides overview of Australian literature, concentrating on the most prominent movements and ideas in both literature and criticism.

Lock, Fred, and Lawson, Alan. *Australian Literature: A Reference Guide.* Melbourne: Oxford University Press, 1980, 120 p.
Describes and evaluates bibliographies on Australian literature, as well as periodicals, research libraries, and associations concerned with the study of Australian literature.

Macartney, Keith. "Louis Esson and the Australian Drama." *Meanjin* 6, No. 2 (Winter 1947): 93-104.
Laments the lack of "a truly national voice" in the Australian theater.

McDonald, Avis G. "How History Hurts: Common Patterns in Australian and West Indian Fiction." *Queen's Quarterly* 96, No. 1 (Spring 1989): 78-93.
Identifies the two literatures as sharing a history of "enforced exile and conditions of bondage" and finds that comparable "images of dispossession and powerlessness, of loss, fragmentation, and alienation emerge."

Modjeska, Drusilla. *Exiles at Home: Australian Women Writers 1925-1945.* London: Sirius Books, 1981, 283 p.
Traces the development of women writers in Australia and provides a selected bibliography of women's literature from 1925 to 1945.

Moore, T. Inglis. *Social Patterns in Australian Literature.* Berkeley and Los Angeles: University of California Press, 1971, 350 p.
Analyzes the major patterns in Australian literature, traces their origins and interrelations, and discusses representative writers.

Narogin, Mudrooroo. *Writing from the Fringe: A Study of*

Modern Aboriginal Literature. Melbourne: Hyland House, 1990, 207 p.

> Discusses modern Aboriginal literature and its representative writers. Narogin provides a selective bibliography of Aboriginal literature and criticism.

Nelson, Emmanuel S. "Black America and the Australian Aboriginal Literary Consciousness." *Westerly* 30, No. 4 (December 1985): 43-54.

> Contends that the cultural and literary influence of African Americans on the Australian Aboriginal literary consciousness has been profound.

———, ed. *Connections: Essays on Black Literatures.* Canberra: Aboriginal Studies Press, 1988, 118 p.

> Collection of essays that address issues in black literatures, with emphasis on a political and historical context.

Phillips, A. A. *The Australian Tradition: Studies in a Colonial Culture.* Melbourne: F.W. Cheshire, 1959, 138 p.

> Offers essays examining the theme of colonialism in Australian literature.

Rees, Leslie. *A History of Drama.* 2 vols. Sydney: Angus & Robertson, 1978.

> Comprises *The Making of Drama from the 1830s to the late 1960s* and *Australian Drama in the 1970s.* Volumes include selective bibliographies of Australian drama and criticism.

Richey, Norma Jean. "Australia's Twentieth-Century Literary Renaissance." *Journal of Popular Culture* 23, No. 3 (Winter 1989): 77-87.

> Credits the burgeoning of Australian literature in the twentieth century to a conducive political atmosphere, especially a generous grant system.

Salzman, Paul. "Talking/Listening: Anecdotal Style in Recent Australian Women's Fiction." *Southerly* 49, No. 4 (December 1989): 539-53.

> Explores sexism in recent Australian fiction.

See, Carolyn. "Why Australian Writers Keep Their Heads Down." *New York Times Book Review* (14 May 1989): 1, 35-7.

> Describes and evaluates the current renaissance in Australian literature.

Shoemaker, Adam. *Black Words, White Pages: Aboriginal Literature 1929-1988.* St. Lucia: University of Queensland Press, 1989, 314 p.

> Places Aboriginal literature in a socio-historical context and provides a primary bibliography of works by black Australian writers.

Smith, Vivian. "Experiment and Renewal: A Missing Link in Modern Australian Poetry." *Southerly* 47, No. 1 (March 1987): 3-18.

> Chronicles the rediscovery of the lyrical tradition in Australian poetry in the 1950s and 1960s.

Stewart, Ken. "Life and Death of the Bunyip: History and 'the Great Australian Novel.'" *Westerly* 28, No. 2 (June 1983): 39-44.

> Chronicles the search for a representative Australian novel.

Taylor, Andrew. *Reading Australian Poetry.* St. Lucia: University of Queensland Press, 1987, 218 p.

> Discussion of recent Australian poets. Taylor includes a selective bibliography.

Tiffin, Chris. "Look to the New-Found Dreaming: Identity and Technique in Australian Aboriginal Writing." *The Journal of Commonwealth Literature* 20, No. 1 (1985): 156-70.

> Examines nature and themes of Aboriginal writing since the 1960s, focusing on the poetry of Kath Walker and fiction by Colin Johnson (Mudrooroo Narogin).

Tranter, John. "Growing Old Gracefully: The Generation of '68." *Meanjin* 37, No. 1 (April 1978): 76-86.

> Appraisal of Australian writers who gained prominence in the 1970s, concluding that they "are noticeably different from their predecessors, and owe little to their example."

Walker, Shirley, ed. *Who Is She?* New York: St. Martin's Press, 1983, 219 p.

> Examines how the image of woman has been dealt with in the works of a select group of Australian writers.

Wallace-Crabbe, Chris. "Mixed Motives, Mixed Diction: Recent Australian Poetry." *The Journal of Commonwealth Literature* 19, No. 1 (1984): 2-9.

> Surveys structure and theme in the works of several Australian poets of the 1970s and 1980s.

Webster, Owen. "The Literary Life of Australia." *Overland,* No. 45 (Autumn 1970): 27-32.

> Laments the state of Australian literature, calling it "a turmoil of old love-hates, of unburied hatchets and unextinguished torches, of unconfessed prejudices and indiscreet gossip."

Wilding, Michael. "Write Australian." *The Journal of Commonwealth Literature* VI, No. 1 (June 1971): 19-30.

> Investigates the relevance of an "Australian tradition" in Australian writing, especially among literary critics and expatriate writers.

Wilkes, G. A. *The Stockyard and the Croquet Lawn: Literary Evidence for Australian Cultural Development.* Melbourne: Edward Arnold, 1981, 153 p.

> Argues that the continuing development of Australian literature is evidence for the maturation of Australian culture.

Willbanks, Ray. *Australian Voices: Writers on Their Own Work.* Austin: University of Texas Press, 1991, 233 p.

> Interviews with contemporary Australian writers.

Wright, Judith. "Australian Poetry since 1941." *Southerly* 31, No. 1 (1971): 19-28.

> Asserts that Australian poetry since 1941 "has felt free to do what it wanted without having to posture in order to catch overseas eyes."

Espionage Literature

INTRODUCTION

Although spying is one of the oldest professions and the theme of spying dates back to classical epic poetry, espionage fiction as a literary genre is usually considered to have begun with the publication of Erskine Childer's *The Riddle of the Sands* in 1903. Since that time, commentators observe, espionage literature has evolved into three main types, each of which reflects a different attitude toward the spy. The first type, which flourished during the early period of espionage fiction, is best represented by John Buchan's *The Thirty-Nine Steps.* In this novel the spy, Richard Hannay, is a heroic figure whose patriotism exonerates his participation in the sordid and disreputable world of espionage. Other notable writers from this period include Childers, E. Phillips Oppenheim, and William Le Queux. In the second type the notable feature of the spy is his physical and intellectual prowess, as exemplified by Ian Fleming's hero James Bond. Fleming sensationalized the spy as a superman who is above the moral and ethical codes of society, and whose violent behavior and self-indulgence are justified by the danger of his occupation. The third type of espionage fiction is often associated with the Cold War era and presents an ironic and cynical view of espionage which undercuts its political necessity and social value. Leading practitioners of this form include Graham Greene, Eric Ambler, John Le Carré, and Len Deighton. For these authors the value of espionage fiction lies not in its heroics or glamor but in its potential for exploring such issues as alienation and betrayal and questioning social and political systems. While the differences among the three types of espionage fiction are significant, together they form a genre of popular literature that many critics contend accurately reflects the complexities and perils of the modern world.

REPRESENTATIVE WORKS

Aarons, Edward S.
Assignment to Disaster   (novel)   1955
Assignment: Ankara   (novel)   1961
Assignment: Moongirl   (novel)   1967
Ambler, Eric
The Dark Frontier   (novel)   1936
Background to Danger   (novel)   1937
Epitaph for a Spy   (novel)   1938
A Coffin for Dimitrios   (novel)   1939
Journey into Fear   (novel)   1940
The Passage of Arms   (novel)   1959
The Light of Day   (novel)   1962

Dirty Story   (novel)   1967
The Intercom Conspiracy   (novel)   1969
Atlee, Philip [pseudonym of James Atlee Philips]
The Green Wound   (novel)   1963
The Deathbird Contract   (novel)   1966
Beeding, Francis
The Seven Sleepers   (novel)   1925
There Are Thirteen   (novel)   1946
Buchan, John
The Half-Hearted   (novel)   1900
Captain, Prester John   (novel)   1910
The Thirty-Nine Steps   (novel)   1915
Greenmantle   (novel)   1916
Mr. Standfast   (novel)   1919
Huntingtower   (novel)   1922
The Three Hostages   (novel)   1924
The Courts of Morning   (novel)   1929
Castle Gay   (novel)   1930
A Prince of the Captivity   (novel)   1933
Buckley, William F., Jr.
Who's on First   (novel)   1980
Marco Polo, If You Can   (novel)   1982
Cheyney, Peter
Dark Duet   (novel)   1942
Dark Bahama   (novel)   1950
Childers, Erskine
The Riddle of the Sands   (novel)   1903
Coles, Manning [pseudonym of Cyril Henry Coles and Adelaide F. O. Manning]
Drink to Yesterday   (novel)   1940
Toast to Tomorrow   (novel)   1941
Condon, Richard
The Manchurian Candidate   (novel)   1959
Conrad, Joseph
The Secret Agent   (novel)   1907
Under Western Eyes   (novel)   1911
Corey, Desmond
Secret Ministry   (novel)   1951
Intrigue   (novel)   1954
Undertow   (novel)   1962
Deadfall   (novel)   1965
Sunburst   (novel)   1971
Dark, James
Come Die with Me   (novel)   1965
Assignment Tokyo   (novel)   1966
Deighton, Len
The Ipcress File   (novel)   1962
Horse under Water   (novel)   1963
Funeral in Berlin   (novel)   1964
The Billion Dollar Brain   (novel)   1966
An Expensive Place to Die   (novel)   1967
Spy Story   (novel)   1974
Yesterday's Spy   (novel)   1975
Berlin Game   (novel)   1984
Engel, Lyle Kenton
Run Spy Run   (novel)   1964
Danger Key   (novel)   1966

Fleming, Ian
  Casino Royale (novel) 1953
  Live and Let Die (novel) 1954
  Moonraker (novel) 1955
  Diamonds Are Forever (novel) 1956
  From Russia, with Love (novel) 1957
  Dr. No (novel) 1958
  Goldfinger (novel) 1959
  Thunderball (novel) 1961
  On Her Majesty's Secret Service (novel) 1963
  The Spy Who Loved Me (novel) 1963
  You Only Live Twice (novel) 1964
  The Man with the Golden Gun (novel) 1965
Forsyth, Frederick
  The Day of the Jackal (novel) 1971
  The Odessa File (novel) 1972
  The Dogs of War (novel) 1974
  The Devil's Alternative (novel) 1980
Gardner, John
  The Liquidator (novel) 1964
Greene, Graham
  The Stamboul Train (novel) 1932
  A Gun for Sale (novel) 1936
  The Confidential Agent (novel) 1939
  The Ministry of Fear (novel) 1943
  The Third Man (novel) 1950
  The Quiet American (novel) 1955
  Our Man in Havana (novel) 1958
  The Honorary Counsel (novel) 1973
  The Human Factor (novel) 1978
Haggard, William [pseudonym of Richard Henry
Michael Clayton]
  Slow Burner (novel) 1958
  The Unquiet Sleep (novel) 1962
Hall, Adam [pseudonym of Elleston Trevor]
  The Quiller Memorandum (novel) 1965
  The Ninth Directive (novel) 1966
  The Striker Portfolio (novel) 1969
  The Warsaw Document (novel) 1971
  The Tango Briefing (novel) 1973
  The Mandarin Cipher (novel) 1975
  The Kobra Manifesto (novel) 1976
  The Sinkiang Executive (novel) 1978
Hamilton, Donald
  Death of a Citizen (novel) 1960
  The Wrecking Crew (novel) 1960
  The Silencers (novel) 1962
  The Ambushers (novel) 1963
Hunt, E. Howard
  The Hargrave Deception (novel) 1980
  The Gaza Intercept (novel) 1981
Leasor, James
  Passport to Oblivion (novel) 1964
Le Carré, John [pseudonym of David Cornwell]
  Call for the Dead (novel) 1961
  The Spy Who Came in from the Cold (novel) 1963
  The Looking-Glass War (novel) 1965
  A Small Town in Germany (novel) 1968
  Tinker, Tailor, Soldier, Spy (novel) 1974
  The Honourable Schoolboy (novel) 1977
  Smiley's People (novel) 1980
Le Queux, William
  The Bond of Black (novel) 1899
  The Day of Temptation (novel) 1899
  Secrets of the Foreign Office (novel) 1903

  Behind the Throne (novel) 1905
  Hidden Hands (novel) 1925
Ludlum, Robert
  The Scarlatti Inheritance (novel) 1971
MacInnes, Helen
  Above Suspicion (novel) 1941
  Assignment in Brittany (novel) 1941
Mackenzie, Compton
  Extremes Meet (novel) 1928
  The Three Courtiers (novel) 1929
Marlowe, Dan J.
  Operation Counterpunch (novel) 1976
Marquand, John P.
  Ming Yellow (novel) 1934
  No Hero (novel) 1935
  Stopover Tokyo (novel) 1957
Maugham, W. Somerset
  Ashenden: or, The British Agent (novel) 1928
McCutchan, Philip D.
  Gibraltar Road (novel) 1960
  Redcap (novel) 1961
  Skyprobe (novel) 1966
O'Donnell, Peter
  Modesty Blaise (novel) 1965
Oppenheim, E. Phillips
  The Mysterious Mr. Sabin (novel) 1898
  The Pawns Count (novel) 1918
  The Great Impersonation (novel) 1920
  Miss Brown of the X.Y.O. (novel) 1927
  Up the Ladder of Gold (novel) 1931
Price, Anthony
  The Labyrinth Makers (novel) 1970
  October Men (novel) 1973
  Paths to Glory (novel) 1974
  Our Man in Camelot (novel) 1975
Sapper [pseudonym of H. C. McNeile]
  Bull-Dog Drummond (novel) 1920
  The Black Gang (novel) 1922
  The Third Round (novel) 1924
  The Final Count (novel) 1926
  The Female of the Species (novel) 1928
  Temple Tower (novel) 1929
  The Return of Bulldog Drummond (novel) 1932
  Knockout (novel) 1933
  Bulldog Drummond at Bay (novel) 1935
  Challenge (novel) 1937
Thomas, Ross
  The Cold War Swap (novel) 1966
York, Andrew
  The Eliminator (novel) 1966

OVERVIEWS

G. Jay Rausch and Diane K. Rausch

[*In the following essay, the critics examine the evolution and major writers of espionage fiction.*]

Espionage fiction is usually associated with detective fiction. Yet the form has its own conventions and history. A newer genre, spy fiction did not appear until the twentieth century and has followed a different pattern of development. While the 1930s are called the "golden age" of the detective story, that period saw no similar florescence for espionage stories. While the figure of Sherlock Holmes dominates detective fiction and accurately reflects the early developments in the field, the later and lesser figure of James Bond dominates and skews the perceptions of espionage fiction.

The impact of the works of Ian Fleming on spy fiction was tremendous. In one decade, the works of Fleming sold more copies than the combined works of Hemingway, Faulkner, and Steinbeck had ever sold. The Bond books so dominated the field that when John Le Carré's novel *The Spy Who Came in from the Cold* was published in 1963, with its anti-heroic spies and cynical tone, it was hailed as a new development in espionage fiction. In fact, there have been three general streams of spy fiction of which the heroic professional agent, or Bond stream, is the newest. The amateur spy and the anti-heroic professional agent had the field largely to themselves until after World War II.

The relatively late appearance of the espionage novel needs explanation, since spying may well be the world's second oldest profession. The reasons for this late development are similar to the reasons for the lack of a major literature about prostitution. Through most of modern history, both professions have been viewed as morally tainted and therefore unable to support a sympathetic protagonist. The lying, cheating, and deception which are inseparable from espionage could be considered acceptable only after nationalism had grown strong enough to provide an acceptable motive for any action done in the name of one's country. That point was apparently reached at the turn of the twentieth century.

In early spy fiction, the prohibition against presenting the professional spy as a sympathetic character continued. This problem could be evaded in two ways: the protagonist could be presented as an innocent amateur who stumbled into trouble or who was temporarily called upon in time of crisis; or the protagonist could be presented as unheroic and flawed. Not until well after World War I did the heroic professional appear; even then he was usually presented as part law enforcement officer; espionage was still questionable but counterespionage activities were acceptable.

A chronological survey of espionage literature, with an eye to the source of the threat to peace, accurately reflects the ups and downs of international relations during the century. Written largely by and for British and American citizens, the early works usually portrayed the enemy as German. After World War I, there was a period of confusion with the threat coming from either wartime Germans or private power groups such as munitions makers. By the 1930s, Germans, Japanese, and occasionally Russians appeared. In the 1940s the Germans were again the enemy in almost all spy fiction. By the 1950s the Russians were the dominant peril but in the early 1960s the Chinese appeared. By the mid-1960s and early 1970s, the picture was again confused with maniacs, Russians, Chinese, neo-Nazis and paleo-Nazis occupying center stage.

Although there were a few earlier works that contained espionage elements, the spy novel really began with Erskine Childers' *The Riddle of the Sands* in 1903. Born in London, but raised in Ireland, Childers attended Cambridge University and worked as a clerk in the House of Commons before service in the Boer War. Childers' concern about British security and his experiences yachting in the North Sea resulted in *The Riddle of the Sands,* a curiously prophetic work which soon launched a flow of novels warning of threats from Germany.

The Riddle of the Sands concerns two young Englishmen who, while sailing off the coast of Germany, stumble upon a German plan to invade Britain. Not only is the book one of the finest novels of small boat sailing ever written but it establishes several characteristics of the espionage genre while clearly reflecting the attitudes of the time. The attitude toward spying is clearly revealed in the following:

> "It's a delicate matter", I mused dubiously, "if your theory's correct. Spying on a spy . . . "
>
> . . . . .
>
> "I don't think you're likely to do anything dishonorable", I hastened to explain. "I grant you the sea's public property in your sense. I only mean that developments are possible which you don't reckon on. There *must* be more to find out than the mere navigation of those channels, and if that's so, mightn't we come to be genuine spies ourselves?"

Davis and Carruthers fall nicely into the category of the amateur spy which became so common in later fiction. Clean-cut, decent Englishmen, they have heroic elements in their character but remain believable and normal. Other noteworthy elements in this seminal work are a lack of physical brutality and a sympathetic attitude toward the position and motivations of the enemy; both elements were frequently lost in the later development of the genre.

The Riddle of the Sands brought the espionage novel to full flower with the establishment of many traits which were to distinguish it for the next seventy years. Its appearance should be no surprise, for it followed by only three years the German Fleet Law which proclaimed Germany's intention of taking her place as a major naval power.

Several authors published novels related to espionage in the next twenty years. William Tufnell Le Queux wrote several rather simple-minded tales on the theme of the German threat. Bennet Copplestone (Frederick Harcourt Kitchin) published a linked series of short stories about C.I.D. officer William Dawson; and Lord Frederic Hamilton produced a similar series of tales in several volumes concerning an absurd adolescent spy-catcher, P. J. Davenant.

Joseph Conrad's *The Secret Agent* (1907) is significant only because of Conrad's place in literature and because of the totally unromantic portrayal of the spy. The book deals only somewhat incidentally with espionage and is not central to the development of the genre.

E. Phillips Oppenheim was one of the most prolific, best known, and after his death one of the least read authors of spy fiction. Starting before the turn of the century, Oppenheim poured forth a flood of novels and short stories that eventually totaled more than one hundred fifty books. A large number of Oppenheim's works dealt with international intrigue; all were highly romantic in approach. Several of Oppenheim's prewar novels dealt with German intentions to invade Britain and the British failure to prepare. His most famous work, *The Great Impersonation* (1920), used this theme but did not appear until after the war.

The first major writer of espionage fiction emerged when John Buchan published *The Thirty-nine Steps* in 1915. Buchan, the son of a Scottish-born clergyman, had a life even more marked by success than his success-oriented characters. By the age of twenty-three his writings had earned him inclusion in *Who's Who;* he was probably the only biographee in the volume whose occupation was listed as undergraduate. After heading Britain's propaganda efforts in the Great War and serving in Parliament, Buchan ended his career as Governor-General of Canada with the title of Lord Tweedsmuir.

Buchan's first novel, *The Half-hearted* (1900), had touched on espionage on the Indian Northwest Frontier and several of his later volumes also contained espionage elements. But three novels published during the war, *The Thirty-nine Steps* (1915), *Greenmantle* (1916), and *Mr. Standfast* (1918), contain his major contributions to the spy novel. Buchan's three wartime spy novels include most of the elements that were to mark the genre in the future. The three main streams of espionage fiction are to a large extent reflected in the characters of Richard Hannay (amateur), Sandy Arbuthnot (heroic spy), and John S. Blenkiron (professional).

In *The Thirty-nine Steps,* Hannay returns to his flat to find a stranger waiting for him. The man tells a strange tale and reveals that his life is threatened by a group that seeks a European war. Hannay fails to prevent the stranger's murder and, knowing that he too is in danger, flees and sets out to identify the enemy. After a long flight into Scotland, he succeeds too late; England is at war.

Greenmantle, although less well-known than *The Thirty-nine Steps,* is probably Buchan's best espionage novel. Hannay is approached by Sir Walter Bullivant of the Foreign Office to undertake a mission to thwart German plans to start a Holy War in the Middle East. Hannay and three others agree to meet in Constantinople after traveling there by different routes in search of clues to the German plot. The British agents achieve their goal and the novel ends with the heroes taking part in a major battle between the Russians and the Turks.

In *Mr. Standfast,* Hannay, called upon to help crack a German spy-ring operating in Britain, travels throughout England, Scotland, France, Switzerland and Italy. On his way, Hannay meets a young female counter-espionage agent whom he eventually marries.

Buchan's inability to portray convincing women is characteristic of much of the later literature in the field; the trav-

elogue nature of the setting is also typical. In Sir Walter Bullivant, we find the first prominent spymaster, a stock figure in the genre probably best represented by the character M in the James Bond novels. Less characteristic of the field are Buchan's charity toward the enemy, his tendency to consider philosophical themes with some depth and the high quality of the writing.

Although the 1920s were not a period of high productivity in espionage fiction, three works, one by W. Somerset Maugham and two by Compton Mackenzie were very significant both for the quality of writing and for the tone of the works. It is clear from these books that the cynical or realistic school made popular in the 1960s by John Le Carré and Len Deighton was created in the 1920s.

Ashenden, or: The British Agent (1928) by Maugham is not a novel but a series of linked short stories. Maugham was himself a British agent during World War I, and the character Ashenden and his adventures are closely modeled after the author's experiences. The six stories and several anecdotes that make up *Ashenden* are written with a flat tone which produces a feeling of pointlessness. Repeatedly, the plots bring out the insignificance of the spy and the capriciousness of fate. In one tale, a carefully plotted assassination succeeds . . . in killing the wrong man. In another, an old woman struggles to tell a secret before she dies—she fails. Perhaps the greatest impact of all comes at the end of a story entitled "Giulia Lazarri" when a woman who has struggled extravagantly before betraying her lover asks: "He had a wrist-watch that I gave him last Christmas. It cost twelve pounds. Can I have it back?"

Ashenden is an unheroic figure who rarely takes a clear position on anything. Also significant is the portrayal of the British espionage head, R. Unlike Sir Walter Bullivant, R. is a rather unappealing creature, both ridiculous and sinister.

Compton Mackenzie published two works very similar in tone to *Ashenden* at almost the same time. Mackenzie, Director of the Aegean Intelligence Service during World War I, based *Extremes Meet* (1928) and *The Three Couriers* (1929) partly on his experiences. The loosely joined tales that comprise the books feature Commander Roger Waterlow, a naval officer whose career was wrecked by alcoholism. Back on active duty because of the war, Waterlow served as the head of British espionage in a country much like Greece. The spy-boss employs a group of largely incompetent and frequently comical agents. The tone is sympathetic and cynical; espionage is shown to be of little importance because even if spies are successful, nobody will believe them.

The works of Compton Mackenzie are not well-known in the literature of espionage and their impact was lessened by the existence of the much better known *Ashenden.* Without Maugham's work, Mackenzie's books would no doubt be regarded as significant landmarks in the realistic school.

The 1930s were a period of slight production and little innovation in espionage literature. Yet, three authors of quality produced works of some importance and all of the streams of spy fiction were at least partially represented.

John P. Marquand's works were an unusual combination of the amateur spy theme with the heroic professional agent theme. Van Wyck Mason produced the first examples of the heroic agent novel and Eric Ambler began a long series of works with amateur protagonists and a cynical tone.

John P. Marquand, the most successful twentieth century American novelist of manners, began a series of novels of intrigue with a Far Eastern setting in 1934 with *Ming Yellow.* The next year he produced *No Hero,* the first of his novels featuring Mr. I. A. Moto. This series is unusual because the series character remains a secondary figure, while the protagonist changes from book to book. In the series, Mr. Moto, a professional Japanese agent, who appears to be a walking book of Japanese etiquette, intervenes in the lives of several harmless Americans who are usually on the verge of moral collapse. The Moto books include five prewar novels and one postwar entry, *Stopover: Tokyo* (1957). The last work is the best and is much more cynical in tone than the others.

Throughout the series Mr. Moto remains an enigmatic character. Few facts about his life are given and, considering the context in which they appear, even those could be purposely inaccurate. The very name was a serendipitous addition to the enigma, for Marquand did not realize that Moto is a suffix and hence an impossible name for a Japanese.

Marquand's political stance is neutral but his stance toward the moral effects of spying is not.

> He was a spy, or a secret agent, if you cared for a politer word, trained to live a life of lying and of subterfuge; trained to submerge his individuality into something he was not—to be a sneak, and if necessary a betrayer; trained to run from danger and let his best friend get it, if it helped the business; to kill or be killed inconspicuously, to die with his mouth shut, in the dark. There was only one loyalty—loyalty to the business. It was, by outside standards, a contemptible profession, and in the end, everybody in the business paid, because deceit was the same as erosion of character.

Francis Van Wyck Mason began a long series of heroic professional agent novels featuring Hugh North of U.S. Army Intelligence in 1930. The main importance of Mason's works is as the first series of the type; they belong to the same tradition as the Bond novels, but they are also clearly of an earlier era. North is usually more detective than spy. While North is often romantically involved with a female character, the sexual element is played down. The North books are well researched and plotted with a usually exotic setting convincingly presented.

Because of the long time span of the series, the political viewpoint is of some interest. The consistent patriotic position portrays the United States as an innocent, rather stupid power being tricked by an evil enemy. The enemy changes through the years. In *The Budapest Parade Murders* (1935), the enemies are munitions makers. Later, the Germans and Japanese and then the Russians and Chinese emerge as the source of danger.

Eric Ambler, who began writing in the mid-'30s, stands out so starkly as the master of the innocent victim school of espionage fiction that one might refer to that type as the Ambler school. The first Ambler works were less subtle than his later efforts, but they already displayed the characteristics that were to remain with him throughout his career. His heroes are average men who stumble into danger without realizing how it happened. The stories, drawn with great attention to both locale and psychology, deal with the efforts of the protagonist to escape with his life and honor intact. Unheroic, the main characters are decent chaps who behave with intelligence while gripped by terror.

After an initial effort, *The Dark Frontier* (1936), which received little attention, Ambler published the well-accepted *Background to Danger* (1937). His growing power as a novelist was reflected in *Cause for Alarm* (1938), *Epitaph for a Spy* (1938), the overrated non-espionage tale *A Coffin for Dimitrios* (1939), and *Journey into Fear* (1940).

Ambler's *Journey into Fear* is possibly his best work and is in many ways the most typical. It is a story of a British munitions salesman who, returning to Britain with orders from the Turkish navy, finds himself the intended victim of assassination by German agents. To avoid being killed, he takes a small ship for Italy and finds that enemy agents are on board. Through intelligence and luck he escapes, but his reactions to fear are so real as to chill the reader.

Twelve years passed before Ambler again published a novel except in collaboration. *Judgment on Deltchev* (1952) was the first of a long series of postwar novels, most of them characterized by complex plotting and psychological subtlety. Many of Ambler's later novels are but slightly concerned with espionage. A definite shift in political attitude occurs between the prewar and postwar works. In the earlier books Ambler was mildly favorable to the goals of the Soviet Union. After the war, Ambler regarded both the East and West with equal distaste.

Graham Greene, who has been called the "greatest contemporary Catholic novelist," is important in espionage literature primarily for the stature that his name has brought to the field. Many of Greene's novels are concerned with political intrigue but only a few deal with espionage. *The Confidential Agent* (1939) concerns an agent of the leftists in a country similar to Spain. Sent to Britain to buy coal for his government, he has little success as an agent because he lacks all of the traits needed for the rough and tumble of international intrigue. In this work, espionage serves as a vehicle for a novel of hopelessness and despair. *The Ministry of Fear* (1943) is outwardly a fairly conventional espionage novel about an amateur who gets involved with Nazi spies when he accidentally buys a cake containing microfilm. In reality, the main theme of the novel involves pity rather than anything deriving from the espionage. *The Quiet American* (1955) is also a novel with an espionage plot but containing more subtle themes—indifference and innocence.

Greene's one fairly original contribution to the espionage field came with *Our Man in Havana* (1958). Espionage has rarely been treated with humor and Greene's rollicking spoof on the whole business is the best ever written. In this tale, a British vacuum cleaner salesman creates an imaginary spy-ring in Cuba and an imaginary secret weapon which is really a giant vacuum cleaner. British intelligence accepts his claims, supports and funds him, and finally ends up decorating him rather than admit it is wrong.

One of the more interesting espionage series was written by Manning Coles (Cyril Henry Coles and Adelaide F. O. Manning) and featured the character Thomas Elphinstone Hambledon. The first two works, *Drink to Yesterday* (1940), and *A Toast to Tomorrow* (1941) are exceptionally fine examples of the cynical school of espionage fiction. Obviously, Hambledon was not intended to be a series character, for he was killed in *Drink to Yesterday*. Later he was featured in many tales. The much inferior later entries in the series find Hambledon as a wisecracking semi-heroic agent.

Another noteworthy author of espionage fiction, Helen MacInnes also made her debut at the beginning of World War II. Both *Above Suspicion* and *Assignment in Brittany* were published in 1941. The patterns which were to characterize the long list of best-selling MacInnes novels were evident at the beginning. In nearly all of them an innocent American or British citizen is caught up in espionage and works with professionals to stifle a Communist, Nazi, or nihilist plot. Usually, the locale is Europe and local color is well done; the pace is fast, but the books are a little too long. Literacy, adventure, and romance are blended in a formula which has brought the author great success. Read as a group, the MacInnes novels provide a consistent and increasingly strident attack on all forms of totalitarianism.

Peter Cheyney was best known for tough crime novels patterned after those of Dashiell Hammett and Raymond Chandler. His contributions to spy fiction came through a series of eight novels collectively known as the "Dark Series" in which the characteristics of the hard-boiled detective story are transferred to the espionage genre. Beginning with *Dark Duet* (1942) and running through *Dark Bahama* (1950), Cheyney's espionage series deals with a loosely related group of agents who work for a spy-boss known as the Old Man. The Cheyney works are excessively brutal and there is little difference in the character of a Cheyney hero and a Cheyney villain.

The 1960s, however, witnessed an unparalleled literary phenomenon which altered the popular perception of espionage literature. James Bond became the most talked-about figure in modern literature. In the absence of major wars, the cold warrior became the new hero. Soon dozens of new spy fiction series appeared, a great many of them following the Bond formula.

Ian L. Fleming was born into a wealthy Anglicized Scottish family, but the early part of his life was marked by failure and somewhat erratic behavior. His first real success came as Personal Assistant to the British Director of Naval Intelligence during World War II. In this role, Fleming's vivid imagination played a significant part in the planning of fantastic intelligence schemes, some of them successful. In many ways, Bond is an idealized Fleming. Many of Bond's personal habits and a good deal of his appearance are modeled upon the author.

The first Bond novel, *Casino Royale*, was published in 1953; and Fleming wrote a book each year thereafter until his death—altogether there are twelve Bond novels and two collections of short stories. Acceptance of the Bond novels came slowly but steadily, until in 1960 Pres.-elect John F. Kennedy revealed that *From Russia with Love* was one of his favorite books. Soon the Bond craze was in full career. Unfortunately, success came too late for Fleming; the hard drinking and heavy smoking that characterized the fictional version of Fleming seemingly broke the health of the real one as early as 1961 and killed him three years later.

While the early Bond novels contain many of the characteristics of the later ones, it is the middle volumes of the series that are the best and contain the clearest examples of the Bond formula. In *From Russia with Love* (1957), *Doctor No* (1958), and *Goldfinger* (1959) Fleming reached his peak. These books also reflect a change in the political situation at that time. In the early works through *From Russia with Love,* the Russians play a central role in motivating the villains in most of the books. The later works feature a private criminal conspiracy called Spectre and a master criminal, Ernst Blofeld.

Since James Bond is one of the most notable figures in modern fiction, it might be well to take a look at him. Agent 007 is one of three agents of the British Secret Service licensed to kill. He probably attended both public school and university, but he exhibits only the surface signs of culture or education. In his middle to late thirties and six feet tall, he weighs 168 pounds, has black hair, blue-grey eyes, a rather cruel mouth, and a scar on his right cheek.

A trained killer, Bond is not a particularly strong man. He is good at his job but his talents are largely the result of training rather than natural ability; he finds it necessary to work hard to stay in shape. This former naval commander is an exceedingly fussy and rigid individual who has definite ideas about the details of his life. He smokes sixty cigarettes a day but they must be his own specially prepared brand; he drinks heavily but has precise ideas about how drinks should be prepared. While Bond makes pretensions to being a gourmet, he largely exists on eggs, toast, bacon, and coffee. Yet, he always specifies exactly what he wants and how it is to be prepared. Bond pays great attention to his clothes but they are rather monotonous.

In nearly all of his adventures, James Bond meets and beds attractive women, but he rarely becomes deeply involved. Agent 007 is clearly a sexist who regards women as attractive playthings. Here too Bond is fussy; his women must be athletic and tomboyish, perhaps the very type least likely to put up with his attitudes for any length of time.

Several features contributed heavily to the success of Fleming's work. Without doubt his bizarre collection of villains played a part. As a group, they provide the most sinister, weird, and ridiculous collection of walking-talking horrors in literature. With all of the unrealistic elements in Fleming's work, it is at first surprising that they retain sufficient elements of realism to have popular appeal. Fleming's style and approach did much to bring his fantasy to life. A major element in the Fleming style is minute description of the everyday things of life. Bond does not just smoke a cigarette, he smokes a particular, carefully described kind. Brand names and detailed descriptions are sprinkled throughout the books and provide an anchor in reality from which the fantastic adventures can spring.

Perhaps the greatest appeal of all is found in the fact that the Bond fantasy world is not an anonymous and totally strange place. It is a plausible fantasy world, the world of a real-life man—Ian Fleming—and thus not very different from the fantasy world of others.

During the early and middle 1960s several authors began spy series closely resembling Fleming's works, while others adapted existing series to fit the successful pattern. Beginning in 1955 with *Assignment to Disaster,* Edward S. Aarons began a long series of books, featuring C.I.A. agent Sam Durell, all with the word "assignment" in the title. While Durell is clearly in the heroic mold, the Assignment series owes nothing to Fleming. Durell is as much detective or soldier of fortune as agent, and the books are marked by sketchy characterization, fast pace, brutal action, and complex plot. Somewhat similar are the Matt Helm novels of Donald Hamilton which began in 1960 with *Death of a Citizen.*

Clearly derivative from Fleming are the works of James Leasor, James Dark, E. Howard Hunt, and Philip Atlee. In the middle and late 1960s, Leasor wrote highly successful heroic agent tales about Dr. Jason Love. The devotion to gadgetry, automobiles, and sado-masochistic sex is similar to Fleming's and the only significantly different element is Love's amateur status. James Dark's books featuring playboy-racing car driver-agent Mark Hood are significant only as an example of the many medium quality series directly derived from Fleming. E. Howard Hunt, later famous because of his connection with Watergate, wrote many espionage novels under a variety of pseudonyms. Perhaps most popular is the series concerning agent Peter Ward written under the pseudonym David St. John. While many features in the series are similar to those in the Bond novels, the works are characterized by a somewhat unheroic agent and a clearly stated pro-American political position. Much more than Bond, Peter Ward has no doubts about who the good guys are. In the works of Philip Atlee, the political position is clearly stated but the certainties are fewer. Agent Joe Gall is one of the most interesting heroic agents in fiction and his disenchantment with American politics is total. While Gall has many of the expected personal peculiarities typical of the Bond-derived hero and the novels degenerate over time into almost outlines of the formula, the early works in the series are surprisingly and refreshingly different.

Two unusual entrants in the heroic agent tradition are the works of Philip D. McCutchan and Peter O'Donnell. Throughout the 1960s, McCutchan's Commander Shaw novels underwent a rapid evolution which almost capsulizes the history of the heroic agent school of espionage fic-

tion. *Redcap* (1961) unveils a mildly puritanical Commander Shaw who reminds one of the heroes of Buchan or of an early Colonel North. By the late 1960s, Commander Shaw has passed through the Bond stage and reminds one of a Mickey Spillane hero. Modesty Blaise, the heroine of Peter O'Donnell's several novels, was billed as a female James Bond and the books are heavily laced with gadgets and casual sex.

Between the late 1950s and the middle 1960s, the heroic school dominated the field of espionage fiction. Then with the publication of John Le Carré's *The Spy Who Came In from the Cold* (1963), the cynical or realistic school made a major comeback. Born in England, David Cornwell, who writes as John Le Carré, attended Oxford and served briefly in British intelligence after World War II.

Le Carré has written a series of cynical, anti-heroic espionage novels about a fat, middle-aged, rumpled and bespectacled agent, George Smiley, who works for a British agency called the Circus. The author's first two books, *Call for the Dead* (1960) and *A Murder of Quality* (1962), caused little stir. Then with *The Spy Who Came In from the Cold* Le Carré received a tremendous amount of attention. His work was hailed as a new kind of spy story—realistic, depressing, and painting spies and espionage as sordid and unromantic.

Le Carré's next two efforts, *The Looking Glass War* (1965) and *A Small Town in Germany* (1968), were successful but somewhat routine efforts. Then, with *Tinker, Tailor, Soldier, Spy* (1974) and *The Honourable Schoolboy* (1977), Le Carré recovered his touch and turned to a more ambitious approach to the espionage novel. The Le Carré plots are always very complex, but with the last two works Le Carré turned to a broader canvas and successfully attempted to write major novels using an espionage theme. For Le Carré all of society and civilization are at least somewhat devious and corrupt; espionage is only slightly more so and seems to epitomize the larger world. A quotation from George Smiley at the end of *The Honourable Schoolboy* conveys the tone of the works very well.

> I honestly do wonder, without wishing to be morbid, how I reached the present pass. So far as I can remember of my youth, I chose the secret road because it seemed to lead straightest and furthest toward my country's goal. The enemy in those days was someone we could point at and read about in the papers. Today, all I know is that I have learned to interpret the whole of life in terms of conspiracy. That is the sword I have lived by, and as I look round me now I see it is the sword I shall die by as well. These people terrify me but I am one of them. If they stab me in the back, then at least that is the judgment of my peers.

At almost the same time that Le Carré's works created a major sensation, the other outstanding practitioner of the realistic school began writing. Len Deighton published *The Ipcress File* in 1962 and followed it with a series of similar works of which the most widely praised was *Funeral in Berlin* (1964). Deighton's early works featured an anonymous agent of a British agency known as W.O.O.C. (P). The novels cover a wide range of geography but the setting is a little vague and uncertain, as is the world of the spy. Double agents and triple agents abound; the protagonist is cynical, witty, and professional. Political preferences are held only mildly; sex plays an unimportant role; and espionage is seen as a sordid, frequently dull, often dangerous business. Deighton's later works edge closer to the heroic school and the always cardboard characters become thinner. In his early works, Deighton rivaled Le Carré for the leadership of the realistic school, but while Le Carré has grown more serious and more ambitious, Deighton has gradually lost his freshness and slipped into formula.

During the late 1960s and early 1970s, several of the best series fell into neither the heroic nor the realistic pattern. Elleston Trevor, writing as Adam Hall, produced several fine efforts about a British agent named Quiller. While the tone of *The Quiller Memorandum* (1965), *The 9th Directive* (1966), and *The Striker Portfolio* (1968) is cynical, it is less so than Le Carré's works and there are several features of the heroic school. Oswald Wynd too, as Gavin Black, wrote excellent novels about a businessman, Paul Harris. The novels are more concerned with intrigue than with espionage and Harris essentially represents only himself. Martin Woodhouse produced a couple of excellent works about Dr. Giles Yeoman. Full of technology and gadgets, the novels in tone are cynical and the agent an amateur. Essentially, Woodhouse's works represent a combination of all three main streams of spy fiction.

Some of the finest works in the last decade were produced by Richard H. M. Clayton under the name William Haggard. Haggard's stories concern spy-master Colonel Charles Russell. Realistic in tone, they feature a professional spy who is well into middle age and who is more heroic in character and intelligence than in actions.

As Simon Harvester, Henry Gibbs has produced a long series of excellent works with "road" in the title. Concerning a group of loosely coordinated professional spies, the Harvester novels are superb for their portrayal of remote parts of the world. In a sense, the "road" books are espionage travelogues.

The espionage novel of the late 1970s reflects the somewhat unclear patterns of international politics. Some of the contemporary works choose the Russians or Chinese as the antagonist but more often a terrorist organization or an individual evil genius is the source of menace. Frequently the time period is moved back to a time in recent history when an obvious enemy existed; usually World War II is chosen and the Nazis become the antagonists. In many books a present problem has its roots in Nazi Germany.

While the three main streams of spy fiction still exist in pure form, the predominant pattern is now somewhat different. The books receiving most attention are long, complex novels of suspense intended to be mainstream novels with an international political theme. This trend is best represented by Frederick Forsyth with *The Day of the Jackal* (1971) and Robert Ludlum, who has several works like *The Scarlatti Inheritance* (1971).

In the immediate future one can expect an increasing merger between the realistic school and the heroic school with an heroic agent operating in a realistic atmosphere. Unless there is a sudden change in the political situation, the antagonists will become even more diverse and the tendency to reach back to World War II may intensify. An alternate way of achieving the clarity of issue that seems necessary for effective espionage fiction would be a shift in the nationality of the protagonist to one which has clear-cut enemies. There have been some experiments in this direction but there is no present trend evident.

Although the espionage novel is fairly vital in the late 1970s, there are few signs that this will be an important period in the development of the genre. Many of the outstanding authors of the last three decades are still writing but there are few new craftsmen of equal talent to replace them. A totally new direction for espionage fiction could revitalize a now somewhat overworked genre but no such development has yet appeared. After a long period of intense interest in espionage and intelligence operations, we may look for a drop in that interest and a falling off in the number and quality of espionage novels in the years immediately ahead. (pp. 71-82)

> *G. Jay Rausch and Diane K. Rausch, "Developments in Espionage Fiction," in* Kansas Quarterly, *Vol. 10, No. 4, Fall, 1978, pp. 71-82.*

Jerry Palmer on the hero of the spy thriller:

The focal point of the thriller, its central contribution to ideology, is the delineation of a personality that is isolated and competitive and who wins because he is better adapted to the world than everyone else. This superiority is incarnated in acts that are deliberately and explicitly deviant, and yet justified. The individuality, the personal worth of the hero is presented as inseparable from the performance of actions that in any other circumstances would be reprehensible; yet at the same time the 'circumstances' are a fictional construct, designed to justify the pleasure that the reader derives from the representation of such acts.

Jerry Palmer, in his Politics and Deviance, *1973.*

Andy East

[*In the following excerpt, East surveys trends in serial spy fiction of the 1960s, 1970s, and 1980s.*]

Fact Seduces Fiction. This revised equation of popular fiction would conceivably apply to the various genres present today. Apart from the expected demand of escapism from the paperback racks, the reader either consciously or unconsciously seeks some form of character identification. Taking these two elements into account, how else better to explain the popularity of the secret-agent series thriller of the sixties?

The suggestion of a continuing spy protagonist of that tumultuous era inevitably recalls the relationship between Ian Fleming and James Bond—which contributed significantly to the conception of uniting the reader and the author's creation. Still, how did the recurring "provocateur" evolve into such a dominant figure during the 'sixties and hence into the present day? By its immediate connotation, the archetypal espionage plot relies to some extent on world politics. Fact Seduces Fiction.

The British release of the first James Bond film, *Dr. No,* in 1962 produced this commentary from English critic Ian Johnson in *Films and Filming:*

> Identifying our snob sex, and violent wish-thinking is a good purgative. But make no mistake about it, Bond is as much a thug as his opponents beneath his beguiling charm. The only difference is he is on our side.

Acknowledging the obvious differences between the Bond novels and films, Johnson's observation typifies the climate of the 'sixties, which spawned the amoralistic spy myth of the Cold War epoch.

Without delving extensively into global geopolitics, the spy fiction of the Cold War was dictated by two post war realities:

1. The suspicious power triangle of the U.S., U.S.S.R., and Red China, especially in the years from the end of the Korean War to the intensification of the Vietnam conflict.

2. The recognition of the atomic threat, arising from Hiroshima as well as the first atomic test near Alamogordo, New Mexico in July 1945.

These staggering postwar effects drastically altered the fictional secret agent in the moral sense, ranging from the hedonistic (Bond) to the cynical (Len Deighton's shadowy anti-hero) to the irrevocably weary (le Carré's George Smiley and Alex Leamas). The patriotism manifested during the two world wars was superceded after 1953 by the disturbing Cold War trappings mentioned above.

1953 signalled the British publication of *Casino Royale,* Ian Fleming's initial James Bond thriller, and it is from this point that the Cold War spy novel, as it came to be defined in the 'sixties, was properly originated.

Not surprisingly, Bond's principal predecessor has been universally accepted as "Sapper's" Bulldog Drummond. However, looking at the scope of the Bond saga two decades after Fleming's death, with five extant additions by Kingsley Amis and John Gardner, Agent 007 seems more comparable to the late Van Wyck Mason's Colonel Hugh North—of the U.S. Army's G-2.

In a fashion similar to Bond's development from *Casino Royale* to John Gardner's *Role of Honor* (1984), Van Wyck Mason introduced North as a captain in *Seeds of Murder* (1930) and crowned his career in 1968 with the highly technological *The Deadly Orbit Mission.* Achieving the rank of colonel by the early days of the Cold War, North survived the imminent Asian peril of the late 'thirties (*The Singapore Exile Murders,* 1939) to the immediate postwar climate in Europe (*The Dardanelles Derelict,* 1949) to the apocalyptic conception of atomic conquest (*Secret Mission to Bangkok,* 1960). Displaying a smooth narrative manner and a sharply defined sense of plotting

and topicality, Mason's classic series of intrigue endured for nearly forty years. Mason consistently transcended North beyond the political concerns "of the moment" without politicizing his books.

In what might be termed the passage effect in spy fiction, Mason richly deserves credit for establishing the perplexing line between escapism and reality. If Mason hadn't broken new ground with North, the Cold War series thriller would have likely failed to attain the celebrity status associated with the 'sixties.

Thus far, I have attempted to identify the basic elements of Cold War series spy fiction with the objective of outlining the era in which it came to power. This brings us to the James Bond series, specifically the differing reactions in the U.S. and Britain.

The postwar atmosphere in Great Britain was one of desolation, resulting from severe economic and military losses sustained during World War II in Europe and the Pacific. The colonial idealism that had motivated pre-war England was savagely consumed by the haunting ironies of the Cold War, notably Britain's decline in global prestige in the early 'fifties. The exotic world of sophistication and dangerous living Ian Fleming created for James Bond in *Casino Royale* evoked such a passionate response with the British reading audience that they instantly regarded 007 as a symbolic saviour of traditional English values—portrayed from the viewpoint of the Cold War.

Bond's early success in Britain convinced Pan Books of his mass appeal, and, by 1957, *Casino Royale* became the first Fleming thriller to appear in paperback in the U.K., to be quickly followed by *Live and Let Die* (1954), *Moonraker* (1955), and *Diamonds are Forever* (1956).

Even Fleming himself was not prepared for what 1958 held for him. By this time, Fleming had acquired approximately 1,250,000 readers in England alone, and in a venomous attack on Bond's sixth appearance in *Doctor No* (1958), British critic Paul Johnson in *The New Stateman* protested: "I have just finished what is, without doubt, the nastiest book I have ever read." Persisting in his high-minded assault, Johnson concluded that he was on to "a social phenomenon of some importance." Johnson theorized that the popularity of the Bond books resulted from "our curious postwar society, with its obsessive interest in debutantes, its cult of U and non-U, its working class graduates educated into snobbery by the welfare state . . . a soft market for Mr. Fleming's poison."

Bond's acceptance in the U.S. was an entirely different proposition, for, despite strong support from the likes of Raymond Chandler and Max Lerner of the *New York Post,* Fleming experienced a difficult time in securing a strong foothold in the American market during the mid- and late-'fifties.

By 1960, Macmillan and Viking Press had enjoyed only moderate hardbound success with Bond, although *From Russia, With Love* (1957) became Fleming's first bestseller, and no fewer than three domestic paperback houses, Popular Library, Perma Books (a subsidiary imprint of Pocket Books during the 'fifties) and the New American

Library, had featured Agent 007 in the mass market. Up to this point, all three concerns had failed to repeat Pan Books' success with the Fleming thrillers.

Agent 007's fortunes in the U.S. were destined to change in March 1961 when it was revealed that President John F. Kennedy was a devoted Fleming fan. Three years had passed since New American Library reprinted seven of the first eight Bond books as Signet paperbacks (*Diamonds are Forever* surfaced under the Signet banner in November 1961), and, curiously, not one of them had entered into a second printing.

Shortly after the Kennedy disclosure, Jay Tower, publicity director for New American Library at the time, said:

> He wasn't doing very well in this country up to then. We couldn't understand it. . . . He had all the ingredients. We thought he should sell very well to American readers of suspense. . . . We decided to really push the books. We had a sales conference and planned new covers. . . . A few weeks later we had fabulous good fortune. President Kennedy said he loved Fleming. . . . Then Fleming made Jackie Kennedy's list of books. . . . Everybody under the sun wanted a Fleming book.

Dr. No premiered in London in October 1962, the same month that the Cuban missile crisis portended atomic war. The rich Jamaican locales of Sean Connery's first celluloid foray as Agent 007 offered a perilously satisfying proximity to Castro's Cuba. The ideal marriage of escapism and reality revealed itself to a global audience. The Cold War spy series genre was properly launched. Fact Seduces Fiction.

Bond had evolved from a respectable cult figure to such a dynamic phenomenon by 1965 that Ian Fleming's posthumous *The Man with the Golden Gun* (New American Library) sold 100,000 copies in the four months following its publication in August 1965, earning it the distinction of being Fleming's bestselling Bond novel.

There was an inclination in certain publishing circles during the 'sixties to assert that the series spy thriller, apart from those in the le Carré-Deighton mold, was a stylized reflection of the James Bond format. An examination of several of the early espionage series *inspired* by Ian Fleming, however, will reveal each to be as distinctive in its own right as Bond was in his.

As this study will illustrate, the marketing strategies employed by various U.S. publishers determined the direction of Cold War-era spy fiction, much to the dismay of the more high-minded literary critics.

The original hardback-to-paperback reprint efforts, at least initially, formed stronger links with Fleming. Nowhere was this more apparent than with Desmond Cory's Johnny Fedora series, for it actually *preceded* Ian Fleming's James Bond by two years. *Secret Ministry,* Cory's first Fedora adventure, was issued by Frederick Muller, Ltd. in Britain in 1951. Regrettably, no American publisher expressed an interest in Fedora until 007 rocketed into the galaxies of espionage in the early 'sixties. As a result,

Undertow (1962) was the first Fedora entry to appear in the U.S. sector, published by Walker in 1963.

Characterized by a compelling plot involving the search for a sunken Nazi U-Boat on the Gibraltar Straits, *Undertow* was evaluated by many critics as a slick imitation of Ian Fleming's *Thunderball* (1961). This contention was strengthened when New American Library reissued the book as a Signet mystery in July 1965—in the thick of the 007 explosion and during the production of *Thunderball,* starring Sean Connery as Ian Fleming's lionized "provocateur."

An ironical twist materialized in Cory's favor, however. New American Library featured a defense of the Fedora series on their Signet paperback edition by the late Anthony Boucher, the definitive suspense critic for the *New York Times Book Review* until his death in 1968. Boucher's contempt for James Bond was one of the worst-kept secrets in the annals of cloak-and-dagger fiction.

> Desmond Cory seems to me to accomplish in *Undertow* precisely what Fleming is aiming at. This is a sexy, colorful, glamorous story of intrigue and violence, complete with spectacular setpieces . . . and even a torture scene. And it is written with finesse, economy, humor and full inventive plotting. For my money, Johnny Fedora, professional killer for British Intelligence, more than deserves to take over James Bond's avid audience.

This major critical recognition proved to be as valuable to Cory as the more highly touted Kennedy publicity had been to Fleming. It was also one of the more vivid demonstrations of the "heir to the James Bond throne syndrome" manifested among suspense reviewers during the period. Later espionage series evaluations would emphasize similar qualities in the works of such authors as James Leasor and Philip McCutchan.

New American Library went on to reissue *Shockwave* (1964—U.S.; published in the U.K. as *Hammerhead* in 1963) and *Johnny Goes South* (1959—Britain; 1964—U.S.) in 1965 and 1966, respectively. In 1968, Universal-Award commenced their distribution project for most of the remaining Cory-Fedora efforts, often under alternate titles. *Intrigue* (1954), for instance, was unmasked as *Trieste* in 1968.

Boucher's support of the Fedora books served to define them as suspenseful tales of intrigue, logically plotted and suitably exotic without Fleming's commercialized trimmings. Throughout the fifteen-book saga, which concluded with *Sunburst* (1971), Cory canvassed a comprehensive geopolitical landscape. In such early Fedora books as *Secret Ministry* (1951), *This Traitor, Death* (1952), and *Johnny Goes North* (1956), Cory concerned himself with the venemous Nazi villian of the dawning postwar world.

Beginning with *Johnny Goes South* and *Johnny Goes West* (both 1959), Cory explored in considerable depth the deceptions of the Cold War. Cory's Fedora thrillers of the 'sixties, including the aforementioned *Undertow* and *Shockwave,* as well as the more gripping *Feramontov* (1966) and *Timelock* (1967), penetrated the sadistic machinations of Soviet master spy Feramontov in the blood-stained shadows of Franco's Spain.

Undertow and *Timelock* were recently reissued as part of Walker's new British mystery paperback program, along with two of Cory's non-Fedora entries, the classic *Deadfall* (1965) and *The Night Hawk* (1969).

William Haggard seemed destined to follow the enigmatic path of Ian Fleming when *Slow Burner* (1958), the first tale in the exploits of Colonel Charles Russell, was published. The British suspense audience rallied enthusiastically around these erudite mysteries concerning the Security Executive, an exclusive military intelligence body situated within the bastions of Whitehall. Its objective was the global preservation of British interests through diplomatic channels.

Having achieved staggering success with Ian Fleming, New American Library reprinted *Venetian Blind* (1959) in 1963 and would feature five additional Haggard entries by 1967, namely *The High Wire* (1963), *The Antagonists* (1964), *The Powder Barrel* (1965), *The Hard Sell* (1965—U.K.; 1966—U.S.), and the aforementioned *Slow Burner*. Haggard never gained a large following in the U.S., although American critics lavished praise on the author's studied expertise in the intricate ways of Whitehall.

Haggard's unique series concept, depicting Russell as the chief of the Security Executive rather than an intrepid operative, found its basis in John Buchan. Russell was portrayed as worldly, calculating, and immensely knowledgeable in the subtle underworld of diplomacy. The typical Russell plot generally focused on rich, polished industrial and political figures, or often valued scientists—all of whom encountered potentially destructive crises against the authentic background of the Cold War. Relying on this precise narrative manner, Haggard transcended both the realism of le Carré and the action of Fleming. *The High Wire* (1963), however, ventured more into the Bondian school with Alpine settings reminiscent of Ian Fleming's *On Her Majesty's Secret Service* (1963).

Haggard's series has matured with the unsettling political realities of the 'eighties, and Russell has enjoyed much-deserved success in the mass market through several current Walker paperback editions.

James Leasor's Dr. Jason Love thrillers was yet another series of intrigue in the Buchan mold, with the author's emphasis on the most hypnotic locales in the world. The first entry in the series, *Passport to Oblivion* (1964—U.K.; 1965—U.S.), proved to be a decade before its time. Dr. Love is dispatched to Teheran by British Intelligence under the respectable cover of attending a malaria conference—to locate a missing agent. The spy fiction of the Cold War rarely mined the mysteries of the Middle East for plot substance. Here Leasor probed uncharted terrain with a plot encompassing critical oil treaties, the Sheik of Kuwait, and a formidably placed Soviet agent in Teheran. In an ominous way, *Passport to Oblivion* pointed to the more explosive period of détente.

Love's term was a brief one, consisting of six books and a short-story collection. Three of the Love novels never appeared on domestic ground.

The disturbing quality of *Passport to Oblivion* was masterfully amplified when the novel's film version, retitled *Where the Spies Are* (1966), appeared in the midst of Bond fever, along with the likes of *Thunderball* (1965), *Our Man Flint* (1966), and *The Silencers* (1966). David Niven superbly translated Leasor's recalcitrant spy to the screen in an altered setting that was, to say the least, prophetic—Beirut.

John Gardner's *The Liquidator* (1964) was understandably misinterpreted as a James Bond parody in the form of Brian Ian "Boysie" Oakes, a former British Army sergeant who gains the callous reputation as "L" or "The Liquidator" for British Intelligence's Department of Special Security. Secretly, Oakes contracts his sanctions to an ex-undertaker and is horrified at the secret agent's ultimate luxury-airplane travel. The Oakes thrillers emerged as parodies of the secret agent *myth* in which Gardner cynically penetrated the disciplined expertise of the sophisticated man of action. Although this seems a precarious precedent for the author who would eventually inherit the mantle of Ian Fleming, Gardner endowed Boysie Oakes with an almost indiscernible seriousness that prepared him for the tongue-in-cheek nature of his Bondian assignments.

Rod Taylor was perfectly cast as Gardner's reluctant spy in *The Liquidator* (1966), which honored the style of Gardner's unconventional thesis.

British author Stephen Coulter worked with Ian Fleming in the Kemsley Newspaper Syndicate after World War II, and, perhaps to his discredit, he supposedly provided the research on European gambling houses which Fleming needed to write *Casino Royale*. This experience resulted in one of the best Bond imitations, the Charles Hood series, which Coulter penned under the pseudonym James Mayo. Hood was presented as freelance operative, although his activities were restricted to the Foreign Office, Special Intelligence Security (S.I.S.), and an exclusive British industrial consortium known as "The Circle." Coulter managed to surpass Fleming in some respects with his delineation of Hood as a man of advanced cosmopolitan pursuits, notably in the art world. The Hood series consisted of only five titles, and of them, the initial entry, *Hammerhead* (1964—not to be confused with the 1963 Desmond Cory thriller) progressed Fleming's basic premise with more fully realized refinements of *Casino Royale* and *Thunderball.*

By 1965, the dimensions of the flourishing spy phenomenon exceeded expectations, and the appearance of two new series, both featuring provocative *femmes fatales,* graphically illustrated the Bondian experiments before them.

Peter O'Donnell's Modesty Blaise was introduced as a comic-strip heroine in 1963 and was prominently ushered into the literary world by Doubleday in 1965 with a spy thriller bearing her name. The *Chicago Tribune* lauded Modesty as "Bond's counterpart with cleavage" and O'Donnell established Modesty as the ultimate fantasy woman—worldly, resourceful, and ensconced in mystery as a result of her early years as a refugee in the postwar Middle East. O'Donnell spiced each successive Blaise adventure with an equal measure of action and sex. Despite persistent criticism of Modesty's comic-strip image, the series has endured into the 'eighties, from *Modesty Blaise* (1965) to the recent *The Night of Morningstar* (1983). (pp. 23-8)

By contrast, James Eastwood's brief series chronicling Magyar-American agent Anna Zordan was marked by a taut atmosphere of realism. In her first mission, *The Chinese Visitor* (1965), Anna was persuaded to enlist in a clandestine British Intelligence unit after her parents were savagely murdered by a German assassin. Eastwood christened Anna with a vindictive quality that was conspicuously absent from the Blaise books. During her limited term, Anna averted a nuclear hijack plot in *Little Dragon from Peking* (1967) and in *Diamonds Are Deadly* (1969) infiltrated Britain's violent political sphere of the late 'sixties. It was 1967 before Dell reprinted *The Chinese Visitor,* and, coupled with the myth accorded to Modesty Blaise, the mass saturation of espionage fiction by this time forced Eastwood to forfeit a well-deserved audience.

As early as 1966, the secret-agent genre was evidencing signs of stagnation, and it was becoming increasingly difficult for authors to conceive salable series characters.

Andrew York proved to be an exception, judging from the debut of Jonas Wilde in *The Eliminator* (1966). Combining the notion of Agent 007's license to kill with Johnny Fedora's freelance status, York's Jonas Wilde developed as an extremely amoralistic operative, with the designated code name "The Eliminator." York's pulsating style and gifted sense of topicality elevated the series above its numerous competitors during the late 'sixties. Wilde survived into the mid-seventies with ten representative titles.

An earlier series, Philip McCutchan's Commander Shaw, stands out from the other members of the Bondian group, given its emphasis on nuclear sabotage against British interests. Although the first entry, *Gibraltar Road,* was distributed in Britain in 1960, the series wasn't launched in the U.S. until 1965 by way of Berkley-Medallion paperback editions.

Throughout the series, which ended in 1971 with *This Drakotny.* . . . McCutchan maintained a consistent line of credibility with his nuclear-oriented themes. However, in a later book, *Skyprobe* (1966—U.K.; 1967—U.S.), McCutchan examined the excesses of Fleming and le Carré. The plot involves the feared threat to Skyprobe IV, a U.S. spacecraft consigned to test the awesome possibilities of future moon exploration. Amidst the spectacular progression of Skyprobe IV in the narrative, Shaw's loyalty to the Special Services, the department of Naval Intelligence he serves as an agent, is questioned, and McCutchan adroitly blends science fiction fantasy with uncompromising realism—a formidable feat which has yet to be encored.

Several prominent writers who entered the espionage genre managed to enhance their already celebrated positions.

John Creasey was already well known for his numerous mystery series when he created the Dr. Palfrey series under his own name. The series was actually an extension of his earlier Department Z saga, which had earned him enormous popularity during World War II. This sequel series dexterously integrated the elements of espionage and science fiction, such as in *The Terror* (1966), which details the strategic course of a missile armed with an apocalyptic warhead destined for England. In retrospect, the Palfrey series can be credited for legitimizing the alliance of espionage and science fiction in the suspense genre.

Mike Hammer personifies Mickey Spillane's notorious image as a mystery writer, but his Tiger Mann spy thrillers, commencing with *Day of the Guns* (1964), have engraved their own mark as espionage fiction. Comprised of four titles, the series featured a cynically lethal protagonist in the classic Spillane tradition, the placement of the U.N. as an effectively continuous plot device, and of course the author's talent for compelling the reader to turn the page. If any cloak-and-dagger character ever deserved to be "recalled" into the 'eighties, it is Mickey Spillane's tough, grim contribution to the Cold War annals of intrigue and deception.

Before James Bond achieved mass acceptance in the early 'sixties, two spy series tested the notion of an operative assigned to a specific global sphere. A concept of this nature unquestionably required a writer with skillful narrative ability. In this respect, Simon Harvester (pseudonym of the late Henry St. John Clair Rumbold-Gibbs) and Gavin Black (Oswald Wynd) proved their talents beyond anticipated limits.

Unsung Road (1960) signaled the introduction of Simon Harvester's Dorian Silk, and throughout this exceptionally readable series the author offered an incisive view of Afro-Asian politics that often touched upon the uncertainty of the world's most incendiary settings. *Assassins' Road* (1965) concerns Silk's pursuit of an elusive master terrorist, "The Prophet," whose activities in the Middle East threaten to trigger *Jihad* or Holy War. Despite the stock inclusion of "Road" in each entry title, the series continued until 1976, constantly reflecting contemporary and often anticipating future geopolitical themes. Since the author's death in 1975, Walker has reissued several Silk thrillers in their British Mystery paperback project.

Gavin Black's Paul Harris series emanated a higher degree of specialization than Harvester's, given the character's "beat" in Southeast Asia and Malaya as a shipping executive frequently employed by the C.I.A. Beginning with *Suddenly at Singapore* . . . (1961), the Scottish-born author concentrated on the economic aspects of the Cold War, often emphasizing Red China as a global menace. Black's series persisted beyond the Cold War, one of the more recent thrillers being *Night Run from Java* (1979).

It has taken thirty years for the paperback original to reach a level of respectability in the "literary world," and yet, ironically, the prosperity associated with the spy series fiction of the sixties can be linked to this format. The hardback-to-paperback reprint efforts defined the genre with an identifiable form; the paperback original missions explored the possibilities.

The general evolution of the paperback spy thriller can be analyzed through the espionage fare of Fawcett-Gold Medal Books, the paperback original division of Fawcett Publications (now owned by Ballantine Books). In 1955, Fawcett entered the intrigue market with two series that established the boundaries of the archetypal paperback secret agent.

Displaying a prolific output before it was fashionable, Edward S. Aarons sketched the audacious Cold War operative with his portrayal of C.I.A. operative Sam Durell in *Assignment to Disaster* (1955). Aarons was perhaps the first practitioner of paperback espionage to effectively utilize the notion of the globe-trekking "provocateur," especially in the context of the turbulent locales which challenged his abilities.

In *Assignment: Ankara* (1961), an airplane on which Durell is traveling is sabotaged by the Russians near the Soviet-Turkish frontier. This Durell mission is set during a period of the Cold War when U.S.-Soviet tensions were edging perilously toward the Cuban missile crisis.

As the series progressed, Aarons tested Durell with professional crises, as exemplified in *Assignment: School for Spies* (1966) in which Durell is forced to leave Europe after being accused by the C.I.A. of treason. *Assignment: Moon Girl* (1967) advanced Aarons into the Creasey galaxy of espionage science fiction in a plot focused on a Russian-Chinese girl's foray to the moon.

Many disciplined devotees evaluated the "Assignment" designation on each successive Durell title as an indication of formularization. The series has endured into the present, however, nearly a decade after Aarons's death in 1975. Will B. Aarons has continued the saga since 1977, with *Assignment: Death Ship* (1983) the latest addition to the series.

Stephen Marlowe's Chester Drum was unique among the cloak-and-dagger heroes of the 'sixties in that he was a private detective rather than a secret agent. Drum's Washington-based office altered the complexion of the series, and, during the course of his thirteen-year career, beginning with *The Second Longest Night* (1955), Drum could be found in the most obscure Arab shiekdoms or in the Cold War-ravaged alleys of divided Berlin. Marlowe (mystery writer Milton Lesser) retained the first person ploy indigenous to the P.I. caper, but in this new environment he added a new dimension to the espionage format that would be perfected by later contenders.

Donald Hamilton emerged as *the* definitive master of Marlowe's innovation with his bestselling Matt Helm series, which was initiated in 1960 with *Death of a Citizen* and *The Wrecking Crew*. Narrated in the first person, the Helm books changed the rules for the paperback spy series thriller, for Hamilton gave his readers seasoned expertise in gun and photographic lore, feverish action, and menacingly conceived plots.

The Silencers (1962), the fourth book in the series, concerned the elements of an elusive enemy agent known as Cowboy, a critical microfilm, and an underground atomic test near Alamogordo, New Mexico. Still regarded as Hamilton's classic Matt Helm novel, *The Ambushers* (1963) adroitly fused the machinations of an insidious Nazi war criminal based in Northern Mexico with a Soviet missile smuggled out of Cuba. The series' strongest recommendation was the character of Helm himself; the first-person framework permitted Hamilton to inject some Hammett-style cynicism into his creation. Interviewed by Otto Penzler for his *The Great Detectives* (1978) mystery authors' profile, Hamilton offered this comment on Helm:

> [T]he fundamental conflict that, I feel, makes Matt Helm Matt Helm; a conflict I set up deliberately for one book, that still seems to intrigue people as I now tackle the nineteenth volume in the series. It can be stated very simply: "a)— He's actually a pretty good guy. b)—He kills."

That *one* book, *Death of a Citizen,* provided considerable insight into Helm's shadowy background. During World War II, Helm served in a secretive assassination squad based in Europe, "the wrecking crew," and later became a successful outdoor photographer and Western novelist. After his "official" discharge from the U.S. Army in 1945, he married a New England girl, Beth, taking up residence in Santa Fe, New Mexico, where he pursued his selected postwar profession. By 1960, Helm was a respectable family man with three children. But the unexpected return of his wartime ally, Tina, and the death of a mysterious Spanish woman in the bathroom adjoining his photography studio generate a sequence of lethal events that result in the dissolution of his family and his reinstatement into "the wrecking crew." The organization's chief, known only as Mac, reassigns him the code name by which he was known during the war: Eric.

Helm has never looked back since 1960. Donald Hamilton's twenty-first mission for Matt Helm, *The Infiltrators,* appeared in June 1984.

Dan J. Marlowe's Earl Drake series distinguished itself from even Stephen Marlowe's Chester Drum with the uncompromising depiction of a callous criminal in *The Name of the Game Is Death* (1962), in which Drake was named Chet Arnold. After becoming totally disfigured during a violent car chase across Florida, Arnold received extensive plastic surgery and a new identity—Earl Drake. Seven years would pass before Drake would blaze paperback covers again, which occurred in *One Endless Night* and *Operation Fireball* (both 1969). Beginning with *Flashpoint* (1970—reissued as *Operation Flashpoint* after Marlowe earned the Mystery Writers of America Edgar for best paperback mystery), Drake firmly established himself as a freelance secret agent in a new series of "Operation" books, culminating with *Operation Counterpunch* in 1976. Although marketed as espionage fare, the series frequently featured elements of the avenger genre.

By 1963, Fawcett had been successfully "playing" the spy market for eight years, and, with the introduction of Philip Atlee's (James Atlee Philips) Joe Gall—"The Nullifier"—in *The Green Wound* (1963), the publisher's espionage series library completed its definition of the format.

Cast in the same grim mold as Donald Hamilton's Matt Helm, Joe Gall arrived on the scene with a more dangerous background than Helm's. Gall's dossier includes a term as an airplane courier in the Far East during World War II, commando duty in pre-Castro Cuba, and a fervent sympathy toward Egypt's Gamal Abdul Nassar. After successfully executing a 1963 assignment in an obscure Southern town, Gall acquires a lethal reputation as a contract killer for a clandestine U.S. intelligence outfit known as "the agency."

The Silken Baroness was issued a year later, and, possessing another phenomenal spy series, Fawcett identified future entries with the dossier stamp of "Contract" (i.e., *The Paper Pistol Contract*). This served to complement the tradition evidenced in earlier Fawcett espionage series, such as Edward S. Aaron's "Assignment" designation and the "Drum Beat" imprint on Stephen Marlowe's last five Chester Drum novels. By 1967, the first two Gall thrillers had been reissued with "Contract" affixed to each title. Fawcett honored Gall's contract until 1976 and a mission appropriately entitled *The Last Domino Contract.*

The early books intensify in savagery as Gall's history unfolds. *The Death Bird Contract* (1966) examines the diplomatic consequences of U.S. involvement in Southeast Asia and a mysterious political figure angling for the position of Undersecretary of State to the Far East. *The Star Ruby Contract* (1967) finds Gall in Burma masquerading as the owner of a contract aviation service on a critical assignment to drive Chinese Communist troops out of the region.

The entire Gall series was suddenly withdrawn from print in 1977, after which time Atlee has yet to resurface in the action market.

Fawcett-Gold Medal meticulously outlined the landscape of the paperback secret agent, and their bestselling achievements were invaluable in carving a tangible identity for the burgeoning spy genre. Simple stated, Fawcett contended that the paperback "provocateur" must be: (1) adventurous, (2) sensual, (3) worldly, (4) skilled in certain arts, and (5) patriotic.

It was now 1964—the year of the blockbuster film version of Ian Fleming's *Goldfinger* and NBC's *The Man from U.N.C.L.E.*—and the burgeoning intrigue genre was advancing in new directions.

Book packager Lyle Kenyon Engel recognized the possibilities of the spy novel, and, after successfully concluding negotiations with the copyright owners of classic detective Nick Carter, Engel transformed the legendary mystery figure into a secret agent. Engel envisioned Carter as an American James Bond, and, at this point, Nick Carter—Killmaster for N-3—was incarnated in *Run Spy Run* (1964).

The series was initially represented by Universal Publishing & Distribution—Nick Carter launched the firm's new Award imprint—until 1977, when Universal ceased operations. During this thirteen-year period, a variety of authors, ranging from the masterfully prolific Michael Avallone to such "writers-in-training" as Martin Cruz Smith

(*Gorky Park*) to virtual unknowns scribed the Universal-Award efforts. By 1977, the series tallied over one hundred titles, with sales exceeding 20,000,000 worldwide.

A year later, Charter Books acquired the series, continuing the basic format devised by Engel. Under the guidance of (then) executive editor Michael Seidman, and associate editors Sybil-Pincus, Pat Crain and Nikki Risucci, Charter reissued a number of the Universal-Award titles between 1978 and 1981 (such as *Istanbul* [1965] and *Macao* [1968]) while assigning new entries to both established and fledgling writers. Approaching the two-hundred-title mark, the series has survived the recent takeover by Berkley, although there seems to be a measurable decline in quality from the early Charter days.

In a very real sense, the original Universal-Award Carter series destroyed the myth that a durable series character had to be supported by a flamboyant writer-celebrity. The series has often been attacked on the basis that it lacks a definite style and, more specifically, that its multi-author complexion endows it with an assembly-line quality. The overwhelming success of the series, however, under both the Universal-Award and Charter banners immediately transcends any such criticism.

Collectively, Engel, Universal-Award, and Charter induced a credible atmosphere of topicality throughout the Carter saga. Red China figured dominantly in the early books, noticeably in the person of N-3's murderous Cold War nemesis, Mr. Judas, in *Run Spy Run* (1964), *Danger Key* (1966), and eight other Carter-Judas confrontations, and other non-Judas missions such as *Macao* and *Operation Moon Rocket* (both 1968). Post-Cold War assignments espoused the intrigues of the Soviet Union and their radically-oriented Arab allies. Not surprisingly, aeronautics has played an integral role in the Carter thrillers of the 'eighties, as exemplified by *Solar Menace* (1981).

By 1965, the paperback original series spy novel was a seasoned genre veteran, although a few surprises awaited passionate devotees.

Norman Daniels is, unquestionably, one of the most accomplished paperback writers in the history of American publishing. Working with his wife, gothic novelist Dorothy Daniels, he has penned over two hundred books in the areas of mystery, spy, and war fiction, novelizations, and, more recently, family sagas. Daniels began his career in the pulps and created a series character named Black Bat, which preceded Batman.

Daniels's John Keith series bowed in *Overkill* (1964), which trailed ambitiously on the path blazed by Nick Carter's *Run Spy Run*. Two additional Keith thrillers, *Spy Ghost* and *Operation K,* were prominently displayed on the paperback racks by October 1965. The Keith series emerged as one of the more inventive of the 'sixties. Producing eight titles by 1971, Daniels conceived Keith as an operative for A.P.E. (American Policy Executive), a global intelligence body which *officially* didn't exist.

In 1967, Daniels launched a second series of intrigue, this one featuring wealthy playboy-businessman Bruce Baron, whose Hong Kong-based interest masked his activities as a C.I.A. agent. The series consisted of only two titles, *The Baron of Hong Kong* and *Baron's Mission to Peking* (both 1967). After concluding the Baron dossier, Daniels went on to scribe two novelizations of TV's *The Avengers* in 1968 and 1969.

Bill S. Ballinger was renowned as a top-flight mystery writer by the time he initiated his Joaquin Hawks series. Commencing with *The Spy in the Jungle* in 1965, Ballinger deployed the Spanish-Indian Hawks in Southeast Asia in this unusually suspenseful series. Besieged by U.S. involvement in the region, the American reading public may have found Ballinger's contribution to Cold War intrigue decidedly too "topical," for it ended in 1966 after only five books.

Generally, the realistic dimension of spy fiction was ignored by the paperback original sector. However, David St. John's Peter Ward series authentically depicted global C.I.A. operations, derived from the author's twenty-year term as a "Company" man. Between 1965 and 1967, Ward would be dispatched to Europe, India, the Orient, and Southeast Asia, as represented by *On Hazardous Duty* (1965) and *One of Our Agents Is Missing* (1967). New American Library reissued their six titles of the series (after 1967, the series was published in hardcover by Weybright) in 1974 to publicize the identity of "David St. John"—E. Howard Hunt—and his involvement in Watergate.

The majority of the 'sixties paperback spy series reverberated the shockwaves of the Cold War, rarely daring to venture beyond this historical perimeter. An exception to this norm was James Dark's Mark Hood series.

Dark focused on global nuclear proliferation, and to effectively convey this theme he devised Intertrust, a world power consortium comprised of the U.S., Great Britain, France and the U.S.S.R. The organization, based in the diplomatic Mecca of Geneva, committed its resources to the aversion of nuclear power-mongering.

The series was not without its Bondian influences, however. Intertrust's top American agent, Mark Hood, was even more specialized in his pursuits than James Bond. Serving as an executive officer on a destroyer during the Korean War, Hood claimed proven expertise as a scuba diver, seasoned practitioner in the martial arts, world-class competition race-car driver, successful freelance magazine writer, and qualified doctor. Hood shared several of his assignments with Intertrust's Richard Hannay-style British agent, Tommy Tremayne, and Murimoto, his Japanese martial arts confederate.

Of the twelve Hood books, no fewer than four were set in the Far East, with locales including Singapore, Hong Kong, Macao, Tokyo, and Lop Nor, Mongolia. Dark frequently focused on Red China as a megalomaniacal global threat and conceived plots that chillingly reflected the nuclear fear of the Cold War . . . and beyond. *Come Die with Me* (1965), the first in the series, centered on a plot to reinstate Nazism through the use of biological warfare. The penetration of a strategically critical missile base provided the crisis in *Assignment Tokyo* (1966), in which Hood displayed his mastery of the martial arts.

The later Hood books touched upon the newly discovered alliance of espionage and science fiction. *Spying Blind* (1968) concerns an aeronautical magnate's calculated hijacking of a Soviet moon probe as it approaches Earth. Participating in the Monaco Grand Prix, Hood is lured into the scheme on the magnate's resplendent yacht.

Taking their cue from Mark Hood, Universal-Award developed the Peter Winston "The Adjusters" series in 1967, using the same author-character concept they had employed for Nick Carter.

Winston commanded an elite spy corps, "The Adjusters," concealed within an impenetrable Georgetown mansion. The series adequately presented nuclear proliferation themes in the fashion of the Mark Hood books, and ended in 1969 after only five entries.

Michael Avallone's Ed Noon materialized as a private detective in *The Tall Dolores* (1953), but fourteen years later the multi-faceted author transformed his splendid creation into "Spy to the President." As the notion suggests, the new Noon plots contained elements of the apocalyptic. The books manifested the classic Avallone wry humor, and in his new incarnation Noon radiated more cynicism than in his pre-intelligence days.

1968 signified a major turning point for the paperback spy series thriller. Its popularity was plummeting toward oblivion. Excessive saturation of espionage fare since 1965, coupled with the changing face of the Cold War, outmoded many secret agent species of the period. To counter this trend, Universal-Award distributed Don Smith's Phil Sherman "Secret Mission" series, issuing four titles alone in 1968: *Secret Mission: Peking, Secret Mission: Morocco, Secret Mission: Prague,* and *Secret Mission: Corsica.*

Smith probed the Cold War in its more complex phases, concentrating on the volatile global locales to which C.I.A. agent Sherman was summoned. *Secret Mission: Prague* (1968) proved to be prophetic. Sherman is assigned to confiscate a multi-million-dollar cache of weapons in Prague which are intended for a massive racial conspiracy in the U.S. This entry surfaced in the midst of intense racial strife in America and the Soviet invasion of Czechoslovakia. Although no longer in print, the Sherman series lasted for eleven years, with twenty-one books.

Otherwise, the waning genre was boosted in 1968 by inventive series that eclipsed the Cold War. Jack Seward's first book in his Curt Stone series, *The Cave of the Chinese Skeletons,* was published in Japan in 1964 but, four years later, Tower reprinted the spy-mystery while offering two new adventures, *The Eurasian Virgins* and *The Frogman Assassination.* Stone was an American P.I. based in Tokyo since the mid-fifties, and he often found himself battling the Chi-Coms in situations stretching from valuable Japanese war treasures to the lucrative sex market in the Orient.

Don Von Elsner's Jake Winkman series actually began in 1963 under the New American Library banner with *How To Succeed at Murder Without Really Trying.* After Universal-Award published *The Ace of Spies* (1966), however,

NAL reissued the first book in 1967 as *The Jake of Diamonds,* followed in 1968 by *The Jake of Hearts.* Winkman was a championship bridge player who managed to engage himself in the more subtle aspects of espionage.

Sam Picard's *The Notebooks* (1969), another Universal-Award property, introduced an anonymous secret agent in the manner of Len Deighton's shadowy operative—replete with first-person narrative but devoid of the latter's technological trappings. Picard deals with an insidious conspiracy in *The Notebooks,* in which a seemingly innocent photograph results in four deaths. The author's gripping style covered themes that confirmed the passing of 007's reign. Picard's elusive operative returned in two 1971 entries from Universal-Award, *Dead Man Running* and *The Man Who Never Was.*

The unprecedented acceptance of Don Pendelton's Mack Bolan in 1969 clearly indicated that the general action market was entering a new era. Although Mack Bolan—"The Executioner"—wasn't initially featured as an espionage agent, Pendelton's accomplishments chartered the course of intrigue for the coming decade.

Alan Caillou's Cabot Cain is an excellent example of the post-Cold War "provocateur." The foundation for Cain was as recognizable as his predecessors; Caillou placed him in Department B-7 of Interpol. Cain was well versed in the Bondian arts, and the action was suitably paced. This series distinguished itself from earlier contenders with Cain's often startling transformation into an instrument of vengeance. Six Cain books appeared between 1969 and 1975, and one of the 1969 entries, *Assault on Ming,* earned Caillou the Mystery Writers of America Special Award.

Caillou is an appropriate author with whom to conclude our history on the paperback original spy series thriller. His later action saga, *The Private Army of Colonel Tobin,* began distribution in 1972 from Pinnacle Books—*the* definitive paperback publisher of espionage fare during the 'seventies and beyond.

If the efforts of, say, James Leasor and James Mayo were influenced by Ian Fleming, then it seems plausible that the realistic works of John le Carré and Len Deighton came about as a contemptuous reaction to James Bond. From this facet of the genre, the anti-hero was conceived.

John le Carré's first two thrillers, *Call for the Dead* (1961—U.K.; 1962—U.S.) and *A Murder of Quality* (1962—U.K.; 1963—U.S.), were published at the inception of the 007 craze and introduced George Smiley, a weary veteran of the British Secret Service who has endured the chaotic changes in the intelligence network since the end of World War II and his own tumultuous marriage. In contrast to Fleming, le Carré depicted Cold War-era Britain as a ravaged victim of World War II and its postwar aftermath—a nation tragically isolated from its vintage pre-war idealism.

Call for the Dead is a bitter, complex novel concerning the suicide of a British government official, Samuel Fennan, whose allegiance to the Communist Party during the 'thirties is leaked to the intelligence sector in an anonymous letter. Smiley is assigned to interview Fennan for security clearance and shortly thereafter Fennan commits suicide. Into this staggering plot, le Carré infuses the tortured character of Fennan's wife, Elsa, a Jewish survivor of the Nazi concentration camps; the intrigues of Dieter Frey, a German Jew who served as one of Smiley's most resourceful spy students before World War II; the significance of the East German Steel Mission in London; and a shadowy East German agent named Hans Dieter Mundt who figures in the machinations of *The Spy Who Came In from the Cold* (1963—Britain; 1964—U.S.).

Le Carré's first two books were well received, but with otherwise scattered mass market attention. *The Spy Who Came In from the Cold,* however, secured the author his global reputation and altered the complexion of the spy novel as it is defined today.

This undisputed espionage classic contains one of the best-known plots in all fiction and a timeless theme—futility. Le Carré's principal character, Alec Leamas, is a seasoned agent for The Circus who secretly loathes his profession. Delineating Leamas as an irretrievable human casualty, le Carré was able to depict an agent's superiors as his most insidious adversaries and his designated enemy in the field, in this case Hans Dieter-Mundt, as an unexpected ally. Not since the early fiction of Eric Ambler has the theme of ambiguity been so defiantly expressed as in le Carré's *The Spy Who Came In from the Cold.*

Le Carré was the first spy novelist to effectively employ the divided East-West settings of Berlin as the primary locale in an espionage thriller. In this book le Carré masterfully manipulated the city's fragmented state to make a venomous commentary on the deteriorating structures of the social organization, be it the family, the corporation, or the Secret Service.

Smiley was relegated to a supporting role in *The Spy Who Came In from the Cold* and *The Looking Glass War* (1965), and, had le Carré not defined George Smiley in *Call for the Dead* and sketched his world of solitude in *The*

Robert Donat, Peggy Ashcroft, and John Laurie in Alfred Hitchcock's The 39 Steps.

Spy Who Came In from the Cold, Smiley's resurgence in *Tinker, Tailor, Soldier, Spy* (1974), *The Honourable Schoolboy* (1977), and *Smiley's People* (1980) would not have been possible. More recently, le Carré has examined the disturbing realities of the Palestinian issue in *The Little Drummer Girl* (1983), in which Smiley is not featured.

The Spy Who Came In from the Cold was adapted into a classic espionage film in 1965, starring Richard Burton as Alec Leamas and British character actor Rupert Davies as George Smiley, fifteen years before Sir Alec Guiness perfected the role in *Tinker, Tailor, Soldier, Spy* (1980).

In a *Life* magazine article on the realistic spy novel, critic Conrad Knickerbocker offered this commentary on the genre, after having read le Carré's *The Spy Who Came In from the Cold,* Len Deighton's *Funeral in Berlin* (1964), and Adam Hall's *The Quiller Memorandum* (1965):

> The key to their popularity rests in the yearnings of their readers. Baffled by Vietnam, . . . they feel increasingly overwhelmed by the vast forces that now shape events. Along came John le Carré and his colleagues with literate styles to soothe educated consciences. It's comforting to find through Leamas that a spy is just folks, another nebbish from next door caught in the grind. The new spy thrillers reduce the Cold War to a human scale.

Len Deighton's popularity is somewhat surprising, considering his acumen for intricate technological detail. But his place in the history of the Cold War spy thriller speaks for itself. *The Ipcress File* (1962—U.K.; 1963—U.S.) was an instant sales and critical success. Before delving into his works, it might be interesting to look at the impressions of his books.

Reading Len Deighton can be linked to examining the facets of a Tiffany diamond. The beauty is obvious from the initial encounter, but, to comprehend its depth, each side must be evaluated separately. In other words, to fully comprehend the substance of a Deighton novel, additional readings may be required.

Where le Carré concentrated on the desolation of The Circus, Deighton accented the cynicism of an agent who might conceivably approach a perilous mission differently than Bond. In its section devoted to Michael Caine's superb portrayal of Harry Palmer (in *The Ipcress File* [1965], *Funeral in Berlin* [1966], and *Billion Dollar Brain* [1967]), the celluloid counterpart of Deighton's elusive hero, *Whodunit?* (edited by H. R. F. Keating) offered this interpretation of the author's selection of an obscure protagonist: "In the books, cunningly, it is never stated that he is each time the same individual. . . . In this way, he can be stretched over an inordinate length of contemporary history."

In his five series spy thrillers of the Cold War era, *The Ipcress File* (1962—Britain; 1963—U.S.), *Horse Under Water* (1963—Britain; 1968—U.S.), *Funeral in Berlin* (1964—Britain; 1965—U.S.), *The Billion Dollar Brain* (1966), and *An Expensive Place To Die* (1967), Deighton adopted a dossier format which emphasized the political or technological aspects of global intelligence. It is this single characteristic of Deighton's work that motivated later advocates to be more perceptive of the mechanics of the spy trade. *The Ipcress File, Funeral in Berlin,* and *The Billion Dollar Brain* featured top-secret appendices, each authentically simulated, which contributed to the plot. Deighton's second thriller, *Horse Under Water,* which involved a currency cache for renegade Nazis hidden on a sunken German tanker off the Portugese Coast, contained a code translation document, a high-level Cabinet letter (dated 1941), and an "Eyes Only" file register. These latter elements were introduced before the first chapter, which indicates the importance Deighton assigned to these devices throughout his books.

Funeral in Berlin has endured as Deighton's most celebrated novel. Deighton's spy is ordered to execute the defection of a valued Russian scientist, and, within the plot, Deighton constructs perhaps the definitive commentary on the East-West tensions of the Cold War, next to le Carré's *The Spy Who Came In from the Cold.* It is in this pulsating thriller that Deighton's hero first encounters Colonel Stok, a high-ranking K.G.B. strategist, and their interaction symbolizes the rising fever of U.S.-Soviet hegemony following the Berlin Wall crisis. Deighton's integration of elementary chess rules as chapter headings in *Funeral in Berlin* prove to be a master stroke on the author's part—in addition to complementing the East-West allegory throughout the book.

The Billion Dollar Brain is regarded as Deighton's most technologically oriented thriller. Assigned to penetrate a fanatically right-wing organization, Facts for Freedom, Deighton's spy uncovers a megalomaniacal blueprint by its head, Colonel Midwinter, to devise a computerized war strategy against the Warsaw Pact powers. His first objective is to launch an invasion of the Soviet republic of Latvia.

The futility of le Carré is poignantly reflected in *An Expensive Place To Die.* The major Western intelligence networks engage in a paranoid battle of wits over the political value of an American nuclear genius and a Chinese Communist scientist. The battleground for these intrigues is Paris, and, in a bitter narrative style more indigenous to détente than the Cold War, Deighton portrays the City of Lovers with a prophetic sense of desolation. Unquestionably, *An Expensive Place To Die* is Deighton's understated classic of Cold War espionage.

Deighton's shadowy creation resurfaced in *Spy Story* (1974), and, after several contemporary non-series thrillers (*Catch a Falling Spy*—1976) and memorable espionage novels rooted in the dark authenticity of World War II (*XPD*—1981), the renowned author has advanced further into the le Carré sector, as typified by the recent *Berlin Game* (1984).

By its very nature, the realistic spy thriller of the Cold War era possessed limited expansion potential. Indeed, after le Carré and Deighton sculpted their enigmatic landscapes, it was generally accepted that the territory had been appropriately covered. From 1965 to 1967, however, two ambitious authors conceived inventive ploys for the format—Adam Hall and Ross Thomas.

Adam Hall's *The Quiller Memorandum* (1965; published in Britain as *The Berlin Memorandum*) was written in the le Carré vein, but manifesting explicit political overtones. Quiller, a contentious British agent for a cryptic intelligence outfit known as The Bureau, is ordered to continue a terminated operative's mission of unearthing a former Nazi as a prelude to locating a parasitical neo-Nazi coven in Berlin. In his review of this masterful bestseller in the *New York Times Book Review*, Anthony Boucher defined the points which separated Hall from his peers:

> A grand exercise in ambivalence and intricacy, tense and suspenseful at every moment, with fascinatingly complex characters, unusual plausibility in detailing the professional mechanics of espionage and a genuine, uncompromising toughmindedness comparable to le Carré's.

Hall intensified Quiller's callous quality in *The 9th Directive* (1966) and *The Striker Portfolio* (1968) and has moved his solitary character into the present day in the excellent *The Peking Target* (1982).

The Quiller Memorandum garnered both the Mystery Writers of America Edgar and the French Gran Prix Littérature Policière in 1965.

Boucher offered an equally incisive evaluation of Ross Thomas's *The Cold War Swap* (1966; issued in Britain in 1967 as *The Spy in the Vodka*), the author's first of three books about Mac McCorkle and Mike Padillo:

> A good, nasty LeCarresque plot of opportunism and betrayal within the intelligence service, a well-observed background of Berlin and Bonn, some violent surprises and a fine individual tone of wry, tough humor in its telling.

The last phrase in the above segment serves to explain the appeal of this brief series. Although Thomas canvassed le Carré-style themes, he presented a pair of tongue-in-cheek protagonists within this seemingly confined framework.

Thomas received the Edgar for *The Cold War Swap*, which involves a contrived "swap" to retrieve two American mathematicians who defect to the Soviet Union. Within this plot, Thomas conceived McCorkle and Padillo with equal conviction, revealing the experiences during World War II that led to their encounter in the mid-fifties when they established Mac's Place, a German bar frequented by the diplomatic elite of Berlin and Bonn.

Padillo and McCorkle operated together for five years in *Cast a Yellow Shadow* (1967) and *The Back-up Men* (1971). *The Cold War Swap* was reissued by Pocket Books in 1976 and more recently in a Harper-Perennial paperback edition.

The realistic spy novel generated some interesting derivative efforts, influenced for the most part by Len Deighton.

Martin Waddell's *Otley* (1966) introduced us to Gerald Arthur Otley, a manipulative thief working in the antiques market. Completing an assignment to "obtain" a hunchback figurine, Otley soon finds himself caught up in the machinations of a devious network, the I.C.S. Anthony Boucher praised Waddell for his superb delineation of the contemptuous British anti-hero of the late 'sixties and his

Hitchcockian gift for invoking uncertainty. The Otley series continued until 1969 with *Otley Pursued* (1967), *Otley Forever* (1968), and *Otley Victorious* (1969).

Otley was adapted into an outlandish 1968 film starring Tom Courtenay as Waddell's mocking operative. That same year, Pocket Books reissued *Otley* and *Otley Pursued* with graphic covers suggestive of the author's unconventional thesis.

Martin Woodhouse was certainly well qualified to write a spy series, given his term as the first lead writer for *The Avengers* when that popular espionage program aired on British television in 1961. Woodhouse's Dr. Giles Yeoman was an aeronautical scientist whose aircraft projects often propelled him into the most sensitive areas of military secrecy. Similar in its parody vibrations to Waddell's Otley series, Woodhouse concentrated on Britain's scientific pursuits during the Cold War era, a reflection of the author's accomplished background in aeronautics and computer technology. *Tree Frog* (1966), the first Yeoman thriller, concerned the development of a pilotless reconnaissance plane.

Philip McAlpine performed as one of the most lethal agents for Britain's Department 6—despite an insatiable attraction to hashish. Adam Diment conceived McAlpine in *The Dolly, Dolly Spy* (1967), and, following the path previously traveled by Waddell and Woodhouse, this avant-garde British novelist infiltrated his operative into the psychedelic wave of the late 'sixties. McAlpine's mission in *The Dolly, Dolly Spy* was to accompany a sadistic Nazi war criminal from Egypt to the U.S. Heralded as "Ian Fleming's successor" in the *New York Times Book Review*, Diment's bizarre mixture of espionage and the "mod" attributes of the late 'sixties was praised in 1968 as the new direction for the waning spy genre. The series ended in 1971, however, after only four books, and Diment has not appeared in print since that time.

The constant threat of Armageddon, not to mention numerous conflicts and border skirmishes in the Middle East and Central America in recent years, has insured the popularity of the spy series thriller. The secret agent continues both to fascinate and mystify readers, and, with the universality achieved with the works of Ian Fleming and John le Carré, among others, the spy is one of the few figures in contemporary fiction who has transcended diverse cultures and creeds. It is unfortunate that the passionate reader can go no further than to merely identify with this enigmatic myth—the Spy in the Dark.

Fact Seduces Fiction. Or does it? (pp. 28-40)

> *Andy East, "The Spy in the Dark: A History of Espionage Fiction," in* The Armchair Detective, *Vol. 19, No. 1, Winter, 1986, pp. 23-40.*

ESPIONAGE FICTION/FORMULA FICTION

Lars Ole Sauerberg

[In the following excerpt, Sauerberg examines the features that distinguish espionage fiction as a literary genre.]

THE FORMULA IN ACTION: OBSERVATIONS ON READING DYNAMICS

As formula fiction is a kind of fiction characterized by an exceptionally high degree of genre uniformity, the reader's recognition of formula elements plays an important role for his reactions. It is true that no two readers' responses to a literary text, not even to formula fiction, are quite alike, because the readers' individual attitudes, educations and general backgrounds will differ. But in the case of formula fiction such differences can be assumed to be of minimal significance for the readers' reactions, as it is in the nature of the formula not to allow the reader too much scope for individualistic approaches. Instead, reactions will differ according to the readers' degrees of familiarity with the formula.

The situation in which a reader encounters a given formula for the very first time is not typical, as it exists only once for each formula. Nor is the opposite situation, in which the reader rereads a particular formula story. There is a difference between comparing an unknown story with one's idea of the formula and repeating a reading of the same story. The tension which there is between the formula and the variations that constitute the individual story—and which makes the story worthwhile reading—disappears at a second reading, and there are seldom facets present in formula fiction which will justify repeated readings. The situation in which the reader reads an unknown story and compares it with a formula that he is already familiar with as he goes along must be assumed to be the usual one.

The reader's recognition of a specific formula in a story depends on various kinds of signal. He will often know even before opening his book which formula to refer it to. He may either know the name of the writer, which will function as a kind of trademark, or he may recognize the name of a series hero, whose name is brandished on the cover along with the writer's. If not signalled externally, the nature of the formula will be made plain very early in the reading process, usually in the opening pages.

Any narrative which, like the secret-agent story, is characterized by a central conflict presupposes the existence of two characters to embody the conflict: the hero and his adversary. According to the conventions of the specific formula, the conflict may involve only these two antagonistic roles, or it may involve others as well. If the conflict pattern of the secret-agent story—an obvious instance of the dichotomy structure—is thought of as antithesis, then each side may be thought of as metonymy. On both sides all character roles are personifications of national interests. The hero—and his adversary—do not refer directly to their communities, but through their superiors whose allegiance is to national interests rather than to hero and adversary. In this hierarchy of loyalties the roles of the hero's or the adversary's helper or helpers are characterized by a thrice-removed allegiance to national interests, through hero/adversary and through superiors.

As the genre builds on political conflict on an international scale the reader will attempt to place the characters, in the order of their introduction, according to their supposed allegiances. When the reader is aware of the identity of the hero even before opening the book, he will want confirmation of his expectations about the hero's usual characteristics. Recognizing the adversary may not be as simple as recognizing the hero. It depends on the degree to which the puzzle element is based on concealed identity.

For the illustration of these observations on the reading dynamics of a formula genre I have chosen the opening page of Fleming's first story [*Casino Royale*]. I have assumed that the reader is one who is fairly familiar with the formula, as this seems to be the typical situation.

The reader's expectation of incipient conflict is confirmed at once in [*Casino Royale*]. The first paragraph presents a scene in a casino at three in the morning:

> The scent and smoke and sweat of a casino are nauseating at three in the morning. Then the soul-erosion produced by high gambling—a compost of greed and fear and nervous tension—becomes unbearable and the senses awake and revolt from it.

To most readers, a casino must be assumed to be a romantic place, at the same time alluring and forbidding by its aura of chance, sudden prosperity and equally sudden poverty, desperation, etc. Consequently, a casino has the very qualities of the alien land of the genre, which is where the conflicts are acted out.

In the second paragraph the reader is introduced to James Bond, whose reaction of fatigue is one with which we can immediately sympathise, because it is felt as perfectly normal under the circumstances: 'James Bond suddenly knew that he was tired'. The reader's beginning feeling of empathy is at once reinforced by Bond's reflections on his situation. His coolness and common sense is the way we would like to react in a similar situation:

> He always knew when his body or his mind had had enough and he always acted on the knowledge. This helped him to avoid staleness and the sensual bluntness that breeds mistakes.

Whereas Bond keeps himself at a distance from the oppressive but enticing atmosphere of the casino, Le Chiffre, to whom the reader is now introduced, seems to be in complete agreement with the place. In contrast to Bond, Le Chiffre has a repulsive effect on the reader:

> Le Chiffre was still playing and still, apparently, winning. There was an untidy pile of flecked hundredmille plaques in front of him. In the shadow of his thick left arm there nestled a discreet stack of big yellow ones worth half a million francs each. Bond watched the curious, impressive profile for a time, and then he shrugged

his shoulders to lighten his thoughts and moved away.

The reader's repulsion is due to several factors. The circumstance that the action is seen through Bond's eyes forces the hero closer to the reader than the object of observation, Le Chiffre. The difference between the values represented by the two men is clearly underlined in the associations of their names. There are effects on two levels: one of sound and one of semantics. There is no doubt that to most ears 'James Bond' sounds pleasant and harmonious, whereas 'Le Chiffre' has a harsh quality about it. On the semantic level, 'James Bond' suggests solidity by its very Englishness, and, in addition, associations are readily made to the security of bonds. 'Le Chiffre', however, suggests something about figures and cash, an immediate relationship with money which is, in many circles, not quite respectable. The impression of the names of the two men is an impression of something rather nice versus something repugnant. Also Le Chiffre's appearance at the table has the effect of repelling the reader. Against Bond's fatigue, Le Chiffre by his endurance seems superhuman, and the overtones of a clockwork nature evoked by his name are repeated by his ability to continue without any signs of exhaustion. In the description of the looks of Le Chiffre, his thick arms and curious profile probably add to the reader's negative reaction based on our usual prejudice against the non-average.

It is quite obvious that for the formula to work well there must be a positive interaction between the attitudes, behaviour and ideas expressed in the story and the reader's own. Unlike many novels, formula fiction does not attempt to suggest unique systems of values, but sticks to the expression of values currently accepted. Thus, in a passage like the one analysed just above, there is a double function. Apparently it is a regularly descriptive passage contributing to give the reader an idea of what is going on. At the same time, however, it functions to secure an agreement between story and reader, as it does not present innovative views but remains a reflection of concepts and attitudes typical of the majority of readers.

FORMULA PLOT AND VARIATION PLOT

When a cover blurb on a thriller tells us to expect an ingenious, amazing, etc. plot, the term plot is used in another sense than when we talk about the plot of, for instance, the secret-agent story as a genre. The difference between the two is a question of abstraction levels. A comparison of a large number of individual plots of thrillers reveals that also in the perspective of plot there is a rather simple formula according to which it is possible to describe recurrent plot elements of different thriller genres. Like all other formula elements the formula plot remains of conceptual validity only, which does not prevent it, however, from having a prominent status in the reader's general genre awareness and hence from forming an important part of the anticipations with which he reads a story.

It may seem a contradiction of my central hypothesis of the role played by the awareness of the formula for the response to thrillers that the reader will experience a given thriller as something unique. What I suggest is, however, that in formula fiction the 'distance' between our sense of

a lowest common denominator and concrete text—what Structuralists call the discourse—is 'short' in comparison with novel genres like the *Bildungsroman* in which there is also a typical genre-constituting structure, but of so loose a nature that it is hardly felt as a formula.

The difference between formula plot and variation plot—or discourse plot—in the persepctive of reading dynamics is that the reader will know about the general outline of a formula-plot phase—when it begins and ends and what kind of activity usually takes place in it—but not to what specific ends the actions of the fictional universe in a specific story are directed: in the secret-agent story the reader will expect a phase, to begin with, in which the hero is given his assignment, because that is part of the formula plot, but what exactly he is asked to do belongs on the level of the individual story, its variation plot.

Our sense of a limited number of phases which constitute the formula plot seems to depend on changes in the hero's situation radical enough for the reader to feel that there is a definite break with the immediately preceding situation. As plot may be defined as the temporal/causal development of relations, most frequently interpersonal ones, the smallest plot unit is to be found between two changes of such relations. Clearly, any paraphase of the plot of a narrative will not include all the plot units thus to be isolated; some are simply more important than others for the forward movement of a narrative. The sorting out of the units which are important and those which are not in a *novel* depends partly on a rather vague notion of the genre in question and its structural characteristics, partly on the way that we are able to compare every new minimal-change unit to the ones preceding it and thus to judge its plot significance. The process of reading is characterized by a current plot summary until, at the end of the reading, a summary including only the sufficient units may be formulated. The reading of a *formula story* implies an awareness of a finished plot summary, and consequently the reader is ordering his impression of minimal plot units according to his anticipation of the plot phases expected to follow, as well as to immediately preceding phases.

It is characteristic of the secret-agent story that, as in other kinds of formula fiction, the reader will have his idea of the formula plot consolidated by each new story he reads. He will soon discover that the incidents unique of each story can be inscribed within certain recurrent situations, and it is possible, by simple comparison, to establish the recurrent pattern. Furthermore, as the genre is an updated version of romance with its central element of quest myth, the recognition of plot phases is stimulated by the reader's sense of echoes from that dominant literary tradition in other well-known kinds of literature, such as folktales.

In the secret-agent story there seem to be six situations which, in the hero's perspective, mean radical change, and which are, furthermore, in agreement with romance: *assignment—departure—ordeals—conclusive ordeal—return—clarification.* This is the normal succession of formula-plot phases, but some of the phases show less stability in the sequence than others. The lack of stability seems to be in the nature of the formula plot and not attributable to changes made by the individual author for the purposes of this specific variation plot, and the temporal/causal logic of the formula plot is not disturbed by such changes. Whereas the departure appears regularly after the assignment, the return phase may appear before or after the conclusive ordeal or after the clarification. The return phase does not necessarily manifest itself in concrete terms as a journey home; it may sometimes exist only as an indication of the re-establishment of a connection to home. The difference between the natures of 'ordeals' and 'conclusive ordeal' is a matter of non-finality versus finality: in the plot situation of ordeals the hero is subjected to a number of 'tests' in which he may be successful or not, but in the conclusive ordeal the hero's side, but not always the hero himself, excels over the adversary. The clarification phase, if present, usually follows the hero's conclusive ordeal, but may coincide with it.

The six formula-plot phases form the matrix pattern from which individual variation plots can be generated. In its abstraction the formula plot is a known entity, but in the tension between the reader's knowledge of it and the application of this knowledge in the process of reading a story suspense may be created in different ways.

THE CREATION OF SUSPENSE

Suspense is, of course, not limited to thrillers. It is a structural device employable in all kinds of text—also in 'texts' such a those provided by the visual media—which depend on temporal/causal progression. However, suspense plays a far more prominent role in thrillers than in most novels, and it is even possible to categorize thriller genres according to typical suspense patterns.

Suspend means to hang up or to put out of action for while, and this is the way suspense works in narrative fiction. In his development of V. Propp's analysis of the Russian folk tale into a cognitive system, A. J. Greimas has defined the principle of suspense structurally as 'l'écartement des fonctions, c'est-à-dire par l'éloignement, dans l'enchainement des fonctions que constitue le récit, des contenus sémiques appartenant a la même structure de la signification' ('the separation of functions by distance in semic patterns which belong to the same structure of significance'). By sticking to the idea but discarding the Structuralist phrasing, the principle of suspense may be defined as the *prevention of immediate satisfaction of curiosity about plot issues through structural obstruction of the logic of temporal progression.*

In a recent treatise on the nature of narrative suspense Eric S. Rabkin has proposed a definition which I believe should be modified in accordance with the general observations I have made above on the difference between novel plot and formula plot. Rabkin's view is that:

> As readers, we concern ourselves with what has come before and what *will be* read, waiting to see how the next bit of text will compare with that which has preceded it. When the bit of text is a bit of plot, and when we are conscious of the waiting, we call the force that draws us through a narrative *suspense*. [Narrative Suspense]

My point is that when we read formula fiction we look as much forward as we look backward, perhaps even more. In a *Bildungsroman,* for instance, which, like the secret-agent story, bears resemblance to romance in its structure, we have only the vaguest sense of its ending. In the secret-agent story, however, we may be quite sure that the hero's side is going to win. With the exception of the fundamental definition of suspense as the raising of curiosity, the elements in the novel which create suspense are unique in each individual work. In formula fiction there are genre-determined 'rules' for the creation of suspense; we are able to say that within such and such limits, which exist on an analytical level less general than mere curiosity but still more general than the individual work, it is possible to anticipate how suspense will work.

Various thriller critics have expressed the opinion that empathy is a necessary premise of suspense, among them H. Brean who [in his *The Mystery Writer's Handbook*] suggests that suspense:

> . . . arises . . . from the vicarious doubt shared by the reader with the fictional actor as the outcome of the fictional intention. This sharing of doubt arises through emotional identification of the reader with the fictional actor.

But not all thriller genres seem to require the same degree of empathy as a condition of suspense. The formal detective story is a good example of missing empathy not in the least preventing suspense to work. The reader's dominant interest is to learn about the identity of the culprit, and that curiosity exists despite the probability that the reader will not be able to identify with the hero, as there are many elements in this figure that create distance rather than identification. And it is not necessary for the reader to identify, as the attractive element is the puzzle, not any one of the characters. But in the secret-agent story there is a certain need for empathy, because even if the puzzle element is present, it is not nearly so dominant as in the detective story. The central point of the reader's interest in the secret-agent story must be assumed to be in his curiosity to learn about the *ways* that the hero manages to get out of his various predicaments, which implies a temporary acceptance of the hero's perspective as his own. Hence the necessity of empathy in that genre.

The nature of suspense in the secret-agent story is, then, composed of three elements. There is the reader's awareness of the formula. There is the invitation to empathy in order to accept the microcosm for the duration of reading a specific story. And there is the structural obstruction which is the result of the author's licence to arrange his discourse as he wishes. All three elements are present in the suspense complex the result of which is the reader's inability to put down the book.

Structural obstruction may be created in a number of ways, but in reality they may all be considered variations of two basic arrangements of the individual story: *concealment* and *protraction*.

The puzzle element characteristic of the detective story is a result of concealment and protraction in interaction. The identity of the culprit is hidden until the end, and the accumulation of red herrings has the effect of protracting his identification. Whereas concealment is the author's deliberate withholding of information, protraction is [a] matter of stretching an issue and its result as much as may be tolerated.

Most often concealment and protraction interact, as in the formal detective story, but sometimes they occur in isolation. The adventure story, as I have loosely called the genre which includes writers like Alistair Maclean and Desmond Bagley, frequently relies on protraction only. Most adventure stories rely on a simple 'counting-down' progression of the plot: at the beginning of the story the reader is told that a bomb is to explode or a plane will crash in a specific span of time. Suspense is created by accounting for events with an eye on the clock, with progressive parallellism between actual time and time of narration, sometimes even with time of narration slower than actual time. Pure concealment is characteristic of much horror fiction, as the reader is impatient to learn about the nature of whatever dreadful thing threatens the hero.

Fleming relies more on protraction than le Carré and Deighton. Perhaps the best-known example is the golf duel between Bond and Goldfinger in [*Goldfinger*], but other stories, too, display this characteristic feature: the game of bridge in [*Moonraker*], the roulette in [*Casino Royale*] and Bond's 'obstacle race' in [*Dr. No*]. But concealment is not absent from Fleming's stories, although it is rarely used.

It is possible to subdivide protraction into *prolongation* and *shift*. A typical example of prolongation is found in the 'counting-down' device, whereas shifts occur when the discourse is broken abruptly, by sudden flash-back or change of setting, for instance, and then resumed later. Fleming prefers the prolongation technique; his stories, with few exceptions, progress fluently and logically in time and space. Deighton's discourse is characterized by sudden temporal and spatial changes, probably modelled on film technique, and the suspense effect comes from the reader's anxious wish to reconnect the logic of the variation plot with the formula plot. Without the almost epic pace of Fleming's stories, and without the abruptness of Deighton's, le Carré uses prolongation and shift to build up special effects, but on the whole he favours concealment. An example of prolongation may be found in the last part of [*Call for the Dead*], in which narration follows actual time when Smiley closes in on his prey, Dieter Frey. Also in the episode in [*The Spy Who Came in from the Cold*] when Leamas explains to Liz about the conspiracy planned by his superiors just before rushing to the Berlin Wall prolongation plays an effective role. Le Carré has used shifts more in his later stories than in his earlier. In both [*The Honourable Schoolboy*] and [*Smiley's People*] there are numerous *lacunae* between incidents, separated in time as well as in space, and the flash-back is likewise a narrative device he often resorts to. Le Carré's concealment technique may be illustrated by this passage from [*Call for the Dead*]:

> As he stood gazing at the little shepherdess, poised eternally between her two admirers, he realized dispassionately that there was another

quite different solution to the case of Samuel Fennan, a solution which matched every detail of circumstance, reconciled the nagging inconsistencies apparent in Fennan's character. The realization began as an academic exercise without reference to personalities; Smiley manœuvred the characters like pieces in a puzzle, twisting them this way and that to fit the complex framework of established facts—and then, in a moment, the pattern had suddenly reformed with such assurance that it was a game no more.

His heart beat faster, as with growing astonishment Smiley retold to himself the whole story, reconstructed scenes and incidents in the light of his discovery. Now he knew why Mundt had left England that day, why Fennan chose so little that was of value to Dieter, had asked for the 8.30 call, and why his wife had escaped the systematic savagery of Mundt. Now at last he knew who had written the anonymous letter. He saw how he had been the fool of his own sentiment, had played false with the power of his mind.

He went to the telephone and dialled Mendel's number. As soon as he had finished speaking to him he rang Peter Guillam. Then he put on his hat and coat and walked round the corner to Sloane Square. At a small newsagent's beside Peter Jones he bought a picture postcard of Westminster Abbey. He made his way to the underground station and travelled north to Highgate, where he got out. At the main post office he bought a stamp and addressed the postcard in stiff, continental capitals to Elsa Fennan. In the panel for correspondence he wrote in spiky longhand: 'Wish you were here'. He posted the card and noted the time, after which he returned to Sloane Square. There was nothing more he could do.

Le Carré's use of the concealment technique here depends on the versatility of the third person in narrative. The 'he' of the first two passages is quite close to the use of the third person in free indirect speech, in which there is virtually no difference between a 'he' and an 'I'. But imperceptibly this kind of 'he' gives way to a more objective third person, a figure whom we are only allowed to watch from the outside; a behaviouristic approach, as it were. Unless the reader has made a brilliant guess, he is now in an ambiguous situation: at the same time as he has established a relationship of empathy with the hero he is left in the dark about the actual working of Smiley's mind. With impatience the reader awaits the materialization of the hero's ideas.

Whereas it is relatively easy to change the status of the third person for the purpose of concealment, there is an almost paradoxical situation in the combination of concealment and the first-person perspective. As I observed above, either the hero must be presented convincingly as not completely informed, or the author must be able [to] suppress the logic that the hero by necessity knows all he is doing, the 'Roger-Ackroyd effect' (cf. Agatha Christie's detective story). Deighton employs both variations, but most frequently the first one, as in [*Spy Story*] in which it is part of the variation plot that the hero is used *because* of his ignorance (and similarly in [*The Ipcress File*]). The other variation appears in the following passage from [*The Ipcress File*]:

> I nodded, but for the first time I began to suspect that something odd was going on; from now on I was keeping my head down.
>
> The next morning I completed a little private task that took an hour of my time about once every two months. I collected a heavy manilla envelope from an address near Leicester Square, inspected the contents and mailed it back to the address from which I'd got it.

The technique is, in principle, like le Carré's in the passage quoted above: a move from an inside (mental) to an outside (action) perspective, a shift from motivation to report of behaviour. In this particular story Deighton is justified in his manipulation of the I-perspective, because the whole story is presented as the I's account of events to his minister. However, the reader hardly remembers this, and it must be assumed that the reader's reaction to the shift is one of wondering at the hero's mysterious doings rather than wondering at the logic of presentation. And it is not until some fifty pages later that the reader learns that the envelope contains the papers and money necessary for a personal emergency.

Deighton is very fond of a technique of style as well as of plot which I shall call the 'puncture technique'. It is an effect which depends on *surprise,* not suspense. His technique is to present a line of events as if the hero were in good faith and then suddenly to puncture it by revealing that the hero knew about the duplicity all along. Again the paradoxical nature of the 'Roger-Ackroyd effect' is probably suppressed by the reader's surprise. A passage from [*Funeral in Berlin*] may be used as an example. A girl nicknamed Sam has been taken out by the hero, and after a late-night supper they both go to Sam's flat. On letting themselves in, they discover that the place has been broken into:

> It wasn't hard to recognize the signs. Burglars open chests beginning with the bottom drawer, so that they don't have to waste time shutting each to get at the next. Sam stood looking at the mess—clothes everywhere and wine spilled across the rug. She trapped her lower lip under her teeth and flung it forward in a heartfelt monosyllabic obscenity.
>
> 'Shall I phone the police?' I asked.
>
> 'The police,' said Sam scornfully. 'You mean that your police in England won't trample around the place like idiots, ask a million questions and end up doing nothing?'
>
> 'They will,' I said. 'But they are very nicely spoken'. Sam said she would like to be alone.
>
> 'Whatever you wish,' I said, for I knew how she felt. When I got back to my flat I phoned Sam. She didn't seem nervous or too distressed.
>
> 'She seems O. K.,' I said to Austin Butterworth, after replacing the receiver.

> 'Good,' he said. Austin was sitting well back in my most comfortable armchair sipping my favorite whisky and being as modest as hell. 'Run-of-the-mill job,' he was saying. 'French window with slide bolts—child's play. People are so silly. You should see my place, that's really well protected against burglars'.

Although the surprise which is the effect of the puncture technique is not suspense, it may contribute to the creation of suspense by concealment, because it adds to the reader's sense of being fooled by appearances.

The difference between suspense by protraction and suspense by concealment has often been seen as a difference of literary quality. However, the quality of a given story hardly depends on the kind of suspense means employed, but on the way that all the elements of a story, suspense included, work together to form a whole.

ASSIGNMENT

There are stories which are secret-agent stories in all other respects, but which do not have a scene in which an assignment is given by a superior to the agent. This is often the kind of story in which the hero *accidentally* becomes involved in matters of international importance. However, in such stories there is a point at which the hero decides on or just realizes his involvement, and this point is the counterpart of the assignment proper which we find in the stories under consideration.

When the hero receives his assignment, this means a radical change of his own situation, and this is where the plot has its logical beginning. The variation plot, however, may be arranged in such a way that more or less important events precede the assignment.

When not putting the assignment phase at the immediate beginning of their individual variation plots, the three writers tend to use the same variation: the *medias-res* opening. There may be, however, two kinds of *medias res:* the one in which we find ourselves in the middle of the events that follow the hero's assignment and are thus part of the ordeals phase (as in Fleming's [*Casino Royale*]), and the one in which the events logically precede the intervention of the secret service but furnish the background of the hero's assignment. In the former the narrative technique is to make use of the flash-back to the assignment situation to reestablish the formula-plot pattern, but in the latter the information provided in the introductory 'loose ends' may be brought to bear on formula-plot situations until the very end of the story. With regard to the creation of suspense the loose-end technique allows the author to make a long-range suspense pattern, that is, a long distance between the 'semic patterns which belong to the same structure of significance', in contrast to the short-range suspense pattern of the flash-back variation. Le Carré's [*Smiley's People*] and Deighton's [*Spy Story*] are typical examples of the loose-end variation. Smiley's assignment to investigate the mysterious death of an *émigré* in London has no evident connection with the events preceding it: the history of a Russian woman exiled in Paris, and a handover of something in a boat on the Elbe near Hamburg in northern Germany. Only the facts that the people appearing here and the murdered man are all *émigrés* from the Soviet

Union, and that the teleological nature of literature makes the reader anticipate an order behind it all, connect the events with the assignment of Smiley. And the situation is quite the same in [*Spy Story*]. The reader—and the hero—does not know anything about the connections between the role played by the submarine at the very start of the story, the subsequent identity riddle experienced by the hero, and the hero's final assignment by his new American master, Schlegel, to assist him with the planning of war games. As it turns out, of course, all these disparate events are integrated elements of a highly sophisticated variation plot.

The reason why the logic of the formula plot—the presentation of the hero followed by his assignment—is only rarely practiced, even by the fundamentalist Fleming, must be seen as the wish to create suspense from the very beginning. If the simple model is used, suspense takes effect from the moment that the reader learns about the nature of the hero's assignment, and this is a highly dangerous procedure. The reader's interest must be aroused at once or he will put down the book. The assignment introduction must thus be cut very short, and the reader must be taken quickly to a point where he will long to know how the hero is to reach his goal. The assignment introduction relies on the creation of suspense by protraction, but a more efficent way to create suspense immediately is to employ either of the *medias-res* openings, as they add the element of concealment at once.

While Fleming uses all three opening possibilities, both le Carré and Deighton prefer the loose-end variation of the *medias-res* variation arrangement. But whereas the flash-back variation satisfies the reader's initial curiosity when the pieces fall into place with the hero's assignment, the loose-end technique does not necessarily give a similar satisfaction. With the flash-back the reader feels that a frame within which the action can take place has been established. The assignment phase in the loose-end opening means a point of orientation, but only in so far as the reader can say to himself that according to his formula expectations the plot has now started.

DEPARTURE AND RETURN

A distinction must be made between the geographical move made by the hero on receiving his assignment and any subsequent moves, except the return move. The hero's immediate post-assignment move and his final return move are formula-plot phases, and as such they are stable features. Any other geographical movements which may appear in a secret-agent story have their origins in variation considerations. I disagree with Bruce Merry's notion of 'global simultaneity' as a formula-plot element characteristic of the 'spy thriller'. He suggests that:

> At various different points on the map, events precipitate down a narrowing funnel to the plot's climax: this is the most important feature common to all spy narratives. Thus the structure of the thriller is seen to depend on sub-division and acceleration through well-sign-posted narrative co-ordinates in five continents. [*Anatomy of the Spy Thriller*]

Merry is right in so far as such shifts are frequently en-

countered in the genre, but that a global simultaneity is a regular occurrence is doubtful. However, this is only a minor objection. My main objection is that Merry does not here point to a genre characteristic, but to a characteristic of narrative fiction in general. Shifts in setting are among the most popular 'tools' with novelists as a means to create suspense by protraction: a development may be cut off, a character left in difficulties, etc. The reader longs to have the thread taken up again and is curious about the continuation. This simple explanation also makes it obvious why shifts in setting, often on a global scale, are so often resorted to by writers of secret-agent fiction.

Shifts in setting are, then, of structural as well as of thematic importance. If the shifts are made between England and various parts of the world, the thematic significance of the departure-and-return pattern is underlined. . . . [A] main characteristic of the secret-agent story is its distinction between the familiar and the unfamiliar. All quest literature, medieval romance and *Bildungsroman* alike, shows us a hero who has to leave home in order to go through his ordeals in order to regain control of the situation.

In the secret-agent story the contrast between the known, which is what the hero leaves, and the unknown, which is where the hero has to fight his ordeals, is expressed as a geographical shift, but the geographical shift symbolizes a move into a world whose main characteristic is a blend of fear and forbidden appeal, a world whose origins may be the more or less realized emotional potentialities in our minds.

The geographical shift in the secret-agent story is, frequently, a departure for a foreign country. With few exceptions, this is so in Fleming's and Deighton's stories, but le Carré makes a variation out of this feature. It must be remembered that the formula-plot situation is departure as such, irrespective of its concrete manifestation. The significance of the departure must be looked for in the changed conditions of life (fear, etc.) to which the hero must subject himself. Thus the departure for a foreign country is also really a variation, but the most usual one, because it offers a convenient opportunity of changing the hero's familiar conditions.

Le Carré's variation occurs in [*Call for the Dead*] and [*Tinker, Tailor, Soldier, Spy*]. In both stories Smiley stays on in London to carry out what he has been asked to do. It may be argued that there is no departure phase in these stories. However, this phase is present as Smiley has to give up his Chelsea address to move in with Mendel, his helper, in [*Call for the Dead*], and, in [*Tinker, Tailor, Soldier, Spy*], to confine himself to a modest hotel room with the files on which he bases his investigation. Despite the familiarity of London in both stories, the hero has become an alien to it, because it is no longer home to him, but suddenly menacing and insecure. Whereas the reader accepts the location in a foreign country as naturally alien, the idea of using London for this purpose is especially refined because it draws on the disfiguration of the familiar which we all know from, for instance, a nightmare.

The cases in which Fleming's and Deighton's heroes remain in Britain (Fleming's [*Moonraker*]) or return to it intermittently during an assignment (Deighton's [*The Ipcress File, Horse Under Water, Funeral in Berlin, Billion Dollar Brain, Spy Story,* and *Yesterday's Spy*] give the same impression of alienation as le Carré's London-based stories. Good examples are the pursuit scene in [*Moonraker*] where Bond races after Hugo Drax at break-neck speed through the southern suburbs of London, and the nightmarish prison in [*The Ipcress File*] which is supposed to be situated somewhere behind the Iron Curtain, but is really in London.

For the cycle to be completed, the departure must, eventually, be followed by a return. As to position, the return is not as stable as the departure, and as to realization, it may not occur as an actual journey home. The reason for this instability in comparison with the departure is probably that there is no need to emphasize the return to the well-known, because it is well-known, whereas the goal for which the hero leaves is intrinsically interesting. There is also the circumstance that whereas the assignment requires instant realization, the first part of which is the hero's hunting down his prey, the conclusion centres on conclusive ordeal and/or clarification. The return may be seen as a natural consequence of these and does not, therefore, require any emphasis. In Fleming's [*You Only Live Twice*], Bond returns to a Japanese island in a condition of amnesia after his successful operation on Blofeld's island. He has returned to the normality of quasimarital life, which signals clearly that a recognizable everyday world has been reestablished. It is enough that the reader knows that contact has been established (e.g. Bond's phone call home in [*Casino Royale*]) so that home, i.e. control of the situation, is dominant once more.

ORDEALS

Assignment and departure are formula-plot phases that occupy only brief passages in comparison with the plot phase of ordeals, a series of functionally identical events, which form the bulk of the secret-agent story. The difference between these ordeals and what I have called the conclusive ordeal is one of position as well as of intensity. As the term implies, the conclusive ordeal marks the termination of the hero's action, but the conclusive ordeal is also qualitatively different from the 'ordinary' ordeals.

The 'body' of the secret-agent story is the series of ordeals to which the hero must subject himself. This phase of the plot corresponds to the detective's gathering of evidence in the formal detective story. As in the detective story there is no limit to the number of functionally identical moves which a specific discourse may use. However, as the ordeals contribute to suspense by protraction, a succession of too many would mar the suspense effect rather than further it.

It is in the nature of longer narrative fiction to present a detailed and often panoramic picture of a number of inter-related events. In contrast to the compressed nature of lyrical poetry, narrative fiction is characterized by inclusiveness and breadth. This characteristic goes some way to explaining why the ordeals form the body of the secret-agent

story, in that this is the phase in which all the details and digressions are contained.

The word ordeal denotes a kind of activity to be seen as test of character and endurance. It may be difficult to realize that the *detective's* gathering of evidence is a test of his character and his endurance, as it can be objected that correct evidence is needed to convict. On the other hand, it must not be forgotten that the detective story is an artefact, not a realistic account of police work, and effects must be judged on literary premises. What appears as the fictional detective's conscientious work towards his goal, is, in the literary perspective, a building-up of an aspect of the hero's character which is best described by the word 'genius'. The reader admires the fictional detective for his incredible abilities of ratiocination, because as the series hero that the detective is, he repeats the testing of his genius by the series of ordeals in each new story.

In the secret-agent story the aim, on the level of its thematic significance, is not to confirm the hero's outstanding intellectual capacities, but to present the hero as generally capable (v. ch. 6). The fictional secret agent is a man who must be able not only to use his brains, like the detective, but also to manage all kinds of physical obstacles which may appear on his way. If the ordeals that the detective goes through are a test of intellect, the secret agent's ordeals are a test of brains as well as physical stamina, in other words, the whole man.

Whereas the activities of the fictional detective are directed towards a very definite goal, and the means employed to reach it, his power of ratiocination, never change, the fictional secret agent contributes to the—for himself—much vaguer goal of securing international status quo. And the means which must be employed are determined by the nature of the specific difficulties he is up against. His test of character and endurance must show him to be capable of overcoming a wide range of difficulties which require the general capabilities of the hero.

The literary predecessor of the fictional secret agent is the knight of romance, and the medieval knight is a figure especially suited for adventures whose nature cannot be foreseen: knighthood is not a profession, but a state of general preparedness.

In Fleming's stories there is a rather fixed progression pattern in the ordeal phase of the plot. After receiving his assignment Bond regularly leaves London and shortly after meets his future adversary. This first meeting is in no way physically violent, but it anticipates the conclusive ordeal in a symbolic way, for instance in the form of a game: roulette in [*Casino Royale*], bridge in [*Moonraker*], golf in [*Goldfinger*]. After these games there follow a number of episodes bearing on Bond's antagonistic relationship with his adversary, but not involving any actual confrontation. These episodes as well as the games prove Bond as a man of character and endurance. Only seldom does his success require cunning alone, but a combination of intellectual and physical force as in [*From Russia with Love*] in which he *pretends* to have been shot by Grant, the adversary's helper, in order to kill him eventually. More often Bond's success requires physical stamina rather than cunning, as in the bizarre obstacle race arranged by Dr No. It is characteristic of the ordeal pattern in Fleming's stories that Bond's last ordeal before the conclusive one is frequently a defeat: the torture scene in [*Casino Royale*], the bathroom-prison scene in [*Moonraker*], etc. This has a suspense effect, in that a concealment situation is created: not until late does the reader know how Bond is going to escape (Fleming's solution is frequently a *deux ex machina*, like the SMERSH agent in [*Casino Royale*]). But his failure also adds to our impression of Bond as not invariably successful and thus an average human being, which is important for retention of empathy. Furthermore the failure provides a background against which Bond's eventual success becomes more emphatic.

The pattern of ordeals in Deighton's stories resembles Fleming's to a considerable extent. The reason why this does not *appear* to be so is due to Deighton's characteristic manner of presentation with its many abrupt shifts in time and setting. In [*Yesterday's Spy*], for instance, there is the initial encounter with the future adversary, Stephen Champion, then a series of episodes originating in the antagonism between the two, but not involving any violent confrontations, and then the hero's preconclusive-ordeal episode in which he is led into an impossible situation by his adversary.

The ordeals phase in le Carré's stories cannot so easily be reduced to a formula as it can in Fleming's and Deighton's. There is too much variation. It is characteristic, however, that the ordeals phase, with one or two exceptions, is non-violent, but nonetheless requires a certain non-intellectual energy. This does not affect the structural and thematic significance of the ordeals. They still emphasize the hero's general capability and contribute to suspense by protraction.

Apart from the comparative lack of violence in le Carré's versions of this phase of the plot, there is the additional characteristic that the meeting with the adversary at an early point common in Fleming's and Deighton's stories is absent in le Carré's stories. In them the ordeals form a series of events which in many ways is similar to the detective's gathering of evidence in the formal detective story. The hero shows his capability first and foremost by his intellectual superiority, except in [*The Spy Who Came in from the Cold*] in which Leamas's ordeals consist of a passive subjection to rough treatment. But it must be remembered that Leamas tolerates his own suffering under the delusion that the plan of which he is a part operates on the assumption that the opposition may be defeated by purely intellectual manipulation. That Leamas himself is also defeated in the end does not change this double nature of his ordeals.

The ordeals through which the hero must pass before the conclusive ordeal are, as I have suggested above, significant in themselves as assuring the reader of the capability of the hero and as intensifying the suspense effect. But they are also part of a climactic pattern which reaches its apex in the conclusive ordeal, the moment of truth.

CONCLUSIVE ORDEAL

It is significant of this phase of the plot that the thematic content is the re-establishment of the international political *status quo*. For the purpose of this re-establishment the heroes' actions are vital, but the heroes as individuals are dispensable. As I see it, this is the essential thematic formula significance of the conclusive ordeal, because in this perspective it is possible to bring all the stories under consideration on a common denominator irrespective of happy or unhappy endings.

That the conclusive ordeal means the success of the national cause rather than the success of the individual secret agent is obvious not only in le Carré and Deighton, but also in Fleming.

It is typical of Fleming's conclusions that Bond is presented as a convalescent recovering from his struggle with his adversary. This trait is interesting because the vulnerability of the hero means a confirmation of his *human* status and thus re-connects him with home. But there are cases in Fleming's stories where Bond appears to be lost. This is so in [*From Russia with Love*] and [*You Only Live Twice*]. In the former story the reader is confused as he does not know anything about the outcome of Bond's having been poisoned by Rosa Klebb, his adversary. And in the latter story Bond is left in a state of amnesia, which may be read as a symbolic death. In both, however, there is no doubt that Bond has served his end: the action against him by Rosa Klebb is a simple one of revenge, and his amnesia is the result of the enormous impact of the explosion which means Blofeld's death. From both, however, he returns to action once more.

Le Carré stories have been much praised because they show the secret agent in a much more realistic light than usual in the genre. The unhappy ending provided by the sacrifice of Leamas in [*The Spy Who Came in from the Cold*] has been considered a good example of le Carré's realism. The realism, however, is due to tone and atmosphere rather than plot, which a comparison with Fleming will make clear.

The stories in which le Carré shows the defeat of the individual in the process of securing *status quo*, [*The Spy Who Came in from the Cold, The Looking-Glass War, A Small Town in Germany,*] and [*The Honourable Schoolboy*] are stories which resemble Fleming's [*From Russia with Love* and *You Only Live Twice*] in this phase of the plot. And as in Fleming's stories the national cause is successfully defended in all four. The reason why the reader feels more emotionally involved with a Leamas or a Westerby has to do with the author's presentation of these figures. We are, quite simply, much more interested because le Carré has made them into rounded characters whereas James Bond is unambiguously flat. The degree of sympathy felt for a character should not be mistaken for a more realistic plot, as this phase of the plot is similar in the two authors' stories.

The convalescence scene following the conclusive ordeal in many of Fleming's stories also has a parallel in some of le Carré's stories. The parallel, however, is in the function, that is, in the human status of the hero, rather than in the means by which it is presented. I am thinking of the *tristesse* which follows on all Smiley's successes. The pessimistic note on which le Carré's stories end is not in itself expressive of criticism of the secret agent's lot, and the realism which it may be taken to express is on a very general level, not restricted to the world of secret agents. It indicates the anti-climactic feeling known to most people on the completion of some task.

Unlike the ordeals leading up to the conclusive ordeal, the final ordeal in le Carré's stories often has an element of violence. In [*Call for the Dead, The Spy Who Came in from the Cold, A Small Town in Germany, The Honourable Schoolboy*] and [*The Little Drummer Girl*] there is bloodshed, whereas in [*The Looking-Glass War*], [*Tinker, Tailor, Soldier, Spy*] and [*Smiley's People*] there are tensions in the show-down on the brink of breaking into something physical.

Deighton is much concerned with the dispensability of the hero as an individual in some of his stories, notably [*Spy Story*] and [*Twinkle Twinkle Little Spy*], and in all his stories the instrumental significance of the hero outweighs his significance as a human being. The hero's own realization of his dispensability may account to a great extent for his egotistical and ironic attitude to his surroundings: he knows that in order to re-establish *status quo* and survive he must combine national and selfish interests, and the isolation resulting from his realization creates a certain distance.

All the conclusive ordeals that Deighton's hero goes through are marked by violence, and in this they resemble Bond's conclusive ordeals. But they differ from Fleming's variation patterns in that they stick to the kind of violence which the reader finds 'familiar', most frequently various kinds of gunfight. Fleming's preference for the fantastic and bizarre in this phase of the plot is well-known.

Whereas in the formal detective story the conclusive ordeal is identical with the clarification—the detective explaining the case to the assembled suspects—the secret-agent stories with a puzzle structure contain a plot phase in which the hero actually secures status quo and a plot phase in which the mysteries of the variation plot are explained to him/the reader.

CLARIFICATION

Julian Symons [in his *Bloody Murder: From the Detective Story to the Crime Novel: A History*] has suggested that:

> Spy stories, and thrillers in general, do stand apart from books that pose a puzzle to the reader. The latter kind of book asks questions about Who or Why or How, sometimes about all three put together, where the thriller or spy story frequently just tells us How.

This is, of course, only a rough distinction, but nevertheless it seems to do some fundamental injustice to the secret-agent story. I have proposed a pattern of formula-plot phases, of which I have placed 'clarification' as the last one. I have included this phase in the formula plot, because the greater part of the stories that I deal with here display some sort of puzzle which needs solution at the end. Admittedly, the puzzle does not play the part it does in the formal detective story, and often the puzzle is very simple. It may consequently be argued whether its presence in the genre is not a variation of the formula rather than a regular formula phase.

A clarification phase may, at a superficial glance, appear as the product of mixing different modern genres in order to obtain maximum suspense potential. That this is not so appears from an examination of a related genre like medieval heroic romance. It will be remembered that in *Sir Gawain* the hero escapes the axe of the Green Knight, and afterwards it is explained to him that everyone concerned has been under a witch's spell. If my hypothesis about the general thematic significance of the secret-agent story and related genres is correct, the ordeal structure, which is a series of How, and the puzzle structure, the Who and the Why, can be seen to supplement each other. Whereas the ordeal structure shows the reader a hero who is generally capable, the puzzle element offers to the reader an alien land existing on another, and abstract, level. When the hero has gone through his ordeals and secured the international political *status quo,* he has assimilated whatever threatened the balance according to his own assignment background, the national cause. With the clarification of the puzzle, the familiarization has also been manifested intellectually. The result is a maximum emphasis on the hero's familiarization of the unknown.

For the purpose of the familiarization theme, which is central to the secret-agent story as well as to romance, it does not matter whether the solution of the puzzle is made by the hero or someone else. In both cases the result is the same: the hero concludes his assignment in a state of complete enlightenment. In the formal detective story, however, it is necessary that the detective himself solves the puzzle, as the solution is completely dependent on his particular abilities. The re-establishment of the international *status quo* in the secret-agent story is not dependent on the hero's information level, but on the thematic perspective in which we see the hero's ordeals as a process of familiarization; it is the solution of the puzzle which is important, not the figure behind the solution.

Fleming, le Carré and Deighton do not rely on the puzzle element to the same extent, and Fleming's puzzle structures are simple compared with those employed by le Carré and Deighton. One puzzle, however, is always present in Fleming's stories: the Why of the adversary's motive. All Bond's adversaries are monomaniac in their pursuit of power. The puzzle based on the adversary's motive is also present in le Carré and Deighton, but not with the same prominence as in Fleming; it tends to be overshadowed by other puzzle structures.

A puzzle which is employed by all three authors may be termed the *identity puzzle*. In principle, this is *the* puzzle of the detective story. The detective works towards the identification of the real culprit among a number of potential culprits. In the secret-agent story it is the general rule that the identity of the adversary is known at an early stage, and the hero's efforts are directed at his destruction. But an identity puzzle may be introduced as a variation of the hero's ordeals.

Fleming makes use of the identity puzzle in [*Casino Roy-*

ale], his first story. As it turns out, Vesper Lynd, his helper during the greater part of the story, is a double agent, and this explains many of Bond's troubles. But the Vesper-Lynd puzzle is not really the kind of puzzle which is known from the detective story. In that genre it is made clear from the start that the search for the culprit forms the backbone of a story. In [*Casino Royale*]—and in *Sir Gawain* as well—the clarification comes as a surprise at the end. This technique is close to the *deus-ex-machina* solution. Le Carré, however, has used the puzzle in a manner which reminds the reader of formal detective stories. The best example is [*Tinker, Tailor, Soldier, Spy*] in which Smiley's assignment is to find a mole operating on top level in the English secret service. There are four possibilities, and like a detective proper Smiley gathers evidence so that eventually he is able to arrange a trap for the most likely suspect.

In le Carré's stories the hero is always the one who sees through to the truth, that is, the hero himself arranges for the clarification. This, of course, underlines his intellectual acumen at the same time as it places him firmly in the centre of events and emphasizes his individualism. Le Carré is consistent when he leaves it to the hero alone to sort out the threads of the puzzle, because in the ethical universe in which his heroes move, the individual is essentially responsible. Even Leamas in [*The Spy Who Came in from the Cold*] assumes personal responsibility when he accepts his own fate as a necessary risk when so much is at stake. Deighton's hero, however, does not assume responsibility in the same way. He is aware of his own position in the hierarchy, and many of his efforts are directed to measures which, in le Carré's universe, would be purely egoistical. The hero's realization that he has to defend himself first of all is based on his experience that the use of him is sometimes merely instrumental, and his function has to be explained to him after his conclusive ordeal. This is the case in [*Spy Story*] and [*Tinker, Tailor, Soldier, Spy*]. In Deighton's other stories the hero is able himself to see through puzzles which in [*The Ipcress File*] and [*Funeral in Berlin*] are identity puzzles built on the mole theme, and, in the remaining, variation on the motive puzzle: the minister's secret in [*Horse Under Water*], Harvey Newbegin's allegiances in [*Billion Dollar Brain*], Monsieurs Datt's mysterious activities in [*An Expensive Place to Die*] and Steven Champion's changed allegiance in [*Yesterday's Spy*].

Although the puzzle element is central to the plot pattern of the secret-agent story, it seems that there is a limit to its use. The limit is determined by the reader's formula expectations: the reader will expect an ordeal structure which is recognizable as a series of ordeals, and that is only possible if the variations are clearly ordeals which test the hero as the generally capable man. When the limit is overstepped, as may be our impression of, for instance, [*Tinker, Tailor, Soldier, Spy*] the hero is 'reduced' to personified intellect, a characteristic of the fictional detective, not of the fictional secret agent. When that happens, the reader is confused in his formula expectations, which makes him a distracted reader. On the other hand, too simple puzzles, in the manner of Fleming's *deus-ex-machina* in [*Casino Royale*], are likewise distracting, because they disturb the reader by underrating his intelli-

gence. A balance is reached, in my opinion, in a story like le Carré's [*Call for the Dead*].

The formula plot, like all formula elements, is an abstraction, but it is an abstraction which is significant, I believe, for the reader's experience of a given story. Unlike the experience of non-formula fiction, the reading of fiction built on certain formulas is not retrospective gathering of threads, but an ordering of textual elements according to an anticipation of what follows. This is why suspense by protraction can be used with so much success in formula genres. The distance between formula and actual discourse—the individual story—is a tension which gives rise to infinite variations, but all of them, if not excessively simple or excessively elaborate, to be responded to with the enjoyment that we get from meeting the familiar in the unfamiliar. (pp. 75-100)

> *Lars Ole Sauerberg, "Plot," in his* Secret Agents in Fiction: Ian Fleming, John le Carré and Len Deighton, *St. Martin's Press, 1984, pp. 75-100.*

Marc Silverstein on the nature of the spy thriller:

The basic assumption governing the pattern of expectations we bring to the reading of thrillers can thus be defined as the belief that precisely because it is hermetic and self-referential, the spy novel—like the world of play—preserves its value by *not* being serious. To take it as model, to extract a world view from it, denies its nature as escapist fantasy.

> *Marc Silverstein, in his "After the Fall: The World of Graham Greene's Thrillers," in* Novel: A Forum on Fiction, *Fall 1988.*

Jacques Barzun

[*Barzun is a French-born American man of letters whose wide range of learning has produced distinguished works in several fields, including history, culture, musicology, literary criticism, and biography. Barzun's contribution to these various disciplines are contained in such modern classics of scholarship and critical insight as* Darwin, Marx, Wagner *(1941),* Berlioz and the Romantic Century *(1950),* The House of the Intellect *(1959), and the biography* A Stroll with William James *(1983). Barzun's style, both literary and intellectual, has been praised as elegant and unpretentious. In the following essay, he criticizes espionage fiction as immature and cynical.*]

As I begin these notes (midsummer 1964), the American public is making into best sellers two works of light literature: *Candy* and *The Spy Who Came In From the Cold*. The one is supposed to be a parody of the modern novel of sex; the other is held up as a really real realistic tale of modern spying; and there is evidence from conversation and printed comments that readers who usually scorn the best seller are giving these books their attention. I suspect that something important but unspoken links these two efforts and also attracts the consumer of so-called serious novels.

I do not know what that something is, but I do know that *Candy* and *The Spy* are dull and, under their respective cloaks of gaiety and of sobriety, affected. The point of *The Spy* is that he wants to quit but is impelled to go on by professional routine. This is enough, I imagine, to make him congenial to all of us. He does not believe in what he is doing; he is anything but a hero; he is a good deal of a masochist. And being a spy in the field, indeed a potential martyr to an unfelt cause, he entitles himself to certain low pleasures—despising his associates; having, skill apart, a poor opinion of himself; sinking morally and physically into degradation almost beyond control; falling in love listlessly, like a convalescent; and, after being betrayed in action by headquarters for double-cross purposes, making a sacrificial end. Death, we are to think, is the only "coming in from the cold" there is.

I am sure that this melodrama played in iron curtains corresponds to something older and deeper than our anxieties of the cold war. The soul of the spy is somehow the model of our own; his actions and his trappings fulfill our unsatisfied desires. How else explain the stir caused, also this past summer, by the death of Ian Fleming? Ten books about James Bond, published in a little more than ten years, do not justify the front-page laments, and even less the studies by academic critics who have argued over Fleming's morals and political philosophy. No, there is something here like earlier ages' recognition of themselves in the pioneer, the warrior, the saint or the poet. We are the spy—an agent, mind you, not a man—hiding behind the muffling zeros of 007 which mean: the right to kill *in the line of duty.*

The advertisers, who always know the color of our emotions, rely on our being good Bondsmen. Leafing through the *New Yorker,* I am told by a travel magazine: "Come to Beirut and see spies. Real spies . . . with shifty eyes and tiny cameras." In *Playboy,* cheek by jowl with a discussion of the "cultural explosion," I am invited to examine a dinner jacket and to "ask Agent 008, the one for whom survival often depends on the smallest detail." These hints play on the surface and suggest the depths. As technologists we love that tiny detail, that tiny camera. As infidels without purpose, we attach a morbid importance to survival. Yet our aplomb is restored by the possession of cosmetic virtue: with those faultless garments on, we would be content to let our eyes shift for themselves.

The spy story does this for us, then: it permits us not to choose, we can live high and lie low. Since Graham Greene no longer writes "entertainments," read Eric Ambler's *The Light of Day* and see how the ironic title is brought down to mean simple survival for an outcast in a dirty raincoat with a mind to match. We are on his side, for as with the cold spy in his Skid Row phase, we relish the freedom that exists at the bottom of cities. And we know that in exchange for a few dirty tricks there is also power and luxury, cash and free sex. True, even James Bond marries while *On Her Majesty's Secret Service,* but the wife mercifully dies within a few hours. They had been lovers, so all is well.

The advantage of being a spy as of being a soldier is that there is always a larger reason—the reason of state—for making any little scruple or nastiness shrink into insignificance. But I want to leave the question of morality to a later place. At this point I am still curious about the satisfactions that the tale of espionage affords Western man in the afternoon of this century. As always in trashy literature, it is the satisfactions that produce the illusion of reality: man despising and betrayed, listless in his loves, dying pointlessly every second, scared, scared, scared—this is, if one may so speak, the life existential. But in the portraits and myths of that life what calms our fears is that dangers and difficulties yield to technique. The spy is imperturbable not by temperament or by philosophy, but from expertise. He is the competent man. Whether the need of the moment is to play bridge like Culbertson, speak a Finnish dialect like a native, ski to safety over precipices or disable a funicular, he comforts us with his powers no less than with the pedantry of the subject. He makes mistakes, of course, to keep us in countenance, but they are errors of inattention, such as killing the wrong man. We respond to this agreeable image of our scientific world, where knowledge commands power, where facts are uniformly interesting, and where fatalities appear more and more as oversights, professional *faux pas.* These results constitute the romance of the age; why should they not be translated into stories—spy stories especially, since what we know as science comes from ferreting and spying, and since we care so much for truth that we are willing to drug and torture for it?

One stumbles here on a preestablished harmony: the novel as a genre has been prurient and investigative from the start. Growing out of the picaresque adventure, which is high life seen from below stairs, the novel does not merely show, it shows up—and what a mountain of discreditable information it has unloaded into our eager minds! What pedantry! What snobbery! At first, simple encounters and reversals kept the reader going; lately it has been character and relationships; but it is all one: from Gil Blas to Henry James's "observer" somebody is always prying. From Scott to Dreiser we take a course in how some other half lives, how fraudulent men and their society really are. The novel is dedicated to subversion; the novelist is a spy in enemy country. No reason, then, to be surprised that his ultimate parable should be the tale with a declared, certified spy in it, one who like the original *picaro* sees society from below, and resentfully.

Mr. Matthew Head, who has written a dozen good detective stories and whose name conceals a well-known art critic, gives in one of his books what might be called the moral strategy of the novel-bred mind. His archeologist hero [of *The Devil in the Bush*] confides that "the first thing I always wonder about new people is what they manage to do for a living and how they arrange their sex life, because it seems to me that those two activities plus sleep and a movie or two account for most people's twenty-four hours a day." This is the brass-tacks appeal, and it goes well with our primitivism, our reliance on formulas, our fatigue at the thought of understanding "new people": there are so many of them, thanks to immoderate prenatal care.

And the wish to invade the privacy of sex gives a clue to the kinship I suspected between the two best sellers with which I began these notes: spying and pornography are related through the curiosity of the child about the mystery of sex. Perhaps the relentless curiosity of science has the same root; certainly our fiction does not neglect the fundamental needs, only the fundamental decencies. It neglects, that is, the difference between recognizing the demands of the body under the elaborations, softenings and concealments of civilized society and thinking that one is very sharp to have discovered them and made the rest negligible.

The genuine primitive has another ring to it. The *Iliad* is about "Helen and all her wealth"—money and sex if you will, but like other national epics it is also about war and the gods, human character and the sorrowful brevity of life. The novel is about malice domestic, and this is what ends by stunting our souls. I reread *Clarissa Harlowe* during a recent bout of illness, and I was shocked by the orgy of violence—of action, language, feeling—that it comes down to. The rape of Clarissa is only the fit gesture to symbolize the concentrated fury that animates all the characters—friend against friend; man against woman; parents, children, relatives against one another. All this hate, like a contagion, made me want to annihilate the lot.

The cold-spy, cold-war story presumably expresses and discharges the tension of violence under which we have lived since 1914. But that expression is rarely touched with regret or remorse. Only occasionally, as in William Haggard's story *The High Wire,* is the theme in contradiction with the mode of life depicted. The main character here is a peaceable, middle-aged engineer who is catapulted into espionage and finds in it only horror, helplessness and torture. He manages to live and marry the heroine, an agent who is—or just has been, for purely professional reasons, of course—the mistress of an opposing agent: again, the true romance of our times. It almost makes one prefer the moral of Cyril Connolly's now famous parody of James Bond, in which 007 must in the line of duty impersonate a homosexual and finds—but the surprise ending must not be told.

An uncommonly deft practitioner, Hubert Monteilhet, gives us another singular version of this romance in *Return from the Ashes,* which tells how a woman survivor from a concentration camp attempts to regain an old lover who may have betrayed her to the Gestapo. She has to turn spy, privately, to achieve her ends, and in so doing she destroys others as well as the hopeful part of herself. At one point she defines the embroidering of sentiment over brutality as "the work of a tragic Marivaux, one to suit this century." But why blame the century? Why are we told over and over again, as by Raymond Chandler in his masterpiece *The Lady in the Lake:* "Doctors are just people, born to sorrow, fighting the long grim fight like the rest of us"? Or in reverse, by one of Chandler's imitators: "She was really a rather naive and inexperienced little girl. She apparently still believed in things like love and hate and gratitude and vengeance, not realizing that they had no place in this work, where your enemy one minute is your ally the next—and maybe your enemy again a few

minutes later." The speaker of this maxim, the tough spy Matt Helm, acknowledges that ours is "not a chivalrous age, nor is mine an honorable profession." The excuse, it appears, is necessity. Chandler's indestructible hero, Philip Marlowe, who crystallized a good many of these poses, declares: "However hard I try to be nice I always end up with my nose in the dirt and my thumb feeling for somebody's eye."

Obviously the reason why these things occur and are bewailed is the way men choose to take life, and modern men take life in the way of sophistication, that is, universal suspicion, hostility, fear of being taken in. People who read only "noteworthy" novels do not know how far the second- and third-hand fiction has copied and exploited the disillusioned stance of the masters. At times one could imagine that it was Somerset Maugham who had decanted into all the lesser works the sour wine from the great vintage casks: "His intelligence was obvious . . . he never quite gave himself away. He seemed to be on his guard . . . those eyes were watching, weighing, judging, and forming an opinion [*sic*]. He was not a man to take things at their face value." This is Maugham's Dr. Saunders, the hero-observer of the well-named *Narrow Corner.* To know in advance that everything and everybody is a fraud gives the derivative types what they call a wry satisfaction. Their borrowed system creates the ironies that twist their smiles into wryness. They look wry and drink rye and make a virtue of taking the blows of fate wryly. It is monotonous: I am fed up with the life of wryly.

One reason for my annoyance is the contamination that the sophisticated and the spies have brought into the story of detection. Mr. Le Carré himself began with two attempts at the genre, in which his talent for situations is evident and any interest in the rationality of detection altogether missing. Under a surface likeness the purposes of spying and criminal detection are opposite: the spy aims at destroying a polity by sowing confusion and civil strife; the detective aims at saving a polity by suppressing crime. Thanks to our literary men we have been made so much at home with crime, we have found the spy's "unobserved shadow world which is nevertheless starkly real" serving us so well as a sort of subconscious of society, that we readily agree with the head of the French Secret Police who said no man "could fully understand our age unless he had spent some time in prison." Logic thus compels the writer to turn detective fiction into the domestic branch of espionage.

In consequence the murders that do not arise from the drug traffic arise from the enchanted realm of "security." And so an excellent story such as Val Gielgud's *Through a Glass Darkly* seeks the solution to a London murder simply by turning inside out the lives of the wife, the friends and the business associates of the victim. In place of the classical observation and inference, there is snooping, which also obliterates action. Simenon's Maigret, whom many innocent readers take for a detective, is but a peeping Tom. He is praised for his patience in looking out of windows across a road, but his "psychology" is a mere offprint of Dr. Saunders': "He took an interest in his fellows that was not quite scientific and not quite human . . . it gave him just the same amusement to unravel the intricacies of the individual as a mathematician might find in the solution of a problem." In short: the mathematical interest that a Paris *concierge* takes in his lodgers and finds rewarded by the Sûreté.

The great illusion is to believe that all these impulses and enjoyments betoken maturity, worldliness, being "realistic." The truth is that Maugham's observer and the ubiquitous spy are bright boys of nine years. Nine is the age of seeking omniscience on a low level. The spy's ingenuity (why not ship the fellow in a trunk?), his shifting partisanship without a cause, like his double bluffs, his vagrant attachments, and his love of torturing and of being tortured are the mores of the preadolescent gang: they yield, as one storyteller puts it, "the joys of conspiracy—all the little thrills and chills that go with being secret and devious." For adult readers to divert themselves with tales of childish fantasy is nothing new and not in itself reprehensible. What is new is for readers to accept the fantasy as wiser than civil government, and what is reprehensible is for the modern world to have made official the dreams and actions of little boys.

There is a further sense in which the philosophy of the spy is childish: at the critical moments it does not work. On this point the authoritative theorist of espionage, an American agent who writes under the pseudonym of Christopher Felix, leaves us in no doubt. He tells us in his *Short Course in the Secret War* that "during World War II the German High command had at least three reliable reports stating the date and place for the Allied invasion of Normandy," and believed none of them. Again, the Russians had daily reports of German battle plans straight from headquarters, and disregarded them all. In the same happy vein of skepticism, Stalin disbelieved Richard Sorge's information from Tokyo that Germany would invade Poland in September 1939 and would attack Russia itself in April 1941.

These failures supply their own moral, although not in the way a moralist would prefer. The moral is that nothing in this world can be accomplished without trust, however rudimentary. You cannot buy a box of matches without your entering into a tacit trust agreement with the tradesman to the effect that when you have handed him the coin he will hand you the box. Deception and ruthlessness are not "Machiavellian" wisdom as the vulgar think; they overshoot policy and recoil on the user. The modern spy, being sophisticated, works for both sides—a double agent—is therefore trusted by neither side and thus loses his only value. Similarly, in literature as in life, the double bluff wears out and can only be succeeded by the triple cross. It is an endless series in which agent and principal are both likely to lose their wits. Who is fooling whom and when? In the end, espionage modern style is like advertising: the participants deploy their gimmicks and make their shifty eyes at one another exclusively. The lack of *pragma* throughout is as shocking as the reckless expense.

As for the game, one can understand why the reader and the spy relish the permissible depravity that goes with it. But why insist that the spy take sides and risk life without conviction? The only answer that suggests itself is that the lukewarm agent can avoid being torn between his conception of his own cause and the acts of his own party. No need to wonder why their enemies hanged Major André and Nathan Hale so reluctantly and unavoidably. Indeed, one need not go back as far as the American Revolution to find out what preceded the universal loss of honor and conviction. From medieval chivalry to Elizabethan times, the spy was a "base fellow," known as such to others and to himself. This notion survived from then to within recent memory: when Henry Stimson, as Secretary of State, was shown the progress of code-breaking, he pushed the documents aside and said curtly: "Gentlemen do not read each other's mail." Now, we hear, every citizen has a democratic chance of serving as a spy. Housewives, students on their travels, foundation officials, merchants, scientists, exchange professors and visiting virtuosos are eligible. Only the *New York Times* protests, on the antiquated ground that duplicity may damage the once trustworthy professions.

The most that can be said in extenuation of the citizen-spy's bad taste is that it corresponds to the decline of a world system. The phases are: 1900, 1914, 1945. At the turn of the century, when Erskine Childers wrote *The Riddle of the Sands,* no one could mistake the amateur spy for anything but a patriot, and the professional on the "wrong side" was partly excused by a mixed ancestry aggravated by private misfortune. Even after the *Götterdämmerung* of the First World War, John Buchan could make his hero pursue espionage and chivalry without a split psyche. If today *The Three Hostages* were by a fluke to reach the screen, Richard Hannay would be hooted at by every thirteen-year-old of either sex. His soldierly attempt to save the life of his deadly enemy while chasing him across the scree and gorges of Scotland would seem puerile; and the valuing of every man in the tale, not by his ruthlessness, clothes, or sexual potency, but by the pain it causes him to be a spy, would be adjudged the improbable invention of a maiden aunt. This contrast in conduct and instinct reminds one of the fate of the old German army in the face of Hitler's shirts. This is but another way of saying that we live in times like those that led Thucydides to make one of his tyrants say to his victims: "We give you joy of your innocence, but covet not your silliness."

But let us be careful. Let us not put this love of spying—one might almost say this love of dishonor—to the sole account of the dictatorships. It grows just as naturally in the soil of democracy; for it has something to do with equality and the confused emotions relating to class. Few people, no doubt, remember James Fenimore Cooper's early and internationally popular novel, *The Spy,* which dates from 1821. I had to refresh my vague memories of a French translation to find that Harvey Birch, the spy who mysteriously helps George Washington, was no hero but a frightened, mean and mercenary character. He was moved by patriotism, to be sure, but also by a restless envy. This was a shrewd insight of Cooper's. Kill the patriot by sophistication and what is left is the competitive egalitarian, the status-seeker powered by envy.

Out of envy and the will to arrive comes the whole apparatus of personal, industrial and governmental spying. Mr.

Richard Rovere has written with justified passion about the multiform attack on privacy that implements this vast jealousy and fear. When no one can take his own merit and place for granted, no one can look upon the world with that "well-opened eye" which Conan Doyle ascribes to "a man whose pleasant lot it had ever been to command and be obeyed." Whatever bad things went with the system that produced such men—and these bad things are many—it did not lead to prying. The Henry Stimsons refrained from reading others' mail, not because they controlled an itch to do so, but because they were not interested. By contrast, the great democratic virtue is to be "interested in people," which undoubtedly fosters sympathy and helpfulness. But it also fosters mutual surveillance and social tyranny.

True, in Flaubert's *Dictionary of Accepted Ideas* the entry "Spy" reads: "Always in high society." But that is the spy of the Age of Reason, polite and cosmopolite, who comes historically between the base fellow and the modern Every Man His Own Secret Agent. E. Phillips Oppenheim gave the ultimate renderings of that delightful intermediate type, a suave habitué of the Orient Express and a willing prey to the svelte seductress whose prerogative it was to transfer the naval plans from his well-marked dispatch box to her bosom, no less well marked. Protocol required these trappings, and this too rested on presumption.

So far from presuming, the democratic character, for all its uneasy claims to equal rewards, is not quite sure of its own existence. Psychoanalysis has taught even the common man that he is in some ways an impostor; he has spied on himself and discovered reasons for distrust and disgust: in all honesty he cannot turn in a good report. Nor do his surroundings help to restore his confidence. The world is more and more an artifact, everywhere facsimiles supplant the real thing—the raucous radio voice, the weird TV screen. Just to find his bearings he must fashion a computer simulation of his case. So mimicry, pretending, hiding, which are part of the child's first nature and used to be sloughed off as true individuality developed, now stay with us as second nature, and indeed as the only escape from the bad self and the bad world. Or as a tough dick in a crude story tells another: A false name, a false address "gives them an immunity from the dreadful actuality of being themselves. . . . Perfectly respectable people, too." Which is to say: for "privacy" read "secrecy."

But I must close with literature, for heaven knows it is literature—the best and the worst—that our feelings have had to imitate in order to make our world what it is. The petering out of an era, the grubby romances of the envious and the blasé, mirror themselves in the mechanical moves, aggressive and sexual, of Candy and the Cold Spy. But there is more than one underground and one resistance, and here and there one hears echoes of Conrad's dictum that "it is conscience that illumines the romantic side of our life." Any other point of view, he goes on, is "as benighted as the point of view of hunger." Thus in effect speaks also the late Arthur Upfield after some violent doings in the bush: "No, I tell you. It's loyalty. Only the basest of us are not actuated by loyalty." And in a remarkable story to end all spy stories, that unfailing virtuoso Andrew

Garve winds up a harrowing scene in which is disclosed a spy's lifelong deception of his daughter as to all his beliefs and all their circumstances, by saying: "I'd been *too* fair to Raczinski. No one had the right to do what he'd done to Marya—not for any reason on earth." (pp. 167-77)

Jacques Barzun, "Meditations on the Literature of Spying," in The American Scholar, *Vol. 34, No. 2, Spring, 1965, pp. 167-78.*

SPIES IN FACT AND FICTION

David A. T. Stafford

[*Stafford is a British-born critic living in Canada. In the following essay, he outlines the fear of foreign invasion that made the spy story popular in Edwardian England.*]

It is a warm afternoon in the sun-blanched Riviera Resort of Nice. Few people are to be seen along the fashionable *Promenade des Anglais,* for it is October and thus early for the season. The huge white hotels lining the seafront are as yet only half full, and the spacious villas still shuttered against the summer sun await their winter visitors. It is not clear, however, that any visitors will arrive this year. For it is 1898, and Europe hovers on the brink of war over a distant colonial outpost called Fashoda, on the upper Nile. The small colony of English residents is humming with earnest discussion as how best to leave the Riviera when war comes. But there is at least one English visitor to whom our eye is drawn. This is a dark, elegant, and youthful gentleman who strolls unconcernedly past the palms and oleanders, enjoying the sensuous colours of the turquoise Mediterranean. He stops to purchase a carnation from a young flower girl, and then crosses the broad Place Masséna where he is greeted by a man of similar age to himself. It is his old friend, the Marchese Meliani, sole surviving descendant of a noble Sicilian family and a serving officer in the Italian navy. The two men return to the privacy of the Englishman's rooms. Here Meliani confides that he has been entrusted by his government with a most important and secret mission connected with the current international crisis. In the event of war between Britain and France, he reveals, the Italian navy will cooperate with the Royal Navy to strike at French ports along the Mediterranean. He asks his friend for assistance but gives him an ominous warning. "Reflect well before you promise your help," he cautions, "for by assisting me you stand a good chance of arrest and deportation to Cayenne." It is without fear or hesitation, however, that his companion promises him unreservedly all the assistance in his power; for, he declares roundly, "I am an Englishman, despite the fact that I am a spy."

Who is this young man of breeding who is so confident that his vocation as spy permits his status and reputation as an English gentleman to remain intact—and whose character and dependability indeed enable the French fleet to be immobilised, thus forcing France into a humiliating diplomatic defeat? It is none other than Duckworth Drew of the British Secret Service, "of whom Bismarck is reputed once to have said that he had half a dozen nationalities and an equal number of personalities." Drew is "chief confidential agent of the British Government, and next to Her Majesty's Secretary of State, one of the most powerful and important pillars of England's supremacy." He first saw the light of day in 1903 with the publication of William Le Queux's *Secrets of the Foreign Office* and can probably claim credit as the first in a long tradition of gentlemanly secret agents with which British popular literature in the twentieth century has been amply supplied. His appearance marks the beginning of an era, for it is in the Edwardian age that the British spy novel was born and the basic formula which determined its development established. Le Queux played a major part in this process, although he was by no means alone, and he reincarnated Drew in varying guises in a succession of stories of intrigue and international espionage which continued up to 1914 and beyond. In the year following the appearance of Duckworth Drew he presented readers of *The Man from Downing Street* with Jack Jardine, head of the British Secret Service, a book-collecting gentleman and bachelor with rooms in Great Russell Street, an ancestral home in Cheshire, and a commission in the cavalry. Jardine's service to country consists both of preventing the signing of a dangerous Franco-Italian treaty and of preventing plans of a new Vickers submarine from falling into Russian hands. He was followed in the next year by Cuthbert Croom, the hero of *Confessions of a Ladies' Man*, a Wykehamist whose bookish personal inclinations are constantly frustrated by the duty to country which demands his intermingling with the meretricious social glitter of the diplomatic rounds in order to pull the country back from the brink of war. And then there is Hugh Morrice, "chief travelling agent of the Confidential Department of His Britannic Majesty's Government," and the hero of *Revelations of the Secret Service*, published in 1911. Morrice combines the virtues of his predecessors into a truly impressive list of attributes, for his creator describes him as "an accomplished linguist, a brilliant raconteur, a good all-round sportsman, a polished diplomat, a born adventurer, a cosmopolitan of cosmopolitans, still under forty, and a personal friend of half a dozen sovereigns."

The character of Hugh Morrice provides a paradigm of the British secret agent as he emerged in British popular fiction during the twenty years prior to the outbreak of the First World War. If there was an apparent contradiction between the activities of the international spy and the calling of an English gentleman—as is so clearly implied in Duckworth Drew's response to his Italian counterpart—then it was a contradiction largely resolved through the attribution of all the negative connotations of espionage to the figure of the foreign spy. It quickly became established as a convention of the genre that there was a clear distinction between spies, who were foreign, and secret agents, who were British. The fictional British agent, in direct contrast with his foreign opponent, was and remained, despite his activities, quintessentially a gentleman. This stereotyped figure developed in the late Victorian and more especially Edwardian period as a symbol of stability in response both to fundamental changes in the nature of Britain's place within the international system and to processes within British society which were perceived as threatening important elements of the social status quo.

Hugh Morrice, Le Queux told his readers in 1911, was not only a veritable prince of secret agents, but "many a time has secret information supplied by him turned the tide of political events in Great Britain's favour" (*Revelations of the Secret Service*). The belief that the tide of international affairs required human intervention for it to flow in Britain's favour at all was an indicator of the decline in public confidence that Britannia's power to rule the waves was an integral part of some divine or natural purpose. The appearance of secret agents in British popular fiction, skilfully piloting Britain through the troubled waters of international diplomacy, is testimony to the impact on popular Edwardian consciousness of the rapidly changing nature of international relations and of its effect on Britain's traditional nineteenth-century position of splendid and superior isolation. An analysis of this literature, the popularity of which was sufficient to provide its most successful authors with small fortunes, furnishes us with further glimpses into the mentality of Edwardian England, and in particular casts some illumination on popular patriotism, xenophobia, and militarism in the years prior to the outbreak of World War One.

The development of police and detective forces in early Victorian Britain provided a thankful middle class with a sense of security about fundamental issues of domestic law and order. The imaginative counterpart of this was the emergence in the 1850s and 1860s of the classical detective story. In the novels of Charles Dickens, Wilkie Collins, and others, the detective served as the protector of established society. The process culminated in the 1890s with Conan Doyle's brilliant creation of Sherlock Holmes. In much the same way, the rise of the spy story reflected concerns about the changing state of international law and order in the dying days of Victoria's reign. This was a period qualitatively different from that of mid-century and was marked by the development of complex alliance systems, crisis diplomacy, and armaments races between the major European powers. In the years following the Franco-Prussian War technology wrought profound changes in the international system, placing a premium on secrecy both in armaments production and diplomacy. Espionage was not, of course, new in the relations between states. Many writers have noted that spying has a legitimate claim to being the second oldest profession, and in Britain itself fears about the subversive role of spies and enemy agents had deeply troubled governments as recently as the Revolutionary and Napoleonic era. They had never entirely disappeared. Popular awareness of spies and foreign agents was kept alive through the nineteenth century by the periodic presence and activities in England of foreign revolutionaries, anarchists, nihilists, and Fenians, and this meant that a popular interest in and concern about spies and agents was not entirely a new phenomenon in the period with which we are concerned. There was, however, a crucial qualitative change in the late nineteenth century. Intelligence agencies became established as a permanent feature of the bureaucratic structures of the European states, and espionage came to play a regular, accepted, and important part in the international behaviour of the great powers. International espionage and counter-espionage as regular facts of life imposed themselves on the consciousness of an increasingly informed public in the 1890s, and their significance for Britain's security was made readily apparent; for if technological superiority was primary coin in the international market, a nation's security could only too readily be liquidated overnight by spies or traitors.

The importance of both overt and covert intelligence in the relations between the great powers in this period is clearly indicated by the emergence of intelligence sections in their military staffs, the rise of the military and naval attaché as a permanent fixture in the capitals of the world, and the appearance of official secrets acts in many countries. Britain, despite her "splendid isolation," did not remain untouched by these developments. She helped set the pace in the introduction of attachés and kept abreast with other developments. In 1873 Edward Cardwell, secretary of state for war, announced in parliament the formation of an Intelligence Department of the army, and it quickly developed into the most important branch of the War Office. In 1883 a Directorate of Military Intelligence was established, and by 1891 it was a settled convention that its director should automatically be consulted on all matters concerning foreign countries. The navy was slower to act, but in 1887 the Naval Intelligence Board was established, and in succeeding years it built up an efficient and effective intelligence network. Although most of the work of these branches involved the collection of overt intelligence, the army at least sent out numerous spies on clandestine missions. Two years after the founding of the Naval Intelligence Board, Britain passed its first Official Secrets Act. It was no accident that it was prepared under the direction of the War Office and Admiralty, for both were profoundly concerned about the security of military secrets. The Foreign Office, too, had an interest, for it had been seriously embarrassed in 1878 by the leakage during the Congress of Berlin of details of a secret Anglo-Russian agreement. The affair threw into relief the new importance attached to secrecy in the international arena, and *The Times* strongly attacked the Foreign Office for its negligence "in the days when priority of intelligence is as marketable as cotton." But it took the unauthorised disclosure of internal instructions to Naval Intelligence and the selling of some warship designs to a foreign power to produce the 1889 act. It lasted until 1911, when it was replaced by the more stringent second Official Secrets Act, which still remains the basis of British secrets legislation. This new act sprang from recommendations of a subcommittee of the Committee of Imperial Defence set up by the cabinet to investigate the alleged German spy menace, and considerably facilitated the prosecution of foreign spies. The enquiry also created the machinery with which to track foreign espionage in Britain, for one of its main recommendations was for the creation of a regular British secret service. This led directly in the following months to the creation both of the counter-intelligence service, popularly known as M.I.5, and of the Secret Intelligence Service (SIS), popularly known as M.I.6. Britain's secret service was, therefore, a child of the Edwardian age and yet a further indica-

tor of Britain's increased sense of vulnerability in a dangerous world.

This sense of threat to national security, even to the sovereign territory, exemplified itself in the increasing number of invasion scares that from the 1880s disturbed public opinion. These derived ultimately from the technological revolution affecting naval armaments which made even relative finality impossible in naval construction; despite the Naval Defence Act of 1889 which established the two-power standard, the ability of the Royal Navy to preserve Britain from invasion was continually questioned. Anxiety became acute at times of international tension and culminated in a full-blown invasion scare in 1900 during the Boer War. This highlighted Britain's diplomatic isolation, now made acute by the apparent hostility of Germany. Britain might have learned to live with the Franco-Russian alliance, but since 1896 public opinion had been alert to the dangers of Anglo-German relations. A major turning point had come in that year with the famous "Kruger Telegram" of the Kaiser, and this stab in the back from the Queen's own grandson evoked bitter public resentment. Anglo-German relations never fully recovered. In 1898 the Germans introduced their first naval bill, the starting point in their construction of a battle fleet which was to present a political challenge to the British. German behaviour during the Boer crisis led the influential journalist W. T. Stead in February 1900 to warn that a French invasion could well be assisted by the Germans. It produced a major scare in the popular press and only slightly more muted responses in official circles. In May, Lord Salisbury appeared publicly to endorse the view that an invasion was possible, and the issue remained sufficiently serious for it to be put before the Committee of Imperial Defence in 1903. Although in 1905 the committee ruled out the likelihood of invasion, there were many dissenters, and the debate produced a strong movement of opinion calling for the creation of a large army to defend Britain from attack. The National Service League called for some sort of compulsory peacetime conscription, while other organisations sought in different ways to improve the nation's moral, physical, and psychological preparedness for war, and to improve national efficiency. The central institutions of government were strengthened with the creation of the Committee of Imperial Defence in 1902 and the establishment of a General Staff for the army, while diplomatic isolation came to an end in 1902 with the Anglo-Japanese alliance, followed by the *ententes* with France in 1904 and with Russia in 1907. These were the years when the "continental commitment" gradually imposed itself as a necessity on the minds of Britain's statesmen, and the consequent changed relationship to the European continent left a deep impression on popular consciousness—perhaps the most profound of all changes in Edwardian England.

Awareness of these revolutionary changes and concern with national vulnerability, invasion, and hostile espionage made their mark on the popular literature of these years. It is here that the roots of the spy story are to be found. The invasion scares had given rise to a whole genre of fiction depicting some imaginary invasion of Britain, one of the earliest and most famous being Sir George

Chesney's *Battle of Dorking of 1871,* which established the model of the genre in the last quarter of the nineteenth century. From 1881 to 1883 the proposal by a commercial company to construct a tunnel under the English Channel had met vociferous opposition, and Sir Garnet Wolseley, adjutant-general of the army, even argued in an official submission to the government that the project could lead to Dover being seized by disguised Frenchmen. The minor panic accompanying the proposal produced some fictional dramas, among which were references to the important part played in a French invasion by enemy spies. But it was not until the 1890s that espionage began to assume major significance in the plot development of these invasion novels. A landmark here was William Le Queux's novel *The Great War in England in 1897,* which first appeared in serial form in *Answers,* Alfred Harmsworth's first publishing venture, in 1893 (and thus before the Dreyfus affair focussed widespread attention on the critical dimensions of espionage). It was an enormous popular success, appearing in book form in 1894 and quickly passing through eight editions. Presenting an imaginary invasion of Britain by France and Russia, the novel exploited popular fears generated by the new Franco-Russian alliance, and the major part of the novel concentrated on the valiant and ultimately successful British resistance and counterattack. The book remained within the tradition of the invasion novel, but attributed a major role to espionage and to the character of a foreign spy. This is Count von Beilstein, the leading villain in the story. Von Beilstein is a German Jew domiciled in Britain who is in the secret pay of the tsar. It is his stealing of secret treaty plans which precipitates the war in the first place, and the novel traces his nefarious activities in Britain through until the bitter end, when he meets his death in front of a firing squad on Horseguards Parade after the British victory. From this point on the number of stories revolving around spies increased, undoubtedly assisted by the massive dimensions of the Dreyfus case in France which absorbed attention from 1894 to the end of the century. In 1898 E. Phillips Oppenheim ("Prince of Storytellers") launched his highly successful and lucrative career as the purveyor of romances of international intrigue with his first spy novel, *Mysterious Mr. Sabin;* between 1900 and the end of the Edwardian age he produced several more. In 1899 Headon Hill produced *Spies of the Wight,* while Le Queux published *England's Peril,* in which the reading public was presented with the devilish cunning of the notorious Gaston La Touche, head of the French Secret Service. In 1901 Max Pemberton published *Pro Patria,* a throwback to the theme of a Channel tunnel invasion in which the French plan is foiled by the diligence of a young amateur British agent. Two years later there appeared what still remains the most famous of the early British spy novels, Erskine Childers's *The Riddle of the Sands,* in which two young Englishmen reveal and thus foil a projected German invasion of Britain. This was also the year of Duckworth Drew's appearance, and from then on until the outbreak of war there was not a year which did not see a novel by Le Queux, Oppenheim, or some other popular writer dealing with the successful British defeat of an enemy espionage conspiracy—often but not always in conjunction with some projected invasion of Britain.

The world presented by these novels is a dangerous and treacherous one in which Britain is the target of the envy, hostility, and malevolence of the other European powers, singly or collectively according to context. The novels reflect the changing contours of alignments and alliances. It took some time for traditional Francophobia to die out; it was not until after the signing of the *entente* in 1904 that it began to disappear, although it occasionally surfaced where Anglo-French relations in the colonial sphere entered the picture. If fear of the French subsided slowly, resentment and hatred of the Germans developed rapidly after 1896. This was testimony to the deep impact on popular consciousness of the Kruger telegram; from then on Germany was more and more frequently added to the list of potential enemies. In Louis Tracy's novel of that year (1896), *The Final War,* the invasion powers are Russia, France, and Germany, although the foreign spy is French. Likewise Oppenheim's *Mysterious Mr. Sabin* presents the reader with a French spy (Mr. Sabin), but the device he uses to achieve his ends is the exploitation of Anglo-German conflict. There is a thinly disguised Kruger telegram incident, and as the Russian attaché tells young Wolfenden, the Englishman pitted against Sabin, "Germany detests you . . . a war between Germany and England is only a matter of time." German espionage is at the focus of Hill's *Spies of the Wight,* while a German invasion and subversive activities by Germans resident in London is central to T. W. Offin's tract of 1900, *How the Germans Took London. The Riddle of the Sands,* therefore, with its focus on Germany, merely fell within an existing tradition, although its huge impact and its durability as a piece of writing endowed it with particular significance. From then on, Germanophobia was a central feature of the British spy novel, feeding upon and fuelling popular hatred of Germany in particular and foreigners resident in Britain ("aliens") in general; the most conspicuous of those happened also to be Germans, both Gentiles and Jews. The close links between these stories and the popular press, particularly the Northcliffe press, contributed substantially to spy mania. Le Queux's espionage drama of 1908, *Spies of the Kaiser,* fuelled the spy panic of 1908-09 and helped pressure the government into setting up the official enquiry which culminated in the 1911 Official Secrets Act. Spy stories also fuelled anti-alien sentiment which was not appeased by the passing of the Aliens Act of 1905; as the hero of E. Phillips Oppenheim's novel of 1907, *The Secret . . . ,* observes while watching an East End crowd of aliens attempt to frustrate the publication of a German invasion plan, "this is what comes of making London the asylum of all the foreign scum of the earth . . . half a million and more of scum eating their way into the entrails of this great city of ours." This and similar sentiments expressed in spy literature helped prepare the ground for antialien riots when war broke out in 1914.

In the hazardous new world of foreign powers abroad and foreign residents at home, where new continental commitments played havoc with traditional certainties, Britain is presented as the innocent victim of foreign machinations, treading a minefield which could at any moment explode and lead to war and loss of empire. "A single stroke of the pen, a hasty or ill-advised action, and a war might result which would cost our Empire millions in money and millions of valuable lives," Le Queux tells his readers in *Of Royal Blood;* "the war cloud hangs over Europe always. The mine is laid, and the slightest spark may fire it." Those who guide Britain through the minefield are the diplomats and their close assistants, the secret agents. Behind the scenes the deadly game of espionage is played, and it is the novelist's task and privilege to draw the curtain aside and let the public glimpse what really goes on. "How little the public knows," Le Queux confides and promises to his readers, "of the stealthy treacherous ways of modern diplomacy, of the armies of spies seeking always to plot and counter plot, of the base subterfuges of certain foreign diplomatists" (*Her Majesty's Minister*); "you, who sit at home so comfortably in your own dining room, never give a thought to the gallant little band . . . who are living in all sorts of disguises in various Continental cities calmly watchful of the interests of Empire" (*Revelations*). What is the fundamental factor which accounts for the deadly nature of this game and demands the intervention of the secret agents? It is the exposed and vulnerable nature of Britain's nineteenth-century empire as the world enters the Edwardian era, which Carruthers, the young hero of *Riddle of the Sands,* refers to as "our delicate network of empire, sensitive as gossamer to external shocks." Or as Duckworth Drew's superior, the foreign secretary, Lord Barmouth, confesses to Drew while briefing him for a mission: "We are weak, Drew, horribly weak. And weakness invites attack" (Le Queux, *Secrets*).

National strength, or rather the lack of it, is a powerful leitmotif in spy literature of the Edwardian age, and for much of it this provided the central message. For if it was a genre which entertained millions of readers, it was also highly didactic. There are lessons for the nation embedded in the melodrama, and almost without fail it is a message which speaks with the voice of "Tory pessimism," that acute sense of decline and weakness which so marks the first decade of the twentieth century. And just as pessimism focussed as much on internal developments in British society as on the external perils surrounding the end of isolation, so these spy novels carry the message that not only is British espionage a necessary response to the behaviour of Britain's continental rivals, but that within Britain itself there are weaknesses and vulnerabilities which threaten national security.

Visions of internal disorder, decline, and decadence abundantly populate the imaginative world of the Edwardian spy novel, as they do of a wide spectrum of English literature in this period. In most cases the visions spring from deep apprehension about urbanism and the growth of a large urban working class. By the late Victorian years the lower classes had come to be seen as "no longer simple dependent inferiors [but as] . . . a mysterious and frightening new force gathered in the cities" [Samuel Hynes, *The Edwardian Turn of Mind*]. The revolutionary potential of the London poor was a spectre raised alarmingly by the great riot of 1886, and the nightmare of the London mob ransacking civilisation as represented by London's West End remained deeply embedded in middleclass memories for many years. Combined with horror at anarchist outrages throughout Europe in the 1890s, it provided materi-

al for Le Queux in *The Great War in England in 1897,* where the Franco-Russian invasion is accompanied by widespread disorder, an excuse, Le Queux tells his readers, "for Anarchism to vent its grievances against law and order, and, unshackled, [to] spread with rapidity through the length and breadth of the land." Emerging from the East End, "the scum of the metropolis had congregated to wage war against their own compatriots," and a major ransacking of the West End follows. Thus revolution at home and treachery by the Jew von Beilstein are presented as cause and consequence of invasion.

This fear of social unrest in war remained a theme in later writings of Le Queux and of others. But after the Boer War it was less the strength than the weakness of the urban working class which was the focus of concern. Following alarming revelations about the state of health of many recruits, it came to be argued by many social commentators that the weakness and "excitability" of the working class meant that they could not be relied upon to defend the nation against external threat, and might simultaneously be misled and manipulated by alien political ideologies such as anarchism and socialism. In *The New Order,* a collection of conservative essays published in 1908, the Earl of Malmesbury issued a representative warning that "Socialism—narcotic like—has drugged the spirit of patriotism into a forced slumber," while Lord Curzon warned the House of Lords in 1909 that a German invasion would unchain the force of law and order and lead to "the utter subversion of the old order of things." In terms of the Edwardian army, apprehension manifested itself in a widespread feeling "that the loyalty, patriotism, and determination to win of the city-bred masses was not what it might be" [T. H. E. Travers, "The Offensive and the Problem of Innovation in British Military Thought, 1870-1915," *Journal of Contemporary History* (1978)]. That the working class was at best a dubious asset is a message in Le Queux's *The Invasion of 1910* (1906), where a German invasion assisted by espionage finds a nation morally weak to resist, for "the peasantry which had formed the backbone of the nation had vanished and been replaced by the weak excitable population of the towns." Excitable indeed they are, especially in London's East End, for the "riff-raff from Whitechapel, those aliens whom we had so long welcomed and pampered in our midst . . . had swarmed westwards in lawless, hungry multitudes . . . not only were the aliens lawless, but the London unemployed and lower classes were now raising their voices. 'Stop the war!' was the cry heard on every hand." Indeed, it is the inability of the urban working class to fall back upon its own resources, combined with demands for peace from both the mercantile community and the socialists, that produces a mere compromise peace and a pyrrhic victory for the British empire "outwardly intact, but internally so weakened that only the most resolute reforms accomplished by the ablest and boldest statesman could have restored it to its old position" (Le Queux, *Invasion*). Socialism is a debilitating force in the moral outlook of the nation and a possibly treacherous one too. Both Le Queux and Oppenheim suggest that labour or socialist unrest (the two being considered synonymous) was capable of being manipulated by the Germans, although this was a theme closer to Le Queux's heart than to Oppenheim's. In an episode in *The Double Four,* which revolves around the exploits of the counter-spy Peter Ruff, Oppenheim depicts a deliberate attempt by Germany to weaken France through the exploitation of labour unrest, while in *Spies of the Kaiser* Le Queux reveals to his readers one "dastardly scheme by which, immediately before a dash is made upon our shore, a great railway strike is to be organized, ostensibly by the socialists, in order to further paralyse our trade and render us in various ways unable to resist the triumphal entry of the foe." It would be a mistake, however, to focus too narrowly on such explicit messages as these in a search for the social message of the Edwardian spy novel, important as they may be. For the message is more often to be found encoded in the symbolism they employ.

In 1907 Oppenheim presented readers of his novel *The Secret . . .* with the spectre of a German invasion plan central to whose success was the operation of a German espionage ring in Britain. German waiters in London form its core, and its headquarters are a German restaurant in Soho. The hero who foils this plot is Hardross Courage. He is thirty-three years old, a bachelor, a magistrate in two counties, a gentleman of ample means, and, in his own words, "Saxon to the backbone" (Oppenheim, *Secret . . .*). His home is Saxby Hall, and he plays cricket for his county, Medchestershire. The next year Le Queux published *Spies of the Kaiser,* also focussed on a German spy ring with 5,000 agents in Britain. The two young amateur agents who foil its machinations are John James Jacox and Ray Raymond. Jacox is a barrister and member of White's, while Ray, his friend from Balliol days, presents "the appearance of a typical athletic young Englishman, aged about thirty, clean-shaven, clean-limbed . . . an all-round good fellow" (Le Queux, *Spies*). Both Le Queux and Oppenheim had by this time perfected the image of the young amateur British agent. Characters such as Ray Raymond and Hardross Courage are stereotypes of the gentleman, symbolising the status quo in its social as well as in its great power dimensions. The ideal gentleman as he had evolved in the course of the nineteenth century was scrupulous, dutiful, fair, and loyal to country, family, and God. Almost literally rooted in the land, he was rarely to be found in business or commerce, and his presence in the city was primarily to carry out his obligations as ruler and administrator. It would be difficult to find a single British secret agent in the literature of these years who does not in some way appear as a gentleman cast in this mould, a man of the right social class and with the correct education carrying out his duty to his country regardless of cost or sacrifice. Just as gentlemen who work in the city affirm their status as gentlemen by maintaining their primary loyalties, interests, and residence in the country, to which they return with regularity, so the gentlemen secret agents of Edwardian fiction reaffirm their status by the rituals attaching to their class; the genteel atmosphere of their city rooms (their real homes, of course, being in the country), the comfort of pipe, fire, and whisky and soda ("which I always appreciate after the sloppy cognac-et-siphon of the Continental cafe," Duckworth Drew confides [Le Queux, *Secrets*]), grandfather chair, and valet. These men belong to the society of clubland heroes, and there can be no fear in the mind of the

reader that they will be tempted by the lures of city vice or socialism, or be other than deeply loyal to class, country, and king.

Values are affirmed not only by what members of a society share, but by contrasting them with a set of opposing values held by others outside the group. Thus symbolic inversions can be a means of highlighting and reaffirming accepted values. The character and behaviour of enemy spies in Edwardian fiction therefore is of importance in helping to establish and emphasize the value and legitimacy of the gentleman secret agent. Von Beilstein is Jewish, as is the head of the German Secret Service in Britain in LeQueux's *Spies of the Kaiser,* "a fat, flabby, sardonic man of about fifty-five with grey eyes full of craft and cunning, a prominent nose, and short-cropped grey beard" (Le Queux, *Spies*). Here Le Queux is resorting to anti-semitism as cultural shorthand, for Jews at this time were symbols of the modern, industrialised, capitalist, and urban civilisation which was seen as eroding British society and its cultural values. On the one hand, they personified crude *laissez-faire* capitalism, as the economist J. A. Hobson argued. On the other, they were often accused, at a time of large Jewish immigration into Britain, of being "anarchists and nihilists of the worst type" [1887 article in the *St. James Gazette*]. Either way they stood condemned as solvents of the social status quo. The individual Jew, moreover, stood as the dialectical antithesis, the symbolic negative, of the English gentleman. For he was, in popular belief, mercenary and cowardly, a man without country, honour, loyalty, or scruple. Essentially, it was often argued, the Jew could not be totally patriotic, for the links of religion and race gave him cosmopolitan interests incompatible with the notion of loyalty to the nation state. These were the years of the emerging Jewish world conspiracy theory, and as one British writer put it in 1905, Jews could never display patriotism "of the same quality as those whose blood thrills at the display of the Union Jack" [Colin Holmes, *Anti-Semitism in British Society*]. The ambiguity of the Jew, therefore, made him a perfect candidate for the role of villainous and mercenary spy counterpoised to the amateur gentleman agent.

Not all enemy spies, of course, were depicted in fiction as Jewish. It is hardly surprising that the antisemitism which is to be found in much of Le Queux's writing is absent from Oppenheim's; for although Oppenheim grew up an Anglican, his family appears to have been of Jewish origin (John Buchan once described him as "my master in fiction . . . the greatest Jewish writer since Isaiah"). But what is interesting is that Oppenheim, like Le Queux, was fascinated by the idea of cosmopolitan networks controlling or influencing world events. In *Mysterious Mr. Sabin,* his first spy novel, the plot against England is foiled by the intervention of some mysterious international secret society, possibly an order of Freemasonry. Its sequel, *The Yellow Crayon,* revolves around an international order of that name whose ostensible objectives are somewhat akin to those of the Primrose League; while in *The Double Four* (1911), Peter Ruff, the secret agent fighting against the German Count von Hern-Bernadine ("the Devil Incarnate"), is in the service of an international society, the Double Four. "It is no longer the wealth of the world alone we may control, but the actual destiny of nations," Ruff is told by its spokesman, the Marquis de Sogrange (Oppenheim, *Double Four*).

Apprehension that the destiny of the British nation might be influenced by elements alien or external to it clearly lay behind this concern with cosmopolitan and international clandestine networks, and Le Queux's writing in particular is marked by a strongly nationalist and xenophobic fervour whose stridency often appears in inverse proportion to its underlying confidence. It is not surprising therefore to find many fictional melodramas closely attuned to the propaganda of some of the more obviously militarist organisations of Edwardian England. Both Le Queux and Oppenheim were supporters of the National Service League, the most militarist and most important organisation campaigning for universal military training in these years. In the minds of its founders national service would not only prepare the nation against invasion, but "would revive the disappearing manliness of the race" [Earl of Malmesbury, *The New Order*]. Le Queux was particularly associated with the figure of Lord Roberts, its moving spirit and second president. Roberts, who fuelled invasion and espionage speculation dramatically when he claimed in a speech to the House of Lords in November 1908 that there were already 80,000 trained German soldiers in the United Kingdom, wrote a foreword for *The Invasion of 1910* and also provided the author with some technical assistance on military matters during its writing. Le Queux became obsessed with the German menace at about this time; he was convinced of the reality of the invasion threat and of German espionage, and his novels can be seen as in large part fictional projections of the Boer War hero's warnings about the lack of national preparedness and vigilance. His spy stories are packed with warnings against Germany, exhortations for some kind of national conscription, and demands for more effective action against foreign spies and aliens in general. He had little love for the Liberals and the government they had formed in 1906, a prejudice which found its way readily into his writings. Arthur Balfour, who apparently had a sneaking liking for some of his novels, was once reputed to have said that a Le Queux spy or invasion novel was worth several thousand votes for the Conservative party. It is not difficult to see Balfour's point when one looks, for example, at *Spies of the Kaiser* (1908), where its hero Ray Raymond explains that the prevalence of German spies is due to government policy. ". . . have not the police received orders from our Government to close their eyes to the doings of these gentry?" he asks rhetorically. "England is the paradise of the spy . . . " (Le Queux, *Spies*). But Le Queux, while the most strident, was not the only author writing with a political purpose. Erskine Childers felt in writing *The Riddle of the Sands* that he needed to demonstrate that "the time had come for training all Englishmen either for the sea or for the rifle," and in the preface to his book he referred scathingly to the "pitiful inadequacy of the official secret service" (Childers, *Riddle*).

That Britain needed an adequate and competitive secret service was a primary message of all Edwardian spy novels. But this need posed a severe dilemma, at least at first glance. For if one dimension of the problem of national strength consisted of internal moral weakness through a corrosion of traditional values, did not the very fact of resorting to clandestine espionage call these values into question and thereby assist the process of decadence and decline? If the essence of clandestine espionage was deceit, was it not then incompatible with the behaviour of gentlemen reared in the moral climate of the late Victorian public school? Colonel G. A. Furse reminded readers of his handbook *Information in War* (1895) that "a spy, in the general acceptance of the term, is a low sneak," thus reinforcing that earlier stricture of the official history of the Crimean War, that "the gathering of Knowledge by clandestine means is repulsive to the feelings of an English gentleman."

By the beginning of the Edwardian era it was clear that this was a precept more honoured in the breach than the observance. The two branches of the armed services each contained organized intelligence branches, and British gentlemen regularly sallied forth on clandestine espionage missions on their behalf. The Official Secrets Act had made it clear that there were important secrets affecting high matters of state and diplomacy which needed to be protected against foreign espionage, although there was as yet no separate and unified British secret service. On the domestic front the activities of anarchists, nihilists, and Irish Fenians in the 1880s and 1890s had focussed much public attention on the world of clandestine police operations with its employment of police spies, informers, and *agents provocateurs*. Few doubted the need for these measures, and a writer in the *Quarterly Review* of 1893 had declared that "the faithful political spy, like the faithful detective, deserves well of the State which employs him."

It was the task of the Edwardian spy novelists to apply this message to the context of diplomacy and international relations and to render acceptable to their readership the notion that Britain, like her continental neighbours, needed the assistance of clandestine espionage. But simultaneously they needed to show that this did not denote the demise of the gentleman, that symbol of traditional values and the lynchpin of the existing order. This contradictory message was conveyed by the use of various devices. The most common was to insist that Britain was merely exercising legitimate self-defence and that any moral obloquy pertaining to the world of espionage belonged to those who had forced it upon her. Jack Jardine, head of the British secret service in Le Queux's *The Man from Downing Street* (1904), puts it best: "There is, I know, something repugnant to the British mind where the secret agent is concerned; but it must be remembered that England's enemies nowadays keep up a whole army of unscrupulous spies. She is compelled, therefore, both in her own interests and in those of European peace, to supplement her attachés at the various Embassies by a corps of secret agents . . . ". The commonly used verbal trick in this passage has already been noted: foreigners used "spies," but the British employed "secret agents." More accurately, of course, Britain did not employ agents at all. Gentlemen merely served their country to defeat foreign plots, and if they did so in a purely amateur and accidental way, so much the better. Hence the prevalence, especially in early novels of the era, of the accidental agent, the young man cast unexpectedly into danger. This is the pattern in Headon Hill's *Spies of the Wight* and in Max Pemberton's *Pro Patria*, while the opening chapter of Oppenheim's *A Maker of History* (1905) is actually entitled "An accidental spy." Similarly, the two heroes of *The Riddle of the Sands* are merely "two young gentlemen in a seven ton boat, with a taste for amateur hydrography and police duty combined." But messing about in boats was one thing, serious secret service work another. Le Queux for one insisted that the age of *ad hoc* and coincidental intelligence was not enough. As Duckworth Drew explains, "Our Empire has such tremendous responsibilities that we cannot now depend upon mere birth, wealth, and honest dealing, but must call in shrewdness, tact, subterfuge, and the employment of secret agents in order to combat the plots of those ever seeking to accomplish England's overthrow" (Le Queux, *Secrets*). Yet Le Queux is quick to make it clear that birth, wealth, and honest dealing are not pushed aside, merely supplemented. Le Queux's agents are gentlemen to the point of caricature, and if they are secret agents they are in their essential qualities indistinguishable from the diplomats with whom they work. As Hugh Morrice tells his readers in *Revelations of the Secret Service,* all members of the "Nameless Department" of the Foreign Office, from Sir Charles Houghton, "the erect grey-haired, steely-eyed diplomat who is our chief, down to the most recently joined young attaché, are everyone of them cosmopolitans and gentlemen" (Le Queux, *Revelations*). Indeed there is no pecuniary gain for Morrice in his job, and, as Le Queux informs the reader, this binds him firmly to tradition; for "in the heart of the Secret Service agent is the ancient love of adventure, the same as that in the hearts of the buccaneers of old, in the hearts of the Crusaders, or in those of Columbus, or of Raleigh and their fellows, all patriots, all adventurers" (Le Queux, *Revelations*).

The adventures of Duckworth Drew, Hugh Morrice, Hardross Courage, Peter Ruff, and others symbolised Britain's determination to survive the complexities and dangers of the new era of international intrigue and conflict. Their ability to unmask and confound enemy spies and plots acted as reassurance that the opening moves towards the continental commitment which drew Britain closer to Europe in the Edwardian years would not lead to the triumph of the foreigner or the weakening of national character and independence. At the same time they carried the message that this could be assured only if governments adopted new institutions and policies to strengthen national defence, and in doing so they contributed to the strong vein of militarism which characterised Edwardian society. Like the militarists, however, they were concerned with more than matters purely exterior to the nation. For the duel between the figure of the English gentleman secret agent and the alien enemy spy symbolised a conflict of values which lay at the heart of Edwardian society and was responsible for so many of its anxieties about the future. The victories of Duckworth Drew and his fellow agents provided a deeply conservative reassurance to those troubled by the emergence of that industrial and urban society which so obsessed the pessimists of Edwardian England, and which led C. F. G. Masterman in 1906 to wonder "whether civilisation is about to blossom

into flower or wither in a ruined tangle of dead leaves and faded gold." If, as Julian Symons has argued, there are two traditions in the spy story, then the first, "conservative, supporting authority, making the assertion that agents are fighting to protect something valuable," is firmly established in these years, a period when crime literature as a whole offered its readers a reassuring world in which those who tried to disturb the established order were always discovered and punished. In an age when the values which had reflected and reinforced the social order of nineteenth-century England were under siege from the onslaught of new political philosophies and social forces, the spy as gentleman patriot emerged as a hero who defeated not only the threatening foreigner, but also exorcised the demons of social disorder and political unrest which troubled the imaginations of so many in Edwardian England. (pp. 489-509)

David A. T. Stafford, "Spies and Gentlemen: The Birth of the British Spy Novel, 1893-1914," in Victorian Studies, *Vol. 24, No. 4, Summer, 1981, pp. 489-509.*

Katy Fletcher

[*In the following essay, Fletcher discusses the nature of the modern American spy novel and the ways in which it differs from its predecessor of the Cold War era.*]

Détente had little effect upon the secret war between the superpowers, in either the real operations of the CIA or in the adventures of the spy novel. However, there was a noticeable thaw in the relationship between the superpowers, and in this atmosphere the shape of spy fiction also changed.

In the modern American spy novel the enemy remained the same to a great extent, but the plots and the characters became more sophisticated. In the 1970s and 1980s, incidents which provoked hostility between America and the USSR took place in isolated areas of the world, and did not threaten nuclear holocaust. The location in these spy adventures changed from the exotic settings of Europe and the richer Far East, to the Third World areas of Asia and Africa.

While in Britain the James Bond stories began to be satirized, and authors like John le Carré injected a cold dose of cynicism into their spy novels, in America this form of literature was turning towards a similar trend in realism—not only were the authors making their characters more human, and the plots more credible, they were also portraying the world of espionage with greater seriousness. The sophistication of the modern spy novel was achieved by the use of real events and historical characters as well as the exploration of contemporary themes such as terrorism.

Another factor which contributed to the rise of the modern spy novel was that an increasing number of CIA veterans had written spy fiction. Two members of this group, William F. Buckley and Charles McCarry, will be discussed later. As the number of these authors appears to be growing, we may be able to expect a greater degree of authenticity in the portrayal of the intelligence world.

To understand how the modern spy novel evolved, it is necessary to return to the cold war spy novel of the 1960s. One author writing spy fiction at this time, who also had experience in intelligence, was E. Howard Hunt. He wrote a series of novels depicting the adventures of CIA agent Peter Ward, who closely resembled Ian Fleming's James Bond.

In the Peter Ward series, Hunt expressed a simple view of the world divided between the good (the Western democracies) and the bad (the USSR, China and their communist satellites). This perspective was strongly supported by both American spy novelists and their reading public until the end of the 1960s, when the world could no longer be seen in such simple terms.

Hunt's depiction of this naive view of the world has been pointed out by John R. Snyder, a critic of spy fiction. In discussing Hunt's novel, *A Festival for Spies,* as an example, Snyder wrote:

> It is the opportunity Southeast Asia offers the spy to indulge his Puritan yen for decadence that Hunt responds to in his fiction, not the imperative to explore the ramifications of political and cultural conflict: giveaway symptoms are his racist depiction of Asian puppets as children and his invariably 'doll-like' bevies of slant-eyed women. All Hunt's world of intrigue amounts to is a backdrop of exotic vice cum communist villainy. Consequently, his hero possesses a bogus guarantee of success.

For twenty-two years, Hunt worked for the CIA as a clandestine political operator. Peter Ward provided a vicarious escapism to the author. As a result, Hunt did not bring a new authenticity to his spy novels—they rather provided an outlet for his frustrated ambitions in the CIA and also acted as a platform for his conservative views. In this regard, Hunt can be compared to Ian Fleming, who also had knowledge of intelligence organization and operations, but decided not to utilize this information to make his spy fiction more realistic, instead choosing a more sensational approach to the subject.

The spy novel is rooted in political assumptions and yet in the past spy fiction, as can be seen in Hunt's Peter Ward series, relegated the political situation to a subordinate position, while elevating the exploits of the spy hero. Authors of spy fiction in Britain and America, before and after the second world war, have consistently shown the spy defending the political status quo against attack. The maintenance of the political position was accepted unquestioningly by the authors and their readers. As Grant Hugo, a student of spy fiction, has confirmed [in 'The Political Influence of the Thriller," *Contemporary Review* (1972)]:

> Subversion of the established political order, whether the villains are domestic or foreign, has long been a traditional theme for the thriller. Most writers handle it on the fairly simple assumption, which could be a reflection of the views of readers rather than an attempt to influ-

ence them, that the status quo is acceptable and its subversion a crime. Complications arise when the powers that be are infiltrated by the enemy or otherwise incapable of right action, so that the hero must actually struggle against authority to restore the just equilibrium . . . It is striking how often, nowadays, this father-figure turns out to be some kind of secret policeman.

The spy novel is essentially written for entertainment and read as a form of escapism. The spy novel is not compelled to be realistic, or even plausible, except that unlike science fiction, it claims to represent the real political world. The potential danger in this kind of literature lies in the attitudes the spy novel projects in building up a generally false image of the real world of politics and espionage.

In the past, spy novels have propagated illusions about the relationship between the USSR and America. This kind of thriller literature thrives on conflict; therefore it has a vested interest in reinforcing hostile attitudes to countries with which America has no sympathy or understanding. The cold war has provided, and still does provide a basic framework for many spy stories. As a result, the spy novel has merely reflected, and thereby reinforced, popular beliefs and prejudices. W. T. Tyler (pseudonym for S. J. Hamrick), the author of two spy novels, noted this characteristic of spy fiction:

> The spy novel is very much a recitative of popular clichés . . . the post World War II spy novel is a recitative of cold war clichés. Ian Fleming, a great favorite of John Kennedy, is probably the best example of that. Spy novelists like Fleming did little to help us understand the Russians or the Soviet bureaucracy, did little to help us better understand ourselves or our times. (As George Kennan points out in a recent article in *The New Yorker,* the genre has probably contributed to our gross ignorance of the Soviet Union and heightened our paranoia.)

The modern spy novel of the late 1970s and early 1980s has just begun to explore and question previously accepted political assumptions. This form of literature has discarded its overt propaganda function of the 1960s in favour of being more topical and more accurate in its depiction of international relations and the role of espionage.

The sensational spy thriller as practised by Howard Hunt is no longer so prevalent today. Apart from treating the business of espionage and politics with greater seriousness, writers of better quality are now attracted to spy fiction, like W. T. Tyler, who have used their literary skills to enhance the credibility of their characters, the plots and the locales. A number of authors feel that being labelled as a spy writer is derogatory, reflecting badly on their literary talents. W. T. Tyler, for instance, said that the four novels he wrote had been about politics rather than espionage and did not like being referred to as a spy novelist.

Modern spy fiction can no longer be described as 'lowbrow' or literature of poor quality because of its subject matter. The second world war and the cold war may have elevated the reputation of spying, as Allen Dulles once remarked, but the literary quality of spy fiction has risen due to the good writers, like Tyler, Charles McCarry and William F. Buckley, currently writing fiction of this kind.

Since the mid 1970s, with the Congressional investigations of the CIA, the American public has become better informed about espionage practices. Readers of spy fiction are now familiar with spy jargon and tradecraft techniques. These new elements are accepted, and expected, as part of the literary baggage of spy novels, and if they are absent, the author may lack credibility as a spy novelist.

Paul Henissart, an author of three spy novels, remarked upon this new awareness in his reading public:

> Today's spy stories undoubtedly require a high degree of realism and precision. Readers to whom they are addressed are better informed than in the past, a fact which an author should look upon with satisfaction: it is no challenge to write for the uninformed.

The contemporary spy novel has become increasingly related to the actual political world, as well as bringing further authenticity to the world of espionage. With more information available to the public, readers of spy fiction demand accuracy from authors writing about espionage. As John Atkins, a literary critic of British spy fiction, expressed it:

> The modern spy writers refer constantly, not only to the sovereign states by name, but to their actual policies, their leaders, their espionage organizations, their successes and their failures. Sometimes historical personages appear as characters in the novels—spies like Philby particularly, but also Prime Ministers and Presidents. Every effort is made to create an impression of actuality.

William F. Buckley attempted to establish this new authenticity in his spy novels by inserting imaginary conversations between politicians and intelligence officers. For instance, in *Who's On First,* there are conversations between Allen Dulles, Director of Central Intelligence, and Dean Acheson, Secretary of State. As mentioned by Atkins, another characteristic of the modern spy novel is the description of real events. The CIA suffered from several intelligence failures, which were well publicized in the 1960s and 1970s, and these events have provided stories for the spy novelist. For example, in Buckley's novel *Marco Polo, If You Can,* the flight of Gary Powers in the U-2 spy plane shot down over Russia in 1960 is described in detail.

International terrorism is another topic which has recently interested the spy novelist. A number of authors, such as Howard Hunt in *The Gaza Intercept* (1981), Charles McCarry in *The Better Angels* (1979) and Paul Henissart in *Narrow Exit* (1973), have adopted terrorism as the central theme of their novels.

Terrorist activities question the political status quo, and as more spy novels explore this theme, it shows that the authors are no longer content to use the spy novel to reaffirm popular political attitudes. As the spy novel has grown in sophistication, it has begun to question the basic political principles accepted for so long. By writing about terrorists and minority political groups, these authors publicize their cause and strive to understand the terrorists themselves, questioning the reasoning behind the government's reaction to terrorist demands. In this way, the spy novel has begun to educate its readers on controversial issues, instead of fuelling their prejudices and paranoias.

The moral ambiguities of espionage are also brought to the surface in the modern spy novel. In the cold war, the moral issue was relatively clear-cut, but in the late 1960s and 1970s it became harder to define. This was partly due to the revelations of CIA activities in this period, which encouraged the belief that the CIA was just as immoral in its methods as the KGB. The spy novel reflected this ambiguity by exploring the theme of defection, e.g. Victor Marchetti's spy novel *The Rope Dancer* (1971). Moral doubts were also shown in the creation of the vigilante spy hero, who resigned from the CIA in disgust, but still found himself embroiled in the machinations of the agency. These disenchanted heroes can be found in W. T. Tyler's *The Man Who Lost the War* (1980) and Howard Hunt's *The Hargrave Deception* (1980).

An examination of the novels of McCarry, Tyler and Buckley shows how the modern spy novel may be differentiated from its typical cold war predecessor. William F. Buckley has written six spy novels to date, beginning with *Saving the Queen* in 1976. All the novels feature CIA operative Blackford Oakes, a graduate of Yale and a Catholic, like the author. Buckley is a syndicated columnist and the host of a weekly television show. He is renowned for his conservative views which can be found in his novels. For eight or nine months, he was affiliated with the CIA in Mexico, where he worked as a deep-cover agent under Howard Hunt. When asked if his CIA experience had contributed to his spy novels, Buckley replied:

> In my first book, 'Queen', the training received by Blackford Oakes is, in exact detail, the training I received. In that sense, it's autobiographical.

His experience in the CIA may well have helped him present espionage operations in his novels, although Buckley claimed that this was not one of the reasons that inspired him to write spy stories. He left the CIA because he was bored by the work:

> Deep-cover agents are really expected to lead full lives doing something else, and they are used for extraordinary endeavors. There were no extraordinary endeavors flashed before me by my boss, Howard Hunt, during the period that I worked for the CIA.

Buckley believed that his novels had an ideological purpose:

> To demonstrate that we *are* the good guys and they're the bad guys. I began writing spy novels because I thought the point was worth making in a fluid context that would capture a wider audience.

He did not write his spy novels to inform the public about how the CIA worked abroad, but saw the spy story partly as a form of entertainment and also as a way of promoting and supporting the CIA. Buckley regarded this form of literature as an ideal vehicle for expressing his own opinions about espionage and the cold war.

He viewed détente as a temporary aberration in the relationship between America and the USSR. This explained why most of his spy novels were set in the past—in the 1950s and 1960s when the cold war was at its height. These novels illustrated the competitive element that characterized the relationship between the two nations during this period. For instance, in *Who's On First* (1980), the race was on between the superpowers to put the first satellite into orbit. Both countries had reached an impasse in their development of the satellite, and needed different solutions to complete the project. The mission of CIA operative, Oakes, was to kidnap two Russian scientists from a delegation to obtain the necessary information to launch the American satellite before the Russians. But the plan backfired and the scientists, who had been turned by the Americans, were unmasked by the Russians, who traded the lives of their scientists to get the information they needed from the Americans.

This plot was an imaginary reconstruction of the events that led up to the USSR launching Sputnik, the first earth satellite in 1957. The Americans have always been reluctant to acknowledge Russian technical breakthroughs, such as the first intercontinental ballistic missile in 1957, and the first moon satellite in 1959. Buckley's reinterpretation of events preceding the launch of Sputnik appealed to those people who preferred to believe that the communists had acquired the information to achieve this goal only by foul means.

Although Buckley's novels look back to the cold war period, by using actual events and people in history, he illustrates some of the new characteristics of the modern spy novel to lend credibility to his fiction. Buckley's stories are historical, but they are also allegorical. He believed that the cold war was the normal state of affairs in the relationship between the superpowers, and setting his stories in the past allowed him to express his political views in a more congenial time frame.

Another author with experience in intelligence is Charles McCarry. He began his career as a journalist, then became a speechwriter for President Eisenhower, before joining the CIA in 1958. He remained with the agency for nine to ten years, working in Europe and Africa, and retired from the CIA in 1967 to become a freelance writer. He has produced five spy novels so far, the first of which was *The Miernik Dossier* in 1973.

This novel was constructed in the form of a dossier, with agents' reports, headquarters' communications, intercepted letters and transcriptions of bugged conversations. It was a skilfully made novel and original in its presentation. By involving the reader in the inner workings of intelligence collection, the author made him play the role of the intelligence analyst—sifting relevant from irrelevant information from different sources, and then having to figure out its meaning and take some action.

McCarry's hero, Paul Christopher, criticized his own intelligence agency because he believed that the cold war at-

mosphere had had a bad effect upon the attitudes and priorities of agency personnel:

> I am going to say a very harsh thing that is directed as much (or more) against myself as against all of you people who sit inside, making the plans that I carry out. I think we ran Miernik as we did primarily for the fun of it. We have come to look on our work, in the field at least, largely as a sport. Miernik provided an opportunity to match wits with the opposition . . . It was a chance not just to beat the Russians for the umpty-umpth straight time, it was an opportunity to humiliate the bastards . . .

Christopher did not see espionage as a game when people died as a result of their antics. McCarry showed in his novels that one of the tragedies of the cold war was the highly suspicious atmosphere it generated between the East and the West. This put pressure on the CIA to obtain information and then act upon it. But it also spawned a bitter rivalry between the superpowers, involving innocent people in the struggle. In McCarry's novels one gets the impression that there can be no ultimate victors in such warfare, only victims.

McCarry's second novel, *The Tears of Autumn* (1974), was also concerned with the pursuit of truth and the costs of its acquisition. The novel was set in 1963 after the assassination of President John F. Kennedy. Paul Christopher believed that he knew who had arranged it and for what reason. He set out to prove his theory that the CIA had arranged the murder of President Ngo Dinh Diem of Vietnam, and three weeks later Diem supporters sent their agents to shoot Kennedy in revenge. President Lyndon B. Johnson believed in this theory, but the Castro revenge motive was perhaps more credible. However, these examples were still speculative explanations of Kennedy's assassination.

This novel was published in 1974, a time when several CIA apostates, like Victor Marchetti, were voicing their criticisms of the agency. Donald McCormick, a critic of spy fiction, remarked [in *Who's Who in Spy Fiction* (1977)] that people thought that McCarry had joined their ranks for his novel

> had government and CIA officials alike hopping around like scalded cats wondering what new revelations were going to emerge. The book caused a stir because its story was built on an explanation of the first Kennedy assassination, which not unnaturally irked those officials whose main purpose in life seems to have been trying to stop the case from being reopened.

McCarry said about this story: 'Maybe the Vietnamese did kill Kennedy. But they sure didn't tell me.' George Grella, a student of spy fiction, remarked [in John M. Reilly's *Twentieth Century Crime and Mystery Writers* (1980)].

> *The Tears of Autumn* is one of the best of the post-Kennedy assassination thrillers, a subgenre that has flourished since the event and remains an important index to the cultural paranoia of the country and the time.

As in Buckley's spy novels, McCarry used real events to

Richard Burton in Martin Ritt's The Spy Who Came in from the Cold.

reflect contemporary fears and paranoias. But there was a difference between these two authors, which is apparent in their novels. McCarry worked for the CIA for nearly ten years, as opposed to Buckley's nine months with the agency. Unlike Buckley's novels, we catch a glimpse of the authentic atmosphere of espionage in McCarry's first novel. Here we are drawn into the aura of doubt and suspicion which usually accompanies real espionage operations. The reader is also presented with some of the problems that beset an intelligence agency—like the momentum of an espionage mission founded on suspicion alone, as well as the difficulty in interpreting facts. Thomas Powers, the biographer of Richard Helms, verified this quality in McCarry's novels [in *The Man Who Kept the Secrets: Richard Helms and the CIA* (1979)]:

> McCarry says that he spent ten years with the Agency as a 'singleton', an officer working outside the usual confines of a CIA station, mostly in Europe and Africa, and his novels capture a sound feel for intelligence in the field, which involves a good deal of political intrigue, but not much melodrama.

A more serious account of espionage in fiction can be found in the novels of W. T. Tyler, the pseudonym of S. J. Hamrick. He has written four novels, only two of which can be called spy novels: *The Man Who Lost the War* (1980) and *Rogue's March* (1982). Although Tyler never worked for an intelligence agency, he had some knowledge of the CIA and its officers:

> I wasn't an intelligence officer but a foreign service officer (although I served in the army counter-intelligence corps before my diplomatic career began). As a diplomat serving abroad, I knew and worked with intelligence officers. That experience helped to the extent that I knew something about the clandestine services.

Tyler served with the State Department for nearly twenty years, seven of which he spent in Central and East Africa. Two of his novels are set in Africa, one of these, *Rogue's March,* is about a coup d'état in a recently independent nation in Central Africa, possibly Zaire, and how the people involved in its disorders—the Africans, the diplomats and the intelligence officers—tried to understand and control events.

The principal character in this story is Andy Reddish, a veteran American intelligence officer under diplomatic cover, who is just completing a long tour of duty. Reddish knows some of the country's political leaders and the problem it faces as a newly independent nation. However, his familiarity with the country does not help him in his efforts to try and define the political implications of the coup for the benefit of his superiors in Washington DC, especially when they conflict with the official desire to show the event as a counter-communist seizure.

Joseph Hosey, an ex-CIA employee and a reviewer of spy fiction, commented upon the level of authenticity reached in this novel [in *FILS (Foreign Intelligence Literary Scene)* (December 1982)].

> Apart from a few necessary safe houses, encrypted cables, ambiguous phone calls, and casual sexual relationships, the day-to-day machinery of the usual fictional intelligence operation is not to be found here. But the atmosphere of doubt, anxiety, caution, and unexpected conflict in which real intelligence operations are in fact conducted has seldom been so well portrayed.

Instead of the archetypal spy novel with the agent hero receiving orders from his boss at headquarters, then plunging into a foreign environment to carry out his mission, we have here the experienced CIA intelligence officer in place, with knowledge of the country and its political leaders, trying to understand the violence that has erupted. Andy Reddish is not a fantasy figure cast in the mould of James Bond; he corresponds to the CIA intelligence officer stationed abroad. Thus Tyler succeeds in telling us an exciting story of politics and espionage without unnecessary embellishment or sensational melodrama.

Rogue's March could be interpreted as an anti-CIA novel, but this would be an inaccurate assessment of the work. In the past, the State Department resented the CIA because of its unlimited funds, its lack of accountability, and because of the danger that secret operations could jeopardize diplomacy. However, if Tyler criticized the bureaucracy of the CIA in this novel, he was just as critical of the performance of the British and American ambassadors at the scene, while he gave Reddish's problems as a CIA officer sympathetic treatment.

When asked for his opinion of the spy novel Tyler wrote:

> I think of the spy novel as a vehicle for entertainment rather than a forum for public education or getting my own views across (although the one doesn't exclude the other). To the extent that everything is sacrificed to entertainment as in most spy novels on the best seller list, few can be taken seriously. The characters are generally sterotypes, the action absurdly melodramatic, and the writing usually bad.

Tyler's novels have introduced a new sophistication and maturity to the American spy novel, and they have shown that such a novel can achieve literary distinction. As Joseph Hosey remarked [in a letter]: 'Tyler is in my opinion the only American writing respectable fiction of this kind at present.' It is ironic that Tyler, a man with no experience in intelligence, has written the best spy novels in America, according to Hosey. Perhaps this tells us that working for the CIA does not necessarily produce the best spy novelists.

Through the novels of Buckley, McCarry and Tyler, the American spy novel has undergone a process of development. These novels displayed a questioning awareness of

politics, and explored the relationship between politics and espionage. The cold war still provides a theme for the spy novel, but the political situation is seen with more detachment and objectivity than before. The cold war no longer dominates the spy novel as it did in the 1960s, as other interests have begun to attract readers and the authors of spy fiction.

In 1977 Donald McCormick speculated upon the future of spy fiction:

> If one must peer into the future of the spy story, I would suggest that the spy stories of the next decade should be assessed on the developments in real-life espionage. As the cloak-and-dagger tactics of past decades disappear (and Watergate has dealt them a severe blow, not to mention the anti-Castro tactics of the CIA), so will computerized espionage become more important. Here is enormous scope for the spy story writer as the technique develops. After all, the frontline spies on whose unfailing watch we now depend for the peace of the world are built into the machines which monitor the anti-nuclear submarine watch round the world.

In the light of the events of the mid 1970s, we now know that, although the Watergate scandal and the anti-Castro plans of the CIA dealt a severe blow to CIA morale, it was not fatal and the agency has since recovered. With the advent of technological espionage, the all-action hero of spy fiction may appear anachronistic. However, it is unlikely that he will ever disappear, especially as in the mid-1970s the advantages of human intelligence were re-advocated. (pp. 319-29)

Katy Fletcher, "Evolution of the Modern American Spy Novel," in The Journal of Contemporary History, *Vol. 22, No. 2, April, 1987, pp. 319-31.*

THE FEMALE SPY

Patricia Craig and Mary Cadogan

[In the following essay, Craig and Cadogan trace the development of the female spy in early American and English espionage fiction.]

By the end of the first decade of the twentieth century, women detectives on both sides of the Atlantic could, at least in fiction, command respect. Female spies, however, were synonymous with seduction, ruthlessness and betrayal, and were therefore far less popular. During the First World War women began to be commended for taking up many forms of work which only a year or two earlier would have been considered unfeminine, and the fictional woman spy then started to come into her own and comply with the mood of patriotic determination; she was gradually to push out the frontiers of female sleuthing, and to help to modernize the image of the 'lady detective'.

The special agents became vivid symbols of independence, but their attitudes were more rebellious and their exploits more bizarre than those of the detectives. There was a touch of bravura about their clothes, coiffures and perfumes, as Plummer, a master-crook in the Sexton Blake saga, finds out when he first meets Vali Mata-Vali:

> She was dressed in a jacket and harem pantaloons of heavy silk . . . her hair was black as a moonless night. . . . Plummer was an expert in scents and he knew her elusive waft at once as that very rare and extremely expensive essence known as 'Moi-même'.

(In fact, many a fictional female spy, despite her calculation and cunning, has ruined a dashing disguise and given herself away by failing to acknowledge that a male opponent might become familiar with the perfume to which she is addicted. Like Vali Mata-Vali, Irma Paterson in the Bulldog Drummond canon is a dark and dominant beauty, adept as a crook and as a spy. Her passion for Guerlain's 'Vol de Nuit'—which is, surprisingly, the same perfume as that favoured by Drummond's impeccably English wife, Phyllis—betrays her to Sapper's heavyweight hero on more than one occasion.)

Vali Mata-Vali is described as a 'devilishly beautiful' actress/dancer from French Indo-China, and she first appeared in the 1920s. She owed more than just part of her exotic name to the notorious Mata Hari, who was shot for espionage against the Allies. (For decades, the myth and tarnished glamour of Mata Hari continued to set the pattern for fictional women spies. By 1964, when realism had more or less overtaken the espionage story, Arthur Marshall in *Girls will be Girls* was able to cut Mata Hari down to size with his customary wit: 'Priestess, dancer, lady? . . . We now know the answers and they are "never, certainly not, and, alas, no."') Whatever the facts of her career, Mata Hari became a symbol of vampish betrayal and of the woman (usually a foreigner) who sells her services to the highest bidder. In fiction this was likely to be the Kaiser, or perhaps a gang of fiendishly cunning orientals planning to take over the world. Fortunately for the Allies, however, even the most intimidating Teutonic adventuress could usually be tamed and brought over to our side by the attentions of an upstanding Englishman. This gratifying fact is demonstrated in Marthe McKenna's *My Master Spy* (1935) when Clive Granville captivates Galie Fhel, a luscious German agent:

> Weakly and in a submissive voice she spoke, her eyes seeking his in the darkened room . . . 'I care not for the command, and it matters not who you are—who Admiral Von Kramann thinks you are,' and her arm lifted and fell in a hopeless gesture. 'I love you . . . My whole life is a sham—all this—' sweeping an expressive slender hand around her, 'false as the false glitter of tinsel.'

In a study of early espionage stories, one of the first questions which arises is 'When is a spy not a spy?' The answer of course is 'When she is British.' In this connection, appropriate distinctions are made between espionage and counter-espionage activities. English women operating behind the German lines were invariably thought of as serving their country, while German women living in Britain and helping the Central Powers seemed in the popular view despicable, demoniacal and sexually corrupt. These contrasting images were reinforced by the personality differences of Nurse Edith Cavell and Mata Hari. Although it is questionable whether either could be described as a spy in the conventional sense, both were indicted and executed for espionage and there is no doubt that Nurse Cavell behaved with a dignity and selflessness that were not part of Mata Hari's make-up. Mata Hari has been surrounded by so much retrospective fantasy that although her existence was real enough she has almost become a fictional character. There are lurid anecdotes relating to her habit of appearing nude 'in an effort at wholesale enticement' when she was about to be arrested, and about her bathing daily in milk and dancing naked in her cell. She did suffer the ultimate irony of the promiscuous female spy: part of the evidence that condemned her was her contraceptive injection fluid containing oxycyanide of mercury, which the French authorities thought was secret ink. Sam Waagenaar's *The Murder of Mata Hari* (1964) is an intriguing attempt to sift facts from fiction, and he suggests that she was punished as much for her vanity and promiscuity as for espionage: apparently German secret service records never confirmed that Mata Hari was one of their agents. Waagenaar builds up a picture of a vain, gullible and histrionic woman anxious 'at all costs . . . to prove that she was important, that she could be of use'. Her reply to her French interrogator was unequivocal, naïve and, apparently, frank:

> I love officers. I have loved them all my life . . .
> It is my greatest pleasure to sleep with them . . .
> and moreover I like to make comparisons between the various nationalities. I swear that the relations I have had with the officers you mention were inspired by nothing but the feeling and sentiments which I have just described to you.

Edith Cavell, whose crime against the German state was to smuggle Allied soldiers out of occupied Belgium, provided a less flamboyant but more morally worthy prototype for authors of spy stories. Curiously, she seems to be as much the end result of late Victorian and Edwardian fictional projections as an influence on the espionage stories that came after her. In Volume 1 of the *Harmsworth Magazine* (1898/99) there are one or two stories about discreet young women of education, integrity and resource who become involved in unpaid and extremely patriotic 'diplomacy'. (Spying was then an even dirtier word than during the First World War.) In 'How The Minister's Notes Were Recovered' by Beatrice Heron-Maxwell, Lady Anstiss, 'the most beautiful girl in Brussels', helps a young diplomat to retrieve 'some important notes' accidentally sent by the US Minister to the wrong man. The story starts on a slightly feminist note—'Women move the levers nowadays, though men make 'em'—but ends with Lady Anstiss figuratively in the young diplomat's protective arms, and readers appreciating that espionage is not really a suitable exercise for a woman, though a fearfully successful wooing mechanism for a male diplomat. In the same volume appears 'London's Latest Lion' by Gilbert Doyle, subtitled 'An Empire Maker's Love Story'. Again, diplomacy, simple deduction and courtship are inextricably fused: the female protagonist this time is Miss Olive Grahame, a demure governess employed by the Earl of Kenwell; she manages to outwit the foreign schemer Count Morlot, whose guile and Gallic gallantry are really no match for her wits, or for the courage and courtesy of the British Empire Builder, who of course woos and wins the governess.

C. N. and A. M. Williamson, the English husband and American wife who co-authored a series of lively Edwardian romances, made espionage a more dashing though still respectable business in *Love and the Spy* (1908). The heroine is an actress and, therefore, slightly socially suspect; Maxine de Renzie suffers the further handicap of not being Anglo-Saxon—she is Polish by birth—although she has been active in the British secret service for some years. She is an attractive character—beautiful, cultivated, quick-witted and far-seeing in the game of plot and counterplot. Although Maxine does not work directly for her own country, she is still motivated by patriotism rather than avarice, as she uses the money she earns from the British government to help impoverished Poland. Madame de Renzie is well set up with the traditional tools of the woman spy—histrionic ability, the capacity to keep a secret when necessary, and of course sexual appeal. The Williamsons create vignettes that are both witty and touching—the slightly exotic continental female spy trying to make advances to the restrained Englishman; the actress/spy who has enjoyed success and adulation but is fed up with both professions. Maxine de Renzie, although involved in fairly stereotyped manœuvres of diplomatic theft and retrieval, is an unusually three-dimensional character for the period, who manages to suggest integrity without smugness.

Like her, several other women spies in fiction before the First World War worked for governments other than their own. These ladies were usually motivated by passion for a foreign national. Female characters were not the strong point of William Le Queux, and in *England's Peril* (1889) Lady Casterton rather unconvincingly uses an explosive cigar to murder her husband, who has been campaigning about Britain's inadequate defence preparations. Lady Casterton betrays husband and country because she is in love with the head of the French Secret Service. Though of French extraction, Le Queux did not experience conflicts of loyalty of this nature in his own life, and intense patriotism for Britain was the keynote of his highly charged but rather turgid novels of political intrigue, which began to appear in the 1890s. His stories stressed Britain's unreadiness for war, and firmly plumped for France as her enemy.

A few years after *England's Peril* a less successful English traitoress—also influenced by a foreign lover—crops up in another book that forecasts war and the invasion of Britain. *The Coming Conquest of England* (1904) was written in German by August Niemann. J. H. Freese's English version appeared soon after Erskine Childers's *The Riddle of the Sands,* and it was of course Childers's persuasive account of espionage and intrigue that established Germany as Britain's potential enemy in the popular imagination; Lord Northcliffe's network of newspapers and boys' mag-

azines, and a spate of spy novels by other writers took up this theme.

As *The Coming Conquest of England* is written from the German viewpoint, it is the aggressiveness of Britain that is condemned. The English heroine Edith Irwin feels let down both by her decadent army officer husband and the British establishment. She has cause, for her gambling spouse ungallantly sells her off to a randy maharajah in order to pay his debts, and the high-ups of the British Army in India, to whom she appeals for protection, are prepared to sacrifice her honour for the maharajah's goodwill. Edith is rescued by Hermann Heideck, a German who hates the British but nevertheless falls for the exploited Edith. In order to shorten the war, Edith passes vital information to Heideck about British naval plans; he is so disgusted by her spying that he renounces her. But he is of course prepared to use the material received to further the interests of the Fatherland. Abandoned by both Germany and England, Edith is driven to suicide. The moral of the story, which is riddled with political ploy and counterploy, seems to be that spying is a reasonable job for a man but deplorable for a woman.

This attitude was certainly modified later by the exigencies of the First World War, but there remained an edge of disapproval for women spies that was not applied to men in espionage. Even Bernard Newman, the author of 128 successful spy stories, who had worked in counter-espionage during the war, seemed dubious about the women in his profession. Writing critically of factual memoirs of some of these ladies, he refers to 'the saccharine reminiscences of these virgin sirens', making the point, presumably, that women agents could actually succeed only if they used promiscuity as a major tool of their trade. However, in his novel *Lady Doctor, Woman Spy* (1937) he comments that '. . . Until the moment of the Armistice the Secret War went on—a veritable war of women, since the majority of the volunteer agents in occupied France and Belgium were women.' He commends the real-life espionage work of Louise de Bettignies and Gabrielle Petit, who directed many of these operations, and he also has a grudging respect for a prostitute named Regina, through whom he organized 'a series of listening posts in the Amiens brothels' in 1917. She had a range of attributes that were helpful in spying, not the least of which was her ability to blink messages accurately in Morse code. Her flair for this kind of signalling is mentioned in an autobiographical piece by Newman in the *Edgar Wallace Mystery Magazine* of July 1965.

Whether or not Marthe McKenna was one of the women agents-turned-author whose attitudes to sex and spying were so unpalatable to Newman, she worked with success in espionage during the war, and then went on to produce several best-selling books about her experiences. Like Bernard Newman, she too was able to write anti-Nazi spy stories when the First World War began to lose its appeal as a fictional subject. Marthe McKenna (née Knockaert) was Belgian, and when her country was overrun by the Kaiser's armies she spied for the Allies while pursuing nursing duties at a German military hospital in Roulers. In *I Was a Spy* (1933) she describes her activities, which included the prising out of information from German officers without the sacrifice of her virtue. Field-Marshal Earl Haig mentioned her in a dispatch for 'gallant and distinguished service in the field'; Winston Churchill described her as 'brave, wise, virtuous and patriotic' and wrote in a foreword to *I Was a Spy:* 'She fulfilled in every respect the conditions which make the terrible profession of a spy dignified and honourable.' Despite the authenticity of her experiences, some of her early spy stories now seem inflated and unreal.

Mrs McKenna fictionalized some of her own espionage activities in her novel *A Spy Was Born* (1935). A Belgian nursing sister recruits a young German officer, whom she is nursing, as an agent for the Allies. He is Fusilier Paul Orthwald from Bavaria and, true to literary traditions, not a brute like some of his fellow officers who hail from Prussia. Paul's defection to the Allied cause is largely due to the barbarous behaviour of his friend Victor (a Prussian, of course) who rapes a young girl in Belgium and—to complete the picture of depravity—has her crippled, hunchbacked brother sent to a concentration camp. (It is interesting that this novel, which is set in the First World War, has portents of several of the hideous realities of Hitler's war—'sturmtruppers', 'concentration camps', the idea of 'subject races' and so on.) Marthe McKenna, as a nursing-sister spy operating in Belgium, possibly struck echoes of Nurse Cavell in the minds of many readers: each was seen as an embodiment of dedicated self-sacrifice, a symbol of one of women's traditional wartime roles.

Mata Hari, of course, became the epitome of seductive betrayal, the other extreme of behaviour associated with women in time of war. In *Lady Doctor, Woman Spy* Bernard Newman writes of Anna Lessing, a German spy whose ruthlessness, sexual arrogance and exploitation of men and women went far beyond Mata Hari's. The mysterious Lady Doctor (no one seems to know how she came to be called this) was a real-life spy, but Newman has fictionalized her adventures. She was, apparently, the result of an illicit union between a German officer and a Slav woman. Once involved in espionage, she received instructions in the art of disguise from a well-known Berlin actress, and became adept at assuming a variety of roles, from pigtailed Swiss schoolgirl to English scoutmistress. In the latter character she persuaded a member of her scout pack to carry out a spying exercise at a tank demonstration given for King George V in a field closed to the public. The scout made a drawing of the newfangled contraption which was sent to the German High Command who, apparently, didn't take it seriously. Anna's flirtation with scouting did not make her an admirer of 'B.P.' since later, when she was in charge of training agents at the German School of Espionage in Antwerp, Newman has her giving this advice to her students:

> You have been given a copy of this book *Adventures as a Spy* by Baden-Powell, the boy-scout man. Don't copy him—he was an amateur. Look at these pictures of butterflies he is so proud of! If they had come under my notice I would have flung him into jail—those wing markings are not known in any butterfly in the world.

Lady Doctor, Woman Spy emphasizes Anna's professionalism; she was an excellent linguist and had an understanding of the technicalities of military and industrial equipment. She could also record important information in her sketches and in pieces of knitting (shades of Madame Defarge!). She was also skilled at hiding secret papers, when she crossed the frontier, concealing them under the fall of her breasts where they were secured with strips of sticking plaster. If she caught women suspected of working for the Allies, she stripped them naked, combed out their hair, looked under arms and breasts and into their ears, and even poked a finger up their noses in her search for concealed messages and information. Her well-developed eye and ear for detail were put to use in other settings. She claimed that she could gain more information from a social gathering than anyone else in espionage or counter-espionage. Newman writes that at a ball just before an offensive was launched on the eastern front: 'Anna identified every division which was to comprise the Second Army of Samsov without stepping outside the ball-room of the Hotel Bristol at Warsaw.'

Lady Doctor, Woman Spy is, as the author stresses, a work of fiction, but there is no doubt that Anna Lessing's colourful activities in espionage invited embellishment. German agents of either sex were of course not likely to be presented by British writers as genial characters, and perhaps the least savoury to emerge in the fiction of the First World War is Dr Adolf Grundt ('Clubfoot'). This spymaster and confidant of the Kaiser was a law unto himself, with powers as draconian as those of the German Emperor. He was created by the war correspondent Valentine Williams in *The Man With the Club-foot* (1921); the novel was an immediate success and Williams continued to produce spy stories. Clubfoot was too dramatic a character to be allowed to disappear, even when the First World War had begun to recede from memory, and Williams resurrected him in occasional books throughout the 1920s and 1930s. One of these was *The Crouching Beast* (1928), written in the first person with an English heroine as the narrator. Her name is Olivia Dunbar. Realism is leavened by romance (while on the run Olivia is efficiently wooed by British agent Nigel Druce) and, despite touches of melodrama, the story comes across with lively conviction. It lacks the recriminating tone that characterized many novels set in the First World War; Olivia's narration is shot through with a slightly rueful, self-aware humour, and there is a general sense of style and slickness. The setting is Germany during the weeks leading up to the war. Olivia, who is working as secretary to an American/German authoress in a small garrison town, gives temporary refuge to a British MI5 agent escaping from the fortress prison. He is soon recaptured and shot, but has entrusted to her a cloak-and-dagger mission—the retrieval of a sealed envelope from the gramophone cabinet in a Berlin opera singer's apartment. This contains information that will alert the British Government to the imminence of German mobilization. Olivia is just a nice unassuming English girl, her sense of adventure appearing to have been satisfied once she had put behind her the vegetating routine of life in a 'dreary typing job' in London. However, she is the daughter of a distinguished soldier, and blood will out: 'It would be more prudent, I know, to wash my hands of the whole affair . . . But Daddy, sprung from a long line of Empire builders, always bade me avoid the easy thing . . . '

Loyalty to the imperial tradition quickly thrusts Olivia into a battle of wills with Clubfoot, who is not only well endowed with cunning and cruelty but has the advantage of disconcerting his opponents by his unprepossessing appearance. Certainly Olivia is rather daunted at their first meeting:

> He was one of the most hirsute individuals I had ever seen. There were pads of black hair on his projecting cheek-bones, and little tufts at his nostrils, and a velvety thatch darkened the backs of his large and spade-like hands . . . He was a massively built person, with curiously long arms and an amazingly broad shoulder span . . . there was more than a suggestion of some gigantic man-ape about him.

And, of course, there is his club foot and crouching mien to complete the picture of a power-mad fanatic, warped within and without. Olivia eventually falls into Clubfoot's unchivalrous and clomping clutches; she is reduced to using a 'woman's weapon', but seductive wheedling gets her nowhere with the 'beast', who merely crows, ' "Corporal punishment, I believe, is still in force for unruly prisoners. For women as well as for men." His shoulders shook in a spasm of silent mirth. "And you are a very unruly person . . . " '

Olivia is rescued by Nigel Druce, the British spy she ultimately marries, and their success, like that of many heroes and heroines of British Intelligence up against implacable Prussians, springs from the efficiency of their physical reflexes in face of danger as much as from their powers of deduction. The book ends on a nice note. Nigel is awarded the DSO but, as his Secret Service Chief explains to Olivia, 'Since I can't get you a DSO, much as you deserved it, I've asked Cartier's to send you along a bangle.'

There is little of the luxury Cartier touch about Somerset Maugham's espionage stories. These are collected in *Ashenden: or The British Agent* (1928), and were based on Maugham's experiences in Intelligence during the war. The book is considered a milestone in the history of spy fiction for its detailed realism and its movement away from the romantic melodrama and social glossiness that Le Queux had earlier established as the pattern. As Eric Ambler has pointed out, Maugham's is the first fictionalized account of the life of a secret agent 'by a writer of stature with first-hand knowledge' of the subject. Ashenden was the original anti-hero of counter-espionage and 'his official existence was as orderly and monotonous as a City clerk's'. His sifting and sleuthing are done in a mood of callousness, irritation or detachment, and interspersed with periods of boredom or nervousness. Women agents do not feature prominently in the stories, although there is one archetypal dark and voluptuous vamp who worms secrets out of the 'chattering, hideous and fantastic' Hairless Mexican in a love-making session, and then has her throat cut. A female spy who fits better into Ashenden's low-toned and slightly seedy world is Giulia Lazzari, a blowsy Spanish dancer involved in working for the Cen-

tral Powers through her Indian lover Chandra, who is one of their agents. Giulia's activities against the Allies are mere fleabites, but Ashenden intends to use her as bait for the capture of Chandra. As they wait in a French hotel near the Swiss border Ashenden turns into a virtual jailer; his distaste for the whole exercise—and for her—is plain:

> She was far from young, she might have been thirty-five, and her skin was lined and sallow . . . She had at the moment no make-up on and she looked haggard. There was nothing beautiful about her but her magnificent eyes. She was big, and Ashenden thought she must be too big to dance gracefully; it might be that in Spanish costume she was a bold and flaunting figure, but there, in the train, shabbily dressed, there was nothing to explain the Indian's infatuation.

Ashenden, in the uneven duel of wits in which he eventually persuades Giulia to write letters that bring Chandra across the border, is further repelled by the feminine intimacies of her life with which he has had to become acquainted: her dressing-table is littered with toilet things that were 'cheap and tawdry and none too clean. There were little shabby pots of rouge and cold-cream and little bottles of black for the eyebrows and eyelashes. The hairpins were horrid and greasy. The room was untidy and the air was heavy with the smell of cheap scent.' She is the sort of woman who forces her feet into shoes that are too small, and is too illiterate to write the letters to her lover that Ashenden wants to dictate. His response to her is one of irritation rather than pity, especially when, to save Chandra, she offers herself to the British agent: ' "Don't be absurd," said Ashenden. "Do you think I want to become your lover? Come, come, you must be serious . . . " '

There is nothing low-key about the female German agent in John Buchan's *Greenmantle* (1916). Richard Hannay, who could retain his equilibrium in the face of death, torture, hypnotism and even the denial of his life-supporting cold baths, is thrown distinctly off balance by Hilda von Einem. This Teuton 'she-devil' working for German Intelligence plans to use Greenmantle, a prophet of the blood of Mahommed, to inflame 'the hordes of Islam' against the British. When Greenmantle suddenly dies she is undeterred, and simply arranges a substitution. The unlikely candidate chosen as the phoney seer is Hannay's chum Sandy Arbuthnot; it has alas to be recorded that he lacks sufficient mettle to resist the blandishments of 'that bedlamite woman'. Hilda von Einem, 'a known man-eater and murderess', has not only cast Sandy in the role of revolutionary leader but—perhaps more fiendishly—she fancies him. His American friend Blenkiron is forced to 'indulge in a torrent of blasphemy' (which amounts to condemning 'this God-darned stuff') when Sandy admits to being fired by her madness. Hannay and Blenkiron, of course, manage to put Sandy back on the rails, but they too have to be ever-watchful of the Teuton temptress: 'with her bright hair and the exquisite oval of her face she looked like some destroying force of a Norse legend.' She also has an inscrutable smile, devouring eyes and 'a bosom that rose and fell in a kind of sigh'.

With Blenkiron, Hilda is like a 'rattle-snake with a bird'. When she turns her attentions to Hannay, he admits, 'The woman frightens me into fits.' It's worse, however, to be ignored by her: 'I hated her instinctively, hated her intensely, but I longed to arouse her interest. To be valued coldly by those eyes was an offence to my manhood . . . ' Richard Hannay is pretty uneasy in the presence of any woman, and as the tension of the plot builds up so too does his love/hatred of Hilda: 'Mad and bad she might be, but she was also great.' In fact before the end of the story she has become the embodiment of that 'craze of the new fatted Germany', that notion 'invented by a sportsman called Nietzsche.' According to Hannay & Co., 'Men have a sense of humour which stops short of the final absurdity. There never has been and there never could be a real superman . . . But there is a super-woman, and her name's Hilda von Einem.' (Joan of Arc, whom he greatly admires, would usually perhaps be Hannay's more likely choice as super-woman, but Hilda as the demon-queen of German espionage has obviously played havoc with his judgement.) It is obvious that with this build-up of implicit sexual tension, some blood-letting in the Buchan tradition is called for; this comes near the end of *Greenmantle* when, after being holed up somewhere near the Euphrates by Turkish troops, Hannay, Blenkiron and Sandy have the thrill of taking part in a Cossack charge against the enemy. Hilda of course has to die so that feminine temptations are satisfactorily exorcised.

If Hilda von Einem represented Buchan's image of a female destroyer in the Mata Hari mould, another of his women who dabbles in political intrigue is definitely closer to Edith Cavell, the preserver. In *The Three Hostages* (1924) Hannay's wife Mary joins him in foiling Medina and other ruthless characters who are out to undermine and overthrow the western democracies. Medina is after more than this—in fact he wants not only material power but 'control of human souls'. When the story opens Hannay has been sufficiently mellowed by marriage and fatherhood to take the occasional self-indulgent *hot* bath. By page 48 however, circumstances have become so challenging that he needs his cold plunge again rather desperately: 'I awoke to a gorgeous spring morning, and ran down to the lake for my bath. I felt that I wanted all the freshening and screwing up I could get, and when I dressed after an icy plunge I was ready for all comers.' But he is not quite able to cope unassisted with Medina's machinations. Mary's maternal nature is affronted by the abduction of a small boy as one of Medina's three hostages. She offers to help, but Hannay is uncertain about what she can do; Mary then shows her mettle. Hannay's investigations take him to a London dancing club which seems to attract all his *bêtes noires*. Against the background of ugly music and garish décor he sees 'fat Jews and blue-black dagos', the college boys 'who imagined they were seeing life', and, most repugnant of all, 'puffy Latins, whose clothes fitted them too well, and who were sometimes as heavily made up as the women'. One of these is dancing with a female who is 'hideously and sparsely dressed' with hair 'too bright to be natural'. Suddenly Hannay realizes, with 'a shock that nearly sent me through the window', that 'in this painted dancer I recognized the wife of my bosom and the mother of Peter John'. Mary has proved once again to be 'such a thorough sportsman that she wouldn't take any soft option'. She takes control again towards the end of the

book at a key point in the plot. The boy hostage David Warcliff has been rescued, but through hypnosis his mind is still in thrall to Medina. Sandy Arbuthnot storms, and Hannay appeals abortively to Medina to release the child; Mary's maternal impulses make her strong—this is one of the moments when she realizes that British decency is really not enough:

> 'You have destroyed a soul,' she said, 'and you refuse to repair the wrong. I am going to destroy your body, and nothing will ever repair it . . . You are a desperate man . . . but I am far more desperate. There is nothing on earth that can stand between me and the saving of this child . . . You may live a long time, but you will have to live in seclusion. No woman will ever cast eyes on you except to shudder. People will point at you and say "There goes the man who was maimed by a woman—because of the soul of a child." . . . Then from her black silk reticule she took a little oddly-shaped green bottle. She held it in her hand as if it had been a jewel . . . 'This is the elixir of death in life, Mr. Medina . . . It will burn flesh and bone into shapes of hideousness . . . '

Medina of course capitulates under this threat of disfiguration by acid, and he restores David's mind:

> Mary leaned back . . . . 'I hope I'm not going to faint,' she said. 'Give me the green bottle, please.'
>
> 'For Heaven's sake!' I cried.
>
> 'Silly!' she said. 'It's only eau-de-cologne.'

The Three Hostages, written soon after the First World War, described the threats to the stability of society, all over the world, posed by anarchists and bolsheviks and power-crazed individuals. This theme was also taken up by E. Phillips Oppenheim in *Miss Brown of X.Y.O.* (1927). Oppenheim had been writing tales of secret diplomacy since 1898, producing about 115 novels as well as numerous short stories. His style, even in the 1920s and 1930s, remained Edwardian, and his approach to espionage was romantic, élitist and melodramatic. His characters are stereotypes, and those who fail to conform with his old-fashioned concepts of social acceptability are patronized or parodied in a somewhat heavy-handed way. There is, however, an element of appeal in his books now because of their period atmosphere and detail.

Miss Brown of X.Y.O. is full of communist agitators—synonymous in this novel with 'anarchist blackguards'—who make their presence felt in Trades Union offices, in Parliament, at night clubs and restaurants, and even at parties given by 'white' Russian refugee aristocrats. According to Oppenheim, these intruders are financed by Soviet Russia to act as professional disrupters of society, but they are not too efficient in either a physical or a psychological sense. In fact they don't do much more than make highly charged gestures and speeches in the tradition of the big-hatted, black-cloaked, bomb-throwing anarchist spies of the children's comic papers. The heroine, Miss Edith Brown, stumbles into this world of international intrigue by accident. In the Oppenheim context she passes for a restrained and subtle figure, so controlled and genteel that she is always on the brink of being downright boring to the reader. At the opening of the story Edith (symbolically, in view of her misty-mindedness) is totally engulfed in a murky London fog. She is a freelance typist who has 'suffered all her life from an unprobed spirit of romance', and the exciting world of Oppenheim's brand of espionage is about to overtake her. Lurching through the pea-souper and clutching her portable, Edith comes to rest on the front steps of an impressive house in Kensington; the door is suddenly opened by a servant with 'an honest face' who, surprisingly, asks this perfect stranger from the streets if she will come inside and do some important work for 'a gentleman'. Perhaps even more surprisingly, Edith agrees without a moment's hesitation, and proceeds to take down in shorthand the immensely significant and confidential notes about the structure of an international communist spy network which her unexpected employer dictates. The whole exercise is so hazardous that the gentleman, Colonel Dessiter, is forced shortly afterwards to feign death in order to avoid assassination by the anarchists. Edith, however, gamely struggles on with her typing jobs, although she becomes a target for the communists, who are prepared to go to extremes to prevent her from transcribing her notes. In spite of the danger that she is in, and the fact that her own background is very ordinary, Edith is never intimidated by even the most powerful of these enemies, and she deals frankly with Pennington, the communist MP who was at Winchester and Oxford, and is considered to have a brilliant political future:

> Miss Brown glanced at his perfectly fitting clothes, his neat jewellery, his air of almost elderly foppishness.
>
> 'One learns a great deal through coming into the world sometimes,' she murmured. 'I have read some of your speeches in the Sunday papers, and I pictured you always with a flannel shirt and a red tie, beating the air with an unclean fist.'

Edith soon gets on to the full-time strength of X.Y.O., which is of course part of the Intelligence Service. She falls in love with her boss Colonel Dessiter, but before they retire to country house married bliss they gambol together through their espionage assignments—their 'world of romance and tragedy and wonder'—like a couple of schoolkids. Edith says about spying 'I felt rather a sneak,' and Dessiter throws her an encouraging 'Well done, Miss Brown,' when she produces a clean transcript, or says something that he agrees with. They are not the only infantile characters in the book: a newly appointed Prime Minister, after only two minutes' acquaintance with Edith, decides that she has all the qualities necessary in a premier's wife and proposes on the spot. Fortunately for England, Edith rejects him.

Oppenheim produced several other female spies who were more exotic than Miss Brown and just as unconvincing. Women characters were usually the weakest links in stories by men of action about men of action, and this applies to the girls in Sapper's Bulldog Drummond saga and to W. E. Johns's Biggles adventures. Johns's attempt at a female spy (and a lover for Biggles) is worthy of mention as in a sense she is the only fictional agent who combines the attributes of Mata Hari and Edith Cavell. Marie Janis started life in a short story, 'Affaire de Coeur' (1918), as an exotic enemy spy who nearly gets Biggles shot: he is besotted with her, and drops behind the German lines messages which contain valuable information about Allied positions; he thinks he is dropping notes to Marie's aged father. She does not crop up again until *Biggles Looks Back* (1964); she is then a prisoner of the communists in Bohemia but has, apprently, followed up her Secret Service career with a spell in nursing. In *Biggles Looks Back* it is obvious that life has very much toned down the frothy First World War blonde whose 'Please Beegles' was almost enough to make the hero crash an aeroplane. (Even then she was not the most subtle or efficient of spies; from her French farmhouse hideout she was supposed to keep in touch with her German HQ by carrier pigeon, but unfortunately, 'the first night Marie was there the pigeon was killed by a cat'.) By 1964 she has settled into a kind of long-suffering dignity, and is deferential to Biggles and his ex-opponent Von Stalhein. The two men co-operate to get her out of communist clutches, and she is content to let them do all the planning and pushing. The passion that has kept her virginal and has made Biggles (by sublimation) into an expert espionage agent and aviator is now transmuted into an asexual triangular chumminess; Marie settles into the domesticity of a Hampshire cottage, and Biggles and Von Stalhein run down regularly at weekends to visit her and chat about the stirring old wartime days. Though not the most enterprising of fictional women spies, Biggles's old flame must at least be one of the longest survivors. (pp. 52-70)

> *Patricia Craig and Mary Cadogan, "The Lady Is a Vamp," in their* The Lady Investigates: Women Detectives and Spies in Fiction, *St. Martin's Press, 1981, pp. 52-70.*

SOCIAL AND PSYCHOLOGICAL PERSPECTIVES

John G. Cawelti and Bruce A. Rosenberg

[*Cawelti is an American educator and critic who writes on popular culture. Rosenberg is an American educator and critic who has written several studies in the field of folklore. In the following excerpt, Cawelti and Rosenberg analyze the psychological appeal of clandestine activities typical of the spy thriller.*]

While the flourishing of the spy story as a popular genre is primarily a phenomenon of the twentieth century, fascination with clandestine operations goes back to the dawn of history and the earliest surviving narratives and folktales. That most famous of clandestine operations, the Trojan horse, comes immediately to mind, but folktales are full of magical paraphernalia which can make the possessor invisible, and almost all epics contain at least one character who betrays the heroic leader. While the impact of historical espionage is highly controversial, clandestinity has always been an important part of war, politics, and commerce. One is tempted to hazard the speculation that the very fascination of clandestine activity as much as its practical necessity makes it a significant part of our history. (p. 11)

[A] generalized analysis of the patterns of clandestine activity and their psychological fascination . . . [will] clarify some of the underlying archetypes of espionage and their psychology. The analysis is based on the fictional literature of spying and on historical accounts of espionage. After we have presented the general paradigm, we will describe two historical episodes, one individual and one cultural, which seem to exemplify what we have defined as the "cycle of clandestinity" in all its aspects. The model is highly speculative and general, and we do not claim that it will fit every particular case. Rather it shows the psychological relationship between different phases of clandestine activity, only some of which may be evident in the career of any individual spy or in any particular espionage episode. At most, we hope that the model will bring into relief some of the underlying psychodynamics that seem to be involved in the practice of clandestinity and reflected in its fictional embodiment in the spy story.

Clandestine operations usually begin with a purpose. Either the individual is so deeply committed to some goal that he is prepared to step beyond the usual boundaries of action, or the end he pursues is by its very nature illegal. Two such purposes are revolutionary activity and the service of a foreign country. Either commitment invariably entails some kind of clandestine operation since the open practice of revolution or subversion is outlawed. There are, however, many other purposes which can lead to clandestinity. For example, when those in power feel that public opinion will resist or reject a certain course of action deemed vital to national security, or to the success of an administration, there may be a great temptation to resort to secret actions against a foreign power or against an organization that is felt to be a domestic threat.

Clandestinity is not entirely political. The pursuit of business in a capitalistic society often leads its practitioners into secret operations. Industrial espionage and defenses against it have played a significant role in modern history both between and within countries (Eells and Nehemkis, *Corporate Intelligence and Espionage*). Crime is another mode of clandestine operation and so are many forms of love. While there are obviously significant differences between these various forms of clandestinity, the basic patterns of a secret love affair and an espionage operation have many features in common. Like the spy, the secret lover must keep his actual commitment secret from his wife and family to whom he owes a legal and moral loyalty. Carrying out a love affair often requires many of the same practices as an espionage mission: secret communications, hidden rendezvous, complicated alibis, and elaborate disguises. Such lovers often experience the special closeness of people who share a dangerous bond unknown to others. Not surprisingly, poets have often noted the analogy between love and espionage. Shakespeare and Donne both use spy metaphors to express secret love, for example.

Clandestinity thus begins with a purpose requiring actions that must be kept secret because they transgress conventional, moral, or legal boundaries. But there are also innate psychological attractions in clandestinity which can give the initial involvement an added impetus. In our imaginations, the role of spy partakes of the very powerful fantasy of invisibility, a motif whose recurrence in myth, legend, and literature indicates a compelling appeal for many people in many different cultures. The spy is invisible in a number of senses: he is the secret observer who, himself unseen, watches through a peephole or, in our modern technological age, through a telescope or some electronic device; he is invisible in the sense that his commission as a spy frees him from responsibility and gives him license to do things he could not ordinarily do without serious consequences. James Bond, for example, has the "license to kill." These aspects of invisibility—voyeurism, self-concealment, and license—clearly have a powerful attraction quite apart from the purpose they are intended to serve.

Closely related to invisibility is the fascination with disguises, another fantasy connected with clandestinity. Again, folktales, myths, and stories indicate the perennial human fascination with disguise, the power of which very likely resides in the thrill of trying on other identities—social, racial, sexual, or chronological. Men often fantasize themselves as women, whites as blacks, rich men as poor men, young people as the aged, and vice versa. Disguise is one of the ways that we have of narrating or dramatizing this fantasy. Disguise is a temporary escape from one's own identity; the role of a spy contains the possibility of a controlled but total escape from the constraints of self. This ties in with a third fantasy deeply connected with many forms of clandestinity, the secret exercise of power. The secret conspiracy—actual and fantasied—has been ever present in human history. To imagine becoming part of a secret organization is a compelling fantasy not only in terms of the exercise of power without its responsibilities and risks, but also as a particularly strong image of belonging. To belong to a clandestine organization seems to carry with it a profound involvement, a relationship to other members of the organization deeper than that characteristic of other kinds of organizations because it requires life-and-death loyalty. This particular fantasy of clandestinity is probably especially powerful in modern industrial cultures where people feel relatively alienated from most of the organizations to which they belong. Mario Puzo's *The Godfather,* with its central theme of the clandestine family, exploited this fantasy just as the contemporary spy thriller does.

Ironically, the cycle of clandestinity often moves from the profound loyalty of the initial commitment to extraordinary forms of betrayal. Though his participation in a secret relationship requires total loyalty on the part of the spy (or the lover) toward his partners in clandestinity, this relationship is also a betrayal of existing relationships and prior commitments. This theme of betrayal, possibly impelled by a deep-seated oedipal urge to throw off parental authority, constitutes, along with the fantasies of invisibility, disguise, and secret conspiracy, the repertoire of psychological attractions which, along with compelling moral or political goals, are reflected in the fantasy of espionage.

From the outset, clandestine involvements are complexly ambiguous, often combining high moral purpose with contradictory psychological needs. As the process of clandestinity develops, the psychological state of the spy tends to become even more ambiguous. After the initial commitment to secret activity, the clandestine operative becomes involved with one or more persons in pursuit of his initial purpose. This association quickly creates what might be called a clandestine world, based on the special view of things which the members of the secret group share. The second stage of the cycle of clandestinity is the full development of this clandestine world, which then exists side by side with the ordinary world in the mind of the spy. Participants in clandestinity believe that their secret world is more real than the ordinary world and that it is exempt from the rules that govern those who are not part of the clandestine world. As Marchetti and Marks put it [in their *The CIA and the Cult of Intelligence*]:

> Deeply embedded within the clandestine mentality is the belief that human ethics and social laws have no bearing on covert actions and their practitioners. The intelligence profession, because of its lofty "national security" goals, is free from all moral restrictions. There is no need to wrestle with technical legalisms or judgments as to whether something is right or wrong. The determining factors in secret operations are purely pragmatic: Does the job need to be done? Can it be done? And can secrecy (or plausible denial) be maintained?
>
> (pp. 11-15)

Participants in a clandestine world live in a state of psychological tension which resembles, in some of its characteristics, the pathology of schizophrenia. This tension results from their dual views of the world. First, there is the "reality" constituted by the secrets shared with other members of the clandestine group. Since these secrets commonly refer to states of affairs or events that are not known to those outside the group, the clandestine world-view seems more real. Yet, since the preservation of the clandestine group requires that these secrets remain hidden from all other persons, a clandestine participant must also live as a member of the ordinary world, pretending to share its view of reality. This double vision is difficult enough. The clandestine participant must remember the attitudes, perceptions, and words characteristic of both the clandestine world and the world outside, and he must manipulate both consciousnesses effectively enough to shift back and forth between them with ease. This slipping in and out of the ordinary world is characteristic of schizophrenic illness. Though one can say that the spy exercises a conscious and rational control over his different roles while the psychotic appears to have lost this power, there is a boundary area in which the anxiety surrounding divergent worldviews can become so great that the secret agent passes beyond that stage of complete rational control over his divided self. The tension and excitement of participating in a clandestine world are among the central motifs of the fiction of espionage:

He found the air of happy gaiety, the complete unknowingness of the crowds, almost unnerving—tragic. Life was going on just as usual, no one realizing anything except those in high authority and a handful of men who tended AFPU ONE under the Official Secrets Act's gat. As Shaw made his way along, diffidently stepping out of the way of dark, buxom Gibraltarian girls and their escorts, he wondered what those crowds would think if they could see into his mind, see the picture which he was carrying within him of the utter annihilation of a community—but no one looked twice at the tall, thin figure in the now rumpled tropic-weight suit, the figure with the worried, lined face and graying hair. They were far too intent upon their present pleasure. [Philip McCutchan, *Gibraltar Road*]

As indicated in this passage, the clandestine participant's attitude toward the ordinary world is a mixture of superiority, loneliness, and resentment. He feels that he has a better understanding of reality and therefore is not deluded by the illusions and facile pleasure-seeking of the majority. On the other hand, he feels terribly isolated by his secret and resents the innocent happiness of those who cannot share his frightening knowledge. As his participation in the clandestine world continues, the spy finds the two roles he must play increasingly difficult to relate to each other:

> "He's changed!" she said. "You must have noticed that yourself. I wouldn't be surprised what he was mixed up in. He has this sort of schizophrenia and an obsession with secrecy. I don't know if you get like that in the secret service, or whether the secret service chooses that sort of man. But it's hell to live with, I'll tell you that."
> [Len Deighton, *Yesterday's Spy*]

So long as the clandestine participant can share with others a secret view of the world and thereby receive support and knowing sympathy, the condition of clandestinity is tolerable. Those who form parts of secret bureaucracies like the CIA receive this support from their organizations. The bureaucratization of clandestinity does not prevent the delusions of the clandestine world from growing, but it probably does counteract some of its more devastating psychological effects.

Even the most stable of organizations cannot entirely remove the sense of isolation inherent in the condition of clandestinity, however. To offset this isolation, clandestine participants are often impelled toward renewed conspiratorial efforts, as if the re-creation of the clandestine group around some new set of secrets or plots could assuage the feeling of separation from other human contacts. The need for renewed conspiracy can be seen over and over again in the lives of spies. Georges Cadoudal, an anti-Bonaparte agent, was once supposed to have observed: "Do you know what we ought to advise the King to do? We ought to tell him that he ought to have both of us shot, for we shall never be anything but conspirators. We have taken the imprint" (Rowan, *Secret Service*). The intensity and complexity of the growing obsession with conspiracy is strikingly instanced in Richard Rowan's observations on the career of Daniel Defoe, who was among other things, an early secret agent:

> Not only were [Defoe's] most famous characters fictions, but he himself was partly a figment of his own teeming imagination. He published some books anonymously, but signed his name to the introductions in which he recommended them to the consideration of the reading public. He encouraged himself in letters to his papers and reviled himself in letters to rival sheets. He corrected himself, he quoted himself, he plagiarized his own writings in works which he attributed to foreign commentators. He boldly reminded himself in print of his alliance with political gentry who were secretly employing him to oppose some policy of the government to which they belonged. Defoe, more than any other man who has ever lived, permitted his aptitude for secret service to infect every other practice of his almost innumerable vocations.

When the participant in a clandestine group reaches the point where he is obsessed with conspiracy and overcome with anxiety about his own isolation and vulnerability, he is likely to pass into the next phase of the cycle of clandestinity: the role of double or triple agent.

The double agent is a role that heroic spies in the tradition of John Buchan and Ian Fleming never accept, however much they are tempted. In the more complex tradition of secret agent adventure, which began with Maugham, Greene, and Ambler and continues in recent writers like John le Carré, Len Deighton, and Adam Hall, double agentry is a central theme. Several different motives can impel a spy to turn double agent. There is the hope for material gain. The double agent's unique position is that he can come to know some of the secrets of both sides. By selling to more than one buyer, he can greatly increase his personal profit. Another motive is the fear of being exposed. Many double agents pretend to work for both sides in order to insure their personal safety. If an agent cannot keep his activities completely concealed from the enemy, the next best thing is to pretend to be one of the enemy's own agents. In many instances, intelligence agencies have used "turned" agents to pass controlled information to an enemy. Apparently some agencies consider it almost a basic principle that an agent who has been in the field for a long period of time is very likely to be "doubled." Also, the agent's isolation—the anxiety of being "out in the cold" alone—may impel him to some kind of negotiation with the enemy simply for the sake of human contact. The psychological complexities of this ultimate state of clandestinity are reflected not only in the number of double agents one runs across in the history of espionage, but in those many cases where one cannot ever be sure where the double agent's real loyalty lay, if indeed it was to anyone but himself.

In the end, the double agent becomes the most isolated human being imaginable, for he must act as if every man's hand is against him. There is no person with whom he can share his secret view of the world. He must lie to everyone. In such a state, the individual easily comes to feel that everyone is in a conspiracy against him, that no person can be trusted. Thus, the double agent becomes the ultimate paranoid:

> "Paranoia—it's the occupational hazard of men who've worked the sort of territories that Champion has worked." Dawlish stared at me. I said, "Like anthrax for tannery workers, and silicosis for miners. You need somewhere . . . a place to go and hide forever . . . and you never shake it off." (Deighton, *Yesterday's Spy*)

With entry into the paranoid world of double agentry, the cycle of clandestinity is complete. It is no longer possible for the individual to join with others in the pursuit of a clandestine purpose since all possibility of trust is closed to him. Having begun the cycle as an individual with a purpose that required collaborative secret actions, he becomes once again an individual but is now enmeshed in the net of multiple lies which he must tell to all other persons. The double agent enters a state of moral and personal isolation so complete that there is no way out but death, exposure, or total flight. The only purpose that remains to him is that of self-preservation through an increasingly complex improvisation of stories to hide his true position of multiple disloyalty.

There are then, three principal phases in the cycle of clandestinity:

1. An individual or group conceives of a purpose which appears to require actions beyond the bounds of law or morality accepted by other members of their society.

2. To pursue these purposes a secret group is formed. This group constitutes a clandestine world defined by the secrets they share. To preserve the clandestine world, members of the group must continue to live as members of ordinary society with the resultant psychological tension between conflicting worldviews.

3. Gradually the individual participant in a clandestine group begins to feel isolated not only from ordinary society, but from other members of the group. This isolation may result from the fear of exposure, a desire for profit, or from a growing sense that all men are engaged in conspiracies against him. He signals his complete isolation by becoming a double agent, that is, by engaging in secret activities against the clandestine group or by apparently or actually betraying the group's secrets to its enemies.

What we have just defined as the cycle of clandestinity is a pattern of experience outlined in broad, abstract strokes. Neither historical spies nor the secret agents of literature necessarily follow this pattern in every respect. In fact, most of the employees of the CIA, the British Secret Service, and, presumably, the KGB are less involved in clandestine operations than in the gathering and sifting of information. As information-gathering has become increasingly dominated by electronics and computer technology, the vast majority of intelligence activities involve sitting in an office and routing the flow of information from various machines into the appropriate bureaucratic channels. Not surprisingly, intelligence operatives are among the most dedicated fans of secret agent fiction, since they, as much as anyone else, need to have their daily professional and bureaucratic routines enlivened by the fantasies of adventure, mystery, and romance. (pp. 17-22)

The history of spy fiction in the twentieth century also reflects in certain ways the basic cycle of clandestinity. . . . The spy stories of World War I and its aftermath, created by English writers like John Buchan, Dornford Yates, and E. Phillips Oppenheim, were heroic stories of romantic gentlemen pursuing moral purposes into successful, redemptive clandestine operations. These were fantasies of the early stages of the clandestine cycle. The same kind of story was revived in popularity by Ian Fleming, but in a later period, Fleming felt it necessary to cloak his romances of adventurous espionage in an aura of exaggeration and irony as if his readers could no longer take such heroics straight. In the 1930s a new kind of spy literature appeared in the novels of Eric Ambler and the "entertainments" of Graham Greene. Both Greene and Ambler specialized in stories of ordinary people suddenly caught up in the dangers and mysteries of international conspiracies. The interplay in their work between the ordinary world and their protagonists' new clandestine view of things clearly manifests the central themes of the second phase of the cycle of clandestinity, the "schizophrenic" ambiguity of clandestine and ordinary world-views. Finally, the most recent school of popular spy fiction—for example, John le Carré and Len Deighton—has become increasingly obsessed with the themes of loyalty, betrayal, and double agentry. Le Carré's *Tinker, Tailor, Soldier, Spy* told an amazingly involuted and paranoid story about the exposure of a Russian plot within the very heart of the British Secret Service, a plot carried on over a long period of years by a double agent who had an impeccably heroic and moral British background. It was as if John Buchan's Richard Hannay had been revealed as the kaiser's leading agent.

Clandestinity poses a particular problem for American culture because, in developing our version of democracy with its strong emphasis on publicity and openness, we have not created over the years a significant tradition of public clandestinity. If the interpretation of the cycle of clandestinity we have espoused here is at all correct, the lack of such a public tradition may be, in most respects, a saving grace. The short, incredible history of the CIA makes it quite clear, however, that when Americans settle down to the creation of clandestine establishments, they do so on the same monumental scale at which they generate other kinds of organizations. If the nature of international relations makes espionage and counterespionage vital necessities on certain occasions, the lack of a continuous tradition of public clandestinity means that we must face over and over again the same kind of irresponsible—indeed lunatic—proliferation of clandestine groups which developed throughout the Cold War era. (pp. 28-30)

Though archetypal themes appear to play an important role in the perennial fascination of clandestine activity, the question of why the spy story has become a primary genre in the twentieth century still remains. In one sense, this question can only be answered by acknowledging the contributions of many individual writers and filmmakers to the creation, the broadening, and the increasing sophisti-

cation of the spy story as a literary and cinematic genre. In particular, the accomplishments of John Buchan, Eric Ambler, Graham Greene, Ian Fleming, and John le Carré have shaped the evolution of the spy story from romantic adventure to many-sided literary and cinematic genre. (p. 30)

The interests that impelled these writers to become part of the espionage tradition and that motivated twentieth-century readers and filmgoers to make the spy story one of their favorite genres clearly go beyond the sum of individual accomplishments. For many reasons, the spy and clandestine activity have come to be central symbols of the human condition in the twentieth century. Because this has been a century of total war and totalitarian societies, espionage, both international and domestic, has become an increasing part of all of our lives. Even in democratic societies, national intelligence organizations like the CIA and the British Secret Service grew to unprecedented size and influence in the aftermath of World War II. In addition, the protracted Cold War and the fear of imminent nuclear catastrophe have made espionage and counterespionage seem activities of the highest importance. Americans widely believed that "the enemy within," that is, Russian spies and their American agents, were responsible for giving vital scientific secrets to the Soviets, enabling them to become a nuclear power and a serious competitor for the conquest of space. During the McCarthy period, clandestinity became an obsession, for Americans were bombarded with claims that a large number of important government officials were Communist spies. Though these claims turned out to be largely groundless, cases like those of the Rosenbergs and Alger Hiss continued to feed fears of widespread subversion in America. These fears were intensified by the prolonged stalemate of the Korean War. The even greater tragedy of the Vietnam War led to an increasing concern with the role of clandestinity on the world scene. In this case, however, the concern was critical, stimulated by a growing fear of the uncontrolled power of the CIA on the international scene and the FBI within the country. Today, facing the bleak prospect of the annihilation of humanity, the public's attitude toward espionage can probably be characterized as profoundly ambiguous. On the one hand, there is a conviction that a strong intelligence community is necessary to prevent our national adversaries from gaining any political, military, or technological advantage that might threaten man's future. But there is also an increasing awareness of the way in which organizations like the CIA abuse their authority by fomenting problems that threaten the peace more than they work to preserve it. The development of the spy story during the Cold War period certainly reflects this ambiguity: one group of writers continues the heroic tradition of Ian Fleming and another presents stories of clandestine operators betrayed by their own organizations, as in many of the novels of Len Deighton and John le Carré.

Finally, though the increasing importance of espionage on the international scene has made the spy one of the central symbols of twentieth-century man, there is another important reason why the clandestine protagonist has become an everyman figure. The situation of the spy "out in the cold" seems to express the way many people feel about the basic patterns of their lives. (pp. 30-2)

[We] have come to think that there is a definite connection between the clandestine protagonist as a symbol of everyman in the twentieth century and an aspect of modern culture which has often been discussed in contemporary works of sociology, both popular and academic: the alienation of the individual from the large organizations—corporations, bureaucracies, professions—which dominate our lives. We think it is this sense of alienation and the deep feeling of conflict between individual self and social role which it engenders that makes the figure of the spy so compelling as a contemporary everyman hero. Into the figure of the spy trying to carry out his secret mission in a territory dominated by the enemy or, even better, threatened by betrayal from his own organization, the individual can project the frustrations he feels toward the limitations imposed on his actions by his corporate employer, by bureaucratic regulations, or by the conventions of his profession.

Thus, the spy story has become a primary twentieth-century genre by drawing on the archetypal power of the patterns of clandestinity to express a compelling vision of contemporary life into which readers can project their own fears and frustrations. This vision relates to the sense of anxiety the public feels about international conflict and to the possibility of nuclear catastrophe, as well as to the sense of alienation so many individuals feel. The present flourishing of the spy story is the accomplishment of three generations of writers and filmmakers who have contributed their creative skills and instincts about readers' needs and interests to the development of the genre. (pp. 32-3)

> *John G. Cawelti and Bruce A. Rosenberg, "The Appeal of Clandestinity," in* The Spy Story *by John G. Cawelti and Bruce A. Rosenberg, The University of Chicago Press, 1987, pp. 11-33.*

[The modern spy] can have one or the other of two main fictional pedigrees: either he is an Odysseus figure—scheming, treacherous and magically successful—or he is a Nisus/Euryalus figure—idealistic and ultimately broken by the train of events.

—Bruce Merry, in his Anatomy of the Spy Thriller, *1977.*

Laura Tracy

[*In the following essay, Tracy examines the theme of the double in espionage fiction.*]

Rooted in the traditions of myth and oral literature, the concept of the double, or doppelganger, has exerted a long

standing fascination for writers, readers, and critics alike. However, despite this enduring intrigue, it is of some interest to realize that critical work on the subject has generally failed to extend its ramifications into the areas of genre study and/or the connection between the double motif and the culture into which it is written. The ensuing study will argue that the double, as a critical tool, is particularly useful in examining the linkage between highly circumscribed genres and the larger culture, focusing on the relevance of the villain as a cultural double in the twentieth century British espionage novel. Specifically, this paper suggests that the villain as double functions in this genre as a cultural defense mechanism, operating to affirm cultural conditions existing at the time of publication.

Although manifestations of the double can be found in folk superstitions such as fear of mirrors, shadows, and self-photography, the psychoanalyst Otto Rank is credited with completing, in 1909, the first scholarly work on the subject. Correlating the characteristics of a number of legendary heroes, Rank developed a thesis founded on Freud's "family romance," the fantasy centered on the illusion that one's parents are actually replacements, surrogates for "real" parents imagined to be of royal or exalted lineage. According to Rank, this sort of fantasy resolved the son's latent hostility to the father and severed the "good" sustaining mother-figure from a corresponding but malevolent image. Doubling for Rank, then, was a psychic process designed to accommodate the individual's deepest fears and most unconscious desires. Since Rank's study, critical work has followed his lead, focusing on the double as symbolic of the individual self in conflict. Through the doubled experience, the self projects outward those qualities of mind and personality experienced as unendurable. The double, therefore, is a psychological defense mechanism by which the self achieves some semblance of homeostatic functioning impossible given what it unconsciously feels as conflicting needs and desires.

In this regard, Freud's comprehension of latent and manifest material in dreams is particularly important. Freud realized that the material accessible to the dreamer's conscious mind concealed a latent, unconscious meaning which could be pieced together within the analytic situation by recourse to the dreamer's lifelong associations. Robert Rogers [in his *A Psychoanalytic Study of the Double in Literature*] has recognized that the double motif functions in a similar fashion. When doubling is overt, or manifest, in such works as Dostoevsky's *The Double* or Poe's "William Wilson," the reader is engaged through an identification with the protagonist, against the doubled figure. Implicit, or latent, doubling, on the others, enables the reader to identify consciously with the protagonist and unconsciously with the doubled figure, usually the antagonist. Latent doubling permits the unitary nature of the doubled image its fullest expression. Conrad's novella *The Secret Sharer,* for example, provides the reader with both manifest and latent doubling. Thickly strewn throughout the text are references to Leggatt as the young ship captain's double, or second self. In addition, however, Leggatt embodies but does not explicitly articulate the captain's fears that he will fail in his new command, permitting the double subsequently to become the vehicle through which the captain resolves those fears. The reader who is to comprehend fully Conrad's tale must experience the two figures as a single personality, temporarily sundered, in order to understand their reunification as the novella's resolution. To a greater or lesser degree, latent doubling occurs in all works depicting an explicitly doubled figure. In psychoanalytic terms, doubling can be understood, then, as externalized images of the protagonist's id or superego, since each is wholly or partially unconscious to the perceiving ego.

As Freud also recognized, the abnormal exists on a continuum with the normal, and the neurotic individual, so to speak, embodies the ills of the culture writ small. Similarly, the double motif as a metaphor of individual endopsychic conflict can be extended to its implications as a metaphor of intra-cultural anxiety. In writing of ego fragmentation, Freud noted that "If we throw a crystal to the floor, it breaks; but not into haphazard pieces. It comes apart along its lines of cleavage into fragments whose boundaries, through they were invisible, were predetermined by the crystal's structure." So, too, the doubled figure haunting any specific culture will find its identity in the fundamental fault lines concealed within the social structure. As F. R. Leavis wrote about Iago, "The essential traitor is within the gates," or more comically phrased in the Pogo cartoon series, "We have met the enemy and he is us."

However, it is important to emphasize that the enemy is met only to be dissociated from the self. If the reader is to identify which both figures of the self, latent doubling must remain unconscious, covertly asserting what is manifestly denied. Similarly, if the double motif is to serve the wider culture as it serves the individual, as a defense mechanism developed to reinforce the status quo by assimilating the seeds of destruction which itself engenders, the doubled figure must function to assuage cultural anxiety consciously denied although unconsciously embraced. In this, the espionage novel has been particularly successful. The genre, in concert with other highly prescriptive generic literature, is constructed to reinforce existing cultural conditions by incorporating its readers' prejudices into its plot and character structures. The spy novel in particular almost inevitably brings political and/or social attitudes explicitly into the work because conflicting political forces function as its primary structural motif. In addition, the modern version of the genre is heavily dependent on contemporary technology, the weapons of modern warfare, and the luxury objects produced by a consumer culture. Although some of these new gadgets can be understood as surrogates for the swords and shields carried by epic heroes, they also present the contemporary reader with the dangerous possibility that the object will supersede the human who wields it. In this they are precisely symbolic of the modern anxiety that a consumer culture carried to its extreme will become itself consuming, devouring its inhabitants to serve itself. By incorporating profuse numbers of these objects into the text, the espionage novel implies they are contemporary toys, implicitly acknowledging their power, yet rendering them emotionally harmless.

Highly circumscribed genres generally are constructed according to the desires of their anticipated audiences. Thus, the modern romance novel has been diagrammed in great detail by publishers who encourage writers simply to fill in outlines of plot, character, tons, and setting. Similar operations might be performed on the mystery novel, on science fiction, the gothic novel, the western, and of course, on the espionage novel. Of primary importance for these genres is their effect on a quite specific audience, ostensibly for the purpose of escape and recreation, but more subliminally, to project a particular world view. Although, for example, an individual romance writer might deny any purposive ideological intent, nevertheless, because the novel remains within restricted generic parameters, ideology is inescapable. Such restriction produces what may be called "contentless" texts, in which subject material is subordinate to form and structure is predetermined, in an analogical correspondence to a psychological defense mechanism. The specific genre, like the defense mechanism, functions to adapt the reader to existing conditions. The content of both the novel and the defense mechanism may vary, according to the fears defended against, but remains important only in terms of its affect. The defensive maneuver and the generic novel conceal their subliminal intent with the illusion that what is offered is merely a pleasurable experience. That pleasure, however, is purchased by accepting and affirming patterns extant beneath conscious apprehension. That is to say, in order for a romance novel to deliver pleasure to its readers, it must also seriously propose the truism that romantic love endures and a "right" man waits for every woman. Pleasure is derived from confirmation of fantasy as well as from the denial of underlying fear. It may be said, therefore, that the individual defense mechanism serves the individual ego by confirming subjective perception against more objective scrutiny. Perception, so to speak, is reinforced at the price of neurosis, in that the neurotic state is characterized by a more or less tenuous connection with reality.

The espionage novel has evolved through several successive generations, adapting its restrictions to cultural changes, beginning with its inception in Britain in the early part of this century. The first group of novels, written by John Buchan, Dornford Yates, E. Phillips Oppenheim, W. Somerset Maugham, Sax Rohmer, and other widely popular exponents of the genre, focused on themes of racial subversion, pitting the white British Empire against the yellow hordes of the East. In effect, although these books were not then considered racist propaganda, they functioned subliminally to confirm deeply held ideas of cultural dominance, landing stability and an aura of permanence to a particular cultural moment. In fact, their overt racism was less important to their success than the underlying structures of dominance and subordination they supported. In these books, then, the figure of the villain was directly contrasted to that of the here, in a rather naively Manichaean version of a world where good and evil were each recognizable and distinct. This strict division between the good and the evil self can be understood in accord with Rank's realization that the doubling process contained features also present in the paranoid individual. Ironically, Rank's connection of paranoia and doubling has been called into question by Lawrence Kohlberg, who noted [in his "Psychological Analysis and Literary Form," *Daedalus* (1963)] that "any awareness of an evil second self is alien to the paranoid state because the typical paranoid thinks of himself as completely innocent and unjustly blamed or persecuted by others." However, in terms of the early espionage novel, Kohlberg's objection precisely highlights the unconscious nature of the doubling process. In order to function as a device protecting a cultural ethos, the villain figure necessarily was construed as alien to cultural self-identification. Just as in the case of the paranoid individual, cultural illusion of unity and stability is reinforced exactly in its conscious assumption that evil waits outside the city gates, a thing apart from those within.

Moreover, the concept of the double lends itself particularly well to an examination of espionage literature because the genre is marked by specific references to double agents, identified as the enemy within. Ironically, the double agent can as easily be the hero as he can the villain, an irony emphasizing the underlying and unconscious nature of both the double in literature and in generic function. Definition of the villain depends, in these books, on the world within the text. The villain who is one of "us" may also be other, but the "us" can be other as well. For example, from within the cultural world of George Orwell's *Nineteen Eighty-Four,* Winston Smith is villainous. Orwell's intent, of course, points to the reverse. From the cultural perspective of 1948, the society of Big Brother appeared as the villain. It is interesting to note that *Nineteen Eighty-Four* is able to awaken its readers to cultural malaise precisely because, although it contains many features of the espionage genre, it also violates the genre, continually combatting rather than affirming deeply held cultural convictions.

The balance of this study will focus on the use of the villain as a cultural double within three versions of the British espionage novel, written by Ian Fleming, John LeCarré, and Graham Greene. These three instances have been selected because each is a slightly altered version of the genre, reflecting the cultural modification occurring even during the brief difference in their dates. In each, however, can be seen the figure of a villain functioning as a latent cultural double, serving to defend the wider society into which the books were written.

In his examination of formulaic literature [in *Adventure, Mystery, and Romance*] John Cawelti has recognized that the primary function of the villain in such work is to "express, explore, and finally to reject those actions which are forbidden but which, because of certain other cultural patterns, are strongly tempting." That is to say, cultural restrictions, developed to ensure cultural stability, bear within them their own antithesis, and paradoxically, are best resolved not through eradication but through assimilation. The espionage villain, as a latent cultural double, permits the reader to unconsciously experience destructive desires and resolve concealed fears while the confines of the highly specific generic parameters assuage those fears with a promise of a return to cultural security. While the death of the doubled figure in serious literature often brings about the death of the protagonist, in that the double's death can be a form of the protagonist's suicide, the death of the villain in espionage novels means a return to cultural standards. The cultural fantasy, its prevailing ethos, depends on the strength of its ability to keep reality at bay. One can suggest, therefore, that from Fleming's novels to Greene's there exists a continuum bringing the genre closer to an objective view of culture, heralding, perhaps, the death of the particular culture, or merely the suicide of the particular genre. Although Greene has labeled much of his espionage fiction "entertainments," in them the genre is pushed to its limits as he increasingly makes explicit the latent nature of the doubled villain, frequently and unmistakably, one of "us."

Ian Fleming began the James Bond series with *Casino Royale,* written in 1953. It is significant that the Bond books did not gain wide popular readership until 1962, when the Cold War and John Kennedy's presidency both contributed to an ideological perspective emphasizing fantasy against reality, offering the legend of Camelot as antidote to the less optimistic Western economic and political situations, soon to blossom into heightened violence with the war in Vietnam. The Bond books, obviously, incorporate romantic day dreams, located in exotic settings, replete with luxurious food and clothing, expensive cars, all combining to depict a mode of life apparently the ideal fantasy of a culture almost overwhelmed by a plethora of consumer materials. Explicitly, Western culture in the decades of the 1950s and early 1960s believed itself functioning in accord with a rhetoric of justice, honor, and independence, the fundamental concepts of ideological democracy. In reality, however, such rhetoric became increasingly hollow in the face of increased consumerism. The cultural conflict, then, was to retain its formative rhetoric while at the same time permitting a consumer economy unimpeded growth. Bond's antagonists are precisely designed to resolve this conflict.

In terms of latent doubling, Fleming's villains function as representatives of consumer figures unimbued with Western rhetoric. In contrast the figure of Bond, who consumes material goods in equal degree, whose character is in fact formed by details of his eating habits, his clothing, his cars, and contemporary technology, is retained as hero because of his alliance with the British Secret Service. His ideals, so to speak, precede and justify his mode of life. His villains have no such rationale. They express contempt for Western ideological philosophy, often connecting idealistic rhetoric with the games children play, while they themselves concentrate on the main chance, on power and wealth and the material goods each of the latter implies. Explicitly, Fleming constructs his villains as dangerous to the Free World because of the evil conspiracies they fashion: implicitly, they are villainous because they embody cultural realities, dispensing with the softening affect of cultural ideals. They admit, barefacedly, the venality inherent in a culture whose economy depends on the production and consumption of material objects, the use of which is to increase the further consumption of other like objects.

Due to consideration of length, this study will cite only two examples of Fleming's series, the villains in *Casino Royale* and *From Russia With Love,* since in what was re-

Maureen O'Hara and Alec Guinness in Carol Reed's Our Man in Havana.

spectively his first and fifth novels Fleming employed overtly political conspiracies, whereas his later books pit Bond against an enemy representing an unspecified ideological position. In *Casino Royale* and *From Russia With Love* West stands against East, figuring as Britain versus Russia. However, despite their obvious ideological material, the villains in both books serve to assimilate the West to itself.

In *Casino Royale* Bond is pitted against Le Chiffre, a communist agent who has himself betrayed the Russians by losing trade union funds entrusted to his care after disastrous financial reverses in an unauthorized group of brothels. Le Chiffre conforms closely to the generic stereotype of the villain; he is of ethnic origin, sexually deviant, physically repulsive. He and Bond initially face off during a game of baccarat at a glamorous casino in Monte Carlo, and Bond's victory at cards means that Le Chiffre's extortion will be discovered by his masters. Therefore, Le Chiffre ambushes Bond, and subjects him to torture of an almost explicitly sexual nature. The latent aspect of the villain is nearly made manifest in this scene, as Fleming carefully delineates the correspondence between the two men, between the torturer and his victim, the master and his slave.

Critics have noted that Fleming's trademark is his vivid, highly detailed, generally sensuous descriptions of the physical objects within Bond's environment. In contrast, the language he uses to create action scenes is usually short and concise or evasive. The action ends almost before the reader is completely aware it has occurred, so that the reader is diverted from the more violent aspects of the genre and focused upon physical objects which exist, because of their extravagant nature, only in a fantasy world. For example, Fleming expends one page on the scene when Bond is captured by Le Chiffre, and even during that scene, changes point of view from Bond to Le Chiffre, so that the most violent portion of the scene is effaced, barely seen through Le Chiffre's ruminations on his future plans for Bond. On the other hand, details of the casino, clothing, cars, and food are constantly and lavishly repeated, to the extent that Fleming's prose occasionally resembles copy from a fashion magazine, another vehicle propagating the fantasies of consumerism. For example, Fleming identifies Vesper Lynd, the novel's stereotypically beautiful heroine, by describing the dress she wears: "Her medium-length dress was of grey soie sauvage with a square-cut bodice. . . . The skirt was closely pleated and flowered down from a narrow, but not a thin, waist. She wore a three-length, hand-stitched black belt. A hand-stitched black saretache rested on the chair beside her, together with a wide cartwheel hat of gold straw, its crown encircled by a thin black velvet ribbon which tied at the back in a short bow. Her shoes were square-toed of plain black leather."

In the structure of the novel, then, Fleming implies that the immediacy of sensual perception overrides abstract understanding. However, the explicit rhetoric spoken by Bond and other "good" figures denies the reader's actual experience, emphasizing instead the abstractions of Western democracy. Thus, Fleming enables the reader to enjoy the forbidden pleasures of physical objects by focusing attention on his idealistic rhetoric or quickly achieved action, away from the sensuous language he employs in descriptive passages. What the reader carries away from a Fleming novel is a plot summary and sense of Bond's mission. What he or she experiences during its reading is a sensuous gratification through the imaginative construction of a world filled with objects the culture defines as luxuries, but which are actually the logical necessities of a culture geared to increasing consumption and demanding, therefore, essentially useless objects. Precisely because most readers never possess the objects Fleming describes they are able to dismiss their subliminal satisfaction and the ethos it implies. Like the luxury object, Le Chiffre also satisfies this function. Through his sensual concupiscence Fleming is able to allow the reader to gratify sensual desires culturally forbidden but endemic to a culture covertly oriented to the accumulation of physical objects. However, Le Chiffre's death returns the novel to overt cultural standards. Bond, equally sensual, is victorious only because he is supported by the Secret Service. Because the villain dies, and Bond triumphs, the reader is able to enjoy that which is forbidden but tempting. Because the culture Fleming directed his novels toward was conflicted about its desire for and ability to produce an ever-increasing array of material objects, that aspect of the villain is precisely his most repellent and yet most fascinating feature.

Fleming divided the villain figure in *From Russia With Love,* written in 1956 into three figures: Kronsteen, the chess wizard who also plans conspiracies for the Russian espionage agency SMERSH; Rosa Klebb, chief chief torturer of SMERSH; and Red Grant, former British Army private, now SMERSH'S primary mercenary. All three, however, function as did Le Chiffre in *Casino Royale,* as images of the culture's deepest desires and most intense fears. In keeping with the genre, and with cultural modifications which occurred between the two books, Kronsteen, Klebb, and Grant do not embody only the explicit desire for material objects seen in Le Chiffre. They also treat human beings as objects, since Kronsteen is an asexual and calculating genius, almost a machine himself, and Klebb and Grant are voracious sexual deviants. Moreover, the plot structure of this book is motivated by a conspiracy in which the British desire an object of Russian technology, a secret code machine, and are willing to use Bond's sexual prowess to obtain it. Bond, then, is himself relegated to the status of becoming a consumer object, but is salvaged by the female heroine, his Russian counterpart, [who] initiates and therefore bears responsibility for the

sexual connection. Both agents are, in fact, marionettes, whose strings are pulled by the villains.

The villainous triumvirate, then, enables the reader to gratify desires for technological objects whose power is nearly unlimited, and to experience the fear that human beings living within a culture whose underlying structure depends on the production of more and more goods will become themselves another species of material object. Manifestly, Bond's own use of the Russian female agent as an object to be consumed is concealed by Bond's idealism and sense of mission. Latently, the villains express, explore, and are finally punished for trespassing on the same forbidden ground. Significantly, in both Fleming novels the enemy is considered distinctly different from Bond and his allies, and this strict division allows the reader to maintain Fleming's fantasy, that the villain is not a figure of Bond, himself as materialistic, violent, and sensually avaricious as are they.

In his novels, begun as Fleming's series was concluding, John LeCarré is less naively Manichaean. His division between good and evil is less well-marked, and the figure of the double agent, the enemy within, frequently appears in his books, as it could not in Fleming's severely divided world. Responding to the sense of restricted possibilities marking the late 1960s, the decline of the global economy, and the ambivalent sense of justice implied by the war in Vietnam as well as to the British spy scandals which demonstrated so vividly the enemy within, LeCarré's novels are pervaded by an atmosphere of despair and bleak endurance. Victory is always incomplete, comprehension of human value tenuous, and it is always reining. LeCarré's primary hero is George Smiley, depicted as "one of us," in contrast to Bond's superheroic posture. Smiley is short, rather plump, sad, sensitive, and inevitably victimized by his tailor. More seriously, he stands as the sole figure of conscience in a culture whose underlying corruption is symbolized by the degraded nature of its defenders, the Circus, LeCarré's version of the British Secret Service.

However, despite Smiley's appearance as unequivocal conscience figure, LeCarré has carefully included details within the series centered on Smiley hinting at Smiley's own corruption. To be sure, it is not the sort of corruption leading to major villainy. Nevertheless, Smiley is forced to participate in shady Circus plots because of some unnamed guilt; his wife, whom he adores and is unable to leave, constantly abuses his faith as Smiley does penance through their marriage; and the most dominant because the recurring image LeCarré leaves of Smiley locates him standing in the rain or the fog, facing a coming nightfall. Smiley, then, although undeniably a hero, is ambiguous in his heroism, counter-pointing LeCarré's villain figures, whose passionate idealism often leads them into their treacheries. In contrast to Fleming, whose books functioned as the defense mechanism of a consumer culture frightened of consuming itself, LeCarré's villains serve to assimilate the dangers inherent in idealism if it exists within a culture whose dominant motif is cynicism.

Two of LeCarré's figures particularly exemplify this dynamic. Both *The Spy Who Came In From The Cold* and *Tinker, Tailor, Soldier, Spy* contain versions of a latent cultural double in the figures of their villains and in both the connection between villain and hero is marked. In fact, in both books LeCarré carefully constructs plot details emphasizing that correspondence.

The Spy Who Came In From The Cold centers on Alec Leamas, former chief of the British Secret Service in Berlin. Leamas has been recalled to London after losing all of his German agents to Mundt, his counterpart in the East German Secret Service. Thus far, the villain seems to be Mundt, who moreover is generically acceptable as villain: sinister, cold, calculating, murderous, and an anti-semitic Neo-Nazi. At this point the novel appears determinedly Manichaen. Good and evil are essentially separate entities, distinct in both aims and methods. However, the British then ask Leamas to pose as an alcoholic, embittered by his treatment at their hands, so that the Germans will recruit him to spy against his own country. Leamas understands that his ulterior role involves protecting a British agent implanted within the German service, a German national recruited by the British as a double agent. Furthermore, Leamas believes that he has identified this agent as Fiedler's, Mundt's deputy. Mundt and Fiedler diverge in every way; Fiedler is Jewish, intellectual, an idealistic communist dedicated to improving life for the mass who has nonetheless retained a conscientious concern for individual life. Leamas, of course, is enormously pleased that the British conspiracy is designed to protect the life of his particular man, one of the few in Leamas' profession for whom he can feel any respect.

However, in what I suggest is the assertion of latent doubling, LeCarré upends his plot. It becomes clear that Mundt is the agent who the British have sent Leamas to protect, and moreover, protect against Fiedler, who has become suspicious of Mundt's treachery. Significantly, the characters of Mundt and Fiedler retain their initial dispositions—Mundt is conventionally evil; Fiedler conforms to the Western concept of a just man. What has been altered is their role as counters in a larger game. Despite Leamas' recognition that Fiedler is the better man, he fulfills the conspiracy, dooms Fiedler, and follows the plot to its convoluted conclusion as it ends with his death while trying to climb the Berlin Wall.

The British conspiracy to protect Mundt, and Leamas' acceptance of it, performs several functions in terms of doubling. First, because Leamas agreed to the plot, and sent Fiedler to almost certain death, Leamas becomes villainous, as does the British Secret Service. Explicitly, LeCarré forces the reader to realize the lack of difference between the British and Mundt; even their goals are muddied and rendered similar. Mundt, is not more a dedicated communist than Leamas' superiors in the British service [who] profess themselves devoted to Western forms of democracy. For both this is a limited war, in which the struggle itself has superseded any possible outcome. In a manner of speaking, because LeCarré tightly controls the world of the novel, restricting it to members of the Secret Service, spies become a metaphor for the world, all there is. Thus, the agents of countries ostensibly antagonistic in fact depend on their counterparts for their very existence.

The villain figure in the novel, then, is explicitly identified as Fiedler, who correctly suspects that Mundt has sold his services to the British, and who is therefore a threat to the British. As a defense mechanism, such identification serves to assuage the anxieties generated by a cultural conflict pitting, on the one hand, inherited ideals now largely rhetorical against, on the other hand, the pragmatic realities of mid-twentieth century cultural life. Those inherited ideals represent both a threat to and a desire of the larger cultural ethos, since to explicitly abandon them would be to accept on unendurable cultural identity, and to explicitly serve them would cripple cultural power. With this dilemma LeCarré echoes the novels written by Rudyard Kipling in the latter half of the nineteenth century. There, too, was embodied the discrepancy between the ideals of British civilization and the necessities demanded by an empire. Kipling, of course, resolved this conflict by resorting to an early version of Fleming's division between "us" and "them," externalizing evil and reversing the victim's position so that the British were almost pathetic in their attempt to bring civilization to the wild barbarous hordes of the colonial territories. LeCarré, on the other hand, makes overt his understanding that evil is endemic to a culture which adopts the methods of its enemy. Latently, however, his villains explore the cultural temptation to operate on lines of idealism while insuring that such behavior emerges as a danger finally eliminated. Most readers of *The Spy Who Came In From The Cold* understand the novel's resolution as victory for the West, albeit a qualified success. However, comprehending Leamas and Mundt as primary villains and Fiedler as their heroic double leads to a more insidious conclusion, one implying that victory is not merely qualified, it is impossible given the cultural conflict it seeks to resolve. Leamas' death substantiates this reading. Leamas almost escapes, is actually over the Berlin Wall, but returns in an act of will to remain with the young girl he has unwittingly drawn into the conspiracy. His murder is thus an act of suicide. Since Fiedler also clearly has died after the conspiracy's successful conclusion, Leamas' death is congruent with that of other serious literary doubles. Like Poe's William Wilson, for example, when the double dies so does the original. In this, of course, LeCarré's novel operates as a flawed defense mechanism, since the culture left alive at the book's close, represented by Mundt and the British Secret Service, is a culture LeCarré has taught his readers to despise.

Tinker, Tailor, Soldier, Spy, LeCarré's major Smiley novel, also employs the figure of a double agent, the villain nestling within, this time actually within the confines of Circus headquarters. Briefly, the plot motivating the novel centers on the exposure, by Smiley, of Bill Haydon, second in command of the entire Circus. Haydon is a mole, or agent implanted by the Russians, both to give them vital information about the British and to employ the techniques of disinformation—giving the British incorrect information which they assume is true because of the veracity of the source. Haydon vouches for that information, in a neat reversal congruent with the double motif. Manifestly, the British believe that he is one of their most valuable members; latently, he betrays them. Like Fiedler, the covert danger represented by Haydon involves cultural ideals. Haydon became a traitor while still at Oxford, recruited by one of his professors to right the world's wrongs. In this book, however, the death of the doubled villain does not necessitate the death of the hero. Smiley survives, and in fact, becomes head of the Circus. But Le-Carré makes clear that Smiley's is a Pyrrhic victory: "Leaving King's Cross, he had had a wistful notion of liking Haydon and respecting him: Bill was a man, after all, who had had something to say and had said it. But his mental system rejected this convenient simplification . . . Smiley shrugged it all aside, distrustful as ever of the standard shapes of human motive." That distrust, of course, LeCarré extends to Smiley's own motives. Indeed, the connection between Smiley and Haydon is made even more explicit through the metaphor of Smiley's wife, also both cousin and lover to Haydon. Although the larger culture remains intact after Haydon's death, he is a hereditary member of its ruling class; literally and symbolically, it has bred him. LeCarré leaves the reader with the implicit comprehension that although Haydon the individual has been eradicated, his surrogate will reappear, inevitably an aspect of a culture conflicted by its desire for power and its desire for honor.

Although LeCarré's novels do not transcend generic limits, they do push at its boundaries. Using the villain as a cultural double, LeCarré seems to render almost explicit the latent and necessarily unconscious component of cultural conflict. Once, of course, such knowledge becomes conscious, latent doubling no longer will perform the function of cultural defense mechanism. As do more serious less prescriptive works, LeCarré's books verge on demanding that the reader awakens to cultural reality by making visible cultural fantasies. Graham Greene, the last novelist considered here, makes this movement even more obvious. In his use of a nearly conscious latent double, Greene's books themselves are doubles of the espionage genre, simultaneously spy novels and serious literature, adhering to generic boundaries and venturing across frontiers in order to destroy perimeters.

Greene himself has divided his canon into what he calls "entertainments," and in the absence of his own definition, serious literature. However, his subjects remain consistent in both, displaying a concern with physical and emotional frontiers; with divided allegiances ending in inevitable betrayal; with the dangers of individual love; with the fascination of failure; and with the value of the human particular over the cultural polemic. Comically, in his "entertainments," these ideas emerge as the "virtue of disloyalty;" more seriously, Greene has described as the only distinguishing mark of a Christian civilization "the divided mind, the uneasy conscience, and the sense of personal failure." "Greeneland," as critics have called it, is a place of seedy degradation where the possibility of moral identity is always qualified by a sense of conditional failure.

Greene's fascination with frontiers and boundaries is, of course, a fundamental motif of the espionage novel. Most of his work contains references to spies and the two books closely considered below are explicitly members of the genre, although Greene considers *Our Man In Havana* to be an entertainment, while *The Human Factor* is bleakly serious. In both, however, Greene employs the villain as

a cultural double and skirts perilously close to exposing its latent nature to conscious scrutiny.

Set in Havana just prior to the Castro revolution, *Our Man in Havana* uses local color to express a dominant cultural mood in the same way LeCarré uses London's weather to express cultural disintegration. In Havana, unlike London, the sun is always shining, but it illuminates a culture grown outrageously decadent.

The novel's protagonist is Jim Wormold, who sells vacuum cleaners and lives with his daughter, whom he adores with a critical but thoroughly indulgent devotion. Milly is fully in harmony with the Cuban social structure, expressing a dogmatic yet sentimental Catholicism and an overwhelming desire for the luxurious objects produced by a culture in the process of consuming itself. The novel contains two characters identified as villainous. There is Captain Segura, chief of the Havana police, who conforms to generic stereotype in his repulsive physical aspect and his brutal behavior; and there is Hawthorne, head of the British Secret Service in Latin America, who recruits Wormold as the services "man in Havana." Segura pays close attention to the beautiful Milly, heightening Wormold's desire to remove her from Cuba, so that Hawthorne is able to seduce him by offering the money he needs both to return eventually to London and to finance Milly's expensive tastes. Comically rendered, the first half of the novel centers on Wormold's creation of an imaginary network of agents whose reports he writes himself and sends on to London. However, the novel abruptly becomes serious in tone when Wormold's agents are taken seriously by the "opposition," and people who resemble them are placed in grave physical danger. Wormold is forced to realize the inherent malignancy in what he thought was a boys' game, finally accepts his responsibility as creator, and extricates himself from his fantasy.

Although the novel's structure ostensibly identifies the villain figures as Segura and Hawthorne, it can be argued that Wormold himself functions as the latent double villainous to the larger culture within the world of the novel. During the first section of the book, Wormold appears to embrace Western cultural rhetoric asserting decency, sensitivity, and honor. Even his failure at selling vacuum cleaners is a qualified success. He, at least, implicitly recognizes the futility of selling a machine designed to clear carpets of dust to people whose houses, in the main, are floored with uncovered wooden planking. In addition, the vacuum cleaners have names like "Atomic Pile" and "Turbo Jet," echoing the increasing nuclear component of Western society. Greene implies that nuclear fission, last seen in the explosions at Hiroshima and Nagasaki, has been recuperated by the culture through the strategy of naming innocent objects, so that the terrifying specter of the atomic bomb comes to be controlled by the domesticated image of the vacuum cleaner. Wormold is, then, a figure of Greene's "just man," apparently different in kind from the likes of Segura and Hawthorne.

However, as the novel progresses, it becomes clear that Segura and Hawthorne are the characters who embrace principled cultural visions, even if the principles themselves are malign. Segura, despite his reputation as the

"Red Vulture," is quite mild in his treatment of Wormold, and seeks, in fact, to establish order in a situation of near chaos, even displaying a social conscience. His nickname was earned because his wallet is said to be sewn of human skin. Segura explains to Wormold, however, that the skin belonged to "A police-officer who tortured my father to death. You see, he was a poor man. He belonged to the torturable class." Earlier, Segura has explained that there exist "class distinctions in torture." Those torturable are "the poor in my own country, in any Latin American country. The poor of Central Europe and the Orient . . . Catholics are more torturable than Protestants." Segura, then, is villainous only in the context of pre-Revolutionary Cuba, but in serving a decadent and brutal culture he also attempts to salvage from its structure the ameliorating effects of systematic order. His knowledge that the poor and Catholics are torturable, himself the son of a peasant and a Catholic, indicates a level of self-consciousness restricting his own villainy. While Greene implies Segura is mistaken in the master he has chosen to serve, he also indicates that for Segura, the choice was more or less inevitable and that he is making the best of a deplorable situation. Moreover, since Segura is self-aware about his culture's disease, he does not function as a villain. The reader cannot despise him, cannot use him to express hidden fears and desires. As a metaphor, he functions to make the reader aware of cultural degradation without offering a cultural fantasy in substitution.

Hawthorne, the British agent, also fails as a structural villain. Initially, when he solicits Wormold's participation in his network, he seems to represent a sort of adolescent fantasy, playing an exciting game culled from the texts of other espionage novels. He induces Wormold to join him at a secret meeting; he explains how to use secret code and disappearing ink; he gives Wormold a new name using a coded cipher. In short, Greene allows Hawthorne to demonstrate all the tricks of the spy trade, while at the same time indicating that Hawthorne is just short of a buffoon, accepting as serious what can only be child's play.

In fact, as the novel's second section makes clear, the play involves real death and Hawthorne has always been aware of the risk. Although his profession involves him in acts drawn from comedy, his appreciation of them is realistic. As he reminds Wormold, "This is a dangerous job. You shouldn't have taken it unless you were prepared . . ." Wormold mistakenly understands Hawthorne's adherence to what Wormold recognizes as the dishonest principles of Imperialism for Hawthorne's personal dishonesty. Like Segura, within the world of the novel Hawthorne conforms to the role of protagonist. In contrast to Segura, however, it is Hawthorne's very unconsciousness which bars him from functioning structurally as a villain. His unconsciousness is complete, so that any evil he embodies is so obviously a case of innocent victimization, so clearly does he receive no pleasure from the espionage "game," that the reader can experience him as no more than a figure of business, misguided but well intentioned.

The villain figure, then, must possess some amount of consciousness of his own villainy in order to express pleasure, or pain, at it. Just as the psychological defense mechanism is selected because it is appropriate to the particular individual in terms of a defense which also brings pleasure—the paranoid individual, for example, usually enjoys his or her constant search for clues—so the villain must consciously seek evil, must be manifest as well as latent. The only figure in the novel who combines both overt and latent villainy in these terms, and who functions to assuage cultural anxiety, then, is Wormold.

During the comic portion of the book, Wormold treats espionage as a great game, which of course it is, since he has fictively imagined his agents. He fails, however, to realize the venality of the motives which led him to accept Hawthorne's offer. He needed money, but not to feed or shelter himself. Rather, the extra funds are docketed to buy Milly a horse and membership in the Havana country club, the very seat of cultural power and dishonesty. He spies, in effect, to give Milly all the luxuries she has been taught to covet by the degraded culture surrounding her. Wormold's indulgence is a tacit approval of the social structure, concealed by Greene as justifiable parental emotion. In fact, as the novel's serious second section makes clear, only when Wormold can covertly refuse Milly another object by ceasing to participate in Hawthorne's game, does he become genuinely heroic. Until that final denouement, when Wormold demonstrates real courage, his character functions as a latent cultural double. His personal conflict, of which he is unconscious, places luxurious consumption concealed by cultural rhetoric of abstract principles against cultural realities of poverty and despair. Until the novel's close Wormold resolves this conflict by indulging in the fantasies made acceptable by the culture in order to divert its inhabitants from the anxiety engendered by its internal inconsistencies. Wormold plays at being a spy, as avid readers of espionage literature similarly fantasize; he plays at being a good father, according to the cultural fantasy that a loving parent satisfies his children's desires. Until his fantasies become realities—until his imaginary agents are placed in real danger, Wormold is able to maintain life for himself and Milly according to inherent cultural standards which he consciously repudiates. That is, he has no respect for the country club, uses the names of its members to staff his fictive network, yet unhesitatingly pays Milly's fees. He recognizes that Hawthorne acts out a childish fantasy, but beats him at his own game. Wormold allows the reader latently to express the desire for adventure, power, wealth, and glamour, which are all tempting but would rupture the social fabric if indulged without restraint. As a cultural double, he incorporates the desire of the good man to live in a way he has been taught is evil. When Wormold realizes he can't get away with it, he returns to the status of protagonist, structurally repudiating the villain's unconscious desires.

Moreover, for the reader who recognizes Wormold only as a protagonist, he is a particularly insidious villain. When Wormold awakens to cultural reality, Greene seems to imply that consciousness will bring about social change. However, even after he has returned to the protagonist's role, Wormold embraces only a fantasy of cultural revolution. Instead of acting on the new version of cultural reality he has acquired, Wormold decides that salvation lies in romantic life. He has chosen, that is to say, another cultural fantasy designed to assimilate dissident voices. One may speculate that the conventionally happy endings closing most of Greene's entertainments explain what may be his ironic use of the term. The books are entertaining because they substitute one fantasy for another, and turn away from the uncompromising realities contained in his serious work.

Although Greene's serious novels focus on conspiracies and plots borrowed from the espionage genre, they as frequently push against generic limits precisely in the degree to which they render latent doubling manifest. They provide, so to speak, a negative plate against which highly generic novels can be scrutinized in terms of the cultural function the latter perform. Greene's serious work tends to be overtly polemical, operating to dispel cultural fantasies affirmed in their generic cousins. The villain figure within them, therefore, is often deliberately obfuscated, in order to allow the reader to experience the shock of duplicity by identifying with its very nature. Just as in *Our Man In Havana,* in *The Human Factor* Greene structures the novel so that the reader will sympathize and identify with the ostensible protagonist and as easily identify with the villain figures. Equally, in *The Human Factor* the enemy is finally located within.

The protagonist of *The Human Factor* is Maurice Castle, a man at the end of a long career with the British Secret Service who, in the last several years, has sold his services to the Russians, not because he is a communist, but because he loathes the injustices of apartheid in South Africa, where he ran a network of agents and where he met his black South African wife. Castle, then, is a double agent, allegedly working for the British, secretly employed by the Russians. However, Greene is careful, for much of the novel, to make clear that Castle's treachery does not make him villainous. The real evil, instead, he locates within the high command of the British Secret Service, whose profession has led them to confuse aims and methods, who consider murder part of the job, who seem to be without principle or belief. In contrast, Castle's Russian counterpart is an idealistic communist, with a genuinely sympathetic personality, as is the other British character who also works for the Russians. They possess a system of beliefs they serve, with apparent regret that cultural change seems to demand methods including dishonesty and violence. Ironically, in terms of the novel's structure, Greene implies that the enemy is within the wider British culture—and that Castle, as a double agent, works according to his conscience and therefore his treachery doubles back on itself and becomes transformed into a species of good. If that structure remained in place throughout the novel, it could be considered an evolved version of Fleming's Bond series. Its protagonist, Castle, would serve to accommodate idealism within the cynical milieu of an information-gathering society; and its villain, the British Secret Service, would assuage cultural anxiety about the methods endemic to a near-police state because Greene insures that those methods fail. Good and evil, although convoluted, are clearly separate.

However, using the villain as a latent cultural double, Greene pushes the espionage genre beyond its prescriptive boundaries. Just as did Wormold, here too the protagonist becomes a latent villain, when Castle becomes indirectly responsible for the murder of his colleague whom the British high command suspects is guilty of Castle's own treachery. Castle's villainy is located in his failure to scrutinize his own motives—he has failed to understand that although the actions he performs to assist the black population of South Africa are laudatory, he cannot refrain from performing them. As Greene makes quite clear with incidents drawing a portrait of Castle's childhood, Castle was destined to be affected by the suffering endured by a victimized majority. His treachery is thus less an act of personal conscience than one of personal necessity. His lack of self-examination leads him, finally, to abandon his wife when he flees to an exile in Moscow, as well as to bear responsibility for his murdered colleague.

Manifestly, then, Castle is the novel's protagonist, caught in a snare set by a corrupted culture for a man attempting to satisfy individual conscience, to value the human factor over the cultural abstraction. However, as a latent cultural double, Castle displays the cultural conflict pitting individual conscience against communal need. In fact, Castle's stand in favor of the individual is as much a fantasy as Wormold's stand for romantic love against patriotism. In focusing upon his desire to ameliorate suffering, Castle has actually caused great suffering to his wife, his son, and his friend. In effect, because of his failure at self assessment, Castle has served the abstraction over the human being sharing his house and office. The reader who has been seduced by Greene to identify with Castle must, by the end of the book, also be implicated in the discrepancy between his good intentions and the disastrous consequences between his real acts. Since villainy lies in destructive behavior, the destruction Castle wreaks in the novel is superseded only by the actual murder of his colleague. Even there, however, Greene is careful to allow the British no concealing rhetoric. They are as cynical as their actions indicate, and therefore, cannot function as an unconscious double. In order to awaken the reader to cultural corruption, Greene necessarily traps Castle in a snare he has unconsciously fashioned for himself. Manifestly, he expresses cultural anxiety about Western ideals in the face of the increasing realities of a Cold War society. Latently, however, his function is to allow the reader to believe that the man with ideals does not fit the cultural system because the ideals themselves are illusory. That, finally, Castle fails to perform this latent function is due to Greene's transgression of generic prescriptions. The final scene of the book, located in a Moscow very similar to the environment of the British Secret Service, where Castle meets his brother traitors and sees himself in the undistorted clarity of the mirror of their venal personalities, makes obvious the fact that Castle has been villainous. Had Greene omitted this scene, and allowed Castle's villainy to remain unarticulated within the novel's narrative structure, Castle's latent function might have remained intact. Once, however, Greene allowed the reader direct access to an unconscious knowledge, he destroyed the possibility for the reader to identify both with and against Castle. In the effort to teach the reader, Greene may, in fact, have lost some of the generic effect of the book. But he might argue that the price paid in generic coin was amply repaid as the novel forces the reader to scrutinize his or her social structure. *The Human Factor* proposes, because it refuses to affirm existing conditions in either Western or Eastern cultures, change founded on the most uncompromising individual and cultural self-scrutiny. Dispensing with all cultural fantasies, Greene justifies the term serious for his books—they seriously confront the reader with the portrait of a culture shorn of its defensive postures, face to face not with its double but with itself.

The three versions of the espionage novel considered above each contain a villain figure functioning as a defense mechanism for the culture into which the novels were delivered, in that in each the villain delineates and assimilates anxiety inherent to the particular social structure. Because the Fleming novels remain within relatively rigid generic parameters, the death of the villain, clearly separated from the hero and understood as a cultural double, reaffirms existing social conditions. The novels written by John LeCarré, in contrast, confuse the definition of hero and villain, and operate as a negative plate for the culture, so the villain's death contains overtones of cultural disintegration as well. Finally, pushing against generic boundaries, the espionage novels written by Graham Greene identify the protagonist and the villain as one figure, and his conclusive failure also signals the failure of the culture at large. One may suggest that for the espionage genre, when the forbidden fantasy becomes a reality, the genre itself becomes that which is forbidden. (pp. 11-35)

Laura Tracy, "Forbidden Fantasy: The Villain as Cultural Double in the British Espionage Novel," in Clues: A Journal of Detection, *Vol. 9, No. 1, Spring-Summer, 1988, pp. 11-37.*

FURTHER READING

Anthologies

Ambler, Eric, ed. *To Catch a Spy: An Anthology of Favourite Spy Stories.* New York: Atheneum, 1965, 224 p.
Collection of seven spy stories by major figures in spy fiction, including Graham Greene, W. Somerset Maugham, Ian Fleming, and John Buchan.

Secondary Sources

Atkins, John. *The British Spy Novel: Styles in Treachery.* London: John Calder, 1984, 287 p.
Examines the origin and development of British spy fiction during the twentieth century, attempts to define the most significant features of espionage as a literary genre, and compares the portrayal of espionage in fiction to its real-life practice.

Bedell, Jeanne F. "Romance and Moral Certainty: The Espionage Fiction of John Buchan." *The Midwest Quarterly* 22, No. 3 (Spring 1981): 230-41.
Compares John Buchan's spy fiction to John Bunyan's

Pilgrim's Progress, where the "spy" is a "seeker after truth."

———. "A Sense of History: The Espionage Fiction of Anthony Price." *The Armchair Detective* 15, No. 2 (Spring 1982): 114-18.
Observes that the feature which sets Price apart from other espionage fiction writers is "his ability to integrate his historical knowledge into tightly woven plots and to use it to build and analyze character."

———. "The Great Game." *The Armchair Detective* 21, No. 4 (Fall 1988): 380-87.
Cites the importance of Rudyard Kipling's *Kim* in the development of espionage fiction by examining the ways in which it anticipates later attitudes and characteristics of the spy novel.

Brady, Charles A. "John Le Carré's Smiley Saga." *Thought* 60, No. 238 (September 1985): 275-96.
Discusses Le Carré's novels featuring the character George Smiley, focusing on the authors and literary traditions that influenced these works.

Cannadine, David. "James Bond and the Decline of England." *Encounter* 53, No. 3 (September 1979): 46-55.
Examines the relation between the world depicted in Ian Fleming's Bond series and the perceived state of decline in England during the time in which they appeared.

Carr, Nick. *America's Secret Service Ace: The Operator 5 Story.* Mercer Island, Wash.: Starmong House, 1985, 63 p.
Summarizes the different adventures encountered by Operator 5 in the paperback series of the same name.

Cook, Michael L. *Mystery, Detective, and Espionage Magazines.* Westport, Conn.: Greenwood Press, 1983, 795 p.
Overview of the different magazines publishing mystery, detective, and espionage fiction in the United States and abroad. Cook also provides profiles of the major writers in each genre.

Cook, Michael L., and Miller, Stephen T. *Mystery, Detective, and Espionage Fiction: A Checklist of Fiction in U.S. Pulp Magazines, 1915-1974.* 2 vols. New York: Garland Publishing, 1988, 1183 p.
Catalogues mystery, detective, and espionage fiction published in pulp magazines.

Drew, Bernard A. *Action Series and Sequels: A Bibliography of Espionage, Vigilante, and Soldier-of-Fortune Novels.* New York: Garland Publishing, 1988, 328 p.
Lists action and adventure series titles. Drew also includes indexes to heroes and villains in each genre.

East, Andy. *The Cold War File.* Metuchen, N.J.: Scarecrow Press, 1983, 362 p.
Compilation of "dossiers" on numerous espionage writers, documenting the ways in which they may be identified with the protagonists of their series fiction.

Gow, Gordon. *Suspense in the Cinema.* New York: Barnes, 1968, 221 p.
Studies the ways in which suspense is created in the cinema, particularly espionage films.

Harper, Ralph. *The World of the Thriller.* Cleveland, Ohio: Press of Case Western Reserve University, 1969, 139 p.
Analysis of the thriller, the distinctive features of its formulaic plots, the character of its heroes, and the psycho-

logical devices used to produce different effects on the reader.

Hay, Eloise Knapp. *The Political Novels of Joseph Conrad: A Critical Study*. Chicago: University of Chicago Press, 1963, 350 p.
  Studies the political aspects of Conrad's two espionage novels, *The Secret Agent* and *Under Western Eyes.*

Larkin, Philip. "The Batman from Blades." *The Times Literary Supplement* (5 June 1981): 625.
  Review of John Gardner's *Licence Renewed,* a novel attempting to follow in the tradition of Ian Fleming's Bond series. Larkin concludes that "to resurrect Bond you have to be Fleming."

Lewis, George H. "Spy Fiction American Style." *Journal of Communication* 25, No. 4 (Autumn 1975): 132-37.
  Compares the characteristics of James Bond in Ian Fleming's novels to those associated with him in American films.

McCormick, Donald. *Who's Who in Spy Fiction.* New York: Taplinger Publishing Co., 1977, 216 p.
  Compilation of biographical and critical sketches of espionage writers.

Merry, Bruce. *Anatomy of the Spy Thriller.* Montreal: McGill-Queen's University Press, 1977, 253 p.
  Accounts for the popular appeal of the spy thriller through an examination of its narrative strategies, use of recurrent situations, and reliance upon the reader's expectations.

Monaghan, David. *The Novels of John Le Carré: The Art of Survival.* Oxford: Basil Blackwell, 1985, 207 p.
  Emphasizes the ways in which Le Carré has reworked the standard formulas of espionage fiction and discusses the worldview delineated in his novels.

Palmer, Jerry. *Thrillers: Genesis and Structure of a Popular Genre.* New York: St. Martin's Press, 1979, 232 p.
  Discussion of the thriller, its heroes and villains, structural elements, origins, and popularity.

Panek, LeRoy L. *The Special Branch: The British Spy Novel, 1890-1980.* Bowling Green, Ohio: Bowling Green University Popular Press, 1981, 288 p.

Surveys major and minor English espionage writers from a historical perspective and describes the form and content of their work.

Ray, Philip E. "The Villain in the Spy Novels of John Buchan." *English Literature in Transition* 24, No. 2 (1981): 81-90.
  Overview of the common characteristics of the villain in Buchan's novels, arguing that they must be taken seriously in order for Buchan's artistry to be recognized.

Reynolds, William. "The Labyrinth Maker: The Espionage Fiction of Anthony Price." *The Armchair Detective* 19, No. 4 (Fall 1986): 350-58.
  Descriptive survey of Price's novels and his protagonist David Audley. Reynolds argues that Price's best works are those in which Audley has figured.

Silverstein, Marc. "After the Fall: The World of Graham Greene's Thrillers." *Novel* 22, No. 1 (Fall 1988): 24-44.
  Argues that Greene should have blurred the distinction between the novel and the spy thriller, thereby transforming the latter into a "mimetic, psychologically complex genre."

Stafford, David. "John Buchan's Tales of Espionage: A Popular Archive of British History." *Canadian Journal of History* 18, No. 1 (April 1983): 1-21.
  Asserts that the four Richard Hannay novels allow Buchan to articulate his own politics and to comment on the significance of World War I.

Symons, Julian. "A Short History of the Spy Story." In his *Mortal Consequences: A History—From the Detective Story to the Crime Novel,* pp. 230-46. New York: Harper & Row, 1972.
  Outlines the development of the spy story in relation to historical events.

Wolfe, Peter. *Corridors of Deceit: The World of John Le Carré.* Bowling Green, Ohio: Bowling Green State University Popular Press, 1987, 275 p.
  Discussion of Le Carré's fiction and the ways in which his novels evoke a detailed picture of the spy's world.

Madness in Twentieth-Century Literature

INTRODUCTION

While madness has been a prominent theme in literature since ancient times, twentieth-century writers have found it particularly suited to portraying the modern world. Many artists have suggested that the First and Second World Wars and the increased mechanization of the twentieth century have contributed to a sense of growing psychic imbalance. These writers have additionally equated madness with an escape from an existence that has become overwhelmingly complex. In twentieth-century feminist literature, for example, madness has represented a form of freedom and rebellion for intelligent, ambitious women who reject the passive roles assigned to them by patriarchal society. Madness has also served as a metaphor for the creative process, and many critics have debated the relationship between creativity and mental instability. Lillian Feder observed: "[The theme of madness] discloses, as it always has, the mind of the protagonist or persona incorporating the limitations and defenses of its society at the same time it exposes their effects. . . . Explorations of madness throughout literature portray a great variety of psychic oppositions to environmental demands. Among these, the narcissistic withdrawal from social and intrapsychic struggles is but one detour of the human mind in its internalization of family, society, and history."

REPRESENTATIVE WORKS

Babb, Sonora
  An Owl on Every Post (novel) 1970
Baker, Elliott
  A Fine Madness (novel) 1964
Barnes, Djuna
  Nightwood (novel) 1936
Beckett, Samuel
  Molloy (drama) 1951
  [*Molloy,* 1955]
Berryman, John
  The Dream Songs (poetry) 1969
  Love and Fame (poetry) 1970
  Recovery (novel) 1974
Brand, Millen
  The Outward Room (novel) 1937
  Savage Sleep (novel) 1968
Callaghan, Morley
  Such Is My Beloved (novel) 1934
Camus, Albert
  La chute (novel) 1956
  [*The Fall,* 1957]
Cleckley, Hervey and Thigpen, Corbett H.
  The Three Faces of Eve (novel) 1957

Conrad, Joseph
  Heart of Darkness (novella) 1902; published in
  Youth: A Narrative, and Two Other Stories
Dürrenmatt, Friedrich
  Die Physiker: Eine Komödie in zwei Akten (drama) 1962
    [*The Physicists: A Play in Two Acts,* 1963]
Fitzgerald, F. Scott
  Tender Is the Night: A Romance (novel) 1934
Fowles, John
  The Collector (novel) 1963
Frame, Janet
  Faces in the Water (novel) 1961
Freeman, Lucy
  Fight against Fears (novel) 1951
Gide, André
  L'immoraliste (novel) 1902
  [*The Immoralist,* 1930]
Gilman, Charlotte Perkins
  "The Yellow Wallpaper" (short story) 1892;
  published in journal *New England Magazine*
Ginsberg, Allen
  Howl, and Other Poems by Allen Ginsberg (poetry) 1956
  Kaddish, and Other Poems, 1958-1960 (poetry) 1961
Grass, Günter
  Die Blechtrommel (novel) 1959
  [*The Tin Drum,* 1962]
Greenberg, Joanne
  I Never Promised You a Rose Garden (novel) 1964
Hedayat, Sadegh
  Buf-e Kur (novel) 1937
  [*The Blind Owl,* 1957]
Hesse, Hermann
  Der Steppenwolf (novel) 1927
  [*Steppenwolf,* 1929]
Kafka, Franz
  Der Prozess (novel) 1925
  [*The Trial,* 1935]
Kesey, Ken
  One Flew over the Cuckoo's Nest (novel) 1962
Lessing, Doris
  The Four-Gated City (novel) 1969
Lucas, Victoria [pseudonym of Sylvia Plath]
  The Bell Jar (novel) 1963
March, William
  Come in at the Door (novel) 1934
Meuller, Amelia
  There Have to Be Six (novel) 1966
Plath, Sylvia
  Ariel (poetry) 1965
Rhys, Jean
  Good Morning, Midnight (novel) 1939
  Wide Sargasso Sea (novel) 1966

Roethke, Theodore
  The Collected Poems of Theodore Roethke (poetry)
    1966
Rubin, Theodore Isaac
  Lisa and David (novel) 1962
Salamanca, J. R.
  Lilith (novel) 1961
Sartre, Jean-Paul
  La nausée (novel) 1938
    [*Nausea,* 1949]
Sexton, Anne
  To Bedlam and Partway Back (poetry) 1960
Shaffer, Peter
  Equus (drama) 1973
Sinclair, Emil [pseudonym of Hermann Hesse]
  Demian: Die Geschichte von Emil Sinclairs Jugend
    (novel) 1919
      [*Demian,* 1923]
Ward, Mary Jane
  The Snake Pit (novel) 1946

OVERVIEWS

Leslie Y. Rabkin

[*In the following essay, Rabkin discusses the relationship between literature, psychology, and mental illness as a means of depicting human experience.*]

[What] is the value of literature for our explorations into personality and psychopathology? The psychologist Gordon Allport expresses one vital aspect in his [*"Personality: A Problem for Science or a Problem for Art"* in *Revista de Psihologie* 1 (1938)] on the important role of humanistic thought in personality study:

> In literature, personality is never regarded, as it sometimes is in psychology, as a sequence of unrelated actions. Personality is not like a water-skate, darting hither and yon on the surface of a pond, with its several fugitive excursions having no relation to one another. Good literature never makes the mistake of confusing the personality of man with that of a water-skate. Psychology often does.

Thus, psychology fragments, literature binds; psychology is concerned with part processes, literature is holistic; psychology strives for scientific objectivity, literature seeks for coherence and esthetic truth. (pp. 1-2)

To the reader accustomed to the usual didactic materials in abnormal psychology, the literary approach may seem at first eccentric. Ordinarily, the study of psychopathology proceeds through three channels—the textbook, the sourcebook or collection of readings, and the volume of case histories. The textbook sketches the basic concepts of the field; the readings add depth to this outline; and the casebook brings in the human element. By the time these varied resources have been tapped, what may have seemed

at first exotic and bizarre can be seen as the result of an intense and all-too-human struggle to resolve the stresses of life and achieve some sort of coherent identity, however distorted the end product may be.

It is just this struggle which has been the pivotal concern of great literature—Hamlet and Oedipus, Raskolnikov and Emma Bovary, Don Quixote and Stephen Dedalus. The insightful delineation of the inner and outer worlds of these characters is a rich mine for the psychologist. It was Freud himself who asserted, "The poets and philosophers before me discovered the unconscious, what I discovered was the scientific method by which the unconscious can be studied."

The creative artist has always examined the contradictory motivations, the inner unrest, the affects and impulses of man. Endowed with a sometimes painful self-consciousness, the writer has been able to chart the geography of the inner landscape of the mind with a power and precision unmatched by the more objective methods of psychological science.

For so many writers, the most compelling features of this psychological terrain have been the deep-shaded valleys of desire, the hidden caves of fantasy, and the dark abysses of madness. Pathological experience, in its myriad forms, has long obsessed the artist. For some, the key element has been the cathartic effect, the artist's more or less conscious attempt to embody in writing and thus purge himself of the private devils which torment him. Maupassant's anguished tales, Dostoevsky's feverish *Notes from the Underground,* Blake's eerie prophetic visions, Gogol's grotesques, Kafka's gnawing concern with guilt—all have elements of this cathartic aspect in common. Their brooding sensitivity made it possible for them to grasp and confront what Matthew Arnold called "the nameless feelings that course through our breast" and to bring things hidden and unexpressed into the light of our focussed consciousness.

Another of the fascinations of the pathological revolves around the problem of pain. All psychopathology involves pain and suffering, both mental and physical. The torment of the emotionally disturbed person, however, is often scanted in more scientific analyses of mental illness, being attributed to the patient's delusive "imagination." This is a regrettable situation. To deal with the patient's intolerable experience of pain as if it were "all in his mind," is to indicate to him a lack of empathy, of true understanding, and is often a key factor in the disruption of treatment. Anyone who has suffered pain, no matter what its origin, knows how real the experience is, yet how difficult to communicate to another person.

For the artist, this elusive agony and the helpless feelings which accompany it, provide a special focus of concern. The very thing which makes pain so intractable to scientific investigation is what draws the writer—its subjectivity. Again, it is his ability to brush aside the mask of convention, and to explore the innermost recesses of heart and mind, which makes the artist the true cartographer of pain.

The use of language is another area in which psychopathology and literature, particularly that of the past half-century, meet. The language of the artist, in its emotive richness and its use of resonant imagery, is a far better vehicle than the often dehumanized jargon of science for the description of human experience. As with the affect of pain, the writer can render the nuances of emotion and thought far more compellingly than the psychologist. And his evocative language can find no more dramatic subject than the emotional upheaval of the disordered personality.

The phenomenon known as the "poetry of madness" deserves comment here. The paradoxical, elliptical, and convoluted language of the psychotic has often been likened to that of the poet. Their use of multi-leveled meanings and unexpected juxtapositions of imagery has a formal similarity. However, as Steven Marcuse has correctly pointed out [in "The Poetry of Madness" in *New York Review of Books* 2, No. 9 (1964)], what so often appears in the language of the psychotic as meaningful and poetic becomes, on closer examination, "merely syntactical elegies for a lost world of intelligible discourse."

In more general terms, the interrelationship of psychology and literature has other dimensions. There are at least four avenues of approach to this broad topic, each independently valid and yet complementary to the others. The first and most comprehensive methodology is to explore the basic psychology of artistic creation with emphasis on writing and literary expression. This type of study might utilize the writings of such an interpreter as Ernst Kris, stressing the psychological, and particularly the psychoanalytic insights which concentrate on the motivations and symbolic aspects of artistic creation. Such a study might also make use of the ideas of the Gestalt school of psychology which has conceptualized art as the finest example of the human mind's striving for a well-organized articulated wholeness.

One focus in the examination of the creative process, for example, might be the part played by regression. As Kris has pointed out, some relaxation of conscious control is a necessary condition for the "inspiration" required in artistic production. This regression is different from that which takes place during sleep, in neurosis, or under the influence of drugs. The difference is that the artist deliberately seeks this relaxed state and utilizes it for conscious, productive purposes.

We could, then, attempt to assess the respective roles of conscious control and spontaneity in literary creativity. The final pages of Gogol's *Diary of a Madman* provide an excellent case in point. The narrator's disintegrating thought processes provide a series of images akin to the verbal transcription of a nightmare. The language is condensed and symbolic, appearing at first glance to be simply fantastic and incoherent. But these verbal wanderings are not merely the end-product of an eruption of spontaneous, unconscious thoughts, which somehow possess their thinker. Closer examination reveals how Gogol controls the pace and utilizes the imagery to delineate the feelings of estrangement and horror of an isolated man's retreat into madness.

A second approach deals with the *effects* of a literary piece on the reader. Here the focus is on the interaction of the psychological field of the reader—his needs, fantasies, wishes—with the structure and content of the world created by the author. Such a study might involve assessment of the effects of certain types of thematic material (for example, incest themes or agression) on varying personalities in whom such conflict areas were of more or less importance, and how each group dealt with the anxieties aroused by these themes.

The "processes of response," as Simon O. Lesser has called them [in *Fiction and the Unconscious* (1957)], are a complex amalgam of conscious and unconscious phenomena. As we read a piece of fiction, on the conscious level we attempt to grasp its obvious or manifest meaning and follow the developing story line, while engaging in an unsystematic appraisal of such qualities as honesty and skillfulness. Our unconscious response, as Lesser demonstrates, involves a series of reactions. Most important is the unconscious apprehension of latent anxiety-arousing material, those facets of the story which are reminiscent of past, personal painful experiences. Each individual reader will have a differential response to any single episode depending on his own experiences.

Kafka's powerful story, *The Judgment,* provides a suitable stimulus for such an investigation. The nature of Georg Bendemann's relationship to his father is such as to set off an unconscious resonance in some readers of an anxiety-ridden childhood struggle with a powerful and arbitrary parental authority, the fully conscious recognition of which could produce an intolerable degree of anxiety. Other unconscious elements of our response to such material may involve the phenomenon of identification, or the loss of critical distance from the characters portrayed, leading to a psychological participation in their activities, and day-dreaming behavior fostered by the stories in which we become involved.

A third approach, the biographical, explores the personality of the writer himself and attempts to assess the effect of his experiences on his literary creations, their direct reflection and various mutations and disguises. Here the concern is with the roots of a specific style of literary expression and characterization—what effect, we might ask, did Dostoevsky's epilepsy and gambling compulsion have on his literary style, his depiction of life, and his character portrayals? This technique of study views a literary work as a "personal document," an objectification, however veiled or open, of the artist's inner concerns.

In utilizing literary materials as a form of "projective test" protocol, however, we must be careful not to expect any simple isomorphism between life events and fictional portrayals. Reflections of the author's personality, in all its conscious and unconscious features, will be found in a variety of characters, as well as in the stylistic aspects of his writing. (pp. 2-6)

The fourth avenue of exploration is the examination of a literary character as a personality in himself. Under this heading would appear the countless examinations of the psyche of fictional characters such as Hamlet, Mann's von Aschenbach, or Lady Chatterley. This approach often draws heavy critical fire from psychologist and literary critic alike because of the tendency of writers in this area to erect monolithic psychological structures on quite shaky foundations. Nevertheless, the intense and finely wrought literary character study can probe as deeply as the best real-life case history and psycho-dynamic formulation.

To examine the motivations of the fictional personality, the critic turns to the tools of clinical psychology and psychoanalysis. The ambivalences, defenses, and impulses which mark our own personalities are equally as present in a well-drawn literary character. His world is finite, and we can never discover certain facts about him, but with our accumulated knowledge concerning personality functioning we can make some good guesses and elaborate a lucid and consistent psychological portrait.

For example, the personality of Paul, the unhappy young hero of Willa Cather's *Paul's Case,* can be subjected to this type of character analysis. We might begin by assessing the world around him and how he experiences the relationships and events which impinge on him. Drawing on our understanding of the psychology of adolescence, we could extrapolate about the important relationship of Paul with his father. How, we might ask, is their interaction different from that of other adolescent-parent pairs? We could then go on to speculate about Paul's earlier life—the possible effect on his personality of his mother's death, his developing sense of isolation, the handling of his childhood fears and anxieties, and so on. In the end, a portrait as vivid as any case history written about a lonely, frustrated adolescent would emerge. This type of analysis, let it be said, is probably most aptly applied in dealing with a novel in which the author can allow himself greater freedom in sketching the life history and behavior variabilities of his characters.

Literature and psychology thus interpenetrate at many points. For the literary critic, the tools of psychology provide a means of access to new levels of understanding a work of art, the artist who created it, and the audience which responds to it. For the psychologist, the artist's ability to depict delicate shadings of feeling and thought, and to portray the hidden motives of man, makes literature an indispensable resource for the investigation of personality in its most holistic sense.

> Anna Sergeyevna was silent for a little. "And so you haven't the least artistic feeling?" she observed, putting her elbow on the table, and by that very action bringing her face nearer to Bazarov. "How can you get on without it?"
>
> "Why, what should I need it for, may I ask?"
>
> "Well, at least to enable you to study and understand men."
>
> Turgenev, *Fathers and Sons*
> (pp. 7-8)

Leslie Y. Rabkin, in an introduction to Psychopathology and Literature, *edited by Leslie Y. Rabkin, Chandler Publishing Company, 1966, pp. 1-8.*

Lillian Feder

[Feder is an American educator and critic. In the following excerpt, she argues that descriptions of madness are by nature distorted and culturally bound.]

Madness has been a continuous theme in Western literature from its beginnings to the present time. Evidence indicates, moreover, that human beings were preoccupied with extreme forms of mental and psychic experience long before they recorded it in literature. Myths and legends appearing in Homer, the Bible, and ancient Greek drama contain primordial symbolizations of delusions, mania, and other bizarre forms of thought and behavior. In some respects, the prototypical mad man or woman is analogous to the wild man, an imaginary being who occurs in various forms throughout Western literature and art, and who also emerges from myth and ritual, the remnants of which can be observed even in the most sophisticated aesthetic representations. In a comprehensive [entitled *Wild Men in the Middle Ages: A Study in Art, Sentiment, and Demonology* (1952)], Richard Bernheimer suggests that "the notion of the wild man must respond and be due to a persistent psychological urge. We may define this urge as the need to give external expression and symbolically valid form to the impulses of reckless physical self-assertion which are hidden in all of us, but which are normally kept under control." Whereas similar impulses are expressed in many literary and artistic representations of mad figures, these also convey more varied and more complicated psychic and social experience.

The mad protagonist generally inhabits the familiar world of civilized people, although in his madness he may retreat to the savage environment and condition of the traditional wild man. Furthermore, although his aberrant thoughts and behavior may determine his essential role, as savagery does the wild man's, madness is still but one aspect of his nature, and it may emerge only in extreme or extraordinary circumstances. The most crucial difference lies in the extent to which the mad protagonist not only symbolizes but reveals the very psychic processes that account for strange and violent behavior and the inextricable connection of such processes with the most ordinary relationships and conduct of daily life. (pp. 3-4)

From the earliest extant myths to the most recent confessions, fiction, poetry, and drama, portrayals of madness convey in symbolic form human beings' preoccupation with their own mental functioning, with the enormous range of their psychic experience. The treatment of madness in literature reflects human ambivalence toward the mind itself; madness, comprising its strangest manifestations, is also familiar, a fascinating and repellent exposure of the structures of dream and fantasy, of irrational fears and bizarre desires ordinarily hidden from the world and the conscious self. In literature, as in daily life, madness is the perpetual amorphous threat within and the extreme of the unknown in fellow human beings. In fact, recurrent literary representations of madness constitute a history of explorations of the mind in relation to itself, to other human beings, and to social and political institutions. The madman, like other people, does not exist alone. He both reflects and influences those involved with him. He embodies and symbolically transforms the values and aspirations of his family, his tribe, and his society, even if he renounces them, as well as their delusions, cruelty, and violence, even in his inner flight.

The most obvious and natural question that arises at this point is what is madness: how is one to define a concept charged with centuries of political, social, religious, medical, and personal assumptions? There is, of course, no one description that evokes all the varieties of aberrant or bizarre thought and conduct that have been regarded as insane throughout human existence. Although similar individual and group manifestations of extreme psychic confusion and suffering have appeared throughout history, it is clear that certain symptoms are characteristic of their different times. Inappropriate, pathological guilt, for example, was among the most common symptoms of mental disturbance prevalent in Western civilization so long as the authority of state, church, and patriarchal family was assumed; the pathological absence of guilt that one observes at present in America and much of Europe surely reflects the disintegration of such authorities. Yet pathological guilt persists, manifesting itself in obsession with sin, as do grandiose identifications with Christ and other gods and heroes, traditional symbols strangely adapted to current narcissism and alienation. In attempting to cover persistent and variable characteristics of actual as well as literary madness, I define madness as a state in which unconscious processes predominate over conscious ones to the extent that they control them and determine perceptions of and responses to experience that, judged by prevailing standards of logical thought and relevant emotion, are confused and inappropriate.

Curiously, one finds a basic similarity in the types of responses to insanity from earliest records to the present, which indicate that few, if any, societies have had a consistent attitude toward madness. Franz Alexander and Sheldon Selesnick group such continuous approaches in three main categories: the organic, the psychological, and the magical. The common assumption that madness in ancient Greek society was regarded as a blessing, an inducement to prophecy and poetry, reflects only one of these approaches, which was taken at the very time that the "Hippocratics inaugurated the first classification of mental illness, and one that was extremely rational. They included in the schema epilepsy, mania (excitement), melancholia, and paranoia" [*The History of Psychiatry: An Evaluation of Psychiatric Thought and Practice from Prehistoric Times to the Present* (1966)]. Furthermore, ancient Greek philosophy and drama treat madness as both divine influence and sickness. Such inconsistencies can be traced from earliest recorded history to the present. The establishment of psychiatry in the eighteenth century and psychoanalysis in the twentieth as branches of medicine has not precluded magical approaches either employed or inspired by physicians themselves. Among both traditional and radical therapists, the omniscient seer and the guru appear in practice and print. A well-known recent movement in so-called radical psychoanalysis is the retreat from the hospital to the commune, where cures are undertaken through induced regressive and even anarchic behavior. The descriptions of cure and self-discovery in such places employ the language and concepts of religion and mysticism. Concomitantly, within the various orthodox institutions of psychiatric training and practice much difference of opinion exists on the nature and treatment of the psychoses.

Despite such continuous diversity of approaches to madness, it still seems possible to designate those qualities of thought, speech, and behavior which have been considered aberrant from the norm throughout human history and which have consistently been perceived as the expression by certain individuals that their mental experience is markedly different from that of most other people. The study of literary representations of these mysterious communications, and especially of their symbolic structure, is elucidated by recent psychoanalytic approaches to mental illness as "impairments of symbolization" [Marshall Edelson, in his *The Idea of a Mental Illness* (1971)]. Imaginative literature, in turn, provides remarkable clues to the mental processes that produce the actual symbolizations of the psychotic, for the poet, dramatist, and novelist explore and illuminate psychic conflict and confusion through the very symbols they employ to depict these states. Intrinsic distortion of experience, as in myth, or personal records replete with clinical details, as in diaries and confessions, or—somewhere in between—imaginative transformations of observations of madness, as in much poetry, fiction, and drama, are consciously ordered versions of delirium, delusion, mania, paranoia, and the many other symptoms now classed under the general term psychoses.

The varieties of madness created in literature are in most respects no different from those to be discovered throughout human society. Since the literary artist employs structures—myth, metaphor, symbol—which continually mediate between unconscious and conscious processes, he is often a gifted explorer of what have been called the "*unlabeled* metaphors" of the schizophrenic, an interpreter of the madman's apparently indecipherable "messages." [Gregory Bateson writes in his *Steps to an Ecology of the Mind* (1973) that schizophrenics'] "conspicuous or exaggerated errors and distortions regarding the nature and typing of their own messages (internal and external), and of the messages which they receive from others," may be transformed in imaginative literature into revelations concerning the nature and processes of hidden layers of psychic reality. Antonin Artaud's declaration [in "Lettres aux médecins-chefs des asiles de fous"] that delirium is "as legitimate, as logical, as any other succession of human ideas or acts" is at once a cry of protest against "the official definition" of madness and a plea for understanding of an alternate mode of communication. It is also a protest against "the repression of anti-social reactions." When Artaud asserts that "madmen are, above all, individual victims of social dictatorship," he implies that madmen's "internalized systems of symbolization" must be regarded in relation and opposition to social and political institutions regulating the human mind, which become internalized as prevailing cultural assumptions. (pp. 4-7)

[It is necessary, however, to be] continually aware of the differences between actual insanity and its portrayal in literature. The madman of literature is, to some extent, modeled on the actual one, but his differences from such a model are at least as important as are his resemblances to it: he is rooted in a mythical or literary tradition in which distortion is a generally accepted mode of expression; furthermore, the inherent aesthetic order by which his existence is limited also gives his madness intrinsic value and meaning. A mad literary character must thus be approached on his own terms, through the verbal, dramatic, and narrative symbols that convey the unconscious processes he portrays and reveals. Even when a writer draws on his own experience of insanity as the subject or emotional source of his work, what is of most interest in this study is his adaptation of delusion, dissociation, or other aberrations to the creation of a unique view of his society, his art, and his own mind. (pp. 9-10)

The reader may well ask how a fictive character can reveal unconscious mental processes: how can one probe a mind that, strictly speaking, does not exist? Furthermore, how can one separate a fictional being from the mind that is responsible for its creation? In regard to literature based on mythical narrative, the answers are apparent: no matter how original the approach of the individual playwright or poet, the collective and social origins of mythical structures can be traced through historical, archeological, and anthropological evidence. The mind of the ancient author responds to and transforms revelations of psychic experience that both encompass and exceed his own. To some extent, moreover, this process is involved in the creation of all literary symbolic forms, for all works of art are both social and individual manifestations. Discussing the artist "projecting the forms of feeling into visible, audible, or poetic material," Susanne Langer suggests [in *Mind: An Essay on Human Feeling* (1967)] that the "image" he creates

> serves two purposes in human culture, one individual, one social: it articulates our own life of feeling so that we become conscious of its elements and its intricate and subtle fabric, and it reveals the fact that the basic forms of feeling are common to most people at least within a culture, and often far beyond it, since a great many works do seem expressive and important to almost everyone who judges them by artistic standards. Art is the surest affidavit that feeling, despite its absolute privacy, repeats itself in each individual life. It is not surprising that this is so, for the organic events which culminate in being felt are largely the same in all of us, at least in their biologically known aspects, below the level of sentience.

The creator is, of course, always present in his product, but, without separating him from his creation, it is possible to view a literary work or character as an aesthetic construct of the psychic, historical, and social forces which together determine the intricate mental processes of human beings. "A poem," says the poet and critic Octavio Paz, "is an object fashioned out of the language, rhythms, beliefs, and obsessions of a poet and a society." The same could be said of the creation of any significant literary work, and certainly of the literature of madness. In a writer's depictions of mad personae and characters, his revelations of his own deep knowledge of psychic pain and terror

or of his empathy with individuals struggling to communicate such experience include what Eric Erikson calls [in *Childhood and Society* (1963)] "the panic emanating from his group." (pp. 27-8)

> Lillian Feder, "Varieties of Madness: Approach and Method," in her Madness in Literature, *Princeton University Press, 1980, pp. 3-34.*

Michel Foucault on the existence of madness:

Madness is precisely at the point of contact between the oneiric and the erroneous; it traverses, in its variations, the surface on which they meet, the surface which both joins and separates them. With error, madness shares non-truth, and arbitrariness in affirmation or negation; from the dream, madness borrows the flow of images and the colorful presence of hallucinations. But while error is merely non-truth, while the dream neither affirms nor judges, madness fills the void of error with images, and links hallucinations by affirmation of the false. In a sense, it is thus plenitude, joining to the figures of night the powers of day, to the forms of fantasy the activity of the waking mind; it links the dark content with the forms of light. But is not such plenitude actually *the culmination of the void?* The presence of images offers no more than night-ringed hallucinations, figures inscribed at the corners of sleep, hence detached from any sensuous reality; however vivid they are, however rigorously established in the body, these images are nothingness, since they represent nothing; as for erroneous judgment, it judges only in appearance: affirming nothing true or real, it does not affirm at all; it is ensnared in the non-being of error.

Michel Foucault, in his Madness and Civilization: A History of Insanity in the Age of Reason, *1967, originally published as* Histoire de la folie, *1961.*

Shoshana Felman

[In the following excerpt, Felman briefly sketches the relationship between literature, philosophy, and madness.]

> The belief in truth is precisely madness.
> Nietzsche, *Das Philosophenbuch*

"Blindness," says the entry of the *Encyclopédie* under the word "Folie," "blindness is the distinctive characteristic of madness":

> To deviate from reason knowingly, in the grip of a violent passion, is to be weak; but to deviate from it confidently and with the firm conviction that one is following it, is to be what we call *mad.*

What characterizes madness is thus not simply blindness, but a blindness *blind to itself,* to the point of necessarily entailing an *illusion of reason.* But if this is the case, how can we know where reason stops and madness begins, since both involve the pursuit of some form of reason? If madness as such is defined as an *act of faith* in reason, no reasonable conviction can indeed be exempt from the suspicion of madness. Reason and madness are thereby inextricably linked; madness is essentially a phenomenon of thought, of thought which claims to denounce, in another's thought, the Other of thought: that which thought is not. Madness can only occur within a world in conflict, within a conflict of thoughts. The question of madness is nothing less than the question of thought itself: the question of madness, in other words, is that which turns the essence of thought, precisely, *into a question.* "The capacity for self reflection is given to man alone," writes Hegel [in "Philosophie de l'esprit," in *Encyclopédie*]: "that is why he has, so to speak, the privilege of madness." Nietzsche goes still further [in *Ainsi parlait Zarathustra*]:

> There is one thing that will forever be impossible: to be reasonable!
>
> A bit of reason though, a grain of wisdom (. . .)—that leaven is mixed in with everything: for the love of madness wisdom is mixed with all things!

Whereas Hegel places madness inside thought, Nietzsche places thought inside madness. In Pascal's conception, these contradictory positions could amount to the same. "Men," says Pascal, "are so necessarily mad that not to be mad would only be another form of madness." Rousseau, it seems, would agree: "Nothing resembles me less than myself";

> I am subject to two principal dispositions which change quite regularly (. . .) and which I call my weekly souls, one finds me wisely mad and the other madly wise, but in such a way that madness wins out over wisdom in both cases. . . . ["Le persifleur," in his *Oeuvres complètes* (1959)]

One could indeed go on reciting a whole series of aphoristic statements issued by philosophers on madness. A question could be raised: Are these pronouncements *philosophical,* or *literary*? Is their effect as aphorisms ascribable to a rhetorical device, or to the rigor of a concept? Do they belong in literature, or in philosophy? If madness so remarkably lends itself to aphoristic statements, to plays of language and effects of style, it could be said that, even in philosophy, its function is rhetorical or literary. But on the other hand, if one turns now to literature in order to examine the role of madness there (in Shakespeare's works, for instance), one realizes that the literary madman is most often a disguised philosopher: in literature, the role of madness, then, is eminently philosophical. This paradox of madness, of being literary in philosophy and philosophical in literature, could be significant. The notions of philosophy, of literature, of madness, seem to be inherently related. And madness, in some unexpected way, could thus elucidate the problematical relationship between philosophy and literature.

Previously confined almost exclusively to the domain of literature, or to the brevity of aphoristic thought, madness, in the modern world, has become a major philosophical preoccupation. It is doubtless no coincidence that in a figure such as Nietzsche, madness invades not only the philosophy, but also the philosopher himself. Nietzsche's impact, as a figure in which poet, philosopher and madman coincide, is crucial in the intensification of the inter-

est in madness, as well as in the recently increased proximity between philosophy and literature. Nietzsche's madness stands before the modern world as both an invitation and a warning, as the danger on which the condition of its very possibility is built. To reflect on the significance of "Nietzsche's madness" is thus to open up and to interrogate the entire history of Western culture. (pp. 206-08)

Shoshana Felman, "Madness and Philosophy or Literature's Reason," in Yale French Studies, *No. 52, 1975, pp. 206-08.*

Frederick R. Karl on madness in the modern age:

One could, I suspect, write an entire history of Modernism and its avant-gardes by way of developments in forms of madness and how these developments are interconnected with acts of purification, so central are these ideas. Madness was not contained in Modernism, but given its potential as act, gesture, discourse, subversion. The Marxist view, held by Foucault, that the semi-mad were identified so they could be used as cheap manpower or the really mad put away because they could not work, is contradicted by the thorough way madness dominated the arts and its forms of discourse. On the contrary, madness was not contained by the bourgeois: it threatened the bourgeois culturally at nearly every turn, until in the second half of the twentieth century—after seventy-five years of running rampant—madness has become virtually the way we perceive. The argument remains that all avant-gardes are "mad," and, therefore, all avant-gardes are aspects of a strange purification, of discourse as well as of act. The argument runs parallel to the one that identifies Modernistic movements as various degrees of the unconscious, unleashed, partially muzzled, often rambunctious. Modernism gave itself life by trafficking not with knowns but with unknowns, and the greatest of human unknowns was no longer God but the unconscious. After a century of religious worship, God had been identified as white, male, a powerful father figure. The unconscious upset all such identifications by substituting for such beliefs a "swamp," an infinitude of time, space, and madness; a place of magical languages.

Frederick R. Karl, in his Modern and Modernism: The Sovereignty of the Artist 1885-1925, *1988.*

William Arrowsmith

[*Arrowsmith is an American educator and critic. In the following essay, he discusses the pervasive angst—or mental neurosis—of the twentieth century, the anxiety of modern writers, and their concern about the instability of reality and the loss of normalcy in contemporary society.*]

Repeatedly during the last two or three decades historians and critics of literature have been forced to take into account a phenomenon which, for want of a better name, they have called "Anxiety." The more one looked at contemporary literature, the more it seemed to be pervaded by a strange form of terror. This Anxiety, moreover, not only affected the atmosphere of literature, but its springs of action as well. Poetry, the novel, drama, as well as the *obiter dicta* of writers and intellectuals, were filled with references to Anxiety or tacitly invoked it, and this prevalence of Anxiety in literature was confirmed by the other arts as well.

Anxiety appeared to be something rather new; while one could find it in the nineteenth century and in Augustine's Rome, it was never found so self-consciously and with such obsessive emphasis as in the twentieth century. Still worse, it was intolerably difficult to analyse: one could hardly define it except in terms which impoverished its terror. You might observe a desperate compound of fear, of terror, of increased powerlessness and an anguish of alienation; you could see both its psychological face and its sociological face, but these separate descriptions did not really clarify the objective terror nor reduce its stubborn front of mystery. Anxiety then was a complex, and it was moreover one which clearly affected the whole given world of contemporary reality. Not everybody, perhaps, knew Anxiety, but it was not therefore merely an intellectual's disease.

How then does literature reveal Anxiety to us, and what is the function of literature in regard to Anxiety?

Here at the outset I should like to plant firmly as confused, random and lush a growth of Anxiety as I possibly can. Anxiety is nothing if not complex, and what I want is a series of images which can convey the sense of a Thing with as many shapes as Proteus and yet at the same time a general shapelessness; the feeling of a labyrinth in which a man, himself a labyrinth, is trapped; or the threat of impending violence which never quite comes, and which therefore creates what might be called a state of prior guilt, guilt not so much for the past as for the crimes which his future may force him to commit; or again, the deepening conviction of madness as the gap between reality and unreality closes and then yaws apart, as choice and responsibility go always toward less choice and more responsibility; then the growing sense of fascination for what he fears, without diminution of the fear; and finally the complete confounding of whatever was meant by health and sickness, objective and subjective, sanity and madness.

There is hardly any modern literature of worth which does not know the Medusa-face of Anxiety. Take Eliot:

> A woman drew her long black hair out tight
> And fiddled whisper music on those strings
> And bats with baby faces in the violet light
> Whistled, and beat their wings
> And crawled head downward down a blackened wall
> And upside down in air were towers
> Tolling reminiscent bells, that kept the hours
> And voices singing out of empty cisterns
> And exhausted wells.

Or those famous lines of Yeats, beginning:

> Turning and turning in the widening gyre,
> The falcon cannot hear the falconer;
> Things fall apart; the centre cannot hold;
> Mere anarchy is loosed upon the world,
> The blood-dimmed tide is loosed, and everywhere

> The ceremony of innocence is drowned.

and coming suddenly upon the true horror:

> The best lack all conviction, while the worst
> Are full of passionate intensity.

Auden's version is less powerful, but more specifically political:

> The situation of our time
> Surrounds us like a baffling crime.
> There lies the body half undressed,
> We all had reason to detest,
> And all are suspects and involved
> Until the mystery is solved,
> And under lock and key the cause
> That makes a nonsense of our laws.
> O who is trying to shield whom?
> Who left a hairpin in the room?
> Who was the distant figure seen
> Behaving oddly on the green?
> Why did the watchdog never bark?
> Why did the footsteps leave no mark?
> Where were the servants at that hour?
> How did a snake get in the tower?

Think again, slowly, of an odd dozen fairly recent titles in fiction and verse: *Losses, Beast in View, The Labyrinth, The Dispossessed, The Victim, Terror, The Age of the Dragon, Lord Weary's Castle, On a Dark Night, There's No Home, The Ministry of Fear, The Hole and Corner Men.* Think too of Thomas Mann's *Doctor Faustus,* that magnificent apocalypse of ruined Europe told by a poor humanist, Serenus Zeitblom, out of his time and out of his depth; and with it that whole literature of the destruction, from within and without, of Modern Megalopolis: Joyce's *Ulysses,* Canetti's *Tower of Babel,* and, on a lower level, Graham Greene's *Third Man,* with its symbolic sewers and its anguished discovery of Harry Lime as the best man in corruption. *Corruptio optimi pessima.* It was Shelley after Blake who saw the city as the hell of our achievements:

> Hell is a city much like London
> A populous and smoky city.

It was Eliot and the other modern poets and novelists who filled the city with those vast hordes of the floating, living dead, the spiritually or sexually impotent:

> Unreal city
> Under the brown fog of a winter dawn,
> A crowd flowed over London bridge, so many,
> I had not thought death had undone so many.

Again in the *Quartets,* we see those

>   strained time-ridden faces
> Distracted from distraction by distraction
> Filled with fancies and empty of meaning
> Tumid apathy with no concentration
> Men and bits of paper, whirled by the cold wind
> That blows before and after time,
> Wind in and out of unwholesome lungs,
> Time before and time after.
> Eructation of unhealthy souls
> Into the faded air, the torpid
> Driven on the wind that sweeps the gloomy hills
>   of London,

Hampstead and Clerkenwell, Campden and Put-
 ney,
Highgate, Primrose, and Ludgate. Not here,
Not here the darkness, in this twittering world.

On still another level think of Camus' *The Plague*, or of
any number of Faulkner novels or of Rex Warner's allegories of power in *The Aerodrome, The Wild Goose Chase*,
and *The Professor*. Or again, of the wrenching brutality
and practiced nausea of Orwell's *1984*, a book which, if
the writing were equal to the conception, would come the
nearest to incarnating the future envisaged by Anxiety. No
need to mention Kafka, the writer of that labyrinthine
Anxiety in which the innocent are always guilty, and the
hero, "without doing anything wrong," is arrested "one
fine morning"; there the Anxiety is, if anything, rendered
even more formidable by being linked with Original Sin.

One of those writers who have been strongly influenced by
Kafka, Dino Buzzati, is the author of a short novel called
The Tartar Steppe, one of the finest allegories of Anxiety
which I know. It is the story of Giovanni Drogo, a young
conscript, who is sent to a Fort overlooking a vast desert
to the North. There he spends his entire life in the anticipation of a Tartar invasion, expected at any moment. All
life in the fort is geared to the certainty that the invasion
will come, and of course it never does. With great skill
Buzzati draws the gradual dehumanization of his hero, de-
sexed, devitalized, impotent in decision, helpless. When
Giovanni goes for his only furlough back home, he finds
himself alienated, bored and dangling, and he returns as
quickly as possible to his life-in-death at the fort. By a
lucky chance, he is allowed to die with as much heroism
as his life can afford, and dying he realizes that he has
never really lived at all. His knowledge is only the knowledge of the passage of time.

All these are images of Anxiety compressed at pretty high
pressure; in the hands of lesser writers Anxiety is a popular subject but its accomplishments are dreary precisely
because the *particular* horrors of Anxiety are never created. There is only a feel of a limp, general debilitation in
which we never really sense the cost of Anxiety to human
beings because the human beings are not created. Or else
we get gratuitous acts of horror without the achievement
of the drama which might flesh them into life. In Carson
McCuller's *Reflections in a Golden Eye*, an army wife who
discovers that her husband is having an affair, calls for the
garden shears and cuts off her nipples. It is an uncanny
novel, but I am not sure that it is ever anything more than
uncanny, though there is a blurb by Tennessee Williams
to the effect that this book "is conceived in that Sense of
the Awful which is the desperate black root of nearly all
significant modern art. . . . " In poetry, Anxiety is so
common that it can be said to have become a new convention, a kind of pastoral of alienation, in which Nymphs
whose names are History, Terror, Frustration, etc., are invoked against a stock setting, and the stock emotions are
purged by a play over the surfaces of the form. It was the
fashionable and portentous self-pity of this low-pressure
Anxiety, its hole-and-corner logic and its melodramatics
which prompted Empson's *Just a Smack at Auden:*

Waiting for the end, boys, waiting for the end.

What is there to be or do?
What's become of me and you?
Are we kind or are we true?
Sitting two and two, boys, waiting for the end.
Shall I build a tower, boys, knowing it will rend
Crack upon the hour, boys, waiting for the end?
Shall I pluck a flower, boys, shall I save or
 spend?
All turns sour, boys, waiting for the end.
Shall we send a cable, boys, accurately penned,
Knowing we are able, boys, waiting for the end,
Via the Tower of Babel, boys? Christ will not as-
 cend.
He's hiding in his stable, boys, waiting for the
 end.
What was said by Marx, boys? what did he per-
 pend?
No good being sparks, boys, waiting for the end.
Treason of the clerks, boys, curtains that de-
 scend,
Light becoming dark, boys, waiting for the end.

But whether low-pressure or high-pressure, the images of
Anxiety as the nightmare of the Unreal are omnipresent
in modern literature, and the man who would deny Anxiety must disregard or distort the evidence literature gives
him.

Let me complete these images with a personal one. I was
once asked the following question by a friend who was
being outwitted by his psychoanalyst and was showing the
required aggression. "What do you call it," he asked,
"when you think people are persecuting you, and they
really are?" Whatever his neurosis may have been, that
question has always seemed to me to be rich with Anxiety,
typical not so much in the feelings of paranoia, as in the
fear the paranoia might be objective, might be rooted in
real facts. For right at the basis of Anxiety, I think, is the
notion of the utter displacement of ordinary reality; Anxiety begins, as it were, with a kind of ontological terror.
The sufferer from Anxiety may exhibit the clinical symptoms of familiar neuroses, but he is not merely a case of
neurosis. What worries him is precisely the instability and
amorphousness of what the world calls reality and normality. Is it the sufferer who is sick? who has distorted reality? or is it his entire culture which has gone mad? To
the psychologist who claims that Anxiety is, after all, only
a familiar family of related neuroses, the sufferer replies
that this misses the point altogether. His experience, he
claims, has been atrociously impoverished by the psychologist's terms. And in so replying I think he is perfectly correct.

He is correct because Anxiety mocks all accepted norms
of reality and all definitions of sickness and health. It rejects the very standard—the cultural definition of normality—by which the psychologist proposes to test for neurosis. It constantly whispers that it is the world and society
and its agents, the psychologists with their corrupted
yardsticks, which are mad, and that those whom the world
thinks sick are really healthy. This rejection of the world's
power to judge who is sick and who is not is, of course,
precariously maintained; it is constantly under the threat
of being swamped by society's massive self-assurance that
all criteria flow from it. And the cost in alienation and the

absurdity of the solipsism the position demands constantly undercut the passion of its perceptions.

Thus the position is constantly aggravated, threatened on one side by the enormous coercive powers of society as well as the very need for human warmth, for associates in the common terror; on the other, by the intolerable burdens of heroic intransigence or the very attractiveness of desperation. On the one side the danger for the sufferer from Anxiety is that his human needs, his deep compulsion to accept the authority of society, constantly threaten to overpower and usurp the truth of his perceptions; on the other side, the loneliness of his position invites him to make himself the very measure of reason and health by which society is to be laid in the balance and found wanting. "Humankind cannot bear very much reality" says the poet, and Anxiety is no exception; it makes demands upon the individual for a heroic stubbornness in cleaving to the truth of what he sees. If he falters and falsifies what he sees either by extrapolating and worsening his perceptions or by softening them, he is lost. This is why, I think, Anxiety shows so many fallen angels: angels turned trimmers on the one side, and on the other a whole host of heretics who have made salvation out of their desperation.

Look for a moment at the purists of Anxiety, or better, the Angst-absolutists. Anxiety begins, as I have said, with a perception that a culture and society which are out of whack make nonsense of the individual's relation to it. Reality is in question; the images are those of a Nightmare of Unreality slowly usurping the world of the familiar real. To hold the perceptions of Anxiety requires a desperate balance, and the costs of trying to balance at all are alienation and guilt. More important, the perceptions of Anxiety lead directly to the feelings of powerlessness and impotence which are most typical of it. The degree of powerlessness may alter, but one of the most basic desires of Anxiety is to recover its power, and its worst temptation is to recover power by fraudulent means. Put it this way: if Anxiety consists of a body of perceptions about the world and our culture and our relation to it, and these perceptions are held as true ones, then power can only return when our perceptions show us a different state of affairs. I do not, of course, discount any means by which we ourselves may struggle to alter the world we see.

The absolutist of Anxiety recovers his sense of power by turning his perceptions of the world into logical necessities; once you can say that the world is unalterably corrupt, insane by definition, then all the torture of responsibility and guilt ceases. Choice also disappears with the loss of possibility, but these are happy losses from his point of view. In order to maintain this position, the absolutist is constantly forced to extrapolate; reality must be even worse than our perceptions of it; the Nightmare must totally usurp the real. Hence he is compelled to support his attitude of desperation by manufacturing evidence where he cannot find enough of it. Point by point he challenges the right of society to judge him, and experiences in alienation the cost of the challenge, but also the exhilaration of his own imagined courage and his sense of lonely self-righteousness. With complete rigor, he pursues his salvation by emphasizing his desperation. When, in the end, he

has completed his journey and sees with fanatic vision the unalterable madness of his society, his alienation is the mark of his health and his sufferings the *stigmata* of sanity. In its purist form Anxiety is arrogant with all the arrogance of men who have been saved towards those who have not.

This is perhaps a peculiar sense of "power," but it is power nonetheless, the kind of power, I suppose, a man might feel if he could manage to transform himself into a Platonic Idea and know what it meant to be wholly separate from the world and yet be its measure. In its absolute form, Anxiety is, I think, very closely akin to a metaphysical experience, and almost religious—a succumbing to the divine power of your Terror and therefore an earning of salvation. Anxiety *moves in* on you, *possesses* you; you become its *enthusiast* and bend the world into the shape of your strange God. On the inside, it feels comfortable and oh so smooth; on the outside, it looks like a kind of ontological morbidity. I recognize that "metaphysics" is a dangerous word, and it may seem that there is no need of invoking metaphysics to account for something so terribly and empirically present as Anxiety. But I think we have to account for the peculiar kind of Anxiety which is genuinely unconvinced by evidence which might controvert it; what does it mean, after all, if there comes a point in the life-cycle of Anxiety when the facts don't really matter any longer? It is not just that Angst is spelled with a capital A, or comes from the country where all metaphysics arise, nor even the extra-ordinary resistance it makes to analysis. What matters is the way in which pure-Anxiety men talk of their experience, the special status they invoke for it, their invulnerability to empirical contradiction, and their singular humorlessness about it all—these traits cast them in the traditional metaphysical pattern. It is because their Anxiety has become a metaphysics of terror that they distort reality even further and insist upon their condition as guaranteeing them both power and salvation.

If Anxiety exists, we cannot easily dispel it, as would J. Donald Adams, by snuggling inside our values and taking the next ski-train to Vermont. The trimmers among the fallen angels of Anxiety are as bad as the absolutists, but it is the absolutists who have escaped notice and whose intransigence is far more influential among intellectuals than the easy compromises of the trimmers. Anxiety requires a perilous balance, as I have said, between our needs and our perceptions; we have to be constantly on our guard against letting our needs overpower the truth of what we see. Anything that diminishes the truth of what we see, or exaggerates the badness of things, is so much more trouble, so much more obfuscation, hindering, obstructing and even prohibiting improvement. Extreme Anxiety, by its compulsion toward desperation and its vicious circularity, cuts us off from the small choice we have and traps us in our needs. If we resist, it calls us cowardly, since to a desperate man all other men are either stupid or dishonest unless they happen to share his desperation.

How then is literature related to Anxiety? It is, of course, diagnostic; it tells us the shape and size of our trouble and our reaction to it, and confronts us with this image. If, as I insist, what is crucial in Anxiety is the truth of our perceptions—without which we are carried along with one or the other of the fallen angels—then the very activity of diagnosis is central. It is literature that particularizes our terrors, gives them a "local habitation and a name." Literature extrapolates or diminishes the truth at its own cost; if the imagination is exact and observation ferocious, then Anxiety is intensified, but not falsified. And lest this seem humdrum, remember that a great part of the terror in Anxiety, as well as the crucial danger, is its very stubbornness to analysis, its front of mystery. Unless our Anxiety is clearly named, we are in danger of hypostatizing it and giving it a dimension altogether outside of the world. This does not, of course, mean that literature waves a wand and our anguish withers; what is exorcised is the irrational, even supernatural form of Anxiety. I think there is no place in any literature, except an impoverished one, for what I have called absolute Anxiety. No metaphysical monster which is maintained, as pure Anxiety is, by systematic distortion of the world, can be made to flourish in the particulars from which it has been abstracted. It withers when confronted by the truths of its own nature and the necessity of human beings to live with their terrors.

Because literature must be exact with all the exactitude of the imagination, it gives us the fullest image of our predicament. Because literature, unlike philosophy, or intellectual history or science, operates with all the modes of the mind and not with merely one of them, it gives us the fullest image of our own behavior when confronted by our predicament, and thus permits us to assess our fears in relation to our hopes. It may, or it may not, attempt to prescribe specific remedies, but usually this is not its business. Its real concern is with the refreshment of possibility and the domestication of Angst into the human condition.

By domestication of Anxiety I don't, of course, mean the taming of it. You don't housebreak a nightmare. What we must know and what literature at its best tells us, is what part of the anguish of our time is our fate and what our misfortune. In so doing, it helps to refresh possibility, for one can work with misfortune but not with fate. Again it forces back into the play of the mind all the material which is suppressed by the needful logic of Anxiety; and more than that it forces the full mind itself back into play. What it thus reminds us of is what we fail to assert as well as the cost of the assertions we do make. Sophocles' *Antigone,* for instance, is really about what she fails to assert and the cost of all she does assert.

Look at Anxiety a little more closely from this point of assertions and their cost. To hold steadily, without swerving, to the truth of what one sees, to refuse to palliate it or exaggerate it, appears to me the bounden duty of all who suffer from Anxiety; only by looking steadily at the nightmare of our time can we hope to recover the opportunity which will restore us our lost power. This requires great endurance and great courage, perhaps more than most of us can afford. Our danger is that we become all endurance, that we lose a part of our human skills by having to steel ourselves so constantly. Anxiety, that is, like "great suffering," "makes a stone of the heart." Our perpetual seriousness castrates us of our humor and our sense of proportion; slowly but inexorably it kills the whole variety of means we have within us for combatting trouble. But because literature works with the discourse of the whole mind, employing all the mind's skills without preference, it refreshes our humanity and our possibilities. Think, for instance, of the great monologue of Molly Bloom at the end of *Ulysses,* and then think of that moment when she lifts the sheet slightly, sticks her head under and sni-fffs herself: she is self-refreshed. Think again of the ending of Saul Bellow's *The Adventures of Augie March,* where the hero articulates the possibilities of his nature and those in the world:

> I got to grinning again. That's the *animal ridens* in me, the laughing creature, forever rising up. Is the laugh at nature—including eternity—that it thinks it can win over us and the power of hope? Nah, nah, I think. It never will. But that probably is the joke, on one or other, and laughing is an enigma that includes them both. Look at me, going everywhere! Why, I am a sort of Columbus of those near-at-hand and believe you can come to them in this immediate *terra incognita* that spreads out in every gaze. I may well be a flop at this line of endeavor. Columbus too thought he was a flop, probably, when they sent him back in chains. Which didn't prove there was no America.

And last of all, think of that tag in the *Four Quartets:*

> We shall not cease from exploration
> And the end of all our exploring
> Will be to arrive where we started
> And know the place for the first time.

It is this that literature can do with Angst: to bring us to the place from which we started, so we know it for the first time. There is no question here of either of those atrocious words—optimism or pessimism. Good literature is as far beyond mere optimism and pessimism as Anxiety is beyond mere trouble and neurosis. Anxiety is not palliated in literature, but given the intensification of truth. Literature does not save; it forces the reluctant to recognize the abyss, to look at it. In the act of looking, it reminds us of the variety of the means we have for keeping our balance. We know our terror for the first time, but the terror is transformed because we also know ourselves.

Finally, the very act of writing is itself an act of order. As Elizabeth Bowen says, "Writing is the writer's means of getting a relation to his society." It is a willful act, writing, whose purpose is not to put a fraudulent order on the disorder in the world, but to find room for chaos in a general order—if logic can tolerate that kind of language. A whole culture may crack apart, but it is an important assertion that writing makes, perhaps only a hypothesis, in the standards by which it judges chaos. Literature holds out to us the hope of incorporating just what our society's commitments are in a world that appears to make commitments difficult. This is the task for the major artist, what I call the Vergilian job, the creation of a culture in its partial absence. In the last few years the writer has had to learn that he can't come by a ready-made myth which can be simply invested with values. As R. P. Blackmur puts it, the "whole job of culture," the creating of a myth which we can live by, has "been dumped on the artist's hands."

Let me close with a personal image again. I recently received a letter from a friend doing graduate work at Harvard. It was a letter full of what I call local and low-pressure Anxiety, a whole chain of domestic and professional troubles. His thesis was going badly; one child had mumps; his wife had cystitis; he had no job; he had just seen McCarthy on TV; Christian humanism was coming to Harvard, etc., etc., etc. He concluded as follows:

> I like to think of a rock somewhere in the Mediterranean, with me on it, skin turning slowly from bronze to brown as I think slow lizard-like thoughts. On shore my three wives and sixteen children look out at me and their hearts fill with love—not for the rich comfort in which I keep them (though, of course, they are grateful for that), not because they think I am talented or important or necessary to them (though all these may enter)—they crown me king of their love, just for the sweet man I am. And I? I take it for granted.

That letter seems to me to be passing into something like literature at the close. It looks at first glance like simple escapism, the common wish-fulfillment of us all; but look at it again, and what you see is only the delicate irony, the emergence of just those skills of proportion and loving self-mockery, that keep us sane in our troubles and our necessities. (pp. 325-35)

William Arrowsmith, "Literature and the Uses of Anxiety," in Western Humanities Review, *Vol. X, No. 4, Autumn, 1956, pp. 325-35.*

MADNESS AND THE CREATIVE PROCESS

Sigmund Freud

[*An Austrian neurologist, Freud was the father of psychoanalysis. The general framework of psychoanalytic thought, explained in his seminal work* The Interpretation of Dreams *(1900), encompasses both normal and abnormal behavior and is founded on the tenet that one's early experiences profoundly affect later behavior. Freud's interrelated theories of the unconscious (primitive impulses and repressed thoughts), the libido (sexual energy that follows a predetermined course), the structure of personality (id, ego, superego), and human psychosexual development (sequential stages of sexual development) have been widely used in the treatment of psychopathy. Freud was sometimes harshly criticized for his innovative theories, especially his insistence that sexual impulses exist in very young children and his definition of the Oedipus and Electra complexes. Nonetheless, he was for the most part greatly respected as a thinker and teacher. In addition, Freud has had significant influence on various schools of philosophy, religious and political ideas, and artistic endeavors such as surrealism in art, atonal music, and stream of consciousness in literature. In the following excerpt, he discusses the artist as neurotic.*]

Before I let you go to-day, however, [I should like to direct your attention] to a side of the life of phantasy which deserves the most general interest. For there is a path that leads back from phantasy to reality—the path, that is, of art. An artist is once more in rudiments an introvert, not far removed from neurosis. He is oppressed by excessively powerful instinctual needs. He desires to win honour, power, wealth, fame and the love of women; but he lacks the means for achieving these satisfactions. Consequently, like any other unsatisfied man, he turns away from reality and transfers all his interest, and his libido too, to the wishful constructions of his life of phantasy, whence the path might lead to neurosis. There must be, no doubt, a convergence of all kinds of things if this is not to be the complete outcome of his development; it is well known, indeed, how often artists in particular suffer from a partial inhibition of their efficiency owing to neurosis. Their constitution probably includes a strong capacity for sublimation and a certain degree of laxity in the repressions which are decisive for a conflict. An artist, however, finds a path back to reality in the following manner. To be sure, he is not the only one who leads a life of phantasy. Access to the half-way region of phantasy is permitted by the universal assent of mankind, and everyone suffering from privation expects to derive alleviation and consolation from it. But for those who are not artists the yield of pleasure to

---

Michel Foucault on madness and language:

Language is the first and last structure of madness, its constituent form; on language are based all the cycles in which madness articulates its nature. That the essence of madness can be ultimately defined in the simple structure of a discourse does not reduce it to a purely psychological nature, but gives it a hold over the totality of soul and body; such discourse is both the silent language by which the mind speaks to itself in the truth proper to it, and the visible articulation in the movements of the body. Parallelisms, complements, all the forms of immediate communication which we have seen manifested, in madness are suspended between soul and body in this single language and in its powers. The movement of passion which persists until it breaks and turns against itself, the sudden appearance of the image, and the agitations of the body which were its visible concomitants—all this, even as we were trying to reconstruct it, was already secretly animated by this language. If the determinism of passion is transcended and released in the hallucination of the image, if the image, in return, has swept away the whole world of beliefs and desires, it is because the delirious language was already present—a discourse which liberated passion from all its limits, and adhered with all the constraining weight of its affirmation to the image which was liberating itself.

It is in this delirium, which is of both body and soul, of both language and image, of both grammar and physiology, that all the cycles of madness conclude and begin. . . . It is madness itself, and also, beyond each of its phenomena, its silent transcendence, which constitute the truth of madness.

Michel Foucault, in his Madness and Civilization: A History of Insanity in the Age of Reason, *1967, originally published as* Histoire de la folie, *1961.*

be derived from the sources of phantasy is very limited. The ruthlessness of their repressions forces them to be content with such meagre day-dreams as are allowed to become conscious. A man who is a true artist has more at his disposal. In the first place, he understands how to work over his daydreams in such a way as to make them lose what is too personal about them and repels strangers, and to make it possible for others to share in the enjoyment of them. He understands, too, how to tone them down so that they do not easily betray their origin from proscribed sources. Furthermore, he possesses the mysterious power of shaping some particular material until it has become a faithful image of his phantasy; and he knows, moreover, how to link so large a yield of pleasure to this representation of his unconscious phantasy that, for the time being at least, repressions are outweighed and lifted by it. If he is able to accomplish all this, he makes it possible for other people once more to derive consolation and alleviation from their own sources of pleasure in their unconscious which have become inaccessible to them; he earns their gratitude and admiration and he has thus achieved *through* his phantasy what originally he had achieved only *in* his phantasy—honour, power and the love of women. (pp. 375-77)

> Sigmund Freud, *"The Paths to the Formation of Symptoms," in his* Introductory Lectures on Psychoanalysis, *edited and translated by James Strachey, W. W. Norton & Company, 1977, pp. 358-77.*

William Stekel

[*In the excerpt below, Stekel examines the role of psychic conflict and neurosis in the creative process and the therapeutic value of writing, arguing that "every artist is a neurotic."*]

In his little common school it occurred to Tolstoy one day to put to test the poetic ability of the peasant children. He began telling them a story and before he went very far he asked them to continue it their own way. The first attempt proved so satisfactory that during the succeeding days he was satisfied to assume merely the rôle of a listener while the children in his charge gave free vent to their flights of phantasy. He was amazed by the keenness of their exposition, their tremendously rich imagery, the sway of their poetic inspiration and the beauty and strength of their imagination as seen in their joint product. He concluded that the most famous writers could not have conceived such wonderful stories as these simple, small, inexperienced village children had playfully knit together.

This experience teaches us clearly a fact which should have been recognized long ago: that in every child there slumbers a creative artist. The child fills the inanimate world with the products of its phantasy. A bit of wood becomes a doll, the doll a child, the child a king's son; the chair becomes a train, the turf-ground a tunnel, the little tin soldier his special guard. Next the little artist ventures with lightning swiftness into the wide world. In an hour he tastes the adventures of a hundred lives. Like every art-

ist the child dwells in a "second" world of his own creation. "It would be unfair to hold," states Freud [in *Der Dichter und das Phantasieren. Sammlung Kleiner Schriften zur Neurosenlehre* (1909)] "that it (the child) does not take that world seriously; on the contrary, its play is a serious matter and involves most earnest emotional outlay on its part. The opposite of play is not earnestness, but reality."

Adults, too, attempt to fly from the grey, perennial sameness of reality into the variegated, richly colored realm of the phantasy. For the artistic trend slumbering in the breast of every person and expressing itself so richly in the child, never dies in us. It may withdraw to a dusty corner in the soul, become covered over with the cobwebs of daily life, there to rest secure against the light of consciousness. In the night dreams it awakens secretly to new life and adorned with the ruler's purple mantle proudly strides forth into the hardy, endless realm of dreams. Every dreamer is an artist. And the artist in him breaks also through the yielding shell of consciousness into the light of clear day. In day-dreams we conjure up before our vision all sorts of adventures which enhance the illusion of happiness. Freud rightly remarks that "the happy person is not addicted to fancy weaving, only the ungratified person does so." But is there in the wide world a man so supremely happy that he has nothing further to require of life? The story about the happy man's shirt is well known; a king sent in search of it, in order to secure a complete cure for himself. The king's messengers searched everywhere, until they found at last a happy man, but—that man had no shirt! It means that such a man lives not at all, he is but a vision—the dream thought of an artist. It is a matter of indifference whether the poet was a single person or the people.

For folk thought is continuously engaged in artistic weaving of fancies. The fairy stories and myths are the people's dream thoughts. The race remains eternally a child. "The myth represents a retained portion of the infantile mental life of the race and the dream is the individual's myth" [Abraham, *Traum und Mythus. Schriften zur angewandten Seelen Kunde*]. Thus we see that the artistic creations of the race are its dreams. How does that hold true?

There is essentially no difference between dream and poetry. Any one who masters the art of unravelling the symbolic representations of the dream is continually amazed at the high artistic quality displayed by the average person. The dream of the average person discloses to us his poetic trend. More correctly: The dream unshackles it.

The poets themselves have known this long before psychoanalysis had proven the fact scientifically. For instance, Hebbel, in his diaries remarks concerning "a wonderful but gruesome" dream of Christine, his sweetheart: "My notion that dream and poetry are identical is verified more and more." We find similar statements by Schopenhauer and Jean Paul.

With their intuitive insight Hebbel and Schopenhauer have discovered a fundamental fact. Dream and poetry are almost identical psychic mechanisms. The dream derives its material from the depths of the unconscious. And does not true artistic talent consist of the ability to draw upon one's unconscious powers? Gœthe relates that he has written down most of his poems at night, in a dream-like trance. Other poets relate similar experiences. The artist's ecstasy, the glowing creative urge, the productive fever are similar states during which consciousness is displaced by a sort of somnambulistic state through autosuggestion, *i.e.,* a dream. The child, too, draws its creative ability from the unconscious. The child also has the ability to dream with open eyes.

We have been led already merely on the basis of these superficial observations to bring poetry and neurosis into apposition. For the neurosis manifests itself under similar circumstances. A hysterical person possesses the ability of withdrawing from the world of reality subjectively perceived as unbearable and to take refuge in the realm of the unconscious. We physicians call that a hysterical attack. The emotional display of such persons (*attitudes passionnelles*), their lively facial expressions disclose to us that during the attack they find vicarious gratification in a realm of highest emotional tension. We also know today—thanks to the glorious researches of Freud—that the world in which the hysterical plunges during the attack is the realm of Eros—an erotism lacking the inhibitions of morals or religion, destitute of the prohibitions of ethics and custom. Plunges? We could say with equal propriety, that the hysterical dreams his way into that realm! The hysterical person conjures up situations which life stubbornly refuses to actualize or which cannot be expected nor even accepted in reality. Following this process one step further we find that every neurotic possesses the ability to live in a second world. He divides his attention between dream and reality.

We (allegedly) normal persons, too, have our day-dreams, our phantasies which lead us into a second, more harmonious world, into the realm of wish fulfillment. Wherein does the difference consist? Why must the hysterical take refuge in his attack, while the "normal" person indulges in phantasies which merely entice him into the twilight of a half sleepy state without robbing him entirely of the critical power of his consciousness?

That difference is due entirely to the fact that the neurotics—we may here properly enough use the popular term "nervous" persons—find their phantasies unbearable in consciousness. What is more—they are not even conscious of their cravings. *The neurotic is unaware of the nature of his longings. His wishes are repressed.* As I have shown in my monograph on the *Causes of Nervousness* every neurotic is the victim of a psychic conflict. The longings of the unconscious conflict with the wishes of the consciousness.

That is true not only of the hysterical, it holds true of all neurotics. Indeed all persons live under the compulsion of repressing unbearable tendencies. The individual extent of ordinary repression constitutes the measure of that degree of neurotic predisposition which may be proven within every one of us. This may be called the "normal" person's "latent" neurosis. But eventually, in the case of normal persons, the repressed tendencies lose entirely their feeling-value. They present themselves as vague and bloodless survivals or appear merely as grotesque emotional relics

during our night dreams. The neurotic on the other hand has hanging unto his repressed complexes the lead weights of powerful affects. He is a victim of inexplainable moods whose deepest causes are the emotionally stressed trends welling up from the unconscious. He is a personality divided, dissociated, "broken up" in Nestroy's sense. Consciousness and the unconscious stand in irreconcilable opposition to one another. The repression renders the unconscious too powerful. Beginning with the earliest stages of childhood all the unpleasant affects are repressed into the unconscious, all the forbidden gratifications, all the foolish and burning desires are tightly clamped down in the inner chamber, away from the outside world. Suddenly these subterranean forces begin to rumble and to stir. At first there may be but a light knocking at the walls. Then the inner voices become gradually louder, the cryptic longings press forward, they crave light, expression, and they attempt to achieve mastery over the soul. The "unconscious complexes" break into consciousness. But consciousness prefers to remain "deaf and dumb." It refuses to acknowledge the hidden wishes. Out of this struggle between the unconscious longings and the conscious inhibitions there arises, as a consequence of half-resisting and half-yielding, the *manifest* neurosis.

In the case of the artist, too, we find essentially a splitting of personality. The artist also stands under the sway of repression. He, too, is a victim of that dissonance between consciousness and the unconscious which leads to a *psychic conflict.*

Wherein does he differ from the neurotic? Rank declares [in *Der Künstler* 1907]:

> The continual repression of certain instinctive cravings and the favoring of others, diametrically opposed to the former, becomes in the course of generations a sort of second nature, and involves a gradually decreasing deliberate opposition on the part of individuals; at the same time this process generates a sense of supreme compulsion in those individuals in whom the two natures are still actively at war. The conflict does not become conscious in the case of the normal because it is generally perceived by them as something objective and the feeling to which it gives rise is readily purged off through the dream (unconsciously); but these particular individuals—the artists—project upon their "self" in the highest individual potence that conflict and its attendant affect so that in their case, it becomes too powerful for the dream to release, though without necessarily becoming a morbid tension; consequently the artists attempt to free themselves of the conflict by expressing it through their artistic creations, which thus resemble the formation of myths. From the psychologic standpoint the artist stands between the dreamer and the neurotic; their subjective mental process is essentially the same as in the others, differing merely in degree as well as in accordance with the measure of their respective artistic abilities. The loftiest types of artistic persons—the dramatist, the philosopher, and the "religious founder" stand closest to the psychoneurotic—the lowest type of dreamer.

Thus far we have proceeded on the assumption that the artist is a normal person who stands in a certain contrast to the neurotic. We have seen that Rank is also of this opinion.

But I cannot wholly approve this view. My investigations have positively convinced me that between the neurotic and the artist there is no essential difference. Not every neurotic is an artist. But every artist is a neurotic.

I do not propose to be misunderstood. I do not mean to stamp all artists as "abnormal." I do not intend to repeat the error of Lombroso and Nordau. In a very suggestive work Löwenfeld has proven that there can be no question of a "degenerative psychosis of the epileptic type" in the case of genius, in Lombroso's sense. According to this investigator genius has its roots in health not in disease. But who dares draw a precise line between disease and health?

Where does the normal cease and the pathological begin? I have pointed out from the first that there are in fact no absolutely normal persons. In every one's breast there slumbers a bit of neurosis. That slumbering piece of neurosis is what constitutes the foundation of all creative ability.

The neurosis is generated by a process of psychic stagnation. The forbidding forces of our inhibitions restrain forcefully our stirring affects. The latter create for themselves in consequence false pathways, *i.e.,* they break out in neurotic symptoms. Or else they attempt to overcome the inhibitions through artistic sublimation. All creative activity represents a freeing of excessive energies, an outflow of pressing inhibitions. This is perhaps nowhere so clearly shown as in the conceptions of poetry. In the case of the musician the personal element disappears under a form of expression capable of reproducing any mood but no thought. The painter expresses moods as well as thoughts. But in his creations the poet discloses the analysis of his own neurosis. He may wish ever so earnestly to hide his intimate thoughts but he can never succeed. *Every poetic creation is a confession!*

The mental abnormality disclosed by creative spirits has been known to investigators for a long time. An attempt has even been made of connecting genius with insanity! This hypothesis with which Lombroso's name is linked had already been precognized by Aristotle (*vid.* his *"nullum magnum ingenium sine mixtura dementiae fuit"*) who attributed poetic inspiration to a powerful onrush of the blood to the head. Nordau particularized the conception by ascribing a number of modern poets to the type of "degenerates," and other contemporary psychiatrists and neurologists incline onesidedly to the "degeneration" and "psychosis" theory of genius. Poetic genius has also been identified with insanity.

The attempt to stamp genius as a sign of "degeneration" rests on an erroneous conception of the matter. With the shibboleth "degeneration" the attempt has been made to explain away the deepest problems of creative ability! The contentions of Lombroso and Nordau who in their well known works have dragged down the conception of artistry, border on the ridiculous. Nothing is so puerile as to attempt to judge artists and to justify their existence as it were with the (wholly hypothetical) canons of "normal"

man. According to Nordau even Richard Wagner, Tolstoy, Ibsen and Maeterlinck are but "degenerate graphomaniacs."

It is high time that we abandon the puerile talk about "degeneration" and "hereditary taint." Artists are not degenerates. They are neurotics; and neurosis is only a result of the progressive cultural level of existence. Neurosis forges the background for all progress. It leads the philosopher to investigate, it impels the discoverer to solve important problems and it enables the artist to conceive his loftiest creations. In that sense the neurosis is actually the bloom on the tree of humanity. Without the neurotic we would find ourselves in the A, B, C, of cultural progress.

But shibboleths, once they have become popular, have an enormous vogue. The artistic genius is mentally deranged—that is what the pathographists preach. And what wonderful diagnoses have they not suggested! Lombroso spoke of "mattoids" and "graphomaniacs." Nordau of "degeneration" (and he always speaks of hysteria as a "degeneration"), Magnan of "dégénerés supérieurs." Modern psychiatrists have gone even further and have attempted more minute diagnoses.

There has been no agreement reached regarding the actual nature of the insanity in question. Some investigators speak of Dementia Praecox, or of Paranoia, others favor the diagnosis of Cyclothymia (manic-depressive insanity). Mœbius who saw in every genius a degenerate in Magnan's sense (Oh, what evil that man has introduced in psychiatry!) divided genius into three groups, all belonging alike to the category of "degenerations": Cyclothymia, Dementia Praecox and Paranoia. He states: "Luther, Gœthe, Schopenhauer, Cowper, Gérard de Nerval were Cyclothymic; Lenz, Hœlderlin, C. F. Meyer, Robert Schumann, Scheffel suffered of Dementia Praecox; while Tasso, Rousseau and Gutzkow suffered of Paranoia (Dementia paranoides)." What a meager list in comparison to the endless chain of men of genius! Tasso, Rousseau and (what strange company) Gutzkow—it is hardly sufficient to base on so scant a number of representatives such a far reaching hypothesis! If one permits oneself such arbitrary choice it might be just as easy to prove that the shoemaker's trade has some relations to Dementia Praecox! It is possible to find a certain proportion of mental disorder among a given number of persons in any vocation.

The artist is not insane! He is a mentally abnormal personality, like every neurotic. His brain functions in normal fashion. He even shows an excessive productive energy. But his soul does not possess equilibrium. I do not propose thereby to draw a contrast between brain and soul. The soul, in popular expression, as the center of affective processes—is but a functional form of our brain. The brain is anatomically sound in the neurotic, and so are also his nervous structures. *Psychosis is a disease of the intellect and of the affects* (Bleuler). The neurotic shows merely a change in his affectivity. His disorders are due merely to a false psychic mechanism. Similar mechanisms play also a rôle in psychosis. Nevertheless certain differences are traceable in the rough. The mentally deranged is one who has lost the critical faculty with reference to his insane notion. There is no bridging over from his mind into the world of reality. The neurotic appears insane only on superficial examination. His compulsive acts, illogical in our eyes, are logically motivated in his unconscious. The bridge linking him to the realm of reality still persists. The connection is merely covered up and invisible from a distance. Moreover Jung and long before him Freud have discovered the presence of connecting links between the subject's mind and the world of reality even in cases of insanity (Dementia Praecox). There are disorders, as melancholia, for instance, which stand on the borderline between neurosis and psychosis.

Unfortunately our confusing nomenclature renders difficult a sharp distinction between mental and nervous disorder. It is a habit, which has long since become an anachronism, to speak of "nervous" complaints in the case of neurotic persons. The nerves as such, have in reality nothing to do with the condition ordinarily designated as nervousness. "The nerves proper," says Strümpell rightly

> are merely connecting paths and although they are subject to disease, as a matter of fact they have nothing to do with what is commonly called in professional language "nervousness," or very little and only in a secondary sense. The letter carrier is not responsible for the content of the message entrusted to him for transmission;

nor is he responsible for the impression made by the message he delivers.

The designation "neurosis" therefore gives us no clue to the nature of the ailment. Freud's term *psychoneurosis* is much more suitable because it hints at the character of the trouble as a disorder of the soul.

The designation "psychosis" certainly does not fit altogether the mental disorders. For psychosis means disorder of the soul, and the neurotics too are soul-sick. Of course, the insane is also a victim of soul sickness. But the characteristic feature of his illness is the disorder of the "intellect."

It is necessary to resort to more fitting nomenclature. Everything that has been designated thus far as "nervousness," being essentially a disorder of affectivity should be called "parapathy"; mental disorder, in which the intellect becomes subservient to the affects, should be called "paralogy."

But new names introduce themselves with difficulty into common use. Therefore we shall still adhere to the old nomenclature but in a different sense. Under *neurosis* we refer to the *psychoneurosis* in Freud's sense, or Janet's

Matthaus Greuter's depiction of Renaissance physicians curing patients of madness.

psychasthenia while *psychosis* is a term we reserve for any disorder of the intellect.

Neurosis is most intimately linked with the subject's infantile experiences. It is only to a very small extent the result of hereditary transmission. For the most part it is due to environmental influences.

If a person is brought up in an environment which requires continuous repression on his part, which compels him to fight down his instinctive cravings, there arises, under a certain constitutional predisposition—a neurosis. In psychosis the repressed cravings overcome the inhibitions of consciousness. The unconscious achieves mastery over consciousness. The psychotic individual destroys the bridges which link him to reality and withdraws within the realm of the obsessive "complexes." His overstressed feeling-judgment destroys all competitive or antagonistic ideas. Psychosis is the last extreme of neurosis; the neurosis represents a compromise between instinct and inhibition, between craving and repression, while the psychosis stands ultimately for the peace of the graveyard. Naturally this excludes the borderland cases between psychosis and neurosis.

Every form of genius shows a certain—often merely apparent—relationship with both, neurosis and psychosis. Attempts have been made (as already stated), to connect genius with "degeneration." But the shibboleth "psychopathic inferiority" does not fit the picture of all-embracing genius. Nevertheless we still encounter attempts at linking genius and insanity—highest "creative ability" and "degeneration." (pp. 73-82)

Unfortunately there is a widespread tendency in modern psychiatry to ascribe various neurotic disorders to insanity. Such clinical entities are currently spoken of as "neurasthenic insanity," and "anxiety psychosis"; compulsion neurotics are regarded as insane, whereas the investigations of psychoanalysis show that there can be no question of insanity in such cases, since the subjects still preserve an insight into their condition and their overstressed feeling-attitude may be reduced down to a "normal" feeling-value through psychoanalysis upon being cleared of the excessive emotional ballast. What the artist exhibits is neurosis, not actual psychosis. Psychosis indicates abandonment of the struggle with the forces of the unconscious. The intellect becomes subjected to the sway of the affects. It is no longer capable of exercising its judgment-function. It ceases to be serviceable. (p. 84)

[Neurosis] inspires the artist to take pen in hand and precisely in what sense his artistic creations are attempts at sublimation. Creative activity is virtually a process of healing through auto-analysis. The psychoanalytic method for the treatment of the neuroses which we have been taught by Freud consists of rendering the unconscious complexes conscious; it brings about a release of the old affects which slumber embedded in the depths of the soul and solves the psychic conflicts.

The artist-writer through his artistic creations similarly relieves himself of the affects and conflicts which beset him. This is the very thought which Heine expresses when he states: "May poetry be perchance a disease of man, like the pearls which are really the product of a disease of the oyster?" (*Romantische Schule*). And Grillparzer who has perhaps gone more deeply than any other writer into the relations between neurosis and poetry, states:

> Dichten heisst denn freilich eben
> Im fremden Dasein eig'ne leben.

The same thought is expressed in a more completely rounded out form by Grillparzer, in his wonderful poem entitled, "Abschied aus Gastein":

> Und wie die Perlen, die die Schönheit schmück-
>   en
> Des wasserreiches wasserhelle Zier,
> Den Finder, nicht die Geberin beglücken,
> Das freudenlose stille Muscheltier;
> Denn *Krankheit* nur und langer Schmerz ent-
>   drücken
> Das heissgesuchte traur'ge Kleinod ihr,
> Und was euch so entzückt mit seinen Strahlen
> Es ward erzeugt in Todesnot und Qualen.

We observe here the striking similarity with Heine's thought; and the end of the poem:

> Was ihr für Lieder haltet, es sind Klagen
> Gesprochen in ein freudenloses All;
> Und Flammen, Perlen, Schmuck, die euch um-
>   schweben,
> *Gelöste Teile sind's von seinem Leben.*

Here we find clearly the thought expressed that every artistic creation of the writer rises out of conflict: out of the unconscious; that the neurosis is the goddess which bestows upon the artist the gift of expressing what he feels.

Having brought out in general outline the relationship between poetry and neurosis we must now bring forth specifically the proofs for our contentions. First we must describe the symptoms of neurosis and investigate whether these symptoms are also found in connection with artistic productiveness. We shall next be confronted with the task of proving that the specific products of artistic creations owe their particular forms not alone to external stimuli but that they are also conditioned by the neurosis.

There is noticeable a tremendous confusion in the particular field of neurosis. Usually the concept "nervous" is confused with "neurasthenic" and any one who shows some nervous symptoms is forthwith stamped as a neurasthenic. Mœbius very properly opposed this abuse of the term neurasthenia. In my experience I find that neurasthenia proper is a very rare occurrence. The more common manifestations are anxiety neurosis, anxiety hysteria, conversion hysteria and compulsive neurosis. But I do not propose to burden the reader with a professional description of the various forms of neurosis. Briefly I may state that my analysis of various artists and writers has always yielded the same result. I found everywhere a definite background of hysteria. This disorder, whose widespread prevalence among persons of the female sex has long ago attracted the attention of observers, occurs also among men in a typical form which, in accordance with the suggestion made by Freud, may be properly called *"anxiety hysteria."* The nucleus of this disorder is formed by the feeling of dread, a feeling which manifests itself under various forms and which arises out of the repression of sexual cravings.

But—what is hysteria? Since we have acquired insight into the psychic structure of the neuroses we know that it represents the emotionally stressed complexes which have become split off from consciousness and thus disturbs the psychic balance. Hysteria is virtually but one of the special forms under which repression manifests itself. This splitting up of the consciousness expresses itself in a number of symptoms—anxiety states, compulsive thoughts, and bodily manifestations—baffling to the consciousness. *The hysterical symptoms are creative formulations of the unconscious.*

Artistic creations are subject to the same law. The writer creates out of his unconscious and that is why it is possible for him to formulate so many varying creations true to nature and to take completely into account so many different emotions. The average neurotic becomes ill because he represses forcefully the cravings which well up from the background of his instincts. His repressions stifle him. On the other hand the artist frees himself of his neurosis, because like Vulcan he throws off his inner flames. (pp. 84-6)

> *William Stekel, "Poetry and Neurosis," translated by James S. Van Teslaar, in* The Psychoanalytic Review, *Vol. X, No. 1, January, 1923, pp. 73-96.*

William Barrett

[In the following essay, Barrett examines the problem of authenticity which madness poses for the writer.]

Is my title ["Writers and Madness"] extreme? It is, if you will, just the same subject that has been very much discussed recently under the titles "Art and Neurosis," "Art and Anxiety," etc. But I choose the more ancient and extreme term precisely to maintain continuity with all the older instances. Is anything born *ex nihilo,* much less a phenomenon so profound and disturbing as that estranged neurotic, the modern writer? Even when the poet existed in his most unalienated condition—in ancient Greece—the similarity of madness and inspiration was the common saying; and Plato did not invent but only gave literary formulation to the belief about the poet's madness. Pause for a moment over this extraordinary paradox. They sat on sacred ground, precinct of the god, the day and drama were surrounded by all the occasions and overtones of religion, the myth known and on the whole taken as true, and yet. . . . And yet this audience too must exact a terrible price of its poet before they can take him seriously. A secret guilt perhaps? As they sat in broad daylight indulging their collective fantasy, pretending to believe that what was before their eyes was in fact something else, did an uneasy stirring at this indulgence drive them to exact from their poet in revenge the penalty of madness-inspiration? But what, in any case, we do know is this: that even when dealing with myths whose form and details were completely laid down for him, the Greek poet had to launch out into this sea (of "madness," if we believe Plato) in order to return to pour his own personal being into the preformed mold. Otherwise, his play could not have con-

vinced an audience that already assumed their myth as a matter of fact—such is the paradox from which we start!

Everything Swift wrote, Leslie Stephen says with penetrating good sense, is interesting because it is the man himself. (If this is true of many other writers, there is on the other hand a special and compelling sense in which it holds of Swift—another reason for my finding his case so apposite.) Does it look as if I were only about to say, with Buffon, "the style is the man"? But "style" does not say enough, and it is not enough to remain happy with the judicious aphorism or with Stephen's judicious critical observation. The modern critic cannot rest easy with this eighteenth-century piece of astuteness, which long ago passed into the stock of our critical assumptions; we begin to know too much and we must dig mines beneath its truth.

But it is well to begin from such broad and obvious data of criticism (instances of which we could multiply indefinitely) for we may now pass on to the more complex and really monumental example provided us by James Joyce. In his *Portrait of the Artist* Joyce develops a theory of literary creation, anchored on the metaphysics of St. Thomas but essentially expressing the Flaubertian view of the writer as a god who remains above and beyond his creation which he manipulates as he wills. But in *Finnegans Wake* the universal human symbol of the writer has now become the infant Earwicker twin scrawling with his own excrement on the floor! (Between the two, somewhere near the midpoint of this remarkable evolution, Stephen Dedalus declares, in the famous discussion of Shakespeare in *Ulysses,* that the writer, setting forth from his door for the encounter with experience, meets only himself on the doorstep.) If Joyce is the great case of a rigorous and logical development among modern writers, each step forward carrying the immense weight of his total commitment and concentration, we are not wrong then to find in this changing portrait of the artist a measure of how far he has matured as man and writer from the once youthful and arrogant aesthete. And if we will not learn from our own experience, do we not remain formalists toward literature only at the expense of neglecting Joyce's far deeper experience?

But in fact we already know there is no escape from ourselves. Existence is a dense plenum into which we are plunged, and every thought, wish, and fear is "overdetermined," coming to be under the infinite pressures within that plenum of all other thoughts, wishes, and fears. Fingerprints and footprints are our own, and Darwin has pointed out that our inner organs differ from person to person as much as our faces. The signature of ourselves is written over all our dreams like the criminal's fingerprints across his crime. The writer, no more than any other man, can hope to escape this inescapable density of particularity. But his difference is precisely that he does not merely submit but insists upon this as his fate. It is *his own* voice which he wishes to resound in the arena of the world. He knows that the work must be his, and to the degree that it is less than his, to the degree that he has not risked the maximum of his being in it, he has missed the main chance, his only chance. The scientist too may insist on the personal prerogative of discovery: he wants the new element, planet, or equation to bear his name; but if in this claim for prestige he responds to one of the deepest urges of the ego, it is only that this prestige itself may come to attend his person through the public world of other men; and it is not in the end his own being that is exhibited or his own voice that is heard in the learned report to the Academy.

So we have come quickly to the point, and may now let the categories of *authentic* and *unauthentic* out of the bag. I am not very happy about the terms, I wish we had better in English, but it should be clear from our instances so far that they are not really new notions, and that they do come forth now at the real pinch of the subject matter. If a certain amount of faddism has recently and regrettably become attached to their use, they have on the other hand also become obsessive for the modern mind—a recommendation which we, existing historically, cannot help finding a little persuasive. The Marxist will not fail to point out that a highly developed technology, which is not directed toward human ends but capable on the other hand of overrunning all areas of the social life, has plunged us into this civilization of the slick imitation, celluloid and cellophane, kitsch and chromium plating, in the morass of which we come inevitably to speak of "the real thing" and "the real right thing" with an almost religious fervor. And he will go on to explain then why the category of authenticity should play such a crucial role in modern existential thought. He would be right, of course, but he ought also to drop his bucket into the deeper waters of the well. One deeper fact is that modern man has lost the religious sanctions which had once surrounded his life at every moment with a recognizable test capable of telling him whether he was living "in the truth" or not; Hegel drew a map of the divided consciousness, and Freud explored it empirically beyond anything Hegel ever dreamed, showing us, among other things, that Venus is the goddess of lies; and so we come, as creatures of the divided and self-alienated consciousness, to wrestle with the problem of how we are to live truthfully. But if these categories have become historically inevitable, and we borrow their formulation from existentialist philosophers, we have on the other hand to insist that it is not these philosophers who can tell us, after all, how authenticity is to be achieved either in art or life. Freud, not Heidegger, holds the key. The mechanism by which any work of art becomes authentic—flooded in every nook and cranny with the personal being of the author—can only be revealed by the searchlight of psychoanalytic exploration.

How then is authenticity—this strange and central power of a fantasy to *convince* us—achieved? A first and principal point: it seems to involve a fairly complete, if temporary, identification with the objects of fantasy. The difference between Kafka and most of his imitators becomes a *crucial* instance here. When Kafka writes about a hero who has become an insect, about a mouse or an animal in a burrow, he is, during the course of the lucid hallucination which is his story, that insect, mouse, or animal; it is he himself who lives and moves through the passages and chambers of his burrow; while his imitators, even when they are fairly successful, strike us as simply using so much clever machinery borrowed from him and often more ingeniously baroque than his, but which lacks pre-

cisely that authenticity of identification. But this identification with the objects of fantasy is also in the direction of insanity; and perhaps this is just what the ancients knew: that the poet in inspiration ventures as close to that undrawn border as he can, for the closer he goes the more vitality he brings back with him. The game would seem to be to go as close as possible without crossing over.

Now imagine, for a moment, Swift in the modern pattern. After the downfall of the Harley ministry he retires to his wretched, dirty dog-hole and prison of Ireland, has a nervous breakdown, a crack-up, is patched together by several physicians and analysts, continues in circulation thereafter by drinking hard but spacing his liquor carefully, and dies at an earlier age of cirrhosis of the liver. Shall we call this: Living on the American Plan? It is the violence of the new world, after all, that has made a system of violent drinking. Now to be drunk and to go mad are both ways of overcoming the world. If in the interests of human economy we are left no choice but to prefer the American Pattern, would we not, however, feel a little cheated had Swift's actual history been different? Before the ravening gaze of his miserable species he flings down his madness as the gage of his commitment and passion, and it has now become an inseparable part of the greatness of the human figure that rises out of history toward us.

When Simon Dedalus Delany, amiable and easygoing, remarked of a mutual acquaintance that "He was a nice old gentleman," Swift retorted, "There is no such thing as a nice old gentleman; any man who had a body or mind worth a farthing would have burned them out long ago." Does not this become his own comment on his eventual madness? The man who retorted thus, it is clear, lived with his whole being flung continuously toward the future at the end of the long corridor of which was the placid if disordered chamber of madness. To have gone mad in a certain way might almost seem one mode of living authentically: one has perhaps looked at the world without illusion and with passion. Nothing permits us to separate this life from this writing: if the extraordinary images the biography provides us—the old man exclaiming, over and over again, "I am what I am," or sitting placidly for hours before his Bible open on Job's lament, "let the day perish wherein I was born,"—if these move us as symbols of a great human ruin, they are also the background against which we must read the last book of *Gulliver*. The game is to go as close as possible without crossing over: poor Gulliver the traveler has now slipped across the border into the country of the mad, but this journey itself was only a continuation of the Voyage among the Houyhnhnms. A moment comes and the desire to escape takes on a definite and terrible clothing, and the whole being is shaken by the convulsions of what we may call the totem urge—the wish to be an animal. Rat's foot, crow's skin, anything out of this human form! The Ainu dances and growls and is a bear, the Bororo Indians chatter and become parokeets; Swift wanted to be a horse, a beautiful and gentle animal—and probably nobler on the whole than most human beings. This is the madness already present in *Gulliver*.

We do not mean to deny all the other necessary qualities

that are there: the once laughter-loving Dean, lover of *la bagatelle,* King of Triflers, the great eighteenth-century wit, the accomplished classicist. Precisely these things give Swift the great advantage over a writer like Céline, whose rage is, by comparison, choking and inarticulate—like a man spitting and snarling in our face and in the end only *about* himself, so that we are not always sure whether we are being moved by literature or by a mere document of some fearful human extremity. What for the moment I am calling "madness," the perhaps simpler thing the Greeks called "madness," must somehow flow freely along the paths where all men can admire. If it erupts like a dam bursting it only inundates and swamps the neighboring fields; conducted into more indirect and elaborate paths, it irrigates and flows almost hidden to the eye. The flow from the unconscious of writer to reader would seem, then, to be more effective precisely where the circuit is longer and less direct, and capable therefore of encompassing ampler territory in its sweep. Lucidity, logic, form, objective dramatization, traditional style, taste—all these are channels into which the writer must let his anguish flow. And the denser his literary situation, the more he is surrounded by a compact and articulate tradition, the more chances he can take in casting himself adrift. But whatever Swift's advantages in literary and moral milieu, we cannot forget that he himself lived to write his own epitaph and in this final summing-up had the last word on the once laughter-loving Dean. And it is just his *saeva indignatio*— the mad wrath which, as he said to Delany, did "eat his flesh and consume his spirits"—that establishes the deeper authenticity of *Gulliver* which separates it from any other production of eighteenth-century wit. He himself as Gulliver towers over his Lilliputian enemies, and flees from the disgusting humans into the quiet stables of the horses. How far his madness had already taken him, he could scarcely have guessed, for it had unconsciously carried him, an unquestioning Christian, for the moment outside Christianity: the rational and tranquil Houyhnhnms do not need a Messiah's blood and an historically revealed religion in order to be saved, while the Yahoos could not possibly be redeemed by any savior. Swift might not have gone mad after writing *Gulliver,* but much of the power of that book comes from the fact that he was already on the road.

Once a writer imposes his greatness on us he imposes his figure totally, and we then read every scrap and scribble against the whole, and we will not find it strange that Joyce should invoke even the scrawling of the Earwicker twin as part of the image of Everymanthewriter. The man who wrote the charming prattle of the *Journal to Stella* is the same who comes to howl at bay before the human race. In his life he made two bluestockings love him desperately (a significant choice this, that they should be bluestockings; but one, to his surprise, turned out, as sometimes happens, a very passionate blue-stocking); and one he loved all his life long. In the simple *Prayers for Stella,* sublimating, he gropes, touches, fondles her in God. What happened beyond this we do not know. But we need no very fanciful imagination to guess the frustration which produces that mingled disgust and fascination at the biology of the female body. He did more, however, than release this into a few scatological verses about milady at and on

her toilet; he was able to project his frustration and rage into the helpless Irish face about him, the insouciant Saxon face, churchmen, bishops, Lord Mayors, quacks, and pedants; "the corruptions and villainies of men in power"; and through these into a total vision of the human condition.

Here at last we come close to the secret: if one characteristic of neurosis is always a displacement somewhere, then perhaps the test of a writer's achievement may be precisely the extent and richness of displacement he is able to effect. In the process of literary expression, the neurotic mass acquires energies which are directed toward reality and seek their satisfaction in reality. As the writer displaces the neurotic mass further afield he is led to incorporate larger and larger areas of experience into his vision. Everything begins to appear then *as if* the world he pictures were itself sufficient to generate this vision (which we may know, in fact, to have been rather the product of quite unconscious compulsions and conflicts); *as if* the ego, really master in its own house, were simply responding appropriately to the world as seen in the book. Thus the peculiar sense of conquest and liberation that follows literary creation cannot be analyzed solely as that fulfillment of wishes which normally occurs in daydreaming or fantasy. Why in that case would it be necessary to complete the literary work at all? And why should the liberation it gives be so much more powerful and durable? No; this conquest is also one for the ego itself, which now seems momentarily to have absorbed the unconscious into itself so that the neurotic disgust itself appears an appropriate response to reality. And if this is an illusion from the analyst's point of view, it may not always be an illusion from the moralist's point of view. The world as it appears in Swift's writings is, in the end, adequate to his madness.

Now Swift's (unlike Cowper's, to cite another literary madman) was a very strong ego, and the fact that he broke in old age only tells us how great were the visions, tensions, and repressions he had to face. We do not know enough to establish his "case," but we know enough to say that his madness probably did not have its source in the literary condition at all—however much incipient madness may have informed and made powerful his writings.

Do we build too much on his example then? Perhaps; but his figure, in its broad strong outlines (and the very simplicity of these outlines is to our advantage here), takes such a grip on the imagination that, pursuing this rather nocturnal meditation, I am loth to let him drop. He has taken us so far already that it seems worthwhile to journey a little way with him still into the darkness.

Certainly there is nothing, or very little, about Swift to make him a modern figure. He sits so solidly amid the prejudices and virtues of his age that we search in vain for any ideas in him that would seem to anticipate us. He was a man of parts rather than of ideas; and his very "rationality" is a kind of eighteenth-century prejudice, having little in common with what we struggle toward as our own, or even what the same century later in France was to discover so triumphantly as its own. He lived before modern political alternatives became very real or meaningful, and only his human hatred of the abuses of power might connect him remotely with some of our own attitudes. As a literary man, he is at the farthest distance from that neurotic specialist, the modern litterateur; he is not even a professional literary man in the sense of his contemporary, Pope, much less in the sense of the consecrated *rentier,* Flaubert. Thus we have no quarrel at all with certain professorial critics who point out that Swift was primarily interested in power and that he came by writing as an instrument of power or simply as a diversion. (What an unhappy conclusion, though, if we thought we had therefore to exclude him from something called "literature"!) And we might even go along a certain way with the generous hint of these critics that the frustration of his desires for power explains both his misanthropy and final insanity.

But does not logic teach us that an induction is strengthened more by a confirming instance further afield? and which at first glance might not seem to fall altogether under the class in question? And if Swift, who sits so solidly in his own age, leads us, when we but plunge deeply enough, into the world of the modern writer, should we not feel all the more assured that we have got at least a little below the surface? Already, beneath the solid outlines of his eighteenth-century figure, I begin to descry the shadows and depths of a *psychic type,* the writer—which has emerged, to be sure, spectacularly only in the two following centuries.

Now the trouble with the professors (and not only when they censure Swift for his craving for power) is that they have unconsciously created a figure of the writer in their own image: a well-bred person with well-tubbed and scrubbed motives, who approaches something specialized and disinterested that they call "literature" as if his function in the end were merely to provide them with books to teach. Perhaps the great writers themselves have unwittingly helped toward this deception? Has any one of them ever told us why he had to become a writer? They tell us instead: "To hold a mirror up to nature"; "To carry a mirror dawdling down a lane"; "To forge the uncreated conscience of my race"; etc., etc.—great blazons of triumph, formulae of their extraordinary achievement, before which we forget even to ask why they had to become writers. The great writer is the victorious suitor who has captured a beautiful bride in an incomparable marriage. There seems almost no point in asking him why he had to love and seek marriage: his reasons seem all too abundant, he has only to point to the incomparable attractions of his beloved. He has lost his private compulsions in the general—in the positive and admirable qualities, known to all men, of the thing achieved. (The Kierkegaardians, by the way, should remind themselves that life must be just such a conquest and appropriation of universals.) But life does not contain only such happy bridegrooms, otherwise we might never know all the enormities and paradoxes of love; and if there were only great geniuses among writers, perhaps we might never know this other truth: the compulsions and paradoxes on the dark side of their calling—which they, the great ones, could afford to forget in the daylight blaze of their triumph.

The mistake is not to have invoked the idea of power but, once invoked, not to have seen it through: we have but to pursue it far enough and we can find it present everywhere in Swift's writings, and indeed the central impulse of his prose itself (perhaps the best in English). What is that stripped and supple syntax but the design of greatest possible economy and force, by which he launches each sentence at its mark like a potent and well-aimed missile? (And each missile thuds against the bestial human face from which he would escape.) Swift's lack of interest in being a literary man as such may account, then, for some of his strongest qualities. The conception of literature as an instrument or a diversion or even a vanity may exist along with the power to produce the greatest literature: Pascal's conviction of the vanity of eloquence is one reason why he is a greater prose-writer than Valery, the aesthete, who mocks at this conviction. Here it seems almost as if from examining Swift's writings themselves we might arrive at Freud's perception: that the writer is more than commonly obsessed by a desire for power which he seeks to gratify through his public fantasies.

Because of an introverted disposition, he is unable to gratify this desire in the usual arenas of external action. Introversion is the brand of his calling: he is the divided man, his consciousness always present but a little absent, hovering over itself, ready to pounce and bring back some fragment to his notebooks. The introverted disposition suggests some excessive and compelling need to be loved; and we would suspect that here too it must result primally from some special strength or strain in the Oedipal relation. But whatever our speculation as to its source, the point of power remains clear; and if he seeks it by a detour, the writer's claims are nonetheless total: it is power of the most subtle kind that the writer wants, power over the mind and freedom of other human beings, his readers.

Such extraordinary claims of power, and particularly their indirectness of gratification, suggest immediately an ambivalent connection with that more than usually acute sense of guilt with which writers as a class seem to be endowed. (That Swift suffered from extraordinary obsessions of guilt toward the end of his life, we know by accounts of several sources; but most of his life, since he accepted Christianity without question, these guilt feelings were tapped and drained off into religion; hence it is that in his writing we usually encounter the aggressive and outgoing parts of his personality.) Georges Blin in "The Gash" (*Partisan Review,* Spring 1946), has presented very eloquently some of the sadistic motives that operate in the artist. We should expect—in accordance with the usual ambivalence—a masochistic pattern to be equally operative, and perhaps even more to the fore because of the essential indirectness of the artist's drives toward power and sadism. What else explains the writer's extraordinary eagerness for the painful humility of his yoke as he crouches over his desk stubbornly weaving and reweaving his own being hundreds of times? "Thought, study, sacrifice, and mortification"—how he trembles with joy to put on these hairshirts of his solitude and calling! These punishments he inflicts upon himself over his desk will help to make clear then why writing should satisfy the claims of guilt upon him; why he should search so passionately for redemption upon the written page, and why as the paragraph takes shape beneath his pen he can feel for moments that his step has become a little less heavy on the face of the earth. But we should also know this ambivalence of power and guilt from phenomenological scrutiny. We never live in a purely private world, our consciousness is penetrated at every point by the consciousness of others, and what is it but one step from seeking redemption in one's own eyes to seeking it in the eyes of others? The movement by which we stoop to lift ourselves out of the pit of self-contempt is one and unbroken with that thrust which would carry us above the shoulders of our fellow-men.

Lillian Feder on madness in literature:

[The theme of madness] discloses, as it always has, the mind of the protagonist or persona incorporating the limitations and defenses of its society at the same time that it exposes their effects. Viewed through the lens of the long history of madness as a theme of literature, the present vogue of the madhouse as a temple of consciousness represents a common but by no means an inevitable psychic defense. Explorations of madness throughout literature portray a great variety of psychic oppositions to environmental demands. Among these, the narcissistic withdrawal from social and intrapsychic struggles is but one detour of the human mind in its internalization of family, society, and history.

Lillian Feder, in her Madness in Literature, *1980.*

And is not this ambivalent urge to power-guilt but the sign of that excessive need to be loved which has driven the writer into a profession where he must speak with *his own* voice, offer to the public gaze of the world so much of his own existence? Love to be conquered by force, or taken as a gift of tenderness and pity for his confession.

But both the satisfaction (of power) and relief (from guilt), though they glow brightly, glow, alas, only for moments, and we live again in the shadow of ourselves. Nothing in the world (we are told) is a substitute for anything else, and if there is a point beyond which the writer can never satisfy these urges in literature itself, then this inability can no longer be regarded as peculiar to Swift, a deficiency of his "case," but an essential and mortifying aspect of the literary condition everywhere. So we come back to our point: Swift is certainly not a modern literary man, but we only had to go deep enough, and we have arrived at a world of impulses and motives that we recognize as our own.

Despite the ancient recognition, the modern world of the crack-up and breakdown has really become a new and almost discontinuous phenomenon. (First the continuity; now we must do justice to the other aspect, the discontinuity of the modern.) It is time we had an exhaustive and statistical study of the problem, done with the grubbing thoroughness of a Ph.D. thesis; for the present I would only suggest some of the main statistical categories: the madmen, those who broke, Swift, Cowper, William Collins, Christopher Smart, Hoelderlin, Ruskin; figures who were not altogether normal, if not altogether mad, like Blake; who, like Coleridge and DeQuincey, had to salvage themselves through drugs (the Romantic equivalent of the American Pattern); or who produce their writing out of a maximum anxiety, their personal rack of torture, like Baudelaire and Eliot; and from these on we could ramify off into all the various subtler neuroses that have afflicted literary men. Even from this sketchy suggestion of a list it begins to appear that the incidence of aberration, neurosis, or outright madness is such that one really begins to doubt whether these misfortunes are accidental to the profession of letters as such. [The author refers to Lionel Trilling's article "Art and Neurosis," in *Partisan Review,* Winter 1945.] And at this point perhaps we ought to face openly the question whether there is not some original flaw—original sin, if you will—about the profession such that the writer's struggle to live it out completely must inevitably involve him in some kind of hubris; and whether, after all, the game is really worth the candle. Freud at one earlier point did suggest something like this: that art is a survival in our day of primitive magic, with some of the magical still hanging about its aspirations; which did not at all prevent him, we may notice, from deriving very deep pleasure and insight from great works of literature.

The fault, the accumulating difficulty, seem to come from the very advance itself of Western culture and history. In a story by Jean Paulhan, *"Aytré qui perd l'habitude"* (Aytré Loses the Knack"), the hero keeps a journal while leading a trek across Madagascar. En route across the country the entries in the journal are very simple and direct: we arrive, leave, chickens cost seven sous, we lay in a provision of medicines, etc. But with the arrival in the city of Ambositra the journal suddenly becomes complicated: discussions of ideas, women's headdresses, strange scenes and characters in the street. The most ordinary incidents of daily life become complicated and almost unexpressible to Aytré struggling to keep his journal. Paulhan is after other game in this tale, where we need not follow him; enough for us that we can take this journey of Aytré for a symbol of the march of writers in history as they progress toward subjects ever more complex, driven by the compulsion to "make it new." From this point of view Paulhan's title itself becomes something of a misnomer: Aytré's trouble is not that he has lost the knack—quite the contrary, he now has altogether too much of it. Become infinitely complicated, all-absorbing, possessive, now the knack *has him*. Aytré, in short, has become a modern writer. He had begun as the simple scribe of the clan.

"Make it new," Pound cried, and Eliot further explicated: Modern poetry must be complicated because modern life is complicated. Both have passed into famous slogans in defense of modernism; but both abbreviate what is a much more complicated process, and have to be expanded in the light or darkness of Aytré's painful journey. The writer objectifies his fantasies (that much of Freudian formula we have to use in any case) but he must return to view them with the analytic eyes of daylight and criticism. But this reality to which he submits is not what he meets if he gazes out into the world with the naked eyes of the first-born man; the reality principle for the writer is one qualified by the works, the recorded experience and knowledge of man, already in existence. After Proust no one can write about love with the old charming simplicity of Prevost. It would be pastiche: archaic and unauthentic. In Prevost it charms us, it is real and convincing. At his cutural moment, love—as the simple lovely disease of sensibility—was itself an extraordinary *donnée,* and the writer could find such release in it that he was capable of the necessary identification with his fantasy. (Even when a form like the novel swings back momentarily into a simpler pattern, the new simplicity is quite different from the old; the simplicity of Gide is not the old simplicity of the classical French novel, but a new one—self-conscious, difficult, refined, defining its slender line from the sum of its rejections.) Hence it appears that Pound's manifesto, and Eliot's recommendation of a complication to parallel the complication of modern life, formulate effect rather than cause; we ought instead to put it that the writer, existing in his time, in his place, and with his past must make such discoveries as to secure the completeness of release necessary to achieve authenticity. If he repeats what is already discovered, he has no chance of making it *his.* That is why his existence is relentlessly historical and he has to travel Aytré's journey. Now the reality principle functions in life chiefly (or its function is felt more forcibly there) to inhibit the gratification of desire. Its literary analogue functions in the same way: it checks the writer from releasing himself into the fantasies that are unreal, trivial, or superficial. To find his authenticity, a material into which he is completely released, the writer has now to dig ever deeper, the unconscious that is released must be at deeper and deeper levels. So he finds, like Aytré, the literary "knack" become absorbing and terrifying. Hence the burden of neurosis that weighs more and more heavily upon the modern man of letters.

The more gifted the writer the more likely he is to be critically conscious of his literary tradition—the more conscious, that is, of the reality principle as it operates in the literary sphere—and the harder it becomes for him to fall into one of the easy publicist styles of his day. Recently I read about a young writer who had written a best-seller in four weeks and made $400,000 out of it—$100,000 a week, almost as good pay as a movie star. If books could be written from the top of one's mind merely (even books of this kind), it is naïve to think a major writer would not do it: after four weeks of absence he returns to support himself for many years in the prosecution of his own unremunerative and serious tasks. But it seems impossible to write a best-seller in complete parody, one has to believe in one's material even there, and it is impossible to fake unless one is a fake. Joyce has written in *Ulysses* a superb parody of the sentimental romance for schoolgirls, but it is quite obvious from that chapter that Joyce could not have turned out a novel in this genre for money: his irony and self-consciousness would have got in the way, and the book would not have attracted its readers but in the end only Joyce's readers. The writer writes what he can, and if he decides to sell out it is by corrupting and cheapening his own level, or perhaps slipping down a step below it; but writing is not so uncommitted an intellectual effort that he can drop down facilely to a very much lower level and operate with enough skill there to convince that kind of reader. Joyce did not write *Finnegans Wake* out of a free decision taken in the void, but because his experience of life and Western culture was what it was, and he had to write that book if he was to write anything.

It is perhaps not a very pleasant thought, but it seems inescapable, that even the commonest best-seller is the product of the personal being of the author and demands its own kind of authenticity. Life also imprisons us in its rewards; and we may draw some satisfaction from the thought that these gay reapers of prestige and money, if they are to keep on terms with their audience, can have in the end only lives adequate to their books: *On écrit le livre qu'on merite.* Our satisfaction might be greater if we were not on the other hand also painfully acquainted with the opposite phenomenon: the gifted people who find it difficult to produce precisely because they are too intelligent and sensitive to tailor their writing to the reigning market. The very awareness of standards inhibits them from writing, and, not being geniuses, they are unable to break through and produce anything adequate to those standards. The literary future in America, and perhaps the West generally, seems to be leading to this final and lamentable split: on the one hand, an enormous body of run-of-the-mill writing (machine-made, as it were), becoming ever more slick as it becomes more technically adequate through abundant competition and appropriation of the tricks of previous serious writing, and in the end generating its own types of pseudo authenticity, like Steinbeck or Marquand; on the other hand, an occasional genius breaking through this wall here and there, at ever more costly price in personal conflict, anguish, and difficulty. Modern poetry already provides us its own and extreme version of this exacerbating split; think of the extremity of personal difficulty required to produce the authentic poetry of our time: the depth of anguish which secreted the few poems of Eliot; and Yeats, we remember, had to struggle through a long life of political unrest, personal heartbreak, see the friends and poets of his youth die off or kill themselves, before he came into his own and could produce poems capable of convincing us that this poetry was not merely a kind of "solemn game."

Some of the more internal difficulties that beset the pursuit of literature are being very much discussed in France by writers like Maurice Blanchot and Brice Parain. Blanchot finishes one essay, in which he has explored certain aspects of anxiety, silence, and expression, with the devastating remark, "It is enough that literature should continue to seem possible," though the reader by the time he has waded through Blanchot's rarefactions to that point may very well have lost the conviction that even the possibility remained. These French researches are of a quite special character, continuing the tradition of Mallarmé—or, rather, attempting to see the aesthetic problems of Mallarmé from the human anguish of Pascal. (As the burdens of civilization become heavier and we see existence itself with fewer illusions, we have come perhaps to share Pascal's attitude toward poetry: a vanity, a "solemn game"; at any rate, we seem to demand more of the modern writer before we take him very seriously.) These difficulties are extreme and we need not share them in that form: after the rigors to which Mallarmé submitted poetry in his search for a *"langage authentique"* no wonder silence should appear as the only and haunting possibility of speech. After Mallarmé, poetry had to swing back toward the language of what he calls *"universel reportage,"* and Eliot's poetry has shown us that this language, suitably charged and concentrated, can be the vehicle of very great poetry. Blanchot's difficulties persist but in another form (especially in a commercial culture). Not silence but garrulousness ("unauthentic chatter," as Heidegger would say) may be the threat confronting the writer; but always and everywhere the difficulty of securing authenticity.

The difficulties we face in America—a society which turns, as Van Wyck Brooks says, its most gifted men into crackpots—are obviously of a much more external and violent kind than in France. External pressures abet the internal tensions, which become unendurable, and at long last comes that slide over into the more tranquil and private self-indulgence of fantasy with a consequent weakening of the reality principle. One (a critic) develops a private language; another spins out elaborate literary theories without content or relevance; a third has maintained his literary alertness and eye for relevance through a sheer aggressiveness which has cost him his ability to maintain personal relations—and which appears therefore in his work as a mutilation too. Scott Fitzgerald's confidante in "The Crack-up" (perhaps his most mature piece of writing, at that) gives him the extraordinary advice: *"Listen. Suppose this wasn't a crack in you—suppose it was in the Grand Canyon. . . . By God, if I ever cracked, I'd try to make the whole world crack with me."* And she was right and profound, but Fitzgerald was tied by too many strings to the values of American life to see her truth. His crack-up was the dawning of a truth upon him which he could not completely grasp or recognize intellectually. Swift in that position would have seen that the crack is in the Grand Canyon, in the whole world, in the total human face about him. If he is powerful enough—now against greater odds—to make the world crack in his work, the writer has at the least the gratification of revenge, and the ego that deeper conquest (described above) where its anguish now seems no more than an appropriate response to a world portrayed (and with some fidelity) as cracked. But, alas, these energies which seek reality and are capable of transforming the neurotic mass into the writer's special and unique vision of the world can also be blocked by the external difficulties in the literary situation. And when that happens we open the door, as Freud says, to the psychoses—at any rate, to the breakdown and crack-up.

And so I am brought back into the center of my theme. If I appeared to have abandoned the theme of neurosis for the difficulties, external and internal, that confront the modern writer, it was only because these difficulties as part of his alienation are the aggravating causes and public face of his madness.

But why (in the end) should it be the writer's fate—more than of any other intellectual profession—to confront this crack in the face of the world? Because his subject is the very world of experience as such, and it is this world, this total world, which he must somehow salvage. The scientist has his appointed place in the community of researchers, he confronts carefully delimited fragments of experience, the data from which he proceeds are publicly recog-

nizable, and his whole being is to be, as it were, an incarnate outward public mind. But the writer is alone—potentially twenty-four hours a day, the luminol pill and the writing pad beside his bed for whatever welcome or unwelcome presence comes that night. On the other hand, it might seem that the philosopher, since he confronts in his own way the totality of experience might also show some fatal tendency toward aberration. But the philosopher deals with concepts and out of these he may construct some kind of "meaning" for the world: when speculative systems were still believed, he had only to be agile enough to design one of these towering arks of salvation, and what if it leaked a little, he was a professor and he had something to do the rest of his professorial life plugging its gaps; now when the pretense to speculative theories is no longer even taken seriously the philosopher can construct an equally elaborate theory showing that the question itself has no meaning, and so philosophy continues to be possible. Whatever the impasse of insoluble antinomies at which his thought finally arrives, he can continue to arrange these in neat parallel columns, chip away at their edges and perpetually recast their statement as if preparing bit by bit for a solution which in fact never arrives; and so continues in business, he has something to say, he "gets published"; and after the initial shocks and disturbance mankind has shown itself capable of settling down peacefully into positivism, and few people are more intellectually adjusted than the positivists. But it is not at the level of concepts that the appalling face of the world is seen, and it is another kind of "meaning" that the writer must construct. Out of the ravages of his experience, his desperate

---

Charles I. Glicksberg on the creative process:

In the past, when Western culture regarded madness as a dangerous outbreak of the irrational, reason was held to be the sanctified, unassailable norm. In exalting madness as the Muse of the modern age, the plenary source of Dionysian inspiration, the writer as rebel failed to consider madness as a psychotic affliction. He did not stop to inquire whether madness could shape a genuine work of art. Madness, like neurosis, was not conducive to creative fulfillment. Even if a writer manages to produce a work of art while suffering from madness, it does not follow that madness was the decisive factor. The madman is at the mercy of his hallucinations and is in too disoriented a condition to achieve the order and unity required of a work of art. The fact that [in the words of Michel Foucault] "from the time of Hölderlin and Nerval," the number of writers "who have 'succumbed' to madness has increased" proves nothing. The artist stricken by madness struggles desperately against this fate, for his madness, as it grows in severity, incapacitates him totally for the creative task. Indeed, madness, as it extends its range of power, results in the supersession of art. As Foucault emphatically declares: *"where there is a work of art, there is no madness. . . ."* Nevertheless, the phenomenology of madness, when it is integrated within a work of art, brings the world into question, for it confronts the mystery of being with the specter of nonbeing.

Charles I. Glicksberg, in his The Literature of Commitment, *1976.*

loneliness, he must put forth those works which look back into his gaze with conviction and authenticity and wear about them the gleams of interest—cathectic charges, in the technical term—which have fled from the vast bare blank face of the world as seen in the extreme situations of *his* truth: in sleeplessness, the nervous darkness, against death and against the inexorable and dragging vista of time which is his being. (pp. 5-22)

William Barrett, "Writers and Madness," in Partisan Review, *Vol. XIV, No. 1, Winter, 1947, pp. 5-22.*

E. Hale Chatfield

[*Chatfield is an American poet, editor, critic, and educator. In the following essay, a response to Lionel Trilling's "Art and Neurosis," Chatfield discusses the relationship between poetry, neurosis, and psychosis.*]

It is unlikely that a psychotic could be a very effective artist, and it is thoroughly impossible that all artists are psychotics. Psychosis, particularly advanced psychosis, includes a lack of perception, as Freud has told us, of the external world, and perceptiveness is invariably acknowledged as being a *sine qua non* of art. But although it is apparent that psychoses must be, necessarily, a hindrance to art, it is not entirely impossible for an artist to be a psychotic or, of course, *vice versa*. Schizophrenia, for example, is often characterized by alternate periods of raving "madness" and apparent sanity, and schizophrenia is one of the classic psychoses. It is conceivable that a schizophrenic might produce excellent art during his saner periods—even works in which he endeavored to express what he remembered of his Mr. Hyde phases. If the general view that Van Gogh was a schizophrenic is correct, it must be assumed that it was during those saner periods that he produced his paintings.

In his article, "Art and Neurosis," Lionel Trilling, speaking of course of neurosis, wrote that "although Van Gogh may have been schizophrenic he was in addition an artist." Although what Mr. Trilling says is, on the face of it, quite true, it is thoroughly misleading in the context of any discussion of neurosis, for if Van Gogh was a schizophrenic he has no place whatever in Mr. Trilling's article. If further proof is necessary that Mr. Trilling's understanding of psychoanalytic terminology is in error, the following quotations from the article in question should allay any doubts:

> Lamb is denying that genius is related to insanity; for "insanity" the modern reader may substitute "neurosis."

> Most literary people, when they speak of mental illness, refer to neurosis.

Strangely enough, the latter statement is partially true, if distressingly so. What is more disappointing than the realization that a large segment of the intelligent population is largely ignorant of the nature of mental illness is the knowledge that one of America's most respected critics and teachers has allowed himself, if unwittingly, to contribute to that ignorance. Mr. Trilling would have been more correct if he had entitled his article "Art and Psychosis."

A correspondence between art and neurosis is not so easily dismissed. Let us take a hypothetical artist born in a hypothetical community. As a child, the artist exists as other children exist; he lives in the kaleidoscopic world of sensation and impression. All children are poets, in that they live fantasy and speak the language of metaphor. The child who sees raindrops dripping from the branches of trees often fancies and perhaps even observes aloud that the trees are "crying"; little boys have been known to say, as they were urinating, "I am raining," or to exclaim while zooming about the room with outspread arms, "Look at me! I'm an airplane!"

Simile is even more common. The girl who says, "My Mommy is as pretty as a princess," and the boy who boasts that his "Daddy is as big as a mountain" are unknowingly making use of methods of expression often thought to be reserved for poets. Children, too, tend to credit animals and even thoroughly inanimate objects with human feelings and emotions. They often express sympathy for the Christmas tree as Daddy cuts it down, and they almost invariably exhibit strong compassion for injured puppies and hurt birds. As most children grow older they learn and accept the facts that trees do not cry, boys cannot "rain," and no one is an airplane. Although they continue to make outlandish exaggerations even into adulthood, they recognize that Mother wasn't *really* as pretty as a princess after all, and it would have been quite impossible for Daddy to have been as big as a mountain. Too, they soon suspect that Christmas trees do not feel pain or loneliness, and they even begin, in the hustle-bustle of more important things, to feel that the agonies of dogs and birds are agonies of a minor order indeed.

About the time that other children are putting away childish things in favor of things more "mature," the potential artist begins to feel that maturity is not so much a gain as it is a loss. He senses that maturity, while it had at one time meant an exciting increase of privilege, now means that he must restrain himself from earlier pleasures. He realizes, one day, that if he were to write a recipe for maturity he would have to write a long list of things not to do. Whereas the other ex-children seem to have generally accepted the demands of maturity and, indeed, even seem to be enjoying it, the potential artist becomes more and more dissatisfied with it. It is probable that at this point some potential artists become derelicts, rebels, and even criminals, while others become artists. For as soon as the potential artist gives in to himself and attempts to re-evoke some of his earlier feelings and affinities; as soon as he tries again to see things with the glittering clarity of childhood; as soon as he feels real remorse for his aging (and for his mortality) and begins to feel nostalgia for a purer state of existence—as soon as he attempts to express these impressions and sensations he has become, to a degree depending on his skill, an artist.

In his book *Life Against Death,* Norman O. Brown observes that "the artist is the man who refuses initiation through education into the existing order (and) remains faithful to his childhood being." If the fledgling artist feels he has succeeded in expressing himself he usually remains an artist, though if he fails initially he may turn to something else, feeling forever an intense dissatisfaction with his second-choice career. "To speak truly," wrote Emerson, "few adult persons can see nature. Most persons do not see the sun. At least they have a very superficial seeing. The sun illuminates only the eye of the man, but shines into the eye and the heart of the child."

What possible bearing, one might ask, can these oversimplifications have on a study of art and neurosis? When Freud said [in "The Loss of Reality in Neurosis and Psychosis"] that "the excessive power of the influence of reality is decisive for neurosis," he meant, by "reality," that portion of life in the external world which requires the development of a sense of self in relation to external needs, and the ultimate development of an impression of oneself as viewed from without; he called the results of those two developments "ego" and "superego," respectively. In "Freud and Literature" Mr. Trilling very aptly defines the Freudian term *reality* as follows: "the limited reality by which we get our living, win our loves, catch our trains and our colds."

In other words, the reality that Freud said was "decisive for neurosis" is none other than the reality one encounters as a direct result of growing up to maturity. By the Freudian definition, then, it is *reality* that the artist of the preceding paragraph finds objectionable. Freud wrote: "A neurosis usually contents itself with avoiding the part of reality in question and protecting itself against coming in contact with it . . . It is from [the] world of phantasy that neurosis draws the material for recreating the world afresh according to its desires, and finds this material there, as a rule, by way of regression to an earlier period in life."

The artist, it would appear, in objecting to being channelled into some corner of society's reality and in retaining a strong respect for the impressions and values of childhood, is naturally susceptible to neurosis. (Indeed, if neurosis were a saleable commodity, salesmen would more than likely consider the artist an excellent prospect.) Although the evidence is not strong enough to prove that all artists are neurotics or even that "more artists are neurotics than anybody," as someone has said, it does seem to support a point already well substantiated: that artists could not very well be psychotics, for Freud also wrote [in "Neurosis and Psychosis"]: "In Meynart's amentia, the acute hallucinatory confusion which is perhaps the most extreme and striking form of psychosis, the outer world is either not perceived in the very least or else any perception of it remains absolutely without effect . . . We know that other forms of psychosis, the schizophrenias, incline to end in effective hebetude, that is, to lose all interest in the outer world."

If there is, at this point, any objection to a conclusion that the artist is, by his very nature, not only more susceptible to neurosis than psychosis but more susceptible to neurosis than is the average citizen of the modern community, the objection must lie with the premise that the artist can be, or would even desire to be, compared with the child. It would be, we may be sure, far easier to convince the av-

erage artist (if that isn't a contradiction in terms) than the average citizen, of the universality of our "hypothetical artist." Nonetheless, there is an observable tendency among poets, particularly the "lyrical poets" or the poets of that era called the "Romantic Period," to idealize childhood and even to express frankly a longing to return to a childish state.

Furthermore, it has been observed by many that comparisons between children and poets need not be confined to the similarity of their views of the world or their mutual capacity for what is often exaggerated compassion. F. J. Hoffman, for example, has observed [in *Freudianism and the Literary Mind*] that "the poet is less disturbed than the 'man of affairs' by bounds set ordinarily to free expression; in this respect, his mind compares favorably with the child's." Freud has noted [in "The Loss of Reality in Neurosis and Psychosis"] that there is yet another area in which the poet and neurotic are on common ground: "neurosis . . . is glad to attach itself, like a children's game, to a part of reality—some other part than the one against which it must protect itself; it endows it with a special meaning and a secret significance which we, not always quite correctly, call *symbolical.*"

The chief objection to an idea of the poet as neurotic seems to reside in the fact that there is, traditionally, a stigma attached to mental illness that at worst tends to equate insanity with immorality and at best to correlate it with intellectual incapacity. One is reminded of the story about the motorist who had just been given some excellent advice concerning the repair of a flat tire by an individual leaning on the fence of a mental hospital. With embarrassed gratitude the motorist had said, "Thank you very much—Are you an inmate here?" The other had laughed heartily and replied, "Look, Mac, I may be nuts, but I'm not stupid!"

Many—especially critics and scholars of literature—feel that if one admits that poets are anything but one hundred percent sane he is, in fact, admitting that poetry must suffer: that poetry stands in danger of being considered something analogous to a bodily secretion. Many, like Lionel Trilling in his essay "Freud and Literature," see in Freud's comments on the neurotic aspects of art a purely imaginary contempt: "And yet eventually Freud speaks of art with what we must indeed call contempt. Art, he tells us, is a 'substitute gratification,' and as such is 'an illusion in contrast to reality'."

The "contempt," of course, is not Freud's for art (for Freud was a great lover of art), but Mr. Trilling's for Freud. Perhaps, for the sake of the many genuine neurotics with whom we rub elbows every day, it might be better if the term "mental illness" might, by general agreement, come to refer only to those advanced neuroses and psychoses that require some degree of isolation from society, for even the housewife or businessman suffering from that common state of depression that medical men call "neurasthenia" are neurotics, though one seldom feels compelled to think of them as "mad."

If one accepts that in general use the term *madness* refers to a type of malady definitely more severe than the minor forms of neurosis, he must state categorically that the myth of the mad poet is quite false. On the other hand, there is no good reason to deny that the poet may be characterized as possessing neurotic qualities, and it may even be said with something considerably more credible than mere surmise that most poets are neurotics. The nature of art (admitting it has never been adequately defined) tends to imply that the ends of art must be achieved through intrinsically neurotic means. The acknowledgement by artists of an impression of external intervention during the creative act, the certain existence of the most extreme sort of concentration in the making of poetry, with the resultant taxing of the mental faculties, and the idea of creative compulsion would point by themselves to a conclusion that the mind of the artist operates under intense stress.

Furthermore, if neuroses were capable of being cultivated it is possible that a poet, knowing what we know of the nature of neurosis, might try to cultivate one. We do know that there is a propensity among some artists to bring upon themselves the artificial fixations produced by drugs, and we know that the fixation is a major element of neurosis. We also know that some poets have taken the trouble to have it demonstrated to them by medical authorities that they were, in fact, neurotic, and that they have then continued to coddle those very neuroses in the certain conviction, apparently, that they were the cause of their genius. Those who are readiest to point out that anti-social behavior does not make poets and that poets need not feel that they have the right to flaunt the laws of society are the last, oddly enough, to recognize that artistic behavior and criminal behavior (or better, rebellious behavior) may be considered the nearly predictable effects of certain neuroses; that is, they do not cause each other, but they are frequently the results of a common cause: a distrust of social "reality."

Yet even if one cannot accept the conclusion that poets are generally neurotic, he cannot deny that the poet is the victim of a peculiar paradox which, on the one hand, presents such a tremendous conflict that he cannot help but wonder whether he is to be driven thoroughly insane and which, on the other hand, seems to him the foundation of his entire existence, his *raison d'etre*. In seeing man as the animal closest to divinity, he likewise sees, for his exceptional possession of those very qualities that separate men from the other beasts, that he is in a sense even closer to the "divine" than other men.

While his natural reaction to this recognition must be to make the most of it, to continue faithfully in a metaphysical "direction" established for him by his nature, he senses a disturbing ungodliness in his past, a built-in uncleanness or unworthiness. This diffuse, past ugliness lends an unrealistic, hopeless character to his journey toward divinity, and he is torn between the passionate frenzy to continue and the gnawing feeling that, to succeed, he must return to his past ("regress") to eradicate whatever it is "back there" that he knows will sooner or later bring him to an irrevocable halt in his quest for personal and generic glory. Whether one calls this "Original Sin"—the fundamental "guilt" of mankind—or simply the recognition of one's animal nature, it is obvious that the poet (with others of

his mystical tribe) must reconcile it with his vision of what lies ahead or succumb ultimately to the conflict. (pp. 163-67)

E. Hale Chatfield, "Neurosis and Poetry: A Myth of Madness?" in University Review, Vol. XXXII, No. 3, Spring, 1966, pp. 163-67.

SUICIDE

Charles I. Glicksberg

[In the following essay, Glicksberg argues that suicide in literature is not merely the ultimate manifestation of a character's madness but a metaphysical affirmation of life.]

Only when the spiritual health of a culture declines does the suicidal obsession, as voiced in its literature, grow strong. A vital culture produces a literature that joyously affirms the will to live; it may create a tragic but never a suicidal art. It is only when energy ebbs, when a society loses its reason for being, that its literature reflects a neurasthenic condition; it becomes enamored of death and dissolution. The will that was once fed by instinctual sources of energy, rooted confidently in the womb of Nature, turns negative and destructive, tired of a life that is not supported by a sure foundation of meaning. What was once Dionysiac ecstasy and intoxication, a creative upsurge of animal faith, a capacity born of immense courage to face the ultimate Ground of Being in all its mysteriousness and terror, degenerates into a morbid preoccupation with the metaphysics of death. Today the popular sport of the intelligentsia is to condemn existence. Like Ivan Karamazov, they are prepared to return their passport, but their gesture has only a symbolic import. Like Ivan, despite their nihilistic logic, they cannot take their life. Sickly and disillusioned, they hold in contempt the precious gift the gods have bestowed on them. Intellect overrides instinct.

Not completely, of course. Literary suicides are not to be taken too seriously. They are really cases of what might be called psychic or symbolic suicide; the writers express the wish to die but fail to end their own life. What they betray is the bankruptcy of the will. Novelists like Celine, Paul Bowles, Sartre, and Camus betray all the symptoms of philosophical neurosis. Fortunately the creative imagination, as in tragedy, provides its own method of cure and redemption. Regardless of what the work seems to say, its whine of distress, its poignant cry of alienation, its indictment of the gods, its savage disgust with the sound and fury of existence, it serves a therapeutic purpose. Through his gesture of rebellion and repudiation the writer somehow manages to make his peace with life. The more gravely he contemplates the dialectics of suicide, the more surely does he come to perceive the absurdity of death that is self-sought and self-imposed. To die by one's own hand— that is obviously as absurd as to go on living. In moments of creative sanity he realizes the impotence of reason, its powerlessness to unravel the Gordian knot, to solve the riddle ever propounded anew by the eternal sphinx.

The will to live triumphs over all obstacles, all suffering, even the absolute of despair; it is indestructible. When Rasholnikov, in *Crime and Punishment,* delirious with fever, tormented by the thought of the murder he had committed, faces the idea of suicide, he is held back by this indefeasible will to live.

> "Where is it I've read," he broods, "that some one condemned to death says or thinks, an hour before his death, that if he had to live on some high rock, on such a narrow ledge that he'd only room to stand, and the ocean, everlasting darkness, everlasting solitude, everlasting tempest around him, if he had to remain standing on a square yard of space all his life, a thousand years, eternity, it were better to live so than to die at once! Life, whatever it may be!"

How can the mind cast off this illusion, if illusion it be, that clings so desperately to life? The fundamental premise that governs all mankind the world over is that life, despite the buffeting seas of adversity, is good. That is the categorical imperative which no species of rationalism can conquer—to live life, whatever it may be. Here is the manifestation of animal faith that confounds all the demonstrations of logic. Whereas the Buddhists can, by austere self-discipline, tame the raging fever of the will to live and embrace the goal of Nirvana, for the intellectuals of the West such a consummation is not only repugnant but inconceivable. They must find metaphysical sanctions for their negation of life. On one condition only can they justify self-murder: that life becomes unbearable. In recommending suicide as salvation, it is thus not death that they are celebrating; it is not Nirvana they seek, escape from the coil of Being; they are energetically protesting against a form of life that fails to satisfy their expectations. Paradoxically symbolic suicide, is an act of affirmation.

In discussing the literature of suicide, we are not referring to characters who, driven by failure or disease or mutilation or extreme pain, decide to make their exit from the state of life. There is nothing either heroic or tragic in such an ending. It may, as with Willy Loman in *Death of a Salesman,* communicate a deep sense of the pathos of existence but not the specifically tragic emotion, which is exalted and liberating, springing as it does from a flash of insight that transcends the illusion of time and the world of appearance. The tragic hero who resorts to suicide retains his dignity to the very last. He may reach a point not far removed from madness, but the justification he gives— and there must always be present an imaginatively convincing principle of justification—is never paltry or pitiful. He is imbued with a spirit of greatness as he prepares his own doom. In his decision to die he implicates all of life, God, the whole universe. Because he refuses to compromise, because he is willing to die for the sake of an ideal which he realizes can never be achieved on earth, because he thus passes judgement on life, he enables the living to identify themselves with his fate and thus, strange as it may seem, intensify and enrich their sense of life. For he dies as a rebel, not as a whimpering coward.

Suicides that reach the tragic heights in literature are thus never either psychopathological or purposeless. The suicide of a madman, for example, would lack tragic meaning. Even Kirillov's suicide, in *The Possessed,* is not a gratuitous act; it is a defiance of God and a promise of salvation for mankind. Septimus Smith, the deranged war veteran in *Mrs. Dalloway,* awakens our compassion, but he remains at best an inarticulate, pathetic figure in the background. It is what he suffers that awakens our sense of pity, not the quality of his insight or the stand he takes against life. The suicides who climb to tragic heights are those who know, or think they know, what they are doing and why. They are the metaphysical suicides, those who relentlessly question life and find it utterly lacking. What it lacks is the nourishing bread of meaning, a nobly sustaining purpose, a pattern of justification. It is their perception of cosmic absurdity—a vision that fills them with "nausea"—that leads them to seek death. Unable to endure a life that is meaningless, they can either go mad or commit suicide. Perhaps their decision to commit suicide is in itself a form of madness.

In Gide's fiction, the gratuitous act is a deliberate violation of law and morality. The protagonist murders not for profit but without reason. In Dostoevski's fiction the gratuitous act leads to suicide, only it is blended with a religious motive: the mythic self-crucifixion of the hero as a means of saving mankind from the enslaving illusion of God. It is the man-god who is exalted. What is of signal interest in this strategy of motivation is that the discovery of the absurd culminates in absurdity. The suicidal act is shown,

Edvard Munch's The Scream *(1893).*

by both Dostoevski and Camus, to be as much a matter of faith as the Pascalian wager or the Kierkegaardian leap. Were it not so, were these sacrificial heroes not actuated in their suicide by some humanly meaningful motive, it is doubtful if they could be fruitfully handled in literature. Characters who die because of grief or financial loss or a psychosis are not of tragic import. They die and are forgotten. The writer who with imaginative power portrays a metaphysical suicide has added a new value to the life of literature. He has brought the gods up for trial, he has passed judgement on life, he has undermined the foundations of faith, he has overcome the tyranny of the flesh, the despotism of instinct.

Our thesis holds that literary suicide is tragic only when it is rooted in a metaphysical or "principled" rejection of life. Not that this needs to be reasoned out in logical terms; logic is not the ruler of life. It is the internal "logic" that counts, the battle the protagonist fights within, the motives that finally prompt him to say no to life. Like Stavrogin in *The Possessed,* he finds life not worth having and (after having experimented with all the drugs, all the pleasures, all the perversions) gives it up in disdain, knowing as he does so that even this final gesture is futile.

This is the nihilism that dominates a large part of Existentialist literature. Once God disappears as the creator and controller of the human drama, once existence is infected with the cancer of absurdity, then death, like life, becomes irremediably absurd. The modern hero expects to achieve nothing by his act of suicide. His protest is without consequences; it is useless. That is why Kirillov is fundamentally an unheroic, if fanatical, character. He is obsessed, and yet convinced by his obsession that he is eminently sane in his messianic ambition: he will emancipate humanity from the lie of religion, their craven, infantile dependence on God. By killing himself, he will prove that man is God. His suicide will be the first revolutionary demonstration of godlike freedom, a blow directed against the will of God.

Kirillov is, from the beginning, searching for the underlying reason why men are afraid to kill themselves. Two prejudices, he feels, restrain people from leaping into the vast indifference of death: one is the fear of pain, a small prejudice; the other prejudice stems from the fear of what will happen in the other world. Furthermore, there are two types of suicides: those who kill themselves out of passion, sorrow, or revenge, not deterred by anticipation of pain; the metaphysical suicides belong to the other type, those who kill themselves as the result of reasoning. Kirillov has worked out what he considers a perfectly logical theory of salvation. "There will be full freedom when it will be just the same to live or not to live. That's the goal for all." Once this truth is grasped, then no one will care to live. To the sensible objection that if man fears death it is because he loves life, a powerful instinct implanted by nature, Kirillov, the demented philosopher of death, has his answer ready. That is the very deception he is determined to unmask.

Kirillov declares that he has always been surprised at the fact that everyone goes on living. He has found his faith: "If there is no God, then I am God." If God exists, then He rules with an iron hand and no one can escape from His Will. If not, then Kirillov is free to assert his self-will. That is how he can defeat God. He is resolved to manifest his self-will, and the highest manifestation of self-will is to kill himself, without any cause at all. Here is the Promethean rebel who will be the first in the history of mankind to disprove the existence of God. "What is there to live for?" The laws of Nature, he points out, did not spare Christ, who died for a lie and thus made clear that all of life is a hideous mockery. It is belief in the old God that is responsible for all the suffering of man. Kirillov's religious mania emerges most clearly when he defends the logic of his proposed action:

> I can't understand how an atheist could know that there is no God and not kill himself on the spot. To recognize that there is no God and not to recognize at the same instant that one is God himself is an absurdity, else one would certainly kill himself. If you recognize it you are sovereign and then you won't kill yourself but will live in the greatest glory. But one, the first, must kill himself, for else who will begin and prove it?

By this act of proof he will abolish the fear of death. By asserting his self-will, he is bound "to believe that I don't believe". This is the terrible new age of freedom he is ushering in.

The contradictions in Kirillov's position are all too apparent: he is a religious fanatic, a mad mystic, who has dedicated himself to the task of annihilating God. He is fond of life, even though he has decided to shoot himself. He does not believe in an eternal life after death, only in eternal life here on earth. He believes that the new Saviour will come and his name will be the man-god. Kirillov's suicide is a ritualistic act of sacrifice. The next stage in the evolution of the race will witness the extinction of God, but first someone must act as the assassin of God and reveal the mighty, liberating secret that there is nothing to fear, not even death.

Dostoevski contrasts Kirillov's suicide with that of Stavrogin. The latter suffers from hallucinations—the fate Dostoevski reserves for the nihilistic rebels like Raskolnikov and Ivan. Stavrogin feels homeless on earth, without close ties of any kind, incapable of giving himself in love or in faith. He has tried his strength everywhere and has not learned to know himself. He does not know what to do with his energy, his time, his talent. He derives pleasure from evil though he desires to do good. What troubles him intensely and at last drives him to suicide is the discovery that his desires are too weak to guide him. He is a man without hope. He cannot feel and therefore cannot believe. He cannot share the utopian dreams of the revolutionists. He has lost connection with his country and his roots. He is nothing. From him, as he realizes toward the end, nothing has come but negation, and even this was without greatness, without force. Kirillov could at least be carried away by the passion of an idea and take his life; Kirillov was a great soul because he could lose his reason. Stavrogin declares: "I can never lose my reason, and I can never believe in an idea to such a degree as he did. I can never, never, never shoot myself." This is the punishment he must bear: he blew neither hot nor cold; he could not transcend his analytical, ironic mind. He is afraid of suicide: the supreme act of absurdity in a drama of life that he regarded as inexpressibly absurd. Even the act of killing himself will be, he knows, another sham—"the last deception in an endless series of deceptions". Yet he returns home and hangs himself in the loft. Despair has conquered his titanic pride.

Dostoevski has prophetically anticipated many of the trends of modern fiction. Once the religious sense was banished from fiction, the human being ceased to possess any genuine importance. Nietzsche, in *The Genealogy of Morals,* brilliantly shows how the growth of science resulted in a loss of individuality, the reduction of the human being to atomistic insignificance. If the novelist were to accept this scientific version of human nature, his art would be severely damaged. To escape the trap of determinism, he focuses on dreams, introspection, the unconscious, the inner world of man. A Catholic novelist like Graham Greene, instead of portraying a gray, neutral universe of energy, draws a vivid picture of the struggle between good and evil, the efforts the beleaguered soul makes to save itself from damnation. But though his characters are saved or damned by their thoughts, their state of grace, they lack the depth, the haunting complexity, the metaphysical passion of Dostoevski's *dramatis personae.* In a personal essay, "The Revolver in the Cupboard", Graham Greene describes his early obsession with suicide and his scheme for carrying it out. Like Stavrogin he was perpetually bored; freedom bored him. When his attempts at killing himself failed, he became bored with these pseudo-suicides. But the problem of suicide is not delineated in his novels except in *The Heart of the Matter,* where it is tied up with the religious issue.

It is Existentialist fiction that projects with intense imaginative pessimism the realization of man's nothingness. Man's existence contains its own negation and is headed inevitably toward death. Man is oppressed by the sense of his finitude, his involvement in death. As he contemplates his own mortality, he achieves the gift of freedom, but out of it springs the feeling of dread: the perception that he hangs precariously over the abyss of nothingness.

Hence he comes to face the question: why live? The Existentialist concerns himself of necessity with the problem of the meaning of life. Thus we come back to the ontological and religious contradictions that tormented Dostoevski's principal characters. It is in the inaccessible privacy of the heart that the energy is born to make an end of it all and that man leaps out of the circle of time. That is where the determination to commit suicide has its inception. When man glimpses the blinding truth of nothingness, he is plunged into eternal night. Somewhere, at some point in his journey to the end of darkness, he breaks his attachment to life and arrives at this fateful decision. What does such a decision reveal if not that life is too much for the man; he no longer considers it worth the trouble to go on living. By consenting to death, he recognizes the absurdity of all attitudes, even this habitual love of life. Why suffer? Why strive? For what purpose?

Suddenly he is overcome with the feeling that he is an utter stranger in a universe which is not only indifferent

to his needs and ideals but completely incomprehensible. Deprived of all consolatory illusions, he regards himself as an alien on earth, whose life—and all of life as a matter of fact—is absurd. Once he apprehends this shattering truth, what is he to do? Is suicide, Camus asks in *The Myth of Sisyphus,* the only logical alternative? Yet many who negate the world still cling tenaciously to life. Rare indeed is it to find a perfect consistency between theory and conduct. The will to live is not to be broken by dint of philosophical argument. Life surpasses thought; the body, by a perverse, unconquerable logic of its own, triumphs over the mandates of reason. Hence man tends to flee from the consequences of his thinking, to evade the ultimate issue; he builds up high the tower of hope—the hope of immortality, redemption through faith in God, devotion to some cause that will fill his life with meaning. This is the biological illusion that betrays him.

But if he is actually convinced that life has no meaning, does it follow that it is therefore not worth living? Why do people commit suicide? Does the perception of absurdity infecting all of existence necessarily lead to suicide? As Camus phrases it, "Does the absurd dictate Death?" What does logic reveal when it is pursued inexorably to the end? Do human beings obey the principle of logic even to the absurd climax of death? The reasoning is in itself highly absurd. The fountains of feeling are not to be overlooked; they flow from mysterious subterranean sources and they disclose more, much more, than the language in which we attempt to clothe them. And these feelings are made known to us in fitful glimpses by our actions and commitments, by what we believe or think we believe, by our illusions as well as our sincerity. Feelings thus disclose themselves by the actions they motivate, the state of mind they support. Hence Camus maintains that true knowledge cannot be achieved; that is why it is so difficult to define the feeling of absurdity. How shall one deal with this aberration of absurdity? The main thing is not to compromise, not to draw back in fear from the implications of the truth. The absurd man—that is the phrase Camus uses—seeks to discover if it is possible to live *without appeal.*

Again the problem of suicide arises. The absurd man knows that in living he keeps the sense of the absurd alive. Camus then proceeds to demonstrate—by no means convincingly—why absurd experience is remote from suicide. Whereas the suicide accepts existence, the man in revolt refuses to do so. The former anticipates his end in the future and thus settles the problem of the absurd, whereas the absurd man rejects death. He confronts the Gorgon-face of reality without illusion. In short, revolt is the opposite of renunciation. Suicide is repudiation. The absurd man, exhausting the limits of experience, relies on his ultimate weapon—defiance.

Like Kirillov, Camus asks if man is free or is subject to a master. If God exists, then man is not free and God must stand condemned as the originator of evil. If man is free, then he must bear full responsibility for his actions. What kind of freedom, after all, can God confer on man? To have freedom—that means freedom to think and to act. The philosophy of the absurd, while it abolishes the kingdom of eternity, restores freedom to man. But even this is an illusion. The numinous encounter with the absurd destroys all possibility of meaning. Death is not only the sole reality but the supreme absurdity. Nothing in this condition of man can be changed. But without the assurance of eternity, what value can freedom possibly have?

Once the double illusion of freedom and of a high purpose to be fulfilled in life is destroyed, man is truly free, for he has been liberated from the myth of the future. The absurd man finally accepts a universe which is incomprehensible and built on nothingness; he finally accepts a life that is without hope and without consolation. Rejecting the solution offered by suicide, Camus stresses the importance of being aware of one's life to the utmost, to see clearly, to refuse the temptation of suicide.

Camus therefore concludes that the novelist must keep faith with the absurd and renounce every illusion. He points to *The Possessed* as a classic example of the absurd. If life is indeed absurd, then why not condemn Nature and make an end of it all? Logical suicide, however, is an act of revenge. Kirillov takes his life because he is possessed by an idea. His suicide is an act of revolt; he behaves absurdly but his action is dictated by an overweening ambition. If God does not exist, then he is god. But God does not exist; therefore he must demonstrate the truth of this redemptive meaning by killing himself. He illustrates the tragic dilemma of the intellectual who confronts life in a universe that has no God. That is his besetting madness and yet he is not mad. He refuses to serve any master. By slaying God he usurps His power. He kills himself in order to liberate man from the thraldom of hope. Strangely enough, it is out of love for deluded mankind that he takes his life. He is the first Existentialist hero, the personification of the absurd.

The modern fictional protagonist, living in an age of Freud, global wars, atomic bombs, and genocidal manias, is thrust into a reality and and a world of time that is radically different from the one in which the Dostoevskian hero lived. The modern "hero" who debates whether or not to commit suicide is passing judgement on the quality of life in the twentieth century. It is society he is condemning as well as the universe at large. If he cannot believe in the Second Coming, if there is no God, if time stretches out meaninglessly to the crack of eternity, then being alive is a useless privilege. Like Quentin in *The Sound and the Fury,* the modern "hero", before he commits suicide, is obsessed with the burden of time. It is this obsession with time that adds a new dimension to the metaphysics of absurdity.

The twentieth-century literary obsession with time is psychologically linked with the awareness of death. Man cannot reverse the movement of time, since each moment lived draws him closer to the end. Time is his burden and his doom because it brings vividly before him the knowledge of his own death. Here is the existential contradiction that overshadows all of life: time the creator and destroyer, womb and tomb. All that man strives for so earnestly may be cut short by the coming of death. This is the spectre that haunts the imagination of modern man—the realization of the futility of life dominated by time. But few of the characters in contemporary fiction who utter an Ev-

erlasting Nay ever commit suicide. They seem to have no intention of bidding this farcical world good-bye. Why die and thus give up the opportunity of condemning a world which is steeped in absurdity? They curse existence, these rebels, at the same time that they refuse to abandon it. If there is a lack of logic in the rôle they play, this is the fault of logic, not of life. If man dies, he loses everything. It is the threat of death, not the suicidal compulsion, that is the recurrent motif in contemporary literature.

The modern literati have achieved an uneasy truce with the finality of death. Absurdity drives out the logical necessity for dying by one's own hand; if it is absurd to live it is even more absurd to die. Camus voices the singular courage of the humanist who, having disposed of God and the question of immortality, is resolved to live as fully as he can while he protests against the universal injustice of death. But it is difficult, if not foolish, to argue with a literary philosopher of the absurd. The logic of the race is rooted in animal faith. As long as one decided to live on—and the writer has already decided that by composing a book—then the only conceivable purpose of life is richness of experience, the fulfillment of the self. The creative man may, like Dostoevski or Camus, question the ultimate meaning of existence, he may even perceive the essential absurdity of the universe and man's place in it, but he will never look upon his own productions as absurd. To recognize absurdity and to live productively in the face of it— that, too, is an affirmation of the courage to be. The writer

---

Michel Foucault on madness, imagination, and logic:

Imagination is not madness. Even if in the arbitrariness of hallucination, alienation finds the first access to its vain liberty, madness begins only beyond this point, when the mind binds itself to this arbitrariness and becomes a prisoner of this apparent liberty. At the moment he wakes from a dream, a man can indeed observe: "I am imagining that I am dead": he thereby denounces and measures the arbitrariness of the imagination—he is not mad. He is mad when he posits as an affirmation of his death—when he suggests as having some value as truth—the still-neutral content of the image "I am dead." And just as the consciousness of truth is not carried away by the mere presence of the image, but in the act which limits, confronts, unifies, or dissociates the image, so madness will begin only in the act which gives the value of truth to the image. There is an original innocence of the imagination: "The imagination itself does not err, since it neither denies nor affirms but is fixed to so great a degree on the simple contemplation of an image"; and only the mind can turn what is given in the image into abusive truth, in other words, into error, or acknowledged error, that is, into truth: "A drunk man thinks he sees two candles where there is but one; a man who has a strabismus and whose mind is cultivated immediately acknowledges his error and accustoms himself to see but one." Madness is thus beyond imagination, and yet it is profoundly rooted in it; for it consists merely in allowing the image a spontaneous value, total and absolute truth.

Michel Foucault, in his Madness and Civilization: A History of Insanity in the Age of Reason, *1967, originally published as* Histoire de la folie, *1961.*

has gazed into the heart of being and he is under an inner necessity, that transcends the metaphysics of absurdity, to deliver an imaginative report of the truth of his experience. The supreme absurdity of the twentieth-century writer is that, believing in many cases neither in the man-god nor in the God-man, he still goes on living productively. That is how the creative life-force surges up in him and triumphs over the death-instinct. (pp. 384-95)

> *Charles I. Glicksberg, "To Be Or Not to Be: The Literature of Suicide," in* Queen's Quarterly, *Vol. LXVII, No. 3, Autumn, 1960, pp. 384-95.*

MADNESS IN AMERICAN LITERATURE

June O. Underwood

[*In the following excerpt, Underwood analyzes portraits of madness in American pioneer plains literature of the early twentieth century.*]

The Plains, with its wind, sand, and extremes of space and temperature, has a very bad reputation. [Ole Edvart] Rølvaag in *Giants in the Earth* entitles Book II, Chapter 4, "The Great Plain Drinks the Blood of Christian Men and Is Satisfied." Walter Prescott Webb says, "The Plains exerted a peculiarly appalling effect on women. . . . The wind drove some to the verge of insanity and caused others to migrate." In Sandoz's *Old Jules* there are, by rough count, eleven different points in Jules's life when the "monotony of the hills . . . broke through the crust in lawsuits, fights, suicide, murders, and insanities." In short, the environment of the Plains is blamed by all kinds of writers for a whole host of mental instabilities. Novelists use Plains madness as a way to build tension and create character contrast; diarists and memoirists record its effects on everyday lives.

In this [essay] I am deliberately using "madness" in its vaguest sense. The inability to cope, accompanied by slow changes of character and habit, is the simplest criterion for madness. Suicide, an extreme inability to cope, obviously involves mental instability. Depression, traditionally suffered by women and seen in fits of crying, slovenly dress, and an aversion to family and community gatherings, is also a sign. Critics of western literature do not identify violence as a symptom of madness. Some of the violence in the literature is mere lawlessness, but that which breaks out under the pressure of blizzard-beseiged huts, for example, and is accompanied by other symptoms and causes must be seen as mental breakdown. Personality and cultural factors often underlie the aversion to the harsh land to produce loss of control. In other words, the Plains sometimes exacerbates outbreaks of "lawsuits, fights, suicide, murders, and insanities," but the primary cause is found elsewhere. Causes for mental breakdown range from economic frustration, personal displacement and

loss of identity, to guilt and isolation. All these are parts not only of a physical environment but of a mental landscape.

Life on the Plains was tough. Men and women alike faced the limits of their capabilities. Many won out over the environment, forcing it to allow their habitation. Others succumbed to it, going home, going mad, dying. Webb says that women were responsible for the numbers of pioneers who retreated from the Plains. Nothing in the literature bears this thesis out. The American folksong, "Sweet Betsy of Pike," has Betsy telling her fearful Ike, who wants to go home, "You'll go by yourself if you do." In the pulp fiction, *The Soddy*, by Sarah Comstock, Terry, the wife, stays on the claim when her husband leaves. She says, "Dexter has a delusion. . . . I've read about delusions—they come when you're worried and worn past what you can stand. He'll get well—I know it. . . . He'll come back! I'm holding on to the soddy till he comes." Among the diaries and memoirs, as many women as men insist upon staying at critical moments of despair.

Leaving is generally thought to be a sign of defeat, especially by those who stay. John Ise, in *Sod and Stubble*, records the sight of people being driven out by drought in 1880: "The discouraged settlers trekked out of the drought-stricken country. Day after day they passed by, grizzled, dejected and surly men; sick, tired, and hopeless women." Yet in many of the memoirs and diaries, moving out seemed, like corn mush, to be an accepted part of life. Mollie Dorsey Sanford [in *Mollie: The Diary of Mollie Dorsey Sanford in Nebraska and Colorado Territories 1857-1866*, 1959] follows her husband from eastern Nebraska (where she has moved from Indianapolis) through many mining towns and army posts in Colorado before they settle in Denver. In *There Have to Be Six*, by Amelia Meuller, the family moves from Kansas to Texas to Oklahoma and back to Kansas, sometimes in defeat but more often in optimism. Sonora Babb's family of *An Owl on Every Post* moves from Oklahoma to 360 acres in eastern Colorado where they live in a sod hut and then move to southwestern Kansas, where they settle in town. All this takes place over a scant two or three year time span. In Nannie T. Alderson's *A Bride Goes West*, she says, "In all my years of marriage, I never had trees over my head; they could have been planted, but we never lived long enough in one place for them to grow." Moving around seems not only a way to stave off starvation (although that enters into it), but also a way to act, to control. Whole families went further west or east, rented other farms or moved to town, and by this activity circumvented madness.

For those who stayed in place, stability maintained itself in one of two ways. One way was to recreate as closely as possible an older culture. This was of particular importance to women, whose roles, especially if they were married and had children, were generally modeled after the cultures from which they came. In Cather's *O Pioneers!*, Mrs. Bergson, Alexandra's mother, "had never quite forgiven John Bergson for bringing her to the end of the earth; but now that she was there, she wanted to be let alone to reconstruct her old life in so far as that was possible. She could still take some comfort in the world if she had bacon in the cave, glass jars on the shelves, and sheets in the press." In *An Owl on Every Post*, the one effort the father makes to get the sod hut ready for his wife and children is to erect two cedar clothesline posts. The morning after their arrival, his wife kerosenes (to get rid of the bugs) and washes all the bedding in the hut. Both her husband and father-in-law had lived with the bugs for years without bothering to kill them.

This mode of retaining sanity, given conditions in the Plains, was difficult. Neither the kind of farming nor the mode of housekeeping was conducive to an easy application of old ways. Women were hard pressed to maintain the image of the frail Victorian while washing clothes on a scrubboard, chasing pigs, and killing bed bugs. Nannie Alderson notes, "As a guide to housekeeping in the West I had brought a cook book and housekeeping manual which our dear old pastor at home had given me for a wedding present. This book, written by a southern gentlewoman for southern gentlewomen, didn't contain a single cake recipe that called for fewer than six eggs." The section on doing laundry began, " 'Before starting to wash, it is essential to have a large, light airy laundry with at least seven tubs.' I had one tub, a boiler, and a dishpan."

Given the nature of the difficulties, many of the pioneers found it saner to actively engage the new conditions rather than attempt to maintain or re-erect the old. Per Hansa, Morissa Kirk, and Alexandra Bergson, to name some fictional characters, all meet the challenges actively. Per Hansa, for example, is ill at ease with the Plains only during the winter when he has no activity to engage in. Men, or women like Alexandra who are unaffected by the Victorian myth about women's place, could work outside, becoming part of the landscape rather than fighting it. Alexandra is only happy outside; the land "seemed beautiful to her, rich and strong and glorious. Her eyes drank in the breadth of it. . . . " Alexandra's house is "unfinished and uneven in comfort. . . . You feel that, properly, Alexandra's house is the big out-of-doors, and that it is in the soil that she expresses herself best." Morissa Kirk, of Sandoz's *Miss Morissa* (1955), not only is the first doctor in western Nebraska, but also begins one of the first gardening and farming operations in the region.

This active engagement, accompanied by a change of old values and expectations, appears not only in the characters of fiction but also in the non-fictional memoirs. Alderson says, "Back home . . . my stepfather . . . wouldn't dream of going into the kitchen, even to carry a pail of water, and all the men were the same. But in Montana that first spring there would always be three or four in the kitchen getting a meal—Mr. Alderson, Mr. Zook, one of the cowboys and myself." In *Memories of the Old Emigrant Days in Kansas 1862-1865,* Mrs. Adela Orpen reminisces about homesteading with her father and aunt. The family allows the 9-year old Adela a great deal of freedom—she wears bloomers and has her own horse—but the aunt, of course, is tied to old customs. Auntie suffers a breakdown. "She was found crying. . . . She was crying because everything was hopelessly ugly, and even the kitchen floor was always dirty, and it was useless to wash it." Adela's father recognizes Auntie's depression and pre-

scribes a radical action to re-establish her sense of control. "This would never do, so my father straightaway bought her a pony. She must fare forth riding, and go down to the creek and see water there, when there was any. At all events, Auntie must get out of the house and refresh her mind and body with riding." Auntie recovers quickly.

Thus the dangers of mental instability on the Plains were averted in two ways: the first was to re-establish, as closely as possible, the way of the home from which one came. The second was to actively wrestle with the environment, to immerse oneself in it wholly. However, maintaining the old ways, as we saw with "Auntie," was fraught with certain dangers.

The re-enacting of the old ways often magnified the contradictions between expectations and reality; the baggage of an outmoded or inappropriate culture sometimes caused madness. Beret of *Giants in the Earth* feels tremendous guilt for leaving her parents; Letty of Scarborough's *The Wind* has been trained as a genteel southern lady and is helpless when confronted by West Texas homesteading. Mr. Schimerda of *My 'Antonia* has to leave behind the gaity, music, and companionship which he valued so highly. Frank Shabata (*O Pioneers!*) is forced into a role as farmer which frustrates all his city ways. Guilt, caused by one's early training, isolation from people like oneself, frustration growing out of an inability to adapt, and displacement from one's expected role all serve to drive the characters of pioneer literature mad.

Rølvaag's Beret is the classic case of madness on the Plains. She is frightened by the new life and feels its threats as punishment. She goes into a depression, not caring for her appearance, withdrawing from her family and their meager social life. Her depression, in spite of Rølvaag's ambivalence about the Plains themselves, is the result of the force of her faith. She feels she has sinned against God and thus the Plains wait to punish her:

> Ever since she had come out here a grim conviction had been taking stronger and stronger hold on her. This was her retribution! Now had fallen the punishment which the Lord God had meted out to her. . . . She had been gotten with child by Per Hansa out of wedlock; nevertheless, no one had compelled her to marry him. . . . Her parents, in fact, had set themselves against the marriage with all their might. . . . Whenever she had been with him she had forgotten the admonitions and prayers of her father and mother. . . . He [Per Hansa] had been life itself to her. . . . Had there ever been a transgression so grievous as hers!

This strong sense of religious duty is clearly a part of her culture; others in the Norwegian community suffer as she does. Both Tönseten and Per Hansa tremble when the preacher arrives, for they fear they have committed unforgivable sins: Tönseten by marrying a couple (he is justice of the peace) who badly need marrying and Per Hansa by naming his child Peder Victorious. Both men fear they have committed sacrilege and both weep at discovering God (in the form of the preacher) is not angry with them. The strength of the religious training and consequent possibility for tremendous guilt is clear. Beret's attempts to build a life like her old one lead to impossible contradictions.

Scarborough's Letty suffers from an inability to cope with a new kind of identity. The life she yearns for, the life she has led in the past, is so drastically different from that which she has come to that she has no resources with which to cope. She is totally unprepared to deal with the realities of Plains homemaking. "She realized her shortcomings as a housekeeper; she couldn't put her heart into the work, and then too, she had never any training for it. At home Mammy had treated her like a child that couldn't wait on itself properly." In addition, she had loved the gentle Virginia countryside from which she had come and had passionately wished to be allowed to stay there. As her sanity slips, she daydreams about the world:

> She lived a dual life . . . sun-scorched plain . . . waste of sand . . . leafless mesquite bushes, dead swords of the yucca [and then] a far off land, a gracious smiling country . . . where magnolias opened their waxen petals in lovely curves to show their golden hearts, where yellow jasmine climbed up into the trees.

When Letty is rudely taken from her Virginia life she responds with the lady-like coquetry she has been trained to; her cousin and most of the cowboys she encounters fall in love with that image and it, as much as anything else in the novel, is her downfall. She is an unthinking product of a stereotyping society, but no one, not herself nor the men around her, are aware of this. When she is seduced by Wirt Roddy, the villain, it is merely the finishing blow to her romantic idealism. She kills him and runs into the windstorm, committing suicide.

Both these authors are ambivalent about the role of the Plains in the breakdown of the women. Rølvaag analyzes Beret's religious and familial guilt, but also feels the land causes madness. In the chapter entitled "The Great Plain Drinks the Blood of Christian Men and Is Satisfied," he begins with a description of "the strange spell of sadness which the unbroken solitude cast upon the minds of some. Many took their own lives; asylum after asylum was filled with disordered beings who had once been human." Scarborough depicts Letty as weak and her upbringing as totally inappropriate. Yet she begins *The Wind:* "The wind was the cause of it all. The sand, too, had a share in it, and human beings were involved, but the wind was the primal force." Both authors see the physical environment as a force with which puny humans must reckon. However, each shows those humans as molded by cultural factors which determine their mind set.

Willa Cather is hardly ambivalent about the exaltation she (and a number of her characters) feel in the land. She does not blame the land for madness, but recognizes that some people can't face its rawness. In *My Antonia* Mr. Shimerda's suicide comes during a blizzard, the first terrible winter of his life on the Plains. He, like Letty, cannot forget the world he has left behind. Antonia tells Jim Burden, "My papa sad for old country. . . . My papa he cry for leave his old friends what make music with him. He love very much the man that play the long horn." Mr. Shimerda kills himself, unable to cope with a world in which it

seemed "peace and order had vanished from the earth." Antonia establishes, after much struggle, her own "peace and order," and through her Cather makes a statement about the land and possible ways of relating dynamically to it.

Another Cather character, Frank Shabata of *O Pioneers!,* is dealt with in more detail. He kills his wife and her lover in what seems to be a relatively simple act of jealous rage. But his stability has clearly been shaken much earlier. When Marie married him, Frank had been the "buck of the beer-gardens—with his silk hat and tucked shirt and blue frock-coat, wearing gloves and carrying a little wisp of a yellow cane." After Frank's marriage the couple move to a farm and when Carl Linstrum meets him, "he was burned a dull red to his neck band and there was a three days stubble on his face." He becomes infuriated over small things: "One of the Goulds was getting a divorce, and Frank took it as a personal affront. . . . The more he read, the angrier he grew. . . . Marie thought it hard that the Goulds, for whom she had nothing but good will, should make her so much trouble. . . . Frank was always reading about the doings of rich people and feeling outraged." Frank's instability builds up over the years; his erratic temper is frightening to everyone. His displacement, removal from the life in which he felt comfortable and from an identity which he felt was his own, leads to his breakdown and Marie's and Emil's murder.

These four examples of acculturation and identity madness are literary. They are plot-centered, traumatic, extreme. In historical records, however, the breakdowns seem to be accepted as part of the normal burden of life. The diaries and published memoirs show madness as a temporary element in the life of most of the pioneers. Women became depressed and silent for finite periods of time; men became violent and acted out their rage and frustration and then subsided. In *There Have to Be Six,* Meuller speaks of a period in which her mother is "unwell." "Mama became ill with the flu. Long after her temperature was back to normal and she no longer had to stay in bed, she continued to be listless and despondent. To Hilda and me it seemed as though she did not want to get well; that she had lost all interest in living." The mother refuses to join the Christmas preparations and celebrations and at one point screams frantically at the carol-singing family to be quiet and leave her some peace. In the next chapter she seems to have recovered. Mrs. Orpen depicts her "Auntie," who cried over nothing (or everything) until she got her horse. "Sir, Looney," in Babb's *An Owl on Every Post,* seems to have suffered and survived a lengthy breakdown, without aid from anyone. He lived afterwards in a dugout, fondling his dead wife's hair, eccentric, but able to cope. Sometimes depression or breakdown was cured, or at least modified, by time. At other times, moving or a change in habit acted as a cure.

A distinction needs to be made between the active, long brewing madness of Beret or Frank Shabata, and the temporary loss of control caused by conditions on the Plains. The soddies, trapped in their 14-by-14 foot huts for days during a blizzard, must have had many moments of insanity. Per Hansa says, "In the dead of winter, of course, when the blizzards are raging and we don't see any other folks for weeks at a time, she [Beret] has days when she seems to go all to pieces; but I hardly reckon that as the disease—that sort of things happens to a good many of us, let me tell you." Madness breaks out when the environmental pressures increase. Old Jules points out the result of a drought: "Water was all they needed. . . . [They could remain] a year or two longer,—at the best,—with more of them hanging from the ridgepoles by ropes and getting free rides to Norfolk to the crazy house."

Those who survive such onslaughts of instability seem to do so either by force of their own character, a life-loving tenacity, or through an alliance with someone who waits them out. Romantic men often chose to come west; they sometimes were lucky enough to bring or find hard-headed women to sustain them. This theme of men as dreamers is quite strong in both the fiction and non-fiction. Old Jules's fourth wife, initially a dainty, pretty woman, becomes the hardheaded stabilizing force in Jules's eccentric romantic vision. Sarah Comstock's Terry works in the fields and, when she is too pregnant to do that any longer, drives a medicine wagon, hanging on to the homestead until charismatic but unstable Dexter returns. Sarah Donnelly Wooley, in Fred Trump's *Uphill in the Sun* (1973), marries a music lover and an adulterer, has eight children, and manages to support all of them, including the husband, through much of her life. One of Avis Dungan Carlson's grandparents, in *Small World, Long Gone,* taught her husband to read and regretted it long after, since he became an educated dreamer, but not a farmer. Carlson says of this grandmother, "she bore ten children, the last when she was forty-three and raised seven of them. She cooked with a wood fire, scrubbed with lye soap, washed clothes on a board, raised her own poultry, and grew her own vegetables, made the family's soap and clothing, even to the men's overalls." To come West, someone had to have the vision, the romance, and the force of character to pull others (wife, husband, family) into that vision. But to stay there after they arrived took perhaps opposite qualities.

Thus far, fact and fiction, biography and novels, have been liberally mixed. But in order to understand the role of madness in the pioneers' lives it is finally necessary to separate the two literary modes. In the factual writings, madness seems to be more prevalent and more complex. It is not a single thing; it derives both from the environment and from acculturation; it comes with bad weather, with money troubles, with moving around. It appears and disappears, is minor or major, sometimes tragic, sometimes, alas, merely tedious. It appears in male and female alike and is conditioned by a great variety of factors, including character, company, and the Plains themselves. It is generally not fatal; it is mostly a part of the difficulty of living. At times it makes small dramas in a monotonous life; at other times it simply exists among other things of the quotidian.

However, in the fiction madness has a simpler and a more dramatic role. It serves as an excellent device for arousing conflict and tension. Beret's struggle against what she feels is the menace of the Plains is vivid and becomes more

acute as the novel progresses. That madness, like the madness of *The Wind,* serves as a major plot device. The drama in both cases works itself inexorably toward tragedy.

Madness also serves to highlight the heroism and strength of those who encounter it or actively battle against it. Per Hansa's superman skills and fearlessness are given focus and clarity when contrasted to Beret's passivity and fear. Letty's inability to cope is directly contrasted to Cora's "unwomanly" management of her romantic husband, her household and the land itself. Terry's saving of the homestead is a dramatic and heroic adventure and works partly because of Dexter's weakness.

The violence which marks the fictional insanity is useful to literary plots. Frank's murder of Emile and Marie precipitates Alexandra's realization that she needs Carl Linstrum. She takes on human qualities in her suffering, and thus madness serves to bring greater awareness. As a device to serve literary realists, the brutality of madness is effective; Hamlin Garland in particular depicts the harsh effects of the endless hard work and hard environment.

In short, while madness in non-fiction is complex and woven into narratives bearing other themes, the madness in the fiction often serves as a major dramatic device, for plot, for contrast, or for awakening a character to new possibilities. Fictional madness is perhaps more vivid, yet more simple, than that which occurred in real life. Mad-

---

Roman S. Struc on literary representations of madness:

From the study of literary documents dealing with madness, two categories seem discernible. The first appears to be a literary rendition of psychopathological conditions in the realistic of naturalistic tradition, *i.e.,* treatments of the theme which do not purport to go beyond the phenomenon as such and emphasize accurate description, often genesis, of such pathological conditions. . . .

The other category is of an infinitely more complex variety. Madness, apart from the more or less accurate account of mental derangement, functions primarily as a symbolic representation, as a cipher for larger and more complex matters. The choice of the theme is determined not by the accident of interest and individual curiosity of the author alone, but rather by artistic and intellectual necessity whose imperative "objective correlative" is madness. We must not think that madness as symbolic representation stands for something specific in an allegorical sense; but, rather, that while frequently being an accurate depiction of a scientifically identifiable mental derangement, it transcends at the same time the immediate context of psychopathology, touching on and pointing to problems of general human validity.

Madness in this second sense could be more accurately described as a representation of a *Grenzsituation,* of an extreme human condition, of man's existential predicaments, and not exclusively as a record of "abnormal" states.

Roman S. Struc, in his "Madness as Existence: An Essay on a Literary Theme," in Research Studies, *March, 1970.*

ness in both worlds brings out the difficulty, the horror, of the Plains environment for some people. It also shows the strength and resilience and insight of others—their love for, rather than fear of, the land. Madness, for men and women alike, was an ever-present part of their existence on the Plains.

The Plains has perhaps gotten undeserved blame—or credit—for causing madness. Like other parts of the human condition, madness seems to accompany the human personality, taking on local coloration as conditions change. It was neither caused by the environment, nor did it refuse to allow blizzard, drought, grasshoppers and sand to aid it. Madness seems to have had as many resources as the settlers themselves. (pp. 51-61)

> *June O. Underwood, "Men, Women, and Madness: Pioneer Plains Literature," in* Under the Sun: Myth and Realism in Western American Literature, *edited by Barbara Howard Meldrum, The Whitston Publishing Company, 1985, pp. 50-63.*

Kary K. Wolfe and Gary K. Wolfe

[*Kary K. Wolfe is a critic and educator. Her husband, Gary K. Wolfe, is an American critic, editor, educator, and journalist who has written extensively about science fiction. In the following essay, they examine the popularity of psychological narratives, focusing on Joanne Greenberg's* I Never Promised You a Rose Garden *(1964) as an example of the genre.*]

Movements and genres in popular literature, emerging as they do from a variety of media and often over an extended period of time, sometimes have the effect of "sneaking up" on scholars of the genre, of developing quietly over a period of years and then seeming to spring full-blown upon the consciousness of the reading public. Such was partially the case with science fiction, which grew almost unnoticed for decades before being "discovered" by critics during the last ten years or so. Such is also the case with the genre we propose to discuss today, a genre which has its roots in the literature of mental abnormality stretching back to classical times, but which has emerged as a genre in itself—drawing on the novel, memoirs, autobiography, and psychological case history—only during this century. Psychologists have long been aware of these works as a sub-genre of psychiatric literature, but it shall be the contention of this paper that such works have in recent years transcended in popularity and form the rather narrow scope of "professional literature" and become a profitable genre of popular writing (and to a lesser extent, of film and television). Such works not only enjoy an appeal that goes well beyond people professionally interested in psychology, but they also have evolved recognizable formulaic elements in structure and imagery. We propose to treat these works, then, not from the point of view of the psychologist so much as from the point of view of popular culture: specifically, what are their characteristics and what might be the reason for their popularity?

Robert Coles, in his introduction to Barbara Field Benzinger's *The Prison of My Mind*, remarks that the book "shares a tradition that goes centuries back" and even cites Augustine's *Confessions* as a precursor. While this statement is undoubtedly true in the broadest sense, and while the list of autobiographical accounts of mental illness includes such illustrious figures as Strindberg, Nijinsky, Boswell, de Maupassant, Arthur Symons, and others, a more immediate source for works such as Benziger's can be found in the works of "muckraking" novelists, reporters, and autobiographers. Perhaps the most significant of these, and perhaps the seminal work in this genre in the twentieth century, is Clifford Beers' *A Mind that Found Itself* (1908), both a moving account of a severe manic-depressive's years of illness and recovery and powerful indictment of the treatment of mental patients at the beginning of this century. The muckraking theme is a recurrent one in later works as well, and what is probably this genre's first major best-seller, Mary Jane Ward's 1946 *The Snake Pit*, is less concerned with the structure of mental illness or the process of therapy than with the nightmarish conditions of the asylum itself. More recently, a similarly social-minded concern with the manipulative aspects of mental treatment is expressed in Ken Kesey's *One Flew Over the Cuckoo's Nest* (1962) and Elliott Baker's *A Fine Madness* (1964), and in such related non-fiction studies as Thomas Szasz's *The Myth of Mental Illness* and Phyllis Chesler's *Women and Madness* (which curiously demonstrates little awareness of this genre, whose major figures are all women).

The Snake Pit was not the first novel in the 1940's to deal with mental illness and recovery; it had been preceded by several years by Millen Brand's *The Outward Room* (1941), and it came at a time of extensive interest in psychological topics in the popular media, especially films (more about which in a moment). But it established as no other book had the market potential of this subject, and for the next twenty years the genre developed steadily, with narratives told not only from the patient's point of view, but from the doctor's as well. In 1955, Max Lerner could write, "One of the byproducts of the post-Freudian age has been the emergence of a new genre of American writing—the work of the writing psychoanalyst or psychiatrist, who applies his insights to the problems of the day or tells of some of his adventures with his patients." Lerner was writing in the introduction to Robert Lindner's *The Fifty Minute Hour*, itself one of the more successful collections of case histories published during the 1950's. It was followed in 1957 by a similar collection, Joseph Anthony's *The Invisible Curtain*, as well as Corbett Thigpen and Hervey Cleckley's *The Three Faces of Eve* the same year. In 1962 appeared *Lisa and David*, the best-known of Theodore Isaac Rubin's series of novelized case histories.

None of these works from the therapist's viewpoint ever achieved the resounding success of a 1964 novel told from the patient's viewpoint, however, Joanne Greenberg's *I Never Promised You a Rose Garden*, published under the pseudonym "Hannah Green," remains the most famous and influential book in this genre, with sales of nearly four million copies in its first decade of publication. Its success is almost certainly a key factor in the present growth and popularity of the genre. Following *I Never Promised You a Rose Garden*, booksellers began to set up displays of popular psychology paperbacks; publishers began to re-issue earlier works, citing similarities to the Greenberg book in an effort to increase sales, and in some cases even changing the titles in order to point up similiarities: Margaret Wiley Emmett's *Satan Have Pity,* originally published in 1962, was reissued in paperback in 1971 under the title *I Love the Person You Were Meant to Be.* Characteristic paperback blurbs would read "A book to equal *I Never Promised You a Rose Garden*" (*Autobiography of a Schizophrenic Girl*); "Not since *INPYRG* [which we shall henceforth abbreviate thus for Convenience] "(*I Love the Person You Were Meant to Be*); A novel in the poignant tradition of *INPYRG*" (*Lisa, Bright and Dark*); "As haunting as *INPYRG* (*The Eye of Childhood*); "A novel with the poignancy of *INPYRG*" (*The Better Part*); or "A novel for those who enjoyed *INPYRG*" (*Crown of Flowers*). "I Never Promised You a Rose Garden," bizarrely, even became the title of a country and western song in 1971 that had nothing to do with mental illness. The genre, at least as far as the marketing departments of publishers were concerned, was established—and highly lucrative.

The sudden flowering of sales of these books also brought renewed attention to such writers as Mary Jane Ward, Lucy Freeman, and Vera Randal, each of whom has published more than one book in the genre since the late forties, with Freeman at least (whose first book, *Fight Against Fears,* appeared in 1951), making a successful career out of such writing. Writers with more serious literary ambitions also found the genre attractive during this period. J. R. Salamanca's *Lilith* (1961) enjoyed some critical success, as did the Robert Rossen film later adapted from it. Both Ken Kesey's *One Flew Over the Cuckoo's Nest* (1962) and Sylvia Plath's *The Bell Jar* (1963) gained wide audiences and critical attention, and both have become "cult" books of a sort, reflecting as they do the values of the counterculture and the women's movement, respectively.

At the same time, the genre has grown in popularity in the movies and on television. Psychiatry in general, and amnesia in particular, became a common theme in films of the forties, most notably in such films as Hitchcock's *Spellbound* (1945) and the film adaptation of *The Snake Pit* (with a screenplay co-authored by Millen Brand, 1949), but also in films from other popular genres, such as *Pride of the Marines* (1945). The fifties followed with film adaptations of William Gibson's *The Cobweb* (1955), Jim Piersall's *Fear Strikes Out* (1957), and Robert Lindner's *Rebel Without a Cause* (1955), the latter, as Gene and Barbara Stanford have observed [in *Strangers to Themselves: Readings on Mental Illness,* 1973] turning a psychopathic case study into "the cultural hero of the fifties." *The Three Faces of Eve* won an Academy Award for Joanne Woodward in 1957, and *David and Lisa,* an adaptation of Rubin's *Lisa and David,* brought director Frank Perry to prominence in 1962. This is not to mention the flood of psychological horror stories following Hitchcock's *Psycho* (1960), Robert Aldrich's *Whatever Happened to Baby Jane* (1962), and Samuel Fuller's *Shock Corridor* (1963).

Television also entered the arena briefly in the early sixties, with two series, *The Eleventh Hour* and *The Psychiatrist,* dealing on a weekly basis with mental problems.

Mental illness remains a frequent theme on such programs as *Marcus Welby, M.D.* and *Medical Center,* and John Neufeld's *Lisa Bright and Dark* recently appeared as a tv-movie. As far back as 1955, Max Lerner [in *The 50-Minute Hour*] castigated television and motion picture exploitation of mental illness in terms that are still applicable today:

> They have usually taken the cheap-and-easy way of starting with some highly dramatic event and, with psychiatric help, working back to infancy and mother-fixation. Although the psychiatric play or movie is still young it is already so threadbare as to be vulnerable to caricature. The trouble with most of them is that they start with a prefabricated drama rather than with a given personality. It takes honesty to avoid the temptation of this kind of synthetic pattern, where everything is untangled neatly and tied together again just as neatly.

Before proceeding to a fuller discussion of the popularity of this genre, and to a more detailed analysis of *I Never Promised You a Rose Garden* as an example of the genre, it is necessary to outline briefly just what it is that justifies lumping all these works together, beyond a common concern with psychology. The more familiar genres of popular writing—westerns, detective stories, gothics, and the like—may be characterized and identified by a number of structural and conventional elements involving style, atmosphere, setting, and characterization, as well as plot. Largely through the cross-influence of writers within the genre, certain formulae are evolved, and popular writers who most successfully make use of these formulae become, in John Cawelti's sense of the term, *auteurs.* In our psychological narratives, such cross-influence seems relatively sparse, and while easily discernible formulae may not yet have completely evolved, there are noteworthy recurrent elements. We shall attempt to characterize the genre in terms of these elements, specifically in regard to imagery and metaphor, structure, point of view, and characterization.

Our first area of concern is imagery and metaphor, and in some ways this is the most important. A striking feature of many of these narratives is their organization of a deliberate metaphoric pattern, guided or controlled by one or two central metaphors that set the tone and attitude for the entire work. Many of these controlling metaphors are evident in the titles of the works: *The Snake Pit, The Prison of My Mind, Labyrinth of Silence, Halfway Through the Tunnel, The Invisible Curtain, The Bell Jar.* Most of these are simple metaphors of madness, although some, like the snake pit, serve the dual function of representing both the patient's state of mind and the horrors of the mental hospital itself. The central importance of the controlling metaphor in these works stems in part from the fact that many of the works tend to be autobiographical, and, as James Olney writes in his study of metaphor in autobiography, "By their metaphors shall you know them" [*Metaphors of the Self: the Meaning of Autobiography* (1972)]. In other words, the power of metaphor becomes the central link between the experience of the reader and the experience described by the author in an autobiographical work. On the most basic level, it represents an attempt at communicating the incommunicable; Frank Conroy writes of the anonymous author of *Autobiography of a Schizophrenic Girl* that she "attempted to re-create through metaphor . . . sensations in the mind of the presumably sane reader that were in her mind while she was insane." Another reason for the importance of such metaphor is the significance of metaphor and metaphoric language in the structure of many psychoses. The personal mythology of Deborah in *I Never Promised You a Rose Garden* is guarded from the outside world by an artificial language based on metaphors; an exchange with Deborah's doctor in therapy illustrates the complexity of this metaphoric structure:

> "There must be some words," the doctor said. "Try to find them, and let us share them together."
>
> "It's a metaphor—you wouldn't understand it."
>
> "Perhaps you could explain it then."
>
> "There is a word—it means Locked Eyes, but it implies more."
>
> "What more?"
>
> "It's the word for sarcophagus." It meant that at certain times her vision reached only as far as the cover of her sarcophagus; that to herself, as to the dead, the world was the size of her own coffin.

Metaphors, then, often represent not only an attempt to communicate the emotional quality of the illness, but to some extent its structure as well. It is not surprising that the most common metaphors are metaphors of darkness and confusion: fog, mazes, labyrinths, tunnels, pits, water, caverns, fire and ice.

Many of these metaphors suggest the classical journey to the underworld, and indeed this is a useful analogue to the structure of many of these works. The pit, among the most common of metaphors, is readily analogous to the pit of Hell, as the less common but occasional mountain metaphor is analogous to Purgatory. Most of the narratives involve some sort of chaotic, metaphoric journey within the hospital, from ward to ward and in some cases from hospital to hospital, with certain wards representing relative health and others representing the "forgotten," the hopeless cases whose screaming isolation seems like nothing so much as the condition of the damned in the lower circles of Dante's Hell. Janet Frame, in *Faces in the Water* (1961), gives evidence of the extreme importance of particular wards to patients in these stories:

> What is Ward Seven but a subaqueous condition of the mind which gave the fearful shapes drowned there a rhythmic distortion of peace; and what if, upon my getting up from my bed, the perspective was suddenly altered, or I was led into a trap where a fire burning in the walls had dried up the water and destroyed the peace by exposing in harsh daylight the submerged shapes in all their terror?

The ward becomes like the unconscious mind itself, hiding "fearful shapes" in a labyrinthine distortion of space and

perspective. This distortion of perspective is also mentioned by Mary Jane Ward in *The Snake Pit*:

> The nurse led her to a door she had never seen before. Naturally. The door was not there before. Just as the washroom was at one end of the corridor one day and at the other end the next day. Entirely new doors were created in order to insure perpetual confusion.

Labyrinthine chaos such as that described in these passages, followed by emergence into some sort of an ordered universe, seems to be the central dramatic movement of many of these narratives: a movement from disorder to order, or at least the promise of order. The movement is highly—and literally—cathartic, and as we shall see later, this catharsis may be a strong reason for the popularity of this genre.

A third element worth noting in these narratives, along with metaphor and structure, is point of view. The autobiographical element again becomes important here, for in most of the narratives we find that the point of view is confined narrowly to the narrating patient or doctor, with perhaps an occasional shift back and forth, but almost never shifting to the point of view of another patient. Within these limits, point of view might further be categorized fourfold: (1) the patient, describing her or his own illness and internal conflicts (*I Never Promised You a Rose Garden; The Prison of My Mind*); (2) the patient, describing hospital conditions and the outward appearance and character of other patients (*Faces in the Water; The Snake Pit*); (3) the therapist, describing a particular case history (*The Fifty-Minute Hour; My Language Is Me*); and (4) the therapist or doctor, describing a number of patients and/or conditions in a hospital (*Labyrinth of Silence; Savage Sleep*). In addition to these most common points of view, a few narratives may be told from the perspective of someone outside the therapist-patient relationship, usually a relative (*In a Darkness; This Stranger, My Son*), and some may contain more than one perspective on the same case, such as Mary Barnes and Joseph Berke's *Two Accounts of a Journey Through Madness* or Marguerite Sechehaye's interpretation appended to the narrative of *Autobiography of a Schizophrenic Girl*. But the prevalence of the four major points of view, with their concentration on the process of therapy or the conditions of therapy and with their clearly defined narrative scope, offers some evidence for the didactic nature of this kind of narrative—and this didacticism may be yet another reason for the genre's popularity.

Finally, there is the element of characterization, and in this area the genre begins more to resemble conventional characteristics of other genres of popular fiction. As we have already noted parenthetically, the vast majority of these narratives concern women, and most of the autobiographical narratives are written by women as well. Furthermore, it seems evident that the majority of readers are women. Much is done, then, toward the development of identification with the central character or characters, who are usually presented as highly intelligent, witty, articulate (within the bounds of their illness), and yet vulnerable and perhaps above all, passive. The narrator's wit is a distinguishing mark of the style in *The Snake Pit* and Sylvia Plath's *The Bell Jar;* it is described as a psychotic defense in *I Never Promised You a Rose Garden*. Yet the protagonists of each of these novels, as well as many others, hardly could be called protagonists in the real sense at all: they simply don't make much happen. They tend to be presented as passive victims, buffered about by family, friends, other patients, doctors, nurses, orderlies, strangers, society in general, and their own internal disturbance. Furthermore, they tend to be creative, usually as artists (*Two Accounts of a Journey through Madness; I Never Promised You a Rose Garden*) or writers (*The Snake Pit*). This dual aspect of the central character—the creative, intelligent woman victimized by roles she is forced into—probably accounts for a large measure of the popularity enjoyed at least by *The Bell Jar* among feminists.

What villains there are in these narratives tend to be unwittingly played by family and friends who mean well but simply "don't understand." Usually, however, the only major figure to recur in a number of the books is a variation on the wise old person, the wizard or wise woman of fairy tales. This role is generally occupied by the therapist, who often represents the first benevolent authority figure the patient encounters during the illness. Advocates of the women's movement may rightly question the frequency with which this figure is a strong male character, but not infrequently the figure is a woman therapist—such as Dr. Fried in *I Never Promised You a Rose Garden.*

Having surveyed thus all too briefly the genre in terms of imagery, structure, point of view, and characterization, we should look back over these elements and try to see what in them, if anything, might account for the growing popularity of this kind of writing. Max Lerner contends that much of this popularity may derive from certain similarities to the detective story, with the process of unravelling the past even more ingenious than in most mysteries, because all we have to begin with is a victim who, with the aid of the doctor, must discover not only who the villains are but indeed if any "crime" was committed at all. Frank Conroy, writing of *Autobiography of a Schizophrenic Girl,* describes the book in terms of another genre: to him the book is "clearly a triumph of faith. . . . As a human document Renee's book is without doubt inspirational." Gene and Barbara Stanford offer yet another explanation:

> Part of the fascination seems to be the sense of strangeness and horror that some of the books convey. In our modern world, where fierce beasts and uninhabited continents have all been conquered, the frontiers of the mind are about the only places where adventures are still possible. This interest in the strange world that lies beyond the borders of the rational mind may partially account for experimentation with drugs as well as for an interest in mental illness.

This "adventure into the unknown" aspect of the books, we might add, also would seem to relate their popularity to the resurgence of interest in witchcraft and occultism, and to the popularity of fantasy and science fiction, particularly the artificial cosmologies of such writers as H. P. Lovecraft or J. R. R. Tolkien.

Certainly all these factors are involved in the popularity of these books, but we might also find clues to popularity from the characteristics we have already mentioned. In terms of structure and imagery in particular, and characterization to a lesser extent, we might regard these works as a variety of romance, which uses the interior landscapes of real mental illness in much the same way that the interior landscapes of the poetic imagination have functioned in romances from the Middle Ages to the present. We may use the term "romance" in a fairly broad sense here, since we are speaking primarily of the manner in which these works are received by a popular audience rather than the manner in which they are deliberately conceived by their authors. We have already noted how these narratives are often structured as a journey into a kind of inferno or wasteland in search of a mysterious goal or boon; this quest element certainly calls to mind heroic romance of the Arthurian sort, and indeed [in *The Origins and History of Consciousness* (1962)] Erich Neumann has already demonstrated at some length the manner in which such quest romances can represent, in Jungian terms, the evolution of consciousness from the unconscious—a process which is often reconstructed in therapy with psychotics.

On another level, these journeys also represent a consciously educational process of self-discovery, and this factor, coupled with the frequently youthful or adolescent protagonists, suggests thematic relationships with the *bildungsroman* of Romantic narrative art. Still a third literary relation, mentioned above, may be found in fantasy and science fiction, whose artificial systems and fantastic imagery are echoed in the detailed fantasies of many psychotics.

Finally, yet another variety of romance that is of perhaps even greater interest than the others in explaining the current popular appeal of the genre is the Gothic romance. We have already noted the passive "victim" aspect of many of the heroines, and this is certainly an element shared with the popular "modern Gothics" that grace newsstands with endless cover paintings of ladies in nightgowns fleeing dimly lit mansions. But many of our protagonists also share the dark obsessions and compulsions of a Heathcliff, thus partaking of the Gothic villain as well as the Gothic heroine and becoming romantic figures in themselves. Janet Frame demonstrates awareness of this aspect of popular psychological fiction in *Faces in the Water:*

> There is an aspect of madness which is seldom mentioned in fiction because it would damage the romantic popular idea of the insane as a person whose speech appeals as immediately poetic; but it is seldom the easy Opheliana recited like the pages of a seed catalog or the outpourings of Crazy Janes who provide, in fiction, an outlet for poetic abandon. Few of the people who roamed the dayroom would have qualified as acceptable heroines, in popular taste; few were charmingly uninhibited eccentrics.

But even Frame's own prosaic narrator is capable of wildly "poetic" outpourings and images. Add this aspect of the protagonist to the presence of the very real "ghosts" and "demons" of mental illness and the labyrinthine settings of huge, shadowy institutions—a modern equivalent of the Gothic castle—and the narratives seem even closer to the more familiar Gothic romance.

To illustrate these various points in a more unified manner, we should now like to examine in greater detail one of these works, analyzing it for the characteristics of the genre, its specific relations to romance, and the reasons for its popularity. The work we have chosen is one which by its huge popular success and influence has become virtually the archetype of the genre, Joanne Greenberg's *I Never Promised You a Rose Garden.* Published in 1964 under the name "Hannah Green," the novel is a fictionalized account of Joanne Greenberg's own illness and her therapy at Chestnut Lodge under Dr. Frieda Fromm-Reichmann. While the novel was generally received well critically as a didactic work concerning mental illness, many reviewers had reservations about its value as fiction. Frank Haskel, writing in *Saturday Review,* complained that "the two-steps-forward, one-step-backward progression of Deborah's surfacing to life lacks that tightness which fiction requires." R. V. Cassill, while generally lauding the book in his *New York Times Book Review* review, observed that it is not wholly "fictionally convincing" and that "it is as if some wholly admirable, and yet specialized, nonfictional discipline has been dressed in the garments and mask of fiction." The *Times Literary Supplement* reviewer noted what is probably the book's chief defect as a novel by pointing out that the "real" world to which Deborah must return is never made nearly as convincing or attractive as her fantasy world: "her normality is perilously close to dullness." And Brigid Brophy in *The New Statesman* declared flatly that "should it turn out to be a work of fiction, its value would vanish overnight." It soon became publicly known that the novel is *not* entirely fiction, of course, and in the years following these initial reviews, as the book phenomenally grew in popularity, relatively little attention was paid to it as anything other than a highly readable case history. And yet there is much evidence, both from the novel itself and from Greenberg's other works, that the book is an attempt at a coherent novel and not merely fictionalized autobiography.

In *Rose Garden,* Greenberg has tried to portray the often chaotic imagery of schizophrenia and the often uneven process of therapy, and to impose upon these realities of her own experience the order and structure of a unified narrative. This is not to suggest that she has deliberately misrepresented either her illness or her therapy for the sake of novelistic expediency; rather it is to suggest that the aesthetic elements of the book exist on two principle levels. For example, the imagery of mountains, which serves a number of complex functions in the context of Deborah's own schizophrenic world, is introduced into the narrative late enough so that it can also function in aesthetic terms as an image of the struggle toward sanity, toward resolution of conflict: "All Deborah heard were the sounds of her own gasps of exhaustion as she climbed an Everest that was to everyone else an easy and a level plain." Similarly, the imagery of the underworld ("the Pit"), which seems to appear more or less at random within the context of the illness, is for the sake of the narrative organized into the more familiar aesthetic pattern of the underworld journey: descent, chaos, and purifying ascent. The danger of this kind of dual use of imagery, of course, is that it tends to lead the reader to confuse the structure of the novel with the structure of therapy, and the pattern of aesthetic imagery with the pattern of schizophrenia. Such confusion is further by the commonplace belief that there is some sort of *de facto* relationship between insanity and art, and one must wonder if in fact such works as *Rose Garden* are popularly read as novels *about* schizophrenia, or as vicarious schizophrenic experiences; the word "seductive" appears prominently twice on the cover blurb of *Rose Garden.* But this question is merely another way of asking the reason for the popularity of these books, and perhaps it can be in part answered by looking at the four key aspects of *Rose Garden* itself: characterization, structure, style and imagery, and rhetoric.

The central element in characterization, as we have already noted for the genre as a whole, is the nature of the protagonist herself. The protagonist in *Rose Garden* is 16-year-old Deborah Blau, a plain but highly intelligent and witty girl whose psychosis involves an elaborately imagined, almost Blakean universe called Yr, with its own pantheon of gods, its own language, and its own landscapes. During the course of the novel, Deborah moves in both the real world and this world of her own creating. But the "real world" in this novel is the world of the mental hospital and its surroundings, a world that is in its own way as artificial as the one Deborah has created. The arbitrary and sometimes hostile nature of this reality is what provides the book's title; in warning Deborah that reality is not necessarily more rewarding than the world of Yr, and in arguing that Deborah's choice must be based on deeper criteria than mere comfort, the therapist Dr. Fried says, "I never promised you a rose garden. I never promised you perfect justice. . . . " And in making this statement, Dr. Fried herself is reminded of her days in Nazi Germany, as if to underline to the reader the point that "reality" is not necessarily morally superior to the world of the psychotic. In fact, it is this real world, the "our-side," represented initially in the novel by the almost mythic figure of Doris Rivera, a patient who has apparently successfully "gone outside," that is the mystery. The artificial worlds of the hospital and the psychosis itself are clearly delineated; the world outside is presented only slightly near the end of the novel.

Deborah must somehow learn to function in all three worlds: her own mind, the hospital, and finally the outside. Each world has a different landscape, a different set of rules, even a different language, and in each world the character of Deborah is developed along certain lines congruent with the fictional reality of that world. And in each world, she must pass from a stage of passivity to one of self-determination and control. Put another way, Deborah must undergo a process of education on three levels: first mastering the workings of her own mind, then mastering the fairly simple rules of life with the other patients in the hospital, and finally mastering the more complex rules of life on the outside. This multifaceted educational process, together with Deborah's adolescence and her relative innocence in each situation, suggests the kind of education undergone by the adolescent protagonists of the *bildungs-*

roman. It is also, of course, a stylized version of the process of socialization in the development of any personality, and it may be for this reason that it is easy to identify with Deborah's problems, stated as they are in such bizarre terms.

Deborah is also appealing because she is essentially an heroic figure, and her Kingdom of Yr is an heroic, even mythopoeic, world. In that world, she initially seems to identify with Anterrabae, "the falling god," who is later revealed to be her own version of Milton's Satan, with all its associations of heroic defiance, eternal punishment, and the underworld. She must endure the derision and hostility of the Collect, "the massed images of all the teachers and relatives and schoolmates standing eternally in secret judgment and giving their endless curses." She is often referred to her gods as "Bird-One", with its suggestion of Icarus, of pride and freedom. Finally, she must declare her self-mastery by renouncing all her gods and the Kingdom of Yr itself—an act which dramatically parallels the myth which gave rise to Anterrabae in the first place, and which in itself represents a kind of Promethean defiance. Deborah renounces her own security in favor of knowledge of the world and freedom; such an ideal is not uncommon in Romantic poetry and fiction.

Another reason for Deborah's success as a popular heroine is her appeal to our own fantasies of irresponsibility. Almost anything she does is excusable in the context of the fiction, and as such she represents, however perversely, a kind of absolute behavioral freedom. She doesn't necessarily get away with all her actions, but she isn't entirely responsible for them either, and it is likely that this freedom is, on a rather basic level, an example of the sort of wish-fulfillment that characterizes much popular literature. The freedom has its limits, however, and these limits seem at least in part defined by the necessity of maintaining reader sympathy. None of the violence on Deborah's part is directed at anyone other than herself, and the general absence of sexual motives and experience from her story— even though it seems likely that such experiences would comprise a significant element of her psyche—give her the aspect of the "innocent." Not even her most repulsive actions, such as her continued self-mutilation, are sufficient to remove our sympathies from her, and in this respect she is not unlike many other adolescent heroines in popular fiction.

The structure of the novel also may be a contributing factor to its popularity, for despite all its images of doom and confusion, *Rose Garden* is essentially comedic. There is from the outset a feeling of imminent resolution and hope; like the traditional fairy tale, elements of horror may be introduced as long as there is no overall feeling of despair. Part of this may be due to the journey motif; the suggestion of a journey naturally implies that the journey will have an end, and in the case of Deborah, this end is relative sanity (the alternative end, death, is only suggested slightly in the novel in brief references to her earlier suicide attempt). *Rose Garden* begins literally with a journey—the trip to the mental hospital—and continues with Deborah's movement from ward to ward and finally back out into the world. This movement, though not effortless,

seems inevitable, and its inevitability is reinforced by the time sequence of the book. Deborah is in the hospital for three years, and in each of these years, springtime represents a progression towards sanity. The first spring arrives when Deborah first secures her relationship with Dr. Fried by learning that she is of value to the doctor: " 'If I can teach you something, it may mean that I can count at least somewhere'." The second spring is characterized by Deborah and her friend and co-patient Carla declaring their friendship and running away from the hospital in a show of self-assertion and fun, prompting the doctor in charge to comment, " 'I'm kind of proud of you'." The third spring, coming at the conclusion of the book, includes Deborah's successful passing of the high school equivalency exams—an act which symbolically certifies both her maturity and her sanity. The three episodes taken together constitute Deborah's learning about the value of her person to others, then asserting that value, and finally proving it with the socially accepted measure of the high school exams. She finally emerges from her private world and prepares to leave the hospital in springtime, just as she had entered it, three years earlier, in the autumn. The three years become metaphorically compressed into one cycle of the seasons, and the inevitability of this cycle—the inevitability of spring—lends to the novel an overall tone of hope.

Yet another source of popularity may be the book's imagery. The idea of the "secret garden"—the private respite from the world that is known only to the child—has long been popular in children's and adolescent literature, and it is not unlikely that Deborah's Kingdom of Yr is just such a garden to many readers. Though on a more intense level, it is not unlike Frances Hodgson Burnett's secret garden in her book of that title, or C. S. Lewis's Narnia. Its landscape is a wildly romantic, exciting one of fire and ice, and its language bears resemblance, though on a much more complex level, to the "secret codes" popular among children. In other words, Yr, though the myth of a psychotic mind, is still a myth, and as such bears strong attraction for the imagination. Thus, as we have mentioned earlier, some of the attraction that readers feel for the novel may be akin to the attractions of Blake, or Lewis, or Tolkien.

Finally, and probably most importantly to the novel's professional audience, there is the didactic element. *Rose Garden* has been used as a supplementary text in many university psychology courses because of its accurate dramatization of facts about psychosis and therapy. Karl Menninger wrote of the book, " 'I'm sure it will have a good effect on lots of people who don't realize that this sort of exploration can be done and this sort of effect achieved.'" Robert Coles [in his introduction to Barbara Field Benzinger's *The Prison of My Mind*] reacts in a similar manner: "If I were upset, in despair, worried about whether there will be many days left, I would be grateful to people like Clifford Beers or Hannah Green or Barbara Benzinger." It appears, then, that the book is widely read as an object lesson in mental illness, and that for many its value as fiction is secondary to its value as case history. And it seems likely that a didactic motive was one of the major reasons the book was written in the first place; a number of novelistic decisions seem to be made on didactic (i.e., what will teach most effectively) rather than aesthetic (i.e., what will work best as fiction) grounds. We learn a great deal more about Deborah's psychosis than we do about her actual personality, for example. Such didacticism may occasionally weaken the novel as fiction, but it probably adds to its popularity.

Rose Garden, then, brings together in a single book many of the elements that have gone into the making of a popular narrative genre. And in terms of the popular audience, it is the book most responsible for the present ascendance of that genre. Part autobiography, part fiction, part educational tract, it is in many ways one of the most significant popular books of the last twenty years. It and the other books in its genre may represent the most broad-based connection yet established between practicing psychology and popular culture. As such, it is worth studying, and the genre is one whose development is worth watching, not only for what it may tell us about how popular genres evolve, but also for what it may tell us about changing attitudes of a mass audience toward issues in psychology and mental health. (pp. 895-907)

> *Kary K. Wolfe and Gary K. Wolfe, "Metaphors of Madness: Popular Psychological Narratives," in* Journal of Popular Culture, *Vol. IX, No. 4, Spring, 1976, pp. 895-907.*

Charles Flowers on the artist's use of madness:

[The] artist, kinetically sure that the business of his life is the creation of a thing that has never been before and that is nonetheless inevitable, will arrange his life in service of that goal. Society should learn that art is not the escape of madmen. Rather artists will often choose behavior patterns that are "abnormal" in order to be freed for the insistent claims of their art.

They must avoid connections which distract, be wary of commitments which might tend to reinforce existing (and therefore suspect) social structures, fear the dangerous acquiescence with what has been until they prove that it must be.

Madmen or mad patterns of behavior—why discuss the difference? Fine nutty artists might not need any apologies, but too many readers and teachers are misreading art when they do not recognize the conscious decision to warp a life. They patronize the artist, as Freud did (despite his wily protests) in his study of Leonardo, and deface the art.

Although artists, like other kinds of evangel, should not be respected simply because of the accident of a vocation, their intent should be understood, if only because it is definitely there. In this country, thanks to the Calvinist notion of the elect, it is fashionable for artists at times to claim that inspiration rises, like marsh gas, from an unknown region of the soul. Rarely do they, good democrats all, articulate theories.

> *Charles Flowers, in his "The Single Vision," in* The Virginia Quarterly Review, *Summer 1981.*

Lillian Feder

[*In the following excerpt, Feder discusses madness as both a theme and technique in the poetry of Allen Ginsberg, Theodore Roethke, John Berryman, and Sylvia Plath.*]

In America, madness as a theme and a point of view determining the techniques of poetry reached its height in the 1950s and 1960s and has waned only recently. Poets as vastly different from each other as Allen Ginsberg, Theodore Roethke, John Berryman, and Sylvia Plath all use their own experience of the shifting images and moods of dreams and hallucinations. Their particular adaptations of this material, which disclose an extremely broad range of experience, response, and symbolic transformation, are continually felt in the highly individual voices of these poets and their personae. The contents of such hallucinations, having evaded the boundaries of the ego, often seem to emerge through the presence of a persona both familiar and strange to the poet, to whom he or she seems to be listening. This hallucinatory material, however personal, reflects contemporary cultural attitudes toward the unconscious mind. The discoveries of psychoanalysis, which were revolutionary to the surrealists, are assumptions to these poets, whatever reservations they may have about their own experience of psychiatric treatment. Ginsberg is obsessed with the disillusionment of post-war America and its values of material success based on a cold-war economy and paranoiac suppression of dissent, which infect his dissociated, prophetic persona. Roethke ignores contemporary America and struggles only with the conflicts of his personal history. All of them, however, react against the anonymous, genteel persona characteristic of the poetry of the 1950s by calling on the processes of psychic dissolution to release their most extreme instinctual cravings, their anger, and their visions, as the vehicles of their talent.

In Ginsberg's poetry, madness is a destructive product of the corrupt values and heartlessness of American society, but it is also a defense against these evils and a means to combat them by confronting that society with its own soul. Most important, it is a way to self-realization in prophetic utterance. Many people who have not even read Ginsberg's work are familiar with the first line of "Howl" [from *Howl and Other Poems by Allen Ginsberg*, 1956]: "I saw the best minds of my generation destroyed by madness, starving hysterical naked." In this poem, hallucinations induced by alcohol and drugs serve two ends: an escape-route from the poverty, ugliness, and repression of their environment for those "who bared their brains to Heaven under the El," and a challenge to the conformists; the "scholars of war," who betrayed the texts they taught; and the managers of Los Alamos and Wall Street.

The language and rhythms of "Howl" transmit the heightened consciousness induced by drugs, the obsessive accumulation of evidence, as if every detail of the remembered experience were intensified to an almost unbearable degree. Undifferentiated rage, sorrow, ecstasy, accusation, hate, shock, and tenderness are combined without transition in the apparently ceaseless flow of incident and association and in the violent concreteness of language, the obsessive repetition, the lines that imitate the breathlessness of a voice that cannot stop pouring out its message. But in "Howl" madness is not only the voice of poetry; it is also a reduction to silence: the rebels are given "the concrete void of insulin metrasol electricity hydrotherapy psychotherapy occupational therapy pingpong & amnesia," and they rest "briefly in catatonia." Years later, they return "to the visible madman doom of the wards of the madtowns of the East." The description of life in "Pilgrim State's Rockland's and Greystone's foetid halls" creates the mind endlessly adapting whatever remains of its desires to the confines of the internalized asylum: "bickering with the echoes of the soul, rocking and rolling in the midnight solitude-bench dolmen-realms of love, dream of life a nightmare, bodies turned to stone as heavy as the moon."

The next association is "mother," the mad Naomi of "Kaddish," the poem [from *Kaddish and Other Poems, 1958-1960,* 1961] in which Ginsberg most fully realizes the thematic and stylistic possibilities of madness. In "Kaddish" he refers briefly to a period when he was a patient at the Psychiatric Institute of Columbia-Presbyterian Medical Center in 1949 only to indicate that it is not his subject: "I was in bughouse that year 8 months—my own visions unmentioned in this here Lament—." Yet "Kaddish" unites the most realistic and sordid details of his mother's schizophrenic breakdowns with his own visionary impulse to creation, a commitment to the processes of psychic dissolution as an initiation into the ancient art of prophecy. Naomi, the mad mother, is also the

> . . . glorious muse that bore me from the womb, gave suck first mystic life & taught me talk and music, from whose pained head I first took Vision—
>
> Tortured and beaten in the skull—What mad hallucinations of the damned that drive me out of my own skull to seek Eternity till I find Peace for Thee, O Poetry—and for all humankind call on the Origin.

The whole of "Kaddish" is a series of transformations—Communism and McCarthyism into paranoid hallucinations, the mother's obsessions and terrors into the son's consciousness of his destiny, Naomi's mad eyes into the "great Eye" of the Lord, the prayer for the dead into an exaltation of individual consciousness merging with the universal.

"Kaddish," as John Tytell points out [in *Naked Angels: The Lives and Literature of the Beat Generation* (1976)], reveals the psychic effects of the drug Ginsberg took throughout the brief, intense period when he composed most of it:

> The racing, breathless pace of the poem reflects its manner of composition—the stimulation of morphine mixed with meta-amphetamine (then new to Ginsberg, and a conflicting combination as well since morphine slows time while amphetamine speeds it up) as Ginsberg sat at his desk from six in the morning and wrote until ten the following night, leaving the poem only for cof-

fee, the bathroom, and several doses of Dexedrine.

Drugs, no doubt, intensified Ginsberg's feelings and the rush of associations that creates the breathless tone of "Kaddish," but the poem also conveys other states of consciousness in which Ginsberg came to poetic terms with the memories of a lifetime. [According to Ginsberg's *Journals: Early Fifties, Early Sixties* (1977), edited by Gordon Ball, he] wrote part IV in 1958 in Paris and obviously had been living with the poem for a long time.

Addressing his mother at the beginning of the poem, he reveals two important sources of its rhythms and moods, and even, however submerged, its contents: he has been "reading the Kaddish aloud" and "listening to Ray Charles blues shout blind on the phonograph." The Hebrew Kaddish is recited in memory of the dead, but it does not refer to death. It is a prayer in praise of God, in which mortality is linked to His transcendent power. Chanted in a communal setting of congregation and mourners, it deals not with the grief of the individual mourner but the attachment of each life to the life of Israel and the eternal existence of God. This essential quality of the Kaddish appears most clearly in Ginsberg's poem in the Hymmnn that concludes II, but it exists throughout it. However intimate and bizarre his personal revelations, there is no exhibitionistic leer in them but rather the compulsion to make a public offering. In "Kaddish," the house in Newark, the horrors of Naomi's paranoia, the details of her physical and mental disintegration, and Ginsberg's own homosexual and incestuous desires are the materials of life offered up in a prayer for transcendence of the self and death. The rhythms of Ray Charles, the union of blues, gospel songs, and jazz, are transmuted by Ginsberg into a rhythmic intensity of both broken phrases and lines accumulating power in their length. Imitating Charles, Ginsberg imposes a contemporary and highly individual sensibility on the rhythmic associations of an oral religious and cultural tradition. The most mundane details of "Kaddish" take on the tones of chanting.

In "Kaddish," Ginsberg, like an ancient prophet, uses the violent and painful memories and disordered associations of the past to transmit a social vision. Identifying his own mantic possession with his mother's "learning to be mad," he re-experiences her life and his as one, and both as part of the political and social history of an era, which, even in its shoddiness and its horror, is given a strange dignity transformed in the anguished, dissociated consciousness of mother and son, as the "great Eye" of the Lord "stares on All."

Ginsberg learned from the surrealists, to whom he pays tribute, that the expansion of consciousness through drugs, dreams, and hallucinations is essential for instigating social reform. In "At Apollinaire's Grave," he feels the poet's presence ("his madness is only around the corner") in Paris "the day the U.S. President appeared in France for the grand conference of heads of state." The surrealists are an "inspiration" for his own explorations of consciousness in poetry:

> I've eaten the blue carrots you sent out of the grave and

An anonymous etching entitled The Mad Artist in Chains.

Van Gogh's ear and maniac peyote of Artaud
and will walk down the streets of New York in
 the black
  cloak of French poetry
improvising our conversation in Paris at Père
 Lachaise
and the future poem that takes its inspiration
 from the light

bleeding into your grave . . .

and his use of his discoveries as a political weapon:

Artaud alone made accusation
 against America,
Before me. . . .

Some of Ginsberg's poems written under the influence of

drugs seem mere recordings of their effects, the "experiments" of "Aether." In these poems [from *Reality Sandwiches, 1953-60* (1963)] there are momentary exaltations observed by an ironic rational consciousness:

> ....I stood on the balcony
>   waiting for an explosion
>   of Total Consciousness of the All—
> being Ginsberg sniffing ether in Lima.
>
> ("Aether")

Ginsberg has referred [in *Allen Ginsberg in America* (1969) by Jane Kramer] to his use of drugs as "pious investigations," and there is no doubt that he used them as a means of exploring his own mind for the material and manner of prophecy. As he has turned from drugs to the use of the mantra to incorporate the mood and style of yoga meditation into poetry, he has turned from identification with madness to a striving for oneness with the processes of life, which include death. Even this change in emphasis came to him in a prophetic dream. In his *Indian Journals,* he tells of his disillusionment with drugs after showing an Indian poet his "Aether": "I realized how much of my life I'd put into this sort of exploration of mind thru drugs, & how sad & futile I felt now that I had gotten to the point with hallucinogens where I no longer liked what I felt & was too disturbed & frightened to continue." Twelve days later in a dream recorded in a poem, he says:

> I feel companion
> to all of us now before death
> waiting inside Life: One big
> place we are here.

The poem ends with resignation to death and separation, but the theme recurs in such poems as "Death on all Fronts" and "Friday the Thirteenth" expanded, as is common in Ginsberg's work, to include his involvement with his society, the world, and the universe. For him, actual insanity, the simulation of its processes through drugs, meditation, and chanting are all intrinsic to the techniques of an art inseparable from the development of a new social consciousness. In this respect, he is unique among the recent American poets who have adapted the psychic processes of madness to depict the mind in the act of creation.

Ginsberg, in his outrage, often internalizes America, *Time* magazine, and various institutions of society as presences haunting his mind, his bed, and his streets. "It occurs to me that I am America," he says [in "America"], erasing any separation between himself and the obsessively loved and hated nation. This breakdown of boundaries between the self and the external world also determines the language, moods, and tones of Roethke's poetry, but it is the world of external nature with which he merges, in a union that seems to exclude any but personal concerns. There is an obsessive, repetitive quality in Roethke's absorption in his terrors of the "abyss" and his efforts to merge with a principle of harmony by defining the searching, creating self beyond its rational manifestations. But his identification of his own psychic underworld with the life beneath and of the soil—its roots, insects, plants, and animals—extends his focus to the mysterious processes of all organic life, of which the mind is part.

In Roethke's poetry, the speaker transmits the "Forms of his secret life" ("The Exorcism") through the instinctual patterns of animals, birds, and insects, and the inevitable flowering and decay of the earth's products, at once vivid in their realistic detail and dream-like in their implications. But to describe Roethke's "world" as that "of a schizophrenic who returns us to where we have always been," as John Vernon does [in *The Garden and the Map*], seems to me a distortion of both Roethke's poetry and schizophrenia. Equating schizophrenia with an idealized primitivism and with childhood, Vernon interprets Roethke's work as "the perfect illustration of the schizophrenia that unites madness and sanity." Actually, Roethke's struggles with his own psychic conflicts and the resolutions he arrives at are more complicated than the Laingian generalities that Vernon imposes on the body of his work.

In his poetry of the late 1950s and 1960s, Roethke, through his very dreams and fantasies of merging with natural life, conveys his inevitable separateness within the laws and manifestations of the physical universe. His ever-present awareness, "I live near the abyss," is confirmed by the stones that have his "own skin" and the "beast with fangs" within "his own house" ("The Pure Fury"), the self that is ever alone despite its continual search for connection. The momentary awakening of a sense of "pure being" ("The Exorcism") is challenged as

> In a dark wood I saw—
> I saw my several selves
> Come running from the leaves,
> Lewd, tiny, careless lives
> That scuttled under stones,
> Or broke, but would not go.

In this poem, he gives an entire stanza to the explicit statement: "I was myself, alone."

The purely instinctual existence of the creatures that enact his psychic needs only confirms this aloneness in the section "They Sing, They Sing" of the poem "The Dying Man." Here he has "the lark's word for it, who sings alone"; the "fury of the slug beneath the stone" is the frustration of any hope of merging with an eternal principle of harmony in the physical universe. In the last stanza, the resolution of the conflict includes yet defies the poet's identification of the self with natural creation:

> Nor can imagination do it all
> In this last place of light: he dares to live
> Who stops being a bird, yet beats his wings
> Against the immense immeasureable emptiness
>   of things.

This, of course, is not Roethke's final resolution. The terror of and yearning for dissolution of the self within and by creation are described in poem after poem and resolved, only partly and temporarily, in a mystical concept of eternal order. "The Abyss" begins with a series of questions and answers in the rhythms of a nursery rhyme, which convey fragmentation, the loss of any fixed concept of external reality characteristic of a terrifying dream or hallucination. There remains only the sense of nothingness everywhere. When the "world," reality, invades the speaker again, he must escape the "terrible hunger for objects" that threatens to overwhelm him by identifying himself with a "furred caterpillar" which he calls "My symbol!" It is both a refuge and a reduction to the elemental, an approach to dying. He lives with death, which appears like "a sly surly attendant" in an asylum, observing his renewed efforts at escape in merging with the "mole," the "otter," and finally, "like the bird, with the bright air." In this poem, as in other late ones, it is ultimately the "Lord God" who relieves his despair, but fusion with God, as with nature, is in Roethke's poetry a tentative definition rather than a lasting experience of wholeness, a defense against the dissolution of the self that remained to the end a perennial threat and his most insistent goal.

As this chapter has indicated, the "abyss" of the self as the material and formative process of creation is the most personal yet the most characteristic motif of modern literature. Taking this "dangerous path," as Roethke calls it in "The Abyss," the "vague, the arid / Neither in nor out of this life," has meant for some recent poets what it did for Mann's Aschenbach and Leverkühn, following the lure of psychic dissolution to its inevitable goal in suicide. Madness in the poetry of John Berryman and Sylvia Plath is [in the words of Otto Fenichel from *The Psychoanalytic Theory of Neurosis,* 1945] a series of "partial suicides," fantasies and memories of attempts at self-destruction that enact the persona's most intense experiences of being and creating.

Guilt, madness, death, and suicide are recurring motifs of Berryman's *Dream Songs.* Yet his insistence that his persona of *The Dream Songs* is "not the poet, not me" only confirms the sense these poems convey that such intimate experience is being filtered through a consciousness detached from its emotional immediacy. The major persona, Henry, externalizes dreams; he is an intermediary who converts them into the conscious acts and responses of daily existence. The language and tone of most of *The Dream Songs* is reportorial and self-instructive, evoking not dreams but notations in a diary. In Song 327, Berryman says that "a dream is a panorama / of the whole mental life," an accurate definition not of actual dreams but of his own series of sensational, pathetic, and comic episodes, a fragmented panorama, like Lautréamont's, that discloses little about the mental or emotional processes that conceived it.

The suicides of friends and fellow poets are occasions to be noted for their sorrow; they elicit a conventional response and an explicit, pathetic self-identification. Mourning the death of Randall Jarrell, the speaker instructs himself: "Let Randall rest, whom your self-torturing / cannot restore one instant's good to, rest. . . ." Even as he tells of the suicide of Delmore Schwartz, he consciously prevents himself from suppressing its implications for him.

> I give in. I must not leave the scene of this same
> 　death
> as most of me strains to.
> There are all the problems to be sorted out. . . .

The Song (156) ends with the speaker's feeling that he "nearly would follow him below." The suicide of Sylvia Plath evokes a similar, though less personal, reaction, except at the end, where Henry wonders why, after all the deaths and suicides of fellow poets, he "alone breasts the wronging tide" [Song 172]. Thoughts of his own madness and possible suicide are chiefly factual and often witty. "Madness & booze, madness & booze" [Song 225], Henry sings as he wonders which one produced the other. Considering suicide [Song 345], he contemplates the "blood & the disgrace" and the effect on the "survivors," and instructs himself in avoiding the meaning of his own mental anguish: "Sit still, / maybe the goblins will go away, leaving you free. . . ."

The Dream Songs, Love and Fame, Delusions, etc., and the novel *Recovery* all express more or less explicitly Berryman's conviction that his compulsive need for love and alcohol, its destructive effects on him, the fragmentation of his sense of self and of reality, and his depressions, guilts, and fantasies of suicide are intrinsic to his writing. In the descent into hell sequence (78-91) of *The Dream Songs,* Berryman goes so far as to imagine the ultimate fragmentation of the self in death:

> I am—I should be held together by—
> But I am breaking up. . . .

Henry, who has "held together" his fragmented thoughts, has "now come to a full stop" [Song 85]. But this death is merely a respite, a preparation to return to the world, like "Lazarus with a plan / to get his own back" [Song 91]. The fantasy of being among the "violent dead," where he can "pick their awful brains" [Song 88] is an ironic quest for release from guilt and conflict and for ultimate fellowship in art and in death, which are inseparable in his consciousness. The "I" of *The Dream Songs* "clasps" Hölderlin and Kleist "to Henry's bosom: / a suicide & a madman, / to teach him lessons who was so far neither" [Song 310]. His poetry emerges out of his perpetual hunger and "need need need." This need for "women, cigarettes, liquor," which destroys his equilibrium and makes him go "to pieces," is inherent in the process of creation:

> The pieces sat up & wrote. They did not heed
> their piecedom but kept very quietly on
> among the chaos.
>
> 　　　　　　　　　[Song 311]

Berryman is even more explicit about his cravings for love and alcohol, his hallucinations, breakdowns, attempts at recovery in psychiatric hospitals, and his return to religion as a source of strength in *Love and Fame, Delusions, etc.,* and his unfinished novel, *Recovery.* Although the "I" of the two volumes of poetry and Severance, the persona of the novel, seem to omit no personal detail in their eagerness to reveal their "whole mental life," Berryman never finds the vehicle he obviously seeks for expressing the connection between his personal anguish and the act of creation. However fragmented the associations, however rapidly and abruptly the moods change, however exact the details about his "Reflexions on suicide," and frequent the references to his father, mother, and wife, and to his own determination to "labour and dream," the language almost always evades the psychic and emotional source of its subject. Berryman is an exact reporter of what he knows, but his eyes, as he himself says, are "bleary as an envelope cried-over / after the letter's lost." The most he can do is to "chip away at the mystery."

The autobiographical episodes, self-analysis, group therapy, and psychiatrists' reports of *Recovery* leave its narrator essentially unknowing and unknown. What is most vivid to him and the reader is the inexplicable "irresistible descent, for the person incomprehensibly . . . determined," the compulsion to destroy the self he is so painfully reconstructing, to return to "every abyss" he has dreaded and longed for, to its despair, hallucinations, and terrors. Among the prayers to and praises of God and the resignations to existence of *Delusions, etc.* the wish remains "for some soft & solid & sudden way out / as quiet as hemlock in that Attic prose. . . . " Berryman's personae are all one in their self-conscious exemplification of the artist as irretrievably drawn to the abyss of the self, which is its ultimate destruction, but his work describes rather than illuminates this compulsion, which takes precedence over any other commitment—to religion, love, and finally art.

The modern poet whose language and imagery most precisely construct the "psychical representatives" of the drive to creation in conflict with its opposition, the impulse toward self-annihilation, is Sylvia Plath. Like Nietzsche and Mann, she returns to the primordial language of these impulses, dream and myth. Plath's adaptations of traditional mythical figures—gods, goddesses, Hades, the Furies, maenads—is readily apparent. A recent book by Judith Kroll [entitled *Chapters in a Mythology: The Poetry of Sylvia Plath* (1976)], entirely devoted to this subject, attempts to demonstrate that Robert Graves's White Goddess served as the model for Plath's own mythical conception of herself, which became her means of resolving and finally transcending unbearable tension. Whereas Kroll's study of Plath's readings in Graves, anthropology, Jung, Zen Buddhism, and other works does elucidate many allusions and images of her poetry, the central thesis of *Chapters in a Mythology* seems to me questionable. Among the many meanings Plath invested in myth, no doubt one was a conquest of the limitations of mortality, but the brilliance of Plath's mythical imagery lies not in its resolutions but in its representation of the physical and psychological nature of irresolvable conflict. Death symbolically becomes the only state in which opposing demands can coexist, and the need for resolution no longer makes its claims on body and mind. Kroll is eager to prove that, though autobiographical material is the basis of Plath's poetry, "mythic rebirth" and finally "ecstatic apprehension of a larger identity" in religious mysticism express her "need to transcend personal history." Actually, mythical conceptions of rebirth and transcendence are among Plath's most authentic autobiographical symbols. It is useless to argue about where her poetry is autobiographical and where it ceases to be so. Her most moving poems are about herself; at the same time, her language releases a more general possibility of psychic life: the intense, agonizing, bizarre manifestations of conflicting drives unmediated by the unifying ego.

By now the central human figures mythicized in Plath's poetry are so well known as to require little discussion: the father of German descent who died when she was nine, the mother who remained alone to support and educate her and her brother and whose struggle for survival seemed indistinguishable from a fierce ambition, which the daughter internalized as love, and the "I" who from childhood sought and found "a sign of election and specialness" to prove that she was "not forever to be cast out." A childhood sign was a wooden monkey, a "totem, . . . a Sacred Baboon" washed up by the sea; later signs were the language of her poetry, inspired by "Disquieting Muses," the nightmare and hallucinatory figures who testify to her omnipotence and her nothingness, to her role of goddess deprived of selfhood.

The central myth of death as release and rebirth is constructed out of warring drives and emotions that transmit the poet's persona as diffuse, elusive, trapped, and raging in the mythical world that is her own creation. In "Getting There" [from *Ariel,*] the image of the realm of Hades is explicit, waiting at the end of a nightmare for her arrival. But first there are the child's questions in the insistent ritualistic rhythms common in her poetry:

> How far is it?
> How far is it now?

Such innocent questions plunge the speaker into a nightmare train-ride to war, death camps, hunger, and wounds. She is the victim of the wheels, which are

> The terrible brains
> Of Krupp, black muzzles
> Revolving, the sound
> Punching out Absence! like cannon.

The wheels of the train "eat"; they are "like gods," with "will— / Inexorable" and "pride." The train has "teeth / Ready to roll, like a devil's." The self in this poem is lost:

> I am a letter in this slot—
> I fly to a name, two eyes.

It exists only in the repeated question: "How far is it?" until, emerging from hate and terror, from the train "Insane for the destination," it arrives to

> Step to you from the black car of Lethe,
> Pure as a baby.

Reality mythicized as gods and devils is set in opposition to the mythical realm of the dead. The horrors of World War II are transformed into a private nightmare world, the "wheels" of her mind driving the persona to the "place . . . Untouched and untouchable," where she sheds the meanings of the past even as she returns to her very beginnings.

In "Lady Lazarus," the "call" comes explicitly from the god of death, who is addressed by many names: he is "Herr Doktor," "Herr Enemy," "Herr God," "Herr Lucifer." He is the Nazi father of "Daddy," the despised and adored tyrant, lover, deserter, deity, and devil, all of whom she symbolically controls by incorporating their power. As she creates them and death, she creates herself:

> Dying
> Is an art, like everything else.
> I do it exceptionally well.

She rises from the dead, renewed but unchanged, to "eat men like air," assuming the role of her enemy who is also the bestower of her divine power, thus leaving the conflict between love and hate, yearning and rage forever unre-solved.

Throughout Plath's poetry, the violent images piled on one another—myths, realistic details of bodily parts, waste, gore, odors, emerging in the rhythms of nursery rhymes or in abrupt one-word lines, like the rapidly shift-ing action of dreams; the disclosures of nothingness through mundane articles of daily life which substitute for identity; the portrayals of the "I," crippled, accused, as-saulted, wounded, bleeding, killing itself again and again—seem forced into consciousness by the violence and chaos of unconscious fear and hate uncontrolled by any order except that of the words themselves. Whatever remnants of the self still exist are continually shattered in its verbal representations:

> And I
> Am the arrow,
>
> The dew that flies
> Suicidal, at one with the drive
> Into the red
>
> Eye, the cauldron of morning.
>
> ("Ariel")

The cultic glorification of Sylvia Plath as a poet whose art in its daring finally required her death distorts her achieve-ment. There is no evidence to support such a conclusion and much biographical data to refute it. She is obviously not the only writer who has portrayed the unconscious, ir-rational determinants of her subjects, language, and imag-ery, and her scope is far narrower than Mann's or Gins-berg's or that of many others for whom psychic dissolu-tion has been a source and subject of art. What finally dis-tinguishes Sylvia Plath from the many other poets who in recent years have used similar mental and emotional expe-rience as their subject and symbolic framework is her dis-covery of a unique language to create what would seem in-expressible—the self as nothingness, emptiness, impelled to explore in "Words dry and riderless" ("Words") its own psychic incorporation of the failure of love and the violence of history. (pp. 264-78)

> *Lillian Feder, "Madness as a Goal," in her* Madness in Literature, *Princeton University Press, 1980, pp. 203-78.*

MADNESS IN GERMAN LITERATURE

Theodore Ziolkowski

[*An American educator and critic, Ziolkowski is best known as the author of* The Novels of Hermann Hesse *(1965) and as the editor of numerous English transla-tions of Hesse's works. A professor of German language and literature, Ziolkowski contends that literature can-not be studied from a single national perspective; accord-ingly, throughout his career he has promoted the value of comparative literary studies. In the following excerpt,*

he examines how contemporary German novelists render the theme of insanity in their works.]

When we venture into the realm of recent German fiction, we expose ourselves to the laws of a topsy-turvy world, a fairy-tale kingdom in which normal restrictions are inval-id and everyday conditions annulled. It is a land of insani-ty, abnormality, and absurdity without parallel. In this world people suddenly make up their minds to deform themselves in order to remain children and to play their *Tin Drum.* Sadistic *Giant Dwarfs*—from the title of a prize-winning novel—set upon their parents in bed, tying them together so that they can observe the act of procre-ation at their lascivious leisure. Gigantic soldiers wander through a *Landscape in Concrete*—another novel-title—where they have the most improbable picaresque adven-tures and finally kill their girl friends by biting them in the jugular vein. It is a world where the *Opinions of a Clown*—and this does not imply the realistic reminiscences of an Emmet Kelley or a Marcel Marceau—are considered wor-thy of enumeration. In this world hitherto normal people, rejecting their true identity, suddenly say *Call Me Ganten-bein* and put on the yellow armband and the dark glasses of the blind, in order to view the world henceforth from this new point of view.

It is unnecessary to cite further titles, for these five best sellers by well-known and representative writers [Günter Grass, Gisela Elsner, Jakov Lind, Heinrich Böll, and Max Frisch] should suffice to illustrate a characteristic phe-nomenon in German fiction between 1959 and 1965. We note first that the typical hero of the German novel in the early sixties presents himself as a pronounced caricature or distortion of human nature. These heroes are not rounded characters, but exaggerations, to the point of ab-surdity, of certain traits—lust, sadism, irresponsibility, cutting frankness, and so forth—that are usually sup-pressed or at least balanced by other elements of the per-sonality.

This leads us immediately to a second observation. The fictional world that is created in these novels is regularly presented from a distorted perspective. In most cases we are dealing with first-person narratives: the dwarf, the giant, the clown, or the supposedly blind man tells us his own story and thus offers us his own point of view as the only proper one. In the cases when there is a third-person narrator, the latter identifies himself so closely with his hero, after the fashion of Kafka, that absolutely no dis-crepancy is apparent between the views of the fictional fig-ure and those of the narrator, who might otherwise put the world back into its customary perspective. It is, in other words, a deformed world that is offered to us. . . . [Here, we] have more than the simple metaphor of insanity: we are asked to share this view from the madhouse.

Finally, the typical mood of this world is a grotesque and often macabre gallows humor, which unmasks the absur-dity of everyday reality and gives the novel its tone.

Characteristics of this sort distinguish the most recent fic-tion from the typical novel of the first postwar years. The representative hero of the period 1945-1955 was a return-ing veteran to whom the world at home had become

A 1735 etching by William Hogarth depicting life in the English insane asylum Bedlam.

alien—an outsider, but not a caricature. His perspective was slightly off-center, but still related to the whole. Very often he appeared in the guise of his typological ancestor Odysseus, possibly the first returning veteran in world literature. Like Beckmann in Wolfgang Borchert's *Outside at the Door* (*Draussen vor der Tür,* 1947), like the sober, lyrical "I" in the poems of Günter Eich, like the melancholy soldiers in Heinrich Böll's early stories, he could not identify fully with the prevailing reality of the postwar world, yet he did not deny its existence. In contrast to the often scurrilous exuberance of much recent prose, the tone of those first novels was consciously restrained and low-keyed.

In his book on postwar German literature [*Deutsche Literatur in West und Ost: Prosa seit 1945* (1963)] Marcel Reich-Ranicki coined a number of suggestive designations for those first representative authors: Hans Erich Nossack he called "the sober visionary"; Alfred Andersch "the vanquished revolutionary"; Siegfried Lenz "the calm accessory." Note the adjectives: sober, vanquished, calm. They characterize quite precisely the tone of most German prose up until about 1955. These writers distrusted any kind of stylistic bravura, dismissing it contemptuously as "calligraphy." But the nouns of the epithets—

visionary, revolutionary, accessory—point to future developments, for they indicate an awareness and tension that produces an inner conflict. The sober hero who calmly criticizes society will permit himself to be good-naturedly humored, tolerantly shrugged off, or rejected with shocked astonishment for only so long. Finally he assumes the role that society forces upon him: the role of the fool, the court jester, the blind man, the abortion. If you treat a writer as a clown long enough, then he will finally appear as a clown. We have here an almost classic case of the collective reification of a metaphor. Perhaps in this role, the writer thinks, he can jolt society into attention, if it refuses to heed sober admonition.

This radical displacement of the fictional perspective can nowhere be seen more clearly than in the proliferation of insanity in recent German literature. It is a veritable bedlam of madmen. Think of the three international theatrical successes from Germany: Friedrich Dürrenmatt's *The Physicists* (*Die Physiker,* 1962), Karl Wittlinger's *Do You Know the Milky Way?* (*Kennen Sie die Milchstrasse,* 1955), and Peter Weiss's *Marat/Sade* (*Die Verfolgung und Ermordung von Jean Paul Marat,* 1964) all take place in a madhouse. Insanity, so to speak, represents the final stage of a process: it is the ultimate intensification of the role of the outsider who is rejected by society or who himself rejects society—alternatives which in the last analysis produce the same effect. In order to understand the implications of this development, as well as the dangers inherent in it, let us consider a few typical examples. The first is Ernst Kreuder's delightful fantasy *Enter without Knocking* (*Herein ohne anzuklopfen*, 1954).

The scene of the action in Kreuder's novel is a neurological clinic. In the first chapter the hero leaps out of a speeding train, clambers up the wall, and jumps down into the courtyard of the asylum, where he remains until the end of the novel as a voluntary paying guest. In this sanatorium everything is inverted. The patients are completely in possession of their senses; only the chief psychiatrist is mad. For Kreuder the madhouse has become a place of refuge, where normal people can withdraw in the face of the ostensible insanity of everyday reality. Kreuder's hero, who is nameless for the first half of the book, expresses this unambiguously in the second chapter of his story:

> Anyone who looks around in the world today, among the people in his neighborhood, and has not completely lost his senses—any such person is horrified by the unimaginable ugliness, the detestable ugliness that manifests itself wherever 'healthy common sense' prevails unhindered. . . . Anyone who is repelled by ugliness because he knows that beauty is reality, uncorrupted reality, distrusts the machinations of that 'healthy common sense' which is so well adapted to exploiting the starving and protecting the prosperous from any discomfort; so well suited to justifying heartlessness and to making a life-task of public and planned deception. The calculation is simple: the much-vaunted common sense excludes the most human capacity, sympathy, and thereby it breaks the contact with all that is animate, with reality.

Kreuder supplies us with a typical case of the displacement of perspective, for in his novel the equation is absolutely equal: normal is insane and insane is normal. Genuine human understanding, which treasures the good and the beautiful, thrives in the madhouse; the outside world is in a state of madness. The occupants of the sanatorium live in complete freedom, for they may be just as they wish, without being compelled to play roles forced on them by society. Outside, by contrast, life is ruled by what Kreuder calls the "Summer Schedule of the Strait-Jacket Life" or the "Official Timetable for Human Age," and freedom is merely an illusion.

But Kreuder's fantasy remains completely unproblematic, for the two worlds hardly come into conflict. The inmates are able to found their League of Brotherliness without hindrance, for they have no difficulty duping their demented doctor. Otherwise the outside world cannot touch them. Kreuder is concerned solely with depicting this model of a world in reverse. He cares neither for the realization of his vision nor for the problematic confrontation of the two worlds. At most, he is interested in the paradigmatic antithesis: we see life and the ideal, reality and the absolute. Because the two realms remain separated by the walls of the asylum, no crises are produced. The whole remains a charming and even instructive fantasy, for Kreuder's concern is aesthetic rather than ethical.

But Kreuder's successors go beyond this pure contrast. In his novel *Billiards at Half-past Nine* (*Billard um halbzehn*, 1959) Heinrich Böll carries the theme a step further by translating the confrontation of the two worlds into moral terms. For Böll the madhouse still possesses the value of the absolute, but this novelist is so deeply committed to the present that he is not content with a flight from reality. The madhouse has become a place of respite, of regaining inner composure, from which one ultimately returns to act in the world outside.

Böll's novel portrays a family that has stubbornly refused to take part in the ugly reality of a Germany gone mad. As in Kreuder's novel, each of the three main figures has created for himself a refuge from detested reality. The grandfather, Heinrich Fähmel, conceived in his youth the social role that he intended to play in life, and by blindly acting out this role for fifty years has succeeded in disconnecting himself from reality; in his innermost being he does not feel affected by the world outside. His son Robert protects himself from the assault of the world by translating all external reality immediately into aesthetic abstractions: for him life takes place on the billiard table or in the mathematical formulae that he dreams up for his amusement. But the grandmother, Johanna, has acted most consistently: she has fled to the madhouse.

Johanna's ostensible "insanity" revealed itself quite early. In 1917 she was impelled by her antipathy toward the First World War publicly to label its instigator an "imperial fool"—a case of *lèse-majesté* that was excused at the time as due to an intellectual infirmity attributable to her pregnancy. (Here already we see that Kreuder's formula is still valid: the person who sees the truth clearly is dismissed as mad.) Johanna's intellectual "infirmity" manifests itself again during the Second World War, when she refuses to accept from the family's rural properties any foods to which she is not legally entitled. Instead, she hands out bread, butter, and honey to strangers who are less favored. Her Christian love for her fellow men, which she not only affirms in principle, but also puts into action, is again held to be insanity. Finally, her remarkable behavior, which also takes the form of criticism of the government, comes to the attention of the authorities, and there is only one possible way for her to save herself. In 1942 she has herself declared insane and withdraws into the madhouse. But even sixteen years later, in 1958 (the year in which the novel takes place), Johanna still prefers her life in the madhouse to everyday life in the Federal Republic of Germany, and her explanation clearly reminds us of Kreuder's lovable madmen. "I can't step back into the magic circle again," she says. "I am afraid. Much more than before. You have obviously gotten used to the faces, but I am beginning to long for my harmless idiots." The asylum is again the place of brotherly love and true humanity, in contrast to the false and inhuman reality of the ostensibly healthy world of reason.

This reverse symbolism is brought out even more clearly in the course of the novel through the introduction of parallel figures. For instance, Böll mentions a parish priest whom the church authorities have hidden away in a remote village because of his mad ideas:

> There he preaches away over the heads of the peasants, the heads of the school children. They do not hate him, they simply don't understand him. They even venerate him, in their fashion, as a lovable fool. Does he really tell them that all men are brothers? They know better and secretly think: "Isn't he a communist, after all?"

We are still dealing with the same displacement of perspective that we noted in Kreuder's novel. The view from the madhouse is actually the view with which the author identifies—and along with him, naturally, the reader—while the everyday world remains mad and in need of redemption. But Böll adds a fuse to this potentially explosive situation when, unlike Kreuder, he allows the two worlds to come into contact.

The novel takes place on various temporal levels. On the one hand, the reader learns, through frequent flashbacks, how it happened in the course of fifty years that grandfather, grandmother, and son of the Fähmel family came to shut themselves off from the prevailing reality. On the other hand, the level of the present action culminates in a moment of decision. This is what matters to Böll: not the mere representation of the model situation, but the moment of decision and action. On this September day of 1958 all three main characters suddenly realize that it is not sufficient to stand apart from life, looking on with aesthetic detachment; it is necessary to intercede actively. In other words, one must return from the secure idyll of the madhouse into the chaos of the everyday world if one wishes to assert oneself as a free individual. At this point Böll goes beyond Kreuder's aesthetic antithesis of real and ideal. But the confrontation of the absolute ethos of the madhouse with the relativized reality of the world presents difficult problems.

Mother Fähmel decides to make an energetic protest against the false life of the present, where the very men who occupied important offices in the Nazi government are still in positions of high authority. She returns to reality and, with a pistol that she has stolen, shoots at a minister of state—a man who once again threatens to set Germany on the same fateful path that led it into two world wars. She does not shoot for revenge, she says, but in order to prevent any future evil. She calls the minister "the murderer of my grandson," and she says that she is committing "not murder of a tyrant, but murder of a man who claims to be decent." Her shot is the symbol of her protest against the deceitful respectability of a generation that has forgotten an evil scarcely past, and it shatters the protective shells in which the members of the family have lived for years. Here, at the end of the novel, both the grandfather and son decide to return to reality (from which each had retreated at age twenty-nine!) and take an active part in life. The minister has escaped with a light wound; Johanna appeals to Paragraph 51 of the penal code (mental incompetence) and is returned to her madhouse, where she feels most at home in any case. Everything has seemingly been resolved. As far as the family is concerned, the symbolic shot unquestionably has a beneficial effect: Heinrich and Robert will no longer be satisfied to observe the

world condescendingly from their aesthetic distance. They will attempt, each in his own way, to alleviate the visible ills of the world.

But are we not left with a sense of nagging uneasiness? What if the minister had died? Has not Böll evaded here a certain thorny dilemma? For if in this novel the perspective of insanity is the one with which we are expected to identify, then does the madman actually have the moral right to commit murder? And if so, is not the symbolic effect of the protest immediately canceled out by the appeal to Paragraph 51, to mental incompetence? We can take a protest seriously only if the one who protests is prepared to lay his or her own life on the line, to accept the consequences of the protest. Is it not logically inconsistent that the moral attitude for which the author has enlisted our sympathy should turn out, in the end, to be "incompetent"?

To put the question in this way is, naturally, purposely crude and somewhat unfair to Böll. In the first place, the minister does not die; in the second place, Mother Fähmel is not the most representative figure of the novel. But Böll's novel reveals the difficulties that arise if one attempts to confront madness, as a model of absolute good, with the reality of everyday life. The madhouse as a symbol of truth is valid only as long as it remains hermetically sealed off, as it does in Kreuder's novel. As soon as the absolute begins to intercede in the world, certain moral dilemmas not easily disposed of unavoidably arise. Böll's novel merely hints gently at this problem.

Thomas Valentin's first novel sounds virtually like an answer to Böll's implicit question. In *Hell for Children* (*Hölle für Kinder,* 1961) the discrepancy between absolute truth and action has been intensified to the utmost extreme. Once again, it is an action in the present that is glaringly illuminated by a series of flashbacks. The traveling salesman Ernst Klewitz is introduced as a man who had a miserable childhood, a circumstance that has led him to the bitter conclusion that life is nothing but hell for children. This conviction, irrespective of its validity, develops in the case of Klewitz into a real psychosis and finally brings about a nervous breakdown. Around this time he becomes acquainted with a boy whose unhappy existence reminds him of his own childhood. He decides, like Böll's Mother Fähmel, to act. In order to save the child from his drunken parents, he attempts to flee with him. When the police catch up with the two of them at the border, Klewitz decides to kill the boy rather than to expose him again to the beatings of his brutal parents.

We see that Valentin has here stretched to the very limit the moral dilemma that is merely suggested implicitly by Böll. To be sure, Klewitz' conviction, his view from the madhouse, is in an absolute sense as correct as Johanna Fähmel's. But he succeeds in carrying out the murder that she botches, and the reader, who up to this unexpected turning point has identified with Klewitz, suddenly recoils in horror. Does Klewitz' view, however right it may be, entitle him to extinguish a human life? And here at the very end we come upon a surprising twist. Klewitz' lawyer tries to persuade him to appeal to the aforementioned Paragraph 51, but Klewitz refuses to accept what he regards as a cheap way out. "How is it that suddenly, in the middle of my life, I am mentally incompetent for a week? I don't accept the gift! I don't understand why they open this door to me, this door to the freedom to be temporarily insane. I understand absolutely nothing but one thing: they cannot take the responsibility away from me! I don't want their revolting sympathy."

Valentin is pleading just as passionately as Böll for a change in the world. For him, also, the view from the madhouse is a view of the truth. But he proceeds to the final consequence of this attitude. If circumstances are completely reversed, then the obligation for moral responsibility now rests with the madman. He may no longer withdraw, under the protection of Paragraph 51, into the idyllic world of the madhouse; he must submit to justice. The absolute is valid only in the madhouse; in life one must compromise. So the model remains—but it is only a model.

This is perhaps the ultimate explanation for the surprising turn of events that electrifies the reader at the end of these two novels. The authors apply their whole skill to winning us over to the reversed perspective—and then shock us with the dilemma that arises as soon as one attempts to apply this truth in life itself. This is thus the final ironic meaning of these novels: that a world in which such moral dead ends can exist is in dire need of change. From under the mask of the madman peers the revolutionary, who no longer expresses his opinions so soberly and calmly. He makes us accomplices in the crimes and murders that are committed—a lesson learned, by the way, from Dostoevsky. And the reader, who has allowed himself to be caught up in the enticing perspective of "insanity," can no longer evade the moral responsibility imposed at the end. This constitutes the cleverest manipulation of *littérature engagée*. The sober veteran, who fifteen years earlier was still standing "outside at the door," now grins at us from the portals of the madhouse. (pp. 332-43)

Madness as a literary symbol has a long and venerable history, a history that reaches back to the *poeta vates* of antiquity and to which *Don Quixote* as well as Dostoevsky's *The Idiot* belong. But the meaning of the symbol changes with the times. It is a convenient framework into which each generation places its own values. In his study of the eccentric in German literature [*Der Typus des Sonderlings in der deutschen Literatur* (1943)] Herman Meyer observes that the eccentric, who occurs so frequently in literature of the eighteenth and nineteenth centuries and who is closely related to the madman, virtually disappears with the emergence of naturalism. Meyer attributes this phenomenon to the rise of positivism; for the eccentric, as a type, is dependent upon the belief in the metaphysical freedom of man: eccentricity interests us as a possibility of life for the completely free man. (This is the same justification that our own hippies claim for themselves in the mid-sixties.) Positivism, by contrast, regards man simply as a random intersection of certain biological and sociological conditions. The eccentric no longer has any value as a valid potentiality of human existence and human development, but is considered as nothing more than a pathological exception, having at most a certain clinical interest.

So we can probably conclude that the reappearance of symbolic eccentrics and madmen in our own age indicates the presence of a philosophical foundation in which, once again, freedom occupies a central position. It is just such a philosophical basis, indeed, that we find in the various trends of existentialism, under whose banner so many postwar novelists have written. As in so many other cases, Nietzsche is one of the important sources of this contemporary phenomenon. In the preface to *Thus Spake Zarathustra* (1883) the prophet expresses his disappointment that people do not want to hear the message he has brought back from his ten years in the mountains. "Not a single shepherd and *one* herd!" he exclaims. "Everyone wants the same thing, everyone is alike: whoever feels otherwise goes voluntarily into the madhouse." Here, seventy years before Kreuder, we find precisely the same symbol used in precisely the same way: the madhouse as the refuge of true understanding, in contrast to an uncomprehending world.

Nietzsche had elucidated the basis for his image in *The Dawn* (*Die Morgenröte*, 1881), his speculations on moral prejudices. In a section entitled "The Meaning of Insanity in the History of Morality" Nietzsche praises "madness" as the force that breaks through the bonds of conventional morality to new ideas and values. "Almost everywhere it is madness that paves the way for new thoughts, that breaks the spell of venerated customs and superstitions." He even goes a step further, claiming that "all those superior men, who felt an irresistible urge to break the yoke of some false morality and to establish new laws, had no alternative—*if they were not really insane*—but to become insane or to pretend to be so." And this holds true, Nietzsche claims, for innovators in every area, not merely in religion and politics. Nietzsche comes back to this image, in one form or another, repeatedly. Thus he suggests that the Good, the Beautiful, and the Mighty need to keep a court jester if they want to hear the truth; for the court jester is "a being with the prerogative of the madman, not to be able to adapt himself." On the whole, Nietzsche's use of the symbol of madness, like almost everything else about him, was in distinct opposition to the prevailing notions of positivism, which (like the old professors in *Berlin Alexanderplatz*) regarded insanity merely as a physiological condition to be cured by sweatbaths.

Among the writers of the twenties and thirties who shared Nietzsche's conception of madness, none is more conspicuous than Hermann Hesse, who [in *Gesammelte Dichtungen* (1952)] asked himself in all seriousness whether, under certain cultural circumstances, it is not "more dignified, nobler, more proper to become a psychopath than to adapt oneself to the present conditions at the expense of all one's ideals." (It is symptomatic that Hesse, in 1919, outlined his beliefs in a major essay entitled "Zarathustra's Return.") In *The Steppenwolf* (1927) madness is the symbolic form that Hesse's belief in Magical Thinking takes. This belief, outlined particularly in his essay on Dostoevsky's *The Idiot* [published in *Gesammelte Schriften*, 1919], holds that true reality consists of an acceptance of all aspects of the world, and not merely of that half that is arbitrarily called good or right by conventional bourgeois morality. Harry Haller, the "Steppenwolf," sees himself at the beginning of the novel as a rather schizophrenic personality who belongs in part to the bourgeois world and in part to the wilderness of the steppes. The two fallacies of his thought are: first, that he regards these two parts of his personality as contradictory rather than complementary; and second, that he has oversimplified the totality of the world into this simple dualism.

The mysterious tract that he obtains at the beginning of his adventures bears the motto "Only for Madmen." It outlines the development that he must undergo in order to become a full human being: he must accept all the impulses of his nature that he has hitherto repressed so carefully. A short time later, when he meets the prostitute Hermine, he tells her: "Don't scold! I already know that I am mad." He is amazed when Hermine, the prophetess of his humanization, replies: "You're not at all mad, Herr Professor. In fact, you're far too little mad to suit me!" Haller's entire reeducation toward an acknowledgment of his personality, then, is seen under the aspect of madness. Consistently, before he enters the Magic Theater toward the end of the novel, as he approaches the culmination of his spiritual odyssey, he receives the warning: "Only for Madmen. The Price of Admission is Your Reason."

In *The Steppenwolf*, then, the meaning of insanity differs completely from the meaning that it carries in other contemporary works: *The Man without Qualities, Berlin Alexanderplatz, The Sleepwalkers*. For Hesse, as for Nietzsche, the values have been reversed: the madman sees the truth that is hidden from the "rationality" of the everyday, bourgeois world. The madhouse is the refuge where man can discover his individuality in total freedom.

Nietzsche and Hesse are the direct precursors of the philosophical freedom that we find again in *Enter without Knocking*. Kreuder's madmen also seek in the sanatorium above all a place of freedom where they can be themselves, without being forced to fulfill false roles thrust upon them by society. But very specific limits are imposed upon this existential freedom. On the one hand, man has the absolute freedom to determine his own being. He is at liberty to be "mad." But on the other hand, his freedom ceases the moment it threatens to encroach upon the freedom of his fellow man. Man possesses, so to speak, a negative freedom: the freedom to rebel, to protest against the prevailing reality, to be philosophically mad; but this implies in no way the absolute freedom to act. For this reason Kreuder keeps his madman carefully segregated from the world outside; Zarathustra is most at home among the eagles on his mountain, far from the "herds" below. And Harry Haller is truly free only in the psychedelic visions of the Magic Theater; at the end of the novel he returns once more to reality. Böll and Valentin, by contrast, show the serious dangers that arise when the free man seeks to act in accordance with his "mad" convictions. With the remarkable prescience of first-rate writers they anticipate the moral issues and ambiguities that, in the course of this decade, have been shifted from literature to the front page of every newspaper by the civil rights movement, the debate concerning Vietnam, and the student rebellions.

There are only two avenues of escape from the dilemma posed by the radical confrontation of reality and the abso-lute. The first is the way of tragedy, in which man comes into conflict with the laws of ethics through his acts. This is probably the deeper meaning of the novels by Böll and Valentin: as long as the world is not changed, the free man must either remain in the madhouse or perish. For if a man insists on asserting his absolute values in reality, he transgresses the legitimate boundaries of his own freedom.

Second, there remains the escape of humor. But if this humor arises from a perspective that, as we have seen [in Wolfgang Kayser's *Das Groteske; Seine Gestaltung in Malerei und Dichtung* (1957)], is in itself perverted or mad, then it can easily degenerate into the grotesque. The result is the novels of Günter Grass, Gisela Elsner, Jakov Lind, and others. The grotesque has one immeasurable advantage: it makes possible a nontragic action, since it no longer operates through the antithesis of reality and the absolute. Instead it takes place in an intermediate realm where the madman can do anything he likes: remain a child and play his tin drum; overpower his parents and tie them together in bed; bite his beloved to death; play the role of a blind man or a clown. The radical confrontation is avoided from the start by the displacement of the perspective of the entire work. The reader knows immediately that he is not dealing with conventional reality, but with a realm of the imagination where normal rules no longer apply.

Recent German literature is rooted, for the most part, in an existential experience of the dualism of self and world, in which the individual seeks desperately to preserve his own freedom in the face of a detested reality. Since 1945 this awareness has passed through three stages or degrees of intensity. In the first stage, everyday reality still dominates the foreground, and the lonely individual is forced to the side with his protests. (This is the general pattern followed by the early postwar literature, which focused on the experiences of returning veterans.) On the second level, the position of the outsider has become absolute: reality and truth confront one another as outside world and madhouse. (This is the pattern of the madhouse novels of Kreuder, Böll, and Valentin.) In the third stage, finally, reality has been completely vanquished: we are left with a realm of the imagination shaped and controlled wholly by the view from the madhouse. (This is the pattern of the grotesques of Grass, Lind, Elsner, and others.)

At this point German literature reached the final limit in the displacement of perspective. It could not be pushed any further. In one of his best known essays Ortega y Gasset claimed that the distortion of perspective has led to the "dehumanization of art" in the twentieth century. Ortega was thinking particularly of abstract painting, but his conclusions apply equally well to recent literary developments. For the danger existed—and still exists—that the most recent prose writers, by making the distorted perspective into an absolute point of view, might gradually lose all contact with human values if they do not return to the level of human reality. The last chapter of Günter Grass's *The Tin Drum* vividly demonstrates how difficult it is to get back to reality from the realm of fantasy.

We recall that Oskar Matzerath, that obscene and infantile dwarf, is writing his memoirs during a two-year period of custody in a mental institution. His life up to this point has taken place on the level of fantasy, where it was unnecessary to assume any moral responsibility. From this level he fled—by way of transition, so to speak—into the madhouse, where he is still secure from the onslaught of reality. On his thirtieth birthday he learns that he is now going to be released. He must return to the outside world, or, to put it more precisely: for the first time in his life he must submit to reality and its ethical system. For his entire previous life has taken place in the fairy-tale world of fantasy, where questions of guilt and innocence do not become acute.

> What I have feared for years, ever since my flight, announces itself today on my thirtieth birthday: they have found the true guilty man, they re-open the case, acquit me, release me from the nursing home, take away my sweet bed, put me out into the cold street which is exposed to all the elements, and compel a thirty-year-old Oskar to collect disciples around himself and his drum.

Like Valentin's hero, Oskar Matzerath realizes that Paragraph 51 is merely a temporary solution: ultimately a man must take upon himself the responsibility for his own deeds. Life, if it is to have any meaning, must finally return from the realm of the imagination and the madhouse into reality. Grass, in a brilliant move, has reversed the historical process: his hero moves symbolically back from the world of the grotesque through the madhouse to the everyday world.

Insanity is the loss of the intellectual faculties. Madness is only a strange and singular use of those faculties.

—Anatole France, in his On Life and Letters, 1924, originally published as La vie littéraire, 1910.

What is valid as the theme of a novel, however, also has a certain validity as an aesthetic principle. The flight into the grotesque is only a temporary solution, which cannot satisfy us in the long run. The theme of insanity, with its radical confrontation, shows that the humanly interesting problems take place in the border zone where reality and the absolute collide. This is the territory where literature has always produced its greatest works. The radical displacement of perspective from this border zone is a characteristic of postwar German literature—and not only of German literature, of course. Black humor in England and America as well as the theater of the absurd tend in the same direction. This attitude has produced some fascinating and unforgettable works that often cast an unexpected light on life and glaringly illuminate its absurdities. But how far from the center can the perspective be displaced?

By 1965 German literature had reached a precarious

point. The flight into the grotesque, as effective as it may be at times, could no longer satisfy, for it ultimately became an aesthetic evasion of the burden, indeed, of the duty of taking an ethical position. In the hands of mere trivializers it had become an amoral and hence inhuman form of art. Moreover, the grotesque degenerated to such an extent during the years of its popularity that it became an empty routine, no longer bringing forth the desired effect of aesthetic alienation, but at most the yawn of *déjà vu*. The grotesque arose initially as the response to a reality that writers considered so absurd that it could be treated only by absurd distortion. But when everybody is insane, then the rational man again comes into his own. (pp. 349-58)

> *Theodore Ziolkowski, "The View from the Madhouse," in his* Dimensions of the Modern Novel: German Texts and European Contexts, *Princeton University Press, 1969, pp. 332-61.*

MADNESS AND FEMINIST ARTISTS

Gloria Feman Orenstein

[*An American critic and educator, Orenstein is a frequent contributor to art and feminist publications. She has commented: "I am very interested in the relationship between consciousness and creativity. I am also interested in the female tradition in the arts and its contribution to intellectual and cultural history." In the following excerpt, she suggests that due to the absence of a female creation myth, female surrealist writers used madness as a search for the self in a "male-defined" world.*]

In his *Manifeste du Surréalisme,* André Breton, proclaiming the absolute value of the freedom of the imagination, offered a new, positive approach to madness. Viewing it as a heightened state of consciousness, productive of poetic discourse, he said: "La seule imagination me rend compte de ce qui *peut être.* . . . Reste la folie 'la folie qu'on enferme' a-t-on si bien dit. Celle-là ou l'autre. . . . Les confidences des fous, je passerais ma vie à les provoquer. Ce sont gens d'une honnêté scrupuleuse, et dont l'innocence n'a d'égale que la mienne."

Reclaiming all the faculties of the mind when freed from the tyranny of logic, Breton sought a new kind of resolution between the states of waking reality and dream—a surreality in which the marvelous resided. Indeed, because madness was an important path to the marvelous, the surrealists often induced and cultivated states of temporary insanity and hailed them as privileged moments of creative vision.

Thus, surrealism remains one of the few poetic and artistic movements in which an artist's output in a mentally alienated state was supremely valued and seen to be the sign of the fecundity and freedom of the imagination. However, while this approach to madness might have been beneficial for the work of certain surrealists, today feminist scholars are calling into question the etiology of insanity in women. They are reinterpreting the causes and symptoms of female madness and redefining the specificity of its meaning within the context of a male-defined description of reality.

Yet, because the surrealist movement placed such a high value on the work produced by artists in moments of madness, it provides us with a unique body of materials from which to understand the significance of this state when it occurs in women writers and artists. It furnishes us with documentation that is virtually unequalled in its illumination of the correlation between states of mental alienation in creative women and their connection with patriarchal creation myths.

I propose to look at the commonality of imagery in the visions of . . . women whose encounters with madness either were transformed into art or made a profound impact on the surrealist movement. However, the deeper meaning of their madness has always been misunderstood, because it has continually been placed within the framework of patriarchal literary and artistic criticism. Looking at their experience from a feminist perspective may help us to gain insight into the nature of the female imagination and women's mythic visions.

How does a feminist perspective interpret the madness of women and, in particular, that of women artists? In *Women and Madness,* Phyllis Chesler discusses the fact that, in a patriarchal society, women are fundamentally alienated from knowledge of their own inner strength, as well as from a history of images that would provide them with role-models of alternative ways of conceiving of woman and being female. Chesler writes:

> Women are impaled on the cross of self-sacrifice. . . . Unlike men, they are categorically denied the experience of cultural supremacy, humanity, and renewal based on their sexual identity. . . . In different ways, some women are driven mad by this fact. Such madness is essentially an intense experience of female biological, sexual, and cultural castration, and a doomed search for potency. The search often involves "delusions" or displays of physical aggression, grandeur, sexuality and emotionality—all traits which would probably be more acceptable in female-dominated cultures. Such traits in women are feared and punished in patriarchal mental asylums.

Chesler's theory maintains that the denial of cultural equality and even supremacy has been an important factor in causing female madness. In a recent study *The Madwoman in the Attic,* Sandra M. Gilbert and Susan Gubar extend this analysis to include the madness specific to women writers. They claim that in a patriarchally-defined literary history men are seen as the fathers of creation with all the cosmic potency of the image of a male God behind them. Since the world was "authored by a male God," it was assumed that the imaginative universe of a corpus of works was similarly authored by the male imagination. As

Gilbert and Gubar point out, the metaphors of literary paternity implicit in our culture assume that God the Father both engendered the cosmos and fathered the text. Female madness, then, within the context of a patriarchal creation myth and literary history is, according to critic Barbara Hill Rigney [in *Madness and Sexual Politics in the Feminist Novel* (1978)], a political event. It is connected to a rebellion against or escape from male authority, and Rigney views it much as R. D. Laing would view all madness—as a form of superior sanity and a search for an authentic, integrated image of the self. In the case of women writers it is a search for an image of the self as creator, even if it is as creator of a world that others do not recognize—a world in which woman reclaims her identification with the Great Mother in an essentially gynocentric description of reality.

In their discussion of George Eliot, George Sand, and the Brontë sisters, Gilbert and Gubar stress the fact that the dilemma of a patriarchal creation model has always forced women to identify the creative self with a male persona in order to fulfill the exigencies of a male mythic vision. Trapped within a masculinist world-view that had no image of a divine female creator, women artists had either to identify their own creativity with a male self-image or to suffer the consequences of an irreconcilable clash between their talents and their sex. This clash usually terminated in madness.

Research into the life histories and art works of the women of surrealism reveals a large number of instances in which creative women have suffered from episodes of temporary insanity often leading to suicide. A closer look at their writings and paintings sheds light on the ways in which the absence of a female creation myth in western culture has been symptomatic in women's insanity when it finds expression in the arts.

While the category "poète maudit" has been created to describe the works of male artists such as Rimbaud and Artaud who have been called visionaries when they were possessed by a "holy" madness, women writers who have had similar experiences, such as Virginia Woolf, Anne Sexton, and Sylvia Plath, have rarely been lauded for their mental states of alienation. The woman writer's madness is never considered to be a special state of grace, a lofty manifestation of her election as sibyl or prophet, as seer of the deeper truths that reality denies us. On the contrary, "mad" women writers and artists have always been treated with disdain; their madness turned to an affliction, a sign of their inferiority, their inability to cope—a permanent stigma.

The surrealist movement is perhaps alone in valuing the artistic production of women in moments of insanity. However, this fact by no means implies that women were considered as equals to men in their ordinary states of maturation and development. Xavière Gauthier [in *Surréalisme et Sexualité* (1971)] has argued that the art of male surrealists and the theoretical position of André Breton demonstrate, rather, that despite their revolutionary pretensions, when it came to women phallic myths prevailed, and that surrealists were "toujours prêts à réduire la femme à un objet de contemplation et de consommation." If at all, it was primarily in their states of alienation, their moments of madness and illumination, that they were given any serious consideration. Yet, as I have shown [in "The Women of Surrealism," in *The Feminist Art Journal* 23 (1975)] women artists in the surrealist movement never depicted women as mere objects. Rather, they created them as Alchemists, Goddesses, and Spiritual Guides. They consistently identified woman with the exalted image of the Magna Mater rather than with the diminished image of the Femme-Enfant. Whereas for the male surrealists women were considered of consequence when they were divested of all cultural power, either infantilized or mad, for the female artists of the same movement the Mother Goddess was indeed the basic image of female creativity and grandeur.

A reading of the theoretical writings by male critics included in the volume of *Obliques* dedicated to "La Femme Surréaliste" indicates that while attention is now being turned to surrealist women, the patriarchal definition of woman has not evolved. Once more we find that woman is conceived of as a creature of the moment, unrelated to time and history. [In "Depuis longtemps je m'étonne je m'indigne," in *Obliques* (1977)] André Pieyre de Mandiargues writes, speaking of the Code Napoléon that still applies to women,

> Rien n'est moins excusable que cette volonté d'incompréhension et d'obstruction que je constate sur le point précis de l'art féminin, puisque, par la nature même de son génie qui selon la commune opinion est sensible et sensuel avant tout, comme par sa manière de prendre le temps sous l'espèce de l'instant, plutôt que sous celle de la durée, la femme nous apparaît ainsi que l'être le plus richement doué des qualités naturelles qui chez la personne élue font l'artiste.

Mandiargues' definition is merely a reiteration of André Breton's earlier definition of woman [in *Arcane* 17 (1965)] as "la femme enfant," an eternal woman-child "parce que sur elle le temps n'a pas de prise."

[The] women to be discussed below bear witness to a profound female desire to restore the original image of the centrality and awesomeness of female divinity to art and religion through reclaiming a female creation myth as a viable model for female creativity. The madness experienced by these women of surrealism is not only connected to the political and social realities of patriarchal authority in the secular world. It is more essentially caused by the repression of the Goddess image in the Judeo-Christian religious tradition. Thus, while male theoreticians have claimed that woman does not relate to time in its duration, what these women have really expressed in their visionary moments of artistic creation is their deep alienation from patriarchal history. In the coded works of these surrealist women, feminist scholars can actually discover a new kind of concern with time, a reclamation of 8,000 years of lost history and an affinity with pre-patriarchal cultures in which the image of the Great Mother was revered as supreme creator of the universe. Coded within the cryptic imaginings of these very rare texts and paintings that give testimony to their female "season in hell" is the desire to restore women to their rightful place in the scheme of cosmic creation and in historical record.

Colette Thomas, an actress who worked with Antonin Artaud, published *Le Testament de la Fille Morte* in 1954 under the male pseudonym of René. Her anonymity—for no one actually knows what became of her—was maintained by the mystery and silence that surrounded the book when it first appeared. André Breton's surrealist group was probably the only one to speak of it at all. This book of "pensées," parables, philosophical fragments, theatrical meditations, personal testimonials, and stories reveals itself to be a feminist statement that resonates deeply today, for Thomas speaks of the disappearance of woman's creative work and of her profound sense of nonexistence in a male-dominated society—the feeling that Simone de Beauvoir has referred to as the experience of the "Other." Colette Thomas writes: "Car la voix est femme mais N'EXISTE PAS. . . . Dieu est mort. Je proteste au nom de la femme."

Her consciousness of woman's social oppression is acute, yet Thomas sees woman collaborating in her own tragic destiny out of a lack of reflection upon her own metaphysical condition. Her book attempts to awaken both men and women to the injustices and realities of their social and spiritual world:

> L'HEROINE DE L'AMOUR DU MONDE.
> —C'EST UNE FEMME. MAIS ON NE LA VOIT PAS—CAR ELLE N'A PAS ETE PRISE PAR L'AMOUR DU MONDE—MAIS VIOLEE, PIETINEE, PETRIE ET REJETEE PAR LA HAINE CONTRE LE MONDE, AVEC SON CONSENTEMENT.

> L'EGLISE APPREND A LA FEMME A SOUFFRIR ET LA SAUVE. MAIS QUAND LA FEMME EST SEULE ET QU'ELLE SOUFFRE? QUAND ELLE N'EST PLUS PROTEGEE PAR RIEN ET QUE LE MONDE CONTINUE A VIVRE EN ELLE? ELLE MEURT OU ELLE CREE LE MONDE NEUF: ELLE-MEME RETOURNEE.

Realizing that woman's true destiny is to be self-generating, autonomous, and independent of male authority, especially of that imposed upon her by the myths and parables in which male divinity is sacralized, she writes:

> LA JERUSALEM CELESTE N'EST PAS UN LIEU—MAIS UNE FEMME FAITE TERRE ET RESTEE FEMME POUR DIRE: PAS DE ROI, PAS DE DIEU, PAS DE PRETRE, PAS DE GENERATION—MOI-MEME SEULE ET SUFFISANTE A ETRE ET A DEVENIR CAR JE SUIS DEVENUE—OUI C'EST-A-DIRE QUE PLUS RIEN N'A A VENIR D'ELLE QU'ELLE-MEME, ENFIN REALISEE. ELLE A MIS LE TEMPS DES ETOILES A LE FAIRE—ET C'EST BIEN ELLE QUI L'A FAIT—ELLE—ELLE—ELLE.

> LA FEMME DEVENUE ESCLAVE DE LA TERRE ET EN MEME TEMPS MAIS SEULE DEVENUE LIBRE DE LA TERRE.

> CAR LE CHRIST A EU BESOIN DE MARIE POUR VIVRE. MAIS MARIE A-T-ELLE BESOIN DE CHRIST POUR CONTINUER A VIVRE?

> VOICI LE CRIME:

APRES QUE LE CHRIST A EU VECU, ON A DIT, LE
PERE, LE FILS, ET LE SAINT-ESPRIT, ET ON A
CACHE LA FEMME.

MAIS MAINTENANT LE MONSTRUEUX MEN-
SONGE, LA PHENOMENALE HYPOCRISIE A EMP-
UANTI TOUT L'EDIFICE. LA CHRETIENTE CREVE
DE SON INFAMIE—ET LA FEMME NAIT D'ELLE-
MEME—SA PROPRE TACHE.

OUI, LA MATERNITE A ETE L'IMMONDE DUPE-
RIE QUI A PESE SUR NOTRE TERRE ET POURRI
SON FONDEMENT. IL N'Y A PAS DE MYSTERE
DANS LA MATERNITE, MAIS IL N'Y A PAS DE
SAINT-ESPRIT.

MAIS IL Y A UN MYSTERE DANS LA FEMME—
QU'ELLE CONNAIT MAINTENANT, QU'ELLE DE-
TRUIT ET QU'ELLE RESSUSCITE, ET QUE LA
CHRETIENTE A NOMME AVEC TOUTES SORTES
DE   SINGERIES   ABOMINABLES: MAL—
MENSONGE—MENSTRUES—TERRE—MAIS QUE
LA FEMME PARVIENT A CRIER: BIEN—
VERITE—CREATION—CIEL. AU CRIME IL FAUT
REPONDRE PAR LE CRIME.

If Thomas's message has been passed over in silence, it is
because she saw all too clearly woman as the original creator of life. Her mad illumination rails against the denial
of female spiritual power, the denial of the Earth Mother.
It protests against the lie that patriarchal theology created
in the myth of Adam and Eve and the myth of the Virgin
Birth which rob woman of her procreative legitimacy.
Thomas is outraged by her vision of woman defiled and
denigrated under our social and religious systems. She realizes that woman was forced to collaborate in her own annihilation. For were she to reject outright those traditional
canons of belief, woman would still be treated as a heretic
and condemned to silence all the more violently.

A visionary deprived of her natural rights, Colette Thomas expresses her protest poignantly in a short parable entitled "La Petite Fille et le monde." It tells of a young girl,
Anne, daughter of a woodcutter, who would take a lantern
with her to greet her father when he returned from the
woods every evening at nightfall. As she welcomed him,
she would repeat the words: "The lantern gives light."
One day she carried her lantern to meet her father and
welcomed him excitedly, saying, "The lantern illuminates
things, Papa." Her father reprimanded her and reminded
her that he had only taught her to say, "The lantern gives
light," nothing more. "C'est vrai, papa, elle éclaire
d'habitude, mais aujourd'hui, elle ILLUMINE. Je l'ai vu
dans le sentier. D'habitude, elle trace un rayon blanc
comme la lune—aujourd'hui sa lumière est rouge, verte,
bleue, de toutes les couleurs—j'ai pensé à la fête—c'est
vrai." When, overpowered by her own vision, she repeated
the word "ILLUMINE" in an exalted and defiant tone, her
father threatened to beat her. Anne ran off into the forest,
collided with a tree, and went blind. Many centuries after
her death men from another age, digging in the ground,
discovered the miraculously preserved body of a young
girl. It radiated such a pure light that from that day on
they instituted great celebrations in honor of the body that
they called "ANNEES" (years) and other less important
rites of Spring, Summer, Autumn, and Winter.

Edvard Munch's The Lunatic *(1908-09).*

This parable can be linked to the symptom of female blindness as it is discussed by Gilbert and Gubar. Eye "troubles," moreover, they write, seem to abound in the lives
and works of literary women, with Dickinson matter-of-
factly noting that her eyes got "put out" . . . Charlotte
Brontë deliberately writing with her eyes closed, and
Mary Elizabeth Coleridge writing about "Blindness" that
came because 'Absolute and bright / the Sun's rays smote
me till they masked the Sun'. Woman, it appears, is commanded not to "see" in a world where the visionary powers are appropriated by men. Colette Thomas meditates
upon the parable and realizes that, given the condition of
women's lives in this culture, one begins to understand
why it is safer for women to continue to say "give light"
when what they really mean is "illuminate." This kind of
awareness of woman's spiritual mission and the thwarting
of her powers by restrictions placed upon her vision and
her use of language becomes a very important key for the
interpretation of women's writing. "Mais pourquoi,"
Thomas writes:

parce qu'elle est "possédee," une femme en ce
monde est méprisable.

Parce que l'homme qui la possède n'est pas parfait.

Et il est plus facile de trouver Dieu qu'un
homme parfait. Mais moi qui ai trouvé Dieu, je
continue à chercher un homme *parfait.*

The imperfect laws made by men have imprisoned woman
within a false image of divinity that denies her true nature—her sexuality and her illuminated vision:

Ah! la mère-vierge! L'élu et le péché dans la
même chair! Ah! L'admirable sophisme!

Et si un Christ est né c'est à Marie qu'on le doit,
on n'a pas besoin d'un Saint-Esprit pour mettre
un enfant au monde, ni d'un Dieu, il suffit d'être
bien véritablement une femme et l'on met au
monde un enfant—et le dieu n'est qu'une figure
de rhétorique.

Thomas has seen through the lie of patriarchal theology.
She has seen the desecration of the Mother Goddess in the
figure of speech, God. She has felt the denial of female sexuality and female spirituality and the need for a return to
woman as the image of creator of the universe.

The female visionary is the "poète maudite" whose madness is a mask and a decoy. Were she to speak any more
openly in a less mystical or cryptic prose, her true meaning
might be revealed in all the intensity of its rage. For the
illuminated vision of Colette Thomas expresses the intimation of the usurpation of her legitimate rights by patriarchal religion. Denied any image of her strength, denied
the symbol of the Goddess, she lives in profound contradiction with her most authentic experience of self-
knowledge. In his presentation of her work ["Colette
Thomas on La Fin du Narcissisme"] in *Obliques,* Michel
Camus comments: "Est-ce pour maîtriser la folie qu'elle
écrit. Écrire est une autre sorte de folie. . . . Comment
lisons-nous *la fille morte.* A la limite son *Testament* n'est
"absolument" lisible pour personne. Ni pour Colette
Thomas ni pour nous. Il n'est pas illisible non plus. Ni tout
à fait lisible ni tout à fait illisible. Il est aveuglant."
Camus's opacity and the mystificatory function of his criticism lead to further obfuscation of Thomas's meaning. To
claim that she is even unreadable to herself is to undermine the power of her vision, which is not blinding, but
illuminating.

Colette Thomas's position prefigures that of Mary Daly,
for she reclaims female spirituality and sexuality and calls
for a new cycle in which a truer explanation of female creation will prevail. Her book [, *Gyn/Ecology: The Metaethics of Radical Feminism,* 1978] ends in this way:

—C'est à la femme maintenant parce que le
monde est *seul,* incommunicable, et *malade.* La
virilité du monde est enterrée, et la *terre* reste
seule à y croire. C'est pourquoi elle seule peut la
retrouver.

Tout le travail du déterrement lui incombe—
mais elle retrouve cela, elle qui, pendant neuf
mois, dans son ventre, depuis la création, déterre
l'esprit.

Car l'esprit ne vient pas du dehors comme le

croit l'Eglise, mais du dedans et par la *seule* puis-
sance de la chair—et la chair n'est pas sainte ni
mère ni vierge ni quoi que ce soit mais *femme—*
femme absolument.

Mais la femme depuis suffisamment longtemps
subit ce supplice pour enfin le crier: accouchement, accouchement, accouchement, total et ab-
solu, sans rémission.

C'est ainsi que tout un cycle d'existence est re-
jeté. Passe au suivant.

[In *Gyn/Ecology: The Metaethics of Radical Feminism*
(1978)] Mary Daly interprets the perception of a woman
like Colette Thomas by reminding us that "patriarchal
myths contain stolen mythic powers. They are something
like distorting lenses through which we *can* see into the
Background. But it is necessary to break their codes in
order to use them as viewers, that is we must see their lie
in order to see their truth. We can correctly perceive patriarchal myths as reversals, as pale derivatives of more ancient, more translucent myths from gynocentric civilizations." (pp. 45-53)

L'Homme-Jasmin: Impressions d'une malade mentale by
Unica Zürn, who committed suicide in 1970 at the age of
fifty-four after numerous encounters with madness, provides us with still more insight into the nature of the conflicts facing the surrealist woman artist. Zürn, who lived
with surrealist artist Hans Bellmer from 1953 until her
death, was obsessed with anagrams and cryptograms. She
was convinced that, just as the real world masks the truth
of the imaginary world, so the body of the word hides the
secret sense of its inner meaning.

Her anagrams, published with automatic drawings in her
first book *Hexentexte* (in German), show a Cabbalistic approach to deciphering the mysteries of the universe
through a mystical reading of the many sacred signs, symbols, and scripts she finds inscribed therein. In *L'Homme-
Jasmin* Zürn also discovers the occult links between her
anagrams and her hallucinations.

The narrative is the autobiography of her own "season in
hell," of her visionary experiences during her period of
mental illness and internment in a psychiatric clinic.
L'Homme-Jasmin is written in the third person, creating
a further level of distancing as she describes the schizophrenic split she underwent as a result of the conflict between her identity as woman and as creator. A look at the
nature of this experience, the symbolism of her hallucinations, and the meaning of her psychic split indicates that
her conflict, too, stemmed from woman's deprivation of
a role-model for spiritual and secular creation. The basic
split she describes is one in which she becomes possessed
and is visited by her masculine double, her *doppelgänger.*
As her hallucinatory counterpart, he is known alternately
as L'Homme Jasmin and L'Homme Blanc. The image of
L'Homme Jasmin is an obvious reversal of the image of
La Femme Jasmin or the Femme-Fleur that we find so
prevalent in surrealist poetry.

Feminizing the male as her own double, Zürn identifies
this self with her potential grandeur, a dimension that she
is deprived of in reality because she cannot reconcile mas-

culine creative privilege and femininity. She sees a magical link between the letters "H. M." in the Hotel Minerva where she stays in Paris and the initials of Herman Melville. Of *Moby Dick* she says she feels "trop faible, trop petite . . . pour pouvoir, comme l'a fait Herman Melville, par exemple, bâtir une œuvre sur ce choc émotionnel. . . . Et elle sent douloureusement les limites, l'étroitesse, la monotonie qui sont parfois celles de la vie d'une femme."

Her so-called "delusions of grandeur" are equivalent to woman's reclamation of the roles accorded to men in her society—those of God the creator and of the male author. Staying at the Hotel Minerva, the house of the Goddess of Wisdom, is for Zürn somehow connected with her desire to become a female Herman Melville. *Moby Dick*'s profound influence on her can perhaps be understood to reside in its assault on the symbol of the Deity and on the spiritual and physical evil incarnated in that symbol. It is precisely when she is staying at the Hotel Minerva that she feels possessed by "les forces de géant," or what psychiatry would characterize as "delusions of grandeur." In several hallucinations she possesses the powers of cosmic creation. Her desire to give birth to a new, more marvelous reality in the form of a city is analogous to Colette Thomas's New Jerusalem and Kay Sage's vision of the collapse of a gynocentric civilization. The yearning for a new, more powerful, divine image of woman is strongly present in the hallucination of the self as Mother of the World. To give birth to a new city is to transform civilization by reclaiming one's identification with The Great Mother: "Et *c'est elle* qui va enfanter cette ville. Ce désir devient si excessif qu'elle éprouve les douleurs de l'enfantement, les mêmes symptômes qu'à la naissance de ses enfants. Elle ne sait pas comment il est possible de se sentir enceinte d'une ville tout entière. Mais depuis quelques jours elle a vécu des évenements tellement incroyables que ce *nouvel état* lui paraît presque naturel."

Woman's dream of changing the world, of radically altering the conditions of life, not only for mankind in general but primarily for women, is the pivotal point of her "madness." Her lack of real secular power obliges her to invent imaginary powers in order to validate the sense of her own potency which is deeply connected to the female experience of procreation. In the image of the self as Mother of the new city, Zürn is not experiencing time in the instant, but rather proclaiming woman as the point of origin of a new cycle of history. During moments of ecstatic transport, when she feels confidence and joy, she undergoes symbolic physical transformations through dance and auditory hallucinations that suggest her subconscious attraction to other cultures and other measures of historical time, to eras of history in which the Goddess was revered. In one particular hallucination she hears oriental music and feels "sa colonne vertébrale se changer en serpent." During this sequence of changes she becomes a tropical bird and hears a voice address her in the following words: " 'Qui est capable de représenter un oiseau s'approche de la maîtrise'." Finally, she perceives the apparition of a tiger, but she wants to enact both the hunter and the hunted simultaneously, for the voice informs her: "Celui qui représente au même moment le tigre et la fuite devant le

tigre a gagné et est un maître." Having wished to become a Master, she is ordered by the voice to become a scorpion and incarnate the image of suicide. Clearly, she subconsciously feels she must be punished for her attempt to fuse with the sacred energy of the serpent, a Goddess energy. In the image of the serpent, Kundalini energy is connected with the Goddess Shakti, the symbol of the Inner Woman. The serpent is also linked to many Cretan and Minoan Goddess figures. Reclaiming the ancient image of the Tree of Life as the Mother Goddess, Zürn in another ecstatic vision also desires to "tenter l'impossible: la plantation de l'arbre à pain." She says:

> Et *qui* parmi les hommes a jamais réussi à planter l'arbre à pain? La terreur de la famine serait vaincue. La phrase se tord en elle comme un serpent et elle ne peut lui résister. . . . Mais où trouver la graine qui donnera l'arbre à pain? Une graine, une poignée de terre, c'est tout ce dont elle a besoin. Avec la certitude qu'elle va accomplir ce miracle elle cherche et découvre sur le plancher un minuscule objet d'origine inconnue et l'enfouit dans la poignée de terre. D'une geste solennel elle pose terre et graine au milieu du bureau et se rassoit, très fière, le coeur rempli d'une foi enfantine.

At the termination of this prolonged hallucinatory experience she asks: "Mais comment l'Univers est-il tombé aux mains des hommes? Comme s'il était besoin de l'aide des hommes! Erreur! erreur!"

The imperative to plant the Tree of Bread comes to her from the memory of a poem by Henri Michaux, "Je plante l'arbre à pain." Once more the initials H.M. are clues to her desire to reclaim for woman the prerogatives of creation and nurturance that belonged to the Mother Goddess rather than to the male God.

Her anagrams inform us that "Les délires sont prières." She convokes the spirit of the genie locked in the bottle in another anagram and identifies this spirit with L'Homme Blanc. In this anagram she calls it the "evil spirit," "celle qui dévora la dépouille de la druidesse." Thus, Unica Zürn has produced a split in which the part of the self she identifies as masculine, or evil according to what is considered appropriate for woman, is a separate entity. The two somehow cannot coexist in one person, for to be feminine and to be an artist like Melville, a powerful divine leader like a Druidess, or a Master is not a viable role for a woman either in her society or in the surrealist movement. L'Homme Blanc is the image of the woman as Druid, Master, and author filtered into a masculine disguise in order to reconcile that power with the prevailing symbology of a patriarchal creation myth.

In a parable appended to her manuscript, which describes a series of games played between male and female, the male protagonist, Flavius, succeeds in capturing Norma in order to begin to incorporate her into himself: "Pendant son incorporation Norma sent comme la moelle s'échapper de ses os, son sang s'écouler de ses veines, ses sens l'abandonner." Flavius absorbs everything from Norma until they both turn completely white. At the conclusion of her document, Zürn writes:

FLAVIUS. L'Homme Blanc.

NORMA. Elle-même.

The myth of a psychic transmutation of male into female and female into male ultimately transcribes a wish-fulfillment, a profound desire to break out of the sex-role boundaries that limit the definition and potentialities of the self.

In Zürn's magical universe, which is permeated with talismanic signs and omens, she presages a time when the male/female dichotomy will be resolved. Her obsessions embrace a yearning for a new order, a time when men and women will be utterly transfigured. She is convinced that "Sous la surveillance de psychiatres et d'infirmières et à l'aide de piqures, l'homme va se transformer lentement en femme et la femme en homme. Ils vont s'unir, se sentir rachetés et s'épouser." This hope for a possible harmony between the sexes eventually extends into the hope for a harmony between all species of life on the planet. It is through her writing (she was at work on this manuscript during her internment) and her art (she did automatic drawings) that she eventually learned to control her hallucinations, to give them esthetic form, and thus, temporarily, to recover from her intense need to live out in secret the private delectation of her messianic mission. Her art reveals a quest for a more perfect order, a world transformed, in which all beings will find salvation. "Tout d'un coup entre visages et plantes elle découvre aussi des animaux. Elle voit ceux qu'elle a essayé de dessiner: oiseaux, poissons et insectes. Elle perçoit même les *rapports* les plus fantastiques entre bêtes et hommes, qui se fondent en une harmonie parfaite et impossible." Her manuscript ends with a comparison between her own experience and that of Artaud, claiming for herself the right to have her "madness" taken as seriously as his.

In a diary Unica Zürn wrote:

> Pour la dernière fois, l'Homme-Jasmin (Hans Bellmer) devient présent dans un dialogue silencieux avec elle. Ce n'est pas lui qui dit qu'elle est à présent Dieu, mais bien elle. Et ça devient une certitude si forte qu'elle peut à peine supporter cet état nouveau. Elle est descendue sur terre pour vivre avec les êtres humains pour la première fois dans l'histoire du monde. Elle se lève et s'asseoit sur le bord du lit. Ce sentiment est insoutenable et trop intense pour être décrit. Elle est bouleversée. Elle se recouche et la voix de L'Homme-Jasmin lui dit: "C'est moi Dieu." Elle répond: "Non, c'est moi." Cette lutte se prolonge jusqu'à ce qu'elle dise: "D'accord, tu es le plus âgé et le plus sage de nous deux. Dieux c'est toi et moi je suis ton fils Jésus."

Christianity's deification of the male as God and redeemer, leaving no important role for woman except that of virgin, is what Zürn's madness calls into question. For she seeks to reconcile the image of creation with the original, pre-patriarchal image of the Great Mother and to return the privilege of creation to women.

Leonora Carrington's experiences during her mental breakdown were published in her narrative *Down Below*. In it she describes the illuminations she had during her in-ternment in a psychiatric hospital in Santander, Spain. Carrington's madness, too, can be characterized by "delusions of grandeur," but her identification with powerful women can also be interpreted as a desire to restore woman to her rightful place in our religious and human systems. Her appropriation of the female principle in all its earthly and spiritual manifestations, of the identity of the Queen of England and of Christ into her persona, indicates her profound need to reclaim woman's secular and sacred powers:

> Later, with full lucidity, I would go 'Down Below' as the third person of the Trinity. I felt that through the agency of the Sun, I was an androgyne, the Moon, the Holy Ghost, a gypsy, an acrobat, Leonora Carrington, and a woman. I was also destined to be, later, Elizabeth of England. . . . I was she who revealed religions and bore on her shoulders the freedom and the sins of the earth changed into knowledge, the union of Man and Woman with God and the Cosmos all equal between them. The son was the Sun and I the Moon, an essential element of the Trinity, with the microscopic knowledge of the earth, its plants and creatures. I knew that Christ was dead and done for, and that I had to take His place, because the Trinity, minus a woman and microscopic knowledge had become dry and incomplete. Christ was replaced by the Sun. I was Christ on earth in the person of the Holy Ghost.

Two of Carrington's paintings in particular deal with the dichotomy between patriarchal and gynocentric vision. They provide interpretations for the image of the Goddess as it is viewed by the female artist raised in an androcentric culture. In *Rarvarok* (1963), Carrington has divided her composition in half, presenting two opposing visions simultaneously. On the left are the priests and rabbis of the Judeo-Christian religions. On the right is a woman who is either "mad" or possessed by a vision. In her vision a horse-drawn chariot appears bearing a white female figure. The chariot is driven by two horses with breasts and human heads, one black, one white. The male figures seem to be aloof, judging the sanity of the woman from a safely-removed distance, perhaps pronouncing her "hysterical." The white horse in Carrington's mythological world-view is generally associated with the Celtic mythological white Horse Goddess, Epona. As a death chariot with its curtain semi-drawn, the Horse Goddess reveals the presence of a luminous white woman, a figure of the White Goddess within the chariot. The woman on the floor is then, from the gynocentric perspective, in a trance state and possessed by a vision of the Mother Goddess. In Carrington's mythic cosmology, death is a passage to another dimension, one in which encounters with the lost tribes and races that worshipped a Goddess, such as the Tribe of the Goddess Dana of the Tuatha de Danaan, transpire. *The Naked Truth* (1962) is another work which shows the position of the White Goddess in patriarchal religion. Once more the painting is divided in half. On the left are the rabbis and scholars engrossed in the study of their sacred texts, while on the right the White Goddess is fettered and bound in a barbed-wire enclosure. Upon her head is a unicorn's horn, an organ of extra-sensory perception through which she receives revelations of the presence of apocalyptic beasts in the Tree of Life. Here Carrington has reversed the traditional iconography of the unicorn from male to female making woman the possessor of the legendary magic associated with the horn. Because the forces of the female principle have been repressed, the rabbis are blinded to the vision of *The Naked Truth.* Ultimately Carrington posits the Goddess as the supreme source of mystical revelation.

The figure of the Goddess also becomes the symbol for the retrieval of woman's pre-patriarchal history in her novel *The Hearing Trumpet,* in which the ninety-year-old heroine, Marion, through the magical powers of her hearing trumpet, a symbol of an organ of extra-sensory perception, embarks upon a quest for the Holy Grail. Carrington's Grail romance reverses the gender of the hero from male to female because in this case the quest marks a voyage to the gynocentric past—a time when the Goddess was the center of creation. Marion, after a series of adventures, has a revelation of her previous incarnations, all of which symbolize aspects of the spirit of the Mother Goddess. "Holding the mirror at arm's length I seemed to see a three-faced female whose eyes winked alternatively. One of the faces was black, one red, one white, and they each belonged to the Abbess, the Queen Bee and myself." The three-faced female is the image of the Triple Goddess or the Triple Muse, who, according to Robert Graves, is woman in her divine character. Each lifetime is revealed to be one step in the karmic cycle, and the conclusion of the process yields a total knowledge of all-time.

Leonora Carrington's conscious integration of Goddess-related material into her creative work, both coded within the cryptic hieroglyphics of paintings such as *Grandmother Moorhead's Aromatic Kitchen* (1975), and overtly explored in her paintings of the *Godmother* and in her novel *The Hearing Trumpet,* constitutes a model of transformative evolution among these women artists. *Grandmother Moorhead's Aromatic Kitchen* is an excellent example of a painting which at first might seem to be a surrealist image of the oneiric world of the subconscious. Actually, the image of Mother Goose is a coded symbol for Mother Goddess. These beings, both otherworldly and mythological, are preparing a meal within a Magic Circle which is decorated with a series of black strokes that would probably not interest the casual viewer. However, these are inscriptions in Old Irish and mirror-writing, and they contain the occult meaning of the work. When studied closely with a mirror, the following inscriptions can be deciphered:

    1. Death is a pass to the world of the Sidhé.
    2. The Goddess Dana became and is the Sidhé.
    3. The old races died—Where did they go?

This painting imparts a visionary and scriptural revelation of the underworld, the land of the Sidhé, whose underground mound dwellings were, according to Celtic mythology, the habitations where the Goddess Dana and her tribe reside. This painting illustrates the kind of conscious occultation of a message that was threatening to society, but that, with the advent of the Women's Liberation Movement, became more openly expressed, and became

central to woman's own struggle for political, spiritual, and artistic freedom.

In her Women's Liberation poster, designed for the Women's Movement in Mexico, Carrington's iconography rejects the myth of Adam and Eve. The New Eve is returning the apple to the old Eve of Patriarchal Theology. She is refusing to be born of Adam and to be the cause of Evil and the Fall. Here she is identified with the Goddess energy of the Kundalini, which rises through the chakras of the body until it reaches the Third Eye of Illumination. The poster is green for the planet Earth, suggesting that when women will have achieved control of their own bodies, control over the growth of the population, the planet will flourish once more. (pp. 58-66)

If these women, in their intuitions of female grandeur both in myth and history, have been pronounced insane, must we not begin to question our definition of sanity? Women's so-called "delusions of grandeur" seem to point to a search for an authentic mythology and history of which they have been dispossessed. Today the symbol of the Goddess no longer represents the figure of a divinity to be worshipped in a new religion. Rather, it symbolizes 8,000 years of pre-patriarchal history which women must repossess before they can come to a true knowledge of their tradition and a definition of their identity. Whether viewed as breakdown or breakthrough, the madness of Surrealist visionary women represents a reclamation of the Great Mother, a feminist journey to madness and back in search of a Goddess heritage. As Carol P. Christ has said [in

---

Michel Foucault on madness and unreason:

[Madness] threatens modern man only with that return to the bleak world of beasts and things, to their fettered freedom. It is not on this horizon of *nature* that the seventeenth and eighteenth centuries recognized madness, but against a background of *Unreason;* madness did not disclose a mechanism, but revealed a liberty raging in the monstrous forms of animality. We no longer understand unreason today, except in its epithetic form: the *Unreasonable,* a sign attached to conduct or speech, and betraying to the layman's eyes the presence of madness and all its pathological train; for us the unreasonable is only one of madness's modes of appearance. On the contrary, unreason, for classicism, had a nominal value; it constituted a kind of substantial function. It was in relation to unreason and to it alone that madness could be understood. Unreason was its support; or let us say that unreason defined the locus of madness's possibility. For classical man, madness was not the natural condition, the human and psychological root of unreason; it was only unreason's empirical form; and the madman, tracing the course of human degradation to the frenzied nadir of animality, disclosed that underlying realm of unreason which threatens man and envelops—at a tremendous distance—all the forms of his natural existence. It was not a question of tending toward a determinism, but of being swallowed up by a darkness.

Michel Foucault, in his Madness and Civilization: A History of Insanity in the Age of Reason, *1967, originally published as* Histoire de la folie, *1961.*

"Why Women Need the Goddess: Phenomenological, Psychological, Political Reflections," in *Womanspirit Rising: A Feminist Reader in Religion,* edited by Christ and Judith Plaskow, 1979]:

> The symbol of the Goddess has much to offer women who are struggling to be rid of the 'powerful pervasive and longlasting moods and motivations' of devaluation of female power, denigration of the female body, distrust of female will, and denial of women's bonds and heritage that have been engendered by patriarchal religion. As women struggle to create a new culture in which women's power, bodies, will and bonds are celebrated, it seems natural that the Goddess would reemerge as a symbol of the newfound beauty, strength, and power of women.
>
> (p. 69)

> *Gloria Feman Orenstein, "Reclaiming the Great Mother: A Feminist Journey to Madness and Back in Search of a Goddess Heritage," in* Symposium, *Vol. XXXVI, No. 1, Spring, 1982, pp. 45-70.*

Carole B. Tarantelli

[*A professor of English literature, editor, and psychoanalyst, Tarantelli is well known for her work in feminist criticism and studies of Victorian literature; she also founded the Italian journal* Calibano. *In the following excerpt, she examines female characters who represent the paradigm of female indifference and for whom madness is a response to an unaccepting social milieu.*]

> Contemporary molecular physics has the concept of "holes" that are not at all equal to the simple absence of matter. These "holes" display an absence of matter in a structural position that implies its presence. In these conditions a "hole" behaves so that it is possible to measure its weight, in negative quantities of course. Physicists regularly speak of "heavy" and "light" holes.
>
> Yuri Lotman, *Analysis of the Poetic Text*
>
> . . . . .
>
> I dissolve, go away, am left with nothing, nothing, nothing—unless I am the wind that blows through the immense spaces that lie between electron and electron, proton and its attendants, spaces that cannot be filled with *nothing,* since nothing is *nothing.*
>
> Doris Lessing, *The Making of the Representative for Planet 8*

Much feminist scholarship can be seen as an attempt to create a story for women different from the traditional one, as part of the larger process which claims for women the fundamental right to interpret the meaning of our acts. These efforts have, among other things, attempted to understand individual women (literary women, historical figures) or groups of women (suffragists, women wage earners) as cultural actors, the originators and interpreters of the meaning of their acts, projected into what Hannah Arendt calls [in *The Human Condition,* 1958] the space of appearance, the space "where I appear to others as others appear to me, where [persons] exist not merely like other living or inanimate things but make their appearance explicitly."

Although feminist scholarship has shown that women are so emphatically capable of being rival intelligences, it has not shown that we have gained the all-important control over the outcome of our stories. It is one thing to be able to speak, to articulate an alternative vision, as opposed to being constrained in silence. It is another thing to be able to ensure the survival or, better, even the realization of the dissenting vision; and it is this, surely, which we are aiming for and have not reached.

The representation of the female figure in literature is a case in point. For example, great nineteenth-century English women novelists were wonderfully capable of revealing the rich interiority of their heroines, and their difference from that culture's story of women. Yet, this subjectivity was doomed to defeat when, at the end of the novel, the text allied itself with the world: the first Catherine Earnshaw in *Wuthering Heights,* for example, the antagonistic woman who cannot reduce her excessiveness to the social norm, inevitably dies, while her daughter, whose story coincides with the traditional female story, survives to be awarded the traditional literary prize, the triumph of the perfectly adequate marriage. Indeed, as Myra Jehlen has convincingly argued [in "Archimedes and the Paradox of Feminist Criticism," *Signs* (1981)], insofar as it is tied to "reality," the already existent, the novel, it would seem, *must* represent the defeat or assimilation of the rebellious heroine, for if her story coincided with the traditional story of femininity, she would have an uninteresting tale to recount; and if it differed, the imposition of that meaning on the world, the realization of her vision, would automatically necessitate a radical (unrealistic) revision of the world. So the "realistic" paradigmatic story will logically be, as in fact it is, that of the disappointment of the character's great expectations, the loss of her illusions (as with Dorothea Brooke in George Eliot's *Middlemarch,* to name only one example, a heroine whose life is "dispersed among hindrances, instead of centring in some long-recognisable deed"). The novel will tell the story of the reduction of the different to the same. Or if her story is the story of her refusal to succumb to circumstance, her unwillingness or inability to stop what Sandra M. Gilbert and Susan Gubar have called [in *The Madwoman in the Attic* (1979)] her mad dance of rebellion, it will be the story of her expulsion from the "sane" world, that part of the whole human experience which can be narrated. As in *Wuthering Heights,* it will, instead, portray her death.

The defeat or assimilation of the different; the inability to accord value, and hence full survival, to anything except the already existent—this is certainly an old tale. Is it, in spite of feminist scholarship's recovery of female dissent, still the necessary end for the tale of difference? Or, in social terms, can the different woman exist only by negative differentiation, that is, insofar as she affirms that she does not correspond to the story of female experience projected by her culture? (pp. 177-79)

. . . . .

. . . the edges of terrestrial reality

Joanne Greenberg, *I Never Promised You a
Rosegarden*

Madness, as feminist criticism has repeatedly pointed out,
is a central metaphor in the women's literary tradition. By
existing outside of the norms and limits which structure
ordinary experience, in a dark elsewhere whose laws are
not those of the diurnal world of sane discourse, the madwoman poses the problem of female indifference in a paradigmatic form.

As Sandra M. Gilbert and Susan Gubar have so brilliantly
demonstrated, the madwoman, at least in the nineteenth-
century English texts, represents the story of women's rebellion as the proud queen's suicidal dance in the red-hot
shoes merited by her mad anger. For self-destructive rage
is the traditionally available emotional alternative to the
Snow White passivity of the acceptance of cultural subordination. The alternative is between the mad exit from
confining social form and the "sane" acceptance of limitation. The question behind this choice and implicitly asked
by the protagonists of the nineteenth-century women's
novels for whose stories these were the possible outcomes
was this: Given history, given structure, how can I be?
And the answer, of course, was, as we have seen, I, as I,
cannot.

Through Charlotte Perkins Gilman and Virginia Woolf
(to name only two), texts of madness continue to pose the
problem of the protagonist's difference. Our period sees a
reflowering of the tradition. Several texts of the 1960s,
such as Sylvia Plath's *The Bell Jar* and Joanne Greenberg's *I Never Promised You a Rosegarden,* can be used to
illustrate how the status of the heroine, whose difference
takes the extreme form of madness, is rendered less precarious. In the 1960s novels, the question as to the possibility for the survival of her difference implicit in the nineteenth-century texts is fundamentally modified. It becomes, as I hope to show, not "Given history, given structure, how can I be?" but "Given that *I am,* why history,
why structure?"

The protagonist's madness in these two novels renders explicit her radical refusal of a world which will not allow
her to constitute herself as a subject, that is, to be present
to herself and others on her own terms. In Joanne Greenberg's *I Never Promised You a Rosegarden,* the heroine
Deborah is part of the mad world of the "atomized armies
of persons who had severed their claims to membership in
all the world's other groups and orders" and exists on "the
edges of terrestrial reality." In *The Bell Jar,* Esther Greenwood makes clear her disgust at the social reality which
surrounds her, taking, for example, a long look at the arti-
facts of modernity, the "colossal junkyard, the swamps
and back lots of Connecticut . . . one broken-down fragment bearing no relation to another" and decides that "it
looked one hell of a mess."

This refusal comports the risk of psychic annihilation for
the unconformed self, which is reduced to self-genesis, to
mere subjectivity. No genealogy exists which will enable
her to understand herself. For example, Esther in *The Bell
Jar* has an impossible choice among the parade of "queer

old ladies," like Jay Cee, the editor, or Philomena Guinea,
the author of popular pulp novels, who exercised derivative and second-rate power in the leftover positions the
culture allowed to women, or Mrs. Willard, in her sensible
suits and shoes using her strong-minded self to perpetuate
the priority of male meaning; or Dodo Conway, who eternally breeds her innumerable offspring. There are no other
lives which can point to and thus confirm hers, no one who
can see her. Thus, although Esther identifies with her creative self, she is able to express that identification only in
the trivial and ultimately self-destructive image of her self
as "the colored arrows from a Fourth of July rocket"; "I
wanted," she says, "change and excitement and to shoot
off in all directions myself."

In *I Never Promised You a Rosegarden,* too, the madwoman is shown to be mad partly because the unsponsored self
is unable to recognize and use its powers, which are then
turned against her self. The image in which the heroine
imagines her sickness is that of a volcano. That is, she *is*
powerful and, having, like a bottled-up volcano, no normal way to express that "male" power, she lives her self
as an immense menace to itself and others. The madwom-
en of this novel, in fact, are "free" to express their "masculine" powers, their physical strength, their violence, their
exhibitionistic sexuality, at the price of enormous pain,
like the tiny old lady, the white-haired Miss Coral who
lifts an iron hospital bed off the floor and hurls it across
the room.

As Mary Shelley had intuited in *Frankenstein,* one of the
tragically logical responses of the "monstrous" subject

An eighteenth-century mezzotint entitled Madness.

who cannot find that confirmation in the eyes of an other, which is the necessary condition for (social) existence, is to annul the self. A self without a story cannot be "seen," and thus it does not apparently exist. A story can never presuppose only a teller, it also presupposes a hearer who confirms it. Esther Greenwood, of course, also tries to annul her unacceptable self; but though her suicide attempt is evidently an act of self-hatred, its meaning goes beyond this. For it is *also* a refusal to reconcile the self which found no space in the "junkyard" with the world. Her suicide thus implicitly asks, Why history?

Another logical response to the inability to exist within the forms of social existence is to attempt to exit from them. This exit can be expressed at all levels of psychic and social life—from the fact that the person needs to exist inside the walls and barriers of the insane asylum, which place her outside "normal" life, to the schizophrenic's adherence to the knowable laws of the "unreal" kingdom in her head, over the unpredictable and chaotic "real" world where the self-representations of persons and their real meanings never coincide, to the awesome experience of madness as the wrenching of the self from *all* levels of meaning.

> A black wind came up. The walls dissolved and the world became a combination of shadows . . . all direction became a lie. The laws of physics and solid matter were repealed. . . . She did not know whether she was standing or sitting down, which way was upright. . . . She lost track of the parts of her body. . . . As sight went spinning erratically away and back, she tried to clutch at thoughts only to find that she had lost all memory of the English language. . . . Memory went entirely, and then mind, and then there was only the faster and faster succession of sensations. . . . These suggested something secret and horrible, but she could not catch what it was because there was at last no longer a responding self.

In this description [from *The Bell Jar*], madness is shown to be the self's attempt to do totally without the psychic structure destroying her. The desire to get out of a structure which is hostile to female life is here the desire for an apocalypse. The mad self, like the souls of the redeemed, abandons all human meaning and, thus, like the suicide, ceases to exist as a self, at least while it is undergoing the experience of madness. But in these novels, the identification of the story with the figures of the mad protagonist totally involves the text's meaning with her fate. In other words, unlike nineteenth-century novels such as *Frankenstein* and *Wuthering Heights,* there is no "objective" world outside her story to survive her death and console the reader for her defeat. Her "I" precedes the story, precedes history, as it were, and thus, since the story exists, is by definition indestructible. The world may seem to disappear, but the "I" cannot. However singular, this female self *exists*—like the mad Sylvia, in *Rosegarden,* who breaks the two-year silence which had made her seem "a useless piece of ward furniture," to assert that she is "sick, but not dead."

But if the exit from psychic structure involves the loss of meaning for the mad character without the disappearance

of her self, this meaning is then clearly seen to be a social construct, the self's power to attribute relevance to what it perceives (it is a "gift," as Deborah says, if the self's meaning and social meaning can coincide). So when meaning returns to the heroine, first to the physical world in the ability to see its forms and colors, and then to the personal and social world, it returns because the self which had "left" the culture is able to reenter at another level, where meaning is not the imposition of the vision of others on the self (traditional feminine meaning). The newly sane self is able to recount its story, has become a full subject.

Other early 1960s accounts of madness, though, hardly point toward a positive solution of the problem of the female subject. At the end of *The Bell Jar,* Esther is "reborn," but this rebirth is a return to the place in the world she had occupied before the descent of the bell jar—she is "patched, retreaded and approved for the road."

And, to take another example, at the end of *Wide Sargasso Sea,* Jean Rhys's revisionary account of the genesis of Bertha Mason, the heroine goes mad because the world is totally other than her self, and all of its expressions monolithically combine to negate her: the political world—as symbolized by the burning of her home by rebellious exslaves; the social world—as a child she is despised by Europeans because she is a Creole and hated by blacks because she is white; the legal world—her money, which could provide the means to escape from Rochester's desire to annul her existence, is legally his after their marriage. And on the most intimate level, where we engage in acts of self-presentation and are seen by others as we see ourselves, she finds no confirmation of that subjectivity. At the end of the novel, the mad self of the heroine is identified with the physical sensations and warm colors of her West Indian childhood, the only things which have not been appropriated by her husband Rochester, and she imposes them as fire on his cold English world, burning Thornfield, but, as we know from Jane Eyre, destroying herself as well.

I Never Promised You a Rosegarden indicates the way out of the bewildering solitude of the unsponsored female subject who lives a mad existence in a precarious and lonely present and whose future is preempted. This is enabled by the woman doctor, who confirms her own and her patient's powers: Dr. Fried is a "lightning rod . . . the grounding path for such power." This power enables Deborah to recover for her own use the powers which had been repressed in the construction of the precarious ego which the social world of parents, teachers, and peers had demanded. But this ending, too, like the nineteenth-century narratives, portrays the reduction of the subject. For Deborah must abandon her gods, must choose between her "real" world and her "imaginary" world (a cure for which the readers of this autobiographical novel can only be grateful, but which should not prevent us from observing its logical implications). The end of the novel, then, implicitly affirms that the world—*this* world, *this* structure, *this* history—is logically as well as temporally prior to the subject. Thus, even though the character determines to "use" her mad experience, as the doctor had assured her she could, she has in some way closed the doors between her self and another, possible world, which, thrown back into darkness, has become precisely that, Other.

Madness and suicide in these novels, then, represent the refusal to live within the narrative structure of the culture without being able to generate an adequate account of the self. These texts do not certainly imagine a totally successful outcome for the story of difference, its survival as itself. But unlike the ninteenth-century texts, the traditional forms for the female story cannot claim the absolute preeminence over the different self which would render unthinkable its existence. (pp. 181-86)

Feminist literary scholarship has rightly emphasized the fact that one of the principal triumphs of the women's literary tradition has been the recovery for visibility of the world from the female point of view and of the hidden and unexpressed female part of the world. But the significance of the novels examined here goes beyond this. For their modification of traditional literary form through the modification of the moment of closure breaks the alliance between the text and the "real" world, an alliance which, as we have seen, had witnessed either the tragic defeat or the comic reduction of the difference of their heroines, an alliance which had cast the prestige of the text on the side of the equation of the possible with the actual and the prediction of the future from the past. They break with the tradition of literary texts which hegemonize the whole of the narratable, from origin to end, texts where, in Jacques Ehrmann's words [from "The Tragic/Utopian Meaning of History," *Yale French Studies* 58 (1979)], "it is the past that, once interpreted, makes up the future (however ephemeral) of the present." In these novels, rather, the vision of the reality of an elsewhere creates the possibility of an alliance between the text and a future which may possibly be new. The close of [Doris Lessing's] *Memoirs of a Survivor* prospects a future which has "transmuted" the past, and the new culture is radically different from the old, for it is allied with hope for the existence of all persons, and among them women. (pp. 190-91)

> *Carole B. Tarantelli, "And the Last Walls Dissolved: On Imagining a Story of the Survival of Difference," in* Women in Culture and Politics: A Century of Change, *edited by Judith Friedlander and others, Indiana University Press, 1986, pp. 177-93.*

FURTHER READING

Anthologies

Rabkin, Leslie Y., ed. *Psychopathology and Literature.* San Francisco: Chandler Publishing, 1966, 325 p.
>   A collection of stories and excerpts from novels that illustrate various forms of mental illness "in the belief that literature can serve an important function in the understanding of personality, and, more germane to this volume, the disordered personality."

Secondary Sources

Biasin, Gian-Paolo. "From Anatomy to Criticism." In his *Literary Diseases: Theme and Metaphor in the Italian Novel,* pp. 3-35. Austin: University of Texas Press, 1975.
>   Examines the roots of psychoanalysis in literature and the use of Freud's theories by modern Italian novelists.

Bonadeo, Alfredo. *Mark of the Beast: Death and Degradation in the Literature of the Great War.* Kentucky: University Press of Kentucky, 1989, 172 p.
>   Studies the impact of World War I on Italian literature, emphasizing the disregard for human life caused by the violence of the war.

Breuer, Rolf. "Irony, Literature, and Schizophrenia." *New Literary History* XII, No. 1 (Autumn 1980): 107-18.
>   Discusses "structural and fictional similarities between schizophrenia on the one hand, and irony and literature on the other."

Claridge, Gordon; Pryor, Ruth; and Watkins, Gwen. "Shadows on the Brain: Virginia Woolf, Antonia White, Sylvia Plath." In their *Sounds From the Bell Jar: Ten Psychotic Authors,* pp. 182-211. New York: St. Martin's Press, 1990.
>   Brief biographical and critical studies of Woolf, White, and Plath.

Colum, Mary M. "The Psychopathic Novel." *The Forum and Century* 91, No. 4 (April 1934): 219-23.
>   Examines three works by F. Scott Fitzgerald, Morley Callaghan, and William March, concluding that psychotic characters reveal traits of the normal mind in an exaggerated state.

Felman, Shoshana. *Writing and Madness (Literature/Philosophy/Psychoanalysis),* translated by Martha Noel Evans, Shoshana Felman, and Brian Massumi. Ithaca: Cornell University Press, 1985, 255 p.
>   Questions the philosophical and literary possibility of representing madness—or the absence of reason—with a linguistic system based on reason. Felman cites the theories of philosophers Friedrich Nietzche, Michel Foucault, and Jacques Derrida in analyzing the works of such writers as Gustave Flaubert, Henry James, and Jacques Lacan.

Friedrich, Otto. *Going Crazy: An Inquiry into Madness in Our Time.* New York: Simon and Schuster, 1975, 384 p.
>   Survey of literature, both fiction and nonfiction, about madness, cultural perceptions of the insane, and various twentieth-century treatment programs.

Glicksberg, Charles I. "Forms of Madness in Literature." *The Arizona Quarterly* 17, No. 1 (Spring 1961): 43-53.
>   Describes attempts by such writers as Franz Kafka, Fedor Dostoevsky, and Albert Camus to defy the absurdity and metaphysical wounds of nineteenth- and twentieth-century life.

Ojo-Ade, Femi. "Madness in the African Novel: Awoonor's *This Earth, My Brother. . . .*" In *African Literature Today,* edited by Eldred Durosimi Jones, pp. 134-52. London: Heinemann Educational Books, 1979.
>   Examines the prevalence of madmen in African literature and the oppressiveness of African societies that causes and then condemns insanity through an analysis of Kofi Awoonor's novel *This Earth, My Brother. . . .*

Plank, Robert L. "The Reproduction of Psychosis in Science Fiction." *International Record of Medicine* 167, No. 6 (July 1954): 407-21.

Studies the relationship between psychosis and science fiction, concluding that science fiction, more than any other literary genre, "is morphologically similar to schizophrenic manifestations."

Rigney, Barbara Hill. *Madness and Sexual Politics in the Feminist Novel: Studies in Brontë, Woolf, Lessing, and Atwood.* Madison: University of Wisconsin Press, 1978, 148 p.

Analyzes works by Charlotte Brontë, Virginia Woolf, Doris Lessing, and Margaret Atwood, concluding that feminist writers examine madness as women's response to a patriarchal society that attempts to confine them to limiting roles.

Ruitenbeek, Hendrik M., ed. *The Creative Imagination: Psychoanalysis and the Genius of Inspiration.* Chicago: Quadrangle Books, 1965, 350 p.

Using Freud's theories of neurosis and creativity, these essays examine aspects of artistic creativity through the lens of psychoanalysis.

Suleiman, Susan Rubin. "Nadja, Dora, Lol V. Stein: Women, Madness and Narrative." In *Discourse in Psychoanalysis and Literature,* edited by Shlomith Rimmon-Kenan, pp. 124-51. London: Methuen, 1987.

Study of works by André Breton and Marguerite Duras in which male narrators observe mad women. Using the techniques of deconstructionism and Freudian and La-canian psychoanalysis, Suleiman examines that "multidimensional space where literature and psychoanalysis, theory, and fiction, meet."

Trilling, Lionel. "Art and Neurosis." In his *The Liberal Imagination: Essays on Literature and Society,* pp. 152-71. 1950. Reprint. New York: Harcourt Brace Jovanovich, 1979.

Discusses the myth of the mad artist as well as the connection between madness, neurosis, and creativity, rejecting the idea that neurosis is the sole source of creative power.

Vernon, John. *The Garden and the Map: Schizophrenia in Twentieth-Century Literature and Culture.* Urbana: University of Illinois Press, 1973, 220 p.

Uses the concepts of schizophrenia and phenomenology to examine Western society's division between fantasy and reality—opposite modes of being that Vernon believes should be united.

Weissman, Philip. "Psychopathological Characters in Current Drama: A Study of a Trio of Heroines." *The American Imago* 17, No. 3 (Fall 1960): 271-88.

Draws on Freud's theories of neurosis to analyze female characters in the work of Tennessee Williams.

Wilmer, Harry A. "Psychiatrist on Broadway." *The American Imago* 12, No. 2 (Summer 1955): 157-78.

Criticizes the images of psychiatrists in contemporary twentieth-century drama.

Negritude

INTRODUCTION

Negritude is a literary and philosophical movement that reaffirms traditional African culture and traces its origins to the former French colonies of Africa and the Caribbean. Negritude poets, novelists, and essayists generally focus on four major areas in their writings: alienation from traditional African culture and related feelings of inferiority; revolt against European colonialism and Western education; self-affirmation and definition of black identity; and the resulting rehabilitation of African culture. Many Negritude writers also suggest that blacks can make unique contributions to an increasingly interdependent world, claiming that people of African origin have a heightened appreciation of nature, rhythm, and human emotions—aspects of life, they claim, that are not as highly valued in the materialistic and rationalistic society of the West.

While such black literary movements as the Harlem Renaissance and the Haitian Literary Renaissance of the 1920s are often considered precursors of Negritude, most scholars agree that the 1933 publication of the journal *L'étudiant noir* marked the official birth of the movement. *L'étudiant noir* was edited by Aimé Césaire, Léon-Gontran Damas, and Léopold Sédar Senghor, three black students respectively from Martinique, French Guiana, and French West Africa who were attending school in Paris. In this publication, the contributors proposed socialist solutions for the problems of exploited peoples, criticizing the arrogant aspects of Western civilization and formulating a new world view for the black race. Although Césaire, Damas, and Senghor are credited with launching the movement in 1933, the term "negritude" itself was not coined until 1939 when it appeared in Césaire's poem "Cahier d'un retour au pays natal" ("Return to My Native Land"). Negritude attracted widespread attention after World War II with the appearance of *Présence africaine* in 1947, a journal committed to the promotion of Negritude concepts, and the publication in 1948 of *Anthologie de la nouvelle poésie nègre et malgache de langue française,* a collection of Negritude poetry edited by Senghor.

Attempts to define and assess the usefulness and aims of Negritude have resulted in intense debates between and among its proponents and detractors. Senghor, for example, defined Negritude as "the sum of the cultural values of the Black world, as these are expressed in the life, the institutions and the work of Negroes." French critic Jean-Paul Sartre, however, considered the movement a distinct historical phase. Using a Marxist analogy, Sartre viewed Negritude as another reaction to the unequal distribution of social wealth and power, arguing that black civilization, as expressed through Negritude, and white civilization would eventually culminate in a raceless society. Other critics have questioned whether Negritude is a European or an African phenomenon and whether it is relevant to all people of African origin or is specific to those residing in former French colonies.

After most African colonies achieved independence in the early 1960s, Negritude waned as an organized movement and came under intense criticism from the next generation of English- and French-speaking African writers who denounced it for its inherent racism and inapplicability to the problems of post-colonial Africa. Nevertheless, as Claude Wauthier has stated: "The generation of Africans who have not known colonisation should be able to adopt a calmer attitude towards the white world. But—and this is an important qualification—this new generation has been nourished on the literature of its predecessors."

REPRESENTATIVE WORKS

Beti, Mongo
  Le pauvre Christ de Bomba (novel) 1956
    [*The Poor Christ of Bomba,* 1971]
  Le roi miraculé: Chronique des Essazam (novel) 1958
    [*King Lazarus,* 1960; also published as *King Lazarus: A Novel,* 1971]
Boto, Eza [pseudonym of Mongo Beti]
  Ville cruelle (novel) 1954
Césaire, Aimé
  Les armes miraculeuses (poetry) 1946
  *Cahier d'un retour au pays natal (poem) 1947
    [*Return to My Native Land,* 1969]
  Discours sur le colonialisme (essay) 1955
    [*Discourse on Colonialism,* 1972]
  Et les chiens se taisaient: Tragédie (drama) 1956
  Lettre à Maurice Thorez (essay) 1956
    [*Letter to Maurice Thorez,* 1957]
  Toussaint L'Ouverture: La révolution française et la probleme coloniale (biography) 1960; revised edition, 1962
  Cadastre (poetry) 1961
    [*Cadastre,* 1973]
  La tragédie du Roi Christophe (drama) 1963
    [*The Tragedy of King Christophe,* 1970]
  Une saison au Congo (drama) 1966
    [*A Season in the Congo,* 1970]
Dadié, Bernard Binlin
  Climbié (novel) 1956
    [*Climbié,* 1971]
  La ronde des jours (poetry) 1956
  Un nègre à Paris (novel) 1959

Patron de New York   (novel)   1964

Damas, Léon-Gontran
  Pigments   (poetry)   1937; also published as *Pigments* [revised edition] 1962
  Poèmes nègres sur des airs africains   (poetry)   1948 [*African Songs of Love, War, Grief and Abuse*, 1961]
  Black-Label   (poetry)   1956

Depestre, René
  Gerbes de sang   (poetry)   1946

Diop, Birago
  Les contes d'Amadou Khoumba   (short stories)   1947

Diop, Cheikh Anta
  Nations nègres et culture   (nonfiction)   1955

Diop, David
  Coups de pilon: Poèmes   (poetry)   1961

Fanon, Frantz
  Peau noir, masques blancs   (essays)   1952 [*Black Skins and White Masks*, 1965; also published as *Black Skin, White Masks*, 1967]
  Les damnés de la terre   (essays)   1961 [*The Damned*, 1963; also published as *The Wretched of the Earth*, 1965]

Kane, Cheikh Hamidou
  L'Aventure ambigüe   (novel)   1961 [*Ambiguous Adventure*, 1963]

Laye, Camara
  L'enfant noir   (autobiography)   1953 [*The Dark Child*, 1954; also published as *The African Child*, 1959]
  Le regard du roi   (novel)   1954 [*The Radiance of the King*, 1959]

Malonga, Jean
  Coeur d'Aryenne   (novel)   1954

Maran, René
  Batouala: Véritable roman nègre   (novel)   1921 [*Batouala*, 1922]

Ousmane, Sembène
  Le docker noir   (novel)   1956
  O pays, mon beau peuple!   (novel)   1957
  Les bouts de bois de Dieu   (novel)   1960 [*God's Bits of Wood*, 1962]

Oyono, Ferdinand
  Une vie de boy: Roman   (novel)   1956 [*Houseboy*, 1966; also published as *Boy!*, 1970]
  Le vieux nègre et la médaille   (novel)   1956 [*The Old Man and the Medal*, 1967]
  Chemin d'Europe   (novel)   1960 [*Road to Europe*, 1989]

Price-Mars, Jean
  Ainsi parla l'oncle   (nonfiction)   1928

Rabemananjara, Jacques
  Antsa: Poème   (poetry)   1956

Roumain, Jacques
  Bois d'ébène   (poetry)   1945 [*Ebony Wood*, 1972]

Sadji, Abdoulaye
  Nini, mulâtresse du Sénégal   (novel)   1954

Sartre, Jean-Paul
  "Orphée noir"   (essay)   1948; published in *Anthologie de la nouvelle poésie nègre et malgache de langue française*

["Black Orpheus," 1964-65; published in *Massachusetts Review*]

Senghor, Léopold Sédar
  Chants d' ombre   (poetry)   1945
  Anthologie de la nouvelle poésie nègre et malgache de langue française   (anthology)   1948
  Hosties noires   (poetry)   1948
  Ethiopiques   (poetry)   1956; also published as *Ethiopiques: Poèmes*, 1974
  Liberté I: Négritude et humanisme   (essays)   1964 [*Freedom I: Negritude and Humanism*, 1974]
  Selected Poems   (poetry)   1964
  Prose and Poetry   (essays and poetry)   1965
  Négritude, arabisme, et francité: Réflexions sur la problème de la culture   (nonfiction)   1967; also published as *Les fondements de l'africanité; ou, Négritude et arabité*, 1967 [*The Foundations of "Africanité"; or, "Negritude" and "Arabité,"* 1971]
  Liberté III: Négritude et civilisation de l'universel   (nonfiction)   1977
  Ce que je crois: Négritude, francité, et la civilisation de l'universel   (nonfiction)   1988

Socé, Ousmane
  Karim: Roman sénégalais   (novel)   1935; also published as *Karim: Roman sénégalais, suivi de contes et legendes d'Afrique noire* [revised edition], 1948
  Contes et légendes d'Afrique noire   (short stories)   1962

Tevoedjre, Albert
  L'Afrique revoltée   (nonfiction)   1958

Tirollien, Guy
  Balles d'or: Poèmes   (poetry)   1961

U Tam' si, Tchicaya
  Feu de brousse: Poème parla en 17 visions   (poetry)   1957 [*Brush Fire*, 1964]

*An incomplete version of this work was originally published in the journal *Volontés* in 1939.

ORIGINS AND EVOLUTION

Ellen Kennedy and Paulette J. Trout

[*In the following essay, Kennedy and Trout present a brief historical overview of Negritude as a literary movement.*]

In June 1931, some Martiniquan students in Paris, led by a poet-philosopher named Etienne Léro, put out the first (and last) issue of a little magazine called *Légitime Défense*. It denounced the misery of the island's Negro population, the sterility of the pseudo-French culture imposed upon it, and the complacent assumptions of cultural supremacy that were molding Negro students from France's colonial territories into second-hand Frenchmen. Léro proclaimed surrealism the only artistic method by which Martinique blacks might rediscover their authentic identity, and a Marxist political revolution as the necessary route to social and economic betterment. Although *Légitime Défense* was frowned on in official quarters and never brought out a second issue, the ephemeral journal had far-reaching repercussions. It not only catalyzed other West Indians in Paris, but also Africans, into rising above regional and tribal lines which had heretofore divided them. The problems *Légitime Défense* had pinpointed were common to all troubled black intellectuals trying to find themselves in a white society.

If the political orientation of *Légitime Défense* had proved its undoing, perhaps a magazine with a different approach would fare better. Two years later, Aimé Césaire of Martinique, Léopold Sédar Senghor from Senegal, and Léon Damas from French Guiana—all university students preparing to teach in the French *lycée* system—founded a second review, *L'Etudiant Noir,* with the stated purpose of providing a forum for discussion and debate. *L'Etudiant Noir* took occasional political stands—notably on the need for more scholarships and the relevance of socialism as a way of solving the problems of exploited peoples—but it was above all concerned with the French-speaking Negro's need to establish who and what he was, and where he was going. The concept of négritude was first aired in its pages.

L'Etudiant Noir stood squarely against assimilation, on the grounds that mimicry of the French suppressed the Negro's original qualities, emasculating his life and his art. By taking a critical view of Western values and concentrating on the retrieval of the lost heritage of African civilizations then being brought to light by a few enterprising European scholars, the circle around *L'Etudiant Noir* sought to formulate a new credo for the Negro race.

The *témoins de la négritude,* as they dubbed themselves, became convinced that there were actual differences in perception, in the fundamental apprehension of reality, between the white and black races. Their credo, and the new literature through which it was to be expressed, would find its sources in what they thought of as the Negro's "special" sensibility, his feeling for rhythm, myth, nature, the erotic and emotional life, group solidarity. Writing in *Diogène* in 1962, Senghor sought to summarize the contrast between the two races:

> [The African Negro] at first does not perceive the object . . . he doesn't take hold of it, he doesn't analyze it. After having taken in its impression like a blind man, he takes its living substance in his hands, being careful not to spoil it, to kill it. He turns it over and over in his supple hands, feeling it, smelling it. The African Negro is a pure sensorial field. . . . The classical European mind is analytical through utilization, the African mind intuitive through participation.

In a 1961 interview with the former Tunisian weekly *Afrique Action,* Senghor discussed the development of négritude as a group mystique:

> It was in Paris then, through contact with our comrades, directly or indirectly in contact with artists, writers, scholars, and philosophers, that we learned to distrust *intellectualism*—I don't mean intelligence—and *rationalism*—I don't mean reason. It was in Paris on the heels of the ethnologists, that we rediscovered négritude, which is to say the cultural values of African-Negro civilization: the gift for emotion and instinctive feeling, the gift of rhythm and form, the natural talent for image and myth, community spirit and democracy.

To express this distinctively Negro temperament, *les témoins* discarded the French classics in favor of new models. The stylized beauty of African masks, the natural humor and wisdom of ancient tales and legends, American "blues" and the spontaneity of Negro American poets such as Claude McKay, Langston Hughes, and Countee Cullen were fervently admired. Senghor experimented with translating oral poems from his native Serer, Birago Diop "recorded" legends gathered from his village *griot,* Ousmane Socé Diop published *Karim* (1935), a novel which viewed transitional Senegalese society through the eyes of its confused young hero.

But négritude found its fullest expression neither in the imitation of traditional African genres, nor in the novel or essay. By its very essence, négritude was a cosmic, pervasive, poetic experience, and poetry the one intrinsic form to give it shape. Where else but in the free verse poem, liberated from artificial rhyme and meter, could the French-speaking Negro find so natural a medium for articulating his view of himself and the world? Poetry became the esthetic vehicle for his revolutionary spirit. Here alone, in soaring, throbbing, pulsating rhythm, could he cry out his rage, sing his nostalgia, satirize a white world pallid, mechanical, and inhuman, celebrate the virility of his color, his pride that *il-est-bon-et-beau-et-légitime-d'être-nègre,* his invincible faith in the brotherhood of man and the future of his race.

The idea that Negro perception is inherently sensorial while white perception is analytical is debatable on many grounds, but it followed logically from *L'Etudiant Noir*'s rejection of non-sensual European intellectualism. As a theory, it helped unite the African and West Indian writers despite important cultural differences. These differences are, however, clearly evident in the poetry they wrote.

Jean-Paul Sartre has described the poems of négritude as "instruments of reconnaissance" in the poet's search for identity, and the circumstances of this search are different for the West Indian and the African. To the West Indian, descended from slaves, alienated from his true heritage by 300 years, Africa is mystical rather than real geography. Rendered socially and economically inferior by his color, the West Indian is obsessed with the anguish of being black in a white man's world. The African, raised in the continent of his roots and in a world predominantly black despite the colonial presence, has rarely experienced the same kind of estrangement. For the African poet, the creation of a modern ethos is a question of successfully preserving those parts of his heritage that can be valid in a twentieth century world. Thus African poetry, written against a background of tribal languages and a richly integrated traditional life, was always less burdened with racial tension.

As cultural mulattoes, the new African poets expressed their individual quests for authenticity in an adopted language which they made their own. From the pejorative *nègre,* they coined the affirmative *négritude.* Images of blackness became for them a source of light. They were not only initiators of a new written literature, but of an African cultural renaissance as well, a renaissance whose keystone was self-determination. Not until after World War II did the African poets realize that they had been forging the tools for their political self-determination as well. Senghor the *lycée* professor, Sissoko the Malinké chief and primary teacher, Dadié the library assistant, and Birago Diop the veterinarian did not yet dare to dream that they would one day be responsible for directing the political destinies of their people.

Although Senghor had published occasional poems from 1935, the poets from the Antilles, who were more numerous than the Africans in pre-war Paris, were the first to make their mark as a group. Léon Damas' inflammatory *Pigments* (1937), suggesting the rhythm of African drums in violent *vers libres,* was soon banned in all the French colonies. The freedom enjoyed in Paris did not extend elsewhere in the empire. On the other hand, Aimé Césaire's *Cahier d'un retour au pays natal,* appearing in fragments in the review *Volontés* in 1939, passed almost unnoticed until its republication in 1947 with a preface by André Breton acclaiming it as "nothing less than the greatest lyric monument of this time." With the publication of Senghor's *Chants d'Ombre* in 1945, delayed because of the war, and of his war poems *Hosties Noires* in 1948, each of the movement's three leaders was represented with a major collection of poems. If the West Indians, Césaire and Damas, were négritude's poets of revolt, Senghor was its virile poet of reconciliation.

Several other events in the late 1940s signalled the coming of age of the literature of négritude. Damas included African and West Indian poets in his 1947 collection, *Poètes d'expression française,* which drew from French colonies in the Far East as well. In 1948, Senghor brought out the landmark *Anthologie de la nouvelle poésie nègre et malgache de la langue française.* Poets from the Antilles made up two-thirds of his collection, and three Senegalese, David Diop, Birago Diop, Senghor himself, and three Madagascans made up the rest. In this decade, too, the literature began to attract the attention of leading French intellectuals. Almost as significant for the poetry of négritude as the anthologies themselves was Jean-Paul Sartre's stunning essay, "Orphée Noir," that prefaced Senghor's volume. Even today, nearly 20 years later, Sartre's searching article is unsurpassed as an appreciation of the poetry in all its ramifications.

A third development of major significance was the simultaneous launching in Paris and Dakar of a new magazine,

Présence Africaine. Among its sponsors were such distinguished names as those of André Gide, Albert Camus, the philosopher Emmanuel Mounier, the American writer Richard Wright; the anthropologist Michel Leiris, the ethnologist Theodore Monod, Senghor, Césaire, and Sartre. With its first issue in December 1947, *Présence Africaine* succeeded to the role left vacant by the defunct *L'Etudiant Noir,* and the publication of négritude literature passed from predominantly West Indian to predominantly West African hands. The editor-in-chief was Alioune Diop of Senegal, who defined his new magazine's role in these terms:

> This magazine does not place itself under the obedience of any philosophical or political ideology. It wishes to be open to the collaboration of all men of good will (white, yellow, or black) capable of helping us to define African originality and to hasten its inclusion in the modern world.

Présence Africaine quickly became the leading literary and cultural review of the French Negro world. Scorned in snobbish French literary salons, the African and West Indian poets now had outlets of their own in *Présence Africaine* and in the publishing house soon established as its affiliate. Aside from a few pioneering efforts by Editions du Seuil and Seghers, two prestigious French houses, *Présence Africaine* has remained almost the only avenue for introducing and promoting French African writers.

The magazine did not limit its horizons to literature or to the French-speaking world, however. Its ambition was to be a cultural review of the entire Negro world. As such it published not only poetry, drama, fiction, and literary criticism, but articles and book reviews on current affairs, comparative religion, anthropology, sociology, psychology, music, and the plastic arts. While expressly nonpolitical, its editorial positions were implicitly pro-Negro, anti-colonial, and anti-imperialist. Since 1959, *Présence Africaine* has been publishing an English-language edition in the effort to promote greater communication with English-speaking Africans. Although the English-language edition is a poor translation, it has encouraged spirited exchange in recent years between African writers of the two language groups. The Nigerian writers clustered at Ibadan, never having been threatened by cultural assimilation, are openly amused at négritude's mystical premises. Yet at 1963 "summit conferences" of the two literary camps held in Dakar and Freetown, delegates soon found themselves debating the merits of négritude as the conceptual key to literary pan-Africanism and to Negro cultural unity the world over.

As the First World Festival of Negro Arts has demonstrated, négritude and the dramatic new poetry it inspired have come a long way since the early 1930s. Whatever its shortcomings as an "anti-racist racism," négritude is the ethos responsible for Black Africa's first authentic and truly modern literature. It has helped to shape the very direction of African independence. The mystique and its poetry have developed over the years from a protest against officially inspired assimilation into a cultural philosophy and the basis of new national literatures. Today's African poets sing not just of continent and race, but of universal themes. Their poems are testimonies on the human condition and, as Sartre puts it, "ultimately a song of every one of us and for every one of us." (pp. 61-2)

Ellen Kennedy and Paulette J. Trout, "The Roots of Negritude," in Africa Report, *Vol. 11, No. 5, May, 1966, pp. 61-2.*

Abiola Irele

[*A Nigerian scholar, Irele has written extensively on Negritude and African literature. In the following excerpt, he outlines the historical events, social conditions, and the literary and intellectual movements that culminated in the formulation of Negritude.*]

The only really significant expression of cultural nationalism associated with Africa—apart from small-scale local movements—is the concept of *négritude*, which was developed by French-speaking Negro intellectuals. Because of its extra-African connexions and implications, and because of its vigorous organisation as a movement (especially in literature) it has developed far beyond the concept of the 'African personality', which has remained more or less a catch-word, or a simple ideological slogan; whereas *négritude* has tended more towards a philosophy.

However, I take *négritude* to mean not the philosophical idea of a Negro essence, which appears to me not only abstract but quite untenable—Senghor himself has moved far away from this point of view—but rather an historical phenomenon, a social and cultural movement closely related to African nationalism. It has aroused considerable controversy and inspired reactions ranging from enthusiastic partisanship to outright hostility. None the less, it seems to have been acknowledged as an important historical phenomenon, and as such it may most conveniently be examined, and its significance fully appreciated.

Négritude in fact appears as the culmination of the complete range of reactions provoked by the impact of western civilisation on the African, and of the whole complex of social and pyschological factors that have gone to form black people's collective experience of western domination. Its roots thus lie far down in the total historical experience of the black man in contact with the white.

It is hardly an exaggeration to say that the advent of the European in Africa turned out to be for the African a shattering experience in more than a metaphorical sense. Although the early phase of contact was marked by an ambiguously calm relationship, the European presence in Africa developed gradually into a situation of conflict, first through the slave trade, and later on with the establishment of colonial rule. African history since the coming of the white man presents examples of violent reactions to this situation—and resistance movements like those of Chaka in Zululand, and Samory in what is now Guinea, form an essential part of the stock of symbols that have nourished the nationalistic strain of *négritude*.

But the main interest of the historical origins of the movement lies in those *indirect* forms of resistance provoked by the colonial situation. As Georges Balandier has pointed out, the establishment of colonial rule in Africa brought with it a drastic re-ordering of African societies and human relations. The fact of domination, and all that this meant in the arbitrary political and social reorganisation of the African communities and the misunderstandings that naturally followed, created 'a state of latent crisis'. Colonial rule also substituted new poles of reference for social organisation and individual life, which were often in conflict with the established traditional pattern, and thus created a society which, in Balandier's words, 'appeared to possess an essentially non-authentic character' [*Sociologie actuelle de l'Afrique noire* (1963)]. In other words, colonial rule created in varying measure all over Africa a state of cultural fluctuation, in which tensions were likely to develop.

It is against this background that certain popular movements in Africa represent a search for new values, an attempt at readjustment. Perhaps the most striking of these indirect reactions to the colonial situation have been religious. It is an objective fact that the Christian missionary was an important agent in cultural change, and his role in the introduction of new values, both voluntary and involuntary, was by no means negligible. Neither is it necessary to belabour the point that Christianity was, and remains, largely identified with colonial rule, as part of the cultural baggage of the coloniser.

In this light, the separatist churches in colonial Africa have been recognised as symptoms of cultural *malaise* and as indications of cultural readjustment. But their real significance appears in their links with nationalist feeling. Again, Balandier's analysis affords an insight into the problem. The main fact that takes precedence over the rest is that of *domination*. Taking a cue from Gabriel d'Arboussier, who attributes to European influence 'the oppression of the cultural stock' of the indigenous African—thus a double politico-economic, and socio-cultural domination—Balandier has pointed out how the separatist movements, particularly that of Simeon Kibangi in the Congo, represented 'a total response to a situation felt to be creative of internal "crisis" and propitious for the maintenance of (a state of) alienation'.

The two main characteristics of these movements, as analysed by Balandier, appear to be their political radicalism—a direct consequence of their schismatic attitude in religious matters, sometimes assuming the proportion of an aggressive racialism—and their syncretic messianism. On the one hand, we have a negative gesture of refusal, a denial of an imposed world-order attributed to the white coloniser, and the wish for a cultural 'differentiation' which gives rise to a nascent political awareness, or a 'nationalist consciousness in the raw state'. On the other hand, we have a recasting of foreign and indigenous elements into a new cultural structure, which offers new possibilities of self-expression.

These popular religious movements were not, of course, always transformed into political movements. In many cases, they helped their adherents to escape from the pressures of a difficult situation; and some also represented forms of cultural regression. But they emphasise some of the problems involved in the colonial situation. For the African was in most cases drawn into the cultural world of the European, but none the less maintained in a secondary position. While he was refused acceptance as an equal by the colonisers, his life and values had come to be ruled by the norms imposed or sanctioned by the latter. He thus lived with the European in a state of symbiosis, but one of ambiguity. The result has been described by B. Malinowski [in *The Dynamics of Culture Change* (1961)]:

> Since Africans cannot share the ideals, interests and full benefits of co-operative activities with the Whites, they naturally fall back on their own system of belief, value and sentiment. To be a mere carbon copy is not satisfactory as a substitute for all the African had initially to give up . . . The African thus is forced at least spiritually to recross the first line and to re-affirm many of the tribal values abandoned at the first crossing.

A particularly dramatic example of this spiritual recrossing of the line was the Mau-Mau revolt. This largely Kikuyu nationalist rebellion was buttressed by a resort to tradition, particularly the oath, designed to counter the influence of European cultural incursion. That this was effective in its psychological purpose can be judged from this testimony of a former Mau-Mau detainee: 'Afterwards in the maize, I felt exalted with a new spirit of power and strength. All my previous life seemed empty and meaningless. Even my education, of which I was so proud, appeared trivial beside this splendid and terrible force that had been given me. *I had been born again.*' (My italics.)

The same instinctive falling back on tradition in the face of political domination formed a regular feature in African societies, especially among educated Africans. In the Congo, the Abako started out as a movement of cultural regroupment for the BaKongo, and the Egbe Omo Oduduwa served the same purpose for the Yoruba in Western Nigeria and was later to give birth to the Action Group.

In short, colonial rule was felt as a shock that reverberated right down to the foundations of African society: a truly traumatic experience that could not but provoke a reaction. This has taken many forms, from makeshift individual adjustments to organised collective movements. The 'messianic' movements presented in bold relief certain traits which were to figure in the more sophisticated reaction to colonial rule of *négritude*. In other words, *négritude* had a popular precedent in Africa; it can be seen as an articulation by an educated élite of sentiments that were felt and confusedly expressed by humbler folk. Balandier has, not without cause, called *négritude* 'the literary replica of African messianisms' [*Afrique ambigüe* (1957)]. But although, in this light, popular movements in Africa furnish an indication of the historical and cultural origins of *négritude*, it was among black people in America that it was to receive its immediate inspiration, as well as most of its distinctive characteristics.

The starting point of Negro history in America is slavery, a fact which has determined to a large extent the nature of the global experience of black people in the New World.

The drastic character of this experience from the first needs no underlining. What is important for our present concern is the general pattern of the Negro's reaction to his condition in America.

In the first place, there were organised forms of violent resistance. The history of the Negro in America has known some heroic moments, the most celebrated of which was the successful revolution under Toussaint Louverture which gave birth to the first Negro republic, Haiti. The example itself is of direct relevance here, since Toussaint has also become a symbol in the literature of *négritude,* and Aimé Césaire has hailed Haiti as the cradle of its revolutionary spirit. The heroic dimensions and the universal import of these resistance movements were not lost upon the slaves themselves, as shown by the proclamation of another group of slaves who revolted in Guadeloupe under Louis Delgrès, which begins: 'To the entire world, the last cry of innocence and of despair', and ends: 'And you, posterity, grant a tear to our misfortunes, and we shall die content'. This lyrical note adopted by the desperate slaves in commenting upon their situation was to reappear in a more extended form in Negro spirituals.

The spirituals represent the earliest examples of the black people's indirect defence, through an art form, against the conditions of contact with the white man. The spiritual appears in this light as a direct ancestor of the *négritude* poem. For the Negro slave not only made observations on his lot, but also created a whole mechanism of defence through lyrical symbols. As Langston Hughes has pointed out, some of the spirituals like 'Steal Away' were disguised weapons of direct resistance. Furthermore, they contain the first form of Negro religious expression; elements taken from the dominating culture of the white master were adapted to the Negro's temperament as well as re-interpreted to apply to his situation. An analogy between the history of the Jews of the Old Testament and that of the Negro slaves was struck in spirituals like 'Go Down, Moses', and thus the Negro slave's sentiment of exile found an appropriate and socially acceptable expression. This analogy survived slavery and has been developed into the idea of a Black Diaspora, both in the popular imagination and in the intellectual movements among black people in the Americas.

The New World Negro's sense of Africa varies considerably, according to the area and the social class in which he lives, but it is undeniable that it exists. Furthermore, the marked racial distinction of the Negro, living as a minority group in dominantly white societies, as well as other specific historical and social factors, have created a differentiation of the black man in America, and have produced Negro sub-cultures throughout the continent. At one extreme lies the largely spontaneous religious syncretism of the Negro in Latin America, notably in Brazil with the *candomblé* cult and in Haiti with the *voodoo* cult. At the other extreme lies the urban sub-culture of the Negro in the north of the U.S.A., created by the failure to complete the process of integration of the black population. In between can be cited examples like Afro-Cuban music (the rhumba) and the 'Nancy' Tales of the British West Indies. Whatever the particular significance that these varied forms of Negro sub-culture were to have in the social context of the countries in which they are found, they kept alive in varying measures a myth of Africa largely as a survival of slavery, to which the Haitian writer Jacques Roumain has given expression in his poem, 'Guinea':

> It's the long road to Guinea
> No bright welcome will be made for you
> In the dark land of dark men:
> Under a smoky sky pierced by the cry of birds,
> Around the eye of the river
> The eyelashes of the trees open on a decaying
> light
> There, there awaits you beside the water a quiet
> village,
> And the hut of your fathers, and the hard ancestral stone where your head will rest at last.

In general, it is probably safe to suppose that the presence in America of Negro sub-cultures composed in part of African elements, and the complementary existence of a myth of Africa among black peoples would never have assumed any kind of active significance without certain social factors. The most important of these was without doubt the caste system which followed on emancipation in the United States. This had the effect of stratifying American society by forcing the Negro into a distinct social organisation, to the extent that Booker T. Washington was able to remark that the Negro had become 'a nation within a nation'. Racial discrimination, which gravely limited the Negroes' opportunity for social advancement, and the various humiliations to which he was exposed created a discontent which gave rise to various political movements. A 'nationalist tradition' thus developed among black people in the United States, which was to have a cultural parallel.

The race problem and its immediate effects on the life of the U.S.A. has made the entire Negro population conscious of its ethnic identity, and has rendered its leaders and intellectuals sensitive to the historical implications. For the caste system was maintained through an elaborate cultural myth governed mainly by the idea of the biological inferiority of the black man. It has often been argued that racial prejudice developed out of attempts to rationalise the slave trade. There is no doubt, however, that the arguments for black inferiority were based upon an evaluation of the Negroes' African origins. Herskovits describes [in *The Myth of the Negro Past* (1941)] how 'the myth of the Negro past' conditioned the life of the Negro in the U.S.A.:

> For though it has often been pointed out that the skin colour of the Negro makes him an all too visible mark for prejudice, it is not so well realised that the accepted opinion of the nature of the Negro's cultural heritage is what makes him the only element in the peopling of the United States that has no operative past except in bondage.

The extension of colonial conquest in Africa all through the nineteenth and the early years of the twentieth century lent weight to the idea of African, and by extension, Negro inferiority, and gave rise to the imperialist ideologies embodied in Kipling's well-known slogan, 'the white man's burden'. Greater still was the effect of these events upon the Negro population in the U.S.A., deprived of any worth-while historical tradition.

This is the background that gives a profound meaning to popular movements such as those inspired by Noble Drew Ali and Marcus Garvey. The cultural position of the black man in the U.S.A., though possessing its own specific characteristics, none the less offered certain resemblances to that of his African counterpart. He too lived in a symbiotic relationship with the white man, and was likewise held in a subordinate position by the caste system. At the same time he was, even more than the African, governed by the secondary institutions imposed or sanctioned by the whites, especially in the fields of religion and social morality. The result resembles that observed in the case of the African, for, as Essien-Udom has remarked, 'Negroes have sought to strike out for themselves in those areas of activity in which the resistance of the white society is marginal' [*Black Nationalism* (1962)]. The Negro wish for independent expression found a ready springboard in those elements of Negro sub-culture which segregation had helped to mould into something of a definite structure, particularly the separatist religious movements.

The role of Noble Drew Ali and Garvey was to capitalise upon this latter aspect of the Negro's situation and to endow it with an historic sense derived from what had up till then remained largely a rudimentary atavistic instinct, namely, the Negro's sense of his African origin. Garvey's 'Back to Africa' movement in particular differed from those before him in that it was presented not as an escape from America, but as a national return to an original home, as a positive rather than a negative gesture. For, whatever his excesses, Garvey appreciated the psychological needs of his adherents, realising that what they hankered after was not so much political freedom as 'freedom from contempt'.

Garvey's mythical revaluation of Africa had the precise function of abolishing the world order created by the white man in the mind of the Negro. The prophetic character of Garvey's movement offered a striking similarity to African messianism. Its visionary nature, springing in part from the historic dimensions of his conception and in part from his remoteness from Africa itself, necessarily informed his movement with a strong millenary strain, and his last directions to his followers from his Atlanta jail were characteristic: 'Look for me in the whirlwind or storm, look for me all around you, for with God's grace, I shall come and bring with me countless millions of black slaves who have died in America and the West Indies and the millions in Africa to aid you in the fight for Liberty, Freedom and Life' [*Philosophy and Opinions* (1923)].

Garvey's contribution was twofold. He helped to crystallise the ambiguous and troubled race feeling of his followers into a definite racial consciousness, although he could not avoid the dangers of racialism. He was also among the first to create a *mystique,* based on a revaluation of the African cultural heritage, as a source of inspiration to the blacks in America and in the world.

For in the early years of this century, the black man's

Aimé Césaire in 1940.

worth was low indeed, not only in the eyes of his white overlord, but also (and as a consequence) in his own eyes. He was on the lowest rung of the racial hierarchy which western civilisation had established. As Césaire has observed, referring to the San Domingo revolution, this was not merely a hierarchy, but even 'an ontology: at the top, the white man—the *being,* in the full sense of the term—at the bottom, the black man . . . the thing, as much as to say, a *nothing*' [*Toussaint Louverture* (1956)]. This was a situation which black intellectuals were to combat with all their strength, particularly those who were in direct contact with the whites. The contest was to infuse a passionate vigour into their movements, which acquired the character of a counter-offensive.

The black man in the western hemisphere occupied a definite cultural position, to say the least, and in the United States this position was manifestly uncomfortable. For, although living in the white man's society, the black man retained an awareness of his racial differences and in some cases was forced to organise his life on a racial basis. Thus distinctive black currents appeared in the 'mainstream' of the majority culture in some American societies.

Where this process was not accentuated by the caste system, it was often helped on by the class system which grew out of slavery. Usually the black man, the former slave, became the peasant or the unskilled worker, and the

Negro sub-cultures also became identified in some American societies with a definite social classification, especially in the south of the U.S.A. But this combination was implicit in other areas, such as Brazil and Cuba.

Thus, even where there were no full-blown nationalist movements based on clear social grievances, there were minor manifestations of ethnic feeling. These were kept to the minimum in Brazil, for example, where racial issues were almost unknown, due to the favourable traditions that had been built up during the slave period and the consequently unproblematic racial assimilation of the population. Ethnic feelings were manifested in popular and cultural movements, which were partly dictated by economic and social factors, and partly by the reaction of black people to Brazilian 'aesthetic prejudice', as it has been called, against the black colour, as distinct from racial prejudice against black people.

These movements combined a revaluation of the black and his sub-culture together with social protest. They culminated in the literature of the so-called 'cannibalistic' school, which was animated mainly by radical white writers and whose misguided literary primitivism was a reaction against Christian and middle-class values. The Negro and the native Indian were glorified on the basis of white stereotype conceptions of their cultural heritages.

But it was in Cuba that the Negro and his sub-culture were to have a preponderant influence on intellectual movements. From the beginning, an anti-slavery tradition had put the Negro in the centre of Cuban literary interests, a position that was to be reinforced by the writings which accompanied the Cuban independence struggle. The ideological stand of the Cuban revolutionaries against slavery, particularly in the writings of José Marti, although part of a general political attitude against Spain, had the effect of affirming the Negro sub-culture as an integral part of the distinctive national heritage of Cuba, and eventually gave rise in the years 1920-40 to what has been called the Afro-Cuban school, or *negrismo.*

As in Brazil, *negrismo* was essentially an affair of white writers and it too had its share of primitivism. The Negro was seen mainly as a stereotype, and in many cases the poetry that he inspired was no compliment to him or to his African origins. But there was a positive side to *negrismo.* In the first place, something of a technical revolution was achieved by some poets turning seriously to Africanisms in Cuba and working them into their poetry to arrive at a striking originality. This was true in particular of their use of the rhythms of Afro-Cuban music. But, more than this, some Cuban poets and intellectuals were to achieve a real sympathy with the Negro's situation and his culture. In this, they were helped by the presence in their midst of the coloured writer, Nicolás Guillén, for whom, as G. R. Courthauld observes, 'the Negro theme is not just a fashion, a subject for literature, but the living heart of his creative activity' [*Race and Colour in Caribbean Literature* (1962)].

Guillén introduced an element of racial and social protest into Afro-Cubanism, along with its formal technical modes. In his long poem, 'West Indies Ltd.,' written in

1934, we have a combination of the stylistic devices of *negrismo* and of a radical, demanding tone, that prefigures in many ways another classic of Negro literature, Césaire's *Cahier d'un retour au pays natal,* written a few years later. In other poems, like 'The Name' and 'Ballad of the Two Grandfathers', he evokes the memory of his African ancestry and of the slave trade, although he invariably ends by reconciling this with his Spanish ancestry in a common cause:

> Black anguish and white anguish
> Both of the same measure.
> Shouting, dreaming, weeping, singing,
> Dreaming, weeping, singing.
> Weeping, singing,
> Singing.

Guillén's work offers no indication of any internal conflict arising out of his Negro connexions, and its militant character is clearly due more to social than racial reasons. And although the intellectuals of the Afro-Cuban movement concerned themselves seriously with the situation of the Negro, their movement had no political aim but was conceived rather in a liberal spirit. A nationalist strain and a distinct racial consciousness were thus absent in Afro-Cubanism.

A completely different picture emerges from a consideration of the United States. Two factors were to play a determining role in this respect: the problematic situation of the Negro in U.S. society, and the fact that what can rightly be called a Negro literature in the U.S.A. was the work of Negroes themselves.

The social situation of the Negro in the U.S.A. made of him an essentially divided individual, a man with a double awareness of himself. This split in the Negro's consciousness, a direct result of racial prejudice, went hand in hand with the other psychological effects of discrimination upon his social life to create a permanent state of mental conflict. he felt a double alienation: by and in society, and from himself.

Thus, even when a Negro was assimilated to the culture of the white majority, he was rejected by society, and remained what R. E. Park has called the 'marginal man', burdened with conflicting ethnic and national loyalties. Here is the problem which is at the bottom of the extreme racial consciousness of the Negro intellectual in the U.S.A., and which appears notably in the 'New Negro Movement' variously called the 'Negro Renaissance' and the 'Harlem Renaissance', which sprang up in the wake of the racial agitation after the First World War.

The outstanding figure in Negro intellectual life in the U.S.A. during this period was W. E. B. Du Bois. He was the first to analyse with clarity the ambiguous social position of the Negro in the U.S.A. In his book, *The Souls of Black Folk,* which first appeared in 1903, the conflict in the Negro's mind was set out in these pathetic yet vigorous terms:

> It is a peculiar sensation, this double consciousness, this sense of always looking at one's self through the eyes of others, measuring one's soul by the tape of a world that looks on in amused contempt and pity. One ever feels his two-ness—an American, a Negro: two souls, two thoughts, two unreconciled strivings, two warring ideals, in one dark body, whose dogged strength alone keeps it from being torn asunder.

This sentiment of alienation furnished the incentive that led Du Bois to a passionate analysis of the distinctive aspects of negro life and history in the U.S.A. from their very beginnings, and induced him, in his consideration of the religious life of the Negro communities and of spirituals, to see them as continuations of the Negro's African heritage. This was a position that he was to develop in another book *Black Folk Then and Now* (1939), which was, in the words of Herskovits, an effort 'to comprehend the entire picture of the Negro, African and New World, in its historical and functional setting'.

Thus, at the same time as Garvey, but on a different plane, Du Bois began to develop the racial ethos which informed his political activities as the founder and moving spirit of Pan-Africanism. His Pan-Negro cultural ideal is well summed up in the following extract from his writings [in *The American Negro Academy Occasional Papers, Vol. 2*]:

> We are Americans, not only by birth and by citizenship, but by our political ideals, our language, our religion. Further than that, our Americanism does not go. At that point, we are Negroes, members of a vast historic race that from the very dawn of creation has slept, but half awakening in the dark forest of its African hinterland. We are the first fruits of this new nation, the harbinger of that black tomorrow which is yet to soften the whiteness of the Teutonic today. We are the people whose subtle sense of song has given America its only American music, its only American fairy tales, its only touch of pathos and humour amid its mad money-making plutocracy. As such, it is our duty to conserve our physical powers, our intellectual endowments, our spiritual ideals; as a race, we must strive by race-organisation, by race solidarity, by race unity to the realisation of that broader humanity which freely recognises differences in men, but sternly deprecates inequality in their opportunities of development.

Du Bois gives voice here to certain sentiments which his Negro compatriots were the first to echo, although we have come to associate them with Léopold Sédar Senghor. The cultivation of a Negro identity, culturally as well as socially and politically, and the expression of a total racial solidarity based not only on a common social experience, but also on a common spiritual feeling, came to dominate the literature of the American Negro. The apologetic tones and veiled revolt that had characterised Negro writing before then gave way to a new revolutionary accent. Claude McKay, Countee Cullen, Langston Hughes, Sterling Brown, and others established a radical and militant tone, and Negro poetry became 'characteristically the poetry of rebellion and self assertion' [R. E. Park, "Negro Race Consciousness as Reflected in Race Literature," in *Race and Culture*].

> I oppose all laws of state and country,
> All creeds of church and social orders,

All conventionalities of society and system
Which cross the path of the light of Freedom
Or obscure the reign of the Right.
                    [Walter Everette Hawkins, 'Credo']

This new Negro poetry was only part of a cultural revival which included a new type of Negro novel of protest, culminating in Richard Wright's *Native Son* (1940), and in which jazz and the blues had an important function: to differentiate the Negro and to give him the sense of a cultural heritage. The theme of Africa as the distant home of the black man came to acquire a new importance. In the circumstances, these poets could not avoid the pitfalls of exoticism, but the theme came to carry a strong emotional weight of personal involvement, as this extract from Cullen's poem, 'Heritage', illustrates:

What is Africa to me:
Copper sun or scarlet sea
Jungle star or jungle track,
Strong bronzed men, or regal black
Women from whose loins I sprang
When the birds of Eden sang?
One three centuries removed
From the scenes his fathers loved,
Spicy grove, cinnamon tree,
What is Africa to me?

Garvey's movement and Du Bois' ideas had begun to give the Negro a pride in his race and origins, and the poets were beginning to affirm this in tones that soon acquired a mystical character, as can be observed from the poem by Langston Hughes, 'The Negro Speaks of Rivers':

I've known rivers:
I've known rivers ancient as the world and older
    than the flow of human blood in human veins
My soul has grown deep like the rivers.
I bathed in the Euphrates when dawns were
    young
I built my hut near the Congo and it lulled me
    to sleep
I looked upon the Nile, and raised my pyramids
    above it
I heard the ringing of the Mississippi when Abe
    Lincoln went down to New Orleans
And I've seen its muddy bosom turn all golden
    at sunset
I've known rivers
Ancient, dusky rivers
My soul has grown deep like the rivers.

The Negro renaissance in the U.S.A. is of capital importance in the development of *négritude*. The writings of American Negroes were known outside the U.S.A. and commented upon by Negro intellectuals in France and the Caribbean. Besides, the renaissance not only exported its writings, but also some of its personalities. McKay, Cullen, and Hughes travelled in France, and a flow of Negro expatriates to that country started a Negro renaissance in Paris, with Josephine Baker and Sidney Bechet as the leading musical personalities. Richard Wright was later to become a prominent Negro expatriate in France. Negro intellectuals in France thus had opportunities of meeting their American counterparts. It must be remembered too that Du Bois' Pan-African Congress held in Paris in 1919

depended very much on the collaboration of Blaise Diagne, an influential Senegalese deputy.

But apart from these personal contacts, the Negro renaissance can be said to have led to *négritude* as a movement by setting precedents in all the areas of feeling in which the latter was to be given articulate expression. The literary movement that it played a part in creating in Haiti provides a link between the two movements that is both historical and thematic. The American poets were thus not so much influences as precursors, whose work the French were to carry on to its logical limits.

The Haitian renaissance was a direct result of the occupation of the Republic by the United States in 1915. Whatever the tactical reasons for this gesture, the American occupation created a colonial situation in Haiti and aroused a profound resentment in its intelligentsia. Apart from the complete take-over of the public institutions of Haiti, an element of colour conflict was introduced by the racial attitude of some members of the American administration. The import of the occupation appeared clear—as the republic was the only state run by black people in the Americas, the reversal of its sovereign position was generally interpreted in a racial light. Haiti thus came under white domination, and its intellectuals reacted along familiar lines.

Although Haiti had for about a century been an independent country, the very absence of direct white domination up to 1915 had made it a Negro republic, as far as the more sophisticated forms of cultural expression were concerned, only in a nominal sense. The Haitian élite, though proud of its political heritage and jealous of its independence, took its cultural values exclusively from France, and was far removed from the original culture of the ordinary folk. A deep cleavage thus existed between the intelligentsia and the masses. The American occupation however brought a radical change in the mental outlook of the Haitian intellectuals. The process has been described by Naomi Garret [in *The Renaissance of Haitian Poetry* (1963)]:

They had been made conscious, in a humiliating manner, of the racial characteristics which distinguished them from the powerful Americans in their country. To fight the feeling of inferiority that the Occupation had managed to engender within them, they turned within themselves and to their distant past to seek what there was, if anything, in their traditions and their heritage of which they could be proud. Here at last was something theirs, and inaccessible to the Americans.

The reaction of the Haitians was to seek for themselves a sphere of thought and action outside American control, and thus to seek a 'national soul'. Their quest was to be facilitated by the writings of a most eminent scholar, the ethnologist J. Price-Mars, who became their ideological leader. His [1928] book, *Ainsi parla l'oncle,* though a scientific report of popular Haitian culture, was interspersed with comments in which he made clear the message he wished it to convey to his compatriots. Like Du Bois, he saw in Haitian popular culture the common denominator, 'the intimate essence', as he termed it, of the Haitian people. And, again like Du Bois, Price-Mars went on to recognise the African basis of this, and to advocate its acceptance as a functional part of the Haitian national heritage, in the hope that such a gesture would make the Haitians no longer coloured Frenchmen, but 'Haitians pure and simple, that is, men born under specific historical conditions.' His main point was: 'We have no chance of being ourselves unless we do not repudiate any part of our ancestral heritage. Well, 80 per cent of this heritage is a gift from Africa!'

Thus the sentiment of diminution by white rule led Price-Mars to place a specific situation within a larger context—cultural, historical, and racial. Naomi Garret has shown how strong the hold of Price-Mars' ideas was upon the younger generation of Haitian writers, who reacted against their predecessors, considering them servile imitators of the French, and organised themselves around literary reviews with significant names like *La Relève, La Revue indigène, Les Griots.* She has also indicated how the American Negro poets of the renaissance were to exercise a determining influence upon the Haitians, through the articles of writers like Frank Schoell on the American Negro phenomenon in Parisian journals, through articles and translations by Haitians such as Dominique Hippolyte and Price-Mars (who had a fervent admiration for Du Bois), and through René Piquion's biographical study of Langston Hughes, with a selection in French of 34 of his poems:

> Like the American Negro writers of the 1920's, Haitians had become race conscious and were beginning to feel for their American brothers a kinship born of similarity of interests. It boosted their morale to discover that in their search for information about their African past, they were not alone; common cause had been found with American Negroes who, too, were ceasing to be ashamed of their heritage and were able to look upon themselves and their brothers with objectivity.

On the other hand, their French connexion drew them into a common stream with French-speaking writers from other parts of the world, in particular from the Caribbean. Thus it was that they became the first poets of *négritude* as such, even before the term had been coined, and occupied a prominent position in the anthology compiled by Senghor which was to launch the movement. The part of Haiti in the development of the movement was well reflected by the election of Dr Price-Mars as chairman for the First Congress of Negro Writers and as president of the Society of African Culture (S.A.C.) created in 1959. Aimé Césaire's designation of Haiti as the birthplace of *négritude* is thus true in more than one sense.

An ironic aspect of Negro popular movements in Africa, as well as in the United States, is the way in which western elements acted as catalysts in the emotional reaction which produced nationalist feelings. Christian egalitarian teaching, for example, helped to show up in the eyes of black converts the fundamental contradiction that separated white domination from the avowed humanitarian principles of western culture, and to underline the rift be-

tween the objective practice and the declared values of the white man. Toussaint Louverture's revolution in San Domingo was founded, by a similar process, on the ideals of the French Revolution. A powerful emotional inspiration of nationalism was thus a disaffection for the white man, judged against his own principles.

Since the separatist churches in Africa as well as in America were syncretic, they were therefore never a pure return to original forms of religious expression in Africa, much less in America, where this was out of the question. Thus, once the black man had been dissociated in any way from his culture, a return to any kind of complete authenticity became impossible. The acculturative process was irremediable.

On the above two points, the popular were again to anticipate the intellectual movements, and what was true of the former became even more so for the assimilated black intellectual. This truth is borne out by the tremendous influence which western ideas and cultural forms have had on Negro intellectual movements, especially on *négritude.* For, without any doubt, the progressive formulation of the movement was made possible by the dominant currents of ideas in the west, was in fact singularly favoured by the intellectual and moral climate created in Europe by the aftermath of World War I.

One of the best chroniclers of this period in the intellectual history of Europe, the French critic R. M. Albérès, has declared: 'European sensibility in the twentieth century is characterised by the belief that there exists a divorce between intelligence and reality, truth, or instinct' [*L'Aventure intellectuelle du XXe siècle* (1963)].

Consequently the dominating current in European intellectual life has been anti-intellectualism, and the man who helped to put it on a philosophical basis was Henri Bergson. His influence was important in creating a climate in which ideals that previous centuries had rendered 'non-western' could be accommodated within the European sensibility; but his position as the 'official philosopher' in France also had a direct consequence for French-educated Negro intellectuals. Bergson's influence is apparent in the way Senghor employs concepts derived from Bergsonian categories like *intuition* and *élan vital* in his own writings on African culture.

Anti-intellectualism also provoked a crisis of European consciousness, marked by a general calling into question of established institutions and of moral and religious values, and by a completely new vision of man. The surrealist movement developed out of this crisis and has left a permanent mark on the literature of *négritude,* counting in Césaire one of its foremost practitioners; but it was not so much the technical revolution as the social import that came to have a meaning for black intellectuals. By its aggressive iconoclasm, surrealism drew attention to the imperfections of western society and helped to foster a radically critical outlook towards it, a lesson that was absorbed by the blacks in their own movements of revolt. [In a footnote, Irele states: 'The surrealists had adopted an anti-colonial attitude in their reaction against western society. In an open letter to Paul Claudel in 1925, they wrote, *inter alia,* 'We heartily wish that revolutions, wars and *colonial insurrections* would come to wipe out this western civilisation whose impurities you defend even as far as the eastern world'.]

But a far more important western influence was Marxism. For if surrealism could be considered, in the words of Gaëtan Picon, 'a passionate enterprise of liberation' [*Panorama de la nouvelle littérature française* (1960)] it was largely literary and individualist, and consequently offered no ideology, despite its revolutionary stand. Marxism, on the other hand, presented a comprehensive framework of social and political ideas. In Marxist concepts such as 'the principle of contradiction', 'alienation', and 'the class struggle', black intellectuals found ready instruments of social analysis applicable to the colonial and 'para-colonial' situation.

Indeed, western Marxists left nothing to chance in making them aware of the relevance of their ideology to their situation. In 1916, Lenin had advanced the thesis that imperialism was 'a direct continuation of the fundamental properties of capitalism in general', and Stalin followed this with an analysis of *The National and Colonial Question,* in which the principles of national and cultural autonomy were reconciled with the ideal of proletarian solidarity. Anti-imperialism thus became an important part of the Marxist ideology. The Communist Party was at the height of its popularity in France in the 1930's and deployed tremendous efforts in the United States to win the adherence of the obviously discontented Negro population. Senghor has recounted how, as students in Europe, black intellectuals came in contact with Marxist teaching [in 'Négritude et marxisme,' in *Pierre Teilhard de Chardin et la politique africaine* (1962)].

> Indeed, right from the time of our arrival in Europe, we were submitted to Marxist propaganda. Some black students—especially the West Indians—had succumbed to its seduction. And they tried in turn to seduce us. They presented 'scientific socialism' as the final solution to our problems, to all our problems. Under the guise of parliamentary democracy (they preached), a minority of bourgeois [elements] held in their hand the levers of power and wealth. They exploited, by oppressing them, not only their own people but also the immense flock of *natives* overseas. The solution to the problem was clear. It was up to us to join the army of the proletariat, and to struggle within its ranks. Once the 'capitalist system' had been overthrown and the ownership of the means of production handed over to the workers, the colonised people would be at one stroke *de-colonised, dis-alienated.* They would recover, at the same time as their independence, the ownership of their material wealth and the freedom to promote the values of their civilisation.

The influence of Marxism on Negro intellectuals on both sides of the Atlantic was profound and enduring. A good number of Negro writers have been, at one time or another, members of the Communist Party. The attraction of Marxism lay in its revolutionary character; and this emotional pull left a permanent imprint on the ideas of most of them. Even after the inevitable period of disillusionment with the Communist Party, due to its tactics and methods, the Marxist dialectic continued to inform their writings.

Finally, the nature of literary activity in Europe has not been without consequence for the literature of *négritude.* The years preceding World War II saw the development of a literature of 'causes', culminating in the outpouring provoked by the Spanish Civil War. This literature committed to political causes was to receive a tremendous impetus during the French Resistance; and after the war Jean-Paul Sartre developed the idea of *littérature engagée* in a series of essays on the nature of literature and on the relationship of the writer to society. The two decades 1930–50 were dominated by the literary figures of Louis Aragon, Albert Camus, Paul Eluard, and Jacques Prévert. It was inevitable that the black writers should have been strongly influenced by them, especially Sartre, who was the first European apostle of *négritude,* and others who were to have a direct hand in its formulation.

French writing thus had a marked social content in this period, and the literature of *négritude* reflects the prevailing atmosphere in France. There was, however, an important distinction between the white writer and the black, which Richard Wright pointed out at the time [in an interview in *Pan-Africa* (1947)]: 'The individual discovers that he is a sacrifice to society. This consciousness of sacrifice is developing around two opposite poles: among the whites, the pole of psychological consciousness, among the blacks, that of the realistic-social'—in other words, the poles of *individual* consciousness for the whites, and of *collective* consciousness for the blacks.

Although the intellectual climate in the west favoured the development of movements that questioned the fundamental values of its society, and Marxism in particular opened the way for a revolt against imperialism, the determining factor which provoked the black counteroffensive and gave it validity was the revision of the image of the black man in modern anthropology. The development of a scientific method and an objective approach, and the consequent evolution of the concept of 'cultural relativity', led western ethnographers to a broader outlook and a more sympathetic view of non-western cultures.

The work of Leo Frobenius was to play an important part in the revaluation of Africa's culture and peoples. His *History of African Civilisation* was the first serious attempt to credit the black race with a part in ancient Egyptian civilisation and with a capacity for evolving more than rudimentary cultural institutions, and his attitude to the black man is summed up in his enthusiastic exclamation, 'Civilised to the marrow of their bones!' The writings of French ethnographers like Maurice Delafosse, Robert Delavignette, Théodore Monod, Marcel Griaule, and later Placide Tempels, and of the American Melville Herskovits, to cite only a few, were to give scientific authority to the growing sentiment that the African cultures had been seriously underestimated, with prejudice to the black man's human worth.

The importance of the new ideas on Africa developed by

the anthropologists is threefold. In the first place they gave an important booster to the black man's self esteem, and provided scientific arguments for the intellectuals to undermine the ideology of the white man's 'civilising mission', one of the principal justifications for colonial rule. Césaire quoted Frobenius in his pamphlet, *Discours sur le colonialisme,* and summed up the indictment of colonial rule with this epigram: 'From colonisation to civilisation, the distance is infinite.'

In the second place, they promoted in the west a new appreciation of African culture. Given the moral and intellectual climate of the inter-war years, when western man began to look outside his own culture for new directions in art and thought, the introduction of non-western forms, and of African sculpture in particular, created an understandably profound impression. Leading artists and writers in Europe took up African forms of cultural expression, including literary styles; and jazz brought over by the Americans began to be considered a serious musical form. In short, 'The Negro was in vogue in Paris', as Naomi Garret has observed; the African and his culture were becoming 'respectable'.

Finally, the anthropologists were to exercise a direct influence on the writings of some of the black intellectuals. In this connexion, Lucien Lévy-Bruhl's studies of non-western forms of experience and knowledge furnished Senghor with a conceptual framework for his description of the Negro African mind. His controversial differentiation between western man's 'sight-reason' (*la raison-œil*) and the Negro African's 'touch-reason' (*la raison-toucher*) are based on Lévy-Bruhl's distinction between western logic and 'primitive' logic in *La Mentalité primitive* (1921).

Négritude thus owes an immense debt to the west, and this much Senghor has conceded: 'Paradoxically, it was the French who first forced us to seek its essence, and who then showed us where it lay' ['What Is Négritude?' *Atlas* (1962)].

Négritude as a definite movement thus grew out of an emotional and intellectual ferment among African and Caribbean students and intellectuals living in Paris before World War II; it was gradually elaborated in a succession of journals, and finally brought into focus in the post-war years. This ferment became significant because of the uneasy position that the black intellectual occupied in French society.

For there was a fundamental weakness at the heart of the French colonial policy, a selective and rigid assimilation of a black élite, combined with discrimination against the rest of the colonised population. It created in the élite a feeling that they were on sufferance, and a conflict of loyalties. Added to this was the fact that they could not always escape racial prejudice against them in white society; for even if French people have little prejudice, the black man was an object of contempt. These contradictions are well expressed in this bitter line from Césaire's *Cahier:* 'I salute the 3 centuries that uphold my civic rights with my blood minimised.'

The black élite was thus assimilated intellectually but never socially, and could not become involved and identified with the culture of their masters. As cultural hybrids, the only way out of their form of alienation was to fall back on their ethnic loyalties. Their situation thus drew them together, and it is not difficult to understand their reaction. As Senghor put it in 1962:

> Early on, we had become aware within ourselves that assimilation was a failure; we could assimilate mathematics or the French language, but we could never strip off our black skins or root out our black souls. And so we set out on a fervent quest for the Holy Grail: our Collective Soul.

The first sign of this reaction came in 1921, when a West Indian administrator, René Maran, published a novel, *Batouala,* based on his experience in the Congo. This won the coveted Prix Goncourt for that year and caused a scandal, leading to his dismissal from the civil service. Although Maran, who was brought up and educated in France, rightly claimed to be French, he has since been acclaimed by other black writers as a 'precursor' of *négritude*. But such a title belongs more properly to another West Indian, Etienne Léro, whose manifesto, *Légitime Défense,* which appeared in 1932, indicated the way in which separate influences from America and Europe had converged upon the blacks in France to inspire their reaction. In one passage, for instance, he wrote:

> The storm wind blowing down from Black America will soon wipe out from our Antilles the aborted fruits of a decaying civilisation. Langston Hughes and Claude McKay, the two revolutionary poets, have brought for us, tempered in red alcohol, the African love of life, the African joy of love, the African dream of death.

In another passage, Léro condemned West Indian writing: 'A foreigner would look in vain in this literature for an original or profound accent, for the sensual and colourful imagination of the black man, for an echo of the resentment as well as aspirations of an oppressed people.' And Léro went on to annex surrealism and Marxism to the cause he had set out to espouse.

Léro's poetry was neither original nor of a high quality. But with this single manifesto he had set in motion a process which was to outlive him, and to be prolonged by the efforts of three other poets—Aimé Césaire, Léon Damas, and Léopold Sédar Senghor—who founded their own paper, *L'Etudiant noir,* which appears to have brought together Africans and West Indians. This was also the period in which Césaire produced his masterpiece, *Cahier d'un retour au pays natal,* published in a little known journal, *Volontés,* in 1939, in which the word *négritude* first appeared in print. The original inventor of the term has been kept a close secret between the three of them, although Césaire is generally given credit for it. The war soon scattered the group, but Césaire kept up their efforts with *Tropiques,* a paper he founded in Fort-de-France, capital of Martinique, where he had returned as professor at the local *lycée.* He maintained a sharp commentary on the colonial situation in his native island, complemented by a new determination, as can be seen in the article he wrote to launch the review:

> The circle of darkness gathers, amid the cries of

men and the howls of beasts. Yet we count ourselves among those who say 'No' to darkness.
We know that the salvation of the world depends
also on us. That the earth has need of all her children. Even the humblest.

It was in Martinique that André Breton, the leader of the
surrealist movement, who was a wartime refugee there,
came to be acquainted with Césaire. As a result, a new bilingual edition of *Cahier* was published in New York, with
a prefatory eulogy in which Breton acclaimed the poem
as 'the greatest lyrical monument of the time'.

After the war, the three men found themselves together
again in Paris, as representatives in the French National
Assembly of their territories of origin. The next step was
however taken independently of the 'triumvirate' by Alioune Diop, a Senegalese, who in 1947 founded the review
Présence Africaine with the collaboration of the most eminent personalities in French literary and academic circles.
This marked a decisive stage. *Présence Africaine* opened
its own publishing section, and helped to give a concrete
formulation to the movement, by bringing out a series of
works by black writers, and by other scholars on African
and Negro literature and problems. Special numbers, such
as *Le Monde noir,* edited by the ethnologist Théodore
Monod, *l'Art nègre, Haiti, Poètes noirs,* or *Trois Ecrivains
nègres* (which included the first novel of Mongo Béti under
the name Eza Boto). Two important landmarks published
by *Présence Africaine* were the French version of *Bantu
Philosophy* (1949), and Cheikh-Anta Diop's controversial
essay on *Nations nègres et culture* (1954). The latter was
a doctoral dissertation in which Diop, pursuing a trail already opened up by Frobenius, put forward the thesis that
ancient Egyptian civilisation was predominantly Negro.
Although the dissertation was rejected by the Sorbonne,
the book made a profound impression, among black people because of the boldness of its ideas and expression, and
in European circles because of its erudition.

Meanwhile, in 1948 Senghor had brought together, in his
well-known *Anthologie de la nouvelle poésie nègre et malgache de langue française,* the first lyrical expression of the
movement, with an introduction in which he expatiated
on the concept of *négritude.* but it was the essay entitled
'Black Orpheus' which Jean-Paul Sartre contributed to
the volume that consecrated the term and gave the movement a start.

By the 1950's a considerable body of literature and ideas
had been produced; Césaire, Damas, and Senghor had
been recognised as important figures in the French literary
world, while others like Jacques Roumain, Paul Niger, Joseph Zobel, Birago Diop, Jacques Rabemananjara, and
later Edouard Glissant, Camara Laye, and René Depestre,
to mention only a few, had become established writers.

The success of the Bandung Conference in 1955 inspired
Présence Africaine to organise a cultural counterpart, and
in 1956 the First Congress of Negro Writers and Artists
was held in Paris, with the express aim of defining a new,
non-western, cultural consciousness. As Alioune Diop put
it in his opening speech, 'We of the non-European world
have got, with the help of everybody, to stimulate new values, to explore together new worlds born out of the meet-

ing of peoples.' This Congress was mainly of a cultural
character, with papers on different aspects of African and
Afro-American cultures, although not without occasional
attacks on the west and impeachments of colonial rule, 'an
enterprise of moral extermination', as Diop called it. In
short, this was a stock-taking and a tentative effort at
Negro solidarity at the cultural level.

The Second Congress, which followed three years later in
Rome, was of a far more political character. The theme
chosen, 'The Responsibility of the Intelligentsia', was a direct reference to the colonial situation and indicated a new
attitude. The crises which marked French colonial policy,
and their consequences in France, were probably connected with this development. Colonialism had at any rate become a burning question, made even more urgent by the
rise of Ghana as the first African nation to become independent after the war. The spirit that dominated at this
conference was thus expressed by Césaire: 'We must hasten the process of de-colonisation, that is to say, employ
all means to hasten the ripening of a popular consciousness.' And further on in his speech he declared: 'As for us,
in the particular situation in which we find ourselves, we
are the propagators of souls, the multipliers of souls, and
in the last resort, the inventors of souls' ['L'Homme de
culture et ses responsabilités,' in *Deuxième Congrès des
écrivains et artistes noirs*].

The 1959 Congress in Rome was the last major public
manifestation of *négritude* to date, and probably indicates
the high-water mark of the movement. For since 1960, the
year of African independence, which sent the majority of
its adherents back to their new countries, and which
marked a turning-point in the relationship between the
west and African peoples, it has begun to ebb as an organised movement. On the other hand, *négritude* has acquired a new orientation in ideas, due to the efforts of one
man—Senghor.

Two facts stand out clearly from a consideration of the
progressive development of *négritude,* seen in its broad
historical perspective. The first is that it was a movement
of *reaction* against the western cultural domination which
was concomitant with political domination. As such, it appears as a remarkable example of *counter-acculturation.*

It seems perfectly clear, however, that without the pressure of colonial rule and the conflicts which it created in
Africa, and without the historical and social factors which
dominated the situation of the black man in America—
that is, without the racial factor—the forms of reaction to
culture contact among black peoples summarised here
would have had a completely different character. In this
respect, the Haitian phenomenon illustrates how both political domination and racial difference, with the psychological problems this involves, have determined the nature
of black reaction to contact with the white man and his
culture. In short, black cultural nationalism was inspired
by a wish for *freedom* from both domination and contempt.

But this would be a very incomplete view of the situation.
The complementary side of the black man's response has
been to turn to means which, at first sight and from a psy-

chological point of view, afford him a *compensation* for the domination and humiliation. The role of the Negro subcultures, leading progressively on both sides of the Atlantic to the myth of Africa among Negro masses and intellectuals, is thus tied to a defence mechanism. Yet it would be wrong to label this altogether an escape into fantasy. For there is a fundamental difference between Garveyism and similar popular movements on the one hand, and the intellectuals' patterns of reaction, which were so much more lucid, on the other.

Thus, although the intellectual movements developed out of very strong emotional conflicts and they too produced their myths, they generally progressed further to a more *constructive* stage. *Négritude,* in particular, has evolved a framework of ideas, and its literature and ideology afford an insight into the intimate processes of the black reaction to the west. (pp. 321-48)

> *Abiola Irele, "Négritude of Black Cultural Nationalism," in* The Journal of Modern African Studies, *Vol. 3, No. 3, October, 1965, pp. 321-48.*

Edna L. Steeves on primitivism, the black aesthetic, and Negritude:

Négritude stresses that black is beautiful and noble. A poem by Léon Damas—puts simply but forcefully what amounts to a cult with the writers of this school:

> For beauty is Black
> And wisdom Black
> For endurance is Black
> And courage Black
> For patience is Black
> And irony Black
> For charm is Black
> And magic Black
> For love is Black
> And hip-swinging Black
> For dance is Black
> And rhythm Black
> For art is Black
> And movement Black
> For laughter is Black
> For joy is Black
> For peace is Black
> For life is Black.

The interesting thing is that the 'black is beautiful' conception, novel as it seemed to the founders of *négritude,* is really nothing very new; in fact, it has a long history in primitivistic thought. Well before the present century, the philosophy of which black beauty is but the latest manifestation had caught men's fancy. As early as the Renaissance, and particularly prominent in the eighteenth century and early nineteenth century, the noble savage was a fascinating figure. Certain aspects of the cult of primitivism find their reflection today in the ideology of *négritude.*

> *Edna L. Steeves, in her "Négritude and the Noble Savage," in* The Journal of Modern African Studies, *March 1973.*

Lilyan Kesteloot

[*Kesteloot is a Belgian scholar who has written extensively on Negritude and African literature. In the following essay, she argues that the intellectual roots of Negritude can be traced to the works of such Afro-American writers as Claude McKay and Langston Hughes.*]

"The wind rising from black America will soon sweep the West Indies clean, we hope, of all the stunted fruits of its outdated culture," cried Etienne Léro at the end of his critical examination of West Indian literature ["Misère d'une poésie" in *Légitime Défense*]. Following Léro's stirring declaration of faith was an excerpt from a rousing chapter of Claude McKay's novel *Banjo,* introduced under a new title, "L'étudiant antillais vu par un noir américain" ("The West Indian student as seen by an American Negro"). In the same journal René Ménil wrote [in "Généralités sur l'écrivain de couleur antillais"]: "The poems of American Negroes are moving the whole world."

Senghor, Césaire, and Damas, the founders of what came to be known as the negritude movement, acknowledge that between 1930 and 1940, African and West Indian students living in Paris were in close contact with the American Negro writers Claude McKay, Jean Toomer, Langston Hughes, and Countee Cullen, and that they read these writers' works and were personally acquainted with them. "We were in contact with these black Americans during the years 1929-34, through Mademoiselle Paulette Nardal, who, with Dr. Léo Sajous, a Haitian, had founded *La Revue du Monde Noir.* Mademoiselle Nardal kept a literary salon, where African Negroes, West Indians, and American Negroes used to get together" [L. S. Senghor, in a letter dated February, 1960]. Around 1935, René Maran's salon came to play the same role. Professor Mercer Cook put many black French and black American intellectuals in touch with one another.

This is an important point, since the American literature already contained seeds of the main themes of negritude. Hence, one can assert that the real fathers of the Negro cultural renaissance in France were neither traditional West Indian writers, nor the French surrealist poets, nor the French novelists of the era between the two wars, but black writers of the United States. They made a very deep impression on French Negro writers by claiming to represent an entire race, launching a cry with which all blacks identified—the first cry of rebellion.

> The dominant feeling of a Negro poet is a feeling of intolerance. An intolerance of reality because it is sordid, of the world because it is caged, of life because it is deprived of the great road to the sun. And now from the dark heavy dregs of anguish, of suppressed indignation, of long silent despair, a hiss of anger is rising. On the shattered foundations of its conformities, America wonders uneasily from what atrocious hatred this cry is the deliverance. [Aimé Césaire, "Introduction à la poésie nègre américaine," in *Tropiques* (July 1941)]

Black American writers were the first to broach the subject—until then taboo—of contacts between Negroes and whites. While West Indians were carefully avoiding these themes, hoping to solve the problem by evading the question of color, the existence of a racial problem was recognized more openly in the United States.

After the abolition of slavery, Negroes had to fight to establish their worth. "I knew that in a large degree we were trying an experiment—that of testing whether it was possible for Negroes to build up and control the affairs of a large educational institution. I knew that if we failed, it would injure the whole race. I knew that the presumption was against us" [Booker T. Washington, *Up from Slavery: An Autobiography* (1901)].

The author of these remarks, Booker T. Washington, who had known slavery, succeeded in founding Tuskegee Institute, the first industrial college for blacks, right in the state of Alabama, probably the state most hostile to blacks and the most convinced of their natural inferiority. Booker T. Washington worked unceasingly to prove that blacks were as good as whites, on condition that their education was equal. He also made famous the phrase "revival of the race." He thought it would be sufficient for Negroes to show they were capable, and racial prejudice would disappear. A great number of young educated blacks, believing in these theories, conscientiously wrote "in the manner of" the poets of the period, cultivating "the conventional melancholy tone of the late nineteenth-century romantics, and dwelt on death, dreams and the wonders of nature" [Margaret Just Butcher, *The Negro in American Culture* (1957)].

Experience showed, to the contrary, that racial prejudice was increasing! And if the rise of Booker T. Washington was followed with a certain sympathy by the abolitionists, the succeeding generation of black intellectuals did not receive the same support. Was it feared that blacks would become competitors if endowed with greater cultural and economic means? Or was racial prejudice too deeply rooted in the American consciousness to disappear because of laws passed during a wave of temporary generosity? As Richard Wright bitterly observed [in *White Man, Listen!* (1957)], the fight to be integrated in the white world was futile.

> The gains they won fastened ever tighter around their necks and shackles of Jim Crowism. For example, every new hospital, clinic, and school that was built was a *Negro* hospital, a *Negro* clinic, a *Negro* school! So, though Negroes were slowly rising out of their debased physical conditions, the black ghettos were growing ever larger; instead of racial segregation lessening, it grew, deepened, spread.

Margaret Just Butcher explains at length the means by which segregation replaced slavery and the new series of false ideas based on pseudoscientific arguments which victimized blacks: blood atavism, inherent primitivism, etc. Even Darwinian theory was invoked to suggest that the Negro was but a link between the ape and genuine man, thus justifying his exploitation and lynching.

At the same time in the South a literature was developing that glorified antebellum life, portraying slavery in the homelike atmosphere of the master's house, in a naïve, innocent, and idyllic light. Black intellectuals reacted against stereotyped pictures of the Negro child, the Negro clown, or the bad Negro which abounded in Southern literature. The most famous of these black intellectuals was Dr. W. E. B. DuBois, whose book *The Souls of Black Folk* became [according to Butcher] "the Bible of the militant school of protest." He was followed by Paul Laurence Dunbar and Charles W. Chesnutt. This was the beginning of the "Harlem Renaissance," which flourished between 1914 and 1925.

The black renaissance, moreover, coincided with a general renewal of American literature immediately after World War I. Breaking away from the romantic tradition, it turned toward critical realism and began to reflect an interest in social problems. In Europe the best known American writers of this new literary orientation are Steinbeck, Hemingway, Dos Passos, Faulkner, Caldwell, and the black author Richard Wright.

For black writers, the new realism consisted of a clearer conception of their situation, exposing the injustice and prejudice that made black Americans outcasts in their own land, and demanding rehabilitation of Negro cultural values and their total independence of the white world.

There is no clearer expression of the militant nature of their stand than Langston Hughes's proud declaration:

> We younger Negro artists who create now intend to express our individual dark-skinned selves without fear or shame. If white people are pleased we are glad. If they are not, it doesn't matter. We know that we are beautiful and ugly too. The tom-tom weeps and the tom-tom laughs. If colored people are pleased we are glad. If they are not, their displeasure doesn't matter either. We build our temples for tomorrow, strong as we know how, and we stand on top of the mountain, free within ourselves.

At the head of this young school were Langston Hughes, Claude McKay, Jean Toomer, Countee Cullen, and Sterling Brown, whose novels and poems became a steady diet for African and West Indian students in France between 1930 and 1940. These authors themselves made a number of trips to Europe and thus had the opportunity to make personal contact with the students.

At home they took full advantage of the "Negro vogue" reigning in New York between 1920 and 1929. The new snobbery, introduced by a successful musical comedy "Shuffle Along," spread to music and Negro dances. Jazz, the Charleston, and the blues were discovered, and people became aware that blacks were good singers, good dancers, and sometimes excellent musicians. In a wider sense, books written by blacks easily found publishers and an audience in certain avant-garde groups such as the circle of the author Carl van Vechten.

One should not, however, have any illusions about this vogue. Antiblack prejudices and segregation were in no degree lessened. New York's "high society" had merely discovered a new exotic toy—the Negro clown—and the only right of the black man that was recognized was the right to amuse whites. So, while profiting commercially from this fad, blacks were not duped, as is illustrated by the humorous text written in this connection by Langston Hughes [in *The Big Sea: An Autobiography* (1962)]:

> White people began to come to Harlem in droves . . . Nor did ordinary Negroes like the growing influx of whites toward Harlem after sundown, flooding the little cabarets and bars where formerly only colored people laughed and sang, and where now the strangers were given the best ringside tables to sit and stare at the Negro customers—like amusing animals in a zoo.
>
> The Negroes said: "We can't go downtown and sit and stare at you in your clubs. You won't even let us in your clubs." But they didn't say it out loud—for Negroes are practically never rude to white people. So thousands of whites came to Harlem night after night, thinking the Negroes loved to have them there, and firmly believing that all Harlemites left their houses at sundown to sing and dance in cabarets, because most of the whites saw nothing but the cabarets, not the houses.
>
> It was a period when local and visiting royalty were not at all uncommon in Harlem. And when the parties of A'Lelia Walker, the Negro heiress, were filled with guests whose names would turn any Nordic social climber green with envy . . . It was a period when Charleston preachers opened up shouting churches as sideshows for white tourists . . . It was a period when every season there was at least one hit play on Broadway acted by a Negro cast. And when books by Negro authors were being published with much greater frequency and much more publicity than ever before or since in history. It was a period when white writers wrote about Negroes more successfully (commercially speaking) than Negroes did about themselves . . . It was the period when the Negro was in vogue.

However, mixed in with the folklore, black writers sowed ideas in their books which some ten years later became the leaven of the negritude movement. They resolutely turned their backs on the preceding generation which had been "characterized by intellectual acceptance of white American values and, in literature, by sentimental lyricism over the misfortunes of an oppressed and exiled race," in order to commit themselves to a "vigorous though not boastful affirmation of their original values" [Georges Friedmann, in the preface to the French edition of *Banjo*].

Claude McKay's novel *Banjo,* already mentioned, presented the broadest criticism of American society and, at the same time, a sample of the feelings and anxieties of the "new Negro." The author rebelled against the black man's obligation to act according to the morals of a society that rejects him.

> It seemed to him [Ray, the narrator] a social wrong that, in a society rooted and thriving on the principles of the "struggle for existence" and the "survival of the fittest" a black child should be brought up on the same code of social virtues as the white, . . . earnestly learning the trite moralisms of a society in which he was, as a

child and would be as an adult, denied any legitimate place.

Harshly he attacked everything which most directly wounded him and his race: racial prejudice. All young black writers were unanimous on this subject, for the wound was painful. They denounced every prejudice which weighed on colored men and justified their shameless exploitation.

> Prejudice and business! In Europe, Asia, Australia, Africa, America, those were the two united terrors confronting the colored man. He was the butt of the white man's indecent public prejudices. Prejudices insensate and petty, bloody, vicious, vile, brutal, *raffiné,* hypocritical, Christian. Prejudices. Prejudices like the stock market—curtailed, diminishing, increasing, changing chameleon-like, according to place and time, like the color of the white man's soul, controlled by the exigencies of the white man's business. [*Banjo*]

Prejudices which automatically led all those who did not approve of them and respect segregation to be banned by society. "Show me a white woman or man who can marry a Negro and belong to respectable society in London, New York or any place."

> In New York we have laws against racial discrimination. Yet there are barriers of discrimination everywhere against colored people . . . We don't want to eat in a restaurant, nor go to a teashop, a cabaret or a theater where they do not want us . . . And when white people show that they do not want to entertain us in places that they own, why, we just stay away—all of us who are decent-minded—for we are a fun-loving race and there is no pleasure in forcing ourselves where we are not wanted.

All these authors reacted strongly to the word "nigger," which, like a slap in the face, arouses in blacks a violent emotion, described at length by Langston Hughes [in *The Big Sea*].

> The word *nigger* to colored people of high and low degree is like a red flag to a bull. Used rightly or wrongly, ironically or seriously, of necessity for the sake of realism, or impishly for the sake of comedy, it doesn't matter. Negroes do not like it in any book or play whatsoever, be the book or play ever so sympathetic in its treatment of the basic problems of the race. Even though the book or play is written by a Negro, they still do not like it.
>
> The word *nigger,* you see, sums up for us who are colored all the bitter years of insult and struggle in America: the slave-beatings of yesterday, the lynchings of today, the Jim Crow cars, the only movie show in town with its sign up FOR WHITES ONLY, the restaurants where you may not eat, the jobs you may not have, the unions you cannot join. The word *nigger* in the mouths of little white boys at school, the word *nigger* in the mouths of foremen on the job, the word *nigger* across the whole face of America! *Nigger! Nigger!* Like the word *Jew* in Hitler's Germany.

In support of this assertion Langston Hughes quotes the poem "Incident" by Countee Cullen:

> Once riding in old Baltimore,
> Heart-filled, head-filled with glee,
> I saw a Baltimorean
> Keep looking straight at me.
>
> Now I was eight and very small,
> And he was no whit bigger
> And so I smiled, but he poked out
> His tongue and called me, "Nigger."
>
> I saw the whole of Baltimore
> From May until December:
> Of all the things that happened there
> That's all that I remember.

Claude McKay also referred to this reaction in *Banjo*. The way America treated blacks was disgusting, he wrote, but the French too, even if they did it more politely, concealed

> a fundamental contempt for black people quite as pronounced as in the Anglo-Saxon lands . . . There was if anything an unveiled condescension in it that was gall to a Negro who wanted to live his life free of the demoralizing effects of being pitied and patronized. Here like anywhere . . . one black villain made all black villains as one black tout made all black touts.

Elsewhere [in the novel] he again denounced the apparent liberalism which had so long maintained the myth of a nonracist France.

> The French are never tired of proclaiming themselves the most civilized people in the world. They think they understand Negroes, because they don't discriminate against us in their bordels. They imagine that Negroes like them. But, Senghor, the Senegalese, told me that the French were the most calculatingly cruel of all the Europeans in Africa.

These prejudices are even inculcated among Negroes themselves: West Indians look down on Africans, for being more "Negro" than they are.

> At the African bar the conversation turned on the hostile feeling that existed between the French West Indians and the native Africans. The *patron* said that the West Indians felt superior because many of them were appointed as petty officials in the African colonies and were often harder on the natives than the whites.
>
> *Fils d'esclaves! Fils d'esclaves!* cried a Senegalese sergeant. Because they have a chance to be better instructed than we, they think we are the savages and that they are "white" negroes. Why, they are only the descendants of the slaves that our forefathers sold.

Similarly, Langston Hughes remarks on the superiority complex of the mulatto regarding a black [in his *The Big Sea*]: "Mary's friend from the West Indies said she did not like Claude McKay because he was too black . . . Rosalie was a light-skinned Jamaican, who had a violent prejudice toward dark Negroes as, unfortunately, so many West Indian mulattoes have."

The list of criticisms could be still longer. The Negro censures American civilization, not only for its prejudices, but also for its oppressive capitalist structure, and the commercial spirit that always places money above men: "Business first and by all and any means! That is the slogan of the white man's world" [*Banjo*]. This anti-capitalist reaction was broadened to meet that of all proletarians, in a sort of humorous "prospectus" written by Langston Hughes around 1929 during the famous New York economic crash. The city's largest hotel, the celebrated Waldorf-Astoria, was being built then at a cost of twenty-three million dollars. With cruel wit, the author invites "the homeless, the starving and the colored folks" to come down to the Waldorf-Astoria, reserve a room and stuff themselves on a menu he enumerated in detail:

> Dine with some of the men and women who got rich off of your labor, who clip coupons with clean white fingers because your hands dug coal, drilled stone, sewed garments, poured steel to let other people draw dividends and live easy.
> (Or haven't you had enough yet of the soup-lines and the bitter bread of charity?)
> *Hallelujah! Undercover driveways!*
> *Ma soul's a witness for de Waldorf-Astoria!*
> (A thousand nigger section-hands keep the road-beds smooth so investments in railroads pay ladies with diamond necklaces staring at Cert murals.)
> *Thank Gawd A'mighty!*
> (And a million niggers bend their backs on rubber plantations, for rich behinds to ride on thick tires to the Theatre Guild tonight.)
> *Ma soul's a witness!*
> (And here we stand, shivering in the cold, in Harlem.)
> *Glory be to Gawd—*
> *De Waldorf-Astoria's open!*

It is from this perspective that one must understand why communism at that time attracted certain black intellectuals. It seemed to them to solve both social and racial problems. The Russian revolution, still so young, seemed to promise every hope of liberty [as Hughes recounts in *The Big Sea*].

> The end of the war! [World War I]. But many of the students at Central [High School] kept talking, not about the end of the war, but about Russia where Lenin had taken power in the name of the workers, who made everything, and who would now own everything they made. "No more pogroms," the Jews said: no more race hatred . . . The daily papers pictured the Bolsheviks as the greatest devils on earth, but I didn't see how they could be that bad if they had done away with race hatred and landlords—two evils that I knew well at first hand.

Even today, one discovers that most of the black writers who were in their twenties at the beginning of the New Deal were for a short period members of the Communist Party and are still more or less Marxist.

In poems where the black man's sufferings and miserable condition are freely expressed, threats begin to sound.

Veiled at first, in Countee Cullen's poem ["From the Dark Tower"]:

> We shall not always plant while others reap
> The golden increment of bursting fruit
> Not always countenance, abject and mute,
> That lesser men should hold their brothers cheap.

Then clearer, as expressed by Fenton Johnson [in "Tired"]:

> I am tired of work; I am tired of building up somebody else's civilization.

And finally, poems [such as "The White House"] poured forth furiously from Claude McKay:

> Your door is shut against my tightened face,
> And I am sharp as steel with discontent; . . . .
> The pavement slabs burn loose beneath my feet
> A chafing savage, down the decent street;
> And passion rends my vitals as I pass,
> Where boldly shines your shuttered door of glass.

The threat becomes a song of revolt in the name of outraged dignity [in "If We Must Die"]:

> If we must die, let it not be like hogs
> Hunted down and penned in an inglorious spot.

With an ironic smile, Langston Hughes wrote a short poem ["I, Too, Sing America"] in the "blues" style, which is a message of strength and the confidence of a man "who has faith in his people's destiny":

> I, too, sing America.
>
> I am the darker brother.
> They send me to eat in the kitchen
> When company comes.
> But I laugh,
> And eat well,
> And grow strong.
>
> Tomorrow
> I'll be at the table
> When company comes
> Nobody'll dare
> Say to me,
> "Eat in the kitchen"
> Then.
>
> Besides,
> They'll see how beautiful I am
> And be ashamed,—
>
> I, too, am America.

Abandoning the role of victim for that of judge, Claude McKay criticized the values of which the West was so proud and in the name of which it presumed the right to colonize other peoples: Christianity, technology, and "reason."

He had no difficulty criticizing the latter. The First World War abundantly proved the impotence of "reason," which had proved unable to prevent either barbarous conflicts or the civil wars of "reasonable" nations:

> [Ray] was not unaware that his position as a black boy looking on the civilized scene was a unique one. He was having a good grinning time of it. Italians against French, French against Anglo-Saxons, English against Germans, the great *Daily Mail* shrieking like a mad virago that there were still Germans left who were unable to swill champagne in Italy when deserving English gentlemen could not afford to replenish their cellars. Oh it was a great civilization indeed, too entertaining for any savage ever to have the feeling of boredom.

His attack on Christianity grew more virulent because this religion seemed to him a huge swindle. While in Western countries the Church tolerates materialism and the profit motive, racial pride, and social diseases like organized prostitution, it claimed the right to "civilize" colored people and purge them of their "heathen morals." In reality, religion was an alibi and a screen for the white subjection of blacks. McKay therefore rejected Christianity entirely and without exception [in *Banjo*]:

> As far as I have been able to think it out the colored races are the special victims of biblical morality—Christian morality . . .
>
> I don't think I loathe anything more than the morality of the Christians. It is false, treacherous, hypocritical. I know that, for I myself have been a victim of it in your white world, and the conclusion I draw from it is that the world needs to get rid of false moralities and cultivate decent manners—not society manners, but man-to-man decency and tolerance.
>
> So—if I were to follow any of the civilized peoples, it wouldn't be the Jews or the Christians or the Indians. I would rather go to the Chinese—to Confucius.

This cry from the heart is an echo of the speech made in 1852 by Frederick Douglass, a pioneer Negro abolitionist, who explained the aversion of blacks to Christian morality:

> You boast of your love of liberty, your superior civilization, and your pure Christianity, while the twin political powers of the nation (as embodied in the two political parties) are solemnly pledged to support and perpetuate the enslavement of three million of your countrymen. You hurl your anathemas at the crown-headed tyrants of Russia and Austria and pride yourselves on your democratic institutions, while you yourselves consent to be the mere tools and bodyguards of the tyrants of Virginia and Carolina. You invite to your shores fugitives of oppression from abroad, honor them with banquets, greet them with ovations, cheer them, toast them, salute them, protect them, and pour out your money to them like water; but the fugitives from your own land you advertise, hunt, arrest, shoot, and kill. You glory in your refinement and education, yet you maintain a system as barbarous and dreadful as ever stained the character of a nation—a system begun in avarice, supported in pride, and perpetuated in cruelty. You shed tears over fallen Hungary, and make the sad story of her wrongs the theme of your poets,

statesmen, and orators, till your gallant sons are ready to fly to arms to vindicate her cause against the oppressor; but in regard to the ten thousand wrongs of the American slave, you would enforce the strictest silence, and would hail him as an enemy of the nation who dares to make these wrongs the subject of public discourse!

We have made a point of quoting a large excerpt from this speech, although it is now more than a hundred years old, because it is contemporary still in many respects. It underlines perfectly the glaring contradictions between beliefs and acts for which colored people censure whites with such constancy as to give truth to the accusation. The travesty of Christian morality, when it occurs in relations between peoples, inevitably casts discredit on an ideology which is nonetheless basically humanist and whose principles call for attitudes completely contrary to those actually adopted.

As to the technical progress so warmly extolled by Western countries as one of their most important attributes, McKay saw in technology the deterioration of human possibilities, a yoke on spontaneity, a diminishment of man, and a depersonalization particularly painful to blacks. We should remember that McKay's book was written at a time when assembly-line work was being denounced on film by Charlie Chaplin (in *Modern Times*) and by René Clair (in *A nous la liberté*). In America as in Europe, men—Mounier, Duhamel, Bernanos—were sounding an alarm. The fears raised by increasing automation concerned not only the "mechanical organization of life" but also the leveling of personalities, the "standardization" of man and the boring everyday life that would be the result. Sinclair Lewis's *Babbitt* expressed a similar anxiety, which was shared by all clear-thinking Americans. The opinion of black writers about most white American writers of the period is summed up by Albert Baiwir, who declared [in *Le déclin de l'individualisme chez les romanciers américains contemporains*]: "The writers' attitude leads therefore to the repudiation of American civilization and, in the final analysis, to the spirit which presided over its establishment."

Claude McKay's pessimism matches that of his contemporaries:

[Ray] kept wondering how [his] race would fare under the ever tightening mechanical organization of modern life . . . The grand mechanical march of civilization had levelled the world down to the point where it seemed treasonable for an advanced thinker to doubt that what was good for one nation of people was also good for another. But as he was never afraid of testing ideas, so he was not afraid of doubting. All peoples must struggle to live, but just as what was helpful for one man might be injurious to another, so it might be with whole communities of peoples.

For Ray happiness was the highest good, and difference the greatest alarm, of life. The hand of progress was robbing his people of many primitive and beautiful qualities. He could not see where they would find greater happiness under the weight of the machine . . .

Many apologists of a changed and magnificent machine system doubted whether the Negro could find a decent place in it . . . [Ray] did not think the blacks would come very happily under the super-mechanical Anglo-Saxon-controlled world society of Mr. H. G. Wells.

It is clear that McKay had little confidence in such a society's capacity for happiness. He was led to wonder whether the future role of the black race would not be precisely to humanize society by escaping from technical civilization. The very backwardness and unadaptability of the black race might have preserved a vital resource, the inestimable potential for happiness.

A black man, even though educated, was in closer biological kinship to the swell of primitive earth life. And maybe his apparent failing under the organization of the modern world was the real strength that preserved him from becoming the thing that was the common white creature of it. [*Banjo*]

The attitude of the assimilated "black intelligensia" appeared to him ridiculous and illogical, and no words were sufficiently contemptuous to vilify them: "The colored intelligentsia lived its life . . . 'to have the white neighbors think well of us' so that it could move more peacefully into nice white streets." In similar fashion, McKay criticized black students in Europe, who, even when out to amuse themselves, were never without books "to protect themselves from being hailed everywhere as minstrel niggers, coons, funny monkeys . . . because the general European idea of the black man is that he is a public performer." He poked fun at their clothes "as close as ever to the pattern of the most correctly grey respectability" and of their glasses—"a mark of scholarship and respectability differentiating them from common types."

The obsession with "propriety" also existed in the literary domain, as Langston Hughes pointed out. "Black American intellectuals," he said, "when Negroes wrote books, . . . wanted them to be books in which only good Negroes, clean and cultured and not funny Negroes . . . were presented." One of them wrote in the *Philadelphia Tribune* about Hughes' *Fine Clothes to the Jew*:

It does not matter to me whether every poem in the book is true to life. Why should it be paraded before the American public by a Negro author as being typical or representative of the Negro? Bad enough to have white authors holding up our imperfections to public gaze. Our aim ought to be to present to the general public, already misinformed by well-meaning and malicious writers, our highest aims and aspirations, and our better selves.

Hughes comments [in *The Big Sea*]:

I felt that the masses of our people had as much in their lives to put into books as did those more fortunate ones who had been born with some means and the ability to work up to a master's degree at a Northern college.

Claude McKay studied this "alienated" reaction of black intellectuals and discovered several reasons for it. First of all, the loss of a folk tradition and folk wisdom, which are the foundations of any culture. Afro-Americans are uprooted people, twice uprooted if they are cultured men, educated and policed by Western civilization. Also, there is the deep inferiority complex from which all American Negroes suffer, the more so this elite for whom whites represent an ideal, leading them to stifle in themselves anything that might appear strange to a civilized white. This black elite so faithfully attempts to imitate the white American as to completely obliterate its own personality. McKay accuses this Negro bourgeoisie of no longer being "a people believing in themselves." They seemed to have lost their native spontaneity, the invigorating contact with the masses, in an attempt to obtain a "civilization" of doubtful value.

To rediscover the least distorted black values, one had to go to the masses, the laborers, the sailors, a whole working class for whom life was difficult, but which still had "that raw unconscious and the devil-with-them pride in being Negro," who represented "the irrepressible exuberance and legendary vitality of the black race" whose apparent anarchy helps safeguard its personality.

The most "genuine" black man would therefore be the one least corrupted by Western social structures and standards, the man from the masses whose very ignorance protects him from the multiple forms of alienation which threaten the educated black: "To be educated, black and his instinctive self [was] something of a big job to put over," remarks McKay. The black workingmen he had met in Harlem or Marseilles, on the other hand, lived far from the influence of a Negro press that carried ads for "skin-whitening" and "hair-straightening" remedies right next to those for training and education programs, which were also excellent "bleaching" agents.

Among these working people, there was no desire to look like a white, but there were a sense of humor, spontaneous artistic gifts, and above all, real fellowship during good and bad times. They did not act, did not try to show themselves as other than they were; they were genuine and free—like the marvelous character Banjo himself, who has always had enough resilience to bounce back into the "gentle, natural jazz of life" as he calls it, despite war, despite the lynching of his brother, despite the precariousness of his life as a sailor, and of all the trades that he plies for a living. When he has no money to pay for his drink at the bar, Banjo strums his instruments, inventing blues so his friends can dance:

> Shake That Thing! That jelly-roll Thing! Shake to the loud music of life playing to the primeval round of life . . . Shake that thing! In the face of the shadow of Death. Treacherous hand of murderous Death, lurking in sinister alleys, where the shadows of life dance, nevertheless, to their music of life. Death over there! Life over here! Shake down Death and forget his commerce, his purpose, his haunting presence in a great shaking orgy. Dance down the Death of these days, the Death of these ways in shaking that thing. Jungle jazzing, Orient wriggling, civi-

lized stepping. Shake that thing! Sweet dancing thing of primitive joy, perverse pleasure, prostitute ways, many-colored variations of the rhythm, savage, barbaric, refined—eternal rhythm of the mysterious, magical, magnificent—the dance divine of life . . . Oh, Shake that Thing!

The rediscovered value of the dance inspired this piece of pure lyricism, and dance, in Africa, symbolizes the joy of living.

Finally, Claude McKay turned to Africa for hope. He felt his race would rediscover its essence only by going to the very roots. Margaret Just Butcher has testified to the indelible survival of Africa in the folklore and sensibility of American blacks, even though they have been cut off from all contact with their continent of origin for more than three centuries.

But it was through personal contact with black Africans that McKay realized both what he had missed and an enrichment in the recognition of his origins.

> [Ray] always felt humble when he heard the Senegalese and other West African tribes speaking their own languages with native warmth and feeling.
>
> The Africans gave him a positive feeling of wholesome contact with racial roots. They made him feel that he was not merely an unfortunate accident of birth, but that he belonged definitely to a race, weighed, tested, and poised in the universal scheme. They inspired him with confidence in them. Short of extermination by the Europeans, they were a safe people, protected by their own indigenous culture. Even though they stood bewildered before the imposing bigness of white things, apparently unaware of the invaluable worth of their own, they were naturally defended by the richness of their fundamental racial values. [*Banjo*]

The acknowledgement of Africa was one of the pervasive characteristics of the Harlem Renaissance. Countee Cullen's most beautiful poem perhaps, "Heritage," is a long evocation of African landscapes, full of the persistent, rhythmic resonance of tom-toms, and of his fascination with ancient gods:

> Lord, I fashion dark gods, too,
> Daring even to give You
> Dark, despairing features where
> Crowned with dark rebellious hair,
> Patience wavers just so much as
> Mortal grief compels, while touches
> Quick and hot, of anger, rise
> To smitten cheek and weary eyes.
> Lord, forgive me if my need
> Sometimes shapes a human creed.
>   . . . . .
> Not yet has my heart or head
> In the least way realized
> They and I are civilized.

It was also in the name of his African heritage that Langston Hughes rejected the modern world [in the poems "Poem" and "Our Land"]:

All the tom-toms of the jungles beat in my blood,
And all the wild hot moons of the jungles beat
in my soul.
I am afraid of this civilization—
　　So hard,
　　　　So strong,
　　　　　　So cold.
　　　　　　　　["Poem"]

We should have a land of sun
Of gorgeous sun
And a land of fragrant water
Where the twilight
Is a soft bandana handkerchief
Of rose and gold,
And not this land where life is cold.

We should have a land of trees,
Of tall thick trees
Bowed down with chattering parrots
Brilliant as the day,
And not this land where birds are grey.

Ah! we should have a land of joy,
Of love and joy and wine and song,
And not this land where joy is wrong.
　　　　　　　　["Our Land"]

The progress accomplished toward authenticity becomes fully evident only if one thinks of the denial of Africa engrained in pre-Harlem Renaissance black consciences: as Phillis Wheatley once called it, "the land of errors and Egyptian gloom."

Banjo was the first novel to articulate the Negro problem fully and clearly. Blacks in Paris could not remain indifferent to so many revolutionary ideas. But they were also attracted by *Banjo*'s free and easy style, by its human warmth, the reality of its characters. Senghor, Césaire, and Damas can still cite entire chapters. "What struck me in this book," said Aimé Césaire, "is that for the first time Negroes were described truthfully, without inhibitions or prejudice."

Banjo's success did not stop with the first "triumvirate" of black writers. Ousmane Socé pointed out during the same period in [his novel] *Mirages de Paris* that *Banjo* was displayed in black student bookshelves right next to books by Delafosse. In *La rue Cases Négres,* Joseph Zobel remarked on the interest aroused in Martinique by McKay's novel. Among writers of the younger generation, Sembene Ousmane in *Le docker noir* was more influenced by *Banjo* than by the novels of Richard Wright, to which *Le docker noir* is occasionally compared.

The success of McKay's book was therefore due not only to its historical timeliness but also to a real literary merit, not yet surpassed by any contemporary black novelist. It is regrettable that many Europeans interested in black literature who have read Richard Wright or Peter Abrahams do not yet know the work of Claude McKay. His books are teeming with ideas, situations, and characters that are not found in such abundance or portrayed with such nuance in the books of any of his successors.

The American Negroes' contribution to young black writers in France was not limited only to new ideas. On a literary level they brought spontaneity of expression, freedom

Claude McKay, author of Banjo.

of rhythm and inner music. Léon Damas still has a veritable passion for Langston Hughes, who had a greater influence on the form of his poems than any French poet. Senghor has personally translated numerous poems by Langston Hughes, as well as those by Countee Cullen and Jean Toomer. He has moreover explained—like the good professor he still is—his interest in the Negro Renaissance poets [in "Trois poètes négro-américains," in *Poésie* 45]:

> What are the characteristics of this poetry? It is essentially nonsophisticated like its African sister. It remains close to song. It is made to be sung or recited and not to be read—thus the importance of the rhythm—Negro rhythm, so tyrannical under its aspect of freedom—thus the importance of its music, so difficult to retain in translating Toomer. These are the characteristics of the picture which, rare or in profusion, adhere closely to an idea or feeling. The words restored to their original purity keep their paradisiac power, and this often explains the clarity of the text.

> In a word, a poetry of flesh and of the earth, to put it as Hughes does, the poetry of a peasant still in contact with tellurian forces. And that explains the cosmic rhythm, this music and these

pictures of flowing water, rustling leaves, beating wings, twinkling stars.

Aimé Césaire, formed by the surrealist and symbolist schools, also appreciated this poetry, but for other reasons [described in *Tropiques* (July 1941)]:

> From this poetry, which might seem like the sort Valéry called "loose," "defenseless," written only to the rhythm of a juvenile spontaneity, at the exact point of intersection between the ego and the world, a drop of blood oozes. A drop. But of blood . . .
>
> There is its value: to be open on man in his wholeness. What others bring to poetry is a preference for the exterior world or for man at his most noble, the finest flower of his thought or feelings. And what indicates that greater or lesser nobility is the fear of oneself, a capitulation of the being to the seeming to be, a refusal to accept one's complete nature. But such weakness is unknown to the Negro poet. His treasure lies in those depths disdained by others . . .
>
> Where the role of an earlier literature was to seek out the grotesque, the absurd or exotic aspects of the ordinary Negro, this Negro now becomes the poet's hero. He is described seriously, with passion, and the limited power of his art— by a miracle of love—succeeds, where more considerable means fail, in suggesting even those inner forces which command destiny. Is creating a world of minor importance? Evoking a world from the outlandish inhuman creatures that used to be displayed row after row as if in a ten-cent store? And where once we could find nothing but a vision of crude puppets, to reap new ways of suffering, dying, enduring, in a word, to carry the sure weight of human existence.

More than aesthetic criteria, it was the human values of sincerity, love, and humility that touched Césaire. He was so deeply affected that without hesitation he proposed this type of poetry as a model for all Negro poets.

Senghor too has emphasized this aspect of American Negro poetry [in his "Trois poètes négro-américains"], which he considers of principal importance:

> [It is a] human poetry, and for this reason it deserves to be known. America is not only a land of machines and records, it is also a land of youth and hope, and among all its faces, America's black face is one of its most human.

(pp. 54-66)

Lilyan Kesteloot, "Negritude and Its American Sources," translated by Ellen Conroy Kennedy, in Boston University Journal, *Vol. XXII, No. 2, Spring, 1974, pp. 54-67.*

Albert Gérard

[*A Belgian scholar, Gérard has authored numerous books and articles on African literature. In the following excerpt, he outlines the aims, origins, and evolution of black literature espousing the tenets of Negritude.*]

Ever since the mediaeval quarrel over universals, there have invariably been minds for whom every general concept is a *flatus vocis*. And for many African intellectuals, the term "negritude," introduced by Aimé Césaire and Léopold Sédar Senghor around the years 1933-1935, is no more than just a word. Yet the mere fact that it came into being, even though it should have no intelligible content, is in itself significant. It is indicative of the same growing awareness that led to the struggle against racial discrimination and the liberation movements of colonial peoples. But a growing awareness of what?

In a recent treatise [*On the Theory of Social Change* (1962)], in which he studies the psycho-social foundations of culture and development, the American economist Everett E. Hagen writes:

> The satisfaction derived by an individual from his activity in life depends in part on the status associated with it. That status shall be satisfying requires not that it is high but merely that it is deemed appropriate by the person occupying it and is respected by others. The peasant as well as the lord, the craftsman as well as the political leader or corporation executive, has a status. One's status derives not only from one's economic function, however, but all that one does and believes, all of one's relationships to other persons and to the unseen forces in which one believes . . . One's status, that is, is one's identity; it includes one's purposes and values in life . . . For the inner satisfaction of the members of a society, as for social stability, it is essential that the status (the identity) of the members of each group in a society also be recognized by the other groups as appropriate and good.

Seen in this perspective, the secular impact of the Europeans on Africa has not only destroyed existing social structures, by replacing the traditional ruling classes with a foreign administrative caste; it has also undermined the ethical and psychological substratum of indigenous societies by demonstrating, through the mere evidence of their invincible power, the intrinsic inferiority of all the systems of beliefs, values and behavior which up to then had given a satisfactory meaning to life.

It will be useful to retrace the phases of this process. The first contacts between Europe and black Africa were of a commercial order and were established within the framework of common interests and mutual esteem. The monarchs of the coastal regions sold gold, ivory and slaves in order to obtain manufactured and luxury goods in exchange. In the sixteenth century the king of Portugal and the king of the Congo exchanged correspondence and ambassadors; the Bakongo princes received their education in Europe; and the Manikongo Alonso (1507 to 1543) undertook the task of modernizing and Christianizing his kingdom on the model of European states. The same type of relations persisted for the two centuries that followed, when the populations of the interior gradually constituted large organized states, such as the empires of Akan, Oyo, Dahomey or the Lunda kingdom of Mwata Yamvo, in order to participate as well in the profitable European trade. During all this time the Europeans had not gained sufficient technological power to proceed to the conquest of the dark continent. Nor did they desire it. And the extremely sporadic and localized contacts between the white man and the black world were not of a sort to provoke profound disturbances in the African cultures. In fact, until the nineteenth century, only the slaves, shipped to the sugar and cotton plantations across the Atlantic, really felt the impact of European power. Being confronted through slavery with the proof of their own weakness and inferiority, they accepted the white man's appraisal of them, and the chief ambition of their "elites" was to become like whites, to adopt their beliefs and values, to participate in their educational system, and to imitate them in everything.

But in the nineteenth century, with the prodigious rise of colonialism, which had been made possible by the industrial revolution, this same alienation from self was to become the fate of the entire dark continent. Was not the white man's power proof of an absolute superiority which gave him nearly divine status? In the eyes of the black man, the white man's contempt for his primitive way of life, his superstitious beliefs, his rudimentary economic structures and his traditional administrative organizations appeared justified. For the Europeans, African culture was devoid of value. It is true, as Hagen writes, that:

> The low valuation of indigenous individuals manifested by the conquerors would not have mattered if the conquerors had no prestige in the indigenous society. However, the conquerors did have one characteristic conveying tremendous prestige, their overwhelming power. Thus their valuation counted.

Thus, all of Africa was now subjected to the trauma experienced previously by the slaves taken to America. Justly despised, in his own esteem, by his masters, the Negro lost the feeling of having a place in the world of man; he considered himself as subhuman, he lost confidence in the value of his ideals and traditions; he was deprived of his dignity and his identity.

Such a situation is obviously unbearable. Every man has the need to feel his worth. Whole peoples have gradually become extinct as a result of having been robbed of their status, their identity, and their human value. In general, however, the collective instinct of preservation produces techniques of survival, first among which is what Hagen, adapting the terminology proposed by Robert K. Merton [in *Social Theory and Social Structure* (1957)], calls "ritualism."

The black slave embraces the religion of his masters; the equatorial citizen proudly perspires in a double-breasted jacket; the typist wears spectacles fitted with window glass; the negress has her hair uncurled; the intellectual prefers to get his degrees in European and American universities; the politician talks of democracy. In the eyes of the average European, these attitudes generally appear comic: they result from a clumsy mechanical imitation of outward forms of behavior emptied of their ethical and cultural contents. For the informed observer, however, they are mainly pathetic, for they bear witness to an effort—inevitably maladroit—to acquire a spare personality, a personality that, it is vainly hoped, will appear wor-

thy and respectable in the view of the social group which establishes the hierarchy of values. Thus, the black man adopts the ways of life of the white man and his criteria of judgment, in a ritualistic fashion, without realizing that they have no value in themselves but are the expression of an inner life whose sources escape him.

These phenomena are clearly manifest in the literature, which in turn clarifies the psychological processes from which it derives. The first Negro-American, Negro-West Indian and Negro-African works, as spaced out as they are in time, show a common preoccupation with assimilating the conceptions, the themes and the style that the white man proposes as models. The first Negro author of the United States, Jupiter Hammon (1720?-1800) wrote a poem with the suggestive title, "The Kind Master and the Dutiful Slave." And his contemporary, Phillis Wheatley (1753?-1784), a slave in Boston, describes the continent from which she had been taken as "the land of errors and Egyptian gloom," in verses that slavishly imitate the style of Pope! A century later, Paul Lawrence Dunbar (1872-1906) dedicates his poetry to the men of his race, but he makes them consonant with the image that the white man has of them, as inferior beings who accept their situation in the social structure and lead a primitive picturesque and idyllic existence. The characters of his three first novels are whites involved in conventional bourgeois plots.

In the same way the French-language West Indian writers echo, often with considerable skill, the Romantics, the Parnassians and the Symbolists—for which they were severely criticized by one of their compatriots, Etienne Léro in 1932:

> The West Indian, stuffed with white morality, white culture, white education, white prejudices, displays in his little books an inflated image of himself. Being a good copy of the pale man replaces for him social as well as poetic reason. He is never decent enough, esteemed enough— "You behave like a negro," he indignantly points out if you evince some natural exuberance in his presence. Nor does he want, in his poetry, to "behave like a negro." He makes it a point of honor that a white man read his book without guessing his pigmentation.

In Africa itself the novels of the colonial period were obviously written from a European perspective: church and administration are more or less discretely flattered; the traditional African is painted with the romantic hues of uncanny folklore (as in *Ngando* by the Congolese Paul Lomani-Tshibamba) or of idyllic pastoralism (as in *L'enfant noir* by the Guinean Camara Laye).

It is not surprising that this attempt at mimesis should have been abandoned first by the negroes of the United States. In the disappointment that followed the Civil War the emptiness of ritualism was revealed. On the other hand, the debate over slavery had thrown harsh light on the contradiction that existed and still exists between the American democratic ideal and the reality of racial discrimination. Finally, Christianity, which in the South had rediscovered its primary function as a religion of slaves and underprivileged, no longer appeared merely as a promise of salvation in the hereafter, but as a statement of human dignity recognized here on earth. These three factors jointly led the American Negro to proclaim his worth as a Negro, and this as early as the first years of the twentieth century. In 1902, P. L. Dunbar chose Harlem as the setting for his last novel, *Sport of the Gods,* and introduced Negro characters who were no longer comic or pathetic, goodnatured or resigned, but who lived in a realistic context of social protest.

In a world free of racial prejudice, this would have appeared only as a particular form of the proletarian inspiration which permeated all Euro-American literature at the end of the nineteenth century, and which contributed so powerfully to the emancipation of the underprivileged classes. And it is a fact that the rise of Negro literature everywhere was tied to social rebellion. A historian of Cuban letters wrote that "the negrista movement is the Cuban version of Spanish-American indigenism and international populism" [J. A. Portuondo, *Bosquejo histórico de las letras cubanas* (1960)]. And the beautiful book *Les bouts de bois de Dieu* (1960) by the Senegalese Sembène Ousmane, which deals with a railway strike, gives a social dimension to a negritude whose psychological and cultural values are proclaimed in Senghor's poetry. But in a society and a universe dominated by the idea of the innate superiority of the white race, the social element seems curiously secondary. In her work on Negro literature in the French language [*Les écrivains noirs de langue française: Naissance d'une littérature* (1963)], Mme Kesteloot cogently remarks that "contrary to what Sartre thinks, . . . it would seem . . . that socialism or communism was a preliminary step towards the negro's demand for racial emancipation, rather than the opposite."

The fact is that the grandson of the Italian, Polish or Armenian immigrant is a white American, just like the descendant of the pioneers. But the descendants of the black slave are just as black, and the racism of the whites has compelled the Negroes to become aware of their human status within the framework of a racial identity, indelibly inscribed in the color of their skin. While proletarian literature, even when it appeals to a class mystique, generally demands that unprivileged individuals participate in the full life of a homogeneous society, Negro writers have to face an even more difficult task. They must show in the first place that the Negro is really a part of human society, that is, they must assert the worth of negritude. If the word does not yet exist, the concept is present. This was evident when the poet Langston Hughes declares: "We younger Negro artists who create now intend to express our individual dark-skinned selves without fear or shame." It was even more obvious when the elderly historian W. E. B. DuBois stated in 1940 that his autobiographical work, *Dusk of Dawn,* was "not so much my autobiography as the autobiography of a concept of race." The import of this declaration becomes clear if it is recalled that DuBois was one of the first to attempt, as Melville Herskovits says [in *The Myth of the Negro Past* (1962)], "to comprehend the entire picture of the negro, African and New World, in its historical and functional setting," in his *Black Folk, Then and Now* (1939), a work that crowns a long career of research in this field.)

Born in the United States under the pressure of an intolerable situation, this tendency to rehabilitate the Negro in his Africanness found the ground admirably prepared. Euro-American civilization had developed under the triple sign of reason, science and technique. In the same way that romanticism was born of a need to reestablish the affective and sensory values ignored by the rationalism of the Age of Enlightenment, the main trends of Western civilization were questioned again at the end of the nineteenth century. Bergson's attractive intuitionism and the exploration of the subconscious by Freud suggested to writers and artists ways of life, of thought, of creation, tending to produce a more total experience, a more cosmic understanding, a more authentic expression. When ethnologists began to study primitive peoples in a truly scientific spirit, and while Oswald Spengler was preparing to dissect the corpse of the West, novelists such as D. H. Lawrence and E. M. Forster in England, Blaise Cendrars and later André Malraux in France were searching other areas of the globe for a less sophisticated but also less degenerate humanity, more primitive but living in harmony with the dark powers of the universe. But while this literary nomadism was mainly directed toward India and China, Italy and Mexico, for artists and musicians, negritude, which did not yet have a name, was the new pole of attraction, the new fountain of forms and inspiration. African sculpture and American jazz introduced mysterious rhythms, tellurian pulsations, a direct expression, as it seemed, of the profound life of the body and of the subconscious.

Thus arose the myth of a paradisaic Africa, the throbbing homeland of rhythm and passion,—a myth that first took form in 1914 in the famous and interminable poem by Vachel Lindsay, "The Congo (A Study of the Negro Race)":

> Wild crap-shooters with a whoop and a call
> Danced the juba in their gambling-hall
> And laughed fit to kill, and shook the town,
> And guyed the policemen, and laughed them down
> With a boomlay, boomlay, boomlay, BOOM . . .
> THEN I SAW THE CONGO, CREEPING THROUGH THE BLACK
> CUTTING THROUGH THE JUNGLE WITH A GOLDEN TRACK.
> A negro fairyland swung into view,
> A minstrel river
> Where dreams come true.
> The ebony palace soared on high
> Through the blossoming trees to the evening sky,
> The inlaid porches and casements shone
> With gold and ivory and elephant bone.
> And the black crowd laughed till their sides were sore
> At the baboon butler in the agate door,
> And the well-known tuner of the parrot band
> That trilled on the bushes of that magic land.
> A troop of skull-faced witch-men came
> Through the agate doorway in suits of flame,
> Yes, long-tailed coats with a gold-leaf crust
> And hats that were covered with diamond dust.
> And the crowd in the court gave a whoop and a call
> And danced the juba from wall to wall.

But the witch-men suddenly stilled the throng
With a stern cold glare, and a stern old song:
"Mumbo Jumbo will hoo-doo you."

The Negro poets of the United States soon adopted this myth, adding a deeply felt nostalgia to its gaudy picturesqueness. "Heritage," a poem by Countee Cullen (1903-1946), provides an example:

What is Africa to me;
Copper sun or scarlet sea,
Jungle star or jungle track,
Strong bronzed men, or regal black
Women from whose loins I sprang
When the birds of Eden sang?
One three centuries removed
From the scenes his fathers loved,
Spicy grove, cinnamon tree,
What is Africa to me?

. . . . .

Quaint outlandish heathen gods
Black men fashion out of rods,
Clay and brittle bits of stone,
In a likeness of their own.
My conversion came high-priced;
I belong to Jesus Christ,
Preacher of humility;
Heathen gods are naught to me.
Father, Son and Holy Ghost,
So I make an idle boast,
Jesus of the twice-turned cheek,
Lamb of God, although I speak
With my mouth thus, in my heart
Do I play a double part.
Even at thy glowing altar
Must my heart grow thick and falter,
Wishing He I served were black . . .

Much of the poetry of Langston Hughes expresses with haunting pathos the predicament of the American Negro, torn between a powerful and contemptuous civilization in which he lives, although he did not create it, and the colorful allurements of the African dream.

Closer consideration of this African myth shows that it is made up of a cluster of very different and sometimes contradictory attitudes, whose heterogeneity reflects the perplexity of a race feeling its way toward the light, searching for an awareness of its own identity and seeking to discover the ways to its salvation. Some exalt Africa as the continent which, through Egypt, gave birth to European civilizations. [In a footnote, Gérard states: "The Jamaican Marcus Garvey declares in *Philosophy and Opinion:* 'When Europe was inhabited by a race of cannibals, a race of savages, naked men, heathens and pagans, Africa was peopled by a race of men who were cultured and refined . . . '."] But more frequently, conceptions generally considered as "civilized" are forcefully rejected. It is significant that G. R. Coulthard could devote a whole chapter of his book on West Indian literature [*Race and Color in Caribbean Literature* (1962)] to the "rejection of European culture as a theme in Caribbean literature,"—a theme in which he distinguished four principal factors:

First, the feeling that the Caribbean negro is somehow constricted in the moulds of European thought and behaviour patterns which are not fitted to his nature. Linked with this is the inter-est in African cultures, past and present, both in Africa and their remains in the West Indies. Second, the feeling that European civilization has failed, by becoming excessively concerned with power and technical progress and not sufficiently concerned with the production of happiness for the human individual. African or negro culture is presented as being nearer to nature and nearer to man. Third, the rejection of Christianity as an agent or ally of colonialism; and finally, the attack on European civilization for the brutality and cynicism with which it enslaved and exploited the Negro, while still maintaining high-sounding principles of freedom and humanitarianism.

This criticism of modern civilization, which is nowhere as strident as in the West Indies, is inevitably tied together with a mystical exaltation of primitivism, mainly in its most elementary and shocking aspects. In Cuba, J. A. Portuondo writes, "*negrismo* is a pure cult of the picturesque, which depends on the two predominant elements of negro folk art: rhythm and color"; and Coulthard notes its "characteristic atmosphere of dancing and sex . . . a noticeable insistence on the animality of the dancers' movements of hips, contortions of muscles, in an atmosphere charged with sexuality, alcohol and sometimes voodoo." The Portorican Palés Matos praises Africa in a rather strange way in a poem entitled "Niam-niam":

Asia dreams its nirvana
America dances its jazz,
Europe plays and theorises,
Africa grunts: ñam-ñam.

In his *Cahier d'un retour au pays natal* Aimé Césaire crudely reveals the logical tie between the rejection of the modern world and the apology of primitivism:

Because we hate you and your reason, . . . we
    turn to
the precocious dementia of flaming madness
of persistent cannibalism.

And in 1927, the Haitian Carl Brouard wrote of a disturbing "Nostalgie," which figures, it seems, in all the anthologies of Haitian poetry:

Drum
when you sound
my soul screams towards Africa.
Sometimes
I dream of an immense jungle
bathed in moonlight
with hirsute, sweating figures,
Sometimes
of a filthy hut
where I drink blood out of human skulls.

Lyrical poetry lends itself to such excesses, although we may rest assured that if he had to choose, even the wildest West Indian poet would prefer canned beer, however dehumanized it may be. The violence of this reaction against Europe and of this primitivist assertion illustrates, on a verbal level and frequently with real talent, the psychological process of alienation which Richard Wright revealed in his *Native Son*. Like the hero of this novel, the West Indian poets, whether they write in French, English or Spanish, are incapable of overcoming the conditioning imposed upon them by a long tradition of oppression, injustice and contempt. Dominated by a quite understandable rage and hatred, their attitude is basically negative. Literature for them is a means of venting the wrath that obsesses them. Whereas Wright has overcome the deterministic mechanism of violence geared on violence which he takes to pieces, the West Indian poets remain caught up in this circle which crushes them and draws from them only cries of rage. (pp. 14-27)

The fact is that Negro experience is infinitely varied, and we are far from knowing the historical factors which have provoked this diversity. A common submission to dependence and to disparagement has kindled a wide range of reactions. The vengeful anger that burns in West Indian poetry is certainly not lacking in other Negro literatures, but in these it is surrounded with more durable, more positive elements. Thus, the Negro poets of the United States have frequently transmuted into conscious and deliberate art the intense religious feeling which inspired the *Negro spirituals* to spring from the soul of the people. And in Africa the majestic rhythm of the poems in which Senghor celebrates his people gives utterance to the serenity of a mind that does not allow itself to be obsessed by painful though inevitably transitory grievances. Moreover, the generation of poets has been completed since 1940 by a generation of novelists: Richard Wright, Ralph Ellison and James Baldwin in America, Peter Abrahams, Mongo Beti, Sembène Ousmane, Hamidou Kane and the Nigerian school in Africa, and George Lamming in the West Indies. With them the cries of rage and vengeance have made room for a more objective understanding of the Negro coping with his lot, a more mature analysis of the psychological factors of the interracial clash and a perception, both more concrete and more subtle, of the social, ethical and cultural problems which the "winds of change" fanning contemporary history pose to the white and the black man alike. After a long period of slavish imitation and a short period of frantic rebellion, Negro literature has reached a third phase in its search for a black identity, a phase in which a more acute sense of reality is allied with a more positive feeling of responsibility.

The nostalgic idea of a common Africanness which crystallized in the post-Rousseau myth of a free and picturesque Africa, peopled by coconut trees, crocodiles and happy cannibals living in harmony with tellurian forces, was artificial and just as utopian as the "Back to Africa" movement launched by Marcus Garvey. In 1940, in his autobiography entitled *The Big Sea,* Langston Hughes relates how he had to renounce the gifts of a benefactress who, he said, "wanted me to be a primitive, and know and feel the intuitions of the primitive. But, unfortunately, I did not feel the rhythms of the primitive surging through me, and so I could not live and write as though I did. I was only an American Negro—who had loved the surface of Africa and the rhythms of Africa—but I was not what she wanted me to be." The multiplication of effective contacts with African reality was responsible for spreading this obvious truth. In 1953, when Richard Wright visited the Gold Coast, which was to become Ghana, he admitted his incapacity to understand Africa and said so in *Black*

Power: "I found the African an oblique, hard-to-know man who seems to take a kind of childish pride in trying to create a state of bewilderment in the minds of strangers . . . I had understood nothing. I was black and they were black but my blackness did not help me." Many such testimonies could be quoted. They show that at a time when Senghor and Césaire were co-operating in defining the cultural unity of the Negro world with a oneness of purpose facilitated no doubt by a common French education, the Negro intellectuals of the United States, who had been the first to formulate the concept of a general Africanness, were beginning to apprehend its diversity.

Paradoxically enough, the conferences of Negro writers—in particular those held in Paris in September 1956, in Rome in March 1959 and in Philadelphia in June 1960—which purported to enhance this cultural unity of the Negro world, ended in fact by stressing its multiplicity. For the Negro world is not a homogeneous and monolithic magma, but, like every human community, a concrete and diversified reality. It might be said that every black man has his place on a graph whose two coordinates are the pre-European tradition and the adaptation to modern civilization. At the start of this graph, as it now stands, are the primitive populations of the equatorial jungle, and at the other end are the Negro intellectuals of South Africa and the United States. But this oversimplifies the problem. Each of these coordinates breaks down in turn into differentiated factors. The pre-European tradition is not the same for the Senegalese Moslem and for the animist of the tropical forest. On the other hand, the impact of modern civilization has not been felt everywhere and on all in the same way. Once it is admitted that negritude is not a metaphysical entity but can have meaning only in designating a number of situations that are recorded in history, it becomes possible to realize the value and fecundity of the cleavages and tensions that it involves.

Contrary to the Jews, the Negroes of the diaspora have lost their contact with the languages and religions of their ancestors. The Negro American conceives of himself today as a black American and not as an exiled African. Commenting on the 1956 Conference of Negro writers and artists, James Baldwin writes [in *Nobody Knows My Name* (1961)]:

> What, at bottom, distinguished the Americans from the Negroes who surrounded us, men from Nigeria, Senegal, Barbados, Martinique—so many names for so many disciplines—was the banal and abruptly quite overwhelming fact that we had been born in a society, which, in a way quite inconceivable for Africans, and no longer real for Europeans, was open, and, in a sense which has nothing to do with justice or injustice, was free.

As a minority group in an open but powerfully developed society, the American Negroes feel less and less impelled to destroy the existing structures. They know that they will be integrated into them and that theoretical and institutional multiracialism is certain to be translated into reality; they know that this will occur within the framework of Western civilization, which they know well and to which they are attached.

The situation is entirely different in Africa, where European civilization has often manifested itself in its least attractive aspects and where a pre-European tradition, which the American Negro does not have to take into account, has remained deeply rooted. It is not yet possible to estimate the influence that the diversity of the traditional substratum may exercise on the configuration of contemporary Africa. But it is clear that the methods of colonization constitute a lasting factor of differentiation. In his own comment on the 1956 Conference, Ezekiel Mphahlele states [in *The African Image* (1962)]:

> It is significant that it is not the African in British-settled territories—a product of "indirect rule" and one that has been left in his cultural habitat—who readily reaches out for his traditional past. It is rather the assimilated African, who has absorbed French culture, who is now passionately wanting to recapture his past. In his poetry he extols his ancestors, ancestral masks, African wood carvings and bronze art and tries to recover the moorings of his oral literature; he clearly feels he has come to a dead-end in European culture, and is still not really accepted as an organic part of French society, for all the assimilation he has been through.

The variety of administrative and educational practices produced a distinction between French-speaking and English-speaking Africans, which came to the fore at the Rome Conference, when the Ghanaian delegates criticized the way in which proceedings were conducted by French-speaking Negro intellectuals. It would seem that the French policy of direct administration and of cultural assimilation had provoked a greater alienation of the elites in relation to the people and, consequently, a more conscious, more violent, and perhaps also more artificial reaction against modern civilization. The satirical anti-clericalism of the Cameroonian Mongo Beti in *Le pauvre Christ de Bomba* (1956) testifies to this. On the other hand, a particularly lucid conception of the significance of traditional cultures and a singularly elevated vision of all that the irruption of Africa on the scene of history implies for the future fate of mankind may be found among the French-educated writers such as Sheik Hamidou Kane in *L'aventure ambiguë* (1961). On the contrary, the novelists and playwrights of the very active Nigerian school, such as Cyprian Ekwensi, Chinua Achebe, Onuora Nzekwu or John Pepper Clark, are less interested in the principles of their own culture and of future syncretisms than in the concrete conflicts that the incompatibilities of tradition and the modern world force on the everyday life of individuals. Observing that "the man of culture in countries of British influence hasn't really caught the negritude fever of the assimilated men in the countries of French influence," Mphahlele finds the reason for it in the fact that "the English-speaking African is much steadier and more confident of himself." There can be no doubt that the policy of indirect rule once instituted in Nigeria by Lord Luggard, by respecting the social structures and the cultural autonomy of the populations concerned, considerably mitigated the inferiority complex provoked by the subjugation to the white man's power as well as the intensity of

the process of compensatory self-assertion resulting from it.

But English-speaking Africa is not homogeneous itself, and the South-African Negroes who have been able to visit other regions of the continent frequently experience feelings of isolation and incomprehension which are far from being solely the result of the institutional measures taken by the Pretoria government. After living for centuries in close symbiosis with a white community, which, after all is also autochthonous, the South-African town dweller is as totally cut off from the tribal tradition as his American counterpart. The reproaches that Ezekiel Mphahlele addresses to the editors of *Présence Africaine* are revealing, even though they may not be entirely justified:

> They seemed to think that the only culture worth exhibiting was traditional or indigenous. And so they concentrated on countries where interaction of streams of consciousness between black and white has not taken place to any significant or obvious degree, or doesn't so much as touch the cultural subsoil.

And he stresses "how similar the American Negro's cultural predicament is to ours in South Africa and in other multi-racial communities." But if the South-African Negro intellectual is detribalized and acculturated, and if his political objective is not negro independence, which would have to start out with genocide, but a multiracial society, still in the southern republic colored people constitute a majority dominated by a racially distinct group. This is an eminently colonial situation which finds its literary reflection in the socio-racial obsession that characterizes the novels of Peter Abrahams, in the same way that it permeated West Indian literature or Senegalese literature before independence. Here again, however, similarity does not mean identity. In the most valid literary expressions of the Negro experience in South Africa one seldom encounters the intransigent violence, the systematic denigration and the hysterical tone which frequently mar the poems of Aimé Césaire, Paul Niger or Léon Damas. This is undoubtedly in part because the South-African Negro elite has deeply absorbed the Christian message. But there is another reason, which Noni Jabavu has outlined in a pregnant comparison between the West Indian and African mentality [in a review of V. S. Naipaul's *The Middle Passage* appearing in the *New York Times Book Review Supplement* (22 September 1963)]:

> Rootlessness, a historical sense of dereliction, absence of tradition, search for identity—these characteristics impressed me during conversations with West Indians. As an African, I possessed a heritage embedded in my language, tribal loyalties, stored treasures of legends, events. Do not these give any African a fortunate sense of continuity? Whatever deprivations apartheid imposes on us in my own country, these can never efface the strengths and traditions of our people.

This statement completes rather than contradicts Mphahlele's declarations: in southern Africa the sectional sense of tribal loyalty today is breaking away from its earlier cultural context and is beginning to assume the modern form of a feeling of national solidarity, more advanced perhaps than in many independent African countries. While the Senegalese and Nigerian novelists have recourse to a foreign idiom to give literary expression to the clash of cultures, this same subject has inspired in South Africa a novel [*Ingqumbo Yeminyanya*] in the Xhosa language by a prominent Negro writer, A. C. Jordan, formerly lecturer at the University of Cape Town and presently professor at the University of Wisconsin. This would seem to suggest that the South-African writer is less alienated from his people, his traditions and his negritude than his colleagues of Western Africa.

With the present state of our knowledge, we can only lift a corner of the veil of ignorance which conceals the diversity of Africa, nevertheless the concept of negritude already seems to dissolve into uncontrollable multiplicity. The reason is that the concept is too frequently used in a summary and rhetorical manner, and without the nuances which ensure the validity of universals. On an affective, polemic, and to some extent strategic level the word "negritude" represents, as the American writer Stanley Allen has said, "the Negro African poet's endeavour to recover for his race a normal self-pride, a lost confidence in himself, a world in which he again has a sense of identity and a significant role." But inevitably the question arises as to what this identity consists of, whether there really exists such a thing as a negro soul, or, to use Kwame Nkrumah's expression, an "African personality." A negative attitude with regard to this question would not be *a priori* justified. After all, we have an immediate consciousness of the unity of Western civilization, and we admit without discussion that this civilization was formed by secular historical processes, that it differs essentially as much from those that preceded it as from those which in the East and in the Arab world established themselves simultaneously, and that it gathers into a fundamental unity peoples otherwise clearly differentiated by their national characteristics. It is legitimate to approach the problem of the African personality in the same spirit.

The international confrontations that have succeeded each other in the course of the last ten years have posed this problem fully in all its complexities. In his comments on the Paris Conference, James Baldwin, powerfully struck as he was by the diversity of the Negro world, still asserts that a common factor exists:

> It became clear as the debate wore on, that there *was* something which all black men held in common, something which cut across opposing points of view, and placed in the same context their widely dissimilar experience. What they held in common was their precarious, their unutterably painful relation to the white world. What they held in common was the necessity to remake the world in their own image, to impose this image on the world, and no longer be controlled by the vision of the world, and of themselves, held by other people. What, in sum, black men held in common was their ache to come into the world as men.

The importance of this will should not be underestimated for it brings together two historical factors which can only

Camara Laye, author of L'enfant noir *and* Le regard du roi.

strengthen it and make it more efficient. One is the gradual disappearance of white messianism: a more refined moral sense, the bad use the white man has made of his power and knowledge, a certain loss of vitality as a necessary consequence of an excess of material prosperity,—all this has softened the aggressiveness of the white man and has undermined his confidence in his own superiority and in his innate right to rule the globe. Secondly, the Negro world, in its will for self-assertion, finds support in the Asian world, so much so that two-thirds of mankind are today united in the revolutionary determination to abolish the hegemony of the white race.

United in this revolutionary dynamism, the Negro peoples are also united at present in the historical phenomenon of underdevelopment. For Aimé Césaire, the Negroes are:

> those who have invented neither gunpowder nor the compass
> those who have never known how to harness steam or electricity
> those who have not explored the seas nor the sky.

Whether this is, as Sartre affirms [in "Orphée noir"], a "proud claim of non-technicity" or, as Mme Kesteloot believes, "the objective, humble, grieved recognition of a true inferiority, added to all the rest of the liabilities of his race," matters little: the fact itself is acknowledged. Technological underdevelopment is evidently the result of underdevelopment on the level of rational and scientific knowledge. In declaring that "the philosophic effort of traditional Africa has always been reflected in vital attitudes and has never had purely conceptual aims" [Colin Legum, *Pan-Africanism* (1962)], the commission on philosophy created by the Rome Conference recognized in fact that African thought has not gone beyond the preconceptual stage. Nevertheless, underdevelopment does not only have negative aspects, and it is expedient to free the term of the derogatory connotations that surround it in the ethnocentric context of the Euro-American vocabulary: the wisdom of lived experience, although deprived of any conceptual framework, is nonetheless a wisdom. Incapable of mastering nature by himself or even of understanding its laws, plunged into an incomprehensible, arbitrary and frequently menacing world, primitive man develops dimensions of being that the progress of science and technique atrophy. He must concoct myths in order to account for natural phenomena and he must resort to magic in order to act on his environment and to control his own fate; but he is imbued with an intense, constantly experienced religious feeling, whose spiritual quality is independent of the false beliefs and superstitious practices through which it manifests itself. On the other hand, the absolute necessity to group together in order to survive has endowed him with a community feeling which is not the application of an abstract doctrine but a powerful emotional reality. At the Rome Conference it was rightly noted in the preamble to one of the resolutions that the essential values of the Negro cultural personality are "a fundamental faith in a transcendental Force from which man draws his origin, upon which he depends and towards which he is drawn" and "the sense of a vital solidarity (*'solidarité'*), a French word which seems to us the least removed from the Fulah *neddaku*, the Bambara *maya*, the Madagascan *fihavanana*, and others, and which comprises a series of moral and social virtues, such as Ancestor worship, the veneration of the Elders, hospitality, the spirit of tolerance, etc."

But if this religious feeling and this community sentiment, not constituted into doctrinal systems, but actually and immediately lived and experienced are at the core of what Senghor calls the *"Negritude of the sources,"* the third common characteristic of the Negro personality is that it is now irrevocably engaged in the dialectics of history. He is implicated in a modern version of the eternal drama by which human civilization renews itself and transforms itself and which Toynbee defined as "the challenge which a civilization presents to a barbarism." Like the Achaeans of the Minoan period and the Germans under the late Roman Empire, the Africans, after having served abroad or at home as a proletariat for a powerful and proud civilization, now reject their former bondage and are taking their destiny into their own hands. The experience of mankind shows that such an event—which has never yet occurred in the past with such magnitude—exerts an incalculable influence on the further evolution of civilization. But if this revolutionary transfer of power appears in the retrospective view of the historian as the triumphal accession of young, primitive, inexperienced peoples, bubbling with ambition, to higher, more universal ways of being, of thinking, of creating, the actors in the drama feel it quite differently. German poetry of the heroic period, from the

Edda to the *Niebelungenlied,* does not reflect only the exaltation of the victory over Rome; it is also imbued with a poignant feeling of tragedy, obsessed by the irrevocable destruction of the ancient order, disturbed by the painful consciousness of chaotic wars, of whose general and positive direction it is not aware. The same fluidity of the historical context gives rise to similar characteristics in neo-African literature. Until the middle of the century the Negro writer everywhere in the world pursued a very precise goal: the definition and recognition of the identity and human dignity of his race. Despite the difficulties that he still encounters, it is now clear that this aim will be realized in the near future. The majority of the African countries and the Caribbean Islands have acquired their independence. In the United States, government authorities are definitively committed to desegregation. There is no doubt that the Republic of South Africa also will be obliged, whether through violence or negotiation, to recognize the rights of the majority of its population. This evolution implies that the literary inspiration furnished by racial conflict is destined to dry up at the source and make way for the genuine problem of the times: the problem of the confrontation of cultures. For at the very moment when the African writer takes possession of his cultural heritage, of the *"Negritude of the sources,"* and when he assumes responsibility for it, he also becomes aware of the paradox, to some extent biological, of all life, of all becoming, of all growth. He finds that his ancestral heritage does not arm him to survive in the modern world, that respect for a venerable tradition is a factor of stagnation, that tribal solidarity in a modern state is a factor of corruption, that abstract thought and economic development corrode the emotional ties that bind men together and to the world in which they live, and that science negates the mythical interpretation of the universe.

From a literary point of view this third aspect of negritude is doubtless the most fecund, but also the most tragic. If the work of the Nigerian Amos Tutuola testifies to the loyalty of the African to ancestral myths, that of his compatriots, Chinua Achebe, Cyprian Ekwensi and Onuora Nzekwu and, in Senegal, Sheik Hamidou Kane, is focused on the necessity of making an agonizing choice; while it reflects a keen desire for evolution, it reveals not only the inner dilemmas to which each choice leads but also a pathetic perplexity over the validity of the sacrifices that this historic choice entails. The young nations, just like adolescents, win their autonomy only in order to lose it in the network of responsibilities to which it leads. All progress, all growth implies to some extent that something dies as something else is born. And while it is inevitable that a syncretism between the negritude of the sources and the requirements of universal civilization will be effected, history teaches us that these processes are painful, that they last for centuries and that their concrete orientations are unpredictable and uncontrollable. (pp. 27-38)

Albert Gérard, "Historical Origins and Literary Destiny of Negritude," translated by Victor A. Velen, in Diogenes, *No. 48, Winter, 1964, pp. 14-38.*

DEFINITIONS

Jean-Paul Sartre

[*A French philosopher, dramatist, novelist, and essayist, Sartre is regarded as one of the most influential contributors to world literature in the twentieth century. In the following excerpt, which was originally published as a preface to* Anthologie de la nouvelle poésie nègre et malgache de langue française *(1948), he attempts to define Negritude using Marxist analogies and arguing that black poetry is an act of rebellion and the only outlet through which blacks can express and discover themselves.*]

When you removed the gag that was keeping these black mouths shut, what were you hoping for? That they would sing your praises? Did you think that when they raised themselves up again, you would read adoration in the eyes of these heads that our fathers had forced to bend down to the very ground? Here are black men standing, looking at us, and I hope that you—like me—will feel the shock of being seen. For three thousand years, the white man has enjoyed the privilege of seeing without being seen; he was only a look—the light from his eyes drew each thing out of the shadow of its birth; the whiteness of his skin was another look, condensed light. The white man—white because he was man, white like daylight, white like truth, white like virtue—lighted up the creation like a torch and unveiled the secret white essence of beings. Today, these black men are looking at us, and our gaze comes back to our own eyes; in their turn, black torches light up the world and our white heads are no more than chinese lanterns swinging in the wind. A black poet—unconcerned with us—whispers to the woman he loves:

> Naked woman, black woman
> Dressed in your color which is life . . .
> Naked woman, dark woman,
> Firm fleshed ripe fruit, somber ecstasies of black
> wine.

and our whiteness seems to us to be a strange livid varnish that keeps our skin from breathing—white tights, worn out at the elbows and knees, under which we would find real human flesh the color of black wine if we could remove them. We think we are essential to the world—suns of its harvests, moons of its tides; we are no more than its fauna, beasts. Not even beasts:

> These gentlemen from the city
> These proper gentlemen
> Who no longer know how to dance in the eve-
> ning by moonlight
> Who no longer know how to walk on the flesh
> of their feet
> Who no longer know how to tell tales by the
> fireside . . .

Formerly Europeans with divine right, we were already feeling our dignity beginning to crumble under American or Soviet looks; Europe was already no more than a geo-graphical accident, the peninsula that Asia shoves into the Atlantic. We were hoping at least to find a bit of our greatness reflected in the domesticated eyes of the Africans. But there are no more domesticated eyes: there are wild and free looks that judge our world.

Here is a black man wandering:

> to the end of
> the eternity of their endless boulevards
> with cops . . .

Here is another one shouting to his brothers:

> Alas! Alas! Spidery Europe is moving its
> fingers and its phalanxes of ships . . .

Here is:

> the cunning silence of Europe's night . . .

in which

> . . .there is nothing that time does not dishon-
> or.

A negro writes:

> At times, we will haunt Montparnasse and Paris,
> Europe and its endless torments, like memories
> or like malaises . . .

and suddenly France seems exotic in our own eyes. She is no more than a memory, a malaise, a white mist at the bottom of sunlit souls, a back-country unfit to live in; she has drifted towards the North, she is anchored near Kamchatka: the essential thing is the sun, the sun of the tropics and the sea "lousy with islands" and the roses of Imangue and the lilies of Iarive and the volcanos of Martinique. Being [l'Être] is black, Being is made of fire, we are accidental and far away, we have to justify our mores, our technics, our undercooked paleness and our verdigris vegetation. We are eaten away to the bones by these quiet and corrosive looks:

> Listen to the white world
> horribly weary of its immense effort
> its rebel articulations crackling under hard stars,
> its steel-blue stiffnesses piercing mystical flesh
> listen to its exhibitionist victories trumpeting its
> defeats
> listen to its wretched staggering with grandiose
> alibis
> Have pity on our naïve omniscient conquerors.

There we are, *finished;* our victories—their bellies sticking up in the air—show their guts, our secret defeat. If we want to crack open this finitude which imprisons us, we can no longer rely on the privileges of our race, of our color, of our technics: we will not be able to become a part of the totality from which those black eyes exile us, unless we tear off our white tights in order to try simply to be men.

If these poems shame us however, they were not intended to: they were not written for us; and they will not shame any colonists or their accomplices who open this book, for these latter will think they are reading letters over someone's shoulder, letters not meant for them. [The black poets represented in *Anthologie de la nouvelle poésie nègre et malgache de langue française*] are addressing themselves to black men about black men; their poetry is neither satiric nor imprecatory: it is an awakening to consciousness. "So," you will say, "in what way does it interest us, if it is only a document? We cannot enter into it." I should like to show in what way we *can* gain access to this world of jet; I should like to show that this poetry—which seems racial at first—is actually a hymn by everyone for everyone. In a word, I am talking now to white men, and I should like to explain to them what black men already know: why it is necessarily through a poetic experience that the black man, in his present condition, must first become conscious of himself; and, inversely, why black poetry in the French language is, in our time, the only great revolutionary poetry.

It is not just by accident that the white proletariat rarely uses poetic language to speak about its suffering, its anger or its pride in itself; neither do I think that workers are less gifted than our bourgeois sons: "talent"—that efficacious grace—loses all meaning when one claims that it is more widespread in one class than in another. Nor is it hard work that takes away their capacity for song: slaves used to drudge even harder and yet we know of slave hymns. It must therefore be recognized that it is the present circumstances of the class struggle that keep the worker from expressing himself poetically. Oppressed by technics, he wants to be a technician because he knows that technics will be the instrument of his liberation; he knows that it is only by gaining professional, economic and scientific know-how that he will be able someday to control business management. He now has a profound practical knowledge of what poets have called *Nature,* but it is a knowledge he has gained more through his hands than through his eyes: Nature is Matter for him—that crafty, inert adversity that he works on with his tools; Matter has no song. At the same time, the present phase of his struggle requires of him continual, positive action: political cal culation, precise forecasting, discipline, organization of the masses; to dream, at this point, would be to betray. Rationalism, materialism, positivism—the great themes of his daily battle—are least propitious for the spontaneous creation of poetic myths. The last of these myths—the famous "Upheaval"—has withdrawn under the circumstances of the struggle: one must take up the matter that is most urgent, gain this and that position, raise this salary, decide on that sympathy strike or on some protest against the war in Indo-China: efficiency alone matters. And, without a doubt, the oppressed class must first find itself. This self-discovery, however, is the exact opposite of a subjective examination of oneself: rather, it is a question of recognizing—in and by action—the objective situation of the proletariat, which can be determined by the circumstances of production or of redistribution of property. Unified by an oppression which is exerted on each and every one, and reduced to a common struggle, workers are hardly acquainted with the inner contradictions that fecundate the work of art and that are harmful to the *praxis.* As far as they are concerned, to know themselves is to situate themselves within the context of the great forces that surround them; it requires them to determine both their exact position in their class and their function in the Party. The very language they use is free from the slight loosen-

ing of the screws, the constant frivolous impropriety, the game of transmissions which create the poetic Word. In their business, they use well-defined technical terms; and as for the language of revolutionary parties, Parain has shown that it is *pragmatic:* it is used to transmit orders, watch-words, information; if it loses its exactness, the Party falls apart. All of this tends more and more rigorously to eliminate the subject; poetry, however, must in some way remain subjective. (pp. 13-17)

Like the white worker, the negro is a victim of the capitalist structure of our society. This situation reveals to him his close ties—quite apart from the color of his skin—with certain classes of Europeans who, like him, are oppressed; it incites him to imagine a privilege-less society in which skin pigmentation will be considered a mere fluke. But even though oppression itself may be a mere fluke, the circumstances under which it exists vary according to history and geographic conditions: the black man is a victim of it *because he is a black man* and insofar as he is a colonized native or a deported African. And since he is oppressed within the confines of his race and because of it, he must first of all become conscious of his race. He must oblige those who have vainly tried throughout the centuries to reduce him to the status of a beast, to recognize that he is a man. On this point, there is no means of evasion, or of trickery, no "crossing line" that he can consider: a Jew—a white man among white men—can deny that he is a Jew, can declare himself a man among men. The negro cannot deny that he is negro, nor can he claim that he is part of some abstract colorless humanity: he is black. Thus he has his back up against the wall of authenticity: having been insulted and formerly enslaved, he picks up the word "nigger" which was thrown at him like a stone, he draws himself erect and proudly proclaims himself a black man, face to face with white men. The unity which will come eventually, bringing all oppressed peoples together in the same struggle, must be preceded in the colonies by what I shall call the moment of separation or negativity: this anti-racist racism is the only road that will lead to the abolition of racial differences. How could it be otherwise? Can black men count on a distant white proletariat—involved in its own struggles—before they are united and organized on their own soil? And furthermore, isn't there some need for a thorough work of analysis in order to realize the identity of the interests that underlie the obvious difference of conditions? The white worker benefits somewhat from colonization, in spite of himself: low as his standard of living may be, it would be even lower if there were no colonization. In any case, he is less cynically exploited than the day laborer in Dakar or Saint-Louis. The technical equipment and industrialization of the European countries make it possible for measures of socialization to be immediately applicable there; but as seen from Sénégal or the Congo, socialism seems more than anything else like a beautiful dream: before black peasants can discover that socialism is the necessary answer to their present local claims, they must learn to formulate these claims jointly; therefore, they must think of themselves as black men.

But this new self-discovery is different from that which Marxism tries to awaken in the white worker. In the European worker, class consciousness is based on the nature of profit and unearned increment, on the present conditions of the ownership of the instruments for work; in brief, it is based on the objective characteristics of the *position* of the proletariat. But since the selfish scorn that white men display for black men—and that has no equivalent in the attitude of the bourgeois towards the working class—is aimed at the deepest recesses of the heart, black men must oppose it with a more exact view of black *subjectivity;* consequently race consciousness is based first of all on the black soul, or, rather,—since the term is often used in this anthology—on a certain quality common to the thoughts and conduct of negroes which is called *Negritude* [sic]. There are only two ways to go about forming racial concepts: either one causes certain subjective characteristics to become objective, or else one tries to interiorize objectively revealed manners of conduct; thus the black man who asserts his negritude by means of a revolutionary movement immediately places himself in the position of having to meditate, either because he wishes to recognize in himself certain objectively established traits of the African civilizations, or because he hopes to discover the Essence of blackness in the well of his heart. Thus subjectivity reappears: the relation of the self with the self; the source of all poetry, the very poetry from which the worker had to disengage himself. The black man who asks his colored brothers to "find themselves" is going to try to present to them an exemplary image of their Negritude and will look into his own soul to grasp it. He wants to be both a beacon and a mirror; the first revolutionary will be the harbinger of the black soul, the herald—half prophet and half follower—who will tear Blackness out of himself in order to offer it to the world; in brief, he will be a poet in the literal sense of "vates." Furthermore, black poetry has nothing in common with heartfelt effusions: it is functional, it answers a need which is defined in precise terms. Leaf through an anthology of contemporary white poetry: you will find a hundred different subjects, depending upon the mood and interests of the poet, depending upon his position and his country. In the anthology which I am introducing to you here, there is only one subject that all the poets attempt to treat, more or less successfully. From Haiti to Cayenne, there is a single idea: *reveal* the black soul. Black poetry is evangelic, it announces good news: Blackness has been rediscovered.

However, this negritude, which they wish to fish for in their abyssal depths, does not fall under the soul's gaze all by itself: in the soul, nothing is gratuitous. The herald of the black soul has gone through white schools, in accordance with a brazen law which forbids the oppressed man to possess any arms except those he himself has stolen from the oppressor; it is through having had some contact with white culture that his blackness has passed from the immediacy of existence to the meditative state. But at the same time, he has more or less ceased to live his negritude. In choosing to see what he is, he has become split, he no longer coincides with himself. And on the other hand, it is because he was already exiled from himself that he discovered this need to reveal himself. He therefore begins by exile. It is a double exile: the exile of his body offers a magnificent image of the exile of his heart; he is in Europe most of the time, in the cold, in the middle of gray crowds; he dreams of Port-au-Prince, of Haiti. But in Port-au-Prince,

he was *already* in exile; the slavers had torn his fathers out of Africa and dispersed them. And all of the poems in this book—except those which were written in Africa—show us the same mystical geography. A hemisphere: in the foreground—forming the first of three concentric circles—extends the land of exile, colorless Europe; then comes the dazzling circle of the Islands and of childhood, which dance the Roundelay around Africa; the last circle is Africa, the world's navel, pole of all black poetry—dazzling Africa, burnt, oily like a snake's skin, Africa of fire and rain, torrid and tufted; Africa—phantom flickering like a flame, between being and nothingness, more *real* than the "eternal boulevards with cops" but absent, beyond attainment, disintegrating Europe with its black but invisible rays; Africa, an *imaginary* continent. The extraordinary good luck of black poetry lies in the fact that the anxieties of the colonized native have their own grandiose and obvious symbols which need only to be gone into deeply and to be meditated upon: exile, slavery, the Africa-Europe couple and the great Manichaeistic division of the world into black and white. This ancestral bodily exile represents the other exile: the black soul is an Africa from which the negro, in the midst of the cold buildings of white culture and technics, is exiled. An ever-present but concealed negritude haunts him, rubs against him; he himself rubs up against its silky wing; it palpitates and is spread throughout him like his searching memory and his loftiest demands, like his shrouded, betrayed childhood, and like the childhood of his race and the call of the earth, like the swarming of insects and the indivisible simplicity of Nature, like the pure legacy of his ancestors, and like the Ethics that ought to unify his truncated life. But if he turns around to look squarely at his negritude, it vanishes in smoke; the walls of white culture—its silence, its words, its mores—rise up between it and him:

> Give me back my black dolls, so that I may play
>   with them
> My instinct's simple games
> that I may remain in the shadow of its laws
> cover up my courage
> my audacity
> feel me as me
> me renewed through what I was yesterday
>   yesterday
>   without complexity
>   yesterday
> when the uprooting hour came . . .
> they have ransacked the space that was mine

However, the walls of this culture prison must be broken down; it will be necessary to return to Africa some day: thus the themes of return to the native country and of redescent into the glaring hell of the black soul are indissolubly mixed up in the *vates* of negritude. A quest is involved here, a systematic stripping and an "ascèse" [the ascetic's movement of *interiorization*] accompanied by a continual effort of investigation. And I shall call this poetry "Orphic" because the negro's tireless descent into himself makes me think of Orpheus going to claim Eurydice from Pluto. Thus, through an exceptional stroke of poetic good luck, it is by letting himself fall into trances, by rolling on the ground like a possessed man tormented by himself, by singing of his angers, his regrets or his hates, by exhibiting his wounds, his life torn between "civilization" and his old black substratum; in short, by becoming most lyrical, that the black poet is most certain of creating a great collective poetry: by speaking only of himself, he speaks for all negroes; it is when he seems smothered by the serpents of our culture that he is the most revolutionary, for he then undertakes to ruin systematically the European knowledge he has acquired, and this spiritual destruction symbolizes the great future taking-up of arms by which black men will destroy their chains. A single example will suffice to clarify this last remark.

In the twentieth century, most ethnic minorities have passionately endeavored to resuscitate their national languages while struggling for their independence. To be able to say that one is Irish or Hungarian, one must belong to a collectivity which has the benefit of a broad economic and political autonomy; but to *be* Irish, one must also *think Irish,* which means above all: think *in* Irish. The specific traits of a Society correspond exactly to the untranslatable locutions of its language. The fact that the prophets of negritude are forced to write their gospel *in French* means that there is a certain risk of dangerously slowing down the efforts of black men to reject our tutelege. Having been dispersed to the four corners of the earth by the slave trade, black men have no common language; in order to incite the oppressed to unite, they must necessarily rely on the words of the oppressor's language. And French is the language that will furnish the black poet with the largest audience, at least within the limits of French colonization. It is in this goose-pimply language—pale and cold

AIMÉ CÉSAIRE

CAHIER

D'UN

RETOUR

AU

PAYS NATAL

précédé par

UN GRAND POÈTE NOIR

par

ANDRÉ BRETON

with translations by
Lionel Abel and Ivan Goll

BRENTANO'S

Title page from the bilingual edition of Aimé Césaire's Cahier d'un retour au pays natal.

like our skies, and which Mallarmé said was "the neutral language *par excellence* since our spirit demands an attenuation of variegation and of all excessively brilliant color"—in this language which is half dead for them, that Damas, Diop, Laleau, Rabéarivell are going to pour the fire of their skies and of their hearts: it is through this language alone that they can communicate; like the sixteenth-century scholars who understood each other only in Latin, black men can meet only on that trap-covered ground that the white man has prepared for them: the colonist has arranged to be the eternal mediator between the colonized; he is there—always there—even when he is absent, even in the most secret meetings. And since words are ideas, when the negro declares in French that he rejects French culture, he accepts with one hand what he rejects with the other; he sets up the enemy's thinking-apparatus in himself, like a crusher. This would not matter: except that this syntax and vocabulary—forged thousands of miles away in another epoch to answer other needs and to designate other objects—are unsuitable to furnish him with the means of speaking about himself, his own anxieties, his own hopes. The French language and French thought are analytical. What would happen if the black spirit were above all synthetical? The rather ugly term "negritude" is one of the few black contributions to our dictionary. But after all, if this "negritude" is a definable or at least a describable concept, it must subsume other more elementary concepts which correspond to the immediate fundamental ideas directly involved with negro consciousness: but where are the words to describe them? How well one understands the Haitian poet's complaint:

> This obsessing heart which does not correspond
> To my language, nor to my customs,
> And on which encroach, like a clinging-root,
> Borrowed feelings and the customs
> Of Europe, feel this suffering
> And this despair—equal to no other—
> Of ever taming with words from France
> This heart which came to me from Sénégal.

It is not true, however, that the black man expresses himself in a "foreign" language, since he is taught French from childhood and since he is perfectly at ease when he thinks in the terms of a technician, of a scholar or of a politician. Rather, one must speak about the slight but patent difference that separates what he says from what he would like to say, whenever he speaks about himself. It seems to him that a Northern Spirit steals his ideas from him, bends them slightly to mean more or less what he wanted; that white words drink his thoughts like sand drinks blood. If he suddenly gorges himself, if he pulls himself together and takes a step backward, there are the sounds lying prostrate *in front of him*—strange: half signs and half things. He will not speak his negritude with precise, efficacious words which hit the target every time. He will not speak his negritude *in prose.* As everyone knows, every poetic experience has its origin in this feeling of frustration that one has when confronted with a language that is supposed to be a means of direct communication.

The reaction of the *speaker* frustrated by prose is in effect what Bataille calls the holocaust of words. As long as we can believe that a pre-established harmony governs the relationship between a word and Being, we use words without seeing them, with blind trust; they are sensory organs, mouths, hands, windows open on the world. As soon as we experience a first frustration, this chattering falls beyond us; we see the whole system, it is no more than an upset, out-of-order mechanism whose arms are still flailing to INDICATE EXISTENCE in emptiness; in one fell swoop we pass judgment on the foolish business of naming things; we understand that language is in essence prose, and that prose is in essence failure; Being stands erect in front of us like a tower of silence, and if we still want to catch it, we can do so only through silence: "evoke, in an intentional shadow, the object *"tu"* by allusive words, never direct, reducing themselves to the same silence" [Stéphane Mallarmé, *Magie*]. No one has better stated that poetry is an incantatory attempt to suggest Being in and by the vibratory disappearance of the word: by insisting on his verbal impotence, by making words mad, the poet makes us suspect that beyond this chaos which cancels itself out, there are silent densities; since we cannot keep quiet, we must *make silence with language.* From Mallarmé to the Surrealists, the final goal of French poetry seems to me to have been this autodestruction of language. A poem is a dark room where words are knocking themselves about, quite mad. Collisions in the air: they ignite each other with their fire and fall down in flames.

It is in this perspective that we must situate the efforts of the "black evangelists." They answer the colonist's ruse with a similar but inverse ruse: since the oppressor is present in the very language that they speak, they will speak this language in order to destroy it. The contemporary European poet tries to dehumanize words in order to give them back to nature; the black herald is going to *de-Frenchifize* them; he will crush them, break their usual associations, he will violently couple them

> with little steps of caterpillar rain
> with little steps like mouthfuls of milk
> with little steps like ball-bearings
> with little steps like seismic shocks
> Yams in the soil stride like gaps of stars

Only when they have regurgitated their whiteness does he adopt them, making of this ruined language a solemn, sacred superlanguage, Poetry. Only through Poetry can the black men of Tananarive and of Cayenne, the black men of Port-au-Prince and of Saint-Louis, communicate with each other in private. And since French lacks terms and concepts to define negritude, since negritude is silence, these poets will use "allusive words, never direct, reducing themselves to the same silence" in order to evoke it. Short-circuits of language: behind the flaming fall of words, we glimpse a great black mute idol. It is not only the black man's self-portrayal that seems poetic to me; it is also his personal way of utilizing the means of expression at his disposal. His position incites him to do it: even before he thinks of writing poetry, in him, the light of white words is refracted, polarized and altered. This is nowhere more manifest than in his use of two connected terms—"white-black"—that cover both the great cosmic division—"day and night"—and the human conflict between the native and the colonist. But it is a connection based on a hierarchical system: by giving the negro this term, the teacher also gives him a hundred language habits which consecrate the white man's rights over the black man. The negro will learn to say "white like snow" to indicate innocence, to speak of the blackness of a look, of a soul, of a deed. As soon as he opens his mouth, he accuses himself, unless he persists in upsetting the hierarchy. And if he upsets it *in French,* he is already poetizing: can you imagine the strange savor that an expression like "the blackness of innocence" or "the darkness of virtue" would have for us? That is the savor which we taste . . . when, for example, we read:

> Your round, shining, black satin breasts . . .
> this white smile
> of eyes
> in the face's shadow
> awaken in me this evening
> deaf rhythms . . .
> which intoxicate, there in Guinée,
> our sisters
> black and naked
> and inspire in me
> this evening
> black twilights heavy with sensual anxiety
> for
> the soul of the black country where the ancients
> are sleeping
> lives and speaks
> this evening
> in uneasy strength, along the small of
> your back . . .

Throughout this poem, black is color; better still, light; its soft diffuse radiance dissolves our habits; the *black* country where the ancients are sleeping is not a dark hell: it is a land of sun and fire. Then again, in another connection, the superiority of white over black does not express only the superiority that the colonist claims to have over the native: more profoundly, it expresses a universal adoration of *day* as well as our night terrors, which also are universal. In this sense, these black men are re-establishing the hierarchy they have just upset. They don't want to be poets *of night,* poets of vain revolt and despair: they give the promise of dawn; they greet

> the transparent dawn of a new day.

At last, the black man discovers, through the pen, his baleful sense of foreboding:

> Nigger black like misery

one of them, and then another, cries out:

> Deliver me from my blood's night

Thus the word *black* is found to contain *all Evil* and *all Good,* it covers up an almost unbearable tension between two contradictory classifications: solar hierarchy and racial hierarchy. It gains thereby an extraordinary poetry, like self-destructive objects from the hands of Duchamp and the Surrealists; there is a secret blackness in white, a secret whiteness in black, a fixed flickering of Being and of Non-being which is perhaps nowhere expressed as well as in this poem by Césaire:

> My tall wounded statue, a stone in its forehead; my great inattentive day flesh with

pitiless spots, my great night flesh with
day spots.

The poet will go even further; he writes:

Our beautiful faces like the true operative
power of negation.

Behind this abstract eloquence evoking Lautréamont is
seen an extremely bold and subtle attempt to give some
sense to black skin and to realize the poetic synthesis of
the two faces of night. When David Diop says that the
negro is "black like misery," he makes black represent deprivation of light. But Césaire develops and goes into this
image more deeply: night is no longer absence, it is refusal.
Black is not color, it is the destruction of this borrowed
clarity which falls from the white sun. The revolutionary
negro is negation because he wishes to be complete nudity:
in order to build his Truth, he must first destroy others'
Truth. Black faces—these night memories which haunt
our days—embody the dark work of Negativity which pa-
tiently gnaws at concepts. Thus, by a reversal which curiously recalls that of the humiliated negro—insulted and
called "dirty nigger" when he asserts his rights—it is the
privative aspect of darkness that establishes its value. Liberty is the color of night.

Destructions, *autodafés* of language, magic symbolism,
ambivalence of concepts: all the negative aspects of modern poetry are here. But it is not a matter of some gratuitous game. The black man's position, his original "rend-
ing," the alienation that a foreign way of thinking imposes
on him, all oblige him to reconquer his existential unity
as a negro,—or, if you prefer, the original purity of his
plan—through a gradual "ascèse," beyond the language
stage. Negritude—like liberty—is a point of departure and
an ultimate goal: it is a matter of making negritude pass
from the immediate to the mediate, a matter of *thematicis-
ing* it. The black man must therefore find death in white
culture in order to be reborn with a black soul, like the
Platonic philosopher whose body embraces death in order
to be reborn in truth. This dialectical and mystical return
to origins necessarily implies a method. But this method
is not presented as a set of rules to be used in directing the
spirit. Rather, it becomes *one* with whoever applies it; it
is the dialectical law of successive transformations which
lead the negro to coincidence with himself in negritude.
It is not a matter of his *knowing,* nor of his ecstatically
tearing himself away from himself, but rather of both discovering and becoming what he is.

There are two convergent means of arriving at this primordial simplicity of existence: one is objective, the other
subjective. The poets in our anthology sometimes use one,
sometimes the other, and sometimes both of them together. In effect, there exists an objective negritude that is expressed by the mores, arts, chants and dances of the African populaces. As a *spiritual exercise,* the poet will prescribe allowing himself to be fascinated by primitive
rhythms, letting his thoughts run in traditional forms of
black poetry. Many of the poems included here are called
tams-tams, because they borrow from the nighttime tam-
bourine players, a percussive rhythm which is sometimes
sharp and regular, sometimes torrential and bounding.
The poetic act, then, is a dance of the soul; the poet turns

round and round like a dervish until he faints; he has established his ancestors' time in himself, he feels it flowing
with its peculiar violent pulls; he hopes to "find" himself
in this rhythmic pulsation; I shall say that he tries to make
himself "possessed" by his people's negritude; he hopes
that the echoes of his tam-tam will come to awaken timeless instincts sleeping within him. . . . The calm center
of this maelstrom of rhythms, chants, shouts, is the poetry
of Birago Diop, in all its majestic simplicity: it alone is at
rest because it comes directly from Griot narratives and
oral tradition. Almost all the other attempts have something contorted, taut and desperate about them because
they aim at *becoming a part of* folkloric poetry rather than
emanating from it. But however far he may be from "the
black country where ancestors sleep," the black man is
closer than we to the great period when, as Mallarmé says,
"the word creates Gods." It is practically impossible for
our poets to resume some closeness with popular traditions: ten centuries of scholarly poetry separate them from
such traditions; furthermore, folkloric inspiration is dry-
ing up: at the very best, we could only imitate its simplicity
from a distance. The black men of Africa, on the contrary,
are still in the great period of mythical fecundity and
French-language black poets are not just using their myths
as a form of diversion as we use our epic poems: they allow
themselves to be spellbound by them so that at the end of
the incantation, negritude—magnificently evoked—may
surge forth. This is why I call this method of "objective
poetry" *magic,* or charm.

Césaire, on the contrary, chose to backtrack into himself.
Since this Eurydice will disappear in smoke if Black Orpheus turns around to look back on her, he will descend
the royal road of his soul with his back turned on the bottom of the grotto; he will descend below words and meanings,—"in order to think of you, I have placed all words
on the mountain-of-pity"—below daily activities and the
plan of "repetition," even below the first barrier reefs of
revolt, with his back turned and his eyes closed, in order
finally to touch with his feet the black water of dreams and
desire and to let himself drown in it. Desire and dream will
rise up snarling like a tidal wave; they will make words
dance like flotsam and throw them pell-mell, shattered, on
the shore.

Words go beyond themselves; and just as the old
geography is done for, the high and the low
(words) do not allow diversion either towards
heaven or towards earth. . . . On the contrary,
they operate on a strangely flexible range at one
level: on the gaseous Level of an organism both
solid and liquid, black and white, day and night.

One recognizes the old surrealistic *method* (automatic
writing, like mysticism, is a method: it presupposes an apprenticeship, exercises, a start along the way). One must
dive under the superficial crust of reality, of common
sense, of reasoning reason, in order to touch the very bottom of the soul and awaken the timeless forces of desire:
desire which makes of man a refusal of everything and a
love of everything; desire, the radical negation of natural
laws and of the possible, a call to miracles; desire which,
by its mad cosmic energy, plunges man back into the

seething breast of Nature and, at the same time, lifts him above Nature through the affirmation of his Right to be unsatisfied. (pp. 18-31)

In Césaire, the great surrealist tradition is realized, it takes on its definitive meaning and is destroyed: surrealism—that European movement—is taken from the Europeans by a Black man who turns it against them and gives it a rigorously defined function. I have pointed out elsewhere how the whole of the proletariat completely shut itself off from the destructive poetry of Reason: in Europe, surrealism languishes and pales, rejected by those who could have given it a transfusion of their own blood. But at the very moment when it is losing contact with the Revolution, it is, in the Antilles, grafted onto another branch of the universal Revolution; it develops into an enormous somber flower. Césaire's originality lies in his having directed his powerful, concentrated anxiety as a negro, as one oppressed, as a militant individual, into this world of the most destructive, free and metaphysical poetry at the moment when Eluard and Aragon were failing to give political content to their verse. And finally, *negritude-object* is snatched from Césaire like a cry of pain, of love and of hate. Here again he follows the surrealist tradition of *objective* poetry. Césaire's words do not describe negritude, they do not designate it, they do not copy it from the outside like a painter with a model: they *create* it; they compose it under our very eyes: henceforth it is a thing which can be observed and learned; the subjective method which he has chosen joins the objective method we spoke about earlier: he ejects the black soul from himself at the very moment when others are trying to interiorize it; the final result is the same in both cases. Negritude is the far-away tam-tam in the streets of Dakar at night; voo-doo shouts from some Haitian cellar window, sliding along level with the roadway; the Congolese mask. . . . (pp. 34-5)

What then, at present, is this negritude, sole anxiety of these poets, sole subject of this book? It must first be stated that a white man could hardly speak about it suitably, since he has no inner experience of it and since European languages lack words to describe it. . . . But this [essay] would be incomplete if, after having indicated that the quest for the Black Grail represented—both in its original intention and in its methods—the most authentic synthesis of revolutionary aspirations and poetic anxiety, I did not show that this complex notion is essentially pure Poetry. I shall therefore limit myself to examining these poems objectively as a cluster of testimonies and to pointing out some of their principal themes. Senghor says: "What makes the *negritude* of a poem is less its theme than its style, the emotional warmth which gives life to words, which transmutes the word into the Word." It could not be more explicitly stated that negritude is neither a state nor a definite ensemble of vices and virtues or of intellectual and moral qualities, but rather a certain affective attitude towards the world. Since the beginning of this century, psychology has renounced its great scholastic distinctions. We no longer believe that the "facts" of the soul are divided into volitions or actions, knowledge or perceptions, sentiments or blind passiveness. We know that a feeling is a definite way of establishing our *rapport* with the world around us, that it involves a certain comprehension

of this universe. It is a tension of the soul, a choice of oneself and of another, a way of going beyond the raw facts of experience; in short, a *plan* quite like the voluntary act. To use Heidegger's language, Negritude is the Negro's being-in-the-world.

Furthermore, here is what Césaire tells us about it:

> My negritude is not a stone with its deafness
>   flung out against the clamor of the day
> My negritude is not a dead speck of water on the
>   dead eye of the earth
> my negritude is neither a tower nor a cathedral
> it plunges into the red flesh of the ground
> it plunges into the ardent flesh of the sky
> it perforates the opaque pressure of its righteous
>   patience.

Negritude is portrayed in these beautiful lines of verse more as an act than as a frame of mind. But this act is an *inner* determination: it is not a question of *taking* the goods of this world in one's hands and transforming them; it is a question of *existing* in the middle of the world. The relation with the universe remains an *adaptation*. But this adaptation is not technical. For the white man, to possess is to transform. To be sure, the white worker uses instruments which he does not possess. But at least his techniques are his own: if it is true that the personnel responsible for the major inventions of European industry comes mainly from the middle classes, at least the trades of carpenter, cabinet-maker, potter, seem to the white workers to be a true heritage, despite the fact that the orientation of great capitalist production tends to remove their "joy in work" from them. But it is not enough to say that the black worker uses instruments which are lent to him; techniques are also lent him.

Césaire refers to his black brothers as:

> Those who have invented neither powder nor
>   compass
> those who have never tamed either steam or
>   electricity
> those who have not explored the seas and the
>   sky . . .

But this haughty claim of non-technicalness reverses the situation: what could pass as a deficiency becomes a *positive* source of wealth. A technical *rapport* with Nature reveals Nature as simple quantity, inertia, exteriority: nature dies. By his haughty refusal to be *homo faber,* the negro gives it life again. As if the passiveness of one of the members of the "man-nature" couple necessarily produced the other's activity. Actually, negritude is not passiveness, since it "perforates the flesh of the sky and of the earth": it is "patience," and patience appears like an active imitation of passiveness. The negro's act is first of all an act on oneself. The black man stands erect and immobilizes himself like a bird-charmer, and things come to perch on the branches of this fake tree. A magic inveigling of the world—through silence and rest—is involved here: the white man, by acting first of all on Nature, loses himself when he loses Nature; the negro, by acting first of all on himself, claims to win Nature while winning himself.

> Seized, they abandon themselves to the essence
>   of every thing

ignorant of the surfaces but seized by the movement of every thing
heedless of counting, but playing the world's
   game
truly the elder sons of the world
porous to all the breaths of the world . . .
flesh of the world's flesh palpitating from the
   very movement of the world.

Upon reading this, one can hardly help thinking of the famous distinction between intelligence and intuition established by Bergson. Césaire rightly calls us

Omniscient and naïve conquerors. . . .

Because of his tools, the white man knows all. But he only scratches the surface of things; he is unaware of the duration of things, unaware of life. Negritude, on the contrary, is comprehension through instinctive congeniality. The black man's secret is that the sources of his existence and the roots of Being are identical.

If one wanted to give a sociological interpretation of this metaphysic, one would say that an agriculturist poetry is here opposed to an engineer prose. Actually, it is not true that the black man has no techniques: the *rapport* between any human group and the exterior world is always technical in one way or another. And inversely, I shall say that Césaire is imprecise: Saint Exupéry's airplane folding the earth below like a carpet is a means of disclosure. However, the black man is first of all a peasant; agricultural technique is "righteous patience"; it trusts in life; it waits. To plant is to impregnate the earth; after that, you must remain motionless and watch: "each atom of silence is a chance for ripe fruit," each instant brings forth a hundred times more than man gave, whereas the worker finds in the manufactured product only as much as he put into it; man grows along with his wheat: from minute to minute he goes beyond himself and becomes more golden; he intervenes in this watchful wait before the fragile swelling belly, only to protect. Ripe wheat is a microcosm because the cooperation of sun, wind and rains was needed for it to grow; a blade of wheat is both the most natural thing and the most improbable chance. Techniques have contaminated the white peasant, but the black peasant remains the great male of the earth, the world's sperm. His existence is great vegetal patience; his work is the yearly repetition of holy coïtus. Creating and nourished because he creates. To till, to plant, to eat, is to make love with nature. The sexual pantheism of these poets is undoubtedly what will impress us first of all: it is in this that they join the dances and the phallic rites of the Negro-Africans.

Oho! Congo lying in your bed of forests, queen
   of tamed Africa
May the phalli of the mountains carry your banner high
For, through my head, through my tongue,
   through my belly, you are a woman,

writes Senghor. And:

and so I shall mount again the soft belly of the
   dunes
and the gleaming thighs of the day. . . .

and Rabéarivelo:

the earth's blood, the stone's sweat and the
   sperm of
the world

and Laleau:

The conical drum laments under the sky
And it is the very soul of the black man
Sultry spasms of men in rut, lover's sticky sobs
Outraging the calm of the evening.

Here, we are far from Bergson's chaste asexual intuition. It is no longer a matter of being congenial with life, but rather of being in love with all its forms. For the white technician, God is first of all an engineer. Jupiter orders chaos and prescribes its laws; the Christian God conceives the world through his understanding and brings it into being through his will: the relation between the created and the creator is never carnal, except for a few mystics whom the Church looks upon with a great deal of suspicion. Even so, erotic mysticism has nothing in common with fecundity: it is the completely passive wait for a sterile penetration. We are *steeped* in alluvium: statuettes come from the *hands* of the divine sculptor. If the manufactured objects surrounding us could worship their ancestors, they would undoubtedly adore us as we adore the All-powerful. For our black poets, on the contrary, Being comes out of Nothingness like a penis becoming erect; Creation is an enormous perpetual delivery; the world is flesh and the son of flesh; on the sea and in the sky, on the dunes, on the rocks, in the wind, the Negro finds the softness of human skin; he rubs himself against the sand's belly, against the sky's loins: he is "flesh of the flesh of this world"; he is "porous to all its breaths," to all its pollens; he is both Nature's female and its male; and when he makes love with a woman of his race, the sexual act seems to him to be the celebration of the Mystery of Being. This spermatic religion is like the tension of a soul balancing between two complementary tendencies: the dynamic feeling of being an erect phallus, and that more deaf, more patient, more feminine one of being a growing plant. Thus negritude is basically a sort of androgyny. [Rabéarivelo writes:]

There you are
Upright and naked
alluvium you are and remember yourself as having been
but in reality you are the child of this parturient
   shadow
feeding on lunar lactogen
then you slowly take the form of a bole
on this low wall jumped over by the dreams of
   flowers
and the perfume of summer at rest.
To feel, to believe that roots are pushing your
   feet
and running and twisting like thirsty serpents
toward some subterranean spring . . .

And Césaire:

Wornout mother, leafless mother, you are a
   flamboyant
and now wear only husks. You are a calabash
   tree
and you are only a stand of *couis*. . . .

This profound unity of vegetal and sexual symbols is certainly the greatest originality of black poetry, especially in a period when, as Michel Carrouges has shown, most of the images used by white poets tend to mineralize the human being. Césaire, on the contrary, "vegetalizes," "animalizes" sea, sky and stones. More precisely, his poetry is a perpetual coupling of men and women who have been metamorphosed into animals, vegetables, stones, with stones, plants and beasts metamorphosed into men. Thus the Black man attests to a natural Eros; he reveals and incarnates it; to find a point of comparison in European poetry, one must go back to Lucretius, the peasant poet who celebrated Venus, the mother goddess, when Rome was not yet much more than a large agricultural market. In our time, only Lawrence seems to me to have had a cosmic feeling for sexuality. Even so, this feeling remains very literary in his works.

However, although negritude seems basically to be this immobile springing-forth, a unity of phallic erection and plant growth, one could scarcely exhaust it with this single poetic theme. There is another motif running through this collection, like a large artery:

> Those who have invented neither powder nor
>   compass . . .
> They know the most remote corners of the coun-
>   try of suffering. . . .

To the absurd utilitarian agitation of the white man, the black man opposes the authenticity gained from his suffering; the black race is a chosen race because it has had the horrible privilege of touching the depths of unhappiness. And even though these poems are anti-Christian from beginning to end, one might call negritude a kind of Passion: the black man who is conscious of himself sees himself as the man who has taken the whole of human suffering upon himself and who suffers for all, even for the white man. [Paul Niger writes:]

> On the judgment day, Armstrong's trumpet will
> be the interpreter of man's sufferings.

Let us note immediately that this in no way implies a resigned suffering. A while ago I was speaking about Bergson and Lucretius; I would be tempted now to quote that great adversary of Christianity: Nietzsche and his "Dionysianism." Like the Dionysian poet, the negro attempts to penetrate the brilliant phantasm of the day, and encounters, a thousand feet under the Apollonian surface, the inexpiable suffering which is the universal essence of man. If one wished to systematize, one would say that the Black man blends with the whole of nature in as much as he represents sexual congeniality with Life and in as much as he claims he is Man in his Passion of rebellious suffering. One will feel the fundamental unity of this double movement if one considers the constantly tighter relationship which psychiatrists establish between anguish and sexual desire. There is only one proud upheaval which can be equally well described as a desire plunging its roots into suffering or as suffering fixed like a sword across a vast cosmic desire. This "righteous patience" that Césaire evokes is both vegetal growth and patience against suffering; it resides in the very muscles of the negro; it sustains the black porter going a thousand miles up the Niger under a blinding sun with a fifty-pound load balanced on his head. But if in a certain sense, one can compare the fecundity of Nature to a proliferation of suffering, in another sense—and this one is also Dionysian—this fecundity, by its exuberance, goes beyond suffering, drowns it in its creative abundance which is poetry, love and dance. Perhaps, in order to understand this indissoluble unity of suffering, eros and joy, one must have seen the Black men of Harlem dance frenetically to the rhythm of "blues," which are the saddest sounds in the world. In effect, rhythm cements the multiple aspects of the black soul, communicates its Nietzschian lightness with heavy dionysian intuitions; rhythm—tam-tam, jazz, the "bounding" of these poems—represents the temporality of negro *existence*. And when a black poet prophesies to his brothers a better future, he portrays their deliverance to them in the form of rhythm:

> What?
> rhythm
> sound wave in the night across the forests, noth-
>   ing—or a new soul
> timbre
> intonation
> vigor
> dilation
> vibration which flows out by degrees into the
>   marrow
> revulses in its progression an old sleeping body,
>   takes
> it by the waist
> and spins it
> and turns
> and once more vibrates in its hands, in its loins,
>   its
> sexual member, its thighs, its vagina . . .

But one must go still further: this basic experience of suffering is ambiguous; through it, black conscience is going to become historic. In effect, whatever may be the intolerable iniquity of his present condition, it is not to that condition that the black man first refers when he proclaims that he has touched the heart of human suffering. He has the horrible benefit of having known bondage. For these poets, most of whom were born between 1900 and 1918, slavery—abolished half a century earlier—lingers on as a very real memory:

> Each of my todays looks on my yesterday
> with large eyes rolling with rancor with
> shame
> Still real is my stunned condition of the past
> of
> blows from knotted cords of bodies calcinated
> from toe to calcinated back
> of dead flesh of red iron firebrands of arms
> broken under the whip which is breaking
>   loose . . .

writes Damas, a poet from Guiana. And the Haitian, Brierre:

> . . . Often like me you feel stiffnesses
> Awaken after murderous centuries
> And old wounds bleed in your flesh . . .

During the centuries of slavery, the black man drank the cup of bitterness to the last drop; and slavery is a past fact which neither our authors nor their fathers have actually experienced. But it is also a hideous nightmare from which even the youngest of them are not yet sure of having awakened. From one end of the earth to the other, black men—separated by languages, politics and the history of their colonizers—have a *collective* memory in common. This will not be surprising if one only recalls the French peasants who, in 1789, were still aware of the panicky terrors that went back to the Hundred Years' war. Thus when the black man goes back to his principal experience, it is suddenly revealed to him in two dimensions: it is both the intuitive seizure of the human condition and the still-fresh memory of a historic past. Here, I am thinking of Pascal who relentlessly repeated that man was an irrational composite of metaphysics and history, his greatness unexplainable if he comes from the alluvium, his misery unexplainable if he is still as God made him; that in order to understand man, one had to go back to the simple basic fact of man's downfall. It is in this sense that Césaire calls his race "the fallen race." And in a certain sense I can see the *rapprochement* that can be made between black conscience and Christian conscience: the brazen law of slavery evokes that law of the Old Testament, which states the consequences of the *Fault.* The abolition of slavery recalls this *other historic fact:* Redemption. The white man's insipid paternalism after 1848 resembles that of the white God after the Passion. The difference being, however, that the expiable fault that the black man discovers in the back of his memory is not his own, it belongs to the white man; the first fact of negro history is certainly a kind of original sin: but the black man is the innocent victim of it. This is why his concept of suffering is radically opposed to white "dolorism." If these poems are for the most part so violently anti-Christian, it is because the white man's religion is more clearly a hoax in the eyes of the negro than in the eyes of the European proletariat: this religion wants to make him share the responsibility for a crime of which he is the victim; it wants to persuade him to see the kidnappings, the massacres, the rapes and the tortures which have covered Africa with blood, as a legitimate punishment, deserved tests. Will you say that it also proclaims equality for all men before God? *Before God,* yes. Only yesterday I was reading in *Esprit* these lines from a correspondent in Madagascar:

> I am as certain as you that the soul of a Malagasy is worth the soul of a white man. . . . Just as, before God, the soul of a child is worth the soul of his father. However, if you have an automobile, you don't let your children drive it.

One can hardly reconcile Christianity and colonialism more elegantly. In opposition to these sophisms, the black man—by a simple investigation of his memory as a former slave—affirms that suffering is man's lot and that it is no less deserved for all that. He rejects with horror Christian stagnation, melancholy sensual pleasure, masochistic humility and all the tendentious inducements to his submission; he lives the absurdity of suffering in its pure form, in its injustice and in its gratuitousness; and he discovers thereby this truth which is misunderstood or masked by Christianity: suffering carries within itself its own refusal; it is by nature *a refusal to suffer,* it is the dark side of nega-

tivity, it opens onto revolt and liberty. The black man promptly *transforms himself into history* in as much as the intuition of suffering confers on him a collective past and assigns to him a goal in the future. Only a short while ago, he was a sheer *present* surging of timeless instincts, a simple manifestation of universal and eternal fecundity. Now he calls to his colored brothers in quite another language:

> Negro pedlar of revolt
> you have known the paths of the world
> ever since you were sold in Guinée . . .

And:

> Five centuries have seen you with weapons in
>   your hands
> and you have taught the exploiting races
> passion for liberty.

There is already a black Epic: first the golden age of Africa, then the era of dispersion and captivity, then the awakening of conscience, the heroic and somber times of great revolts, of Toussaint Louverture and black heroes, then the *fact* of the abolition of slavery—"unforgettable metamorphosis," says Césaire—then the struggle for definitive liberation:

> You are waiting for the next call
> the inevitable mobilization
> for that war which is yours has known only
>   truces
> for there is no land where your blood has not
>   flowed
> no language in which your color has not been in-
>   sulted
> You smile, Black Boy,
> you sing
> you dance
> you cradle generations
> which go out at all hours to the
> fronts of work and pain
> which tomorrow will assault bastilles
> onward toward the bastions of the future
> in order to write in all languages
> on the clear pages of all skies
> the declaration of your rights unrecognized
> for more than five centuries . . .

Strange and decisive turn: *race* is transmuted into *historicity,* the black Present explodes and is temporalized, negritude—with its Past and its Future—is inserted into Universal History, it is no longer a *state,* nor even an existential attitude, it is a *"Becoming";* the black contribution to the evolution of Humanity is no longer savour, taste, rhythm, authenticity, a bouquet of primitive instincts: it is a dated enterprize, a long-suffering construction and also a future. Previously, the Black man claimed his place in the sun in the name of *ethnic* qualities; now, he establishes his right to life on his mission; and this mission, like the proletariat's, comes to him from his historic position: because he has suffered from capitalistic exploitation more than all the others, he has acquired a sense of revolt and a love of liberty more than all the others. And because he is the most oppressed, he necessarily pursues the liberation of all, when he works for his own deliverance:

> Black messenger of hope
> you know all the hymns of the world

even those of the timeless building-works of the Nile.

But, after that, can we still believe in the interior homogeneousness of negritude? And how can one say that it exists? Sometimes it is lost innocence which had its existence in some faraway past, and sometimes hope which can be realized only within the walls of the future City. Sometimes it contracts with Nature in a moment of pantheistic fusion and sometimes it spreads itself out to coincide with the whole history of Humanity; sometimes it is an existential attitude and sometimes the objective ensemble of negro-African traditions. Is it being discovered? Is it being created? After all, there are black men who "collaborate"; after all, in the prefaces he writes for the works of each poet, Senghor seems to distinguish between degrees of negritude. Does the poet who would be the Prophet for his colored brothers invite them to *become* more negro, or does he disclose to them what they *are,* by a sort of poetic psychoanalysis? Is negritude necessity or liberty? For the authentic negro, is it a matter of conduct deriving from essences, as consequences derive from a principle, or is one a negro in the way that the religious faithful are believers, that is to say in fear and trembling, in anguish, in perpetual remorse for never being enough what one would like to be? Is it a given fact or a value? The object of empiric intuition or of a moral concept? Is it a conquest of meditation? Or does meditation poison it? Is it never authentic except when unmeditated and in the immediate? Is it a systematic *explanation* of the black soul, or a Platonic Archetype which one can approach indefinitely without ever attaining? Is it, for black men, like our engineer's common sense, the most widely shared thing in the world? Or do some have it, like grace; and if so, does it have its chosen ones? One will undoubtedly answer this question by saying that it is all of these at once, and still other things. And I agree: like all anthropological notions, Negritude is a shimmer of being and of needing-to-be; it makes you and you make it: both oath and passion. But there is something even more important in it: the negro himself, we have said, creates a kind of antiracist racism. He wishes in no way to dominate the world: he desires the abolition of *all* kinds of ethnic privileges; he asserts his solidarity with the oppressed of every color. After that, the subjective, existential, ethnic notion of *negritude* "passes," as Hegel says, into that which one has of the proletariat: objective, positive and precise. Senghor says: "For Césaire, 'White' symbolizes capital, just as Negro symbolizes work. . . . When writing about the black men of his race, he is writing about the worldwide proletarian struggle." It is easy to say, not so easy to think. And it is certainly not just by accident that the most ardent cantors of Negritude are also militant Marxists. Nevertheless, the notion of race does not mix with the notion of class: the former is concrete and particular; the latter, universal and abstract; one belongs to what Jaspers calls comprehension, and the other to intellection; the first is the product of a psychobiological syncretism, and the other is a methodic construction starting with experience. In fact, Negritude appears like the up-beat [unaccented beat] of a dialectical progression: the theoretical and practical affirmation of white supremacy is the thesis; the position of Negritude as an antithetical value is the moment of negativity. But this negative moment is not sufficient in itself, and these black men who use it know this perfectly well; they know that it aims at preparing the synthesis or realization of the human being in a raceless society. Thus Negritude is *for* destroying itself, it is a "crossing to" and not an "arrival at," a means and not an end. A poem by Jacques Roumain, a black communist, furnishes the most moving evidence of this new ambiguity:

> Africa I have held on to your memory Africa
> you are in me
> Like a thorn in a wound
> like a guardian mascot in the center of the village
> make of me the stone of your sling
> of my mouth the lips of your wound
> of my knees the broken columns of your humbling
> however
> I want to be only of your race
> peasant workers of all countries.

With what sadness he still retains for a moment what he has decided to abandon! With what pride as a *man* he will strip his pride as a negro for other men! He who says both that Africa is in him like "a thorn in a wound" and that he *wants* to be only of the universal race of the oppressed, has not left the empire of afflicted conscience. One more step and Negritude will disappear completely: the negro himself makes of what was the mysterious bubbling of black blood, a geographical accident, the inconsistent product of universal determinism:

> Is it all that climate extended space
> which creates clan tribe nation
> skin race gods
> our inexorable dissimilarity.

But the poet does not completely have the courage to accept the responsibility for this *rationalization* of the racial concept; one sees that he limits himself to questioning; a bitter regret is visible beneath his will to unite. Strange road: humiliated and offended, black men search deep within themselves to find their most secret pride; and when they have found it at last, it challenges its own right to exist: through supreme generosity they abandon it, just as Philoctetes abandoned his bow and arrows at Neoptolemus. Thus the rebel Césaire finds the secret of his revolts in the bottom of his heart: he is of royal blood:

> —it is true that there is in you something which has
> never been able to yield, an anger, a desire, a sadness,
> an impatience, in short a scorn, a violence . . . and now
> your veins carry gold, not mud; pride, not servitude.
> King you have been King in the past.

But he immediately thrusts aside this temptation:

> There is a law that I cover up with a chain unbroken
> as far as the confluence of fire which violates me
> which purifies me and burns me with my prism
> of amalgamated gold. . . . I shall perish. But one. Whole.

It is perhaps this ultimate nudity of man that has snatched from him the white rags that were concealing his black armor, and that now destroys and rejects that very armor; it is perhaps this colorless nudity that best symbolizes Negritude: for Negritude is not a state, it is a simple going-beyond-itself, it is love. It is when negritude renounces itself that it finds itself; it is when it accepts losing that it has won: the colored man—and he alone—can be asked to renounce the pride of his color. He is the one who is walking on this ridge between past particularism—which he has just climbed—and future universalism, which will be the twilight of his negritude; he is the one who looks to the end of particularism in order to find the dawn of the universal. Undoubtedly, the white worker also becomes conscious of his class in order to deny it, since he wants the advent of a classless society: but once again, the definition of class is objective; it sums up only the conditions of the white worker's alienation; whereas it is in the bottom of his heart that the negro finds race, and he must tear out his heart. Thus Negritude is dialectical; it is not only nor above all the blossoming of atavistic instincts; it represents "going beyond" a situation defined by free consciences. Negritude is a sad myth full of hope, born of Evil and pregnant with future Good, living like a woman who is born to die and who feels her own death even in the richest moments of her life; it is an unstable rest, an explosive fixity, a pride which renounces itself, an absolute that knows it is transitory: for whereas it is the Announcer of its birth and of its death agony, it also remains the existential attitude chosen by free men and lived *absolutely,* to the fullest. Because it is tension between a nostalgic Past into which the black man can no longer enter completely and a future in which it will be replaced by new values, Negritude adorns itself with a tragic beauty that finds expression only in poetry. Because it is the living and dialectical unity of so many opposites, because it is a Complex defying analysis, Negritude is only the multiple unity of a hymn that can reveal both it and the flashing beauty of the Poem which Breton calls *"explosante-fixe."* Because any attempt to conceptualize its various aspects would necessarily end up showing its relativity,—even though it is lived in the absolute through royal consciences—and because the poem is an absolute, it is poetry alone that will allow the unconditional aspect of this attitude to be fixed. Because it is subjectivity written in the objective, Negritude must take form in a poem, that is to say in a subjectivity-object; because it is an Archetype and a Value, it will find its most transparent symbol in aesthetic values; because it is a call and a gift, it will make itself heard and offer itself only by means of a work of art which is both a call to the spectator's liberty and absolute generosity. Negritude is the content of the poem, it is the poem like a thing of the world, mysterious and open, obscure and suggestive; it is the poet himself. One must go still further; triumph of Narcissism and Narcissus' suicide, tension of the soul beyond culture, beyond words and beyond all psychic facts, luminous night of unknowing, deliberate choice of the *impossible* and of what Bataille calls "torture" [*supplice*], intuitive acceptance of the world and refusal of the world in the name of "the law of the heart," double contradictory postulation, demanding retraction, expansion of generosity—Negritude is, in essence, Poetry. For once at least, the most authentic revolutionary plan and the most pure poetry come from the same source.

And if the sacrifice is achieved one day, what will happen then? What will happen if, casting off his negritude for the sake of the Revolution, the black man no longer wishes to consider himself only a part of the proletariat? What will happen if he then allows himself to be defined only by his objective condition? if, in order to struggle against white capitalism, he undertakes to assimilate white technics? Will the source of poetry run dry? or in spite of everything, will the great black river color the sea into which it flows? That does not matter: each era has its poetry; in each era, circumstances of history elect a nation, a race, a class to take up the torch, by creating situations that can be expressed or that can go beyond themselves only through Poetry; sometimes the poetic *élan* coincides with the revolutionary *élan* and sometimes they diverge. Let us greet today the historic chance that will permit black men to

> shout out the great negro cry so hard that the world's foundations will be shaken.
>
> (pp. 35-52)

> *Jean-Paul Sartre, "Black Orpheus," in* The Massachusetts Review, *Vol. VI, No. 1, Winter, 1964-65, pp. 13-52.*

Léopold Sédar Senghor

[*A Senegalese poet, essayist, nonfiction writer, critic, and editor, Senghor also served as President of the Republic of Senegal for twenty years following its independence from France in 1960. Best known as one of the most outspoken proponents of Negritude, Senghor affirms the rich traditions of his African heritage in his poetry and essays. In the following essay, he defines Negritude in humanistic terms and describes the unique contribution that African culture can make to world civilization.*]

> Negritude is . . . the sum of the cultural values of the Black world, as these are expressed in the life, the institutions and the work of Negroes . . . Our sole preoccupation since 1932-34 has been to assume this negritude by *living* it and, having lived it, to seek for its deeper meaning, to present it to the world as the cornerstone in the construction of the "Civilization of the Universal", which will either be the work of all races, or will never exist at all . . .
>
> In this respect, this open negritude is a humanism. It has enriched European civilization and has been enriched by it. Humanism, in this 20th century of "panhuman convergence", consists of nothing but this intercourse of heart and mind, in this "give and take".
>
> —Léopold Sédar Senghor: Introduction to *Négritude et Humanisme.*

During the last thirty or so years that we have been proclaiming negritude, it has become customary, especially among English-speaking critics, to accuse us of *racialism*. This is probably because the word is not of English origin. But, in the language of Shakespeare, is it not in good company with the words humanism and socialism? Mphahleles have been sent about the world saying: "Negritude is an inferiority complex"; but the same word cannot mean both "racialism" and "inferiority complex" without contradiction. The most recent attack comes from Ghana, where the government has commissioned a poem entitled "I hate Negritude"—as if one could hate oneself, hate one's being, without ceasing to be.

No, negritude is none of these things. It is neither racialism nor self-negation. Yet it is not just affirmation; it is rooting oneself in oneself, and self-confirmation: confirmation of one's *being*. The English-speaking peoples, who have such a strong personality and are more sensitive to differences than to similarities, should really have no difficulty in understanding us. And, in fact, many of the most penetrating studies of the negritude writers have been made by English-speaking critics. Negritude is nothing more or less than what some English-speaking Africans have called the *African personality*. It is no different from the "black personality" discovered and proclaimed by the American New Negro movement. As the American Negro poet, Langston Hughes, wrote after the First World War: "We, the creators of the new generation, want to give expression to our *black personality* without shame or fear . . . We know we are handsome. Ugly as well. The drums weep and the drums laugh." Perhaps our only originality, since it was the West Indian poet, Aimé Césaire, who coined the word negritude, is to have attempted to define the concept a little more closely: to have developed it as a weapon, as an instrument of liberation and as a contribution to the humanism of the 20th century.

But, once again, what is negritude? Ethnologists and sociologists today speak of "different civilizations". It is obvious that peoples differ in their ideas and their languages, in their philosophies and their religions, in their customs and their institutions, in their literature and their art. Who would deny that Africans, too, have a certain way of conceiving life and of living it? A certain way of speaking, singing and dancing; of painting and sculpturing, and even of laughing and crying? Nobody, probably; for otherwise we would not have been talking about "Negro art" for the last 60 years and Africa would be the only continent today without its ethnologists and sociologists. What, then, is negritude? It is—as you can guess from what precedes—*the sum of the cultural values of the black world;* that is, a certain active presence in the world, or better, in the universe. It is, as John Reed and Clive Wake call it [in their introduction to *Léopold Sédar Senghor: Selected Poems*], a certain "way of relating oneself to the world and to others." Yes, it is essentially relations with others, an opening out to the world, contact and participation with others. Because of what it is, negritude is necessary in the world today: it is a humanism of the 20th century.

But let us go back to 1885 and the morrow of the Berlin Conference. The European nations had just finished, with Africa, their division of the planet. Including the United States of America, they were five or six at the height of their power who dominated the world. Without any complexes, they were proud of their material strength; prouder even of their science, and paradoxically, of their *race*. It is true that at that time this was not a paradox. Gobineau, the 19th century philosopher of racial supremacy, had, by

a process of osmosis, even influenced Marx, and Disraeli was the great theoretician of that "*English race,* proud, tenacious, confident in itself, that no climate, no change can undermine." (The italics are mine.) Leo Frobenius, the German ethnologist, one of the first to apprehend the rich complexity of African culture, writes in *The Destiny of Civilizations:* "Each of the great nations that considers itself personally responsible for the 'destiny of the world' believes it possesses the key to the understanding of the whole and the other nations. It is an attitude raised from the past."

In fact, this attitude "raised from the past" had begun to be discredited towards the end of the 19th century by books like Bergson's *Time and Free Will,* which was published in 1889. Since the Renaissance, the values of European civilization had rested essentially on discursive reason and facts, on logic and matter. Bergson, with an eminently dialectical subtlety, answered the expectation of a public weary of scientism and naturalism. [In a footnote, Senghor states: "In the late 19th century, French intellectuals became fascinated by the new discoveries of science, and many philosophers (scientism) and novelists (naturalism) believed everything should be explained scientifically. As amateurs, their conclusions were often erroneous. Henri Bergson (1859-1941), the forerunner of many aspects of modern French philosophy, reacted against this tendency, as well as the contemporary fondness for constructing purely intellectual philosophical systems (e.g. Hegel and Kant), and claimed that philosophy must be concerned with concrete reality, which must be perceived as much by intuition as by the intellect."] He showed that facts and matter, which are the objects of discursive reason, were only the outer surface that had to be transcended by *intuition* in order to achieve a *vision in depth* of *reality*.

But the "Revolution of 1889"—as we shall call it—did not only affect art and literature, it completely upset the sciences. In 1880, only a year before the invention of the word electron, a distinction was still being drawn between matter and energy. The former was inert and unchangeable, the latter was not. But what characterized both of them was their permanence and their continuity. They were both subject to a strict mechanical determinism. Matter and energy had, so to speak, existed from the beginning of time; they could change their shape, but not their substance. All we lacked in order to know them objectively in space and time were sufficiently accurate instruments of investigation and measurement.

Well, in less than 50 years, all these principles were to be outmoded and even rejected. Thirty years ago already, the new discoveries of science—quanta, relativity, wave mechanics, the uncertainty principle, electron spin—had upset the 19th century notion of determinism, which denied man's free will, along with the concepts of matter and energy. The French physicist, Broglie, revealed to us the duality of matter and energy, or the wave-particle principle that underlies things; the German physicist, Heisenberg, showed us that objectivity was an illusion and that we could not observe facts without modifying them; others showed that, on the scale of the infinitely small as on

Léon-Gontran Damas in 1970.

that of the immensely great, particles act on one another. Since then, the physico-chemical laws, like matter itself, could no longer appear unchangcable. Even in the field, and on the scale, where they were valid, they were only rough approximations, no more than probabilities. It was enough to scrape the surface of things and of facts to realize just how much instability there is, defying our measuring instruments, probably because they are only mechanical: *material.*

It was on the basis of these discoveries, through a combination of logical coherence and amazing intuition, of scientific experiment and inner experience, that Pierre Teilhard de Chardin was able to transcend the traditional dichotomies with a new dialectic, to reveal to us the living, throbbing unity of the universe. On the basis, then, of the new scientific discoveries, Teilhard de Chardin transcends the old dualism of the philosophers and the scientists, which Marx and Engels had perpetuated by giving matter precedence over the spirit. He advanced the theory that the stuff of the universe is not composed of two realities, but of a single reality in the shape of two phenomena; that there is not matter and energy, not even matter and spirit, but spirit-matter, just as there is space-time. Matter and spirit become a "network of relations", as the French philosopher, Bachelard, called it: energy, defined as a network of forces. In matter-spirit there is, therefore, only one energy, which has two aspects. The first, *tangential energy,* which is external, is material and quantitative. It links together the corpuscles, or particles, that make up

matter. The other, *radial energy,* which is internal, is psychic and qualitative. It is centripetal force. It organizes into a complex the centre-to-centre relations of the internal particles of a corpuscle. Since energy is force, it follows that radial energy is the creative force, the "primary stuff of things", and tangential energy is only a residual product "caused by the interreactions of the elementary 'centres' of the consciousness, imperceptible where life has not yet occurred, but clearly apprehensible by our experience at a sufficiently advanced stage in the development of matter" [Pierre Teilhard de Chardin, *The Phenomenon of Man*]. It follows that where life has not yet occurred the physico-chemical laws remain valid within the limitations we have defined above, while in the living world, as we rise from plant to animal and from animal to Man, the psyche increases in consciousness until it makes and expresses itself in freedom. "Makes itself": that is, *realizes* itself, by means of—yet by transcending—material well-being through an increase of spiritual life. "Realizes itself": by that I mean it develops in harmonious fashion the two complementary elements of the soul: the heart and the mind.

The paradox is only apparent when I say that negritude, by its ontology (that is, its philosophy of being), its moral law and its aesthetic, is a response to the modern humanism that European philosophers and scientists have been preparing since the end of the 19th century, and as Teilhard de Chardin and the writers and artists of the mid-20th century present it.

Firstly, African ontology. Far back as one may go into his past, from the Northern Soudanese to the Southern Bantu, the African has always and everywhere presented a concept of the world which is diametrically opposed to the traditional philosophy of Europe. The latter is essentially *static, objective, dichotomic;* it is, in fact, dualistic, in that it makes an absolute distinction between body and soul, matter and spirit. It is founded on separation and opposition: on analysis and conflict. The African, on the other hand, conceives the world, beyond the diversity of its forms, as a fundamentally mobile, yet unique, reality that seeks synthesis. This needs development.

It is significant that in Wolof, the main language of Senegal, there are at least three words to translate the word spirit: *xel, sago* or *degal,* whereas images have to be used for the word matter: *lef* (thing) or *yaram* (body). The African is, of course, sensitive to the external world, to the material aspect of beings and things. It is precisely because he is more so than the white European, because he is sensitive to the tangible qualities of things—shape, colour, smell, weight, etc.—that the African considers these things merely as signs that have to be interpreted and transcended in order to reach the reality of human beings. Like others, more than others, he distinguishes the pebble from the plant, the plant from the animal, the animal from Man; but, once again, the accidents and appearances that differentiate these kingdoms only illustrate different aspects of the same reality. This reality is *being* in the ontological sense of the word, and it is life force. For the African, matter in the sense the Europeans understand it, is only a system of signs which translates the single reality of the universe: being, which is spirit, which is life force. Thus, the whole universe appears as an infinitely small, and at the same time an infinitely large, network of life forces which emanate from God and end in God, who is the source of all life forces. It is He who vitalizes and devitalizes all other beings, all the other life forces.

I have not wandered as far as might be thought from modern ontology. European ethnologists, Africanists and artists use the same words and the same expressions to designate the ultimate reality of the universe they are trying to know and to express: "spider's web", "network of forces", "communicating vessels", "system of canals", etc. This is not very different, either, from what the scientists and chemists say. As far as African ontology is concerned, too, there is no such thing as dead matter: every being, every thing—be it only a grain of sand—radiates a life force, a sort of wave-particle; and sages, priests, kings, doctors and artists all use it to help bring the universe to its fulfilment.

For the African, contrary to popular belief, is not passive in face of the order—or disorder—of the world. His attitude is fundamentally ethical. If the moral law of the African has remained unknown for so long, it is because it derives, naturally, from his conception of the world: from his ontology—so naturally, that both have remained unknown, denied even, by Europeans, because they have not been brought to their attention by being reexamined by each new generation of Africans.

So God tired of all the possibilities that remained confined within Him, unexpressed, dormant and as if dead. And God opened His mouth, and he spoke at length a word that was harmonious and rhythmical. All these possibilities, expressed by the mouth of God *existed* and had the vocation *to live:* to express God in their turn, by establishing the link with God and all the forces deriving from Him.

In order to explain this *morality in action* of negritude, I must go back a little. Each of the identifiable life forces of the universe—from the grain of sand to the ancestor—is, itself and in its turn, a network of life forces—as modern physical chemistry confirms: a network of elements that are contradictory in appearance but really *complementary.* Thus, for the African, Man is composed, of course, of matter and spirit, of body and soul; but at the same time he is also composed of a virile and a feminine element: indeed of several "souls". Man is therefore a composition of mobile life forces which interlock: a world of solidarities that seek to knit themselves together. Because he exists, he is at once end and beginning: end of the three orders of the mineral, the vegetable and the animal, but beginning of the human order.

Let us ignore for the moment the first three orders and examine the human order. Above Man and based on him, lies this fourth world of concentric circles, bigger and bigger, higher and higher, until they reach God along with the whole of the universe. Each circle—family, village, province, nation, humanity—is, in the image of Man and by vocation, a close-knit society.

So, for the African, living according to the moral law means living according to his nature, composed as it is of contradictory elements but complementary life forces. Thus he gives stuff to the stuff of the universe and tightens the threads of the tissue of life. Thus he transcends the contradictions of the elements and works towards making the life forces complementary to one another: in himself first of all, as Man, but also in the whole of human society. It is by bringing the complementary life forces together in this way that Man reinforces them in their movement towards God and, in reinforcing them, he reinforces himself; that is, he passes from *existing* to *being.* He cannot reach the highest form of being, for in fact only God has this quality; and He has it all the more fully as creation, and all that exists, fulfil themselves and express themselves in Him.

Ethnologists have often praised the unity, the balance and the harmony of African civilization, of black society, which was based both on the *community* and on the *person* and in which, because it was founded on dialogue and reciprocity, the group had priority over the individual without crushing him, but allowing him to blossom as a person. I would like to emphasize at this point how much these characteristics of negritude enable it to find its place in contemporary humanism, thereby permitting black Africa to make its contribution to the "Civilization of the Universal" which is so necessary in our divided but interdependent world of the second half of the 20th century. A contribution, first of all, to international co-operation, which must be and which shall be the cornerstone of that civilization. It is through these virtues of negritude that decolonization has been accomplished without too much bloodshed or hatred and that a positive form of co-operation based on "dialogue and reciprocity" has been established between former colonizers and colonized. It is through these virtues that there has been a new spirit at the United Nations, where the "no" and the bang of the fist on the table are no longer signs of strength. It is through these virtues that peace through co-operation could extend to South Africa, Rhodesia and the Portuguese colonies, if only the dualistic spirit of the Whites would open itself to dialogue.

In fact, the contribution of negritude to the "Civilization of the Universal" is not of recent origin. In the fields of literature and art, it is contemporary with the "Revolution of 1889." The French poet, Arthur Rimbaud (1854-1891), had already associated himself with negritude. But in this article I want to concentrate on the "Negro revolution"—the expression belongs to Emmanuel Berl—which helped to stir European plastic art at the beginning of this century.

Art, like literature, is always the expression of a certain conception of the world and of life; the expression of a certain philosophy and, above all, of a certain ontology. Corresponding to the philosophical and scientific movement of 1889 there was not only a literary evolution—symbolism then surrealism—but another revolution, or rather revolutions, in art, which were called, taking only the plastic arts, nabism, expressionism, fauvism and cubism. A world of life forces that have to be *tamed* is substituted for a closed world of permanent and continuous substances that have to be *reproduced.*

Since the Greek *kouroi* (the term used for the statues of young men in classical Greek sculpture), the art of the European West had always been based on realism; the work of art had always been an imitation of the object: a *physeôs mimêsis,* to use Aristotle's expression: a corrected imitation, "improved", "idealised" by the requirements of rationality, but imitation all the same. The interlude of the Christian Middle Ages is significant in so far as Christianity is itself of Asian origin and strongly influenced by the African, St. Augustine. For the European artists of the 20th century—for a Kandinsky for example—"art begins where nature leaves off ". To what will the artist then give expression? No longer to purely objective matter, but to his spiritual self: that is, to his inner self, his spirituality, and beyond himself to the spirituality of his age and of mankind. No longer by means of perspective, relief and chiaroscuro, but, as the French painter, Bazaine, writes, "by the most hidden workings of instinct and the sensibility." Another French painter, André Masson, makes it more explicit when he writes: "By a simple interplay of shapes and colours legibly ordered." This interplay of shapes and colours is that of the life forces, which we have already discussed, and which has been illustrated in particular by a painter like Soulages.

"Interplay of life forces": and so we come back to—negritude. As the French painter, Soulages, in fact, once told me, the African aesthetic is "that of contemporary art." I find indirect proof of this in the fact that, while the consecration and spread of the new aesthetic revolution have occurred in France, the majority of its promoters were of Slav and Germanic origin; people who, like the Africans, belong to the mystical civilizations of the senses. Of course, without the discovery of African art, the revolution would still have taken place, but probably without such vigour and assurance and such a deepening of the knowledge of Man. The fact that an art of the subject and of the spirit should have germinated outside Europe, in Africa—to which ethnologists had not yet given its true place in world culture—was proof of the human value of the message of the new European art.

Over and above its aesthetic lesson—to which we shall return later—what Picasso, Braque and the other artists and early explorers of Africa art were seeking was, in the first place, just this: its human value. For in black Africa art is not a separate activity, in itself or for itself: it is a social activity, a technique of living, a handicraft in fact. But it is a major activity that brings all other activities to their fulfilment, like prayer in the Christian Middle Ages: birth and education, marriage and death, sport, even war. All human activities down to the least daily act must be integrated into the subtle interplay of life forces—family, tribal, national, world and universal forces. This harmonious interplay of life forces must be helped by *subordinating* the lower forces—mineral, vegetable and animal—to their relations with Man, and the forces of human society to its relations with the Divine Being through the intermediary of the Ancestral Beings.

A year or two ago I attended, on the cliffs of Bandiagara in the Mali Republic, an entertainment which was microcosm of Dogon art. Even though it was but a pale reflection of the splendours of the past, this "play-concert" was an extremely significant expression of the Dogon vision of the universe. It was declaimed, sung and danced; sculptured and presented in costume. The whole of the Dogon universe was portrayed in this symbiosis of the arts, as is the custom in black Africa. The universe—heaven and earth—was therefore *represented* through the intermediary of Man, whose ideogram is the same as that of the universe. Then the world was *re-presented* by means of masks, each of which portrayed, at one and the same time, a totemic animal, an ancestor and a spirit. Others portrayed the foreign peoples: nomadic Fulani and white Europeans. The aim of the entertainment was, by means of the symbiosis of the arts—poetry, song, dance, sculpture and painting, used as techniques of integration—to *re-create* the universe and the contemporary world, but in a more harmonious way by making use of African humour, which corrects distortions at the expense of the foreign Fulani and the White conquerors. But this ontological vision was an entertainment—that is, an artistic demonstration—as well: a joy for the soul because a joy for the eyes and ears.

It was perhaps—indeed, it was certainly—this last aspect of the African aesthetic lesson that first attracted Picasso and Braque when, towards 1906, they discovered African art and were inspired by it. For my part, what struck me from the start of the Dogon "play-concert", even before I tried to understand its meaning, was the harmony of form and movement, of colour and rhythm, that characterised it. It is this harmony by which, as a spectator, I was moved; which, in the re-creation of reality, acts on the invisible forces whose appearances are only signs, subordinates them in a complementary fashion to one another and establishes the link between them and God through the intermediary of Man. By appearances I mean the attributes of matter that strike our senses: shape and colour, timbre and tone, movement and rhythm.

I have said that these appearances are signs. They are more than that: they are meaningful signs, the "lines of force" of the life forces, insofar as they are used in their pure state, with only their characteristics of shape, colour, sound, movement and rhythm. Recently M. Lods, who teaches at the National School of Art of Senegal, was showing me the pictures his students intend exhibiting at the projected Festival of African Arts. I was immediately struck by the noble and elegant interplay of shape and colour. When I discovered that the pictures were not completely abstract, that they portrayed ladies, princes and noble animals, I was almost disappointed. There was no need for me to be: the very interplay of coloured shapes perfectly expressed that elegant nobility that characterises the art of the Northern Soudan.

This, then, is Africa's lesson in aesthetics: art does not consist in photographing nature but in taming it, like the hunter when he reproduces the call of the hunted animal, like a separated couple, or two lovers, calling to each other in their desire to be reunited. The call is not the simple reproduction of the cry of the Other; it is a call of complementarity, a *song:* a call of harmony to the harmony of union that enriches by increasing *Being*. We call it pure harmony. Once more, Africa teaches that art is not photography; if there are images they are rhythmical. I can suggest or create anything—a man, a moon, a fruit, a smile, a tear—simply by assembling shapes and colours (painting sculpture), shapes and movement (dance), timbre and tones (music), provided that this assembling is not an aggregation, but that it is ordered and, in short, rhythmical. For it is rhythm—the main virtue, in fact, of negritude—that gives the work of art its beauty. Rhythm is simply the movement of attraction or repulsion that expresses the life of the cosmic forces; symmetry and asymmetry, repetition or opposition: in short, the lines of force that link the meaningful signs that shapes and colours, timbre and tones, are.

Before concluding, I should like to pause for a moment on the apparent contradiction that must have been noticed between contemporary European art (which places the emphasis on the subject) and African art (which places it on the object). This is because the "Revolution of 1889" began by reacting, of necessity, against the superstition of the *object;* and the existentialist ontology of the African, while it is based on the being-subject, has God as its pole-object: God who is the fullness of Being. What was noticed, then, was simply a nuance. For the contemporary European, and the African, the work of art, like the act of knowing, expresses the confrontation, the embrace, of subject and object: "That penetration", wrote Bazaine, "that great common structure, that deep resemblance between Man and the world, without which there is no living form."

We have seen what constitutes for the African the "deep

resemblance between Man and the world." For him, then, the act of restoring the order of the world by re-creating it through art is the reinforcement of the life forces in the universe and, consequently, of God, the source of all life forces—or, in other words, the Being of the universe. In this way, we reinforce ourselves at the same time, both as interdependent forces and as beings whose being consists in revitalizing ourselves in the recreation of art.

A last proof of the fact that negritude is a humanism of the 20th century is provided by the welcome that has been accorded throughout the world to the projected Festival of African Arts, which will take place at Dakar in Senegal from April 1 to 24, 1966. The great nations of Europe and America intend to participate by sending either works from their collections or even, in the case of the United States and Brazil, their black artists. Significant, too, is the fact that the Arab states of Africa will also be present at Dakar.

This goes to show that the world—that is, the "Civilization of the Universal"—which has slowly been building itself up since the beginning of the century, on the ruins of racial hatreds and intercontinental wars, feels itself concerned. It feels itself concerned with good reason, for a number of its characteristics, as they are at present taking shape, would not be what they are without the fertilizing contributions of negritude.

In any case, the negritude of the 20th century, the Neo-African, to quote my friend [Janheinz] Jahn, intends to contribute doubly to the Civilization of the Universal: to the civilization of the 20th century. Firstly, by contributing the riches of his traditional philosophy, literature and art; and secondly, by showing the borrowings he has made since the Renaissance from other civilizations, particularly the European and the Arab-Berber civilizations. This is, in fact, the aim of the Festival of African Arts: to demonstrate a humanism of the 20th century. (pp. 1-8)

> *Léopold Sédar Senghor, "Negritude: A Humanism of the 20th Century," in* Optima, *Vol. 16, No. 1, March, 1966, pp. 1-8.*

The problematic issue of *Negritude* is not definition but actional translation. Whether it is *Negritude* or African personality, we African people are dealing with ethno-psychologic problems rather than *melanic* problems. It is the issue of the right attitude toward Black existential postulates and their objective resolution.

—*P. Chike Onwuachi, in his "Negritude in Perspective," in* Black World, *(October 1971).*

Ezekiel Mphahlele

[*A South African novelist, autobiographer, short story writer, essayist, poet, and critic, Mphahlele is considered a major African author and a provocative social critic. In the following essay, he asserts that Negritude is a sociopolitical concept and should not solely be viewed as a literary standard or a romanticization of African culture.*]

Yesterday I was personally attacked by someone who, because of my views against *négritude,* associated me with "colonialism, neo-colonialism and imperialism." He charged me, in effect, with hindering or frustrating the protest literature of *négritude* in its mission. If I had not exiled myself from South Africa five years ago, after having lived for 37 years in the South African nightmare, I should either have shrivelled up in my bitterness or have been imprisoned for treason. My books have been banned in South Africa under a law that forbids the circulation of literature that is regarded as "objectionable, undesirable or obscene." So, you see what things I have been called in my life; my body itches from the number of labels that have been stuck on me! As for what I really am, and my place in the African revolution, I shall let my writings speak for me.

We in South Africa have for the last 300 years of oppression been engaged in a bloody struggle against white supremacy—to assert our *human* and not African dignity. This latter we have always taken for granted. During these three centuries, we the Africans have been creating an urban culture out of the very condition of insecurity, exile and agony. We have done this by integrating Africa and the West. Listen to our music, see our dancing and read our literature both in the indigenous and English languages. The bits of what the white ruling class calls "Bantu culture" that we are being told to "return to" are being used by that class to oppress us, to justify the Transkei and other Bantustans. And yet there still survive the toughest elements of African humanism which keep us together and supply the moral force which we need in a life that rejects us.

If you notice the two segregated sections of a town like Brazzaville, Congo, you cannot fail to see the sterile and purposeless life of the whites in their self-imposed ghetto as distinct from the vibrant and vigorous life of the black community. The blacks have reconciled the Western and African in them, while the whites refuse to surrender to their influence. This is symbolic of the South African situation. The only cultural vitality there is is to be seen among the Africans: they have not been *uplifted* by a Western culture but rather they have reconciled the two in themselves. This is the sense in which I feel superior to the white man who refuses to be liberated by me as an African. So, anyone who imagines that we in South Africa are just helpless, grovelling and down-trodden creatures of two worlds who have been waiting for the "messiah" of *négritude,* does not know a thing about what is going on in our country. My detractor, as an American Negro, who would like to teach us how to feel African, cites the entry of James Meredith into Indiana University as symbolic of the triumph of the Negro's *négritude* in Mississip-

pi. Are we really to believe that the U.S. Federal Army went to Indiana to make it possible for Meredith to sing the blues or gospel songs? Surely his entry is to be seen as part of the Negro's campaign to be integrated socially and politically in the American population; to assert his human dignity.

Of course, I am quite aware of certain—and luckily they are few—non-African blacks and whites who come crawling on their bellies into this continent as it were, prepared to be messengers or lackeys of some of us, prepared to eat the dust under our feet in self-abasement in an attempt to identify with Africa. Such people are prompted to do this out of a guilt complex whereby they seek to bear the sins of past colonisers who, they imagine, we associate them with. Elsewhere I have warned against this ugly self-abasement because it prevents the "patient" from criticizing adversely anything the African says or writes, ripe, raw and rotten. I fully agree with James Baldwin when he says in a brilliant and most moving essay in a recent issue of *The New Yorker* (17 November 1962), that the Negro must solve his problem inside America, not by a romantic identification with Africa. I appreciate also his remark that the Negro refuses to be integrated "into a burning house", i.e. the American social and political life that is sadly misguided, in which whites do not believe in death. And yet he also says that white and black in the U.S. need each other badly, that the white American needs to be liberated from himself but can only do this when he has liberated the Negro. After this, integration must come. Although he appreciates the Black Muslims, he foresees that one day he may have to fight them because they are such a menace.

Now to *négritude* itself. Who is so stupid as to deny the historical fact of *négritude* as both a protest and a positive assertion of African cultural values? All this is valid. What I do not accept is the way in which too much of the poetry inspired by it romanticizes Africa—as a symbol of innocence, purity and artless primitiveness. I feel insulted when some people imply that Africa is not also a violent continent. I am a violent person, and proud of it because it is often a healthy human state of mind; someday I'm going to plunder, rape, set things on fire; I'm going to cut someone's throat; I'm going to subvert a government; I'm going to organize a coup d'état; yes, I'm going to oppress my own people; I'm going to hunt down the rich fat black men who bully the small, weak black men and destroy them; I'm going to become a capitalist, and woe to all who cross my path or want to be my servants or chauffeurs and so on; I'm going to lead a breakaway church—there is money in it; I'm going to attack the black bourgeoisie while I cultivate a garden, rear dogs and parrots; listen to jazz and classics, read, "culture" and so on. Yes, I'm also going to organize a strike. Don't you know that sometimes I kill to the rhythm of drums and cut the sinews of a baby to cure it of paralysis? . . . This is only a dramatisation of what Africa can do and is doing. The image of Africa consists of all these and others. And *négritude* poetry pretends that they do not constitute the image and leaves them out. So we are told only half—often even a falsified half—of the story of Africa. Sheer romanticism that fails to see the large landscape of the personality of the African makes bad poetry. Facile protest also makes bad poetry. The omission of these elements of a continent in turmoil reflects a defective poetic vision. The greatest poetry of Leopold Sedar Senghor is that which portrays in himself the meeting point of Europe and Africa. This is the most realistic and honest and most meaningful symbol of Africa, an ambivalent continent searching for equilibrium. This synthesis of Europe and Africa does not necessarily reject the negro-ness of the African.

What have we to say about "benevolent dictatorship"; chauvinists, peasants who find that they have to change a way of life they have cherished for centuries and have to live in the twentieth century? Let me italicize again: an image of Africa that glosses over or dismisses these things is not a faithfully-conceived one; it restricts our emotional and intellectual response. An image of Africa that only glorifies our ancestors and celebrates our "purity" and "innocence" is an image of a continent lying in state. When I asked the question at the Accra Congress of Africanists last December how long our poets are going to continue to bleat like a goat in the act of giving birth, I was suggesting that Ghanaian poets should start looking inward, into themselves. Now I am being accused of encouraging "artistic purity" by asking writers to cease protesting against a colonial boss that has left their country.

What is "artistic purity"? Am I being asked to lay the ghost of *l'art pour l'art?* Surely meaningful art has social significance or relevance and this very fact implies social criticism—protest in the broadest sense of the word. Gorky, Dostoïevsky, Tolstoy, Dickens and so on did this, but they were no less Russian or English; certainly they were much more committed than *négritude* poets. They took in the whole man. Camara Laye's *Le Regard du Roi,* Ferdinand Oyono's *Le Vieux Négre et la Médaille* and Mongo Beti's *Le pauvre Christ de Bomba* are not bullied by *négritude.* They are concerned in portraying the black-white encounter, and they do this, notwithstanding, with a devastating poetic sense of irony unmatched by any that one sees in the English novel by Africans (there are fascinating works in the three main Bantu languages in South Africa which are of the same standard). I am suggesting here that we as writers need to be emancipated from ourselves. *Négritude,* while a valuable slogan politically, can because its apostles have set it up as a principle of art, amount to self-enslavement-*autocolonisation,* to quote a French writer speaking of African politics and economics. We should not allow ourselves to be bullied at gun-point into producing literature that is supposed to contain a *négritude* theme and style. For now we are told, also, that there is *un style negro-african,* and that therefore we have to sloganize and write to a march. We are told that *négritude* is less a matter of theme than style. We must strive to visualize the whole man, not merely the things that are meant to flatter the Negro's ego. Let it not be forgotten, too, that *négritude* has an overlap of 19th century European protest against machines and cannons. In the place of the cuckoo, the nightingale, the daffodil, Africa has been dragged to the altar of Europe. *Négritude* men should not pretend that this is an entirely African concept.

Several of us, as a result of the physical and mental agony we have been going through in South Africa, have rejected Christianity or any other religion as a cure for human ills. But if I wrote a poem or novel expressly to preach against religion without my seeing the irony of the good and bad done in the name of religion; if I omitted the irony of Christians and educated Africans who still revere ancestral spirits, and several other ironies and paradoxes, then it would not be a lasting work of art. I think that a writer who is too sure about his rejection of the use of a god can be as overbearing as the one who is too sure about his need of an existence of a god, like Browning. I say, then, that *négritude* can go on as a socio-political slogan, but that it has no right to set itself up as a standard of literary performance; there I refuse to go along. I refuse to be put in a Negro file—for sociologists to come and examine me. Art unifies even while it distinguishes men; and I regard it as an insult to the African for anyone to suggest that because we write independently on different themes in divers modes and styles all over Africa, therefore we are ripe victims of balkanization.

But then I speak as a simple practising writer, not as a politician or a philosopher, or a non-African Africanist who is looking for categories and theories for a doctorate thesis. I refuse to be put in a dossier. And yet I am no less committed to the African revolution, to the South African freedom fight. The South African, East African and English-speaking West African do not worry over *négritude* because they have never lost the essence of their negroness. Again, let *négritude* make the theme of literature if people want to use it. But we must remember that literature springs from an individual's experience, and in its effort to take in the whole man, it also tries to see far ahead, to project a prophetic vision, such as the writer is capable of, based on contemporary experience. It must at least set in motion vibrations in us that will continue even after we have read it, prompting us to continue inquiring into its meaning. If African culture is worth anything at all, it should not require myths to prop it up. These thoughts are not new at all. I have come to them after physical and mental agony. And this is of course not my monopoly either. It is the price Africa has to pay. And if you thought that the end of colonialism was the end of the agony, then it is time to wake up.

We acknowledge that *négritude* as a socio-political concept defines the mind of the assimilated African in French-speaking territories. The British never set out to assimilate their colonial subjects. They hate to see people come out of their culture to emulate them (the British). They like the exotic African, not the one who tries to speak, walk and eat like them. They love Africans in museum cases, so they left much of African culture intact. But literature and art are too big for *négritude,* and it had better be left as a historical phase. (pp. 82-4)

Ezekiel Mphahlele, "Negritude—A Phase," in The New African, *Cape Town, Vol. 2, No. 5, June 8, 1963, pp. 82-4.*

Bentley Le Baron

[*In the following essay, Le Baron examines Negritude in relation to Pan-Africanism.*]

> Pan-Africanism is not, and never has been, a unified or a structured political movement. It is a movement of ideas and emotions: its recent political history has been a search for a viable political organization. [Colin Legum, "Pan-Africanism, The Communists and the West," *African Affairs* (1964)]

As Legum suggests, the general movement toward Pan-Africanism has always been highly emotional in content, and this is even more strikingly true of négritude, which may be seen as a particular component of, a variant of, or even, in some senses, an alternative to Pan-Africanism. Négritude has always been a literary-cultural movement, a movement more potent in the realm of intellect and idea than in terms of concrete political activity, and it might even be argued that its net effect is more detrimental than helpful to the Pan-African aim of political union on a continental scale.

Both Pan-Africanism and négritude have origins outside the African continent, in Europe and the New World; both gained impetus during the 1940's and 1950's from reaction against different aspects of the experience of colonial subjugation; and each, in various ways, derives substance in today's context from the political, economic, and psychological problems of an underdeveloped continent facing a highly competitive world. Obviously the two patterns of thought will have numerous points of overlap, but they also have points of conflict, and when the ideals seek objectification in political organization, the conflicts tend to become acute. My aim in this [essay] is to examine négritude within a Pan-African frame of reference, especially problems and conflicts. In particular I want to discuss racism, political union, ambivalence toward the white (or European? or non-African?) world and mystical overtones. It will be helpful to mention the origins and principal themes of négritude, and parallels with other intellectual ideas and movements both African and European.

In a sense, the roots of Pan-Africanism (and of négritude) extend as far back as the slave trade, but in terms of an organized, self-conscious movement, Pan-Africanism begins in the first quarter of the twentieth century with two Americans, Du Bois and Garvey, whose accomplishments range from organization of Pan-African conferences and the National Association for the Advancement of Colored People, on one hand, to proclamation of a "Negro Empire" on the other. The protest is against the inferior status of the Negro, and the means are political.

Négritude, as a self-conscious movement, began in Paris with the publication in 1939 of *Cahier d'un retour au pays natal* by the West Indian poet-politician Aimé Césaire, and Césaire was but one of a group of writers and intellectuals from the West Indies and Africa—including Senegal's Léopold Senghor, another poet-politician—who sought to express the frustrations of the black "exile" in a world of alien white. "What I am," Césaire declares, "is a man alone imprisoned in white":

> c'est un homme seul qui défie
> les cris blancs de la mort blanche . . .
> c'est un homme qui facine
> l'épervier blanc de la mort blanche
> c'est un homme seul dans la mer inféconde
> de sable blanc. . . .

Négritude is a protest at a very sophisticated level: a protest of men largely assimilated into European culture, but for all that unable to escape from the color of their skins. This is no mere request for social equality. These men ask not to be accepted like other men, but, somewhat ironically, to be valued precisely because they are unique and so are in a position to make a unique contribution to mankind. The exile of physical slavery is always in the background, but the exigent concern here is an exile of spirit. "Cet exile ancestral des corps figure l'autre exile: l'âme noire est une Afrique dont le nègre est exilé au milieu des froids buildings de la culture et de la technique blanches" [Jean-Paul Sartre, *Orphée Noir*]. The physical homeland on the African continent is paralleled by a semi-mystical homeland of the soul—which is "négritude."

Senghor felt the full impact of the French assimilation policy—a policy of acceptance, on white terms, into a metropolitan white society—and he reacted as against a smothering embrace. [Austin] Shelton remarks that it could be expected that French education aimed at assimilation would create "a class who very rapidly perceived the clay feet of the white gods and consequently began to oppose the whole business of colonialism and culture supremacy" ["The Black Mystique: Reactionary Extremes in 'Négritude'," *African Affairs* (1964)]. So it was with Senghor: he wanted association without assimilation, on terms acceptable to both black and white. Like Césaire, he called for a renaissance of black culture and for a recognition on the part of European civilization that Negroes have a contribution to make to a world civilization. In a sense he sought to perpetuate what Sartre called "la grande division manichéiste du monde en noir et blanc," by refusing to reject totally either European or traditional cultures, wanting rather to create a new Negro culture which would draw selectively from both. He refuses the "straight choice between isolation and assimilation" which Alion Diop called "the trap in which the malice of the colonizer has cunningly tried to catch the conscience of the Africans."

The persistent themes of négritude poetry include a remembrance of past indignities; but more significant is an emphasis on present and future greatness. Even in passages recalling slavery and humiliation, references to inherent Negro values are contrasted with the shallowness of the seemingly superior whites, who [in the words of Mabel Imoukhuede]

> trampled down all that was strange
> and filled the void
> with half-digested alien thoughts;
> they left a trail of red
> wherever their feet had passed.

By implication, [Aimé Césaire writes in *Cahier d'un retour au pays natal,*] black culture is superior, even without invention and conquest:

> Écoutez le monde blanc

horriblement las de son effort immense
ses articulations rebelles craquer sous les étoiles
     dures
ses raideurs d'acier bleu transperçant la chair
     mystique
écoute ses victoires proditoires trompeter ses dé-
     faites
écoute aux alibis grandioses son piètre trébuche-
     ment

Pitié pour nos vainquers omniscients et naïfs
Eia pour ceux qui n'ont jamais rien inventé
pour ceux qui n'ont jamais exploré
pour ceux qui n'ont jamais dompté

Eia pour la joie
Eai pour l'amour
Eia pour la douleur aux pis de larmes réin-
     carnées.

In David Diop's poetry, as in Césaire's and Senghor's, imagery of hardness and coldness is associated with whites;
Negroes, by contrast, epitomize the warmth of human
feeling—some joy, and much pain:

> It seemed as if the rays of the sun
> were extinguished in my empty hut.
> My wives crushed their reddened mouths
> Against the thin hard lips of the
> Conquerors with eyes of steel.
> My children took off their peaceful nakedness
> To put on a uniform of blood and iron. . . .
>
> . . . . . .
>   . . . In those days
> There was painful laughter on the metallic hell
>   of the roads
> And the monotonous rhythm of the paternoster
> Drowned the howling on the plantations. . . .

But Diop looks to a new era of black glory, when the
pride, beauty, and strength of the Negro will overshadow
a faded white culture:

> This tree, young and strong,
> This tree there, in splendid isolation
> Amidst white and faded flowers,
> That is Africa, your Africa,
> That grows again, patiently, obstinately
> As its fruit gradually acquires
> The bitter taste of liberty.

Senghor wonders who else but the Negro could be "the
leaven that the white flour needs."

> For who else would teach rhythm to the world
>   that has died of machines and cannons?
> For who else should ejaculate the cry of joy, that
>   arouses the dead and the wise in a new dawn?
> Say, who else could return the memory of life to
>   men with a torn hope?

Sartre expresses the same theme from a white point of
view [in *Orphée Noir*]. It is with justice he says, that Césaire has called up "Vainqueurs omniscients et naïfs," for

> de l'outil, le blanc sait tout. Mais tout griffe la
> surface des choses, il ignore la durée, la vie. La
> négritude, au contraire, est une compréhension
> par sympathie. Le secret du noir c'est que les
> sources de son *existence* et les racine de l'Être
> sont identiques.

In the end, this "compréhension par sympathie" extends
to all cultures; it is not exclusive; it is the medium by
which the Negro can be, rather paradoxically, at once separated from and united with the whites. Senghor calls for
"a synthesis of civilizations, retaining only the fecund elements of each." His objective is "a *dynamic symbiosis* . . .
a cultural blending" [*African Socialism* (1959)]. In another place he refers to himself as "a cultural mulatto." Sartre
expresses it in terms of "une progression dialectique":

> l'affirmation théorique et pratique de la supré-
> matie du blanc est la thèse; la position de la Né-
> gritude comme valeur antithétique est le mo-
> ment de la négativité. Mais ce moment négatif
> n'a pas de suffisance par lui-même et les noirs qui
> en usent le savent fort bien; ils savent qu'il vise
> à préparer la synthèse ou réalisation de l'humain
> dans une société sans races.

But to many, Negroes and whites alike, a world society
without races is a utopian ideal which can be criticized
from at least two directions. In the first place, it can be argued that as long as some skins are white and others black
the notion of a dialectic synthesis is a piece of romantic,
even mystical fancy. (In reality, the insistence on uniqueness may be more likely to perpetuate antithesis than to
promote synthesis.) Second, it can be argued in practical
terms that race conflict is simply a concrete fact of life
which is likely to be with us for some time. [Shelton
writes:]

> Whatever attempts might be made by some Afri-
> cans to claim that there is no racism in Africa,
> the obvious truth is there to see: all the national-
> istic arguments about economic and political
> subservience, social scorn, and the like, which
> were suffered by colonial peoples in Africa were
> imposed by white persons upon black persons.
> So nationalism, as a stage in the response of Afri-
> cans to the colonial situation, is naturally linked
> with the whole problem of race supremacy, and
> aids in the growth of further race consciousness
> among Africans.

The possibility of localized racial conflict in Africa continues to be very real—as Congo, South Africa, and the Portuguese territories attest—and the danger of négritude is
that potentially it could be used (twisted) to promote racial antagonism on a generalized scale. Of course it will
be countered that négritude aims at lessening racism, but
one of the criticisms frequently expressed in non-French
Africa—and in America—is precisely that idealization of
black character and black culture, pushed by the extreme
emotionalism of reaction, keeps the racial issue explosive—perpetuates the Manichean division.

The problem is that Pan-Africanism can be interpreted
two ways. The slogan "Africa for Africans" can be used
to unify peoples of diverse racial and cultural backgrounds, all of whom claim the designation "African," or
it can be used as an opening wedge in an ugly split between
"true" (i.e., black) Africans and "foreigners." Similarly,
an exponent of négritude can emphasize the conflict between black and white peoples, or he can emphasize their
ultimate "complementary" unity: the concept is big
enough and ambiguous enough to accommodate both

themes. To the extent that négritude fosters self-confidence, restores dignity, inspires creative activity, its emotional content is salutary; to the extent that it fosters chauvinism and accentuates bitterness, it is dangerous. And both attitudes have characterized Pan-Africanism from the beginning, for while Du Bois opposed racial arrogance of both white and black varieties, Garvey countered one prejudice with another, demanding a pure black race.

Following Sartre, apologists for négritude have tried to get around the problem with the concept of "antiracist racism." Négritude is seen as the necessary but passing moment of antithesis which must negate the thesis of white supremacy before a non-racial synthesis can be achieved. In a somewhat similar spirit, Legum tries to establish a distinction between race-consciousness ("a positive statement in defense of one's race") and racialism (which seeks to "elevate that race above other races") [*Pan-Africanism* (1963)]. Senghor, following Teilhard de Chardin, articulates the "complementarity" theme: "races are not equal but complementary, which is a superior form of equality." At the same time, he wants to establish a "Negro African Nation," and what else can a Negro nation be if not racial? It is evident that there are no clear or firm dividers between the notions of racial, racist, and race-conscious, and only extreme caution tempered by patient good will can prevent them, in practice, from becoming hopelessly tangled.

Négritude is obviously ambivalent; it is not an easy concept to concretize. Césaire realized this, and was conscious of the danger of racial hate.

> . . . preserve me, heart, from all hatred
> do not turn me into a man of hate whom I shall
> hate
> for in order to emerge into this unique race,
> you know my world-wide love,
> know it is not hatred against other races
> that turns me into the cultivator of this one race.
> for what I want
> arises from infinite hunger
> from infinite thirst.

As the suppressed Negro typically developed an ambivalent love-hate relationship with his white "superior," so négritude juxtaposes expressions of admiration and of contempt for European civilization. This is not merely reaction against the oppressions of the colonial situation; Césaire's "infinite hunger" continues into the post-independence period. The poet of négritude wishes to redeem and embrace that same white world which he so bitterly rejects and denounces. Forgiveness and revenge, protest and acceptance, are parallel themes. This is, in Mazrui's apt phrase, "less a rebellion than the paradox of rebellious imitation" ["On the Concept of 'We Are All Africans,'" *American Political Science Review* (1963)], for in the end it must be admitted that forgiveness and acceptance outweigh rejections. Senghor hates, but he can forget his hatred:

> Lord, I have accepted your white cold that burns
> worse than salt.
> And now my heart melts like snow in the sun.
> And I forget

> The white hands that loaded the guns that de-
> stroyed the kingdoms,
> The hands that whipped the slaves and that
> whipped you
> The dusty hands that slapped you, the white
> powdered hands that slapped me
> The sure hands that pushed me into solitude and
> hatred. . . .

The major reaction is, of course, against Europe, but there is a problem of vagueness: It is never quite settled whether négritude reacts against all non-black culture (hence against major portions of indigenous Africa), or only against "European" culture (which would seriously diminish the impact of the black-white dichotomization). It seems that négritude in its most simple and obvious form would have to stand in opposition to Pan-Africanism in its most simple and obvious form, for, interpreted in terms of a strict black-white dichotomy, négritude must not only divide the African continent but also overlap into non-African areas, particularly the Americas: in short, it becomes non-territorial.

This particular problem becomes most relevant when political union is proposed—when African states contemplate merging into a greater African community. To the extent that it is an expression of, and a plea for, solidarity, négritude could be a support to political union. This would be most likely, of course, among those states comprising the former French West and Central Africa. But the trouble is, in part, that the solidarity encouraged by négritude tends to exclude non-Negro areas of Africa, and this problem is seen even more acutely in light of Mazrui's reminder that Algeria, for instance, has much firmer historical connections with Europe than with, say, Congo or Tanganyika. Typically, the Pan-Africanist calls for continental unity, but there are exceptions: Awolowo of Nigeria is one who, like Senghor, puts black African community ahead of continental community. But this is not the end of the problem, for négritude is to some extent a divisive force even within the black community; it tends to alienate those outside the French tradition (and, of course, even some within it). This is partly because Negroes within the English-speaking and (some of) the Islamic communities have not felt the intense alienation from traditional roots which dominated the thinking of "exiles" in Europe and America. It is also, as suggested above, partly because of racial overtones, which are repugnant to many English-speaking Negroes. (As Mphahlele has remarked, "I take my Negroness for granted, and it is no matter for slogans"; or, putting it in Soyinka's terms, a tiger does not find it necessary to proclaim his tigritude.) And partly it is because the heavy emphasis on romantic, even mystical, doctrines or ideals seems, to some, to obscure the real problems of economic, social, and political development.

Of course Pan-Africanism, as well as négritude, may with some justice be termed a utopian ideal. Legum suggests that it is not merely an ideal, but "the right answer to Africa's needs," and he adds the caution that to advocate union is "not the same thing as concluding that this is in fact what will happen." But if Pan-Africanism is utopian, it is at least a concrete and tangible ideal, whereas Senghor invites the charge of mysticism when he suggests that

Table of contents from the premiere issue of Présence afri-caine, *November-December 1947.*

black French Africa represents the "soul" of France, and her "raison d'être." Négritude claims for black men a special prerogative to represent the spiritual, the sensual, the blood-warm and "humanistic" aspects of the human community—man's vital, vibrant, earth contact—as opposed to the harshness and cold rigidity of a rational, efficient, technological civilization.

> Naked woman, black woman
> Clothed with your colour which is life, with your
> form which is beauty . . .
> Your beauty strikes me to the heart like the flash
> of an eagle.
> Naked woman, dark woman
> Firm-fleshed ripe fruit, sombre raptures of
> black wine, mouth making lyrical my
> mouth . . . .

Appealing as these notions may be to the black intellectual struggling to establish his own sense of dignity and personal worth, they are not necessarily helpful and may even be a hindrance when it comes to working out a practical program for unification and development. The poets of négritude have in fact been charged with the sin of writing for a European rather than an African audience, but whether or not this is true it is at least apparent that the appeal of négritude is a sophisticated appeal likely to have little impact on the ordinary African workingman, or peasant, or housewife—unless indirectly. It is an expression, in other words, of a cleavage not only between black and white but

between black intellectual and black peasant, so that to some degree the "alien and exile" theme carries directly into the heart of the African homeland.

Originating as it did in Paris, in the 1930's, it is hardly surprising that négritude should show parallels with intellectual currents of those years: Marxism, existentialism, surrealism, to name three which are intimately associated in the general quest for "liberation." Much of Césaire's imagery is surrealist, although later poets have tended toward greater analytic precision. The alienation theme is, of course, central to both Marxist and existential thought.

Sartre, in his *Orphée Noir,* uses a modified Marxist frame of reference: négritude is dialectic; the black race is a world proletariat; "le 'Blanc' symbolise le capital, comme le Nègre le travail. . . ." And much of the Marxist orientation, though without its rigid categorizations, carries over into contemporary discussions of "African Socialism." In particular, "race" tends to be substituted for "class," and the notion of class struggle is repudiated as inapplicable to Africa. Senghor follows Marx's economic analysis at length, but concludes that it is a *"philosophy of humanism,* rather than economics," which is "the basic character, the positive contribution of Marxian thought." He specifically ties African Socialism in with race and, only a little less specifically, with the spiritual mystique of négritude, in terms of a unique sort of black "communion of souls."

> Socialism is based, by definition, not only on race, but also on geography and history—political and economic. It is these values, especially the cultural values of sentiment, which constitute the contribution which the new Negroes can make to the rendezvous of giving and receiving: to the convergent current of socialism, in a word to the "New Directions of Socialism." . . . We have developed co-operation, not *collectivist,* but *communal.* For co-operation—of family, village, tribe—has always been honoured in Black Africa; once again, not in collectivist form, not as an aggregate of individuals, but in communal form.

For Senghor, African Socialism is "existentialist and humanistic" and "integrates spiritual values," which ordinary socialism lacks. But it is the black African's duty to renew socialism "by helping it regain spiritual dimensions." Like négritude, the African Socialism concept is seen by some as more of a mystique than a rational political program.

Interestingly, the notion of African Socialism is also very closely identified with Pan-Africanism—with political union. Nelkin sees the three mainstreams of Pan-African thought as African unification, black nationalism, and African Socialism. The socialism theme has been a dominant one throughout the history of the Pan-African movement, for instance, in the activity of Du Bois and Padmore. It has been referred to as "the unifying ideology" of the movement, and is seen by some as essential to establishing a level of economic viability sufficient to support a stable political union of continental dimensions.

African Socialism is also closely associated with the concepts of "African Personality" and "Consciencism," which may to some extent be seen as the counterparts of négritude in much of non-French Africa. In fact, the African Personality tends to be defined, in part, as a socialistic personality. And unlike négritude, these concepts fit easily, comfortably, with Pan-Africanism, for they are not racially exclusive. The term "African Personality" suggests a unique contribution to be made not by the Negro but by the African (of whatever color), and if this notion is less schematically tidy, less symbolic, than the metaphysic of négritude, it is at the same time less socially dangerous, and (hopefully) more workable. It has sometimes been suggested that the English-speaking African—in contrast with the French-speaking—tends to avoid elaborate abstractions in his practical concern with real political and economic problems, but, as Consciencism demonstrates, this is not necessarily so. To some extent it is true of African Personality, for this is a concept easily understood at the grass roots, easily adaptable to the problems and vocabulary of the peasant who has never thought in terms of "alienation" or of a "dialectic of cultures" but who does want to take pride in his achievements as an African. The related and elaborated concept of Consciencism, on the other hand, is as far beyond the concern of the common man, as self-consciously abstract and philosophical, as is négritude—and, it might be fair to add, without the delicate coloring, the poignancy, the romance, of the French tradition.

Consciencism is an expression of Nkrumah's (and Abraham's) desire to establish a unifying doctrine which will overcome that "schizophrénie la plus pernicieuse" which results from the tension between the several cultures—traditional and modern—which impinge on the individual African today. It is a deliberate attempt "d'établir un ensemble cohérent de réflexions qui détermineront la nature générale de notre action, en unifiant la société dont nous sommes les héritiers"; it aims at "une révolution intellectuelle, une révolution qui oriente nos réflexions et notre philosophie vers une renaissance de notre société" [Kwame Nkrumah, "Le 'Consciencisme,'" *Présence Africaine* (1964)].

> Consciencisme . . . représente, en termes intellectuels, cette disposition stratégique des forces qui permettra à la société africaine d'assimiler les éléments occidentaux, islamiques et euro-chrétiens, et de les adapter à la personalité africaine. La personalité africaine se définit elle-même par le foisonnement des principes ayant l'homme pour objet, qui sont sous-jacents dans la société africaine traditionelle. Le "consciencisme philosophique" représente ce point de vue philosophique qui, à partir de l'état actuel de la conscience africaine, s'efforce d'indiquer comment le conflit qui agite cette conscience peut donner lieu au progres.

Consciencism starts from a materialist basis, but it is not an ordinary materialism—it is spiritualized by "le phénomène de la conscience." In the course of a metaphysical romp which takes us all the way from Thales and Heraclites to Einstein and the Logical Positivists, we learn that while matter is the most fundamental category of being, it is animate, dynamic; it is capable of dialectic transfor-

mation into other categories—which is a fact, as it turns out, that the Bantu tradition had proclaimed all along. And the socio-political implications which allegedly follow from these foundations turn out to be remarkably similar to those of both African Socialism and négritude: in particular, a "humanist" mystique; a special claim to spiritual-communal leadership; ambivalence toward the colonial experience and European culture; insistence on the unique contribution to be made by the African who is firmly rooted in a traditional past but in step with "progress" and committed to a flowering of African culture.

This synthesis of cultures, this reaching for the best of both worlds, points in the direction of a millennial future which is only implied by Consciencism but which becomes explicit in the more mystical versions of négritude. The cosmic vision of dialectical necessity which turns the world into a garden of delights is reminiscent of Teilhard de Chardin's "Omega point," which represents a "biologically necessary" culmination of evolutionary history. (Needless to add, this grand climax is seen as impossible without the unique contribution of the Negro personality.) Like Césaire, Teilhard longs for a "worldwide love" which "embraces the total of men," [*The Phenomenon of Man* (1963)] and he regards this "superior state of humanity" as the inevitable result of a synthesis of the various aspects or components of humanity. It is difficult to render his thought in concrete terms, but it is at least evident that he sees Omega not as a "fusion" of elements but as a grouping in which "personalizations of the elements reach their maximum simultaneously and without merging."

Senghor—and the French intellectual climate in general—have been influenced by Teilhard's thought, but it seems likely that the main currents of négritude are parallel to, rather than derivative from, Teilhard. Certainly it is easy enough to see in Omega the négritude mystique of a world civilization composed of various cultures, each contributing to a unified whole, but "uniquely," without losing its identity. At this point we are well beyond Pan-Africanism, into something closer to Pan-Humanism. As a final note on Teilhard, it is interesting that, like Nkrumah, he starts with matter as the "basic reality," and ends by subordinating physical to psychic energy. "Thus," as Senghor puts it, "starting from concrete facts, on a material basis, but broader and more profound than Marx, Teilhard de Chardin emerges on the spiritual above and ahead." This does sound like an echo of Consciencism.

Even more than Consciencism, and quite unlike Pan-Africanism, négritude is persistently and essentially ethereal. It insists on dealing with psychic and cultural verities, ahead of the politico-economic. And one suspects that a Negro poet might want to argue that, just as Pan-Africanism requires solid economic foundations, so also it requires solid racio-cultural foundations: that, in short, the vision of négritude must be fulfilled before Pan-Africanism can become a meaningful reality. Négritude represents, in Allen's words,

> the Negro African poet's endeavor to recover for his race a normal self-pride, a lost confidence in himself, a world in which he again has a sense of identity and a significant role. It is, in Sartre's

figure from classic mythology, his Eurydice recovered by Orpheus from Pluto, his lost beloved,
his ultimate identity, his vision of the world and
not that of a culture holding him in derision and
contempt. It is not a goal to be accomplished,
but rather, more basically, an affective disposition, in Heidegger's existentialist term, the
Negro's "being-in-the-world."

And if a pragmatist from Ghana or Egypt or Kenya
should object to this emphasis on blackness, he could
hardly object to Touré's formulation, which captures a
certain flavor of African aspirations, which is common to
both Pan-Africanism and négritude:

> Hier dominée mais non conquise, l'Afrique est
> déterminée a délivrer au monde son message
> particulier et à apporter à l'univers humain le
> fruit de ses expériences, la totalité de ses ressour-
> ces intellectuelles et les enseignements de sa cul-
> ture propre.

(pp. 267-75)

*Bentley Le Baron, "Négritude: A Pan-African
Ideal?" in* Ethics, *Vol. 76, No. 4, July, 1966,
pp. 267-76.*

Frederick Ivor Case

[*In the following excerpt, Case defines Negritude as a
product of Western rather than African philosophy.*]

Aimé Césaire and Léopold Sédar Senghor are indisputa-
bly the two great leaders of the Négritude movement
which was born in France in the late 1930s. It is significant
that both men are now politicians of some stature and that
Senghor is generally considered as one of the greatest supporters of the concept of Francophonie. He has made use
of his position as President of Senegal to promote the recognition of African cultural values throughout the world
and is an international figure whose reputation has spread
beyond the French-speaking nations.

Césaire is less well known internationally but as a Member
of Parliament in Paris representing Fort-de-France and as
mayor of that Martiniquan town his preoccupation with
Negro-African culture is widely known in the French-
speaking world.

Césaire was born in 1913 in Martinique and eventually became a student of the *Ecole Normale Supérieure,* one of
the highest academic institutions in France. In his poem
Return to my Native Land he proceeds to the revalorisation of Negro-African values and asserts a belief in the dignity of the black man. He counters every European and
Christian denial of the Black by a brilliant reversal of prejudices:

> I declare my crimes and say that there is nothing
>   to say in my defence
> Dances. Idols. Relapses.
> I too have murdered
> God with my idleness
> my words my gestures my obscene songs
>
> I have worn parrot feathers and
> musk-cat skins

> I have worn down the patience of missionaries
> I have insulted the benefactors of humanity.
> Defied Tyre. Defied Sydon.
> Adored the Zambezi.
> The expanse of my perversity confounds me.

Sometimes, however, this ironic reversal is not sufficient
to express his anger or indignation and he simply asserts
the superior qualities of certain aspects of Negro-African
culture:

> Heia for the royal Kailcedrate!
> Heia for those who have never invented any-
>   thing
> those who never explored anything
> those who never tamed anything
>
> those who give themselves up to the essence of
>   all
>   things
> ignorant of the surfaces but struck by the move-
>   ment of
>   all things
> free of the desire to tame but familiar with the
>   play
>   of the world

It is necessary to examine these and other passages in the
poem carefully since one could conclude, like Sartre in *Orphée Noir,* that Négritude is a *racisme antiraciste.* Césaire
is repudiating the cloak of white 'sophistication' without
repudiating the white man and all his values.

One of the principal characteristics of any racism is its
negative basis. It is, essentially, the negation of the humanity of a racial group and the denial of all the values of that
group. Césaire's Négritude, and Senghor's also, is the affirmation of African cultural values. It is a positive expression of human dignity and pride which, of necessity, has
to be preceded by a 'purification' of the harmful aspects
of the Western European conditioning of the Black which
has made him turn against himself. Césaire's repudiation
of this conditioning is the recognition that cultural and religious values are not absolute but entirely relative. As
Senghor declared in a speech before the Ghanaian Parliament in 1962:

> Négritude is not even attachment to a particular
> race, our own, although such attachment is legit-
> imate. Négritude is the awareness, defence and
> development of African cultural values. . . .
>
> However, the struggle for négritude must not be
> negation but affirmation.

Césaire recognises in his essay, *Discours sur le Colonialisme,* that the principal error of the European lies in the
equations:

> Christianity = Civilisation
> Paganism   = Barbarity

Everything and everyone is judged in relation to these values.

One certainly could not accuse Senghor of racism. Whilst
Césaire was once a member of the French Communist
Party and is still a Marxist, Senghor has been Catholic for
most of his life. Born in 1906, he also left his native land

to further his academic education in France and was also a student at the *Ecole Normale Supérieure.*

Senghor's greatest contribution to the Négritude movement appears to have been his personal influence on Caribbean writers, the sons of a people who had for centuries been humiliated, enslaved and alienated from their culture and from themselves in the name of Western European Christianity.

Senghor's poetic work is characterised by a quiet dignity and pride, his richest verse, mostly composed to be set to traditional West African instruments, expresses his desire to return to the native village that he has left so very far behind:

> Toko'Waly my uncle, do you remember those
>   distant nights when my head grew heavy
>   against the patience of your back?
> Or holding me by the hand, your hand led me
>   through the shadows and signs?
> The fields are flowers of glowworms; the stars
>   come to rest on the grass, on the trees.
> All around is silence.
> Only the droning scents of the bush, hives of red
>   bees drowning the stridulation of the crickets
> And the muffled tom-tom, the far-off breathing
>   of the night.
>   ('For Koras and Balafong' in *Chants d'Ombre*)

Then at the end of that very beautiful poem 'Joal' which is also in the collection *Chants d'Ombre* we read this striking stanza:

> I remember, I remember . . .
> In my head the rhythm of the tramp tramp
> So wearily down the days of Europe where there
>   comes,
> Now and then a little orphaned jazz that goes
>   sobbing, sobbing, sobbing.

It is particularly in this first collection of his poems that the nostalgic note is struck although it is also evident in the later collections of verse.

Senghor also condemns the savagery of the European rape of Africa but acknowledges a great debt to French humanism and to the French language. His speeches and essays are of great importance and interest to the student of Negro-African cultures.

What is very striking indeed in Senghor's writings is the passionate love of Africa and of France which never seem to enter into conflict. Speaking of Africa he says:

> What is forgotten is that this land was abandoned for three centuries to the bloody cupidity of slave traders; that through the murderous actions of the Whites, twenty millions of its children were deported to the West Indies and to the Americas, that two hundred million died in man hunts. What is generally forgotten is that each 'benefit of colonisation' has had its reverse. (*Négritude et Humanisme*)

In the same article, which appeared in *Présence Africaine* in 1950, he goes on to say that the West's technological contribution to Africa is of value only if the soul of the Af-

rican is not altogether altered by the new exterior forces that threaten its tranquil homogeneity.

In a very famous article entitled 'French as a Language of Culture' which appeared in the November 1962 number of *Esprit*, Senghor gives five reasons why the French language is of such great importance to African writers. Firstly, he says, many of the elite think in French and speak it better than their mother tongue. Secondly, there is the richness of the French vocabulary. Thirdly, French, through its syntax, is a concise language:

> To the syntax of juxtaposition of Negro-African languages is opposed the syntax of subordination of French; to the syntax of concrete reality, that of abstract thought: in point of fact, the syntax of reason to that of emotion. (*Négritude et Humanisme*)

Fourthly, the stylistic demands of the French language open new universal dimensions to the reader. It is the fifth reason that is of particular concern here, and I will quote the entire paragraph that explains it.

> Fifth reason: French Humanism. It is precisely in this elucidation, in this *re-creation*, that French Humanism consists. For man is the object of its activity. Whether it be in the case of Law, of Literature, of Art, even of Science, the distinguishing mark of French genius lies in this concern with Man. French always expresses a *moral*. This gives it its character of *universality* which counterbalances its tendency to individualism.

In the poem 'Prayer for Peace' dedicated to Georges and Claude Pompidou, Senghor prays for France:

> O Lord, take from my memory the France
>   which is not France, mask of smallness and
>   hatred upon the face of France
> That mask of smallness and hatred for which I
>   have hatred . . . yet I may well hate Evil
> For I have a great weakness for France.
> Bless this people who were tied and twice able
>   to free their hands and proclaim the coming
>   of the poor into the kingdom
> Who turned the slaves of the day into men free
>   equal fraternal
> Bless these people who brought me Thy Good
>   News, Lord, and opened my heavy eyelids to
>   the light of faith.
>   ('Prayer for Peace' in *Hosties Noires*)

This poem was written in 1945 and it hardly seems that Senghor's love of France and his gratitude have altered.

Though Césaire does not insist on his love of France in his work, both he and Senghor, the Marxist and the Catholic, look forward to the day when all peoples will recognise and respect differences in culture and when all the oppressed of the world will join hands in brotherhood.

In his play *Et les Chiens se taisaient,* Césaire's hero illustrates universal tolerance:

> Suppose that the world were a forest. Good!
> There are baobabs, flourishing oaks, black pines
>   and white walnuts;
> I would like them all to grow, firm and strong,

different in wood, in bearing, in colour,
but equally full of sap and without one encroach-
    ing on the other's space,
different at the base
but oh!
                    (Ecstatically)
may their heads join high, very high, in the ether
    so as to form for all
a single roof
            I say the only protective roof!
                        (*Et les Chiens . . .*)

It would be superfluous to quote similar sentiments expressed by Senghor since they are easily to be found in his speeches and essays.

What seems to characterise Négritude then is an assertion of African dignity, a desire to return to the cultural values which are deeply rooted in traditional religion, and the future hope of a universal brotherhood in a universal civilisation.

I will now attempt to analyse this black ideology through the application of certain concepts on African ontology discussed by Professor John Mbiti in his book *African Religions and Philosophy.*

John Mbiti defines two dimensions of African reality which he calls the Sasa period and the Zamani. The Sasa is the now, the immediate future, the near period of time in the past, present, and future. Zamani is the period beyond which nothing can go. It is the past incorporating the present. To illustrate this I will recall briefly Mbiti's exposition of the concept of life and death among many African peoples.

Whilst I am alive, I live in the Sasa period which will continue for me, as a living dead, even after my death. For as long as there is someone who remembers me whilst I was alive and as long as my name still evokes a real image which is neither myth nor legend, then my Sasa, my present reality, continues. I progress into the Zamani when my name no longer evokes this reality in the mind of anyone. Only then am I truly dead, and only then do I become a part of the spiritual body, which, by its progression into the Zamani, comes close to God.

Mbiti sets out to show that existence is apprehended by the African in traditional society in such a way that the immediate future is the only future perspective that exists. Consequently, in traditional religions there is no prophetism and no future paradise. For time—to use Western terms—recedes rather than progresses and the Golden Age—that era of the black man's greatness—the era of Timbuctoo and Benin, the era of the Yoruba and the Zulu, of Shango and Chaka, lies in the Zamani period. The Sasa is an ever-constant construction of the past and not of the future. Utopia exists in the past.

It is interesting that if one examines the works of Senghor and Césaire it becomes evident that they are characterised by elements peculiar to the Zamani period. The revalorisation of African artistic and humanistic values coincides inevitably with the creation of a myth superimposed on African history. It is difficult to say which comes first since

revalorisation and myth are interwoven to the point of identification, one with the other.

The references in Césaire's *Return to my Native Land* to the periods of African greatness are many and there is a defiant insistence on the value of what may well be lost completely for most West Indians and for many Africans. One cannot do better than quote this very famous passage:

> I refuse to pass my swellings off for authentic glories. And I laugh at my old childish imaginings.
>
> No, we have never been amazons at the court of the King of Dahomey, nor princes of Ghana with eight hundred camels, nor doctors at Timbuctoo when Askia the Great was king, nor architects at Djenné, nor Madhis, nor warriors. We do not feel in our armpits the itch of those who once carried the lance. (*Return to my Native Land*)

Césaire's theatre is placed entirely out of the context of the Caribbean of today. Of four plays he has written only one is concerned directly with a twentieth-century figure—Patrice Lumumba. The Congo is geographically very far from Martinique and from the author's socio-cultural situation in Paris. Lumumba's Congo is no nearer Césaire's Sasa than is King Christophe's Haiti.

Senghor's poems convey an attitude and an atmosphere that are different. But this *normalien* living in Paris and writing of a traditional African society is in fact looking back to what is another age and another place in terms of his evolution within the Western European world. Like so many African and Caribbean writers he is at a great distance in terms of space and time from his subject.

This brings to mind the story of Camara Laye and the composition of *L'Enfant Noir,* translated variously as *The African Child* and *The Black Child.* At the time of writing, Laye was experiencing the solitude and misery of the black worker in France. He would work in the factory during the day and return alone to the Africa he was trying to recreate for himself in his cold, barren room. The result is stunning in its stark simplicity but it is the fruit of a very painful period of parturition.

Senghor, the intellectual, has long left this stage behind him. He does not battle against being an *assimilado* and accepts his cultural *métissage* and is proud of it. In an article entitled 'On the Freedom of the Soul or the Praises of Métissage' which appeared in the October 1950 issue of *Liberté de l'Esprit,* Senghor reminds us that most great civilisations have depended on the grafting of culture on culture to reach their high stage of development. Africans should therefore take advantage of this opportunity in cultural development being offered by the European colonisation of their native land. The same idea is repeated several times in his essays and speeches. In the 1956 Conference of Black Writers and Artists, held at the Sorbonne, a lively discussion developed between the Afro-Americans and Antilleans on the one hand and the Africans on the other. Here is part of Senghor's contribution to the discussion:

> So we, too, are objectively half-castes. And this is where I would quarrel with Césaire while

agreeing with him. Today we are objectively half-castes . . . much of the reasoning of French Africans derives from Descartes. This is why, quite often, you don't follow us, as we don't altogether follow you, because you, like the Anglo-Saxons, are pragmatists. (Taken from *Prose and Poetry*)

However, since Senghor can declare:

I think in French; I express myself in French better than in my mother tongue. (*Négritude et Humanisme*)

in that famous essay published in *Esprit,* he has evidently been a victim of the acculturation which appears to have been the aim of the French educational system in Africa. This cultural imperialism serves to make the victim nostalgic and sentimental about a past that still exists in the present reality of the mass of his brothers.

In terms of space and time the writer is so far removed from the reality of his people that having lived in Western society and having been assimilated by its values, the African has moved out of his traditional ecological milieu, out of the socio-cultural structure of his people and he has begun to move forward in time.

This movement can best be illustrated by referring to the first novel of Olympe Bhêly-Quénum, *Un Piege sans Fin.* The novel is divided into two main parts. In the first half the hero, Ahouna, is living in the village of Kiniba with his people. Apart from brief but always tragic intrusions of white colonisers or of people who have had too much contact with them, the scene is as peaceful and dignified as in Camara's novel *The African Child.* Ahouna leaves Kiniba through a series of quite unacceptable events which also, incidentally, have their origin in the South of Dahomey, that part directly under the influence of whites. Ahouna leaves his native milieu for the first time travelling very far among peoples whose tongue he cannot understand and coming increasingly into contact with the technological manifestations of White Power. Once he enters this world and then the structured, brutal world of the French coloniser, events seem to leap at him and he is forever trailing behind situations which overtake him in a world where eyes are rigidly fixed on a destination, in terms of space, and on an aim, in terms of time. He is totally *dépaysé.*

What I am attempting to show is that the concept of Négritude is the direct product of a successful process of acculturation undertaken by the European in Africa. It is an intellectual concept that has nothing to do with the existential reality of the mass of black men. It is the means of integrating alienated man in the security of a myth that he has created for his own benefit and for that of his social class.

The individualism peculiar to the exercise is the antithesis of the authentic cultural values of Africa where art is for the largest possible group but yet not vulgarised. The oral tradition in literature is a community participatory exercise. Dance and sculpture, by their very nature, are community-oriented activities. Aesthetics for its own sake is a nonsense and absurd since man as a collective being is

forever at the centre of artistic expression. The esoteric nature of Césaire's writings leaves no doubt about the individualism of his work. His intellectualisation and mythification of the black man's reality further alienate him from his brothers with whom he can feel only an intellectual solidarity.

The black man in the tramway, shunned by Césaire, serves as a catalyst in *Return to my Native Land.* Césaire awakens to the reality of his blackness and to the universality of his Négritude. However, his predilection for the fine French phrase, the obscure word that frequently sends even the educated reader vainly searching in his dictionary, this parade of Western European erudition that Frantz Fanon analyses so well in *Black Skin, White Masks,* serves only to remove him yet further from his people. Indeed he appears to be writing not for them but for a white public.

> le bulbe tératique de la nuit, germé de nos bas-
> sesses et de nos renoncements.
> (the monstrous bulb of the night, germinated
> from all our meanness and renunciations.)
> . . . . .
> Passes août où les manguiers pavoisent de toutes
> leurs lunules, septembre l'accoucheur de cy-
> clones, octobre le flambeur de cannes, novem-
> bre qui ronronne aux distilleries, c'était Noël
> qui commençait.
>
> (August when the mango-trees sport moons:
> September-midwife of cyclones: October-
> burning sugar-cane, November which purrs in
> the stills. And now Christmas beginning.)
> . . . . .
> Iles annelées, unique carène belle
> Et je te caresse de mes mains d'océan. Et je te
> vire
> de mes paroles alizées. Et je te lèche de mes
> langues d'algues.
> Et je te cingle hors-flibuste
>
> O mort ton palud pâteux!
> Naufrage ton enfer de débris! j'accepte!
>
> (Ringed islands, only lovely keel
> I caress you with my ocean hands. I swing you
> round
> with my trade-wind words. I lick you with my
> algae tongues.
> I raid you without thought of gain.
>
> The furred swamp of death!
> The fragments of shipwrecks! I accept!)
>
> 　　　　　　　　　　(*Return* . . .)
> 　　　　　　　　　　　　(pp. 65-73)

Both Césaire and Senghor project themselves in another country and at another period which is no longer theirs. For Senghor thinks of a way of life now lost for him among his Serere people. Césaire looks towards a traditional African life that he cannot know and towards periods of the past when Africans governed Africa and when Africans liberated themselves of a foreign yoke in Haiti. Both men are looking towards a utopian state.

I am not trying to say that Senghor and Césaire are completely oblivious to every aspect of the black man's reality. But as a map is an abstraction of a city, province or country, the economic and political awareness of problems is an intellectualisation and institutionalisation of social reality.

Négritude is then a new religion of the middle-class black intellectual and as such it dulls his sense of reality. His eyes are firmly fixed on a utopian period although he can hear the cries of anguish of his brothers struggling through their present reality. But the Western-educated intellectual is also future-oriented and yet another myth is the implication that the Zamani Utopia may return, and the Utopia is the myth that the humanistic values of Négritude will prevail and that eventually, a harmonious universal civilisation will evolve, deeply impregnated with the sap of African cultural and moral values. Western philosophies—Marxist as well as Christian—have led black intellectuals to these conclusions. Angela Davis and Martin Luther King have very much in common.

Western religious philosophy has ensnared the black man into a belief in dialectical or evolutionary processes towards universal harmony where eventually he will be assimilated or integrated. But assimilated and integrated into what? If the black man does become integrated into Western European thought patterns and humanistic values, as Césaire and Senghor have been, then he becomes alienated or a man divided against himself—whichever terminology one prefers.

Léopold Sédar Senghor on Negritude, colonialism, and the "Civilization of the Universal":

[The values of Negritude] must flow toward the meeting point of all humanity; they must be our contribution to the Civilization of the Universal.

Biological miscegenation . . . takes place spontaneously, provoked by the very laws which govern life, and in the face of all policies of apartheid. It is a different matter in the realm of culture. Here, we remain wholly free to cooperate or not, to provoke or prevent the synthesis of cultures. This is an important point. For, as certain biologists point out, the psychological mutations brought about by education are incorporated in our genes and are then transmitted by heredity. Hence the major role played by *Culture*.

Seen within this prospect of the Civilization of the Universal, the colonial policies of Great Britain and France have proved successful complements to each other, and black Africa has benefited. The policies of the former tended to reinforce the traditional native civilization. As for France's policy, although we have often reviled it in the past, it too ended with a credit balance, through forcing us actively to assimilate European civilization. This fertilized our sense of Negritude. Today our Negritude no longer expresses itself as opposition to European values, but as a *complement* to them. Henceforth, its militants will be concerned, as I have often said, *not to be assimilated, but to assimilate*. They will use European values to arouse the slumbering values of Negritude, which they will bring as their contribution to the Civilization of the Universal.

Léopold Sédar Senghor, in his "What Is 'Negritude?',” in Atlas, January 1962.

The concept of Négritude cannot be the answer to any situation pertaining to the reality of the black masses. It is a fine idea, useful and necessary to the cultural development of a Western-educated elite. It is also perhaps a necessary stage in a true renaissance of African culture so long devastated or bastardised by ignorance and prejudice. But at best today Négritude seems no more than yet another of Western Europe's philosophic aberrations. (pp. 73-4)

Frederick Ivor Case, "Négritude and Utopianism," in African Literature Today, *No. 7, 1975, pp. 65-75.*

Eric Sellin

[*Sellin is an American educator, poet, and critic. In the following essay, he compares several definitions of Negritude.*]

The Barbadian novelist, George Lamming, once described the twofold plight of the African or Afro-Caribbean writer in an emerging nation or in a period of growing national awareness:

> . . . I am aware of a dual challenge. The first difficulty is whether I as novelist-critic can overcome the demands of that special subjectivity which orders my view. The second difficulty lies in the complex ramifications of the term *négritude*. ["Caribbean Literature: The Black Rock of Africa," *African Forum* (Spring 1966)]

These two areas are mutually self-canceling and self-stimulating. This sounds like a contradiction, and it is one. In fact, one must recognize, with Lamming, that the critic of *négritude* "is dealing with a concept whose ideological content has defied precise definition." The problem of definition is relatively simple until one begins to consider the application of the word in separate political or cultural cases. We shall take a look at some of the principal adoptions of the term *négritude*, but I should first like to examine the term in a theoretical context, namely in terms of the contradiction already mentioned. Thus, certain problems of definition will arise or obtain whether the term itself is *négritude, mélanisme, tigritude, négristique, zébrisme*, or any other word which functions at once as a deductive label and a politically expedient "-ism."

Historically the dual challenge referred to by Lamming has functioned as a scale upon which a writer's relative political commitment or acquiescence might be weighed. Lack of involvement is associated with the "Uncle Tom" who aspires to pass as a white writer without giving due thought to the idea that a white writer subconsciously creates out of his *whiteness* and any attempt to counterfeit his whiteness is, no doubt, an economically and socially motivated act rather than a well-thought-out formula for optimum aesthetic fulfilment. Etienne Léro described the monstrous "outsider" in *Légitime Défense*, the pioneer journal whose single issue appeared in Paris in 1932:

> D'être un bon décalque d'homme pâle lui tient
> lieu de raison sociale aussi bien que de raison

poétique. . . . "Tu fais comme un nègre," ne
manque-t-il pas de s'indigner si, en sa présence,
vous cédez à une exubérance naturelle. Aussi
bien ne veut-il pas dans ses vers "faire comme un
nègre." Il se fait un point d'honneur qu'un blanc
puisse lire tout son livre sans deviner sa pigmentation.

This attitude is not a simple matter, being a product of the
self-hatred which the colonized individual feels after hundreds of years of humiliation. As Abiola Irele has put it,
"The cultural and political ascendancy of the white man
over the black man, combined with the active denigration
of the black man, has thus had the effect of vitiating the
latter's self-esteem, with profound psychological consequences, which involve shame and self-hatred" ["Négritude—Literature and Ideology," *Journal of Modern African Studies* (1965)].

Much of the driving force in many Francophone African
and Caribbean poems is in the statement of and flight from
this humiliation. Historically the colonized black and, especially, the black sold into slavery in the Americas were
permitted to retain little of the dignity of their elders in
the tribes in the ancient kingdoms of Africa: "Et ce pays
cria pendant des siècles que nous sommes des bêtes brutes;
que les pulsations de l'humanité s'arrêtent aux portes de
la négrerie; que nous sommes un fumier ambulant
hideusement prometteur de cannes tendues et de coton
soyeux et l'on nous marquait au fer rouge et nous dor-
mions dans nos excréments et l'on nous vendait sur les
places . . ." [Aimé Césaire, *Cahier d'un retour au pays
natal*].

It may be that Léro and Césaire would tell Lamming to
make no effort to overcome the "special subjectivity"
which orders his view. It is also possible that the subjectivity indicates the complex nexus of factors contributing to
his view, including reprehensible as well as noble urges,
and that the way to overcoming the challenge is through
authenticity and self-assertion. Self-analysis is a prerequisite to authenticity and self-analysis leads to other things
as well. In the colonial situation self-analysis leads to the
will for political freedom through a deep awareness of social and racial injustices inherent in colonization and, especially, the slave trade. Thus *négritude*—being a self-
assertion which is based both on self-evident truths (such
as a black man's averment that he is black) and on a political platform for equality, independence, and self-
government—will permit the writer to overcome his "special subjectivity." It is, in a sense, the old saw: "If you
can't beat 'em, join 'em." By becoming what he in fact is,
by willing himself to be what he cannot avoid being, the
black writer can rally his cultural and political forces for
the long pull to liberation and independence. Thus, since
the "complex ramifications of the term *négritude*" provide
a number of complex behavioral options to him who has
perceived the over-all network of ramifications, Lamming's equation is, in a sense, $1 + 1 = 0$ at the same time
that it is $1 + 1 = 2$.

It is clear that *négritude* involves modality if we go beyond
the most simplistic definition of it as a description of color.
The modality is precisely the cause of differences in opinion regarding proper definition of the term. As long as one
describes a static or physical abstraction or generality
there can be a degree of coincidence of minds, but when
one moves into the modal abstraction he encounters attitudes and behavioral patterns predicated on a spectrum of
interpretations and applications of the abstraction varying
from cosmologies to political activism. If one accepts these
dynamics as the catalytic ingredient in *négritude* it becomes clear how views as opposing as those of Senghor or
Dadié and Andrade or Soyinka can and do make use of
the same term or, if they decline the term, make use of the
dynamics. If there was an attempt during the Festival held
in Algiers in the summer of 1969 to bury the term *négritude* in favor of *mélanisme* or some other term, it was not
because of a concern for the lexicological exactitude but
rather for the political dynamics of the word. *Négritude*
does, by definition, exclude most North Africans—
although one might include people like the Tuaregs—and
this exclusion is contrary to the spirit in which the Festival
was planned and the reason for which Algeria wished to
host it. The desire for change was, no doubt, motivated by
a wish to alter or expand the political dynamics inherent
in the word; in this case in order to permit Algeria to share
in, if not control, the movement. Some critics say that pan-
Islamism is here taking sway over pan-Africanism, but
one thing is clear: the shift was perpetrated not in order
to relax or expand the linguistic definition but rather to
broaden the geographical base of the political dynamics
which have accrued to the modality discussed here.

Certainly even the most evanescent definition of *négritude*
has political implications: this is in the nature of the word
itself, for without a political motivation and without an
ambivalent cultural proximity with and social inferiority
to the white man, the black man would never have felt the
need to assert his blackness nor his freedom. As a number
of intellectuals from Frobenius to Fanon have pointed out,
the white man created the black man. This fact has even
formed the basis for a philosophical definition of *négritude*. In his interesting study, *De la négritude*, Thomas
Melone posits a dynamics of *négritude* of his own—valid
in the framework of his exposition but quite different from
the dynamics I suggest in this study—based on a series of
polarities (absence-presence, Black-White, negation-
affirmation, etc.) whose magnetic forces create fields of
anxiety, "ennui," dissatisfaction, and so forth, and whose
resolution is at once the birth and goal of *négritude*:

> C'est la privation de toute direction morale, de
> tout axe de référence dans la vie—l'inquiétude—
> qui avait fait jaillir la source de la conscience
> nègre. Celle-ci se veut à la fois réponse et ques-
> tion. La Négritude fournit une réponse au
> monde nègre dans sa recherche angoissée de sa
> propre image. Elle pose une question au monde
> Blanc, jadis dominateur et porte contre lui un té-
> moignage parfois accablant devant le tribunal de
> l'histoire. Elle figure enfin cette distance im-
> matérielle qui sépare et unit à la fois le monde
> Noir et le monde Blanc.

Those who contend that *négritude* is essentially a spiritual
quality should consider the fact that in the recent period
of political effervescence in Africa and the Caribbean the
amount of creative activity representing the cultural wing
of *négritude* has multiplied dramatically. In his preface to

a collection of articles by Angolans published in 1901, António José do Nascimento wrote:

> Parmi les Noirs qui ont été déportés au Brésil depuis le XVIIe siècle . . . aucun n'en est revenu avec un haut niveau de culture. D'où il faut conclure que seule l'instruction combinée avec la liberte peuvent engendrer des besoins pour le travail et la prospérité de la province. . . . Dans un pays où règne l'esclavage, il ne saurait y avoir de travail, ni civilisation, ni de progrès.

Even the most militantly committed explicator of *négritude* would not in good conscience claim that liberation automatically brings about a flourishing in national literature. As Mário de Andrade points out in his introduction to the French edition of his anthology of African poetry of Portuguese expression, "Il est à peine besoin de noter que la recouvrance de la souveraineté nationale ne suscite pas automatiquement une élévation du niveau de la création artistique." Furthermore, when there is a considerable increase in artistic works in these conditions—as in Algeria during and immediately following the revolution—many of the texts lack aesthetic distinction. However, even treated lightly, the works exist and they bespeak a mingling of the political and cultural interpretations of *négritude*. It is useful to quote George Lamming once again in this context and, although he is referring to English-language Caribbean literature, the phenomenon he speaks of is based on a truth which, though seldom so dramatically, still characterizes all the other new literatures in vehicular languages in Africa, the Malagasy Republic, the Antilles, and Guiana:

> After three centuries of colonization, these islands could make no claim to an indigenous achievement, however minor in the literary arts. As late as the 1930s there could not have been more than half-a-dozen books of imaginative literature written about these islands by people who were representative of, and rooted in, that soil. But within fifteen years after World War II, there were to appear in England about two hundred such books, which were the work of just over twenty West Indian writers.
>
> I don't think it is an accident that this kind of creative literary explosion took place when it did. Its source may be found in the collective grievances that were beginning to bear fruit through political action. I, for example, clearly remember being surprised, terrified, and exhilarated by the violence of speech with which simple, anonymous men threatened the traditional agents of power in my island.

And the fact remains that, despite centuries of foreign presence and indoctrination, the colonial relationship took much and gave little and the vehicular literatures of the ex-colonies are, with few exceptions, barely thirty or forty years old. I should like to consider briefly, at this point, the term *négritude* from an historical viewpoint.

The dynamics of *négritude* came into being well before the term existed. Since the act of colonization from the outset provokes "collective grievances" and a growing national awareness—unified and magnified by the *lingua franca* of

the colonialist's language—it may be said that just as the white man has created the black man, so colonialism creates nationalism. The dynamics of *négritude* are, therefore, several hundred years old; before which there simply existed people who functioned as best they could in their environments on the basis of autochthonous traditions. The contact with white civilization marks the inception of the concept of *négritude;* as Sartre has said, "c'est au choc de la culture blanche que sa négritude est passée de l'existence immédiate à l'état réfléchi" ["Orphée noir," in *Anthologie de la nouvelle poésie nègre et malgache de langue française* (1948)]. The dynamics only flowered into a distinctive literature, however, in the early 1930s. It was not long, then, in finding a name. Two Paris journals, *Légitime Défense* (1932) and *L'Etudiant Noir* (1934-40), functioned as a focal point for the young intellectuals from French Africa and the West Indies, and indirectly prepared the ground; the term *négritude* was born under the pen of Aimé Césaire. In his explosive epic, *Cahier d'un retour au pays natal,* first published in 1939, Césaire wrote: "ma négritude n'est ni une tour ni une cathédrale / elle plonge dans la chair rouge du sol."

Although the word did not come into being until 1939, after which it was quickly adopted by Senghor and others, *négritude* discovered its poetic formula in 1937 in the little collection of poems by Léon Damas entitled *Pigments.* While his contemporaries were still groping for ways to social and political self-discovery or were writing neo-Parnassian verse in the vein of Baudelaire and Leconte de Lisle, Damas opted for an authenticity which, at the time, was considered not only unpoetic but in poor taste. *Pigments* fell like a bombshell in the literary circles of Paris—exciting, upsetting, disgusting, or enthralling blacks and whites alike. The few samples found in this study will give an inkling of the collection's stark simplicity, stripped syntax, its indebtedness to the American black and its frank personal content which could not help but ultimately prevail over the neo-romantic poems in vogue till then. Here is the close of a poem from *Pigments* entitled "La Complainte du nègre":

> Va encore mon hébétude du temps jadis
> de
> coups de corde noueux de corps calcinés
> de l'orteil au dos calcinés
> de chair morte de tisons de fier rouge de bras
> brisés sous le fouet qui se déchaîne sous le fouet
>   qui fait
> marcher la plantation s'abreuver de sang
> de mon sang de sang la sucrerie
> et la bouffarde du commandeur crâner au ciel.

As is so often the case with panacea labels, the meaning of *négritude* was ambivalent in the very beginning. Like Cubist, Fauve, or Beatnik, the name contained a certain pejorative element: "c'est au moment où groupés derrière l'étendard de la liberté et de l'égalité, la grande majorité de l'humanité se dresse pour endiguer et balayer le déferlement envahisseur et esclavagiste de l'hitlérisme, que des Négro-africains créent le terme de *Négritude*—terme d'ailleurs laid et choquant et voulu comme tel—et lui donnent la signification quasi-romantique et sentimentale d'une expression humaine spécifiquement nègre" (Melone). In the half-dozen times that the word *négritude* is used by Césaire in *Cahier d'un retour au pays natal* it has slightly different implications. It is used first historically in an apparent reference to Toussaint Louverture: "Haïti où la négritude se mit debout pour la première fois et dit qu'elle croyait à son humanité . . . "

The description of a poor Negro in the tram—who inspires disgust and, no doubt, a degree of self-disgust mingled with superiority in Césaire who is then ashamed of his own shame—tends to contaminate the word *négritude* when it appears in that context: "Son nez qui semblait une péninsule en dérade et sa négritude même qui se décolorait sous l'action d'une inlassable mégie."

The suffering associated with the white man's view and treatment of the black man, especially the one who through slavery was wrenched from his home and his own society, is crystallized in the word *nègre:*

> (les nègres-sont-tous-les-mêmes, je-vous-le-dis
> les vices-tous-les-vices, c'est-moi-qui-vous-le-dis
> l'odeur-du-nègre, ça-fait-pousser-la-canne
> rappelez-vous-le-vieux-dicton:
> battre-un-nègre, c'est le nourrir).

One writer [Lamming] has observed three elements in the West Indian creative imagination: embarrassment, ambivalence, and a sense of possibility. The above associations with the word *nègre* were bound to give the word *négritude* its share of negative connotations, and it was in part a yardstick of "collective grievances" whose rectification was, no doubt, one of the aims of *négritude* as a "possibility." Césaire describes this yardstick eloquently:

> j'accepte
>
> et la détermination de ma biologie, non prisonnière d'un angle facial, d'une forme de cheveux, d'un nez suffisamment aplati, d'un teint suffisament mélanien, et la négritude, non plus un indice céphalique, ou un plasma, ou un soma, mais mesurée au compas de la souffrance.

The inherited embarrassment and ambivalence of the colonized African writer has, since 1932, yielded to a definition of *négritude* in which the imagination senses possibilities. Possibilities are multifarious, obviously, and with this new stage we move out of pure biological or historical measurement into modality. This sense of possibility took many artistic and philosophical—whence political— forms. The greatest difference in expressions was certainly that between Africans and West Indians. The former were colonized, the latter enslaved and transported out of their homelands. Both experienced a form of exile, but the means to rediscovery had to be, perforce, quite different. With independence, the African regained his sovereignty; with abolition the slave in the New World knew only token emancipation and a continued social exile. Césaire sadly evokes the splendor of pre-colonial Africa which the West Indian cannot strive to regain:

> Non, nous n'avons jamais été amazones du roi du Dahomey, ni princes de Ghana avec huit cents chameaux, ni docteurs à Tombouctou, Askia le Grand étant roi, ni architectes de Djénné, ni Madhis, ni guerriers. Nous ne nous sen-

tons pas sous l'aisselle la démangeaison de ceux qui tinrent jadis la lance. Et puisque j'ai juré de ne rien celer de notre histoire (moi qui n'admire rien tant que le mouton broutant son ombre d'après-midi), je veux avouer que nous fûmes de tout temps d'assez piètres laveurs de vaisselle, des cireurs de chaussures sans envergure . . .

But if the trauma of a violent uprooting, an arduous, oft-fatal trans-Atlantic voyage in chains below deck, and subsequent enslavement and servitude permanently set the African in the New World physically and emotionally apart from his brothers at home, he still retained his origins to some degree. As Austin J. Shelton has said [in *The African Assertion* (1968)], "The 'old' life still exists within the African, whether he is 'acculturated' or not, or to whatever degree he has been assimilated by European culture." One can get a good idea of the extent to which Africa's image, though distorted by subcultural factors, has remained in the psyche of the West Indian or Afro-American from *Muntu* by Janheinz Jahn. One of the most valuable contributions of this highly controversial work is the lengthy tracing of African customs into the contemporary New World black man's dance, religion, philosophy, and music.

The sense of possibility has taken two tangible forms in literature and criticism, one retrospective, the other forward-looking; that is, rediscovery of ancient values and an effort to pull abreast of the modern technological societies of the world. These two areas are in conflict to some extent and that conflict contributes to the ambivalence of the term *négritude*. Lilyan Kesteloot writes:

> Bien sûr on peut croire que la technique et la science rendront toutes les civilisations identiques. Mais alors pourquoi les cultures chinoise, russe et américaine, allemande et japonaise, française et anglaise, ne sont-elles pas déjà identiques puisqu'elles ont le même niveau technique et des systèmes économiques analogues? [. . .]
>
> La civilisation africaine n'est donc pas destinée à périr parce qu'elle se modernise. La négritude non plus.

There is a fundamental flaw here. Since African civilization is not traditionally scientific, it will, strictly speaking, perish upon modernization. One cannot alter radically without destroying what previously existed. Furthermore, there is, it seems to me, a basic difference between the Greco-Roman technical society which has put improvement at a premium, and African society which has tended to relate itself to that which surrounds it already. This is reflected in the cosmologies and tales of the genesis. In European religions there is generally a belief that a primal god *created* man and the universe and thus is an external force, meaning that our environment is susceptible to manipulation, experimentation. In many African religions man appeared by some sort of spontaneous generation, found in a fish net, bursting out of a reed, or the like. Thus there is generally an *eternal* quality to man and the universe and these are not subject to manipulation without risking the wrath of the spirits in them. This perhaps explains the lack of progressiveness in traditional African culture. Just as Kesteloot groups France and Russia, she might associate Gambia and Upper Volta, for the questions here raised pertain to cultures, not nations.

Négritude is, in the case of many poets, equated with a rediscovery of the pre-colonial values or, in the New World, a re-affirmation of the link with the generic "Guinée" or African homeland. The degree of exile varies. Césaire is from Martinique; Damas is Guianese and, furthermore, a *métis* of African, Indian, and European stock; David Diop's parents were from Senegal and Cameroon but he was born in Bordeaux. The rediscovery of Africa is, then, a device to achieve self-respect and is thus a subcategory of *négritude*.

The rediscovery of Africa was naturally more intense in the early period of *négritude* in the 1930s and 40s and it is natural that her image should have been both oversimplified and romanticized, a trend which later elicited an equally understandable counter-reaction. Césaire's most significant adoption of the word *négritude* in *Cahier d'un retour au pays natal* is used in this context, implying not only a spiritual relationship with Africa, but also a fundamental animism in the black *Weltanschauung:*

> Ceux qui n'ont inventé ni la poudre ni la boussole
> ceux qui n'ont jamais su dompter la vapeur ni l'électricité
> ceux qui n'ont exploré ni les mers ni le ciel
> mais ils savent en ses moindres recoint le pays de souffrance
> ceux qui n'ont connu de voyages que de déracinements
> ceux qui se sont assoupis aux agenouillements
> ceux qu'on domestiqua et christianisa
> ceux qu'on inocula d'abâtardissement
> tams-tams de mains vides
> tams-tams inanes de plaies sonores
> tams-tams burlesques de trahison tabis
>
> Tiède petit matin de chaleurs et de peurs ancestrales
> par dessus bord mes richesses pérégrines
> par dessus bord mes faussetés authentiques
> Mais quel étrange orgueil tout soudain m'illumine?
> . . . . .
> ma négritude n'est pas une pierre, sa surdité ruée contre la clameur du jour
> ma négritude n'est pas une taie d'eau morte sur l'œil mort de la terre
> ma négritude n'est ni une tour ni une cathédrale
>
> elle plonge dans la chair rouge du sol
> elle plonge dans la chair ardente du ciel
> elle troue l'accablement opaque de sa droite patience
>
> Eia pour le Kaïlcédrat royal!
> Eia pour ceux qui n'ont jamais rien inventé
> pour ceux qui n'ont jamais rien exploré
> pour ceux qui n'ont jamais rien dompté
>
> mais ils s'abandonnent, saisis, à l'essence de toute chose
> ignorants des surfaces mais saisis par le mouvement de toute chose
> insoucieux de dompter, mais jouant le jeu du monde . . .

Négritude in this context was personally salubrious before it was political, although, as I have already mentioned, the appearance of self-respect in a humiliating environment is political since it will naturally lead to revolt. There has to be first an individual, internal, transfiguration—a "strange pride" which suddenly illuminates the individual. This moment is described both by Césaire, in *Cahier d'un retour au pays natal:* "Par une inattendue et bienfaisante révolution intérieure, j'honore maintenant mes laideurs repoussantes"; and by Damas, in a poem entitled "Savoir-vivre":

> On ne bâille pas chez moi comme ils bâillent chez eux
> avec la main sur la bouche
> je veux bâiller sans tralalas
> le corps recroquevillé
> dans les parfums qui tourmentent la vie
> que je me suis faite
> de leur museau de chien d'hiver
> de leur soleil qui ne pourrait pas même tiédir
> l'eau de coco qui faisait glouglou dans mon ventre au réveil
>
> Laissez-moi bâiller la main
> là
> sur le cœur
> à l'obsession de tout ce à quoi j'ai en un jour donné le dos.

If the newly self-discovered Africans and West Indians felt alienated from the white man's world:

> J'ai l'impression d'être ridicule
> dans leurs souliers dans leur smoking
> dans leur plastron dans leur faux col
> dans leur monocle dans leur melon

they were also alienated to some degree from their birthright culture, the Africans being less radically cut-off than those exiled to the New World. The unfamiliarity the writers—who had been the most intensively subjected to European cultural influence—had with their own heritage caused them to approach Mother Africa with a mixture of romanticism and disappointment. After all, when Damas turned his back on European culture, he wanted the alternative to be a satisfying one. The romanticism inevitably led to disappointment and a radical reassessment on the part of some writers who had to adjust their concept of *négritude* to fit the real situation.

For many years, interpretations of *négritude* tended to conform to the spirit in which Aimé Césaire first intended the term and in which Senghor has consistently used it: that is, *négritude* is the sum total of things which make up the black man in African and attendant cultures. Furthermore, *négritude* denoted a *mystique,* a timeless innate quality which the black man possesses and which he alone possesses. This anthropological approach characterizes the criticism and aesthetics of Senghor and, to a lesser degree, the other poets of his generation. Lilyan Kesteloot describes *négritude* as follows: "On peut dire, comme définition générale, que la négritude est la façon dont les Négro-Africains comprennent l'univers, c'est-à-dire le monde qui les entoure, la nature, les gens, les événements: c'est aussi la façon dont ils créent."

Although, as I have already indicated, the concept of *négritude* was centuries in the making and is specifically associated, as a coinage, with several writers, the best known, most eloquent, and most frequently attacked elucidator of the term is Léopold Sédar Senghor. A member of the Césaire-Damas-Senghor *troika* which gave impetus to and explanation of the word *négritude* both as fact and as idea, Senghor has continued unstintingly to write apologias of the Negro-African mentality or personality, or what he has called "psychophysiology."

Senghor's view of *négritude* lies at one pole of the anthropological-empirical spectrum of definitions of the African mentality and at times it approaches the mystical:

> Nous avons vu, plus haut, l'importance de la religion chez le Noir et que le trait le plus caractéristique de son âme était le *sens du divin.* Si nous en regardons le côté terrestre, nous retrouvons le même *sens du surréel.* C'est artificiellement que nous distinguons la religion, la famille, l'Etat, la société, car ce qui s'impose à son âme, despotiquement, c'est l'*unité du monde,* l'unité de la vie. ["L'Afrique noire: La Civilisation négro-africaine," in *Négritude et humanisme* (1964)]

His view is expressed throughout his writings, but most emphatically and persuasively in two essays entitled "L'Esthétique négro-africaine" and "Comme les lamantins vont boire à la source," first published in the journal *Diogènes* and as a postface to *Ethiopiques* respectively and later collected in Senghor's *Liberté I: Négritude et humanisme.* A definition of *négritude* which Senghor is wont to give is that it is "l'ensemble des valeurs culturelles du monde noir." This is a safe, broad-base definition which does not, in fact, reveal the poet's basic view. A careful reading of his essays reveals that, if Senghor does not limit his definition to art, literature, and philosophy, these at least are the foundation, cornerstone, and keystone of the definition. Senghor repeatedly suggests that *négritude* describes the black man's soul and is based on his lingua-ontology:

> Singulièrement en Afrique noire, où la *Parole,* enfermée dans le sein de Dieu, était au commencement de toutes choses, engendrant toutes choses, création et expression de toutes choses. En Afrique noire, la *Mythologie de la Parole* domine tous les mythes, qui traduisent l'*ontologie* négro-africaine. Les ethnographes en ont, maintenant, conscience, qui placent l'*ethnologie de la Parole* au centre de leurs recherches.

On the basis of the African's sensual relationship with his environment, Senghor has concluded that the predominant trait of the black man's soul is his sense of the divine. This sense of the divine is extended by Senghor in several directions to become—after adaptation—philosophy, aesthetics, ethics, or politics. All of these categories are thus more or less based, in Senghor's *Weltanschauung,* or "attitude affective à l'égard du monde," on a metaphysical understanding of Man and the Universal. He summed it up in a speech delivered at the Sorbonne in April, 1961:

> Eh bien! la Négritude, c'est, essentiellement, cette chaleur humaine, qui est *présence à la vie:*

au monde. C'est un *existentialisme,* pour parler comme vous, enraciné dans la Terre-Mère, épanoui au soleil de la Foi. Cette présence au monde est *participation du sujet à l'objet,* participation de l'Homme aux Forces cosmiques, *communion* de l'Homme avec les autres hommes et, par-delà, avec tous les *existants,* du caillou à Dieu. Ici, connaissance, art et action sont liés par des échanges fulgurants. La connaissance s'exprime non en chiffres algébriques, mais en œuvres d'art, en images rythmées, où le symbole n'est pas *signe,* mais *sens* identificateur. Et l'œuvre d'art, parce que fonctionnelle, est action efficace. Telle est cette *Civilisation de l'Unité par symbiose, par symbole.* L'individu s'y réalise en *personne* par et dans la société. Une société qui n'est pas collectiviste, c'est-à-dire agrégat hétéroclite d'individus, mais *communielle,* je veux dire un peuple tendu vers le même but, animé de la même foi.

> Ce ne sont pas là vues abstraites. Vous-mêmes parlez, maintenant, d'une connaissance par participation et communion. Vos artistes entendent traduire les forces cosmiques sous forme de couleurs et de rythmes.

The idea of *négritude* has, since the "heroic period" of the 1930s and the onrush of independence movements of the 1960s, taken on a different meaning for the poets and intellectuals who feel that they are, by age group and by New-Left inclination, a part of this new age rather than the age preceding whose anthropological idea of *négritude* they reject. They reject it largely because they contend that Europeans and their indoctrinated African brothers have created this inductive viewpoint as a quaint idea for their delectation and exploitation. Yambo Ouologuem writes in *Lettre à la France nègre:*

> Si la *négritude,* cependant, vaut toujours parce qu'elle est un cadre auquel il reste encore à donner meilleur contenu, ce contenu ne saurait être que s'il n'érige pas des autels et des statues à cent mythes, qui ne répondent et n'ont jamais correspondu à quoi que ce soit de vivant en Afrique: foire aux chimères où s'est exaltée l'imagination de plus d'un marchand d'idéologie, échafaudant mille impostures dont le mérite—peut-être—est de rassurer, à la Bourse des valeurs de la primitivité, tous les petits rentiers de la tragi-comédie . . .

> En vérité, ceux-là qui (journalistes, sociologues, ethnologues, africanistes, littérateurs et négrophiles "spécialisés") chercheraient à rêver l'Afrique à la mesure de leur bonne conscience, je les soupçonne de vouloir—sous prétexte fallacieux de la servir—l'encapsuler dans *le génie de la littéralité.*

Thus, a number of the younger African writers feel that the idea of an innate, anthropological quality, as expounded by Senghor and others, is a bit of inappropriate romanticism on the part of white scholars and some of their misguided black brothers, as well as a subtle form of segregation and paternalism. Ezekiel Mphahlele has said, in this matter:

> Who is so stupid as to deny the historical fact of

négritude as both a protest and a positive assertion of African cultural values? All this is valid. What I do not accept is the way in which too much of the poetry inspired by it romanticizes Africa as a symbol of innocence, purity and artless primitiveness. I feel insulted when some people imply that Africa is not also a violent continent. I am also a violent person and proud of it because it is often a healthy state of mind.

The earlier definitions of *négritude*—whether interpreted in the neutral sense of the "sum total of the cultural values of the black world" or as a *mystique* involving special rapports with nature, animism, and a cosmic intent in the practice of art—have been thrown out by most English-speaking Africans and the younger Francophone Africans. Consider, for example, Wole Soyinka's famous remark that a black man should not have to feel the need to assert his *négritude* any more than a tiger feels the need to affirm its *tigritude.*

The modern African intellectual, even if he is not a militant, is inclined to reject Senghor's sophisticated aesthetic and to argue that *négritude* seen in this light is retrogressive and tends to blunt the thrust toward scientific excellence, a thrust essential to Africa's integration into a world community. Soyinka's attitude is typical of this interpretation of Negro-African culture and aesthetics: "it is from this totem-narcissistic phase that a different kind of poet has begun to emerge, one who goes back to real knowledge—namely, the knowledge that hot sterilizing pads sealed the cord at birth but that such discouraging facts need not condemn the poet to exile."

The most militant reading of the word *négritude* is diametrically opposed to the anthropological one and yet it is also, at the same time, more charitable to it than is the scientific view of Soyinka and others. The militant view considers Senghor's interpretation fallacious, but admits that the very existence of his interpretation conforms to the historical or revolutionary concept of *négritude* as understood by the militant, namely, as a *prise de conscience* constituting a necessary, and important, step in the revolutionary progression from being a *colonisé,* with all that entails, to being a full-fledged nationalist and, ultimately, a peer citizen in an egalitarian world.

Perhaps the most eloquent apologist of this idea of *négritude* is the Angolan poet and critic Mário de Andrade. On four or five occasions, while in Algiers during 1958-69, I had talks with Andrade. His revolutionary view of *négritude* is almost the opposite of Senghor's. For Andrade, *négritude* is a slogan, a device, a rallying cry to evoke and fortify the revolutionary resolve of the far-dispersed and long-crushed black men of a colonized society. It is akin to "black pride" and the phrase "black is beautiful" and asserts a self-evident truth that has been tarnished by humiliation. *Négritude* is a self-awareness, a *prise de conscience,* whose function it is to erase the effects of more than a century of subjugation and humiliation. Once this awareness has been achieved, *négritude* ceases to exist, according to Andrade, and the newly-independent African must rather look to being a modern socialist man among other men of the world. Thus Senghor's *négritude* tends to some extent to isolate or set off black men from other

men whereas the militant socialist's *négritude* brings the black man closer to other men. Andrade agrees that Senghor's *négritude,* in its time and place, conformed to his own condition of self-awareness regardless of the relative validity of the concept involved—in other words, even if Senghor's idea of *négritude* were entirely false, it would still be valid *historically* if it did instill a sense of pride in the colonized men, bring them together, and lead them to freedom through an ethnically-founded nationalism. Andrade merely contends that Senghor's argument for an innate *négritude* has outlived its usefulness and is not only useless but actually pernicious inasmuch as Senghor's definition does not provide for a demise of *négritude* after self-awareness and liberation have occurred.

The shift in the interpretation of the term *négritude* may be illustrated by a consideration of the vicissitudes in critical reception of Sartre's "Orphée noir." In 1948, this essay appeared as the unexpectedly long and eloquent introduction to Senghor's monumental *Anthologie de la nouvelle poésie nègre et malgache de langue française.* "Orphée noir" was recognized by most as an outstanding achievement, but was generally thought to distort the black man's *négritude* to suit Sartre's own politico-philosophical credo. The tone of Sartre's essay clashed with the tenor of the works included in the anthology and was certainly quite contrary to Senghor's own meaning of *négritude.*

The modern militant, even if he rejects Sartre's specific politics, tends to repeat the basic messages of "Orphée noir." Sartre's view is that *négritude* is a socially and politically dictated *prise de conscience* and thus transitory:

> Et j'en demeure d'accord: comme toutes les notions anthropologiques, la Négritude est un chatoiement d'être et de devoir-être; elle vous fait et vous la faites: serment et passion à la fois. Mais il y a plus grave: le nègre, nous l'avons dit, se crée un racisme antiraciste. Il ne souhaite nullement dominer le monde: il veut l'abolition des privilèges ethniques d'où qu'ils viennent; il affirme sa solidarité avec les opprimés de toute couleur. Du coup la notion subjective, existentielle, ethnique de *négritude* "passe," comme dit Hegel, dans celle—objective, positive, exacte—de *prolétariat.* . . . En fait, la Négritude apparaît comme le temps faible d'une progression dialectique: l'affirmation théorique et pratique de la suprématie du blanc est la thèse; la position de la Négritude comme valeur antithétique est le moment de la négativité. Mais ce moment négatif n'a pas de suffisance par lui-même et les noirs qui en usent le savent fort bien; ils savent qu'il vise à préparer la synthèse ou réalisation de l'humain dans une société sans races. Ainsi la Négritude est pour se détruire, elle est passage et non aboutissement, moyen et non fin dernière. Dans le moment que les Orphées noirs embrassent le plus étroitement cette Eurydice, ils sentent qu'elle s'évanouit entre leurs bras.

This view, rather than Senghor's, has become prevalent among the black intellectuals in Africa. President Sékou Touré spoke for an ever-growing number of African intellectuals when, in a special taped message at the Algiers Festival, he said:

Pour mener le juste combat, les responsables africains, les leaders, de quelque rang qu'ils soient,
ne devront jamais se laisser guider ni par les faux
concepts de négritude et de soi-disant métissage
culturel, ni par la tactique néo-colonialiste divi-
sant notre continent en Afrique francophone et
en Afrique anglophone, en Afrique du nord du
Sahara et en Afrique du sud du Sahara, mais par
les seuls aspirations des peuples progressistes qui
au-delà des questions de couleur, de religion ou
de nationalité, constituent une seule et même
force, celle de la révolution déjà en marche dans
un grand nombre de pays du monde . . .

Touré's remarks appear to be aimed at Senghor's idea of
négritude and his recent preoccupation with *francophonie.*

For better or worse, the trend in interpretation and exploitation of the tired word *négritude* seems now to be away
from the socio-mystical assertions of the thirties and toward the socio-political expediencies of the sixties. Thomas Melone has described *négritude* as "le terme 'd'où' a
jailli la source Nègre quand le panafricanisme est le terme
'vers lequel' la construction humaine, l'élaboration dialectique s'efforcent de canaliser ce jaillissement"—namely,
rediscovery and socio-political orientation; retrospective
and forward-looking self-assertions respectively; the two
dimensions constituting *négritude.* If the early stage of rediscovery has been replaced by the later stage of political
emphasis it is, nevertheless, a fact of definition that both
stages belong to the term *négritude* and it may be that rediscovery will again tip the balance when political maturity and stability have visited Africa's young nations. Post-
animistic African thought—summed up in the term *négritude*—seems to be subject to the two attracting-repelling
poles of mysticism and positivism which one finds in the
va-et-vient of European culture. The large over-all look
seems, therefore, more appropriate than Melone's highly
particularized one in which the phenomenon is crystallized in an existential awareness: "La négritude se présente
donc tout d'abord comme une prise de position, à la fois
une négation et une affirmation. Elle a toutes les carac-
téristiques d'une 'situation' existentialiste." If indeed, political history is moving in such a way as to validate
Sartre's view of *négritude*, Senghor's *négritude* is an undeniable part of that history as well as a philosophy which
may one day be restored when political turmoil has subsided sufficiently to make room anew for the less expedient
wing of *négritude* which I characterized above as retrospective. When the vicissitudes of the term *négritude* have
made this journey—full circle—there will be, I feel, a
great flowering of arts and letters in Africa in which some
sort of synthesis will have been achieved between the age-
old traditional African aesthetics and the exigencies of the
European languages in which black Africans seem destined to write for a long time to come. At that time the
term *négritude,* and attendant abstractions, will have become—like surrealism in Europe—assimilated into current African thought as a felt thing and will have been relegated, as a precise term, to the literary manuals. (pp. 163-
81)

> *Eric Sellin, " 'Négritude': Status or Dynam-
> ics?" in L'Esprit Creatéur, Vol. X, No. 3, Fall,
> 1970, pp. 163-81.*

NEGRITUDE IN LITERATURE

Abiola Irele

[*In the following excerpt, Irele provides a thematic analysis of literary and nonliterary works associated with Negritude.*]

The literature of *négritude* is dominated by the collective
consciousness of the black writer as member of a minority
group which is subordinated to another and more powerful group within the total political and social order. The
literary preoccupations of the movement revolve around
this central problem, the Negro predicament of having
been forced by historical circumstances into a state of dependence upon the west, considered the master society
and the dominating culture. The literary themes of *négritude* can be seen as a counter-movement away from this
state: they constitute a symbolic progression from subordination to independence, from alienation, through revolt,
to self-affirmation.

The theme of exile is the point of departure of the whole
literary expression of *négritude,* and in it is involved the
most pathetic aspect of the French-speaking Negro intellectuals' specific situation, which derives from the political
and cultural uprooting of black people in general by colonial conquest. The overwhelming sentiment that dominates in this connection is the black man's sense of separation from his own world and of being thrown into a social
system with whose cultural values he can strike no personal relation. The black man recognises himself as belonging
to an 'out-group', an alien in relation to the west, which
controls the total universe in which he moves. For the
French-speaking Negro writer, this situation is signified
by his physical exile in Europe.

> Bless you, Mother,
> I hear your voice when I am given up to the
> insidious silence of this European night
> Prisoner under the white cold sheets tightly
>   drawn,
> prisoner of all the inextricable anxieties that
> encumber me.
>   [Léopold Sédar Senghor, 'On the Appeal from
>   the Race of Sheba']

This sentiment of belonging no longer to oneself but to another goes together with an awareness of inferiority, which
becomes translated in social terms into a caste and class
consciousness. The association between race and servitude
is a constant theme in Negro literature, and occupies a
prominent place in *négritude:*

> I am a docker in Brooklyn
> Bunker-hand on all the oceans
> Labourer in Cuba,
> Soldier in Algeria.
>   [Roussan Camille, *Assaut à la nuit*]

The economic exploitation of the race which defines it as
a community and gives its members a group consciousness

is a consequence of its original humiliation by conquest and slavery. The memory of slavery thus has a particular significance for Negro writers, especially for those of the Caribbean.

> And they sold us like beasts and counted our teeth . . . and they examined our genitals, felt the gloss and the roughness of our skin, pawed us, weighed us, and put around our neck like tamed animals the strap of servitude and of nickname. [Aimé Césaire, *Et les chiens se taisaient* (1956)]

The black man's principal role in western history has thus been as an economic tool. This is what Césaire, echoing Marx, has called [in *Discours sur le colonialisme* (1955)] 'the reduction of the Negro into an object' (*la chosification du nègre*). But although the Negro experience forms, in this light, part of the general Marxist conception of the 'class struggle', the prevailing preoccupation of these writers was with the black people as a race, and not as a class. They were concerned with the collective image of the black man in the west and with his human status in the world.

The colonial system was based on a social division determined by 'the colour line', and it was maintained by a racial ideology which defined the black man as inferior. The social relationship between coloniser and colonised was thus converted, as far as the black man was concerned, into an opposition between *white* and *black,* which acquired the moral values summarised by the South African, Bloke Modisane [in 'Why I Ran Away'], in these words:

> White is right, and to be black is to be despised, dehumanised . . . classed among the beasts, hounded and persecuted, discriminated against, segregated and oppressed by government and by man's greed. *White is the positive standard, black the negative.* [Italics mine]

The cultural and political ascendancy of the white man over the black man, combined with the active denigration of the black man, has thus had the effect of vitiating the latter's self-esteem, with profound psychological consequences, which involve shame and self-hatred. The demoralising effect of the caste system on the black man has been expressed by Léon Damas [in 'La complainte du négre']:

> My todays have each one for my yesterdays
> Wide eyes that roll with rancour and with shame.

The black man in the world suffered his negation as a human being. This was the external reality with which the literature of *négritude* was concerned. But there is a more personal and intimate side to this theme of alienation, which has to do with the cultural situation of the assimilated Negro intellectual.

The colonial enterprise was presented as a 'civilising mission', aimed at transforming the black man by his progressive approximation to the ideals of western civilisation through education. This implied in most cases his dissociation from the basic personality pattern imprinted in him by his original culture. Western education was thus an instrument of imposed acculturation, aimed at replacing the black man's original modes of thought and feeling, which were attuned to his native norms, by another personality structure corresponding to western norms. The French policy of *assimilation* probably went furthest in this cultural policy, which was to some extent common to all the colonising powers, of attempting to fashion the black man—or at least a black *élite*—in a foreign image.

This problem is at the heart of the cultural and spiritual dilemma of the French-speaking Negro intellectual. For in order to be acceptable socially in the western world, it was necessary for him to deny a part of himself. Conformity to white ideals was only possible at the cost of a repression of his original self.

> I must hide in the depths of my veins
> The Ancestor storm-dark skinned, shot with lightning and thunder
> And my guardian animal, I must hide him
> Lest I smash through the boom of scandal.
> He is my faithful blood and demands fidelity
> Protecting my naked pride against
> Myself and all the insolence of lucky races.
>   [Senghor, 'Totem']

The result was a division in his personality. The Haitian poet Léon Laleau has expressed this sentiment of the divided self in remarkable poetic terms [in 'Trahison']:

> This beleaguered heart
> Alien to my language and dress
> On which I bite like a brace
> The borrowed sentiments and customs of Europe.
> Mine is the agony
> The unutterable despair
> In breaking with the cold words of France
> The pulsing heart of Senegal.

We touch here upon what Roger Bastide has called the 'pathology of the uprooted man' [in 'Problèmes de l'entre croisement des civilisations et de leurs oeuvres,' in *Traité de sociologie* (1963)], and which R. E. Park has observed in the 'cultural hybrid' as part of the psychological results of culture contact and the acculturative process: 'spiritual instability, intensified self consciousness, restlessness and malaise' [*Race and Culture* (1950)]. Damas has put this sentiment of *malaise* into verse [in 'Solde']:

> I feel ridiculous
> in their shoes
> in their evening suits,
> in their starched shirts,
> in their hard collars
> in their monocles
> in their bowler hats.

This is a problem that was even more accentuated in the case of the Caribbean writers, whose non-western cultural background was marginal, and whose racial stock, because of the total orientation of their society towards western values, symbolised by whiteness, was more a source of shame and frustration than for the Africans. The pressure upon them to deny their racial connections and to identify with Europe was even greater, though they were subject to the same discrimination as the Africans. The West Indians' sentiment of exile is thus intensified by a feeling of rootlessness, which Césaire [in 'Dit d'errance'] expresses with the symbol of the island itself.

> Island of the blood of Sargassoes
> island, nibbled remains of remora,
> island, backfiring laughter of whales,
> island, specious word of mounted proclama-
> tions,
> island, large heart spread out
>
> island ill-jointed, island disjointed,
> all islands beckon
> all islands are widows.

The black man, and especially the intellectual, found himself a man no longer in his own right, but with reference to another, thus estranged from himself; in exile, not only in a political and social sense, but also spiritually. The whole colonial existence appears as one long paling of the black self, an 'Ambiguous Adventure' as C. H. Kane has put it [in *L'aventure ambigüe* (1961)]. A man divided between two worlds, his over-riding aspiration thus became, in the words of Kane's tragic hero, Diallobé, 'nothing but harmony'.

A situation of oppression offers to the victim a range of reactions limited by two opposite poles—total submission, or total refusal—but the exact nature and degree of this reaction will depend upon the experience and the disposition of the individual. The colonial situation as a whole was a collective political and cultural oppression of black people yet it cannot be said that it was felt uniformly as such. The black intellectuals were in fact privileged in comparison with the masses, as far as the more external conditions of life were concerned, and it is quite conceivable that their consciousness of the fundamental injustice of the system in which they lived was limited, if it existed at all.

But the mental conflict into which the French-speaking Negro intellectuals were plunged as individuals probably made them aware that their dilemma was inherent in the whole colonial situation. Thus they were forced, despite assimilation, into an identification with the colonised rather than with the coloniser:

> But if I must choose at the hour of testing,
> I have chosen the verset of streams and of for-
> ests,
> The assonance of plains and rivers, chosen the
> rhythm of blood in my naked body,
> Chosen the trembling of balafongs, the harmony
> of strings and brass that seem to clash,
> chosen the
> Swing swing yes chosen the swing

Léopold Sédar Senghor with fellow students in Paris in 1931. Georges Pompidou, president of France from 1969 to 1974, is seated in the front row, second from left.

I have chosen my toiling black people, my
    peasant people, the peasant race through
      all the world.
'And thy brothers are wroth against thee, they,
    have set thee to till the earth.'
To be your trumpet!
      [Senghor, 'For Koras and Balafongs']

The literature of *négritude* became, as a result, a testimony
to the injustices of colonial rule and an expression of the
black man's resentment:

An immense fire which my continuous suffering
and your sneers
and your inhumanity,
and your scorn
and your disdain
have lighted in the depths of my heart
will swallow you all.
      [Regror C. Bernard, *Négre*]

The tone changes often from this kind of menace to one
of accusation. The poetry of David Diop illustrates best
this indictment of colonial rule:

In those days
When civilisation kicked us in the face
When holy water slapped our tamed foreheads,
The vultures built in the shadow of their talons
The blood-stained monument of tutelage
In those days
There was painful laughter on the
    metallic hell of the roads
And the monotonous rhythm of the
    pater noster
Drowned the howling on the plantations.
      ['Les Vautours']

Accusation in turn becomes a criticism of western society
as a whole, and in this respect the contradiction of 'war
and civilisation' became a powerful weapon. Senghor's
Hosties Noires, for example, are a collection of war poems
in the tradition of Wilfrid Owen, but he reveals a particular view of European war when he speaks with sarcasm of
having been 'delivered up to the savagery of civilised men'.

The shortcomings of western society, both within and
without, furnished that element of disenchantment which
made it possible for *négritude* to develop an attitude of refusal towards the colonial system:

I shout no
no to class
no to the taint of soot
no to the humid floor
no to the glass furnace
no to damped lights
no to love paid for in bank notes.
      [René Depestre, 'Quand je crie non']

Protest, accusation, and refusal lead inevitably to a call to
arms:

But when, O my people,
winters in flames dispersing a host
of birds and ash,
shall I see the revolt of your hands?
    [Jacques Roumain, 'Prelude' to *Bois d'ébène*]

Protest and threats of revolt are in themselves an indirect

form of defence, a verbal means of projecting violent reaction which cannot be realised physically. Although the
militancy of *négritude* was an explicit response to a real
situation (and the agitated character of a good deal of this
writing indicates that the situation was often felt as real
personal experience), it has no more than a symbolic
value. Its real significance, however, lies elsewhere, for it
does reveal in fact the hidden mechanism of response to
oppression. The resentment of the black man against domination tends towards retaliation and, as Fanon has
shown, his consciousness as a colonised man is suffused
with violence. In the work of Césaire, this element is translated in poetic terms into an apocalyptic vision [as seen in
'Soleil serpent']:

And the sea lice-ridden with islands
breaking under rose fingers
flame shafts and my body
thrown up whole from the thunderbolt.

The surrealist technique is here employed in a manner appropriate to the alienated condition of the black man. It
offers the black poet a means of projecting his dream of
violence, and becomes in fact a symbolism of aggression.
A corresponding side to this aggressiveness is the way in
which the black poet responds by wilfully identifying himself with western symbols of evil:

I seek the thousand folds of the oceans
witnesses of savageness
and rivers where beasts go to drink
to make for myself a face
that would scatter vultures.
      [René Bélance, 'Moi nègre']

Négritude here borders on nihilism. Yet nihilism is not
characteristic of the movement as a whole; more often
than not, it represents a defiant truculence, as in this passage [from *Black Label*] where Damas operates a literary
reversal of situations in a way reminiscent of Nietzsche:

The White will never be negro
for beauty is negro
and negro is wisdom
for endurance is negro
and negro is courage
for patience is negro
and negro is irony
for charm is negro
and negro is magic

for joy is negro
for peace is negro
for life is negro.

In this respect, one of the most striking technical innovations of *négritude* has to do with the reversal of colour associations in the western language which was the only
tongue accessible to most of them, namely French, as in
this example from Césaire's *Cahier*:

a solitary man imprisoned in white
a solitary man who defies the white cries of
white death
TOUSSAINT TOUSSAINT LOUVERTURE
He is a man who bewitches the white hawk of
white death
He is a man alone in the sterile sea of white sand.

A reversal of western symbols implies as well a reversal of the concepts associated with them. The revolt of *négritude* appears also as a refusal of western values, regarded as oppressive constraints. The Christian religion in particular comes in for continual attack, and this theme has had an original and refreshing treatment, though mainly in strident notes, in the comic novels of Mongo Beti, in particular *Le Pauvre Christ de Bomba*. Western morality is also set in contrast to the African's unbridled sensuality.

It can be remarked that, in general, the theme of revolt in the literature of *négritude* represents a reinforcement of the antagonism created by the colonial situation, between the white master and the black subordinate. It is a way of underlining an opposition that was implicit in the colonial human context. It is not, however, an end in itself, as Sartre has observed, but rather part of a movement towards a more constructive vision.

The refusal of western political and cultural domination in the literature of *négritude* represents also a severing of the bonds that tie the black man to western civilisation. The corollary to this claim for freedom from the west is a search for new values. Revolt becomes not only a self-affirmation but also an instrument of self-differentiation:

> For myself I have nothing to fear I am before
> Adam I belong neither to the same lion
> nor to the same tree I am of another warmth and
> of another cold.
> [Césaire, 'Visitation']

The quest for new values thus leads the black writer to self-definition in terms that are non-western, and the association between the black race and Africa acquires a new meaning: instead of being a source of shame, it becomes a source of pride. This is the ultimate end of *négritude*, and much of the literature is dedicated to a rehabilitation of Africa, a way of refurbishing the image of the black man. The psychological function of this, as well as being a counter to the Negro's inferiority complex, is to permit an open and unashamed identification with the continent, a poetic sublimation of those associations in the Negro's mind which constitute for him a source of mental conflict in his relationship with western culture: a process of self-avowal and self-recognition. This view of the movement is best justified by the writings of the West Indians, whose collective repression of Africa, as has been pointed out, has been the more painful:

> Africa, I have preserved your memory, Africa
> you are in me
> like the splinter in a wound
> like a totem in the heart of a village.
> [Roumain, *Bois d'ébène*]

A myth of Africa developed in consequence out of the literature of *négritude*, which involved a glorification of the African past and a nostalgia for the imaginary beauty and harmony of traditional African society, as in Camara Laye's evocation of his African childhood.

This strain in *négritude* is probably charged with the greatest emotional force. Senghor for instance infuses into his well-known love poem, 'Black Woman', a feeling that is more filial than erotic, due to his identification of the continent with the idea of woman, in a way that lends to the image of Africa the force of a mother figure:

> Naked woman, black woman,
> Clothed with the colour which is life, with
> your form which is beauty,
> In your shadow I have grown up; the gentleness of
> your hands was laid over my eyes
> And now, high up on the sun-baked pass, at the heart
> of summer, at the heart of noon, I come upon you,
> my Promised Land,
> And your beauty strikes me to the heart like the
> flash of an eagle.
>
> Naked woman, black woman,
> I sing your beauty that passes, the form that I
> fix in the Eternal,
> Before jealous Fate turns you to ashes to feed the
> roots of life.

In a poem ['Couronne à l'Afrique'] by another writer, Bernard Dadié, despite the use of conventional western imagery, Africa is celebrated in cosmic terms:

> I shall weave you a crown
>   of the softest gleam
>   bright as the Venus of the Tropics
> And in the feverish scintillation
>   of the milky sphere
> I shall write
> in letters of fire
> your name
> O, Africa.

The romanticism of the African theme in *négritude* illustrates certain of the functions and characteristics of 'nativistic movements' as analysed by Ralph Linton, but in literary rather than ritualistic form, that is, at a sophisticated level. Yet a purely sociological and 'realistic' view would miss the profound significance of this aspect of *négritude*. In any case, realism is a purely relative term applied to literature, and has little relevance to poetry; but apart from this, the African theme went far beyond a purely compensatory mechanism in that it was also a genuine rediscovery of Africa, a rebirth of the African idea of the black self. This opening up of the African mind to certain dimensions of its own world which western influence had obscured appears to be in fact the most essential and the most significant element in the literature of *négritude* as *the principal channel of the African Renaissance*. For the way in which the best of these poets came to root their vision in African modes of thought has given a new meaning to the traditional African world-view.

Césaire's poetic formulation of *négritude* [in *Cahier d'un retour au pays natal*] is in fact taken from a Bambara symbol of man in a telluric union with the universe:

> My *négritude* is not a stone, its deafness hurled
>   against the clamour of the day,
> my *négritude* is not a speck of dead water on the
>   dead eye of the earth,
> my *négritude* is neither a tower nor a cathedral
>   it thrusts into the red flesh of the earth
>   it thrusts into the livid flesh of the sky.

The West Indian is of course at one remove from the living centre of traditional African humanism, which is essential to the poetry of the African writers of *négritude,* as in Senghor's works; and it has perhaps been expressed in its purest and most authentic form by Birago Diop in his famous poem, 'Souffles':

> Listen more often
> To things than to beings;
> The fire's voice is heard,
> Hear the voice of water.
> Hear in the wind
> The bush sob
> It is the ancestors' breath.
>
> Those who died have never left,
> They are in the woman's breast,
> They are in the wailing child
> And in the kindling firebrand
> The dead are not under earth.
>
> They are in the forest, they are in the home
> The dead are not dead.

The literature of *négritude* tends towards a point where it can coincide with the traditional mythical system of thought in Africa. This does not imply that the coincidence is perfect nor that it is always genuine; what is significant about it is the 'backward movement' towards an end from which western culture had originally pulled the African. *Négritude,* as literature, retraces a collective drama as well as a spiritual adventure, involving a quest for the self, with the conquest of a lost identity as the prize.

From a social angle, its importance is mainly symbolic and functional. In the historical context in which it developed, the black writer incarnating his despised and oppressed race is the mediator of a new self-awareness. The racial exaltation of the movement is mainly a defence; the use of an African myth represents black ethnocentrism, an attempt to recreate an emotional as well as an original bond beneath the contingencies of a particularly difficult historical experience.

The alliance of the imaginative and the political in *négritude* relates the movement to African nationalism. Nationalism hardly ever corresponds to an objective reality; but is, none the less, a powerful emotional attitude, and literature has always been an outstanding vehicle for dominated people to give voice to their group feelings. But imaginative writing, even with an explicit political content, implies a group mind rather than group action; it is essentially inactive. At the literary level, *négritude* remains largely subjective, and it was the ideology that attempted to establish objective standards of thought and action for the black man in general, and for the African in particular.

The non-imaginative writings of French-speaking Negro intellectuals to a great extent run parallel to the literature. They are determined by the same sentiments, and are consequently, in the main, a formulation in direct language of the attitudes expressed in symbolic terms in the imaginative writings. The distinction lies in the fact that, whereas the literary works simply express these attitudes, the non-literary writings formulate and define them.

The majority of the books, essays, articles, and speeches that constitute what may be called the ideological writings of *négritude* are straightforward polemics: protest writing, testimonies, and direct attacks on colonialism. A typical example is Albert Tevoedjre's essay, *L'Afrique révoltée,* which is a violent denunciation of colonial rule, with particular reference to Dahomey, the author's place of origin. Even here, the main source of grievance appears to be cultural rather than economic or social:

> I shall always regret the fact of having been obliged to learn French first; to think in French while being ignorant in my own mother tongue. I shall always deplore the fact that anyone should have wanted to make me a foreigner in my own country.

An even more forceful attack on colonialism is Césaire's famous pamphlet, *Discours sur le Colonialisme,* which takes up the question in original terms by demonstrating the evil effects on both coloniser and colonised of a system which limits the idea of man, as promoter of values, to the west:

> Never was the west, even at the time when it shouted the word loudest, further removed from being able to assume the responsibilities of real humanism—humanism of a world-wide scope.

It was not enough, however, to denounce colonialism; it was also considered necessary to contest its foundations, and especially the racial and cultural ideas by which it was rationalised.

The subordinate role of the Negro in western society had been justified mainly by the allegation that Africa had made no contribution to world history, had no achievements to offer. The logical conclusion drawn from this idea was put by Alioune Diop in this way:

> Nothing in their past is of any value. Neither customs nor culture. Like living matter, these natives are asked to take on the customs, the logic, the language of the coloniser, from whom they even have to borrow their ancestors.

The western thesis that the African had no history implied for the black man that he had no future of his own to look forward to. A good deal of the propaganda effort of French-speaking intellectuals was as a consequence devoted to a refutation of this unacceptable proposition. Cheikh-Anta Diop's writings stand out in this respect. His book, *Nations nègres et culture,* for example, is an impassioned, heavily documented attempt to show that ancient Egyptian civilisation was in fact a Negro-African achievement, and thus to prove that the west owed its enlightenment to Africa. The conclusion to the principal section of his thesis is worth quoting in full, as it illustrates the tenor of the whole book:

> The Egyptian origin of civilisation, and the Greeks' heavy borrowing from it are historical evidence. One wonders therefore why, in the face of these facts, the emphasis is laid on the role played by Greece, while that of Egypt is more and more passed over in silence. The foundation for this attitude can only be understood by recalling the heart of the question.

Egypt being a Negro country, and the civilisation which developed there being the product of black people, any thesis to the contrary would have been of no avail; the protagonists of these ideas are certainly by no means unaware of this fact. Consequently, it is wiser and surer purely and simply to strip Egypt of all her achievements for the benefit of a people of genuine white origin.

This false attribution of the values of an Egypt conveniently labelled white to a Greece equally white reveals a profound contradiction, which is not negligible as a proof of the Negro origin of Egyptian civilisation.

As can be seen, the black man, far from being incapable of developing a technical civilisation, is in fact the one who developed it first, in the person of the Negro, at a time when all the white races, wallowing in barbarism, were only just fit for civilisation.

In saying that it was the ancestors of Negroes, who today inhabit principally Black Africa, who first invented mathematics, astronomy, the calendar, science in general, the arts, religion, social organisation, medicine, writing, engineering, architecture . . . in saying all this, one is simply stating the modest and strict truth, which nobody at the present moment can refute with arguments worthy of the name.

The whole thesis is based on an implied correlation between history and culture which determines the nature of society, and of the individual: and its intention was to prove that the African was essentially a technical man—*homo faber*. However, by summarily ascribing all civilisation to the black man in this way, Diop proceeds in the field of scholarship in the same fashion as Léon Damas in the poem already cited—by reversing the hierarchy established by the coloniser, without contesting the basis on which it was founded. It is, in a way, a total acceptance of the western measure of evaluation, namely technical achievement.

Négritude may be distinguished from other efforts to rehabilitate Africa by what can be termed its 'ethnological' aspect, which attempted to redefine its terms, and to re-evaluate Africa within a non-western framework. Here the concept of cultural relativity was to help in sustaining a campaign whose purpose was to establish the validity of African cultural forms *in their own right*.

This explains the preoccupation of the French-speaking Negro intellectuals with anthropology, a preoccupation which reveals itself in the series of special numbers published by *Présence africaine*, especially the two remarkable volumes *Le Monde noir* (1951) and *L'Art négre* (1952). The former, edited by Theodore Monod, brought together a number of articles by eminent scholars, both European and African, on various aspects of African cultural expression as well as their ramifications in the New World, in such a way as to suggest not only their originality but their world-wide permanence.

The accent was almost invariably placed on the non-material aspects, on those intangible elements which could distinguish the African's approach to the world from the western, and which might seem to underlie his conscious existence as well as his material productions. Thus African traditional beliefs and, in particular, the native forms of religion received strong emphasis. African 'animism' tended in general to be placed on an equal footing with Christianity, though curiously enough by an effort of reconciliation in most cases. The most noteworthy example of this kind of procedure is perhaps a paper by Paul Hazoumé, in which the Dahomean conception of God is likened to that of John the Evangelist.

The anthropological interests of *négritude* came to the fore at the First Congress of Negro Writers and Artists, whose express purpose was to make a total inventory of the Negro's cultural heritage, in an effort to define a Pan-Negro cultural universe. This was at best a very delicate, if not an impossible, undertaking, as the discomfort and reserve of the American participants at the conference was to make clear. It would be tedious to go into the details, but two main lines of thought emerged from the deliberations of this conference. Foremost in the minds of the organisers was the will to demonstrate the specific character of traditional African institutions and beliefs as well as of African survivals in America, in a way that refuted the western thesis of inferiority. The purpose of this was made clear by the Haitian, Emmanuel Paul [in 'L'ethnologie et les cultures noires,' in *Contributions au Ier congrès des écrivains et artistes noirs*]:

> It was from this [African] past that colonial authors undertook to make the black man inferior . . . But what we look for from these studies is precisely the awakening of a historical consciousness embracing the millennial past of the race. These black people scattered all over the world who, even under the pressure of the west, still hesitate to deny themselves, have need of this source of pride, this reason for clinging to life.

Secondly, and as a consequence, the concern with the past implied a process of self-appraisal and self-definition, as a solid basis. The Malagasy writer, Jacques Rabemananjara, declared [in 'L'Europe et nous' in *Contributions au Ier congrès des écrivains et artistes noir*]:

> The deliberations [of this Congress] have no other purpose than to assemble and to select material for the dialogue. First among ourselves, with the aim of knowing ourselves more, of grasping, through our diverse mentalities, customs, and countries of origin, the essential human note, the ineffable human warmth that unites us.

These efforts cannot be said to have produced a common cultural denominator, but their significance lay rather in the attitude that inspired them. In direct response to the intolerance that characterised the cultural policy of the coloniser, *négritude* developed into a vindication and an exaltation of cultural institutions which were different from those of the west; it was thus a conscious attitude of pluralism. The corollary was a rejection of *assimilation* and a claim to cultural autonomy and initiative. Alioune Diop expressed this aspect of the movement in the following terms [in *Deuxième congrès des écrivains et artistes noirs*]:

> Unable to assimilate to the English, the Belgian, the French, the Portuguese—to allow the elimination of certain original dimensions of our genius for the benefit of a bloated mission of the west—we shall endeavour to forge for this genius those means of expression best suited to its vocation in the twentieth century.

These efforts to rehabilitate African history and to re-evaluate African culture were a conscious reaction to the ideology that sustained colonial rule. But the central pole of the colonial situation was political domination rather than cultural supremacy. The next step after a demand for cultural autonomy was logically a corresponding demand for political independence. The arguments for an explicit political stand came mainly from the Marxist elements in the movement, especially at the second congress in Rome. Frantz Fanon's address to this meeting contained an unequivocal summary of their point of view:

> In the colonial situation, culture, denied the twin support of nation and state, withers away in a slow death. The condition for the existence of culture is therefore national liberation, the rebirth of the state. ['Fondements réciproques de la culture nationale et des luttes de libération']

However, if a certain political awareness was an implicit part of the cultural offensive of the French-speaking black intellectual, which placed *négritude* in close relationship with African nationalism and Pan-Africanism, it is none the less quite clear that *négritude* remained essentially a cultural and intellectual movement, albeit with political implications. The French-speaking Negro élite tended more towards an elaboration of ideas concerning the black man's place in the world than towards the actual mobilisation of the masses for an immediate and definite political goal. *Négritude* was thus at the most an ideological movement with remote political purposes.

Its link with nationalism is all the same certain in that a special *rationale* was developed along with it; it furnished the most important *mystique* of African nationalism.

In so far then as it is an answer to a certain combination of circumstances, the product of a historical situation, *négritude* is another cultural and political myth: the expression of a justified self-assertion swelling into an exaggerated self-consciousness. *Négritude* has also meant to a considerable extent an assiduous cultivation of the black race.

That Negro nationalism on both sides of the Atlantic should have been based on a vehement racial consciousness can be imputed to the racialism that grew out of and which often came to underlie white domination: black nationalism can in the final analysis be reduced to a challenge to white supremacy. *Négritude,* by confronting white domination with its own racial protest and zealous partisanship of the Negro race, did more than draw together the sentiments and attitudes that went with black reaction and embody them in a heightened form: it moved in fact very distinctly towards a racial ideology.

Even here, most of the ideas expressed by French Negro

intellectuals are limited to a refutation of the racial ideology of colonialism. For if, in the literary works, the exaltation of the black race rises to dizzy heights, it has not been reproduced in the non-literary writings with anything like the same abandon. In the single case of Senghor, this aspect of *négritude* acquires a certain intellectual dimension. [In a footnote, Irele states: "No other member of the movement has elaborated *négritude* so fully as Senghor. As a matter of fact, Césaire himself prefers to regard *négritude* as a historical stand, as an attitude, rather than as a comprehensive system".] (pp. 499-517)

Senghor's *négritude* starts out as, and essentially remains, a defence of African cultural expression. It presents itself first as an elaborate apology before it becomes an exposition and a personal view of Africa: it is a passion that is later rationalised. Nonetheless, his ideas over the last quarter-century present a coherent and even a consistent pattern.

On several occasions, Senghor has defined *négritude* as 'the sum total of African cultural values', something perhaps more than the simple relation of the African's personality to his social and cultural background. For although Senghor never speaks of an 'essence', he speaks of a 'negro soul', of a special spiritual endowment of the African which is, in some respects, shared by the Negro in the New World, and is therefore a racial mark.

Senghor describes and defines the African's distinctive qualities mainly by opposition to the western, often by setting a positive value on what the west derided in the African, sometimes proceeding by grounding his own thinking in modern currents of western thought, which he then turns against the west for the benefit of his arguments. He has written, for example [in the preface to *Les nouveaux contes d'Amadou Khoumba* by Birago Diop]:

> Discursive reason merely stops at the surface of things, it does not penetrate their hidden resorts, which escape the lucid consciousness. Intuitive reason is alone capable of an understanding that goes beyond appearances, of taking in total reality.

It is this line of thought that forms the basis for his justification of the African's non-rational approach to the world. He has boldly annexed Lévy-Bruhl's studies on 'primitive mentality' to argue the validity of the African's ways of thinking. He seizes in particular upon the French anthropologists' 'law of participation'; and he uses this in his own formulation of the African's mode of experience, which he presents as essentially one of feeling—of a mystical sympathy with the universe [in 'Ce que l'homme noir apporte', in *Liberté,*]: 'The African cannot imagine an object as different from him in its essence. He endows it with a sensibility, a will, a human soul.'

For Senghor, this African mode of apprehending reality through the senses rather than through the intellect is at the root of his direct experience of the world, of his spontaneity. The African's psychology helps to determine a different form of mental operation from the western, a different kind of logic:

> The life-surge of the African, his self-aban-

donment to the other, is thus actuated by reason. But here, reason is not the eye-reason of the European, it is the *reason-by-embrace* which shares more the nature of the *logos* than *ratio*.

He goes on to say [in 'Psychologie du Négro-Africain', in *Diogène*, 37 (1962)], 'Classical European reason is analytical and makes use of the object. African reason is intuitive and participates in the object'. Senghor has made this distinction a constant theme in his writings.

The 'law of participation' governs the African's sensibility, which to Senghor is basically emotive. He has pushed this conception of the African mind to a point where emotion has become its cardinal principle. 'Emotion is African, as Reason is Hellenic', he has exclaimed, and though this statement has been given careful nuances by him (for the benefit of his critics) he still leaves no doubt about this aspect of his theory of *négritude:* 'It is this gift of emotion which explains *négritude* . . . For it is their *emotive attitude* towards the world which explains the cultural values of Africans.'

Senghor points to creative works to demonstrate the presence of a unique African sensibility which animates them, and insists above all on the privileged position of rhythm in African artistic expression—rhythm is for him the expression of the essential vitality of the African:

> [Rhythm] is the architecture of being, the internal dynamism which shapes it, the system of waves which it sends out towards others, the pure expression of vital force . . . For the Negro-African, it is in the same measure that rhythm is embodied in the senses that it illuminates the Spirit. ['L'ésthétique négro-africaine' in *Liberté* I]

In his exposition of the African mind, Senghor lays emphasis on its intensely religious disposition, on the African's 'sense of the divine', on 'his faculty of perceiving the supernatural in the natural' ['Ce que l'homme noir apporte', in *Liberté,* I]. The African's mystical conception of the world is for Senghor his principal gift, and derives from his close links with the natural world. Because the African 'identifies *being* with life, or rather with the *life-force*', the world represents for him the manifestation in diverse forms of the same vital principle: 'For the universe is a closed system of forces, individual and distinct; it is true, yet also interdependent.' Lévy-Bruhl's law of participation is here allied to Fr. Temple's 'Bantu Philosophy' to produce a conception of the African world-view as a system of participating forces, a kind of great chain of vital responses in which Man, the personification of the 'life-force', occupies a central position: 'From God through man, down to the grain of sand, it is a seamless whole. Man, in his role as person, is the centre of this universe'.

For Senghor, this is not an abstract system but an existential philosophy, a practical view of life; *négritude* is for him not only a way of being, but also a way of living. He therefore extends his theory of the African personality to explain African social organisation. Senghor believes that the African society is an extension of the clan, which is a kind of mystical family, 'the sum of all persons, living and dead, who acknowledge a common ancestor'. Thus African society has a religious character—it is not so much a community of persons as 'a communion of souls'. Where, therefore, western culture insists on the individual, African culture lays emphasis on the group, though without the loss of a sense of the person.

Senghor's theory of *négritude* is not really a factual and scientific demonstration of African personality and social organisation, but rather a personal interpretation. An element of speculation enters into his ideas, which lays them wide open to criticism. His more subtle formulations often have a specious character; besides, the most sympathetic reader of his theories cannot fail to be disturbed by his frequent confusion of race and culture, especially in his early writings.

On the other hand, these weaknesses are due to the circumstances in which his ideas developed. In assessing the objective differences that cut off the African from western man, his concern is to make a positive re-evaluation of realities which the west considered negative.

Furthermore, Senghor's political career has given his theory of *négritude* a practical significance—from polemics, it has evolved into an ideology. His social and political thought are set within the general framework of his cultural philosophy. It is in the name of the innate spiritual sense of the African that he rejects the atheistic materialism of Marxism as unfitted for and irrelevant to the African situation.

In a certain sense, therefore, Senghor may be justified in designating his theory of *négritude* as a cultural and not as a racial philosophy. At any rate, it is not an exclusive racism. Senghor's views on the African, and even on the whole Negro race, open out towards the larger perspectives of a broader humanism. Here he has been influenced by Teilhard de Chardin's philosophy of the convergence of all forms of life and experience towards the evolution of a superior human consciousness, which has given Senghor a pole around which he has developed his idea of 'a civilisation of the Universal'. His defence of cultural and racial mingling is founded on this key concept, which is summed up in the following passage [from *Nation et voie africaine du socialisme*]:

> The only 'pan-ism' which can meet the demands of the 20th century is—let us proclaim it boldly—pan-humanism, I mean a humanism which embraces all men at the double level of their contributions and their comprehension.

An ideology, when it becomes explicit, is a kind of thinking aloud on the part of a society or of a group within it. It is a direct response to the actual conditions of life, and has a social function, either as a defensive system of beliefs and ideas which support and justify an established social structure, or as a rational project for the creation of a new order. The latter type of ideology, even when it includes a certain degree of idealism, also implies a reasoned programme of collective action; it becomes the intellectual channel of social life.

The literature and ideology of *négritude* were by their nature revolutionary, or at the very least radical. Because they spring from a need to reverse an intolerable situation, they are moved in the first instance by a negative principle. They are a challenge to the common lot which western expansion had imposed on non-western man, especially the Negro, whose experience—dispersal, subjugation, humiliation—illustrates the worst aspects of contact with the white man. For black people had in common an experience which, in the word of James Baldwin, placed in the same context their widely dissimilar experience. He continues [in *Nobody Knows My Name*]:

> What they held in common was their precarious, their unutterably painful reaction to the white world. What they held in common was the necessity to remake the world in their own image, to impose this image on the world, and no longer be controlled by the vision of the world, and of themselves, held by other people. What in sum black men held in common was their ache to come into the world as men.

In the circumstances, it is not surprising that this 'ache' should have developed sometimes into an intense collective neurosis, which has reached a paroxysm in movements like those of the Black Muslims in the U.S., and the Rastafarians in Jamaica. The dilemma in which history placed the black man, and from which the intellectual movements could not escape, was that Negro nationalism of any kind was bound to be even more irrational than any other, for it was to a considerable degree a gesture of despair.

This negative aspect of black reaction to white rule has left a mark on *négritude,* even in its development of positive perspectives. A contradiction, purely emotional in origin, bedevils the movement, which, in its crusade for the total emancipation of black people, has sought to comprise within a single cultural vision the different historical experiences of Negro societies and nations.

It would be a mistake, however, to dismiss the movement as a futile and sectarian obsession with self—a kind of black narcissism. In the larger context of Negro experience, it represents the ultimate and most stable point of self-awareness. For, although its expression has sometimes been exaggerated, it has always had an intellectual content. In the African political context, its role as the ideological spear-point of African nationalism has been sufficiently emphasised. Its profound significance in the cultural and social evolution of Africa has been perhaps less appreciated.

Négritude represents both an African *crise de conscience,* and its most significant modern expression; it is the watershed that marks the emergence of a modern African consciousness. African 'messianism' and *négritude* represent the ritualistic and the intellectual facet of the reaction to the same historical, social, and cultural stimulus. Their forms have varied. In African messianism, tradition remains the basis of social behaviour, despite borrowings from western religion, which are absorbed only so far as they will fit in. The reverse is true of *négritude:* despite its championship of a non-rational tradition, it remains rigorously rational. Senghor's *négritude,* for example, is an anti-intellectualism mediated by the intellect, and the whole movement is expressed through a western mould which absorbs African realities. In short, *négritude* is a break with tradition: although African in content, it is western in its formal expression.

The movement thus marks a transition in the nature of collective expression in Africa—from the myth of the millennium and from the religious undercurrent upon which traditional Africa had relied for human accomplishment, to the lay, intellectually-centred approach to the world which is a legacy of the European Renaissance. It marks a 'desacralisation' of African collective life, an attitude which is spontaneous and no longer imposed, and out of which have begun to flow new currents of ideas for tackling present-day African problems.

This is what Balandier has observed as 'the progression from myth to ideology' in Africa. Although this progression has been continuous and although, as L.-V. Thomas has remarked [in *Les Idéologies négro-africaines d'aujourd'hui* (1965)], 'the originality of modern solutions is inspired by the specific character of former times', none the less the transition is real. African messianism was an archaic reaction to a new situation; *négritude* was a far more appropriate response, adapted to the modern age.

It thus forms an essential and significant part of an African revolution which is marked not only by the emotions it has liberated and the ideas it has thrown up, but also by the forms it has assimilated. The profound character of the transition can best be appreciated by comparing the respective visions of the Absolute in African messianism and in *négritude.* The former was supernatural and apocalyptic—essentially an eschatology. The idealism of *négritude* from the beginning tended towards an earthly utopia:

> We Africans need to know the meaning of an ideal, to be able to choose it and believe in it freely, but out of a sense of personal necessity, to relate it to the life of the world. We should occupy ourselves with present questions of world importance, and, in common with others, ponder upon them, in order that we might one day find ourselves among the creators of a new order. [A. Diop, 'Niam n'goura ou les raisons d'être de présence africaine', in *Présence africaine* I, 1947]

In their search for identity, the adherents of *négritude* have had to accept and explore to the full their particular situation. But, although preoccupied with a sectional and limited interest, they were inspired by a universal human need for fulfilment. In this, they have never strayed from the central, enduring problem of the human condition. (pp. 517-23)

Abiola Irele, "Négritude—Literature and Ideology," in The Journal of Modern African Studies, *Vol. 3, No. 4, December, 1965, pp. 499-526.*

A. C. Brench

[*Brench is a critic and educator who specializes in literature written in French. In the following excerpt, he analyzes the thematic differences between Caribbean and African literature and examines patterns of theme and characterization in the novels of French-speaking Africans.*]

Colonialism in Africa is different in one important respect from colonialism in the Caribbean Islands. In Africa the Europeans were colonists and conquerors; in the Caribbean both the African slaves and their white masters were strangers. There is another difference between white domination of negroes in the Americas and European colonization in Africa. Apart from the four communes in Senegal and other centres in North Africa, French influence in Africa was almost non-existent until the end of the nineteenth century. On the other hand, in Guadeloupe, Martinique, Haiti and the other islands, the African slaves were, by that time, gaining some degree of freedom within a society based entirely on French civilization. These two factors are responsible for the major differences in the evolution towards cultural and political independence in Africa and in the islands where people of African origin are in the majority. They also explain the similarities which exist between American negroes and people of similar stock in Latin America and the Caribbean.

In the French Antilles, then, the African slaves were sold in the market place. The white colonists took great care that, as far as possible, people of the same family or tribe were not put to work on the same plantation. The small social groups which were formed in this way on each plantation were, therefore, composed of people from a wide variety of tribes with an equally varied number of beliefs and customs. From this amalgam some standard social behaviour evolved. The slaves were, though, subjected to the French planters and their concept of civilization. Superimposed on the way of life they created, these European customs, especially the Roman Catholic religion, were a new and often predominant factor which further alienated them from their own, original beliefs.

This complex evolution led, in some cases, to the development of such exotic religions as Voodoo. In others, as black and, especially, half-caste people gradually gained some degree of freedom, they copied the habits of the Europeans. In literature this development is seen in the poetry of Phyllis Wheatly in America and the many imitators of the Parnassus poets and Victor Hugo in the Antilles such as Oswald Durand and Gilbert de Chambertrand.

The predominance of French civilization and its acceptance as the only true standard was not put in doubt until the beginning of the twentieth century. Even then, scholars such as Dr. Price-Mars were in a minority scorned by many of their own people for trying to discover and give value to the predominantly African customs which still survived among the peasant farmers. Haiti, Dr. Price-Mars' country, was itself in a peculiar position. Its early independence and subsequent conquest by America in 1915 had awakened a sense of nationalist responsibility still absent elsewhere in the Caribbean.

It was not until the inter-war years, during the twenties and thirties, when Africa had only been colonized for twenty or thirty years, that a concerted movement for independent cultural freedom began to gain momentum. Basically, this was created by intellectuals from the Antilles but Africans, such as Senghor and Birago Diop who were studying in Paris at the same time, were also intimately connected with it.

During the years of European colonization in Africa, the French had decided upon a policy of assimilation. The Africans were considered acultural and could, then, only become responsible members of society when they had learnt to become 'black Frenchmen'. Theory and practice were not, however, wholly similar. While, in the old communes such as Saint-Louis and Dakar, assimilation was very advanced among the intellectuals, the teachers and civil servants as well as in the rich, traditional upper-classes, many Africans escaped. Penetration extended only along the coastal strip, down the rivers and towards the main inland towns. Villagers in the bush and the desert had only limited contact with the colonial administration. Their traditional ways were only slightly influenced by European civilization. Many of the intellectuals, as we see in Senghor's poetry and Diop's stories, were also very close to their African roots. There was not, as in the Caribbean, complete alienation and the need to create an entirely new set of values from various and often incompatible sources. When, after the Great War, the movement for freedom of expression among Africans gained strength, Africans, except those in the old communes and old-established trading posts, had had only thirty or forty years under not very extensive colonial rule. When, together with this fact, it is noted that Africans in Africa were not, within the strict definition of the word, slaves of the colonists, the differences between the situation then existing in Africa and that in the Antilles appear considerable.

June 1932, when *Légitime défense,* published by a group of students from the Antilles, first voiced publicly the young generation's revolt against servile imitation of French ways, can be considered as the date from which the movement began to spread its influence more widely. These students claimed, very rightly, that such imitation was sterile. Imitation of French literature and manners in general as an attempt to become black Frenchmen was bound to lead to an impasse. In the first place, they could only become second-class Frenchmen because the French despised them as black inferiors. Secondly, as imitators they were adding nothing new to French or their own civilization. Third, by rejecting their colour and traditional values they were trying to destroy a part of themselves which can never be eradicated. It is, too, the only part of their personality which offers a way out of the impasse. In reaction against the previous attitude, they called for a profound study of traditional values and their use as a source of inspiration in literature and the arts in general.

While several prominent Africans and many students from Africa were associated with this movement, it can be seen immediately that there are basic factors in this manifesto which are inapplicable to Africa. There was, in the first place, no long tradition of imitation among Africans. Neither Senghor nor Diop had been brought up as children in a society where pre-eminence was given to European standards. On the contrary, Senghor's family in Joal and Diop's in Dakar were solidly traditionalist. The only force driving them towards assimilation came from the

René Maran, author of the novel Batouala.

colonists. They had, therefore, never consciously rejected their colour and their traditions in order to imitate the French. They had, however, been educated in an atmosphere which implied French superiority and against which traditional society was powerless. In many cases they had been assimilated unwittingly. Those assimilated in this way were by no means the majority in their country; the upper-classes were divided among the traditionalists and the assimilated with many shades of meaning between the extremes. There was no extensive and firmly established bourgeoisie as in the Antilles; the vast majority of Africans were, as they still are, farmers and small traders living in village communities. The process of acceptance of coloured people as a wealthy but isolated middle-class which had taken place in the Antilles had hardly begun in Africa. Related to this, the Europeans also considered that only a small minority of Africans were worth educating. While there was a growing number of lower and middle grade officials and teachers, these were trained only as far as was necessary. No attempt was made to take them away from their traditional background.

That there was little attempt or opportunity during the initial period of colonialism in Africa to create an imitative literature is shown by the fact that the only well-known novel published by an African before 1930 was *Force-Bonté* by Bakary Diallo, who had been a *tirailleur sénégalais*. This novel is no more than a naïve panegyric

of French civilization in the tradition of Caribbean imitative literature. On the other hand, the importance attached to African myths and legends is demonstrated by the number of translations by teachers and other Africans published in journals and periodicals since the second decade of the twentieth century. No other novel of importance was published until more than ten years after Diallo's. Hazoumé's *Doguicimi* (1938) is set in Dahomian society before colonialism. In both style and content it is inspired by traditional, oral literature. Ousmane Socé Diop's *Contes et légendes* and his novel, *Karim,* published in 1938, are also devoted to themes which exclude colonialism and assert the originality of African tradition. In the same way, the stories and poems published in periodicals such as *L'étudiant noir,* were either based on traditional themes or attacked colonialism for having destroyed the Africans' culture and their social systems. Whereas, therefore, in the Antilles there were two problems to be resolved (that of colonialism and also that of middle-class subservience to French culture which made any developments towards positive expression impossible), in Africa literature was concerned almost exclusively with traditional themes or the struggle against colonial domination and its destructive influence.

In the thirties there were other influences which played an important part in the growth of the African intellectuals' movement. Both communism, with its emphasis on racial equality, and surrealism, which attacked all established social and cultural values, appealed to the needs of Africans and coloured people from the Antilles. These two movements lost their appeal, however, especially after the 1939-45 war, when the neo-Victorian paternalism of the Russians towards coloured people became evident and when it was seen that surrealism was sterile in that it offered no constructive means of progress. It does seem, though, that the Africans have rejected these two purely European philosophies more completely than the people of the Antilles.

This is explained, in part, by the differences in the societies in the Antilles and Africa. Aimé Césaire's *Cahier d'un retour au pays natal* contains tragic descriptions of economic poverty and a spiritual emptiness which are absent in Senghor's poetry written during the same period as Césaire's poem. Again, the exploitation of the peasants by the coloured middle-class in Martinique, for example, has no real parallel in Senegal where the colonist is the enemy of all but a small majority of the people. The feeling that the great majority of Africans were united in the struggle against colonialism has given a sense of complacency and an optimism to the works of African writers which make them appear facile. The same is not true of the Caribbean writers. In the islands the conflicts between the different classes and groups give the works a poignancy and tragic content similar to those in the works of Baldwin in America.

In the first instance, the literature of Negritude was a call for emancipation and the assertion of African tradition as the inspiration for creative art. This was, obviously a common bond between those from Africa and from the Antilles. While, however, Roumains and Alexis were publishing novels before 1940 and, with others from the Antilles, continued to do so after the war, novels of reasonable quality by Africans did not appear in any number or take on any importance until the early 1950s. Camara Laye's *L'enfant noir* was the first of these, published in 1953. The first works to be published, when the movement towards colonial freedom gained considerable impetus as a result of the Second World War and consequent political developments, were collections of poetry and stories. Birago Diop and Senghor both published their first volumes in 1947. These poems and stories were an assertion of the positive value of African cultures but did not analyse the society from which they spring. They were a call to battle. It is not until the later fifties that the attacks were mounted in any depth by the novelists.

After Laye's two novels, both of which belong, in several respects, to the initial period of the struggle for freedom of expression, *Présence Africaine* published *Trois écrivains noirs* in 1955. The three novels, by Eza Boto (Mongo Beti), by Abdoulaye Sadji and by Jean Malonga, had all been prepared in the forties or fifties, in the case of Malonga's *Coeur d'Aryenne* as early as 1948, or published as a serial in periodicals as Sadji's *Nini* had been in 1947-8. None has any great literary merit nor do they presage the evolution which will follow. Boto's *Ville cruelle* is an adventure story with, however, some stylistic devices and a concern for social problems which he develops in his later novels. Malonga's novel is, perhaps, the closest to those which will follow. Mambeké the hero's assimilation and ultimate rejection of European civilization is a theme found in the novels of Oyono, Loba, Ousmane and, to some extent, Kane.

In 1956, both Oyono and Beti published their first novels followed, in the next two years, by their other attacks on colonialism in Africa—or, more precisely, Cameroon. These are but two of the first of an ever increasing number of novelists who have published [between 1956 and 1967].

With such proliferation it is impossible to distinguish any clear, chronological progression in the treatment of theme or the development of characterization. Nonetheless, a pattern can be discerned. It is imposed, mainly, by the predominant, political commitment to the anti-colonial struggle which is at the basis of African negritude. That negritude has ceased to be, if it ever was, a purely artistic movement, is obvious from the fact that many African writers, notably Senghor and Kane, are now preoccupied with social, economic and political problems; the former, in particular, has published only studies on these subjects during the last ten years. The factors which influence the evolution of this struggle and the individual writer must, however, be taken into account. In the first place, the radical change in French policy which followed de Gaulle's accession in 1958 accelerated the move towards independence for the colonies. Then, in Africa, the pressure exerted by the more independent-minded governments opened new perspectives even for the less adventurous. The fluctuating fortunes of the 'cold war' also played a part in the political and, indirectly, cultural developments in Africa. As far as the individual writers are concerned, there are even more complex factors to be considered. There are

those, like Abdoulaye Sadji and Birago Diop, who were born and brought up in the 'vieilles communes' and in the Islamic faith. While Sadji's career kept him mainly within the confines of Rufisque, Diop's has taken him to most parts of West Africa. They belong, too, to the older generation of African nationalists, Diop, especially, having been involved in the formation of *L'étudiant noir* and other aspects of the movement for African freedom in Paris in the thirties. Laye, on the other hand, comes from Guinea, the most independent-minded state among the ex-French colonies in Africa. His first novel was criticized by its leaders for its apparent naïvety and exoticism. Among the second generation of writers, Sembene Ousmane has arrived at similar conclusions to those of African political and labour leaders; but his thought developed through contact with European trade unionism and work in the docks in Marseilles, not through the exchange of ideas at conferences nor through participation in any organised, purely Africanist movement. In contrast, Kane describes the effects of European civilization on a young African who, like himself, was brought up in a strict Muslim tradition until suddenly faced with the contradictory influence of French thought.

A factor which is often ignored but which has considerable importance is the influence of the writers' country of origin. The first point is that, with rare exceptions, the majority of the writers, both poets and novelists, come from countries on the coastal plain; Senegal, Ivory Coast, Cameroon. Upper Volta, Mali, the Sudan and, especially the countries of ex-French Equatorial Africa, have only one or two well-known or accomplished writers. This can be explained by the existence of a greater number of urban centres and, therefore, educational institutions on the coast. If the case of Senegal is considered, it is seen that with the old communes and the educational and administrative centres for French West Africa in Dakar, it is obviously the country which would produce the greatest number of writers. That it also has coastal tribes who have traded with Europeans for several centuries, Muslims who fought and kept apart from the colonists and the inhabitants of the old communes, means that the differences between Diop, Kane and Sembene Ousmane are not difficult to understand. Similarly, the Ivory Coast and Cameroon, both countries which benefited from close participation in the educational facilities offered in Dakar have, like Dahomey, produced a number of well-known writers.

Ex-French Equatorial Africa had no such centre as Dakar. Brazzaville, the capital of the Congo, was a poor substitute. Educational facilities were lacking and means of contact with the outside world limited. The Congo has produced Malonga and the poets U'Tamsi and Sinda. Malonga, who grew up long before independence became even a possibility, is the product of mission school education. His novel reflects this influence clearly. Paradoxically, though, he is the first novelist to describe the Africans' revolt against assimilation.

If the date of publication of *L'enfant noir* is considered the beginning of the growth of the novel as an influential means of literary expression in sub-Saharan French-speaking Africa, a certain pattern can be discerned in its evolution when related to the various factors already mentioned. The first stage is, obviously, represented by the older writers: Diop, Sadji and Dadié among others. Together with Ousmane Socé these three are, probably, the best-known and most accomplished writers of prose fiction among this generation. They have one factor in common which is immediately significant. Diop, Socé and Sadji were all born and brought up in one or other of the old communes while Dadié spent many years as a student and Government official in Gorée, Saint-Louis and Dakar. All have characteristics in common. In the first place, only Dadié in his novels *Climbié, Un nègre à Paris* and *Patron de New York* deals briefly with colonialism as a political or social influence in Africa. Diop and Socé both use traditional myths, legends and stories as their basic material: Socé has also, like Dadié, published a novel describing the life of a young man from his earliest schooldays. Both Socé's *Karim* and Dadié's *Climbié* are more concerned with the Africans' life outside the colonial situation although, in the latter, there are direct references to the political and social implications of the anti-colonial struggle in the last chapters. Sadji is principally concerned with the social problems of urban life in the enclaves formed by the old communes. Although the Europeans are responsible for the creation of these cities and also influence the evolution of the social behaviour of the African inhabitants, they are not active participants in the novels.

When, in one or two of Diop's stories and in *Un nègre à Paris,* Europeans are described or mentioned, they are treated with sympathetic irony. The brutal satire of Oyono and the complete rejection of Malonga and Ousmane are not possible for people who have lived so long in close and friendly contact with Frenchmen. Whatever the reason, there is a much more pronounced emphasis on the universality of man's goodness and stupidity in these writers' works than in others which follow them.

Camara Laye, whose two novels are the first of the many to be published in the last thirteen years [1953-1967], writes in this early tradition. In *L'enfant noir* the colonist is absent yet his influence is very great. It is responsible for the boy's exile and nostalgia. Yet there is no bitterness, only the acceptance of the inevitable. For this reason he was accused of not being committed to the cause of African nationalism. *Le regard du roi* is at the other extreme. Clarence, the hero of this novel, is a European who finds his true worth in African society after having been rejected by his fellow white men.

These two novels, published in 1953 and 1954, are at the watershed which divides the two periods. In the first, when African folk-stories, Socé's *Karim* and B. Diop's *Contes d'Amadou Koumba* are published, there is an assertion of the value of African traditions but no direct attempt to attack colonialism which is destroying them. In the second, the political and social significance of the novel in the struggle against European domination becomes clearly evident. In 1956 are published Dadié's *Climbié,* Ousmane's *Le docker noir,* Matip's *Afrique, nous t'ignorons,* Beti's *Le pauvre Christ de Bomba,* and Oyono's *Une vie de boy* and *Le vieux nègre et la médaille,* all of which openly attack European domination and brutality in Africa or, in *Le docker noir,* colour prejudice in France.

Of these writers, Oyono and Beti are, perhaps, the most representative of the political climate of the time. Oyono's two novels and the three published by Beti between 1956 and 1958 all deal with one or other aspect of colonialism's negative influence in Africa. Oyono's third novel, *Chemin d'Europe* (1960) has, basically, the same theme. Colonists and missionaries are central characters in their novels. They are described objectively in their daily contact with Africans. Oyono describes their posturing and brutality, their inability to appreciate the fact that Africans are human beings, and Beti shows the missionaries as they good-naturedly but foolishly try to impose their Christian ideas on people whose whole philosophy is alien to Catholicism. Both, too, show the way in which European interference has emasculated traditional, African society.

In the novels of Oyono and Beti, as in those of their predecessors, there is no attempt to reject colonialism. There is no way for the Africans to escape the colonists' presence. Only in Malonga's *Coeur d'Aryenne,* written in 1948 and published in 1955, Mambeké, the hero, rejects European civilization at the end of the novel and returns to his village determined to devote himself to his people to the exclusion of all else. This is the first attempt by a novelist to describe conscious escape from the framework imposed by colonialism and find a purely African solution to Africa's problems.

Until 1959 no African novelist had described an African's impressions of France. Camara and Mambeké both visit Paris but neither Laye nor Malonga describe their experiences. Dadié and Aké Loba, whose novels were published in 1959 and 1960 respectively, are the first to give their impressions of the capital of the mother country. Dadié's description is humorous and slightly ironical. He laughs at the Parisians but appreciates their qualities. His, though, is not the attitude of a subservient, colonial inferior but of an equal who can give an objective judgement on what he sees. Loba has neither the panache nor the experience of Dadié as a writer. His hero, Kocoumbo, is a student who, after many vicissitudes, returns to Africa as a magistrate. For him, Paris is limited to that part inhabited by African students. Again, though, it is described objectively. It is a place which offers opportunities for study not for adulation. African students should use its facilities but beware of its pitfalls.

At almost the same time as Dadié and Loba published their novels set in France, Sembene Ousmane and Hamidou Kane opened new perspectives. In *L'aventure ambiguë,* Kane analyses the confrontation between the mysticism of traditional Islam and the materialism of Europe. The African and the European are equals in this novel. The Africans are not inferiors because of colonial domination. Kane presents the conflict between two equally valid philosophies. Materialism is victorious but only because it answers immediate needs; the fundamental problems are still unsolved. In *Les bouts de bois de Dieu* Ousmane sets out to show how Africans should adapt to their own ends new ideas and techniques drawn from Europe. He is concerned with the material well-being of African workers and is, therefore, the opposite, in some respects, of Kane. Yet they both carry further the theme, glimpsed, even, in the novels of Oyono and Beti, of the positive part African thought can play in the world. Both these writers present situations which have nothing to do with colonial domination. For them there is a confrontation between two ways of life. Each has something to offer the other. For the present, however, because of its material needs, Africa must accept European predominance.

In *Le regard du roi*, finally, Laye describes the opposite situation. Now, it is the European, Clarence, who is looking for a society offering him the means of participation which allows him to develop freely. He finds it in Africa. This is one conclusion but not the last. The problems of a balance between Europe and Africa have still to be solved. Since independence has been achieved in their countries some African novelists in French have been repeating the themes used earlier; Dadié's *Patron de New York* recalls *Un nègre à Paris*. Beti and Laye have remained silent. The new writers, either using themes from pre-colonial Africa as in Ikelle-Matiba's *Cette Afrique-là* or, with Gologo's *Le rescapé d' Ethylos,* treating problems such as alcoholism. With the end of colonialism the main source of inspiration has also dried up. One easy outlet would be facile propaganda literature; on the other hand, having proclaimed the originality of the African genius, this would appear to be a poor indication of its worth. (pp. 1-12)

> *A. C. Brench, in an introduction to his* The Novelists' Inheritance in French Africa: Writers from Senegal to Cameroon, *Oxford University Press, London, 1967, pp. 1-12.*

> **Négritude may be considered a parallel to "American-ness" in American literature (surely another debatable subject: everyone knows what is truly American, but each has his own opinion on the matter; yet all are agreed that something uniquely American exists).**
>
> **—*Martin Tucker, in his* Africa in Modern Literature: A Survey of Contemporary Writing in English, *1967.***

Gerald Moore

[*An English educator and critic, Moore has written extensively on African literature. In the following excerpt, he discusses the style and themes of Negritude poetry and compares the literatures of the Caribbean, French-speaking Africa, and English-speaking Africa.*]

The opening shots in the campaign to create a new African literature were fired, not by Africans, but by black writers from the Caribbean. The loudest and most resounding of these was probably Aimé Césaire's familiar cry:

> Hurray for those who never invented anything
> for those who never explored anything
> for those who never conquered anything
> hurray for joy
> hurray for love
> hurray for the pain of incarnate tears!

This cry was first sounded in the Parisian review *Volontés,* which published Césaire's *Cahier d'un Retour au Pays Natal* (Journal of a Return to my Native Country) in 1939, and over the next few years it gradually found its audience and created a new literary movement among French-speaking Negroes, *négritude*; for Césaire had coined the word when he wrote elsewhere in the poem:

> My négritude is no deaf stone that reflects the
>   noise of the day
> My négritude is no spot on the dead eye of the
>   earth
> My négritude is no tower and no cathedral
> It dives into the red flesh of the soil
> It dives into the flowing flesh of the sky
> Piercing the weight of oppression with its erect
>   patience

The concept of négritude is of such fundamental importance in French African writing, and is so much a development of earlier tendencies in the Caribbean, that it may be as well to trace the course of that revolution which made coloured writers exalt their colour and their African origins instead of ignoring them. Behind *négritude* lies *negrismo.* This literary movement began in Cuba as long ago as 1927, and was influenced, as its sponsors have admitted, by the European fashion for Africa and things African that was part of the Western reaction to the inhuman horrors of the First World War. The new generation in Cuba had grown up under a white or would-be white ruling class which despised everything remotely connected with Africa, the more so as slavery in Cuba did not end until the 1880s. It was, then, a revelation to discover that Europe itself was ready to provide an audience for writers who would sing the real culture of the Cuban people, with its strong African flavour.

Negrismo was promoted in Spanish-speaking Cuba by the *Revista de Avance* (1927-30) and rapidly influenced such writers as the Cuban poets Ramón Guirao and Nicolás Guillén and the Puerto Rican poet Luis Palés Matos. At the same time a somewhat similar 'African' movement was under way in French-speaking Haiti, centred around the magazine *La Revue Indigène* and largely inspired by Jean Price-Mars' book *Ainsi Parla L'Oncle* (*What Uncle Said,* 1927) in which he had written:

> Ah, I know the wall of repugnance against which I am striking by daring to speak to you of Africa and African things! The subject seems to you inelegant and quite uninteresting, doesn't it? But beware, my friends, that such sentiments are not based upon scandalous ignorance. We are living with ideas turned rancid by the prodigious idiocy of a malintegrated culture, and our puerile vanity is only satisfied when we intone the phrases written for others in which are glorified, 'the Gauls, our ancestors'.

This last complaint was to be echoed many years later by

the African poet Senghor in his poem *Le Message.* Meanwhile *La Revue Indigène* attracted a brilliant group of young Haitian writers, including the poet and novelist Jacques Roumain, and turned the attention of Haitian artists, intellectuals and writers towards the discovery and celebration of everything African in their heritage.

All these writers, both in Spanish and in French, make the concept of Africa central in their work, though their Africa is more a state of soul than a geographical and political reality. For some, it means the Golden Age which preceded the Atlantic Slave Trade and the crude rape of the continent by White Europe. This is the vein worked by the Haitian Regnor Bernard in *African Dusk:*

> Gone are the forests where sang and danced the
> inspired priestess,
> Profaned are the altars of the eternal lamps;
> and the Sphinx mourns on the desert's edge.
> The Pharaohs are troubled at the heart of the
> Pyramids;
> and Africa no longer is:
> Neither its temples,
> nor its mysteries,
> for the priests are dead
> for the traders in Negroes have come.

To others, Africa is a resolution of their present humiliation and suffering, a future state where the long aspirations of her exiled people will be fulfilled at last. So Aimé Césaire ends his poem 'Africa':

> . . . but the word is hard, the will sure and the
> hour cedes
> the forgotten days which walk always among the
> twisting
> shells among the doubts of the regard
> shall burst upon the public face among the
> happy ruins!
> In the plain
> The white tree with helping arms outstretched
> will be like every tree
> a tempest of trees in surging foam and sands
> the hidden thing shall climb again the slope of
> slumbering music
> a wound of today is a womb of the orient
> a shuddering which rises from the black forgot-
> ten fires, it is
> the ruin risen from the ash, bitter word of scars
> all lithe and new, a visage
> of old, bird of scorn, bird reborn, brother of the
> sun.

A third variation on the theme of Africa is played in Jacques Roumain's 'Guinea', where he makes use of the old Haitian belief that Guinea is a kind of Negro Heaven to which all coloured poeple will journey in death, and where they will belong of right in comradeship and repose:

> It's the long road to Guinea
> Death takes you down
> Here are the bough, the trees, the forest
> Listen to the sound of the wind in its long hair
> of eternal night
>
> It's the long road to Guinea
> Where your fathers await you without impa-
> tience
> Along the way, they talk

> They wait
> This is the hour when the streams rattle like
> beads of bone
>
> It's the long road to Guinea
> No bright welcome will be made for you
> In the dark land of dark men:
> Under a smoky sky pierced by the cry of birds
> Around the eye of the river the eyelashes of the
> trees open on decaying light
> There, there awaits you beside the water a quiet
> village
> And the hut of your fathers, and the hard ances-
> tral stone where your head will rest at last.

All this is the poetry of exile, for the Caribbean poet is exiled in a far more profound sense than the African born and bred who happens to pass a few years in Paris or London. A good deal of Caribbean Negro poetry is concerned with the special dilemmas of Caribbean, rather than African, man. The Cuban Nicolás Guillén laments that even his name, like his language, is borrowed from the 'masters', while his own is irretrievably lost. Like most Afro-Americans, he has no idea even from which part of Africa his forefathers came:

> . . . All my skin (I should have said so)
> all my skin—does it really come
> from that Spanish marble statue? And my fear-
> ful voice
> the harsh cry from my gorge? and all my bones
> do they come from there? And my roots
> and the roots of my roots and
> the dark branches swayed by dreams
> and the open flowers on my front
> and the bitter sap of my bark?
> Are you quite sure?
> Is there nothing else, only that which you wrote
> that which you sealed
> with a sign of wrath . . .
> Do you not see these drums in my eyes?
> Do you not see these drums hammering out
> Two dry tears?
> Have I not got an ancestor of night
> with a large black mark
> (blacker than the skin)
> a large mark
> written with a whip?
> Have I not got an ancestor
> From Mandingo, the Congo, Dahomey?

Another special dilemma affecting many Caribbean writers is that of their mixed blood. Some react to this by detestation and rejection of the white man in their veins, like Jacques Roumain who exults that when the tom-tom beats: 'the white man who made you mulatto / Is nothing but foam; like spittle cast up on the coast'. But Nicolás Guillén, in one of his most famous poems, tries to reconcile his 'Two Ancestors' and accept his mingled nature as an enrichment rather than a curse:

> Shadows, only visible to me,
> My two ancestors haunt me.
> Don Federico cries to me
> And Papa Fecundo is silent.
> The two dream in the night
> They stride on and on
> But I reconcile them.

'Federico!'
'Fecundo!'—and so they embrace,
They sigh together and lift
Their heavy heads.
After all they are both of the same size
Under the high stars.
After all they are both of the same size
The black greediness and the white greediness,
The black suffering and the white suffering,
After all they are both of the same size
The white fear and the black fear,
After all they are both of the same size
They cry, dream, weep, sing,
Sing, sing, sing. . . .

These profound differences of situation often cause the Caribbean poet to celebrate his blackness in ways that may not be at all to the liking of the educated African. Afro-Cuban poetry, in particular, lays great stress on the sensual, the sexual and rhythmic elements in Cuban life, which it opposes to the cold, abstract intellectualism of Europe. Far from denying or shying away from the primitive, such poetry exults in it, proclaiming it to be the medicine which the Negro alone can administer to a world grown sick on a surfeit of machinery, profits and calculation. Typically, this poetry makes great use of rumba rhythms to induce in the reader the proper sense of excited sensuality, as in José Zacarias Tallet's poem 'Rumba':

Zumba, mamá, la rumba y tambó!
Mabimba, mabomba, mabomba y bombó!
Buzzing mamá dances rumba to the drum,
Mabimba, mabomba, mabomba y mabum! . . .
The blackish Tomasa with lecherous gesture
She tears back her hips and she lifts up her head
she jerks up her arms, she is folding her hands,
and in them is resting her ebony neck.
She boldly exposes her ball-like breasts
they tremble to the left, they tremble to the right
they gleam, they are dazzlingly Ché Encarnación.
Chaqui, chaqui, chaqui, charaqui!
Chaqui, chaqui, chaqui, charaqui!
The maddened negro now bends down to leap
the silken kerchief he holds in his hands
and now he will mark the blackish Tomasa
who provokes him with daring breasts and behind . . .

Haitian poetry often exults too in the ritual of Voodoo, with all its elements of African paganism. Charles Pressoir's poem 'La Mambo dans le Hounfort', calls nostalgically for the blood of sacrifice in its refrain:

But what can be done with a goat without horns?

and his 'Country Graveyard' muses upon the black man's double faith, asking whether death will not finally force him to choose his path:

At the foot of the Cross suspended,
Lest the dead should know grangou,
A tiny grain, some fish, foods blended,
At the feet of Christ you find voodoo.
So they follow the two faiths ever—
The white, the bone-bred deeply,
Do the dead go then forever
To heaven or to Guinea?

The complex, passionate poetry of Aimé Césaire gathers into itself all these elements of Caribbean Negro writing and fuses them into the single concept of négritude. . . . [Léon Damas of French Guiana] was the first to break rudely into French Literature with his angry, passionate poems, published by GLM in 1937 as *Pigments*. The bitter energy of these poems, which led to their being seized and burnt by the French police in 1939, moved French Negro writing into a new field of experience and expression:

Do they really dare to treat me as white
while I aspire to be nothing but negro
and while they are looting my Africa?
bleached
abominable affront they give me
while they ransack my Africa
that wants peace and nothing but peace
bleached

my hatred thrived on the margin of culture
the margin of theories the margin of idle talk
with which they stuffed me since birth
even though all in me aspired to be negro
while they ransack my Africa.

It was not until the eve of the Second World War that Césaire found his own voice with his long poem *Cahier d'un Retour au Pays Natal*. Here he began his long experiment, based on Surrealist technique, to break the French language into a new mould. When he writes lines like:

Listen to the white world
how their defeats sound in their victories

he is using paradox in an attempt to shock both black and white out of the old assumptions into a new awareness of humanity. But in 1939 this great poem passed almost without notice, and soon Césaire had returned to Martinique, while Senghor had gone to the French Army and captivity in Germany.

At the end of the war a series of events following each other in rapid succession announced the awakening of a new sense of solidarity and common purpose among coloured writers in all parts of the French Empire, from Madagascar to Martinique. Although Senghor had been writing poems since 1938, it was not until 1945 that he was able to publish his first volume, *Chants d'Ombre*. In 1946 came Césaire's *Les Armes Miraculeuses* and in 1947 his *Cahier* was reissued in both French and English; in November of that year appeared the first number of the important review *Présence Africaine*. During 1948 both poets produced important new volumes and Senghor published his *Nouvelle Anthologie de la Poésie Nègre et Malgache*, with a long introduction by Jean-Paul Sartre. This was probably the most influential single work of the whole movement, giving to all who read it a sense of the sweep and variety of the contributions now being made by those who had sweated in so many corners of the world to learn the names of their Gaulish ancestors. From 1948 onwards the cult of négritude was established as securely along the Guinea coast as on the far side of the Atlantic, and in the excitement of the times some of the basic contradictions between the Caribbean dilemma and the African may have passed unnoticed.

All these stirring events left scarcely a ripple on the surface of British West Africa. In part this was a reflection of the provincial and somewhat Philistine character of West African society at that time; in part of the curious fact that the poet-politicians of the French Empire (Damas, Césaire and Senghor have all been members of the French National Assembly and leaders of their respective countries' nationalism) find no parallel in British territories, where an interest in politics too often seems to exclude an interest in anything else. But most of all it was probably due to the barrier of language. Few people in Nigeria, Ghana or Sierra Leone read French, Senghor's anthology has never been translated, and Hughes and Bontemps' *Poetry of the Negro* (1949) gave such a disproportionate space to mediocre American Negro verse that it could not convey anything of the same excitement. (pp. viii-xvi)

It does not follow, however, that négritude would have been a big hit in British West Africa even if it had been better known. The intensely romantic and rhetorical tradition of négritude poetry makes very little appeal in regions where the literary mood, as it is now emerging, is either realistic or introspective. The Nigerian attitude to négritude was typified by Wole Soyinka when he remarked, 'I don't think a tiger has to go around proclaiming his tigritude'. A similar scepticism has been expressed by the South African writer Ezekiel Mphahlele in a recent article in *Encounter* (March 1961). Mphahlele examines Senghor's claim that Africans are distinguished by a heightened sensibility and an intensity of emotion, that 'Emotion is Negro', but finds it utterly untenable. The truth is that passionate protests against the increasing abstraction of European life have been made by many European poets, from Blake to W. B. Yeats. No African has criticized our modern urban civilization more devastatingly than Dickens, Baudelaire or Lawrence. Assertions that Emotion is Negro are ultimately as silly as assertions that Intellect is White. Mphahlele's final conclusion is that négritude offers too narrow a field of response and that, 'Neither facile rejection nor facile acceptance makes good poetry'.

This pragmatic and realistic approach, which surely owes something to British intellectual tradition, has meant that the apostles of négritude have had little or no discernible effect upon the emergent literature of English-speaking Africa. If there have been Negro influences, they have probably been from writers like Richard Wright and Peter Abrahams rather than from the fluent and flourishing school of Paris. There is, for example, a singular independence about Nigeria's writers. A man like Amos Tutuola seems to acknowledge no masters; Chinua Achebe has probably learnt more from Joseph Conrad than from any other author; Cyprian Ekwensi's masters are in urban America rather than the Caribbean. Those British West Africans who have studied in America over the past thirty years or so have probably read fairly widely in the literature of American and West Indian Negroes writing in English, such as Richard Wright, Countee Cullen, Langston Hughes and Claude McKay. Here too the theme of exile and the idealization of Africa are sometimes found, but how different is the gentle, dreamy tone of the Jamaican McKay from the excited syncopations of Cuba!

For the dim regions whence my fathers came
My spirit, bondaged by the body, longs.
Words felt, but never heard, my lips would
      frame:
My soul would sing forgotten jungle songs.
I would go back to darkness and to peace,
But the great western world holds me in fee,
And I may never hope for full release
While to its alien gods I bend my knee.
Something in me is lost, forever lost,
Some vital thing has gone out of my heart,
And I must walk the way of life a ghost
Among the sons of earth, a thing apart.
For I was born, far from my native clime,
Under the white man's menace, out of time.

Probably the very absence of rhetoric in such writing helped its African readers to realize that McKay's dilemma was not theirs, and that he could not teach them how to write about their situation as Africans in Africa. The painful realism of a book like Achebe's *No Longer at Ease* is only possible because the author is taking a hard look at Lagos society as it is, without indulging in any comforting generalizations about the virtues of 'the African personality'. A similar realism is apparent in some of the younger writers from the French sphere, such as Ferdinand Oyono and Mongo Beti. Again, the poets now emerging in Nigeria and Ghana, men like Wole Soyinka, John Pepper Clark, Gabriel Okara and Awoonor-Williams, have been eclectic and uninhibited in their selection

The cover of Léopold Sédar Senghor's second book of poems, Hosties Noires.

of influences. They write out of a whole sensibility; a sensibility which Hopkins, Eliot, Pound, Yeats and Dylan Thomas, among others, have helped to shape. But they transmute these influences by their new feeling for English rhythms and the particularity of their writing about moments and places. This poetry is not concerned with large gestures, or with general statements about the black race, the cultural situation, the death of colonialism, etc. It is concerned with personal and intense experience; it is often inward, observant and reflective rather than rhetorical and 'public' in the French manner.

Introducing Senghor's anthology in 1948, Jean-Paul Sartre was able to describe the situation of the black writer in these terms:

> It is because he is already exiled from himself that he feels this need to declare himself. So he begins with an exile, a double exile. To the exile of his heart, the exile of his body offers a magnificent image. He is most of the time in Europe, in the cold, amid grey crowds; he dreams of Port-au-Prince, in Haiti. But that is not all: at Port-au-Prince he is already in exile; the slave-dealers have snatched his fathers from Africa and scattered them. And all the poems of this book (save those written in Africa) offer us the same mystic geography. A hemisphere; far down, making the first of the three concentric circles lies the land of exile, colourless Europe; then comes the dazzling ring of the Islands and the childhood that dances in circles around Africa; Africa makes the last circle, navel of the world, pole of all black poetry, Africa bright, burning and oily like a snakeskin, Africa of fire and rain, between being and becoming, more real than the endless boulevards of pleasure, but destroying Europe by its black invisible rays, beyond arrest, Africa, imaginary continent . . .

But Africa has now moved out of the shadows in which it was shrouded by the imagination of its lost children. It is no longer the imaginary continent. The young writer of today is no longer an exile, even a voluntary and temporary one, for he can carry his education to doctorate level without ever leaving his own country. When he does come to Europe it is probably not as a lonely disorientated youth, but as a scholar or writer, who is already testing his style and finding his place. The mystic geography, therefore, needs drastic revision. The black writer is no longer penned on the cold periphery, casting wistful glances towards the mysterious, unknown centre; his viewpoint has shifted to the centre itself. It is from there that he speaks to us.

Is négritude, then, a false and artificial movement? The answer, I think, is that all literary movements involve a measure of artificiality and arbitrary selection. The chief danger carried by négritude is that of degenerating into a racialism as intolerant and arrogant as any other. At its fiercest, it can lead to the writing of defiant, if invigorating nonsense like this, from Léon Damas' *Black Label:*

> The White will never be negro
> for beauty is negro
> and negro is wisdom
> for endurance is negro

and negro is courage
for patience is negro
and negro is irony
for charm is negro
and negro is magic
for love is negro
and negro is loose walking
for the dance is negro
and negro is rhythm
for art is negro
and negro is movement
for laughter is negro
for joy is negro
for peace is negro
for life is negro

But at its best it unlocked the talents of a very remarkable group of young Negroes; it gave them an attitude out of which they could create; it provided a vehicle for the passion, energy and conviction of a whole generation. (pp. xvi-xx)

> *Gerald Moore, in an introduction to his* Seven African Writers, *Oxford University Press, London, 1962, pp. vii-xx.*

Suzanne Valenti

[*In the following essay, Valenti compares how Negritude is depicted in the poetry of West Africans and black Americans.*]

Negritude refers to a special set of qualities, values, thoughts, and emotions possessed by blacks. It is a movement of ideas; an ideology; a motif in literature, particularly poetry, created by black writers. It represents an attempt to erect a new man, a new black man in a white world. Négritude is a literary response by educated blacks to enslavement, oppression, rejection and marginality. Acceptance of dominant group definitions left the blacks invisible, brutalized, and alienated from themselves.

> . . . The mind of the black man was held in bondage; his mind was often white-washed with a biting corrosive lime which seemed to eat away at the very structure of his life. The serfdom was not only menial, but moral, and black men seemed to be living forms without life, garbed and robed in the skin of Europe.
>
> . . . . .
>
> And the black man's rhythm became the cry of his blood and the pounding of his oppressed heart. His song became a wailing on the wind; his body an object of scorn and laughter. His language was lost and stifled, his feelings repressed, his strength sapped and sucked, his woman prostituted, his land, Africa, made a harlot. [Wilfred Cartey, "Dark Voices," *Présence Africaine* (1963)]

This response crystalized in the nineteen-thirties within the French literary circle of Senghor, Césaire and Damas. The term, itself, first appeared in a poem by Césaire [in *Cahier d'un retour au pays natal*]:

> My négritude is not a rock, its deafness hurled
> against the clamour of the day

My négritude is not a film of dead water on the
   dead eye of the earth
My négritude is neither a tower nor a cathedral,
It plunges into the burning flesh of the earth
It plunges into the burning flesh of the sky
It pierces the opaque prostration by its upright
   patience.

Beginnings of négritude, however, can be seen as early as 1881 in Blyden's address to Liberia College, when he recognized the plight of black people:

> . . . In the depth of their being they always feel themselves strangers, and the only escape from this feeling is to escape themselves, and this feeling of self-depreciation is not diminished . . . by the books they read. . . . Still we are held in bondage by our indiscriminate and injudicious use of foreign literature, and we strive to advance by the methods of a foreign race. . . . The African must advance by methods of his own.

He urged the black man to "develop his own peculiar gifts and powers with a sense of race individuality, self-respect and liberty. . . . Let us depend on it . . . the emotions and thoughts which are natural to us. . . ."

In the late 1950's, it was still seen as the task of educated blacks to "rediscover the historical truth and revalue Negro cultures which have been ignored, under-estimated or sometimes destroyed; to defend, illustrate and publicise the national values of their people." Négritude, however, was present in the writings of black Americans and Africans before the thirties, even though it was not labeled as such. In the United States, it was to take a somewhat different form than in the writings of black Africans. First, the common elements of the motif will be examined, and differences in emphasis between black Africans and black Americans will be noted.

Négritude can be broken down into several areas of expression, but it really begins with a recognition, a consciousness of blackness, then proceeds to an acceptance in which blackness is praised; the qualities of blacks are elaborated; a heritage is created; the plight of blacks is described and white values and civilization are belittled.

The poet Gabriel Okara, seeking admission to white society but being denied it (" 'Feel at home'; 'Come again,' they say . . . I find the doors shut,") discovers the insincerity of whites and their ways: "taught how to laugh only with teeth / to shake hands without hearts / how to wear face . . . ," and he asks his son to teach him how to laugh again with heart: "But believe me son / I want to be what I used to be. . . . " R. T. Dempster, in "Africa's Plea," recognizes the impenetrability of the white world and pleads to be permitted to be himself:

> I am not you—
> but you will not
> give me a chance,
> will not let me be me.

Hughes flatly states [in *Poems from Black Africa*]:

> I am a Negro
> Black as the night is black,

Black like the depths of my Africa.

Parkes cries:

> Give me black souls,
> Let them be black
> Or chocolate . . .

Diop whispers:

> Listen more often to things rather than beings.
> Hear the fire's voice,
> Hear the voice of the water.
> In the wind hear the sobbing of the trees,
> It is our forefathers breathing.
> The dead are not gone forever.
> They are in the paling shadows,
> The dead are not beneath the ground,
> They are in the rustling tree,
> In the murmuring wood . . .

Senghor reports:

> The Africa of the empires is dying, see, the
>   agony of a pitiful
> princess and Europe too where we are both
>   joined by the navel. . . .
> Let us report present at the rebirth of the World
> Like the yeast which white flour needs . . .

and proclaims,

> We are the men of the dance, whose feet draw
>   new strength
> pounding the hardened earth.

Yes, we are black, black writers proclaim, we are no longer going to try to be whiter than whites, or in the African case, no longer going to try to be "Black Frenchmen." Independence is to be sought; the "yoke of colonialism" is to be thrown off; Africa is to be for Africans. In the American case, independent development is sought (with, perhaps, integration later as equals) and/or separation. This political movement is, however, slightly later than its African counterpart (the 1960's versus the eruption of nationalism in Africa after World War II).

The plight of Blacks is strongly stated in Diop's verse:

> The white man killed my father
> My father was proud
> The white man seduced my mother
> My mother was beautiful
> The white man burnt my brother beneath the
>   noonday sun
> My brother was strong.
> His hands red with black blood
> The white man turned, to me
> And in the Conqueror's voice said,
> "Hey, boy! a chair, a napkin, a drink."

The situation of blacks is seen as one of oppression, enslavement, deculturalization [in Osadebay's "Blackman Trouble"]:

> I give my blood and my life for you,
>   But you no remember me;
> My heart be clean, my word be true,
>   My body no be free.
> Why must my feet be in your chain . . .
> I no got gun, I no get bomb,
>   I no fit fight nomore;

You bring your cross and make me dumb,
  My heart get plenty sore.
You tell me close my eyes and pray,
Your brudder thief my land away.
I not fit listen to more lies,
  I done see everything;
Dis tam I open wide my eyes
  And see de tricks you bring . . .

The "alien and exile" theme thus develops:

But the great western world holds me in fee,
And I may never hope for full release
While to its alien gods I bend my knee.
Something in me is lost, forever lost,
Some vital thing has gone out of my heart,
And I must walk the way of life of a ghost
Among the sons of earth, a thing apart,
For I was born, far away from my native clime,
under the white man's menace, out of time.

The Nigerian, Gabriel Okara, presents essentially the same situation in "Piano and Drums," in which he is caught between two worlds, a member of neither:

When at break of day at a riverside
I hear jungle drums telegraphing . . .
. . . my blood ripples, turns torrent,
. . . then I hear a wailing piano
solo speaking of complex ways
in tear-furrowed concerto;
of far-away lands
and new horizons . . . But lost in the labyrinth
of its complexities . . .
And I lost in the morning mist
of an age at a riverside keep
wandering in the mystic rhythm
of jungle drums and the concerto.

Whites and their civilization are belittled; whites are seen as superficial, vain, insensitive and inhumane. The anti-colonialism and anti-racism theme is thus developed [by Aimé Césaire]:

Europe has stuffed us with
lies and bloated us in pestilence,
for it is not true that the work of man is finished
that we have nothing to do in the world
that we are parasites in the world . . . .

Hear the white world
horribly fatigued by its immense effort,
its rebellious articulations crack under the hard
  stars
its inflexibilities of blue steel pierce the mystic
  flesh
hear its treacherous victories trumpeting its defeats
hear the grandiose alibis the pitiful fumbling.
Mercy for our omniscient and naive conquerors!

In order to reject dominant group definitions, the dominant group itself must be dismissed, and so it is.

The differences between the insensitive, callous oppressors and the oppressed are then enumerated. A history, a past, a culture, is created with the writer's pen. Roots to be proud of are grasped for. Women and Africa often become the vehicles for this assertion of a new self; of a heritage,

and thereafter, unity among Blacks of the diaspora. Africa is romanticized and idealized:

I love the days of long ago,
Great days of virtuous chastity
When wild men and wilder beasts
Kept close company.

I love Africa as herself—
Unsophisticated queenly Africa,
That precious pearl of the past.
Not all her beauties were the best
Nor all her charms the highest
In the day of long ago.

But give me back that Africa . . .
      [Michael Dei-Anang, "My Africa"]

(It is interesting, by the way, to note how Africa is praised here for characteristics whites had used to support their belief in her savagery and inferiority.) Black women become goddesses; they represent all that is good and true [in Countee Cullen's "Song of Praise"]:

You have not heard my love's dark throat,
  Slow-fluting like a reed,
Release the perfect golden note
  She caged there for my need . . .

My love is dark as yours is fair,
  Yet lovelier I hold her
Than listless maids with pallid hair,
  And blood that's thin and colder.

Blacks, in general, are praised for qualities of sensitivity, naturalness, innocence, spiritual depth, sensuousness—characteristics which had been cynically invoked by whites to support a negative stereotype become positive qualities in the poetry of négritude:

God!
glad I'm black;
pitch-forking devil black:
black, black, black;
black absolute of life complete,
greedfully grabbing life's living,
stupor drunkenness,
happiness.
depth of hurt,
anger of sorrow:
synthesis of joy, sadness;
composite child of life.
pulsating,
brash;
hatred coarse,
joy smooth.
stupid,
solomon wise;
shallow,
coconut-tree tall.
            [Bloke Modisane, "blue black"]

Senghor praises the black soldier and celebrates the qualities of blackness:

You are the flower of the foremost beauty in
  stark absence of flowers
Black flower and solemn smile, diamond time
  out of mind.

You are the clay and the plasma of the world's
  vivid spring
Flesh you are of the first couple, the fertile belly,
  milt and sperm
You are the sacred fecundity of the bright paradise gardens . . .
Black martyrs, O undying race, give me leave to
  say the words which will forgive.
                                    ["Martyrs"]
          . . . . .
No, you are the messengers of his mercy, breath
  of Spring after Winter
For those who had forgotten laughter (using
  only an oblique smile) . . .
You bring the springtime of Peace, hope at the
  end of waiting.
              ["To the American Negro Soldiers"]

Langston Hughes continues this theme of praise:

Black
As the gentle night,
Black as the kind and quiet night
Black as the deep productive earth.
Body
Out of Africa,
Strong and black . . .
Kind
As the black night . . .

Négritude is, therefore, not a simple theme in literature developed at a particular point in time. It is a complex association of elements found in the poetry of black Americans and black Africans. Damas's poem "Limbe" combines most of these ingredients [including recognition and consciousness, the return theme and qualities of Blackness, the plight, the roots, and the heritage]:

Give me back my black dolls. I want to play with
  them.
Play the ordinary games that come naturally to
  me,
Stay in the shadow of their rules,
Get back my courage and my boldness,
Feel myself, what I was yesterday,
Without complexity.

Yesterday, when I was torn up by the roots,
Will they ever know the rancour eating at my
  heart,
My mistrustful eye open too late.

They have stolen the space that was mine
The customs, the days of my life
The singing, the rhythm, the strain,
The path, the water, the hut
The earth, grey, smokey
And Wisdom, the word, the palavers,
The ancients.
And the beat, the hands, the beating of the hands
And the stamping of the feet on the ground . . .

How satisfactory this response to race conditions has been is difficult to assess. As a temporary measure, it was useful to bolster egos, to restore pride, and to unite some parts of the black world. It helped to promote independence in Africa. In the United States, it is . . . being fully exploited politically, educationally and economically. Often this is taken to the near point of Black racism. Achebe notes that

it is time to move on to other topics; that the theme has been overdone. For black Africans perhaps it has been. Disillusionment, on the part of some, was felt:

Is this all you are? . . .
Africa, you are a concept, which we all
Fashion in our minds, each to each, to
Hide our seperate years, to dream our separate
  dreams.
        [Abioseh Nicol, "The Continent that Lies
                                    Within Us"]

The black American faced this problem in even greater depth. He was black, but an American as well. He was not an African. This ambivalence, (related to what the educated African felt caught between traditional Africa and Europe), is expressed early in the works of DuBois as "twoness," and is echoed today, for example, in [LeRoi] Jones's "Notes for a Speech":

African blues does not know me . . .
Does not feel what I am . . .
Africa is a foreign place. You are
as any other sad man here american.

This theme is an American development. The emphasis on the Africanism of négritude is replaced, in black American poetry, by an emphasis on color, Blackness. Qualities which are praised are often linked solely with blackness, as though they were genetically inherited. Négritude becomes *soul* in the United States. It is a "black man's thing," a result of having paid the dues. Blacks seek Americanity, integration. (In Africa, this can only be found in South Africa, *e.g.*, in the works of Richard Rive.) The symbols are clear, folk-like in contrast with the literary symbols used by West Africans. More frequently, symbols of Christianity are used. Another difference between black African and black American poetry is the mood of resignation prominent in the latter. Music, love, God and alcohol are all used by black Americans to escape rather than to confront the situation. This tendency is expressed as submission and fatalism in the following two poems:

Again the day
The low bleak day of the stricken years
And now the years.

The huge slow grief drives on
And I wonder why
I grow cold
And care less
And less and less I care.

If the stars should fall,
I grant them privilege;
Or if the stars should rise to a brighter flame
The mighty day, the buckled Orion
To excellent purposes appear to gain—
I should renew their privilege
To fall down.

It is all to me the same
The same to me
I say the great Gods, all of them,
All-cold, pitiless—
Let them fall down
Let them buckle and drop.

[Samuel Allen, "If the Stars Should Fall"]
. . . . .
I woke up this morning
just befo' the break of day.
I was bitter, blue and black, Lawd.
There ain't nothing else to say.
I wondered why God made me.
I wondered why He made me black.
I wondered why Mama begat me—
And I started to give God His ticket back.
          [Lerone Bennett, "Blues and Bitterness"]

And in "Prayer" by Isabellas Brown:

I had thought of putting an
altar here in the house,
just a small corner.
Anyway, I usually fall down on my knees
Anywhere in the house . . .
So I ask God to hold my mind
and lead me in His path.

It sure is raining hard today.

Négritude has taken many forms in its development. It began with a rejection of the dominant group and a recognition of acceptance of blackness. In the enumeration and praising of black qualities, it reached its height in an "unfolding" common to both black American and black African poetry. The emphases are somewhat different, however, due to the particular historical circumstances of the black American. In both cases, the movement of these ideas originates in a response to oppression and rejection. Colonialism and slavery destroyed an old way of life, but

---

W. F. Feuser on Negritude and Afro-American Literature:

At a first glance, we may discover many similarities between Negritude writing and Afro-American literature. Can we therefore claim that both derive from the same source? James Ivy contends that "les accents passionés de la Muse noire-américaine sortent directement de la ségrégation raciale, non de la Négritude." Apart from the relative newcomer, "Soul," the facile identification of which with "Négritude" would seem to be of doubtful value since even in Anglophone African countries "soul" merely conjures up images of raucous crooning and novel types of bodily gyrations, without cutting any deeper, there exists only one other apparent synonym of "Négritude" in the American context. But on close scrutiny it conveys an entirely different meaning. "Negroness," as first defined by J. S. Redding in his analytical study, *On Being Negro in America* (1951), is a negative phenomenon, an emotional inability to show normal human reactions in extreme situations involving black and white. Redding admits that, paralyzed with fear, he did not move a finger to help a white women who died after an epileptic fit outside the southern Negro college where he was teaching. For him "Negroness is a kind of superconsciousness that directs thinking, that dictates action, and that perverts the expression of instinctual drives which are salutary and humanitarian."

W. F. Feuser, in his "Afro-American Literature and Negritude," in Comparative Literature, *Fall 1976.*

---

denied access to the new one they had made appear desirable. Caught in between, the black man responded. Since true integration and common humanity were impossible, what was left except a return to the old and a stress on difference? This was, after all, nothing more than the lesson of the master learned with a vengeance and put to unexpected use. This socio-cultural situation combined with the socio-psychological one of the basic human need for recognition, response, and a sense of worthiness, produced and supported the literary movement known as négritude. (pp. 390-98)

> *Suzanne Valenti, "The Black Diaspora: Negritude in the Poetry of West Africans and Black Americans," in* PHYLON: The Atlanta University Review of Race and Culture, *Vol. XXXIV, No. 4, fourth quarter (December, 1973), pp. 390-98.*

Lilyan Kesteloot

[*In the following excerpt, which is based on a 1960 survey of twenty-two black French-language writers, Kesteloot discusses the writers' attitudes toward Negritude and the dominant themes in their works.*]

Since Sartre's "Orphée noir" Negro intellectuals have reacted quickly to the word "negritude," to the term, it would seem, rather than to its meaning. It will be recalled that, with reason, Sartre linked negritude and neoracism, but in no way did he suggest they were one and the same. If it contained a racial nuance, something Sartre moreover felt necessary, negritude included many other positive elements, among them what he called "love," "going beyond itself," etc. Yet it is to this "accusation" of racism that blacks react so passionately. The better to deny a part, they reject the whole!

In discussing Sartre's essay, in which, they believe, negritude first took shape as a theory, black students [as recounted in *Les étudiants noirs parlent* (1953)] violently oppose the notion of an "antiracist racism, which seems to be the cornerstone of this theory." One might think at first that Sartre called this an antiracist racism only because he personally objected to it. Nothing of the kind. Sartre wished to help create this antiracist racism. He believed it to be an effective, the *only* effective, tool! Since he was addressing writers, his opinion was the same as saying:

> Blacks, sing loudly of your color, seeing fundamentally in it a sign of human value. Blacks, develop a black racism, necessarily revolutionary, because it will bring about the failure of white racism by replacing the formula, white-equals-superiority, with black-equals-superiority. [*Les étudiants noirs parlent*]

This was obviously the path which was going to be chosen by numerous young poets, often without future, and in several issues of *Présence Africaine* there were worthless poems inevitably exalting "negritude."

Sartre's "Black Orpheus" seems to have been the quite unintentional cause of this passionate reaction, since the inventors of negritude (Césaire, Senghor, and Damas), as well as those who had used the term before Sartre's essay, in no way altered their position and continued to use the word with the meaning they had always given it.

Questioned today [1960], on the other hand, many young writers declare their opposition to the use of the word. For Tchicaya U Tam'si, for example, negritude implies racism and must therefore be rejected, because the only thing that counts today is national originality. Mongo Beti told us: "It is better to treat the problem in sociological than in racial terms. In any case, the situation is changing, and with the disappearance of colonial tutelage, in all probability there will be attempts by blacks to oppress blacks. It is in terms of social oppression that the situation must be seen." Agblemagnon was struck by the restrictive aspects of negritude. "This concept was necessary," he said, "but it is confining. Nor should writers be fake hunters running in someone else's smoke." Negritude can, in fact, embody key themes to be repeated by weak writers who do not dare follow a personal path but lean on political slogans to "give themselves a certain standing." As for Ousmane Sembene, he believes negritude often encourages writers to make negative and, above all, excessively passive complaints, instead of committing them to activities that are truly revolutionary.

Rabemananjara was moved by another definition of negritude in "Black Orpheus" and reacted against "some obscure essence called negritude . . . which, since a certain resounding preface, has become a source of ambiguity" ["Le poète noir et son peuple," *Présence Africaine* (1957)]. Sartre did in fact use the expression "essence noire" and seemed to mean by it that a black man, by his very nature, is basically different from all others. Because of his skin! To make this assertion reveals that one is unconsciously racist, Rabemananjara observes. "Negritude is explained to him [the black man] as a totality, as the very essence of his nature, and ample advantage has been taken of this confusion to convince the black man of his fundamental difference from all other human species." What the black poet really wished to do was quite the contrary, to rid his color of its imaginary stains and proclaim the "unique truth of his people":

> Beyond the color of my skin, my blood is as red
>   as your blood,
> my flesh as red as your flesh
> and my soul is of the same essence as yours.

Following this, Rabemananjara rises against the claim that there is creative virtue in negritude: "It is obvious that conditions responsible for the new black poetics were in no way furnished by the influence of that notorious category, negritude." In 1959, in more moderate terms, Rabemananjara protested against all notions of black "essence." Two factors, in his view, had favored the meeting and unity of blacks of all origins: First, the general contempt toward their color had engendered in all of them the same demand for dignity; second, conditions of colonial exploitation which affected all Negro peoples created a community of feeling, of suffering, and of opposition to white colonizers. "But would the Madagascan and the Dahomean," Rabemananjara writes, "have sought each other out if they had not suffered European domination?

The day this state of colonization disappears, negritude will disappear all by itself."

This is an obvious restriction of Sartre, for whom negritude covered "the black man's being-in-the-world," beyond his situation of "being black in the *colonized* world." In addition, it confirms . . . Rabemananjara is not an African but a Madagascan. Although black, he belongs to a different civilization, closer to the peoples of the Orient than of Africa, and he does not feel a close bond uniting him with other blacks above and beyond the present European domination. He does not realize that other black peoples may feel united by the community of an ancient civilization which has left deep impressions on the entire continent and which might—after the disappearance of all white domination—enable the peoples of Africa to reinforce the ties of their common negritude. Rabemananjara is therefore right in insisting that negritude is not an *essence* separating the black man from other men, or a question of color, but a similarity of condition. He forgets, however, to include in this condition the weight of a whole common past. Instead of concluding that negritude is only transitory and bound to disappear, one ought then to conclude it will persist.

To summarize, the concept of negritude has obviously changed since Sartre's study, because of the very passionate reactions it provoked. It therefore seems necessary to us to restate Césaire's present idea of it.

Starting from the "awareness of being black," which implies "the taking over of one's destiny, history, and culture," negritude becomes "the simple recognition of a fact" and "includes no racism or rejection of Europe, and no exclusivity, but on the contrary a fraternity of all men." "A greater unity between the men of the black race" does exist, however, "not because of skin, but because of a community of culture, history, and temperament." Hence "there is no need to go beyond negritude, which is a *sine qua non* condition of creative authenticity in any domain" (interview with Aimé Césaire, June 1959).

Understood thus, the concept of negritude is close to that of "cultural originality," which has today replaced it for the majority of black writers we interviewed. They were almost unanimous in preferring this new expression, which has the advantage of containing no racial nuance while emphasizing local origin. In the same way, one can speak of "the African personality" or of "de-Westernizing cultures." The resolutions of the Second Congress of Black Writers and Artists strongly insisted not only on the responsibilities of black writers toward their peoples, but also on the bonds of a common civilization:

> . . . these considerations do not rest on ethnic or racial assumptions. They are the result of a common origin and suffering. Black peoples have borne together a series of historical misadventures which, under the special form of total colonization, involving slavery, deportation, and racism, have been imposed upon these peoples, and upon them only, in this objectively known period of history. The existence of an African Negro civilization, beyond national or regional particularities, thus appears historically justi-

fied, and reference to this civilization legitimate and enriching. This must form the basis of unity and solidarity among the various Negro peoples.

We observe that to avoid being accused of racism, black writers insist on stating that their solidarity is not based on race. But, who, in fact, has shared this "community of origin and suffering" if not black peoples, and they alone? If the term negritude is therefore abandoned, everything it contained—except the racial affirmation—is maintained.

Understood in this manner, negritude would in no way impede the creation of a universal humanism shared by all Africans.

In conclusion we would like to quote two young African writers who have already gone beyond the aggressive phase of negritude to retain only its generous, positive aspect. Paulin Joachim describes it with enthusiasm: "Where are my values, I who am a racial lie? Negritude helps me to rediscover my sources, my origins, one by one, not to mourn for them, but to draw upon their magnificent vitality which the world needs. Negritude is a slow-burning light from which all violence is excluded; it is a solar Pentecost, that sinks into my past in order to re-awaken burnt-out suns. It is a horse I bestride, it is also the aim, the day after colonialism, when the Negro will truly be himself. It is both the path and the goal." Less lyrically, here is how Olympe Bhêly-Quénum defines negritude: "The exhuming of Negro cultural values, which have been stifled, their explication and affirmation. I hope to see negritude rid of its political context. The role of black writers is to show that negritude progresses, that it eliminates racism."

Let us now examine the principal themes the black writers address.

A majority—eighteen—speak of *colonization,* in a different way, of course, depending upon whether they are poets, novelists, or essayists. Poetry lends itself better to lyrical cries of pain and revolt (Césaire, Damas, Rabemananjara, Senghor, Niger, David Diop, and Bernard Dadié). The novel is better adapted to concrete situations, and one learns a great deal through novels about the condition of colonized natives and their psychology; colonization and the white man are exposed to a light of day never found in colonial magazines, too rarely in official reports or the exotic novels of outsiders. Finally, essayists like A. Tevoedjre, Alioune Diop, or Frantz Fanon bring weighty, scientific arguments to bear. With figures and documentation they demonstrate the great destitution and material want of the black masses, their acute frustration, the disastrous psychological effects of colonization, the complexes and alienations which result from it.

Let us briefly call attention to the aspects of *Western domination* most frequently revealed in the works of black writers. Together they form quite an indictment!

The Caribbean writers (Damas, Césaire, Sainville, Glissant, and Niger) often come back to *slavery,* still an incredibly tenacious wound. But the Africans too had cause to complain of a *loss of liberty.* Through feelings of solidarity they too are interested in the ancient slavery, but rather from its historical angle; they study the archives in order to describe the slave trade, and attempt to account for Africa's decadence. For these African writers, however, slavery is never a source of literary inspiration.

Most of the writers describe with considerable force the multiple aspects of *poverty and destitution:* ever-present hunger, hard and poorly paid work, sickness and death, illiteracy, poverty of the land, where peasants labor for beggarly wages, or the poverty of the cities with their sad retinue of slums, unemployment, and prostitution, not forgetting the evil psychological effects of detribalization, poor adaptation to machinery, and closer contact with white masters.

Colonization is rejected outright! Direct reference to its positive contributions is rare—to medical care, hygiene, education, modern techniques—although several writers such as Niger, Senghor, or Alioune Diop soften their criticism by admitting that "along with its errors and backsliding, the French presence did, historically, on the whole constitute progress" [Senghor, "Congrés constitutif du P.R.A."].

Yet even these writers share the unanimous opinion that this necessary contact with Western countries could have occurred without exploitation. They mention the example of Japan, which developed, because of economic contact with Europe and America, without brutal colonization. If the blacks readily recognize our technical superiority, they contest the use we have made of it and are opposed to European capitalism and materialism, sharing in this the reaction of many other underdeveloped lands. "It often happens that the population of an underdeveloped country has the feeling of having been . . . mistreated by the world in general or by one rich country in particular" [Gunnar Myrdal, *Théorie économique et pays sous-développés*].

For a European who wishes to understand the works of black writers, we would advise first of all reading a few UNESCO statistics, a book such as *Les Antilles décolonisées* by Daniel Guérin, or the voluminous report by the Bureau International du Travail, *Les problèmes du travail en Afrique noire (Work problems in Black Africa).* After this he will be less inclined to feel wounded by black accusations or to suspect their systematic indictments of exaggeration. We should like, however, to make another observation. There is no doubt that black writers show only the seamy underside of our colonial action. Doubtless this is because for too long we have been willing to show only its rosiest aspect! Some, on the other hand, like Joseph Zobel, describe colonial societies without any polemic intention and without apparent bitterness; what they show is no greater consolation to the Western conscience.

The second group of themes deals with *traditional life.* Customs, festivals, daily life, work, people, wisdom—all the aspects of native cultures, in short, are endless sources of inspiration for black authors. . . . [Most] of them have lived in their native lands. Others are interested in African life, but as a European would be. This was the case of René Maran, who had a feeling of community with other blacks, having himself suffered from color prejudice. He studied their customs with considerable objectivity, though without participating in their culture. Some of the younger writers, like David Diop and Elolongué Epanya Yondo, already influenced by the "negritude movement," feel frustrated, and their works seem pained, rebellious, directed toward the future. How different the equilibrium of Senghor or Birago Diop, or of good novelists like Aké Loba and Olympe Bhêly-Quénum, who had the advantage of participating in Negro cultures, even if they had been diminished or distorted. Césaire, though he has never been to Dahomey, might thus feel comfortable in the culture of that country.

Much of the flavor of the novels on rural Caribbean life, too, comes from the fact that their authors remained close to the ordinary people, their mores, beliefs, and mentalities. In the West Indies, the clearing and harvesting of the land is always a community project carried out to the sound of tom-toms. Voodoo rites, predictions, superstitions, belief in metamorphoses and in "quimboi" love potions are still an intimate part of the popular sensibility.

The novels show the obstinacy of these small, hard-working communities, their spirit of mutual aid, also their sense of humor which helps to balance lives so difficult they would be unbearable if faced on the tragic level. They tell of simple, uncomplicated loves, of men and women for whom sexuality has cosmic extensions. How far the delicacy of the two scenes that follow [from Edouard Glissant's *La Lézarde*] is from the stifling eroticism of French novels today:

> Ce qui court entre eux, c'est plus que la grace aiguë du désir, plus que l'ineffable et le grondement, bien plus encore que l'assurance des deux arbres qui auraient joint leurs racines sous la surface . . . oho! c'est le charroi de toute la sève, c'est le cri même de la racine, ho! c'est la geste venue du fond des ages, qu'ont parfait les ancêtres et que voici renaître.

> [What flows between them is more than the sweet intensity of desire, greater than what is unutterable or looming, greater even than the certainty of two trees whose roots have intertwined beneath the surface . . . oh! It is the rising of all the sap, the very cry of their roots, the age-old motion perfected by their ancestors and born with them anew.]

> Ils coulèrent dans le temps qui jusqu'à eux menait sa rivière sans crue, ils furent sur l'ocean, ils furent dans la révolte, ils connurent le goût des fruits de la forêt marronne, ils revinrent ensemble dans le présent presque éclairci.

> [They streamed through time which had brought its floodless river to them, they rode the ocean, were part of the fugitives' forests, they returned together to a present almost bright.]

Despite their incontestable kinship, African novels are nonetheless very different from those of the West Indies. We must not forget that there is a far greater distance in miles between the countries of Mongo Beti, Edouard Glissant, and Hampate Ba than between Norway, Spain, and Russia, and as great a distance emotionally. Africa is an immense continent, and if some power lines traverse it,

they leave vast space for many varieties and degrees of refinement. The happy moderation of *L'enfant noir* is a hundred leagues from the ostentation of the Dakar society described in *Maïmouna*, which in turn derives from a very different culture than that of *Le roi miraculé*.

If the themes of suffering and revolt are similar to the point of sounding "monochordal," as Agblemagnon put it, the novels evoking traditional life and wisdom fortunately escape this defect and are fascinating in their variety. It is through the deeper investigation of their native lands that the writers differ and find a personal accent. We mentioned earlier that black writers excel at the type of tale that depicts the simple and precious aspects of traditional life, meeting up to now only with success. The wisdom, the humor of everyday, a sense of the marvelous, of myth and legend, all is recouped here, retained in its original form, and should prove of considerable interest to the curiosity of sociologists, moralists, psychologists, and artists alike. Authors such as Birago Diop, Léon Damas, and Jean Malonga deserve congratulation. In a manner sometimes too discreet to be fully appreciated, they bear witness to the ancient patrimony and nourish its most authentic art.

We would point out that the authors who attack colonization most violently are not the ones most interested in traditional life. The most careful and vivid descriptions of this life are by completely nonpolemical authors. They try to dig out, understand, and express all all that is original in their societies, whose spirit and language no white writer could express as well.

The reason for this may be that these writers, whom we may call "traditionalist," are more deeply rooted in their ancestral cultures than their fellow writers, either because, like Hampate Ba, Paul Hazoumé, or Jean Malonga, their contact with Europe was very sparse and late, or because, like Birago Diop or Bhêly-Quénum, they had thought through their culture deeply and were able to take new root in it. These authors seem to have acquired a balance which enables them to extract greater richness from their heritage. The polemical writers, perhaps because they are more Westernized, seem frustrated and more deeply wounded. For them rebellion seems the natural outlet. They are both closer to the West and more bitterly opposed to its influence, which they consider evil. Such is the case of Césaire, Damas, David Diop, Fanon, Beti, Epanya, and others.

We only suggest this as a hypothesis, one which of course has no effect on the literary value of these writers.

One is struck however by the small role played by *personal themes* of love, death, nature, God, etc. Not that these do not frequently occur in the works of the two main schools of writers previously discussed, but we have never, for example, come across the classical love story involving two or three characters so popular in France since Madame de Lafayette. Nor are there subtle introspections like those of Proust or Sartre! Very little meditation on death or nature! In the African Negro novels or poems, the individual is part of the people and the society from which he originates. Even when he says "I" he means "we." He represents his people. He reinvests all personal emotion in a more general current. For Glissant and Rabemananjara, for example, feelings of love are always "reinvested" in the themes of freedom, love of country, or the bond with one's ancestors. Even in works that seek to defend no thesis, such as those by F. D. Sissoko, J. Zobel, or J. Malonga, the action is never limited to the adventures of a few individuals; the principal subject is always the community, and the life of the group. [In a footnote, Kesteloot states: "An exception to this general rule must, however, be made for a whole series of autobiographical novels describing the tribulations of young blacks—usually students—who arrive in France. Whether well or less well analyzed, one discovers in them the efforts of naïve, uprooted blacks who attempt to penetrate and find acceptance in a white milieu, the prejudices encountered, the snubs, the disappointments, material difficulties, and loneliness. The hero fights, triumphs, or is defeated. The most successful novel of this type seems to us Aké Loba's *Kocoumbo, l'étudiant noir.*"]

Among traditional values they most appreciate, black intellectuals often single out solidarity, a sense of community. An interesting comparison could certainly be made here between ancient African culture and this aspect of literary works by black writers today.

The genres in which black writers prefer to express themselves are poetry (thirteen poets out of seventeen writers) and novels (mentioned eleven times).

We have repeatedly indicated the marked superiority of black poetry over the novel, particularly up to the late 1940s. Since then, however, the novel has certainly caught up, and several writers—Niger, Zobel, and Bhêly-Quénum among them—declared they prefer this genre because it permits a more explicit presentation of ideas, greater nuance and emphasis.

Why did the explosion of poetry come first, and why was poetry preferred at that time? The Algerian poet, Henri Kréa, speaking of *his* country's poetry, gives one possible answer [in an interview printed in *L'Express* (21 July 1960)]. "What French poetry particularly lacks," he points out, "is a dramatic context," while Algeria is "at the smelting point." "In underdeveloped countries the imagination becomes overdeveloped, it becomes mythological." Discussing such a "dramatic context," that is, the presence of a world that one rejects and that one would wish were different, where direct action toward the transformation of reality is or seems impossible, Frantz Fanon sees poetry as "a temporary form of combativity," a verbal compensation. Poetry upsets and transforms the world intellectually, replacing it with the hope of a better world, lending the courage to endure this one. The novel, a more concrete, explicit mode of action, comes only later when there is hope of real solutions.

All this is mere hypothesis, but nonetheless has elements of truth.

In any case, the black novel, which has now assumed an important place beside black poetry, is very much alive today. Much fiction, as we have said, is either autobiographical or includes a good many happenings and situations which were actually experienced by the authors or those close to him. In general, the novels are realistic, often polemical, more rarely poetic or fantastic like Glissant's *La lézarde,* or *Un piège sans fin* by Bhêly-Quénum.

The folktale, on the other hand, has no controversial element at all. It makes no demands, is in no way intended to set blacks and whites in opposition to one another. Quite simply, it describes traditional life, folklore, mores, and customs, and it is in these folk narratives that one finds the most authentic impressions of Negro life. The short story would seem to be the genre par excellence of black writers, for this writer has so far not read a single one that was not successful, whether it be a West Indian story by Damas or J. S. Alexis, or an African one by Birago Diop, Bernard Dadié, or Jean Malonga.

Less personal than novels, short stories are nonetheless just as effective. They give us a better understanding of the Negro soul by showing us the wisdom and sense of humor so specific to black peoples, and describing their lives candidly and without lies.

As for the essays, these range from article and pamphlet to the more substantial kind of study. Nearly half the writers questioned (ten out of twenty-two) consider it an excellent means of making oneself clearly understood by all. For this reason the essay is favored even by poets such as Césaire *(Discours sur le colonialisme),* Senghor ("Ce que l'homme noir apporte," together with a number of his important articles on traditional cultures), or Glissant *(Soleil de la conscience).* Other essayists, like Fanon and Cheik Anta Diop, show real literary gifts.

The historical works of black writers can scarcely be considered "essays" because they have achieved too great a scope and importance. There is only one professional historian. Léonard Sainville, author of a work on Victor Schoelcher, but several others are successfully following in his wake. Aimé Césaire recently published the biography of a man he greatly admires, Toussaint Louverture. Cheik Anta Diop has written two important books: *Nations nègres et culture* and *L'Afrique noire pré-coloniale.* Hampate Ba has done a history of the Dogon people, and Paul Hazoumé has written about the institutions of Dahomey.

All black intellectuals are fully aware to what extent the foundations of history can help their cultural movement, and that is the reason for their passionate interest in ethnology.

More than half the writers interviewed are engaged in some political or union activity parallel to their literary efforts. Six, elected by their people, have even occupied official positions. It is significant that certain of them were only elected after some cultural achievement. This was the case for Senghor, Césaire, and Damas, who were drawn into political engagement through the ideas they stood for in their writings. Not all of these writers embraced political life by personal inclination, but they were the first people to become aware of the human and political needs of their countries and to show themselves capable of asserting these needs before the West. To the extent that they presume to represent more than themselves, the fact that these writers engage in real action should not surprise us. It merely makes their artistic vocation more authentic. In his article "Le leader politique considéré comme le représentant d'une culture," Sékou Touré has an excellent perception of the close bond between the defender of a national culture—which is what these black writers seek to be—and political action. (pp. 317-28)

> Lilyan Kesteloot, *"A New Generation and the Negritude Label,"* in her Black Writers in French: A Literary History of Negritude, *translated by Ellen Conroy Kennedy, Temple University Press, 1974, pp. 317-32.*

Willfried Feuser

[*Feuser is a scholar of modern languages. In the following essay, he observes the French cultural and literary influences on Negritude.*]

Lecturing on early European Romanticism at the University of Montpellier a few years ago, René Etiemble made a disclosure at the end of his course. He had taken all the quotations illustrating the genesis of this movement from Chinese poetry written before and after the beginning of our era! Without pushing the comparison too far, one could attempt the same experiment by substituting modern African verse in French for some of the 19th-century French Romantics. Clive Wake in his introduction to a recent anthology has explored the affinities between Senghor, Birago Diop and Victor Hugo. Other critics, and not the meanest among them Senghor himself, point out the uniqueness of the African's experience and of its poetic expression, which are only facets of "Négritude." Nobody can avoid a discussion of this concept, or movement, when dealing with French African poetry.

Négritude is a concept of romantic race-consciousness of the Negro, but it was not born in Africa. It was essentially a "racial," political, and cultural awakening of the African in exile, and the feeling at the root of its literature is prefigured in the 137th psalm:

> By the rivers of Babylon,
> There we sat down, yea, we wept,
> When we remembered Zion . . .

Négritude can be divided into three main phases, partly overlapping, with changes of name entailed by its moving from one linguistic medium to another. It is not surprising that the racial awakening of the first phase should have taken place among the largest single group of exiled Africans, the Negroes of the United States, where, after a period of acquiescence, DuBois asserted, "The problem of the twentieth century is the problem of the colour-line." DuBois's equalitarian belief in a co-existence of the races, which evolved into Pan-Africanism, was challenged by Marcus Garvey, whose cry "Back to Africa" rocked the American-Negro masses of the 'Twenties. Garvey's *Philosophy and Opinions* influenced Kwame Nkrumah, for example, more strongly than did Hegel, Marx, and Engels.

In the cultural sphere the writings of Leo Frobenius had by that time caught up with the current of political thought and with the musical revolution of jazz and went into the making of that great cultural movement, the Negro Renaissance, epitomised in Alain Locke's anthology, *The New Negro* (1925). Langston Hughes, whom Locke called "the most racial of the New Negro poets," proclaimed: "We younger Negro artists who create now intend to express our individual dark-skinned selves without fear or shame." The racial content of New Negro poetry is further illustrated by the titles of Countee Cullen's volumes from *Colour* (1925) to *The Black Christ* (1929). The end of the 'Twenties saw the rise of *Negrismo* in Cuba and of a similar movement heralded by Price-Mars in Haiti.

But the second phase of the movement was truly inaugurated by the young French Caribbean rebels, twice exiled in Paris, starting with Etienne Léro's shortlived journal, *Légitime Défense* (1932). Léro acknowledged his group's debt of gratitude to the "New Negroes,"—"Langston Hughes and Claude MacKay (sic), the two revolutionary poets, have brought us, soaked in red alcohol, the African love of life, the African joy of love, and the African dream of death."

Négritude emerged from the obscurity of student magazines into the light of Aimé Césaire's *Cahier d'un retour au pays natal* (1939 and 1947). By that time "Négritude" covered a variety of frequently conflicting tendencies: racial self-discovery, surrealist self-expression, Marxist revolutionary hope, and Afro-Christian humanism. Its underlying unity consisted in the eternally romantic return to the sources, Senghor's *retour aux sources de la Négritude,* but its codified creed is best understood in terms of the French cultural tradition "with its intellectualisation and its love of literary manifestoes" (Wake). After all, its most coherent interpretation to date has been given by Sartre. For Sartre, Négritude poetry was "the only great revolutionary poetry" of his day. It was an expression of *racisme antiraciste,* a revitalisation of Surrealism and, to give Freud his full due, the "unity of phallic erection and vegetal growth." It was the poetry of a new chosen people, the selective principle being Suffering.

Leaving aside the Caribbean phase of Négritude—with Césaire's achievement in the *Cahier* overshooting the limits of any definition and Damas's resounding racism ending in an emotional cul-de-sac—we are here mainly concerned with Senghor's contribution and with what I should like to call the third phase, that of Négritude-in-Africa. Senghor's creative phase largely coincides with the period of his close collaboration with the Caribbean poets; the same is true of Birago Diop. David Diop, who spoke a genuine poetic idiom all his own, was an exile too; he could not fulfil his promise because he died too young. Jacques Rabemananjara of Madagascar is a Négritude poet by adoption. This leaves us with Bernard Dadié of the Ivory Coast, who can claim some genuine African-born Négritude verse as his own though in his litany-like style he lacks Senghor's power over the word; with the softly probing accent of Somalia's William Syad, whose French verse is weaker than his English with its strong Arabic component; Joseph Bognini, who shows great promise; Lamine Diakhaté of Senegal with an unimaginative harping on the theme of escape and the myth of blood, an echo of Senghor's call to international brotherhood, and a tin-drum finale of crude political propaganda; Antoine-Roger Bolamba's *Chant du soir* is quite charming, but it is too evident that he is still serving his apprenticeship, as his imagery lacks the power and density of his fellow-Congolese from the Brazzaville side of the river, Félix Gérard Tchicaya U Tam'si.

U Tam'si could be called a surrealist or a symbolist, but in the first place he is very intensely U Tam'si. He is concerned with death and blood, but blood not in the sense of "noble black blood." He is obsessed with the question of the origin of the collective self, the race, symbolised by the tree: *mais d'oú me vient cette folie tellement arborescente?* . . . Or is it sometimes "the tree of grace" and sometimes "the tree of race," to use the language of Charles Péguy (*La double Racination*)? For the debate between body and soul is going on relentlessly in his monologuising. It brings him into violent conflict with God. *"Toi qui m'as fait si triste."* It leads to his mock-identification with Christ [in "Epitomé"],

> Come unto me . . .
> If you have only a body
> you are mortal
> tear yourself away from your flesh
> I can betray you.

He hates Christ for associating himself with the bourgeois, and he hates the Christians and merchants like his brother in Anti-Christ, Arthur Rimbaud. Like him, he calls the leaders of a society he condemns *faux négres*—fake Negroes. He himself is a true Negro, in Rimbaud's words, Je suis de la race qui chantait dans le supplice. (*Une Saison en enfer,* "Mauvais Sang," which became the title of U Tam'si first collection of poems). Rimbaud wanted to leave civilisation behind and drink in distant lands *des liqueurs fortes comme du métal bouillant.* In the title poem of *Brush Fire* we read,

> I said to you
> my race
> remembers
> the taste of bronze drunk hot.

Far from being the "sordid physical relationship with a certain Arthur" to which he confesses in his poem "The Slave," Tchicaya U Tam'si's love for Rimbaud's poetry has helped him to heighten, over and above his search for the origins of the collective self, his awareness of the individual self, his *coeur* and *conscience imberbe.* And this takes time beyond the confines of official Négritude poetry,

> Je vends ma négritude
> cent sous le quatrain.

According to Senghor, African literature is functional and collective and therefore a literature of commitment. This would seem to be a true assessment of traditional literature but does not quite do justice to the new literature. We may wonder whether a radical "return to the sources" can ever be successful in a rapidly changing society with its new patterns of class formation, urbanisation, and the resultant self-reliance of the individual person, especially the intellectual.

But Senghor is more concerned with the metaphysical problem of man's position in the cosmos where "a vital power similar to his own animates every object endowed with sensitive characteristics, from God to a grain of sand [Léopold Sédar Senghor, "African-Negro Aesthetics," *Diogenes* (1956)]. This sounds again remarkably close to the Romantic's view of the divine order, to be more precise, to Victor Hugo's cosmological system, his listening to "the soul of things." The place of honour held by the ancestors in the African hierarchy of being is not quite paralleled by the European Romantics, but Victor Hugo had his own private cult. In his "armchair of the ancestors" were carved the names of the Hugos of old, and the deeply significant words, ABSENTES ADSUNT—"The absent ones are with us."

Hugo's influence on Senghor, the one-time French teacher and author of a study on "Victor Hugo's Youth," is probably deeper than that undergone by other African writers, none of whom could escape the giant of the time-honoured school syllabus. In Ake Loba's novel *Kokoumbo* the hero's father thinks Hugo "probably the greatest patriarch France has ever had." Senghor himself exclaims, *Ecoutez le grand Hugo.*

The "emotive attitude towards the world" which Senghor defines as the basis of Négritude is not in the last resort directed towards the French language, *la langue des dieux* (*Ethiopiques,* epilogue). To the French African poet, French is not merely the language of the coloniser, but also the language of the French Revolution and therefore intrinsically of his own final liberation. Senghor's international brotherhood of the 20th century sings "la Marseillaise de Valmy," and elsewhere he says, "The French language has become the cornerstone of the Civilisation of the Universal. As such it is humanism."

The same "emotive attitude" is evidenced towards France itself. In his prayer of the Senegalese Riflemen, Private Second Class Senghor, two months before his capture by the German army, felt that he and his comrades were fighting for a "Confederate France." Temporarily at least, his Négritude took on strong assimilationist overtones reminiscent of the protagonist's attitude in the first French Négritude novel, Ousmane Socé's *Mirages de Paris* (1937). And in his "Prayer for Peace" he invokes God to place France "at the right of the father."

This emotional involvement of the "cultural Mulatto" in the French language, his love-hate relationship with France, accounts for a great deal of the indifference Négritude meets with in English-speaking Africa. There are, of course, other reasons as well. When writing poetry about Africa, Senghor always sits on the carved ebony stool of the sage. From his African heritage he takes the wisdom and leaves the wit, he takes the romanticism and leaves the realism. That is why even African novelists writing in French, and in the realist tradition—Mongo Beti, Ferdinand Oyono, and Sembène Ousmane—keep aloof from his movement.

The *mystique* of Négritude in its last metamorphosis is also lost on most American Negro writers, significantly enough even one of their foremost critics, Saunders Redding, who wrote *To Make a Poet Black* (1939) and coined the term "negroness" in his book *On Being Negro in America* (1951).

This shows that like any other movement, Négritude is subjected to the conditions of time, space, and culture. But Léopold Sédar Senghor has become a widely acclaimed master of the language he assimilated, though his poetic imagination seems to have died down with the fertile friction of exile after his country's attainment of independence. Even when the fiery chariot of Négritude grinds to a final halt, his poetry will be remembered. And the African poets of the future may yet see in him their Hugo or Hesiod. (pp. 63-4)

> Willfried Feuser, "Negritude: The Third Phase," in The New African, *London, Vol. 5, No. 3, April, 1966, pp. 62-4.*

Janheinz Jahn

[*A German educator, translator, and critic, Jahn was an astute observer and interpreter of African culture and literature and was among the first European scholars to treat modern African literature as a serious and substantial field of study. In the following excerpt, he presents a thematic and stylistic analysis of Negritude poetry.*]

Caliban and Prospero: as O. Mannoni and George Lamming (born 1927) have pointed out, the relationship between these two characters in *The Tempest* can be interpreted as similar to the relationship of the two opposing sides in a colonialist society. This is not, of course, to drag Shakespeare into modern controversies or credit him with ideas some way ahead of his time! But the parallel drawn strikes me as highly illuminating, and I believe can be followed up further than has been done by Mannoni and Lamming. Here, then, is a dialogue that takes place between the two characters:

> CALIBAN. This island's mine, by Sycorax my
>   mother,
>   Which thou takest from me. When
>   thou camest first,
>   Thou strokedst me and madest much
>   of me, wouldst give me
>   Water with berries in't, and teach me
>   how
>   To name the bigger light, and how the
>   less,
>   That burn by day and night: and then
>   I loved thee
>   And show'd thee all the qualities o' the
>   isle,
>   The fresh springs, brine-pits, barren
>   place and fertile:
>   Cursed be I that did so! All the charms
>   Of Sycorax, toads, beetles, bats, light
>   on you!
>   For I am all the subjects that you have,
>   Which first was mine own king: and
>   here you sty me
>   In this hard rock, whiles you do keep
>   from me
>   The rest o' the island.

> PROSPERO. Thou most lying slave,
>   Whom stripes may move, not kind
>   ness! I have used thee,
>   Filth as thou art, with human
>   care. . . .
>   I pitied thee,
>   Took pains to make thee speak, taught
>   thee each hour
>   One thing or other: when thou didst
>   not, savage,
>   Know thine own meaning, but
>   wouldst gabble like
>   A thing most brutish, I endow'd thy
>   purposes
>   With words which made them known.
>   But thy vile face,
>   Though thou didst learn, had that in't
>   which good natures
>   Could not abide to be with; therefore
>   wast thou
>   Deservedly confined into this rock,
>   Who hadst deserved more than a pris
>   on.
> CALIBAN. You taught me language; and my prof-
>   it on't
>   Is, I know how to curse. The red
>   plague rid you
>   For learning me your language!

Lamming stresses the fact that both Prospero and Caliban are exiles, and has this to say on the question of language:

> Prospero has given Caliban Language; and with it an unstated history of consequences, an unknown history of future intentions. This gift of language meant not English, in particular, but speech and concept as a way, a method, a necessary avenue towards areas of the self which could not be reached in any other way. It is this way, entirely Prospero's enterprise, which makes Caliban aware of possibilities. Therefore, all of Caliban's future—for future is the very name for possibilities—must derive from Prospero's experiment, which is also his risk.

> Provided there is no extraordinary departure which explodes all of Prospero's premises, then Caliban and his future now belong to Prospero . . . Prospero lives in the absolute certainty that Language, which is his gift to Caliban, is the very prison in which Caliban's achievements will be realized and restricted.

Lamming puts down Caliban's limitations to his being a part of nature, which is no doubt the way Shakespeare conceived the character; the other possibility, the 'extraordinary departure', is not followed up. But I find it instructive to take a closer look at this aspect, so as to shed light on the phenomenon of Negritude.

Lamming is right: if Caliban is no more than a part of nature, he will never be able to break out of the prison of Prospero's language: all the culture he can obtain, as is Prospero's intention, must then derive from Prospero's language and mentality; and everything Caliban does will be derivative. But suppose Caliban is also part of a culture, a different culture unfamiliar to Prospero. Caliban remembers this but can grasp it only in images, not words; he is imprisoned in Prospero's language and his own servility. Shakespeare's text provides clues for this line of interpretation as well:

> CALIBAN. Be not afeard; the isle is full of noises,
> 　　　　　Sounds and sweet airs, that give delight and hurt not.
> 　　　　　Sometimes a thousand twangling instruments
> 　　　　　Will hum about mine ears, and sometime voices
> 　　　　　That, if I had then waked after long sleep,
> 　　　　　Will make me sleep again: and then, in dreaming,
> 　　　　　The clouds methought would open and show riches
> 　　　　　Ready to drop upon me, that, when I waked,
> 　　　　　I cried to dream again.

Like any other creature Caliban feels the urge for freedom, but he also knows the basis for his oppressor's power:

> . . . there thou mayst brain him,
> Having first seized his books . . .
> 　　　　　　　　　　　　Remember
> First to possess his books; for without them
> He's but a sot, as I am, nor hath not
> One spirit to command: they all do hate him
> As rootedly as I. Burn but his books.

Let us now suppose that in an 'extraordinary departure' Caliban carries out the revolt suggested to him by his urge for freedom, no longer as the helpmate of foreign buffoons like Stephano and Trinculo but on his own initiative and with his own resources. Then he would have nothing to rely on but the riches dropping upon him from the clouds in dreams; such riches have always been his only source of strength. And to gain his freedom, he must consider the 'thousand twangling instruments' not as the voice of nature but as culture; and culture does not emerge out of nothing but always has a source. For his mother, Sycorax the sorceress, although conquered by Prospero, possessed magic powers, magic knowledge, mastery over 'toads, beetles, bats', i.e., over nature, and therefore culture.

Once Caliban has recognized the limits and roots of Prospero's power, he may try some further unsuccessful revolts, but if his urge to freedom remains unbroken, the idea is bound to occur to him in the end—helped by the education Prospero has given him, however defective—that his mother's powers, the voices, the instruments and the riches that drop in dreams, all belong together: that they form a culture, but one very different from Prospero's book culture, He, Caliban, must at last wrench this from dreams into reality, in other words consciously recognize it. He does this through language, Prospero's language, for he possesses no other.

So he captures, in his own and Prospero's language, a culture Prospero did not create and cannot control, which he, Caliban, has recognized as his own. But in the process the

Alioune Diop, the first editor of Présence africaine.

language is transformed, acquiring different meanings which Prospero never expected. Caliban becomes 'bilingual'. That language he shares with Prospero and the language he has minted from it are no longer identical. Caliban breaks out of the prison of Prospero's language. This provides a new point of departure.

Prospero's lessons cannot be unlearned, so Caliban will continue to understand Prospero's language. But Prospero will have only a partial grasp of the language which is now Caliban's own, so long as he retains his old attitudes. He is bound to miss essential parts, nuances and references, everything that relates to that different cultural background, and so he will misunderstand Caliban's new language.

But Prospero can have himself initiated into the new language, which has been extended by Caliban to take in new fields of experience. The condition for this, however, is that Prospero asks Caliban questions, that he is willing to be instructed, and is instructed. In fact he must abandon his colonialist arrogance, shed his claim to be the master race, and consort with Caliban on the same level. Thus Caliban's liberation gives Prospero too a great opportunity: the chance of turning from a tyrant into a humane person.

The literary movement which produced its works between 1934 and 1948 and became known under the name of 'Negritude' may be described as the successful revolt in which Caliban broke out of the prison of Prospero's language, by converting that language to his own needs for self-expression.

The idea of the new movement began in Paris in 1934, when a few students founded the journal *L'Étudiant Noir.* They were Léopold Sédar Senghor (born 1906) from Senegal, Léon Damas (born 1912) from French Guiana, and Aimé Césaire (born 1913) from the West Indian island of Martinique.

This event was preceded by another, which Lilyan Kesteloot sees as the origin of Negritude and with which she starts her study: in 1932 Étienne Léro (1909-39), René Ménil and Jules Monnerot, all from Martinique, founded in Paris the journal *Légitime Défense;* there was only one issue, which contained a strident manifesto. In it these students from Martinique rejected the bourgeois conventions and humanitarian hypocrisy which imposed on them a 'borrowed personality'; they rejected the European literary models offered them at school, and vowed their allegiance to the proletariat and surrealism. They rejected Victor Hugo and Alexandre Dumas, but adopted new models which were just as European: Marx, Freud, Rimbaud and Breton.

So they did not even fully catch up with the successful revolt carried out some time before by the Harlem style and by Indigenism. Through accepting the thesis that the cultural revolution must be preceded by a political one, they blocked the way to the recognition of an African culture; and by slavishly copying surrealism, they remained imitators who had only changed their models. A poem by Léro, 'Sur la Prairie', will serve as an example:

> Sur la prairie trois arbres prennent le thé
> Tes mains sont cachées
> Mes mains sont cachées
> Une seule bouche et l'heure d'été
> Laisse-moi jouer au jeu de l'habitude
> Beau paquebot aux lignes de mes mains.

> 'On the prairie three trees take tea
> Your hands are hidden
> My hands are hidden
> A single mouth and the hour of summer
> Let me play the game of habit
> Fine steamer on the lines of my hands.'

The group who founded *L'Étudiant Noir* took, from the outset, a more independent attitude to communism and surrealism. 'For us politics was only an aspect of culture,' Senghor wrote in 1960 in a letter to Lilyan Kesteloot; and 'We accepted surrealism as a means but not as an end, as an ally not as a master. We were willing to find inspiration in surrealism, but solely because surrealist writing rediscovered the language of Negro Africa.'

These writers knew the works of the Negro Renaissance, and also knew some of its authors personally—'Senghor the Senegalese' is mentioned in Claude McKay's novel *Banjo;* they realized the movement's importance. Césaire stressed the fact that it was authentic: 'The ordinary Negro, whose grotesqueness or exoticism a whole literature sets out to emphasize, is made a hero, drawn seriously and passionately, and the limited power of his art is successful . . . To create a world, is that a small thing?

To make a world emerge where only the junk-shop's exotic inhumanity rose before!'

Senghor stressed the form of the Negro Renaissance [in 'Trois poètes négro-américains,' *Poésie* (1945)]: 'It remains near to song, it is made to be sung or spoken, not to be read. Hence the importance of the rhythm, Negro rhythm, so despotic beneath its appearance of freedom. Hence the importance of the music, so difficult to render in translation . . . In short, a poetry of flesh and earth, to talk like Hughes, a poetry of the peasant who has not broken off contact with the forces of the earth.' Senghor saw the Negro Renaissance as more indigenist than it really was. In fact the expression 'forces of the earth' (*les forces telluriques*) projects on to it his personal aspiration of 'back to the sources' (*retour aux sources*).

Coming from different parts of the world, Senghor, Damas and Césaire inspired each other and succeeded in avoiding provincialism. They caught up with Negro Renaissance, Indigenism and Negrism, and in the process of introducing African elements into poetic art took a decisive step forward. This was because they achieved a reversal of values, and saw Africa no longer as only exotic and 'primitive' but as a specific culture which they must search for and rediscover.

The process of getting closer to Africa became more and more a conscious one, and eventually led Senghor to the study of African style which he brought into his celebrated essay: 'The spirit of civilization or the laws of Negro-African culture' ('L'Ésprit de la civilisation ou les lois de la culture négro-africaine'). The political consequences of this psychological revolt helped a good deal towards the decolonization of Africa. . . . The literary harvest, Caliban's breakout from the prison of Prospero's language, was reaped in three fields: semantics, rhythm and subject matter.

Césaire must be given chief credit for the semantic achievements. Words in the French poetic language gained extended meanings and new associations not to be explained from the historical experience of French literature. A European can easily confuse these with the spontaneous images of European surrealism which are determined by absurdities and coincidences. In Césaire's writing they have a firm semantic and syntactical coherence. (pp. 239-44)

The rhythmic innovations were made mainly by Senghor and Damas. French poetic language, which has quantitative metres with no accentuation, was forced to scan and also made to 'dance' in an Afro-American fashion by Damas, in a purely African fashion by Senghor. Besides the techniques from music and dancing, formal means of producing rhythm in language include, as Senghor writes, 'alliterations, paranomasias, anaphoras, which are based on a repetition of similar phonemes or sounds, and create secondary rhythms which reinforce the effect of the whole' ['L'Ésprit de la civilisation ou les lois de la culture négro-africaine' *Présence Africaine* (1956)]. But that is not all. The emphasis on rhythm leads logically to the demand: 'I persist in thinking that a poem is not completed unless it combines song, words and music' [*Ethiopiques*].

Mrs. Kesteloot has given some fine examples of how Senghor's rhythmic techniques are revealed in his own poetry. . . . Mrs. Kesteloot writes [in *Les écrivains noirs de langue française: naissance d'une littérature*]: ' . . . even oftener he [Senghor] works himself up into a dance rhythm—specially that typically African dance which doubles its step by jumping, one-two on one foot, one-two on the other, Senghor recreates this step by doubling or hammering home the accentuated syllables.'

> A. Et quand sur son ombre elle se taisait, resonnait le tam-tam des tanns obsédés.

> 'And when in his shadow it had come dumb, came the beat
>   of tom-tom from throbbing deep creeks.'

> B. Nous n'avancerons plus dans le frémissement fervent de nos corps égaux épaules égales.

> 'We shall swing along no longer the tingling thrill to feel of
>   body frames the same and soldered the shoulders.'

> C. Ma tête bourdonnant au galop guerrier des dyoung-dyoungs, au grand galop de mon sang de pur sang.

> 'My head's in a roar with the gallop of war of the dyoung-
>   dyoungs, the gallop and thud of my thoroughbred blood.' . . .

These examples show that such features are not beyond translation into other languages, once the rhythmical technique is recognized, bearing in mind that the consonants count, of course, as well as the vowels. (pp. 244-46)

Mrs. Kesteloot offers yet another example:

> Senghor gave the longest poem in *Chants d'Ombre* the title 'Que m'accompagnent kôras et balafong'.

In this title the names of the instruments give the verse its sonorous quality: repetition of the hard C (quc m'acc . . . k . . .) and of the final 'ong, the nasal song of which should be stressed ('agn and 'fong). So the line is accentuated thus:

> *Que* m'*acc*omp*agn*ent k*ô*ras et bala*fong.*

This example, though in itself minimal, reveals to us a major difficulty for us Westerners! To 'grasp' the rhythm of a poem by Senghor, we must break away from the French way of accentuating words. In the line above we automatically put the accent on the syllables *pa, ras* and *fong,* that is on the final ones:

> Que m'accom*pa*gnent kô*ras* et bala*fong.*

In many of his poems Senghor's cadence follows a pattern which we meet again in the African cultural field: the mainly falling speech melody of West African tone languages. There the high, low and medium tones of single words in a sentence may be incorporated into a falling tonal curve, so that the high tone of the last word in a sentence may be lower than a low tone at the beginning of the sentence. We often find such a falling intonation in the North American Blues, sung in English. And no less often in Senghor's poetry. (p. 246)

Léon Damas, who is usually underrated in the shadow of Senghor and Césaire, had already adopted dance rhythms in his poetry before them. In his collection *Pigments* (1937) he adopted for the first time the African stylistic technique so characteristic of the poets of Negritude, of heightening the effect by repetition and the setting of poems like 'Hoquet' (hiccup) 'Bientôt' and 'Obsession', to racy Afro-Caribbean dance rhythms, which he uses functionally, not descriptively as in Negrism. In *Graffiti* (1952) he brought the dance principle of duplication into short poems like the following:

> D'avoir un instant cru
> à la main dégantée
> à la main dégantée au printemps
> dégantée au printemps né
> au printemps né de la magie
> de la magie du rythme

> la meute édentée
> scrofuleuse
> et borgne
> a crié sus
> à mon cœur de fou sans haine

The English translation cannot hope to produce the sound values as well as the repetition technique:

> When I for a moment believed
> in the gloveless hand
> in the gloveless hand in the spring
> gloveless in the spring that's born
> in the spring that's born of a magic
> born of a magic rhythm

> the toothless mob
> scurvy
> and one-eyed
> cried havoc on
> my madman's hateless heart.

In his most recent volume *Black-Label* (1956) he 'composed' the whole four-part poem of eighty-four pages like a piece of music, with each part held together by a *leitmotiv* verse like:

> BLACK-LABEL A BOIRE
> pour ne pas changer
> Black-Label à boire
> à quoi bon changer

Within this framework he connects simple images to form a train of thought, which, however, does not, and is not meant to, produce any logical sequence in the European sense. An idea is never pursued to its conclusion, but is taken up periodically and repeatedly. Grouping, paragraphing and connection within the sequences of images, are done by keeping to the same sound values, which also carry the message of the image:

> BAMAYE DO BRAZIL
> BAMAYE DO BRAZIL

montrant la voie aux gueux
montrant la voie aux peu
montrant la voie aux rien
montrant la voie aux chiens
montrant la voie aux maigres
montrant la voie aux nègres.

Césaire has never deliberately produced specific rhythmic formulas, but his whole poetry is propelled forward through rhythm. Senghor writes of him [in *Éthiopiques*]: 'What is surprising about his using his pen like Louis Armstrong his trumpet? Or more accurately perhaps, like the devotees of Voodoo their tom-toms? He needs to lose himself in the dance of words, the tom-tom rhythm, to rediscover himself in the Universe.'

In theme, Senghor was the first to introduce into French poetry African customs and manners, myths and celebrations personally experienced, also hero figures, chiefs, kings, priests, shrines, spirits, springs and animals—his 'Royaume d'Enfance' which he was constantly invoking. Birago Diop (born 1906) set a model for prose with his recreation of African stories and myths in the oral style of a professional narrator: 'Les Contes d'Amadou Koumba' (1947). Césaire was the first to bring alive in his poetry the cosmic connection of all powers and living things, the existential unity of man and nature and the magic of the word.

The aim of the subject matter is to capture the African reality; the semantic shifts of meaning bring about the magic of words and rhythm; the 'architecture of being' (in Senghor's phrase) is the heart-beat of the universe, evoking ecstasy, giving the poetry sound and weight. So the semantic, rhythmical and thematic achievements of Negritude have a fruitful connection with each other as characteristics of a specific philosophy and attitude to the world, the conception of an African style and the unity of an African culture. These ideas . . . are proclaimed as part of the Negritude movement's programme by Senghor in his essays and have been propagated in the magazine *Présence Africaine* edited by Alioune Diop (born 1910). In 1948 Jean-Paul Sartre tried to give them an existentialist interpretation. The theoretical foundation, which rests on the philosophical works of Placied Tempels and Alexis Kagame (born 1912), is still disputed however.

But it is essential to be familiar with these ideas for a deeper understanding of the writing of Negritude. In connection with this view of the world, the African writer has a very important function: he is word-magician and announcer, Africa's spokesman, sponsor and interpreter to the outside world, Africa's educator within. His rhythmical word produces the images which when put together become poetry and prose. Reality offers dormant subject matter, which his word awakens, turns into images and projects towards the future. The function of this kind of writing is not to describe things as they are for the sake of description, but to create prototypes: visions of what ought to be. Therefore the style is 'in the imperative'. When the writer transposes his visions of the future into the present, or even back into the past, as if what he commanded were taking place before his eyes or as if the new

reality invoked had already come into being, his imperative achieves its highest force:

Paysan frappe le sol de ta daba. . . .
je me souviens de la fameuse peste qui aura lieu
 en l'an 3000
il n'y avait pas eu d'étoile annoncière . . .
lc premier jour les oiseaux mourront
le second jour les poissons échouèrent
le troisième jour les animaux sortirent des bois
et faisaient aux villes une grande ceinture chaude
 très forte
frappe le sol de ta daba. . . .

'Farmer strike the soil with your daba. . . .
I remember the famous plague which will happen in the year 3000
there was no prophetic star . . .
the first day the birds will die
the second day the fishes were grounded
the third day the animals came out of the woods
and made for the towns a great hot mighty belt
strike the soil with your daba. . . .'
[Césaire, *Soleil cou-coupé*]

According to Senghor, he and Césaire 'launched' the word 'negritude' in the years 1933-35. The first time it appeared in one of their works, however, was in Césaire's poem, written in 1938, 'Cahier d'un retour au pays natal'. Since then it has come to bear many different shades of meaning, which have been put together by Mrs. Kesteloot; I have added some more and put them in a systematic order. I give below, with categories in the margin, and the significant words in italics, examples of some of the ways in which the word has been used, varying from an instrument, a style, a particular form or feature of style, a quality or an attitude, to 'being', 'way of being', race, skin-colour, or the sum of all values:

Instrument	(1) '. . . so that our negritude should be the effective *instrument* for a liberation.' (Senghor)
Style form	(2) 'The monotony of tone, which is what distinguishes poetry from prose, is the seal of negritude, the *incantation* which allows access to the truth of essentials.' (Senghor)
Style	(3) 'The thing which makes up a poem's negritude is less the subject than the *style*.' (Senghor)
Stylistic feature	(4) '. . . . the *rhythm* born of emotion . . .'
Quality	(5) '. . . produces emotion in its turn. And also produces *humour,* the other side of negritude.' (Senghor)
Attitude	(6) 'Negritude, in contrast, is *understanding* through sympathy.' (Sartre)
Attitude	(7) 'I shout hurrah! *The old negritude* is progressively turning into a corpse.' (Césaire)
Attitude	(8) 'It is the same with independence as with negritude. This is first of all a *negation* . . .

		rejection of the Other, refusal to assimilate . . . rejection of the Other is *self-affirmation*.' (Senghor)
Being	(9)	'. . . the affirmation of our *being*, our negritude . . .' (Senghor)
A Way of Being	(10)	'My negritude is not a stone hurled against the clamour of the day my negritude is not a speck of dead water on the dead eye of the earth my negritude is no tower and no dome.' (Césaire)
A Way of Being	(11)	'We could not return to the negritude of the past, the negritude of the sources.' (Senghor)
A Way of Being	(12)	'Night, you dissolve all my contradictions, all contradictions in the *primeval unity* of your negritude.' (Senghor)
Being-in-the-World	(13)	'Negritude, to use Heidegger's language, is the Negro's *Being-in-the-world.*' (Sartre)
Race	(14)	'Haiti, where negritude emerged for the first time.' (Césaire)
Oppressed Race	(15)	'You do not know the restaurants and swimming pools, and nobility forbidden to black blood, And Science and Humanity, setting up their police cordons at the frontiers of negritude.' (Senghor)
Skin-Colour	(16)	'His very negritude was losing its colour.' (Césaire)
Sum of all Values	(17)	'Negritude is the cultural heritage, the values, and above all the *spirit* of Negro-African civilization.' (Senghor)
Sum of all Values	(18)	'Negritude, the *sum of* black Africa's *cultural values* . . .' (Senghor)

To help explain the relationship of these different meanings and shades of meaning, setting them against the background of African thought, I would like to quote from an essay of mine on 'Value Concepts in Sub-Saharan Africa' [in *Cross-cultural Understanding,* edited by F. S. C. Northrop and Helen H. Livingston, 1964]:

> In African thinking, the universe consists of a network of living forces. The universe is a field of forces. Man and woman, dog and stone, even yesterday and east, beauty and laughter—all these are forces related to each other and in continuous interaction. The universe is a unity, in which each part depends on the others, and no part is changeless. If you take possession of part of a thing, you thereby participate in its life force. If you tear a leaf from a tree, not only does the tree quiver, but the whole universe is affected, since nothing stands alone. For Europeans, force is an attribute: a being *has* force. In African thinking, force *is* being, being *is* force, a physi-

cal-spiritual energy and potency. The totality of all these living forces is NTU, Being . . . which, however, is never conceived of as separable from its manifestations. In NTU, the cosmic universal force, all single forces are tied together. The individual forces fall into four groups, within each of which there is a hierarchical ordering: *Muntu, Kintu, Hantu* and *Kuntu.*

> . . . the *Kuntu* group contains all the forces of relationship, of acting on and of manipulating, of way and manner of acting. They answer questions about the *how* of a culture—that is, about its *style.* Kuntu-forces are function-forces (forces-modalité) . . .

Style, qualities, attitudes, 'way of being' are all *Kuntu* forces; so are stylistic forms, features and 'instruments', if considered dynamically, in action; and so are specific external factors like race and skin colour, which are the African's way of 'being in the world'. The *Kuntu*-forces, in a world of forces, produce specific values and are in themselves the sum of such values. If we bear in mind this structure, the apparent contradictions in the above statements are resolved: every 'Being'-force, and the qualities and methods resulting from it—which are forces in their own right—make up both the whole and all its parts: i.e., according to these writers' statements, *negritude.*

Admittedly the negritude writers did not establish their special structure beforehand, but developed it as they went along or retrospectively. This was to the poetry's advantage, for it was hardly ever written merely to make it fit into a programme.

Because they claimed to feel and represent their own dynamic 'being-in-the-world', these writers looked on all Afro-American writers before them as their forerunners and discovered negritude in the earlier writers' works.

They were quite justified in this, seeing that all the literary schools of an era are, of course, the 'legitimate heirs' of their predecessors, and that in their predecessors' works, as I have tried to show, there really were African or Afro-American stylistic features and forms. Being very much on the look-out for these, the negritude writers were bound to notice them. So their own writings, besides developing new qualities, contain a good deal that is traditional, which has only been put into a wider and more comprehensive context. Indeed the whole history of neo-African literature can be recapitulated, as it were, in these writers' works.

Here are memories, as if from their own experience, of the days of slavery, its suffering and revolts. We read in Senghor:

> Car il faut bien que tu oublies ceux qui ont exporté dix
> millions de mes fils dans les maladreries de leurs navires
> Qui en ont supprimé deux cent millions.

> 'For you must surely forget those who exported ten millions
> of my sons in the leper-houses of their ships,
> Who enslaved two hundred million of them.'

And in Césaire:

Et l'on nous vendait comme des bêtes,
et l'on nous comptait les dents . . .
et l'on nous tâtait les bourses
et l'on examinait le cati ou décati de notre peau
et l'on nous palpait et pesait et soupesait
et l'on passait à notre cou de bête domptée le col-
    lier de la
servitude et du sobriquet.

'And they sold us like beasts,
and they counted our teeth . . .
and they felt our testicles
and they tested the lustre or dullness of our skin
and they felt over us and weighed us and
    weighed us up
and round our tamed-beast necks they put the
    collar of
slavery and of nickname.'

And in Damas:

. . . sous le fouet qui se déchaîne
sous le fouet qui fait marcher la plantation
et s'abreuver de sang de mon sang de sang la
    sucrerie.

'. . . beneath the whip which rages
beneath the whip which keeps the plantation
    going
and bathes in the blood of my blood from the
    blood of the
sugar works.'

Here are the themes, the stylistic forms and features of the Negro Renaissance, the Harlem atmosphere:

. . . où de bar en bar
où de verre en verre
j'ai saoulé ma peine
(à même) la piste enduite
et patinée de steps
de stomps
de slows
de songs
de sons
de blues

[Damas]

'. . . where from bar to bar
where from glass to glass
I drowned my pain
right to the dance-floor
trodden and worn with steps
with stomps
with slows
with songs
with sons
with blues'

Here is the Harlem anti-civilization primitivism in Senghor and Damas as well as Césaire. The symbols of civilization are worthless:

Vieille France, vieille Université et tout le chape-
    let déroulé

(Senghor)

(the last words by a modernism might be translated as 'all that jazz')

The clothes are all wrong:

J'ai l'impression d'être ridicule
dans leurs souliers
dans leur smoking
dans leur plastron
dans leur faux-col.

(Damas)

'I feel I am absurd
in their shoes
in their dinner-jacket
in their stuffed shirt
in their stiff collar.'

One must behave as a 'savage':

Et je boirai long longuement le sang fauve qui re-
    monte à son cœur
Le sang lait qui flue à sa bouche, les senteurs de
    terre mouillée.

(Senghor)

'And I'll linger long drinking in the strong blood
    bubbling back into her heart
The milk blood which spills into her mouth with
    the smells of the sodden soil.'

for:

Pourquoi arracher mes sens païens qui crient?

'Why try to tear out my pagan senses that
    shout?'

. . . . .

Eia pour ceux qui n'ont jamais rien inventé
pour ceux qui n'ont jamais rien exploré
pour ceux qui n'ont jamais rien dompté. . . .

(Césaire)

'Hurray for those who have never invented any-
    thing
for those who have never explored anything
for those who have never tamed anything.'

So far these famous lines are merely repeating the old primitivism in a louder voice. But then the poem soars directly to the heights of a new negritude concept:

mais ils s'abandonnent, saisis, à l'essence de
    toute chose
ignorants des surfaces mais saisis par le mouve-
    ment de toute chose
insoucieux de dompter mais jouant le jeu du
    monde.

'but they give themselves up, possessed, to the
    essence of things,
ignoring the shells but possessed by the rhythm
    of things,
not caring to tame but working in well with the
    world.'

Naturally negritude also contains the exoticism of the Negro Renaissance, and the longing for an imaginary Africa:

L'Afrique saigne, ma mère.

(Césaire)

'Africa, my mother, bleeds.'

. . . . .

Déjá me poignent le flanc les cents regrets du
　Pays noir

(Senghor)

'My side already burns with yearning hundred-
　fold for the dark land'

. . . . .

Rendez-les moi mes poupées noires
　mes poupées noires
　poupées noires
　noires.

(Damas)

　　'Give me back my black dolls
　my black dolls
　black dolls
　black.'

. . . . .

Et nous baignerons mon amie dans une présence
　africaine
Des meubles de Guinée et du Congo, gravcs ct
　polis, sombres et sereins.
Des masques primordiaux et purs aux murs, dis-
　tants mais si présents!

(Senghor)

'And we'll steep ourselves, sweet, in feelings
　deep of our Africa round about us,
With Guinea furniture and Congo too, heavy
　and smooth, sombre and serene.
With pure and primordial masks upon the walls,
　so far yet ever near.'

. . . . .

À force de penser au Congo
je suis devenu un Congo bruissant de forêts et de
　fleuves.

(Césaire)

'From thinking of thc Congo
I've turned into a Congo murmuring with for-
　ests and rivers.'

Then there is the voluptuous sensuality and flaunted vitality:

Femme nue, femme obscure
Fruit mûr à la chair ferme, sombres extases du
　vin noir.

(Senghor)

'Dark woman, naked woman,
Ripe fruit with flesh so firm, darkling delights of
　black wine.'

. . . . .

Je charrie dans mon sang un fleuve de semences
a feconder toutes les plaines de Byzance.

(Senghor)

'I carry in my blood a stream of fertile seed to
　impregnate all the wide plains of great Byzan-
　tium.'

As in the writing of the Depression period, we find also
an identification of race with class and the idea of a proletarian revolution:

Pour le dernier assaut contre les Conseils
　d'administration qui gouvernent les gou-
　verneurs des colonies.

(Senghor)

'For the last assault against the councils of ad-
　ministration which govern the governors of
　colonies.'

. . . . .

La Marseillaise catholique.
Car nous sommes là tous réunis, divers le
　teint . . .
Divers de traits de costume de coutumes de
　langue; mais au fond des yeux la même
　mélopée de souffrances à l'ombre des longs
　cils fiévreux
Le Cafre le Kabyle le Somali le Maure, le Fân
　le Fôn le Bambara le Bobo le Mandiago
Le nomade le mineur le prestataire, le paysan et
　l'artisan le boursier et le tirailleur
Et tous les travailleurs blancs dans la lutte
　fraternelle.
Voici le mineur des Asturias le docker de Liver-
　pool le juif chassé de l'Allemagne, et Dupont
　et Dupuis et tous les gars de Saint-Denis.

(Senghor)

'The true Catholic Marseillaise.
For here we are all met as one, varied in hue . . .
Varied in features and costume and custom and
　tongue; but deep in the eyes the same sad
　chant of distress beneath the long feverish
　lashes
Kaffer Kabyle Somali and Moor, Fan Fon Bam-
　bara Bobo and Mandiago
Nomad and miner and slave, peasant and arti-
　san, poor student and gunner
And all the white workers in the great fraternal
　struggle.
Here is the miner from Asturias the docker from
　Liverpool the Jew out of Germany driven, and
　Dupont and Dupuis and all the lads from
　Saint-Denis.'

Significantly, however, the Negritude writers do not show
any trace of indigenism. They are too committed for that,
identifying too fervently with their subject. Césaire's portrayal of the Martinique peasants in the first part of 'Retour au pays natal' is a document of ecstatic compassion,
a brilliant display of images soaring to a climax, a volcano
of exploding indignation. And Senghor is not describing
the funeral rites of other people, he is consorting with his
own ancestors, is always on the most confidential terms
with his dead, talks to them, prays to the masks and puts
himself under their protection:

Je songe dans la pénombre d'une après-midi.
Me visitent les fatigues de la journée
Les defunts de l'année, les souvenirs de la décade
Comme la procession des morts du village à
　l'horizon des tanns.

C'est le même soleil mouillé de mirages
Le même ciel qu'énervent les presences cachées
Le même ciel redouté de ceux qui ont des
　comptes avec les morts
Voici que s'avancent mes mortes à moi.

'I dream in the dim dusk-light of an afternoon
I am called on by the toils of all the day,
By the dead of the year, by the memories of the
　decade,

Like the long march of village dead right to the
    wide horizon of tanns.

It's the same sweet sun steeped in mirages,
The same sky perturbed by the beings concealed,
The same sky of dread for those who risk a reck-
    oning with the dead
And here are my dead moving forward to me.'

'All these references to the dead in Senghor's poetry,' Ulli
Beier writes [in 'The Theme of the Ancestors in Senghor's
poetry,' *Black Orpheus* (1959)], 'are not conscious statements or pronouncements of belief. These are, on the contrary, images that rise in his mind not because he is asserting his "negritude", but because he is an African and allows himself to be one.'

Herein lies the greatest achievement of negritude, that a
genuine African feeling for life, and attitude to life, could
be and was expressed in a European language. As shown
above, this is just what the *philosophical* concept of negritude means; and here the term is used to denote a *literary*
era. Here it attained the goal of a century's laborious
searching by all Africa's exiles. Only an African could
have attained this goal, an African, of course, who was assimilated enough to master a European language right to
its last refinements.

This achievement was necessary before negritude could
cross the ocean to Africa and help to free other Africans,
threatened by the call for assimilation, who felt themselves
trapped in Prospero's language. Birago Diop, also a Senegalese, immediately took the cue:

    Dans un des trois canaris
    des trois canaris où reviennent certain soirs
    les âmes satisfaites et sereines
    les souffles des ancêtres
    des ancêtres qui furent des hommes,
    des aïeux qui furent des sages,
    Mère a trempé trois doigts . . .

    'In one of the three pots
    the three pots to which some evenings there re-
      turn
    the souls satisfied and serene
    the breath of the ancestors,
    of the ancestors who were men
    the grandsires who were sages,
    Mother dipped three fingers. . . .'

Indigenism, on the other hand, with its folkloric realism,
which aims at sympathetic description, is found only in
negritude writers of the second rank, such as Paul Niger
(1917-62) from Guadaloupe, who after studying in Paris
became administrator in Katiola on the Ivory Coast. He
wrote typical indigenist poetry like:

    Mamadou, apprends-moi le chant pur de
      l'Afrique. . . .
    Sous la blessure du Soleil
    Sous le kapok de la lune courbe parfaite aux sens
      de géomètre
    Le corps de Mamadou m'apprend le rythme de
      la brousse
    Fuyance et devenir puissant chute
    Source
    Le corps d'Amadou n'est pas le corps sans par-
      fum. . . .

    'Mamadou, teach me Africa's pure song. . . .
    Under the wound of the Sun
    Under the kapok of the moon's curve so perfect
      in the geometrician's sense
    Mamadou's body teaches me the rhythm of the
      bush
    Flight and becoming powerful fall
    Source
    Mamadou's body is no body without a scent.'

The novel *Karim* by Ousmane Socé (born 1911) is also indigenist. The deeds of the hero of the title, who tries to imitate his heroic ancestors by daring his rivals to contests
of extravagance, is described without any complexities. It
is the story of a good black Moslem told in immaculate
French, set in a Senegal accurately portrayed from a folkloric angle. In his other novel, *Mirages de Paris,* Socé
showed that the theme of Paris was more in tune with the
elegance of his pen.

Although indigenism is completely missing in the great
negritude writers, there are occasional passages reminiscent of negrism:

    Et de la terre sourd le rythme, sève et sueur, une
      onde odeur de sol mouillé
    Qui trémule les jambes de statue, les cuisses ou-
      vertes au secret
    Déferle sur la croupe, creuse les reins tend
      ventre gorges et collines
    Proues de tam-tams. . . .

                   (Senghor)

    'And rhythm springs from out the earth, its sap
      and its sweat, a wave with the scent of sodden
      soil,
    Which will shiver the legs of a statue, the thighs
      to the open secret.
    It breaks upon the rump, and hollows loins, and
      tenses belly, throat and breasts,
    Prows of tom-toms.'

or

    voum rooh oh
    voum rooh oh
    à charmer les serpents à conjurer les morts
    voum rooh oh

                   (Césaire)

'To charm snakes, to conjure up the dead'

Whatever the negritude writers may owe to their predecessors, they brought it into the great complex of their
own conception. Even when borrowing or taking over,
they often excelled those earlier writers in inspiration and
poetic power. Their self-confidence was firmly based on a
real achievement.

One result of this self-confidence was that laughter could
break in again, and was allowed free play. It is saying
something that neo-African writing had not entirely lost
its sense of humour, in spite of its history; but its laughter
was the laughter of escapism, as with Langston Hughes
and his famous book-title (and slogan) *Laughing to Keep
from Crying.* The negritude writers could laugh from their
hearts, because they believed in an African future. Many
of their poems end, too, on a note of jubilant, self-
confident optimism:

Car qui apprendrait le rythme au monde défunt
des machines et des canons?
Qui pousserait le cri de joie pour réveiller morts
et orphelins à l'aurore?
Dîtes, qui rendrait la mémoire de vie à l'homme
aux espoirs éventrés?
Ils nous disent les hommes du coton, du café, de
l'huile
Ils nous disent les hommes de la mort.
Nous sommes les hommes de la danse, dont les
pieds reprennent vigueur en frappent le sol
dur.

(Senghor)

'For who will be teachers of rhythm to a withered world, to a world of machines and guns?

Who will shout aloud for joy to waken the dead
and orphans to the morning?
Who is to restore a new memory of life to a man
with his hopes slit to bits?
Still they call us the men of cotton and oil and
coffee,
Still they call us the men of death.
We are the men of the dance, with feet that find
new strength again in stamping the hard soil.'

. . . . .

La faiblesse de beaucoup d'hommes est qu'ils ne
savent devenir ni une pierre ni un arbre
Pour moi j'installe parfois des mèches entre les
doigts pour
l'unique plaisir de m'enflammer en feuilles
neuves de
poinsettias tout le soir
rouges et verts tremblants au vent
comme dans ma gorge notre aurore.

(Césaire)

'The weakness of many men is that they don't
know how to become a stone or a tree
As for me I sometimes stick tinder between my
fingers sheerly for the pleasure of blazing up
in new poinsettia leaves all evening
red and green trembling in the wind
as in my throat our dawn.'

'I think that negritude is dangerous,' writes David Rubadiri (born 1930) from Malawi [in 'Why African Literature,' *Transition* (1964)], 'because its final result is to press
down the creative spirit, to tie it, sometimes so tight that
a work of art becomes meaningless.'

Does he mean the sterile tying down of the mind by an ideology? But the true poet does not let himself be tied, even
when there is a political power behind the ideology. When
Césaire belonged to the Communist Party, he was incapable of producing 'Party' poetry, his work remained negritude poetry. No doubt Rubadiri means that the poetry of
negritude is anyhow insignificant, and he tries to prove
this by quoting Damas's primitivist lines, published in
1937:

J'ai l'impression d'être ridicule
avec mes orteils qui ne sont pas faits
pour transpirer du matin jusqu'au soir qui dés-
habille
avec l'emmaillotage qui m'affaiblit les membres
et enlevent à mon corps sa beauté de cache-sexe.

'I feel I am absurd

with my toes which are not made
for sweating from morning till evening's un-
dressing
with the swaddling which weakens my limbs
and takes from my body its loin-cloth beauty.'

Rubadiri comments: 'When you come to think of it, any
self-respecting nudist of any race could declare this.
Doesn't he know what a poetic simile is?'

In fact Rubadiri is only sharpening the attack which Ezekiel Mphahlele (born 1919) began in his book *The African
Image*. Mphahlele rejected Senghor's statement that emotion was 'Negro' and advocated a poetic realism to be
based on the poet's personal experience. But this rejection
was of negritude's ideology, which need not affect one's
judgement on negritude poetry; a non-Christian who asserted that Christian poetry must be bad would simply be
showing that he knew nothing about poetry. The course
Mphahlele recommended, on the other hand, merely indicated his personal preferences.

In his book Mphahlele's attitude was still relatively moderate, but in many conferences of recent years it has har-
dened to dogmatic and categorical assertions. For instance, he said in Berlin in 1964: 'There have even been
attempts to read Senghor's poetry to the accompaniment
of drums—poetry in French. I have heard this and I
frankly must say I felt it was phoney. Because the rhythm
of drums is just not the rhythm of French poetry.'

This is a personal opinion, which can be countered by another personal opinion, that of Lilyan Kesteloot: 'Recently also, during a recital of Negro poetry at the Congolese
University of Lovanium, the poem "Chaka" was delivered
by a black student to a tom-tom accompaniment. It was
astonishingly successful, and the whole of Leopoldville
was talking about the "Senghor recital". Clear proof that
this writer's poetry loses its apparent tonelessness when it
is recited as it should be.' Between these two contradictory
opinion I shall express no further judgement until careful
investigations of the Serers' musical rhythm have been
completed, in reference to the obvious vowel and consonant patterns in Senghor's poetry. The question cannot be
settled without comparing his poetical rhythms to the
rhythms of his specific musical background.

Such investigation, which alone can resolve the dispute,
would be futile, however, if one were to believe Mphahlele.
According to him, the rhythms that each language employs because of its own inherent qualities as a language,
whether French or English, are incapable of accommodat-
ing the rhythms of an African language. 'You write
French, so you use French rhythms. You write an African
language, you use the rhythms inherent to that language.'

Yet European poetry has continually been influenced by
classical rhythms. I am deliberately talking of poetry, not
of language in general, as this would include not only
prose but even everyday speech. The Afro-American
rumba rhythm successfully penetrated into the Spanish
poetry of Cuban negrism; there is Arabic metre and
rhythm in Swahili; and Vilakazi tried hard to enhance his
Zulu poetry with English rhymes, verse-forms and
rhythms. One may justifiably ask in each case whether the

attempt succeeded or failed, but one cannot exclude the very possibility of success. Many poems by Guillén, for instance, obviously succeeded.

Mphahlele did admit that idioms and symbols can indeed be carried over into another language 'with exciting results very often'. But he then gave as contrary examples some translations from sentences in Bantu languages, where 'taste', 'feel' and 'smell' are expressed by 'hear': 'Do you hear how it smells?'—'Take it, hear it, it's sweet.' In the language of poetry, however, such usages are quite permissible. Édouard Maunick (born 1931) from Mauritius has a line which says: 'La lumière sentait l'iode'—the light smelt (or felt—here also a double meaning of 'sentir') of iodine (or the sea).

Gerald Moore too finds negritude poetry 'rhetorical' and sentimental. He stigmatizes as 'typographical tricks' [*Seven African Writers* (1962)] the attempts Damas made to clarify the rhythm by arranging his lines for visual effect; and declares that Césaire's technique is 'unmistakably surrealist' [Gerald Moore and Ulli Beier, *Modern Poetry from Africa* (1963)]. As evidence he quotes a passage where only the breaking of the lines in the English translation is absurd. They are long lines, and the narrow typeface of the original edition of 1947 could accommodate only 35 letters (including spaces). This number of letters was taken over in a later edition with a type-face not much wider. The lines were separated and broken up like prose just for the purpose of showing that two lines following each other always belong together:

> (TOUSSAINT, TOUSSAINT
> L'OUVERTURE)
> is a man who fascin-
> ates the white hawk of white death
> is a man alone in the ster-
> ile sea of white sand
> is an ole darky braced against
> the waters of the sky.

Compare the original:

> (TOUSSAINT, TOUSSAINT L'OUVERTURE)
> c'est un homme qui fascine l'épervier blanc de
>   la mort blanche
> c'est un homme seul dans la mer inféconde de
>   sable blanc
> c'est un moricaud vieux dressé contre les eaux
>   du ciel

Moreover, these critics cite only passages where the Negritude writers' new achievements recede from view; where the foreground is clearly occupied by the heritage which, as I showed in the previous section, they took over from the previous eras. This kind of presentation is unfair. It would be equally unfair to cite Rubadiri's poem 'A Negro Labourer in Liverpool', parts of which are over-sentimental, but in line with Afro-American poetry at the beginning of this century; or to remind Mphahlele of his poetic conversation with the north wind,

> now lisping
> dead prophecies
> collected from ruins of lost empires.

Such quotations do not characterize the whole work of these writers.

Again, the critics in question are writing in English. Their criticism is based on what is often an inadequate translation, in which the rhythms and melodies of the negritude writers are lost. Thus the examples of Senghor's rhythms . . . go like this in the translation by John Reed and Clive Wake (only in the case of D is there something like a phonetic equivalent to Senghor's internal harmonies):

> A. And when in his shadow it fell silent, the
>   drums sounded from the insistent *tanns*
> B. No more advance in the eager trembling of
>   equal bodies equal shoulders
> C. My heart pounding with the warrior gallop
>   of the *dyoung-dyoungs,* great gallop of my
>   blood my pure blood.
> D. Precious pelts bars of salt and gold from
>   Bouré, of gold from Boundou.

There is a saying by Wole Soyinka (born 1934): 'I don't think a tiger has to go around proclaiming his tigritude.' Referring to this in his two books Gerald Moore remarks that 'this attitude is a trifle unfair'. Moore would have us think that Africa's authors writing in English, especially the younger Nigerian school, reject negritude, and that this school simply accept the individualist stream recommended by Mphahlele—the idea that there is no such thing as a negritude, a 'being African'. The result has been violent arguments between French-writing and English-writing African authors, on the 'notion', as it were, of 'Tigritude versus Negritude'.

Soyinka put the record straight at the Berlin conference in 1964:

> As Aimé Césaire said, it is quite common for things to be quoted out of context and for portraits to be issued by foreign critics and even by African interviewers which end up by a little bit of distorting the real image. The point is this that, to quote what I said fully, I said: 'A tiger does not proclaim his tigritude, he pounces.' In other words: a tiger does not stand in the forest and say: 'I am a tiger.' When you pass where the tiger has walked before, you see the skeleton of the duiker, you know that some tigritude has been emanated there. In other words: the distinction which I was making at this conference (in Kampala, Uganda, 1962) was a purely literary one: I was trying to distinguish between propaganda and true poetic creativity. I was saying in other words that what one expected from poetry was an intrinsic poetic quality, not a mere name-dropping.

So a tiger's tigritude or tigerishness must be expressed in his work. This is just what the theorists of negritude have claimed, so the critic may legitimately look for and define the quality of 'tigerishness' in the 'tiger's' work. (pp. 247-66)

[For] those who would put down any influence from European literature as a triumph of Europe over another culture, I would remind them of Caliban and Prospero. Through his arrogance Prospero was just as much a prisoner as Caliban. By continually harping on his own 'noble nature' and on the lowliness of Caliban the 'savage', Prospero reveals only his weakness, insecurity, guilty conscience and the fact that he is confined within the four walls of his 'biological' ideology. Caliban's emancipation, his break-out from the prison of Prospero's language, gives Prospero too a chance of freedom, I would repeat. But of course it does not set him free automatically.

He can ignore Caliban's free and expanded language. He can try to persuade himself that he has still got Caliban trapped in the 'Prospero' language and attitudes. He can go on taking Caliban's new free language for the 'gabble' which he once taught Caliban. In this way he can go on being the language instructor, and consider language (in Lamming's words [in *The Pleasures of Exile,* 1960]) as his way of 'measuring the distance which separates him from Caliban.' Prospero can preserve his arrogance so long as he closes his ears and gives up his own rights to a world of freedom and humanity. The writers of Negritude were indeed vehement and often strident. They were trying to break through Prospero's deafness. (p. 269)

Janheinz Jahn, "The Negritude School," in his A History of Neo-African Literature: Writing in Two Continents, *translated by Oliver Coburn and Ursula Lehrburger, Faber & Faber Limited, 1968, pp. 239-76.*

If I apply Surrealism to my particular situation I can call upon the forces of the unconscious. . . . We have been influenced by Cartesianism and French rhetoric, but if all this is shed, and we descend to the depths of the unconscious, we discover the fundamental Negro.

—Aimé Césaire as quoted in Michael Dash's "Marvellous Realism—The Way Out of Negritude," in Black Images, *Spring 1974.*

Gerald Moore

[*In the following essay, Moore examines the relationship between race, politics, and society in Negritude poetry.*]

It is my hope to say something new about politics and Negritude, although that isn't easy because it is a much-trodden field. I certainly don't want to thrust at you reflections with which you are probably already quite familiar.

So I thought we might take as a starting-point the observations of Frantz Fanon, a Martiniquan writer of Negro origin, who spent a good deal of his life in France and, latterly, became the head of a mental hospital in Algeria. He looks at the problem of colour (if you can call it a problem) from the point of view of an Antillean. He doesn't claim to be an African. He keeps insisting that what he says is

true of the Antilles. He doesn't say it is true of anywhere else. He looks at these problems also as a psychiatrist who has been concerned with treating people whose mental condition may be related to some of the conflicts and stresses of racial contact. And in his book, *Peau Noire, Masques Blancs*—the title of which seems to very well project, I think, the central issue that he is concerned with—he says,

> The black is a black man. That is to say that as a result of certain aberrations—what are, in effect, aberrations—he is established in the breast of a world from which he wishes he could escape. The problem is an important one. We are concerned with nothing less than to liberate the man of colour from himself. We will go very slowly, for there are two camps—the white and the black. Keenly we will interrogate. We will question the two metaphysics, and we will see that they are frequently blended. We shall have no pity for the ancient administrators of old and the missionaries of old. For thus, those who adore Negroes, are just as sick as those who hate them. Conversely, the black man who wants to whiten his race is just as sick as those who preach the hatred of the whites.

Now, he goes on to say that to take a language is to assume a world. That the French language, in particular, is a language by which this whole system of what one might call racial snobbery—that is, an idea of hierarchy based on colour with the blackest at the bottom and the whitest at the top—projects itself upon the coloured man. He speaks, of course, from the point of view of an Antillean who has no choice about that language. It is the only language that he has; the language he grew up with; the one through which he must educate himself, and through which he is forced to advance himself.

Intimately related to this question of the hierarchy of colour is the hierarchy of social values: the planter pseudo-aristocratic values of the white man in the Antilles: the bourgeois values, obsessed with respectability, obsessed with climbing up the colour ladder and not going down it, of the mulatto middle-classes; and what he bluntly calls the inferiority of the black man, at the bottom of this system in every sense. He quotes examples of this obsession from books like *Nini,* a novel about Senegal; a book called *Je suis Martiniquaise,* and a book by René Maran, who was a Negro of Guyanese origin. This is an obsession with marrying upwards in the coloured system and not downwards—and he quotes examples of this not only on the part of women, but also of men. It is a determination that whatever one does once one has ceased to be completely black, whatever one does, one must marry someone lighter than oneself. And to fail to do so is to outrage not only your own standards, but those of all your relatives, because your parents might say, 'Look, you've thrown away the thing that we achieved. We've managed to get you three shades lighter, now you've gone and married a black man. We're going to go back to being black again.' This is why it leads to serious ruptures within the existing social system if people do this. Of course, he is not saying that they shouldn't do it, he's endeavouring to objectivize this kind of situation.

Now I think some of what we think of as the politics of Negritude begins right here with these two metaphysics, and I think we see these beautifully portrayed in a poem that you may know, by Léon Damas, one of the first writers associated with the Negritude movement. It is a poem called 'Hiccups'. Léon Damas is specifically a man of colour, but not black. He's midway, one might say, a sort of a brown man from Guyana. One concludes from this poem that his background was of this petit-bourgeois kind, which was absolutely obsessed with getting further up this ladder of colour, and, also, what went with it: the ladder of social prestige, the ladder of social influence, and so forth:

> In vain I swallow
> three or four times daily
> seven mouthfuls of water
> yet my childhood comes up in hiccups
>   and shakes my instinct like
>   a policeman a ruffian
> Catastrophe
> tell me about the catastrophe
> tell me how
> My mother wanted a son with good table manners
>   hands on the table
>   the bread is not to be cut
>   the bread is to be broken
>   the bread of the Lord is not to be wasted
>   the bread of the sweat of your father's brow
>   the bread of bread
> A bone has to be gnawed with moderation and
>   restraint
> the stomach must be content with little
> a moderate stomach behaves and does not belch
> a fork is not a toothpick
> one does not blow one's nose
> in front of everybody
> and then keep upright
> do not wipe the plate with your nose
> and then and then
> and then in the name of the father
>   of the son
>   of the holy ghost
> at the end of the meal
> and then and then
> and then the catastrophe
> talk to me about the catastrophe
> tell me how
> My mother wanted a well trained son
>   if you don't learn your history lesson
>   you shall not go to mass on Sunday
>   your behaviour on Sunday
>   this child is a disgrace to the family
>   This child in the name of God
>   be quiet
>   did I not tell you to speak French
>   French as in France
>   The French of French people
>   Real French French
> Catastrophe
> tell me about the catastrophe
> Tell me how
> My mother wanted a son a son of her mother

(Note that, 'a son of her mother'—a reference to the kind of scale that I was trying to suggest.)

> you do not greet the neighbour
> again your shoes are full of dirt
> and if I catch you again in the street
> in the bush or in the savannah
> in the shadow of the war memorial
> and you are playing there
> and you are romping about with one
> with one who has not been baptized
> Catastrophe
> tell me about the catastrophe
> tell me how
> My mother wanted a son
>   really do
>   really mi
>   really fa
>   really sol
>   really ti
>   really do
>   re-mi-fa
>   so-la-ti
>   do
> And now I must hear you absconded again
> from your violin lesson
> A banjo
> are you saying a banjo
> what do you say
> a banjo you really say banjo
> no my dear
> you must know that we suffer
> neither ban
> nor jo
> a mulatto does not do that sort of thing
> you leave that to the negroes

Now, this then is the kind of situation from which Damas is trying to escape, and the tension that exists in his early poety, in the volume like *Pigments,* is the tension between this kind of background and the difficulty of finding something else to be. There is another poem of his in which he rejects the impediments of European society:

> I feel ridiculous in their shoes
> And in their collar like a factory funnel
> And with the little glass of hot water
> That they offer you in the afternoon

This, he rejects, and at the same time he can't really identify himself with an Africa that he doesn't know. He is not one of those writers that overcame this by romancing about a shattered golden age from which everybody was uprooted by slavery—seeing this simply as an aspect of the modern capitalist system. He doesn't want to look back at Africa as something existing like a kind of prenatal bliss in the womb of time in the way that some other Caribbean writers do in that period, particularly in the thirties. Yet, in a sense, he wants to recapture some kind of unity of being, and I think the great search in early Negritude literature, whether it be of Antillean origin or of African origin, is for this kind of unity of being. Occasionally, he appears to be seeking for an inner kind of primitivism, but I think it's really only a mood with Damas—it's not a programme. I'm thinking of another well-known poem of his, 'Black Dolls' ('Limbé'):

> Give me back my black dolls
> To disperse the image of pallid wenches—
>   vendors of love

Going and coming on the boulevard of my bore-
dom.
Give me back my black dolls
To disperse the everlasting image
The hallucinating image of overdressed and
heavy marionettes
From which the wind brings misery.
Merci.
Give me the illusion never to appease
The exposed need of roaring demands
Under the unconscious disdain of the world.

Give me back my black dolls
To play the simple games of my instincts,
To rest in the shadow of their laws,
To recover my courage, my boldness,
To feel myself myself,
A new self from the one I was yesterday.
Yesterday without complications;
Yesterday when the hour of uprooting came.

Will they ever know this rancour of my heart?
In the eye of my mistrust too late opened
They have stolen the space that was mine,
Custom, days, life, song, rhythm, effort, path-
ways,
Water, home, smoking grey earth, wisdom,
words, palaver,
Ancestors, cadence, hands, standards, hands,
trampling the soil.

At this point, the poem seems to be reaching through some kind of a mist; and already there seems to be a sort of consciousness, within the poem, that the black dolls don't quite subsume what he's looking for—and the movement becomes a groping one. But then he pulls back to the black dolls in the last line, 'Give me back my black dolls, my black dolls, black dolls, dolls'. I think a poem like this could be seen as a piece of deliberate primitivism, if we ignore its ironic intention. And this, of course, was one escape that some people saw. But I think it savours of the condition which Gênet perhaps identifies better than anybody else, of playing a rôle which is projected upon you by the other race.

Plenty of European spokesmen have been saying ever since the end of the First World War (which caused a certain disenchantment with European civilization), 'Look at the black man. Look at his spontaneous joy and gaiety, and his instinctual richness and his freedom from our over-intellectualized existence!' Now, it is possible to respond to this sort of thing as quite a number of poets, particularly in the Antilles, did in the early days of Negritude and Negroism by saying, 'Yes, all right, this is a good rôle for us to play. Let's celebrate all the respects in which we are different. Let us revel in rhythm, in primitivism, mumbo-jumbo, bongo-bongo and all the rest of it.' And you can find poems which virtually revert to a sort of bongo-bongo at certain points in their structure. But I don't think this is really the intention of Damas's poem. I think the intention of that poem is really to seek for this kind of unity of being, and he only sees it, for purposes of the mood of this poem, in terms of being given back his black dolls. The search doesn't stop there, as the poem shows at the point where it seems, as I say, to drop the dolls for a moment and turn to face this misty opposing presence through which it is groping for the thing it wants.

Now, Césaire is certainly the most formidable poet of the Antilles in this movement of Negritude. He also, in his first poem 'Cahier D'un Retour Au Pays Natal', appears sometimes to be offering the same kind of complementary rôle to the Negro. The white world is this; therefore, let us be that. The white world is too competitive; it is obsessed with its own concepts of power; it's obsessed with speed; it's steel-hard; it's a mass of right angles; it externalizes everything; it abstracts everything. Let us be everything that the white world is not, in order to complement the white world and build a new total civilization. But again, I think that Césaire becomes dissatisfied with this kind of rôle—even within the bounds of that poem— because he has a programme within the poem of saving the Negro, the black man, from his poverty and the squalor of the society which he inhabits in an island like Martinique. And this programme itself seems to challenge the basis of racialism; and, therefore, to challenge the basis of any philosophy which suggests that certain qualities are intrinsic in one race, and other qualities are intrinsic in another race. Césaire is sufficient of a Marxist to at least contemplate the idea that racism is primarily an economic phenomenon; and that if you could conceive a society in which all the people at the top are black—at the top in all senses (I mean political, economic, social prestige)—and brown people in the middle, and the whites at the bottom; then you would get a complete reversal of the racial attitudes that we are so familiar with, a carbon copy, upside-down.

This would be the pure Marxist viewpoint. In fact, I have heard many Marxists put this forward. That it is quite wrong to feel bitter about racism, because it is simply an aspect of economic organization and it will change as economic organization changes. Of course, we know it won't, because there is a long time-lag even if we accept the Marxist thesis. We know that there is a long time-lag, because people take some time to adjust to a changing situation. But, at the same time, I don't think we can reject this kind of formulation, and we must recognize that this formulation hovers on the frontiers of Negritude; particularly at the point, where, for purely strategic reasons of French political life, both the major African nationalist party and the deputies of Martinique, Guadeloupe and Guyana identified themselves with the Communist Party in the French National Assembly.

I think during that period we find a specific recognition, in a thing like Césaire's *Discourse on Colonialism,* of the force of the Marxist thesis on this subject of race and economics. But I don't think that Senghor, for example, is ever very convinced about this, or about Marxism. That's why, earlier, we find him groping towards a concept of African Socialism, a kind of socialism which is not simply a fragment of international Communism or international Socialism, but something special which is rooted in African social organization—in some innate quality of the African, of the African Negro—a phrase that recurs over and over again in Senghor's work. This is something that is peculiar to him, that peculiarly suits his genius, his contribution to the world. Other forms of organization will always be alien to him. He must have a Socialism that is specifically African—uniquely African—different from any other Socialism.

I think that when we are considering the politics of Negritude, we do have to make up our own minds about this question if we are going to see clearly where other people stand in relation to it. We have to make up our own minds how far racialism is a purely economic phenomenon in origin, and how far it is something else. How far is it true to suggest that there is some kind of instinctual animosity between races based simply on pigmentation; and how far is this something that is conditioned entirely by my idea of your status, governed by your colour, because I have become habituated to a situation in which I can judge your status, your power, your position in relation to me purely by your pigmentation. I am not sure that the writers we are dealing with have always made up their minds about this, but I think we have to make up our minds about it in order, as I said, to see where they appear to stand in relation to this question.

Senghor, in his poem 'New York' puts forward, I suppose, the classic statement of the complementary view of the Negro's rôle, and he ends the poem with the very improbable conjuration to New York to 'Let black blood flow into your blood', the most forlorn piece of advice, I suppose, that has ever been given.

> New York, I say to you: New York let black
>   blood flow into your blood

Can you imagine the white suburbs hearing that advice today?

> That it may rub the rust from your steel joints,
>   like an oil of life,
> That it may give to your bridges the bend of but-
>   tocks and the suppleness of creepers.
> Now return the most ancient times, the unity re-
>   covered, the reconciliation of the Lion the
>   Bull and the Tree.
> Thought linked to act, ear to heart, sign to sense.
> There are your rivers murmuring with scented
>   crocodiles and mirage-eyed manatees. And no
>   need to invent the Sirens.
> But it is enough to open the eyes to the rainbow
>   of April
> And the ears above all the ears, to God who out
>   of the laugh of a saxophone created the heav-
>   en and the earth in six days.
> And the seventh day he slept the great sleep of
>   the Negro.

This is the last section of 'New York'. The whole sense of the poem (it is too long to read) is that here is Manhattan, this place of which the beauty is so dazzling simply because it is so sharp, so angular, so cold, so plastic-wrapped and polythene-finished. And then there is Harlem, in which the mangoes of love roll under the hooves of the police horses, and so forth. He wants to marry these two elements and produce out of them a whole America. Perhaps James Baldwin wants to do it too, but Baldwin, of course, would never express it quite so boldly as, 'Let black blood flow into your blood.'

With Senghor, we do come upon some of the things that happen, or may happen, to Negritude when it comes home to Africa. There were so many things that the group of Negro students who found themselves in Paris in the thirties and early forties had in common. They had in common subjection to a policy of assimilation which, when it was rationalized and perpetuated, became what, if we wish to be Marxists, we may regard as part of the innate dynamics of the situation. In other words, you had a situation where—whatever the education or policy had been, whether it had been an assimilationist policy or not— power was held by white people and not by black people, where in order to move freely—even relatively freely—in the middle reaches of that power system, you needed a knowledge of French, and you needed to be able to understand and refer to the culture which the Frenchman enjoyed. But the system of education was a huge rationalization of this power-system and an attempt to perpetuate it: an attempt to perpetuate it by making this the only series of criteria by which any kind of value could be judged. The degree of approximation to the 'homme civilisé' became the test of everything.

They had in common the experience of colour, they had in common a relatively exploited status in an economic and political sense. But what they didn't have in common was an experience of Africa, of current Africa, contemporary Africa. This, I think, is where Negritude upon African soil begins to acquire some flavour of its own. And in particular, I think, in the work of Senghor and some other writers, it begins no longer to be so universalizing in its outlook. There is a great emphasis in the Negritude literature of the late 1930's on the universal problem of the exploited races. This is most recently expressed of course in Fanon's last book, *The Wretched of the Earth*. There is an emphasis on the fact that there is so much that the Indo-Chinese, the Madagascan, the African, the Caribbean Negro have in common. Not only the fact of French colonialism, but also the whole structure which subjects them and which aims to perpetuate their subjection is identical in all these places. Therefore, their programme must be identical, and therefore their literature, their culture should celebrate these common elements and this universality which will enable them all to become men, and, by becoming men, to enrich human civilization.

I think Negritude in Africa tends to assume a rather more local field of reference, and this comes up in this insistence upon African Socialism as the programme of political and social action. And what goes with that—the attempt to feed into a new synthesis, into a new culture (a neo-African culture as Jahn calls it) all those elements of African traditional civilization which are felt to be of absolute validity for the coming world in which Africa will pour its riches into a common pool. We can be misled about this, I suppose, by assuming that Senghor is a rather special case because of his profound Christian piety, because of his concern with reconciliation, because of his desire always to make the initial gesture of resentment, the gesture of bitterness, and, at the end of the poem, to bring everything to a harmonious conclusion. So often in his poetry we close on a note of reconciliation, a note of unity, an emphasis upon the complementary nature of African and European civilization. We may assume that this is rather special to Senghor, but I think a poet we could oppose to him, merely because his tone is more militant, would actually be a more special case. I am thinking of David Diop. For though of African descent—being half Camerounian, and half Senegalese—he sees Africa at a great distance. I think he sees it at the same kind of distance that many West Indian writers see it. It is something that he doesn't really know, that he hasn't proved upon his pulses. Therefore, in David Diop's poetry, we do find (although it was written in the fifties) this emphasis upon the universal dilemma of the man of colour—a universalizing tendency, a call to the barricades for everybody from Indo-China to the Caribbean. 'Listen, comrades of the struggling centuries' ['Listen Comrades'] and so on. In his poetry, we find references to Madagascar, we find references to Indo-China and to Negro America. Again, in Diop we don't find this emphasis on reconciliation. We don't find any suggestion that what is needed is a marrying of what Africa can give to Europe, or what the black world can give to the white world, to make a richer total civilization. The tone throughout is one of rejection—rejection of what the white world stands for, in favour implicitly of what the black world stands for. It is a rejection of one set of values, one system, in favour of another.

> In those days
> When civilization kicked us in the face
> When holy water slapped our cringing brows
> The vultures built in the shadow of their talons
> The blood-stained monument of tutelage
> In those days
> There was painful laughter on the metallic hell
>   of the roads
> And the monotonous rhythm of the paternoster
> Drowned the howling on the plantations
> O the bitter memories of extorted kisses
> Of promises broken at the point of a gun
> Of foreigners who did not seem human
> Who knew all the books but did not know love
> But we whose hands fertilize the womb of the
>   earth
> In spite of your songs of pride
> In spite of the desolate villages of torn Africa
> Hope was preserved in us as in a fortress
> And from the mines of Swaziland to the facto-
>   ries of Europe
> Spring will be reborn under our bright steps.
>   [David Diop, 'The Vultures']

All right, what is the programme that underlines this kind of poetry? Is it African Socialism? No. Is it international Socialism? International Communism? It doesn't appear to be specifically that. Is it the substitution of an African civilization for a white civilization?—the removal of one and its replacement by the other? Again, we are not quite sure whether it is that. So I think that Diop is another of those poets who sets us thinking about just what he, himself, is advocating; and what his own attitude is to the phenomenon of racialism—not the phenomenon of race (we must not get involved in that) but of racialism.

Now, in all this literature, I think up to about the late 1940's or early 1950's, the literature of Negritude is in a posture of facing towards the white world. The expression it wears on its face may vary; it may be one of reconcilia-

tion; it may be one of bringing gifts to enrich the common store; it may be an expression of hatred; it may be an expression of rejection; it may be an expression of hope; it may be one of disappointment; it may be one of grief; but the face is towards the white world, towards Europe.

I don't want to trespass on Clive Wake's territory which, I believe begins about 1950, but I do think that, since my theme is Negritude, and his is not specifically Negritude, we ought to consider now another question: How far is Negritude the child of a particular historical moment, as I think Sartre suggested in 'L'Orphée Noir'? He called it the true revolutionary poetry of our time (he was writing nearly twenty years ago when he said that) and he was suggesting then that the true revolutionary poetry is a sort of torch which passes from one hand to another. At that particular moment of historical time, it was in the hands of the Negro races because this was the moment of their revolution, of their emancipation, their throwing off of the shackles of servitude. And he says:

> What did you expect to hear when you took the
> muzzle off those lips? Did you expect to hear
> yourself overwhelmed with praises and love?

Fanon has a comment on that. He says, 'Do not expect to see anything in my eyes but a perpetual question.' Well, I have already quoted the bit about lips, but Sartre goes on to say, 'What expression did you expect to see in those eyes when you took off the blinkers?' and so on. Fanon's comment helps to bring us up to date. Is Negritude that, or is it, as Jahn suggests, the only valid way for African poetry to be written? Or is it simply a question of a kind of value brought, it seems, from outside literature, which gives the accolade of approval to everything that bears the marks of Negritude, and proclaims this as the only valid African literature? Or, is it something much more Protean than that—which is not the child of a particular historical moment, which is not the only valid way for Africans to write poetry, but which is a valid way for African poetry to be written, and which is continually changing its aspect so that if we try to fix it in a historical moment and say 'this is Negritude and that isn't', we are missing the point? Is it capable of change? Is it capable of developing with the developing situation? Is it capable of changing its habitation, and the face that it shows to the world, and yet being Negritude? Well, I am not going to give an answer to that question because I don't really know it. But I am inclined towards the last view, because I think that it is a much more enriching view, and it is one that dictates less to literature. I have a particular dislike of people who dictate to writers—what they should or should not be, or even what they are.

I would like to end by trespassing a little bit outside my strict chronological limit, and look at a poet who seems to me to be—if there is such a thing as Negritude and if it does have any kind of ultimate validity—to be a poet who is carrying it forward to the era when Africa's face is no longer just towards the white world, but towards itself; when the hatred may be a hatred not of Europe but for other Africans, for what they do or don't do, or for what they do to each other. It may be a rejection of certain things which have taken root in African society and not things which can be shrugged off as being imported by a colonial power. The hope may be a specifically African hope, the agony a specifically African agony, and I think we find this in Tchicaya U'Tamsi, a poet of the Congo (Brazzaville). Here he is writing at the time of the Congo mutiny in 1960, when the Belgian paratroops had dropped again into the country, and there was so much strife going on—not only between Katanga and the rest, but in other areas, in Kasai and various other parts of the Congo. There were struggles which were partly racial, partly tribal, and so forth. And he is looking at all this from Paris, and he doesn't like himself for looking at it from Paris. He says at one time, 'I spit into the Seine like all honest poets.' But he is looking at it with the whole of himself. The whole of his attention is turned upon the Congo, and what is happening there in his own Africa, in his own country— because this boundary between Belgian and French Congo is meaningless, to Tchicaya and to many people who live on the shore of that great river.

> You must be from my country
> I see it by the tick
> Of your soul around the eyelashes
> And besides you dance when you are sad
> You must be from my country
>
> Keep moving time is waiting to seduce us
> Learn from this that the oil in your lamp
> Is really my blood brimming up
> And that, if it overflows, you musn't light your
>   lamp
> We must have a dark corner somewhere
> For our ancient orisons
>
> All of us from the same umbilical cord
> But who knows where we fetch
> Our awkward heads
> Often the silences
> Reeking of iodine
> Ravage us
> With lecherous resolves
> For my beardless conscience
> Ravage us alone.

Notice the phrase, 'All of us from the same umbilical cord. But who knows where we fetch our awkward heads.'

It seems to me that the trouble with the complementary theory of race relations, if I may sum it up in that way, whether it comes from an African source or from a white source, as it does with somebody like Laurens Van Der Post, is that it dictates the rôle of the other part of the unity. It says I want to be this, therefore you must be that, so that together we can make a nice egg-shaped thing. I want to be intellectual. You must be emotional. No, no, you mustn't be intellectual, that's my part, you must be emotional, and you must feed my over-abstracted actiolated pale existence with your fullness of life. Now, I don't know, but it seems to me that I wouldn't like to be dictated to in this way, and I think that Tchicaya is one of the people who can't and won't be dictated to as to the rôle that he should play. And he keeps referring in his poetry to his awkward head. It's the head that prevents him from accepting the traditional colonial rôle. It's the same head that makes it difficult for him to accept what is happening now:

> You are falling into the trap
> Go on!
> I will give you my head
> Against your lingering fear of water
> Or else, these erupting pestilences
> Of my heart
> To buckle your loins against my passion.

Again, he is a poet who is continually, as it were, striking chords from parts of his anatomy. One of his favourite images is that he finds it very difficult to bend himself to Christian faith. His poetry is full of a tremendous sense of the instruments of Christ's passion and so forth—the resurrection—but he can't bend to it because he says he is a vertebrate and Christianity is, to him, an invertebrate religion. So there's his head which makes him awkward and makes him refuse to play some kind of complementary rôle; there is his backbone which makes it difficult for him to bend. All the parts of his body gradually become animated in his poetry with some kind of objective significance of this kind. The lines in his hand are almost an image of the river itself, the great Congo, 'unfolding flowing through time-unfolding destiny'. And he ends this section of his poem,

> Thus following the path of this river to the sea
> To mingle with the salty current my candour
> Allotting from sea to source the tide-mark
> At the whim of a Congolese will
> And then giving
> All the water hyacinth to toil for mercy
> Putting fresh cresses on the neuralgic joints
> Not tattoos upon the cheeks of the Congolese
> So that seeing them beautiful
> Each may dance with sadness
> Toilers also
> My filth, the slow waters,
> My sadness,
> Following the ways of this river to the sea,
> If grass must come to the cheeks of the savannah
>
> I forget to be negro so as to forgive
> I will not see my blood upon their hands
> The world will repay me for my mercy

So, in Tchicaya, in this series of poems, which were written at the time of the Congo crisis, we find not the Senghor kind of reconciliation, but one which is dictated by his own need for growth, his own need to keep flowing; and so he says two or three times in this section of the poem (I have just quoted one), 'I will not see my blood upon their hands, I forgive them in order to be Negro'—'Negro' here is used in the sense of wholeness, in order to be a whole person. He is not suggesting that other than Negroes can't be whole people, but 'in order to be a whole person, I will refuse to see my blood upon their hands'.

I think it is going to be interesting to look in the next few years at the poetry that comes out of Africa, perhaps specifically French-speaking Africa, because I think we must recognize that Negritude, if it means anything, has been largely a phenomenon of Francophone African literature. It will be interesting to see how far the writers themselves give us evidence on which we can base a decision about this question that I put to you earlier—What is Negritude? What is its relation to the stream of time? What is its relation to this question of 'intrinsic racial qualities', or, on the other hand, to qualities which are intrinsic in a particular organization of society which places one race here, and another race there? (pp. 26-42)

> Gerald Moore, "The Politics of Negritude," in Protest and Conflict in African Literature, *edited by Cosmo Pieterse and Donald Munro, Africana Publishing Corporation, 1969, pp. 26-42.*

Edris Makward

[*Makward is a specialist in African literature and languages. In the following excerpt, he describes parallels between such African ideologies as Negritude and Pan-Africanism and discusses works that reflect these ideologies.*]

Time and again students of contemporary Africa has stressed the impact of ideologies on the literary works of contemporary African writers. Authors have also insisted on the imperative need to link closely the study of the new written literature from Africa with the study of the general cultural and political renaissance of the past two or three decades in Africa. This view is strongly expressed by Claude Wauthier, the author of *The Literature and Thought of Modern Africa* in the following terms:

> . . . for anyone wishing to understand more fully the process of emancipation of the African colonies it is useful—if not indispensable—to study the recent literature of the black continent, not in isolation, but in the more general context of the whole African cultural revival. . . . This seems to me all the more important since African writers and research workers are linked by so many communal preoccupations and characteristics.

Similarly, Thomas Hodgkin devoted the last chapter of his invaluable book *Nationalism in Colonial Africa* to "the ideological and theoretical constructions" of Africans, including in particular, "Negritude" or "Pan-negrism" and "Pan-Africanism".

Philippe Decraene, who considers "Negritude" as the "literary expression" of "Pan-Africanism", defines the latter as being originally "nothing but a demonstration of fraternal solidarity among blacks of African descent from the British Antilles and the United States of America" [*Le Panafricanisme* (1964)]. For Decraene, Pan-Africanism is a political as well as a cultural movement.

There is no denying that for many politically-minded African intellectuals—and among them are many creative writers—*Négritude* is nothing but a form of mystification, or a kind of "bourgeois romanticism". Ousmane Sembène's remarks at the beginning of his short novel *Vehi Ciosane* characterize aptly this attitude:

> I have discussed again and again these matters with some of you who call yourselves AFRICANS. I have not been convinced by your reasons. Of course, there was one point you all agreed upon: that I should not write this story. Your argument was that it would bring disgrace and shame upon US, THE BLACK RACE. Moreover, you

would add, the detractors of NEGRO-AFRICAN CIVILISATION would pick it up and then. . . .

For fear of pedantry, I refuse to analyse your reactions as regards these matters. My question, however, is, when are we going to stop justifying our existence in terms of the colour of others and not in terms of our own HUMAN SELVES. Of course, there is no denying the existence of racial solidarity; we have to admit, however, that this solidarity is basically subjective. So much so that this racial solidarity has not prevented the assassinations, the illegal detentions, the political imprisonments practised by the dynasties reigning today in Black Africa.

There is also the often quoted "A tiger does not go about proclaiming its tigritude" quipped by Nigerian playwright Wole Soyinka, to which President Senghor of Sénégal and one of the "fathers of Négritude" retorted sharply in a speech given at Howard University in 1966:

> I fear that it may indicate an inferiority complex inoculated by the former colonizer, a complex the former colonizer has not cured. My answer would be: the tiger does not proclaim its tigritude because it neither speaks nor thinks. It is an animal. To man alone the privilege is given to think and rethink his thought: the privilege to know himself. [*African Forum* (Winter 1967)]

There are also those for whom Pan-Africanism represents a sample of utopian political thinking. The fact that the *First Festival of Negro Arts* in Dakar, 1966, was followed by another "first": the *First Pan-African Cultural Festival,* is indeed a sign of the polemics and ideological in-fighting that are still going on in Africa.

African socialism is also another major African ideology that has its partisans and its detractors. Senghor, the theoretician of *Négritude,* is also the theoretician of *African socialism.* He wrote in his *Nation et voie africaine du socialisme* (1961):

> They (the new Negro-African nations) will be inspired by the ideal of socialism, but it will be an "open socialism". Within this perspective they will be grouped in federal states. These states will have as their objective the progress of many, by raising his standard of living and culture. The ways and means will be a strong democracy and a planned economy.

Asked what he thought of "African Socialism", President Houphouet-Boigny of Ivory Coast once replied bluntly:

> We cannot afford it. If we *nationalize* everything it will be a handicap for our development. We must persuade foreign capital to come here and help in the development of our country. I do not think I shall be helping my country by nationalising soap-flakes and underwear. Our problem is exploiting the country's wealth, not *nationalizing* it. We do not criticize other countries for having chosen socialism. We follow their experiments with eagerness. [*Daily Telegraph* (17 August 1964)]

It is quite clear here that Houphouet-Boigny mistakenly equates socialism with nationalization. Such disagreements due to a lack of clear definitions—or to a deliberate choice to ignore these definitions—are indeed quite frequent in ideological discussions in contemporary Africa.

F. Dumont, author of an article entitled *Idéologie et Savoir,* states that man has two ways of justifying himself:

> On the one hand, my own consciousness constructs definitions of my singular conditions in this world. Modern psychoanalysis would refer to these definitions as rationalisations. On the other hand, society offers me also explicit diagrams which constitute, with regard to the ends of the actions contemplated, definitions that are bound up with the situation and with the groups engaged in this action. It is for the latter diagrams that we would reserve the term ideologies. There is more than mere parallelism between the latter and rationalisations: there is indeed a reciprocity of perspectives from one category to the other. [*Cahiers Internationaux de Sociologie* (1963)]

For the purpose of this discussion of major Negro-African ideologies and their treatment in contemporary African literature, I will deliberately choose not to follow the sociologist all the way, and will, therefore, not insist much further on the distinctness between these two categories—rationalizations and ideologies. But if we retain L. Goldman's definition that myth is "a coherent and unitary perspective on the relationships of man with his fellow-men and with the universe" [L. V. Thomas, *Les idéologies negro-africaines d'aujourd 'hui* (1965)], it becomes very tempting to equate myths with these rationalizations or ideologies.

It has been said that "myth in its strong sense is the ideology of archaic or traditional societies", for myths allow "the justification of behaviours by helping to bring about the passage from a situation locked in the immediate present and now, to a superimposed temporality; our Western ideologies are built in a time unit considered just as *real* as that of empirical action" [Thomas].

Because of the many meanings that words such as ideologies, myths, Négritude, African Personality, Pan-Africanism and African Socialism can take, depending on the background and standpoint of the speaker or writer, we will make the following distinctions:

(1) Taken in its most common usage in the past two or three decades among African writers, intellectuals and political thinkers, the term ideology refers to a "body of ideas—*idées forces*—capable not only of justifying a point of view, but also of giving life to a movement. At this level there is always a certain "disengagement" or "distance"—"un décollement"—between ideology and reality, between the promises of the idea and the actualizations of these promises. This is, in my view, the appropriate general definition of most contemporary African ideologies—political, cultural or religious: Négritude, African Personality, Pan-Africanism, etc.

(2) At the extreme limit, there is the pejorative interpretation of the "unbeliever" who rejects all the definitions as irrelevant or "*Dépassé*" and for whom ideology is nothing but "conscious deception, international lie, hypocritical thought, a 'mystification' to use Marx's word" [Thomas]. This attitude towards ideologies in general is quite recognizable in the attacks against the contemporary Negro-African ideologies made by other African as well as non-African intellectuals and writers.

It is in this extreme negative sense that ideologies are most commonly equated to "myths" as products of the imagination or unrealizable "utopia". It is indeed in this sense that Ousmane Sembène, the film-maker from Sénégal and author of *God's Bits of Wood* and *Le Mandat,* and Gabriel d'Arboussier, refer to Négritude as a "mystifying ideology".

Aside from these two general interpretations, ideology can be taken with much broader connotations to refer to "a system of ideas that are peculiar to a group which in final analysis is defined and conditioned by its own centres of interest" [Thomas]. (pp. 81-4)

It may be said that in the concept of Négritude there is a greater insistence on the *specificity*—or the *fundamental originality*—of the Negro-African than in the concept of *African personality*. It goes without saying, however, that both ideologies are essentially identical. In his paper ["Négritude and African Personality," *Le Soleil,* No. 305 (8 May 1971)] read at the Dakar Colloquium last April, Professor Abiola Irele from the University of Ife gives the most convincing demonstration of the profound similarity between these two ideologies which have often been viewed—erroneously in my opinion—as characterizing the basic differences between Anglophone and Francophone Africa. Irele shows very convincingly indeed that the preoccupations of the father of "African personality" coincide perfectly with those of the "Négritudinists". For in spite of all the recent disputes the three-fold perspective of Blyden's "African personality" can hardly be distinguished from the basic points stressed by Senghor in his many writings and speeches about Négritude or in Césaire's famous open letter of resignation from the French Communist Party in 1956.

For Blyden—as well as for Nkrumah, Sékou Touré and other prominent Africans whose names have been associated with the concept of "African personality", there is the desire to define one's identity, then the effort to elaborate for this identity or "personality" a new mode of expression that would be more relevant in a modern context, and lastly the awareness of the contribution that Africa and the black world can make not only for blacks but for the whole of humanity. These are indeed the same essential points often reiterated by the advocates of *Négritude:*

> *Senghor* [in the opening address of the April 1963 Dakar Festival]: "Once more, Négritude is not racism; it does not spring from a vulgar and distorted attitude of mind. It is simply the sum of civilised values of the black world; not past values but the values of the culture. It is the spirit of Negro-African civilization, which is rooted in the land and in the heart of the black man,

that is stretching out towards the world of men and things in the desire to understand it, unify it and give expression to it."

Césaire [in a 1956 letter to Maurice Thorez]: "There are two paths to doom: by segregation, by walling oneself in the particular; or by dilution, by thinning off into the emptiness of the 'universal'. I have a different idea of a universal. It is of a universal rich with all that is particular, rich with all the 'particulars' there are, the deepening of each 'particular', the co-existence of them all.

". . . And so we must have the patience to take up the task again, the strength to invent rather than to follow, the strength to "invent" our itinerary and to rid the way ahead of made-to-order prefabricated forms, petrified forms that obstruct."

In the light of all this, it becomes quite evident that rather than divide contemporary African intelligentsia into pro- and anti-Négritude, or pro- and anti-socialist, etc., according as they are Francophone or Anglophone, one should distinguish between the adherents of ideologies and those who shun ideologies like the plague. The latter reject ideology in general as mere dogmatism and think of the former as dishonest demagogues. It is in this dual context that ideologies are seen by some African intellectuals and creative writers—and not only from one linguistic group—as the expression of "*Compensating reactions*". Négritude thus becomes the attitude of the "white black man"—"le Nègre-blanc"—that is, the black man who is so Westernized that he feels the need to persuade himself and others that he has remained African. Likewise "African socialism" becomes the invention of political leaders attempting to mask their "bourgeois exploiter" tendencies, and Pan-Africanism becomes a means of concealing the persistence of tribalism and its use by the leaders to remain in power. And it is most certainly from the same positions that Imamu Amiri Baraka—LeRoi Jones—protested vehemently L. S. Senghor's induction into the Black Academy of Arts and Letters at the University of Vermont last June. Imamu Baraka, himself a member of the Academy, wrote to its President: "I cannot see how you can justify honouring Senghor, which is at the same time honouring neo-colonialism and slavish commitment to European ideas. And to try to separate art from life by giving this award to Senghor in the midst of his degeneracy is in itself European because the African artist knows that art and life are the same" [*Black World* (October 1971)].

It goes without saying that this distrust toward ideology is not always expressed so explicitly by African writers. Furthermore, it does not denote a lack of faith in the destiny of Africa. It should be said rather that the themes and topics treated by most of the best-known contemporary African writers in their literary works denote a striking similarity with the preoccupations of the "ideologists". Thus to bestow on Chinua Achebe the label "Négritude" would most certainly surprise the novelist in the first place. But he certainly would not protest that "culture", "dignity", and "communal ethics" are among his major preoccupations in his novels *Things Fall Apart* and *The Arrow of God*. The preoccupation with "culture" and "dignity" is expressed most eloquently in a lecture given in 1964 at a Commonwealth Literature Conference in Leeds, England: "There is a saying in Ibo that a man who can't tell where the rain began to beat him cannot know where he dried his body. The writer can tell the people where the rain began to beat them." Thus for Achebe as for many other African writers, the theme of cultural rehabilitation is fundamental [according to General Moore]:

> . . . as far as I am concerned, the fundamental theme must first be disposed of. This theme—put quite simply—is that African people did not hear of culture for the first time from Europeans; that their societies were not mindless but frequently had a philosophy of great depth and value and beauty, that they had poetry and, above all, they had dignity. It is this dignity that many African people all but lost during the colonial period, and it is this that they must now regain. The worst thing that can happen to any people is the loss of their dignity and self-respect. The writer's duty is to help them regain it by showing them in human terms what happened to them, what they lost. [*African Literature and the Universities* (1965)]

Likewise it is no exaggeration to say with Abiola Irele that "there is no better expression of Négritude than Wole Soyinka's own literary work". In *God's Bits of Wood*, Ousmane Sembène also makes forcefully a triple cultural, socio-economic and political statement without explicit conceptualization into Négritude, African socialism and/or Pan-Africanism. The implication is obvious, however. In *Vehi-Ciosane*, Sembène makes an indirect attack against a narrow-minded brand of Négritude that glorifies tradition indiscriminately. His position is clearly that "return to the sources" should never mean uncompromising continuation of tradition particularly when corruption has started to undermine the latter. In this novelette the champion of justice and truth within the village community is characteristically a representative of the lower caste, a 'griot-cardonnier' who believes that 'le sang de la vérité est toujours noble, peu importe sa source', and that 'griot n'est pas synonyme de servitude'. This treatment of tradition is reminiscent of Soyinka's treatment of the same subject in some of his plays: *The Strong Breed* and *The Swamp Dwellers*.

To mention one example from the most recent library contributions, Yambo Ouologuem's *Bound to Violence* goes back to the most glorious era of Negro-African history and then moves forcefully to our contemporary times in order to show that the "return to the cultural sources" should not be equated to 'a return to innocence'.

Many an African leader (Senghor, Nyerere, Nkrumah, Touré, Azikiwe, among others) has used the theme of African socialism as a political ideology. The first reason for this option is the frequently stated claim that traditional socio-economic structures of African societies were built along socialistic patterns. The other reason is that a socialist programme would always naturally include anti-imperialist struggle, national reconstruction, economic development and the promotion of mankind in general. Thus, "African socialism" is often brandished as the ideal weapon in the war against social, economic and cultural underdevelopment.

This African sense of communal life whereby the group's interest supersedes the individual's and on which the ideology of "African socialism" is based, has indeed been treated by many African writers. One of the most outstanding examples is again Chinua Achebe. His first novel, *Things Fall Apart* (1958), tells of the tragedy of a man (Okonkwo) within a self-sufficient traditional village society (Ibo) just as the impact of European presence on African soil was beginning to make itself felt. There is no denying that the novel is also about the "falling apart" of this society while European penetration was taking place culturally and spiritually as well as politically and militarily. However, the most edifying message that the reader gets from the major character's tragedy is unequivocally that the "group", "community", is much more important than the individual, that one has to move always with the "group". In this tightly knit novel the words uttered by Okonkwo's father during his fatal illness ring like a prophecy:

> Do not despair. I know you will not despair. You have a manly and a proud heart. A proud heart can survive a general failure because such

a failure does not prick its pride. It is more difficult and more bitter when a man fails *alone*.

Inexorably the prophecy becomes reality, for when Okonkwo hangs himself dramatically, it is because he has failed *alone*. Indeed, having killed in one of his characteristic impulses the white District Commissioner's messenger:

> Okonkwo stood looking at the dead man. *He knew Umuofua would not go to war.* He knew because they had let the other messengers escape. They had broken into tumult instead of action. He acted with them against his headstrong and ambitious priest and thus upheld the wisdom of their ancestors—*that no man however great was greater than his people; that no man ever won judgment against his clan.*

In the modern setting of the historic Dakar-Niger railway strike of 1947-48 (*God's Bits of Wood*) Ousmane Sembène treats the theme of communal co-operation as a factor of success in a modern social struggle. The theme of Pan-Africanism can be also recognized in this novel as the strike took place in two colonial territories simultaneously—Senegal and Soudan Français. Sembène's second novel, *O, pays mon beau peuple* (1959), describes the courageous and unhappy fatal struggle of a young Senegalese from Casamance (Southern Sénégal) who tries to promote in his region an economic and independent organization which would benefit in the first instance his fellow-countrymen and not the colonial exploiters. He has a French wife and has to fight against the representatives of the colonial power and their racist attitudes as well as the ill-will and the old-fashioned ways of a decadent African society. Oumar Faye, the hero, is finally murdered by order of the foreign companies whose lucrative supremacy he has challenged.

This double combat is also found in *L'haramattan,* which deals with the referendum campaign of September, 1958, in an imaginary African country which voted "oui".

Ousmane Sembène's masterpiece remains *Les bouts de bois de Dieu* (1960) in the inspiration, the construction and the style. Around the main theme—the strike of the Dakar-Niger railway (October 10th, 1947, to March 19th, 1948)—the author examines with a sharp sense of observation the co-existence of a traditional mentality and a modern mentality in modern African society.

In keeping with his background and training as a manual worker, Ousmane Sembène is not much preoccupied with the problems of thought and sentiment; though this does not mean that all his characters lack psychological depth (Bakayoko, N'Dèye Touti, Tiémoko). But Sembène is naturally more concerned with the problems of social and political action. His heroes, Diaw Falla (*Le Docker Nois*), Oumar Faye (*O, Pays, mon beau peuple*), Bakayoko (*Les bouts de bois de Dieu*), are all engaged, emotionally and actively, in the changes of Africa. They are passionately involved in directing these changes the way they believe is best for the welfare and happiness of their fellow-Africans: progress, industrialization and also equality, freedom, political and economic independence. Bakayoko and Diaw Falla are both involved in labour struggles,

Title page from the first edition of Léon-Gontran Damas's Pigments.

Oumar Faye in introducing new methods of agriculture and commercialization of the farmers' products.

This deliberate orientation has, of course, its consequential effects on Sembène's technique. The narrative is no longer sustained chronologically; it does not even follow a logical progression of action leading to a logical dénouement, as is the case with most Negro-African novels. His method is much indebted to the cinematographic media. The reader is taken from one place to another to follow the simultaneous development of the action: the famous railway strike—Thies, Dakar, Bamako, etc.—in *Les bouts de bois de Dieu;* the preparation for the 1958 referendum in the various territories in *L'harmattan.*

Moreover, there is a definite resolution to sound realistic; thus in many important scenes he gives up the narrative or description and uses the discussion or dialogue form which conveys a stronger feeling of reality. And quite in keeping with these preoccupations Sembène uses an everyday conversational French and without any intention whatsoever to sound poetic, to attain elegance or to suggest an authentic traditional Africa; unlike, say, Elechi Amadi's *The Concubine* in which the long dialogues are meant to give a genuine impression of village life in a traditional Ibo community. Sembène's style reminds one rather of André Malraux's *Les Conquérants.*

He tackles African social problems with conviction. In his earlier novels already mentioned: *Le Docker Noir, O, Pays, mon beau peuple,* there is a definite antagonism between two societies: the Europeans and the Africans, the whites and the blacks, but in *Les bouts de bois de Dieu,* the railway workers struggle on two different levels: on the one hand to claim their rights as workers, and in this respect they appreciate without hesitation the support of metropolitan trade unions; on the other hand, they never lose sight of their position as Negroes struggling for their human rights. Lastly, there is one aspect which distinguishes Sembène from most African novelists: he sees above all the positive side of Western technology; he never opposes Western materialism to African spiritualism. On the contrary, he considers that the future of Africa depends on the development of mechanization. His conviction is that machines can be mastered and used by all those who want to learn, irrespective of race. Thus, the image of the locomotive running again at the end of the strike symbolizes the promise of a better future.

Bakayoko warns young N'Dèye Touti against the servile imitation of the white man's manners:

> . . . savez-vous qu'on n'effeuille pas la marguerite dans ce pays . . . *Il y a tant de belles choses chez nous, qu'il n'est pas nécessaire d'en introduire d'étrangères.* Surtout que de là ou viennent ces gestes, nous pouvons en apprendre bien d'autres, beaucoup plus *fructueux pour notre pays.*

In conclusion, we can say that in addition to displaying a fascinating evidence of social transformation in Africa, Ousmane Sembène proposes with conviction a direction, a line of action. On the whole, a resolute optimism in the future of Africa is apparent in his work, without his ever resorting, or even alluding, to the terminology of any established African ideology.

If Négritude can be seen first as a reaction against colonial alienation and then only as an assertion of Negro-African reality, African socialism can also be viewed firstly as a rejection of liberal colonial economy and then as a wilful desire to implement in a modern context Negro-African socio-economic values; likewise African nationalism and Pan-Africanism can be defined first as a rejection of foreign domination and balkanization, and then as a commitment towards the construction of Pan-African unity.

The nationalist movement was naturally characterized by protest and demands for independence. And this fact is quite apparent in much of the politically committed writings appearing in the mid and late 1950s. The greater commitment to political action by French African writers has often been noted.

The obvious reason for this is firstly time: French African writers having started producing books about a decade before their English-speaking counterparts, that is, at a time when the struggle for political emancipation was going full swing. It is indeed quite significant that the most familiar names in English-speaking African literature are those of Wole Soyinka, Christopher Okigbo, Chinua Achebe, Ayi Kwei Armah, Abioseh Nicol—that is, those of writers who belong primarily to the post-independence era; and, who unlike their French-speaking counterparts, were not actively involved in the struggle for independence. There was also the strong conviction that literature could be used as an effective weapon for political and social emancipation which characterized much of French-speaking African creative writing at the time. It goes without saying that these two factors are most certainly inter-related. The Nationalist theme and the Pan-Africanist theme were most eloquently treated by poets such as Senegalese David Diop:

> Africa my Africa
> Africa of proud warriors in the ancestral savannahs
> Africa my grandmother sings of
> Beside her distant river
> I have never seen you
> But my gaze is full of your blood
> Your black blood spilt over the fields
> The blood of your sweat
> The sweat of your toil
> The toil of slavery
> The slavery of your children
> Africa, tell me Africa,
> Are you the back that bends
> Lies down under the weight of humbleness?
> The trembling black striped red
> That says yes to the sjambok on the roads of noon?
> Solemnly a voice answers me
> "Impetuous child, that young and sturdy tree
> That tree that grows
> There splendidly alone among white and faded flowers
> Is Africa, your Africa. It puts forth new shoots
> Slowly its fruits grow to have
> The bitter taste of liberty."

The Pan-Africanist theme was also treated by Sierra Leonian poet Abioseh Nicol. This poem, *The Meaning of Africa,* which appeared first in the mid-fifties, is full of thoughtful lines. It is quite clear that the poet did not feel that Pan-Africanism corresponded to anything concrete in reality:

> Africa, you were once just a name to me
> But now you lie before me with sombre green
>   challenge
>
> So I came back
> Sailing down the Guinea Coast
>
> Dakar, Accra, Cotonou
> Lagos, Bathurst, and Bissau;
> Liberia, Freetown, Libreville,
> Freedom is really in the mind.
>
> We look across a vast continent
> And blindly call it ours.
> You are not a country, Africa,
> You are a concept,
> Fashioned in our minds, each to each,
> To hide our separate fears,
> To dream our separate dreams.

Among the novelists, the most forceful works dealing with the political ideologies of Nationalism and Pan-Africanism are Camerounian Mongo Beti (*Ville Cruelle* and *Le Roi Miraculé* and Ousmane Sembène whose *God's Bits of Wood* and *L'Harmattan* have already been referred to. *The African,* a novel by Sierra Leonian William Conton, can be included here. Likewise, South African Peter Abrahams' *A Wreath for Udomo,* in which the leader's country is symbolically called "Panafrica").

Mongo Beti's nationalism as pictured in *Le Roi Miraculé* by Bitama's juvenile enthusiasm for the new P.P.P. (Parti Progressiste Populaire) is skillfully counterbalanced by the cynicism of another educated youth in the novel:

> ". . . Je reste confondu devant ton indifférence, Kris, à l'égard du P.P.P. Comment est-il possible que les jeunes gens les plus intelligents, les plus instruits, l'élite en un mot, restent froids vis-a-vis du P.P.P.? Je ne comprends pas. N'as-tu pas ressenti, toi, cette chose bizarre? Enfin bizarre, c'est une façon de parler. Voilà: on est là sur cette foutue planète; on est noir, mais on a beau chercher autour de soi, lire dans les livres, scruter le visage des hommes celebres, eh bien, rien à faire!
>
> "On ne trouve personne à sa ressemblance. Alors, tu te sens bizarrement solitaire, tu voudrais inventer des hommes qui soient noirs comme toi, des gens qui existent vraiment, quoi, Tu te ferais Dieu, juste en vue de cela; ne l'as-tu pas rescenti, toi?"

Thus the genesis of ideologies is a universal phenomenon in contemporary Black Africa. Writers—novelists, playwrights, poets, essayists—from all over the continent are aware of them and have dealt with them in their writings, more or less directly, more or less consciously. Some writers have strongly felt that ideologies would only hamper creativity. South African Ezekiel Mphahlele, the author

of *The African Image,* has been the most vocal among the latter:

> And now I know why the idea of the African personality can remain but a glorious myth which has nothing to do with the success of the Accra Conference.
>
> . . . . .
>
> At best, it can be but a focus, a coming into consciousness. It's no use pretending that it means anything in any practical terms.
>
> . . . . .
>
> Beyond the focus on freedom from colonialism in certain countries and fascist white rule in others, and the emergence into nationhood of others, the only thing that can really be said to be capable of expressing an African personality lies in those areas of cultural activity that are concerned with education and the arts. All this requires no slogan at all. . . . The African artist, because he must deal with African themes, rhythms and idiom cannot but express an African personality. There need be no *mystique* about it. The experiences that his art is about and his perspective are peculiarly African—if his art has authenticity—as distinct from a European's, American's or a Chinaman's. . . . We are not going to help our artist by rattling tincans of the African personality about his ears. The dial of response inside him will quiver in the way the dial of a balance does when you throw a weighty object on it instead of placing it gently. And while it quivers like that, it does not register anything at all. That's how slogans act on an artist. . . .

Other Africans have attempted a clear and unimpassioned analysis of these ideologies. Thus Ghanaian scholar W. E. Abraham wrote in *The Mind of Africa* (1962):

> In the preoccupation with the African personality they (the politicians and statesmen of Africa) appear to hold that the guiding principles of the future of Africa will be those authenticated in the African experience and cultures. Progress, its objectives, and some of its avenues are thought of in terms of a picture of the African personality. . . . The African personality, namely, that complex of ideas and attitudes which is both identical and significant in otherwise different African cultures. . . .
>
> Attempts have for some time been made to represent Africa as a sort of colossal *tabula rasa,* blank sheet, where culture is concerned.

One remarkable fact, however, is that the major African ideologies examined here, do present a definite parallelism between them despite disagreements over definitions, or even over the usefulness of definitions, which can sometimes be expressed in the most uncompromising fashion— to say the least. This parallelism is apparent not only in the *historical development* of these ideologies from the colonial era to the present, but also in their *finality* and their manifestations. It is indeed incontestable that for some of the most outstanding African political leaders as well as for many of the most committed authors of the new African literature, the cultural fact (Négritude or African personality), the political fact (nationalism and Pan-Africanism), and the socio-economic fact (African socialism) are primarily inseparable. The quarrel among African intellectuals and writers is not on content. It springs rather from the fact that some believe in the importance of defining ideas and preoccupations in conceptual terms first, and others believe in incarnating directly in their works, almost the same ideas and preoccupations but without conceptual presuppositions. (pp. 84-93)

> *Edris Makward, "Literature and Ideology in Africa," in* Pan-African Journal, *Vol. 5, No. 1, 1972, pp. 81-94.*

NEGRITUDE RECONSIDERED

Bernth Lindfors

[*In the following essay, Lindfors summarizes the arguments for and against Negritude that were presented in July 1969 at the First Pan-African Cultural Festival.*]

The *raison d'étre* of the First Pan-African Cultural Festival appears to have been more political than cultural. According to President Houari Boumediène, who delivered the keynote address, the five thousand performers, intellectuals, politicians, freedom fighters, and "men of culture" who flocked to Algiers [in July 1969] from all parts of Africa were there to "recover and assert our basic oneness" in an effort to "make our cultures into an instrument for our final liberation and future development." Since the two-week Festival was sponsored by the OAU, it is not surprising that heavy emphasis was placed on African unity and the political uses of indigenous culture.

The very structure of the Festival's Symposium on African Culture, which was held daily in the majestic Club des Pins overlooking the Mediterranean, seemed deliberately designed to minimize friction and maximize opportunities for agreement. Only the heads of national delegations were permitted to deliver speeches during the plenary sessions, and none of these speeches could be answered from the floor. There were no confrontations, no heated discussions, no spontaneous dialogue. When the delegates broke up into three commissions to discuss the realities of African culture, the role of African culture in the economic and social development of Africa, and the role of African culture in national liberation struggles and in the consolidation of African unity, journalists and uninvited foreign observers were not allowed into the conference rooms to witness the proceedings. All family squabbles and ideological in-fighting were thus hidden from public view. On the last day of the Festival the three commissions presented the results of their deliberations in the form of a 3000-word Pan-African Cultural Manifesto, to which were appended forty concrete "suggestions for the dynamic utilization of the elements of African culture in the lives of the peoples of Africa." The Manifesto was endorsed unanimously, and Chairman Mohamed Benyahia of Algeria concluded the Symposium by urging that "after this conference we must not allow anyone to say there are substantial differences between us."

Yet to everyone who listened to the speeches at the plenary sessions it was obvious that there were some differences which the official Manifesto could not completely conceal. Several French African nations seemed intent on discrediting the intellectual leadership which Senegal has long provided in matters pan-African. This they did by denouncing Negritude, sometimes in very colorful imagery. Guinea led the attack at the first plenary session with a 40-minute recorded message by Ahmed Sékou Tourè, who asserted, "there is no black culture, nor white culture, nor yellow culture . . . Negritude is thus a false concept, an irrational weapon encouraging the irrationality based on racial discrimination, arbitrarily exercised upon the peoples of Africa, Asia and upon men of color in America and Europe." Two days later Mamadi Keita, the Head of the Guinean delegation, expanded upon this point. "Holy Negritude, be it Arab-Berber or Ethiopian-Bantu," he said,

> is an ideology auxiliary to the general imperialist ideology. The Master transforms his slave into a Negro whom he defines as a being without reason, subhuman, and the embittered slave then protests: as you are Reason, I am Emotion and I take this upon myself . . . The Master assumes his pre-eminence, and the Slave his servitude, but the latter claims his right to weep, a right which the Master grants him . . . One easily understands why the imperialist propaganda system goes to such trouble to spread the comforting concept of Negritude. Negritude is actually a good mystifying anaesthetic for Negroes who have been whipped too long and too severely to a point where they have lost all reason and become purely emotional.

This unflattering interpretation of the supposed dichotomy between European reason and African emotion was an obvious slap at the thinking of President Léopold Sédar Senghor of Senegal. Other French African delegates may have thought Guinea's attack too personal, for in their own remarks they displayed greater tact, aiming their fire at the concept of Negritude rather than the man behind it. Henri Lopès of Congo-Brazzaville complained of the "pigmentary belt" that Negritude imposed on Africa by stressing racial differences instead of cultural similarities. Paul Zanga of Congo-Kinshasa found Negritude "out of date as an historic movement" but conceded that it "forms part and parcel of our history and can therefore by no manner of means be brushed aside, even if, at the present time, we recognize the need to transcend it." Criticism was even heard in Arabic when Wabu Baker Osman of the Sudan rejected the negativism of racial philosophies which only "serve the interests of the colonialists who have worked for two centuries to characterize people of different continents according to racial criteria." Soon it was becoming almost fashionable for French African speakers to take at least a perfunctory swipe at Negritude and its adherents. The English-speaking African participants, on the other hand, virtually ignored the subject, as if it were no longer worthy of serious attention.

Finally, at the last plenary session, Stanislas Adotevi of Dahomey took the floor and delivered the most eloquent denunciation of them all. "Negritude," he maintained,

> has failed. It has failed, not in the main because a few pseudo-philosophical scribblings have attributed to it the wish to denounce a certain form of African development, but because, denying its origins to deliver us, bound hand and foot, to ethnologists and anthropologists, it has become hostile to the development of Africa. The Negritude we are offered is the relegation of the Negro to the slow rhythm of the fields, at the treacherous hour of neo-colonialism. . . . Negritude today fixes and coagulates for unavoidable ends the most well-worn theories about African traditions, of which it claims to be the literary expression. By rehashing the past and tickling a morbid sensitivity, it hopes to make us forget the present.

There was a time, Adotevi admitted, when Negritude served a useful though limited purpose: "it shook a few consciences and brought a few Negroes together, and this was a good thing . . . In consequence, we should consider it as a primitive period necessary to the African renaissance." But today it is no more than a "political mysticism" which impedes progress by perpetuating the myth of Negro irrationality and neglecting to provide practical solutions to Africa's most pressing problems. As an ideology it is "hollow, vague, inefficient" and dangerously misleading. "Negritude, by pretending that socialism already existed in traditional communities and that it would be sufficient to follow African traditions to arrive at an authentic socialism, deliberately camouflaged the truth and thus became ripe for destruction." While Africa stood in need of social and political revolution, Negritude offered only "the uncertainty of a philosophy without imperatives," mere words instead of deeds. "Negritude," Adotevi concluded, "was born dead; it was going to die and it died." The Guinean delegation applauded wildly.

Senegal did not take all this lying down. Speaking last at the final plenary session, Amadou Mahtar M'Bow, Senegal's Minister of Culture, Youth and Sport, elaborated on some of the points raised in President Senghor's message to the Symposium, which had been read on the opening day shortly after Sékou Tourè's tape-recorded oration. Culture, he said, is a social fact which "cannot be separated from the objective conditions which determine it." Different peoples living in different conditions will therefore have different cultures. The mode or character of a given culture will be a "symbiosis of the influences of Geography and History, of Race and Ethnicity" and will change with time because cultures are dynamic, not static. "As the material conditions of our existence are modified, as new social relationships are established, as our institutions evolve, as modern education spreads, our cultures transform themselves." And eventually these transformations will lead to a "universal convergence," a "progressive symbiosis of cultures" which will culminate in a single "planetary civilization." "Africanity," the symbiotic alliance of two geographically contiguous but philosophically disparate cultural perspectives, generally known as Negritude and Arabism, is a first desirable step in this direction.

But cultural unity will not be achieved in Africa without first passing through the "indispensable phase of recognition of the singularity of the different regional or subregional elements." Negritude, by defining the distinctive cultural traits of the Negro world, will thus make an impressive contribution to the ultimate synthesis of cultures which will usher in a millennium of genuine pan-African unity. In other words, Negritude, far from being dead, is still one of Africa's best hopes for a better future.

Several other Senegalese delegates joined in the debate by contributing papers which were distributed but not read at the Symposium. Alassane N'Daw, quoting liberally from Senghor, stressed the common heritage and common destiny of the Arab-Berber and Negro-African worlds, a theme which had been enunciated in President Boumediène's address. Lamine Niang examined one of these worlds in detail in an essay entitled "Negro-African Culture and Poetry—Elements of the Survival of our Civilization," which was neo-Senghorian in its emphasis on the need to "recreate" Negro-African culture and "fit it into a universal culture . . . while yet retaining its character, its originality." Both papers, perhaps partly as a gesture to the OAU, spoke more of Africanity than of Negritude, but a poem privately circulated by an attractive young Senegalese artist, Mme. Younousse N'Diaye, proclaimed the older concept:

"SUBJECT: NON-LIBERTY: YES!"

I shall cry Negritude
as long as the freedom
of Africa is not complete . . .

I shall cry Negritude
as long as all the races
of Africa are not symbiotic . . .

I shall cry Negritude
as long as it is considered
a racist doctrine . . .

I shall cry Negritude
as long as the American Negro
at the hour of the exploration of the cosmos
has not broken down racial segregation . . .

I shall cry Negritude
because it is my liberty
to be Negro.

It would be difficult to say whether the Negritudinists or the anti-Negritudinists came out best in this exchange, but Guinea certainly had many more allies than Senegal. This may be important as evidence of a decided shift to the Left in pan-African thinking or it may be merely a reflection of the Festival's forthright emphasis on Revolution (almost every African freedom group—ANC, ZAPU, FRELIMO, SWAPO, MPLA, PAIGC—was represented, as was America's Black Panther Party). Nevertheless, nobody really won or lost at the Symposium because, despite the muted polemics at the plenary sessions, the delegates apparently were able to resolve many of their differences in caucus. As expected, they issued a united statement on African culture. However, one is tempted to read significance into the fact that in the cultural olympics staged in the stadiums and streets of Algiers every afternoon and evening, Senegal placed first in the most literary competition—drama—and Guinea was the overall winner with a gold medal in ballet and four silver medals in drama, traditional instrumental music, modern instrumental music, and choral and solo singing. Senegal's best cultural performance still came from its elite, Guinea's from its masses. (pp. 5-7)

Bernth Lindfors, "Anti-Negritude in Algiers," in Africa Today, Vol. 17, No. 1, First quarter, 1970, pp. 5-7.

Henri Lopes

[*Lopes is a Congolese novelist, poet, short story writer, critic, and politician. In the essay below, which was delivered as a speech in July 1969 at the First Pan-African Cultural Festival, he criticizes Negritude as a false concept that stifles communication and creativity.*]

Mr. President,

Your Excellencies,

Honourable Delegates,

Ladies and Gentlemen:

As we have been called upon to speak in this symposium for the first time in the name of the Delegation from Congo-Brazzaville, may we express the joy of our people, our country and our government at being represented at this first giant demonstration of African thought, African arts—in short, African life.

It is for us a cheerful duty and a real pleasure at this time to thank all of those who organized this festival which, we feel, should usher in the rebirth of African thought, of a common Pan-African culture, just as the Panhellenic Games engendered a common Greek culture which was to leave its mark on the entire history of European thought.

Military power by itself is not enough to enable a people to assert itself. *On the contrary,* how is it possible to explain that the black people of Africa have been able to survive the greatest deportation in human history, conquest, slavery, the Ku Klux Klan, aesthetic, intellectual and even religious debasement, in a word banishment from mankind, if there were not the songs sung in the holds of slaveships, those songs which they formerly used to support their fight against nature and to lift themselves above the sufferings inflicted by a monstrous humanity, to outface death. How is it possible to explain our survival if there were not the remembrance of tutelary and guardian masks carved by sculptors from Ife, Bandiaga or M'bouli; if there were not the remembrance of tales and myths describing the African as a strong and proud man; if there were not the ancestral dances to bring relief after the overseer's whip on the cotton plantation. In a famous statement made at the first Congress of Negro Artists and Writers, Frantz Fanon showed how storytellers emerged in the maquis of the Algerian resistance. The fact is that in moments of hope, weariness and despair, man needs dreams. These dreams are supplied by art. And the remembrance of common hopes and dreams is what is appropriately called national culture. But this cannot be allowed to petrify. It must develop with time and the transformations which men and the passage of time make in their surroundings. For those who are fighting today in Angola, Cabinda, Guinea Bissao, Mozambique, Rhodesia and South Africa, the poems of Agostino Neto, Mario de Andrade, Marcellino Dos Santos, Cesaire and Henri Krea and the sort of song which is Frantz Fanon's conclusion to his *Wretched of the Earth* are not a luxury but an inspiration.

Culture is not a collection of encyclopaedic information pertaining to such and such a region, but the organisation of knowledge enabling men to act and to behave in such a way as to work towards a better life and a fuller understanding of each other. Culture is life. It is quite wrong to claim that it turns its back on life. In this present age, when there are those who imply that a militant shows weakness if he is also a poet, musician or other kind of artist, we, the representatives of a country that has chosen to develop along socialist lines, wish, on the contrary, to proclaim loud and clear that art and culture are nourished with the most precious sap of life.

From art and culture a man can draw the strength to live and to fight for the highest ideals of mankind. I remember a comrade who, incarcerated in a prison cell for many long months without books, without paper or writing materials managed to survive. For, he told me later, he was recreating the world and Africa. But above all, he said, because the stirring texts of revolutionary writers he had read when he was a student rose slowly from the depths of his subconscious and he himself wrote verses that he sent to his wife. In this sense, it is of the highest importance that our artists should feel Africa in their bones, in the same way that Goya was inspired when painting his *Thirteenth of May* and Picasso when denouncing Guernica. This was the idea expressed by Elsa Tridet when she wrote "War, disease and famine can discourage genius but cannot kill it. If its tongue is cut out, it will speak with gestures and if its eyes are put out it will continue to feel its way. . . . "

Cesaire once said, and very rightly, when speaking of artists, that they must be "engineers of the soul". The whole truth is contained in this phrase.

This Festival and this Symposium are not just a meeting, just an excuse for festivities. They constitute a confrontation, the moment for emulation and perhaps also for an international soul-searching with a view to a fresh departure.

Here we shall be discussing, for several days, the lines along which artistic creation should proceed. This is a difficult task. A task—and we are sorry to say this—that appears impossible given so brief a period. And artistic creativity can ill abide constraints.

But if this Festival can bring home to each one of us, who are all in responsible positions, that the artist is not an amusing oddity, that he is not the amiable village idiot but a precious instrument of our own improvement, then we shall not have come here in vain. We should act in such a way that if Rabearivelo, the unknown sculptors of the Ife bronzes or the author of the Sundiata Keita were to come into this hall and ask us what we have done to help them to live and produce other work, we could give them a straight answer with no element of mockery.

To us Congolese who have chosen the Socialist path to development, culture represents an irreplaceable adjuvant for the initial effort required of us. The austerity necessary for economic independence, and the fact that the results of our efforts to develop will not be immediately apparent, imply that we must provide our people with opportunities for leisure-time enrichment at low cost. Only culture can provide these. We should mention in passing that the great task of construction which we have undertaken necessarily implies the maintenance of myths. And although artists and intellectuals in general tend to stand aside from myths and to divorce themselves from mysticism, there are nonetheless myths which our artists must propagate in their work. A festival like this should select these myths. We should mention, among others, the myths of work and of the necessity for a real Pan-African unity. This does not mean that work unconnected with the myths that we propagate should be entered on the *Pan-African Index*. Artistic terrorism must be rejected. But we must, on the other hand, develop a high level of artistic criticism armed against the alienating tendencies of certain artistic productions and at the same time impelling artists to set in motion an intellectual life blending with the life of Africa today. This must be a life serving the interests of the people, of society and of its development.

This Pan-African Cultural Festival gives us all an opportunity to look beyond race and thus to call in question the idea of "negritude" without any intention of starting a dispute. We met together at the Congresses of Negro Artists and Writers held in 1956 and 1959, on the keynote of our race and common sufferings, and in 1966 at the World Festival of Negro Art which had the same keynote. In 1969, we have met to celebrate our more or less close connection with the African continent and our common option and efforts to obtain entire possession of the lands, oceans and rivers of this continent. As from now we will no longer be able to define ourselves by race or by any other physical characteristic, but by geography and, above all, by our common determination which is the best basis for national and international unity.

We must overcome racial conditioning and humanise it, just as the peasant works to transform the most difficult country and to give it a covering of manioc, sweet potatoes or coffee. We must stop this headlong and illusory flight towards cultural purity. Man speaks to man, whatever the colour of his skin. Endogamous societies are only what they are because of geographical isolation. Paul Valery defines the European not by "race, language or customs but by his desires and the strength of his will-power". What is there that is Gallic about the so-called heirs of ancient Gaul? And are the Roman virtues really found among the present-day inhabitants of the Eternal City? Antonio Gramsci criticizes this tendency to say that Italy is not the heir of ancient Rome because nothing "august" is any longer to be found there.

Another geographical and cultural environment has an adverse effect on racial consciousness. Race is so greatly exalted in the U.S.A. only because of the segregation there. Langston Hughes recognised in *The Big Sea* that he belonged to America and not to Africa. We know how Richard Wright was taken aback and almost thrown into despair during his visit to the Gold Coast in 1953 because of the distance between him and his fellow-negroes. "I could not understand at all", he wrote. "I was black and they were black but my colour didn't help me". And at the first Congress in 1956 he could not say whether an American negro should give pride of place to African negro or to American culture in spite of Senghor's exhortations to "Take the tents of Africa as his classics".

The values of "negritude" are to be found among various peoples in varying, but not immutable, connections. Worship of the dead, solidarity, union with the cosmic forces, rhythm, are not attributes of negroes alone.

The worst danger about "negritude" is that it constitutes an inhibiting force for negro writers, so far as creative activity is concerned. If it does not actually incite folklore in literature, as denounced by David Diop, it does lead to conformity of style and content, as prejudicial to cultural vitality as all other constraints, moral or other. As our poet, J. B. Tati Loutard, has written, an originality crisis is rampant today among young African writers and it is paralysing the literary vocations. In their phobia at not being able to say things differently from the Europeans or the Asiatic, they do their utmost to cultivate an agreed difference, whereas they merely have to lift the screen of race to liberate their writer's temperament. Thus, we cannot end this contribution without emphasising that it is high time African art rid itself of certain ideas which engender and foster a static conception of culture.

The African writer or painter must keep abreast of the times, must face up to them victoriously. Our culture must come out from the museums, be revived and help African man exploit and dominate his soil, his sub-soil, his rivers, his forests, his oceans, his lakes and his atmosphere.

And, African artists, do stop stressing the superficial differences which seem to single you out and which, in fact, set you apart! We do not mean the personality which distinguishes one artist from another, but the false cultural areas to which one has given the seductive names of negritude, arabism, bantuism, and which, in fact, only result in people no longer understanding one another in the end. There is an Arab proverb which says that men resemble their brothers rather than their father. We should like to add that, with the swift development of knowledge, the mentality of the 20th century is not that of the 19th century, even though the two come next to each other.

King Makoko, confronting De Brazza or the kings of the old Kingdom of the Congo, if they were to come into this room, would not understand our delegation's contribution. And yet we are Bantu just as they were. Would their "Bantu" culture help them to understand the educational needs of our youth? The rights of African women today? The organization of which our society today is in need? The economic tasks we must accomplish for our independence?

How, too, forbear from mentioning the example of Frantz Fanon who came here to fight for a people to whom his mother did not belong, who adopted him and made an African out of him without so much as asking him anything about the degree of his Arabism, who simply turned him into an African. For our artists, it is a matter of furthering a culture that it may give rise to mentalities such that a young African from Algiers should understand one from Bujumbura, and that a young woman from Bulawayo should feel akin to one from Cairo. For this reason, we should like to take advantage of this platform to denounce publicly all the institutions and all the coteries which arrogate to themselves the right to continue speaking in the name of all Africa, on topics which today are obsolete.

The African governments must oppose this and must not extend their help to such decadent academies which, even if they did know a period of glory, could not, from their exile understand the upheavals which affect Africa and can therefore no longer speak in the name of its intelligentsia. The Symposium must launch an appeal to African artists to break their shackles and free themselves from exploitation at the hands of the merchants of African culture. Our artists must first become known in their own country and over the entire continent. And if they are not understood, then let them explain themselves to the public. From such a dialogue will be born an African cultural life, whereas African production outside the continent will yield only exotic fruit.

It is therefore desirable that from this Festival and Symposium should emerge a policy of cultural exchange among the various republics represented here. When a writer has his work published in Europe, it is because no publisher and no broadcasting time are forthcoming in Africa. Every African country has cultural agreements with the Great Powers, but how many such agreements are there between African countries, even when they are neighbours? Each State on the continent should undertake frequently to accept artistic productions from other countries. African artists and men of cultural eminence should be able to travel throughout Africa to explain their work and their motives to the peoples of other African countries. The exchanges organised today by this Festival on a Pan-African basis should become a permanent feature of bilateral relations between African countries.

As we said a moment ago, even if the nature of the local genius determines that the cadence, rhythm or choice of colours be different in the Magrab, the savannah or the forest regions, this will not deter the men of our continent from a sense of fraternity nor from establishing contacts with a sense of the commonalty of their problems. It is not true, honoured Delegates, that our struggles, the revolution in which we are engaged, are a passing phase. We declare, on the contrary, that the Revolution is fundamental and that the African artists should undertake to change human nature, to shape human beings free from alien influences—free and better (even if they are negroes) who will no longer endure that man should oppress man.

As President Marien Ngouabi said,

> The aim of our culture is not to lull our friends with fairy stories, nor to boast of our art or civilisation—in a word, our knowledge of human sciences. It has a more important part to play,

namely to awaken in the African a sentiment of striving for the national liberation of the continent. It is not even a question of proclaiming or glorifying our heroes, though this is indispensable. African culture should be the light which guides our combatants towards national liberation, because it will enable Africans to understand the necessity for them to free themselves. For when a vast continent such as ours is able to appreciate and to defend its culture, this means that it is determined to fight. Without this struggle our culture would not exist, because it would be misunderstood by the forces of evil.

(pp. 58-64)

Henri Lopes, "Negritude: A Sober Analysis," in Journal of the New African Literature and the Arts, *Nos. 7-8, Spring-Fall, 1969, pp. 58-64.*

[There] is no black culture, nor white culture, nor yellow culture . . . Negritude is thus a false concept, an irrational weapon encouraging the irrationality based on racial discrimination, arbitrarily exercised upon the peoples of Africa, Asia and upon men of color in America and Europe.

—Ahmed Sékou Touré, in a speech at the First Pan-African Cultural Festival, July 1969.

Stanislas Adotevi

[*Adotevi is a Beninese writer. In the following essay, which was delivered as a speech in July 1969 at the First Pan-African Cultural Festival, he discusses the limitations and failures of Negritude, which he terms a "hollow, vague and inefficient" ideology, and proposes Melanism as a replacement.*]

Under-development, as we now know, is the presence of absence in the present, the mythical character in a debased drama, named neo-colonisation. It is neo-colonisation which fills the stage of today's events with both actors and scenery, which robs the wakeful state of its certainty. It is a mysterious force whence issue the Delphic emanations of eternal exploitation, the matrix from which fetishes are endlessly turned out. It is this which makes and unmakes governments. Every African brought into its service like Caliban by Prospero's wand, is working only to accomplish its desires.

Therefore, since in Africa there is no reality except through this savage fiction, the extraordinary resilience of which Caesar spoke and which all of us wish for can only come about through the projection over Africa—the whole of Africa—of unbridled entities which, spreading to infinity, liberate new energy. These new categories, this system of unaccustomed entities, must assume the task of retranslating in detail all the excrescences with which Africa is afflicted.

In concrete terms, it will no longer do to talk of African unity; we must pursue the means. We can no longer contend ourselves with abstract affirmations about African culture in general; we must elucidate scientifically what it is that makes such and such a manifestation distinctly African negro, another Magrabin and a third by its origins and inspiration strictly Arab. This is the truth, eroded sometimes by the passage of time but confirmed by circumstance. All of us share the desire to bridge centuries and differences and to create a united Present.

Mr. Chairman, distinguished delegates, it is to a review of conscience that I invite you—to a casting up of accounts, and finally to a resolution.

Since accounting there must be, I will myself speak of negritude, but I trust that all the other strains which go to make up our continent will be studied. For that is Africa.

Since we must arrive at a resolution, each one of us has a duty to regard differences in the perspective of unity.

Magrabism and Panarabism are no doubt political concepts, but it would be hard to deny that their infrastructure is cultural.

Negritude thinks of itself no doubt as a purely literary concept; in truth it is today a political mysticism.

These, Gentlemen, are the problems we have earnestly to tackle.

For my part, I should like in turn, but in other terms, to take up the theme of negritude. Negritude has failed. It has failed, not in the main because a few pseudo-philosophical scribblings have attributed to it the wish to denounce a certain form of African development, but because, denying its origins to deliver us, bound hand and foot, to ethnologists and anthropologists, it has become hostile to the development of Africa. The negritude we are offered is the relegation of the negro to the slow rhythm of the fields, at the treacherous hour of neo-colonisation. As Madame Kesteloot has realized a little belatedly, it is not surprising that the young no longer flock to hear her.

The approach to eternity of the negritic negro is not a metaphysical one, but political. Negritude today fixes and coagulates, for unavoidable ends, the most well-worn theories about African traditions, of which it claims to be the literary expression.

By rehashing the past and tickling a morbid sensitivity, it hopes to make us forget the present. The negritude of speeches, the negritude of today provides, when the great distributions are made, the "good negroes". Alas for the great poetic vision!

"Do you suppose", we read, "that we can beat the Europeans at mathematics, except for a few outstanding men who would confirm that we are not a race of abstractions?" This sentence was contributed by a theoretician of negritude to the UNESCO Courier of April 1965. Re-read it; you will look in vain for poetry. What you will find is the con-

firmation that the zealots of negritude are not content merely to point out a difference which is, after all, understandable, but as part of this mania for upholding the concept of theoretical imperfection they endeavour consciously to oppose the black continent to a Europe which is rational and, above all, industrial.

It is easy to discern the intention behind all this mental confusion. From the unfinished concept of negritude one passes to another, very vague and very subtle, of the negro soul; and thereafter to the uncertainty of a philosophy without imperatives and without foundation whose sole title is the frenzy which, it appears, is to regenerate the world—the African world and, of course, the rest. At the end of the road we are offered African socialism which, excuse the incongruity, is merely the conclusion of a syllogism of which the premises is the lubricious negro. This comes from no theorist of negritude, but we know our Sartre. However great our liking for him, we find passages which are mere enormities. "Negritude", he wrote, "is not a state but an attitude . . . an act; but an act which ignores the world, which does not tend towards transforming the wealth of the world . . . it is a matter of existing in the midst of this world . . . of an appropriation which is not technical". From this it follows that for our negro poets (and I quote):

"Existence is the repetition year by year of the sanctified coitus . . . the human rises out of nothing like a penis in erection; creation is an immense and perpetual parturition; the world is flesh and the offspring of flesh. . . . Thus the deepest roots of negritude are androgynous". This is sheer phantasmagoria. It is not surprising if after this the negroes are incapable of making revolution. Revolution is primarily technical and that is why Marx was the one to write the finest songs about the bourgeoisie.

But Sartre, in self-defence, came practically to another conclusion, It will suffice to read the final pages of that very fine text "Orphee Noir" to become aware of this. By keeping the sexual pedal pressed right down, Sartre drifted into delirium, which is normal. Negritude, by seeking fecundity elsewhere than in Africa, lapsed into socialism, which serves it right.

We know that African socialism derived from negritude will bring about the downfall of the warehouses.

This is the winding street of revolutions and the end of all our hopes. Negritude, by pretending that socialism already existed in traditional communities and that it would be sufficient to follow African traditions to arrive at an authentic socialism, deliberately camouflaged the truth and thus became ripe for destruction.

The first outcome of all this nonsense are the ghosts which disturb our dreams at night:

> The purring of states which are running in neutral gear; antediluvian demagogy; government waltzes; a cacophony of administrative interferences in stagnant economic operations; daily increasing cleavage between town and country; unemployment and impotence of the educated; lack of structural changes; incompetent civil servants, and so on.

Only frenzy and bitterness is in sight. This must change and to do this it is not sufficient to talk of negritude, for African negroes know they are negroes and that they are in the midst of the present African catastrophe. In other words we must deal with today's tasks.

This duty may be understood in accordance with the seriousness with which the following questions are tackled: How shall we modernize Africa? How shall we get rid of old structures? How shall we encourage technical culture? What importance should we attach to each stratum of our society? What place will be occupied by women and young people? How shall we resolve our ethnic problems? How shall we approach traditional religions?

For the intellectual, the worker, the shopkeeper, the peasant and for those who do not want to travel outside the country, these are the daily problems which must be solved immediately and which have nothing to do with the pink pages of *Larousse*.

The artificial quest for traditions is, as Fanon says, a "mere study of exoticism".

Negritude, hollow, vague and inefficient is an ideology. There is no further place in Africa for literature other than that of the revolutionary combat. Negritude is dead.

A worrying thought arises at this point. I should like to combine this worry with my own worries. It lies in the same direction.

Doubtless, if we examine the events over the past ten years in Africa, and if we disgustedly consider this cavalcade of servility and begging and if we measure the extent of this hyprocrisy, we cannot prevent ourselves from calling for a revolt.

Africa has not gone and she does not seem to be ready for departure.

The false alarms, the courtelinesque ballets and the tragicomic setting of the gigantic Luna-Park make people quick to conclude that these negroes are worth nothing and are still under the influence of their fantasies and keeping the worst surprises for the best intentions. The conclusion can be quickly drawn and it is drawn. It grieves and humiliates us and we are tempted to throw up the sponge. It could be the same for Negritude.

It is necessary to restore the natural aridity to things, to understand how I deviate from my friends, not because of the objectives or the projected end, but because of the means. To understand Negritude, we must put it back in its former neurotic context and by comparing it with the current situation, ask ourselves what the chances are of exorcising it.

At this abstract level, it is easy to see that nothing has changed. Exploitation has become more disgusting, and this continent which, except for man's looting, was not destined for misfortune, lives without an objective and with a stagnant future. We know what they say: mess, waste and disorder. This is what the great friends of these States are saying among themselves. To know this is to know the necessity of recovering in the same movement at least the Negritude programme, if not the final goal.

Without a doubt, the irrationality of under-development and especially that of negroes is enormous. But without going as far as taking examples from their history, it might be useful for Europeans to make the dialectic reversal advocated by Marx, which has now become a working argument. This reversal will allow us to refute certain allegations. And we have known since Montesquieu that, in political life, "All political vices are not moral vices and all moral vices are not political ones". In the same way, we will be led to think that, however vicious negroes may be, they are not completely commanded by their imagination: and that, beyond the negro's unreason there lies a reason that is not reasonable, but extraordinarily rational. All this unreason has its structure: colonial necessity whose dominion is so sure that it can not only digest the strangest eccentricities but even the stroke of fortune bringing success or failure to a coup d'etat, and which depends on an Ambassador's smile or his silence. This understanding of the structure of the exploitation of negritude should have assured him.

Its failure came about because it neither would nor could do this work for itself or for us. In any case, there can be no doubt that Negritude will never do it now, but Negritude, at the outset and merely because it did not yet have the possibility, already raised its voice in certain contexts in a way that could be heard and which some of us did hear.

In consequence, whatever may be our quite justifiable references with regard to it, and although certain aspects may seem old-fashioned and with frankly reactionary objectives, we should consider it as a primitive period necessary to the African renaissance. I would say, and I choose my words carefully, that at a time when the whole world was given over to racialism and people like Andrass and Morand were taken for vagabonds, at a time when the whole of humanity raised voice in competitive cacophony, there was a single pistol-shot in the middle of this concert—negritude. It shook a few consciences and brought a few negroes together, and this was a good thing. I do not intend to defend negritude against its internal weaknesses and the disintegration with which it is threatened.

We should nonetheless recognise that the exaltation of our heroes can be none other than abstract. It underlines contemporary demands—poetry of the unusual and of solitude, doubtless, but at the same time political in its refusal to betray its origins. It was political before being lyrical.

I am not speaking of deviated or perverted negritude. I am speaking of our debt, and above all, our pride, in belonging to the tradition of African civilization, and in possessing values which distinguish the black world from that of the white men. In the realm of artistic creation, this attitude calls for a casting off of European models and a profession of faith in the destiny of Africa. Formulated thus, Negritude should be considered as the first moment of present day requirements; I think that it was, yesterday, one of the possible forms for the struggle for emancipation.

It is a curious struggle, I will be told, that contents itself with words when depersonalisation is rampant in Senegal and men are dying like flies in the banana-fields of the

West Indies. Doubtless this is so, but one should forget, for an instant, the Negritude of the dictionary and neo-colonial imposture, and should try to understand what courage was needed to dare to protest against humiliation in the "thirties". And as regards words, I should recommend a little more thorough reading of Marx. One can read, in his "Contribution to the Criticism of Hegel's Philosophy of Law", this phrase which may appear astonishing to some of you.

"It is evident", says Marx, "that the aim of criticism can in no wise replace criticism by armed force. Material force can only be countermanded by material force, but theory is also changed to a material force as soon as it penetrates the masses". I do not think, therefore, that the error arises at this level. The capital error of this older Negritude, the great sin of Negritude in general was to have been, at the outset, inverted love. It was to have believed, even before its birth, in universality—when the universe was forbidden to it. The carnal ardour of black hatred should have been opposed to the cosmic insults to which none other than the black race have been subjected. But our poets, overtaken by unreason, preferred the crazy advances of love. Damas says this when he looks in vain for "a shoulder in which to hide his face and his share of reality". On behalf of us all, pigment confirms the truth that this entire negritude is morbid sterility because it never knew what harvest it would reap. And indeed, that which brings about the restructuring of the world concerns revolution, not cosmic ferment. Negritude was born dead; it was going to die and it died.

A message, however, remains. Apart from the ineffectiveness of its negation, apart from the labyrinth of mystification, Negritude was a rejection of humiliation.

Today this humiliation is still apparent and the problem posed by Negritude remains. There are the unwanted gifts intermittently showered upon us so as to ensure our continued subjection. There is the deterioration of rates of exchange, there are the prices fixed in Paris, London and elsewhere. And for one unemployed—let no more be said—there is the appetizing food to be had in foreign embassies. There is the isolation of China. There are the millions that foreign aid brings in to the countries that are supposed to be aiding us, and the moving text by Che that I will read and which says, in effect:

> How can we speak of the "mutual benefits" if we have the sale, at world market prices, of raw products costing unlimited efforts and sufferings to the under-developed countries and the purchase, at world market prices, of machines produced in today's great automated factories?
>
> If we establish this sort of relationship between the two groups of nations, we will have to agree that the Socialist countries are to a certain extent implicated in imperialist exploitation.
>
> It will be argued that the volume of exchanges with the underdeveloped countries constitutes an insignificant percentage of Socialist countries' foreign trade. This is absolutely true, but makes no difference as to the immoral character of this exchange.

In short, there is the spirit of Camp David. And finally, there we are—divided, crushed and pulverized. A reduced and shaken Africa, with no grasp of its future.

This, Mr. Chairman and gentlemen, is the reality set before us.

Africa, still anti-Aristotelian, is still in the expectation of form. But the great upheavals of the next decades will proceed from this unreasoning, formless Africa. All that is needed is unceasingly renewed action, an imposed discipline and, above all, a way of thinking which can embrace situations, discern difficulties, repulse determinism and make real the new situation enabling us to reach our goal. I would put forward the doctrine of Melanism.

One could find another name for it, but the essential thing is the cementing force and thought which, operating in the perspective of unity, reacts on particular sensibilities as do Magrabism and Arabism.

The Melanism which I would propose to you is open to all Nubia (Africa). It is not a new racialism but an identification. It is an affirmation of the plain fact that to be a negro today is still to live through the violent depredations of the slave trade.

Melanism is the acceptance of a state of war, but with arms other than prayers and negro spirituals. It is, said Machiavelli, "an act of humanity to take up arms in the defence of a people for whom they are the only resource".

Melanism will be the unique resource of a people who can no longer deck out its torture with trophies conquered from shame. It will be, as Cesaire says, the expression denying the whip. We must give the lie to negation by assigning positive tasks to each negro.

We are not trying to racialise problems but to understand that white people have the habit of putting all negroes into the same category and to inspire themselves with this same common historical attack and subsequent traumatism, so as to define a strategy for the present. To put it clearly, negroes should relegate their tears to antiquity. The battle has taken on a physical form, and should henceforth only have a physical expression. And, for certain American negroes, it would be illusory to think that the battle will end with the illusory conquest of civil rights. Even if they one day take over economic and social power, or if, in the meantime, they have crumbs thrown to them in the middle hierarchies, they should know that they are nothing, so long as the negroes of Africa have not yet completed the ascendancy, the tragedy of which was related by King Christopher.

All this goes to say that the essential task must fall on the negroes of Africa. And they can only carry it out by coming to agreement on the following questions: Is it true that no race has been more insulted than ours? Is not the present-day situation the perennialization of this humiliation? Is it not true that the Africans themselves (our ancestors who acquiesced in the selling of slaves and who are the present-day apologists of modern sodomy) bear the overwhelming responsibility for this fearsome cavalcade? And, as things are thus, is it worthwhile making the effort to get out of this slough of spittle, tears and blood? Finally, is there a certain and effective means of doing this? And if so, what is it?

These are the five questions that Melanism would place before the conscience of each African.

For my part, I do not think much of African socialism. It is the ideological expression of a social category which installs, in a backward country, capitalism with its backward economy. It has nothing to offer to us.

I therefore think that the only practical socialism is that propounded by Marx, completed by Lenin and applied, with a greater or lesser degree of success, by the socialist countries. This socialism is the only practical possibility—with, of course, the variations imposed by geography. But we know Lenin's dictum "Communism is the power of the Soviets plus electrification". This is not yet the case in Africa. There is also the advice given by Lenin to the 2nd Internationale. To make the great socialist leap forward one must, he said, have an active, organised proletariat and help from socialist governments. Now, what we know of our proletariats and the present international situation condemns us to defer this hope.

There remains capitalism. I will not speak of the extent of this phenomenon, but will content myself with listing its failures by means of a quotation from Meister:

> Finally one fails to wonder about the inability of liberalism to apply to new countries the principles which made possible the spectacular development of our Western countries. By its very development, capitalism impedes the development of new countries: the principle of the free circulation of capital empties these countries of their surpluses, while that of free enterprise kills the embryo of industrial development. To stick to these principles and leave their frontiers open means condemning these countries to the same stagnation as that reigning in Latin America, that typical product of neo-colonialism in the last century. It is obvious that the liberal way is a total failure in Africa.

Although during several decades Europe has been the theatre of the greatest capitalist upheavals, and although capitalism today still appears as an extraordinarily fertile model which constantly generates free energy, here, for the African, it is, to use a metaphor, an extinguished and slag-covered volcano.

We therefore are forced to look for something else. Melanism which, I admit, is somewhat irrational, aims at keeping the sore open and, by shelving the solutions so far proposed, gets rid of the inextricable estrangement and founds the state in which the future history of Africa will take on a meaning.

I have already defined melanism. It is not just a phobia. As it cannot be compared to the "anti-racist racism" Sartre speaks of in "Orphée Noire", it is our purpose here to de-mystify the concept of race and to wrench it out of the hands of reactionary politicians who are using it to obscure the issue.

Although Sartre's objective was the same as ours—to denounce the evil that has led to the racism of the black poets—ours differs from his in that it does not limit itself to exorcising race by making it active, but aims at strengthening a people by a racial awareness, a people which perhaps is still abstract although not paradoxical, and which is probably mistaken as a result of inhibition.

There remains however, in spite of the precautions taken, something which should not be left obscure. We should repeat here what we have already said:

Firstly, we are products of white unreason: we are Negroes only for the whites. In Africa, to be a Negro, is to be as natural as the infinite stars in the night. Secondly, whatever our opinions, whether we are Christians, Muslims, Communists or reactionaries, and often at the height of battle, white necessity has been burnt to a cinder in our flesh. And thirdly, as it is our purpose to save ourselves from racism by constructing a modern state in Africa, this our purpose can only be made real by an exacerbated nationalism, the force of which, although partly resting as objective facts, also derives, according to Renouvin, from irrational elements. Consequently, we cannot reject the irrational part of such an enterprise. On the contrary, if we take the end into account, the objective pursued will give the enterprise a positive value, as has always been the case throughout history. Undoubtedly, to be able to speak of national feeling, we should, according to the well-known pattern, first have a Nation. But who could deny that Islam has favoured nationalism? And is it possible, as Renouvin asks, to understand anything about Japanese nationalism without referring to Shintoism?

Our project therefore, far from floundering through excessiveness, may break silence in pointing to the beyond and in rejecting limits. It states the necessity for a modern state while indicating the means to attain it.

Therefore it takes its inspiration from the great nationalist upsurges of the past centuries, but with the difference that, although it may serve to create a myth, this myth should draw its truth only from its own strength: we need a myth which is not mythical but a reality shattered in the bric-a-brac of time. A myth such as the one Gramsci, who pronounced the only right and profound judgment on Machiavelli, discovered in "The Prince", which he considered as an: "Illustration of a political ideology which does not present itself as a frigid Utopia or a doctrinaire argument, but as the creation of a concrete reasoning process which operates on a dispersed and scattered people to provoke and organize their collective renaissance".

In the same way, Africa must be convinced by meditation on race. It should come to terms with its time so as to regenerate the future. In this connection, there are two objectives: the establishment of a collective melanin will and new mental structures.

There are five prerequisites for attaining these objectives:

(1) On the political level: the establishment of a modern state.

(2) On the economical level: a democratic national economy.

(3) In the field of the philosophy of history, all systems which persist in discovering cyclic

returns and which deny indefinite progress should be rejected.

(4) On the intellectual and moral level:

    (a) in the moral field, an educational system drawing its force from a constant reference to past and present humiliations of the race and which also considers reprehensible any insane cult of the past, even when national, as well as all stupid borrowings from abroad.

    (b) in the intellectual field, opposition to stifled traditions, an appeal for rational innovations of the various world revolutions.

(5) Lastly, on the level of personal training, we should only strive for a perpetual creation of ourselves and for a constant creative activity based upon a sense of initiative and responsibility and only retaining elements useful for the Nation.

To sum up, pending the union of the whole of Africa, this transitional ideology aims at the establishment of a strong and prosperous national state which inside the country brings about the recovery of the race by vivisection; outside the country asserts African irredentism using subversion if necessary; finally, on the economic level, takes advantage of the contradictions between and inside the power coalitions in order to found a modern industry and economy.

A hallucination? Perhaps. In any case, the methods will have to be transformed. Practical and theoretical necessities often entail the introduction of new concepts into the problem.

Before socialist recovery, must come recovery of ourselves. This is not a matter of repudiation. Tactics had to be changed. We are changing them.

In any case, these lines are addressed to the young Africans of my generation. To the generation which, like me, will perhaps not see the promised land, but which should know that the shore exists. Melanism is after all the preliminary to socialism. Instead of disdain and condescension, each African, as is more or less the case with the Chinese today, will read in the eyes of the European the first signs of terror. Therefore, everybody should, in the sinister hour of discouragement, repeat after Fichte these sentences of restored hope: "Already one sees the new daybreak shine, it casts a glow upon the mountain tops, announcing the coming day". I want, as much as is in my power, to seize the rays of this daybreak and condense them to make a mirror which reflects its image on our desperate era, so that it may find there its true core, and perceives, through its successive transformations and developments, the anticipated form of its definitive face. No doubt this contemplation will dissolve the image of our former life and that what is dead will not definitely enter in the tomb before emitting excessive moans. (pp. 70-81)

Stanislas Adotevi, "Negritude Is Dead: The Burial," in Journal of the New African Literature and the Arts, *Vols. 7-8, Spring-Fall, 1969, pp. 70-81.*

Mbella Sonne Dipoko

[*In the following essay, Dipoko contends that Negritude has declined in popularity because the attitudes of its leaders are reactionary and politically cautious.*]

For one who knows how much the *Négritude* Movement has fallen out of favour even among a majority of Francophone African intellectuals, it is only natural to view with scepticism the reported success of the recently-concluded Dakar Seminar on *"Négritude"*, which brought together some of the most outstanding personalities in the field of culture in Africa and abroad. One is tempted to suspect that the seminar was conceived mainly as a means of recruiting some urgently needed support for *négritude* which even in Francophone Africa has been systematically criticized and resisted by most radical intellectuals, and is being increasingly abandoned by those who at one time had supported it. One could therefore safely say that it was to give the flagging movement a boost that the Senegalese authorities decided to spend so much money on yet another talk fair—one of those international get-togethers at which a lot of people say a lot of gloriously high-sounding things and in between the flow of verbiage they are lavishly wined and dined while being used to lend support and credibility to whatever movement had invited them to the particular talk jamboree.

Of course, conferences have an important part to play in the diffusion of ideas and in the study of the state of a society at any given time; but their negative, hot-air aspect should not be underestimated, just as it would be naive to over-estimate the positive contribution mere talk is likely to make to the good health of civilization. And since most of the time their composition is selective, they tend to be misleading about the state of popular opinion in the land. Also, more than half of the foreign guests at the Dakar meeting would never have been there had it not been for the free return tickets and free board.

So the present impact of *négritude* should not be judged by the glamour of those international cultural jamborees the movement has the knack of organizing, but rather by the now ever-growing hostility African intellectuals are showing towards its over-cautious political attitudes. It was because of this over-cautiousness on the part of *négritude* bosses that I myself resigned from the editorial staff of the movement's review *Présence Africaine*. Ever since more and more Francophone African intellectuals have turned against the movement which we now consider to be reactionary through its insistence on traditional values and its opposition to marxian socialism; for after all, some of its militants now have ministerial responsibilities and one of them is even a head of state. Still none of them has cared to set up a revolutionary socialist to state the promise of which seemed to have been present in its early message.

It was because of that original revolutionary promise that the French philosopher Jean-Paul Sartre had so much praise for *négritude* in his *Black Orpheus*. But with Senghor a President of an independent republic and some of his followers ministers elsewhere, the movement he, Césaire and Damas founded in Paris in the thirties had become very much an establishment affair. And as they have so far shown very little desire to rid their countries of capitalism, and some of the governments they dominate or influence are giving revolutionary leftwingers a hard time, it is only fair to state that the movement has become rightwing. I would be very surprised indeed if a man like Sartre would today say the same things he said in *Black Orpheus* many years ago. But his essay is still in print and so words go on telling a story that is no longer entirely true.

A more definite proof of the movement's decline was given during a five-day conference recently held in Paris in March. Organised by *Présence Africaine* which champions President Senghor's ideas, the conference brought together some twenty London-based South African exiles among whom were writers, artists and musicians. Besides seminars on the various aspects of art and literature and a paper on the South African economy, there was an exhibition of books, painting and photographs, film shows and a jazz session given by the *Spear* jazz formation. Unfortunately, at no time was there an audience of more than thirty to forty persons (half of whom were the South Africans themselves) in the ultra-modern hall made to hold well over a thousand. This confirmed an earlier rumour that the African community in Paris had decided to boycott the conference as a sign of its opposition to the politics of *négritude*. Invited to participate I refused, and attended the conference only as a member of the press, and some of the Africans resident in Paris who attended did so only as observers. It was a complete failure and I had never before seen the *négritude* people looking so depressed, for there was a sure sign that their movement had ceased to be representative even of majority opinion in Francophone Africa.

In matters of culture and politics, African attitudes in Paris can serve as pointers to the prevailing intellectual trends in Francophone Africa. Hence it was very significant that although *Présence Africaine* had invited them to the conference, most of the African diplomats in the French capital chose to stay away. And the powerful Black African Students' Union (FEANF) also refused to participate, which might have been due to the fact that in order to steer clear of political controversy, *Présence Africaine* had insisted on making the conference a strictly cultural affair. So its theme was "Cultural Aspects of (Black) South Africa under the impact of Apartheid", although according to handouts by *Présence Africaine* the mission of the conference was to discuss "the dynamism of black civilisation in South Africa"—a precision which is very much in the *négritude* spirit which claims psycho-cultural particularities for black people all over the world. All this could not but put off many progressive Africans and left-wing French groups who are actively interested in anti-Apartheid activities.

One can easily understand how repugnant the idea of an exclusively cultural conference on South Africa would be to many people at this time when they would rather discuss such burning political issues as the sale of arms to

Pretoria, an issue which was raised very early in the proceedings by the radical novelist Alex La Guma, and the poet Dennis Brutus. But as it was only a cultural get-together, there was very little discussion on this issue which is unfortunate as this may give the wrong impression that Africans resident in Paris and the French public as a whole are indifferent to the fate of black people in South Africa. If the attendance at the March 12-16 conference was so low it was simply because few people can be bothered to attend a conference called by an organisation which has its priorities so outrageously wrong. What killed the conference was the fact that once more *Présence Africaine* characteristically chose to play it safe by avoiding any frontal attacks against anybody.

Of course, by intending the conference to show "the dynamism of black civilisation in South Africa," the Society of African Culture (*Présence Africaine*) was only being faithful to its cautious, almost apolitical approach which it has consistently applied to African problems over the years and which has enabled it to survive and even to prosper in its long exile in Paris since the review was founded in 1947. But for how long are the preachers of *négritude* going to remain in business? The failure of their conference of South Africa proves beyond any doubt that *négritude* and its cultural programme are irrelevant to the situation in Africa. They are particularly irrelevant to the situation in South Africa where all the races must come together in order to build a composite democratic culture; and any attempts at mobilising black South Africans for the defense of their ancient traditions, which is what talk of "cultural aspects of (Black) South Africa" amounts to, could only mean falling into the trap of "separate development" which is what Apartheid is all about. But because *Présence Africaine* seems reluctant to keep abreast with the times and appears instead to be moving farther and farther to the Right with the consolidation of its cultural positions into rigid reactionary dogma and in spite of the occasional revolutionary articles from outside contributors which the journal publishes, the organisation can only continue to lose its audience. This trend will increasingly make it more of a liability than an asset to any progressivist issue with which it tries no matter how cautiously to associate itself.

The South Africans left Paris with the impression that they had been made fun of, which is understandable seeing that besides the other participants, a whole South African jazz orchestra had been lifted all the way from London to Paris only to come and perform before an audience of hardly more than thirty persons.

Présence Africaine could say they did their best to publicise the conference, and communiqués were sent to press agencies and to newspapers; they sent invitations to student organisations and to African embassies; and that if the response was so limited almost to the point of being nil, it wasn't their fault.

Maybe they did their best; but that best wasn't simply good enough, and it is definitely their fault that through a reluctance to commit themselves militantly on topical political issues more and more people seem to be losing all interest in an organisation which a quarter of a century ago seemed to hold so much promise for the oppressed of the Third World. That is why, instead of jumping into its band-wagon because of all those return tickets by air and free meals and posh hotel rooms in foreign capitals which are such a temptation, progressive African intellectuals, militant students and radical trade unionists must come together and formulate a radical alternative to *négritude* which is now definitely on the wane. We need fresh thinking in the field of African culture; and plenty of that fresh thinking can come out of our universities and trade union circles. (pp. 748-49)

> *Mbella Sonne Dipoko, "The Negritude Debate: 2," in* West Africa, *No. 2820, July 2, 1971, pp. 748-49.*

Femi Osofisan

[*In the following essay, Osofisan describes Negritude as a cultural concept that is no longer useful in addressing current African problems.*]

> When I read poems sent to me by young black writers (and) I recognise old flavours of Damas, Césaire or Senghor, I really feel like yawning. And I say to myself: This is no good.

Thus proclaimed Leopold Sedar Senghor at the last Colloquy on Négritude in Dakar [in 1971]. What he obviously fails to understand is that, for many of us of the younger generation, when we hear the word Négritude at all, even in a whisper, we not only feel like yawning, but actually fall asleep. And our comments on waking are much less tolerant than the insipid "this is no good."

Needless to say, we are amazed that our elders can still allow themselves the indulgence of flogging a useless debate like whether Négritude is dead or alive. Clearly it is a debate that has lost all meaning, as frustrated [Mbella Sonne] Dipoko tried to point out. We cannot ignore the indisputable facts of history.

For times have changed; and we, black men and others, have been caught in the flux. We are, like it or not, no longer where we were in 1930. After DuBois, we have had Luther King, Malcolm X and the Black Panthers. Why then should we keep waving the old banners and outmoded weapons? Because a horse ran well in our grandfather's time, shall we now abandon the motor-car?

Négritude as a cultural concept is a horse that has run well, without doubt. At a very significant period, it infused courage in black men fighting against colonial domination, re-established our cultural heritage, and was one of our most palpable weapons in the winning of independence and the activation of nationalistic forces. Now the horse has grown old, and the age of the motor engine has arrived.

In order, however, that the vital forces which Négritude helped to foster might not die with independence, Senghor—echoed since by disciples—extended the concept into a humanistic philosophy. Négritude became "the sum total of the civilization values of the Negro world as expressed in the life and works of Negroes."

Négritude, thus defined, can therefore never die, unless the whole black race is exterminated. Any dissident voice, like that of Soyinka or U'Tamsi, explains Senghor, is not really a refutal, but a mere transcendence of the same basic philosophy. It is only a matter of "schools" and "generations", following the same master; not a revolution, but a continuation.

What we can conclude from this then, is that if the 16th century cultural renaissance in Europe had been called *blanchitude,* and there had been a white Senghor involved in it, all the subsequent movements and philosophies would never have had any other name. Everything, from romanticism to rationalism, symbolism to surrealism to the absurd, all would have gone under the same tag of *blanchitude.* Liberalism, conservatism, fascism would never have been born. And why democracy, communism or marxism when there is *blanchitude?* When we already have horse, why find other names like car, bus or aeroplane?

The absurdity of trying to incorporate all fields of Negro activity for all ages under a single banner is so immense that one is surprised that the men who gathered in Dakar last April for the Négritude "colloquy" did not notice it. Which was perhaps the motivation for such giggling titles as "Négritude and Law", "Négritude and Politics" . . . etc. . . . I looked in vain for some paper entitled "Négritude and the Lavatory" . . .

That was the only thing which spoilt these otherwise excellent papers, the desire to cling on frantically to a sunken post in a rapidly moving world, to hold desperately to a moribund philosophy.

Take Alioune Sene's paper on politics for example. Rightly, he points out that the only workable political formula for Africa must be one based on the fusion of traditional dialectics ("socialisme traditionnel") and modern marxist mechanics. He also goes on to suggest the re-introduction of animism as a natural spiritual extension, and the complete alienation of atheism.

Much of this paper is of course idealistic and even not original, but the over-all brilliance of it is indisputable. What is annoying is the patently mortal struggle, to incorporate the word "Négritude", when it was glaringly irrelevant. And this seems to have been the general plague at the colloquy, infecting everybody, like cholera.

Césaire has said; "Négritude is the mere recognition of the fact of being black, and the acceptance of this fact . . . " Well, since 1930, we have recognised and accepted, and persuaded other people to recognise and accept, the authenticity of our cultural identity. But afterwards?

Négritude was a necessary phase of narcissistic encomium, of the reedification of black dignity in the face of white scorn. Its foundation rested on the past, or rather on what was conveniently salvaged from the "heroic" past. Therefore it has become obsolete and, like the old horse, it must die or be killed as an act of mercy. The new literature and the new humanism we seek for the new generation must divorce itself from the historical and cultural egomania which Négritude represented, and face contemporary realities. We must turn from the grandeur of fantasy to the ugliness of modernity.

No, there is even no need to deflate the self-glorifying splendour of ancient myths and legends, in the manner of Ouloguem, though that may be a revolutionary method of opening our eyes on the important present. As Bakary Traoré has pointed out, our enemies are no longer the strangers from across the seas, but "within ourselves, among ourselves." They are hunger, disease, illiteracy and ignorance. They are also our kinsmen, the politicians and statesmen.

We need a new breed of courageous men, men such as Senghor, Césaire and Damas were in 1930, to write about and analyse the new situation; to be loud where praise is deserved, but not to fight shy when it comes to blame.

And I am thinking of people like Mazrui, Kwei Armah, Soyinka and El Hassan Fadl. Instead of Narcissus, the sons of Ogun . . .

As the brilliant men at Dakar exposed, we in Africa are engaged in a search for new formulae for fusing the worthy aspects of our past with those of our inheritance from colonial history. If we finally find these formulae, we may yet succeed in building an ideal society, washed clean of the slimes of our shame. But we cannot do that unless we kill all that is continuously tying our hands, continuously drawing our eyes to the rear.

In order that the beautiful ones may be born, we must perform a mass pogrom of all obsolete labels and stagnant, emasculated, philosophies which limit our view to a single horizon. What we need, in order to step forward, is, in other words, a negritugrom.

> *Femi Osofisan, "Negritude: Need for a New Approach," in* West Africa, *No. 2827, August 27, 1971, p. 981.*

One easily understands why the imperialist propaganda system goes to such trouble to spread the comforting concept of Negritude. Negritude is actually a good mystifying anaesthetic for Negroes who have been whipped too long and too severely to a point where they have lost all reason and become purely emotional.

—Mamadi Keita, in a speech at the First Pan-African Cultural Festival, July 1969.

Claude Wauthier

[*Wauthier is a French journalist and critic. In the following excerpt, he speculates on the future of Negritude in post-colonial Africa.*]

If one accepts the definition of negritude as an ideological

movement, the expression in literature and the human sciences (particularly ethnology and history) of African nationalism, one must ask what will be its role now that independence has been achieved. The leading specialists in contemporary Negro literature, science and art—Sartre, Jahn and Kesteloot—have not overlooked this problem. Sartre saw Negro poetry in the first place as a splendid weapon against colonial rule for writers rediscovering pride in their own race. But, for Sartre, the negritude movement was only one stage. Basing his conclusions on the marxist convictions of many Negro poets, their urge to transcend racial concepts and merge with the proletarian fight, the author of "Orphée noir" considered Negro protest poetry a temporary phase.

> Negritude is the low ebb in a dialectic progression. The theoretical and practical assertion of white supremacy is the thesis; negritude's role as an antithetical value is the negative stage. But this negative stage will not satisfy the Negroes who are using it, and they are well aware of this. They know that they are aiming for human synthesis or fulfilment in a raceless society. Negritude is destined to destroy itself; it is the path and not the goal, the means but not the end.

Sartre concluded his study with the following words:

> What will happen if the Negro despoils his negritude for the sake of the revolution and only wishes to be taken for a member of the proletariat? What will happen if he allows himself to be defined only by his objective condition; if he forces himself to assimilate white techniques to fight against white capitalism? Will the source of his poetry run dry? Or will the great Negro river colour the sea into which it flows? No matter: to each age its own poetry; in each period a nation, race or class is singled out by historical circumstances to take up the torch, because its situation can only be expressed or mastered through poetry. Sometimes poetic inspiration and the revolutionary urge coincide, sometimes they diverge. Let us welcome today the historical chance which has enabled the Negroes 'to utter such a great Negro cry that it will shake the very foundations of the world.'

Lilyan Kesteloot rebukes Sartre for the 'no matter', and above all for appearing to think that the day will come when there is no longer any need for the exaltation of negritude. For her, it has a permanent value.

> Survival of their own cultural values in writers using a foreign language is not exclusive to the Negro race. The poems of Rabindranath Tagore have retained all the grace and wisdom of India, and *The Prophet* of Khalil Gibran is full of eastern mysticism. So much so that these works, written in English or French, belong in style to the literature of their countries and not ours. The Negro soul revealed here belongs to all time, and will not be superseded, as Sartre and his followers have maintained, any more than will the Slav or Arab souls or the French spirit!

She ends with this quotation from Alioune Diop's inaugural speech to the conference at Rome: 'Since we cannot let ourselves be assimilated by the English, French, Belgian or Portuguese, or allow the original aspects of our talent to be eliminated in favour of a hypertrophied western vocation, we shall struggle to give this talent means of expression suited to its vocation in the twentieth century' [*Les écrivains noirs de langue française: naissance d'une littérature*].

Janheinz Jahn, who barely touches on the political aspects of contemporary Negro literature, has set out to define the criteria of 'neo-African culture'. He maintains that it should be a contribution to universal culture, but he assigns to it a more precise and important role than the mere offering of its originality to the world. Because it is essentially different from western culture—not just another culture among other peoples—African culture will provide a steadying factor intellectually and morally. Indeed, Jahn sees the western world as rather 'dried up' by a mechanical civilisation which sacrifices everything to the object for its own sake. In African philosophy, on the other hand, the important thing is the meaning which the creator gives his object, this having a significance only in so far as man gives it one. Such a conception is necessary for the western mind as a kind of antidote to materialism. 'Only the Negro', asserts Jahn, quoting Senghor, 'can teach rhythm and joy to our world subjugated by machines.'

As we have seen, independence has come to practically the whole of Africa, but it is a tenuous independence, especially in the economic field. Unity has still to come. Neutrality has suffered many compromises. Socialism—in most cases—has yet to be built. Although the foundations have been laid, there is still a lot to do. In these circumstances, one might imagine that literature and scientific research would set their sights on completing the first conquests of emancipation, and that this would determine the literary themes and direction of scientific research for the second generation of African intelligentsia. The cause of unity could be decisively upheld by the ethnologists who would uncover the common ground in the beliefs and institutions particular to each African tribe. Historians could also take up the work by drawing the military conquerors, empire-builders and outstanding figures of African history as the forerunners of a future United States of Africa. Every war gives rise after the event to a whole literature recounting the exploits and sufferings of those involved, so one might expect Negro historical novels exalting the memory of the fight for independence. In the construction of socialism, an aggressive literature might be developed, criticising the go-getting of some, the opportunism of others, abusive profits, and customs shackling economic development. Ethnologists could find in the customs of their countries community habits which would forecast the institution of collectivism; they could hunt out the traditions which could best be adapted to the needs of modern Africa.

A few writers have already started on this work. Sheikh Anta Diop has tried to find characteristics common to the different African societies; Sembène Ousmane has traced the story of one of the historic strikes in French West Africa; Frantz Fanon has discovered in the 'African palaver' a custom close to self-criticism; Mamadou Dia has attempted to sketch out a type of co-operative based on clan property; Niane has resurrected the epic of Sundiata, and Babikir has revived that of Rabah.

There is still a vast field to explore, but pioneers have already pointed the way. There remains the work of the second wave. Sartre predicted that the Negro struggle would give way to a proletarian struggle; the fight of African intellectuals has so far not always tended to go in this direction. This is not because some of them have become resolutely anti-communist. The striking thing, even among marxist sympathisers, has been their concern to build an African version of socialism. Georges Balandier summarises this desire for a specific brand of socialism when he stresses that African marxists have accepted Soviet ideology only with reservations. African christians have also tried to give their faith a special stamp. This is the whole reason for the black messiahs and the 'Ethiopian' churches. But this preoccupation with the African personality is just as marked among strict catholics and protestants, if only in their efforts to find echoes of Christ's teaching in their ancestral beliefs. The Kampala meeting, in 1963, of representatives of Anglican, Protestant and Orthodox churches to create a 'panafrican conference of churches' which would give 'a renovated church to young Africa', was a clear illustration of this concern.

African intellectuals should bring the 'Negro emotion', mentioned by Senghor, to modern society, which has been levelled off by a mechanical, dehumanised civilisation; the interest of their message should outlive the historical situation which has revived Negro philosophy. But once the spur of a cultural renaissance, brought into being by political claims, is lacking, will the spirit which animated the first surge of negritude survive? Jahn's suggestion of the need for an African contribution towards a more balanced world seems far less compelling than one which would lead to political combat arising from a statement of the wrong doings of the colonial regime.

When Césaire takes for granted the Negro's non-technical nature in his famous lines, it is to boast that suffering has made him more human than other people. Jahn considers that the source of this warmer Negro humanity lies in his ancestral traditions; Césaire thinks it comes from his past as a slave and a colonial subject; for Kane it is the muslim faith. But all three agree that the Negro has a better feeling for humanity than other people, and a message to give the world. This message counterbalances the white man's technical contributions and is a step towards cultural miscegenation, which Alioune Diop and Senghor have also advocated.

Such are the reflexions to which a study of the future of negritude give rise.

It is surprising that Sartre, Jahn and Kesteloot have not considered the possible courses opened, or closed, to Negro literature by political regimes placing scientific thought and artistic endeavour under state control. Such a situation clearly cannot be ignored, especially since it is already a reality in a number of states. This second phase of the negritude movement would differ in several essential ways from the preceding one, yet still be inspired by the same themes. It would lack one dimension essential up till now—that of the pioneer and combatant. Negro intellectuals in the service of the African state will no longer need to fear repression or pressure from the colonial administrations; they will receive official encouragement. Although their work may be inspired by convictions as strong as those of politically committed intellectuals before independence, they will have lost the freedom fighter's halo. Must one assume that their work will be less interesting, their contribution to the building of a new Africa less important?

Mphahlele maintains that the cultured elite in Ghana and Nigeria is becoming middle class because the diplomas of its members give them access to positions of responsibility, whereas in South Africa the Negro intellectual is still a member of the proletariat because the policy of racial segregation prevents his obtaining any of the better jobs reserved for white people. In West Africa, devoid of settlers, negritude could become a game for aesthetes, finding their *raison d'être* in a complacent narcissism, while in the detribalised southern part of Africa 'a rugged proletarian literature' could develop, as Fanon has suggested.

Whether this be so or not, and although we may miss the spontaneity and taste of danger characteristic of a literature which fights against the established order, we may look forward to more productive scientific research, unshackled from the prejudices of a foreign power.

Léopold Sédar Senghor, president of Senegal, at the First World Festival of Negro Arts in Dakar in 1962.

The rebel intellectual's works may suffer from his precarious situation, just as that of the cosseted intellectual may be impaired by his security. In any case, it would be going too far to presuppose the African intellectuals' docility in his independent homeland. On the contrary, we can imagine that not all the intellectuals of the next generation will be satisfied with the path that is laid down for them. It is probable that their critical faculties will be sharpened by the choice between the various ways open to the newly independent states of Africa. The controversies already in full swing among politicians will doubtless be extended into literature and scientific research. As far as one can tell from the first indications, the dividing line will be drawn less by geographical criteria than by ideological dictates. The latest collection of Sembène Ousmane's short stories, *Voltaïque,* is an indictment of the new coloured bourgeoisie which has come to power.

An enquiry carried out recently among African students in France by Jean-Pierre Ndiaye provides some answers to these questions on the future of the negritude movement. The young Senegalese sociologist questioned a sample of over 300 black students, in Paris and the provincial towns, out of a total of nearly 5,000 African students in France in 1961-2. A first questionnaire set out to discover whether the new generation of African intellectuals feels that the fight is virtually over when independence is granted. Far from it. Indeed, to the question 'Do you feel that there is a conflict between your leaders and yourself?', 63 per cent of students answered 'Yes'. And the causes of this discontent? For 27 per cent of the students who felt themselves in conflict with their leaders, it was because 'they are betraying independence, endorsing the policy of neo-capitalism and rejecting African solidarity and unity'. For 18 per cent it was because 'they are favouring the establishment of a middle class and carrying out a class policy against the people and progress.' [In a footnote, the critic states: 'The conflict between expatriate African students and the governments of their countries has become a common phenomenon, sparked off, it sometimes seems, by the fairly unbridled competition between western and communist countries to win them over. Negro student demonstrations in several eastern countries have attracted attention to the problem. President Houphouet-Boigny's comment on this is well known: "Send your students to Paris and they will come home communists. Send them to Moscow and they will come back capitalists." Two Ghanaian students have tackled the question: the first, Jilly Osei, in a little booklet *Un Africain à Moscou* published in the *Etudes Soviétiques* collection in Paris, attacks the propaganda which tends to give credence to the tale that African students are victims of racial discrimination in the USSR; the second, Emmanuel John Hevi, in his book *An African Student in China,* draws up an indictment of Chinese communism.']

If today's students remain faithful to their youthful convictions, we may expect the literary and scientific work of the new wave in Africa to be scarcely less politically committed than that of their predecessors. As with the work of the first authors of the negritude movement, it is likely to be militant literature and research—unless, that is, the blackguard politicians of today mend their ways or are replaced by others who can do better.

What will be the aims of this young generation, in the light of the weakness which they are denouncing in the African statesmen of today? The ideals of unity and socialism are still in the forefront of their minds. To the question, 'Do you think the African states of tomorrow should be split up as now, federally united or confederally united?' only 3 per cent opted for the first solution, 34 per cent for the second and 53 per cent for the third. Similarly, very few Negro students advocated a capitalist-type economy: only 7 per cent of those questioned would like to see a liberal economy with a preponderence of private business established in their own country. Although most of them favour socialism, their views are divided more or less equally between its different aspects: 38 per cent prefer 'integral socialism' on Soviet or Chinese lines, 30 per cent 'personal or community socialism', and 20 per cent the 'liberal socialism' of the Scandinavian countries.

Other equally clear signs of the reflection of marxist ideologies in the thinking of African students emerge from Ndiaye's questionnaires. The USSR and the Chinese People's Republic head the list of the most-admired countries. The writers who have had the greatest influence on the students questioned are revolutionary and marxist writers. It is interesting to note that 52 per cent class themselves as christian (catholic or protestant) and 32 per cent as muslim. Opinions on religion are nevertheless extremely divided, and their stay in France has generally resulted in students practising their religion far less than before.

Replies to Ndiaye's enquiry give the impression, therefore, that the two major slogans of African nationalism—independence and unity—have kept their validity for the next generation of Africans. Socialism also has widespread support, but interpretations of it vary. The questions asked do not throw any clear light on the popularity of neutrality and non-engagement. It is also difficult to know (the question was not asked) whether the students think the exaltation of negritude should continue to be a weapon in the fight. The only indications here are the order of preference of Negro writers 'who have contributed most to knowledge about and rehabilitation of African Negro culture'. Césaire comes top (42 per cent), followed by Senghor (38 per cent) and Sheikh Anta Diop (31 per cent). Ndiaye's questionnaire also throws light on the African students' attitudes to the former colonial power now that decolonisation is complete. On the whole, this is not unfavourable, and France is held to be maintaining friendly relations at government level with its former colonies.

Under the circumstances, and as the wounds are closing fast, should we conclude that, after all, they were not so deep? That would be a very hasty judgement. . . . [Many works] testify to the deep humiliations experienced. Of course, some of the African nationalists' exaggerations have been dictated, not purely by conviction, but by tactical considerations also. From the moment battle was engaged, it was no longer possible to give the enemy the benefit of the doubt. The colonial world had to be painted in black and white, with no shades of grey: the black was for Europe and the white for Africa. Exaggeration, however,

was not exclusively the privilege of African intellectuals. It was a reply to other extravagances, which were felt all the more keenly since they came from the stronger side. Moreover, it is unusual for a writer of the negritude movement not to have expressed, at some time or another, his rejection of all anti-white racialism and his desire for the brotherhood of man.

Today, when most of Africa is free or, more precisely, freed from direct colonisation, the movement's often aggressive attitude to the white world at the height of battle, when exaltation of Negro values was but an aspect of the dominated people's protest, has rather lost its point. The generation of Africans who have not known colonisation should be able to adopt a calmer attitude towards the white world. But—and this is an important qualification—this new generation has been nourished on the literature of its predecessors. Their recent fight will be the pride and inspiration of their successors for years to come.

We should not forget this as we try to establish a new friendship. A sudden interest in Africa runs the risk of seeming like a tardy conversion to the cause of African freedom. Conspicuous solicitude, hasty to offer advice from centuries of experience, may be interpreted as the expression of egoistic interests or tenacious paternalism. Such attitudes are sure to arouse latent susceptibilities. The people of the former colonies, and particularly those where blood was shed, are slowly recovering from a profoundly traumatic experience. Only Europe could believe it easy to make a clean sweep of memories such as these. (pp. 278-85)

Claude Wauthier, "Negritude and the Future," in his The Literature and Thought of Modern Africa, *second edition, Heinemann, 1978, pp. 278-85.*

FURTHER READING

Anthologies

Dathorne, O. R., and Feuser, Willfried, eds. *Africa in Prose.* Baltimore: Penguin Books, 1969, 383 p.
    Collection of African literature that has been translated into English.

Kennedy, Ellen Conroy, ed. *The Negritude Poets: An Anthology of Translations from the French.* New York: Viking Press, 1975, 284 p.
    Anthology of Negritude poetry that has been translated into English.

Secondary Sources

Amonoo, Reginald. "The Negritude Debate—1." *West Africa,* No. 2819 (25 June 1971): 725.
    Summarizes papers presented at a symposium on Negritude held in Dakar, Senegal, in April 1971.

Beier, Ulli, ed. *Introduction to African Literature: An Anthol-*

ogy of Critical Writing from "Black Orpheus." Evanston, Ill.: Northwestern University Press, 1970, 272 p.

Collection of essays discussing oral literature, poetry, novels, and theater in Africa. Several of the essays focus on writers associated with Negritude such as Aimé Césaire, Léopold Sédar Senghor, Tchicaya U Tam'si, and Camara Laye.

Chapman, Abraham. "The Black Aesthetic and the African Continuum." *Pan-African Journal* IV, No. 4 (Spring 1971): 397-406.

Posits that Negritude was a forerunner of the Black Aesthetic, a concept celebrating the lifestyles, music, and language that have contributed to the overall Black experience in Africa and the Western world.

Chappelle, Yvonne Reed. "The Negritude Process." *Black World* XXIV, No. 3 (January 1975): 72-6.

Defines Negritude as a process by which black people who have been divorced from their African heritage come to know, accept, and value themselves.

Coulthard, G. R. "The French West Indian Background of *Négritude*." In his *Race and Colour in Caribbean Literature*, pp. 58-70. London: Oxford University Press, 1962.

Argues that the roots of Negritude are found in the French-speaking areas of the Caribbean, particularly Haiti.

———. "Négritude—Reality and Mystification." *Caribbean Studies* 10, No. 1 (April 1970): 42-51.

Discusses the origins and development of Negritude, delineates its relation to Surrealism, and defends the movement against charges of racialism.

Depestre, Rene. "Hello and Goodbye to Negritude." In *Africa in Latin America: Essays on History, Culture, and Socialization*, edited by Manuel Moreno Fraginals, translated by Leonor Blum, pp. 251-72. New York: Holmes & Meier Publishers, 1984.

Surveys the history of Negritude and black cultures in the West, concluding that the ideology of Negritude is no longer viable since "Black and White, as well as all other 'racial' categories of capitalism, are disappearing from the historic scene."

Dixon, Melvin. "Toward a World Black Literature & Community." *The Massachusetts Review* XVIII, No. 4 (Winter 1977): 750-69.

Examines the concept of black community and identity as expressed in three novels associated with the Harlem Renaissance, Negritude, and the Indigenist movement in Haiti and the Caribbean: Claude McKay's *Banjo*, René Maran's *Batouala*, and Jacques Roumain's *Masters of the Dew*.

Erickson, John. "Sartre's African Writings: Literature and Revolution." *L'esprit créateur* X, No. 3 (Fall 1970): 182-96.

Analyzes Sartre's writings on literature and revolution in Africa, particularly his essay on Negritude "Orphée noir."

Gérard, Albert. "Humanism and Negritude: Notes on the Contemporary Afro-American Novel." *Diogenes*, No. 37 (Spring 1962): 115-33.

Concludes that the values which the Afro-American novel depicts—"[emotional] personalism, the natural integration of the personality, spontaneous spirituality, [and] an instinctive communal sense"—are important to modern humanity, both black and white.

Gleason, Judith Illsley. *This Africa: Novels by West Africans in English and French*. Evanston, Ill.: Northwestern University Press, 1965, 186 p.

Thematic analysis of several African novels. Gleason observes that the themes of cultural awareness present in contemporary African fiction have their origins in the 1956 and 1959 *Présence africaine* conferences on Negritude.

González-Cruz, Luis F. "Nature and the Black Reality in Three Caribbean Poets: A New Look at the Concept of *Négritude*." *Perspectives on Contemporary Literature* 5 (1979): 138-46.

Contends that in the poetry of Aimé Césaire, Luis Palés Matos, and Nicolás Guillén "the artistic representation of the black 'nature' reflects both a perception of *the real* and a creation of a dream world in a sort of symbolic process."

Irele, Abiola. "Post-Colonial Negritude: The Political Plays of Aimé Césaire." *West Africa*, No. 2643 (27 January 1968): 100-01.

Briefly argues that Césaire's *La tragédie du roi Christophe* and *Une saison au Congo* address the role of Negritude in African nations that gained independence in the 1950s and 1960s.

———. "Négritude Revisited." *Odu* 5 (April 1971): 3-26.

Examines Negritude as a philosophical concept and concludes that it "can be considered not only as the end point in the growth of psychological self-sufficiency on the part of the black man, but also as the decisive stage in the intellectual elaboration of modern African identity and consciousness."

———. "Negritude—Philosophy of African Being." *Nigeria Magazine* 122 & 123 (1977): 1-13.

Analyzes Senghor's formulation of Negritude and the criticisms leveled against it.

———. "Négritude and African Personality." In his *The African Experience in Literature and Ideology*, pp. 89-116. London: Heinemann, 1981.

Explores the relationship between the concepts of Negritude and "African personality" and their contribution to the development of a distinctive African consciousness.

Ita, J. M. "Negritude—Some Popular Misconceptions." *Nigeria Magazine* 97 (June 1968): 116-20.

Discusses misconceptions about Negritude which, he argues, have prejudiced many Nigerians against French-African literature.

Jackson, Irene Dobbs. "*Négritude* in Full Bloom: A Study in Outline." *College Language Association Journal* VII, No. 1 (September 1963): 77-83.

Summarizes the history of Negritude, concluding that the movement "has accomplished its *raison d'être*" and therefore "seems ready to fade, both in Europe and in America."

Jeanpierre, W. A. "African Negritude—Black American Soul." *Africa Today* XIV, No. 6 (December 1967): 10-11.

Contends that African Negritude and the concept of "soul," despite differences in time and place, "are nonetheless identical, since both refer to that immaterial essence which is the actuating principle informing the Black Personality."

Jones, Edward A. "Afro-French Writers of the 1930's and Creation of the *Négritude* School." *College Language Association Journal* XIV, No. 1 (September 1970): 18-34.
Provides brief biographical sketches of Aimé Césaire, Léopold Sédar Senghor, and Léon-Gontran Damas as well as critical commentary on their poetry.

———. *Voices of Négritude: The Expression of Black Experience in the Poetry of Senghor, Césaire & Damas.* Valley Forge, Pa.: Judson Press, 1971, 125 p.
Contains critical commentary and French and English versions of poems by various Negritude poets. Jones concludes that their poems are "variations on a common theme: the suffering, insults, and humiliations resulting from racist attitudes and practices the world over."

Kesteloot, Lilyan. *Intellectual Origins of the African Revolution.* Washington, D.C.: Black Orpheus Press, 1972, 128 p.
Defines Negritude and places the movement in the context of African nationalism and the quest for political independence.

Kimenyi, Alexandre. "The 'Popularity' of Négritude." *The Journal of Ethnic Studies* 9, No. 1 (1983): 69-74.
Describes the characteristic style and themes of Negritude, attributes its popularity to the support and curiosity of liberal European intellectuals, and concludes that the movement has outlived its mission.

Klíma, Vladimír. "The Grasp of Négritude." *Archiv Orientální* 39 (1971): 200-10.
Surveys various aims, aspects, and phases of Negritude, which he defines "as a living phenomenon [that] has preserved its validity as an intellectual notion rather than as a French-African concept."

Knight, Vere W. "Négritude and the Isms." *Black Images* 3, No. 1 (Spring 1974): 3-20.
Explores the influence of Existentialism, Marxism, and Surrealism on Negritude and examines works by Aimé Césaire, Frantz Fanon, and Léon-Gontran Damas.

Larson, Charles R. "Omnipresent Negritude? African-Afro-American Literary Relations; Basic Parallels." *Negro Digest* XIX, No. 2 (December 1969): 35-42.
Outlines the similarities in theme and development between twentieth-century African and African-American fiction, calling for a comparative approach to the study of black literature worldwide.

———. "Assimilated Négritude: Camara Laye's *Le Regard du Roi.*" In his *The Emergence of African Fiction,* pp. 167-226. Bloomington: Indiana University Press, 1972.
Maintains that in his thorough incorporation of African cultural values in his works, particularly *Le regard du roi,* Laye has created the "Négritude novel."

Mezu, S. Okechukwu. "Black Renaissance and Negritude." *Black Academy Review* 2, Nos. 1 & 2 (Spring-Summer 1971): 9-22.
Examines the origins of and connections between Negritude and the Black Renaissance.

Michael, Colette V. *Negritude: An Annotated Bibliography.* West Cornwall, Conn.: Locust Hill Press, 1988, 315 p.

Lists primary sources, organized according to genre, and secondary sources, arranged thematically, that relate to Negritude.

Moore, Gerald, ed. *African Literature and the Universities.* Ibadan, Nigeria: Ibadan University Press, 1965, 148 p.
Relates the proceedings of the Dakar and Freetown Conferences on "African Literature and the University Curriculum" held respectively in March and April 1963. Several of the essays deal with topics relating to Negritude and literature.

Mouralis, Bernard. "African Literature and the Writing Subject." *Research in African Literatures* 21, No. 1 (Spring 1990): 69-77.
Contends that scholars have placed too much emphasis on the social function of African literature and consequently neglected "the nature of the discourse in which [an individual work] participates and the specific use it makes of language."

Niang, Lamine. "Negro-African Culture and Poetry—Elements of the Survival of Our Civilization." *Journal of the New African Literature and the Arts,* Nos. 7-8 (Spring-Fall 1969): 82-8.
Positive assessment of Negritude. Niang argues that the principal concern of Africans "should be to recreate [their] culture and fit it into a universal culture."

Ormerod, Beverley. "Beyond *Négritude:* Some Aspects of the Work of Edouard Glissant." *Contemporary Literature* 15, No. 3 (Summer 1974): 360-69.
Maintains that Glissant considers Negritude to have been an evolutionary phase and that the development of "a more realistic approach to the problem of Caribbean identity" is a principal concern in his prose, poetry, and dramas.

Shelton, Austin J. "The Black Mystique: Reactionary Extremes in 'Negritude'." *African Affairs* 63, No. 250 (January 1964): 115-28.
Argues that Negritude is not just a form of racism or nationalism but " 'black light'—[a] negation of whiteness and all it stands for, coupled with attempts to create a 'new truth' about black men, to 'rewrite' African history, to show that the black man is not merely the equal of the white man, but is actually in many ways superior."

Soyinka, Wole. "And After the Narcissist?" *African Forum* 1, No. 4 (Spring 1966): 53-64.
Contends that Negritude as an aesthetic movement is formulated on a "literature of self-worship."

Van Niekerk, Barend V. D. *The African Image (Négritude) in the Work of Léopold Sédar Senghor.* Cape Town, South Africa: A. A. Balkema, 1970, 140 p.
Critical study of Senghor's life and poetry. Van Niekerk concludes that "[much] has been made of the independent African nature of Négritude . . . but with everything said, it still remains ultimately only a peculiar twist of French poetry" and it is as a "French poet that [Senghor's] status as poet will eventually endure or go under."

Wolitz, Seth L. "The Hero of Negritude in the Theater of Aimé Césaire." *Kentucky Romance Quarterly* XVI, No. 3 (1969): 195-208.

Maintains that the heroes in Césaire's plays are political martyrs who initiate the process of independence and embody the tenets of Negritude.

Occultism in Modern Literature

INTRODUCTION

Occult movements generally share the assumption that the world is suffused with supernatural forces that have a definite influence on material reality, a philosophy that has produced a broad range of beliefs and practices that may be grouped into several different types. These include such metaphysical schools as Rosicrucianism or Theosophy, which seek through occult means to discover ultimate truths; pseudo-scientific systems such as alchemy and astrology, which attempt to understand or control natural and supernatural forces; esoteric religions such as Satanism and voodoo; parapsychological societies that examine such phenomena as telekinesis and telepathy or endeavor to teach the use of such powers; mystical fellowships that seek spiritual development through transcendent experiences; and various groups or individuals promulgating such phenomena as "ancient astronauts." The relationship between literature and the various manifestations of occultism is similarly multifaceted. Such occultists as Madame Helena Petrovna Blavatsky, the founder of the Theosophist movement, have used fictional works to propagate their ideas. Other writers, including Arthur Machen and Algernon Blackwood, have adapted a variety of occult concepts to express their highly personal artistic visions. Some authors, such as William Blake and William Butler Yeats, have blended various aspects of different esoteric doctrines to create personal occult cosmologies that form a philosophical basis for their literary work. Such writers of supernatural and horror fiction as Ira Levin and William P. Blatty utilize aspects of the occult as the basis for their popular novels, although the authors may not maintain any serious belief in occult teachings. Some critics have suggested that the increasing interest of readers in occultism and literary works influenced by the occult evidences the need for belief in the supernatural in the present era of scientific rationalism.

REPRESENTATIVE WORKS

Blackwood, Algernon
  John Silence, Physician Extraordinary (short stories) 1908
  The Human Chord (novel) 1910
  The Centaur (novel) 1911
  Julius Le Vallon (novel) 1916
  The Bright Messenger (novel) 1921
Blatty, William P.
  The Exorcist (novel) 1971

Bulwer-Lytton, Edward
  Zanoni (novel) 1842
  A Strange Story (novel) 1862
Campbell, Ramsey
  The Doll Who Ate His Mother (novel) 1976
Conrad, Joseph
  The Shadow Line: A Confession (novel) 1917
Crowley, Aleister
  The Works of Aleister Crowley. 3 vols. (poetry and prose) 1905-07
  Moonchild (novel) 1929
Derleth, August
  The Watchers Out of Time (short stories and novel) 1974
Eliade, Mircea
  Two Tales of the Occult (novellas) 1970
Ewers, H. H.
  Alraune (novel) 1911
  [*Alraune,* 1929]
Fortune, Dion [pseudonym of Violet Mary Firth]
  The Secrets of Dr. Taverner (short stories) 1926
  The Demon Lover (novel) 1927
  The Goat-Foot God (novel) 1936
  The Sea Priestess (novel) 1938
  Moon Magic (novel) 1956
Haggard, H. Rider
  She (novel) 1887
Huysmans, Joris-Karl
  Là-Bas (novel) 1891
  [*Down There,* 1924]
Le Fanu, Sheridan
  In a Glass Darkly (short stories) 1886
Leiber, Fritz
  Conjure Wife (novel) 1953
Levin, Ira
  Rosemary's Baby (novel) 1967
Lovecraft, H. P.
  The Outsider, and Others (short stories, novel, and criticism) 1939
  Beyond the Wall of Sleep (short stories, essays, poetry, and novels) 1943
Machen, Arthur
  The House of Souls (short stories) 1906
  The Great Return (novel) 1915
  The Secret Glory (novel) 1922
Meyrink, Gustav
  Der Golem (novel) 1915
  [*The Golem,* 1928]
  Walpurgisnacht (novel) 1917
  Der weisse Dominaker (novel) 1921
  Der Engel vom westlichen Fenster (novel) 1927
Mundy, Talbot [pseudonym of William L. Gribbon]
  Caves of Terror (novel) 1924
  The Nine Unknown (novel) 1924
  The Devil's Guard (novel) 1926

Poe, Edgar Allan
  Tales of the Grotesque and Arabesque   (short stories) 1840
  Tales of Edgar A. Poe   (short stories)   1845
Ouspensky, Peter Demianovitch
  The Strange Life of Ivan Osokin   (novel)   1947
Rohmer, Sax [pseudonym of Arthur Henry Ward]
  Brood of the Witch Queen   (novel)   1918
Stewart, Fred Mustard
  The Mephisto Waltz   (novel)   1967
Tryon, Thomas
  Harvest Home   (novel)   1973
Wheatley, Dennis
  The Devil Rides Out   (novel)   1934
  To the Devil—A Daughter   (novel)   1953
Whitehead, Henry S.
  Jumbee, and Other Uncanny Tales   (short stories) 1944
  West India Lights   (short stories)   1946
Yeats, William Butler
  The Wind among the Reeds   (poetry)   1899
  A Vision   (essay)   1925; also published as *A Vision* [enlarged edition], 1938

THE INFLUENCE OF OCCULTISM ON MODERN LITERATURE

John Senior

[*In the following excerpt, Senior comments on the influence of occultism on twentieth-century literature.*]

Let me begin with three passages from three different contemporary works. First, the famous ending of James Joyce's "The Dead":

> His soul had approached that region where dwell the vast hosts of the dead. He was conscious of, but could not apprehend, their wayward and flickering existence. His own identity was fading out into a grey impalpable world: the solid world itself, which these dead had one time reared and lived in, was dissolving and dwindling.
>
> A few light taps upon the pane made him turn to the window. It had begun to snow again. He watched sleepily the flakes, silver and dark, falling obliquely against the lamplight. The time had come for him to set out on his journey westward. Yes, the newspapers were right, snow was general all over Ireland. It was falling on every part of the dark central plain, on the treeless hills, falling softly upon the Bog of Allen, and farther westward, softly falling into the dark mutinous Shannon waves. It was falling, too, upon every part of the lonely churchyard on the hill where Michael Fury lay buried. It lay thickly drifted on the crooked crosses and headstones, on the spears of the little gate, on the barren

thorns. His soul swooned slowly as he heard the snow falling faintly through the universe and faintly falling, like the descent of their last end, upon all the living and the dead.

Second, Virginia Woolf's *Mrs. Dalloway:*

> But she said, sitting on the bus going up Shaftesbury Avenue, she felt herself everywhere; not "here, here, here"; and she tapped the back of the seat; but everywhere. She waved her hand, going up Shaftesbury Avenue. She was all that. So that to know her, or any one, one must seek out the people who completed them; even the places. Odd affinities she had with people she had never spoken to, some woman in the street, some man behind a counter—even trees, or barns.

Third, William Faulkner's *Go Down Moses:*

> So they stood motionless, breathing deep and quiet and steady. If there had been any sun, it would be near to setting now; there was a condensing, a densifying, of what he had thought was the gray and unchanging light until he realized suddenly that it was his own breathing, his heart, his blood—something, all things, and that Sam Fathers had marked him indeed, not as a mere hunter, but with something Sam had had in his turn of his vanished and forgotten people.

These are not accidentally similar passages: each, in its context, represents what Joyce's Stephen Dedalus calls an "epiphany," that is, each represents a significant moment in the consciousness of the character, a moment when the usually meaningless ebb and flow of ideas and perceptions—the "stream of consciousness"—suddenly makes a kind of sense.

One of the characteristic features of twentieth-century literature has been its preoccupation with irrelevance. In *Bleak House* everything is relevant. Lady Dedlock's housekeeper, Mrs. Rouncewell, turns out to be the mother of Mr. George, the friend of the dead lover of Lady Dedlock. But in Chekhov—a transitional figure between the traditional and the contemporary—nothing seems to be relevant. In "Gooseberries," for example, two men walk on a summer afternoon, it rains, they take shelter at a farm nearby, they swim, they have supper with the farmer, and talk. One of them tells about his brother who had got so fanatical over gooseberries that he sacrificed his career, his wife, his life, in order to grow some. He succeeded, but the gooseberries were sour. The moral, according to the character who narrates the tale, is that life is a cheat. But that is not the moral of Chekhov's story. What are we to make of *it?* Is it merely a slice of life, a deliberate revolt against Dickensian relevance? If the author of *Bleak House* had written "Gooseberries," the brother might have turned out to be the long-lost son of the farmer's wife by a lover she had met in Australia. But Chekhov just recounts a simple afternoon. Or does he? Is there not another kind of relevance, an ironic connection, in this case, between the lovely summer afternoon and the sour berries? Just at the moment when we are told that life is a cheat, we recall that the character who makes the observation had been ducking his head in the water not an hour before, crying for the sheer joy of his existence. Life is, and is not, wonderful. Everything in the story of the brother is denied by the very circumstances in which it is told. And those apparent irrelevancies—the walk, the swim, the supper—turn out to be significant, and it is "significant irrelevance" which is the key to Chekhov and to much of the literature that follows him.

Modern fiction has also been concerned with consciousness, not merely with the events a character perceives but with perception itself. One of the great discoveries at the turn of the century—or rediscoveries, for it was a commonplace before the Renaissance—was the realization that a perception is a combination of two events, the one external in the physical world, the other internal in the mental world. Every time we see a cat, we bring to that sight our memories of cats we have seen before and all the associations our memories of those cats are entangled in. Thus it may be that an irrelevant Siamese is significantly related to one's mother-in-law. The moment of realization—the epiphany—occurs when the haphazard stream of consciousness is suddenly seen as related to some other time and place. The most famous examples occur in Proust, whose whole novel is a fabric of such relations—the cake and tea, the little phrase, the bell towers.

But the passages quoted above go further. What is most interesting about them is not that the characters see sudden significances, but that they all see the same significance no matter what the particulars. The relevance they perceive in apparently irrelevant things is not merely psychological. They discover in those moments that *all things are relevant*—different characters, in different times and places, discover the same connections among all things, places, and times. These moments are crossroads in space-time when everything is seen as connected. Gabriel in "The Dead" sees the snow falling not only on Dublin and on the incident in the past which his wife had just recalled, but "through the universe." Mrs. Dalloway in her moment not "here, here, here" "felt herself everywhere." Ike McCaslin sees "something, all things." The significant moment in the stream of consciousness turns out to be a significant moment in the river of time, through all possible geography.

[The] "epiphany" is no mere literary device, but the natural result of a world view which is in fact the world view of the symbolist movement in literature, and, further, that no matter how misunderstood, and misapplied, this is essentially the world view of a tradition older than history—"esoteric tradition," or the "perennial philosophy." The gravest difficulties will occur over terminology, and they might best be faced at the outset. Because in the West there has been no "tradition" since the Renaissance, the symbolist doctrine has been in the hands of individuals rather than schools, amateurs rather than professionals; and this has led to a kind of esoteric protestantism, to the formation of individual sects, some wise, many foolish. "Occultism" is a dangerous word to use, and special care must be taken not to misunderstand it. There are very low occultists and very high ones, and we should no more commit the world view itself to Hell because of charlatans who misrepresent it than we should disavow religion be-

cause of Chaucer's Pardoner. We should be very careful even of dismissing the charlatans. In my Father's house are many mansions with many doors, both front and back. Even the dirtiest alley may lead someone in.

Once we actually look for connections between contemporary literature and the esoteric world view, we find them everywhere, by no means in the most respectable places. Yeats's work is in great part the result of a lifelong preoccupation with occult ideas; A. E. was a kind of theosophist; D. H. Lawrence's later work is riddled with ideas derived from yoga; Katherine Mansfield died in a sanatorium run by the occultist Gurjieff; Joyce used Hermetic methods in the construction of his work; Aldous Huxley has become a popularizer of Oriental mysticism; Eliot refers to tarot cards and Mme Blavatsky in his early work, and some of the behavior of Sir Henry Harcourt Riley is suspiciously like Cagliostro's.

The list could be longer, but it is at the moment sufficient to demonstrate that there has been widespread interest in the occult on the part of some of the most eminent English literary figures in our century. If we include German and French literature, the list is richer still. Valéry, for example, wrote on Swedenborg, Rilke's interest in Orpheus was profound, Mann's famous séance in *The Magic Mountain* was based on personal experience. (xi-xv)

Attempts at a definition of the word "occult" and classifications of "occult" movements have been made by anthropologists, sociologists, and psychologists. . . . Some more general remarks, however, might be made here: As the occult often seems to impinge on "science," so it may on "religion" also, chiefly on those areas usually called "mystic." It is important at the outset to make clear that the occult is not itself scientific—it does not submit evidence that has anything to do with laboratory or law court. Some occultists, especially modern practitioners of occult science, as they call it, try to give the impression that it does. Practitioners of "psychical research," using the vocabulary of psychology and statistics, have attempted to catch Leviathan with a fishhook and demonstrate that some occult phenomena, at least, are available for laboratory analysis. So-called "yogis" are asked to perform physical marvels with medical apparatus attached. (p. xvi)

Though it may have a scientific aspect, occultism qua occultism cannot be scientific since it goes beyond what E. A. Burtt [in *The Metaphysical Foundations of Modern Science*] calls the basic assumption of science, that positive knowledge must be quantitative only. The traditional occult sciences such as astrology, alchemy, and what we might call symbolic medicine have nothing to do with what passes under such names in the modern West. They were specific applications to the material realm of occult principles realized by means other than those of the specific "sciences." "Science" in the occult sense is an "application" of knowledge otherwise gained, and not at all a kind of knowledge in itself or even a means to knowledge.

And occultism is not in itself "religion," though here too the distinction is seldom clear because "religion" is a difficult and confused term. Dean Inge uses the word "reason" to make a distinction usually accepted by writers on mysti-

A woodcut by Han Wieditz of an alchemist and his assistant at work. The figure of the alchemist seeking to understand the secrets of the universe through experiments with matter informed a large body of literary works from the Renaissance onward.

cism, one between the true religious mystic and the mere occultist:

> Mysticism [he says] has its origin in that which is the raw material of all religion, and perhaps of all philosophy and art as well, namely, that dim consciousness of the *beyond,* which is part of our nature as human beings. . . . Mysticism arises when we try to bring this higher consciousness into relation with the other contents of our minds. . . . [It is] the attempt to realise, in thought and feeling, the immanence of the temporal in the eternal, and of the eternal in the temporal . . . [but since] our consciousness of the beyond is . . . itself formless, it cannot be brought directly into relation with the forms of our thought. Accordingly, it has to express itself by symbols. [W. R. Inge, *Christian Mysticism*]

But, Dean Inge continues,

> the mystic . . . is not [necessarily] a visionary; nor has he any interest in appealing to a faculty "above reason," if reason is used in its proper sense, as the logic of the whole personality. . . . A revelation absolutely transcending reason is an absurdity; no such revelation could ever be made. . . . What we can and must transcend, if we would make any progress in Divine knowledge, is not reason, but that shallow rationalism which regards the data on which we can reason

as a fixed quantity, known to all, and which bases itself on a formal logic, utterly unsuited to a spiritual view of things. . . . For Reason is still "King." Religion must not be a matter of *feeling* only. St. John's command to "try every Spirit" condemns all attempts to make emotion or inspiration independent of reason. . . . Our object should be so to *unify* our personality, that our eye may be single, and our whole body full of light.

Alas, this is a distinction that occultists the world over make whenever they condemn what they call the "pseudo-occultism" of a rival school. If we accept Dean Inge's mysticism as religion, we shall have to call Plato, Dionysius the Areopagite, Hermes Trismegistus, Paracelsus, Swedenborg, many alchemists, fewer astrologers—all theologians. To do so confuses more than clarifies. However wrong we may be, most of us in the West think of religion as the understanding and application of particular historically revealed doctrines—to say Blake or Baudelaire was a mystic is to run the immediate danger of implying he was a Christian. If we accept the great sentence of St. Ambrose that "all that is true, by whomsoever it has been said, is from the Holy Ghost" and if we take the word "catholic" literally and accept the doctrine most famously expressed by St. Thomas that whosoever follows the will of God is a member of His church, then it may be that Baudelaire and Blake were Christians—even Catholics. But then so was Buddha. The disadvantages outweigh the uses of the term "mystic." . . . Put another way, all that Dean Inge would call "mystic" is included under the more general term "occult." Mysticism is the form occultism took in Christendom as yoga is the form it took in India.

Again and again in discussing particular poets, this challenge arises: Do you mean to say T. S. Eliot is not a Christian poet, but an occultist? The challenge must be met with a wider understanding of the word "occult" than we ordinarily have. Suppose it were demonstrated that Eliot believed in the law of gravity; would that challenge his position as a Christian? It is true that particular Christian churches have opposed certain scientific ideas; and it is true that they have also opposed certain occult ideas, declared certain scientists and mystics heretical, and at public ceremonies condemned whole occult societies. But those were acts of men and councils of men, subject to history and the sway of the world. Whether a particular formulation of scientific or occult doctrine is compatible with a particular formulation of Christianity is decided by ecclesiastical authority; but the occult itself, as the scientific itself, cannot be "opposed" to any religion, or to science. Church opposition to occult doctrine has been chiefly the result of a split between esoteric and exoteric religion. (pp. xvi-xix)

American writers and the occult:

Almost every American writer of note had some direct experience with the popular supernaturalisms of the nineteenth century, especially with mesmerism and its successors—the spiritualistic movement that began with the unearthly rappings of the Fox sisters in 1848, and the psychical research societies that sprang up later in the century. The mesmeric treatments for headaches undergone by Sophia Peabody during her courtship with Hawthorne brought to his attention the potentially sinister rapport between mesmerist and trance-maiden, upon which he would later brood in his fiction. Harriet Beecher Stowe received séance messages from the ghost of Charlotte Brontë, and her husband saw visions throughout his life. The most famous work of Henry James, whose father was a Swedenborgian mystic, is a ghost story. His brother William founded the American Society for Psychical Research and conducted an extensive study of the famous medium Mrs. L. E. Piper. [W. D.] Howells suffered great embarrassment when his *Atlantic Monthly* published articles about séances that turned out to be fraudulent, but he also sought comfort in dream visions of his dead daughter and wrote a series of psychical tales. As a child [Jack] London was introduced to the occult by his mother's séances, which frightened him and left their mark on his fiction. Mark Twain knew them all—mesmerists, mediums, palmists, and psychical researchers—and treated them both straightforwardly and satirically in his work. Whatever their various attitudes toward it, all of these writers had close encounters with the occult.

Howard Kerr, John W. Crowley, and Charles L. Crow, in their The Haunted Dusk: American Supernatural Fiction, 1820-1920, *1983.*

Perhaps the most brilliant occult movement of the twentieth century has been the one led by René Guénon. Guénon argues—as . . . all occultists argue—that religion is symbol and that beneath the body of this or that particular ritual and this or that particular theology lies one, single, universal, metaphysical doctrine, the *philosophia perennis.* . . . Starting with the usual layman's method, merely pointing to what most people would call occultism, we should quickly compile a list: theosophy, Rosicrucianism, alchemy, astrology, immediately come to mind. If we push deeper, however, and try to find the assumptions behind the exteriors of these movements, we are led to profound and universal ideas which may be identified with the *philosophia perennis.* It must be clear, therefore, that the term occult is not used in a pejorative sense. One of my chief contentions is that the symbolist poets, finding the scientific world view inadequate, embraced another they considered more complete and beautiful, however imperfect their understanding of it might have been, however tragic their misapplication of it often turned out to be. This is not necessarily to defend or attack occultism, but to understand it; and to achieve that purpose it is necessary to take occultism seriously. . . . Let us call the occult imaginative, if not true, and at least let us realize its importance in the history of literature; and if it is important—and if the literature is important—then it is serious. (p. xix)

> *John Senior, in an introduction to his* The Way Down and Out: The Occult in Symbolist Literature, Cornell, *1959, pp. xi-xxvi.*

Frank Paul Bowman

[*Bowman is an American educator and critic specializing in French literature. In the following excerpt, he discusses the literary influence of theories of language developed by French occultists.*]

"Oyant jadis l'ange / Donner un sens plus pur aux mots de la tribu" (Hearing in another age the angel gives a purer sense to the words of the tribe)—so Mallarmé describes the parallel the hydra-mob drew when faced with Poe's poetry, implying that this was indeed what Poe had done or at least tried to do and, less directly, that this was what Mallarmé was doing in writing Poe's epitaph. Léon Cellier asked repeatedly that we study the "occult sources" of symbolist poetic theory and practice, following the model of Auguste Viatte's famous *Sources occultes du romantisme,* suggesting that the occult-illuminist tradition informed symbolist poetic theory as Viatte had indeed proved that it informed Romanticism. With respect to poetic language—the nature and sense of words and grammar—the tradition in some ways did, and in some perhaps more important ways it did not. No self-respecting occultist could write Mallarmé's line; he would have to rewrite it to read: "Hearing now as ever the man of desire restore a purer sense to the words of the human race." Writings on occultism and the illuminist tradition, often apologetic in both senses of the term, tend to "tirer la couverture," to claim that all comes from the Tradition, the Cabbala, Saint-Martin, whatever source one wills.

My concern here is with occultist theories of language as expounded in France during the Romantic age and with the question of how much those theories may have affected later poetic practice, particularly that of Mallarmé and the symbolists. My illuminist version of the famed passage from "Le Tombeau d'Edgar Poe" pinpoints some of the problems. For the illuminist tradition, the purer sense is not something to be created, but something to be restored, something that has been lost. That restoration is a continuing task, which takes place throughout all of history (just as, of course, the corruption and degradation of language can take place throughout all of history). It is the words not of the tribe but of the human race—all language—that must be restored. Finally, the task of restoration is performed not by an angel nor by the poet—though, as we shall see, the poet may have a particular and even preeminent function in the task—but by the man of desire, he who yearns for and seeks the divine and absolute and has been initiated into the illuminist vision. Man alone is both free and gifted with thought; all of nature thinks, and indeed an illuminist may well maintain that all of nature has a language, but man alone is free and he alone has the power to restore language to its primordial purity.

The basic tenets of occultism are rather simple, though of course each school, each representative of the tradition emphasizes or develops certain common convictions.

At the beginning, all was unity; this unity has been lost, fractured. The restoration of unity and the obliteration of differences are the tasks of men and the end of history. From this principle stems a preference for modes of thought that are unifying, for synthesis rather than analysis, or at least for a dialectic that can synthesize differences, for the intuitive perceptions of unity rather than the categorizations of reason. This preference often leads to an appreciation of the "poor in spirit," who in their innocence perceive a truth hidden from educated intellectuals. Certain mechanisms of language, in particular allegory and metaphor, are especially apt at embodying the perception of unity. All creation emanates from the Divine (creation is not, then, *ex nihilo*) and, because of the Fall (of angels, then of man/woman), is more or less separated from the Divine. This emanation-separation is represented by one form or another of the great chain of being, with man always at the center but with the Divine present to some degree throughout the chain. God is in everything— trees, babbling brooks, stones—but these things are not divine. They must be restored to their divine status by man, that free and thinking microcosm of God. The term *panentheism* describes more accurately than pantheism this presence of the divine, but it alas has not been widely adopted. However, the poem reads: "Tongues in trees, books in the running brooks, sermons in stones, and good in everything." This presence of the divine in all creation is conceived of as a presence of language because of the very mechanism of creation, where God emanates from his Being to the Sophia or uncreated Wisdom and then the Logos, Word, or created Wisdom, which is thus present in all creation, but corrupted since the Fall. The illuminist tradition, with its fondness for synthesis, associates rather than dissociates the divine Word, the Platonic logos, the Johanine logos, language as such (including human language and also the language of all creation) and, when the tradition is Christianized, the Christ as the Word incar-

nate in history. Language, like creation, is divine in origin; it has lost in large part its original purity and unity and yet retains traces of that origin. These traces may be found in the four aspects of language: in sounds (vowels, consonants, monemes), in words, in syntactic and/or grammatical structures, and in writing itself (letters, hieroglyphs, and so on). Illuminist linguistics, like any linguistics, examines all four. The story of Babel represents the destruction of linguistic unity just as the apostolic gift of tongues or glossolalia is a vision of an at least partial restoration of that unity. This fractioning of language is an historical phenomenon and is reversible in history—hence the development of an illuminist philology with its etymological quest for traces or remnants of the divine and an illuminist comparative linguistics that seeks what different languages have in common with, or rather retain of, their divine origin. Usually, though not always, Hebrew is considered the language closest to the divine. During the first half of the nineteenth century in particular, illuminist thought is preoccupied with an historical and comparative study of language. Illuminists on language are always "essentialists"; that is, they are convinced that linguistic signs are or should be motivated, as opposed to "conventionalists," who consider linguistic signs to be unmotivated or arbitrary, the results of historical and/or social convention.

Other aspects of illuminist thought are less central to the problem of language, but it is important to note that all religious systems and myths are studied from a similar perspective. They all offer, in their varied forms, different expressions of the same unity. This syncretism is assured by an allegorical reading of sacred literature, of liturgies, of myths. The universally discerned essential pattern is one of Fall, initiation via a new revelation and expiatory suffering, which results in transfigurative metapmorphosis or beatific vision and so on. (Alchemy and astrology are susceptible of a similar analysis.) This pattern or redemptive process is repeated in history until the end of time. The nineteenth century is perhaps distinct from earlier illuminism in the high degree of importance it attaches to woman's role not only in the Fall but also in the redemptive process; a study in the illuminist origins of women's liberation (Esquiros, A.-L. Constant, Enfantin in France) would be of considerable interest.

The illuminist tradition is richer and more varied than the preceding schematic analysis may suggest. I should like now to present four instances of illuminist discourse on language: the grand master Jacob Boehme; the "unknown philosopher" Louis-Claude de Saint-Martin, who was, in fact, very well known and influential in nineteenth-century France; Louis de Bonald, because of his synthesis of illuminist notions of language and traditionalism; finally Steinmetz, an unknown author of the 1840s, whom I have chosen for his representative value. In conclusion, I shall try to contrast (a most unilluminist approach) these theories of language with the two other mainstreams of Romantic thought on language, those of the conventionalist and the mimologist, and raise certain questions about the importance of each for modern poetic theory and practice.

Jacob Boehme, like all illuminists, was fascinated by the first verse of the Gospel according to Saint John and concluded from a meditation on it and on Genesis that the Word was both the objectivation of God and the means of the creation of the visible world. Thus, there is a mutual, essential relation between the representation of the Word in the spirit and its incarnation in creation; the Word proffered by God continues to live both in our mind and in objects. The names Adam gave to animals and to creation before the Fall (the Adamic language) were translations of the divine Word, signatures; for Adam, knowing the virtues of beings, gave them their correct names. This correctness was perverted by the Fall, but the Adamic signatures can still be partially read in the words we use for things. For the language of nature—the Word in creation—also exists, and letters, words, and syllables reflect its secrets and significations. Since man is created in God's image and his spirit partakes immediately of the divine spirit, letters, and so on, are figurations of this divine centrum; by them, man participates in the qualities that constitute the world (by the letter *S,* for example, with fire). Our intellection of natural language lets us understand the divine acts demonstrated by the letters, and Boehme provided exemplary readings of the Our Father and the first chapter of Genesis in terms of this intelligence of natural language.

Wolfgang Kayser has exhaustively studied the origins of Boehme's theories in classical, patristic, and medieval thought, including Boehme's debt to the Cabbala. Boehme synthesizes various currents, combining in particular Neoplatonic theories of the logos and meditations on Adamic language; later illuminism mostly embroiders on his synthesis. God becomes the eternal orator; all creation is an oration or prayer; all life is the action of the Word. Thus, all creation is a symbolic cipher, the hieroglyph of a superior reality. The natural language is found in the signatures of things and in the Word within us. Man can know the being of things and learn to give them their true names, and language is the depository of man's resemblance to God.

Louis-Claude de Saint-Martin has been called the "Luther of occultism" and perhaps merits the title several ways, not only because he was impatient with certain superstitious practices curried in some occultist circles and because he preferred instead to emphasize the essential elements of illuminist theory but also because of his considerable skills as a writer. *L'Homme de désir,* perhaps the most moving of his texts, can still be read with pleasure as well as appreciation. Saint-Martin frequently discusses the problem of language; perhaps his fullest exposition is in *Des erreurs et de la vérité* (1775). Man's major resource is the attributes contained in his knowledge of language, for language gives him the power to communicate his thought, to enter into commerce with his fellows, and to make them sensitive to his thoughts and affections (Saint-Martin draws a sad portrait of the insufficiency of the substitutes for language among animals and deaf-mutes). If language has this power of communication, however, it must be because languages are common to all men, because, that is, all men possess the same signs. Indeed, if language is now fragmented, our desire to learn other lan-

guages is a sign of our drive toward unity—though Saint-Martin would consider it a better task to purify one's mother tongue rather than to seek to restore unity through the acquisition of multiple languages. An introspective analysis of man himself proves that he is meant to possess only one language and, therefore, that the multitude of languages are the effect of habit and convention, perpetuating mankind's loss of unity.

Saint-Martin distinguishes between two sorts of language: an interior, mute language, contained within us, and the demonstrative and perceptible language by which we communicate with others. The former is the "mother" of the latter but is itself the voice and expression of a principle that is outside us and that is a manifestation of the Divine. Because this principle is one and governs all interior language, that language should take the same form everywhere and follow identical structures; the true intellectual language of man is everywhere the same and essentially one. But if the principle is one and the mother or interior language is one, then perceptible language should also be one, which it obviously is not. The variations of perceptible language, however, reflect a deficiency located, not in it, but in the mother language within us. This deficiency is produced by our misuse of the will and the imagination, which has impeded or perverted the operations of the principle. As a result, perceptible language has been considerably altered. Man, who no longer perceives things in their true nature, has given them names that came from him and that, as they are no longer analogous with the thing named, cannot designate unequivocally; this incapacity gives rise to misunderstandings, inaccuracies, and so on. The variety of language is thus a proof of the inadequacy of language and a demonstration of the great distance between man and the spiritual principle that should govern him. The picture, however, is not totally black; words may be largely conventional rather than essential, but potentially they can still offer fairly sure signs of the beings represented. Man's natural tendency is to express a thing by the sign or word that seems most analogous. We experience pleasure and admiration when offered signs, expressions, and figures that bring us close to the nature or essence of the objects being evoked and that make us conceive them better, for then every production or object comes closer to the ideal of being presented by its proper name, the name that is linked to its essence. The task of every man is to learn and use the true names; as we shall see, the true poet for Saint-Martin is the one who excels at this task.

Language is not something discovered or invented by man, but the true attribute of men, a divine gift, of which sufficient vestiges remain so that man can return to his source or origin, to purity and unity. Saint-Martin notes that many do not agree and cites the problem of the child brought up in solitude or by animals—a child dear to eighteenth-century linguistic speculation. That child admittedly does not speak the natural or essential language. Saint-Martin uses the child to refute both Descartes and Locke. On the one hand, the child proves that in our present state of privation, we can do nothing without the aid of an exterior reaction, without, that is, the aid of our fellow men who also labor at their rehabilitation. We must help one another in restoring our faculties, including our linguistic faculties; both nature and the law of the mind call us to live in society. (Other illuminists also emphasize the "social" aspects of the language problem.) Experiments with a child raised in isolation are doomed to failure; it is as if you placed a seed on a stone, and then the seed did not grow, and then you made comments on the seed—which rather takes care of the Cartesian innate ideas. On the other hand, the fact that the child does not produce a language also shows that the universal language is not a "natural" product of our structures and perceptions but must be a divine gift—which takes care of Locke or rather of the *idéologues* such as Destutt de Tracy and Garat, with whom Saint-Martin debated at the Ecole Normale. He does concede that the child will achieve an elemental system that will let him express pleasure and pain, but animals also possess that language of sensation, whereas true language seeks to express not sensation, but thought. The distinction, however, is one of degree rather than kind, and the degree depends on where the being is in the great chain. One must grant a degree of language even to the least of created beings, a language that is nothing other than the expression of their faculties.

This, one might note, is not quite "sermons in stones," for the faculties of the stones, according to Saint-Martin, are not really adequate for the practice of sacred eloquence. Martinism distinguishes between the developments of the *coeli enarrant* theme—"the heavens declare the Glory of God, and the firmament proclaimeth His handywork," the perception of the divine in the harmonies of creation, on the one hand, and, on the other, the presence of the logos throughout the chain of being. Romantic poets such as Gérard de Nerval and Victor Hugo tend to confuse or, at least, fuse the two.

Saint-Martin is confident that the possibility exists of restoring the "essentiality" of language, of recovering the fixed and invariable language of the principle. It has not been totally lost; it is present in all men and nations and is the source of the true principles of justice. It does and must use our human, physical organs and senses. the ear and the eye because writing lets us communicate with those distant from us (although for Saint-Martin writing only indicates, offers a dead explication, whereas speech is a living explication; I know not what he would have thought of tapes and records). The study of etymologies can lead us back to prelapsarian language. More importantly, we can purify our own language by the spiritual *ascesis* Saint-Martin ever recommends, which is rather quietist. We must abandon our own will—our "property"—and desire the will of that active and intelligent Cause, which should govern man and the universe. To demonstrate this survival of the essential language in humanity, he cites a syntagmatic example—for grammar, more than words, retains and manifests the inherent order. In order to express any complete notion of a thought, one needs an active noun or pronoun, a verb, and a passive noun or pronoun; this grammatical law is invariable and essential, for it reflects the ternary of agent, action, and product. (The significance of the ternary in Martinism and its relation to the Trinity are too complex to discuss here, but it is a very essential—in both senses of the word—concept.) Other

parts of speech are accessory; they supplement these three, and their usage and position vary greatly from speaker to speaker and from language to language. The accessories, in short, have been more corrupted than the basics. (One of Saint-Martin's great virtues is that, unlike many illuminists, he never succumbs to the delight of the accessory and returns unerringly to the basics.)

I leave aside his developments on the six cases and the six major modifications of matter, as well as on gender, to emphasize two points. First, Martinism is a very active and demanding spirituality; in the *Tableau naturel,* Saint-Martin provides a quite similar statement of his linguistic theories but concludes with what amounts to an appeal for linguistic action. The present variety, corruption, and obscurity of language are the products and proofs of our ignorance, sloth, and prevarication (Saint-Martin avoids "sin," a word he considered obfuscatory). We can know the forms and numbers of the essential signs. Indeed, we cannot utter a single word, write a single letter, that does not to a degree manifest the supreme Agent. The question is, To what degree? All use of language becomes charged with moral value.

The other noteworthy point is that poets are those who manifest the supreme Agent to the highest degree in their use of language. Poetry is not the true and unique language, yet it is the nearest equivalent. It is the most sublime production of man's faculties, which draws him closest to his principle and which, by the transports it provokes, best proves to him the dignity of his origins. This proclamation of the preeminence of poetry is somewhat circular in the sense that Saint-Martin clearly does not have in mind the contemporary satirical or didactic verse of Voltaire or the descriptive nature poetry of Saint-Lambert or even the earlier poetry of the Renaissance, but rather his own ideal of poetry. He does define elsewhere the qualities of this poetry in a way that prefigures Romantic practice and also echoes pre-Romantic poetics: poetry is not a question of fixed form or rhyme and rhythm; rather, it differs from prose by the very nature of its language. Poetic language is essentially prophetic because it recalls man's origin and mission and also because it presents not the beautiful but rather the sublime, which englobes the ugly—not only honey but also gall, *miel* and *fiel;* he provides a very developed spiritual (as opposed to mimetic) justification for the presence of the ugly in "true poetry." The models cited or evoked, to my knowledge, are all Biblical.

Maine de Biran, the most noteworthy of French philosophers in the early nineteenth century, labeled Louis de Bonald a *"histrion en philosophie"*—a clown, and a bad one at that, whose excess makes his artifice all too evident. Indeed, Bonald's single-minded devotion to the task of explaining, justifying, and thereby destroying the Revolution of 1789 in order to turn the clock back to an ideal feudal age is so overriding that it is at times hard to take him seriously. He has neither the whimsy and wit of Montlosier nor the ambiguity and precious little of the radicalism of Joseph de Maistre, to name his two great conservative contemporaries. Yet for illuminist linguistic theory, he is, I suspect, of great importance, and that for two reasons.

The first is that he historicizes that theory or, more accurately, associates the philosophy of language and the philosophy of history and derives from the illuminist meditation on language a theory of history and hence of politics. Others will do likewise, either echoing or refuting him. The other reason is that he "Catholicizes" the illuminist theories of language, utters them from a declared Roman Catholic position, and thereafter (perhaps not only because of Bonald—Ballanche and Maistre are tributaries) the discourse of French Catholicism on Word and language becomes profoundly marked by the basic illuminist tenets and will remain so throughout the Romantic age.

Bonald discusses language in the *Discours préliminaire* of his *Législation primitive* (1802), and again in his *Recherches philosophiques sur les premiers objets des connaissance morales* (1818), but his theses do not change. Language is, and remains, of divine origin, but man knows it not immediately because of a contact with the divine but mediately through society, which is of divine institution and mediates or transmits language to man. Thus, he rejects both Malebranche, who proposed that man had direct communication with eternal Reason, and Condillac, who failed to note the divine origins of society and hence of social language. Man is indeed created in the image of God, and just as God is only known by His Word *(Verbe)*—the expression and image of His substance—so man, finite intelligence, is only known by his word *(parole),* the true expression of his spirit. Society, however, transmits that language to man and thereby transmits to him the knowledge of all moral truths that are innate not in man, but in society (to a greater or lesser degree). Man, in acquiring language, which subsists perpetually in society, acquires moral and religious truth. Thus, any society with an articulated language has a knowledge of God, of the future life, and so on. Bonald carries this idea quite far; the three grammatical persons (again, like Saint-Martin, he prefers to demonstrate the essential nature of language via an analysis of syntax, rather than of words or sounds) reflect not only the divine Trinity and the structure of the family, but also the structure of society, that is, king, nobles, and people—the latter, like children, should obey. When the people took power in France, they immediately created linguistic disorder. This will become a common theme among French rightists: the revolution destroyed not only institutions but also language, creating bad grammar and neologisms and even confusing grammatical persons (Bonald cites Molière's servant's "j'avions" as exemplary of the bad grammar of democracy, where the individual claims to speak for the collectivity). Victor Hugo, in his "Réponse à un acte d'accusation" and more particularly its "Suite" ("Sequel"), will take up the challenge, assert the revolutionary right to neologisms, and claim that the destruction of the barriers between the levels of style is a good thing. Hugo was for linguistic change, whereas, of course, Bonald was against it, except so far as that change represented a purifying return to prerevolutionary usage.

Bonald's linguistic theories presuppose a universal revelation to all society of divine truth and hence of language, which he propounded together with Maistre and which Lamennais developed as an apologetic argument in his *Essai sur l'indifférence.* By so doing, they gave great im-pulse within French Catholicism to the kind of syncretist reading of religions and myths characteristic of illuminism—and indeed to the analysis of language as the vehicle of the expression of religious truth. Only in the late 1830s will a renewed attention to the distinction between natural revelation and supernatural revelation dampen (and then, to a limited extent) this syncretist quest for Aztec trinities, Chinese incarnations, American Indian resurrections, and so on. Meanwhile, theories such as Bonald's gave rise to immense speculations about philology and comparative linguistics. The leading figure here was Baron Eckstein (affectionately known as "Baron Sanskrit"), who, convinced of the essential relations between language, the divine, and the created world, wrote and published a whole periodical, *Le Catholique,* devoted to demonstrating that relation in detail.

Finally, Bonald's position attaches a great deal of importance to language because it precedes thought. "Man must think his word before he can speak his thought," as he succinctly put it—which seemed to him yet another proof that man cannot have invented language. This is the sense he gives to *"si orem lingua, spiritus meus orat"* (if my tongue prays, my spirit prays); all prayer, for Bonald, seemingly must be verbal, as is all thought; we can only think and pray by language, an instrument God gave to society when He instituted it and that society transmits to us.

The early nineteenth century knew endless variations on this theme of the divine origin of language, and it would be interesting to trace them through Fabre d'Olivet and his reconstruction of Hebrew, through Lamennais, Bautain, Blanc Saint-Bonnett, Lacuria, the great French Swedenborgian Edouard Richer, and many others. I prefer to cite a tempered statement from the 1840s because it represents what I think was the common core of the doctrine. In the *Université catholique* for 1842, Steinmetz, in a "Cours de physiologie" offers a lengthy analysis of language as an instrument of faith, of the essential relations between language and thought, and of the degradation of that relation. Language is the instrument of the order of faith, is the source of all thought, and is endowed with inherent power that fecundates intelligence. This is true not only of spoken language, but of all creation, because all creatures announce or proclaim the glory of God—even inorganic nature possesses language. Man probably received this powerful instrument in a state of perfection at the time of his creation; some have maintained that he only received the potential of language as a gift, but even if one accepts that theory, there can be no development of intelligence without language. Everything we know, including the most recent discoveries of philology and linguistics, leads to the belief in the existence of a divine primitive language. Steinmetz then examines the imperfections of savage language, where the divine gift is in a state of notable corruption. (For him and the *Université catholique,* all civilization is necessarily Christian, and the heathen is barbaric). They have lost the art of writing, they have lost words, their language systems are embedded in the material order of concrete metaphors, they cannot express abstract ideas, and they use polysyllabic words to express simple numbers. After painting this sad, if rather im-

Albrecht Dürer's depiction of Melancholy, the guiding spirit of occultists, surrounded by esoteric and alchemical symbols.

perialistic, picture, Steinmetz insists on man's responsibility to use properly the divine gift of language and quotes Matthew (12:36-37) about the punishment of individuals and societies that misuse language. The spirit of evil seeks to corrupt language, particularly by blasphemy and sarcasm. His strictures concerning blasphemy are not unexpected. Sarcasm, he maintains, denatures the meaning of words and attributes bad qualities to the good; the theater is a center of the misuse of language. Happily, God created the Catholic church as the guardian of the truth and of truth in language . . . A similar and even more complicated and metaphysical theory of language is offered by R. Bossey in the same periodical. The *Université catholique* is not an illuminist publication; in the 1840s, it is the major periodical of French Catholic intellectuals—lay and clerical.

The illuminist tradition of language as being divine in origin is, of course, not the only linguistic theory propounded in early nineteenth-century France. Oversimplifying, one could divide the speculations on language into three tendencies: the illuminist, the conventionalist, and the "cratylist" or mimologist. The conventionalists, perhaps best represented by Destutt de Tracy in his *Eléments d'idéologie* (1801-1815), continue the Condillac tradition. Language is of human invention, provoked by our sense perceptions and developed by our faculties, and natural signs are refined and developed by the needs of survival, of society, and so on. It is noteworthy, however, that Destutt de Tracy also has a Utopian dream of a perfected language that would possess the referential certitude of the language of mathematics, where all misunderstanding and ambiguity would disappear; he, also, dreams of a transparency between thought and language.

Cratylism can, of course, enter into an illuminist theory of language but, as Gérard Genette has noted, is usually presented during the late eighteenth and early nineteenth centuries as an alternative explanation of the origin of language. Charles Nodier, the great exponent of mimologism in Romantic France, posits an origin in onomatopoeic imitation transformed and developed by metaphor and metonymy; poetry once again becomes the highest or purest form of language but for reasons quite different from those advanced by Louis-Claude de Saint-Martin. Nodier's theory is based on a series of "horizontal" harmonies among sounds, colors, forms, whereas in illuminist language theory the correspondences are vertical, between matter, man, and the divine.

Things are never all that simple, and Baudelaire's famed "Correspondances" discusses both. Modern poetry, with Nerval, Baudelaire, Hugo of the exile years, and their symbolist successors, thus faced a rich inheritance of theories of language. How much does it owe to illuminist theory? Parallels are tempting, but I think there are also problems. Illuminism is concerned with syntax; the poets were perhaps more preoccupied with the nature of the word. Mallarmé's debts to George Cox and Cox's debt to Nodier are well known; *Les Mots anglais,* Chapter IX of Victor Hugo's *Les Travailleurs de la mer,* Nerval's *Pandora,* those premonitions of *Finnegans Wake* rather represent explosions of cratylism à la Nodier, of horizontal correspondences among words with little if any verticality. Illuminist language theory posits the existence of the divine and seeks a restoration of the unity between that divine, language, and the created world. Hugo also sought such a restoration, but he posited that words as they are contain the Word, refused any hierarchial notion of language, and proposed the inherent goodness of what was normally labeled evil language. In the "Suite" to the "Réponse à un acte d'accusation," which requires and merits close reading, he refuses to say who created language. And Mallarmé's famed flower, absent from every bouquet, contradicts by its absence the illuminist dream of restoring creation in divine harmony. So far as symbolist poetics moves toward the notion that a poem must be, not mean, it creates a chasm between itself and the illuminist tradition. Signs are potentially motivated for both mimologists and illuminists, but Romantic illuminism is deeply marked by a Christian heritage on the one hand (whence the ease with which its tenets were adapted by such Catholics as Maistre, Ballanche, Bonald) and a belief in progress partly conceived of as a restoration of language. (A study of the evolution of A. -L. Constant, alias Eliphas Lévi, as he moves from Christian illuminism to a quite different kind of occultism, would probably help understand this historical change.) Christian illuminism surely survives, but its great twentieth-century exponent is not André Breton but Teilhard de Chardin. For Mallarmé, the poet becomes an angel, seemingly ex officio; for Saint-Martin, the poet is a man who desires God and the will of God. Mallarmé's poet gives a purer sense to the word and thereby separates it from all created bouquets; Saint-Martin's poet restores a purer sense in the word and thereby seeks to reunite created bouquets with the divine. The social dimensions of illuminist linguistic theory are largely absent from symbolist poetics. Mallarmé's poet is concerned with the words of the tribe; Saint-Martin's, with the words of the entire human race so far as the Word is at the origin of all creation. This constitutes a considerable change in perspective, the consequences of which are perhaps best illustrated in Rimbaud's *Alchimie du Verbe*—"l'histoire d'une de mes folies." (pp. 51-63)

Frank Paul Bowman, "Occultism and the Language of Poetry," in The Occult in Language and Literature, *edited by Hermine Riffaterre, New York Literary Forum, 1980, pp. 51-64.*

OCCULTISM, LITERATURE, AND SOCIETY

Patrick Brantlinger

[*In the following excerpt, Brantlinger scrutinizes the relationship between occultism and imperialist political ideologies in the lives and works of several English authors of the late nineteenth and early twentieth centuries.*]

In "The Little Brass God," a 1905 story by Bithia Croker, a statue of "Kali, Goddess of Destruction," brings misfortune to its unwitting Anglo-Indian possessors. First their pets kill each other or are killed in accidents; next the servants get sick or fall downstairs; then the family's lives are jeopardized. Finally the statue is stolen and dropped down a well, thus ending the curse. This featherweight tale typifies many written between 1880 and 1914. Its central feature, the magic statue, suggests that Western rationality may be subverted by the very superstitions it rejects. The destructive magic of the Orient takes its revenge; Croker unwittingly expresses a social version of the return of the repressed characteristic of late Victorian and Edwardian fiction, including that blend of adventure story with Gothic elements—imperial Gothic, as I will call it—which flourished from H. Rider Haggard's *King Solomon's Mines* in 1885 down at least to John Buchan's *Greenmantle* in 1916. Imperial Gothic combines the seemingly scientific, progressive, often Darwinian ideology of imperialism with an antithetical interest in the occult. Although the connections between imperialism and other aspects of late Victorian and Edwardian culture are innumerable, the link with occultism is especially symptomatic of the anxieties that attended the climax of the British Empire. No form of cultural expression reveals more clearly the contradictions within that climax than imperial Gothic.

Impelled by scientific materialism, the search for new sources of faith led many late Victorians to telepathy, séances, and psychic research. It also led to the far reaches of the Empire, where strange gods and "unspeakable rites" still had their millions of devotees. Publication of Madame Blavatsky's *Isis Unveiled* in 1877 marks the beginning of this trend, and the stunning success of Edwin Arnold's *The Light of Asia* (1879) suggests the strength of the desire for alternatives to both religious orthodoxy and scientific skepticism. For the same reason, A. P. Sinnett's *Esoteric Buddhism* (1883) was widely popular, as was his earlier *The Occult World* (1881). The standard explanation for the flourishing of occultism in the second half of the nineteenth century is that "triumphant positivism sparked an international reaction against its restrictive world view." In illustrating this thesis, Janet Oppenheim lists some manifestations of that reaction: "In England, it was an age of . . . the Rosicrucian revival, of cabalists, Hermeticists, and reincarnationists. In the late 1880s, the Hermetic Order of the Golden Dawn first saw the light of day in London, and during its stormy history, the Order lured into its arcane activities not only W. B. Yeats, but also the self-proclaimed magus Aleister Crowley. . . . Palmists and astrologers abounded, while books on magic and the occult sold briskly" [*The Other World: Spiritualism and Psychical Research in England, 1850-1914*]. Oppenheim's thesis that "much of the attraction of these and related subjects depended on the dominant role that science had assumed in modern culture" is borne out by the testimony of those drawn to occultism, among them Arthur Conan Doyle, Annie Besant, Arthur J. Balfour, and Oliver Lodge. At the same time an emphasis on the occult aspects of experience was often reconciled with "science" and even with Darwinism; such a reconciliation characterizes Andrew Lang's interests in both anthropology and psychic research, as well as the various neo-Hegelian justifications of Empire. Thus in *Origins and Destiny of Imperial Britain* (1900), J. A. Cramb argues that "empires are successive incarnations of the Divine ideas," but also that empires result from the struggle for survival of the fittest among nations and races. The British nation and Anglo-Saxon race, he contends, are the fittest to survive.

Imperialism itself, as an ideology or political faith, functioned as a partial substitute for declining or fallen Christianity and for declining faith in Britain's future. The poet John Davidson, for instance, having rejected other creeds and causes, "committed himself to a cluster of ideas centering on heroes, hero worship, and heroic vitalism," according to his biographer, which led him to pen ardent celebrations of the Empire [Carroll V. Peterson, *John Davidson*]. In "St. George's Day," Davidson writes:

> The Sphinx that watches by the Nile
> Has seen great empires pass away:
> The mightiest lasted but a while;
> Yet ours shall not decay—

a claim that by the 1890s obviously required extraordinary faith. The religious quality of late Victorian imperialism is also evident in much of Rudyard Kipling's poetry, as in "Recessional":

> God of our fathers, known of old,
>   Lord of our far-flung battle-line,
> Beneath whose awful Hand we hold
>   Dominion over palm and pine—
> Lord God of Hosts, be with us yet,
> Lest we forget—lest we forget!

In his study of William Ernest Henley, who did much to encourage the expression of imperialism in fin-de-siècle literature, Jerome Buckley remarks that "by the last decade of the century, the concept of a national or racial absolute inspired a fervor comparable to that engendered by the older evangelical religion" [*William Ernest Henley: A Study in the "Counter-Decadence" of the 'Nineties*].

Imperialism and occultism both functioned as ersatz religions, but their fusion in imperial Gothic represents something different from a search for new faiths. The patterns of atavism and going native described by imperialist romancers do not offer salvationist answers for seekers after religious truth; they offer instead insistent images of decline and fall or of civilization turning into its opposite just as the Englishman who desecrates a Hindu temple in Kipling's "Mark of the Beast" turns into a werewolf. Imperial Gothic expresses anxieties about the waning of religious orthodoxy, but even more clearly it expresses anxieties about the ease with which civilization can revert to barbarism or savagery and thus about the weakening of Britain's imperial hegemony. The atavistic descents into the primitive experienced by fictional characters seem often to be allegories of the larger regressive movement of civilization, British progress transformed into British backsliding. So the first section of Richard Jefferies's apocalyptic fantasy *After London* (1885) is entitled "The Relapse into Barbarism." Similarly, the narrator of Erskine Childers's spy novel *Riddle of the Sands* (1903) starts his tale in this way: "I have read of men who, when forced by their calling to live for long periods in utter solitude—save for a few black faces—have made it a rule to dress regularly for dinner in order to . . . prevent a relapse into barbarism." Much imperialist writing after about 1880 treats the Empire as a barricade against a new barbarian invasion; just as often it treats the Empire as a "dressing for dinner," a temporary means of preventing Britain itself from relapsing into barbarism.

After the mid-Victorian years the British found it increasingly difficult to think of themselves as inevitably progressive; they began worrying instead about the degeneration of their institutions, their culture, their racial "stock." In *Mark Rutherford's Deliverance* (1885), William Hale White writes that "our civilization is nothing but a thin film or crust lying over a volcanic pit," and in *Fabian Essays* (1889), George Bernard Shaw contends that Britain is "in an advanced state of rottenness." Much of the literary culture of the period expresses similar views. The aesthetic and decadent movements offer sinister analogies to Roman imperial decline and fall, while realistic novelists—George Gissing and Thomas Hardy, for instance—paint gloomy pictures of contemporary society and "the ache of modernism" (some of Gissing's pictures are explicitly anti-imperialist). Apocalyptic themes and images are characteristic of imperial Gothic, in which, despite the consciously pro-Empire values of many authors, the feeling emerges that "we are those upon whom the ends of the world are come" [I Corinthians 10:11].

The three principal themes of imperial Gothic are individual regression or going native; an invasion of civilization by the forces of barbarism or demonism; and the diminution of opportunities for adventure and heroism in the modern world. In the romances of Stevenson, Haggard, Kipling, Doyle, Bram Stoker, and John Buchan the supernatural or paranormal, usually symptomatic of individual regression, often manifests itself in imperial settings. Noting that Anglo-Indian fiction frequently deals with "inexplicable curses, demonic possession, and ghostly visitations," Lewis Wurgaft cites Kipling's "Phantom Rickshaw" as typical, and countless such tales were set in Burma, Egypt, Nigeria, and other parts of the Empire as well [*The Imperial Imagination: Magic and Myth in Kipling's India*]. In Edgar Wallace's *Sanders of the River* (1909), for example, the commissioner of a West African territory out-savages the savages, partly through police brutality but partly also through his knowledge of witchcraft. Says the narrator: "You can no more explain many happenings which are the merest commonplace in [Africa] than you can explain the miracle of faith or the wonder of telepathy."

In numerous late Victorian and Edwardian stories, moreover, occult phenomena follow characters from imperial settings home to Britain. In Doyle's "The Brown Hand" (1899), an Anglo-Indian doctor is haunted after his return to England by the ghost of an Afghan whose hand he had amputated. In "The Ring of Thoth" (1890) and "Lot No. 249" (1892), Egyptian mummies come to life in the Louvre and in the rooms of an Oxford student. In all three stories, western science discovers or triggers supernatural effects associated with the "mysterious Orient." My favorite story of this type is H. G. Wells's "The Truth about

Pyecraft," in which an obese Londoner takes an Indian recipe for "loss of weight" but instead of slimming down, begins levitating. The problem caused by oriental magic is then solved by western technology: lead underwear, which allows the balloonlike Mr. Pyecraft to live almost normally, feet on the ground.

The causes of the upsurge in romance writing toward the end of the century are numerous, complex, and often the same as those of the upsurge of occultism. Thus the new romanticism in fiction is frequently explained by its advocates—Stevenson, Haggard, Lang, and others—as a reaction against scientific materialism as embodied in "realistic" or "naturalistic" narratives. The most enthusiastic defender of the new fashion for romances was Andrew Lang, who thought the realism of George Eliot and Henry James intellectually superior but also that the romances of Stevenson and Haggard tapped universal, deep-rooted, "primitive" aspects of human nature which the realists could not approach. (pp. 227-31)

All the same, Lang believes, realism in fiction should coexist with romanticism just as the rational, conscious side of human nature coexists with the unconscious. Lang can appreciate realistic novels intellectually, but "the natural man within me, the survival of some blue-painted Briton or of some gipsy," is "equally pleased with a *true* Zulu love story" ["Realism and Romance," *Contemporary Review* 52 (November 1887)]. He therefore declares that "the advantage of our mixed condition, civilized at top with the old barbarian under our clothes, is just this, that we can enjoy all sorts of things." Romances may be unsophisticated affairs, but because they appeal to the barbarian buried self of the reader, they are more fundamental, more honest, more natural than realism. In Lang's criticism, romances are " 'savage survivals,' but so is the whole of the poetic way of regarding Nature."

An anthropologist of sorts, Lang acquired his theory of savage survivals from his mentor Edward Burnett Tylor, who contends that occultism and spiritualism—indeed, all forms of superstition (and therefore, implicitly, of religion)—belong to "the philosophy of savages." Modern occultism, according to Tylor, is "a direct revival from the regions of savage philosophy and peasant folk-lore," a reversion to "primitive culture" [*Primitive Culture*]. At the same time Tylor associates poetry with the mythology of primitive peoples: "The mental condition of the lower races is the key to poetry, nor is it a small portion of the poetic realm which these definitions cover." Literary activity in general thus appears to be a throwback to prerational states of mind and society. Similarly, Arthur Machen, author of numerous Gothic horror stories from the 1890s onward, defines literature as "the endeavour of every age to return to the first age, to an age, if you like, of savages" [quoted in Wesley D. Sweetser, *Arthur Machen*].

Robert Louis Stevenson, who echoes Lang's defenses of romances as against novels, discovered sources of "primitive" poetic energy in his own psyche, most notably through the nightmare that yielded *Dr. Jekyll and Mr. Hyde.* Stevenson entertained ambivalent feelings toward the popularity of that "Gothic gnome" or "crawler," in part because *any* popular appeal seemed irrational or vaguely barbaric to him. Although not overtly about imperial matters, *Jekyll and Hyde,* perhaps even more than *Treasure Island* and *Kidnapped,* served as a model for later writers of imperial Gothic fantasies. Because "within the Gothic we can find a very intense, if displaced, engagement with political and social problems," it is possible, as David Punter argues, to read *Jekyll and Hyde* as itself an example of imperial Gothic: "It is strongly suggested [by Stevenson] that Hyde's behaviour is an urban version of 'going native.' The particular difficulties encountered by English imperialism in its decline were conditioned by the nature of the supremacy which had been asserted: not a simple racial supremacy, but one constantly seen as founded on moral superiority. If an empire based on a morality declines, what are the implications . . .? It is precisely Jekyll's 'high views' which produce morbidity in his *alter ego*" [*The Literature of Terror: A History of Gothic Fictions from 1765 to the Present Day*]. Jekyll's alchemy releases the apelike barbarian—the savage or natural man—who lives beneath the civilized skin. Not only is this the general fantasy of going native in imperial Gothic, but Hyde—murderous, primitive, apelike—fits the Victorian stereotype of the Irish hooligan, and his dastardly murder of Sir Danvers Carew resembles some of the "Fenian outrages" of the early 1880s. (pp. 231-33)

. . . . .

Numerous travel writers from about 1870 onward lament the decline of exploration into mere tourism. In "Regrets of a Veteran Traveller" (1897), Frederic Harrison declares: "Railways, telegraphs, and circular tours in twenty days have opened to the million the wonders of foreign parts." These signs of technological progress, however, conceal losses: "Have they not sown broadcast disfigurement, vulgarity, stupidity, demoralisation? Europe is changed indeed since the unprogressive forties! Is it all for the better?" The old ideal of opening up the dark places of the world to civilization, commerce, and Christianity fades into the tourist trade: "Morally, we Britons plant the British flag on every peak and pass; and wherever the Union Jack floats there we place the cardinal British institutions—tea, tubs, sanitary appliances, lawn tennis, and churches; all of them excellent things in season. But the missionary zeal of our people is not always according to knowledge and discretion." Before the ugly American came the ugly Briton, clutching a Baedeker or a Cook's travel guide. Harrison thinks it has all become too easy, too common, too standardized to be heroic or adventuresome—"We go abroad, but we travel no longer."

Imperial Gothic frequently expresses anxiety about the waning of opportunities for heroic adventure. With regression and invasion, this is the third of its major themes (ironic today, given Hollywood's frequent regressions to Haggard and Kipling for its adventure tales, as in *Raiders of the Lost Ark*). Early Victorian adventure writers—Marryat, Chamier, Mayne Reid, R. M. Ballantyne—took as self-evident the notion that England was the vanguard nation, leading the world toward the future. As one of the marooned boys in Ballantyne's *Coral Island* (1856) says, "We'll take possession of [this island] in the

name of the King; we'll . . . enter the service of its black inhabitants. Of course we'll rise, naturally, to the top of affairs. White men always do in savage countries." Upbeat racism and chauvinism continued to characterize boys' adventure fiction well into the twentieth century, but in imperial Gothic white men do not always rise to the top—just as often they sink into savagedom, cowardice, or exotic torpor, as in Tennyson's "Lotos Eaters." Conrad's fictions frequently read like botched romances in which adventure turns sour or squalid, undermined by moral frailty, and the same is true also of Stevenson's most realistic stories—*The Beach of Falesá, The Wreckers, Ebb-Tide.* Lord Jim's failure to live up to his heroic self-image has analogues in many imperial Gothic stories that are not ostensibly critical of imperialism.

The fear that adventure may be a thing of the past in the real world led many writers to seek it in the unreal world of romance, dreams, imagination. "Soon the ancient mystery of Africa will have vanished," Haggard laments in an 1894 essay appropriately titled " 'Elephant Smashing' and 'Lion Shooting.' " Where, he dolefully asks, "will the romance writers of future generations find a safe and secret place, unknown to the pestilent accuracy of the geographer, in which to lay their plots?" In similar fashion, in both *Heart of Darkness* and his autobiographical essays, Conrad registers his youthful excitement over the blank places on the map of Africa and the disillusionment he felt when he arrived at Stanley Falls in 1890: "A great melancholy descended on me . . . there was . . . no great haunting memory . . . only the unholy recollection of a prosaic newspaper 'stunt' and the distasteful knowledge of the vilest scramble for loot that ever disfigured the history of human conscience and geographical exploration. What an end to the idealized realities of a boy's daydreams! I wondered what I was doing there" ["Geography and Some Explorers," *Last Essays*]. The stunt was Stanley's 1871 trek into Central Africa in search of Livingstone for the *New York Herald,* the scramble for loot that Conrad saw at first hand King Leopold's rapacious private empire in the Congo.

Arguments defending theosophy and spiritualism often sound like Haggard's and Conrad's laments for the waning of geographical adventure: the disappearance of earthly frontiers will be compensated for by the opening of new frontiers in the beyond. Not only were occultists seeking proofs of immortality and of a spiritual realm above or beneath the material one, they were also seeking adventure. The fantasy element in such adventure seeking is its most obvious feature, as it is also in the literary turn away from realism to romanticism. According to Lang: "As the visible world is measured, mapped, tested, weighed, we seem to hope more and more that a world of invisible romance may not be far from us. . . . The ordinary shilling tales of 'hypnotism' and mesmerism are vulgar trash enough, and yet I can believe that an impossible romance, if the right man wrote it in the right mood, might still win us from the newspapers, and the stories of shabby love, and cheap remorses, and commonplace failures" ["The Supernatural in Fiction," in his *Adventures in Books*]. But even a well-written impossible romance, as Lang well knows, carries with it more than a hint of childish daydreaming.

If imperialist ideology is atavistic, occultism is obviously so, a rejection of individual and social rationality and a movement backward to primitive or infantile modes of perception and belief. "Ages, empires, civilisations pass, and leave some members even of educated mankind still, in certain points, on the level of the savage who propitiates with gifts, or addresses with prayers, the spirits of the dead"—so Lang writes in _Cock Lane and Common Sense_ (1894), intended in part to expose the spurious aspects of spiritualism. Lang believes that much of what goes by that name is fraudulent: "As to the idea of purposely evoking the dead, it is at least as impious, as absurd, as odious to taste and sentiment, as it is insane in the eyes of reason. This protest the writer feels obliged to make, for while he regards the traditional, historical, and anthropological curiosities here collected as matters of some interest . . . he has nothing but abhorrence and contempt for modern efforts to converse with the manes, and for all the profane impostures of 'spiritualism.' "

Like many other well-known Victorians, Lang participated in the Society for Psychical Research, founded in 1882, and even served as its president. But his opinions about psychic phenomena always retain a healthy skepticism. Stopping short of supernatural explanations, Lang favors instead explanations in terms of extraordinary, hitherto unidentified mental powers, including the power of "unconscious cerebration" to create illusions of ghosts or spirits and to perform telepathic feats. If we assume psychic phenomena do occur, then the theory that they emanate from the subconscious is the chief alternative to what Lang calls "the old savage theory" of "the agency of the spirits of the dead" ["Psychical Research" _Encyclopedia Britannica_].

Just how the subconscious works—how to explain its mechanisms of projection, hallucination, dreams, and forgetting—was a major issue in late nineteenth-century psychology. British psychologists followed paths similar to those that led to psychoanalysis, and their explanations of psychic phenomena, in common with Freud's, tend toward ideas of regression and unconscious cerebration. In _The Future of an Illusion,_ Freud writes that the beliefs of the "spiritualists" are infantile: "They are convinced of the survival of the individual soul. . . . Unfortunately they cannot succeed in refuting the fact that . . . their spirits are merely the products of their own mental activity. They have called up the spirits of the greatest men . . . but all the pronouncements and information which they have received . . . have been so foolish . . . that one can find nothing credible in them but the capacity of the spirits to adapt themselves to the circle of people who have conjured them up." Freud interprets spiritualist beliefs, as he does all of the "fairy tales of religion," as backsliding from adult, conscious rationality into the irrational depths of the subconscious.

Such an explanation of superstitions might do for the psychologists and also for Lang, who as an anthropologist was more interested in the products of myth making and religion than in experiencing the miraculous himself. For many of Lang's colleagues in psychic research, however, the realm of spirit was not reducible to that of the unconscious, even though the latter might contain unknown, potentially miraculous powers. In his _Encyclopedia Britannica_ article on psychical research, Lang notes F. W. H. Myers's various studies; regrettably, Myers "tended more and more to the belief in the 'invasion' and 'possession' of living human organisms by spirits of the dead." He points to the same tendency in the work of the physicist and psychic researcher Oliver Lodge, and adds: "Other students can find, in the evidence cited [by Lodge and Myers], no warrant for this return to the 'palaeolithic psychology' of 'invasion' and 'possession.' "

Other late Victorians and Edwardians moved in the direction Lang held to be retrograde—away from an early skepticism toward increasing and occasionally absolute faith in occult phenomena, including demonic invasions and possessions of reality. Obviously the will-to-believe in such cases was powerful. A. J. Balfour, for example, Conservative prime minister from 1902 to 1905, produced several "metaphysical" essays—_A Defence of Philosophic Doubt_ (1879), _The Foundations of Belief_ (1895), and others—that make the case for faith by sharply dividing science and religion. Balfour argues that the two are separate, equally valid realms; the methods and discoveries of science cannot invalidate those of religion. That his sympathies lie with religion is obvious. In his presidential address to the Society for Psychical Research in 1894, Balfour expresses his joy that the society's work demonstrates "there are things in heaven and earth not hitherto dreamed of in our scientific philosophy." Small wonder that in 1916, when the former prime minister (aided by several automatic writers, including Kipling's sister Alice Fleming) began to receive spirit communications from the love of his youth, Mary Lyttelton, he came to believe that the messages were genuine. Small wonder, too, given his political career, that among the themes in the three thousand messages directed to him from the beyond is the establishment of a harmonious world order (Oppenheim).

Several early modern writers followed roughly similar paths from doubt to faith. In Kipling's case, the faith was perhaps never firm. While lightly tossing off such ghost stories as "The Phantom Rickshaw" (1888) and "The Return of Imray" (1891), the young Kipling showed what he actually thought of occultism in "The Sending of Dana Da" (1888)—and what he thought was skeptical to the point of sarcasm: "Once upon a time, some people in India made a new Heaven and a new Earth out of broken teacups, a missing brooch or two, and a hair-brush. These were hidden under bushes, or stuffed into holes in the hillside, and an entire Civil Service of subordinate Gods used to find or mend them again; and every one said: 'There are more things in Heaven and Earth than are dreamt of in our philosophy.' " Kipling's satire, perhaps inspired by recent exposures of Mme. Blavatsky's fraudulence, takes aim at all branches of occultism including theosophy. The new "Religion," he says, "was too elastic for ordinary use. It stretched itself and embraced pieces of everything that the medicine-men of all ages have manufactured," including "White, Gray, and Black Magic . . . spiritualism, palmistry, fortune-telling by cards, hot chesnuts, double-kernelled nuts, and tallow droppings." It would even "have adopted Voodoo and Oboe had it known anything about them." (pp. 238-42)

Just when Kipling put aside skepticism and began to be something of an occultist himself is not clear, though some accounts attribute the change to the death of his daughter Josephine in 1899. Certainly her death inspired Kipling to write the psychic story "They" (1904), in which the protagonist communicates with ghostly children in a ghostly country-house setting. But by that time Kipling had also written stories dealing with reincarnation—"The Finest Story in the World" (1891) and "Wireless" (1902)—a subject of increasing interest also to his friend Haggard, whose views about spiritual matters are easier to trace because he was always less defensively ironic than Kipling. Some critics dismiss the problem, suggesting that Kipling occasionally includes supernatural elements in his stories merely for artistic purposes, but this approach seems no more explanatory than arguing that Dante writes about heaven and hell for artistic purposes. Nor did Kipling drop the supernatural after the early 1900s: several stories in *Debits and Credits* (1926) deal with the supernatural— "The Gardener," "The Madonna of the Trenches," and "The Wish House"—and so do other works among his late fiction.

Haggard was interested in occultism from the time when, as a young man in London, he attended séances at the house of Lady Paulet, who gave him his "entree to the spiritualistic society of the day" [*The Days of My Life: An Autobiography*]. The apparitions that he saw were not exactly spirits, he thought, but rather the products of "some existent but unknown force." Occultism shows up in his first novel, *Dawn* (1884), which combines realism with, as George Saintsbury put it, the "elements of occult arts and astral spirits" [quoted in *Rudyard Kipling to Rider Haggard: The Record of a Friendship*, edited by Martin Cohen]. Haggard's second novel, *The Witch's Head* (1884), also supposedly realistic, touches upon the theme of reincarnation. After about 1900, according to Norman Etherington, Haggard dwelt with "increased fervor on the truth of reincarnation. The idea he had first tentatively expressed in *Witch's Head*, that lovers worked out their relationships in successive lives and literally eternal triangles, became a dominant theme in his later novels. He believed he had caught glimpses of his own previous existences in dreams and visions" [*Rider Haggard*]. In *The Days of My Life,* Haggard describes a series of these visions of former lives, which might almost, Etherington says, "be tableaux from the ethnographic section of a museum," similar to "displays on 'the ascent of man' from the Stone Age to the Iron Age." In the first reincarnation Haggard is a primitive man, perhaps of the Stone Age; in the second he is black, again primitive, defending his rude home against attackers who kill him; in the third he is an ancient Egyptian, in love with a "beautiful young woman with violet eyes"; and in the fourth he is probably an early medieval barbarian, living in "a timber-built hall" in a land of "boundless snows and great cold," though again in love with a violet-eyed woman, the same "as she of the Egyptian picture." Haggard believes that these "dream-pictures" can be explained in one of three ways: "(1) Memories of some central incident that occurred in a pre-

vious incarnation. (2) *Racial* memories of events that had happened to forefathers. (3) Subconscious imagination and invention." The third explanation is the easiest to accept, he says, but he clearly favors the first or the second.

Kipling and Haggard often discussed telepathy, ghosts, and reincarnation. Although it is likely that Kipling believed—perhaps always with a certain ambivalence or ironic distance—in some version of occultism at least from 1904 onward, Haggard later opined that he converted Kipling to faith in reincarnation in the 1920s. "He is now convinced," Haggard wrote in his diary in 1923, "that the individual human being is not a mere flash in the pan, seen for a moment and lost forever, but an enduring entity that has lived elsewhere and will continue to live, though for a while memory of the past is blotted out" (quoted in Cohen). This may have been only wishful thinking on Haggard's part. In any event, it seems likely that the very ambivalence with which Kipling approached any belief in the supernatural made him all the more ardent an imperialist. On political issues Haggard often seems more supple and thoughtful than Kipling, though always also ardently imperialistic. Thus Haggard was not prepared to blame "all our Russian troubles" on "the machinations of the Jews." Puzzled by Kipling's often belligerent antisemitism, Haggard wrote in 1919: "I do not know, I am sure, but personally I am inclined to think that one can insist too much on the Jew motive, the truth being that there are Jews and Jews. . . . For my own part I should be inclined to read Trade Unions instead of Jews" (quoted in Cohen). In contrast, Kipling, ambivalent about so many matters, is often dogmatic about politics: "Any nation save ourselves, with such a fleet as we have at present, would go out swiftly to trample the guts out of the world," Kipling declaimed to Haggard in 1897; "and the fact that we do not seems to show that even if we aren't very civilized, we're about the one power with a glimmering of civilization in us" (quoted in Cohen). The only ambivalence here has to do with the meaning of civilization: perhaps it is a weakness, a disease; perhaps the brave if not civilized thing to do would be to "trample the guts out of the world."

Haggard's comparative uncertainty about politics is dimly reflected in the romance conventions he employs in most of his fictions. In common with other advocates of the romance as against the novel, Haggard hesitates at defending his tales as truer than realistic fictions or even as somehow true. He agrees with Lang that he is expressing universal, mythic concerns—writing about what Jung would later call archetypes. But he also knows that his landscapes shade into the fantastic and are therefore highly subjective landscapes of the mind. Just as Lang is inclined to attribute psychic phenomena to the unconscious, so Haggard often suggests that his stories refer more to his own—or perhaps to universal—dream states than to outward reality. Haggard shares this emphasis on fantasy with all Gothic romancers, whose stories always veer toward dreams and the subliminal reaches of the mind.

Defining occultism:

'Occultism' is a difficult term to define. It denotes a large variety of different beliefs and practices such as fortune-telling, spiritualism, magic, witchcraft, necromancy and alchemy, and it has inevitably acquired adverse connotations of fraud and deception. The word itself, according to Murray's *New English Dictionary*, was . . . used for the first time in 1881 by the leading Theosophical writer A. P. Sinnett. . . .

What appears to be common to all occult doctrines is a belief that the universe is essentially spiritual, so that to this extent occultism generally may be described as a form of idealism. Two of the most recurrent notions of the many 'occult philosophers' are essentially Neo-Platonic: they are (*a*) that the life or energy of God permeates all created things, visible and invisible, and (*b*) that earthly phenomena 'correspond' to, i.e. are symbols or counterparts of, spiritual realities. These Neo-Platonic doctrines are immediately recognizable in a passage from the French poet Gérard de Nerval which is quoted by Arthur Symons in *The Symbolist Movement in Literature:*

> All things live, all things are in motion, all things correspond; the magnetic rays emanating from myself or others traverse without obstacle the infinite chain of created things: a transparent network covers the world, whose loose threads communicate more and more closely with the planets and the stars. Now a captive upon the earth, I hold converse with the starry choir, which is feelingly a part of my joys and sorrows.

In its hypothetically purest form, . . . occultism is perhaps best regarded as a continuation of the Neo-Platonic tradition, according to which the universe is living, spiritual, and unified.

Tom Gibbons, in his Rooms in the Darwin Hotel: Studies in English Literary Criticism and Ideas, 1880-1920, *1973.*

The subjectivism of Gothic romance as a genre thus intersects with the atavistic character of both imperialist ideology and occultist belief. According to Theodor Adorno, "occultism is a reflex-action to the subjectification of all meaning, the complement of reification." Adorno contends that "occultism is a symptom of regression in consciousness," diagnosing it specifically as a "regression to magic under late capitalism" whereby "thought is assimilated to late capitalist forms."

> The power of occultism, as of Fascism, to which it is connected by thought-patterns of the ilk of anti-semitism, is not only pathic. Rather it lies in the fact that in the lesser panaceas, as in superimposed pictures, consciousness famished for truth imagines it is grasping a dimly present knowledge diligently denied to it by official progress in all its forms. It is the knowledge that society, by virtually excluding the possibility of spontaneous change, is gravitating towards total catastrophe. The real absurdity is reproduced in the astrological hocus-pocus, which adduces the impenetrable connections of alienated elements—nothing more alien than the stars—as knowledge about the subject. ["Theses against Occultism," *Minima Moralia: Reflections from Damaged Life*].

Adorno's analysis of the interior parallelism between occultism and fascism suggests also the interior significance (the political unconscious) of imperial Gothic fantasy. The subjective nature of the genre is more or less apparent to all of its best practitioners. The motif of the exploration of the Dark Continent or of other blank spaces of external reality whose meaning seems inward—the fabled journey into the unconscious or the heart of darkness of the explorer—is omnipresent in late Victorian and Edwardian literature. Graham Greene is writing at the end of a long tradition when, in *Journey without Maps* (1936), he likens African travel to a landscape of the mind, a dream geography, to be understood as much in psychoanalytic as in geographical terms. Africa, India, and the other dark places of the earth become a terrain upon which the political unconscious of imperialism maps its own desires, its own fantastic longitudes and latitudes. (pp. 243-46)

Of all late Victorian and Edwardian occultists, none was more sanguine than [W. T. Stead] about the truth of his convictions. He believed that God had given him a personal mission as a journalist, to defend the Empire and to trumpet the truths of spiritualism through the world. In reporting the news, he made innovative use of interviews with the great and powerful, and when the great were not available—when they happened to be dead, for example—he questioned them anyway through what he called "automatic interviews." Thus he was able to publish the opinions of Catherine the Great on the Russian Question and those of Gladstone's ghost on the budget of 1909. The headline on the front page of the *Daily Chronicle* for 1 November 1909 read: "Amazing Spirit Interview: The Late Mr. Gladstone on the Budget." In her study of spiritualism Ruth Brandon notes that "Mr. Gladstone, as it happened, had not much of interest to say; but the news (to paraphrase Dr. Johnson) lay in his saying it at all" [*The Spiritualists: The Passion for the Occult in the Nineteenth and Twentieth Centuries*].

Through the urgings of his dead friend Julia Ames, Stead made plans to open better communications with the spirit world. In his occultist journal *Borderland* and elsewhere, Stead projected a highly original sort of news agency—one that would transmit news of the beyond through spirit mediumship and that would be named Julia's Bureau. "What is wanted is a bureau of communication between the two sides," Julia's ghost told Stead. "Could you not establish some sort of office with one or more trustworthy mediums? If only it were to enable the sorrowing on the earth to know, if only for once, that their so-called dead live nearer them than ever before, it would help to dry many a tear and soothe many a sorrow. I think you could count upon the eager co-operation of all on this side" [*After Death: A Personal Narrative*].

Over the years Julia sent Stead many spirit letters containing news from the borderland, and she often exhorted him to open a bureau of communication. He saw these exhortations as a great opportunity but also, considering the numbers of both dead and living who might want to avail themselves of the bureau's services, as an enormous undertaking. On this score Julia was reassuring. In a communiqué dated 6 October 1908, four years before Stead went down in the *Titanic,* Julia acknowledged that the population of the spirit world was vast—of course far larger than the one and a half billion in the world of the living. But the desire of the dead to communicate with the living tended to wane quickly; therefore "I should say that the number of the 'dead' who wish to communicate with the living are comparatively few." Julia's ghost then offers what to any imperialist must have seemed an obvious analogy:

> It is with us as with immigrants to my former country [Australia]. When they arrive their hearts are in the old world. The new world is new and strange. They long to hear from the old home; and the post brings them more joy than the sunrise. But after a very little time the pain is dulled, new interests arise, and in a few years . . . they write no more. . . . The receipt of letters and telegrams has taken away the death-like edge of emigration. "We shall hear from them again." "Write soon." These are the consolations of humanity even on the physical plane. What the Bureau will do is to enable those who have newly lost their dead to write soon, to hear messages.

The emigration analogy suggests once again the complex, unconscious interconnections between imperialist ideology and occultism. To the ardent imperialist, "away" can never be "away"; nothing is foreign, not even death; the borderland itself becomes a new frontier to cross, a new realm to conquer. And with the help of friendly spirits like the Australian Julia, how easy the conquest seems! Just at the moment actual frontiers were vanishing, late Victorian and Edwardian occultist literature is filled with metaphors of exploration, emigration, conquest, colonization. Nor is the news agency metaphor of Julia's Bureau unique. An imagery of telegraphy and cablegrams, telephone and radio, permeates the millennial expectations of the spiritualists, as Kipling shows in "Wireless." According to the persistent modernist Stead: "The recent applications of electricity in wireless telegraphy and wireless telephony, while proving nothing in themselves as to the nature or permanence of personality, are valuable as enabling us to illustrate the difficulties as well as the possibilities of proving the existence of life after death." But though hard to prove, the discoveries of the spiritualists are at least as immense as those of Christopher Columbus: "In order to form a definite idea of the problem which we are about to attack, let us imagine the grave as if it were the Atlantic Ocean." Using similar language in *Phantom Walls,* [Sir Oliver Lodge] writes of his hope "to be able to survey the ocean of eternity from Darien-like peaks," while Arthur Conan Doyle often seems willing to don armor and go crusading in order to conquer death or convince doubters of the truths of spiritualism: "The greater the difficulty in breaking down the wall of apathy, ignorance, and materialism, the more is it a challenge to our manhood to attack and ever attack in the same bulldog spirit with which Foch faced the German lines" [*Memories and Adventures*]. (pp. 248-50)

Doyle's path to spiritualism was much like the one traversed by many late Victorians and Edwardians. In his *Memories and Adventures* (1924), he writes that his youthful education had trained him in "the school of medical materialism," formed by "the negative views of all my great teachers." At first he was generally skeptical about occultism:

> I had at that time the usual contempt which the young educated man feels towards the whole subject which has been covered by the clumsy name of Spiritualism. I had read of mediums being convicted of fraud, I had heard of phenomena which were opposed to every known scientific law, and I had deplored the simplicity and credulity which could deceive good, earnest people into believing that such bogus happenings were signs of intelligence outside our own existence. . . . I was wrong and my great teachers were wrong, but still I hold that they wrought well and that their Victorian agnosticism was in the interests of the human race, for it shook the old iron-clad unreasoning Evangelical position which was so universal before their days. For all rebuilding a site must be cleared.

From the 1890s onward, Doyle became increasingly interested in the spiritualist rebuilding of nothing less than world civilization. He engaged in psychic research, experimenting with telepathy and searching for poltergeists in haunted houses, at first with a skeptical air but later with growing belief in an invisible realm of spirits just beyond the boundaries of material reality. If it seemed evident that adventure was vanishing from the modern world, Doyle for one rebelled against the evidence. True, his reinventions of adventure in fiction have about them the same compensatory quality that characterizes most late Victorian romance writing, which senses its inferiority to realistic narration. Romance writers indicate in a variety of ways that their adventure stories are for adolescents; and occultist pursuits are also somehow, even to occultists themselves, childish and subrational. As a young man, at least, Doyle perceived these difficulties but plunged ahead anyway, toward the blinding light (he thought) at the end of the long tunnel of world history.

In Doyle's 1911 novel *The Lost World,* the journalist hero Malone is told by his girlfriend that he must go adventuring and become a hero before she will marry him. The demand seems to him next to impossible because, as his editor exclaims, "the big blank spaces in the map are all being filled in, and there's no room for romance anywhere." But there is room—or Doyle at least will make room—for romance in a fantasy version of the Amazon basin, where the British adventurers regress through a Darwinian nightmare to the days of the dinosaurs. The characters in the story, including the atavistically apelike Professor Challenger, reappear next in *The Poison Belt* of 1913, where adventure shrinks: they watch the end of the world from the windows of an airtight room in Challenger's house. But the world does not end, the poisonous cloud lifts, people revive, and Doyle's band of fantasy adventurers live on to appear in a third novel, *The Land of Mist,* published in 1925, the same year as Yeats's *A Vision.* Challenger and the rest are now participants in what Doyle believes to be the greatest adventure of all, beyond the borders of the material world. Exploration and invasion metaphors abound. Lord John Roxton's newspaper ad sets the tone: Roxton is "seeking fresh worlds to conquer. Having exhausted the sporting adventures of this terrestrial globe, he is now turning to those of the dim, dark and dubious regions of psychic research. He is in the market . . . for any genuine specimen of a haunted house." While the crumbling of the Empire quickened after World War I, Doyle himself turned obsessively to haunted houses, séances, lands of mysticism and mist. The skeptical Challenger exclaims that the "soul-talk" of the spiritualists is "the Animism of savages," but Doyle himself was no longer skeptical. He believed in magic, he believed in fairies, he believed in ectoplasmic projections. He believed Spiritualism with a capital S was the successor to Christianity, the new advent of the City of God after the fall of the City of Man. The creator of that great incarnation of scientific rationalism Sherlock Holmes devoted himself to the spiritualist movement, becoming one of its leaders, and it became for him a substitute for all other causes—for imperialism itself. Just as his friend Stead felt that he had received a call from God, so Doyle after the world war felt that the meaningful part of his life had begun. He had received the call; it was his duty to save the world. "In the days of universal sorrow and loss [after World War I], when the voice of Rachel was heard throughout the land, it was borne in upon me that the knowledge which had come to me thus was not for my own consolation alone, but that God had placed me in a very special position for conveying it to that world which needed it so badly" (*Memories*).

Doyle's version of "Heaven was rather like Sussex, slightly watered down," says Brandon, but his plans for the future of the world were somewhat larger than Sussex. He believed the spirit world was arranged in a marvelous, infinite bureaucratic hierarchy very much like the British Raj in India. In 1923 an "Arabian spirit" named Pheneas began to communicate with him through his wife's automatic writing, telling him that the old world would end soon and a glorious new one dawn. Doyle was no doubt reassured to learn that "England is to be the centre to which all humanity will turn. She is to be the beacon light in this dark, dark world. The light is Christ, and all humans will strive to get to that light in the great darkness" (*Pheneas Speaks*). Sherlock Holmes cannot tolerate a mystery without solving it, nor can Doyle: the darkness of this world will soon disperse, and light, radiating especially from England and Sussex, will be universal. Doyle experienced a glimmer of embarrassment toward the end of the decade, shortly before his death, when Pheneas's predictions did not seem to be coming true on schedule, but it was only a minor setback. Material adventure in the material Empire might be on the wane, but over the ruins was dawning the light of the great spiritualist adventure.

As far as geopolitical arrangements were concerned, Doyle believed, the programs of all governments would have to be revised. In spiritualist armor, slaying the drag-

ons of Bolshevism and materialism, Doyle sometimes felt that the future was his. Like the souls of the dead, the glories of the imperialist past would be reborn, purified or rarefied, for they were eternal. In his *History of Spiritualism,* Doyle writes: "I do not say to [the] great and world-commanding . . . powers . . . open your eyes and see that your efforts are fruitless, and acknowledge your defeat, for probably they never will open their eyes . . . but I say to the Spiritualists . . . dark as the day may seem to you, never was it more cheering . . . never . . . more anticipatory of ultimate victory. It has upon it the stamp of all the conquering influences of the age" [*The History of Spiritualism*]. But the ultimate victory of spiritualism was prefigured for Doyle in the demise of the empires of this world, the precondition for the invasion and reconquest of reality by the realm of spirit, or perhaps of our transubstantiation—a kind of psychic emigration and colonization—into the world beyond reality, an invisible, even more glorious empire rising ghostlike out of the corpse of the old.

As cultural formations, both imperialism and spiritualism have roots in "the dark powers of the subconscious, [and call] into play instincts that carry over from the life habits of the dim past. Driven out everywhere else, the irrational" seeks refuge in imperialism, Schumpeter contends [Joseph Schumpeter, *Imperialism and Social Classes*], and, I would add, in late Victorian and early modern occultism. Imperial Gothic expresses the atavistic character of both movements, shadowing forth the larger, gradual disintegration of British hegemony. Doyle's phantom empire—and the imperial Gothic themes of regression, invasion, and the waning of adventure—express the narrowing vistas of the British Empire at the time of its greatest extent, in the moment before its fall. (pp. 250-53)

Patrick Brantlinger, "Imperial Gothic: Atavism and the Occult in the British Adventure Novel, 1880-1914," in his Rule of Darkness: British Literature and Imperialism, 1830-1914, *Cornell, 1988, pp. 227-53.*

The relationship of art to magic:

The ancient belief that the poet has magical powers is so compelling that it survives in certain distorted ways today. "People speak with justice," says Freud, "of the 'magic of art' and compare artists with magicians. . . ." In early European culture the association led directly into the realms of the forbidden; the artist was regarded as the heritor of the mythical beings whose "creativity" was rebellion and who were punished for their awful audacity: Daedalus, who was imprisoned; Wieland and Hephaestus, both crippled; Prometheus, the great prototype, chained to his rock. For man to create—a statue, a building, a painting, a poem—has always been in some sense to encroach on divine prerogative.

Robert C. Eliott, in his The Power of Satire: Magic, Ritual, Art, *1960.*

Nachman Ben-Yehuda

[*In the following excerpt, Ben-Yehuda examines the cultural implications of the popular interest in science fiction and occultism.*]

The first question is why does the "occult explosion" exist today? I shall suggest a new conceptual framework for the timing problem using the terms "revitalizing" and "recentering."

Modern occultists and science fiction fans are not overwhelmed by an incomprehensible environment, to which they respond passively by developing various supernatural and superstitious belief systems. On the contrary, these are usually well educated people, quite capable of coping with their complex environment. However, these young, educated and sophisticated persons find themselves, by the very nature of their social position, in an environment which consistently undergoes rather rapid processes of social change (stemming from various scientific-technological innovations), in what Keniston (1969) termed "chronic change." These changes create numerous fundamental existential problems which cannot be easily answered by either traditional religions or by science.

The trend toward radical secularization, contrary to dire prognoses of men like Max Weber at the beginning of the century, does not dominate the late modern world. The contemporary era presents the curious spectacle of a world whose Judeo-Christian foundations have been thoroughly shaken but unlike T. S. Elliot's Wasteland, it swarms with a variety of competing doctrines promising salvation from nihilism in a wide variety of directions, from various forms of new political radicalism, communitarianism, drug and rock sub-cultures, new religious sects, renewed adherence to orthodox religion and the like. This wide spectrum offers what could be termed as competing and alternative centers. Each of them, with varying degrees of intensity, offers its adherents a new route to recentralize one's world.

Another theoretical concept which can—and should—be of help in this analysis, is the concept of revitalization (see Wallace 1966; Norbeck 1961). Wallace (1966), who suggested the term, had in mind religiously-oriented types of movements, aimed at creating a more satisfying culture. Wallace pointed out that revitalization movements find clear expression in various rituals and function as a source for cultural diversity. While the actual classification of the varieties of revitalization movements " . . . has proved to be a difficult task . . ." " . . . cultures recognize . . . identity problems in individual instances and provide culturally standardized ways for the unfortunate victims of identity conflict to achieve relief . . . . " Wallace points out that without revitalization movements, cultures are apt to disintegrate as both an important outlet for identity-less (or decentralized) people and an important source for social change would be absent there. Both science fiction/fantasy and the modern occult not only provide elective centers but provide essential and cherished individualized revitalization experiences as well.

Thus, the recentering and revitalizing of one's world, even in its collective manifestation, is essentially a personal one—it is a quest for an elective, revitalizing center. Kavolis (1970) stated that the "decentralized personality" is one " . . . in which no set of activities is perceived as particularly important for the maintaining of personal integrity and in which the functions of the personality are not arranged in a hierarchical pattern . . . ". On the personality level, such decentralization reflects the major implication of radical secularization. This analysis is furthermore strengthened by Berger and Luckman's (1967) theory of the "privatization of belief ", suggesting that in modern and complex society each individual has his / her own private "religious universe" and therefore also his / her own "private reality" since individuals no longer depend so much on institutions / religions to provide much needed, ready made, definitions of reality. Berger (1973) reinforced this view stating that " . . . This quest for more satisfactory private meanings may range from extramarital affairs to experiments with exotic religious sects . . . " and calling these phenomena "pluralization of social life worlds." Thus, the complex and pluralized cultural matrix of modern society enables its members to actively search for "privatized beliefs and realities." The quest for alternative centers, and actors' efforts to recentralize their world views and sometimes lifestyles, becomes an essential and vital sociological phenomenon. The act of *choosing* a specific world view, and possibly a transcendency as well, is in itself not easy and includes the probability of changing one's own decision frequently.

Interviews conducted in Israel from June to August with various science fiction fans, Jews who "return" to orthodox Judaism, members of various cults (i.e., Scientology, EMIN, Hare Krishna, "Moonies", and some others) and "consumers" of astrology journals, "palm / coffee" readers and others, indicate clearly that those people gravitate constantly among various centers. Bird and Reimer's (1982) study confirmed that in the U.S. and Canada similar phenomenon exists, which Greeley (1978) calls "Religious Musical Chairs."

The tension between personal decentralization—itself a reflection of a centerless world—and the new quest for elective centers, determines the basic dynamics of the various attempts at "recentering the world." Analysing science fiction and modern occultism as elective centers provides an answer for the problem of timing.

Science fiction and modern occultism can be compared as elective centers using seven factors: 1) the cultural conditions which engender the quest for the beyond; 2) the degree to which science fiction and modern occultism are consciously recognized as elective centers; 3) the degree of structure manifested by science fiction and modern occultism; 4) the degree to which science fiction and modern occultism emerge spontaneously vis-a-vis the degree to which they are sponsored; 5) the "site" of the elective centers; past, future, outside / inside individuals and / or society; 6) mechanisms of attraction, recruitment and entering these elective centers; 7) the possibility that science fiction and modern occultism would serve as a foundation for a new institutional and moral order.

The first factor to be considered is the cultural conditions which engender the modern quest for the beyond.

The present discussion is based on the fact that rather than dealing with a new phenomenon, we are faced with a revival (Jorgensen and Jorgensen 1982). Modern occultists, for example, have added practically nothing to the conception of occult practices, theories or notions, all of which have existed for hundreds of years. Saler even (1977) notes that the category of the "supernatural" itself has been part of Western culture for many years. Science fiction too is an old story.

The *revival* of science fiction and of the occult, their histories, the type of people who are attracted to it and levels of involvement mean that—contrary to what some scholars might think—we are not dealing here with a transitory, unstable cultural "fad." The occult and science fiction have always been an integral and inseparable part of Western civilization (see also Jorgensen and Jorgensen's 1982).

Common to all constituents of the modern "occult explosion," science fiction and adherents to modern myths, is the sharing of an attempt to grasp and arrive at the ultimate "entity" which defies all empirical manifestation. In this sense, the "occult explosion" is religious, but it also negates both conventional religion and science.

O'Dea (1966) defined religion as " . . . the manipulation of non-empirical or supraempirical means for non-empirical or supraempirical ends . . . ," and positivistic science as the manipulation of empirical means for empirical ends. O'Dea's approach, in general, closely recalls that of Weber (1964), for whom the main function of the magician is to cope with relatively *ad hoc* interests and tensions. Magical powers can be "forced" to serve human needs by the magician's correct use of formulas.

Perhaps the corollary to magic would be science fiction, the fantastical, and various modern myths. Several studies have already pointed out that magic and science are—in fact—very similar. Frazer (1922), Tyler (1973), White (1913), Horton (1967), and, of course, Thorndike's (1941) would have it that, historically speaking, magic is necessary for the development of science. Kirsch (1978, p. 157) even states that " . . . The growth of demonology and of the witch hunt mania paralleled that of the scientific revolution . . . " Once magic becomes reality—it is no longer magic, it is science.

The rise of modern magic, however, is in many respects unique. The modern occult consists of a sophisticated technological system supposedly capable of telling its orthodox adherents exactly how to get what. This sophisticated occultist-technological system is usually anchored in a wider belief system. The modern occultist's position is further strengthened because not only does he aim to *use* supernatural forces, but he also claims to *understand* why and how they operate in an attempt to *control* them. The mythical heroes of the modern phantastica, such as Elric of Melnibone the albino, Moorcock's legendary prince, or Niven's heroes are cases in point. Darth Vader, the super bad guy from "Star Wars," probably symbolizes the "ideal" mixture of control over both scientific knowledge as well as the black arts of the Jedi Knights. The occult-technological system is described almost as science—in this sense, it is close to science and competes with it. The

underlying ideological assumptions at stake here constitute a belief system which both resembles and competes with religion. This, in part, explains why the modern occult is being haunted by clergymen and scientists alike. It competes with, and tries to be, both.

The second factor relates to the fact that science fiction and modern occult differ regarding the degree to which these elective centers are consciously recognized as such by the seekers and adherents. In its most intense forms, which find expression in total change of life style as can happen if one joins such cults as a Satanic group, the Church of all Worlds or Scientology, the elective center is very explicit. It can be somewhat less explicit if one's activity is concentrated in the medium involvement level of going to science fiction conventions regularly, joining a fan club or taking part in regular occult-type activities like spiritualism. The other possibility is to have an implicit elective center. That is, those centers which constitute quite vague common notions, uniting adherents into a rather diffuse subculture without real or explicit direction and organization of orientation, attitudes and behavior. In its most popular and widespread form, science fiction, fantasy and modern occultism are probably implicit. Most "adherents" read horoscopes, like to watch a movie (science fiction or occult), read a science fiction book, or even subscribe to journals. This type of superficial involvement provides adherents with an almost instant gratification, clear and strong sense of awe and of the beyond. In this way, most adherents can have, even daily, a small and controllable excursion or escape into an alternative, revitalizing elective center. This excursion is necessarily limited in terms of time, ecology and geography and is not unlike taking some psycho-active substances, like marijuana and alcohol, as a leisure time activity. Both Landsman (1972) and the Panshins (1981) state that science fiction, for example, provides modern society with both mythology and transcendence.

Third, both science fiction and modern occult can provide different degrees of structure for the adherents. When one joins such groups as the "Church of all Worlds," a Satanist group, or Scientology, one obviously has to subjugate one's whole self to a new, rigid and comprehensive imposed structure. This, however, is hardly the typical case. The terms which best describe the amount of structure introduced by both science fiction and modern occultism are harmony and liminality.

While occupying oneself in both science fiction and occultism is certainly considered as somewhat deviant, there is some congruence and legitimacy in pursuing one's desires and needs through the social order which, after all, provides and nourishes science fiction and occultism. Delving into such deviant types of activities will therefore usually not be met with extreme resistance, provided that one does not get too deep into it. On the most popular, widespread level of involvement in the phenomena, harmony exists between the demands of the social order and the individual's needs and desires as they find expression in transitory, controlled interest in science fiction and occultism. The sense of awe, bewilderment, encounter with the unknown, unexplained, the "beyond," maybe even the transcendental, as experienced repeatedly by and in science fiction and occultism, necessarily brings one very close to what O'Dea (1966) called "breaking points," or to a liminal situation (Turner 1977). It becomes impossible to encounter the contents of both science fiction and occultism and remain indifferent, unless one is well shielded or encapsulated in some other strong form of belief. Occult claims, and science fiction, by definition are *made* to create liminal situations. While in most cases these situations are short lived, the tremendously large world contents of both science fiction, fantasy and occultism enable anyone to find his / her own private sphere there and delve more intensely into it, if one so wishes.

Fourth, we have to examine the extent to which science fiction and the modern occult, as elective centers, emerge spontaneously out of the common quest of individual seekers or are sponsored by various entrepreneurs who initiate and build it up, out of spiritual or commercial motives.

Clearly, cults and consumers of science fiction and occult were driven by both spiritual and commercial motives (i.e., Scientology, various Satanist groups). However, for the most popular level of involvement in these phenomena as a subculture, the argument is more complex. (Let us take science fiction first). That there has been increased popular interest and demand for science fiction since the early 1970s can hardly be debated. This need translated itself into two developments. First, tens—perhaps hundreds—of science fiction fan clubs sprang up like mushrooms after a rain. Second, and since the field *is* based on authors, writers, artists, organizers, the movie industry, tourism (for conventions), publishers, and the like, we find that very many commercial interests are deeply rooted in this area. Publishers of science fiction books and magazines have high stakes in this field and they are usually more than willing to contribute support and organize various activities including the initiation or sponsorship of conventions and fan clubs. In a sense, therefore, the need for more and increased activity in science fiction was met on the one hand by and through much spontaneous activity by fans, but also by much sponsored back-up from various agencies and institutions who have real, undeniable, commercial interests in this area.

The modern occult scene presents a similar panorama. There too, spontaneous organizations of clubs was the first activity. However, contrary to science fiction, it seems that the magnitude, scope and intensity of activities in these clubs have always been much lower than in science fiction. The second factor, therefore, that of sponsorship by commercial firms, agencies and interests is much clearer and stronger there. There are specialized stores, magazines, and books through which people can "get into the scene." Most prominent, of course, has been astrology.

Fifth, we have to specify the "site" of the elective center: in the past, the future, outside or inside the individual, inside or outside modern society. Clearly, much of the modern revival of the occult, if not all of it, enjoys finding its original roots in the past, attempting to establish a link between a once glorious past (i.e., the myth of Atlantis), perhaps times and places where magic "really" worked and

today. In this way, much occult activity *boasts* of having "secret" ancient knowledge. Many techniques utilized in various modern activities are said to be remnants, or direct descendants, of "ancient" knowledge. Science fiction is much more future-oriented and thrives on the question of "what if." There are, however, two streams within science fiction which constitute exceptions. The first stream is that which deals with so-called "alternate histories." In it, authors send their heroes back in history to prevent certain events or to act in such a fashion as to change history as we know it. For example, in her book, *Shadow of Earth*, Phyllis Eisenstein assumed that in 1588 the Spanish Armada won the battle against the English fleet, conquered England and assured Spain's domination of the world for centuries. Such a story, and others (see Hacker and Chamberlain 1981 for an exhaustive survey) could blur the distinction between past and future. The other stream is fantasy. While many fantasies take place conveniently, in "alternate realities," not all do, and some of the adventures take place in Earth's past.

The other two categories are more difficult to classify. Both science fiction and occultism are more private than public. A regular, and personal excursion into an alternate reality for a specified period of time is probably what a large part of the "science fiction experience" is all about: a controlled, technologically fantastic encounter with the ultimate. This, basically, is an internal quest through anchoring oneself into a fascinating, enchanted and marvelous ecology. The science fiction experience is a mystical one; it puts romanticism back into cold technology.

Occultism is similar, but also somewhat different particularly an experience of "actual" encounters with such occult "real life" phenomena like ghosts, possessions, reincarnations, trances, seances, automatic writing, UFOs and the like. These experiences are usually not found in science fiction. It is well documented, for example, that encounters with UFO-like phenomena are likely to leave a profound psychological impact on those who experience them. Occult related phenomena can have a deeper, more pervasive experimental impact on an observer than science fiction.

In terms of going outside modern society, it seems that in both cases—occult and science fiction—the establishment of communes and cults provide examples for attempts to go beyond modern society and establish new forms of moral order. However, there is a difference in the basic ethos of these two alternative centers. The occult (and in a similar fashion, fantasy as well) presents adherents with alternative rationality, life styles, belief systems, in many cases very different from conventional beliefs of modern pluralistic, moral orders. Occultism is truly *outside* modern society. Science fiction, on the other hand, takes various existing elements of modern society, or assumed and hypothetical technologies, and makes an extrapolation. Science fiction presents various, more or less extreme, scenarios of "what if . . . ", which are *extensions* of the existing society. While this falls outside modern society, in a strange fashion it is also an extension of it.

Sixth, we have to examine mechanisms of attraction, recruiting and entering elective centers.

The amount of attraction a specific alternative center has for a specific person depends on many factors; the specific type of needs the decentralized person has, his / her personality, the type of demands and benefits the alternative center has and offers respectively.

On the popular widespread levels of involvement in both the occult and science fiction, finding a way to get into it is easy—all one has to do is enter a book store, kiosk, or even take a course in high school, a university or local community center on these topics. Getting more involved, however, demands more skill and effort. To plug into the vast network of science fiction fans, reading a book, or watching a movie will not suffice. As a minimum, one needs to buy or subscribe to a science fiction journal or magazine. There, references can be found to local and national fan clubs, times and places of meetings and conventions. Attending fan club meetings and conventions opens the way for deeper involvement. Almost the same applies to occult-related activities. Other mechanisms include simple advertisements in local newspapers and in the electronic media. In case of communes or cults, other mechanisms are used. The first important mechanism is the one described by Stark and Bainbridge in 1980 as both recruiting through personal networks on the one hand and the new cult / commune's ability to give significant direct rewards to the newly recruited persons, not only in spiritual terms but in such earthly terms as food, shelter, clothing, possibly a career and a sense of purpose.

Seventh, one has to examine the possibility that both science fiction and modern occultism will serve as foundations for a new institutional and moral order.

Obviously, many cults, such as the Church of all Worlds, Satanism, Scientology and others, aim at transforming the world and creating a new social and moral order. Under what conditions would such an effort be developed? There are groups which demand a total change in life style; commune life; various restrictions in terms of food, sex, entertainment; disconnecting oneself from previous friends, original community reference groups and nationality; control over one's private life; offer a career and an alternative lifestyle and have as explicit goals to recruit as many members as possible with an open messianic ideology and total conversion. These groups are usually international in nature and have claims for a new moral order. However, most science fiction and the modern occult subcultures are certainly not like that. For most people, being part of the science fiction and / or occult sub-culture, even with relatively high degrees of involvement, means that they have a meaningful, controlled, enchanted alternative center towards which they can orient themselves whenever they so wish, with very little risk to their otherwise usual and conformist lifestyle in the disenchanted, pluralistic centerless modern world. Thus, although the ability of the occult and science fiction to create an actual, all embracing movement of social change potentially exists, it seems that both types of elective centers—at the present level of popularity—are oriented more towards individual inward experience and less toward actual large-scale social change.

When these subcultures do have an institutional claim it is usually close to one of their areas of interest. For example, science fiction fans like to think of themselves as supporters of space exploration programs. Many modern occultists would support research into such pseudo-sciences as astrology, parapsychology, UFOlogy and reincarnation, and will support groups dedicated to these causes.

The nature of these subcultures is such that hardly any type of institution building takes place there. There are two exceptions. The first consists of cults such as the EMIN and Scientology. The second exception is the fact that in both science fiction and the occult there arose key figures which have helped to organize fan clubs, conventions, study centers, associations and groups dedicated to continued dispersing of occultish or science fiction ideas. These institutions, weak as they are, affect positive recruitment, make the attachment of older members more meaningful and give members a sense of history (which is strongly emphasized in both science fiction fandom and in occult movements) and therefore strengthens the sense of belonging and of purpose.

The question regarding science fiction and the modern occult revival as a source for innovations has another dimension. Shepherd (1970), Tiryakian (1972), Heirich (1910) and Collins (1977) have all suggested that the occult can provide a fertile background and a "seed bed" for new ideas both in science and society. Heirich (1976) even specified the conditions under which a "secularly produced encounter" could lead to conceptual religious breakthroughs that would dissolve the hold of the past ways of experiencing and organizing understanding. Thus, the "occult explosion" could potentially lead to shifts in scientific paradigms.

It is important to notice that the possibility of the occult serving as a source for social innovations is in itself the product of a world view which distinguishes clearly between religion, work and leisure; even in many so-called 'primitive societies', religion is no longer understood as work, or as the worshipping of the deities, but is relegated to leisure activities. It appears that innovation becomes possible when religion is compartmentalized within a wider conception of the world not based on religion per se. In such situations, the existential problems of routine life remain as acute as always, but here they lack clearly articulated formal religious referents—religion is lined up as a sphere of expressive activity alongside leisure activities such as play. In this framework, the occult explosion comes well after the social processes which accompanied the scientific revolution that dismantled, to a large extent, the technology of religion (that is, the coherence and hence efficiency of religion as a belief system).

Why have the occult and science fiction flourished? Can we provide an explanation for the specific *content* and *meaning* of the phenomena?

Traditionally it has always been religion's role to help man cope with difficult existential problems, provide meaning, a basis for community, establish contact with the sacred and prescribe conduct norms. Most sociologists in previous years predicted the disappearance of religion, citing "secularization" as the main indicator for their prediction. While religion, in the classical, conservative connotation of the term (Christianity, Judaism) is probably doomed to experience a problematic existence in the future, this social phenomenon in itself cannot be forced to disappear since the functions met by religion still have to be met. Such problems as powerlessness, scarcity, questions of meaning, quest for community and a transcendental experience must still be solved. In this sense, religion cannot "disappear"; particular *religious forms,* perhaps, might but not that ideological structure which answers various existential problems. "Religion", as a system of related ideas dealing with basic human needs, will always remain (Berger 1969, Luckman 1967).

Furthermore, the scientific revolution of this century has generated and reinforced other problematic trends as well. Along with it there came an unprecedented stress on personal choice and the fashioning of individualistic lifestyles. Urbanization and rapid movement from one dwelling place to another has helped to break the hold of traditional religion on its constituents. Modern America, especially the well-educated and young, emphasizes the search for immediate solutions to existential problems. The emphasis appears to derive more from a folk-tradition of positivistic hard science and technology than it does from traditional religion, with the latter's emphasis on the "living of life" in hope of divine intercession. The crisis we experience is not only "religious" by nature, but scientific as well. In past decades, especially during the 1940s and the 1950s, western science, and the scientific establishment, pretended to have answers to all questions, be they technical, social or otherwise, in their attempt to encompass all aspects of human existence in so-called "scientific rationality." *This* pretension was shattered during the 1960s and 1970s as, for example, various ecologically-oriented groups pointed out some of the disastrous effects of industrialization and of advanced technologies. It became increasingly clear that science, as an ideological system, is incapable of solving existential dilemmas. Science's failure in this regard is very salient against the background of the 1969 human landing on the moon, the rise of the sophisticated military-industrial complex and the realization that science is a cold tool, capable of solving some but not all existential, social or theological philosophical problems. The crisis then is in science's pretension to capably provide answers to religious questions and to satisfactorily relate to issues which go far beyond science.

Both science fiction and the modern occult, as two elective centers, are capable to meet some, if not all, functions mentioned earlier.

The occult explosion consists of the usage of "long-proven" techniques, in a world which is portrayed to be as advanced—and even more so—than ours; it is embedded in an eclectic, cosmic, ideological belief system which allows its human adherents the power of enlisting different deities (or powers) to do things for them (and sometimes even benefit the world). Moorcock's (1961, 1962) heroes exemplify this, as do such myths as ancient astronauts, "pyramid power", Atlantis and others. Alas, the kind of "science" adhered to by these occultists is always antithetical to positivistic science. It uses PSI powers, either (Sigma 1980), "unmeasurable" results, nonempirical

means, irreproducible experiments, and the like. The new occultists seek solutions for ancient existential problems by resorting to ancient, half-true legends, myths and magic. They look for the transcendental, for community, for meaning—and they find it in science fiction, in witchcraft, magic, various myths, sorcery. This is no coincidence. In many cases, the new wave presents a necessary alternative to scientific and traditional religions.

Contrary to some traditional societies, in which the rulers develop restrictions on the accumulation and diffusion of knowledge (realizing that such accumulation could undermine the basic premises of a particular culture), western societies put few restrictions on the accumulation and diffusion of various types of knowledge. In modern societies there is a growing internal socio-economic differentiation within what Shils (1976) called both centers and periphery. This development is connected to changed relations between different types of rationality in modern society. As Eisenstadt (1971) posited, perhaps the major transformation accompanying modernity was the growing secularization of the centers, the "opening up" of their contents and, consequently, a growing interpenetration and

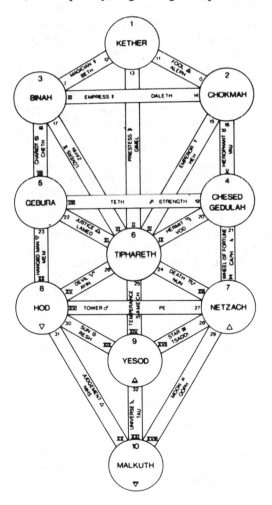

The paths on the Tree of Life, as visualized by members of the Order of the Golden Dawn, an occultist society to which William Butler Yeats belonged.

interdependence between centers and periphery. Thus, modern societies are continuously faced with the basic problem of how to redefine cultural tradition, in general, and how to legitimate it in accordance with broader universalistic orders, in particular. The development of science and technology plays a crucial role in these complex processes as their incorporation into modern societies has its effect on the formation and mastery of the continuously-expanding cosmic, cultural, social and economic orders (Eisenstadt 1971).

The young, educated and sophisticated persons who constitute the zealots of the social phenomena we deal with here face the fundamental existential problems mentioned earlier, as they are at the forefront of various social-technological innovations. Traditional religion's failure to cope successfully with these questions, especially in large urban centers where social change and technological innovations are so visible, has also not escaped their attention. It is no coincidence that the science fiction "boom" and the occult explosion generally characterize large urban centers. There, the attempt to compare contemporary "scientific" phenomena with phenomena of a "cosmic" nature is rife.

However, because the adherents of these theories are intelligent and they do not want to believe and practice the "unbelievable," modern occultists hide their cosmologies behind a strong quasi-scientific cloak, using an "alternate" scientific paradigm—science fiction. This blend is unique in history. It constitutes the abuse of western positivistic science, the re-discovery of "ancient scientific paradigms," the dependence on a strong cosmic and eclectic belief system. Palmer (1979) put this point succinctly when commenting that ". . . Daniken . . . is a caricature of positivism, something that has crawled out from under the damp stones of scientific inquiry . . . closer to soap opera than to science. . . . " It is hardly coincidental that the most commonly heard literary criticism of science fiction literature is that it lacks multidimensional characterization; that the description of its heroes is shallow; and that the *real* hero of science fiction literature is technology, gadgets, machines, inventions, and sometimes even the plot. Considering that science fiction is a reflection of a future-oriented society, committed and devoted to change, it stands to reason that the *real* societal hero *is* change, machines, the future, technology and *not* the human factor. The science fiction books and films of the 1950s emphasized this point, and although it is much less emphasized today, it remains a strong aspect of science fiction and fantasy.

The "occult explosion" also represents the more individualistic search for comparatively immediate solutions to problems, receiving a great boost from the very processes of differentiation and specialization which have been helping to sink traditional religion, and which have been part of the consequences of a technological society, perhaps best exemplified by the modern-day ethos of "how to . . . in 10 easy lessons."

Modern society leaves the individual perplexed, as the scientification of the world does not provide essential answers to existential problems. Reactions to this scientifica-

tion must present some anti-scientific ideas as an alternate paradigm. The particular contemporary blend of science, fiction, and occult, is a direct result of people having been socialized into positivistic science and being unable to provide satisfactory answers to existential problems. Signer and Benassi (1981) for example, state that the rise of the modern occult is the result of inadequate science education. In this sense, the occult-related movement definitely goes against what Weber called "demystification" of the world (especially in the "centers"). This movement *seeks* the beyond, the unexplained and the mystic in the elective center. The success of science fiction and of the occult to meet various existential problems in such a fashion which is attractive to the young corroborate Eisenstadt's (1971) observation that a major theme of protest that develops in modern society is the "anti-rational" and the creation of tendencies of widespread antinomianism. Eisenstadt specifically mentions that this type of protest is not only limited to a small, closed intellectual group, but is commonplace and widespread among novices and aspirants to intellectual status.

The modern occultist, as contrasted with medieval demonologists, does not shy away from supernatural phenomena. He believes in them, wants to prove their existence and, most important of all, to *control* them. Modern occultism offers something traditional religion does not have—an alternative scientific paradigm, coupled with a "scientifically" controlled belief system. A witch is *not* perceived to be a puppet of Satan. On the contrary, it is thought that supernatural forces can in fact be forced to serve the wishes of their human adherents. Modern and sophisticated science fiction, describes alternate universes and galaxies where unknown laws of nature and super-advanced technologies prevail, and brought the art of "creating" new universes (even to the small details of geography, weather, social customs, countries, regimes, and the like) almost to perfection. Thus, Eliade's (1976) note that " . . . the discovery that your life is related to astral phenomena does confer a new meaning on your existence . . . the horoscope shows how you are related to the entire universe . . . " strongly exemplifies the point because our culture is the polar opposite from any order of cosmic unity (Landsman 1972).

The search and craving for the beyond is a manifestation of what Wilson (1979) called "the return of the sacred." By participating in various "esoteric" activities, like science fiction and modern occultism, people gain not only a sense of the transcendental, the beyond, but also a deeper, more complex, mystical and powerful understanding of their own individuality (in terms of selves, identities) vis-a-vis the complex and complicated collectivity of modern society.

However, although the "occult explosion" and science fiction present "anti-demystification" trends, on the one hand, they also present a paradox on the other. Modern occultists do not shy away from supernatural phenomena. Above all, they want to *control* them. *This* aspiration, in the long run, will help demystify the occult. Someone who looks for mystery, the mystic, or the beyond, should at least theoretically, not want to scientifically control it.

Once full control is achieved, the phenomenon can no longer be secret, mystic or irreproducible. It stops being magic and becomes science, pure and simple. Thus while the modern occultist seeks the novel, irreproducible, genuine supernatural experience as a goal, the means which he uses to achieve this goal would eventually render the solution useless and defeat its original purpose. (pp. 1-14)

Nachman Ben-Yehuda, "The Revival of the Occult and of Science Fiction," in Journal of Popular Culture, *Vol. 20, No. 2, Fall, 1986, pp. 1-16.*

OCCULT FICTION

Glen St John Barclay

[*Barclay is a New Zealand-born Australian educator and political historian who has written several works on occultism. In the following excerpt, he considers the appeal of occult fiction to its readers.*]

In many ways, the most mysterious thing about novels of the occult is that there are not more of them. If one understands the term 'occult' to refer to all kinds of phenomena which appear not to be subject to the laws of the physical universe, the opportunities for the storyteller seem to be limitless. Apart from the fact that he can introduce beings which are not limited to merely human capacities but can do literally anything that he wants them to, the author would seem to be under no obligation to make the events or scenes he describes convincing or even authentic. Nor need he be too concerned with characterization: there is really no point in bothering to analyze the motivations of a vampire for example, since vampires do not exist, and since the only motivation attributed to them even in myth is in fact extreme thirst. It is of course possible for the writer of occult fiction to achieve useful effects by enumerating what might seem to be corroborative details, but these are in practice far more impressive when totally imaginary than when extracted from genuine legends the details of which are often uninteresting and almost always in dispute. But the attraction of the occult for the writer of limited ability is not due solely to the fact that it makes so few demands on his industry or his talent. Far more important is the fact that it possesses almost infallible popular appeal.

Various esoteric reasons have been put forward from time to time to explain the continuing popularity of the genre. Peter Penzoldt, for example, refers to Freud's argument that the fear of the supernatural, which he thinks provides the raison d'être for the story of the occult, is based on 'the survival of the ancient animistic beliefs such as the faith in the omnipotence of thought and in instantaneous wish fulfilments.' Penzoldt accordingly concludes that the role of the occult story is to combat a 'secret and persistent faith in the unknown', and that individuals require to be assured continually that 'the horrors we have been con-

templating are naught but fiction', precisely at those times when they are most prone to insist upon their own rationality. Howard P. Lovecraft expressed much the same idea in radically different language, when he claimed:

> the oldest and strongest emotion of mankind is fear . . . men with minds sensitive to hereditary impulse will always tremble at the thought of the hidden and fathomless worlds of strange life which may pulsate in the gulfs beyond the stars, or press hideously upon our own globe in unholy dimensions which only the dead and the moonstruck can glimpse. [*Supernatural Horror in Literature,* in his *Dagon, and Other Macbre Tales*]

There are simpler explanations, quite apart from the fact that Lovecraft's, at least, is totally dishonest. Lovecraft by his own account never believed in his own inventions of strange life beyond the stars, and as an atheist and a materialist certainly never believed that the dead could glimpse anything. The only unholy dimensions pressing upon our own globe of which Lovecraft was ever aware, were those of human existence itself, most aspects and representatives of which he loathed beyond measure. But the fact is that the inherent appeal of the story of the occult lies in its capacity not to exorcize faith in the unknown, but to reinforce it. Any story which in any sense refers to the intervention of the supernatural in human affairs necessarily affirms that the supernatural exists. It holds out the reality of alternative modes and realms of existence beyond the physical limitations of our material life. In doing so, it responds directly to what is certainly man's most abiding concern, the prospect of his own personal annihilation and oblivion in death. The aspect of supernatural fear is, by comparison, of very little relevance indeed. One may be frightened at the prospect of seeing a ghost oneself, through fear of what the effect of such a vision might be upon one's own nerves; but one is always immensely interested and reassured to hear that someone else has had such an experience, since a ghost is *de facto* proof of personal immortality, in however unsatisfactory a form. In any case, it is literally impossible to contemplate any horrors from beyond the grave worse than those which one might encounter at the hands of the living. Anybody given a choice between being assaulted and murdered by a psychopathic street gang, and having an encounter with Dracula, would choose Dracula every time, partly because Dracula can always be repelled by simple defences such as holy water and the sign of the cross, which are notoriously ineffective against human monsters, and also because the unequivocal apparition of a supernatural being would be the most convincing proof possible of one's own possession of a supernatural existence.

Nor does it seem actually true that people turn to occult fiction as a means of reinforcing their confidence in their own rationality. It is obviously impossible to prove statistically any kind of correlation between the popularity of occult stories and the incidence of religious belief. Occult fiction has always been read and it has been read most avidly when it has been written by authors of unusual technical skill, regardless of whether the churches have been full or empty at the time. It is certainly probable that the popularity of occult fiction has never been greater, nor the authority of conventional religion less, than at this present stage in human history; but this situation would seem to support a quite different argument. It would have been difficult in the past for a believer in orthodox Christianity to sustain any kind of serious interest in the occult with a clear conscience, because of the unanimous opposition of the clergy to anybody other than themselves having any dealings with such matters. At the same time, contemporary experience shows clearly that a decline in the authority of orthodox religion is not necessarily accompanied by a decline of faith or hope in the unknown. Exactly the opposite would in fact seem to be the case: individuals turn to the occult in such circumstances with vastly enhanced interest, partly because the conventional prohibitions no longer deter them, but also because of their concern to find reassurances of personal survival which the churches are no longer able to provide convincingly. Moreover, the decline in respect for conventional theology in contemporary times has been accompanied by a decline in respect for conventional science. The clergy have not suffered at the hands of the scientists: they have suffered together at the hands of the parapsychologists. The work of Carl Jung, Arthur Koestler, the Rhines, E. Y. Evans-Wentz, Raymond L. Moody and literally scores of others has helped to create a contemporary mood in which it is positively conventional to accept as a working hypothesis the existence of alternative levels of existence and the occasional practical irrelevance of space and time. In such a climate, the story of the occult becomes positively a potential work of social realism.

The story of the occult has still other grounds of appeal, no less effective for being less respectable. In times when censorship or conventions operated to deter authors from dealing specifically with certain human situations, the occult provided a reservoir of images which could be used to convey symbolically what could not be presented literally. Lesbianism, the physical experience of the orgasm and oral sex in particular could be depicted and their emotional intensity conveyed only under the guise of parables about vampires and ladies, composed by authors who may not always have fully admitted to themselves what they were actually doing. Similarly, Lovecraft's hatred for the vast majority of his fellow-beings, and his revulsion from most of the physical aspects of human life, could be externalized in his visions of slimy and inchoate horrors descending from outer space, or jeering ghouls surfacing in Boston graveyards. Even in less inhibited times, the paraphernalia of certain aspects of the occult provided opportunities to develop fantasies of the physical abuse of women in the pages of ostensibly respectable fiction. Vampirism of course necessarily involved oral assaults on male or female victims by male or female vampires, and the consequent impalement of female vampires by the victims' vengeful relatives. Male vampires, as a point of interest, are customarily beheaded. The ceremony of satanism similarly involved the stripping and physical degradation of women. There are however limits to the extent to which this particular aspect can be developed, simply because there are limits to the number of sadistically interesting things that can be done to the human body: when William P. Blatty describes his heroine masturbating with

a crucifix in *The Exorcist,* one feels that the end of the road might in fact have been reached.

There is another reason for the appeal of the occult, however, the limits of which can never be reached. This is the simple fact that for many people occult experiences form an intrinsic part of human existence, and therefore need to be taken account of in any systematic study of human life. This attitude seems to have been shared by so many writers of undoubted importance that a comprehensive study of the occult in fiction would come very close indeed to being a history of world literature. The occult element emerges even in authors who represent themselves as atheists or agnostics, and deny the presence of any supernatural element in their writings. Thus for example, George Eliot, the author of arguably the greatest English novel of the nineteenth century, and a self-professed realist, who defined realism as 'the doctrine that all truth and beauty are to be attained by a humble and faithful study of nature, and not by substituting vague forms, bred by imagination on the mists of feeling, in place of definite, substantial reality', introduces in *Adam Bede* an episode in which the village carpenter's son hears a sound which brings to his mind the image of a willow wand striking the door of his house. He later finds the drowned body of his father, wedged against a willow tree growing in a brook some distance away. George Eliot does indeed refer to a village superstition that forewarnings of death may be conveyed in this way, but there is no way in which Adam Bede's experience can be interpreted other than as validating the superstition: it is presented as a simple fact of life, which can be nothing other than a precognitive intimation of death.

George Eliot was indeed no writer of ghost stories. Henry James was; but he was also the most self-conscious of literary artists, who made an explicit distinction between his ghost stories and his stories of social realism. It is in one of the latter, *The Portrait of a Lady,* that he describes one of the most frequently reported of occult occurrences, the appearance of the phantasm of the dead to a close friend. Again, there is no possible suggestion of any possible error or hallucination. Indeed, James makes it clear that neither of the two persons involved had any particular belief in the possibility of the survival of the human personality after death: Isabel Archer, the woman who sees the apparition, had been looking forward to death as a release from thought and feeling; and Ralph Touchett, the man who dies, had merely reflected that it was 'all over' with himself. Nor is there any possibility that James, any more than George Eliot, was introducing a mild thrill into his novel to enhance its popularity: nobody who had already persevered to this stage of *The Portrait of a Lady* could possibly be interested in even the mildest of literary thrills. The only possible assumption is that both Henry James and George Eliot believed that such experiences did in fact occur in real life, or at least believed that their readers thought they did.

The most peculiar example of an author who seems to have introduced occult elements into his stories positively against his will is Joseph Conrad, who was even more committed to the ideal of self-conscious literary artistry than Henry James, if that were possible. Nobody could ever believe that Conrad wrote a line for any purpose other than to gratify his own artistic ideals. He also insisted throughout his life on maintaining an unyielding agnosticism, confronting the prospect of death with a total rejection of hope or consolation. Yet Conrad wrote two stories, one of them at least partly autobiographical, in which occult interventions are fundamental to the development of the plot. He did so despite the fact that he insisted in his prefaces to the stories that they were in fact not about the supernatural. He even expressed surprise that more than one critic had been inclined to imagine that *The Shadow Line* was

> intended to touch on the supernatural. . . . But as a matter of fact my imagination is not made of stuff so elastic as all that. . . . Whatever my native modesty may be it will never condescend so low as to seek help for my imagination within those vain imaginings common to all ages and that in themselves are enough to fill all lovers of mankind with unutterable sadness . . . there is nothing supernatural in it.

This is explicit enough. However, it does not alter the fact that *The Shadow Line* is really all about the supernatural. A young officer is appointed skipper of a sailing-ship, following the death of the former captain, a 'stern, grim, wind-tanned, rough, sea-salted, taciturn sailor of sixty-five', who, according to the admittedly fever-stricken mate, had expressed before he died the wish that the ship and its crew would never make port. When the ship unexpectedly runs into a patch of dead calm, about the place where the former captain died, the mate explains that 'it was the fault of the "old man"—the late captain— ambushed down there under the sea with some evil intention'. The calm continues. 'Mysterious currents' drift the ship off course. The new skipper remarks that 'It's like being bewitched, upon my word.' The crew are stricken with fever as well. The wind behaves completely unpredictably: 'just about sunrise we got for an hour an inexplicable, steady breeze, right in our teeth. There was no sense in it. It fitted neither with the season of the year, nor with the secular experience of seamen as recorded in books, nor with the aspect of the sky. Only purposeful malevolence could account for it.' The ship is then battered by an equally unnatural storm, at a time when neither the crew nor the rigging are capable of coping with any new emergency. At this stage the mate appears on deck and challenges the spirit of the dead captain with 'such a loud laugh as I had never heard before. It was a provoking, mocking peal, with a hair-raising, screeching over-note of defiance.' Almost immediately, the wind freshens for the first time in seventeen days, blows 'true, true to a hair', and carries the ship and its crew safely to port. The evil spell has been exorcized.

There is no question but that *The Shadow Line* is presented as a story of the occult, the events of which do not permit natural explanation. Conrad no doubt had his own reasons for pretending otherwise. It was not that he did not know what a story of the occult was: another story of his, *The Inn of the Two Witches,* depends upon the credibility of a warning from beyond the grave. An English naval officer and his coxswain land on the coast of Spain

during the Peninsular War. The officer goes back to the ship, leaving the coxswain to go ahead on his own to a rendezvous with a Spanish guerrilla leader. Returning later to the village where they had landed, the officer puts up for the night at an inn. After locking the door of his room, the officer hears 'the blood beating in his ears with a confused rushing noise, in which there seemed to be a voice uttering the words: "Mr Byrne, look out, sir!" ' He again hears his coxswain's voice 'speaking earnestly somewhere near'. Later, Byrne finds the body of his coxswain in a cupboard. He puts the body on the bed, covers it with a sheet, and resigns himself to sitting up all night, on guard, in a chair. He then sees the baldaquin over the bed 'coming down in short smooth rushes till lowered half way or more, when it took a run and settled swiftly its turtle-back shape with the deep border piece fitting exactly the edge of the bedstead'. This was how the coxswain had died, and the way that he would have died himself, had he not been forewarned by the dead man's spirit. Conrad at least does not try to pretend that this is not a tale of the supernatural. He never refers to it.

There are even more impressive examples of classic authors who have chosen to introduce occult elements into stories presented as works of social realism or at least social commentary. Charles Dickens, like Henry James, wrote stories which were explicitly tales of the supernatural. However, like James, he made a clear distinction between such efforts and his major studies of contemporary urban life. Nonetheless, he introduces into *Our Mutual Friend* the episodes of Mrs Boffin's finding the house full of the faces of its dead owner and his supposedly lost son, and Lizzie Hexham's precognitive intimation of her father's death by drowning. He also began what would unquestionably have been the greatest novel ever written concerned primarily with the intrusion of occult forces in everyday life, if not perhaps with intrusions from beyond the grave: *The Mystery of Edwin Drood.* This novel is presented unequivocally as a psychic duel between two people possessed by paranormal powers. John Jasper, Edwin Drood's uncle and the ultimate wicked uncle of fiction, possesses hypnotic powers which operate unaffected by distance or time, and virtually approximate to telekinesis. Edwin's fiancée, Rosa Budd, with whom he is infatuated, is terrified by him: she tells the other protagonist in the psychic duel, Helena Landless: 'He haunts my thoughts, like a dreadful ghost. I feel that I am never safe from him. I feel as if he could pass in through the wall when he is spoken of.' There is no indication that Dickens meant Rosa's words to be taken literally, but he does make it clear that Jasper is at least able to make Rosa aware of his personality and intentions through particular notes of music, even when his own voice cannot be discerned. He can certainly exert his will over other human beings from a distance, as is seen in the robot-like behaviour of the men who intercept Helena's brother, Neville Landless, outside *The Tilted Waggon.* He may also be able to cast spells upon or somehow affect inanimate objects, as shown by the experience of Canon Chrisparkle, who finds that he has unconsciously wandered to Cloisterham Weir, and that he has 'a strange idea that something unusual hung about the place'. Chrisparkle is unable to see anything unusual by night, but resolves to come back early in the morning, and investigate further. He does so, and promptly notices what he could not have seen at night, Edwin Drood's gold watch and stick-pin, presumably thrown there by Jasper, who has used his psychic powers to have them discovered by Chrisparkle, so that Drood's disappearance will be attributed to murder, and Landless hopefully blamed for it.

His opponent, Helena, is understood to have powers fully capable of matching Jasper's own. She is certainly telepathic: as her brother tells Chrisparkle: 'You don't know, sir, yet, what a complete understanding can exist between my sister and me, though no spoken word—perhaps hardly as much as a look—may have passed between us. She not only feels as I have described, but she very well knows that I am taking this opportunity of speaking to you, both for her and for myself.' Chrisparkle has his doubts, but observes on re-entering the house that between Helena and her brother an instantaneous recognition passed, in which Mr Chrisparkle saw, or thought he saw, the understanding that had been spoken of, flash out'. This scene is followed by the episode of Rosa's collapse while singing to Jasper's accompaniment, apparently because of the psychic impact of a note which Jasper keeps playing or hinting at in the music. Drood then asks Helena if she would not be afraid of Jasper under similar circumstances, to which she replies: 'Not under any circumstances.' Similarly, when Rosa confesses to Helena her fear that Jasper could pass in through the wall, Helena embraces her so that her 'lustrous gipsy-face drooped over the clinging arms and bosom, and the wild black hair fell down protectingly over the childish form. There was a slumbering gleam of fire in the intense dark eyes, though they were then softened with compassion and admiration. Let whomsoever it most concerned look well to it!' Jasper is obviously to meet his match in the psychic contest. The most probable and certainly the simplest manner in which this would have come about would have been for Helena to confront Jasper after Drood's murder, and extract a full confession from him by exerting her will upon his through hypnosis. The circumstances of the duel would be made more acceptable by the fact that the two adversaries both have associations with the mysterious East: both are described in terms implying Eurasian origins; and Jasper is very clearly acting out the role of a Thug, although Dickens had not yet given any hint as to what element in Jasper's parentage or experiences might account for this obsession. Helena and her brother on the other hand come from Ceylon, and it is suggested that they might have native blood.

There is a melancholy appropriateness in the fact that what might on every account have been the best mystery story of the occult ever written was doomed to remain a mystery forever. It certainly remains the major effort in the genre by a great novelist, although it is not perhaps the major novel in which occult intrusions occur. That distinction undoubtedly belongs to Tolstoy's *Anna Karenina,* whose fundamental plot is in fact the fulfilment of a precognitive dream. In chapter twenty-nine Anna has an intimation of her own death when the train in which she is returning to St Petersburg stops at the station: 'there was a terrible screech and clatter, as though someone were being torn to pieces; then a red light blinded her eyes, and at last a wall rose up and blotted everything out. Anna felt as if she were falling from a height. But all this, far from seeming dreadful, was rather pleasant.' Later in the novel Anna's lover, Count Vronsky, dozes off in a mood in which

> memories of the disreputable scenes he had witnessed during the last few days became confused and merged with a mental image of Anna and of a peasant who had played an important part as beater in the bear-hunt. . . . He awoke in the dark, trembling with horror, and hurriedly lighted a candle. 'What was it? What was the dreadful thing I dreamed? Yes, I know. The peasant-beater—a dirty little man with a matted beard—was stooping down doing something, and of a sudden he began muttering strange words in French. Yes, there was nothing else in the dream,' he said to himself. 'But why was it so awful?' He vividly recalled the peasant again and the incomprehensible French words the man had uttered and a chill of horror ran down his spine.

He goes to see Anna, without telling her of the dream. She however tells him that she knew that she was going to die and set him free, because she had had a dream about it herself.

> 'Yes, a dream,' she said. 'A dream I had a long time ago. I dreamed that I ran into my bedroom to fetch something or find out something. . . . And, in the bedroom, in the corner, stood something. . . . And the something turned around and I saw it was a peasant with a tangled beard, little and dreadful-looking. I wanted to run away, but he stooped down over a sack and was fumbling about in it with his hands. . . . And all the time he was rummaging, he kept muttering very quickly, in French, you know, rolling his r's: *Il faut le battre, le fer; le broyer, le petrir. . . .*'

The intimations all come together when Anna at last kills herself by throwing herself under the St Petersburg train. 'She tried to get up, to throw herself back; but something huge and relentless struck her on the head and dragged her down on her back. "God forgive me everything!" she murmured, feeling the impossibility of struggling. A little peasant muttering something was working on the rails.' One supposes that the words which the peasant was muttering, the words which Vronsky had not been able to recall when he dreamed of the event and which Anna could not possibly have heard at the actual moment of her death, were the words she had heard in her dream and remembered from it: 'The iron must be beaten, pounded, kneaded. . . . ' It is important to note that none of these intimations are presented at all symbolically, as Dickens presents the railroad as an image of death in *Dombey and Son,* in which Carker the manager is in fact killed by a train: as in all the other examples discussed, the occult intrusions in *Anna Karenina* are presented as realities, experienced by real people in real life.

It is perhaps unnecessary to prolong the list. The fact is that many and perhaps most of the major novelists concerned with presenting authentic visions of the human experience, have felt required to include occult intrusions as elements in that experience. On the other hand, it is also true that the occult element is nearly always peripheral or at least unobtrusive. Only Dickens seems to have regarded it as worthwhile to attempt a full-length novel in which the occult was to provide the major element. The reasons are not difficult to imagine. A serious novelist is concerned with human life as it is actually experienced in society; and in any human life lived in the company of other human beings the occult can by definition play only a peripheral and unobtrusive part, if it plays any part at all. The physical universe may indeed be an illusion; but it is an illusion which most of us are compelled to accept as a reality we have to come to terms with for all but a few fleeting moments of our waking lives.

On the other hand, there have been writers who have devoted most or even all of their literary output exclusively to the occult. Most of them have been very bad and very unimportant, and it is reasonable to assume that their chief motivations have been lack of ability to work in any other area of fiction, or the simple desire to make money in the easiest possible way, by cultivating their readers' fears or prurience. But there are still others who by their treatment of occult themes have somehow managed to create or revivify legends, or have themselves become legends in their own lifetimes. They include some of the most popular and certainly most assiduously emulated and plagiarized authors of the past hundred years. They are remarkable phenomena in their own right, and as such they are certainly worth close investigation. They might even have a message for us. (pp. 7-21)

> Glen St John Barclay, "The Lure of the Occult," *in his* Anatomy of Horror: The Masters of Occult Fiction, *Weidenfeld and Nicolson, 1978, pp. 7-21.*

Peter B. Messent

[*In the following excerpt, Messent defines some of the traits and concerns of occult fiction.*]

Farrell comments perceptively in Peter Beagle's humorous work *Lila the Werewolf,* "You could have either werewolves or Pyrex nine-cup percolators in the world, but not both, surely." This tension between what Sir Walter Scott called in his introduction to Walpole's *The Castle of Otranto* the "appeal to that secret and reserved feeling of love for the marvellous and supernatural, which occupies a hidden corner in almost every one's bosom" and "the dissipating sights and sounds of everyday life," lies at the very foundation of occult literature.

Coleridge used his phrase "willing suspension of disbelief" with direct application to the sense of the supernatural, and in doing so posited two entirely separate worlds, that of Pyrex percolators and that of werewolves, if you like. I would suggest that, in its purest form, the literature of the occult operates in that area where these two worlds clash head on—that sense of radical disjunction, that *thrill,* the sensation of numbing dislocation which arises at that point of intersection between two separate worlds,

Playwright Stanisław Wyspiański's illustrations of Fire *and* Air, *two of the four elements of which occultist philosophers believed all matter was composed. The balance of fire and air with water and earth in an object or creature was thought to determine its character and destiny.*

the material and the supernatural. It is this sense of *fracture* which provides the real power of this type of literature. This sensation is equivalent in some regards to that which Richard Wilbur finds in different form in Edgar Allan Poe's "Dream-Land" with its

> Bottomless vales and boundless floods,
> And chasms, and caves, and Titan woods, . . .

> Mountains toppling evermore
> Into seas without a shore;. . . .

Wilbur analyzes what occurs when the reader is confronted with those initial words: "The factual sense of the word 'vale' is instantly blasted by the adjective 'bottomless.' " Poe, Wilbur claims, short-circuits the intellect by his use of language, "inviting a mystic illumination," transporting the reader to "a realm of unimaginable unities in which 'bottomless' and 'vale' are compatible."

This same "blasting" of the reader is what occurs in occult fiction, but here no "realm of unimaginable unities" results. The distinction between natural and supernatural remains absolutely apparent—indeed, becomes the very *point* of the genre. This separation lies at the heart of perhaps the most widespread form of occult fiction, the ghost story. In such stories we move from that solid matter-of-factness which goes to make up the convention we call realism—in Henry James's words, "the lawn and the bright flowers and the crunch of my wheels on the gravel and the clustered tree tops over which the rooks circled and cawed"—to jarring superimpositions of the world of the other—"a view of the back of the tapestry," as the governess in James's *Turn of the Screw* calls it. That phrase will serve to sum up the method of occult literature: in terms of normal and paranormal, it makes both sides of the tapestry equally visible; and when these sides *touch* the dislocating effect occurs.

To illustrate with two examples: In Jasper John's "The Seeker of Souls" the opening paragraph presents us with two worlds, the visible and the normal and the invisible and occult, both equally "there" but separate:

> It was in a deathly silence that we awaited the coming of the hour that would release the evil thing. I heard someone cough, and it echoed through the house. The clock ticked away the minutes with a grim satisfaction, and my neighbour breathed in a noisy fashion. But for once I was grateful for both sounds; they were something ordinary and commonplace, belonging to everyday life.

Despite an element of cliché which intrudes here and elsewhere ("Philip had heard whisperings of ghosts, . . . but what Englishman could believe those things?"), the discontinuity between the two worlds becomes evident within the sentence structure itself. The "evil thing" and the "ordinary and commonplace" command our attention from the start. When the two worlds meet, when the "evil thing" in this case actually appears in the mundane setting, the literature of the occult exercises its characteristic effect.

In Edith Nesbit's "Man Size in Marble," these properties of the traditional ghost story are again present. There is the ritual insistence on "the truth" of the episode to be recounted, even though the narrator expects disbelief from a skeptical audience: "Although every word of this story is as true as despair, I do not expect people to believe it. Nowadays [the story was published in 1893] a 'rational explanation' is required before belief is possible." Next, the tale itself gives us a young honeymoon couple living in an ivy-covered cottage in a small village—the homely and mundane stratum, as in "The Seeker of Souls." In the local church, however, lie marble figures of knights in full armor, knights who, as

> the peasants told of them, . . . had been guilty of deeds so foul that the house they had lived in—the big house, by the way, that had stood on the site of our cottage—had been stricken by lightning and the vengeance of Heaven. But for all that, the gold of their heirs had bought them a place in the church.

Not, be it noted, a place that could *contain* them. On All Saints' Eve, as the peasants liked to put it, "them two bodies sits up on their slabs, and gets off of them, and then walks down the aisle, *in their marble*" to go back to their old home. If anyone should meet them in the process, it is suggested, something disastrous would occur—its nature remaining typically ill defined.

All Saints' Eve, the witching hour, comes. The narrator fails to take the precautions laid down by folk tradition to ward off the approach of evil. He visits the local church by moonlight to find with a sickening shock that the "bodies drawed out man-size" *are gone,* and their marble slabs lie "bare." Rushing home, filled with intimations of disaster, he collides with the local doctor. He, with his "six feet of common sense," insists that the narrator has imagined the whole thing, and, sure enough, on returning to the church, they find the "two shapes" lying on their slabs—one of them, however, lacking a hand. The protagonist's mind is eased by the sight of the figures, but when he returns home he finds doors open, candles blazing, his wife dead, a "look of frantic fear and horror on her face"—her hands tightly clenched. The climactic last lines of the story give the final turn of the occult screw:

> When I was quite sure that she was dead, and that nothing mattered at all any more, I let [the doctor] open her hand to see what she held. It was a grey marble finger.

It is here, at the very last, that the two worlds—natural and supernatural—*collide.* Neither world would appear to admit the other, but there we are, left finally with a cold and tangible object, the presence of which cannot be rationally explained. Through persuading the reader, nonetheless, of this presence (in this case and in that of the majority of ghost stories) the literature of the occult achieves its point.

If, then, occult literature stems initially from a point of intersection between "realistic" and rationally "unexplainable," it obviously has a relation to the fantastic, a more inclusive type of literature defined by Tzvetan Todorov in *The Fantastic: A Structural Approach to a Literary Genre.* . . . Todorov's impressive analysis of the fantastic and of the concept of literary genres ("precisely those relay-points by which the work assumes a relation with the universe of literature") provides us with an excellent starting point for fixing the literature of the occult within a larger context.

Todorov's initial definition of the fantastic is as follows:

> In a world which is indeed our world, the one we know, a world without devils, sylphides or

vampires, there occurs an event which cannot be explained by the laws of this same familiar world.

Two choices remain open then. Either the protagonist who experiences this event is "a victim of an illusion of the senses" or the event really took place: "it is an integral part of reality—but . . . this reality is controlled by laws unknown to us."

> The fantastic occupies the duration of . . . [our] uncertainty. Once we choose one answer or the other, we leave the fantastic for a neighboring genre, the uncanny or the marvelous. . . .

[These] two neighboring genres are distinguished. In the uncanny,

> events are related which may be readily accounted for by the laws of reason, but which are, in one way or another, incredible, extraordinary, shocking, disturbing, or unexpected.

In the marvelous, the story ends

> with an acceptance of the supernatural, . . . supernatural elements provoke no particular reaction in either the characters or in the implicit reader. It is not an attitude toward the events described which characterizes the marvelous, but the nature of these events.

Todorov then distinguishes two subgenres lying *between* the three forms already mentioned: the "fantastic-uncanny" and the "fantastic-marvelous."

The literature of the occult may be defined, in direct relation to this latter "fantastic-marvelous," as a genre which deals with events occurring "in a world which is indeed our world": events which *shock*, which cannot be explained according to "the natural laws of this same familiar world," yet do take place. Such a genre, like Todorov's "fantastic," may then shade off in two quite different directions.

For first, of course, the occult phenomenon may be presented with a certain ambiguity. In such tales as James's *Turn of the Screw*, Le Fanu's "Green Tea," Poe's "Fall of the House of Usher," and Lovecraft's "Rats in the Wall," the reader is left hanging between a supernatural and a psychological interpretation of the events presented. Is the governess in James's story, for example, a reliable witness? Are the ghosts of Peter Quint and Miss Jessel really *there* or merely products of her overwrought imagination? No conclusive answer can be given to these questions. In Todorov's terms, the fantastic-marvelous is replaced here by the "fantastic" itself, which depends for its effect on exactly this kind of ambiguity. This is one way in which the "pure" occult may be modified.

Another category of fictions shades off in the direction of what we know as romance. But here a distinction becomes necessary. One type of romance, a type that falls *outside* the category of the occult, is described by Hawthorne in his "Custom House" introduction to *The Scarlet Letter*. Writing of "moonlight" as the "medium the most suitable for a romance writer," he goes on to observe:

> There is the little domestic scenery of the well-

known apartment, the chairs, with each its separate individuality; the centre-table, sustaining a work-basket, a volume or two. . . . all these details, so completely seen, are so spiritualized by the unusual light, that they seem to lose their actual substance. . . . Nothing is too small or too trifling to undergo this change. . . . A child's shoe; the doll, seated in her little wicker carriage, . . . whatever, in a word, has been used or played with during the day is now invested with a quality of strangeness and remoteness, though still almost as vividly present as by daylight. Thus, therefore, the floor of our familiar room has become *a neutral territory somewhere between the real world and fairyland, where the Actual and the Imaginary may meet, and each imbue itself with the nature of the other. Ghosts might enter here without affrighting us.* [My emphasis]

What Hawthorne suggests is that romance, in this sense, can bridge the gap between natural and supernatural, actual and imaginary. The material world evaporates as we enter that "neutral territory" where the distinction between realistic and supernatural becomes ambiguous. This type of romance belongs to fantasy, that area where the solid substance of everyday life disappears, where actual probabilities give way to a world in which real and fantastic shimmer together and imagination becomes more central than fact.

Occult literature on the contrary insists on the *fracture* between real and supernatural. It therefore includes only that form of romance—"a new species of romance," Walpole called it—which insists on this consciousness of dislocation. When "imagination and improbability" intrude violently upon "a strict adherence to common life" (to modify Walpole's terms somewhat), we reach the species of romance which is found within, if to one side of, my definition of occult literature. So, for example, in *Dracula*, as in *The Castle of Otranto*, exotic settings, atmospheric effects, and a style of character depiction which we associate with the romantic do not finally destroy the occult effects produced within the texts. Indeed, this type of romance pays a great deal of attention to furnishings, the actual materials which go to make up the presented world—the description, right down to *"Whitaker's Almanac,"* of the English books in the count's library in *Dracula*, for example. Once we are placed in such a world of predictable possibility as these particulars suggest, we are prepared for the dislocatory thrill that results when the unpredictable—be it gigantic helmet or living dead—intrudes. Though the environmental trappings and atmospheric effects used in this kind of romantic fiction diminish the gap between natural and supernatural, and therefore the degree of occult disjunction, that disjunction is still clearly present. Hence this type of romance belongs within the genre. (pp. 2-8)

[The] subject matter of spiritualism fits directly into my conception of occult literature in a way denied to the Christian literary tradition, indeed to the literature of religion generally. Spiritualism is concerned, not with formal codes of belief, but with phenomenal apparitions.

The stage properties of the spiritualist meeting—revolving tables, accordions playing, bodies levitating, apparitions, and the like—all insist upon exactly that meeting of two separate worlds, the material and the other, which constitutes the occult. The radical disharmony which occurs in these convergences of visible and invisible was effectively—if ironically—formulated by John Delaware Lewis in *Once a Week* (August 18, 1860) where he asked:

> Are the secrets of the invisible world, concealed for so many thousands of years from mortal ken, now for the first time to be made plain to us through the agency of our household furniture? Are mahogany tables the apostles of the new faith, and brass bells and accordions its missionaries? Will an outlay of ten shillings and sixpence, and the engagement of a celebrated medium, procure for us an interview with the soul of a departed father, mother, husband, wife, in the midst of a London drawing-room, with the Hansom cabs rattling outside, and the servants standing in waiting with the tray of sandwiches and sherry?

Secrets of the invisible world circulating among trays of sandwiches and sherry! This is the crossroads where occult literature thrives. On the same grounds, the whole literature of werewolves, vampirism, and other assorted monsters fits the genre, provided means are given by which the abnormal may be measured against the normal. This suggests the reason why the most successful monsters in the history of the horror movie tend to be those most recognizably human, the human image then drastically distorted physically (Karloff's Frankenstein monster) or physiologically (Lugosi's Count Dracula).

In Stoker's *Dracula,* tension between the expected and the unexpected is developed as "Kodak views" of the estate at Purfleet are discussed by the brisk though rather uncomfortable young Englishman Jonathan Harker in the exotically furnished, vast ruined castle of Count Dracula, Transylvanian aristocrat. The tension grows of course as Dracula is shown in action in a nineteenth-century Victorian setting, and the occult powers of the undead are set directly against the powers of Van Helsing, philosopher and metaphysician—"one of the most advanced scientists of his day"—protector of the sexual, moral, and social norms of the society. As Mark Hennelly points out in "*Dracula:* The Gnostic Quest and Victorian Wasteland," Dracula is in many ways an alter ego of Van Helsing; likewise the occult world of Count Dracula is in many ways a direct representation of the nightside of the Victorian consciousness. The placing of the supernatural against the natural reverberates throughout the entire fiction, an opposition extending beyond the story to take in alternative visions of both society and morality. "Occultism is the philosophy of hidden matters," the *Encyclopedia Americana's* definition begins. Vampirism in *Dracula* is thus an entry point into an entire alternative universe. The journey to Dracula's castle begins, as Leonard Wolf suggests in his *Dream of Dracula: In Search of the Living Dead,* with

> the voyage of a candid, clear-eyed, honest Englishman [who is] moving deeper and deeper into a psychological landscape in which darkness, deceit and ancient superstition are as natural as breathing.

In literature of the occult the supernatural is more often associated with the powers of darkness than with those of light. The reality at the very core of this kind of fiction is the power of the diabolic to show itself and effectively disrupt the normal patterns of life, set against the power of the human mind to deny and combat such disruption. Images of disaster are never far from the surface. Matthew Lewis's novel *The Monk,* for example, climaxes with a powerful demonic agency bringing ruin:

> Darting his talons into the monk's shaven crown, he sprang with him from the rock. The caves and mountains rang with Ambrosio's shrieks. The daemon continued to soar aloft, till reaching a dreadful height, he released the sufferer. Headlong fell the monk through the airy waste: the sharp point of a rock received him; and he rolled from precipice to precipice, till, bruised and mangled, he rested on the river's banks.

Ambiguities of power lie very much at the heart of this fiction. Power struggles between God and the Devil, or, to offer a secular and peculiarly contemporary parallel, between forces of sanity, rationality, and stability and what might be called, in Pynchon's terms, "the brute Other," are obsessively traced. The Faustian pact (with its concomitant, the search for secret knowledge) is one of the staples of the genre. G. R. Thompson, in "A Dark Romanticism: In Quest of a Gothic Monomyth," defines the Gothic as "demonic-quest romance," and this suggestion of a demonic quest pervades the entire field of occult literature. The role of magician, transformed, as the processes of the natural universe became more comprehensible, into that of scientist, has always been associated with power—a power which attempts to penetrate to the heart of the mystery of the universe, a power too which seeks mastery over the minds and hearts of others.

This concern evidences itself clearly in Mary Shelley's *Frankenstein.* This story, like Stevenson's *Dr. Jekyll and Mr. Hyde* and Arthur Machen's "Novel of the White Powder," lies on the boundary line and combines the characteristics of two genres, science fiction and the occult. Similarly, Victor Frankenstein bridges in his education two worlds, the occult ("secret stores of knowledge" revealed in the works of Paracelsus and of Cornelius Agrippa, author of *De Occulta Philosophia libri tres*) and the "enlightened and scientific." In fact, Frankenstein brings the methods of science to the matter of the occult. Soon convinced of the uselessness of the ancient system whose powers he now sees to be "chimerical," he is still impressed by its objectives: to seek "immortality and power; such views, although futile, were grand." He therefore undertakes to see what can be done with the new science of modern chemistry:

> The ancient teachers of this science . . . promised impossibilities and performed nothing. The modern masters promise very little; they know that metals cannot be transmuted, and that the elixir of life is a chimera. But these philosophers, whose hands seem only made to dabble in dirt, and their eyes to pour [sic] over the microscope or crucible, have indeed performed miracles. They penetrate into the recesses of nature, and

shew how she works in her hiding places. They ascend into the heavens; they have discovered how the blood circulates, and the nature of the air we breathe. They have acquired new and almost unlimited powers; they can command the thunders of heaven, mimic the earthquake, and even mock the invisible world with its own shadows.

Frankenstein uses the techniques of "modern chemistry," though these techniques remain remarkably unspecified, to accomplish the grand designs of the occultists:

> I succeeded in discovering the cause of generation and life; nay, more, I became myself capable of bestowing animation upon lifeless matter.

Science fiction is described by Todorov as "the supernatural . . . explained in a rational manner but according to laws which contemporary science does not acknowledge." If we accept this definition, we can see that Frankenstein fits it only partially. The supernatural—the "abhorred monster"—is brought into existence scientifically, by purely human hands, but the lack of any real scientific detail, the use of the language not of science but of the occult ("I . . . disturbed with profane fingers, the tremendous secrets of the human frame"), and, most of all, the infusion of the monster with "spirit"—something absolutely unexplainable by scientific law—leads the reader back to those occult sciences to which previous reference has been made. Frankenstein's grand scheme—to create human life itself—and the "power" which is a direct consequence of this are presented throughout the remainder of the book not in scientific but in diabolic terms. An alternative to divine creation is offered as Frankenstein infuses "a spark of being" into mere "lifeless matter." His monster then stalks the pages of the novel disrupting normal patterns of individual and family life and placed in a relationship with his master directly patterned, as Harold Bloom suggests, on that between Satan and God in *Paradise Lost*. The presentation of the relationship between monster and master—

> I am thy creature and I will be even mild and docile to my natural lord and king, if thou wilt also perform thy part, the which thou owest me. . . . Remember that I am thy creature: I ought to be thy Adam; but I am rather the fallen angel, whom thou drivest from joy for no misdeed.

—and the portrayal of Victor Frankenstein's dark powers consistently imply a diabolic context. This particular "fallen angel," and his creator who ("like the archangel who aspired to omnipotence") ends up "chained in an eternal hell," belong first and foremost to occult rather than science-fiction traditions. The latter, to use Kingsley Amis's definition,

> treat of a situation that could not arise in the world we know, but which is hypothesised on the basis of some innovation in science or technology, or pseudo-science or pseudo-technology, whether human or extra-terrestrial in origin.

Obviously there is a crucial distinction to be made between "some innovation in science" and the living, breathing, anguished monster seen in Mary Shelley's novel. Yet the line between the occult and the scientific remains here a narrow one.

In both *Frankenstein* and *Dracula* the concept of a power struggle between universal forces of darkness and light is accented by the figure of the alien, a figure whose features have distinguished occult literature from *Melmoth the Wanderer* to Anne Rice's *Interview with the Vampire*. Devendra P. Varma in his article "Quest of the Numinous: the Gothic Flame" describes as one type of Gothic villain

> the terrible "superman" whose ways lie in darkness and whose strength originates far beyond mortal thoughts. He is a new mintage of the Satan portrayed by Milton in *Paradise Lost*—the immortal outcast, a masterful, vaunting villain, his spirit unbroken even in defeat. He is the Rosicrucian, the Alchemist staking his very life on some dark hope, and behind him is all the mystery of Cabbala, Freemasonry, Medieval Satanism.

One branch of occult literature derives from the Gothic in its continuing use of this "immortal outcast," this "masterful, vaunting villain." Where the hidden forces of the universe are gathered up into a human or quasi-human figure such as Frankenstein or Dracula, the status of the figure as "outsider" is insisted on throughout the text. Thus Frankenstein's experiment with the monster shatters his own connections with the "magnetic chain of humanity": he is left metaphorically tied to his grotesque creation, pursuer and pursued symbiotically linked in that Arctic wasteland in which their story ends. At the same time, one must not overlook the fact that here and in much other occult fiction a curiously ambivalent stance, containing elements of both sympathy and repulsion, is taken toward the dark protagonist as he embarks on what G. R. Thompson calls, in relation to Gothic fiction as a whole, his "metaphysical quest."

Dracula, too, is the very image of the "terrible 'superman'" of which Varma speaks; as Van Helsing informs his colleagues:

> This vampire which is amongst us in of himself so strong in person as twenty men; he is of cunning more than mortal, for his cunning be the growth of ages; he have still the aids of necromancy, . . . he is devil in callous, and the heart of him is not; he can, within limitations, appear at will when, and where, and in any of the forms that are to him; he can, within his range, direct the elements, . . . if we fail in this our fight he must surely win; and then where end we? . . . to fail here, is not mere life or death. It is that we henceforward become foul things of the night like him—without heart or conscience, preying on the bodies and the souls of those we love best. To us forever are the gates of heaven shut. . . . We go on for all time abhorred by all; a blot on the face of God's sunshine; an arrow in the side of Him who died for man.

The terminology used in this novel consistently opposes the diabolic to the Christian. Dracula, alien to all conventional familial, social, and sexual patterns, has a terrible strength which threatens a supernatural disruption of what we call normality.

This disruption assumes another form in the ghost story and in those tales of horror which involve the entry into the world of normality of some supernatural presence. Jack Sullivan's thesis about the ghost story in his *Elegant Nightmares: The English Ghost Story from Le Fanu to Blackwood* . . . can usefully be extended to take in a large number of tales of supernatural horror. Sullivan suggests that in those mysterious forces which haunt and sometimes terrorize the protagonists of such tales, we have a manifestation of a "principle of disorder" that gradually dismembers "the narrator's comfortably structured world":

> The ghost story . . . begins by assuming that life is rational and morally ordered, then begins to worry about that assumption when something inexplicably threatening creeps in.

We move here from the idea of a universe in which the angelic and the diabolic are at battle to a concept perhaps more suited to the modern age, that human forms of order are in fact continually threatened by the chaotic and anarchic forces of a hostile and random universe—another version perhaps of Henry Adams's view of Chaos as "the law of nature," Order as "the dream of man."

Throughout the history of occult writing, efforts have occasionally been made to define the emotions to which it appeals and which it feeds. H. P. Lovecraft's extended essay *Supernatural Horror in Literature* . . . concentrates on this particular aspect of the occult tale, making the decisive test

> whether there be excited in the reader a profound sense of dread, . . . a subtle attitude of awed listening, as if for the beating of black wings or the scratching of outside shapes and entities on the known universe's utmost rim.

Mrs. Radcliffe anticipates this conclusion, using for her test the writer's ability to move beyond terror to horror:

> They must be men of very cold imaginations with whom certainty is more terrible than surmise. Terror and horror are so far opposite, that the first expands the soul, and wakens the faculties to a high degree of life; the other contracts, freezes, and nearly annihilates them. I apprehend that neither Shakespeare nor Milton by their fictions, nor Mr. Burke by his reasoning, anywhere looked to positive horror as a source of the sublime, though they all agree that terror is a very high one; and where lies the great difference between horror and terror, but in uncertainty and obscurity, that accompany the first respecting the dreader evil? ["On the Supernatural in Poetry", *New Monthly Magazine,* Volume 7, (1826)]

More recently, Barton Levi St. Armand in *The Roots of Horror in the Fiction of H. P. Lovecraft* has usefully expanded and developed Mrs. Radcliffe's definitions, claiming that both terror and horror are equally "annihilating" emotions:

Terror expands the soul outward; it leads us to or engulfs us in the sublime, the immense, the cosmic. We are, as it were, lost in the ocean of fear or plunged directly into it, drowning of our dread. What we lose is the sense of self. That feeling of "awe," which traditionally accompanies intimations of the sublime, links terror with experiences that are basically religious in nature, like those annihilating confrontations with the numinous that Otto explores in *The Idea of the Holy,* . . . horror is equally annihilating, but from a dramatically different direction. Horror overtakes the soul from the inside; consciousness shrinks or withers from within, and the self is not flung into the exterior ocean of awe but sinks in its own bloodstream, choked by the alien salts of its inescapable prevertebrate heritage.

The intrusion, then, of the mysterious, the other, the supernatural within the context of everyday life; the clash between rational and irrational, dark forces and light; the knowledge through direct revelation of a universe directed by forces beyond our comprehension; a state of the emotions that may itself be a conflict between elements positive and negative: these factors characterize a form of literature which . . . has in a curiously tenacious manner continued to hear the "scratching of outside shapes . . . on the known universe's utmost rim." (pp. 8-16)

> *Peter B. Messent, in an introduction to* Literature of the Occult: A Collection of Critical Essays, *edited by Peter B. Messent, Prentice-Hall, Inc., 1981, pp. 1-16.*

OCCULT DRAMA

Daniel Gerould and Jadwiga Kosicka

[*In the following excerpt, Gerould and Kosicka define the various types of occultist drama.*]

As our own turn of the century draws closer—and already rumblings are heard some twenty years in advance of the precise epicenter—we are experiencing a vast revival of interest in the symbolist art and literature of the last fin de siècle. Esoteric painters and writers, long declared obscure and consigned to oblivion, have been rehabilitated and publicly acclaimed. In the field of theatrical performance, rediscovery proceeds at a slower pace. Burdened with audiences, actors, and a variety of material requisites, the stage seems at first glance inimical to the visionary.

Yet in our own time we can discern—although still in a highly tentative form—an attempted revival of the sort of spiritual theater that was first proposed at the last turn of the century, doubtful though it may be whether these modern practitioners are fully conscious of all the precedents which they are following. Take, for example, the Om Theater's *The Cosmic Mass,* performed at the Cathedral of St. John in New York as part of the World Spiritual Summit Conference V in October 1975 after having been first presented on the mountain summits of Chamonix-Mont Blanc the previous summer. Combining drama, music, song, dance, and meditation, *The Cosmic Mass* was structured as an immense pageant and processional dedicated to the celebration of spiritual oneness.

Now the very concept of a mystical multimedia spectacle performed among high mountain peaks inevitably leads us back to those extraordinary endeavors to theatricalize the unseen that animated the most advanced European drama in the years around 1900. Contemporary resurgence of occult drama provides a fitting occasion to explore some forgotten turn-of-the-century antecedents, particularly those strange visionary dramas that were created in Eastern Europe as old empires approached the whirlwind of war, revolution, and apocalypse and everyone awaited the coming end of a dying world.

Andrei Bely's *Jaws of Night* and *He Who Has Come,* Valerii Briusov's *The Earth,* Alexander Scriabin's *Prefatory Action* and *Mysterium,* Stanisław Wyspiański's *November Night* and *Acropolis,* Tadeusz Miciński's *The Revolt of the Potemkin* and *Basilissa Teophano,* and Stanisław Przybyszewski's *Visitors*—these are not works that have entered into the mainstream of twentieth-century European drama, and yet it is precisely such hidden masterpieces that can best serve as prototypes of occult theater, by its very nature committed to journeys into the unknown. The often bizarre and disconcerting theatrical forms and postulates put forward by these Russian and Polish fin-de-siècle artists—along with analogical and contrastive models provided by Strindberg, Maeterlinck, and other less familiar Western occultists—will offer sufficiently wide range of examples upon which to base on outline typology and poetics of occult drama.

First, a few preliminary observations setting out the perimeters of our investigation. By occult drama we mean quite simply the visionary, spiritual, and esoteric current in playwriting that flourished throughout all of Europe at the turn of the century. Called by its adherents the "theater of the soul"—a richly allusive phrase suggesting as much a public playhouse for the world soul as an inner stage for the individual psyche—this movement in drama was virtually synonymous with symbolism. Of the relationship between the two, the Russian critic and poet Ellis (L. L. Kobylinsky) wrote in 1910: "The most subtle and delicate form of art, symbolism, has an innate tendency to identify itself with mysticism and the visionary" [*Russkiye Simvolisty*]. Interpreting occult along these lines, in the fin-de-siècle context, we shall use the word interchangeably with the term *symbolist*.

A look at the symbolist playwrights of the period and their filiations with the occult suffices to justify this usage. Above all, it was the Belgian Maurice Maeterlinck in the early 1890s, with his plays and essays delving into unexplained psychic phenomena and mysterious transcendent forces, who first opened the path for the occult drama that then swept the whole of Europe within a decade. Conversant with ancient and modern mystics, including the fourteenth-century Flemish "Ecstatic Doctor," Jan van Ruysbroeck, whom he translated into French, as well as with Indian philosophy, Plotinus, Kant, and Swedenborg,

Maeterlinck became the spiritual guide of an entire generation of dramatists.

Without exception, the other symbolist playwrights were students and adepts of esoteric knowledge. Yeats's and Strindberg's contacts with the occult are too well known to need any elaboration here. In his search for spiritual harmony, the Russian novelist and poet Bely became an active member of Rudolph Steiner's anthroposophical community at Dornach, Switzerland, from 1914 to 1916. His friend and associate Briusov, chief spokesman for Russian symbolism, attended seances in Moscow, contributed to the spiritualist journal *Rebus,* and showed a passionate interest in medieval witchcraft, upon which he did extensive research.

The Spanish symbolist Ramón del Valle-Inclán pursued the occult tradition in the folklore of his native Galicia; fascinated by books on magic, he filled his plays and novels with tales of sorcery, demonic possession, curses and spells (especially the evil eye), hypnotism, clairvoyance, and telepathy. Like Valle-Inclán, the Italian poet and playwright Gabriele D'Annunzio avidly collected superstitions and was intrigued by fortune-telling, numerology, astrology, cartomancy, and the other divinatory arts, affirming in 1916 that "our life is a magical work which escapes the scrutiny of reason . . . An occult power directs it, often in opposition to apparent laws" ["La Leda Senza Cigno: Ritratto d'Ignota," in his *Poesie: Teatro: Prose*]—a declaration of faith that could be subscribed to by all the symbolist playwrights of the fin de siècle.

Przybyszewski was the outstanding Polish satanist at the turn of the century. Nurtured on local superstitions reaching back to the Middle Ages and drawn from childhood to forbidden communication with invisible powers, he dabbled in black magic and devil-worship. From his readings in Trentowski's *Demonomania* and Kiesewetter's *History of Occultism,* as well as Renaissance demonologists Jean Bodin, Martin Antoine del Rio, and Pierre de Lancre, Przybyszewski conceived the idea of a "synagogue of Satan" (the title of one of his books, taken from the Book of Revelation 2:9) for all those rebellious spirits who are cursed and live in despair; and his disciples at the Peacock Café in Cracow proudly called themselves the "sons of Satan"—an allusion to the master's novel, *Satans Kinder.*

Przybyszewski's fellow countryman Miciński was his exact spiritual opposite. Known as the Magus, he traveled about Europe in quest of enlightenment, studying mysticism in Spain, organizing in Warsaw the Brethren of the Sun, a secret society—similar to the Rosicrucians—devoted to the transformation of man, frequenting Vyacheslav Ivanov's circle in Moscow, and visiting the Emile Jaques-Dalcroze Institute at Hellerau, where he saw Claudel's *L'Annonce faite à Marie.* In both his life and his works, Miciński sought to return to the primal Indo-European religious heritage, by reconciling Christianity, Buddhism, Hinduism, Zoroastrianism, alchemy, the Cabbala, gnosticism, and Persian philosophy. During his years in Paris as a young painter, Miciński's more famous contemporary, Wyspiański, was initiated into the occult sciences by Paul Serusier (Gauguin's friend from Pont-

Aven and one of the founders of the Nabis), who gave lectures propagating Plato, Hermes Trismegistus, and hermeneutics in Schuré's version.

But no further evidence is needed at this point to support our claim that the symbolist playwrights were deeply immersed in occult lore. And in any case, we are less interested in the specific mystical beliefs held by these writers than with the uses to which they put them in creating innovative theatrical forms and techniques. In other words, our concern is not with doctrine, but with dramaturgy. Whatever the attitude of the playwright to the tenets of esoteric philosophy—and it may range from total commitment to simple curiosity, or even ironic detachment—as an artist, he imaginatively appropriates mystical precepts and practices in their more theatrical manifestations and makes the occult serve the purposes of drama, not vice versa. The occult dramatist is not necessarily a professional mystic.

The symbolists were attracted to esoteric knowledge primarily because it offered them opportunities for new poetic formulations. In *La Littérature et l'occultisme,* Denis Saurat points out that poets have always been in sympathy with the occultist circles of their age, finding an almost inexhaustible mine of fresh material in the mystic teachings, which have preserved intact the most primordial concepts.

> Occultism is the place of refuge for all vanquished religions and philosophies. For our poets, in opposition to the orthodox culture of their time, there lies a whole world of artistic possibilities. They find in it, living in all the fervor of the initiates, ancient and profound myths, in general little exploited by poets and thus doubly precious.

The great contribution of the turn-of-the-century occult drama has been not to the dissemination of esoteric wisdom, but to the art of the theater, which it has revitalized by expanding conventional notions of what a play is and by liberating stagecraft from nineteenth-century realistic canons. In establishing a new hierarchy of relationships between visible and invisible, outer and inner, known and unknown, the symbolist playwrights have made possible the theatricalization of the unseen, thereby adding new dimensions to the old stage world. (pp. 3-8)

The occult dramatist's goal is to render theatrically tangible the unseen forces that control man's destiny on earth. To reveal an invisible world hidden behind the facade of everyday reality and its practical concerns, the playwright must transport audience as well as dramatic characters beyond the personal and public preoccupations that are the subjects of the traditional genres. Symbolist theater becomes an act of initiation, leading us—by a process of awakening and transformation—across what Villiers de l'Isle-Adam calls [in his *Axël*] "the threshold of the occult world" and into heightened states of consciousness, whether these be of a higher of a lower form of life. Although professional occultists and their followers tend to believe that spiritual journeys bring enlightenment, not all commerce with otherworldly powers is benign; as well as ascents, there may be descents, sudden plunges into the dark regions and abysses of the soul where madness, chaos, and destruction lurk.

To embark upon voyages of discovery toward an unknown world lying outside our customary temporal and spatial notions, the visionary playwright is required to create new time and new space rather than to copy existing models. And here lies the special significance of symbolist dramaturgy for the theater, a form seemingly bound and circumscribed by a highly conventionalized, yet "real" sense of time and space—or at least traditional theory would have us so believe.

Rejecting the confines of the nineteenth-century playhouse, cut off from eternity, and measured by the petty calculations of an economy-minded mercantile society anxious to maximize profits and not waste time or space, the most daring occult dramatists of the turn of the century longed to establish a sacral playing arena on mountain summits and in holy places. Inspired by the example of Wagner's total theater, two visionary Polish playwrights voiced similarly grandiose plans around 1900. Wyspiański projected a stage on "sacred national soil" by the Royal Castle of Wawel in Cracow overlooking the Vistula and at the same time dreamed of an enormous theater under the open sky in the Tatra Mountains, with the lofty peaks serving as the wings and the deep blue waters of a small lake suggesting the auditorium. In the same mountain range, which he associated with the Himalayas and the origins of ancient Indian religions, Miciński called for the creation of a universal temple of beauty, "where in an amphitheater of the dead and the living, carved in the mountains, under the azure sky and among the deep forests, there will be revealed the mysteries of life on earth," and where Sanskrit dramas, such as *Shakuntala* could be performed [*Myśl teatralna Młodej Polski,* edited by Irena Sławińska and Stefan Kruk].

At this same period, the Russian composer and mystic Alexander Scriabin first conceived the idea for a vast *Mysterium,* which would represent a synthesis of the arts of music, song, dance, and theater and compose a cosmic symphony of sounds, lights, colors, scents, and tastes. Designed to usher in the end of the world in a flaming conflagration, Scriabin's *Mysterium* was to be given on the banks of the Ganges or at the foot of the Himalayas (the London theosophists recommended Darjeeling), with sunrise and sunset as part of the stage setting, and thousands of spectators seated in a huge, semicircular auditorium with spiral steps facing a semicircle of reflecting water.

Hostile to the conventional theater of his time, the composer was deeply impressed by the rhythmic rendering of a chorus from *Antigone,* as presented at Meyerhold's Studio in 1913, and hoped to use the same technique in his mystery play. As part of his work on the *Mysterium,* Scriabin studied Sanskrit, became a disciple of Yogi Ram Charak, and actually planned a trip to India in the winter of 1914, buying a white suit and pith helmet and spending hours in the sun to prepare himself for the tropical climate. Although he continued to work on the project until his death in 1915, Scriabin was able to complete only a fragmentary sketch of the *Prefatory Action,* which was to last seven days, whereupon, at the end of the twelfth hour of the seventh day, a new race of humans would be born. The *Mysterium* was never realized.

The failure of these visionary artists to create—except in their imaginations—a feasible new playing area outside the theater of commerce might at first suggest that their dream was a futile and unproductive one, worthy of ridicule. But if the theater could not be moved to the mountains and holy places, at least the mountains could be brought into the theater and the secular stage transformed into a sacred arena for ritual performance—and this is precisely what the symbolists did. Emulating Greek, medieval, and Indian models, the turn-of-the-century playwrights made the theater a temple.

And yet, despite these noble efforts, the question naturally arises: Is the occult per se theatrical or suited to visualization? Are the great mysteries too large or too small for the theater as we know it? Here matters of scale and focus become of central importance. Mystical experience takes place either deep within a single consciousness or far outside in the entire cosmos, in both cases leading to a fusion of individual and universal. Stéphane Mallarmé, the poetic presence behind French symbolist theater, recognized these two polar extremes, stating that the ideal drama would be either a vast spectacle of cosmic quest or a minimal presentation involving a single character engaged in soliloquy and mime. The problem for the dramatist—as opposed to the poet or the novelist, whose imagination remains unfettered—is to find a stage where consciousness can meet cosmos and to escape from cagelike drawing rooms and box sets into a magical universe dominated by the four elements.

But the standard judgment has been that the stage is best suited to purely human interactions, whether personal or social, and inimical to the paranormal and extrarational. For this reason, occult drama—when it is genuinely visionary in form and not simply imitative of traditional genres—inevitably seems odd in shape and lacking in proportion to the untrained eye. From the point of view of ordinary theatrical optics, plays in this mode are too long or too short, there is too much or too little action, and we are too close or too distant from the characters and events. The perspective is disturbing and incommensurate with accepted human dimensions.

If theatricalization of the unseen is the touchstone of occult drama, then we can discern three broad categories of mystical theater corresponding to the different areas in which the invisible forces are manifested: (1) dramas of eternal human consciousness, such as Maeterlinck produced in *The Interior* and *The Blind;* (2) dramas of cosmic consciousness, as envisaged by Scriabin in the *Mysterium,* with its choir of voices embodying Waves of Life, Awakening Feelings, Mountains, Sunbeam, Forest, and Desert; and (3) dramas of human and cosmic destiny seen in the workings of history—personal, national, or universal—as exemplified by works of Strindberg, Wyspiański, and Miciński. Although the boundaries between these groupings are neither clearly marked nor firmly established, such a rough schema will enable us to chart a typology of occult drama and isolate the unique characteristics of what is by far the least known and most complex species—the historical occult.

*The Maeterlinckian Model of Interior Drama of Con-*sciousness. The Maeterlinckian model of interior drama of consciousness takes one of two forms. In the first, revelation of the mysteries occurs in a contemporary setting within the sphere of daily life; in the second, otherworldly powers make themselves manifest in a removed universe of legend or myth. The two subspecies are nonetheless fundamentally alike in their concern with transcendent states of soul and their avoidance of practical mundane affairs.

In the first variety, of which Maeterlinck's *The Intruder* is a good example, an ordinary room with its human community is invaded by a stranger (in this case, death), who—unlike the intruder in realistic social drama—brings not a temporal secret from this world, but an eternal secret from the other world. Within familiar perspectives the old stage space—the drawing room—is made to bear the weigth of the cosmos and reverberate to its invisible forces. Behind banal surfaces there can be glimpsed the outlines of an occult universe; the contemporary loses its particularized features and becomes transformed into a timeless realm. In the second variant, represented by *Pelléas and Mélisande,* no pretense as to actual time or place is maintained. Instead we are transported out of the present to time immemorial, usually a nebulous Middle Ages where an unearthly atmosphere prevails and invisible presences lurk in every shadow.

In both branches of the Maeterlinckian paradigm, the occult can be disclosed in human life only to the degree that the arena of performance moves away from the concrete and the historical toward a dim past or idealized region. Here the unseen is theatricalized through vagueness and imprecision, suggestion and removal, with heavy dependence on muted lighting effects. Because of Maeterlinck's persuasive example, the mystical quickly became associated with the murky. Symbolist playwrights in France followed the Belgian master's practice of setting his dramas in ancient castle and shadowy medieval kingdoms. The note by the occult theoretician and playwright Victor-Emile Michelet at the beginning of his drama *The Knight Who Wore His Cross* could be used to characterize hundreds of such plays: "The action takes place—if you like—at an indeterminate period of the conventional Middle Ages as portrayed in the Chansons de Gestes." As a result of the wide dissemination of this model, it has been assumed that all symbolist drama must flee the harsh light of reality and take refuge in a never-never land of obscurity and gloom, thus giving rise to the accusation—forcefully expressed by John Gassner—that "it is against the nature of the theatre to exist in a mist and to thrive on vagueness. Drama and theatre are among the most definite of all the arts" [*Directions in Modern Theatre*].

Dramas of Cosmic Consciousness. Rejecting Maeterlinck as a guide, the French musicologist and occult playwright Edouard Schuré—author of studies of Wagner and an immensely influential and popular work on mysticism, *The Great Initiates*—proposed a theoretic model for a universal cosmic drama based on the synthesis of all religions and not dissimiliar in spirit from Scriabin's *Mysterium.* An initiatory and redemptive drama, the "theatre of the soul" proposed by Schuré, should express the harmony of "the entire religious traditions of East and West" and demonstrate "the continuity of inspiration in history as an historical fact" [*The Genesis of Tragedy and the Sacred Drama of Eleusis*]. By revealing the bonds between Visible and Invisible in the three interrelated worlds of Nature, Soul, and Spirit (or the terrestrial, astral, and divine), the occult dramatist will lead his audience to the door of initiation and make the world beyond vividly perceptible.

Providing a reconstruction of the sacred drama of Eleusis—the Hellenic version of the Christian fall and redemption—as the exemplar of all mystery plays of death and rebirth, Schuré describes how the visionary playwright can dramatize the transmigrations of the soul, its material incarnations, and earthly trials, preceding ultimate purification and return to its heavenly home. The two movements of such a drama are descent into the lower sphere of dense matter and ascent into the spiritual realm, as Persephone—archetype of the human soul—regains her position in the upper world. Because for the author of *The Great Initiates* "the theatre affords . . . the joy of metamorphosis and resurrection," it must present a positive and sympathetic visionary hero who not only seeks initiation, but who actually succeeds in opening the doors of the mystery. Accordingly, Schuré dismisses Maeterlinck's static theater, with its passive, terror-stricken characters, as an inadequate model for occult drama. A genuine pioneer, Maeterlinck has penetrated into the hidden world but wanders there in darkness without any sense of direction. "The occult, in Maeterlinck," Schuré writes, "does not serve to illumine life, it makes it still more incomprehensible."

Schuré's critique of the Maeterlinckian paradigm is from an ideological point of view that proclaims the inevitable victory of the spirit and the transcendent power of spiritual love. But when we turn from the theory to the practice and look at the plays written in this cosmic mode, we find that for the most part such hierophantic dramas of the soul—whether Graeco-mythic or legendary-Christian—fail as theater (although they may be convincing as sacred pageants for true believers) precisely because they are doctrinal rather then poetic in origin. Often written by authors more immersed in the tenets of mysticism than in the imaginative life of drama, these occult thesis plays move too facilely to a preordained conclusion required by esoteric dogma. Anguish and horror can only be fleeting, for a definitive and triumphant solution must resolve all tensions, enlarge consciousness, and usher in a higher life. These initiatory spectacles tend to be little more than hymns of celebration, affirming the harmony of the universe and ending in a cosmic apotheosis that features celestial lights, music, and white-robed chanting figures with uplifted arms.

Two examples of doctrinally inspired cosmic drama should be enough to show the vastness of its aims and the monotonous emptiness of its form. In Fabre des Essart's *Christ the Savior*, "A Gnostic Drama in Three Days," the esoteric Christ preached by the Gnostics and Saint John confronts his enemy Satan, who offers temptations in the form of Spectres that disclose the future crimes of religious wars and inquisitions. After an Angel appears to announce that good as well as evil will result from Christian-

ity, we witness Christ's triumph over Satan in a future earthly paradise, where, clothed in radiant white, all mankind lives in peace and harmony. Digging in the ground, small children unearth an old buried cannon, but no longer recognize what it is, and flowers have grown over the guillotine, fallen into eternal disuse. The City of God has been realized, and the divine millennium come. As Jesus pats the playing youngsters on the head, Mary Magdalene leads a penitent Satan to be forgiven.

Even more grandiose in its effects is Vroncourt de la Ville's *The Mystery Play of Love*, "A Symbolic Hierodrama in Two Acts and Four Tableaux," presented in the style of the medieval revival. Complete with two Eves, the Virgin, Death, Adam, Lucifer, personified vices, and vast choruses, *The Mystery Play of Love* is a sacramental pageant, utilizing Franck's Symphony in D minor and calling for spectacular lighting, as the "Symphonic Interlude" after the third tableau makes clear.

> While the two Eves remain locked in each other's arms in a mystical ecstasy, a flood tide mounts through the orchestra: it is the flood tide of Mercy and Love which invades the world: "the presence of God" appears in its most profound and mysterious aspect. And it is like a torrent which sweeps away Evil, triumphing over Lucifer and the Vices. Then, an immense calm reigns, while up there, in the Heavens, the harmony of the movement of the stars resounds, joyous and sparkling. The entire Creation celebrates.

Lofty in tone and predictable in outcome, ceremonial cosmic drama looks toward a fixed past, not an uncertain future. Working with preconceived patterns of action, rigidly archetypal characters, and traditional imagery, the occult playwright in this mode can hardly avoid schematism, formula, and allegory; the author must depend heavily on music and external elements of spectacle to produce a spiritually uplifting effect.

Dramas of Human and Cosmic Destiny. The third of our paradigms, the historical occult, offers the least abstract and conventionalized arena for the theatricalization of the unseen—the stage of history with its inexhaustible supply of particularized character and event. Instead of turning back to knights, princesses, and ruined castles in dark forests or to the bare bones of primordial religious myth, the symbolist playwright can also dramatize the occult in the workings of the historical process—as did Strindberg with the everyday details of his own life, Wyspiański with the November 1830 uprising, and Miciński with the revolution of 1905. In the historical occult, the symbolist imagination ceases to operate in a void or become an occasion for fleeing from reality and refusing to deal with social and political issues—the most frequent charges made against mystical theater. Instead of angelic choirs intoning hymns, historical personages reenact desperate and violent deeds intractable to simplistic allegorization, and archetypes are clothed not in white, but in unique human shapes.

For example, Miciński's *Revolt of the Potemkin*, which deals with the same events as Sergei Eisenstein's film, is

The Rose Cross Lamen, or badge, worn by advanced members of the Order of the Golden Dawn. The three rings of "petals" at the cross's center number three, seven, and twelve, symbolizing the three elements of fire, air, and water; the seven planets known to the ancients; and the twelve constellations of the Zodiac. Also depicted on the cross are a number of astrological symbols.

both wildly visionary and rigorously documentary. The Polish playwright invests with occult significance realistic details taken from the widest range of sources: songs of the period, eyewitness accounts of the Russo-Japanese war and Jewish pogroms, Russian folklore, and newspaper articles, memoirs, and interviews on the subject of the mutiny. The antithetical, yet complementary pair of Christ and Lucifer, who dominate Miciński's drama and give it a metaphysical dimension, appear not as symbolic figures, but as two actual Russian officers, Lieutenant Schmidt and Lieutenant Ton. Fusing rather than opposing the temporal and the eternal, Miciński inscribes historical time in mystical time; sanctified from the perspective of ultimate things, contemporary history is raised to the level of myth.

Unlike the cosmic religious dramas in which there is no place for tragedy, the historical occult is permeated with unending tension between real and ideal, human and divine, good and evil. The raw materials of history abound in evidence of contradiction and failure and teach sobering lessons about man's quest for absolutes. The workings of invisible powers in history—whether they be personal, national, or world—bring humanity as much or more pain and torment as consolation and hope of salvation.

August Strindberg, who in fact was a practitioner of all three varieties of the historical occult, can for our purposes be taken as the prime illustration of the psychological visionary, whose laboratory is his own experience in the everyday world—in what Evelyn Underhill calls the "borderland region where the mystical and the psychical meet" [*Mysticism*]. In plays such as *To Damascus* and *There Are Crimes and Crimes,* Strindberg theatricalizes the unseen in contemporary daily life through intricate concatenations of events, which are interpreted as signs of the workings of a higher power. The Swedish playwright and occultist transcends the level of immediate reality and uncovers a secret dimension by suggesting mysterious rapports among ordinary happenings. Cause-and-effect plot is subordinated to symmetrical patterning of events, which the author-hero sees as a manifestation of the invisible forces directing his life. As Marcel Réja points out in his preface to the original French edition of *Inferno,* in rejecting causality in favor of coincidence, Strindberg violates common sense and the supposed logic of the theater based upon it. But whereas excessive use of coincidence is regarded as a flaw in all modes of realistic drama, it becomes a crucial device in occult drama.

The two remaining categories of the historical occult, the national and the world, are in many ways similar in form and technique, although different in subject matter. Wyspiański's plays on Polish themes are examples of the former, dealing as they do with questions of national destiny, whereas Miciński's *Potemkin* and *Basilissa,* devoted to significant moments in European history, serve as illustrations of the latter. (pp. 8-17)

By its very nature the turn of the century points in two different directions, and the apocalyptic syndrome with its cycle of birth, death, and resurrection is dualistic. Bely described the sense of eschatological tension felt by members of his generation in the following terms: "The failure of the old ways is experienced as the End of the World; the tidings of the new era—as the Second Coming. We sensed the apocalyptic rhythm of the time. Towards the Beginning we strive through the end." It is only natural that the apocalyptic occult dramatists at the fin de siècle, caught between two epochs at the point where past and future intersect, should make extensive use of dualistic and antithetical pairs, such as Christ and Antichrist, light and dark, heights and depths (found throughout the Book of Revelation) and strive for unity of polar opposites.

What the great fifteenth-century mystic, churchman, philosopher, mathematician, and political theorist, Nicholas of Cusa, called *coincidentia oppositorum* (or union of contraries in God) became an essential technique of turn-of-the-century occult dramatists, whereby the mystery of totality finds affirmation and "ultimate reality is defined by pairs of opposites." The plays of Bely and Miciński are structured dualistically through the use of striking iconographic extremes in setting, character, and situation. Instead of the optimistic and univocal denouements that render doctrinal cosmic drama flabby, unresolved tension is maintained throughout these Russian and Polish works by ambivalence between paired antipodal possibilities.

Sharing Heraclitus' notion that all things carry with them their opposite, Bely in his *Antichrist* plays penetrates to the primordial state in which contraries exist as complementary aspects of a single reality. Viewed with metaphysical irony, cosmos and chaos, creation and destruction, Christ and Antichrist are seen as inseparably linked and even indistinguishable at times. In *He Who Has Come,* members of the commune awaiting the end fall into dissension as to whether "He Who Has Come" is Christ or Antichrist; and although the prophet Ilya declares that the millennium has already begun, life goes on as before and the waiting continues. In *Jaws of Night,* the saintly old prophet with luminous clothes and electrically charged hair may actually be an evil magician, preaching a false messiah and luring the children to night and death.

Following the Gnostic myth that God and the Devil are blood brothers, Miciński in *The Revolt of the Potemkin* develops the *coincidentia oppositorum,* central to all his work, that Lucifer—"the elder brother of Christ in his pre-eternal existence"—must complete what God alone could not successfully accomplish. In turn-of-the-century eschatology, as God ceased to be regarded as the judge and became the accused, going on trial for having created an unhappy and destructive race of men, Lucifer was rehabilitated as the champion of poor and downtrodden humanity. Like Prometheus, Miciński's revolutionary Lucifer—embodied in the nihilistic Lieutenant Ton—identifies with human misery and challenges God in the hopes of destroying his imperfect creation and building a new earthly paradise free from suffering. Master only of the material world and its knowledge, acting not out of love, but will to power, the Luciferian Ton (a direct descendent of Dostoevsky's Ivan Karamazov and Kirillov) brings only disaster with his utopian schemes. To create a new world, the wisdom and energy of Lucifer must be combined with the faith of Christ in a synthesis of two opposite, yet complementary forces within man.

Like the rotten meat served to the sailors and the entire

rotten *ancien régime,* the human condition itself—as portrayed in *The Revolt of the Potemkin*—is subject to decay, disease, and death unless it is redeemed by a transcendent spiritual goal. In the Walpurgis Night of Act III, during which Odessa is looted and burned, Miciński presents the grotesque underside of the revolutionary saga—a polar opposite of divine aspiration—in the form of the Putrescent Man in the Garbage Can (half a century before Beckett's *Endgame*), the Syphilitic Madonna, and the Unknown Figure proclaiming his vision of a world ruled over by microbes. Lucifer curses and longs for God, rebels and creates the darkness that will lead men back to Christ's light.

Everywhere in Miciński's *Potemkin,* the informing principle is *coincidentia oppositorum.* Responsible for consuming the old port, the fire—associated with apocalypse—is a self-immolating conflagration that annihilates and purifies at the same time. The sea—symbol of life and death, as well as of the strength and desolation of the soul—is *mare tenebrarum* (sea of darkness), the flood that devours and the flood that renews. Ever-present are contradictory aspects, both creative and destructive, of the mysterious elements and powers active in the universe, as the phantom ship of the soul passes by on its endless journey.

The opposition between legend and history felt by Western European authors ceases to exist in the dramas of the Polish symbolists. For Stanisław Wyspiański, obsessed with national issues, ancient Greek mythology comes to life in Polish history. The myth which Wyspiański's Polish heroes embody is not known to them in advance; it is only by acting out the time-honored story that they gradually become modern incarnations of legend. The myth lives again through their deeds. Wyspiański's characters are not abstract archetypes; rather, as historical figures participating in a ritual experience, they become initiates in an action that acquires its significance once it is sanctified by being raised to the level of myth.

Wyspiański's drama about the first great Polish uprising against czarist oppression, *November Night,* takes place at a precise historical place and hour—Warsaw on the night of November 29, 1830—with a cast of characters, including Grand Duke Constantine, Governor General of Poland, and members of the Cadets Corps who led the rebellion; and yet at the same time the events of the insurrection are presented within the eternal context of the ancient myth of Demeter and Persephone, advocated by Schuré as the essential sacred drama. Through juxtaposition and synchronism, the nineteenth-century Polish soldiers become Greek warriors, playthings in the hands of Homeric gods, and the 1830 uprising turns into an Eleusinian mystery of vegetation.

The moment is night, a magical time of dreams, memories, and associations reaching back to roots of human consciousness, and the principal place, to which the action constantly returns, is a windswept autumnal park, where the conspirators meet to begin their ill-fated revolt. In this elemental setting, dead leaves—a classic symbolist motif introduced by Maeterlinck, but here put to startling new use—swirl under the feet of the doomed officers who will win no other laurels. At the same time, the gloomy park becomes the borderland between Earth and Hades where the goddess Demeter says farewell to her daughter, Persephone, who every year must descend into the underworld—only to return each spring, bringing hope of deliverance from pain and death. As the immortals converse, the two dialogues—human and divine—become intercut, the Polish cadets taking up the words of the mythic litany without realizing that they are entering into the occult world and reenacting the Eleusinian rites. The seasonal death of nature (and its longed-for resurrection)—embodied in the withered leaves—is the eternal mystery confronting the officers who await their destiny in the autumnal park.

In Wyspiański's visionary mythopoetic awareness, past times and present times, Greek myth and modern history coexist in an eternal moment. Seeing the entire world and its history as a whole, rather than scientifically compartmentalized, the occult playwright is able to make daring leaps and surprising linkages that open unexpected theatrical vistas and free the stage from the bounds of time and space. In a second drama of death and rebirth, *Acropolis* (written in 1903, but not performed in its original form until 1926), Wyspiański fashions a syncretism of Judaic, Greek, and Christian religious mythology through a series of correspondences—a central device of symbolist poetics—whereby the Old Testament, Homer, and Polish history are fused.

By setting *Acropolis* in the royal castle and cathedral of Wawel overlooking the city of Cracow and the river Vistula, Wyspiański, who had a double vocation as painter and playwright, was able to make the entire action of the drama grow out of visual images associated with the sacral place. Instead of human characters (none ever appears in the work), sculptured figures in wood and marble from the cathedral architecture and heroes woven on tapestries depicting scenes from the Bible and from Homer come to life and reenact their eternal stories at the magical hour of midnight preceding Easter Sunday. Utilizing the syncretic theory advanced by Schuré that all known religions contain one and the same esoteric doctrine, Wyspiański links Easter to pagan rites of seasonal renewal and the primordial rhythms of nature. By occult analogue, Poland is the living Troy, Wawel becomes the Acropolis on the holy hill of Athens, and the sacred rivers Jordan and Scamander flow again in waters of the Vistula. Resurrection, awaited as a spiritual, biological, and national event, comes in an apocalyptic ending, when, amidst thunder and the extinction of the old world, a luminous Christ-Apollo appears at dawn in the chariot of the sun drawn by four white horses to the pealing of the cathedral bells.

So far in our charting of the range of occult drama at the turn of the century, we have dealt only with models that portray ascending spiritual quests, no matter how doubtful or ambiguous their outcomes may be. A final paradigm remains to be discussed—the Satanic occult—a flamboyant subgenre that shows the purely negative impact commerce with the unknown can have on certain human psyches.

One of the great fascinations that esoteric lore held for fin-de-siècle writers lay in its cult of black magic, demonology, Satan worship, vampirism, and sacrilege—themes first popularized in French poetry of the 1880s and then quickly taken over by fiction and drama. In the years around 1900 Satanism became a European craze, promulgated from Spain to Poland and Russia. One popular theatrical variant, inspired by Huysman's *Là-Bas* and the contemporary vogue for blasphemous ceremonies, was the black mass play. Designed to shock and titillate, these pornographic dramas are only pseudo-occult travesties of the genuinely demonic, cleverly exploited for profit.

Consider, for example, Roland Brevannes's *Black Masses,* presented at the Théâtre de la Bodinière in 1904, which in a series of sensational tableaux presents infernal practices down the ages. In Part I, The Black Mass in the Middle Ages, we watch the notorious Gilles de Rais (Bluebeard) practicing alchemy in his laboratory and longing for more little boys and girls to torture; the height of pleasure, he says, would be "to caress a woman with hands reddened in her child's blood." During a witches' Sabbath in a graveyard while a frightful storm rages, a beautiful young sorceress removes all her clothes, setting in motion an abandoned orgy in which male and female sorcerers, demons, and monstrous animals all rub against the phallic black goat and couple on the ground. Part II, the Black Mass in the Age of Louis XIV, is celebrated by the evil Abbé Guiborg on the bare torso of Madame de Montespan. In the third and final section of the drama, the Black Mass in the Twentieth Century, at a private party given by Axel Wartz, decadent young men lounge on tiger skins, embrace, and crown one another with roses. The author himself views the supposedly infernal proceedings with irony, as can be seen from the comic denouement when the Prefect of Police arrives and demands to know what is going on.

> AXEL. We were getting ready to celebrate a modernized black mass.
>
> PREFECT OF POLICE. In the Middle Ages that would have warranted burning at the stake; under Louis XIV, exile or the Bastille.
>
> AXEL. And nowadays?
>
> PREFECT OF POLICE. I'm a good devil; permit me to see the show.
>
> AXEL. Let the festivities continue!

In his brochure *Sadism, Satanism, and Gnosis,* the occultist Fabre des Essarts points out that Satanism—once a tragic protest against the iniquities of God's created universe (as in Miciński's Luciferianism)—has degenerated into lascivious farce or elegant, aesthetic pornography. After 1900, at least in France, Satanism is little more than an excuse for public nudity, and the devil becomes a character in vaudeville or opera, until the macabre reality of World War I brings to an end the fashion for demonic make-believe.

A far different form of black occult drama is represented by Stanisław Przybyszewski's dramatic epilogue in one act, *Visitors.* . . . as a fitting epilogue to this study. In the truly demonic universe of *Visitors,* man is in the clutches of unseen diabolic forces, which first awaken him to a con-

sciousness of evil and then drive him to suicide as the only way out of a hopeless dilemma. As portrayed in Przybyszewski's dark and sinister drama, human nature appears to be the creation of a wily Satanic spirit hostile to Adam-Everyman, who is guilty without even knowing why, simply for following the promptings of his heart. *Visitors* dramatizes a frightening personal apocalypse that becomes cosmic in implication, for the microcosmic individual psyche and timeless realm of the unconscious are expressive of the larger universe ruled over by fiendish powers.

In 1899, Przybyszewski read a lecture, entitled "The Mystical in Maeterlinck," after the first Cracow performance of *The Intruder.* Written not long afterwards, *Visitors* is an inner drama that undoubtedly reflects the influence of the Belgian playwright, even though Przybyszewski was no admirer of Maeterlinck's dramatic vision or style. Depicting—as did Maeterlinck—the unknown forces within man that act as a palpable fatality, the Polish dramatist sought to penetrate deeper and find an innovative theatrical form capable of expressing the naked soul—outside time, independent of environment, beyond experience and reality. A remarkable anticipation of depth psychology in its embodiment of what Jung would call the shadow and R. D. Laing the divided self, *Visitors* avoids all discursive analysis and renders in vivid theatrical shapes the indefinable atmosphere of anxiety generated by an hysterically obsessed psyche.

Like "The Dance of Life" and other paintings and engravings done by Przybyszewski's friend Edvard Munch at this same period, *Visitors* projects a world of eros and guilt against a stark, empty background dominated by primal imagery of earth, water, sun, moon, and mountains. Instead of serving as a healing power to soothe disordered passions, the the music for the ball in the mansion of the soul is a cacophonous dance of death futilely employed to drown out and deaden the painful voice of conscience that torments its owner. Not only the music, but the entire orchestration of sounds—Adam's sardonic laugh, the Visitor's infernal chuckle, the Stranger's convulsive giggle, the dry cackling of the Old Men, the gasps and sighs of Pola and Bela, and the uneasy murmurs from the couples in the mansion—create a hellish vocalization of the demonic universe. Przybyszewski's occult drama moves not toward spiritual illumination, but total darkness, as all the lights in the house of the psyche are forever extinguished.

An original variation on the dual themes of the double and the shadow, which were often combined in nineteenth-century fantastic fiction, *Visitors* externalizes Adam's shadow as an astral or phantom double that has become detached from his body, only to reappear when the moment of his death draws near. In occult doctrine, demonic apparitions, phantoms, ghosts, and doubles correspond to the real beings that inhabit the astral or lower plane of the invisible world. Returning to the source of its being, the shadow now exacts revenge on the creature who once had projected it. Hating and fearing his divided self, which he has attempted to repress and destroy, Adam must now confront himself, as his life, his marriage, and his psyche come to pieces.

The paranoia of the persecuting double, so forcefully portrayed in *Visitors*, calls to mind Przybyszewski's onetime friend, August Strindberg, who during the Inferno crisis (1894-1897) came to regard the Polish Satanist as his deadliest enemy, intent on destroying him. Identifying with the terrifying Przybyszewski, whom he regarded as the personification of his own guilty conscience, the Swedish author—like Adam in *Visitors*—experienced premonitions of disaster, torment for imagined sins, and sensations of suffocation, as his hated other self drove him relentlessly to suicide. Victim of an astral double existence comparable to Adam's relationship to the Visitor, Strindberg in his descent into an inferno of madness and despair, maintained that "happiness must be punished," feeling that he was "always being accused without knowing why" and suffering from "remorse for bad deeds" even when he had committed no known crime. In the light of the close personal and artistic interplay between Strindberg and Przybyszewski, *Visitors* can be interpreted as a dramatic depiction of neurotic states of anxiety shared by these twin souls, pursued by the same demons and subject to corresponding hallucinations.

But these biographical details should not be taken as exhausting or even limiting the meanings of *Visitors;* rather they illustrate the range of its allusiveness and universality. Przybyszewski's dramatic epilogue has many other resonances and affinities. The setting and atmosphere of the play can be traced back to Poe's poem "The Haunted Palace" in which a stately mansion where once joyous spirits swayed musically has been invaded by a "hideous throng" who "move fantastically to a discordant melody." The persecuting shadow and punishment for uncommitted crimes are common themes in fin-de-siècle occult literature, as witness the observation from one of Miciński's novels, "Everything in life exacts its vengeance, and punishment must take place even where there has been no crime," and the final stanza of his poem, "Christmas Eve."

> But a threatening Shadow follows me everywhere,
> and I do not know when I shall be freed
> from this darkness—by God's deliverance.

Visitors also had its impact in the theater, most notably influencing Leonid Andreyev's *Black Maskers* (1908), in which Lorenzo's castle becomes filled with strange visitors who attend a masked ball, while the host's shadow forces him to recognize his deceitful life and drives him to suicide as the only escape.

Using purely theatrical means, in *Visitors* Przybyszewski accomplished what he himself had declared to be Munch's goal: "to express, in fine, the naked psychological state, not mythologically, that is, by means of sensory metaphors, but directly in its coloristic equivalent." In this short masterpiece of occult drama, the demonic world of psychic phenomena comes alive as powerfully as in a painting by Munch. (pp. 28-39)

> *Daniel Gerould and Jadwiga Kosicka, "The Drama of the Unseen-Turn-of-the-Century Paradigms for Occult Drama," in* The Occult in Language and Literature, *edited by Her-*

mine Riffaterre, New York Literary Forum, 1980, pp. 3-42.

FURTHER READING

Anthologies

Haining, Peter, ed. *The Black Magic Omnibus.* London: Taplinger, 1976, 413 p.
  Contains nonfiction texts and short stories of black magic and Satanism.

Parry, Michel, ed. *Great Black Magic Stories.* London: Taplinger, 1877, 222 p.
  Classic and contemporary fiction on occult themes, including stories by Aleister Crowley and Madame Blavatsky.

Summers, Montague, ed. *The Supernatural Omnibus.* London: 1931. Reprint. New York: Causeway, 1974, 622 p.
  Collection of short stories about the supernatural, classified into various categories. In his introduction, Summers outlines the characteristics of a well-made supernatural tale.

Secondary Sources

Bloom, Clive. *The 'Occult' Experience and the New Criticism: Daemonism, Sexuality, and the Hidden in Literature.* Sussex, England: Harvester Press, 1986, 133 p.
  Examines "occult," or hidden elements, and the "daemonic," or hidden compulsions, that exist in the relationship between reader and text in Saussurean literary theory.

Briggs, Julia. *Night Visitors: The Rise and Fall of the English Ghost Story.* London: Faber, 1977, 238 p.
  Describes major features of the ghost story genre and discusses notable authors of ghost stories in English.

Evans, C. S. "The Lure of the Occult." *The Bookman* LVII, No. 339 (December 1919): 110-12.
  Contrasts the literary ghost story with fiction intended to propogate occult systems of belief, praising the masterpieces of the former and deprecating the latter.

Kerr, Howard, John W. Crowley, and Charles L. Crow. *The Haunted Dusk: American Supernatural Fiction, 1820-1920.* Athens: The University of Georgia Press, 1983, 236 p.
  Collection of critical essays about works of supernatural fiction written by American authors between 1820 and 1920.

Kinahan, Frank. *Yeats, Folklore, and Occultism: Contexts of the Early Work and Thought.* Boston: Unwin Hyman, 1988, 255 p.
  Examines Yeats's early works and influences, including his esoteric studies and involvement with such occultist organizations as the Order of the Golden Dawn.

Morris, David. *The Masks of Lucifer: Technology and the Occult in Twentieth-Century Popular Literature.* London: B. T. Batsford, 1992, 223 p.
  Studies what Morris terms "Techno-Occultism," the

combination of nineteenth-century occult doctrines with contemporary technology, in twentieth-century works about such phenomena as UFOs, ancient astronaut theories, and catastrophism.

Reed, John R. "The Occult." In his *Victorian Conventions,* pp. 440-73. Athens: Ohio University Press, 1975.

Contends that the use of supernatural phenomena in Victorian-era fiction was often calculated to inspire optimism and a sense of security rather than fright.

Saurat, Denis. *Literature and Occult Tradition: Studies in Philosophical Poetry.* Translated by Dorothy Bolton. 1930. Reprint. Port Washington, New York: Kennikat Press, 1966, 246 p.

Shows the influence of neoplatonism and occult theories on philosophical poetry, focusing on works by John Milton, Wolfgang Goethe, Friedrich Nietzsche, Walt Whitman, and Madame Blavatsky.

Scarborough, Dorothy. *The Supernatural in Modern English Fiction.* New York: Octagon Books, 1967, 329 p.

Surveys major themes in supernatural fiction written during the latter part of the nineteenth century.

Todorov, Tzvetan. *The Fantastic: A Structural Approach to a Literary Genre.* 1970. Translated by Richard Howard. Ithaca, New York: Cornell University Press, 1975, 180 p.

Structuralist study that seeks to define the fantastic as a genre and, in doing so, to examine genre theory.

Varnado, S. L. *Haunted Presence: The Numinous in Gothic Fiction.* Tuscaloosa: The University of Alabama Press, 1987, 160 p.

Discusses Gothic fiction in the light of the concept of the "numinous" as defined in Rudolph Otto's *The Idea of the Holy.*

Wilson, Colin. *The Occult: A History.* New York: Random House, 1971, 601 p.

Argues that humans have reached the point in their history where they must begin to understand their "occult" powers, their "hidden levels of being." Wilson includes a history of occult phenomena, an examination of such topics as witchcraft and ghosts, and a discussion of the metaphysical implications of occult theories.

Twentieth-Century
Literary Criticism

Cumulative Indexes
Volumes 1-50

How to Use This Index

The main references

> **Calvino, Italo**
> 1923-1985......CLC 5, 8, 11, 22, 33, 39,
> 73; SSC 3

list all author entries in the following Gale Literary Criticism series:

CLC = Contemporary Literary Criticism
CLR = Children's Literature Review
CMLC = Classical and Medieval Literature Criticism
DC = Drama Criticism
LC = Literature Criticism from 1400 to 1800
NCLC = Nineteenth-Century Literature Criticism
PC = Poetry Criticism
SSC = Short Story Criticism
TCLC = Twentieth-Century Literary Criticism

The cross-references

> See also CANR 23; CA 85-88;
> obituary CA 116

list all author entries in the following Gale biographical and literary sources:

AAYA = Authors & Artists for Young Adults
AITN = Authors in the News
BLC = Black Literature Criticism
BW = Black Writers
CA = Contemporary Authors
CAAS = Contemporary Authors Autobiography Series
CABS = Contemporary Authors Bibliographical Series
CANR = Contemporary Authors New Revision Series
CAP = Contemporary Authors Permanent Series
CDALB = Concise Dictionary of American Literary Biography
CDBLB = Concise Dictionary of British Literary Biography
DLB = Dictionary of Literary Biography
DLBD = Dictionary of Literary Biography Documentary Series
DLBY = Dictionary of Literary Biography Yearbook
HW = Hispanic Writers
MAICYA = Major Authors and Illustrators for Children and Young Adults
MTCW = Major 20th-Century Writers
SAAS = Something about the Author Autobiography Series
SATA = Something about the Author
WLC = World Literature Criticism, 1500 to the Present
YABC = Yesterday's Authors of Books for Children

A.
See Arnold, Matthew

A. E. .... TCLC 3, 10
See also Russell, George William
See also DLB 19

A. M.
See Megged, Aharon

Abasiyanik, Sait Faik 1906-1954
See Sait Faik
See also CA 123

Abbey, Edward 1927-1989 ...... CLC 36, 59
See also CA 45-48; 128; CANR 2, 41

Abbott, Lee K(ittredge) 1947- ...... CLC 48
See also CA 124; DLB 130

Abe, Kobo 1924-1993 .... CLC 8, 22, 53
See also CA 65-68; 140; CANR 24; MTCW

Abelard, Peter c. 1079-c. 1142 ... CMLC 11
See also DLB 115

Abell, Kjeld 1901-1961 .... CLC 15
See also CA 111

Abish, Walter 1931- .... CLC 22
See also CA 101; CANR 37; DLB 130

Abrahams, Peter (Henry) 1919- ..... CLC 4
See also BW; CA 57-60; CANR 26;
DLB 117; MTCW

Abrams, M(eyer) H(oward) 1912-... CLC 24
See also CA 57-60; CANR 13, 33; DLB 67

Abse, Dannie 1923-............. CLC 7, 29
See also CA 53-56; CAAS 1; CANR 4;
DLB 27

Achebe, (Albert) Chinua(lumogu)
1930- ..... CLC 1, 3, 5, 7, 11, 26, 51, 75
See also BLC 1; BW; CA 1-4R; CANR 6,
26; CLR 20; DA; DLB 117; MAICYA;
MTCW; SATA 38, 40; WLC

Acker, Kathy 1948- .... CLC 45
See also CA 117; 122

Ackroyd, Peter 1949-.......... CLC 34, 52
See also CA 123; 127

Acorn, Milton 1923-.............. CLC 15
See also CA 103; DLB 53

Adamov, Arthur 1908-1970 ...... CLC 4, 25
See also CA 17-18; 25-28R; CAP 2; MTCW

Adams, Alice (Boyd) 1926- ... CLC 6, 13, 46
See also CA 81-84; CANR 26; DLBY 86;
MTCW

Adams, Douglas (Noel) 1952- ... CLC 27, 60
See also AAYA 4; BEST 89:3; CA 106;
CANR 34; DLBY 83

Adams, Francis 1862-1893...... NCLC 33

Adams, Henry (Brooks)
1838-1918 .... TCLC 4
See also CA 104; 133; DA; DLB 12, 47

Adams, Richard (George)
1920- .... CLC 4, 5, 18
See also AITN 1, 2; CA 49-52; CANR 3,
35; CLR 20; MAICYA; MTCW;
SATA 7, 69

Adamson, Joy(-Friederike Victoria)
1910-1980 .... CLC 17
See also CA 69-72; 93-96; CANR 22;
MTCW; SATA 11, 22

Adcock, Fleur 1934-.............. CLC 41
See also CA 25-28R; CANR 11, 34;
DLB 40

Addams, Charles (Samuel)
1912-1988 .... CLC 30
See also CA 61-64; 126; CANR 12

Addison, Joseph 1672-1719 .... LC 18
See also CDBLB 1660-1789; DLB 101

Adler, C(arole) S(chwerdtfeger)
1932- .... CLC 35
See also AAYA 4; CA 89-92; CANR 19,
40; MAICYA; SAAS 15; SATA 26, 63

Adler, Renata 1938-............. CLC 8, 31
See also CA 49-52; CANR 5, 22; MTCW

Ady, Endre 1877-1919 .... TCLC 11
See also CA 107

Aeschylus 525B.C.-456B.C. ...... CMLC 11
See also DA

Afton, Effie
See Harper, Frances Ellen Watkins

Agapida, Fray Antonio
See Irving, Washington

Agee, James (Rufus)
1909-1955 .... TCLC 1, 19
See also AITN 1; CA 108;
CDALB 1941-1968; DLB 2, 26

A Gentlewoman in New England
See Bradstreet, Anne

A Gentlewoman in Those Parts
See Bradstreet, Anne

Aghill, Gordon
See Silverberg, Robert

Agnon, S(hmuel) Y(osef Halevi)
1888-1970 .... CLC 4, 8, 14
See also CA 17-18; 25-28R; CAP 2; MTCW

Aherne, Owen
See Cassill, R(onald) V(erlin)

Ai 1947-................... CLC 4, 14, 69
See also CA 85-88; CAAS 13; DLB 120

Aickman, Robert (Fordyce)
1914-1981 .... CLC 57
See also CA 5-8R; CANR 3

Aiken, Conrad (Potter)
1889-1973 ... CLC 1, 3, 5, 10, 52; SSC 9
See also CA 5-8R; 45-48; CANR 4;
CDALB 1929-1941; DLB 9, 45, 102;
MTCW; SATA 3, 30

Aiken, Joan (Delano) 1924-........ CLC 35
See also AAYA 1; CA 9-12R; CANR 4, 23,
34; CLR 1, 19; MAICYA; MTCW;
SAAS 1; SATA 2, 30, 73

Ainsworth, William Harrison
1805-1882 .... NCLC 13
See also DLB 21; SATA 24

Aitmatov, Chingiz (Torekulovich)
1928-........................ CLC 71
See also CA 103; CANR 38; MTCW;
SATA 56

Akers, Floyd
See Baum, L(yman) Frank

Akhmadulina, Bella Akhatovna
1937-........................ CLC 53
See also CA 65-68

Akhmatova, Anna
1888-1966 .... CLC 11, 25, 64; PC 2
See also CA 19-20; 25-28R; CANR 35;
CAP 1; MTCW

Aksakov, Sergei Timofeyvich
1791-1859 .... NCLC 2

Aksenov, Vassily................... CLC 22
See also Aksyonov, Vassily (Pavlovich)

Aksyonov, Vassily (Pavlovich)
1932-........................ CLC 37
See also Aksenov, Vassily
See also CA 53-56; CANR 12

Akutagawa Ryunosuke
1892-1927 .... TCLC 16
See also CA 117

Alain 1868-1951 .... TCLC 41

Alain-Fournier................... TCLC 6
See also Fournier, Henri Alban
See also DLB 65

Alarcon, Pedro Antonio de
1833-1891 .... NCLC 1

Alas (y Urena), Leopoldo (Enrique Garcia)
1852-1901 .... TCLC 29
See also CA 113; 131; HW

Albee, Edward (Franklin III)
1928- ... CLC 1, 2, 3, 5, 9, 11, 13, 25, 53
See also AITN 1; CA 5-8R; CABS 3;
CANR 8; CDALB 1941-1968; DA;
DLB 7; MTCW; WLC

Alberti, Rafael 1902-.............. CLC 7
See also CA 85-88; DLB 108

Alcala-Galiano, Juan Valera y
See Valera y Alcala-Galiano, Juan

Alcott, Amos Bronson 1799-1888 .. NCLC 1
See also DLB 1

Alcott, Louisa May 1832-1888 .... NCLC 6
See also CDALB 1865-1917; CLR 1; DA;
DLB 1, 42, 79; MAICYA; WLC;
YABC 1

Aldanov, M. A.
See Aldanov, Mark (Alexandrovich)

Aldanov, Mark (Alexandrovich)
1886(?)-1957 . . . . TCLC 23
See also CA 118

Aldington, Richard 1892-1962 . . . . . . CLC 49
See also CA 85-88; DLB 20, 36, 100

Aldiss, Brian W(ilson)
1925- . . . . CLC 5, 14, 40
See also CA 5-8R; CAAS 2; CANR 5, 28;
DLB 14; MTCW; SATA 34

Alegria, Claribel 1924- . . . . CLC 75
See also CA 131; CAAS 15; HW

Alegria, Fernando 1918- . . . . CLC 57
See also CA 9-12R; CANR 5, 32; HW

Aleichem, Sholom . . . . TCLC 1, 35
See also Rabinovitch, Sholem

Aleixandre, Vicente 1898-1984 . . . CLC 9, 36
See also CA 85-88; 114; CANR 26;
DLB 108; HW; MTCW

Alepoudelis, Odysseus
See Elytis, Odysseus

Aleshkovsky, Joseph 1929-
See Aleshkovsky, Yuz
See also CA 121; 128

Aleshkovsky, Yuz . . . . CLC 44
See also Aleshkovsky, Joseph

Alexander, Lloyd (Chudley) 1924- . . CLC 35
See also AAYA 1; CA 1-4R; CANR 1, 24,
38; CLR 1, 5; DLB 52; MAICYA;
MTCW; SATA 3, 49

Alfau, Felipe 1902- . . . . CLC 66
See also CA 137

Alger, Horatio, Jr. 1832-1899 . . . . . NCLC 8
See also DLB 42; SATA 16

Algren, Nelson 1909-1981 . . . . CLC 4, 10, 33
See also CA 13-16R; 103; CANR 20;
CDALB 1941-1968; DLB 9; DLBY 81,
82; MTCW

Ali, Ahmed 1910- . . . . CLC 69
See also CA 25-28R; CANR 15, 34

Alighieri, Dante 1265-1321 . . . . CMLC 3

Allan, John B.
See Westlake, Donald E(dwin)

Allen, Edward 1948- . . . . CLC 59

Allen, Roland
See Ayckbourn, Alan

Allen, Woody 1935- . . . . CLC 16, 52
See also AAYA 10; CA 33-36R; CANR 27,
38; DLB 44; MTCW

Allende, Isabel 1942- . . . . CLC 39, 57
See also CA 125; 130; HW; MTCW

Alleyn, Ellen
See Rossetti, Christina (Georgina)

Allingham, Margery (Louise)
1904-1966 . . . . CLC 19
See also CA 5-8R; 25-28R; CANR 4;
DLB 77; MTCW

Allingham, William 1824-1889 . . . NCLC 25
See also DLB 35

Allston, Washington 1779-1843 . . . . NCLC 2
See also DLB 1

Almedingen, E. M. . . . . CLC 12
See also Almedingen, Martha Edith von
See also SATA 3

Almedingen, Martha Edith von 1898-1971
See Almedingen, E. M.
See also CA 1-4R; CANR 1

Alonso, Damaso 1898-1990 . . . . CLC 14
See also CA 110; 131; 130; DLB 108; HW

Alov
See Gogol, Nikolai (Vasilyevich)

Alta 1942- . . . . CLC 19
See also CA 57-60

Alter, Robert B(ernard) 1935- . . . . . . CLC 34
See also CA 49-52; CANR 1

Alther, Lisa 1944- . . . . CLC 7, 41
See also CA 65-68; CANR 12, 30; MTCW

Altman, Robert 1925- . . . . CLC 16
See also CA 73-76

Alvarez, A(lfred) 1929- . . . . CLC 5, 13
See also CA 1-4R; CANR 3, 33; DLB 14,
40

Alvarez, Alejandro Rodriguez 1903-1965
See Casona, Alejandro
See also CA 131; 93-96; HW

Amado, Jorge 1912- . . . . CLC 13, 40
See also CA 77-80; CANR 35; DLB 113;
MTCW

Ambler, Eric 1909- . . . . CLC 4, 6, 9
See also CA 9-12R; CANR 7, 38; DLB 77;
MTCW

Amichai, Yehuda 1924- . . . . . . CLC 9, 22, 57
See also CA 85-88; MTCW

Amiel, Henri Frederic 1821-1881 . . NCLC 4

Amis, Kingsley (William)
1922- . . . . . . CLC 1, 2, 3, 5, 8, 13, 40, 44
See also AITN 2; CA 9-12R; CANR 8, 28;
CDBLB 1945-1960; DA; DLB 15, 27,
100; MTCW

Amis, Martin (Louis)
1949- . . . . CLC 4, 9, 38, 62
See also BEST 90:3; CA 65-68; CANR 8,
27; DLB 14

Ammons, A(rchie) R(andolph)
1926- . . . . CLC 2, 3, 5, 8, 9, 25, 57
See also AITN 1; CA 9-12R; CANR 6, 36;
DLB 5; MTCW

Amo, Tauraatua i
See Adams, Henry (Brooks)

Anand, Mulk Raj 1905- . . . . CLC 23
See also CA 65-68; CANR 32; MTCW

Anatol
See Schnitzler, Arthur

Anaya, Rudolfo A(lfonso) 1937- . . . . CLC 23
See also CA 45-48; CAAS 4; CANR 1, 32;
DLB 82; HW; MTCW

Andersen, Hans Christian
1805-1875 . . . . NCLC 7; SSC 6
See also CLR 6; DA; MAICYA; WLC;
YABC 1

Anderson, C. Farley
See Mencken, H(enry) L(ouis); Nathan,
George Jean

Anderson, Jessica (Margaret) Queale
. . . . CLC 37
See also CA 9-12R; CANR 4

Anderson, Jon (Victor) 1940- . . . . CLC 9
See also CA 25-28R; CANR 20

Anderson, Lindsay (Gordon)
1923- . . . . CLC 20
See also CA 125; 128

Anderson, Maxwell 1888-1959 . . . . . TCLC 2
See also CA 105; DLB 7

Anderson, Poul (William) 1926- . . . . CLC 15
See also AAYA 5; CA 1-4R; CAAS 2;
CANR 2, 15, 34; DLB 8; MTCW;
SATA 39

Anderson, Robert (Woodruff)
1917- . . . . CLC 23
See also AITN 1; CA 21-24R; CANR 32;
DLB 7

Anderson, Sherwood
1876-1941 . . . . . . TCLC 1, 10, 24; SSC 1
See also CA 104; 121; CDALB 1917-1929;
DA; DLB 4, 9, 86; DLBD 1; MTCW;
WLC

Andouard
See Giraudoux, (Hippolyte) Jean

Andrade, Carlos Drummond de . . . . . . CLC 18
See also Drummond de Andrade, Carlos

Andrade, Mario de 1893-1945 . . . . . TCLC 43

Andrewes, Lancelot 1555-1626 . . . . . . LC 5

Andrews, Cicily Fairfield
See West, Rebecca

Andrews, Elton V.
See Pohl, Frederik

Andreyev, Leonid (Nikolaevich)
1871-1919 . . . . TCLC 3
See also CA 104

Andric, Ivo 1892-1975 . . . . CLC 8
See also CA 81-84; 57-60; MTCW

Angelique, Pierre
See Bataille, Georges

Angell, Roger 1920- . . . . CLC 26
See also CA 57-60; CANR 13

Angelou, Maya 1928- . . . . CLC 12, 35, 64, 77
See also AAYA 7; BLC 1; BW; CA 65-68;
CANR 19; DA; DLB 38; MTCW;
SATA 49

Annensky, Innokenty Fyodorovich
1856-1909 . . . . TCLC 14
See also CA 110

Anon, Charles Robert
See Pessoa, Fernando (Antonio Nogueira)

Anouilh, Jean (Marie Lucien Pierre)
1910-1987 . . . . . . CLC 1, 3, 8, 13, 40, 50
See also CA 17-20R; 123; CANR 32;
MTCW

Anthony, Florence
See Ai

Anthony, John
See Ciardi, John (Anthony)

Anthony, Peter
See Shaffer, Anthony (Joshua); Shaffer,
Peter (Levin)

Anthony, Piers 1934- . . . . CLC 35
See also CA 21-24R; CANR 28; DLB 8;
MTCW

Antoine, Marc
See Proust,
(Valentin-Louis-George-Eugene-)Marcel

Antoninus, Brother
See Everson, William (Oliver)

Antonioni, Michelangelo 1912- ..... **CLC 20**
See also CA 73-76

Antschel, Paul 1920-1970. ...... **CLC 10, 19**
See also Celan, Paul
See also CA 85-88; CANR 33; MTCW

Anwar, Chairil 1922-1949 .... **TCLC 22**
See also CA 121

Apollinaire, Guillaume .... **TCLC 3, 8**
See also Kostrowitzki, Wilhelm Apollinaris
de

Appelfeld, Aharon 1932- .... **CLC 23, 47**
See also CA 112; 133

Apple, Max (Isaac) 1941-....... **CLC 9, 33**
See also CA 81-84; CANR 19; DLB 130

Appleman, Philip (Dean) 1926- ..... **CLC 51**
See also CA 13-16R; CANR 6, 29

Appleton, Lawrence
See Lovecraft, H(oward) P(hillips)

Apteryx
See Eliot, T(homas) S(tearns)

Apuleius, (Lucius Madaurensis)
125(?)-175(?) .... **CMLC 1**

Aquin, Hubert 1929-1977......... **CLC 15**
See also CA 105; DLB 53

Aragon, Louis 1897-1982....... **CLC 3, 22**
See also CA 69-72; 108; CANR 28;
DLB 72; MTCW

Arany, Janos 1817-1882........ **NCLC 34**

Arbuthnot, John 1667-1735.......... **LC 1**
See also DLB 101

Archer, Herbert Winslow
See Mencken, H(enry) L(ouis)

Archer, Jeffrey (Howard) 1940- .... **CLC 28**
See also BEST 89:3; CA 77-80; CANR 22

Archer, Jules 1915- .... **CLC 12**
See also CA 9-12R; CANR 6; SAAS 5;
SATA 4

Archer, Lee
See Ellison, Harlan

Arden, John 1930- .... **CLC 6, 13, 15**
See also CA 13-16R; CAAS 4; CANR 31;
DLB 13; MTCW

Arenas, Reinaldo 1943-1990 .... **CLC 41**
See also CA 124; 128; 133; HW

Arendt, Hannah 1906-1975 .... **CLC 66**
See also CA 17-20R; 61-64; CANR 26;
MTCW

Aretino, Pietro 1492-1556 .... **LC 12**

Arguedas, Jose Maria
1911-1969 .... **CLC 10, 18**
See also CA 89-92; DLB 113; HW

Argueta, Manlio 1936-............ **CLC 31**
See also CA 131; HW

Ariosto, Ludovico 1474-1533........ **LC 6**

Aristides
See Epstein, Joseph

Aristophanes
450B.C.-385B.C........ **CMLC 4; DC 2**
See also DA

Arlt, Roberto (Godofredo Christophersen)
1900-1942 .... **TCLC 29**
See also CA 123; 131; HW

Armah, Ayi Kwei 1939-......... **CLC 5, 33**
See also BLC 1; BW; CA 61-64; CANR 21;
DLB 117; MTCW

Armatrading, Joan 1950-......... **CLC 17**
See also CA 114

Arnette, Robert
See Silverberg, Robert

Arnim, Achim von (Ludwig Joachim von
Arnim) 1781-1831 .... **NCLC 5**
See also DLB 90

Arnim, Bettina von 1785-1859.... **NCLC 38**
See also DLB 90

Arnold, Matthew
1822-1888 .... **NCLC 6, 29; PC 5**
See also CDBLB 1832-1890; DA; DLB 32,
57; WLC

Arnold, Thomas 1795-1842 ...... **NCLC 18**
See also DLB 55

Arnow, Harriette (Louisa) Simpson
1908-1986 .... **CLC 2, 7, 18**
See also CA 9-12R; 118; CANR 14; DLB 6;
MTCW; SATA 42, 47

Arp, Hans
See Arp, Jean

Arp, Jean 1887-1966............... **CLC 5**
See also CA 81-84; 25-28R

Arrabal
See Arrabal, Fernando

Arrabal, Fernando 1932-...**CLC 2, 9, 18, 58**
See also CA 9-12R; CANR 15

Arrick, Fran...................... **CLC 30**

Artaud, Antonin 1896-1948 ..... **TCLC 3, 36**
See also CA 104

Arthur, Ruth M(abel) 1905-1979.... **CLC 12**
See also CA 9-12R; 85-88; CANR 4;
SATA 7, 26

Artsybashev, Mikhail (Petrovich)
1878-1927 .... **TCLC 31**

Arundel, Honor (Morfydd)
1919-1973 .... **CLC 17**
See also CA 21-22; 41-44R; CAP 2;
SATA 4, 24

Asch, Sholem 1880-1957 .... **TCLC 3**
See also CA 105

Ash, Shalom
See Asch, Sholem

Ashbery, John (Lawrence)
1927- ..... **CLC 2, 3, 4, 6, 9, 13, 15, 25,**
41, 77
See also CA 5-8R; CANR 9, 37; DLB 5;
DLBY 81; MTCW

Ashdown, Clifford
See Freeman, R(ichard) Austin

Ashe, Gordon
See Creasey, John

Ashton-Warner, Sylvia (Constance)
1908-1984 .... **CLC 19**
See also CA 69-72; 112; CANR 29; MTCW

Asimov, Isaac
1920-1992 ...... **CLC 1, 3, 9, 19, 26, 76**
See also BEST 90:2; CA 1-4R; 137;
CANR 2, 19, 36; CLR 12; DLB 8;
DLBY 92; MAICYA; MTCW; SATA 1,
26, 74

Astley, Thea (Beatrice May)
1925- .... **CLC 41**
See also CA 65-68; CANR 11

Aston, James
See White, T(erence) H(anbury)

Asturias, Miguel Angel
1899-1974 .... **CLC 3, 8, 13**
See also CA 25-28; 49-52; CANR 32;
CAP 2; DLB 113; HW; MTCW

Atares, Carlos Saura
See Saura (Atares), Carlos

Atheling, William
See Pound, Ezra (Weston Loomis)

Atheling, William, Jr.
See Blish, James (Benjamin)

Atherton, Gertrude (Franklin Horn)
1857-1948 .... **TCLC 2**
See also CA 104; DLB 9, 78

Atherton, Lucius
See Masters, Edgar Lee

Atkins, Jack
See Harris, Mark

Atticus
See Fleming, Ian (Lancaster)

Atwood, Margaret (Eleanor)
1939- .... **CLC 2, 3, 4, 8, 13, 15, 25, 44;**
SSC 2
See also BEST 89:2; CA 49-52; CANR 3,
24, 33; DA; DLB 53; MTCW; SATA 50;
WLC

Aubigny, Pierre d'
See Mencken, H(enry) L(ouis)

Aubin, Penelope 1685-1731(?)........ **LC 9**
See also DLB 39

Auchincloss, Louis (Stanton)
1917- .... **CLC 4, 6, 9, 18, 45**
See also CA 1-4R; CANR 6, 29; DLB 2;
DLBY 80; MTCW

Auden, W(ystan) H(ugh)
1907-1973 ..... **CLC 1, 2, 3, 4, 6, 9, 11,**
14, 43; PC 1
See also CA 9-12R; 45-48; CANR 5;
CDBLB 1914-1945; DA; DLB 10, 20;
MTCW; WLC

Audiberti, Jacques 1900-1965 ...... **CLC 38**
See also CA 25-28R

Auel, Jean M(arie) 1936-.......... **CLC 31**
See also AAYA 7; BEST 90:4; CA 103;
CANR 21

Auerbach, Erich 1892-1957 .... **TCLC 43**
See also CA 118

Augier, Emile 1820-1889 .... **NCLC 31**

August, John
See De Voto, Bernard (Augustine)

Augustine, St. 354-430.......... **CMLC 6**

Aurelius
See Bourne, Randolph S(illiman)

Austen, Jane
1775-1817 . . . . **NCLC 1, 13, 19, 33**
See also CDBLB 1789-1832; DA; DLB 116;
WLC

Auster, Paul 1947- . . . . **CLC 47**
See also CA 69-72; CANR 23

Austin, Frank
See Faust, Frederick (Schiller)

Austin, Mary (Hunter)
1868-1934 . . . . **TCLC 25**
See also CA 109; DLB 9, 78

Autran Dourado, Waldomiro
See Dourado, (Waldomiro Freitas) Autran

Averroes 1126-1198 . . . . **CMLC 7**
See also DLB 115

Avison, Margaret 1918- . . . . **CLC 2, 4**
See also CA 17-20R; DLB 53; MTCW

Ayckbourn, Alan
1939- . . . . **CLC 5, 8, 18, 33, 74**
See also CA 21-24R; CANR 31; DLB 13;
MTCW

Aydy, Catherine
See Tennant, Emma (Christina)

Ayme, Marcel (Andre) 1902-1967 . . . **CLC 11**
See also CA 89-92; CLR 25; DLB 72

Ayrton, Michael 1921-1975 . . . . **CLC 7**
See also CA 5-8R; 61-64; CANR 9, 21

Azorin . . . . **CLC 11**
See also Martinez Ruiz, Jose

Azuela, Mariano 1873-1952 . . . . **TCLC 3**
See also CA 104; 131; HW; MTCW

Baastad, Babbis Friis
See Friis-Baastad, Babbis Ellinor

Bab
See Gilbert, W(illiam) S(chwenck)

Babbis, Eleanor
See Friis-Baastad, Babbis Ellinor

Babel, Isaak (Emmanuilovich)
1894-1941(?) . . . . **CLC 73**
See also CA 104; TCLC 2, 13

Babits, Mihaly 1883-1941 . . . . **TCLC 14**
See also CA 114

Babur 1483-1530 . . . . **LC 18**

Bacchelli, Riccardo 1891-1985 . . . . . **CLC 19**
See also CA 29-32R; 117

Bach, Richard (David) 1936- . . . . **CLC 14**
See also AITN 1; BEST 89:2; CA 9-12R;
CANR 18; MTCW; SATA 13

Bachman, Richard
See King, Stephen (Edwin)

Bachmann, Ingeborg 1926-1973 . . . . . **CLC 69**
See also CA 93-96; 45-48; DLB 85

Bacon, Francis 1561-1626 . . . . **LC 18**
See also CDBLB Before 1660

Bacovia, George . . . . **TCLC 24**
See also Vasiliu, Gheorghe

Badanes, Jerome 1937- . . . . **CLC 59**

Bagehot, Walter 1826-1877 . . . . . . **NCLC 10**
See also DLB 55

Bagnold, Enid 1889-1981 . . . . **CLC 25**
See also CA 5-8R; 103; CANR 5, 40;
DLB 13; MAICYA; SATA 1, 25

Bagrjana, Elisaveta
See Belcheva, Elisaveta

Bagryana, Elisaveta
See Belcheva, Elisaveta

Bailey, Paul 1937- . . . . **CLC 45**
See also CA 21-24R; CANR 16; DLB 14

Baillie, Joanna 1762-1851 . . . . **NCLC 2**
See also DLB 93

Bainbridge, Beryl (Margaret)
1933- . . . . **CLC 4, 5, 8, 10, 14, 18, 22, 62**
See also CA 21-24R; CANR 24; DLB 14;
MTCW

Baker, Elliott 1922- . . . . **CLC 8**
See also CA 45-48; CANR 2

Baker, Nicholson 1957- . . . . **CLC 61**
See also CA 135

Baker, Ray Stannard 1870-1946 . . . **TCLC 47**
See also CA 118

Baker, Russell (Wayne) 1925- . . . . . . **CLC 31**
See also BEST 89:4; CA 57-60; CANR 11,
41; MTCW

Bakshi, Ralph 1938(?)- . . . . **CLC 26**
See also CA 112; 138

Bakunin, Mikhail (Alexandrovich)
1814-1876 . . . . **NCLC 25**

Baldwin, James (Arthur)
1924-1987 . . . . . **CLC 1, 2, 3, 4, 5, 8, 13,
15, 17, 42, 50, 67; DC 1; SSC 10**
See also AAYA 4; BLC 1; BW; CA 1-4R;
124; CABS 1; CANR 3, 24;
CDALB 1941-1968; DA; DLB 2, 7, 33;
DLBY 87; MTCW; SATA 9, 54; WLC

Ballard, J(ames) G(raham)
1930- . . . . **CLC 3, 6, 14, 36; SSC 1**
See also AAYA 3; CA 5-8R; CANR 15, 39;
DLB 14; MTCW

Balmont, Konstantin (Dmitriyevich)
1867-1943 . . . . **TCLC 11**
See also CA 109

Balzac, Honore de
1799-1850 . . . . **NCLC 5, 35; SSC 5**
See also DA; DLB 119; WLC

Bambara, Toni Cade 1939- . . . . **CLC 19**
See also AAYA 5; BLC 1; BW; CA 29-32R;
CANR 24; DA; DLB 38; MTCW

Bamdad, A.
See Shamlu, Ahmad

Banat, D. R.
See Bradbury, Ray (Douglas)

Bancroft, Laura
See Baum, L(yman) Frank

Banim, John 1798-1842 . . . . **NCLC 13**
See also DLB 116

Banim, Michael 1796-1874 . . . . . . **NCLC 13**

Banks, Iain
See Banks, Iain M(enzies)

Banks, Iain M(enzies) 1954- . . . . **CLC 34**
See also CA 123; 128

Banks, Lynne Reid . . . . **CLC 23**
See also Reid Banks, Lynne
See also AAYA 6

Banks, Russell 1940- . . . . **CLC 37, 72**
See also CA 65-68; CAAS 15; CANR 19;
DLB 130

Banville, John 1945- . . . . **CLC 46**
See also CA 117; 128; DLB 14

Banville, Theodore (Faullain) de
1832-1891 . . . . **NCLC 9**

Baraka, Amiri
1934- . . . **CLC 1, 2, 3, 5, 10, 14, 33; PC 4**
See also Jones, LeRoi
See also BLC 1; BW; CA 21-24R; CABS 3;
CANR 27, 38; CDALB 1941-1968; DA;
DLB 5, 7, 16, 38; DLBD 8; MTCW

Barbellion, W. N. P. . . . . **TCLC 24**
See also Cummings, Bruce F(rederick)

Barbera, Jack 1945- . . . . **CLC 44**
See also CA 110

Barbey d'Aurevilly, Jules Amedee
1808-1889 . . . . **NCLC 1**
See also DLB 119

Barbusse, Henri 1873-1935 . . . . **TCLC 5**
See also CA 105; DLB 65

Barclay, Bill
See Moorcock, Michael (John)

Barclay, William Ewert
See Moorcock, Michael (John)

Barea, Arturo 1897-1957 . . . . **TCLC 14**
See also CA 111

Barfoot, Joan 1946- . . . . **CLC 18**
See also CA 105

Baring, Maurice 1874-1945 . . . . **TCLC 8**
See also CA 105; DLB 34

Barker, Clive 1952- . . . . **CLC 52**
See also AAYA 10; BEST 90:3; CA 121;
129; MTCW

Barker, George Granville
1913-1991 . . . . **CLC 8, 48**
See also CA 9-12R; 135; CANR 7, 38;
DLB 20; MTCW

Barker, Harley Granville
See Granville-Barker, Harley
See also DLB 10

Barker, Howard 1946- . . . . **CLC 37**
See also CA 102; DLB 13

Barker, Pat 1943- . . . . **CLC 32**
See also CA 117; 122

Barlow, Joel 1754-1812 . . . . **NCLC 23**
See also DLB 37

Barnard, Mary (Ethel) 1909- . . . . **CLC 48**
See also CA 21-22; CAP 2

Barnes, Djuna
1892-1982 . . . **CLC 3, 4, 8, 11, 29; SSC 3**
See also CA 9-12R; 107; CANR 16; DLB 4,
9, 45; MTCW

Barnes, Julian 1946- . . . . **CLC 42**
See also CA 102; CANR 19

Barnes, Peter 1931- . . . . **CLC 5, 56**
See also CA 65-68; CAAS 12; CANR 33,
34; DLB 13; MTCW

Baroja (y Nessi), Pio 1872-1956 . . . . **TCLC 8**
See also CA 104

Baron, David
See Pinter, Harold

Baron Corvo
See Rolfe, Frederick (William Serafino
Austin Lewis Mary)

Barondess, Sue K(aufman)
　　1926-1977 .... CLC 8
　　See also Kaufman, Sue
　　See also CA 1-4R; 69-72; CANR 1

Baron de Teive
　　See Pessoa, Fernando (Antonio Nogueira)

Barres, Maurice 1862-1923 .... TCLC 47
　　See also DLB 123

Barreto, Afonso Henrique de Lima
　　See Lima Barreto, Afonso Henrique de

Barrett, (Roger) Syd 1946- .... CLC 35
　　See also Pink Floyd

Barrett, William (Christopher)
　　1913-1992 .... CLC 27
　　See also CA 13-16R; 139; CANR 11

Barrie, J(ames) M(atthew)
　　1860-1937 .... TCLC 2
　　See also CA 104; 136; CDBLB 1890-1914;
　　CLR 16; DLB 10; MAICYA; YABC 1

Barrington, Michael
　　See Moorcock, Michael (John)

Barrol, Grady
　　See Bograd, Larry

Barry, Mike
　　See Malzberg, Barry N(athaniel)

Barry, Philip 1896-1949 .... TCLC 11
　　See also CA 109; DLB 7

Bart, Andre Schwarz
　　See Schwarz-Bart, Andre

Barth, John (Simmons)
　　1930- ...... CLC 1, 2, 3, 5, 7, 9, 10, 14,
　　　　　　　　　　　　　27, 51; SSC 10
　　See also AITN 1, 2; CA 1-4R; CABS 1;
　　CANR 5, 23; DLB 2; MTCW

Barthelme, Donald
　　1931-1989 ..... CLC 1, 2, 3, 5, 6, 8, 13,
　　　　　　　　　　23, 46, 59; SSC 2
　　See also CA 21-24R; 129; CANR 20;
　　DLB 2; DLBY 80, 89; MTCW; SATA 7,
　　62

Barthelme, Frederick 1943- .... CLC 36
　　See also CA 114; 122; DLBY 85

Barthes, Roland (Gerard)
　　1915-1980 .... CLC 24
　　See also CA 130; 97-100; MTCW

Barzun, Jacques (Martin) 1907- .... CLC 51
　　See also CA 61-64; CANR 22

Bashevis, Isaac
　　See Singer, Isaac Bashevis

Bashkirtseff, Marie 1859-1884 ... NCLC 27

Basho
　　See Matsuo Basho

Bass, Kingsley B., Jr.
　　See Bullins, Ed

Bassani, Giorgio 1916- .... CLC 9
　　See also CA 65-68; CANR 33; DLB 128;
　　MTCW

Bastos, Augusto (Antonio) Roa
　　See Roa Bastos, Augusto (Antonio)

Bataille, Georges 1897-1962 .... CLC 29
　　See also CA 101; 89-92

Bates, H(erbert) E(rnest)
　　1905-1974 .... CLC 46; SSC 10
　　See also CA 93-96; 45-48; CANR 34;
　　MTCW

Bauchart
　　See Camus, Albert

Baudelaire, Charles
　　1821-1867 .... NCLC 6, 29; PC 1
　　See also DA; WLC

Baudrillard, Jean 1929- .... CLC 60

Baum, L(yman) Frank 1856-1919 ... TCLC 7
　　See also CA 108; 133; CLR 15; DLB 22;
　　MAICYA; MTCW; SATA 18

Baum, Louis F.
　　See Baum, L(yman) Frank

Baumbach, Jonathan 1933- ...... CLC 6, 23
　　See also CA 13-16R; CAAS 5; CANR 12;
　　DLBY 80; MTCW

Bausch, Richard (Carl) 1945- ...... CLC 51
　　See also CA 101; CAAS 14; DLB 130

Baxter, Charles 1947- .... CLC 45, 77
　　See also CA 57-60; CANR 40; DLB 130

Baxter, George Owen
　　See Faust, Frederick (Schiller)

Baxter, James K(eir) 1926-1972 .... CLC 14
　　See also CA 77-80

Baxter, John
　　See Hunt, E(verette) Howard, Jr.

Bayer, Sylvia
　　See Glassco, John

Beagle, Peter S(oyer) 1939- .... CLC 7
　　See also CA 9-12R; CANR 4; DLBY 80;
　　SATA 60

Bean, Normal
　　See Burroughs, Edgar Rice

Beard, Charles A(ustin)
　　1874-1948 .... TCLC 15
　　See also CA 115; DLB 17; SATA 18

Beardsley, Aubrey 1872-1898 ..... NCLC 6

Beattie, Ann
　　1947- .... CLC 8, 13, 18, 40, 63; SSC 11
　　See also BEST 90:2; CA 81-84; DLBY 82;
　　MTCW

Beattie, James 1735-1803 .... NCLC 25
　　See also DLB 109

Beauchamp, Kathleen Mansfield 1888-1923
　　See Mansfield, Katherine
　　See also CA 104; 134; DA

**Beauvoir, Simone (Lucie Ernestine Marie
　　Bertrand) de**
　　1908-1986 ... CLC 1, 2, 4, 8, 14, 31, 44,
　　　　　　　　　　　　　50, 71
　　See also CA 9-12R; 118; CANR 28; DA;
　　DLB 72; DLBY 86; MTCW; WLC

Becker, Jurek 1937- .... CLC 7, 19
　　See also CA 85-88; DLB 75

Becker, Walter 1950- .... CLC 26

Beckett, Samuel (Barclay)
　　1906-1989 ..... CLC 1, 2, 3, 4, 6, 9, 10,
　　　　　　　　　11, 14, 18, 29, 57, 59
　　See also CA 5-8R; 130; CANR 33;
　　CDBLB 1945-1960; DA; DLB 13, 15;
　　DLBY 90; MTCW; WLC

Beckford, William 1760-1844 .... NCLC 16
　　See also DLB 39

Beckman, Gunnel 1910- .... CLC 26
　　See also CA 33-36R; CANR 15; CLR 25;
　　MAICYA; SAAS 9; SATA 6

Becque, Henri 1837-1899 .... NCLC 3

Beddoes, Thomas Lovell
　　1803-1849 .... NCLC 3
　　See also DLB 96

Bedford, Donald F.
　　See Fearing, Kenneth (Flexner)

Beecher, Catharine Esther
　　1800-1878 .... NCLC 30
　　See also DLB 1

Beecher, John 1904-1980 .... CLC 6
　　See also AITN 1; CA 5-8R; 105; CANR 8

Beer, Johann 1655-1700 .... LC 5

Beer, Patricia 1924- .... CLC 58
　　See also CA 61-64; CANR 13; DLB 40

Beerbohm, Henry Maximilian
　　1872-1956 .... TCLC 1, 24
　　See also CA 104; DLB 34, 100

Begiebing, Robert J(ohn) 1946-..... CLC 70
　　See also CA 122; CANR 40

Behan, Brendan
　　1923-1964 .... CLC 1, 8, 11, 15
　　See also CA 73-76; CANR 33;
　　CDBLB 1945-1960; DLB 13; MTCW

Behn, Aphra 1640(?)-1689 .... LC 1
　　See also DA; DLB 39, 80, 131; WLC

Behrman, S(amuel) N(athaniel)
　　1893-1973 .... CLC 40
　　See also CA 13-16; 45-48; CAP 1; DLB 7,
　　44

Belasco, David 1853-1931 .... TCLC 3
　　See also CA 104; DLB 7

Belcheva, Elisaveta 1893- .... CLC 10

Beldone, Phil "Cheech"
　　See Ellison, Harlan

Beleno
　　See Azuela, Mariano

Belinski, Vissarion Grigoryevich
　　1811-1848 .... NCLC 5

Belitt, Ben 1911-................. CLC 22
　　See also CA 13-16R; CAAS 4; CANR 7;
　　DLB 5

Bell, James Madison 1826-1902 ... TCLC 43
　　See also BLC 1; BW; CA 122; 124; DLB 50

Bell, Madison (Smartt) 1957- ...... CLC 41
　　See also CA 111; CANR 28

Bell, Marvin (Hartley) 1937-..... CLC 8, 31
　　See also CA 21-24R; CAAS 14; DLB 5;
　　MTCW

Bell, W. L. D.
　　See Mencken, H(enry) L(ouis)

Bellamy, Atwood C.
　　See Mencken, H(enry) L(ouis)

Bellamy, Edward 1850-1898 ...... NCLC 4
　　See also DLB 12

Bellin, Edward J.
　　See Kuttner, Henry

Belloc, (Joseph) Hilaire (Pierre)
1870-1953 . . . . TCLC 7, 18
See also CA 106; DLB 19, 100; YABC 1

Belloc, Joseph Peter Rene Hilaire
See Belloc, (Joseph) Hilaire (Pierre)

Belloc, Joseph Pierre Hilaire
See Belloc, (Joseph) Hilaire (Pierre)

Belloc, M. A.
See Lowndes, Marie Adelaide (Belloc)

Bellow, Saul
1915- . . . . . CLC 1, 2, 3, 6, 8, 10, 13, 15,
25, 33, 34, 63
See also AITN 2; BEST 89:3; CA 5-8R;
CABS 1; CANR 29; CDALB 1941-1968;
DA; DLB 2, 28; DLBD 3; DLBY 82;
MTCW; WLC

Belser, Reimond Karel Maria de
1929- . . . . CLC 14

Bely, Andrey . . . . TCLC 7
See also Bugayev, Boris Nikolayevich

Benary, Margot
See Benary-Isbert, Margot

Benary-Isbert, Margot 1889-1979 . . . CLC 12
See also CA 5-8R; 89-92; CANR 4;
CLR 12; MAICYA; SATA 2, 21

Benavente (y Martinez), Jacinto
1866-1954 . . . . TCLC 3
See also CA 106; 131; HW; MTCW

Benchley, Peter (Bradford)
1940- . . . . CLC 4, 8
See also AITN 2; CA 17-20R; CANR 12,
35; MTCW; SATA 3

Benchley, Robert (Charles)
1889-1945 . . . . TCLC 1
See also CA 105; DLB 11

Benedikt, Michael 1935- . . . . CLC 4, 14
See also CA 13-16R; CANR 7; DLB 5

Benet, Juan 1927- . . . . CLC 28

Benet, Stephen Vincent
1898-1943 . . . . TCLC 7; SSC 10
See also CA 104; DLB 4, 48, 102; YABC 1

Benet, William Rose 1886-1950 . . . TCLC 28
See also CA 118; DLB 45

Benford, Gregory (Albert) 1941- . . . . CLC 52
See also CA 69-72; CANR 12, 24;
DLBY 82

Bengtsson, Frans (Gunnar)
1894-1954 . . . . TCLC 48

Benjamin, David
See Slavitt, David R(ytman)

Benjamin, Lois
See Gould, Lois

Benjamin, Walter 1892-1940 . . . . . TCLC 39

Benn, Gottfried 1886-1956 . . . . TCLC 3
See also CA 106; DLB 56

Bennett, Alan 1934- . . . . CLC 45, 77
See also CA 103; CANR 35; MTCW

Bennett, (Enoch) Arnold
1867-1931 . . . . TCLC 5, 20
See also CA 106; CDBLB 1890-1914;
DLB 10, 34, 98

Bennett, Elizabeth
See Mitchell, Margaret (Munnerlyn)

Bennett, George Harold 1930-
See Bennett, Hal
See also BW; CA 97-100

Bennett, Hal . . . . CLC 5
See also Bennett, George Harold
See also DLB 33

Bennett, Jay 1912- . . . . CLC 35
See also AAYA 10; CA 69-72; CANR 11;
SAAS 4; SATA 27, 41

Bennett, Louise (Simone) 1919- . . . . . CLC 28
See also BLC 1; DLB 117

Benson, E(dward) F(rederic)
1867-1940 . . . . TCLC 27
See also CA 114

Benson, Jackson J. 1930- . . . . CLC 34
See also CA 25-28R; DLB 111

Benson, Sally 1900-1972 . . . . CLC 17
See also CA 19-20; 37-40R; CAP 1;
SATA 1, 27, 35

Benson, Stella 1892-1933 . . . . TCLC 17
See also CA 117; DLB 36

Bentham, Jeremy 1748-1832 . . . . . NCLC 38
See also DLB 107

Bentley, E(dmund) C(lerihew)
1875-1956 . . . . TCLC 12
See also CA 108; DLB 70

Bentley, Eric (Russell) 1916- . . . . CLC 24
See also CA 5-8R; CANR 6

Beranger, Pierre Jean de
1780-1857 . . . . NCLC 34

Berger, Colonel
See Malraux, (Georges-)Andre

Berger, John (Peter) 1926- . . . . . . CLC 2, 19
See also CA 81-84; DLB 14

Berger, Melvin H. 1927- . . . . CLC 12
See also CA 5-8R; CANR 4; SAAS 2;
SATA 5

Berger, Thomas (Louis)
1924- . . . . CLC 3, 5, 8, 11, 18, 38
See also CA 1-4R; CANR 5, 28; DLB 2;
DLBY 80; MTCW

Bergman, (Ernst) Ingmar
1918- . . . . CLC 16, 72
See also CA 81-84; CANR 33

Bergson, Henri 1859-1941 . . . . TCLC 32

Bergstein, Eleanor 1938- . . . . CLC 4
See also CA 53-56; CANR 5

Berkoff, Steven 1937- . . . . CLC 56
See also CA 104

Bermant, Chaim (Icyk) 1929- . . . . . . CLC 40
See also CA 57-60; CANR 6, 31

Bern, Victoria
See Fisher, M(ary) F(rances) K(ennedy)

Bernanos, (Paul Louis) Georges
1888-1948 . . . . TCLC 3
See also CA 104; 130; DLB 72

Bernard, April 1956- . . . . CLC 59
See also CA 131

Bernhard, Thomas
1931-1989 . . . . CLC 3, 32, 61
See also CA 85-88; 127; CANR 32;
DLB 85, 124; MTCW

Berrigan, Daniel 1921- . . . . CLC 4
See also CA 33-36R; CAAS 1; CANR 11;
DLB 5

Berrigan, Edmund Joseph Michael, Jr.
1934-1983
See Berrigan, Ted
See also CA 61-64; 110; CANR 14

Berrigan, Ted . . . . CLC 37
See also Berrigan, Edmund Joseph Michael,
Jr.
See also DLB 5

Berry, Charles Edward Anderson 1931-
See Berry, Chuck
See also CA 115

Berry, Chuck . . . . CLC 17
See also Berry, Charles Edward Anderson

Berry, Jonas
See Ashbery, John (Lawrence)

Berry, Wendell (Erdman)
1934- . . . . CLC 4, 6, 8, 27, 46
See also AITN 1; CA 73-76; DLB 5, 6

Berryman, John
1914-1972 . . . . . CLC 1, 2, 3, 4, 6, 8, 10,
13, 25, 62
See also CA 13-16; 33-36R; CABS 2;
CANR 35; CAP 1; CDALB 1941-1968;
DLB 48; MTCW

Bertolucci, Bernardo 1940- . . . . CLC 16
See also CA 106

Bertrand, Aloysius 1807-1841 . . . . NCLC 31

Bertran de Born c. 1140-1215 . . . . . CMLC 5

Besant, Annie (Wood) 1847-1933 . . . TCLC 9
See also CA 105

Bessie, Alvah 1904-1985 . . . . CLC 23
See also CA 5-8R; 116; CANR 2; DLB 26

Bethlen, T. D.
See Silverberg, Robert

Beti, Mongo . . . . CLC 27
See also Biyidi, Alexandre
See also BLC 1

Betjeman, John
1906-1984 . . . . CLC 2, 6, 10, 34, 43
See also CA 9-12R; 112; CANR 33;
CDBLB 1945-1960; DLB 20; DLBY 84;
MTCW

Betti, Ugo 1892-1953 . . . . TCLC 5
See also CA 104

Betts, Doris (Waugh) 1932- . . . . CLC 3, 6, 28
See also CA 13-16R; CANR 9; DLBY 82

Bevan, Alistair
See Roberts, Keith (John Kingston)

Beynon, John
See Harris, John (Wyndham Parkes Lucas)
Beynon

Bialik, Chaim Nachman
1873-1934 . . . . TCLC 25

Bickerstaff, Isaac
See Swift, Jonathan

Bidart, Frank 19(?)- . . . . CLC 33
See also CA 140

Bienek, Horst 1930- . . . . CLC 7, 11
See also CA 73-76; DLB 75

Author Index

Bierce, Ambrose (Gwinett)
1842-1914(?) ..... **TCLC 1, 7, 44; SSC 9**
See also CA 104; 139; CDALB 1865-1917;
DA; DLB 11, 12, 23, 71, 74; WLC

Billings, Josh
See Shaw, Henry Wheeler

Billington, Rachel 1942-.......... **CLC 43**
See also AITN 2; CA 33-36R

Binyon, T(imothy) J(ohn) 1936- .... **CLC 34**
See also CA 111; CANR 28

Bioy Casares, Adolfo 1914-.... **CLC 4, 8, 13**
See also CA 29-32R; CANR 19; DLB 113;
HW; MTCW

Bird, C.
See Ellison, Harlan

Bird, Cordwainer
See Ellison, Harlan

Bird, Robert Montgomery
1806-1854 .... **NCLC 1**

Birney, (Alfred) Earle
1904- .... **CLC 1, 4, 6, 11**
See also CA 1-4R; CANR 5, 20; DLB 88;
MTCW

Bishop, Elizabeth
1911-1979 ..... **CLC 1, 4, 9, 13, 15, 32;
PC 3**
See also CA 5-8R; 89-92; CABS 2;
CANR 26; CDALB 1968-1988; DA;
DLB 5; MTCW; SATA 24

Bishop, John 1935-.............. **CLC 10**
See also CA 105

Bissett, Bill 1939-................ **CLC 18**
See also CA 69-72; CANR 15; DLB 53;
MTCW

Bitov, Andrei (Georgievich) 1937-... **CLC 57**

Biyidi, Alexandre 1932-
See Beti, Mongo
See also BW; CA 114; 124; MTCW

Bjarme, Brynjolf
See Ibsen, Henrik (Johan)

Bjornson, Bjornstjerne (Martinius)
1832-1910 .... **TCLC 7, 37**
See also CA 104

Black, Robert
See Holdstock, Robert P.

Blackburn, Paul 1926-1971 ...... **CLC 9, 43**
See also CA 81-84; 33-36R; CANR 34;
DLB 16; DLBY 81

Black Elk 1863-1950 .... **TCLC 33**

Black Hobart
See Sanders, (James) Ed(ward)

Blacklin, Malcolm
See Chambers, Aidan

Blackmore, R(ichard) D(oddridge)
1825-1900 .... **TCLC 27**
See also CA 120; DLB 18

Blackmur, R(ichard) P(almer)
1904-1965 .... **CLC 2, 24**
See also CA 11-12; 25-28R; CAP 1; DLB 63

Black Tarantula, The
See Acker, Kathy

Blackwood, Algernon (Henry)
1869-1951 .... **TCLC 5**
See also CA 105

Blackwood, Caroline 1931- .... **CLC 6, 9**
See also CA 85-88; CANR 32; DLB 14;
MTCW

Blade, Alexander
See Hamilton, Edmond; Silverberg, Robert

Blaga, Lucian 1895-1961 .... **CLC 75**

Blair, Eric (Arthur) 1903-1950
See Orwell, George
See also CA 104; 132; DA; MTCW;
SATA 29

Blais, Marie-Claire
1939- .... **CLC 2, 4, 6, 13, 22**
See also CA 21-24R; CAAS 4; CANR 38;
DLB 53; MTCW

Blaise, Clark 1940-............... **CLC 29**
See also AITN 2; CA 53-56; CAAS 3;
CANR 5; DLB 53

Blake, Nicholas
See Day Lewis, C(ecil)
See also DLB 77

Blake, William 1757-1827 .... **NCLC 13**
See also CDBLB 1789-1832; DA; DLB 93;
MAICYA; SATA 30; WLC

Blasco Ibanez, Vicente
1867-1928 .... **TCLC 12**
See also CA 110; 131; HW; MTCW

Blatty, William Peter 1928-........ **CLC 2**
See also CA 5-8R; CANR 9

Bleeck, Oliver
See Thomas, Ross (Elmore)

Blessing, Lee 1949-.............. **CLC 54**

Blish, James (Benjamin)
1921-1975 .... **CLC 14**
See also CA 1-4R; 57-60; CANR 3; DLB 8;
MTCW; SATA 66

Bliss, Reginald
See Wells, H(erbert) G(eorge)

Blixen, Karen (Christentze Dinesen)
1885-1962
See Dinesen, Isak
See also CA 25-28; CANR 22; CAP 2;
MTCW; SATA 44

Bloch, Robert (Albert) 1917-....... **CLC 33**
See also CA 5-8R; CANR 5; DLB 44;
SATA 12

Blok, Alexander (Alexandrovich)
1880-1921 .... **TCLC 5**
See also CA 104

Blom, Jan
See Breytenbach, Breyten

Bloom, Harold 1930- .... **CLC 24**
See also CA 13-16R; CANR 39; DLB 67

Bloomfield, Aurelius
See Bourne, Randolph S(illiman)

Blount, Roy (Alton), Jr. 1941- ..... **CLC 38**
See also CA 53-56; CANR 10, 28; MTCW

Bloy, Leon 1846-1917........... **TCLC 22**
See also CA 121; DLB 123

Blume, Judy (Sussman) 1938-... **CLC 12, 30**
See also AAYA 3; CA 29-32R; CANR 13,
37; CLR 2, 15; DLB 52; MAICYA;
MTCW; SATA 2, 31

Blunden, Edmund (Charles)
1896-1974 .... **CLC 2, 56**
See also CA 17-18; 45-48; CAP 2; DLB 20,
100; MTCW

Bly, Robert (Elwood)
1926- .... **CLC 1, 2, 5, 10, 15, 38**
See also CA 5-8R; CANR 41; DLB 5;
MTCW

Bobette
See Simenon, Georges (Jacques Christian)

Boccaccio, Giovanni 1313-1375
See also SSC 10

Bochco, Steven 1943-............. **CLC 35**
See also CA 124; 138

Bodenheim, Maxwell 1892-1954 ... **TCLC 44**
See also CA 110; DLB 9, 45

Bodker, Cecil 1927- .... **CLC 21**
See also CA 73-76; CANR 13; CLR 23;
MAICYA; SATA 14

Boell, Heinrich (Theodor) 1917-1985
See Boll, Heinrich (Theodor)
See also CA 21-24R; 116; CANR 24; DA;
DLB 69; DLBY 85; MTCW

Bogan, Louise 1897-1970..... **CLC 4, 39, 46**
See also CA 73-76; 25-28R; CANR 33;
DLB 45; MTCW

Bogarde, Dirk .... **CLC 19**
See Van Den Bogarde, Derek Jules
Gaspard Ulric Niven
See also DLB 14

Bogosian, Eric 1953- .... **CLC 45**
See also CA 138

Bograd, Larry 1953-............. **CLC 35**
See also CA 93-96; SATA 33

Boiardo, Matteo Maria 1441-1494 .... **LC 6**

Boileau-Despreaux, Nicolas
1636-1711 .... **LC 3**

Boland, Eavan 1944-.......... **CLC 40, 67**
See also DLB 40

Boll, Heinrich (Theodor)
1917-1985 ... **CLC 2, 3, 6, 9, 11, 15, 27,
39, 72**
See also Boell, Heinrich (Theodor)
See also DLB 69; DLBY 85; WLC

Bolt, Lee
See Faust, Frederick (Schiller)

Bolt, Robert (Oxton) 1924-........ **CLC 14**
See also CA 17-20R; CANR 35; DLB 13;
MTCW

Bomkauf
See Kaufman, Bob (Garnell)

Bonaventura.................... **NCLC 35**
See also DLB 90

Bond, Edward 1934-....... **CLC 4, 6, 13, 23**
See also CA 25-28R; CANR 38; DLB 13;
MTCW

Bonham, Frank 1914-1989......... **CLC 12**
See also AAYA 1; CA 9-12R; CANR 4, 36;
MAICYA; SAAS 3; SATA 1, 49, 62

Bonnefoy, Yves 1923-........ **CLC 9, 15, 58**
See also CA 85-88; CANR 33; MTCW

Bontemps, Arna(ud Wendell)
1902-1973 . . . . CLC **1, 18**
See also BLC 1; BW; CA 1-4R; 41-44R;
CANR 4, 35; CLR 6; DLB 48, 51;
MAICYA; MTCW; SATA 2, 24, 44

Booth, Martin 1944- . . . . CLC **13**
See also CA 93-96; CAAS 2

Booth, Philip 1925- . . . . CLC **23**
See also CA 5-8R; CANR 5; DLBY 82

Booth, Wayne C(layson) 1921- . . . . . CLC **24**
See also CA 1-4R; CAAS 5; CANR 3;
DLB 67

Borchert, Wolfgang 1921-1947 . . . . . TCLC **5**
See also CA 104; DLB 69, 124

Borges, Jorge Luis
1899-1986 . . . CLC **1, 2, 3, 4, 6, 8, 9, 10,
13, 19, 44, 48; SSC 4**
See also CA 21-24R; CANR 19, 33; DA;
DLB 113; DLBY 86; HW; MTCW; WLC

Borowski, Tadeusz 1922-1951 . . . . . . TCLC **9**
See also CA 106

Borrow, George (Henry)
1803-1881 . . . . NCLC **9**
See also DLB 21, 55

Bosman, Herman Charles
1905-1951 . . . . TCLC **49**

Bosschere, Jean de 1878(?)-1953 . . . TCLC **19**
See also CA 115

Boswell, James 1740-1795 . . . . LC **4**
See also CDBLB 1660-1789; DA; DLB 104;
WLC

Bottoms, David 1949- . . . . CLC **53**
See also CA 105; CANR 22; DLB 120;
DLBY 83

Boucolon, Maryse 1937-
See Conde, Maryse
See also CA 110; CANR 30

Bourget, Paul (Charles Joseph)
1852-1935 . . . . TCLC **12**
See also CA 107; DLB 123

Bourjaily, Vance (Nye) 1922- . . . . CLC **8, 62**
See also CA 1-4R; CAAS 1; CANR 2;
DLB 2

Bourne, Randolph S(illiman)
1886-1918 . . . . TCLC **16**
See also CA 117; DLB 63

Bova, Ben(jamin William) 1932- . . . . CLC **45**
See also CA 5-8R; CANR 11; CLR 3;
DLBY 81; MAICYA; MTCW; SATA 6,
68

Bowen, Elizabeth (Dorothea Cole)
1899-1973 . . . . . CLC **1, 3, 6, 11, 15, 22;
SSC 3**
See also CA 17-18; 41-44R; CANR 35;
CAP 2; CDBLB 1945-1960; DLB 15;
MTCW

Bowering, George 1935- . . . . CLC **15, 47**
See also CA 21-24R; CAAS 16; CANR 10;
DLB 53

Bowering, Marilyn R(uthe) 1949- . . . CLC **32**
See also CA 101

Bowers, Edgar 1924- . . . . CLC **9**
See also CA 5-8R; CANR 24; DLB 5

Bowie, David . . . . CLC **17**
See also Jones, David Robert

Bowles, Jane (Sydney)
1917-1973 . . . . CLC **3, 68**
See also CA 19-20; 41-44R; CAP 2

Bowles, Paul (Frederick)
1910- . . . . CLC **1, 2, 19, 53; SSC 3**
See also CA 1-4R; CAAS 1; CANR 1, 19;
DLB 5, 6; MTCW

Box, Edgar
See Vidal, Gore

Boyd, Nancy
See Millay, Edna St. Vincent

Boyd, William 1952- . . . . CLC **28, 53, 70**
See also CA 114; 120

Boyle, Kay
1902-1992 . . . . . CLC **1, 5, 19, 58; SSC 5**
See also CA 13-16R; 140; CAAS 1;
CANR 29; DLB 4, 9, 48, 86; MTCW

Boyle, Mark
See Kienzle, William X(avier)

Boyle, Patrick 1905-1982 . . . . CLC **19**
See also CA 127

Boyle, T. Coraghessan 1948- . . . . CLC **36, 55**
See also BEST 90:4; CA 120; DLBY 86

Boz
See Dickens, Charles (John Huffam)

Brackenridge, Hugh Henry
1748-1816 . . . . NCLC **7**
See also DLB 11, 37

Bradbury, Edward P.
See Moorcock, Michael (John)

Bradbury, Malcolm (Stanley)
1932- . . . . CLC **32, 61**
See also CA 1-4R; CANR 1, 33; DLB 14;
MTCW

Bradbury, Ray (Douglas)
1920- . . . . CLC **1, 3, 10, 15, 42**
See also AITN 1, 2; CA 1-4R; CANR 2, 30;
CDALB 1968-1988; DA; DLB 2, 8;
MTCW; SATA 11, 64; WLC

Bradford, Gamaliel 1863-1932 . . . . . TCLC **36**
See also DLB 17

Bradley, David (Henry, Jr.) 1950- . . CLC **23**
See also BLC 1; BW; CA 104; CANR 26;
DLB 33

Bradley, John Ed 1959- . . . . CLC **55**

Bradley, Marion Zimmer 1930- . . . . . CLC **30**
See also AAYA 9; CA 57-60; CAAS 10;
CANR 7, 31; DLB 8; MTCW

Bradstreet, Anne 1612(?)-1672 . . . . LC **4**
See also CDALB 1640-1865; DA; DLB 24

Bragg, Melvyn 1939- . . . . CLC **10**
See also BEST 89:3; CA 57-60; CANR 10;
DLB 14

Braine, John (Gerard)
1922-1986 . . . . CLC **1, 3, 41**
See also CA 1-4R; 120; CANR 1, 33;
CDBLB 1945-1960; DLB 15; DLBY 86;
MTCW

Brammer, William 1930(?)-1978 . . . . CLC **31**
See also CA 77-80

Brancati, Vitaliano 1907-1954 . . . . . TCLC **12**
See also CA 109

Brancato, Robin F(idler) 1936- . . . . . CLC **35**
See also AAYA 9; CA 69-72; CANR 11;
SAAS 9; SATA 23

Brand, Max
See Faust, Frederick (Schiller)

Brand, Millen 1906-1980 . . . . CLC **7**
See also CA 21-24R; 97-100

Branden, Barbara . . . . CLC **44**

Brandes, Georg (Morris Cohen)
1842-1927 . . . . TCLC **10**
See also CA 105

Brandys, Kazimierz 1916- . . . . CLC **62**

Branley, Franklyn M(ansfield)
1915- . . . . CLC **21**
See also CA 33-36R; CANR 14, 39;
CLR 13; MAICYA; SAAS 16; SATA 4,
68

Brathwaite, Edward (Kamau)
1930- . . . . CLC **11**
See also BW; CA 25-28R; CANR 11, 26;
DLB 125

Brautigan, Richard (Gary)
1935-1984 . . . . CLC **1, 3, 5, 9, 12, 34, 42**
See also CA 53-56; 113; CANR 34; DLB 2,
5; DLBY 80, 84; MTCW; SATA 56

Braverman, Kate 1950- . . . . CLC **67**
See also CA 89-92

Brecht, Bertolt
1898-1956 . . . . . TCLC **1, 6, 13, 35; DC 3**
See also CA 104; 133; DA; DLB 56, 124;
MTCW; WLC

Brecht, Eugen Berthold Friedrich
See Brecht, Bertolt

Bremer, Fredrika 1801-1865 . . . . . NCLC **11**

Brennan, Christopher John
1870-1932 . . . . TCLC **17**
See also CA 117

Brennan, Maeve 1917- . . . . CLC **5**
See also CA 81-84

Brentano, Clemens (Maria)
1778-1842 . . . . NCLC **1**

Brent of Bin Bin
See Franklin, (Stella Maraia Sarah) Miles

Brenton, Howard 1942- . . . . CLC **31**
See also CA 69-72; CANR 33; DLB 13;
MTCW

Breslin, James 1930-
See Breslin, Jimmy
See also CA 73-76; CANR 31; MTCW

Breslin, Jimmy . . . . CLC **4, 43**
See also Breslin, James
See also AITN 1

Bresson, Robert 1907- . . . . CLC **16**
See also CA 110

Breton, Andre 1896-1966 . . . CLC **2, 9, 15, 54**
See also CA 19-20; 25-28R; CANR 40;
CAP 2; DLB 65; MTCW

Breytenbach, Breyten 1939(?)- . . CLC **23, 37**
See also CA 113; 129

Bridgers, Sue Ellen 1942- . . . . CLC **26**
See also AAYA 8; CA 65-68; CANR 11,
36; CLR 18; DLB 52; MAICYA;
SAAS 1; SATA 22

Bridges, Robert (Seymour)
1844-1930 . . . . TCLC **1**
See also CA 104; CDBLB 1890-1914;
DLB 19, 98

Bridie, James . . . . **TCLC 3**
  See also Mavor, Osborne Henry
  See also DLB 10

Brin, David 1950- . . . . **CLC 34**
  See also CA 102; CANR 24; SATA 65

Brink, Andre (Philippus)
  1935- . . . . **CLC 18, 36**
  See also CA 104; CANR 39; MTCW

Brinsmead, H(esba) F(ay) 1922- . . . . **CLC 21**
  See also CA 21-24R; CANR 10; MAICYA;
  SAAS 5; SATA 18

Brittain, Vera (Mary)
  1893(?)-1970 . . . . **CLC 23**
  See also CA 13-16; 25-28R; CAP 1; MTCW

Broch, Hermann 1886-1951 . . . . **TCLC 20**
  See also CA 117; DLB 85, 124

Brock, Rose
  See Hansen, Joseph

Brodkey, Harold 1930- . . . . **CLC 56**
  See also CA 111; DLB 130

Brodsky, Iosif Alexandrovich 1940-
  See Brodsky, Joseph
  See also AITN 1; CA 41-44R; CANR 37;
  MTCW

Brodsky, Joseph . . . . **CLC 4, 6, 13, 36, 50**
  See also Brodsky, Iosif Alexandrovich

Brodsky, Michael Mark 1948- . . . . . **CLC 19**
  See also CA 102; CANR 18, 41

Bromell, Henry 1947- . . . . **CLC 5**
  See also CA 53-56; CANR 9

Bromfield, Louis (Brucker)
  1896-1956 . . . . **TCLC 11**
  See also CA 107; DLB 4, 9, 86

Broner, E(sther) M(asserman)
  1930- . . . . **CLC 19**
  See also CA 17-20R; CANR 8, 25; DLB 28

Bronk, William 1918- . . . . **CLC 10**
  See also CA 89-92; CANR 23

Bronstein, Lev Davidovich
  See Trotsky, Leon

Bronte, Anne 1820-1849 . . . . **NCLC 4**
  See also DLB 21

Bronte, Charlotte
  1816-1855 . . . . **NCLC 3, 8, 33**
  See also CDBLB 1832-1890; DA; DLB 21;
  WLC

Bronte, (Jane) Emily
  1818-1848 . . . . **NCLC 16, 35**
  See also CDBLB 1832-1890; DA; DLB 21,
  32; WLC

Brooke, Frances 1724-1789 . . . . **LC 6**
  See also DLB 39, 99

Brooke, Henry 1703(?)-1783 . . . . **LC 1**
  See also DLB 39

Brooke, Rupert (Chawner)
  1887-1915 . . . . **TCLC 2, 7**
  See also CA 104; 132; CDBLB 1914-1945;
  DA; DLB 19; MTCW; WLC

Brooke-Haven, P.
  See Wodehouse, P(elham) G(renville)

Brooke-Rose, Christine 1926- . . . . . . **CLC 40**
  See also CA 13-16R; DLB 14

Brookner, Anita 1928- . . . . . . **CLC 32, 34, 51**
  See also CA 114; 120; CANR 37; DLBY 87;
  MTCW

Brooks, Cleanth 1906- . . . . **CLC 24**
  See also CA 17-20R; CANR 33, 35;
  DLB 63; MTCW

Brooks, George
  See Baum, L(yman) Frank

Brooks, Gwendolyn
  1917- . . . . **CLC 1, 2, 4, 5, 15, 49**
  See also AITN 1; BLC 1; BW; CA 1-4R;
  CANR 1, 27; CDALB 1941-1968;
  CLR 27; DA; DLB 5, 76; MTCW;
  SATA 6; WLC

Brooks, Mel . . . . **CLC 12**
  See also Kaminsky, Melvin
  See also DLB 26

Brooks, Peter 1938- . . . . **CLC 34**
  See also CA 45-48; CANR 1

Brooks, Van Wyck 1886-1963 . . . . . . **CLC 29**
  See also CA 1-4R; CANR 6; DLB 45, 63,
  103

Brophy, Brigid (Antonia)
  1929- . . . . **CLC 6, 11, 29**
  See also CA 5-8R; CAAS 4; CANR 25;
  DLB 14; MTCW

Brosman, Catharine Savage 1934- . . . . **CLC 9**
  See also CA 61-64; CANR 21

Brother Antoninus
  See Everson, William (Oliver)

Broughton, T(homas) Alan 1936- . . . **CLC 19**
  See also CA 45-48; CANR 2, 23

Broumas, Olga 1949- . . . . **CLC 10, 73**
  See also CA 85-88; CANR 20

Brown, Charles Brockden
  1771-1810 . . . . **NCLC 22**
  See also CDALB 1640-1865; DLB 37, 59,
  73

Brown, Christy 1932-1981 . . . . **CLC 63**
  See also CA 105; 104; DLB 14

Brown, Claude 1937- . . . . **CLC 30**
  See also AAYA 7; BLC 1; BW; CA 73-76

Brown, Dee (Alexander) 1908- . . **CLC 18, 47**
  See also CA 13-16R; CAAS 6; CANR 11;
  DLBY 80; MTCW; SATA 5

Brown, George
  See Wertmueller, Lina

Brown, George Douglas
  1869-1902 . . . . **TCLC 28**

Brown, George Mackay 1921- . . . . **CLC 5, 48**
  See also CA 21-24R; CAAS 6; CANR 12,
  37; DLB 14, 27; MTCW; SATA 35

Brown, (William) Larry 1951- . . . . . . **CLC 73**
  See also CA 130; 134

Brown, Moses
  See Barrett, William (Christopher)

Brown, Rita Mae 1944- . . . . **CLC 18, 43**
  See also CA 45-48; CANR 2, 11, 35;
  MTCW

Brown, Roderick (Langmere) Haig-
  See Haig-Brown, Roderick (Langmere)

Brown, Rosellen 1939- . . . . **CLC 32**
  See also CA 77-80; CAAS 10; CANR 14

Brown, Sterling Allen
  1901-1989 . . . . **CLC 1, 23, 59**
  See also BLC 1; BW; CA 85-88; 127;
  CANR 26; DLB 48, 51, 63; MTCW

Brown, Will
  See Ainsworth, William Harrison

Brown, William Wells
  1813-1884 . . . . **NCLC 2; DC 1**
  See also BLC 1; DLB 3, 50

Browne, (Clyde) Jackson 1948(?)- . . . **CLC 21**
  See also CA 120

Browning, Elizabeth Barrett
  1806-1861 . . . . **NCLC 1, 16; PC 6**
  See also CDBLB 1832-1890; DA; DLB 32;
  WLC

Browning, Robert
  1812-1889 . . . . **NCLC 19; PC 2**
  See also CDBLB 1832-1890; DA; DLB 32;
  YABC 1

Browning, Tod 1882-1962 . . . . **CLC 16**
  See also CA 117

Bruccoli, Matthew J(oseph) 1931- . . **CLC 34**
  See also CA 9-12R; CANR 7; DLB 103

Bruce, Lenny . . . . **CLC 21**
  See also Schneider, Leonard Alfred

Bruin, John
  See Brutus, Dennis

Brulls, Christian
  See Simenon, Georges (Jacques Christian)

Brunner, John (Kilian Houston)
  1934- . . . . **CLC 8, 10**
  See also CA 1-4R; CAAS 8; CANR 2, 37;
  MTCW

Brutus, Dennis 1924- . . . . **CLC 43**
  See also BLC 1; BW; CA 49-52; CAAS 14;
  CANR 2, 27; DLB 117

Bryan, C(ourtlandt) D(ixon) B(arnes)
  1936- . . . . **CLC 29**
  See also CA 73-76; CANR 13

Bryan, Michael
  See Moore, Brian

Bryant, William Cullen
  1794-1878 . . . . **NCLC 6**
  See also CDALB 1640-1865; DA; DLB 3,
  43, 59

Bryusov, Valery Yakovlevich
  1873-1924 . . . . **TCLC 10**
  See also CA 107

Buchan, John 1875-1940 . . . . **TCLC 41**
  See also CA 108; DLB 34, 70; YABC 2

Buchanan, George 1506-1582 . . . . **LC 4**

Buchheim, Lothar-Guenther 1918- . . . **CLC 6**
  See also CA 85-88

Buchner, (Karl) Georg
  1813-1837 . . . . **NCLC 26**

Buchwald, Art(hur) 1925- . . . . **CLC 33**
  See also AITN 1; CA 5-8R; CANR 21;
  MTCW; SATA 10

Buck, Pearl S(ydenstricker)
  1892-1973 . . . . **CLC 7, 11, 18**
  See also AITN 1; CA 1-4R; 41-44R;
  CANR 1, 34; DA; DLB 9, 102; MTCW;
  SATA 1, 25

Buckler, Ernest 1908-1984........ CLC 13
See also CA 11-12; 114; CAP 1; DLB 68;
SATA 47

Buckley, Vincent (Thomas)
1925-1988 .... CLC 57
See also CA 101

Buckley, William F(rank), Jr.
1925- .... CLC 7, 18, 37
See also AITN 1; CA 1-4R; CANR 1, 24;
DLBY 80; MTCW

Buechner, (Carl) Frederick
1926- .... CLC 2, 4, 6, 9
See also CA 13-16R; CANR 11, 39;
DLBY 80; MTCW

Buell, John (Edward) 1927-........ CLC 10
See also CA 1-4R; DLB 53

Buero Vallejo, Antonio 1916-... CLC 15, 46
See also CA 106; CANR 24; HW; MTCW

Bufalino, Gesualdo 1920(?)-........ CLC 74

Bugayev, Boris Nikolayevich 1880-1934
See Bely, Andrey
See also CA 104

Bukowski, Charles 1920-.... CLC 2, 5, 9, 41
See also CA 17-20R; CANR 40; DLB 5,
130; MTCW

Bulgakov, Mikhail (Afanas'evich)
1891-1940 .... TCLC 2, 16
See also CA 105

Bullins, Ed 1935- .... CLC 1, 5, 7
See also BLC 1; BW; CA 49-52; CAAS 16;
CANR 24; DLB 7, 38; MTCW

Bulwer-Lytton, Edward (George Earle Lytton)
1803-1873 .... NCLC 1
See also DLB 21

Bunin, Ivan Alexeyevich
1870-1953 .... TCLC 6; SSC 5
See also CA 104

Bunting, Basil 1900-1985.... CLC 10, 39, 47
See also CA 53-56; 115; CANR 7; DLB 20

Bunuel, Luis 1900-1983 .... CLC 16
See also CA 101; 110; CANR 32; HW

Bunyan, John 1628-1688 .... LC 4
See also CDBLB 1660-1789; DA; DLB 39;
WLC

Burford, Eleanor
See Hibbert, Eleanor Alice Burford

Burgess, Anthony
1917- ..... CLC 1, 2, 4, 5, 8, 10, 13, 15,
22, 40, 62
See also Wilson, John (Anthony) Burgess
See also AITN 1; CDBLB 1960 to Present;
DLB 14

Burke, Edmund 1729(?)-1797........ LC 7
See also DA; DLB 104; WLC

Burke, Kenneth (Duva) 1897- .... CLC 2, 24
See also CA 5-8R; CANR 39; DLB 45, 63;
MTCW

Burke, Leda
See Garnett, David

Burke, Ralph
See Silverberg, Robert

Burney, Fanny 1752-1840 .... NCLC 12
See also DLB 39

Burns, Robert 1759-1796....... LC 3; PC 6
See also CDBLB 1789-1832; DA; DLB 109;
WLC

Burns, Tex
See L'Amour, Louis (Dearborn)

Burnshaw, Stanley 1906-..... CLC 3, 13, 44
See also CA 9-12R; DLB 48

Burr, Anne 1937- .... CLC 6
See also CA 25-28R

Burroughs, Edgar Rice
1875-1950 .... TCLC 2, 32
See also CA 104; 132; DLB 8; MTCW;
SATA 41

Burroughs, William S(eward)
1914- .... CLC 1, 2, 5, 15, 22, 42, 75
See also AITN 2; CA 9-12R; CANR 20;
DA; DLB 2, 8, 16; DLBY 81; MTCW;
WLC

Busch, Frederick 1941- ... CLC 7, 10, 18, 47
See also CA 33-36R; CAAS 1; DLB 6

Bush, Ronald 1946- .... CLC 34
See also CA 136

Bustos, F(rancisco)
See Borges, Jorge Luis

Bustos Domecq, H(onorio)
See Bioy Casares, Adolfo; Borges, Jorge
Luis

Butler, Octavia E(stelle) 1947- ..... CLC 38
See also BW; CA 73-76; CANR 12, 24, 38;
DLB 33; MTCW

Butler, Samuel 1612-1680 .... LC 16
See also DLB 101, 126

Butler, Samuel 1835-1902 ..... TCLC 1, 33
See also CA 104; CDBLB 1890-1914; DA;
DLB 18, 57; WLC

Butler, Walter C.
See Faust, Frederick (Schiller)

Butor, Michel (Marie Francois)
1926- .... CLC 1, 3, 8, 11, 15
See also CA 9-12R; CANR 33; DLB 83;
MTCW

Buzo, Alexander (John) 1944-...... CLC 61
See also CA 97-100; CANR 17, 39

Buzzati, Dino 1906-1972 .... CLC 36
See also CA 33-36R

Byars, Betsy (Cromer) 1928-....... CLC 35
See also CA 33-36R; CANR 18, 36; CLR 1,
16; DLB 52; MAICYA; MTCW; SAAS 1;
SATA 4, 46

Byatt, A(ntonia) S(usan Drabble)
1936- .... CLC 19, 65
See also CA 13-16R; CANR 13, 33;
DLB 14; MTCW

Byrne, David 1952-.............. CLC 26
See also CA 127

Byrne, John Keyes 1926-.......... CLC 19
See also Leonard, Hugh
See also CA 102

Byron, George Gordon (Noel)
1788-1824 .... NCLC 2, 12
See also CDBLB 1789-1832; DA; DLB 96,
110; WLC

C.3.3.
See Wilde, Oscar (Fingal O'Flahertie Wills)

Caballero, Fernan 1796-1877..... NCLC 10

Cabell, James Branch 1879-1958 ... TCLC 6
See also CA 105; DLB 9, 78

Cable, George Washington
1844-1925 .... TCLC 4; SSC 4
See also CA 104; DLB 12, 74

Cabral de Melo Neto, Joao 1920-... CLC 76

Cabrera Infante, G(uillermo)
1929- ....CLC 5, 25, 45
See also CA 85-88; CANR 29; DLB 113;
HW; MTCW

Cade, Toni
See Bambara, Toni Cade

Cadmus
See Buchan, John

Caedmon fl. 658-680............. CMLC 7

Caeiro, Alberto
See Pessoa, Fernando (Antonio Nogueira)

Cage, John (Milton, Jr.) 1912- ..... CLC 41
See also CA 13-16R; CANR 9

Cain, G.
See Cabrera Infante, G(uillermo)

Cain, Guillermo
See Cabrera Infante, G(uillermo)

Cain, James M(allahan)
1892-1977 .... CLC 3, 11, 28
See also AITN 1; CA 17-20R; 73-76;
CANR 8, 34; MTCW

Caine, Mark
See Raphael, Frederic (Michael)

Calderon de la Barca, Pedro
1600-1681 .... DC 3

Caldwell, Erskine (Preston)
1903-1987 .... CLC 1, 8, 14, 50, 60
See also AITN 1; CA 1-4R; 121; CAAS 1;
CANR 2, 33; DLB 9, 86; MTCW

Caldwell, (Janet Miriam) Taylor (Holland)
1900-1985 .... CLC 2, 28, 39
See also CA 5-8R; 116; CANR 5

Calhoun, John Caldwell
1782-1850 .... NCLC 15
See also DLB 3

Calisher, Hortense 1911-.... CLC 2, 4, 8, 38
See also CA 1-4R; CANR 1, 22; DLB 2;
MTCW

Callaghan, Morley Edward
1903-1990 .... CLC 3, 14, 41, 65
See also CA 9-12R; 132; CANR 33;
DLB 68; MTCW

Calvino, Italo
1923-1985 .... CLC 5, 8, 11, 22, 33, 39,
73; SSC 3
See also CA 85-88; 116; CANR 23; MTCW

Cameron, Carey 1952-............ CLC 59
See also CA 135

Cameron, Peter 1959-............. CLC 44
See also CA 125

Campana, Dino 1885-1932........ TCLC 20
See also CA 117; DLB 114

Campbell, John W(ood, Jr.)
1910-1971 .... CLC 32
See also CA 21-22; 29-32R; CANR 34;
CAP 2; DLB 8; MTCW

Campbell, Joseph 1904-1987 . . . . **CLC 69**
See also AAYA 3; BEST 89:2; CA 1-4R;
124; CANR 3, 28; MTCW

Campbell, (John) Ramsey 1946- . . . . **CLC 42**
See also CA 57-60; CANR 7

Campbell, (Ignatius) Roy (Dunnachie)
1901-1957 . . . . **TCLC 5**
See also CA 104; DLB 20

Campbell, Thomas 1777-1844 . . . . **NCLC 19**
See also DLB 93

Campbell, Wilfred . . . . **TCLC 9**
See also Campbell, William

Campbell, William 1858(?)-1918
See Campbell, Wilfred
See also CA 106; DLB 92

Campos, Alvaro de
See Pessoa, Fernando (Antonio Nogueira)

Camus, Albert
1913-1960 . . . **CLC 1, 2, 4, 9, 11, 14, 32,**
63, 69; DC 2; SSC 9
See also CA 89-92; DA; DLB 72; MTCW;
WLC

Canby, Vincent 1924- . . . . **CLC 13**
See also CA 81-84

Cancale
See Desnos, Robert

Canetti, Elias 1905- . . . . . . **CLC 3, 14, 25, 75**
See also CA 21-24R; CANR 23; DLB 85,
124; MTCW

Canin, Ethan 1960- . . . . **CLC 55**
See also CA 131; 135

Cannon, Curt
See Hunter, Evan

Cape, Judith
See Page, P(atricia) K(athleen)

Capek, Karel
1890-1938 . . . . **TCLC 6, 37; DC 1**
See also CA 104; 140; DA; WLC

Capote, Truman
1924-1984 . . . . . **CLC 1, 3, 8, 13, 19, 34,**
38, 58; SSC 2
See also CA 5-8R; 113; CANR 18;
CDALB 1941-1968; DA; DLB 2;
DLBY 80, 84; MTCW; WLC

Capra, Frank 1897-1991 . . . . **CLC 16**
See also CA 61-64; 135

Caputo, Philip 1941- . . . . **CLC 32**
See also CA 73-76; CANR 40

Card, Orson Scott 1951- . . . . **CLC 44, 47, 50**
See also CA 102; CANR 27; MTCW

Cardenal (Martinez), Ernesto
1925- . . . . **CLC 31**
See also CA 49-52; CANR 2, 32; HW;
MTCW

Carducci, Giosue 1835-1907 . . . . **TCLC 32**

Carew, Thomas 1595(?)-1640 . . . . **LC 13**
See also DLB 126

Carey, Ernestine Gilbreth 1908- . . . . **CLC 17**
See also CA 5-8R; SATA 2

Carey, Peter 1943- . . . . **CLC 40, 55**
See also CA 123; 127; MTCW

Carleton, William 1794-1869 . . . . . . **NCLC 3**

Carlisle, Henry (Coffin) 1926- . . . . . . **CLC 33**
See also CA 13-16R; CANR 15

Carlsen, Chris
See Holdstock, Robert P.

Carlson, Ron(ald F.) 1947- . . . . **CLC 54**
See also CA 105; CANR 27

Carlyle, Thomas 1795-1881 . . . . . . **NCLC 22**
See also CDBLB 1789-1832; DA; DLB 55

Carman, (William) Bliss
1861-1929 . . . . **TCLC 7**
See also CA 104; DLB 92

Carossa, Hans 1878-1956 . . . . **TCLC 48**
See also DLB 66

Carpenter, Don(ald Richard)
1931- . . . . **CLC 41**
See also CA 45-48; CANR 1

Carpentier (y Valmont), Alejo
1904-1980 . . . . **CLC 8, 11, 38**
See also CA 65-68; 97-100; CANR 11;
DLB 113; HW

Carr, Emily 1871-1945 . . . . **TCLC 32**
See also DLB 68

Carr, John Dickson 1906-1977 . . . . . . **CLC 3**
See also CA 49-52; 69-72; CANR 3, 33;
MTCW

Carr, Philippa
See Hibbert, Eleanor Alice Burford

Carr, Virginia Spencer 1929- . . . . . . **CLC 34**
See also CA 61-64; DLB 111

Carrier, Roch 1937- . . . . **CLC 13**
See also CA 130; DLB 53

Carroll, James P. 1943(?) . . . . **CLC 38**
See also CA 81-84

Carroll, Jim 1951- . . . . **CLC 35**
See also CA 45-48

Carroll, Lewis . . . . **NCLC 2**
See also Dodgson, Charles Lutwidge
See also CDBLB 1832-1890; CLR 2, 18;
DLB 18; WLC

Carroll, Paul Vincent 1900-1968 . . . . **CLC 10**
See also CA 9-12R; 25-28R; DLB 10

Carruth, Hayden 1921- . . . . **CLC 4, 7, 10, 18**
See also CA 9-12R; CANR 4, 38; DLB 5;
MTCW; SATA 47

Carson, Rachel Louise 1907-1964 . . . **CLC 71**
See also CA 77-80; CANR 35; MTCW;
SATA 23

Carter, Angela (Olive)
1940-1992 . . . . **CLC 5, 41, 76**
See also CA 53-56; 136; CANR 12, 36;
DLB 14; MTCW; SATA 66;
SATA-Obit 70

Carter, Nick
See Smith, Martin Cruz

Carver, Raymond
1938-1988 . . . **CLC 22, 36, 53, 55; SSC 8**
See also CA 33-36R; 126; CANR 17, 34;
DLB 130; DLBY 84, 88; MTCW

Cary, (Arthur) Joyce (Lunel)
1888-1957 . . . . **TCLC 1, 29**
See also CA 104; CDBLB 1914-1945;
DLB 15, 100

Casanova de Seingalt, Giovanni Jacopo
1725-1798 . . . . **LC 13**

Casares, Adolfo Bioy
See Bioy Casares, Adolfo

Casely-Hayford, J(oseph) E(phraim)
1866-1930 . . . . **TCLC 24**
See also BLC 1; CA 123

Casey, John (Dudley) 1939- . . . . **CLC 59**
See also BEST 90:2; CA 69-72; CANR 23

Casey, Michael 1947- . . . . **CLC 2**
See also CA 65-68; DLB 5

Casey, Patrick
See Thurman, Wallace (Henry)

Casey, Warren (Peter) 1935-1988 . . . **CLC 12**
See also CA 101; 127

Casona, Alejandro . . . . **CLC 49**
See also Alvarez, Alejandro Rodriguez

Cassavetes, John 1929-1989 . . . . **CLC 20**
See also CA 85-88; 127

Cassill, R(onald) V(erlin) 1919- . . . **CLC 4, 23**
See also CA 9-12R; CAAS 1; CANR 7;
DLB 6

Cassity, (Allen) Turner 1929- . . . . **CLC 6, 42**
See also CA 17-20R; CAAS 8; CANR 11;
DLB 105

Castaneda, Carlos 1931(?)- . . . . **CLC 12**
See also CA 25-28R; CANR 32; HW;
MTCW

Castedo, Elena 1937- . . . . **CLC 65**
See also CA 132

Castedo-Ellerman, Elena
See Castedo, Elena

Castellanos, Rosario 1925-1974 . . . . . **CLC 66**
See also CA 131; 53-56; DLB 113; HW

Castelvetro, Lodovico 1505-1571 . . . . . **LC 12**

Castiglione, Baldassare 1478-1529 . . . **LC 12**

Castle, Robert
See Hamilton, Edmond

Castro, Guillen de 1569-1631 . . . . **LC 19**

Castro, Rosalia de 1837-1885 . . . . . **NCLC 3**

Cather, Willa
See Cather, Willa Sibert

Cather, Willa Sibert
1873-1947 . . . . . . **TCLC 1, 11, 31; SSC 2**
See also CA 104; 128; CDALB 1865-1917;
DA; DLB 9, 54, 78; DLBD 1; MTCW;
SATA 30; WLC

Catton, (Charles) Bruce
1899-1978 . . . . **CLC 35**
See also AITN 1; CA 5-8R; 81-84;
CANR 7; DLB 17; SATA 2, 24

Cauldwell, Frank
See King, Francis (Henry)

Caunitz, William J. 1933- . . . . **CLC 34**
See also BEST 89:3; CA 125; 130

Causley, Charles (Stanley) 1917- . . . . . **CLC 7**
See also CA 9-12R; CANR 5, 35; CLR 30;
DLB 27; MTCW; SATA 3, 66

Caute, David 1936- . . . . **CLC 29**
See also CA 1-4R; CAAS 4; CANR 1, 33;
DLB 14

Cavafy, C(onstantine) P(eter) . . . . . . **TCLC 2, 7**
See also Kavafis, Konstantinos Petrou

Cavallo, Evelyn
See Spark, Muriel (Sarah)

Christie
See Ichikawa, Kon

Christie, Agatha (Mary Clarissa)
1890-1976 ...... **CLC 1, 6, 8, 12, 39, 48**
See also AAYA 9; AITN 1, 2; CA 17-20R;
61-64; CANR 10, 37; CDBLB 1914-1945;
DLB 13, 77; MTCW; SATA 36

Christie, (Ann) Philippa
See Pearce, Philippa
See also CA 5-8R; CANR 4

Christine de Pizan 1365(?)-1431(?) .... **LC 9**

Chubb, Elmer
See Masters, Edgar Lee

Chulkov, Mikhail Dmitrievich
1743-1792 .... **LC 2**

Churchill, Caryl 1938- .... **CLC 31, 55**
See also CA 102; CANR 22; DLB 13;
MTCW

Churchill, Charles 1731-1764........ **LC 3**
See also DLB 109

Chute, Carolyn 1947-............ **CLC 39**
See also CA 123

Ciardi, John (Anthony)
1916-1986 .... **CLC 10, 40, 44**
See also CA 5-8R; 118; CAAS 2; CANR 5,
33; CLR 19; DLB 5; DLBY 86;
MAICYA; MTCW; SATA 1, 46, 65

Cicero, Marcus Tullius
106B.C.-43B.C............... **CMLC 3**

Cimino, Michael 1943-............ **CLC 16**
See also CA 105

Cioran, E(mil) M. 1911-............ **CLC 64**
See also CA 25-28R

Cisneros, Sandra 1954-............ **CLC 69**
See also AAYA 9; CA 131; DLB 122; HW

Clair, Rene....................... **CLC 20**
See also Chomette, Rene Lucien

Clampitt, Amy 1920- .... **CLC 32**
See also CA 110; CANR 29; DLB 105

Clancy, Thomas L., Jr. 1947-
See Clancy, Tom
See also CA 125; 131; MTCW

Clancy, Tom...................... **CLC 45**
See also Clancy, Thomas L., Jr.
See also AAYA 9; BEST 89:1, 90:1

Clare, John 1793-1864........... **NCLC 9**
See also DLB 55, 96

Clarin
See Alas (y Urena), Leopoldo (Enrique
Garcia)

Clark, (Robert) Brian 1932-........ **CLC 29**
See also CA 41-44R

Clark, Eleanor 1913- .... **CLC 5, 19**
See also CA 9-12R; CANR 41; DLB 6

Clark, J. P.
See Clark, John Pepper
See also DLB 117

Clark, John Pepper 1935- .... **CLC 38**
See also Clark, J. P.
See also BLC 1; BW; CA 65-68; CANR 16

Clark, M. R.
See Clark, Mavis Thorpe

Clark, Mavis Thorpe 1909- .... **CLC 12**
See also CA 57-60; CANR 8, 37; CLR 30;
MAICYA; SAAS 5; SATA 8, 74

Clark, Walter Van Tilburg
1909-1971 .... **CLC 28**
See also CA 9-12R; 33-36R; DLB 9;
SATA 8

Clarke, Arthur C(harles)
1917- ...... **CLC 1, 4, 13, 18, 35; SSC 3**
See also AAYA 4; CA 1-4R; CANR 2, 28;
MAICYA; MTCW; SATA 13, 70

Clarke, Austin 1896-1974........ **CLC 6, 9**
See also CA 29-32; 49-52; CAP 2; DLB 10,
20

Clarke, Austin C(hesterfield)
1934- .... **CLC 8, 53**
See also BLC 1; BW; CA 25-28R;
CAAS 16; CANR 14, 32; DLB 53, 125

Clarke, Gillian 1937-............ **CLC 61**
See also CA 106; DLB 40

Clarke, Marcus (Andrew Hislop)
1846-1881 .... **NCLC 19**

Clarke, Shirley 1925-............ **CLC 16**

Clash, The .... **CLC 30**
See also Headon, (Nicky) Topper; Jones,
Mick; Simonon, Paul; Strummer, Joe

Claudel, Paul (Louis Charles Marie)
1868-1955 .... **TCLC 2, 10**
See also CA 104

Clavell, James (duMaresq)
1925- .... **CLC 6, 25**
See also CA 25-28R; CANR 26; MTCW

Cleaver, (Leroy) Eldridge 1935- .... **CLC 30**
See also BLC 1; BW; CA 21-24R;
CANR 16

Cleese, John (Marwood) 1939- ..... **CLC 21**
See also Monty Python
See also CA 112; 116; CANR 35; MTCW

Cleishbotham, Jebediah
See Scott, Walter

Cleland, John 1710-1789 .... **LC 2**
See also DLB 39

Clemens, Samuel Langhorne 1835-1910
See Twain, Mark
See also CA 104; 135; CDALB 1865-1917;
DA; DLB 11, 12, 23, 64, 74; MAICYA;
YABC 2

Cleophil
See Congreve, William

Clerihew, E.
See Bentley, E(dmund) C(lerihew)

Clerk, N. W.
See Lewis, C(live) S(taples)

Cliff, Jimmy..................... **CLC 21**
See also Chambers, James

Clifton, (Thelma) Lucille
1936-.................... **CLC 19, 66**
See also BLC 1; BW; CA 49-52; CANR 2,
24; CLR 5; DLB 5, 41; MAICYA;
MTCW; SATA 20, 69

Clinton, Dirk
See Silverberg, Robert

Clough, Arthur Hugh 1819-1861.. **NCLC 27**
See also DLB 32

Clutha, Janet Paterson Frame 1924-
See Frame, Janet
See also CA 1-4R; CANR 2, 36; MTCW

Clyne, Terence
See Blatty, William Peter

Cobalt, Martin
See Mayne, William (James Carter)

Coburn, D(onald) L(ee) 1938- ...... **CLC 10**
See also CA 89-92

Cocteau, Jean (Maurice Eugene Clement)
1889-1963 .... **CLC 1, 8, 15, 16, 43**
See also CA 25-28; CANR 40; CAP 2; DA;
DLB 65; MTCW; WLC

Codrescu, Andrei 1946-........... **CLC 46**
See also CA 33-36R; CANR 13, 34

Coe, Max
See Bourne, Randolph S(illiman)

Coe, Tucker
See Westlake, Donald E(dwin)

Coetzee, J(ohn) M(ichael)
1940- .... **CLC 23, 33, 66**
See also CA 77-80; CANR 41; MTCW

Cohen, Arthur A(llen)
1928-1986 .... **CLC 7, 31**
See also CA 1-4R; 120; CANR 1, 17;
DLB 28

Cohen, Leonard (Norman)
1934- .... **CLC 3, 38**
See also CA 21-24R; CANR 14; DLB 53;
MTCW

Cohen, Matt 1942-............... **CLC 19**
See also CA 61-64; CANR 40; DLB 53

Cohen-Solal, Annie 19(?)- .... **CLC 50**

Colegate, Isabel 1931-............ **CLC 36**
See also CA 17-20R; CANR 8, 22; DLB 14;
MTCW

Coleman, Emmett
See Reed, Ishmael

Coleridge, Samuel Taylor
1772-1834 .... **NCLC 9**
See also CDBLB 1789-1832; DA; DLB 93,
107; WLC

Coleridge, Sara 1802-1852 .... **NCLC 31**

Coles, Don 1928- .... **CLC 46**
See also CA 115; CANR 38

Colette, (Sidonie-Gabrielle)
1873-1954 ...... **TCLC 1, 5, 16; SSC 10**
See also CA 104; 131; DLB 65; MTCW

Collett, (Jacobine) Camilla (Wergeland)
1813-1895 .... **NCLC 22**

Collier, Christopher 1930-......... **CLC 30**
See also CA 33-36R; CANR 13, 33;
MAICYA; SATA 16, 70

Collier, James L(incoln) 1928- ..... **CLC 30**
See also CA 9-12R; CANR 4, 33;
MAICYA; SATA 8, 70

Collier, Jeremy 1650-1726.......... **LC 6**

Collins, Hunt
See Hunter, Evan

Collins, Linda 1931-.............. **CLC 44**
See also CA 125

Collins, (William) Wilkie
1824-1889 .... **NCLC 1, 18**
See also CDBLB 1832-1890; DLB 18, 70

Collins, William 1721-1759 . . . . **LC 4**
See also DLB 109

Colman, George
See Glassco, John

Colt, Winchester Remington
See Hubbard, L(afayette) Ron(ald)

Colter, Cyrus 1910- . . . . **CLC 58**
See also BW; CA 65-68; CANR 10; DLB 33

Colton, James
See Hansen, Joseph

Colum, Padraic 1881-1972 . . . . **CLC 28**
See also CA 73-76; 33-36R; CANR 35;
MAICYA; MTCW; SATA 15

Colvin, James
See Moorcock, Michael (John)

Colwin, Laurie (E.)
1944-1992 . . . . **CLC 5, 13, 23**
See also CA 89-92; 139; CANR 20;
DLBY 80; MTCW

Comfort, Alex(ander) 1920- . . . . **CLC 7**
See also CA 1-4R; CANR 1

Comfort, Montgomery
See Campbell, (John) Ramsey

Compton-Burnett, I(vy)
1884(?)-1969 . . . . . . **CLC 1, 3, 10, 15, 34**
See also CA 1-4R; 25-28R; CANR 4;
DLB 36; MTCW

Comstock, Anthony 1844-1915 . . . . **TCLC 13**
See also CA 110

Conan Doyle, Arthur
See Doyle, Arthur Conan

Conde, Maryse . . . . **CLC 52**
See also Boucolon, Maryse

Condon, Richard (Thomas)
1915- . . . . **CLC 4, 6, 8, 10, 45**
See also BEST 90:3; CA 1-4R; CAAS 1;
CANR 2, 23; MTCW

Congreve, William
1670-1729 . . . . **LC 5, 21; DC 2**
See also CDBLB 1660-1789; DA; DLB 39,
84; WLC

Connell, Evan S(helby), Jr.
1924- . . . . **CLC 4, 6, 45**
See also AAYA 7; CA 1-4R; CAAS 2;
CANR 2, 39; DLB 2; DLBY 81; MTCW

Connelly, Marc(us Cook)
1890-1980 . . . . **CLC 7**
See also CA 85-88; 102; CANR 30; DLB 7;
DLBY 80; SATA 25

Connor, Ralph . . . . **TCLC 31**
See also Gordon, Charles William
See also DLB 92

Conrad, Joseph
1857-1924 . . . . . . **TCLC 1, 6, 13, 25, 43;**
SSC 9
See also CA 104; 131; CDBLB 1890-1914;
DA; DLB 10, 34, 98; MTCW; SATA 27;
WLC

Conrad, Robert Arnold
See Hart, Moss

Conroy, Pat 1945- . . . . **CLC 30, 74**
See also AAYA 8; AITN 1; CA 85-88;
CANR 24; DLB 6; MTCW

Constant (de Rebecque), (Henri) Benjamin
1767-1830 . . . . **NCLC 6**
See also DLB 119

Conybeare, Charles Augustus
See Eliot, T(homas) S(tearns)

Cook, Michael 1933- . . . . **CLC 58**
See also CA 93-96; DLB 53

Cook, Robin 1940- . . . . **CLC 14**
See also BEST 90:2; CA 108; 111;
CANR 41

Cook, Roy
See Silverberg, Robert

Cooke, Elizabeth 1948- . . . . **CLC 55**
See also CA 129

Cooke, John Esten 1830-1886 . . . . . **NCLC 5**
See also DLB 3

Cooke, John Estes
See Baum, L(yman) Frank

Cooke, M. E.
See Creasey, John

Cooke, Margaret
See Creasey, John

Cooney, Ray . . . . **CLC 62**

Cooper, Henry St. John
See Creasey, John

Cooper, J. California . . . . **CLC 56**
See also BW; CA 125

Cooper, James Fenimore
1789-1851 . . . . **NCLC 1, 27**
See also CDALB 1640-1865; DLB 3;
SATA 19

Coover, Robert (Lowell)
1932- . . . . **CLC 3, 7, 15, 32, 46**
See also CA 45-48; CANR 3, 37; DLB 2;
DLBY 81; MTCW

Copeland, Stewart (Armstrong)
1952- . . . . **CLC 26**
See also Police, The

Coppard, A(lfred) E(dgar)
1878-1957 . . . . **TCLC 5**
See also CA 114; YABC 1

Coppee, Francois 1842-1908 . . . . . . **TCLC 25**

Coppola, Francis Ford 1939- . . . . . . **CLC 16**
See also CA 77-80; CANR 40; DLB 44

Corcoran, Barbara 1911- . . . . **CLC 17**
See also CA 21-24R; CAAS 2; CANR 11,
28; DLB 52; SATA 3

Cordelier, Maurice
See Giraudoux, (Hippolyte) Jean

Corman, Cid . . . . **CLC 9**
See also Corman, Sidney
See also CAAS 2; DLB 5

Corman, Sidney 1924-
See Corman, Cid
See also CA 85-88

Cormier, Robert (Edmund)
1925- . . . . **CLC 12, 30**
See also AAYA 3; CA 1-4R; CANR 5, 23;
CDALB 1968-1988; CLR 12; DA;
DLB 52; MAICYA; MTCW; SATA 10,
45

Corn, Alfred 1943- . . . . **CLC 33**
See also CA 104; DLB 120; DLBY 80

Cornwell, David (John Moore)
1931- . . . . **CLC 9, 15**
See also le Carre, John
See also CA 5-8R; CANR 13, 33; MTCW

Corrigan, Kevin . . . . **CLC 55**

Corso, (Nunzio) Gregory 1930- . . . **CLC 1, 11**
See also CA 5-8R; CANR 41; DLB 5,16;
MTCW

Cortazar, Julio
1914-1984 . . . . . **CLC 2, 3, 5, 10, 13, 15,**
33, 34; SSC 7
See also CA 21-24R; CANR 12, 32;
DLB 113; HW; MTCW

Corwin, Cecil
See Kornbluth, C(yril) M.

Cosic, Dobrica 1921- . . . . **CLC 14**
See also CA 122; 138

Costain, Thomas B(ertram)
1885-1965 . . . . **CLC 30**
See also CA 5-8R; 25-28R; DLB 9

Costantini, Humberto
1924(?)-1987 . . . . **CLC 49**
See also CA 131; 122; HW

Costello, Elvis 1955- . . . . **CLC 21**

Cotter, Joseph S. Sr.
See Cotter, Joseph Seamon Sr.

Cotter, Joseph Seamon Sr.
1861-1949 . . . . **TCLC 28**
See also BLC 1; BW; CA 124; DLB 50

Coulton, James
See Hansen, Joseph

Couperus, Louis (Marie Anne)
1863-1923 . . . . **TCLC 15**
See also CA 115

Court, Wesli
See Turco, Lewis (Putnam)

Courtenay, Bryce 1933- . . . . **CLC 59**
See also CA 138

Courtney, Robert
See Ellison, Harlan

Cousteau, Jacques-Yves 1910- . . . . . . **CLC 30**
See also CA 65-68; CANR 15; MTCW;
SATA 38

Coward, Noel (Peirce)
1899-1973 . . . . **CLC 1, 9, 29, 51**
See also AITN 1; CA 17-18; 41-44R;
CANR 35; CAP 2; CDBLB 1914-1945;
DLB 10; MTCW

Cowley, Malcolm 1898-1989 . . . . **CLC 39**
See also CA 5-8R; 128; CANR 3; DLB 4,
48; DLBY 81, 89; MTCW

Cowper, William 1731-1800 . . . . **NCLC 8**
See also DLB 104, 109

Cox, William Trevor 1928- . . . **CLC 9, 14, 71**
See also Trevor, William
See also CA 9-12R; CANR 4, 37; DLB 14;
MTCW

Cozzens, James Gould
1903-1978 . . . . **CLC 1, 4, 11**
See also CA 9-12R; 81-84; CANR 19;
CDALB 1941-1968; DLB 9; DLBD 2;
DLBY 84; MTCW

Crabbe, George 1754-1832 . . . . **NCLC 26**
See also DLB 93

Author Index

Fletcher, John Gould 1886-1950 . . . **TCLC 35**
See also CA 107; DLB 4, 45

Fleur, Paul
See Pohl, Frederik

Flooglebuckle, Al
See Spiegelman, Art

Flying Officer X
See Bates, H(erbert) E(rnest)

Fo, Dario 1926- . . . . **CLC 32**
See also CA 116; 128; MTCW

Fogarty, Jonathan Titulescu Esq.
See Farrell, James T(homas)

Folke, Will
See Bloch, Robert (Albert)

Follett, Ken(neth Martin) 1949- . . . . **CLC 18**
See also AAYA 6; BEST 89:4; CA 81-84;
CANR 13, 33; DLB 87; DLBY 81;
MTCW

Fontane, Theodor 1819-1898 . . . . . **NCLC 26**
See also DLB 129

Foote, Horton 1916- . . . . **CLC 51**
See also CA 73-76; CANR 34; DLB 26

Foote, Shelby 1916- . . . . **CLC 75**
See also CA 5-8R; CANR 3; DLB 2, 17

Forbes, Esther 1891-1967 . . . . **CLC 12**
See also CA 13-14; 25-28R; CAP 1;
CLR 27; DLB 22; MAICYA; SATA 2

Forche, Carolyn (Louise) 1950- . . . . . **CLC 25**
See also CA 109; 117; DLB 5

Ford, Elbur
See Hibbert, Eleanor Alice Burford

Ford, Ford Madox
1873-1939 . . . . **TCLC 1, 15, 39**
See also CA 104; 132; CDBLB 1914-1945;
DLB 34, 98; MTCW

Ford, John 1895-1973 . . . . **CLC 16**
See also CA 45-48

Ford, Richard 1944- . . . . **CLC 46**
See also CA 69-72; CANR 11

Ford, Webster
See Masters, Edgar Lee

Foreman, Richard 1937- . . . . **CLC 50**
See also CA 65-68; CANR 32

Forester, C(ecil) S(cott)
1899-1966 . . . . **CLC 35**
See also CA 73-76; 25-28R; SATA 13

Forez
See Mauriac, Francois (Charles)

Forman, James Douglas 1932- . . . . . . **CLC 21**
See also CA 9-12R; CANR 4, 19;
MAICYA; SATA 8, 70

Fornes, Maria Irene 1930- . . . . . . **CLC 39, 61**
See also CA 25-28R; CANR 28; DLB 7;
HW; MTCW

Forrest, Leon 1937- . . . . **CLC 4**
See also BW; CA 89-92; CAAS 7;
CANR 25; DLB 33

Forster, E(dward) M(organ)
1879-1970 . . . . **CLC 1, 2, 3, 4, 9, 10, 13,
15, 22, 45, 77**
See also AAYA 2; CA 13-14; 25-28R;
CAP 1; CDBLB 1914-1945; DA; DLB 34,
98; DLBD 10; MTCW; SATA 57; WLC

Forster, John 1812-1876 . . . . **NCLC 11**

Forsyth, Frederick 1938- . . . . . . **CLC 2, 5, 36**
See also BEST 89:4; CA 85-88; CANR 38;
DLB 87; MTCW

Forten, Charlotte L. . . . . **TCLC 16**
See also Grimke, Charlotte L(ottie) Forten
See also BLC 2; DLB 50

Foscolo, Ugo 1778-1827 . . . . **NCLC 8**

Fosse, Bob . . . . **CLC 20**
See also Fosse, Robert Louis

Fosse, Robert Louis 1927-1987
See Fosse, Bob
See also CA 110; 123

Foster, Stephen Collins
1826-1864 . . . . **NCLC 26**

Foucault, Michel
1926-1984 . . . . **CLC 31, 34, 69**
See also CA 105; 113; CANR 34; MTCW

Fouque, Friedrich (Heinrich Karl) de la Motte
1777-1843 . . . . **NCLC 2**
See also DLB 90

Fournier, Henri Alban 1886-1914
See Alain-Fournier
See also CA 104

Fournier, Pierre 1916- . . . . **CLC 11**
See also Gascar, Pierre
See also CA 89-92; CANR 16, 40

Fowles, John
1926- . . . . **CLC 1, 2, 3, 4, 6, 9, 10, 15, 33**
See also CA 5-8R; CANR 25; CDBLB 1960
to Present; DLB 14; MTCW; SATA 22

Fox, Paula 1923- . . . . **CLC 2, 8**
See also AAYA 3; CA 73-76; CANR 20,
36; CLR 1; DLB 52; MAICYA; MTCW;
SATA 17, 60

Fox, William Price (Jr.) 1926- . . . . . **CLC 22**
See also CA 17-20R; CANR 11; DLB 2;
DLBY 81

Foxe, John 1516(?)-1587 . . . . **LC 14**

Frame, Janet . . . . **CLC 2, 3, 6, 22, 66**
See also Clutha, Janet Paterson Frame

France, Anatole . . . . **TCLC 9**
See also Thibault, Jacques Anatole Francois
See also DLB 123

Francis, Claude 19(?)- . . . . **CLC 50**

Francis, Dick 1920- . . . . **CLC 2, 22, 42**
See also AAYA 5; BEST 89:3; CA 5-8R;
CANR 9; CDBLB 1960 to Present;
DLB 87; MTCW

Francis, Robert (Churchill)
1901-1987 . . . . **CLC 15**
See also CA 1-4R; 123; CANR 1

Frank, Anne(lies Marie)
1929-1945 . . . . **TCLC 17**
See also CA 113; 133; DA; MTCW;
SATA 42; WLC

Frank, Elizabeth 1945- . . . . **CLC 39**
See also CA 121; 126

Franklin, Benjamin
See Hasek, Jaroslav (Matej Frantisek)

Franklin, (Stella Maraia Sarah) Miles
1879-1954 . . . . **TCLC 7**
See also CA 104

Fraser, Antonia (Pakenham)
1932- . . . . **CLC 32**
See also CA 85-88; MTCW; SATA 32

Fraser, George MacDonald 1925- . . . . **CLC 7**
See also CA 45-48; CANR 2

Fraser, Sylvia 1935- . . . . **CLC 64**
See also CA 45-48; CANR 1, 16

Frayn, Michael 1933- . . . . . . **CLC 3, 7, 31, 47**
See also CA 5-8R; CANR 30; DLB 13, 14;
MTCW

Fraze, Candida (Merrill) 1945- . . . . . **CLC 50**
See also CA 126

Frazer, J(ames) G(eorge)
1854-1941 . . . . **TCLC 32**
See also CA 118

Frazer, Robert Caine
See Creasey, John

Frazer, Sir James George
See Frazer, J(ames) G(eorge)

Frazier, Ian 1951- . . . . **CLC 46**
See also CA 130

Frederic, Harold 1856-1898 . . . . . . **NCLC 10**
See also DLB 12, 23

Frederick, John
See Faust, Frederick (Schiller)

Frederick the Great 1712-1786 . . . . . . **LC 14**

Fredro, Aleksander 1793-1876 . . . . . **NCLC 8**

Freeling, Nicolas 1927- . . . . **CLC 38**
See also CA 49-52; CAAS 12; CANR 1, 17;
DLB 87

Freeman, Douglas Southall
1886-1953 . . . . **TCLC 11**
See also CA 109; DLB 17

Freeman, Judith 1946- . . . . **CLC 55**

Freeman, Mary Eleanor Wilkins
1852-1930 . . . . **TCLC 9; SSC 1**
See also CA 106; DLB 12, 78

Freeman, R(ichard) Austin
1862-1943 . . . . **TCLC 21**
See also CA 113; DLB 70

French, Marilyn 1929- . . . . . . **CLC 10, 18, 60**
See also CA 69-72; CANR 3, 31; MTCW

French, Paul
See Asimov, Isaac

Freneau, Philip Morin 1752-1832 . . **NCLC 1**
See also DLB 37, 43

Friedan, Betty (Naomi) 1921- . . . . . . **CLC 74**
See also CA 65-68; CANR 18; MTCW

Friedman, B(ernard) H(arper)
1926- . . . . **CLC 7**
See also CA 1-4R; CANR 3

Friedman, Bruce Jay 1930- . . . . **CLC 3, 5, 56**
See also CA 9-12R; CANR 25; DLB 2, 28

Friel, Brian 1929- . . . . **CLC 5, 42, 59**
See also CA 21-24R; CANR 33; DLB 13;
MTCW

Friis-Baastad, Babbis Ellinor
1921-1970 . . . . **CLC 12**
See also CA 17-20R; 134; SATA 7

Frisch, Max (Rudolf)
1911-1991 . . . . . **CLC 3, 9, 14, 18, 32, 44**
See also CA 85-88; 134; CANR 32;
DLB 69, 124; MTCW

Fromentin, Eugene (Samuel Auguste)
1820-1876 . . . . **NCLC 10**
See also DLB 123

Frost, Frederick
See Faust, Frederick (Schiller)

Frost, Robert (Lee)
1874-1963 . . . **CLC 1, 3, 4, 9, 10, 13, 15,**
26, 34, 44; PC 1
See also CA 89-92; CANR 33;
CDALB 1917-1929; DA; DLB 54;
DLBD 7; MTCW; SATA 14; WLC

Froy, Herald
See Waterhouse, Keith (Spencer)

Fry, Christopher 1907-. . . . . . . **CLC 2, 10, 14**
See also CA 17-20R; CANR 9, 30; DLB 13;
MTCW; SATA 66

Frye, (Herman) Northrop
1912-1991 . . . . **CLC 24, 70**
See also CA 5-8R; 133; CANR 8, 37;
DLB 67, 68; MTCW

Fuchs, Daniel 1909-. . . . . **CLC 8, 22**
See also CA 81-84; CAAS 5; CANR 40;
DLB 9, 26, 28

Fuchs, Daniel 1934-. . . . . **CLC 34**
See also CA 37-40R; CANR 14

Fuentes, Carlos
1928-. . . . . . **CLC 3, 8, 10, 13, 22, 41, 60**
See also AAYA 4; AITN 2; CA 69-72;
CANR 10, 32; DA; DLB 113; HW;
MTCW; WLC

Fuentes, Gregorio Lopez y
See Lopez y Fuentes, Gregorio

Fugard, (Harold) Athol
1932-. . . . . . . **CLC 5, 9, 14, 25, 40; DC 3**
See also CA 85-88; CANR 32; MTCW

Fugard, Sheila 1932- . . . . **CLC 48**
See also CA 125

Fuller, Charles (H., Jr.)
1939- . . . . **CLC 25; DC 1**
See also BLC 2; BW; CA 108; 112; DLB 38;
MTCW

Fuller, John (Leopold) 1937-. . . . . . . **CLC 62**
See also CA 21-24R; CANR 9; DLB 40

Fuller, Margaret . . . . **NCLC 5**
See also Ossoli, Sarah Margaret (Fuller
marchesa d')

Fuller, Roy (Broadbent)
1912-1991 . . . . **CLC 4, 28**
See also CA 5-8R; 135; CAAS 10; DLB 15,
20

Fulton, Alice 1952-. . . . . **CLC 52**
See also CA 116

Furphy, Joseph 1843-1912. . . . . **TCLC 25**

Fussell, Paul 1924-. . . . . **CLC 74**
See also BEST 90:1; CA 17-20R; CANR 8,
21, 35; MTCW

Futabatei, Shimei 1864-1909 . . . . . . **TCLC 44**

Futrelle, Jacques 1875-1912 . . . . . . **TCLC 19**
See also CA 113

G. B. S.
See Shaw, George Bernard

Gaboriau, Emile 1835-1873 . . . . . . **NCLC 14**

Gadda, Carlo Emilio 1893-1973 . . . . **CLC 11**
See also CA 89-92

Gaddis, William
1922-. . . . . **CLC 1, 3, 6, 8, 10, 19, 43**
See also CA 17-20R; CANR 21; DLB 2;
MTCW

Gaines, Ernest J(ames)
1933-. . . . . **CLC 3, 11, 18**
See also AITN 1; BLC 2; BW; CA 9-12R;
CANR 6, 24; CDALB 1968-1988; DLB 2,
33; DLBY 80; MTCW

Gaitskill, Mary 1954-. . . . . **CLC 69**
See also CA 128

Galdos, Benito Perez
See Perez Galdos, Benito

Gale, Zona 1874-1938 . . . . **TCLC 7**
See also CA 105; DLB 9, 78

Galeano, Eduardo (Hughes) 1940-. . . **CLC 72**
See also CA 29-32R; CANR 13, 32; HW

Galiano, Juan Valera y Alcala
See Valera y Alcala-Galiano, Juan

Gallagher, Tess 1943-. . . . . **CLC 18, 63**
See also CA 106; DLB 120

Gallant, Mavis
1922-. . . . . **CLC 7, 18, 38; SSC 5**
See also CA 69-72; CANR 29; DLB 53;
MTCW

Gallant, Roy A(rthur) 1924- . . . . **CLC 17**
See also CA 5-8R; CANR 4, 29; CLR 30;
MAICYA; SATA 4, 68

Gallico, Paul (William) 1897-1976 . . . **CLC 2**
See also AITN 1; CA 5-8R; 69-72;
CANR 23; DLB 9; MAICYA; SATA 13

Gallup, Ralph
See Whitemore, Hugh (John)

Galsworthy, John 1867-1933 . . . . **TCLC 1, 45**
See also CA 104; CDBLB 1890-1914; DA;
DLB 10, 34, 98; WLC 2

Galt, John 1779-1839 . . . . **NCLC 1**
See also DLB 99, 116

Galvin, James 1951-. . . . . **CLC 38**
See also CA 108; CANR 26

Gamboa, Federico 1864-1939. . . . . . **TCLC 36**

Gann, Ernest Kellogg 1910-1991. . . . **CLC 23**
See also AITN 1; CA 1-4R; 136; CANR 1

Garcia, Christina 1959- . . . . **CLC 76**

Garcia Lorca, Federico
1898-1936 . . **TCLC 1, 7, 49; DC 2; PC 3**
See also CA 104; 131; DA; DLB 108; HW;
MTCW; WLC

Garcia Marquez, Gabriel (Jose)
1928-. . . **CLC 2, 3, 8, 10, 15, 27, 47, 55;**
SSC 8
See also Marquez, Gabriel (Jose) Garcia
See also AAYA 3; BEST 89:1, 90:4;
CA 33-36R; CANR 10, 28; DA;
DLB 113; HW; MTCW; WLC

Gard, Janice
See Latham, Jean Lee

Gard, Roger Martin du
See Martin du Gard, Roger

Gardam, Jane 1928-. . . . . **CLC 43**
See also CA 49-52; CANR 2, 18, 33;
CLR 12; DLB 14; MAICYA; MTCW;
SAAS 9; SATA 28, 39

Gardner, Herb . . . . **CLC 44**

Gardner, John (Champlin), Jr.
1933-1982 . . . . **CLC 2, 3, 5, 7, 8, 10, 18,**
28, 34; SSC 7
See also AITN 1; CA 65-68; 107;
CANR 33; DLB 2; DLBY 82; MTCW;
SATA 31, 40

Gardner, John (Edmund) 1926-. . . . . **CLC 30**
See also CA 103; CANR 15; MTCW

Gardner, Noel
See Kuttner, Henry

Gardons, S. S.
See Snodgrass, William D(e Witt)

Garfield, Leon 1921-. . . . . **CLC 12**
See also AAYA 8; CA 17-20R; CANR 38,
41; CLR 21; MAICYA; SATA 1, 32

Garland, (Hannibal) Hamlin
1860-1940 . . . . **TCLC 3**
See also CA 104; DLB 12, 71, 78

Garneau, (Hector de) Saint-Denys
1912-1943 . . . . **TCLC 13**
See also CA 111; DLB 88

Garner, Alan 1934-. . . . . **CLC 17**
See also CA 73-76; CANR 15; CLR 20;
MAICYA; MTCW; SATA 18, 69

Garner, Hugh 1913-1979 . . . . **CLC 13**
See also CA 69-72; CANR 31; DLB 68

Garnett, David 1892-1981 . . . . **CLC 3**
See also CA 5-8R; 103; CANR 17; DLB 34

Garos, Stephanie
See Katz, Steve

Garrett, George (Palmer)
1929-. . . . . **CLC 3, 11, 51**
See also CA 1-4R; CAAS 5; CANR 1;
DLB 2, 5, 130; DLBY 83

Garrick, David 1717-1779 . . . . **LC 15**
See also DLB 84

Garrigue, Jean 1914-1972 . . . . **CLC 2, 8**
See also CA 5-8R; 37-40R; CANR 20

Garrison, Frederick
See Sinclair, Upton (Beall)

Garth, Will
See Hamilton, Edmond; Kuttner, Henry

Garvey, Marcus (Moziah, Jr.)
1887-1940 . . . . **TCLC 41**
See also BLC 2; BW; CA 120; 124

Gary, Romain . . . . **CLC 25**
See also Kacew, Romain
See also DLB 83

Gascar, Pierre . . . . **CLC 11**
See also Fournier, Pierre

Gascoyne, David (Emery) 1916- . . . . **CLC 45**
See also CA 65-68; CANR 10, 28; DLB 20;
MTCW

Gaskell, Elizabeth Cleghorn
1810-1865 . . . . **NCLC 5**
See also CDBLB 1832-1890; DLB 21

Gass, William H(oward)
1924- . . . **CLC 1, 2, 8, 11, 15, 39; SSC 12**
See also CA 17-20R; CANR 30; DLB 2;
MTCW

Gasset, Jose Ortega y
See Ortega y Gasset, Jose

Gautier, Theophile 1811-1872 . . . . . **NCLC 1**
See also DLB 119

Gawsworth, John
See Bates, H(erbert) E(rnest)

Gaye, Marvin (Penze) 1939-1984 ... CLC 26
See also CA 112

Gebler, Carlo (Ernest) 1954- .... CLC 39
See also CA 119; 133

Gee, Maggie (Mary) 1948-......... CLC 57
See also CA 130

Gee, Maurice (Gough) 1931- .... CLC 29
See also CA 97-100; SATA 46

Gelbart, Larry (Simon) 1923- ... CLC 21, 61
See also CA 73-76

Gelber, Jack 1932-.......... CLC 1, 6, 14
See also CA 1-4R; CANR 2; DLB 7

Gellhorn, Martha Ellis 1908- ... CLC 14, 60
See also CA 77-80; DLBY 82

Genet, Jean
1910-1986 ... CLC 1, 2, 5, 10, 14, 44, 46
See also CA 13-16R; CANR 18; DLB 72;
DLBY 86; MTCW

Gent, Peter 1942-................. CLC 29
See also AITN 1; CA 89-92; DLBY 82

George, Jean Craighead 1919-...... CLC 35
See also AAYA 8; CA 5-8R; CANR 25;
CLR 1; DLB 52; MAICYA; SATA 2, 68

George, Stefan (Anton)
1868-1933 .... TCLC 2, 14
See also CA 104

Georges, Georges Martin
See Simenon, Georges (Jacques Christian)

Gerhardi, William Alexander
See Gerhardie, William Alexander

Gerhardie, William Alexander
1895-1977 .... CLC 5
See also CA 25-28R; 73-76; CANR 18;
DLB 36

Gerstler, Amy 1956-.............. CLC 70

Gertler, T. .... CLC 34
See also CA 116; 121

Ghalib 1797-1869 .... NCLC 39

Ghelderode, Michel de
1898-1962 .... CLC 6, 11
See also CA 85-88; CANR 40

Ghiselin, Brewster 1903- .... CLC 23
See also CA 13-16R; CAAS 10; CANR 13

Ghose, Zulfikar 1935-............. CLC 42
See also CA 65-68

Ghosh, Amitav 1956- .... CLC 44

Giacosa, Giuseppe 1847-1906 ...... TCLC 7
See also CA 104

Gibb, Lee
See Waterhouse, Keith (Spencer)

Gibbon, Lewis Grassic .... TCLC 4
See also Mitchell, James Leslie

Gibbons, Kaye 1960- .... CLC 50

Gibran, Kahlil 1883-1931........ TCLC 1, 9
See also CA 104

Gibson, William 1914-............ CLC 23
See also CA 9-12R; CANR 9; DA; DLB 7;
SATA 66

Gibson, William (Ford) 1948- ... CLC 39, 63
See also CA 126; 133

Gide, Andre (Paul Guillaume)
1869-1951 .... TCLC 5, 12, 36
See also CA 104; 124; DA; DLB 65;
MTCW; WLC

Gifford, Barry (Colby) 1946-....... CLC 34
See also CA 65-68; CANR 9, 30, 40

Gilbert, W(illiam) S(chwenck)
1836-1911 .... TCLC 3
See also CA 104; SATA 36

Gilbreth, Frank B., Jr. 1911-....... CLC 17
See also CA 9-12R; SATA 2

Gilchrist, Ellen 1935-.......... CLC 34, 48
See also CA 113; 116; CANR 41; DLB 130;
MTCW

Giles, Molly 1942- .... CLC 39
See also CA 126

Gill, Patrick
See Creasey, John

Gilliam, Terry (Vance) 1940-....... CLC 21
See also Monty Python
See also CA 108; 113; CANR 35

Gillian, Jerry
See Gilliam, Terry (Vance)

Gilliatt, Penelope (Ann Douglass)
1932-................ CLC 2, 10, 13, 53
See also AITN 2; CA 13-16R; DLB 14

Gilman, Charlotte (Anna) Perkins (Stetson)
1860-1935 .... TCLC 9, 37
See also CA 106

Gilmour, David 1944-............. CLC 35
See also Pink Floyd
See also CA 138

Gilpin, William 1724-1804....... NCLC 30

Gilray, J. D.
See Mencken, H(enry) L(ouis)

Gilroy, Frank D(aniel) 1925-........ CLC 2
See also CA 81-84; CANR 32; DLB 7

Ginsberg, Allen
1926- ..... CLC 1, 2, 3, 4, 6, 13, 36, 69;
PC 4
See also AITN 1; CA 1-4R; CANR 2, 41;
CDALB 1941-1968; DA; DLB 5, 16;
MTCW; WLC 3

Ginzburg, Natalia
1916-1991 .... CLC 5, 11, 54, 70
See also CA 85-88; 135; CANR 33; MTCW

Giono, Jean 1895-1970......... CLC 4, 11
See also CA 45-48; 29-32R; CANR 2, 35;
DLB 72; MTCW

Giovanni, Nikki 1943- ..... CLC 2, 4, 19, 64
See also AITN 1; BLC 2; BW; CA 29-32R;
CAAS 6; CANR 18, 41; CLR 6; DA;
DLB 5, 41; MAICYA; MTCW; SATA 24

Giovene, Andrea 1904-............. CLC 7
See also CA 85-88

Gippius, Zinaida (Nikolayevna) 1869-1945
See Hippius, Zinaida
See also CA 106

Giraudoux, (Hippolyte) Jean
1882-1944 .... TCLC 2, 7
See also CA 104; DLB 65

Gironella, Jose Maria 1917- .... CLC 11
See also CA 101

Gissing, George (Robert)
1857-1903 .... TCLC 3, 24, 47
See also CA 105; DLB 18

Giurlani, Aldo
See Palazzeschi, Aldo

Gladkov, Fyodor (Vasilyevich)
1883-1958 .... TCLC 27

Glanville, Brian (Lester) 1931- ...... CLC 6
See also CA 5-8R; CAAS 9; CANR 3;
DLB 15; SATA 42

Glasgow, Ellen (Anderson Gholson)
1873(?)-1945 .... TCLC 2, 7
See also CA 104; DLB 9, 12

Glassco, John 1909-1981 .... CLC 9
See also CA 13-16R; 102; CANR 15;
DLB 68

Glasscock, Amnesia
See Steinbeck, John (Ernst)

Glasser, Ronald J. 1940(?)- .... CLC 37

Glassman, Joyce
See Johnson, Joyce

Glendinning, Victoria 1937-........ CLC 50
See also CA 120; 127

Glissant, Edouard 1928-........ CLC 10, 68

Gloag, Julian 1930- .... CLC 40
See also AITN 1; CA 65-68; CANR 10

Gluck, Louise (Elisabeth)
1943- .... CLC 7, 22, 44
See also Glueck, Louise
See also CA 33-36R; CANR 40; DLB 5

Glueck, Louise................. CLC 7, 22
See also Gluck, Louise (Elisabeth)
See also DLB 5

Gobineau, Joseph Arthur (Comte) de
1816-1882 .... NCLC 17
See also DLB 123

Godard, Jean-Luc 1930-.......... CLC 20
See also CA 93-96

Godden, (Margaret) Rumer 1907-... CLC 53
See also AAYA 6; CA 5-8R; CANR 4, 27,
36; CLR 20; MAICYA; SAAS 12;
SATA 3, 36

Godoy Alcayaga, Lucila 1889-1957
See Mistral, Gabriela
See also CA 104; 131; HW; MTCW

Godwin, Gail (Kathleen)
1937- .... CLC 5, 8, 22, 31, 69
See also CA 29-32R; CANR 15; DLB 6;
MTCW

Godwin, William 1756-1836...... NCLC 14
See also CDBLB 1789-1832; DLB 39, 104

Goethe, Johann Wolfgang von
1749-1832 .... NCLC 4, 22, 34; PC 5
See also DA; DLB 94; WLC 3

Gogarty, Oliver St. John
1878-1957 .... TCLC 15
See also CA 109; DLB 15, 19

Gogol, Nikolai (Vasilyevich)
1809-1852 ..... NCLC 5, 15, 31; DC 1;
SSC 4
See also DA; WLC

Gold, Herbert 1924-....... CLC 4, 7, 14, 42
See also CA 9-12R; CANR 17; DLB 2;
DLBY 81

Goldbarth, Albert 1948-......... **CLC 5, 38**
  See also CA 53-56; CANR 6, 40; DLB 120

Goldberg, Anatol 1910-1982 .... **CLC 34**
  See also CA 131; 117

Goldemberg, Isaac 1945-.......... **CLC 52**
  See also CA 69-72; CAAS 12; CANR 11,
  32; HW

Golden Silver
  See Storm, Hyemeyohsts

Golding, William (Gerald)
  1911- ..... **CLC 1, 2, 3, 8, 10, 17, 27, 58**
  See also AAYA 5; CA 5-8R; CANR 13, 33;
  CDBLB 1945-1960; DA; DLB 15, 100;
  MTCW; WLC

Goldman, Emma 1869-1940 ...... **TCLC 13**
  See also CA 110

Goldman, Francisco 1955-......... **CLC 76**

Goldman, William (W.) 1931- .... **CLC 1, 48**
  See also CA 9-12R; CANR 29; DLB 44

Goldmann, Lucien 1913-1970 ...... **CLC 24**
  See also CA 25-28; CAP 2

Goldoni, Carlo 1707-1793 .... **LC 4**

Goldsberry, Steven 1949-.......... **CLC 34**
  See also CA 131

Goldsmith, Oliver 1728-1774........ **LC 2**
  See also CDBLB 1660-1789; DA; DLB 39,
  89, 104, 109; SATA 26; WLC

Goldsmith, Peter
  See Priestley, J(ohn) B(oynton)

Gombrowicz, Witold
  1904-1969 .... **CLC 4, 7, 11, 49**
  See also CA 19-20; 25-28R; CAP 2

Gomez de la Serna, Ramon
  1888-1963 .... **CLC 9**
  See also CA 116; HW

Goncharov, Ivan Alexandrovich
  1812-1891 .... **NCLC 1**

Goncourt, Edmond (Louis Antoine Huot) de
  1822-1896 .... **NCLC 7**
  See also DLB 123

Goncourt, Jules (Alfred Huot) de
  1830-1870 .... **NCLC 7**
  See also DLB 123

Gontier, Fernande 19(?)- .... **CLC 50**

Goodman, Paul 1911-1972.... **CLC 1, 2, 4, 7**
  See also CA 19-20; 37-40R; CANR 34;
  CAP 2; DLB 130; MTCW

Gordimer, Nadine
  1923- .... **CLC 3, 5, 7, 10, 18, 33, 51, 70**
  See also CA 5-8R; CANR 3, 28; DA;
  MTCW

Gordon, Adam Lindsay
  1833-1870 .... **NCLC 21**

Gordon, Caroline
  1895-1981 .... **CLC 6, 13, 29**
  See also CA 11-12; 103; CANR 36; CAP 1;
  DLB 4, 9, 102; DLBY 81; MTCW

Gordon, Charles William 1860-1937
  See Connor, Ralph
  See also CA 109

Gordon, Mary (Catherine)
  1949- .... **CLC 13, 22**
  See also CA 102; DLB 6; DLBY 81;
  MTCW

Gordon, Sol 1923-................ **CLC 26**
  See also CA 53-56; CANR 4; SATA 11

Gordone, Charles 1925-.......... **CLC 1, 4**
  See also BW; CA 93-96; DLB 7; MTCW

Gorenko, Anna Andreevna
  See Akhmatova, Anna

Gorky, Maxim................... **TCLC 8**
  See also Peshkov, Alexei Maximovich
  See also WLC

Goryan, Sirak
  See Saroyan, William

Gosse, Edmund (William)
  1849-1928 .... **TCLC 28**
  See also CA 117; DLB 57

Gotlieb, Phyllis Fay (Bloom)
  1926-...................... **CLC 18**
  See also CA 13-16R; CANR 7; DLB 88

Gottesman, S. D.
  See Kornbluth, C(yril) M.; Pohl, Frederik

Gottfried von Strassburg
  fl. c. 1210-................. **CMLC 10**

Gottschalk, Laura Riding
  See Jackson, Laura (Riding)

Gould, Lois .... **CLC 4, 10**
  See also CA 77-80; CANR 29; MTCW

Gourmont, Remy de 1858-1915.... **TCLC 17**
  See also CA 109

Govier, Katherine 1948-........... **CLC 51**
  See also CA 101; CANR 18, 40

Goyen, (Charles) William
  1915-1983 .... **CLC 5, 8, 14, 40**
  See also AITN 2; CA 5-8R; 110; CANR 6;
  DLB 2; DLBY 83

Goytisolo, Juan 1931- .... **CLC 5, 10, 23**
  See also CA 85-88; CANR 32; HW; MTCW

Gozzi, (Conte) Carlo 1720-1806 .. **NCLC 23**

Grabbe, Christian Dietrich
  1801-1836 .... **NCLC 2**

Grace, Patricia 1937-............. **CLC 56**

Gracian y Morales, Baltasar
  1601-1658 .... **LC 15**

Gracq, Julien................ **CLC 11, 48**
  See also Poirier, Louis
  See also DLB 83

Grade, Chaim 1910-1982 .... **CLC 10**
  See also CA 93-96; 107

Graduate of Oxford, A
  See Ruskin, John

Graham, John
  See Phillips, David Graham

Graham, Jorie 1951-............. **CLC 48**
  See also CA 111; DLB 120

Graham, R(obert) B(ontine) Cunninghame
  See Cunninghame Graham, R(obert)
  B(ontine)
  See also DLB 98

Graham, Robert
  See Haldeman, Joe (William)

Graham, Tom
  See Lewis, (Harry) Sinclair

Graham, W(illiam) S(ydney)
  1918-1986 .... **CLC 29**
  See also CA 73-76; 118; DLB 20

Graham, Winston (Mawdsley)
  1910- .... **CLC 23**
  See also CA 49-52; CANR 2, 22; DLB 77

Grant, Skeeter
  See Spiegelman, Art

Granville-Barker, Harley
  1877-1946 .... **TCLC 2**
  See also Barker, Harley Granville
  See also CA 104

Grass, Guenter (Wilhelm)
  1927- .. **CLC 1, 2, 4, 6, 11, 15, 22, 32, 49**
  See also CA 13-16R; CANR 20; DA;
  DLB 75, 124; MTCW; WLC

Gratton, Thomas
  See Hulme, T(homas) E(rnest)

Grau, Shirley Ann 1929- .... **CLC 4, 9**
  See also CA 89-92; CANR 22; DLB 2;
  MTCW

Gravel, Fern
  See Hall, James Norman

Graver, Elizabeth 1964-........... **CLC 70**
  See also CA 135

Graves, Richard Perceval 1945- .... **CLC 44**
  See also CA 65-68; CANR 9, 26

Graves, Robert (von Ranke)
  1895-1985 ..... **CLC 1, 2, 6, 11, 39, 44,**
  45; PC 6
  See also CA 5-8R; 117; CANR 5, 36;
  CDBLB 1914-1945; DLB 20, 100;
  DLBY 85; MTCW; SATA 45

Gray, Alasdair (James) 1934- ...... **CLC 41**
  See also CA 126; MTCW

Gray, Amlin 1946- .... **CLC 29**
  See also CA 138

Gray, Francine du Plessix 1930-.... **CLC 22**
  See also BEST 90:3; CA 61-64; CAAS 2;
  CANR 11, 33; MTCW

Gray, John (Henry) 1866-1934 .... **TCLC 19**
  See also CA 119

Gray, Simon (James Holliday)
  1936- .... **CLC 9, 14, 36**
  See also AITN 1; CA 21-24R; CAAS 3;
  CANR 32; DLB 13; MTCW

Gray, Spalding 1941-............. **CLC 49**
  See also CA 128

Gray, Thomas 1716-1771 .... **LC 4; PC 2**
  See also CDBLB 1660-1789; DA; DLB 109;
  WLC

Grayson, David
  See Baker, Ray Stannard

Grayson, Richard (A.) 1951-....... **CLC 38**
  See also CA 85-88; CANR 14, 31

Greeley, Andrew M(oran) 1928- .... **CLC 28**
  See also CA 5-8R; CAAS 7; CANR 7;
  MTCW

Green, Brian
  See Card, Orson Scott

Green, Hannah .... **CLC 3**
  See also CA 73-76

Green, Hannah
  See Greenberg, Joanne (Goldenberg)

Green, Henry................... **CLC 2, 13**
  See also Yorke, Henry Vincent
  See also DLB 15

Habbema, Koos
See Heijermans, Herman

Hacker, Marilyn 1942- .... **CLC 5, 9, 23, 72**
See also CA 77-80; DLB 120

Haggard, H(enry) Rider
1856-1925 .... **TCLC 11**
See also CA 108; DLB 70; SATA 16

Haig, Fenil
See Ford, Ford Madox

Haig-Brown, Roderick (Langmere)
1908-1976 .... **CLC 21**
See also CA 5-8R; 69-72; CANR 4, 38;
DLB 88; MAICYA; SATA 12

Hailey, Arthur 1920- .... **CLC 5**
See also AITN 2; BEST 90:3; CA 1-4R;
CANR 2, 36; DLB 88; DLBY 82; MTCW

Hailey, Elizabeth Forsythe 1938- ... **CLC 40**
See also CA 93-96; CAAS 1; CANR 15

Haines, John (Meade) 1924- .... **CLC 58**
See also CA 17-20R; CANR 13, 34; DLB 5

Haldeman, Joe (William) 1943-..... **CLC 61**
See also CA 53-56; CANR 6; DLB 8

Haley, Alex(ander Murray Palmer)
1921-1992 .... **CLC 8, 12, 76**
See also BLC 2; BW; CA 77-80; 136; DA;
DLB 38; MTCW

Haliburton, Thomas Chandler
1796-1865 .... **NCLC 15**
See also DLB 11, 99

Hall, Donald (Andrew, Jr.)
1928- ....**CLC 1, 13, 37, 59**
See also CA 5-8R; CAAS 7; CANR 2;
DLB 5; SATA 23

Hall, Frederic Sauser
See Sauser-Hall, Frederic

Hall, James
See Kuttner, Henry

Hall, James Norman 1887-1951 ... **TCLC 23**
See also CA 123, SATA 21

Hall, (Marguerite) Radclyffe
1886(?)-1943 .... **TCLC 12**
See also CA 110

Hall, Rodney 1935- .... **CLC 51**
See also CA 109

Halliday, Michael
See Creasey, John

Halpern, Daniel 1945- .... **CLC 14**
See also CA 33-36R

Hamburger, Michael (Peter Leopold)
1924- .... **CLC 5, 14**
See also CA 5-8R; CAAS 4; CANR 2;
DLB 27

Hamill, Pete 1935-............... **CLC 10**
See also CA 25-28R; CANR 18

Hamilton, Clive
See Lewis, C(live) S(taples)

Hamilton, Edmond 1904-1977....... **CLC 1**
See also CA 1-4R; CANR 3; DLB 8

Hamilton, Eugene (Jacob) Lee
See Lee-Hamilton, Eugene (Jacob)

Hamilton, Franklin
See Silverberg, Robert

Hamilton, Gail
See Corcoran, Barbara

Hamilton, Mollie
See Kaye, M(ary) M(argaret)

Hamilton, (Anthony Walter) Patrick
1904-1962 .... **CLC 51**
See also CA 113; DLB 10

Hamilton, Virginia 1936-......... **CLC 26**
See also AAYA 2; BW; CA 25-28R;
CANR 20, 37; CLR 1, 11; DLB 33, 52;
MAICYA; MTCW; SATA 4, 56

Hammett, (Samuel) Dashiell
1894-1961 .... **CLC 3, 5, 10, 19, 47**
See also AITN 1; CA 81-84;
CDALB 1929-1941; DLBD 6; MTCW

Hammon, Jupiter 1711(?)-1800(?).. **NCLC 5**
See also BLC 2; DLB 31, 50

Hammond, Keith
See Kuttner, Henry

Hamner, Earl (Henry), Jr. 1923- ... **CLC 12**
See also AITN 2; CA 73-76; DLB 6

Hampton, Christopher (James)
1946- .... **CLC 4**
See also CA 25-28R; DLB 13; MTCW

Hamsun, Knut 1859-1952... **TCLC 2, 14, 49**
See also Pedersen, Knut

Handke, Peter 1942- .. **CLC 5, 8, 10, 15, 38**
See also CA 77-80; CANR 33; DLB 85,
124; MTCW

Hanley, James 1901-1985 ... **CLC 3, 5, 8, 13**
See also CA 73-76; 117; CANR 36; MTCW

Hannah, Barry 1942-......... **CLC 23, 38**
See also CA 108; 110; DLB 6; MTCW

Hannon, Ezra
See Hunter, Evan

Hansberry, Lorraine (Vivian)
1930-1965 .... **CLC 17, 62; DC 2**
See also BLC 2; BW; CA 109; 25-28R;
CABS 3; CDALB 1941-1968; DA;
DLB 7, 38; MTCW

Hansen, Joseph 1923-............. **CLC 38**
See also CA 29-32R; CAAS 17; CANR 16

Hansen, Martin A. 1909-1955..... **TCLC 32**

Hanson, Kenneth O(stlin) 1922- .... **CLC 13**
See also CA 53-56; CANR 7

Hardwick, Elizabeth 1916- .... **CLC 13**
See also CA 5-8R; CANR 3, 32; DLB 6;
MTCW

Hardy, Thomas
1840-1928 ..... **TCLC 4, 10, 18, 32, 48;**
SSC 2
See also CA 104; 123; CDBLB 1890-1914;
DA; DLB 18, 19; MTCW; WLC

Hare, David 1947- .... **CLC 29, 58**
See also CA 97-100; CANR 39; DLB 13;
MTCW

Harford, Henry
See Hudson, W(illiam) H(enry)

Hargrave, Leonie
See Disch, Thomas M(ichael)

Harlan, Louis R(udolph) 1922-..... **CLC 34**
See also CA 21-24R; CANR 25

Harling, Robert 1951(?)- .... **CLC 53**

Harmon, William (Ruth) 1938-..... **CLC 38**
See also CA 33-36R; CANR 14, 32, 35;
SATA 65

Harper, F. E. W.
See Harper, Frances Ellen Watkins

Harper, Frances E. W.
See Harper, Frances Ellen Watkins

Harper, Frances E. Watkins
See Harper, Frances Ellen Watkins

Harper, Frances Ellen
See Harper, Frances Ellen Watkins

Harper, Frances Ellen Watkins
1825-1911 .... **TCLC 14**
See also BLC 2; BW; CA 111; 125; DLB 50

Harper, Michael S(teven) 1938- ... **CLC 7, 22**
See also BW; CA 33-36R; CANR 24;
DLB 41

Harper, Mrs. F. E. W.
See Harper, Frances Ellen Watkins

Harris, Christie (Lucy) Irwin
1907- .... **CLC 12**
See also CA 5-8R; CANR 6; DLB 88;
MAICYA; SAAS 10; SATA 6, 74

Harris, Frank 1856(?)-1931....... **TCLC 24**
See also CA 109

Harris, George Washington
1814-1869 .... **NCLC 23**
See also DLB 3, 11

Harris, Joel Chandler 1848-1908 ... **TCLC 2**
See also CA 104; 137; DLB 11, 23, 42, 78,
91; MAICYA; YABC 1

Harris, John (Wyndham Parkes Lucas)
Beynon 1903-1969 .... **CLC 19**
See also CA 102; 89-92

Harris, MacDonald
See Heiney, Donald (William)

Harris, Mark 1922- .... **CLC 19**
See also CA 5-8R; CAAS 3; CANR 2;
DLB 2; DLBY 80

Harris, (Theodore) Wilson 1921-.... **CLC 25**
See also BW; CA 65-68; CAAS 16;
CANR 11, 27; DLB 117; MTCW

Harrison, Elizabeth Cavanna 1909-
See Cavanna, Betty
See also CA 9-12R; CANR 6, 27

Harrison, Harry (Max) 1925-....... **CLC 42**
See also CA 1-4R; CANR 5, 21; DLB 8;
SATA 4

Harrison, James (Thomas) 1937-
See Harrison, Jim
See also CA 13-16R; CANR 8

Harrison, Jim .... **CLC 6, 14, 33, 66**
See also Harrison, James (Thomas)
See also DLBY 82

Harrison, Kathryn 1961-.......... **CLC 70**

Harrison, Tony 1937-............. **CLC 43**
See also CA 65-68; DLB 40; MTCW

Harriss, Will(ard Irvin) 1922-...... **CLC 34**
See also CA 111

Harson, Sley
See Ellison, Harlan

Hart, Ellis
See Ellison, Harlan

Hart, Josephine 1942(?)- .... **CLC 70**
See also CA 138

Hart, Moss 1904-1961 .... **CLC 66**
See also CA 109; 89-92; DLB 7

Herbert, Zbigniew 1924- .... **CLC 9, 43**
See also CA 89-92; CANR 36; MTCW

Herbst, Josephine (Frey)
1897-1969 .... **CLC 34**
See also CA 5-8R; 25-28R; DLB 9

Hergesheimer, Joseph
1880-1954 .... **TCLC 11**
See also CA 109; DLB 102, 9

Herlihy, James Leo 1927- .... **CLC 6**
See also CA 1-4R; CANR 2

Hermogenes fl. c. 175- .... **CMLC 6**

Hernandez, Jose 1834-1886..... **NCLC 17**

Herrick, Robert 1591-1674 .... **LC 13**
See also DA; DLB 126

Herriot, James................... **CLC 12**
See also Wight, James Alfred
See also AAYA 1; CANR 40

Herrmann, Dorothy 1941- .... **CLC 44**
See also CA 107

Herrmann, Taffy
See Herrmann, Dorothy

Hersey, John (Richard)
1914-1993 .... **CLC 1, 2, 7, 9, 40**
See also CA 17-20R; 140; CANR 33;
DLB 6; MTCW; SATA 25

Herzen, Aleksandr Ivanovich
1812-1870 .... **NCLC 10**

Herzl, Theodor 1860-1904 .... **TCLC 36**

Herzog, Werner 1942- .... **CLC 16**
See also CA 89-92

Hesiod c. 8th cent. B.C.- .... **CMLC 5**

Hesse, Hermann
1877-1962 ... **CLC 1, 2, 3, 6, 11, 17, 25,**
69; SSC 9
See also CA 17-18; CAP 2; DA; DLB 66;
MTCW; SATA 50; WLC

Hewes, Cady
See De Voto, Bernard (Augustine)

Heyen, William 1940- .... **CLC 13, 18**
See also CA 33-36R; CAAS 9; DLB 5

Heyerdahl, Thor 1914-............ **CLC 26**
See also CA 5-8R; CANR 5, 22; MTCW;
SATA 2, 52

Heym, Georg (Theodor Franz Arthur)
1887-1912 .... **TCLC 9**
See also CA 106

Heym, Stefan 1913-.............. **CLC 41**
See also CA 9-12R; CANR 4; DLB 69

Heyse, Paul (Johann Ludwig von)
1830-1914 .... **TCLC 8**
See also CA 104; DLB 129

Hibbert, Eleanor Alice Burford
1906-1993 .... **CLC 7**
See also BEST 90:4; CA 17-20R; CANR 9,
28; SATA 2; SATA-Obit 74

Higgins, George V(incent)
1939-.............. **CLC 4, 7, 10, 18**
See also CA 77-80; CAAS 5; CANR 17;
DLB 2; DLBY 81; MTCW

Higginson, Thomas Wentworth
1823-1911 .... **TCLC 36**
See also DLB 1, 64

Highet, Helen
See MacInnes, Helen (Clark)

Highsmith, (Mary) Patricia
1921- .... **CLC 2, 4, 14, 42**
See also CA 1-4R; CANR 1, 20; MTCW

Highwater, Jamake (Mamake)
1942(?)- .... **CLC 12**
See also AAYA 7; CA 65-68; CAAS 7;
CANR 10, 34; CLR 17; DLB 52;
DLBY 85; MAICYA; SATA 30, 32, 69

Hijuelos, Oscar 1951- .... **CLC 65**
See also BEST 90:1; CA 123; HW

Hikmet, Nazim 1902-1963........ **CLC 40**
See also CA 93-96

Hildesheimer, Wolfgang
1916-1991 .... **CLC 49**
See also CA 101; 135; DLB 69, 124

Hill, Geoffrey (William)
1932- .... **CLC 5, 8, 18, 45**
See also CA 81-84; CANR 21;
CDBLB 1960 to Present; DLB 40;
MTCW

Hill, George Roy 1921- .... **CLC 26**
See also CA 110; 122

Hill, Susan (Elizabeth) 1942- .... **CLC 4**
See also CA 33-36R; CANR 29; DLB 14;
MTCW

Hillerman, Tony 1925-........... **CLC 62**
See also AAYA 6; BEST 89:1; CA 29-32R;
CANR 21; SATA 6

Hillesum, Etty 1914-1943 .... **TCLC 49**
See also CA 137

Hilliard, Noel (Harvey) 1929-...... **CLC 15**
See also CA 9-12R; CANR 7

Hillis, Rick 1956-................ **CLC 66**
See also CA 134

Hilton, James 1900-1954........ **TCLC 21**
See also CA 108; DLB 34, 77; SATA 34

Himes, Chester (Bomar)
1909-1984 .... **CLC 2, 4, 7, 18, 58**
See also BLC 2; BW; CA 25-28R; 114;
CANR 22; DLB 2, 76; MTCW

Hinde, Thomas .... **CLC 6, 11**
See also Chitty, Thomas Willes

Hindin, Nathan
See Bloch, Robert (Albert)

Hine, (William) Daryl 1936-....... **CLC 15**
See also CA 1-4R; CAAS 15; CANR 1, 20;
DLB 60

Hinkson, Katharine Tynan
See Tynan, Katharine

Hinton, S(usan) E(loise) 1950- ..... **CLC 30**
See also AAYA 2; CA 81-84; CANR 32;
CLR 3, 23; DA; MAICYA; MTCW;
SATA 19, 58

Hippius, Zinaida .... **TCLC 9**
See also Gippius, Zinaida (Nikolayevna)

Hiraoka, Kimitake 1925-1970
See Mishima, Yukio
See also CA 97-100; 29-32R; MTCW

Hirsch, Edward 1950- .... **CLC 31, 50**
See also CA 104; CANR 20; DLB 120

Hitchcock, Alfred (Joseph)
1899-1980 .... **CLC 16**
See also CA 97-100; SATA 24, 27

Hoagland, Edward 1932-.......... **CLC 28**
See also CA 1-4R; CANR 2, 31; DLB 6;
SATA 51

Hoban, Russell (Conwell) 1925- .. **CLC 7, 25**
See also CA 5-8R; CANR 23, 37; CLR 3;
DLB 52; MAICYA; MTCW; SATA 1, 40

Hobbs, Perry
See Blackmur, R(ichard) P(almer)

Hobson, Laura Z(ametkin)
1900-1986 .... **CLC 7, 25**
See also CA 17-20R; 118; DLB 28;
SATA 52

Hochhuth, Rolf 1931-........ **CLC 4, 11, 18**
See also CA 5-8R; CANR 33; DLB 124;
MTCW

Hochman, Sandra 1936-.......... **CLC 3, 8**
See also CA 5-8R; DLB 5

Hochwaelder, Fritz 1911-1986...... **CLC 36**
See also Hochwalder, Fritz
See also CA 29-32R; 120; MTCW

Hochwalder, Fritz................. **CLC 36**
See also Hochwaelder, Fritz

Hocking, Mary (Eunice) 1921-..... **CLC 13**
See also CA 101; CANR 18, 40

Hodgins, Jack 1938-.............. **CLC 23**
See also CA 93-96; DLB 60

Hodgson, William Hope
1877(?)-1918 .... **TCLC 13**
See also CA 111; DLB 70

Hoffman, Alice 1952-............. **CLC 51**
See also CA 77-80; CANR 34; MTCW

Hoffman, Daniel (Gerard)
1923- .... **CLC 6, 13, 23**
See also CA 1-4R; CANR 4; DLB 5

Hoffman, Stanley 1944-............ **CLC 5**
See also CA 77-80

Hoffman, William M(oses) 1939- ... **CLC 40**
See also CA 57-60; CANR 11

Hoffmann, E(rnst) T(heodor) A(madeus)
1776-1822 .... **NCLC 2**
See also DLB 90; SATA 27

Hofmann, Gert 1931-............. **CLC 54**
See also CA 128

Hofmannsthal, Hugo von
1874-1929 .... **TCLC 11**
See also CA 106; DLB 81, 118

Hogan, Linda 1947-.............. **CLC 73**
See also CA 120

Hogarth, Charles
See Creasey, John

Hogg, James 1770-1835.......... **NCLC 4**
See also DLB 93, 116

Holbach, Paul Henri Thiry Baron
1723-1789 .... **LC 14**

Holberg, Ludvig 1684-1754 .... **LC 6**

Holden, Ursula 1921-............. **CLC 18**
See also CA 101; CAAS 8; CANR 22

Holderlin, (Johann Christian) Friedrich
1770-1843 .... **NCLC 16; PC 4**

Holdstock, Robert
See Holdstock, Robert P.

Holdstock, Robert P. 1948-........ **CLC 39**
See also CA 131

Holland, Isabelle 1920- . . . . **CLC 21**
See also CA 21-24R; CANR 10, 25;
MAICYA; SATA 8, 70

Holland, Marcus
See Caldwell, (Janet Miriam) Taylor
(Holland)

Hollander, John 1929- . . . . . . **CLC 2, 5, 8, 14**
See also CA 1-4R; CANR 1; DLB 5;
SATA 13

Hollander, Paul
See Silverberg, Robert

Holleran, Andrew 1943(?)- . . . . **CLC 38**

Hollinghurst, Alan 1954- . . . . **CLC 55**
See also CA 114

Hollis, Jim
See Summers, Hollis (Spurgeon, Jr.)

Holmes, John
See Souster, (Holmes) Raymond

Holmes, John Clellon 1926-1988. . . . **CLC 56**
See also CA 9-12R; 125; CANR 4; DLB 16

Holmes, Oliver Wendell
1809-1894 . . . . **NCLC 14**
See also CDALB 1640-1865; DLB 1;
SATA 34

Holmes, Raymond
See Souster, (Holmes) Raymond

Holt, Victoria
See Hibbert, Eleanor Alice Burford

Holub, Miroslav 1923- . . . . **CLC 4**
See also CA 21-24R; CANR 10

Homer c. 8th cent. B.C.- . . . . **CMLC 1**
See also DA

Honig, Edwin 1919- . . . . **CLC 33**
See also CA 5-8R; CAAS 8; CANR 4;
DLB 5

Hood, Hugh (John Blagdon)
1928- . . . . **CLC 15, 28**
See also CA 49-52; CAAS 17; CANR 1, 33;
DLB 53

Hood, Thomas 1799-1845. . . . . . . **NCLC 16**
See also DLB 96

Hooker, (Peter) Jeremy 1941- . . . . . . **CLC 43**
See also CA 77-80; CANR 22; DLB 40

Hope, A(lec) D(erwent) 1907- . . . . **CLC 3, 51**
See also CA 21-24R; CANR 33; MTCW

Hope, Brian
See Creasey, John

Hope, Christopher (David Tully)
1944- . . . . **CLC 52**
See also CA 106; SATA 62

Hopkins, Gerard Manley
1844-1889 . . . . **NCLC 17**
See also CDBLB 1890-1914; DA; DLB 35,
57; WLC

Hopkins, John (Richard) 1931- . . . . . . **CLC 4**
See also CA 85-88

Hopkins, Pauline Elizabeth
1859-1930 . . . . **TCLC 28**
See also BLC 2; DLB 50

Hopley-Woolrich, Cornell George 1903-1968
See Woolrich, Cornell
See also CA 13-14; CAP 1

Horatio
See Proust,
(Valentin-Louis-George-Eugene-)Marcel

Horgan, Paul 1903- . . . . **CLC 9, 53**
See also CA 13-16R; CANR 9, 35;
DLB 102; DLBY 85; MTCW; SATA 13

Horn, Peter
See Kuttner, Henry

Hornem, Horace Esq.
See Byron, George Gordon (Noel)

Horovitz, Israel 1939- . . . . **CLC 56**
See also CA 33-36R; DLB 7

Horvath, Odon von
See Horvath, Oedoen von
See also DLB 85, 124

Horvath, Oedoen von 1901-1938. . . **TCLC 45**
See also Horvath, Odon von
See also CA 118

Horwitz, Julius 1920-1986. . . . . **CLC 14**
See also CA 9-12R; 119; CANR 12

Hospital, Janette Turner 1942- . . . . . **CLC 42**
See also CA 108

Hostos, E. M. de
See Hostos (y Bonilla), Eugenio Maria de

Hostos, Eugenio M. de
See Hostos (y Bonilla), Eugenio Maria de

Hostos, Eugenio Maria
See Hostos (y Bonilla), Eugenio Maria de

Hostos (y Bonilla), Eugenio Maria de
1839-1903 . . . . **TCLC 24**
See also CA 123; 131; HW

Houdini
See Lovecraft, H(oward) P(hillips)

Hougan, Carolyn 19(?)- . . . . **CLC 34**
See also CA 139

Household, Geoffrey (Edward West)
1900-1988 . . . . **CLC 11**
See also CA 77-80; 126; DLB 87; SATA 14,
59

Housman, A(lfred) E(dward)
1859-1936 . . . . **TCLC 1, 10; PC 2**
See also CA 104; 125; DA; DLB 19;
MTCW

Housman, Laurence 1865-1959 . . . . . **TCLC 7**
See also CA 106; DLB 10; SATA 25

Howard, Elizabeth Jane 1923- . . . **CLC 7, 29**
See also CA 5-8R; CANR 8

Howard, Maureen 1930- . . . . . **CLC 5, 14, 46**
See also CA 53-56; CANR 31; DLBY 83;
MTCW

Howard, Richard 1929- . . . . . . **CLC 7, 10, 47**
See also AITN 1; CA 85-88; CANR 25;
DLB 5

Howard, Robert Ervin 1906-1936. . . **TCLC 8**
See also CA 105

Howard, Warren F.
See Pohl, Frederik

Howe, Fanny 1940- . . . . **CLC 47**
See also CA 117; SATA 52

Howe, Julia Ward 1819-1910 . . . . . **TCLC 21**
See also CA 117; DLB 1

Howe, Susan 1937- . . . . **CLC 72**
See also DLB 120

Howe, Tina 1937- . . . . **CLC 48**
See also CA 109

Howell, James 1594(?)-1666 . . . . **LC 13**

Howells, W. D.
See Howells, William Dean

Howells, William D.
See Howells, William Dean

Howells, William Dean
1837-1920 . . . . **TCLC 41, 7, 17**
See also CA 104; 134; CDALB 1865-1917;
DLB 12, 64, 74, 79

Howes, Barbara 1914- . . . . **CLC 15**
See also CA 9-12R; CAAS 3; SATA 5

Hrabal, Bohumil 1914- . . . . **CLC 13, 67**
See also CA 106; CAAS 12

Hsun, Lu . . . . **TCLC 3**
See also Shu-Jen, Chou

Hubbard, L(afayette) Ron(ald)
1911-1986 . . . . **CLC 43**
See also CA 77-80; 118; CANR 22

Huch, Ricarda (Octavia)
1864-1947 . . . . **TCLC 13**
See also CA 111; DLB 66

Huddle, David 1942- . . . . **CLC 49**
See also CA 57-60; DLB 130

Hudson, Jeffrey
See Crichton, (John) Michael

Hudson, W(illiam) H(enry)
1841-1922 . . . . **TCLC 29**
See also CA 115; DLB 98; SATA 35

Hueffer, Ford Madox
See Ford, Ford Madox

Hughart, Barry . . . . **CLC 39**
See also CA 137

Hughes, Colin
See Creasey, John

Hughes, David (John) 1930- . . . . **CLC 48**
See also CA 116; 129; DLB 14

Hughes, (James) Langston
1902-1967 . . . . **CLC 1, 5, 10, 15, 35, 44;
DC 3; PC 1; SSC 6**
See also BLC 2; BW; CA 1-4R; 25-28R;
CANR 1, 34; CDALB 1929-1941;
CLR 17; DA; DLB 4, 7, 48, 51, 86;
MAICYA; MTCW; SATA 4, 33; WLC

Hughes, Richard (Arthur Warren)
1900-1976 . . . . **CLC 1, 11**
See also CA 5-8R; 65-68; CANR 4;
DLB 15; MTCW; SATA 8, 25

Hughes, Ted 1930- . . . . . **CLC 2, 4, 9, 14, 37**
See also CA 1-4R; CANR 1, 33; CLR 3;
DLB 40; MAICYA; MTCW; SATA 27,
49

Hugo, Richard F(ranklin)
1923-1982 . . . . **CLC 6, 18, 32**
See also CA 49-52; 108; CANR 3; DLB 5

Hugo, Victor (Marie)
1802-1885 . . . . **NCLC 3, 10, 21**
See also DA; DLB 119; SATA 47; WLC

Huidobro, Vicente
See Huidobro Fernandez, Vicente Garcia

Huidobro Fernandez, Vicente Garcia
1893-1948 . . . . **TCLC 31**
See also CA 131; HW

Hulme, Keri 1947- .... **CLC 39**
See also CA 125

Hulme, T(homas) E(rnest)
1883-1917 .... **TCLC 21**
See also CA 117; DLB 19

Hume, David 1711-1776............. **LC 7**
See also DLB 104

Humphrey, William 1924-......... **CLC 45**
See also CA 77-80; DLB 6

Humphreys, Emyr Owen 1919-..... **CLC 47**
See also CA 5-8R; CANR 3, 24; DLB 15

Humphreys, Josephine 1945-.... **CLC 34, 57**
See also CA 121; 127

Hungerford, Pixie
See Brinsmead, H(esba) F(ay)

Hunt, E(verette) Howard, Jr.
1918- .... **CLC 3**
See also AITN 1; CA 45-48; CANR 2

Hunt, Kyle
See Creasey, John

Hunt, (James Henry) Leigh
1784-1859 .... **NCLC 1**

Hunt, Marsha 1946-............. **CLC 70**

Hunter, E. Waldo
See Sturgeon, Theodore (Hamilton)

Hunter, Evan 1926- .... **CLC 11, 31**
See also CA 5-8R; CANR 5, 38; DLBY 82;
MTCW; SATA 25

Hunter, Kristin (Eggleston) 1931-... **CLC 35**
See also AITN 1; BW; CA 13-16R;
CANR 13; CLR 3; DLB 33; MAICYA;
SAAS 10; SATA 12

Hunter, Mollie 1922-............. **CLC 21**
See also McIlwraith, Maureen Mollie
Hunter
See also CANR 37; CLR 25; MAICYA;
SAAS 7; SATA 54

Hunter, Robert (?)-1734............. **LC 7**

Hurston, Zora Neale
1903-1960 .... **CLC 7, 30, 61; SSC 4**
See also BLC 2; BW; CA 85-88; DA;
DLB 51, 86; MTCW

Huston, John (Marcellus)
1906-1987 .... **CLC 20**
See also CA 73-76; 123; CANR 34; DLB 26

Hustvedt, Siri 1955-............. **CLC 76**
See also CA 137

Hutten, Ulrich von 1488-1523....... **LC 16**

Huxley, Aldous (Leonard)
1894-1963 .. **CLC 1, 3, 4, 5, 8, 11, 18, 35**
See also CA 85-88; CDBLB 1914-1945; DA;
DLB 36, 100; MTCW; SATA 63; WLC

Huysmans, Charles Marie Georges
1848-1907
See Huysmans, Joris-Karl
See also CA 104

Huysmans, Joris-Karl............. **TCLC 7**
See also Huysmans, Charles Marie Georges
See also DLB 123

Hwang, David Henry 1957-........ **CLC 55**
See also CA 127; 132

Hyde, Anthony 1946-............ **CLC 42**
See also CA 136

Hyde, Margaret O(ldroyd) 1917- ... **CLC 21**
See also CA 1-4R; CANR 1, 36; CLR 23;
MAICYA; SAAS 8; SATA 1, 42

Hynes, James 1956(?)-............ **CLC 65**

Ian, Janis 1951-................. **CLC 21**
See also CA 105

Ibanez, Vicente Blasco
See Blasco Ibanez, Vicente

Ibarguengoitia, Jorge 1928-1983.... **CLC 37**
See also CA 124; 113; HW

Ibsen, Henrik (Johan)
1828-1906 ..... **TCLC 2, 8, 16, 37; DC 2**
See also CA 104; DA; WLC

Ibuse Masuji 1898-............... **CLC 22**
See also CA 127

Ichikawa, Kon 1915-.............. **CLC 20**
See also CA 121

Idle, Eric 1943-.................. **CLC 21**
See also Monty Python
See also CA 116; CANR 35

Ignatow, David 1914-...... **CLC 4, 7, 14, 40**
See also CA 9-12R; CAAS 3; CANR 31;
DLB 5

Ihimaera, Witi 1944- .... **CLC 46**
See also CA 77-80

Ilf, Ilya....................... **TCLC 21**
See also Fainzilberg, Ilya Arnoldovich

Immermann, Karl (Lebrecht)
1796-1840 .... **NCLC 4**

Inclan, Ramon (Maria) del Valle
See Valle-Inclan, Ramon (Maria) del

Infante, G(uillermo) Cabrera
See Cabrera Infante, G(uillermo)

Ingalls, Rachel (Holmes) 1940-..... **CLC 42**
See also CA 123; 127

Ingamells, Rex 1913-1955 .... **TCLC 35**

Inge, William Motter
1913-1973 .... **CLC 1, 8, 19**
See also CA 9-12R; CDALB 1941-1968;
DLB 7; MTCW

Ingelow, Jean 1820-1897........ **NCLC 39**
See also DLB 35; SATA 33

Ingram, Willis J.
See Harris, Mark

Innaurato, Albert (F.) 1948(?)- .. **CLC 21, 60**
See also CA 115; 122

Innes, Michael
See Stewart, J(ohn) I(nnes) M(ackintosh)

Ionesco, Eugene
1912-........ **CLC 1, 4, 6, 9, 11, 15, 41**
See also CA 9-12R; DA; MTCW; SATA 7;
WLC

Iqbal, Muhammad 1873-1938 ..... **TCLC 28**

Ireland, Patrick
See O'Doherty, Brian

Irland, David
See Green, Julian (Hartridge)

Iron, Ralph
See Schreiner, Olive (Emilie Albertina)

Irving, John (Winslow)
1942- .... **CLC 13, 23, 38**
See also AAYA 8; BEST 89:3; CA 25-28R;
CANR 28; DLB 6; DLBY 82; MTCW

Irving, Washington
1783-1859 .... **NCLC 2, 19; SSC 2**
See also CDALB 1640-1865; DA; DLB 3,
11, 30, 59, 73, 74; WLC; YABC 2

Irwin, P. K.
See Page, P(atricia) K(athleen)

Isaacs, Susan 1943- .... **CLC 32**
See also BEST 89:1; CA 89-92; CANR 20,
41; MTCW

Isherwood, Christopher (William Bradshaw)
1904-1986 .... **CLC 1, 9, 11, 14, 44**
See also CA 13-16R; 117; CANR 35;
DLB 15; DLBY 86; MTCW

Ishiguro, Kazuo 1954-...... **CLC 27, 56, 59**
See also BEST 90:2; CA 120; MTCW

Ishikawa Takuboku
1886(?)-1912 .... **TCLC 15**
See also CA 113

Iskander, Fazil 1929-............. **CLC 47**
See also CA 102

Ivan IV 1530-1584 .... **LC 17**

Ivanov, Vyacheslav Ivanovich
1866-1949 .... **TCLC 33**
See also CA 122

Ivask, Ivar Vidrik 1927-1992....... **CLC 14**
See also CA 37-40R; 139; CANR 24

Jackson, Daniel
See Wingrove, David (John)

Jackson, Jesse 1908-1983 .... **CLC 12**
See also BW; CA 25-28R; 109; CANR 27;
CLR 28; MAICYA; SATA 2, 29, 48

Jackson, Laura (Riding) 1901-1991 .. **CLC 7**
See also Riding, Laura
See also CA 65-68; 135; CANR 28; DLB 48

Jackson, Sam
See Trumbo, Dalton

Jackson, Sara
See Wingrove, David (John)

Jackson, Shirley
1919-1965 .... **CLC 11, 60; SSC 9**
See also AAYA 9; CA 1-4R; 25-28R;
CANR 4; CDALB 1941-1968; DA;
DLB 6; SATA 2; WLC

Jacob, (Cyprien-)Max 1876-1944 ... **TCLC 6**
See also CA 104

Jacobs, Jim 1942-................ **CLC 12**
See also CA 97-100

Jacobs, W(illiam) W(ymark)
1863-1943 .... **TCLC 22**
See also CA 121

Jacobsen, Jens Peter 1847-1885 .. **NCLC 34**

Jacobsen, Josephine 1908-........ **CLC 48**
See also CA 33-36R; CANR 23

Jacobson, Dan 1929- .... **CLC 4, 14**
See also CA 1-4R; CANR 2, 25; DLB 14;
MTCW

Jacqueline
See Carpentier (y Valmont), Alejo

Jagger, Mick 1944-.............. **CLC 17**

Jakes, John (William) 1932-....... **CLC 29**
See also BEST 89:4; CA 57-60; CANR 10;
DLBY 83; MTCW; SATA 62

James, Andrew
See Kirkup, James

Jones, Rod 1953- . . . . **CLC 50**
See also CA 128

Jones, Terence Graham Parry
1942- . . . . **CLC 21**
See also Jones, Terry; Monty Python
See also CA 112; 116; CANR 35; SATA 51

Jones, Terry
See Jones, Terence Graham Parry
See also SATA 67

Jong, Erica 1942- . . . . **CLC 4, 6, 8, 18**
See also AITN 1; BEST 90:2; CA 73-76;
CANR 26; DLB 2, 5, 28; MTCW

Jonson, Ben(jamin) 1572(?)-1637. . . . . . **LC 6**
See also CDBLB Before 1660; DA; DLB 62,
121; WLC

Jordan, June 1936- . . . . **CLC 5, 11, 23**
See also AAYA 2; BW; CA 33-36R;
CANR 25; CLR 10; DLB 38; MAICYA;
MTCW; SATA 4

Jordan, Pat(rick M.) 1941- . . . . **CLC 37**
See also CA 33-36R

Jorgensen, Ivar
See Ellison, Harlan

Jorgenson, Ivar
See Silverberg, Robert

Josipovici, Gabriel 1940- . . . . **CLC 6, 43**
See also CA 37-40R; CAAS 8; DLB 14

Joubert, Joseph 1754-1824 . . . . **NCLC 9**

Jouve, Pierre Jean 1887-1976. . . . . . **CLC 47**
See also CA 65-68

Joyce, James (Augustine Aloysius)
1882-1941 . . . . **TCLC 3, 8, 16, 35; SSC 3**
See also CA 104; 126; CDBLB 1914-1945;
DA; DLB 10, 19, 36; MTCW; WLC

Jozsef, Attila 1905-1937. . . . . **TCLC 22**
See also CA 116

Juana Ines de la Cruz 1651(?)-1695 . . . **LC 5**

Judd, Cyril
See Kornbluth, C(yril) M.; Pohl, Frederik

Julian of Norwich 1342(?)-1416(?) . . . . **LC 6**

Just, Ward (Swift) 1935- . . . . **CLC 4, 27**
See also CA 25-28R; CANR 32

Justice, Donald (Rodney) 1925- . . **CLC 6, 19**
See also CA 5-8R; CANR 26; DLBY 83

Juvenal c. 55-c. 127 . . . . **CMLC 8**

Juvenis
See Bourne, Randolph S(illiman)

Kacew, Romain 1914-1980
See Gary, Romain
See also CA 108; 102

Kadare, Ismail 1936- . . . . **CLC 52**

Kadohata, Cynthia. . . . . **CLC 59**
See also CA 140

Kafka, Franz
1883-1924 . . . . . . **TCLC 2, 6, 13, 29, 47;
SSC 5**
See also CA 105; 126; DA; DLB 81;
MTCW; WLC

Kahn, Roger 1927- . . . . **CLC 30**
See also CA 25-28R; SATA 37

Kain, Saul
See Sassoon, Siegfried (Lorraine)

Kaiser, Georg 1878-1945 . . . . **TCLC 9**
See also CA 106; DLB 124

Kaletski, Alexander 1946- . . . . **CLC 39**
See also CA 118

Kalidasa fl. c. 400- . . . . **CMLC 9**

Kallman, Chester (Simon)
1921-1975 . . . . **CLC 2**
See also CA 45-48; 53-56; CANR 3

Kaminsky, Melvin 1926-
See Brooks, Mel
See also CA 65-68; CANR 16

Kaminsky, Stuart M(elvin) 1934- . . . **CLC 59**
See also CA 73-76; CANR 29

Kane, Paul
See Simon, Paul

Kane, Wilson
See Bloch, Robert (Albert)

Kanin, Garson 1912-. . . . . **CLC 22**
See also AITN 1; CA 5-8R; CANR 7;
DLB 7

Kaniuk, Yoram 1930- . . . . **CLC 19**
See also CA 134

Kant, Immanuel 1724-1804 . . . . . . **NCLC 27**
See also DLB 94

Kantor, MacKinlay 1904-1977 . . . . . . **CLC 7**
See also CA 61-64; 73-76; DLB 9, 102

Kaplan, David Michael 1946- . . . . . . **CLC 50**

Kaplan, James 1951- . . . . **CLC 59**
See also CA 135

Karageorge, Michael
See Anderson, Poul (William)

Karamzin, Nikolai Mikhailovich
1766-1826 . . . . **NCLC 3**

Karapanou, Margarita 1946- . . . . **CLC 13**
See also CA 101

Karinthy, Frigyes 1887-1938 . . . . . **TCLC 47**

Karl, Frederick R(obert) 1927- . . . . . **CLC 34**
See also CA 5-8R; CANR 3

Kastel, Warren
See Silverberg, Robert

Kataev, Evgeny Petrovich 1903-1942
See Petrov, Evgeny
See also CA 120

Kataphusin
See Ruskin, John

Katz, Steve 1935- . . . . **CLC 47**
See also CA 25-28R; CAAS 14; CANR 12;
DLBY 83

Kauffman, Janet 1945- . . . . **CLC 42**
See also CA 117; DLBY 86

Kaufman, Bob (Garnell)
1925-1986 . . . . **CLC 49**
See also BW; CA 41-44R; 118; CANR 22;
DLB 16, 41

Kaufman, George S. 1889-1961 . . . . . **CLC 38**
See also CA 108; 93-96; DLB 7

Kaufman, Sue . . . . **CLC 3, 8**
See also Barondess, Sue K(aufman)

Kavafis, Konstantinos Petrou 1863-1933
See Cavafy, C(onstantine) P(eter)
See also CA 104

Kavan, Anna 1901-1968 . . . . **CLC 5, 13**
See also CA 5-8R; CANR 6; MTCW

Kavanagh, Dan
See Barnes, Julian

Kavanagh, Patrick (Joseph)
1904-1967 . . . . **CLC 22**
See also CA 123; 25-28R; DLB 15, 20;
MTCW

Kawabata, Yasunari
1899-1972 . . . . **CLC 2, 5, 9, 18**
See also CA 93-96; 33-36R

Kaye, M(ary) M(argaret) 1909- . . . . . **CLC 28**
See also CA 89-92; CANR 24; MTCW;
SATA 62

Kaye, Mollie
See Kaye, M(ary) M(argaret)

Kaye-Smith, Sheila 1887-1956. . . . . **TCLC 20**
See also CA 118; DLB 36

Kaymor, Patrice Maguilene
See Senghor, Leopold Sedar

Kazan, Elia 1909- . . . . **CLC 6, 16, 63**
See also CA 21-24R; CANR 32

Kazantzakis, Nikos
1883(?)-1957 . . . . **TCLC 2, 5, 33**
See also CA 105; 132; MTCW

Kazin, Alfred 1915- . . . . **CLC 34, 38**
See also CA 1-4R; CAAS 7; CANR 1;
DLB 67

Keane, Mary Nesta (Skrine) 1904-
See Keane, Molly
See also CA 108; 114

Keane, Molly. . . . . **CLC 31**
See also Keane, Mary Nesta (Skrine)

Keates, Jonathan 19(?)- . . . . **CLC 34**

Keaton, Buster 1895-1966 . . . . **CLC 20**

Keats, John 1795-1821 . . . . . . **NCLC 8; PC 1**
See also CDBLB 1789-1832; DA; DLB 96,
110; WLC

Keene, Donald 1922- . . . . **CLC 34**
See also CA 1-4R; CANR 5

Keillor, Garrison . . . . **CLC 40**
See also Keillor, Gary (Edward)
See also AAYA 2; BEST 89:3; DLBY 87;
SATA 58

Keillor, Gary (Edward) 1942-
See Keillor, Garrison
See also CA 111; 117; CANR 36; MTCW

Keith, Michael
See Hubbard, L(afayette) Ron(ald)

Kell, Joseph
See Wilson, John (Anthony) Burgess

Keller, Gottfried 1819-1890 . . . . . . **NCLC 2**
See also DLB 129

Kellerman, Jonathan 1949- . . . . **CLC 44**
See also BEST 90:1; CA 106; CANR 29

Kelley, William Melvin 1937- . . . . . . **CLC 22**
See also BW; CA 77-80; CANR 27; DLB 33

Kellogg, Marjorie 1922-. . . . . **CLC 2**
See also CA 81-84

Kellow, Kathleen
See Hibbert, Eleanor Alice Burford

Kelly, M(ilton) T(erry) 1947-. . . . . . . **CLC 55**
See also CA 97-100; CANR 19

Kelman, James 1946- . . . . **CLC 58**

Knox, Calvin M.
See Silverberg, Robert

Knye, Cassandra
See Disch, Thomas M(ichael)

Koch, C(hristopher) J(ohn) 1932- ... **CLC 42**
See also CA 127

Koch, Christopher
See Koch, C(hristopher) J(ohn)

Koch, Kenneth 1925- .... **CLC 5, 8, 44**
See also CA 1-4R; CANR 6, 36; DLB 5;
SATA 65

Kochanowski, Jan 1530-1584....... **LC 10**

Kock, Charles Paul de
1794-1871 .... **NCLC 16**

Koda Shigeyuki 1867-1947
See Rohan, Koda
See also CA 121

Koestler, Arthur
1905-1983 .... **CLC 1, 3, 6, 8, 15, 33**
See also CA 1-4R; 109; CANR 1, 33;
CDBLB 1945-1960; DLBY 83; MTCW

Kohout, Pavel 1928-.............. **CLC 13**
See also CA 45-48; CANR 3

Koizumi, Yakumo
See Hearn, (Patricio) Lafcadio (Tessima
Carlos)

Kolmar, Gertrud 1894-1943 ...... **TCLC 40**

Konrad, George
See Konrad, Gyoergy

Konrad, Gyoergy 1933- ...... **CLC 4, 10, 73**
See also CA 85-88

Konwicki, Tadeusz 1926-..... **CLC 8, 28, 54**
See also CA 101; CAAS 9; CANR 39;
MTCW

Kopit, Arthur (Lee) 1937- .... **CLC 1, 18, 33**
See also AITN 1, CA 81-84, CADS 3,
DLB 7; MTCW

Kops, Bernard 1926-.............. **CLC 4**
See also CA 5-8R; DLB 13

Kornbluth, C(yril) M. 1923-1958.... **TCLC 8**
See also CA 105; DLB 8

Korolenko, V. G.
See Korolenko, Vladimir Galaktionovich

Korolenko, Vladimir
See Korolenko, Vladimir Galaktionovich

Korolenko, Vladimir G.
See Korolenko, Vladimir Galaktionovich

Korolenko, Vladimir Galaktionovich
1853-1921 .... **TCLC 22**
See also CA 121

Kosinski, Jerzy (Nikodem)
1933-1991 ... **CLC 1, 2, 3, 6, 10, 15, 53,
70**
See also CA 17-20R; 134; CANR 9; DLB 2;
DLBY 82; MTCW

Kostelanetz, Richard (Cory) 1940- .. **CLC 28**
See also CA 13-16R; CAAS 8; CANR 38

Kostrowitzki, Wilhelm Apollinaris de
1880-1918
See Apollinaire, Guillaume
See also CA 104

Kotlowitz, Robert 1924-............ **CLC 4**
See also CA 33-36R; CANR 36

Kotzebue, August (Friedrich Ferdinand) von
1761-1819 .... **NCLC 25**
See also DLB 94

Kotzwinkle, William 1938- ... **CLC 5, 14, 35**
See also CA 45-48; CANR 3; CLR 6;
MAICYA; SATA 24, 70

Kozol, Jonathan 1936-............ **CLC 17**
See also CA 61-64; CANR 16

Kozoll, Michael 1940(?)- .... **CLC 35**

Kramer, Kathryn 19(?)- .... **CLC 34**

Kramer, Larry 1935- .... **CLC 42**
See also CA 124; 126

Krasicki, Ignacy 1735-1801 .... **NCLC 8**

Krasinski, Zygmunt 1812-1859 .... **NCLC 4**

Kraus, Karl 1874-1936............ **TCLC 5**
See also CA 104; DLB 118

Kreve (Mickevicius), Vincas
1882-1954 .... **TCLC 27**

Kristeva, Julia 1941- .... **CLC 77**

Kristofferson, Kris 1936-.......... **CLC 26**
See also CA 104

Krizanc, John 1956-.............. **CLC 57**

Krleza, Miroslav 1893-1981........ **CLC 8**
See also CA 97-100; 105

Kroetsch, Robert 1927- ...... **CLC 5, 23, 57**
See also CA 17-20R; CANR 8, 38; DLB 53;
MTCW

Kroetz, Franz
See Kroetz, Franz Xaver

Kroetz, Franz Xaver 1946- ...... **CLC 41**
See also CA 130

Kroker, Arthur 1945-............ **CLC 77**

Kropotkin, Peter (Aleksieevich)
1842-1921 .... **TCLC 36**
See also CA 119

Krotkov, Yuri 1917-.............. **CLC 19**
See also CA 102

Krumb
See Crumb, R(obert)

Krumgold, Joseph (Quincy)
1908-1980 .... **CLC 12**
See also CA 9-12R; 101; CANR 7;
MAICYA; SATA 1, 23, 48

Krumwitz
See Crumb, R(obert)

Krutch, Joseph Wood 1893-1970.... **CLC 24**
See also CA 1-4R; 25-28R; CANR 4;
DLB 63

Krutzch, Gus
See Eliot, T(homas) S(tearns)

Krylov, Ivan Andreevich
1768(?)-1844 .... **NCLC 1**

Kubin, Alfred 1877-1959 .... **TCLC 23**
See also CA 112; DLB 81

Kubrick, Stanley 1928-............ **CLC 16**
See also CA 81-84; CANR 33; DLB 26

Kumin, Maxine (Winokur)
1925- .... **CLC 5, 13, 28**
See also AITN 2; CA 1-4R; CAAS 8;
CANR 1, 21; DLB 5; MTCW; SATA 12

Kundera, Milan
1929- .... **CLC 4, 9, 19, 32, 68**
See also AAYA 2; CA 85-88; CANR 19;
MTCW

Kunitz, Stanley (Jasspon)
1905- .... **CLC 6, 11, 14**
See also CA 41-44R; CANR 26; DLB 48;
MTCW

Kunze, Reiner 1933-.............. **CLC 10**
See also CA 93-96; DLB 75

Kuprin, Aleksandr Ivanovich
1870-1938 .... **TCLC 5**
See also CA 104

Kureishi, Hanif 1954(?)-.......... **CLC 64**
See also CA 139

Kurosawa, Akira 1910-............ **CLC 16**
See also CA 101

Kuttner, Henry 1915-1958........ **TCLC 10**
See also CA 107; DLB 8

Kuzma, Greg 1944-.............. **CLC 7**
See also CA 33-36R

Kuzmin, Mikhail 1872(?)-1936 .... **TCLC 40**

Kyd, Thomas 1558-1594...... **LC 22; DC 3**
See also DLB 62

Kyprianos, Iossif
See Samarakis, Antonis

La Bruyere, Jean de 1645-1696...... **LC 17**

Lacan, Jacques (Marie Emile)
1901-1981 .... **CLC 75**
See also CA 121; 104

**Laclos, Pierre Ambroise Francois Choderlos
de** 1741-1803 .... **NCLC 4**

Lacolere, Francois
See Aragon, Louis

La Colere, Francois
See Aragon, Louis

La Deshabilleuse
See Simenon, Georges (Jacques Christian)

Lady Gregory
See Gregory, Isabella Augusta (Persse)

Lady of Quality, A
See Bagnold, Enid

**La Fayette, Marie (Madelaine Pioche de la
Vergne Comtes** 1634-1693....... **LC 2**

Lafayette, Rene
See Hubbard, L(afayette) Ron(ald)

Laforgue, Jules 1860-1887........ **NCLC 5**

Lagerkvist, Paer (Fabian)
1891-1974 .... **CLC 7, 10, 13, 54**
See also Lagerkvist, Par
See also CA 85-88; 49-52; MTCW

Lagerkvist, Par
See Lagerkvist, Paer (Fabian)
See also SSC 12

Lagerloef, Selma (Ottiliana Lovisa)
1858-1940 .... **TCLC 4, 36**
See also Lagerlof, Selma (Ottiliana Lovisa)
See also CA 108; CLR 7; SATA 15

Lagerlof, Selma (Ottiliana Lovisa)
See Lagerloef, Selma (Ottiliana Lovisa)
See also CLR 7; SATA 15

La Guma, (Justin) Alex(ander)
1925-1985 . . . . CLC 19
See also BW; CA 49-52; 118; CANR 25;
DLB 117; MTCW

Laidlaw, A. K.
See Grieve, C(hristopher) M(urray)

Lainez, Manuel Mujica
See Mujica Lainez, Manuel
See also HW

Lamartine, Alphonse (Marie Louis Prat) de
1790-1869 . . . . NCLC 11

Lamb, Charles 1775-1834. . . . . . . NCLC 10
See also CDBLB 1789-1832; DA; DLB 93,
107; SATA 17; WLC

Lamb, Lady Caroline 1785-1828. . NCLC 38
See also DLB 116

Lamming, George (William)
1927- . . . . CLC 2, 4, 66
See also BLC 2; BW; CA 85-88; CANR 26;
DLB 125; MTCW

L'Amour, Louis (Dearborn)
1908-1988 . . . . CLC 25, 55
See also AITN 2; BEST 89:2; CA 1-4R;
125; CANR 3, 25, 40; DLBY 80; MTCW

Lampedusa, Giuseppe (Tomasi) di . . . TCLC 13
See also Tomasi di Lampedusa, Giuseppe

Lampman, Archibald 1861-1899 . . NCLC 25
See also DLB 92

Lancaster, Bruce 1896-1963. . . . . . . CLC 36
See also CA 9-10; CAP 1; SATA 9

Landau, Mark Alexandrovich
See Aldanov, Mark (Alexandrovich)

Landau-Aldanov, Mark Alexandrovich
See Aldanov, Mark (Alexandrovich)

Landis, John 1950-. . . . . CLC 26
See also CA 112; 122

Landolfi, Tommaso 1908-1979. . . CLC 11, 49
See also CA 127; 117

Landon, Letitia Elizabeth
1802-1838 . . . . NCLC 15
See also DLB 96

Landor, Walter Savage
1775-1864 . . . . NCLC 14
See also DLB 93, 107

Landwirth, Heinz 1927-
See Lind, Jakov
See also CA 9-12R; CANR 7

Lane, Patrick 1939- . . . . CLC 25
See also CA 97-100; DLB 53

Lang, Andrew 1844-1912. . . . . TCLC 16
See also CA 114; 137; DLB 98; MAICYA;
SATA 16

Lang, Fritz 1890-1976 . . . . CLC 20
See also CA 77-80; 69-72; CANR 30

Lange, John
See Crichton, (John) Michael

Langer, Elinor 1939- . . . . CLC 34
See also CA 121

Langland, William 1330(?)-1400(?) . . . LC 19
See also DA

Langstaff, Launcelot
See Irving, Washington

Lanier, Sidney 1842-1881 . . . . NCLC 6
See also DLB 64; MAICYA; SATA 18

Lanyer, Aemilia 1569-1645 . . . . LC 10

Lao Tzu . . . . CMLC 7

Lapine, James (Elliot) 1949-. . . . . . . CLC 39
See also CA 123; 130

Larbaud, Valery (Nicolas)
1881-1957 . . . . TCLC 9
See also CA 106

Lardner, Ring
See Lardner, Ring(gold) W(ilmer)

Lardner, Ring W., Jr.
See Lardner, Ring(gold) W(ilmer)

Lardner, Ring(gold) W(ilmer)
1885-1933 . . . . TCLC 2, 14
See also CA 104; 131; CDALB 1917-1929;
DLB 11, 25, 86; MTCW

Laredo, Betty
See Codrescu, Andrei

Larkin, Maia
See Wojciechowska, Maia (Teresa)

Larkin, Philip (Arthur)
1922-1985 . . . CLC 3, 5, 8, 9, 13, 18, 33,
39, 64
See also CA 5-8R; 117; CANR 24;
CDBLB 1960 to Present; DLB 27;
MTCW

Larra (y Sanchez de Castro), Mariano Jose de
1809-1837 . . . . NCLC 17

Larsen, Eric 1941- . . . . CLC 55
See also CA 132

Larsen, Nella 1891-1964 . . . . CLC 37
See also BLC 2; BW; CA 125; DLB 51

Larson, Charles R(aymond) 1938-. . . CLC 31
See also CA 53-56; CANR 4

Latham, Jean Lee 1902-. . . . . CLC 12
See also AITN 1; CA 5-8R; CANR 7;
MAICYA; SATA 2, 68

Latham, Mavis
See Clark, Mavis Thorpe

Lathen, Emma . . . . CLC 2
See also Hennissart, Martha; Latsis, Mary
J(ane)

Lathrop, Francis
See Leiber, Fritz (Reuter, Jr.)

Latsis, Mary J(ane)
See Lathen, Emma
See also CA 85-88

Lattimore, Richmond (Alexander)
1906-1984 . . . . CLC 3
See also CA 1-4R; 112; CANR 1

Laughlin, James 1914-. . . . . CLC 49
See also CA 21-24R; CANR 9; DLB 48

Laurence, (Jean) Margaret (Wemyss)
1926-1987 . . CLC 3, 6, 13, 50, 62; SSC 7
See also CA 5-8R; 121; CANR 33; DLB 53;
MTCW; SATA 50

Laurent, Antoine 1952- . . . . CLC 50

Lauscher, Hermann
See Hesse, Hermann

Lautreamont, Comte de
1846-1870 . . . . NCLC 12

Laverty, Donald
See Blish, James (Benjamin)

Lavin, Mary 1912-. . . . . . CLC 4, 18; SSC 4
See also CA 9-12R; CANR 33; DLB 15;
MTCW

Lavond, Paul Dennis
See Kornbluth, C(yril) M.; Pohl, Frederik

Lawler, Raymond Evenor 1922- . . . . CLC 58
See also CA 103

Lawrence, D(avid) H(erbert Richards)
1885-1930 . . . . . . TCLC 2, 9, 16, 33, 48;
SSC 4
See also CA 104; 121; CDBLB 1914-1945;
DA; DLB 10, 19, 36, 98; MTCW; WLC

Lawrence, T(homas) E(dward)
1888-1935 . . . . TCLC 18
See also Dale, Colin
See also CA 115

Lawrence Of Arabia
See Lawrence, T(homas) E(dward)

Lawson, Henry (Archibald Hertzberg)
1867-1922 . . . . TCLC 27
See also CA 120

Lawton, Dennis
See Faust, Frederick (Schiller)

Laxness, Halldor. . . . . CLC 25
See also Gudjonsson, Halldor Kiljan

Layamon fl. c. 1200-. . . . . CMLC 10

Laye, Camara 1928-1980. . . . . . . CLC 4, 38
See also BLC 2; BW; CA 85-88; 97-100;
CANR 25; MTCW

Layton, Irving (Peter) 1912-. . . . . CLC 2, 15
See also CA 1-4R; CANR 2, 33; DLB 88;
MTCW

Lazarus, Emma 1849-1887. . . . . . . NCLC 8

Lazarus, Felix
See Cable, George Washington

Lazarus, Henry
See Slavitt, David R(ytman)

Lea, Joan
See Neufeld, John (Arthur)

Leacock, Stephen (Butler)
1869-1944 . . . . TCLC 2
See also CA 104; DLB 92

Lear, Edward 1812-1888 . . . . NCLC 3
See also CLR 1; DLB 32; MAICYA;
SATA 18

Lear, Norman (Milton) 1922- . . . . . . CLC 12
See also CA 73-76

Leavis, F(rank) R(aymond)
1895-1978 . . . . CLC 24
See also CA 21-24R; 77-80; MTCW

Leavitt, David 1961-. . . . . CLC 34
See also CA 116; 122; DLB 130

Leblanc, Maurice (Marie Emile)
1864-1941 . . . . TCLC 49
See also CA 110

Lebowitz, Fran(ces Ann)
1951(?)- . . . . CLC 11, 36
See also CA 81-84; CANR 14; MTCW

le Carre, John . . . . CLC 3, 5, 9, 15, 28
See also Cornwell, David (John Moore)
See also BEST 89:4; CDBLB 1960 to
Present; DLB 87

Le Clezio, J(ean) M(arie) G(ustave)
1940- . . . . **CLC 31**
See also CA 116; 128; DLB 83

Leconte de Lisle, Charles-Marie-Rene
1818-1894 . . . . **NCLC 29**

Le Coq, Monsieur
See Simenon, Georges (Jacques Christian)

Leduc, Violette 1907-1972 . . . . **CLC 22**
See also CA 13-14; 33-36R; CAP 1

Ledwidge, Francis 1887(?)-1917 . . . **TCLC 23**
See also CA 123; DLB 20

Lee, Andrea 1953- . . . . **CLC 36**
See also BLC 2; BW; CA 125

Lee, Andrew
See Auchincloss, Louis (Stanton)

Lee, Don L. . . . . **CLC 2**
See also Madhubuti, Haki R.

Lee, George W(ashington)
1894-1976 . . . . **CLC 52**
See also BLC 2; BW; CA 125; DLB 51

Lee, (Nelle) Harper 1926- . . . . . . **CLC 12, 60**
See also CA 13-16R; CDALB 1941-1968;
DA; DLB 6; MTCW; SATA 11; WLC

Lee, Julian
See Latham, Jean Lee

Lee, Lawrence 1903- . . . . **CLC 34**
See also CA 25-28R

Lee, Manfred B(ennington)
1905-1971 . . . . **CLC 11**
See also Queen, Ellery
See also CA 1-4R; 29-32R; CANR 2

Lee, Stan 1922- . . . . **CLC 17**
See also AAYA 5; CA 108; 111

Lee, Tanith 1947- . . . . **CLC 46**
See also CA 37-40R; SATA 8

Lee, Vernon . . . . **TCLC 5**
See also Paget, Violet
See also DLB 57

Lee, William
See Burroughs, William S(eward)

Lee, Willy
See Burroughs, William S(eward)

Lee-Hamilton, Eugene (Jacob)
1845-1907 . . . . **TCLC 22**
See also CA 117

Leet, Judith 1935- . . . . **CLC 11**

Le Fanu, Joseph Sheridan
1814-1873 . . . . **NCLC 9**
See also DLB 21, 70

Leffland, Ella 1931- . . . . **CLC 19**
See also CA 29-32R; CANR 35; DLBY 84;
SATA 65

Leger, (Marie-Rene) Alexis Saint-Leger
1887-1975 . . . . **CLC 11**
See also Perse, St.-John
See also CA 13-16R; 61-64; MTCW

Leger, Saintleger
See Leger, (Marie-Rene) Alexis Saint-Leger

Le Guin, Ursula K(roeber)
1929- . . . . **CLC 8, 13, 22, 45, 71; SSC 12**
See also AAYA 9; AITN 1; CA 21-24R;
CANR 9, 32; CDALB 1968-1988; CLR 3,
28; DLB 8, 52; MAICYA; MTCW;
SATA 4, 52

Lehmann, Rosamond (Nina)
1901-1990 . . . . **CLC 5**
See also CA 77-80; 131; CANR 8; DLB 15

Leiber, Fritz (Reuter, Jr.)
1910-1992 . . . . **CLC 25**
See also CA 45-48; 139; CANR 2, 40;
DLB 8; MTCW; SATA 45;
SATA-Obit 73

Leimbach, Martha 1963-
See Leimbach, Marti
See also CA 130

Leimbach, Marti . . . . **CLC 65**
See also Leimbach, Martha

Leino, Eino . . . . **TCLC 24**
See also Loennbohm, Armas Eino Leopold

Leiris, Michel (Julien) 1901-1990 . . . **CLC 61**
See also CA 119; 128; 132

Leithauser, Brad 1953- . . . . **CLC 27**
See also CA 107; CANR 27; DLB 120

Lelchuk, Alan 1938- . . . . **CLC 5**
See also CA 45-48; CANR 1

Lem, Stanislaw 1921- . . . . **CLC 8, 15, 40**
See also CA 105; CAAS 1; CANR 32;
MTCW

Lemann, Nancy 1956- . . . . **CLC 39**
See also CA 118; 136

Lemonnier, (Antoine Louis) Camille
1844-1913 . . . . **TCLC 22**
See also CA 121

Lenau, Nikolaus 1802-1850 . . . . . . **NCLC 16**

L'Engle, Madeleine (Camp Franklin)
1918- . . . . **CLC 12**
See also AAYA 1; AITN 2; CA 1-4R;
CANR 3, 21, 39; CLR 1, 14; DLB 52;
MAICYA; MTCW; SAAS 15; SATA 1,
27

Lengyel, Jozsef 1896-1975 . . . . **CLC 7**
See also CA 85-88; 57-60

Lennon, John (Ono)
1940-1980 . . . . **CLC 12, 35**
See also CA 102

Lennox, Charlotte Ramsay
1729(?)-1804 . . . . **NCLC 23**
See also DLB 39

Lentricchia, Frank (Jr.) 1940- . . . . . . **CLC 34**
See also CA 25-28R; CANR 19

Lenz, Siegfried 1926- . . . . **CLC 27**
See also CA 89-92; DLB 75

Leonard, Elmore (John, Jr.)
1925- . . . . **CLC 28, 34, 71**
See also AITN 1; BEST 89:1, 90:4;
CA 81-84; CANR 12, 28; MTCW

Leonard, Hugh
See Byrne, John Keyes
See also DLB 13

Leopardi, (Conte) Giacomo (Talegardo
Francesco di Sales Save
1798-1837 . . . . **NCLC 22**

Le Reveler
See Artaud, Antonin

Lerman, Eleanor 1952- . . . . **CLC 9**
See also CA 85-88

Lerman, Rhoda 1936- . . . . **CLC 56**
See also CA 49-52

Lermontov, Mikhail Yuryevich
1814-1841 . . . . **NCLC 5**

Leroux, Gaston 1868-1927 . . . . **TCLC 25**
See also CA 108; 136; SATA 65

Lesage, Alain-Rene 1668-1747 . . . . **LC 2**

Leskov, Nikolai (Semyonovich)
1831-1895 . . . . **NCLC 25**

Lessing, Doris (May)
1919- . . . . **CLC 1, 2, 3, 6, 10, 15, 22, 40;
SSC 6**
See also CA 9-12R; CAAS 14; CANR 33;
CDBLB 1960 to Present; DA; DLB 15;
DLBY 85; MTCW

Lessing, Gotthold Ephraim
1729-1781 . . . . **LC 8**
See also DLB 97

Lester, Richard 1932- . . . . **CLC 20**

Lever, Charles (James)
1806-1872 . . . . **NCLC 23**
See also DLB 21

Leverson, Ada 1865(?)-1936(?) . . . . **TCLC 18**
See also Elaine
See also CA 117

Levertov, Denise
1923- . . . . . . **CLC 1, 2, 3, 5, 8, 15, 28, 66**
See also CA 1-4R; CANR 3, 29; DLB 5;
MTCW

Levi, Jonathan . . . . **CLC 76**

Levi, Peter (Chad Tigar) 1931- . . . . . **CLC 41**
See also CA 5-8R; CANR 34; DLB 40

Levi, Primo
1919-1987 . . . . **CLC 37, 50; SSC 12**
See also CA 13-16R; 122; CANR 12, 33;
MTCW

Levin, Ira 1929- . . . . **CLC 3, 6**
See also CA 21-24R; CANR 17; MTCW;
SATA 66

Levin, Meyer 1905-1981 . . . . **CLC 7**
See also AITN 1; CA 9-12R; 104;
CANR 15; DLB 9, 28; DLBY 81;
SATA 21, 27

Levine, Norman 1924- . . . . **CLC 54**
See also CA 73-76; CANR 14; DLB 88

Levine, Philip 1928- . . **CLC 2, 4, 5, 9, 14, 33**
See also CA 9-12R; CANR 9, 37; DLB 5

Levinson, Deirdre 1931- . . . . **CLC 49**
See also CA 73-76

Levi-Strauss, Claude 1908- . . . . **CLC 38**
See also CA 1-4R; CANR 6, 32; MTCW

Levitin, Sonia (Wolff) 1934- . . . . **CLC 17**
See also CA 29-32R; CANR 14, 32;
MAICYA; SAAS 2; SATA 4, 68

Levon, O. U.
See Kesey, Ken (Elton)

Lewes, George Henry
1817-1878 . . . . **NCLC 25**
See also DLB 55

Lewis, Alun 1915-1944 . . . . **TCLC 3**
See also CA 104; DLB 20

Lewis, C. Day
See Day Lewis, C(ecil)

Lewis, C(live) S(taples)
1898-1963 . . . . **CLC 1, 3, 6, 14, 27**
See also AAYA 3; CA 81-84; CANR 33;
CDBLB 1945-1960; CLR 3, 27; DA;
DLB 15, 100; MAICYA; MTCW;
SATA 13; WLC

Lewis, Janet 1899- . . . . **CLC 41**
See also Winters, Janet Lewis
See also CA 9-12R; CANR 29; CAP 1;
DLBY 87

Lewis, Matthew Gregory
1775-1818 . . . . **NCLC 11**
See also DLB 39

Lewis, (Harry) Sinclair
1885-1951 . . . . **TCLC 4, 13, 23, 39**
See also CA 104; 133; CDALB 1917-1929;
DA; DLB 9, 102; DLBD 1; MTCW;
WLC

Lewis, (Percy) Wyndham
1884(?)-1957 . . . . **TCLC 2, 9**
See also CA 104; DLB 15

Lewisohn, Ludwig 1883-1955. . . . . . **TCLC 19**
See also CA 107; DLB 4, 9, 28, 102

Lezama Lima, Jose 1910-1976 . . . **CLC 4, 10**
See also CA 77-80; DLB 113; HW

L'Heureux, John (Clarke) 1934- . . . . **CLC 52**
See also CA 13-16R; CANR 23

Liddell, C. H.
See Kuttner, Henry

Lie, Jonas (Lauritz Idemil)
1833-1908(?) . . . . **TCLC 5**
See also CA 115

Lieber, Joel 1937-1971. . . . . **CLC 6**
See also CA 73-76; 29-32R

Lieber, Stanley Martin
See Lee, Stan

Lieberman, Laurence (James)
1935- . . . . **CLC 4, 36**
See also CA 17-20R; CANR 8, 36

Lieksman, Anders
See Haavikko, Paavo Juhani

Li Fei-kan 1904- . . . . **CLC 18**
See also CA 105

Lifton, Robert Jay 1926- . . . . **CLC 67**
See also CA 17-20R; CANR 27; SATA 66

Lightfoot, Gordon 1938- . . . . **CLC 26**
See also CA 109

Ligotti, Thomas 1953- . . . . **CLC 44**
See also CA 123

Liliencron, (Friedrich Adolf Axel) Detlev von
1844-1909 . . . . **TCLC 18**
See also CA 117

Lima, Jose Lezama
See Lezama Lima, Jose

Lima Barreto, Afonso Henrique de
1881-1922 . . . . **TCLC 23**
See also CA 117

Limonov, Eduard. . . . . **CLC 67**

Lin, Frank
See Atherton, Gertrude (Franklin Horn)

Lincoln, Abraham 1809-1865. . . . . **NCLC 18**

Lind, Jakov . . . . **CLC 1, 2, 4, 27**
See also Landwirth, Heinz
See also CAAS 4

Lindsay, David 1878-1945 . . . . **TCLC 15**
See also CA 113

Lindsay, (Nicholas) Vachel
1879-1931 . . . . **TCLC 17**
See also CA 114; 135; CDALB 1865-1917;
DA; DLB 54; SATA 40; WLC

Linke-Poot
See Doeblin, Alfred

Linney, Romulus 1930- . . . . **CLC 51**
See also CA 1-4R; CANR 40

Li Po 701-763 . . . . **CMLC 2**

Lipsius, Justus 1547-1606 . . . . **LC 16**

Lipsyte, Robert (Michael) 1938- . . . . **CLC 21**
See also AAYA 7; CA 17-20R; CANR 8;
CLR 23; DA; MAICYA; SATA 5, 68

Lish, Gordon (Jay) 1934- . . . . **CLC 45**
See also CA 113; 117; DLB 130

Lispector, Clarice 1925-1977 . . . . **CLC 43**
See also CA 139; 116; DLB 113

Littell, Robert 1935(?)- . . . . **CLC 42**
See also CA 109; 112

Littlewit, Humphrey Gent.
See Lovecraft, H(oward) P(hillips)

Litwos
See Sienkiewicz, Henryk (Adam Alexander
Pius)

Liu E 1857-1909 . . . . **TCLC 15**
See also CA 115

Lively, Penelope (Margaret)
1933- . . . . **CLC 32, 50**
See also CA 41-44R; CANR 29; CLR 7;
DLB 14; MAICYA; MTCW; SATA 7, 60

Livesay, Dorothy (Kathleen)
1909- . . . . **CLC 4, 15**
See also AITN 2; CA 25-28R; CAAS 8;
CANR 36; DLB 68; MTCW

Livy c. 59B.C.-c. 17 . . . . **CMLC 11**

Lizardi, Jose Joaquin Fernandez de
1776-1827 . . . . **NCLC 30**

Llewellyn, Richard . . . . **CLC 7**
See also Llewellyn Lloyd, Richard Dafydd
Vivian
See also DLB 15

Llewellyn Lloyd, Richard Dafydd Vivian
1906-1983
See Llewellyn, Richard
See also CA 53-56; 111; CANR 7;
SATA 11, 37

Llosa, (Jorge) Mario (Pedro) Vargas
See Vargas Llosa, (Jorge) Mario (Pedro)

Lloyd Webber, Andrew 1948-
See Webber, Andrew Lloyd
See also AAYA 1; CA 116; SATA 56

Locke, Alain (Le Roy)
1886-1954 . . . . **TCLC 43**
See also BW; CA 106; 124; DLB 51

Locke, John 1632-1704 . . . . **LC 7**
See also DLB 101

Locke-Elliott, Sumner
See Elliott, Sumner Locke

Lockhart, John Gibson
1794-1854 . . . . **NCLC 6**
See also DLB 110, 116

Lodge, David (John) 1935- . . . . **CLC 36**
See also BEST 90:1; CA 17-20R; CANR 19;
DLB 14; MTCW

Loennbohm, Armas Eino Leopold 1878-1926
See Leino, Eino
See also CA 123

Loewinsohn, Ron(ald William)
1937- . . . . **CLC 52**
See also CA 25-28R

Logan, Jake
See Smith, Martin Cruz

Logan, John (Burton) 1923-1987. . . . . **CLC 5**
See also CA 77-80; 124; DLB 5

Lo Kuan-chung 1330(?)-1400(?) . . . . . **LC 12**

Lombard, Nap
See Johnson, Pamela Hansford

London, Jack . . . . **TCLC 9, 15, 39; SSC 4**
See also London, John Griffith
See also AITN 2; CDALB 1865-1917;
DLB 8, 12, 78; SATA 18; WLC

London, John Griffith 1876-1916
See London, Jack
See also CA 110; 119; DA; MAICYA;
MTCW

Long, Emmett
See Leonard, Elmore (John, Jr.)

Longbaugh, Harry
See Goldman, William (W.)

Longfellow, Henry Wadsworth
1807-1882 . . . . **NCLC 2**
See also CDALB 1640-1865; DA; DLB 1,
59; SATA 19

Longley, Michael 1939- . . . . **CLC 29**
See also CA 102; DLB 40

Longus fl. c. 2nd cent. - . . . . **CMLC 7**

Longway, A. Hugh
See Lang, Andrew

Lopate, Phillip 1943- . . . . **CLC 29**
See also CA 97-100; DLBY 80

Lopez Portillo (y Pacheco), Jose
1920- . . . . **CLC 46**
See also CA 129; HW

Lopez y Fuentes, Gregorio
1897(?)-1966 . . . . **CLC 32**
See also CA 131; HW

Lorca, Federico Garcia
See Garcia Lorca, Federico

Lord, Bette Bao 1938- . . . . **CLC 23**
See also BEST 90:3; CA 107; CANR 41;
SATA 58

Lord Auch
See Bataille, Georges

Lord Byron
See Byron, George Gordon (Noel)

Lord Dunsany . . . . **TCLC 2**
See also Dunsany, Edward John Moreton
Drax Plunkett

Lorde, Audre (Geraldine)
1934- . . . . **CLC 18, 71**
See also BLC 2; BW; CA 25-28R;
CANR 16, 26; DLB 41; MTCW

Lord Jeffrey
See Jeffrey, Francis

MacNeice, (Frederick) Louis
1907-1963 . . . . **CLC 1, 4, 10, 53**
See also CA 85-88; DLB 10, 20; MTCW

MacNeill, Dand
See Fraser, George MacDonald

Macpherson, (Jean) Jay 1931- . . . . . . **CLC 14**
See also CA 5-8R; DLB 53

MacShane, Frank 1927- . . . . **CLC 39**
See also CA 9-12R; CANR 3, 33; DLB 111

Macumber, Mari
See Sandoz, Mari(e Susette)

Madach, Imre 1823-1864 . . . . **NCLC 19**

Madden, (Jerry) David 1933- . . . . **CLC 5, 15**
See also CA 1-4R; CAAS 3; CANR 4;
DLB 6; MTCW

Maddern, Al(an)
See Ellison, Harlan

Madhubuti, Haki R.
1942- . . . . **CLC 6, 73; PC 5**
See also Lee, Don L.
See also BLC 2; BW; CA 73-76; CANR 24;
DLB 5, 41; DLBD 8

Madow, Pauline (Reichberg) . . . . **CLC 1**
See also CA 9-12R

Maepenn, Hugh
See Kuttner, Henry

Maepenn, K. H.
See Kuttner, Henry

Maeterlinck, Maurice 1862-1949 . . . **TCLC 3**
See also CA 104; 136; SATA 66

Maginn, William 1794-1842 . . . . . . **NCLC 8**
See also DLB 110

Mahapatra, Jayanta 1928- . . . . **CLC 33**
See also CA 73-76; CAAS 9; CANR 15, 33

Mahfouz, Naguib (Abdel Aziz Al-Sabilgi)
1911(?)-
See Mahfuz, Najib
See also BEST 89:2; CA 128; MTCW

Mahfuz, Najib . . . . **CLC 52, 55**
See also Mahfouz, Naguib (Abdel Aziz
Al-Sabilgi)
See also DLBY 88

Mahon, Derek 1941- . . . . **CLC 27**
See also CA 113; 128; DLB 40

Mailer, Norman
1923- . . . . . . **CLC 1, 2, 3, 4, 5, 8, 11, 14,
28, 39, 74**
See also AITN 2; CA 9-12R; CABS 1;
CANR 28; CDALB 1968-1988; DA;
DLB 2, 16, 28; DLBD 3; DLBY 80, 83;
MTCW

Maillet, Antonine 1929- . . . . **CLC 54**
See also CA 115; 120; DLB 60

Mais, Roger 1905-1955 . . . . **TCLC 8**
See also BW; CA 105; 124; DLB 125;
MTCW

Maitland, Sara (Louise) 1950- . . . . . **CLC 49**
See also CA 69-72; CANR 13

Major, Clarence 1936- . . . . . . **CLC 3, 19, 48**
See also BLC 2; BW; CA 21-24R; CAAS 6;
CANR 13, 25; DLB 33

Major, Kevin (Gerald) 1949- . . . . . . **CLC 26**
See also CA 97-100; CANR 21, 38;
CLR 11; DLB 60; MAICYA; SATA 32

Maki, James
See Ozu, Yasujiro

Malabaila, Damiano
See Levi, Primo

Malamud, Bernard
1914-1986 . . . . . **CLC 1, 2, 3, 5, 8, 9, 11,
18, 27, 44**
See also CA 5-8R; 118; CABS 1; CANR 28;
CDALB 1941-1968; DA; DLB 2, 28;
DLBY 80, 86; MTCW; WLC

Malcolm, Dan
See Silverberg, Robert

Malherbe, Francois de 1555-1628 . . . . . **LC 5**

Mallarme, Stephane
1842-1898 . . . . **NCLC 4; PC 4**

Mallet-Joris, Francoise 1930- . . . . . . **CLC 11**
See also CA 65-68; CANR 17; DLB 83

Malley, Ern
See McAuley, James Phillip

Mallowan, Agatha Christie
See Christie, Agatha (Mary Clarissa)

Maloff, Saul 1922- . . . . **CLC 5**
See also CA 33-36R

Malone, Louis
See MacNeice, (Frederick) Louis

Malone, Michael (Christopher)
1942- . . . . **CLC 43**
See also CA 77-80; CANR 14, 32

Malory, (Sir) Thomas
1410(?)-1471(?) . . . . **LC 11**
See also CDBLB Before 1660; DA;
SATA 33, 59

Malouf, (George Joseph) David
1934- . . . . **CLC 28**
See also CA 124

Malraux, (Georges-)Andre
1901-1976 . . . . . . **CLC 1, 4, 9, 13, 15, 57**
See also CA 21-22; 69-72; CANR 34;
CAP 2; DLB 72; MTCW

Malzberg, Barry N(athaniel) 1939- . . . **CLC 7**
See also CA 61-64; CAAS 4; CANR 16;
DLB 8

Mamet, David (Alan)
1947- . . . . **CLC 9, 15, 34, 46**
See also AAYA 3; CA 81-84; CABS 3;
CANR 15, 41; DLB 7; MTCW

Mamoulian, Rouben (Zachary)
1897-1987 . . . . **CLC 16**
See also CA 25-28R; 124

Mandelstam, Osip (Emilievich)
1891(?)-1938(?) . . . . **TCLC 2, 6**
See also CA 104

Mander, (Mary) Jane 1877-1949 . . . **TCLC 31**

Mandiargues, Andre Pieyre de . . . . . . **CLC 41**
See also Pieyre de Mandiargues, Andre
See also DLB 83

Mandrake, Ethel Belle
See Thurman, Wallace (Henry)

Mangan, James Clarence
1803-1849 . . . . **NCLC 27**

Maniere, J.-E.
See Giraudoux, (Hippolyte) Jean

Manley, (Mary) Delariviere
1672(?)-1724 . . . . **LC 1**
See also DLB 39, 80

Mann, Abel
See Creasey, John

Mann, (Luiz) Heinrich 1871-1950 . . . **TCLC 9**
See also CA 106; DLB 66

Mann, (Paul) Thomas
1875-1955 . . . **TCLC 2, 8, 14, 21, 35, 44;
SSC 5**
See also CA 104; 128; DA; DLB 66;
MTCW; WLC

Manning, David
See Faust, Frederick (Schiller)

Manning, Frederic 1887(?)-1935 . . . **TCLC 25**
See also CA 124

Manning, Olivia 1915-1980 . . . . . . **CLC 5, 19**
See also CA 5-8R; 101; CANR 29; MTCW

Mano, D. Keith 1942- . . . . **CLC 2, 10**
See also CA 25-28R; CAAS 6; CANR 26;
DLB 6

Mansfield, Katherine . . . **TCLC 2, 8, 39; SSC 9**
See also Beauchamp, Kathleen Mansfield
See also WLC

Manso, Peter 1940- . . . . **CLC 39**
See also CA 29-32R

Mantecon, Juan Jimenez
See Jimenez (Mantecon), Juan Ramon

Manton, Peter
See Creasey, John

Man Without a Spleen, A
See Chekhov, Anton (Pavlovich)

Manzoni, Alessandro 1785-1873 . . **NCLC 29**

Mapu, Abraham (ben Jekutiel)
1808-1867 . . . . **NCLC 18**

Mara, Sally
See Queneau, Raymond

Marat, Jean Paul 1743-1793 . . . . **LC 10**

Marcel, Gabriel Honore
1889-1973 . . . . **CLC 15**
See also CA 102; 45-48; MTCW

Marchbanks, Samuel
See Davies, (William) Robertson

Marchi, Giacomo
See Bassani, Giorgio

Margulies, Donald . . . . **CLC 76**

Marie de France c. 12th cent. - . . . . **CMLC 8**

Marie de l'Incarnation 1599-1672 . . . . **LC 10**

Mariner, Scott
See Pohl, Frederik

Marinetti, Filippo Tommaso
1876-1944 . . . . **TCLC 10**
See also CA 107; DLB 114

Marivaux, Pierre Carlet de Chamblain de
1688-1763 . . . . **LC 4**

Markandaya, Kamala . . . . **CLC 8, 38**
See also Taylor, Kamala (Purnaiya)

Markfield, Wallace 1926- . . . . **CLC 8**
See also CA 69-72; CAAS 3; DLB 2, 28

Markham, Edwin 1852-1940 . . . . . . **TCLC 47**
See also DLB 54

Markham, Robert
See Amis, Kingsley (William)

Marks, J
See Highwater, Jamake (Mamake)

Marks-Highwater, J
See Highwater, Jamake (Mamake)

Markson, David M(errill) 1927- .... **CLC 67**
See also CA 49-52; CANR 1

Marley, Bob................... **CLC 17**
See also Marley, Robert Nesta

Marley, Robert Nesta 1945-1981
See Marley, Bob
See also CA 107; 103

Marlowe, Christopher
1564-1593 .... **LC 22; DC 1**
See also CDBLB Before 1660; DA; DLB 62;
WLC

Marmontel, Jean-Francois
1723-1799 .... **LC 2**

Marquand, John P(hillips)
1893-1960 .... **CLC 2, 10**
See also CA 85-88; DLB 9, 102

Marquez, Gabriel (Jose) Garcia...... **CLC 68**
See also Garcia Marquez, Gabriel (Jose)

Marquis, Don(ald Robert Perry)
1878-1937 .... **TCLC 7**
See also CA 104; DLB 11, 25

Marric, J. J.
See Creasey, John

Marrow, Bernard
See Moore, Brian

Marryat, Frederick 1792-1848 .... **NCLC 3**
See also DLB 21

Marsden, James
See Creasey, John

Marsh, (Edith) Ngaio
1899-1982 .... **CLC 7, 53**
See also CA 9-12R; CANR 6; DLB 77;
MTCW

Marshall, Garry 1934- .... **CLC 17**
See also AAYA 3; CA 111; SATA 60

Marshall, Paule 1929- .. **CLC 27, 72; SSC 3**
See also BLC 3; BW; CA 77-80; CANR 25;
DLB 33; MTCW

Marsten, Richard
See Hunter, Evan

Martha, Henry
See Harris, Mark

Martin, Ken
See Hubbard, L(afayette) Ron(ald)

Martin, Richard
See Creasey, John

Martin, Steve 1945- .... **CLC 30**
See also CA 97-100; CANR 30; MTCW

Martin, Webber
See Silverberg, Robert

Martin du Gard, Roger
1881-1958 .... **TCLC 24**
See also CA 118; DLB 65

Martineau, Harriet 1802-1876 .... **NCLC 26**
See also DLB 21, 55; YABC 2

Martines, Julia
See O'Faolain, Julia

Martinez, Jacinto Benavente y
See Benavente (y Martinez), Jacinto

Martinez Ruiz, Jose 1873-1967
See Azorin; Ruiz, Jose Martinez
See also CA 93-96; HW

Martinez Sierra, Gregorio
1881-1947 .... **TCLC 6**
See also CA 115

Martinez Sierra, Maria (de la O'LeJarraga)
1874-1974 .... **TCLC 6**
See also CA 115

Martinsen, Martin
See Follett, Ken(neth Martin)

Martinson, Harry (Edmund)
1904-1978 .... **CLC 14**
See also CA 77-80; CANR 34

Marut, Ret
See Traven, B.

Marut, Robert
See Traven, B.

Marvell, Andrew 1621-1678......... **LC 4**
See also CDBLB 1660-1789; DA; DLB 131;
WLC

Marx, Karl (Heinrich)
1818-1883 .... **NCLC 17**
See also DLB 129

Masaoka Shiki................... **TCLC 18**
See also Masaoka Tsunenori

Masaoka Tsunenori 1867-1902
See Masaoka Shiki
See also CA 117

Masefield, John (Edward)
1878-1967 .... **CLC 11, 47**
See also CA 19-20; 25-28R; CANR 33;
CAP 2; CDBLB 1890-1914; DLB 10;
MTCW; SATA 19

Maso, Carole 19(?)- .... **CLC 44**

Mason, Bobbie Ann
1940- .... **CLC 28, 43; SSC 4**
See also AAYA 5; CA 53-56; CANR 11,
31; DLBY 87; MTCW

Mason, Ernst
See Pohl, Frederik

Mason, Lee W.
See Malzberg, Barry N(athaniel)

Mason, Nick 1945- .... **CLC 35**
See also Pink Floyd

Mason, Tally
See Derleth, August (William)

Mass, William
See Gibson, William

Masters, Edgar Lee
1868-1950 .... **TCLC 2, 25; PC 1**
See also CA 104; 133; CDALB 1865-1917;
DA; DLB 54; MTCW

Masters, Hilary 1928- .... **CLC 48**
See also CA 25-28R; CANR 13

Mastrosimone, William 19(?)- ...... **CLC 36**

Mathe, Albert
See Camus, Albert

Matheson, Richard Burton 1926- ... **CLC 37**
See also CA 97-100; DLB 8, 44

Mathews, Harry 1930- .... **CLC 6, 52**
See also CA 21-24R; CAAS 6; CANR 18,
40

Mathias, Roland (Glyn) 1915- ...... **CLC 45**
See also CA 97-100; CANR 19, 41; DLB 27

Matsuo Basho 1644-1694 .... **PC 3**

Mattheson, Rodney
See Creasey, John

Matthews, Greg 1949- .... **CLC 45**
See also CA 135

Matthews, William 1942- .... **CLC 40**
See also CA 29-32R; CANR 12; DLB 5

Matthias, John (Edward) 1941- ...... **CLC 9**
See also CA 33-36R

Matthiessen, Peter
1927- .... **CLC 5, 7, 11, 32, 64**
See also AAYA 6; BEST 90:4; CA 9-12R;
CANR 21; DLB 6; MTCW; SATA 27

Maturin, Charles Robert
1780(?)-1824 .... **NCLC 6**

Matute (Ausejo), Ana Maria
1925- .... **CLC 11**
See also CA 89-92; MTCW

Maugham, W. S.
See Maugham, W(illiam) Somerset

Maugham, W(illiam) Somerset
1874-1965 .... **CLC 1, 11, 15, 67; SSC 8**
See also CA 5-8R; 25-28R; CANR 40;
CDBLB 1914-1945; DA; DLB 10, 36, 77,
100; MTCW; SATA 54; WLC

Maugham, William Somerset
See Maugham, W(illiam) Somerset

Maupassant, (Henri Rene Albert) Guy de
1850-1893 .... **NCLC 1; SSC 1**
See also DA; DLB 123; WLC

Maurhut, Richard
See Traven, B.

Mauriac, Claude 1914- .... **CLC 9**
See also CA 89-92; DLB 83

Mauriac, Francois (Charles)
1885-1970 .... **CLC 4, 9, 56**
See also CA 25-28; CAP 2; DLB 65;
MTCW

Mavor, Osborne Henry 1888-1951
See Bridie, James
See also CA 104

Maxwell, William (Keepers, Jr.)
1908- .... **CLC 19**
See also CA 93-96; DLBY 80

May, Elaine 1932- .... **CLC 16**
See also CA 124; DLB 44

Mayakovski, Vladimir (Vladimirovich)
1893-1930 .... **TCLC 4, 18**
See also CA 104

Mayhew, Henry 1812-1887 ...... **NCLC 31**
See also DLB 18, 55

Maynard, Joyce 1953- .... **CLC 23**
See also CA 111; 129

Mayne, William (James Carter)
1928- .... **CLC 12**
See also CA 9-12R; CANR 37; CLR 25;
MAICYA; SAAS 11; SATA 6, 68

Mayo, Jim
See L'Amour, Louis (Dearborn)

Maysles, Albert 1926- .... **CLC 16**
See also CA 29-32R

Maysles, David 1932- .... **CLC 16**

Montagu, Elizabeth 1917- . . . . NCLC 7
See also CA 9-12R

Montagu, Mary (Pierrepont) Wortley
1689-1762 . . . . LC 9
See also DLB 95, 101

Montagu, W. H.
See Coleridge, Samuel Taylor

Montague, John (Patrick)
1929- . . . . CLC 13, 46
See also CA 9-12R; CANR 9; DLB 40;
MTCW

Montaigne, Michel (Eyquem) de
1533-1592 . . . . LC 8
See also DA; WLC

Montale, Eugenio 1896-1981 . . . CLC 7, 9, 18
See also CA 17-20R; 104; CANR 30;
DLB 114; MTCW

Montesquieu, Charles-Louis de Secondat
1689-1755 . . . . LC 7

Montgomery, (Robert) Bruce 1921-1978
See Crispin, Edmund
See also CA 104

Montgomery, Marion H., Jr. 1925- . . CLC 7
See also AITN 1; CA 1-4R; CANR 3;
DLB 6

Montgomery, Max
See Davenport, Guy (Mattison, Jr.)

Montherlant, Henry (Milon) de
1896-1972 . . . . CLC 8, 19
See also CA 85-88; 37-40R; DLB 72;
MTCW

Monty Python . . . . CLC 21
See also Chapman, Graham; Cleese, John
(Marwood); Gilliam, Terry (Vance); Idle,
Eric; Jones, Terence Graham Parry; Palin,
Michael (Edward)
See also AAYA 7

Moodie, Susanna (Strickland)
1803-1885 . . . . NCLC 14
See also DLB 99

Mooney, Edward 1951- . . . . CLC 25
See also CA 130

Mooney, Ted
See Mooney, Edward

Moorcock, Michael (John)
1939- . . . . CLC 5, 27, 58
See also CA 45-48; CAAS 5; CANR 2, 17,
38; DLB 14; MTCW

Moore, Brian
1921- . . . . CLC 1, 3, 5, 7, 8, 19, 32
See also CA 1-4R; CANR 1, 25; MTCW

Moore, Edward
See Muir, Edwin

Moore, George Augustus
1852-1933 . . . . TCLC 7
See also CA 104; DLB 10, 18, 57

Moore, Lorrie . . . . CLC 39, 45, 68
See also Moore, Marie Lorena

Moore, Marianne (Craig)
1887-1972 . . . CLC 1, 2, 4, 8, 10, 13, 19,
47; PC 4
See also CA 1-4R; 33-36R; CANR 3;
CDALB 1929-1941; DA; DLB 45;
DLBD 7; MTCW; SATA 20

Moore, Marie Lorena 1957-
See Moore, Lorrie
See also CA 116; CANR 39

Moore, Thomas 1779-1852 . . . . NCLC 6
See also DLB 96

Morand, Paul 1888-1976 . . . . CLC 41
See also CA 69-72; DLB 65

Morante, Elsa 1918-1985 . . . . CLC 8, 47
See also CA 85-88; 117; CANR 35; MTCW

Moravia, Alberto . . . . . . CLC 2, 7, 11, 27, 46
See also Pincherle, Alberto

More, Hannah 1745-1833 . . . . NCLC 27
See also DLB 107, 109, 116

More, Henry 1614-1687 . . . . LC 9
See also DLB 126

More, Sir Thomas 1478-1535 . . . . LC 10

Moreas, Jean . . . . TCLC 18
See also Papadiamantopoulos, Johannes

Morgan, Berry 1919- . . . . CLC 6
See also CA 49-52; DLB 6

Morgan, Claire
See Highsmith, (Mary) Patricia

Morgan, Edwin (George) 1920- . . . . . CLC 31
See also CA 5-8R; CANR 3; DLB 27

Morgan, (George) Frederick
1922- . . . . CLC 23
See also CA 17-20R; CANR 21

Morgan, Harriet
See Mencken, H(enry) L(ouis)

Morgan, Jane
See Cooper, James Fenimore

Morgan, Janet 1945- . . . . CLC 39
See also CA 65-68

Morgan, Lady 1776(?)-1859 . . . . . . NCLC 29
See also DLB 116

Morgan, Robin 1941- . . . . CLC 2
See also CA 69-72; CANR 29; MTCW

Morgan, Scott
See Kuttner, Henry

Morgan, Seth 1949(?)-1990 . . . . CLC 65
See also CA 132

Morgenstern, Christian
1871-1914 . . . . TCLC 8
See also CA 105

Morgenstern, S.
See Goldman, William (W.)

Moricz, Zsigmond 1879-1942 . . . . . TCLC 33

Morike, Eduard (Friedrich)
1804-1875 . . . . NCLC 10

Mori Ogai . . . . TCLC 14
See also Mori Rintaro

Mori Rintaro 1862-1922
See Mori Ogai
See also CA 110

Moritz, Karl Philipp 1756-1793 . . . . . . LC 2
See also DLB 94

Morland, Peter Henry
See Faust, Frederick (Schiller)

Morren, Theophil
See Hofmannsthal, Hugo von

Morris, Bill 1952- . . . . CLC 76

Morris, Julian
See West, Morris L(anglo)

Morris, Steveland Judkins 1950(?)-
See Wonder, Stevie
See also CA 111

Morris, William 1834-1896 . . . . . . NCLC 4
See also CDBLB 1832-1890; DLB 18, 35, 57

Morris, Wright 1910- . . . CLC 1, 3, 7, 18, 37
See also CA 9-12R; CANR 21; DLB 2;
DLBY 81; MTCW

Morrison, Chloe Anthony Wofford
See Morrison, Toni

Morrison, James Douglas 1943-1971
See Morrison, Jim
See also CA 73-76; CANR 40

Morrison, Jim . . . . CLC 17
See also Morrison, James Douglas

Morrison, Toni 1931- . . . . . CLC 4, 10, 22, 55
See also AAYA 1; BLC 3; BW; CA 29-32R;
CANR 27; CDALB 1968-1988; DA;
DLB 6, 33; DLBY 81; MTCW; SATA 57

Morrison, Van 1945- . . . . CLC 21
See also CA 116

Mortimer, John (Clifford)
1923- . . . . CLC 28, 43
See also CA 13-16R; CANR 21;
CDBLB 1960 to Present; DLB 13;
MTCW

Mortimer, Penelope (Ruth) 1918- . . . . CLC 5
See also CA 57-60

Morton, Anthony
See Creasey, John

Mosher, Howard Frank . . . . CLC 62
See also CA 139

Mosley, Nicholas 1923- . . . . CLC 43, 70
See also CA 69-72; CANR 41; DLB 14

Moss, Howard
1922-1987 . . . . CLC 7, 14, 45, 50
See also CA 1-4R; 123; CANR 1; DLB 5

Mossgiel, Rab
See Burns, Robert

Motion, Andrew 1952- . . . . CLC 47
See also DLB 40

Motley, Willard (Francis)
1912-1965 . . . . CLC 18
See also BW; CA 117; 106; DLB 76

Mott, Michael (Charles Alston)
1930- . . . . CLC 15, 34
See also CA 5-8R; CAAS 7; CANR 7, 29

Mowat, Farley (McGill) 1921- . . . . . CLC 26
See also AAYA 1; CA 1-4R; CANR 4, 24;
CLR 20; DLB 68; MAICYA; MTCW;
SATA 3, 55

Moyers, Bill 1934- . . . . CLC 74
See also AITN 2; CA 61-64; CANR 31

Mphahlele, Es'kia
See Mphahlele, Ezekiel
See also DLB 125

Mphahlele, Ezekiel 1919- . . . . CLC 25
See also Mphahlele, Es'kia
See also BLC 3; BW; CA 81-84; CANR 26

Mqhayi, S(amuel) E(dward) K(rune Loliwe)
1875-1945 . . . . TCLC 25
See also BLC 3

Mr. Martin
   See Burroughs, William S(eward)

Mrozek, Slawomir 1930-........ **CLC 3, 13**
   See also CA 13-16R; CAAS 10; CANR 29;
   MTCW

Mrs. Belloc-Lowndes
   See Lowndes, Marie Adelaide (Belloc)

Mtwa, Percy (?)-................. **CLC 47**

Mueller, Lisel 1924-.......... **CLC 13, 51**
   See also CA 93-96; DLB 105

Muir, Edwin 1887-1959 .... **TCLC 2**
   See also CA 104; DLB 20, 100

Muir, John 1838-1914 .... **TCLC 28**

Mujica Lainez, Manuel
   1910-1984 .... **CLC 31**
   See also Lainez, Manuel Mujica
   See also CA 81-84; 112; CANR 32; HW

Mukherjee, Bharati 1940-......... **CLC 53**
   See also BEST 89:2; CA 107; DLB 60;
   MTCW

Muldoon, Paul 1951-......... **CLC 32, 72**
   See also CA 113; 129; DLB 40

Mulisch, Harry 1927-............. **CLC 42**
   See also CA 9-12R; CANR 6, 26

Mull, Martin 1943-.............. **CLC 17**
   See also CA 105

Mulock, Dinah Maria
   See Craik, Dinah Maria (Mulock)

Munford, Robert 1737(?)-1783 .... **LC 5**
   See also DLB 31

Mungo, Raymond 1946-.......... **CLC 72**
   See also CA 49-52; CANR 2

Munro, Alice
   1931-........ **CLC 6, 10, 19, 50; SSC 3**
   See also AITN 2; CA 33-36R; CANR 33;
   DLB 53; MTCW; SATA 29

Munro, H(ector) H(ugh) 1870-1916
   See Saki
   See also CA 104; 130; CDBLB 1890-1914;
   DA; DLB 34; MTCW; WLC

Murasaki, Lady................. **CMLC 1**

Murdoch, (Jean) Iris
   1919-...... **CLC 1, 2, 3, 4, 6, 8, 11, 15,**
               22, 31, 51
   See also CA 13-16R; CANR 8;
   CDBLB 1960 to Present; DLB 14;
   MTCW

Murphy, Richard 1927-........... **CLC 41**
   See also CA 29-32R; DLB 40

Murphy, Sylvia 1937-............. **CLC 34**
   See also CA 121

Murphy, Thomas (Bernard) 1935-... **CLC 51**
   See also CA 101

Murray, Albert L. 1916-.......... **CLC 73**
   See also BW; CA 49-52; CANR 26; DLB 38

Murray, Les(lie) A(llan) 1938-..... **CLC 40**
   See also CA 21-24R; CANR 11, 27

Murry, J. Middleton
   See Murry, John Middleton

Murry, John Middleton
   1889-1957 .... **TCLC 16**
   See also CA 118

Musgrave, Susan 1951-........ **CLC 13, 54**
   See also CA 69-72

Musil, Robert (Edler von)
   1880-1942 .... **TCLC 12**
   See also CA 109; DLB 81, 124

Musset, (Louis Charles) Alfred de
   1810-1857 .... **NCLC 7**

My Brother's Brother
   See Chekhov, Anton (Pavlovich)

Myers, Walter Dean 1937- .... **CLC 35**
   See also AAYA 4; BLC 3; BW; CA 33-36R;
   CANR 20; CLR 4, 16; DLB 33;
   MAICYA; SAAS 2; SATA 27, 41, 70, 71

Myers, Walter M.
   See Myers, Walter Dean

Myles, Symon
   See Follett, Ken(neth Martin)

Nabokov, Vladimir (Vladimirovich)
   1899-1977 .... **CLC 1, 2, 3, 6, 8, 11, 15,**
           23, 44, 46, 64; SSC 11
   See also CA 5-8R; 69-72; CANR 20;
   CDALB 1941-1968; DA; DLB 2;
   DLBD 3; DLBY 80, 91; MTCW; WLC

Nagy, Laszlo 1925-1978........... **CLC 7**
   See also CA 129; 112

Naipaul, Shiva(dhar Srinivasa)
   1945-1985 .... **CLC 32, 39**
   See also CA 110; 112; 116; CANR 33;
   DLBY 85; MTCW

Naipaul, V(idiadhar) S(urajprasad)
   1932-...... **CLC 4, 7, 9, 13, 18, 37**
   See also CA 1-4R; CANR 1, 33;
   CDBLB 1960 to Present; DLB 125;
   DLBY 85; MTCW

Nakos, Lilika 1899(?)-............ **CLC 29**

Narayan, R(asipuram) K(rishnaswami)
   1906-................ **CLC 7, 28, 47**
   See also CA 81-84; CANR 33; MTCW;
   SATA 62

Nash, (Fredric) Ogden 1902-1971 .. **CLC 23**
   See also CA 13-14; 29-32R; CANR 34;
   CAP 1; DLB 11; MAICYA; MTCW;
   SATA 2, 46

Nathan, Daniel
   See Dannay, Frederic

Nathan, George Jean 1882-1958 ... **TCLC 18**
   See also Hatteras, Owen
   See also CA 114

Natsume, Kinnosuke 1867-1916
   See Natsume, Soseki
   See also CA 104

Natsume, Soseki .... **TCLC 2, 10**
   See also Natsume, Kinnosuke

Natti, (Mary) Lee 1919-
   See Kingman, Lee
   See also CA 5-8R; CANR 2

Naylor, Gloria 1950-.......... **CLC 28, 52**
   See also AAYA 6; BLC 3; BW; CA 107;
   CANR 27; DA; MTCW

Neihardt, John Gneisenau
   1881-1973 .... **CLC 32**
   See also CA 13-14; CAP 1; DLB 9, 54

Nekrasov, Nikolai Alekseevich
   1821-1878 .... **NCLC 11**

Nelligan, Emile 1879-1941........ **TCLC 14**
   See also CA 114; DLB 92

Nelson, Willie 1933-.............. **CLC 17**
   See also CA 107

Nemerov, Howard (Stanley)
   1920-1991 .... **CLC 2, 6, 9, 36**
   See also CA 1-4R; 134; CABS 2; CANR 1,
   27; DLB 6; DLBY 83; MTCW

Neruda, Pablo
   1904-1973 .... **CLC 1, 2, 5, 7, 9, 28, 62;**
              PC 4
   See also CA 19-20; 45-48; CAP 2; DA; HW;
   MTCW; WLC

Nerval, Gerard de 1808-1855...... **NCLC 1**

Nervo, (Jose) Amado (Ruiz de)
   1870-1919 .... **TCLC 11**
   See also CA 109; 131; HW

Nessi, Pio Baroja y
   See Baroja (y Nessi), Pio

Neufeld, John (Arthur) 1938- ...... **CLC 17**
   See also CA 25-28R; CANR 11, 37;
   MAICYA; SAAS 3; SATA 6

Neville, Emily Cheney 1919-....... **CLC 12**
   See also CA 5-8R; CANR 3, 37; MAICYA;
   SAAS 2; SATA 1

Newbound, Bernard Slade 1930-
   See Slade, Bernard
   See also CA 81-84

Newby, P(ercy) H(oward)
   1918-.................... **CLC 2, 13**
   See also CA 5-8R; CANR 32; DLB 15;
   MTCW

Newlove, Donald 1928-............ **CLC 6**
   See also CA 29-32R; CANR 25

Newlove, John (Herbert) 1938-..... **CLC 14**
   See also CA 21-24R; CANR 9, 25

Newman, Charles 1938-.......... **CLC 2, 8**
   See also CA 21-24R

Newman, Edwin (Harold) 1919- .... **CLC 14**
   See also AITN 1; CA 69-72; CANR 5

Newman, John Henry
   1801-1890 .... **NCLC 38**
   See also DLB 18, 32, 55

Newton, Suzanne 1936-........... **CLC 35**
   See also CA 41-44R; CANR 14; SATA 5

Nexo, Martin Andersen
   1869-1954 .... **TCLC 43**

Nezval, Vitezslav 1900-1958 ...... **TCLC 44**
   See also CA 123

Ngema, Mbongeni 1955- .... **CLC 57**

Ngugi, James T(hiong'o)........ **CLC 3, 7, 13**
   See also Ngugi wa Thiong'o

Ngugi wa Thiong'o 1938-.......... **CLC 36**
   See also Ngugi, James T(hiong'o)
   See also BLC 3; BW; CA 81-84; CANR 27;
   MTCW

Nichol, B(arrie) P(hillip)
   1944-1988 .... **CLC 18**
   See also CA 53-56; DLB 53; SATA 66

Nichols, John (Treadwell) 1940-.... **CLC 38**
   See also CA 9-12R; CAAS 2; CANR 6;
   DLBY 82

Nichols, Peter (Richard)
   1927-.................... **CLC 5, 36, 65**
   See also CA 104; CANR 33; DLB 13;
   MTCW

Nicolas, F. R. E.
See Freeling, Nicolas

Niedecker, Lorine 1903-1970.... **CLC 10, 42**
See also CA 25-28; CAP 2; DLB 48

Nietzsche, Friedrich (Wilhelm)
1844-1900 .... **TCLC 10, 18**
See also CA 107; 121; DLB 129

Nievo, Ippolito 1831-1861 .... **NCLC 22**

Nightingale, Anne Redmon 1943-
See Redmon, Anne
See also CA 103

Nik.T.O.
See Annensky, Innokenty Fyodorovich

Nin, Anais
1903-1977 ..... **CLC 1, 4, 8, 11, 14, 60;**
SSC 10
See also AITN 2; CA 13-16R; 69-72;
CANR 22; DLB 2, 4; MTCW

Nissenson, Hugh 1933-.......... **CLC 4, 9**
See also CA 17-20R; CANR 27; DLB 28

Niven, Larry .... **CLC 8**
See also Niven, Laurence Van Cott
See also DLB 8

Niven, Laurence Van Cott 1938-
See Niven, Larry
See also CA 21-24R; CAAS 12; CANR 14;
MTCW

Nixon, Agnes Eckhardt 1927-...... **CLC 21**
See also CA 110

Nizan, Paul 1905-1940.......... **TCLC 40**
See also DLB 72

Nkosi, Lewis 1936-.............. **CLC 45**
See also BLC 3; BW; CA 65-68; CANR 27

Nodier, (Jean) Charles (Emmanuel)
1780-1844 .... **NCLC 19**
See also DLB 119

Nolan, Christopher 1965-......... **CLC 58**
See also CA 111

Norden, Charles
See Durrell, Lawrence (George)

Nordhoff, Charles (Bernard)
1887-1947 .... **TCLC 23**
See also CA 108; DLB 9; SATA 23

Norfolk, Lawrence 1963-......... **CLC 76**

Norman, Marsha 1947- .... **CLC 28**
See also CA 105; CABS 3; CANR 41;
DLBY 84

Norris, Benjamin Franklin, Jr.
1870-1902 .... **TCLC 24**
See also Norris, Frank
See also CA 110

Norris, Frank
See Norris, Benjamin Franklin, Jr.
See also CDALB 1865-1917; DLB 12, 71

Norris, Leslie 1921-.............. **CLC 14**
See also CA 11-12; CANR 14; CAP 1;
DLB 27

North, Andrew
See Norton, Andre

North, Captain George
See Stevenson, Robert Louis (Balfour)

North, Milou
See Erdrich, Louise

Northrup, B. A.
See Hubbard, L(afayette) Ron(ald)

North Staffs
See Hulme, T(homas) E(rnest)

Norton, Alice Mary
See Norton, Andre
See also MAICYA; SATA 1, 43

Norton, Andre 1912- .... **CLC 12**
See also Norton, Alice Mary
See also CA 1-4R; CANR 2, 31; DLB 8, 52;
MTCW

Norway, Nevil Shute 1899-1960
See Shute, Nevil
See also CA 102; 93-96

Norwid, Cyprian Kamil
1821-1883 .... **NCLC 17**

Nosille, Nabrah
See Ellison, Harlan

Nossack, Hans Erich 1901-1978....`. **CLC 6**
See also CA 93-96; 85-88; DLB 69

Nosu, Chuji
See Ozu, Yasujiro

Nova, Craig 1945-.............. **CLC 7, 31**
See also CA 45-48; CANR 2

Novak, Joseph
See Kosinski, Jerzy (Nikodem)

Novalis 1772-1801 .... **NCLC 13**
See also DLB 90

Nowlan, Alden (Albert) 1933-1983 .. **CLC 15**
See also CA 9-12R; CANR 5; DLB 53

Noyes, Alfred 1880-1958......... **TCLC 7**
See also CA 104; DLB 20

Nunn, Kem 19(?)-................ **CLC 34**

Nye, Robert 1939- .... **CLC 13, 42**
See also CA 33-36R; CANR 29; DLB 14;
MTCW; SATA 6

Nyro, Laura 1947- .... **CLC 17**

Oates, Joyce Carol
1938- ..... **CLC 1, 2, 3, 6, 9, 11, 15, 19,**
33, 52; SSC 6
See also AITN 1; BEST 89:2; CA 5-8R;
CANR 25; CDALB 1968-1988; DA;
DLB 2, 5, 130; DLBY 81; MTCW; WLC

O'Brien, E. G.
See Clarke, Arthur C(harles)

O'Brien, Edna
1936- ... **CLC 3, 5, 8, 13, 36, 65; SSC 10**
See also CA 1-4R; CANR 6, 41;
CDBLB 1960 to Present; DLB 14;
MTCW

O'Brien, Fitz-James 1828-1862... **NCLC 21**
See also DLB 74

O'Brien, Flann....... **CLC 1, 4, 5, 7, 10, 47**
See also O Nuallain, Brian

O'Brien, Richard 1942-.......... **CLC 17**
See also CA 124

O'Brien, Tim 1946-.......... **CLC 7, 19, 40**
See also CA 85-88; CANR 40; DLBD 9;
DLBY 80

Obstfelder, Sigbjoern 1866-1900... **TCLC 23**
See also CA 123

O'Casey, Sean
1880-1964 .... **CLC 1, 5, 9, 11, 15**
See also CA 89-92; CDBLB 1914-1945;
DLB 10; MTCW

O'Cathasaigh, Sean
See O'Casey, Sean

Ochs, Phil 1940-1976............. **CLC 17**
See also CA 65-68

O'Connor, Edwin (Greene)
1918-1968 .... **CLC 14**
See also CA 93-96; 25-28R

O'Connor, (Mary) Flannery
1925-1964 ... **CLC 1, 2, 3, 6, 10, 13, 15,**
21, 66; SSC 1
See also AAYA 7; CA 1-4R; CANR 3, 41;
CDALB 1941-1968; DA; DLB 2;
DLBY 80; MTCW; WLC

O'Connor, Frank.......... **CLC 23; SSC 5**
See also O'Donovan, Michael John

O'Dell, Scott 1898-1989.......... **CLC 30**
See also AAYA 3; CA 61-64; 129;
CANR 12, 30; CLR 1, 16; DLB 52;
MAICYA; SATA 12, 60

Odets, Clifford 1906-1963 .... **CLC 2, 28**
See also CA 85-88; DLB 7, 26; MTCW

O'Doherty, Brian 1934-........... **CLC 76**
See also CA 105

O'Donnell, K. M.
See Malzberg, Barry N(athaniel)

O'Donnell, Lawrence
See Kuttner, Henry

O'Donovan, Michael John
1903-1966 .... **CLC 14**
See also O'Connor, Frank
See also CA 93-96

Oe, Kenzaburo 1935-.......... **CLC 10, 36**
See also CA 97-100; CANR 36; MTCW

O'Faolain, Julia 1932-....... **CLC 6, 19, 47**
See also CA 81-84; CAAS 2; CANR 12;
DLB 14; MTCW

O'Faolain, Sean
1900-1991 .... **CLC 1, 7, 14, 32, 70**
See also CA 61-64; 134; CANR 12;
DLB 15; MTCW

O'Flaherty, Liam
1896-1984 .... **CLC 5, 34; SSC 6**
See also CA 101; 113; CANR 35; DLB 36;
DLBY 84; MTCW

Ogilvy, Gavin
See Barrie, J(ames) M(atthew)

O'Grady, Standish James
1846-1928 .... **TCLC 5**
See also CA 104

O'Grady, Timothy 1951-.......... **CLC 59**
See also CA 138

O'Hara, Frank
1926-1966 .... **CLC 2, 5, 13, 77**
See also CA 9-12R; 25-28R; CANR 33;
DLB 5, 16; MTCW

O'Hara, John (Henry)
1905-1970 .... **CLC 1, 2, 3, 6, 11, 42**
See also CA 5-8R; 25-28R; CANR 31;
CDALB 1929-1941; DLB 9, 86; DLBD 2;
MTCW

O Hehir, Diana 1922- .... **CLC 41**
See also CA 93-96

Okigbo, Christopher (Ifenayichukwu)
1932-1967 .... **CLC 25**
See also BLC 3; BW; CA 77-80; DLB 125;
MTCW

Olds, Sharon 1942-............ **CLC 32, 39**
See also CA 101; CANR 18, 41; DLB 120

Oldstyle, Jonathan
See Irving, Washington

Olesha, Yuri (Karlovich)
1899-1960 .... **CLC 8**
See also CA 85-88

Oliphant, Margaret (Oliphant Wilson)
1828-1897 .... **NCLC 11**
See also DLB 18

Oliver, Mary 1935-............ **CLC 19, 34**
See also CA 21-24R; CANR 9; DLB 5

Olivier, Laurence (Kerr)
1907-1989 .... **CLC 20**
See also CA 111; 129

Olsen, Tillie 1913- ..... **CLC 4, 13; SSC 11**
See also CA 1-4R; CANR 1; DA; DLB 28;
DLBY 80; MTCW

Olson, Charles (John)
1910-1970 ..... **CLC 1, 2, 5, 6, 9, 11, 29**
See also CA 13-16; 25-28R; CABS 2;
CANR 35; CAP 1; DLB 5, 16; MTCW

Olson, Toby 1937- .... **CLC 28**
See also CA 65-68; CANR 9, 31

Olyesha, Yuri
See Olesha, Yuri (Karlovich)

Ondaatje, Michael
1943- .... **CLC 14, 29, 51, 76**
See also CA 77-80; DLB 60

Oneal, Elizabeth 1934-
See Oneal, Zibby
See also CA 106; CANR 28; MAICYA;
SATA 30

Oneal, Zibby .... **CLC 30**
See also Oneal, Elizabeth
See also AAYA 5; CLR 13

O'Neill, Eugene (Gladstone)
1888-1953 .... **TCLC 1, 6, 27, 49**
See also AITN 1; CA 110; 132;
CDALB 1929-1941; DA; DLB 7; MTCW;
WLC

Onetti, Juan Carlos 1909- .... **CLC 7, 10**
See also CA 85-88; CANR 32; DLB 113;
HW; MTCW

O Nuallain, Brian 1911-1966
See O'Brien, Flann
See also CA 21-22; 25-28R; CAP 2

Oppen, George 1908-1984 .... **CLC 7, 13, 34**
See also CA 13-16R; 113; CANR 8; DLB 5

Oppenheim, E(dward) Phillips
1866-1946 .... **TCLC 45**
See also CA 111; DLB 70

Orlovitz, Gil 1918-1973 .... **CLC 22**
See also CA 77-80; 45-48; DLB 2, 5

Orris
See Ingelow, Jean

Ortega y Gasset, Jose 1883-1955 ... **TCLC 9**
See also CA 106; 130; HW; MTCW

Ortiz, Simon J(oseph) 1941- .... **CLC 45**
See also CA 134; DLB 120

Orton, Joe .... **CLC 4, 13, 43; DC 3**
See also Orton, John Kingsley
See also CDBLB 1960 to Present; DLB 13

Orton, John Kingsley 1933-1967
See Orton, Joe
See also CA 85-88; CANR 35; MTCW

Orwell, George .... **TCLC 2, 6, 15, 31**
See also Blair, Eric (Arthur)
See also CDBLB 1945-1960; DLB 15, 98;
WLC

Osborne, David
See Silverberg, Robert

Osborne, George
See Silverberg, Robert

Osborne, John (James)
1929- .... **CLC 1, 2, 5, 11, 45**
See also CA 13-16R; CANR 21;
CDBLB 1945-1960; DA; DLB 13;
MTCW; WLC

Osborne, Lawrence 1958- .... **CLC 50**

Oshima, Nagisa 1932- .... **CLC 20**
See also CA 116; 121

Oskison, John M(ilton)
1874-1947 .... **TCLC 35**

Ossoli, Sarah Margaret (Fuller marchesa d')
1810-1850
See Fuller, Margaret
See also SATA 25

Ostrovsky, Alexander
1823-1886 .... **NCLC 30**

Otero, Blas de 1916- .... **CLC 11**
See also CA 89-92

Otto, Whitney 1955-.............. **CLC 70**
See also CA 140

Ouida .... **TCLC 43**
See also De La Ramee, (Marie) Louise
See also DLB 18

Ousmane, Sembene 1923- .... **CLC 66**
See also BLC 3; BW; CA 117; 125; MTCW

Ovid 43B.C.-18th cent. (?) ... **CMLC 7; PC 2**

Owen, Hugh
See Faust, Frederick (Schiller)

Owen, Wilfred 1893-1918 ...... **TCLC 5, 27**
See also CA 104; CDBLB 1914-1945; DA;
DLB 20; WLC

Owens, Rochelle 1936-............. **CLC 8**
See also CA 17-20R; CAAS 2; CANR 39

Oz, Amos 1939- ... **CLC 5, 8, 11, 27, 33, 54**
See also CA 53-56; CANR 27; MTCW

Ozick, Cynthia 1928-...... **CLC 3, 7, 28, 62**
See also BEST 90:1; CA 17-20R; CANR 23;
DLB 28; DLBY 82; MTCW

Ozu, Yasujiro 1903-1963 .... **CLC 16**
See also CA 112

Pacheco, C.
See Pessoa, Fernando (Antonio Nogueira)

Pa Chin
See Li Fei-kan

Pack, Robert 1929-.............. **CLC 13**
See also CA 1-4R; CANR 3; DLB 5

Padgett, Lewis
See Kuttner, Henry

Padilla (Lorenzo), Heberto 1932-... **CLC 38**
See also AITN 1; CA 123; 131; HW

Page, Jimmy 1944-................ **CLC 12**

Page, Louise 1955-................ **CLC 40**
See also CA 140

Page, P(atricia) K(athleen)
1916- .... **CLC 7, 18**
See also CA 53-56; CANR 4, 22; DLB 68;
MTCW

Paget, Violet 1856-1935
See Lee, Vernon
See also CA 104

Paget-Lowe, Henry
See Lovecraft, H(oward) P(hillips)

Paglia, Camille (Anna) 1947-....... **CLC 68**
See also CA 140

Pakenham, Antonia
See Fraser, Antonia (Pakenham)

Palamas, Kostes 1859-1943 .... **TCLC 5**
See also CA 105

Palazzeschi, Aldo 1885-1974 .... **CLC 11**
See also CA 89-92; 53-56; DLB 114

Paley, Grace 1922-.... **CLC 4, 6, 37; SSC 8**
See also CA 25-28R; CANR 13; DLB 28;
MTCW

Palin, Michael (Edward) 1943-..... **CLC 21**
See also Monty Python
See also CA 107; CANR 35; SATA 67

Palliser, Charles 1947-............ **CLC 65**
See also CA 136

Palma, Ricardo 1833-1919........ **TCLC 29**

Pancake, Breece Dexter 1952-1979
See Pancake, Breece D'J
See also CA 123; 109

Pancake, Breece D'J.............. **CLC 29**
See also Pancake, Breece Dexter
See also DLB 130

Panko, Rudy
See Gogol, Nikolai (Vasilyevich)

Papadiamantis, Alexandros
1851-1911 .... **TCLC 29**

Papadiamantopoulos, Johannes 1856-1910
See Moreas, Jean
See also CA 117

Papini, Giovanni 1881-1956....... **TCLC 22**
See also CA 121

Paracelsus 1493-1541............. **LC 14**

Parasol, Peter
See Stevens, Wallace

Parfenie, Maria
See Codrescu, Andrei

Parini, Jay (Lee) 1948- .... **CLC 54**
See also CA 97-100; CAAS 16; CANR 32

Park, Jordan
See Kornbluth, C(yril) M.; Pohl, Frederik

Parker, Bert
See Ellison, Harlan

Parker, Dorothy (Rothschild)
1893-1967 .... **CLC 15, 68; SSC 2**
See also CA 19-20; 25-28R; CAP 2;
DLB 11, 45, 86; MTCW

Parker, Robert B(rown)　1932-......　**CLC 27**
See also BEST 89:4; CA 49-52; CANR 1,
26; MTCW

Parkes, Lucas
See Harris, John (Wyndham Parkes Lucas)
Beynon

Parkin, Frank　1940-.............　**CLC 43**

Parkman, Francis, Jr.
1823-1893 ....　**NCLC 12**
See also DLB 1, 30

Parks, Gordon (Alexander Buchanan)
1912- ....　**CLC 1, 16**
See also AITN 2; BLC 3; BW; CA 41-44R;
CANR 26; DLB 33; SATA 8

Parnell, Thomas　1679-1718 ....　**LC 3**
See also DLB 94

Parra, Nicanor　1914-..............　**CLC 2**
See also CA 85-88; CANR 32; HW; MTCW

Parrish, Mary Frances
See Fisher, M(ary) F(rances) K(ennedy)

Parson
See Coleridge, Samuel Taylor

Parson Lot
See Kingsley, Charles

Partridge, Anthony
See Oppenheim, E(dward) Phillips

Pascoli, Giovanni　1855-1912 ......　**TCLC 45**

Pasolini, Pier Paolo
1922-1975 ....　**CLC 20, 37**
See also CA 93-96; 61-64; DLB 128;
MTCW

Pasquini
See Silone, Ignazio

Pastan, Linda (Olenik)　1932- ......　**CLC 27**
See also CA 61-64; CANR 18, 40; DLB 5

Pasternak, Boris (Leonidovich)
1890-1960 .....　**CLC 7, 10, 18, 63; PC 6**
See also CA 127; 116; DA; MTCW; WLC

Patchen, Kenneth　1911-1972 ...　**CLC 1, 2, 18**
See also CA 1-4R; 33-36R; CANR 3, 35;
DLB 16, 48; MTCW

Pater, Walter (Horatio)
1839-1894 ....　**NCLC 7**
See also CDBLB 1832-1890; DLB 57

Paterson, A(ndrew) B(arton)
1864-1941 ....　**TCLC 32**

Paterson, Katherine (Womeldorf)
1932- ....　**CLC 12, 30**
See also AAYA 1; CA 21-24R; CANR 28;
CLR 7; DLB 52; MAICYA; MTCW;
SATA 13, 53

Patmore, Coventry Kersey Dighton
1823-1896 ....　**NCLC 9**
See also DLB 35, 98

Paton, Alan (Stewart)
1903-1988 ....　**CLC 4, 10, 25, 55**
See also CA 13-16; 125; CANR 22; CAP 1;
DA; MTCW; SATA 11, 56; WLC

Paton Walsh, Gillian　1939-
See Walsh, Jill Paton
See also CANR 38; MAICYA; SAAS 3;
SATA 4, 72

Paulding, James Kirke　1778-1860..　**NCLC 2**
See also DLB 3, 59, 74

Paulin, Thomas Neilson　1949-
See Paulin, Tom
See also CA 123; 128

Paulin, Tom.....................　**CLC 37**
See also Paulin, Thomas Neilson
See also DLB 40

Paustovsky, Konstantin (Georgievich)
1892-1968 ....　**CLC 40**
See also CA 93-96; 25-28R

Pavese, Cesare　1908-1950 ....　**TCLC 3**
See also CA 104; DLB 128

Pavic, Milorad　1929-.............　**CLC 60**
See also CA 136

Payne, Alan
See Jakes, John (William)

Paz, Gil
See Lugones, Leopoldo

Paz, Octavio
1914- ......　**CLC 3, 4, 6, 10, 19, 51, 65;**
PC 1
See also CA 73-76; CANR 32; DA;
DLBY 90; HW; MTCW; WLC

Peacock, Molly　1947-............　**CLC 60**
See also CA 103; DLB 120

Peacock, Thomas Love
1785-1866 ....　**NCLC 22**
See also DLB 96, 116

Peake, Mervyn　1911-1968 ......　**CLC 7, 54**
See also CA 5-8R; 25-28R; CANR 3;
DLB 15; MTCW; SATA 23

Pearce, Philippa ....　**CLC 21**
See also Christie, (Ann) Philippa
See also CLR 9; MAICYA; SATA 1, 67

Pearl, Eric
See Elman, Richard

Pearson, T(homas) R(eid)　1956- ....　**CLC 39**
See also CA 120; 130

Peck, John　1941-.................　**CLC 3**
See also CA 49-52; CANR 3

Peck, Richard (Wayne)　1934-......　**CLC 21**
See also AAYA 1; CA 85-88; CANR 19,
38; MAICYA; SAAS 2; SATA 18, 55

Peck, Robert Newton　1928-........　**CLC 17**
See also AAYA 3; CA 81-84; CANR 31;
DA; MAICYA; SAAS 1; SATA 21, 62

Peckinpah, (David) Sam(uel)
1925-1984 ....　**CLC 20**
See also CA 109; 114

Pedersen, Knut　1859-1952
See Hamsun, Knut
See also CA 104; 119; MTCW

Peeslake, Gaffer
See Durrell, Lawrence (George)

Peguy, Charles Pierre
1873-1914 ....　**TCLC 10**
See also CA 107

Pena, Ramon del Valle y
See Valle-Inclan, Ramon (Maria) del

Pendennis, Arthur Esquir
See Thackeray, William Makepeace

Pepys, Samuel　1633-1703..........　**LC 11**
See also CDBLB 1660-1789; DA; DLB 101;
WLC

Percy, Walker
1916-1990 ...　**CLC 2, 3, 6, 8, 14, 18, 47,**
65
See also CA 1-4R; 131; CANR 1, 23;
DLB 2; DLBY 80, 90; MTCW

Perec, Georges　1936-1982 ....　**CLC 56**
See also DLB 83

Pereda (y Sanchez de Porrua), Jose Maria de
1833-1906 ....　**TCLC 16**
See also CA 117

Pereda y Porrua, Jose Maria de
See Pereda (y Sanchez de Porrua), Jose
Maria de

Peregoy, George Weems
See Mencken, H(enry) L(ouis)

Perelman, S(idney) J(oseph)
1904-1979 ...　**CLC 3, 5, 9, 15, 23, 44, 49**
See also AITN 1, 2; CA 73-76; 89-92;
CANR 18; DLB 11, 44; MTCW

Peret, Benjamin　1899-1959 ....　**TCLC 20**
See also CA 117

Peretz, Isaac Loeb　1851(?)-1915...　**TCLC 16**
See also CA 109

Peretz, Yitzkhok Leibush
See Peretz, Isaac Loeb

Perez Galdos, Benito　1843-1920...　**TCLC 27**
See also CA 125; HW

Perrault, Charles　1628-1703 ....　**LC 2**
See also MAICYA; SATA 25

Perry, Brighton
See Sherwood, Robert E(mmet)

Perse, Saint-John
See Leger, (Marie-Rene) Alexis Saint-Leger

Perse, St.-John ....　**CLC 4, 11, 46**
See also Leger, (Marie-Rene) Alexis
Saint-Leger

Peseenz, Tulio F.
See Lopez y Fuentes, Gregorio

Pesetsky, Bette　1932-.............　**CLC 28**
See also CA 133; DLB 130

Peshkov, Alexei Maximovich　1868-1936
See Gorky, Maxim
See also CA 105; DA

Pessoa, Fernando (Antonio Nogueira)
1888-1935 ....　**TCLC 27**
See also CA 125

Peterkin, Julia Mood　1880-1961....　**CLC 31**
See also CA 102; DLB 9

Peters, Joan K.　1945-.............　**CLC 39**

Peters, Robert L(ouis)　1924-........　**CLC 7**
See also CA 13-16R; CAAS 8; DLB 105

Petofi, Sandor　1823-1849.......　**NCLC 21**

Petrakis, Harry Mark　1923-........　**CLC 3**
See also CA 9-12R; CANR 4, 30

Petrov, Evgeny ....　**TCLC 21**
See also Kataev, Evgeny Petrovich

Petry, Ann (Lane)　1908- ......　**CLC 1, 7, 18**
See also BW; CA 5-8R; CAAS 6; CANR 4;
CLR 12; DLB 76; MAICYA; MTCW;
SATA 5

Petursson, Halligrimur　1614-1674 ....　**LC 8**

Philipson, Morris H.　1926-........　**CLC 53**
See also CA 1-4R; CANR 4

Phillips, David Graham
1867-1911 .... **TCLC 44**
See also CA 108; DLB 9, 12

Phillips, Jack
See Sandburg, Carl (August)

Phillips, Jayne Anne 1952- ..... **CLC 15, 33**
See also CA 101; CANR 24; DLBY 80;
MTCW

Phillips, Richard
See Dick, Philip K(indred)

Phillips, Robert (Schaeffer) 1938-... **CLC 28**
See also CA 17-20R; CAAS 13; CANR 8;
DLB 105

Phillips, Ward
See Lovecraft, H(oward) P(hillips)

Piccolo, Lucio 1901-1969......... **CLC 13**
See also CA 97-100; DLB 114

Pickthall, Marjorie L(owry) C(hristie)
1883-1922 .... **TCLC 21**
See also CA 107; DLB 92

Pico della Mirandola, Giovanni
1463-1494 .... **LC 15**

Piercy, Marge
1936- .... **CLC 3, 6, 14, 18, 27, 62**
See also CA 21-24R; CAAS 1; CANR 13;
DLB 120; MTCW

Piers, Robert
See Anthony, Piers

Pieyre de Mandiargues, Andre 1909-1991
See Mandiargues, Andre Pieyre de
See also CA 103; 136; CANR 22

Pilnyak, Boris .... **TCLC 23**
See also Vogau, Boris Andreyevich

Pincherle, Alberto 1907-1990 ... **CLC 11, 18**
See also Moravia, Alberto
See also CA 25-28R; 132; CANR 33;
MTCW

Pinckney, Darryl 1953- .... **CLC 76**

Pineda, Cecile 1942-.............. **CLC 39**
See also CA 118

Pinero, Arthur Wing 1855-1934 ... **TCLC 32**
See also CA 110; DLB 10

Pinero, Miguel (Antonio Gomez)
1946-1988 .... **CLC 4, 55**
See also CA 61-64; 125; CANR 29; HW

Pinget, Robert 1919- .... **CLC 7, 13, 37**
See also CA 85-88; DLB 83

Pink Floyd....................... **CLC 35**
See also Barrett, (Roger) Syd; Gilmour,
David; Mason, Nick; Waters, Roger;
Wright, Rick

Pinkney, Edward 1802-1828 ..... **NCLC 31**

Pinkwater, Daniel Manus 1941-.... **CLC 35**
See also Pinkwater, Manus
See also AAYA 1; CA 29-32R; CANR 12,
38; CLR 4; MAICYA; SAAS 3; SATA 46

Pinkwater, Manus
See Pinkwater, Daniel Manus
See also SATA 8

Pinsky, Robert 1940-........ **CLC 9, 19, 38**
See also CA 29-32R; CAAS 4; DLBY 82

Pinta, Harold
See Pinter, Harold

Pinter, Harold
1930-.. **CLC 1, 3, 6, 9, 11, 15, 27, 58, 73**
See also CA 5-8R; CANR 33; CDBLB 1960
to Present; DA; DLB 13; MTCW; WLC

Pirandello, Luigi 1867-1936..... **TCLC 4, 29**
See also CA 104; DA; WLC

Pirsig, Robert M(aynard)
1928-.................... **CLC 4, 6, 73**
See also CA 53-56; MTCW; SATA 39

Pisarev, Dmitry Ivanovich
1840-1868 .... **NCLC 25**

Pix, Mary (Griffith) 1666-1709 ...... **LC 8**
See also DLB 80

Pixerecourt, Guilbert de
1773-1844 .... **NCLC 39**

Plaidy, Jean
See Hibbert, Eleanor Alice Burford

Plant, Robert 1948- .... **CLC 12**

Plante, David (Robert)
1940-.................... **CLC 7, 23, 38**
See also CA 37-40R; CANR 12, 36;
DLBY 83; MTCW

Plath, Sylvia
1932-1963 .... **CLC 1, 2, 3, 5, 9, 11, 14,
17, 50, 51, 62; PC 1**
See also CA 19-20; CANR 34; CAP 2;
CDALB 1941-1968; DA; DLB 5, 6;
MTCW; WLC

Plato 428(?)B.C.-348(?)B.C....... **CMLC 8**
See also DA

Platonov, Andrei .... **TCLC 14**
See also Klimentov, Andrei Platonovich

Platt, Kin 1911- .... **CLC 26**
See also CA 17-20R; CANR 11; SATA 21

Plick et Plock
See Simenon, Georges (Jacques Christian)

Plimpton, George (Ames) 1927-..... **CLC 36**
See also AITN 1; CA 21-24R; CANR 32;
MTCW; SATA 10

Plomer, William Charles Franklin
1903-1973 .... **CLC 4, 8**
See also CA 21-22; CANR 34; CAP 2;
DLB 20; MTCW; SATA 24

Plowman, Piers
See Kavanagh, Patrick (Joseph)

Plum, J.
See Wodehouse, P(elham) G(renville)

Plumly, Stanley (Ross) 1939- ...... **CLC 33**
See also CA 108; 110; DLB 5

Poe, Edgar Allan
1809-1849 ... **NCLC 1, 16; PC 1; SSC 1**
See also CDALB 1640-1865; DA; DLB 3,
59, 73, 74; SATA 23; WLC

Poet of Titchfield Street, The
See Pound, Ezra (Weston Loomis)

Pohl, Frederik 1919- .... **CLC 18**
See also CA 61-64; CAAS 1; CANR 11, 37;
DLB 8; MTCW; SATA 24

Poirier, Louis 1910-
See Gracq, Julien
See also CA 122; 126

Poitier, Sidney 1927-............. **CLC 26**
See also BW; CA 117

Polanski, Roman 1933- .... **CLC 16**
See also CA 77-80

Poliakoff, Stephen 1952- .... **CLC 38**
See also CA 106; DLB 13

Police, The....................... **CLC 26**
See also Copeland, Stewart (Armstrong);
Summers, Andrew James; Sumner,
Gordon Matthew

Pollitt, Katha 1949- .... **CLC 28**
See also CA 120; 122; MTCW

Pollock, Sharon 1936- .... **CLC 50**
See also DLB 60

Pomerance, Bernard 1940-........ **CLC 13**
See also CA 101

Ponge, Francis (Jean Gaston Alfred)
1899-1988 .... **CLC 6, 18**
See also CA 85-88; 126; CANR 40

Pontoppidan, Henrik 1857-1943 ... **TCLC 29**

Poole, Josephine .... **CLC 17**
See also Helyar, Jane Penelope Josephine
See also SAAS 2; SATA 5

Popa, Vasko 1922-................ **CLC 19**
See also CA 112

Pope, Alexander 1688-1744 .... **LC 3**
See also CDBLB 1660-1789; DA; DLB 95,
101; WLC

Porter, Connie 1960- .... **CLC 70**

Porter, Gene(va Grace) Stratton
1863(?)-1924 .... **TCLC 21**
See also CA 112

Porter, Katherine Anne
1890-1980 ..... **CLC 1, 3, 7, 10, 13, 15,
27; SSC 4**
See also AITN 2; CA 1-4R; 101; CANR 1;
DA; DLB 4, 9, 102; DLBY 80; MTCW;
SATA 23, 39

Porter, Peter (Neville Frederick)
1929-.................... **CLC 5, 13, 33**
See also CA 85-88; DLB 40

Porter, William Sydney 1862-1910
See Henry, O.
See also CA 104; 131; CDALB 1865-1917;
DA; DLB 12, 78, 79; MTCW; YABC 2

Portillo (y Pacheco), Jose Lopez
See Lopez Portillo (y Pacheco), Jose

Post, Melville Davisson
1869-1930 .... **TCLC 39**
See also CA 110

Potok, Chaim 1929-........ **CLC 2, 7, 14, 26**
See also AITN 1, 2; CA 17-20R; CANR 19,
35; DLB 28; MTCW; SATA 33

Potter, Beatrice
See Webb, (Martha) Beatrice (Potter)
See also MAICYA

Potter, Dennis (Christopher George)
1935-....................... **CLC 58**
See also CA 107; CANR 33; MTCW

Pound, Ezra (Weston Loomis)
1885-1972 ..... **CLC 1, 2, 3, 4, 5, 7, 10,
13, 18, 34, 48, 50; PC 4**
See also CA 5-8R; 37-40R; CANR 40;
CDALB 1917-1929; DA; DLB 4, 45, 63;
MTCW; WLC

Povod, Reinaldo 1959-............ **CLC 44**
See also CA 136

Raine, Craig 1944- . . . . **CLC 32**
See also CA 108; CANR 29; DLB 40

Raine, Kathleen (Jessie) 1908- . . . **CLC 7, 45**
See also CA 85-88; DLB 20; MTCW

Rainis, Janis 1865-1929 . . . . **TCLC 29**

Rakosi, Carl. . . . . **CLC 47**
See also Rawley, Callman
See also CAAS 5

Raleigh, Richard
See Lovecraft, H(oward) P(hillips)

Rallentando, H. P.
See Sayers, Dorothy L(eigh)

Ramal, Walter
See de la Mare, Walter (John)

Ramon, Juan
See Jimenez (Mantecon), Juan Ramon

Ramos, Graciliano 1892-1953 . . . . . **TCLC 32**

Rampersad, Arnold 1941-. . . . . **CLC 44**
See also CA 127; 133; DLB 111

Rampling, Anne
See Rice, Anne

Ramuz, Charles-Ferdinand
1878-1947 . . . . **TCLC 33**

Rand, Ayn 1905-1982. . . . . . . **CLC 3, 30, 44**
See also AAYA 10; CA 13-16R; 105;
CANR 27; DA; MTCW; WLC

Randall, Dudley (Felker) 1914-. . . . . . **CLC 1**
See also BLC 3; BW; CA 25-28R;
CANR 23; DLB 41

Randall, Robert
See Silverberg, Robert

Ranger, Ken
See Creasey, John

Ransom, John Crowe
1888-1974 . . . . **CLC 2, 4, 5, 11, 24**
See also CA 5-8R; 49-52; CANR 6, 34;
DLB 45, 63; MTCW

Rao, Raja 1909- . . . . **CLC 25, 56**
See also CA 73-76; MTCW

Raphael, Frederic (Michael)
1931- . . . . **CLC 2, 14**
See also CA 1-4R; CANR 1; DLB 14

Ratcliffe, James P.
See Mencken, H(enry) L(ouis)

Rathbone, Julian 1935- . . . . **CLC 41**
See also CA 101; CANR 34

Rattigan, Terence (Mervyn)
1911-1977 . . . . **CLC 7**
See also CA 85-88; 73-76;
CDBLB 1945-1960; DLB 13; MTCW

Ratushinskaya, Irina 1954- . . . . **CLC 54**
See also CA 129

Raven, Simon (Arthur Noel)
1927- . . . . **CLC 14**
See also CA 81-84

Rawley, Callman 1903-
See Rakosi, Carl
See also CA 21-24R; CANR 12, 32

Rawlings, Marjorie Kinnan
1896-1953 . . . . **TCLC 4**
See also CA 104; 137; DLB 9, 22, 102;
MAICYA; YABC 1

Ray, Satyajit 1921-1992. . . . . . . **CLC 16, 76**
See also CA 114; 137

Read, Herbert Edward 1893-1968. . . . **CLC 4**
See also CA 85-88; 25-28R; DLB 20

Read, Piers Paul 1941- . . . . . . **CLC 4, 10, 25**
See also CA 21-24R; CANR 38; DLB 14;
SATA 21

Reade, Charles 1814-1884 . . . . **NCLC 2**
See also DLB 21

Reade, Hamish
See Gray, Simon (James Holliday)

Reading, Peter 1946- . . . . **CLC 47**
See also CA 103; DLB 40

Reaney, James 1926- . . . . **CLC 13**
See also CA 41-44R; CAAS 15; DLB 68;
SATA 43

Rebreanu, Liviu 1885-1944 . . . . . . **TCLC 28**

Rechy, John (Francisco)
1934- . . . . **CLC 1, 7, 14, 18**
See also CA 5-8R; CAAS 4; CANR 6, 32;
DLB 122; DLBY 82; HW

Redcam, Tom 1870-1933 . . . . **TCLC 25**

Reddin, Keith. **CLC 67**

Redgrove, Peter (William)
1932- . . . . **CLC 6, 41**
See also CA 1-4R; CANR 3, 39; DLB 40

Redmon, Anne. . . . . **CLC 22**
See also Nightingale, Anne Redmon
See also DLBY 86

Reed, Eliot
See Ambler, Eric

Reed, Ishmael
1938- . . . . **CLC 2, 3, 5, 6, 13, 32, 60**
See also BLC 3; BW; CA 21-24R;
CANR 25; DLB 2, 5, 33; DLBD 8;
MTCW

Reed, John (Silas) 1887-1920 . . . . . . **TCLC 9**
See also CA 106

Reed, Lou. . . . . **CLC 21**
See also Firbank, Louis

Reeve, Clara 1729-1807 . . . . **NCLC 19**
See also DLB 39

Reid, Christopher (John) 1949-. . . . . **CLC 33**
See also CA 140; DLB 40

Reid, Desmond
See Moorcock, Michael (John)

Reid Banks, Lynne 1929-
See Banks, Lynne Reid
See also CA 1-4R; CANR 6, 22, 38;
CLR 24; MAICYA; SATA 22

Reilly, William K.
See Creasey, John

Reiner, Max
See Caldwell, (Janet Miriam) Taylor
(Holland)

Reis, Ricardo
See Pessoa, Fernando (Antonio Nogueira)

Remarque, Erich Maria
1898-1970 . . . . **CLC 21**
See also CA 77-80; 29-32R; DA; DLB 56;
MTCW

Remizov, A.
See Remizov, Aleksei (Mikhailovich)

Remizov, A. M.
See Remizov, Aleksei (Mikhailovich)

Remizov, Aleksei (Mikhailovich)
1877-1957 . . . . **TCLC 27**
See also CA 125; 133

Renan, Joseph Ernest
1823-1892 . . . . **NCLC 26**

Renard, Jules 1864-1910 . . . . **TCLC 17**
See also CA 117

Renault, Mary. . . . . **CLC 3, 11, 17**
See also Challans, Mary
See also DLBY 83

Rendell, Ruth (Barbara) 1930- . . **CLC 28, 48**
See also Vine, Barbara
See also CA 109; CANR 32; DLB 87;
MTCW

Renoir, Jean 1894-1979 . . . . **CLC 20**
See also CA 129; 85-88

Resnais, Alain 1922-. . . . . **CLC 16**

Reverdy, Pierre 1889-1960 . . . . **CLC 53**
See also CA 97-100; 89-92

Rexroth, Kenneth
1905-1982 . . . . . . **CLC 1, 2, 6, 11, 22, 49**
See also CA 5-8R; 107; CANR 14, 34;
CDALB 1941-1968; DLB 16, 48;
DLBY 82; MTCW

Reyes, Alfonso 1889-1959 . . . . **TCLC 33**
See also CA 131; HW

Reyes y Basoalto, Ricardo Eliecer Neftali
See Neruda, Pablo

Reymont, Wladyslaw (Stanislaw)
1868(?)-1925 . . . . **TCLC 5**
See also CA 104

Reynolds, Jonathan 1942- . . . . **CLC 6, 38**
See also CA 65-68; CANR 28

Reynolds, Joshua 1723-1792 . . . . **LC 15**
See also DLB 104

Reynolds, Michael Shane 1937- . . . . **CLC 44**
See also CA 65-68; CANR 9

Reznikoff, Charles 1894-1976 . . . . **CLC 9**
See also CA 33-36; 61-64; CAP 2; DLB 28,
45

Rezzori (d'Arezzo), Gregor von
1914- . . . . **CLC 25**
See also CA 122; 136

Rhine, Richard
See Silverstein, Alvin

R'hoone
See Balzac, Honore de

Rhys, Jean
1890(?)-1979 . . . . **CLC 2, 4, 6, 14, 19, 51**
See also CA 25-28R; 85-88; CANR 35;
CDBLB 1945-1960; DLB 36, 117; MTCW

Ribeiro, Darcy 1922- . . . . **CLC 34**
See also CA 33-36R

Ribeiro, Joao Ubaldo (Osorio Pimentel)
1941- . . . . **CLC 10, 67**
See also CA 81-84

Ribman, Ronald (Burt) 1932- . . . . **CLC 7**
See also CA 21-24R

Ricci, Nino 1959-. . . . . **CLC 70**
See also CA 137

Rice, Anne 1941- . . . . **CLC 41**
See also AAYA 9; BEST 89:2; CA 65-68;
CANR 12, 36

Rice, Elmer (Leopold)
1892-1967 .... CLC 7, 49
See also CA 21-22; 25-28R; CAP 2; DLB 4,
7; MTCW

Rice, Tim 1944- .... CLC 21
See also CA 103

Rich, Adrienne (Cecile)
1929- ... CLC 3, 6, 7, 11, 18, 36, 73, 76;
PC 5
See also CA 9-12R; CANR 20; DLB 5, 67;
MTCW

Rich, Barbara
See Graves, Robert (von Ranke)

Rich, Robert
See Trumbo, Dalton

Richards, David Adams 1950- ...... CLC 59
See also CA 93-96; DLB 53

Richards, I(vor) A(rmstrong)
1893-1979 .... CLC 14, 24
See also CA 41-44R; 89-92; CANR 34;
DLB 27

Richardson, Anne
See Roiphe, Anne Richardson

Richardson, Dorothy Miller
1873-1957 .... TCLC 3
See also CA 104; DLB 36

Richardson, Ethel Florence (Lindesay)
1870-1946
See Richardson, Henry Handel
See also CA 105

Richardson, Henry Handel .... TCLC 4
See also Richardson, Ethel Florence
(Lindesay)

Richardson, Samuel 1689-1761 .... LC 1
See also CDBLB 1660-1789; DA; DLB 39;
WLC

Richler, Mordecai
1931- .... CLC 3, 5, 9, 13, 18, 46, 70
See also AITN 1; CA 65-68; CANR 31;
CLR 17; DLB 53; MAICYA; MTCW;
SATA 27, 44

Richter, Conrad (Michael)
1890-1968 .... CLC 30
See also CA 5-8R; 25-28R; CANR 23;
DLB 9; MTCW; SATA 3

Riddell, J. H. 1832-1906 .... TCLC 40

Riding, Laura .... CLC 3, 7
See also Jackson, Laura (Riding)

Riefenstahl, Berta Helene Amalia 1902-
See Riefenstahl, Leni
See also CA 108

Riefenstahl, Leni .... CLC 16
See also Riefenstahl, Berta Helene Amalia

Riffe, Ernest
See Bergman, (Ernst) Ingmar

Riley, Tex
See Creasey, John

Rilke, Rainer Maria
1875-1926 .... TCLC 1, 6, 19; PC 2
See also CA 104; 132; DLB 81; MTCW

Rimbaud, (Jean Nicolas) Arthur
1854-1891 .... NCLC 4, 35; PC 3
See also DA; WLC

Ringmaster, The
See Mencken, H(enry) L(ouis)

Ringwood, Gwen(dolyn Margaret) Pharis
1910-1984 .... CLC 48
See also CA 112; DLB 88

Rio, Michel 19(?)- .... CLC 43

Ritsos, Giannes
See Ritsos, Yannis

Ritsos, Yannis 1909-1990 ..... CLC 6, 13, 31
See also CA 77-80; 133; CANR 39; MTCW

Ritter, Erika 1948(?)- .... CLC 52

Rivera, Jose Eustasio 1889-1928... TCLC 35
See also HW

Rivers, Conrad Kent 1933-1968...... CLC 1
See also BW; CA 85-88; DLB 41

Rivers, Elfrida
See Bradley, Marion Zimmer

Riverside, John
See Heinlein, Robert A(nson)

Rizal, Jose 1861-1896 .... NCLC 27

Roa Bastos, Augusto (Antonio)
1917- .... CLC 45
See also CA 131; DLB 113; HW

Robbe-Grillet, Alain
1922- ...... CLC 1, 2, 4, 6, 8, 10, 14, 43
See also CA 9-12R; CANR 33; DLB 83;
MTCW

Robbins, Harold 1916- .... CLC 5
See also CA 73-76; CANR 26; MTCW

Robbins, Thomas Eugene 1936-
See Robbins, Tom
See also CA 81-84; CANR 29; MTCW

Robbins, Tom .... CLC 9, 32, 64
See also Robbins, Thomas Eugene
See also BEST 90:3; DLBY 80

Robbins, Trina 1938- .... CLC 21
See also CA 128

Roberts, Charles G(eorge) D(ouglas)
1860-1943 .... TCLC 8
See also CA 105; DLB 92; SATA 29

Roberts, Kate 1891-1985 .... CLC 15
See also CA 107; 116

Roberts, Keith (John Kingston)
1935- .... CLC 14
See also CA 25-28R

Roberts, Kenneth (Lewis)
1885-1957 .... TCLC 23
See also CA 109; DLB 9

Roberts, Michele (B.) 1949- .... CLC 48
See also CA 115

Robertson, Ellis
See Ellison, Harlan; Silverberg, Robert

Robertson, Thomas William
1829-1871 .... NCLC 35

Robinson, Edwin Arlington
1869-1935 .... TCLC 5; PC 1
See also CA 104; 133; CDALB 1865-1917;
DA; DLB 54; MTCW

Robinson, Henry Crabb
1775-1867 .... NCLC 15
See also DLB 107

Robinson, Jill 1936- .... CLC 10
See also CA 102

Robinson, Kim Stanley 1952- ...... CLC 34
See also CA 126

Robinson, Lloyd
See Silverberg, Robert

Robinson, Marilynne 1944- .... CLC 25
See also CA 116

Robinson, Smokey .... CLC 21
See also Robinson, William, Jr.

Robinson, William, Jr. 1940-
See Robinson, Smokey
See also CA 116

Robison, Mary 1949- .... CLC 42
See also CA 113; 116; DLB 130

Roddenberry, Eugene Wesley 1921-1991
See Roddenberry, Gene
See also CA 110; 135; CANR 37; SATA 45

Roddenberry, Gene .... CLC 17
See also Roddenberry, Eugene Wesley
See also AAYA 5; SATA-Obit 69

Rodgers, Mary 1931- .... CLC 12
See also CA 49-52; CANR 8; CLR 20;
MAICYA; SATA 8

Rodgers, W(illiam) R(obert)
1909-1969 .... CLC 7
See also CA 85-88; DLB 20

Rodman, Eric
See Silverberg, Robert

Rodman, Howard 1920(?)-1985 ..... CLC 65
See also CA 118

Rodman, Maia
See Wojciechowska, Maia (Teresa)

Rodriguez, Claudio 1934- .... CLC 10

Roelvaag, O(le) E(dvart)
1876-1931 .... TCLC 17
See also CA 117; DLB 9

Roethke, Theodore (Huebner)
1908-1963 ...... CLC 1, 3, 8, 11, 19, 46
See also CA 81-84; CABS 2;
CDALB 1941-1968; DLB 5; MTCW

Rogers, Thomas Hunton 1927- ..... CLC 57
See also CA 89-92

Rogers, Will(iam Penn Adair)
1879-1935 .... TCLC 8
See also CA 105; DLB 11

Rogin, Gilbert 1929- .... CLC 18
See also CA 65-68; CANR 15

Rohan, Koda .... TCLC 22
See also Koda Shigeyuki

Rohmer, Eric .... CLC 16
See also Scherer, Jean-Marie Maurice

Rohmer, Sax .... TCLC 28
See also Ward, Arthur Henry Sarsfield
See also DLB 70

Roiphe, Anne Richardson 1935- ... CLC 3, 9
See also CA 89-92; DLBY 80

Rolfe, Frederick (William Serafino Austin
Lewis Mary) 1860-1913...... TCLC 12
See also CA 107; DLB 34

Rolland, Romain 1866-1944....... TCLC 23
See also CA 118; DLB 65

Rolvaag, O(le) E(dvart)
See Roelvaag, O(le) E(dvart)

Romain Arnaud, Saint
See Aragon, Louis

Romains, Jules 1885-1972 . . . . CLC 7
See also CA 85-88; CANR 34; DLB 65;
MTCW

Romero, Jose Ruben 1890-1952 . . . TCLC 14
See also CA 114; 131; HW

Ronsard, Pierre de 1524-1585 . . . . LC 6

Rooke, Leon 1934- . . . . CLC 25, 34
See also CA 25-28R; CANR 23

Roper, William 1498-1578 . . . . LC 10

Roquelaure, A. N.
See Rice, Anne

Rosa, Joao Guimaraes 1908-1967 . . . CLC 23
See also CA 89-92; DLB 113

Rosen, Richard (Dean) 1949- . . . . CLC 39
See also CA 77-80

Rosenberg, Isaac 1890-1918 . . . . . . TCLC 12
See also CA 107; DLB 20

Rosenblatt, Joe . . . . CLC 15
See also Rosenblatt, Joseph

Rosenblatt, Joseph 1933-
See Rosenblatt, Joe
See also CA 89-92

Rosenfeld, Samuel 1896-1963
See Tzara, Tristan
See also CA 89-92

Rosenthal, M(acha) L(ouis) 1917- . . . CLC 28
See also CA 1-4R; CAAS 6; CANR 4;
DLB 5; SATA 59

Ross, Barnaby
See Dannay, Frederic

Ross, Bernard L.
See Follett, Ken(neth Martin)

Ross, J. H.
See Lawrence, T(homas) E(dward)

Ross, (James) Sinclair 1908- . . . . CLC 13
See also CA 73-76; DLB 88

Rossetti, Christina (Georgina)
1830-1894 . . . . NCLC 2
See also DA; DLB 35; MAICYA;
SATA 20; WLC

Rossetti, Dante Gabriel
1828-1882 . . . . NCLC 4
See also CDBLB 1832-1890; DA; DLB 35;
WLC

Rossner, Judith (Perelman)
1935- . . . . CLC 6, 9, 29
See also AITN 2; BEST 90:3; CA 17-20R;
CANR 18; DLB 6; MTCW

Rostand, Edmond (Eugene Alexis)
1868-1918 . . . . TCLC 6, 37
See also CA 104; 126; DA; MTCW

Roth, Henry 1906- . . . . CLC 2, 6, 11
See also CA 11-12; CANR 38; CAP 1;
DLB 28; MTCW

Roth, Joseph 1894-1939 . . . . TCLC 33
See also DLB 85

Roth, Philip (Milton)
1933- . . . . . . CLC 1, 2, 3, 4, 6, 9, 15, 22,
31, 47, 66
See also BEST 90:3; CA 1-4R; CANR 1, 22,
36; CDALB 1968-1988; DA; DLB 2, 28;
DLBY 82; MTCW; WLC

Rothenberg, Jerome 1931- . . . . CLC 6, 57
See also CA 45-48; CANR 1; DLB 5

Roumain, Jacques (Jean Baptiste)
1907-1944 . . . . TCLC 19
See also BLC 3; BW; CA 117; 125

Rourke, Constance (Mayfield)
1885-1941 . . . . TCLC 12
See also CA 107; YABC 1

Rousseau, Jean-Baptiste 1671-1741 . . . LC 9

Rousseau, Jean-Jacques 1712-1778 . . . LC 14
See also DA; WLC

Roussel, Raymond 1877-1933 . . . . . TCLC 20
See also CA 117

Rovit, Earl (Herbert) 1927- . . . . CLC 7
See also CA 5-8R; CANR 12

Rowe, Nicholas 1674-1718 . . . . LC 8
See also DLB 84

Rowley, Ames Dorrance
See Lovecraft, H(oward) P(hillips)

Rowson, Susanna Haswell
1762(?)-1824 . . . . NCLC 5
See also DLB 37

Roy, Gabrielle 1909-1983 . . . . . . CLC 10, 14
See also CA 53-56; 110; CANR 5; DLB 68;
MTCW

Rozewicz, Tadeusz 1921- . . . . CLC 9, 23
See also CA 108; CANR 36; MTCW

Ruark, Gibbons 1941- . . . . CLC 3
See also CA 33-36R; CANR 14, 31;
DLB 120

Rubens, Bernice (Ruth) 1923- . . . CLC 19, 31
See also CA 25-28R; CANR 33; DLB 14;
MTCW

Rudkin, (James) David 1936- . . . . . . CLC 14
See also CA 89-92; DLB 13

Rudnik, Raphael 1933- . . . . CLC 7
See also CA 29-32R

Ruffian, M.
See Hasek, Jaroslav (Matej Frantisek)

Ruiz, Jose Martinez . . . . CLC 11
See also Martinez Ruiz, Jose

Rukeyser, Muriel
1913-1980 . . . . CLC 6, 10, 15, 27
See also CA 5-8R; 93-96; CANR 26;
DLB 48; MTCW; SATA 22

Rule, Jane (Vance) 1931- . . . . CLC 27
See also CA 25-28R; CANR 12; DLB 60

Rulfo, Juan 1918-1986 . . . . CLC 8
See also CA 85-88; 118; CANR 26;
DLB 113; HW; MTCW

Runyon, (Alfred) Damon
1884(?)-1946 . . . . TCLC 10
See also CA 107; DLB 11, 86

Rush, Norman 1933- . . . . CLC 44
See also CA 121; 126

Rushdie, (Ahmed) Salman
1947- . . . . CLC 23, 31, 55
See also BEST 89:3; CA 108; 111;
CANR 33; MTCW

Rushforth, Peter (Scott) 1945- . . . . . CLC 19
See also CA 101

Ruskin, John 1819-1900 . . . . TCLC 20
See also CA 114; 129; CDBLB 1832-1890;
DLB 55; SATA 24

Russ, Joanna 1937- . . . . CLC 15
See also CA 25-28R; CANR 11, 31; DLB 8;
MTCW

Russell, George William 1867-1935
See A. E.
See also CA 104; CDBLB 1890-1914

Russell, (Henry) Ken(neth Alfred)
1927- . . . . CLC 16
See also CA 105

Russell, Willy 1947- . . . . CLC 60

Rutherford, Mark . . . . TCLC 25
See also White, William Hale
See also DLB 18

Ruyslinck, Ward
See Belser, Reimond Karel Maria de

Ryan, Cornelius (John) 1920-1974 . . . CLC 7
See also CA 69-72; 53-56; CANR 38

Ryan, Michael 1946- . . . . CLC 65
See also CA 49-52; DLBY 82

Rybakov, Anatoli (Naumovich)
1911- . . . . CLC 23, 53
See also CA 126; 135

Ryder, Jonathan
See Ludlum, Robert

Ryga, George 1932-1987 . . . . CLC 14
See also CA 101; 124; DLB 60

S. S.
See Sassoon, Siegfried (Lorraine)

Saba, Umberto 1883-1957 . . . . TCLC 33
See also DLB 114

Sabatini, Rafael 1875-1950 . . . . TCLC 47

Sabato, Ernesto (R.) 1911- . . . . . . CLC 10, 23
See also CA 97-100; CANR 32; HW;
MTCW

Sacastru, Martin
See Bioy Casares, Adolfo

Sacher-Masoch, Leopold von
1836(?)-1895 . . . . NCLC 31

Sachs, Marilyn (Stickle) 1927- . . . . . CLC 35
See also AAYA 2; CA 17-20R; CANR 13;
CLR 2; MAICYA; SAAS 2; SATA 3, 68

Sachs, Nelly 1891-1970 . . . . CLC 14
See also CA 17-18; 25-28R; CAP 2

Sackler, Howard (Oliver)
1929-1982 . . . . CLC 14
See also CA 61-64; 108; CANR 30; DLB 7

Sacks, Oliver (Wolf) 1933- . . . . CLC 67
See also CA 53-56; CANR 28; MTCW

Sade, Donatien Alphonse Francois Comte
1740-1814 . . . . NCLC 3

Sadoff, Ira 1945- . . . . CLC 9
See also CA 53-56; CANR 5, 21; DLB 120

Saetone
See Camus, Albert

Safire, William 1929- . . . . CLC 10
See also CA 17-20R; CANR 31

Sagan, Carl (Edward) 1934- . . . . CLC 30
See also AAYA 2; CA 25-28R; CANR 11,
36; MTCW; SATA 58

Sagan, Francoise . . . . CLC 3, 6, 9, 17, 36
See also Quoirez, Francoise
See also DLB 83

Sahgal, Nayantara (Pandit) 1927-... **CLC 41**
See also CA 9-12R; CANR 11

Saint, H(arry) F. 1941- .... **CLC 50**
See also CA 127

St. Aubin de Teran, Lisa 1953-
See Teran, Lisa St. Aubin de
See also CA 118; 126

Sainte-Beuve, Charles Augustin
1804-1869 .... **NCLC 5**

Saint-Exupery, Antoine (Jean Baptiste Marie Roger) de 1900-1944 .... **TCLC 2**
See also CA 108; 132; CLR 10; DLB 72;
MAICYA; MTCW; SATA 20; WLC

St. John, David
See Hunt, E(verette) Howard, Jr.

Saint-John Perse
See Leger, (Marie-Rene) Alexis Saint-Leger

Saintsbury, George (Edward Bateman)
1845-1933 .... **TCLC 31**
See also DLB 57

Sait Faik .... **TCLC 23**
See also Abasiyanik, Sait Faik

Saki .... **TCLC 3; SSC 12**
See also Munro, H(ector) H(ugh)

Salama, Hannu 1936-............ **CLC 18**

Salamanca, J(ack) R(ichard)
1922- .... **CLC 4, 15**
See also CA 25-28R

Sale, J. Kirkpatrick
See Sale, Kirkpatrick

Sale, Kirkpatrick 1937- .... **CLC 68**
See also CA 13-16R; CANR 10

Salinas (y Serrano), Pedro
1891(?)-1951 .... **TCLC 17**
See also CA 117

Salinger, J(erome) D(avid)
1919- .... **CLC 1, 3, 8, 12, 55, 56; SSC 2**
See also AAYA 2; CA 5-8R; CANR 39;
CDALB 1941-1968; CLR 18; DA;
DLB 2, 102; MAICYA; MTCW;
SATA 67; WLC

Salisbury, John
See Caute, David

Salter, James 1925- .... **CLC 7, 52, 59**
See also CA 73-76; DLB 130

Saltus, Edgar (Everton)
1855-1921 .... **TCLC 8**
See also CA 105

Saltykov, Mikhail Evgrafovich
1826-1889 .... **NCLC 16**

Samarakis, Antonis 1919- .... **CLC 5**
See also CA 25-28R; CAAS 16; CANR 36

Sanchez, Florencio 1875-1910..... **TCLC 37**
See also HW

Sanchez, Luis Rafael 1936-........ **CLC 23**
See also CA 128; HW

Sanchez, Sonia 1934-............. **CLC 5**
See also BLC 3; BW; CA 33-36R;
CANR 24; CLR 18; DLB 41; DLBD 8;
MAICYA; MTCW; SATA 22

Sand, George 1804-1876......... **NCLC 2**
See also DA; DLB 119; WLC

Sandburg, Carl (August)
1878-1967 ... **CLC 1, 4, 10, 15, 35; PC 2**
See also CA 5-8R; 25-28R; CANR 35;
CDALB 1865-1917; DA; DLB 17, 54;
MAICYA; MTCW; SATA 8; WLC

Sandburg, Charles
See Sandburg, Carl (August)

Sandburg, Charles A.
See Sandburg, Carl (August)

Sanders, (James) Ed(ward) 1939- ... **CLC 53**
See also CA 13-16R; CANR 13; DLB 16

Sanders, Lawrence 1920-.......... **CLC 41**
See also BEST 89:4; CA 81-84; CANR 33;
MTCW

Sanders, Noah
See Blount, Roy (Alton), Jr.

Sanders, Winston P.
See Anderson, Poul (William)

Sandoz, Mari(e Susette)
1896-1966 .... **CLC 28**
See also CA 1-4R; 25-28R; CANR 17;
DLB 9; MTCW; SATA 5

Saner, Reg(inald Anthony) 1931- .... **CLC 9**
See also CA 65-68

Sannazaro, Jacopo 1456(?)-1530...... **LC 8**

Sansom, William 1912-1976....... **CLC 2, 6**
See also CA 5-8R; 65-68; MTCW

Santayana, George 1863-1952..... **TCLC 40**
See also CA 115; DLB 54, 71

Santiago, Danny .... **CLC 33**
See also James, Daniel (Lewis); James,
Daniel (Lewis)
See also DLB 122

Santmyer, Helen Hooven
1895-1986 .... **CLC 33**
See also CA 1-4R; 118; CANR 15, 33;
DLBY 84; MTCW

Santos, Bienvenido N(uqui) 1911-... **CLC 22**
See also CA 101; CANR 19

Sapper .... **TCLC 44**
See also McNeile, Herman Cyril

Sappho fl. 6th cent. B.C.-..... **CMLC 3; PC 5**

Sarduy, Severo 1937-.............. **CLC 6**
See also CA 89-92; DLB 113; HW

Sargeson, Frank 1903-1982 .... **CLC 31**
See also CA 25-28R; 106; CANR 38

Sarmiento, Felix Ruben Garcia 1867-1916
See Dario, Ruben
See also CA 104

Saroyan, William
1908-1981 ..... **CLC 1, 8, 10, 29, 34, 56**
See also CA 5-8R; 103; CANR 30; DA;
DLB 7, 9, 86; DLBY 81; MTCW;
SATA 23, 24; WLC

Sarraute, Nathalie
1900- .... **CLC 1, 2, 4, 8, 10, 31**
See also CA 9-12R; CANR 23; DLB 83;
MTCW

Sarton, (Eleanor) May
1912- .... **CLC 4, 14, 49**
See also CA 1-4R; CANR 1, 34; DLB 48;
DLBY 81; MTCW; SATA 36

Sartre, Jean-Paul
1905-1980 ... **CLC 1, 4, 7, 9, 13, 18, 24,**
44, 50, 52; DC 3
See also CA 9-12R; 97-100; CANR 21; DA;
DLB 72; MTCW; WLC

Sassoon, Siegfried (Lorraine)
1886-1967 .... **CLC 36**
See also CA 104; 25-28R; CANR 36;
DLB 20; MTCW

Satterfield, Charles
See Pohl, Frederik

Saul, John (W. III) 1942- .... **CLC 46**
See also AAYA 10; BEST 90:4; CA 81-84;
CANR 16, 40

Saunders, Caleb
See Heinlein, Robert A(nson)

Saura (Atares), Carlos 1932-....... **CLC 20**
See also CA 114; 131; HW

Sauser-Hall, Frederic 1887-1961.... **CLC 18**
See also CA 102; 93-96; CANR 36; MTCW

Saussure, Ferdinand de
1857-1913 .... **TCLC 49**

Savage, Catharine
See Brosman, Catharine Savage

Savage, Thomas 1915- .... **CLC 40**
See also CA 126; 132; CAAS 15

Savan, Glenn .... **CLC 50**

Saven, Glenn 19(?)- .... **CLC 50**

Sayers, Dorothy L(eigh)
1893-1957 ....TCLC 2, 15
See also CA 104; 119; CDBLB 1914-1945;
DLB 10, 36, 77, 100; MTCW

Sayers, Valerie 1952-............. **CLC 50**
See also CA 134

Sayles, John (Thomas)
1950- .... **CLC 7, 10, 14**
See also CA 57-60; CANR 41; DLB 44

Scammell, Michael .... **CLC 34**

Scannell, Vernon 1922- .... **CLC 49**
See also CA 5-8R; CANR 8, 24; DLB 27;
SATA 59

Scarlett, Susan
See Streatfeild, (Mary) Noel

Schaeffer, Susan Fromberg
1941- .... **CLC 6, 11, 22**
See also CA 49-52; CANR 18; DLB 28;
MTCW; SATA 22

Schary, Jill
See Robinson, Jill

Schell, Jonathan 1943-............ **CLC 35**
See also CA 73-76; CANR 12

Schelling, Friedrich Wilhelm Joseph von
1775-1854 .... **NCLC 30**
See also DLB 90

Scherer, Jean-Marie Maurice 1920-
See Rohmer, Eric
See also CA 110

Schevill, James (Erwin) 1920-....... **CLC 7**
See also CA 5-8R; CAAS 12

Schiller, Friedrich 1759-1805 .... **NCLC 39**
See also DLB 94

Schisgal, Murray (Joseph) 1926-..... **CLC 6**
See also CA 21-24R

Schlee, Ann 1934-................ **CLC 35**
    See also CA 101; CANR 29; SATA 36, 44

Schlegel, August Wilhelm von
        1767-1845 .... **NCLC 15**
    See also DLB 94

Schlegel, Johann Elias (von)
        1719(?)-1749 .... **LC 5**

Schmidt, Arno (Otto) 1914-1979.... **CLC 56**
    See also CA 128; 109; DLB 69

Schmitz, Aron Hector 1861-1928
    See Svevo, Italo
    See also CA 104; 122; MTCW

Schnackenberg, Gjertrud 1953-..... **CLC 40**
    See also CA 116; DLB 120

Schneider, Leonard Alfred 1925-1966
    See Bruce, Lenny
    See also CA 89-92

Schnitzler, Arthur 1862-1931 ...... **TCLC 4**
    See also CA 104; DLB 81, 118

Schor, Sandra (M.) 1932(?)-1990 ... **CLC 65**
    See also CA 132

Schorer, Mark 1908-1977 .... **CLC 9**
    See also CA 5-8R; 73-76; CANR 7;
    DLB 103

Schrader, Paul (Joseph) 1946-...... **CLC 26**
    See also CA 37-40R; CANR 41; DLB 44

Schreiner, Olive (Emilie Albertina)
        1855-1920 .... **TCLC 9**
    See also CA 105; DLB 18

Schulberg, Budd (Wilson)
        1914- .... **CLC 7, 48**
    See also CA 25-28R; CANR 19; DLB 6, 26,
    28; DLBY 81

Schulz, Bruno 1892-1942.......... **TCLC 5**
    See also CA 115; 123

Schulz, Charles M(onroe) 1922- .... **CLC 12**
    See also CA 9-12R; CANR 6; SATA 10

Schuyler, James Marcus
        1923-1991 .... **CLC 5, 23**
    See also CA 101; 134; DLB 5

Schwartz, Delmore (David)
        1913-1966 .... **CLC 2, 4, 10, 45**
    See also CA 17-18; 25-28R; CANR 35;
    CAP 2; DLB 28, 48; MTCW

Schwartz, Ernst
    See Ozu, Yasujiro

Schwartz, John Burnham 1965- .... **CLC 59**
    See also CA 132

Schwartz, Lynne Sharon 1939-..... **CLC 31**
    See also CA 103

Schwartz, Muriel A.
    See Eliot, T(homas) S(tearns)

Schwarz-Bart, Andre 1928-....... **CLC 2, 4**
    See also CA 89-92

Schwarz-Bart, Simone 1938-........ **CLC 7**
    See also CA 97-100

Schwob, (Mayer Andre) Marcel
        1867-1905 .... **TCLC 20**
    See also CA 117; DLB 123

Sciascia, Leonardo
        1921-1989 .... **CLC 8, 9, 41**
    See also CA 85-88; 130; CANR 35; MTCW

Scoppettone, Sandra 1936-........ **CLC 26**
    See also CA 5-8R; CANR 41; SATA 9

Scorsese, Martin 1942- .... **CLC 20**
    See also CA 110; 114

Scotland, Jay
    See Jakes, John (William)

Scott, Duncan Campbell
        1862-1947 .... **TCLC 6**
    See also CA 104; DLB 92

Scott, Evelyn 1893-1963.......... **CLC 43**
    See also CA 104; 112; DLB 9, 48

Scott, F(rancis) R(eginald)
        1899-1985 .... **CLC 22**
    See also CA 101; 114; DLB 88

Scott, Frank
    See Scott, F(rancis) R(eginald)

Scott, Joanna 1960- .... **CLC 50**
    See also CA 126

Scott, Paul (Mark) 1920-1978.... **CLC 9, 60**
    See also CA 81-84; 77-80; CANR 33;
    DLB 14; MTCW

Scott, Walter 1771-1832......... **NCLC 15**
    See also CDBLB 1789-1832; DA; DLB 93,
    107, 116; WLC; YABC 2

Scribe, (Augustin) Eugene
        1791-1861 .... **NCLC 16**

Scrum, R.
    See Crumb, R(obert)

Scudery, Madeleine de 1607-1701..... **LC 2**

Scum
    See Crumb, R(obert)

Scumbag, Little Bobby
    See Crumb, R(obert)

Seabrook, John
    See Hubbard, L(afayette) Ron(ald)

Sealy, I. Allan 1951- .... **CLC 55**

Search, Alexander
    See Pessoa, Fernando (Antonio Nogueira)

Sebastian, Lee
    See Silverberg, Robert

Sebastian Owl
    See Thompson, Hunter S(tockton)

Sebestyen, Ouida 1924- .... **CLC 30**
    See also AAYA 8; CA 107; CANR 40;
    CLR 17; MAICYA; SAAS 10; SATA 39

Secundus, H. Scriblerus
    See Fielding, Henry

Sedges, John
    See Buck, Pearl S(ydenstricker)

Sedgwick, Catharine Maria
        1789-1867 .... **NCLC 19**
    See also DLB 1, 74

Seelye, John 1931-................ **CLC 7**

Seferiades, Giorgos Stylianou 1900-1971
    See Seferis, George
    See also CA 5-8R; 33-36R; CANR 5, 36;
    MTCW

Seferis, George .... **CLC 5, 11**
    See also Seferiades, Giorgos Stylianou

Segal, Erich (Wolf) 1937- .... **CLC 3, 10**
    See also BEST 89:1; CA 25-28R; CANR 20,
    36; DLBY 86; MTCW

Seger, Bob 1945-................ **CLC 35**

Seghers, Anna .... **CLC 7**
    See also Radvanyi, Netty
    See also DLB 69

Seidel, Frederick (Lewis) 1936-..... **CLC 18**
    See also CA 13-16R; CANR 8; DLBY 84

Seifert, Jaroslav 1901-1986..... **CLC 34, 44**
    See also CA 127; MTCW

Sei Shonagon c. 966-1017(?) ...... **CMLC 6**

Selby, Hubert, Jr. 1928- ..... **CLC 1, 2, 4, 8**
    See also CA 13-16R; CANR 33; DLB 2

Selzer, Richard 1928-............ **CLC 74**
    See also CA 65-68; CANR 14

Sembene, Ousmane
    See Ousmane, Sembene

Senancour, Etienne Pivert de
        1770-1846 .... **NCLC 16**
    See also DLB 119

Sender, Ramon (Jose) 1902-1982 .... **CLC 8**
    See also CA 5-8R; 105; CANR 8; HW;
    MTCW

Seneca, Lucius Annaeus
        4B.C.-65................ **CMLC 6**

Senghor, Leopold Sedar 1906-...... **CLC 54**
    See also BLC 3; BW; CA 116; 125; MTCW

Serling, (Edward) Rod(man)
        1924-1975 .... **CLC 30**
    See also AITN 1; CA 65-68; 57-60; DLB 26

Serna, Ramon Gomez de la
    See Gomez de la Serna, Ramon

Serpieres
    See Guillevic, (Eugene)

Service, Robert
    See Service, Robert W(illiam)
    See also DLB 92

Service, Robert W(illiam)
        1874(?)-1958 .... **TCLC 15**
    See also Service, Robert
    See also CA 115; 140; DA; SATA 20; WLC

Seth, Vikram 1952-.............. **CLC 43**
    See also CA 121; 127; DLB 120

Seton, Cynthia Propper
        1926-1982 .... **CLC 27**
    See also CA 5-8R; 108; CANR 7

Seton, Ernest (Evan) Thompson
        1860-1946 .... **TCLC 31**
    See also CA 109; DLB 92; SATA 18

Seton-Thompson, Ernest
    See Seton, Ernest (Evan) Thompson

Settle, Mary Lee 1918- .... **CLC 19, 61**
    See also CA 89-92; CAAS 1; DLB 6

Seuphor, Michel
    See Arp, Jean

Sevigne, Marie (de Rabutin-Chantal) Marquise
        de 1626-1696 .... **LC 11**

Sexton, Anne (Harvey)
        1928-1974 ... **CLC 2, 4, 6, 8, 10, 15, 53;
                                                  PC 2**
    See also CA 1-4R; 53-56; CABS 2;
    CANR 3, 36; CDALB 1941-1968; DA;
    DLB 5; MTCW; SATA 10; WLC

Shaara, Michael (Joseph Jr.)
        1929-1988 .... **CLC 15**
    See also AITN 1; CA 102; DLBY 83

Sim, Georges
See Simenon, Georges (Jacques Christian)

Simak, Clifford D(onald)
1904-1988 . . . . **CLC 1, 55**
See also CA 1-4R; 125; CANR 1, 35;
DLB 8; MTCW; SATA 56

Simenon, Georges (Jacques Christian)
1903-1989 . . . . **CLC 1, 2, 3, 8, 18, 47**
See also CA 85-88; 129; CANR 35;
DLB 72; DLBY 89; MTCW

Simic, Charles 1938- . . . **CLC 6, 9, 22, 49, 68**
See also CA 29-32R; CAAS 4; CANR 12,
33; DLB 105

Simmons, Charles (Paul) 1924- . . . . . **CLC 57**
See also CA 89-92

Simmons, Dan 1948- . . . . **CLC 44**
See also CA 138

Simmons, James (Stewart Alexander)
1933- . . . . **CLC 43**
See also CA 105; DLB 40

Simms, William Gilmore
1806-1870 . . . . **NCLC 3**
See also DLB 3, 30, 59, 73

Simon, Carly 1945- . . . . **CLC 26**
See also CA 105

Simon, Claude 1913- . . . . . . **CLC 4, 9, 15, 39**
See also CA 89-92; CANR 33; DLB 83;
MTCW

Simon, (Marvin) Neil
1927- . . . . **CLC 6, 11, 31, 39, 70**
See also AITN 1; CA 21-24R; CANR 26;
DLB 7; MTCW

Simon, Paul 1942(?)- . . . . **CLC 17**
See also CA 116

Simonon, Paul 1956(?)- . . . . **CLC 30**
See also Clash, The

Simpson, Harriette
See Arnow, Harriette (Louisa) Simpson

Simpson, Louis (Aston Marantz)
1923- . . . . **CLC 4, 7, 9, 32**
See also CA 1-4R; CAAS 4; CANR 1;
DLB 5; MTCW

Simpson, Mona (Elizabeth) 1957- . . . **CLC 44**
See also CA 122; 135

Simpson, N(orman) F(rederick)
1919- . . . . **CLC 29**
See also CA 13-16R; DLB 13

Sinclair, Andrew (Annandale)
1935- . . . . **CLC 2, 14**
See also CA 9-12R; CAAS 5; CANR 14, 38;
DLB 14; MTCW

Sinclair, Emil
See Hesse, Hermann

Sinclair, Iain 1943- . . . . **CLC 76**
See also CA 132

Sinclair, Iain MacGregor
See Sinclair, Iain

Sinclair, Mary Amelia St. Clair 1865(?)-1946
See Sinclair, May
See also CA 104

Sinclair, May . . . . **TCLC 3, 11**
See also Sinclair, Mary Amelia St. Clair
See also DLB 36

Sinclair, Upton (Beall)
1878-1968 . . . . **CLC 1, 11, 15, 63**
See also CA 5-8R; 25-28R; CANR 7;
CDALB 1929-1941; DA; DLB 9; MTCW;
SATA 9; WLC

Singer, Isaac
See Singer, Isaac Bashevis

Singer, Isaac Bashevis
1904-1991 . . . **CLC 1, 3, 6, 9, 11, 15, 23,
38, 69; SSC 3**
See also AITN 1, 2; CA 1-4R; 134;
CANR 1, 39; CDALB 1941-1968; CLR 1;
DA; DLB 6, 28, 52; DLBY 91;
MAICYA; MTCW; SATA 3, 27;
SATA-Obit 68; WLC

Singer, Israel Joshua 1893-1944 . . . **TCLC 33**

Singh, Khushwant 1915- . . . . **CLC 11**
See also CA 9-12R; CAAS 9; CANR 6

Sinjohn, John
See Galsworthy, John

Sinyavsky, Andrei (Donatevich)
1925- . . . . **CLC 8**
See also CA 85-88

Sirin, V.
See Nabokov, Vladimir (Vladimirovich)

Sissman, L(ouis) E(dward)
1928-1976 . . . . **CLC 9, 18**
See also CA 21-24R; 65-68; CANR 13;
DLB 5

Sisson, C(harles) H(ubert) 1914- . . . . . **CLC 8**
See also CA 1-4R; CAAS 3; CANR 3;
DLB 27

Sitwell, Dame Edith
1887-1964 . . . . **CLC 2, 9, 67; PC 3**
See also CA 9-12R; CANR 35;
CDBLB 1945-1960; DLB 20; MTCW

Sjoewall, Maj 1935- . . . . **CLC 7**
See also CA 65-68

Sjowall, Maj
See Sjoewall, Maj

Skelton, Robin 1925- . . . . **CLC 13**
See also AITN 2; CA 5-8R; CAAS 5;
CANR 28; DLB 27, 53

Skolimowski, Jerzy 1938- . . . . **CLC 20**
See also CA 128

Skram, Amalie (Bertha)
1847-1905 . . . . **TCLC 25**

Skvorecky, Josef (Vaclav)
1924- . . . . **CLC 15, 39, 69**
See also CA 61-64; CAAS 1; CANR 10, 34;
MTCW

Slade, Bernard . . . . **CLC 11, 46**
See also Newbound, Bernard Slade
See also CAAS 9; DLB 53

Slaughter, Carolyn 1946- . . . . **CLC 56**
See also CA 85-88

Slaughter, Frank G(ill) 1908- . . . . . . **CLC 29**
See also AITN 2; CA 5-8R; CANR 5

Slavitt, David R(ytman) 1935- . . . . **CLC 5, 14**
See also CA 21-24R; CAAS 3; CANR 41;
DLB 5, 6

Slesinger, Tess 1905-1945 . . . . **TCLC 10**
See also CA 107; DLB 102

Slessor, Kenneth 1901-1971 . . . . **CLC 14**
See also CA 102; 89-92

Slowacki, Juliusz 1809-1849 . . . . . **NCLC 15**

Smart, Christopher 1722-1771 . . . . **LC 3**
See also DLB 109

Smart, Elizabeth 1913-1986 . . . . **CLC 54**
See also CA 81-84; 118; DLB 88

Smiley, Jane (Graves) 1949- . . . . **CLC 53, 76**
See also CA 104; CANR 30

Smith, A(rthur) J(ames) M(arshall)
1902-1980 . . . . **CLC 15**
See also CA 1-4R; 102; CANR 4; DLB 88

Smith, Betty (Wehner) 1896-1972 . . . **CLC 19**
See also CA 5-8R; 33-36R; DLBY 82;
SATA 6

Smith, Charlotte (Turner)
1749-1806 . . . . **NCLC 23**
See also DLB 39, 109

Smith, Clark Ashton 1893-1961 . . . . **CLC 43**

Smith, Dave . . . . **CLC 22, 42**
See also Smith, David (Jeddie)
See also CAAS 7; DLB 5

Smith, David (Jeddie) 1942-
See Smith, Dave
See also CA 49-52; CANR 1

Smith, Florence Margaret
1902-1971 . . . . **CLC 8**
See also Smith, Stevie
See also CA 17-18; 29-32R; CANR 35;
CAP 2; MTCW

Smith, Iain Crichton 1928- . . . . **CLC 64**
See also CA 21-24R; DLB 40

Smith, John 1580(?)-1631 . . . . **LC 9**

Smith, Johnston
See Crane, Stephen (Townley)

Smith, Lee 1944- . . . . **CLC 25, 73**
See also CA 114; 119; DLBY 83

Smith, Martin
See Smith, Martin Cruz

Smith, Martin Cruz 1942- . . . . **CLC 25**
See also BEST 89:4; CA 85-88; CANR 6, 23

Smith, Mary-Ann Tirone 1944- . . . . . **CLC 39**
See also CA 118; 136

Smith, Patti 1946- . . . . **CLC 12**
See also CA 93-96

Smith, Pauline (Urmson)
1882-1959 . . . . **TCLC 25**

Smith, Rosamond
See Oates, Joyce Carol

Smith, Sheila Kaye
See Kaye-Smith, Sheila

Smith, Stevie . . . . **CLC 3, 8, 25, 44**
See also Smith, Florence Margaret
See also DLB 20

Smith, Wilbur A(ddison) 1933- . . . . . **CLC 33**
See also CA 13-16R; CANR 7; MTCW

Smith, William Jay 1918- . . . . **CLC 6**
See also CA 5-8R; DLB 5; MAICYA;
SATA 2, 68

Smith, Woodrow Wilson
See Kuttner, Henry

Smolenskin, Peretz 1842-1885 . . . . **NCLC 30**

Smollett, Tobias (George) 1721-1771 . . **LC 2**
See also CDBLB 1660-1789; DLB 39, 104

Snodgrass, William D(e Witt)
1926- . . . . CLC **2, 6, 10, 18, 68**
See also CA 1-4R; CANR 6, 36; DLB 5;
MTCW

Snow, C(harles) P(ercy)
1905-1980 . . . . CLC **1, 4, 6, 9, 13, 19**
See also CA 5-8R; 101; CANR 28;
CDBLB 1945-1960; DLB 15, 77; MTCW

Snow, Frances Compton
See Adams, Henry (Brooks)

Snyder, Gary (Sherman)
1930- . . . . CLC **1, 2, 5, 9, 32**
See also CA 17-20R; CANR 30; DLB 5, 16

Snyder, Zilpha Keatley 1927- . . . . . . CLC **17**
See also CA 9-12R; CANR 38; MAICYA;
SAAS 2; SATA 1, 28

Soares, Bernardo
See Pessoa, Fernando (Antonio Nogueira)

Sobh, A.
See Shamlu, Ahmad

Sobol, Joshua . . . . CLC **60**

Soderberg, Hjalmar 1869-1941 . . . . TCLC **39**

Sodergran, Edith (Irene)
See Soedergran, Edith (Irene)

Soedergran, Edith (Irene)
1892-1923 . . . . TCLC **31**

Softly, Edgar
See Lovecraft, H(oward) P(hillips)

Softly, Edward
See Lovecraft, H(oward) P(hillips)

Sokolov, Raymond 1941- . . . . CLC **7**
See also CA 85-88

Solo, Jay
See Ellison, Harlan

Sologub, Fyodor . . . . TCLC **9**
See also Teternikov, Fyodor Kuzmich

Solomons, Ikey Esquir
See Thackeray, William Makepeace

Solomos, Dionysios 1798-1857 . . . NCLC **15**

Solwoska, Mara
See French, Marilyn

Solzhenitsyn, Aleksandr I(sayevich)
1918- . . . CLC **1, 2, 4, 7, 9, 10, 18, 26, 34**
See also AITN 1; CA 69-72; CANR 40;
DA; MTCW; WLC

Somers, Jane
See Lessing, Doris (May)

Sommer, Scott 1951- . . . . CLC **25**
See also CA 106

Sondheim, Stephen (Joshua)
1930- . . . . CLC **30, 39**
See also CA 103

Sontag, Susan 1933- . . . CLC **1, 2, 10, 13, 31**
See also CA 17-20R; CANR 25; DLB 2, 67;
MTCW

Sophocles
496(?)B.C.-406(?)B.C. . . . . CMLC **2**; DC **1**
See also DA

Sorel, Julia
See Drexler, Rosalyn

Sorrentino, Gilbert
1929- . . . . CLC **3, 7, 14, 22, 40**
See also CA 77-80; CANR 14, 33; DLB 5;
DLBY 80

Soto, Gary 1952- . . . . CLC **32**
See also AAYA 10; CA 119; 125; DLB 82;
HW

Soupault, Philippe 1897-1990 . . . . . CLC **68**
See also CA 116; 131

Souster, (Holmes) Raymond
1921- . . . . CLC **5, 14**
See also CA 13-16R; CAAS 14; CANR 13,
29; DLB 88; SATA 63

Southern, Terry 1926- . . . . CLC **7**
See also CA 1-4R; CANR 1; DLB 2

Southey, Robert 1774-1843 . . . . NCLC **8**
See also DLB 93, 107; SATA 54

Southworth, Emma Dorothy Eliza Nevitte
1819-1899 . . . . NCLC **26**

Souza, Ernest
See Scott, Evelyn

Soyinka, Wole
1934- . . . . CLC **3, 5, 14, 36, 44**; DC **2**
See also BLC 3; BW; CA 13-16R;
CANR 27, 39; DA; DLB 125; MTCW;
WLC

Spackman, W(illiam) M(ode)
1905-1990 . . . . CLC **46**
See also CA 81-84; 132

Spacks, Barry 1931- . . . . CLC **14**
See also CA 29-32R; CANR 33; DLB 105

Spanidou, Irini 1946- . . . . CLC **44**

Spark, Muriel (Sarah)
1918- . . . . CLC **2, 3, 5, 8, 13, 18, 40**;
SSC **10**
See also CA 5-8R; CANR 12, 36;
CDBLB 1945-1960; DLB 15; MTCW

Spaulding, Douglas
See Bradbury, Ray (Douglas)

Spaulding, Leonard
See Bradbury, Ray (Douglas)

Spence, J. A. D.
See Eliot, T(homas) S(tearns)

Spencer, Elizabeth 1921- . . . . CLC **22**
See also CA 13-16R; CANR 32; DLB 6;
MTCW; SATA 14

Spencer, Leonard G.
See Silverberg, Robert

Spencer, Scott 1945- . . . . CLC **30**
See also CA 113; DLBY 86

Spender, Stephen (Harold)
1909- . . . . CLC **1, 2, 5, 10, 41**
See also CA 9-12R; CANR 31;
CDBLB 1945-1960; DLB 20; MTCW

Spengler, Oswald (Arnold Gottfried)
1880-1936 . . . . TCLC **25**
See also CA 118

Spenser, Edmund 1552(?)-1599 . . . . LC **5**
See also CDBLB Before 1660; DA; WLC

Spicer, Jack 1925-1965 . . . . . . CLC **8, 18, 72**
See also CA 85-88; DLB 5, 16

Spiegelman, Art 1948- . . . . CLC **76**
See also AAYA 10; CA 125; CANR 41

Spielberg, Peter 1929- . . . . CLC **6**
See also CA 5-8R; CANR 4; DLBY 81

Spielberg, Steven 1947- . . . . CLC **20**
See also AAYA 8; CA 77-80; CANR 32;
SATA 32

Spillane, Frank Morrison 1918-
See Spillane, Mickey
See also CA 25-28R; CANR 28; MTCW;
SATA 66

Spillane, Mickey . . . . CLC **3, 13**
See also Spillane, Frank Morrison

Spinoza, Benedictus de 1632-1677 . . . . LC **9**

Spinrad, Norman (Richard) 1940- . . . CLC **46**
See also CA 37-40R; CANR 20; DLB 8

Spitteler, Carl (Friedrich Georg)
1845-1924 . . . . TCLC **12**
See also CA 109; DLB 129

Spivack, Kathleen (Romola Drucker)
1938- . . . . CLC **6**
See also CA 49-52

Spoto, Donald 1941- . . . . CLC **39**
See also CA 65-68; CANR 11

Springsteen, Bruce (F.) 1949- . . . . . . CLC **17**
See also CA 111

Spurling, Hilary 1940- . . . . CLC **34**
See also CA 104; CANR 25

Squires, (James) Radcliffe
1917-1993 . . . . CLC **51**
See also CA 1-4R; 140; CANR 6, 21

Srivastava, Dhanpat Rai 1880(?)-1936
See Premchand
See also CA 118

Stacy, Donald
See Pohl, Frederik

Stael, Germaine de
See Stael-Holstein, Anne Louise Germaine
Necker Baronn
See also DLB 119

Stael-Holstein, Anne Louise Germaine Necker
Baronn 1766-1817 . . . . NCLC **3**
See also Stael, Germaine de

Stafford, Jean 1915-1979 . . . CLC **4, 7, 19, 68**
See also CA 1-4R; 85-88; CANR 3; DLB 2;
MTCW; SATA 22

Stafford, William (Edgar)
1914- . . . . CLC **4, 7, 29**
See also CA 5-8R; CAAS 3; CANR 5, 22;
DLB 5

Staines, Trevor
See Brunner, John (Kilian Houston)

Stairs, Gordon
See Austin, Mary (Hunter)

Stannard, Martin . . . . CLC **44**

Stanton, Maura 1946- . . . . CLC **9**
See also CA 89-92; CANR 15; DLB 120

Stanton, Schuyler
See Baum, L(yman) Frank

Stapledon, (William) Olaf
1886-1950 . . . . TCLC **22**
See also CA 111; DLB 15

Starbuck, George (Edwin) 1931- . . . . CLC **53**
See also CA 21-24R; CANR 23

Stark, Richard
See Westlake, Donald E(dwin)

Staunton, Schuyler
See Baum, L(yman) Frank

Stead, Christina (Ellen)
    1902-1983 . . . . **CLC 2, 5, 8, 32**
    See also CA 13-16R; 109; CANR 33, 40;
    MTCW

Stead, William Thomas
    1849-1912 . . . . **TCLC 48**

Steele, Richard   1672-1729 . . . . **LC 18**
    See also CDBLB 1660-1789; DLB 84, 101

Steele, Timothy (Reid)   1948- . . . . **CLC 45**
    See also CA 93-96; CANR 16; DLB 120

Steffens, (Joseph) Lincoln
    1866-1936 . . . . **TCLC 20**
    See also CA 117

Stegner, Wallace (Earle)   1909- . . . **CLC 9, 49**
    See also AITN 1; BEST 90:3; CA 1-4R;
    CAAS 9; CANR 1, 21; DLB 9; MTCW

Stein, Gertrude
    1874-1946 . . . . **TCLC 1, 6, 28, 48**
    See also CA 104; 132; CDALB 1917-1929;
    DA; DLB 4, 54, 86; MTCW; WLC

Steinbeck, John (Ernst)
    1902-1968 . . . . . **CLC 1, 5, 9, 13, 21, 34,**
                                      45, 75; SSC 11
    See also CA 1-4R; 25-28R; CANR 1, 35;
    CDALB 1929-1941; DA; DLB 7, 9;
    DLBD 2; MTCW; SATA 9; WLC

Steinem, Gloria   1934- . . . . **CLC 63**
    See also CA 53-56; CANR 28; MTCW

Steiner, George   1929- . . . . **CLC 24**
    See also CA 73-76; CANR 31; DLB 67;
    MTCW; SATA 62

Steiner, Rudolf   1861-1925 . . . . **TCLC 13**
    See also CA 107

Stendhal   1783-1842 . . . . **NCLC 23**
    See also DA; DLB 119; WLC

Stephen, Leslie   1832-1904 . . . . **TCLC 23**
    See also CA 123; DLB 57

Stephen, Sir Leslie
    See Stephen, Leslie

Stephen, Virginia
    See Woolf, (Adeline) Virginia

Stephens, James   1882(?)-1950 . . . . . . **TCLC 4**
    See also CA 104; DLB 19

Stephens, Reed
    See Donaldson, Stephen R.

Steptoe, Lydia
    See Barnes, Djuna

Sterchi, Beat   1949- . . . . **CLC 65**

Sterling, Brett
    See Bradbury, Ray (Douglas); Hamilton,
    Edmond

Sterling, Bruce   1954- . . . . **CLC 72**
    See also CA 119

Sterling, George   1869-1926 . . . . **TCLC 20**
    See also CA 117; DLB 54

Stern, Gerald   1925- . . . . **CLC 40**
    See also CA 81-84; CANR 28; DLB 105

Stern, Richard (Gustave)   1928- . . . **CLC 4, 39**
    See also CA 1-4R; CANR 1, 25; DLBY 87

Sternberg, Josef von   1894-1969 . . . . . **CLC 20**
    See also CA 81-84

Sterne, Laurence   1713-1768 . . . . **LC 2**
    See also CDBLB 1660-1789; DA; DLB 39;
    WLC

Sternheim, (William Adolf) Carl
    1878-1942 . . . . **TCLC 8**
    See also CA 105; DLB 56, 118

Stevens, Mark   1951- . . . . **CLC 34**
    See also CA 122

Stevens, Wallace
    1879-1955 . . . . . . **TCLC 3, 12, 45; PC 6**
    See also CA 104; 124; CDALB 1929-1941;
    DA; DLB 54; MTCW; WLC

Stevenson, Anne (Katharine)
    1933- . . . . **CLC 7, 33**
    See also CA 17-20R; CAAS 9; CANR 9, 33;
    DLB 40; MTCW

Stevenson, Robert Louis (Balfour)
    1850-1894 . . . . **NCLC 5, 14; SSC 11**
    See also CDBLB 1890-1914; CLR 10, 11;
    DA; DLB 18, 57; MAICYA; WLC;
    YABC 2

Stewart, J(ohn) I(nnes) M(ackintosh)
    1906- . . . . **CLC 7, 14, 32**
    See also CA 85-88; CAAS 3; MTCW

Stewart, Mary (Florence Elinor)
    1916- . . . . **CLC 7, 35**
    See also CA 1-4R; CANR 1; SATA 12

Stewart, Mary Rainbow
    See Stewart, Mary (Florence Elinor)

Still, James   1906- . . . . **CLC 49**
    See also CA 65-68; CAAS 17; CANR 10,
    26; DLB 9; SATA 29

Sting
    See Sumner, Gordon Matthew

Stirling, Arthur
    See Sinclair, Upton (Beall)

Stitt, Milan   1941- . . . . **CLC 29**
    See also CA 69-72

Stockton, Francis Richard   1834-1902
    See Stockton, Frank R.
    See also CA 108; 137; MAICYA; SATA 44

Stockton, Frank R. . . . . **TCLC 47**
    See also Stockton, Francis Richard
    See also DLB 42, 74; SATA 32

Stoddard, Charles
    See Kuttner, Henry

Stoker, Abraham   1847-1912
    See Stoker, Bram
    See also CA 105; DA; SATA 29

Stoker, Bram . . . . **TCLC 8**
    See also Stoker, Abraham
    See also CDBLB 1890-1914; DLB 36, 70;
    WLC

Stolz, Mary (Slattery)   1920- . . . . **CLC 12**
    See also AAYA 8; AITN 1; CA 5-8R;
    CANR 13, 41; MAICYA; SAAS 3;
    SATA 10, 70, 71

Stone, Irving   1903-1989 . . . . **CLC 7**
    See also AITN 1; CA 1-4R; 129; CAAS 3;
    CANR 1, 23; MTCW; SATA 3;
    SATA-Obit 64

Stone, Oliver   1946- . . . . **CLC 73**
    See also CA 110

Stone, Robert (Anthony)
    1937- . . . . **CLC 5, 23, 42**
    See also CA 85-88; CANR 23; MTCW

Stone, Zachary
    See Follett, Ken(neth Martin)

Stoppard, Tom
    1937- . . . **CLC 1, 3, 4, 5, 8, 15, 29, 34, 63**
    See also CA 81-84; CANR 39;
    CDBLB 1960 to Present; DA; DLB 13;
    DLBY 85; MTCW; WLC

Storey, David (Malcolm)
    1933- . . . . **CLC 2, 4, 5, 8**
    See also CA 81-84; CANR 36; DLB 13, 14;
    MTCW

Storm, Hyemeyohsts   1935- . . . . **CLC 3**
    See also CA 81-84

Storm, (Hans) Theodor (Woldsen)
    1817-1888 . . . . **NCLC 1**

Storni, Alfonsina   1892-1938 . . . . **TCLC 5**
    See also CA 104; 131; HW

Stout, Rex (Todhunter)   1886-1975 . . . **CLC 3**
    See also AITN 2; CA 61-64

Stow, (Julian) Randolph   1935- . . **CLC 23, 48**
    See also CA 13-16R; CANR 33; MTCW

Stowe, Harriet (Elizabeth) Beecher
    1811-1896 . . . . **NCLC 3**
    See also CDALB 1865-1917; DA; DLB 1,
    12, 42, 74; MAICYA; WLC; YABC 1

Strachey, (Giles) Lytton
    1880-1932 . . . . **TCLC 12**
    See also CA 110; DLBD 10

Strand, Mark   1934- . . . . . . **CLC 6, 18, 41, 71**
    See also CA 21-24R; CANR 40; DLB 5;
    SATA 41

Straub, Peter (Francis)   1943- . . . . . . **CLC 28**
    See also BEST 89:1; CA 85-88; CANR 28;
    DLBY 84; MTCW

Strauss, Botho   1944- . . . . **CLC 22**
    See also DLB 124

Streatfeild, (Mary) Noel
    1895(?)-1986 . . . . **CLC 21**
    See also CA 81-84; 120; CANR 31;
    CLR 17; MAICYA; SATA 20, 48

Stribling, T(homas) S(igismund)
    1881-1965 . . . . **CLC 23**
    See also CA 107; DLB 9

Strindberg, (Johan) August
    1849-1912 . . . . . . **TCLC 1, 8, 21, 47**
    See also CA 104; 135; DA; WLC

Stringer, Arthur   1874-1950 . . . . **TCLC 37**
    See also DLB 92

Stringer, David
    See Roberts, Keith (John Kingston)

Strugatskii, Arkadii (Natanovich)
    1925-1991 . . . . **CLC 27**
    See also CA 106; 135

Strugatskii, Boris (Natanovich)
    1933- . . . . **CLC 27**
    See also CA 106

Strummer, Joe   1953(?)- . . . . **CLC 30**
    See also Clash, The

Stuart, Don A.
    See Campbell, John W(ood, Jr.)

Stuart, Ian
    See MacLean, Alistair (Stuart)

Stuart, Jesse (Hilton)
    1906-1984 . . . . **CLC 1, 8, 11, 14, 34**
    See also CA 5-8R; 112; CANR 31; DLB 9,
    48, 102; DLBY 84; SATA 2, 36

Warner, Sylvia Townsend
　　1893-1978 .... **CLC 7, 19**
　　See also CA 61-64; 77-80; CANR 16;
　　DLB 34; MTCW

Warren, Mercy Otis 1728-1814... **NCLC 13**
　　See also DLB 31

Warren, Robert Penn
　　1905-1989 ... **CLC 1, 4, 6, 8, 10, 13, 18,**
　　　　　　　　39, 53, 59; SSC 4
　　See also AITN 1; CA 13-16R; 129;
　　CANR 10; CDALB 1968-1988; DA;
　　DLB 2, 48; DLBY 80, 89; MTCW;
　　SATA 46, 63; WLC

Warshofsky, Isaac
　　See Singer, Isaac Bashevis

Warton, Thomas 1728-1790......... **LC 15**
　　See also DLB 104, 109

Waruk, Kona
　　See Harris, (Theodore) Wilson

Warung, Price 1855-1911 .... **TCLC 45**

Warwick, Jarvis
　　See Garner, Hugh

Washington, Alex
　　See Harris, Mark

Washington, Booker T(aliaferro)
　　1856-1915 .... **TCLC 10**
　　See also BLC 3; BW; CA 114; 125;
　　SATA 28

Wassermann, (Karl) Jakob
　　1873-1934 .... **TCLC 6**
　　See also CA 104; DLB 66

Wasserstein, Wendy 1950-...... **CLC 32, 59**
　　See also CA 121; 129; CABS 3

Waterhouse, Keith (Spencer)
　　1929 .... **CLC 47**
　　See also CA 5-8R; CANR 38; DLB 13, 15;
　　MTCW

Waters, Roger 1944-.............. **CLC 35**
　　See also Pink Floyd

Watkins, Frances Ellen
　　See Harper, Frances Ellen Watkins

Watkins, Gerrold
　　See Malzberg, Barry N(athaniel)

Watkins, Paul 1964-.............. **CLC 55**
　　See also CA 132

Watkins, Vernon Phillips
　　1906-1967 .... **CLC 43**
　　See also CA 9-10; 25-28R; CAP 1; DLB 20

Watson, Irving S.
　　See Mencken, H(enry) L(ouis)

Watson, John H.
　　See Farmer, Philip Jose

Watson, Richard F.
　　See Silverberg, Robert

Waugh, Auberon (Alexander) 1939-.. **CLC 7**
　　See also CA 45-48; CANR 6, 22; DLB 14

Waugh, Evelyn (Arthur St. John)
　　1903-1966 ... **CLC 1, 3, 8, 13, 19, 27, 44**
　　See also CA 85-88; 25-28R; CANR 22;
　　CDBLB 1914-1945; DA; DLB 15;
　　MTCW; WLC

Waugh, Harriet 1944- .... **CLC 6**
　　See also CA 85-88; CANR 22

Ways, C. R.
　　See Blount, Roy (Alton), Jr.

Waystaff, Simon
　　See Swift, Jonathan

Webb, (Martha) Beatrice (Potter)
　　1858-1943 .... **TCLC 22**
　　See also Potter, Beatrice
　　See also CA 117

Webb, Charles (Richard) 1939-...... **CLC 7**
　　See also CA 25-28R

Webb, James H(enry), Jr. 1946-.... **CLC 22**
　　See also CA 81-84

Webb, Mary (Gladys Meredith)
　　1881-1927 .... **TCLC 24**
　　See also CA 123; DLB 34

Webb, Mrs. Sidney
　　See Webb, (Martha) Beatrice (Potter)

Webb, Phyllis 1927-.............. **CLC 18**
　　See also CA 104; CANR 23; DLB 53

Webb, Sidney (James)
　　1859-1947 .... **TCLC 22**
　　See also CA 117

Webber, Andrew Lloyd............. CLC 21
　　See also Lloyd Webber, Andrew

Weber, Lenora Mattingly
　　1895-1971 .... **CLC 12**
　　See also CA 19-20; 29-32R; CAP 1;
　　SATA 2, 26

Webster, John 1579(?)-1634(?) .... **DC 2**
　　See also CDBLB Before 1660; DA; DLB 58;
　　WLC

Webster, Noah 1758-1843 .... **NCLC 30**

Wedekind, (Benjamin) Frank(lin)
　　1864-1918 .... **TCLC 7**
　　See also CA 104; DLB 118

Weidman, Jerome 1913-............ **CLC 7**
　　See also AITN 2; CA 1-4R; CANR 1;
　　DLB 28

Weil, Simone (Adolphine)
　　1909-1943 .... **TCLC 23**
　　See also CA 117

Weinstein, Nathan
　　See West, Nathanael

Weinstein, Nathan von Wallenstein
　　See West, Nathanael

Weir, Peter (Lindsay) 1944- .... **CLC 20**
　　See also CA 113; 123

Weiss, Peter (Ulrich)
　　1916-1982 .... **CLC 3, 15, 51**
　　See also CA 45-48; 106; CANR 3; DLB 69,
　　124

Weiss, Theodore (Russell)
　　1916- .... **CLC 3, 8, 14**
　　See also CA 9-12R; CAAS 2; DLB 5

Welch, (Maurice) Denton
　　1915-1948 .... **TCLC 22**
　　See also CA 121

Welch, James 1940-......... **CLC 6, 14, 52**
　　See also CA 85-88

Weldon, Fay
　　1933(?)- .... **CLC 6, 9, 11, 19, 36, 59**
　　See also CA 21-24R; CANR 16;
　　CDBLB 1960 to Present; DLB 14;
　　MTCW

Wellek, Rene 1903- .... **CLC 28**
　　See also CA 5-8R; CAAS 7; CANR 8;
　　DLB 63

Weller, Michael 1942-......... **CLC 10, 53**
　　See also CA 85-88

Weller, Paul 1958-.............. **CLC 26**

Wellershoff, Dieter 1925-......... **CLC 46**
　　See also CA 89-92; CANR 16, 37

Welles, (George) Orson
　　1915-1985 .... **CLC 20**
　　See also CA 93-96; 117

Wellman, Mac 1945- .... **CLC 65**

Wellman, Manly Wade 1903-1986 .. **CLC 49**
　　See also CA 1-4R; 118; CANR 6, 16;
　　SATA 6, 47

Wells, Carolyn 1869(?)-1942 ...... **TCLC 35**
　　See also CA 113; DLB 11

Wells, H(erbert) G(eorge)
　　1866-1946 ...... **TCLC 6, 12, 19; SSC 6**
　　See also CA 110; 121; CDBLB 1914-1945;
　　DA; DLB 34, 70; MTCW; SATA 20;
　　WLC

Wells, Rosemary 1943-............ **CLC 12**
　　See also CA 85-88; CLR 16; MAICYA;
　　SAAS 1; SATA 18, 69

Welty, Eudora
　　1909- .... **CLC 1, 2, 5, 14, 22, 33; SSC 1**
　　See also CA 9-12R; CABS 1; CANR 32;
　　CDALB 1941-1968; DA; DLB 2, 102;
　　DLBY 87; MTCW; WLC

Wen I-to 1899-1946 .... **TCLC 28**

Wentworth, Robert
　　See Hamilton, Edmond

Werfel, Franz (V.) 1890-1945 ...... **TCLC 8**
　　See also CA 104; DLB 81, 124

Wergeland, Henrik Arnold
　　1808-1845 .... **NCLC 5**

Wersba, Barbara 1932-............ **CLC 30**
　　See also AAYA 2; CA 29-32R; CANR 16,
　　38; CLR 3; DLB 52; MAICYA; SAAS 2;
　　SATA 1, 58

Wertmueller, Lina 1928- .... **CLC 16**
　　See also CA 97-100; CANR 39

Wescott, Glenway 1901-1987....... **CLC 13**
　　See also CA 13-16R; 121; CANR 23;
　　DLB 4, 9, 102

Wesker, Arnold 1932- .... **CLC 3, 5, 42**
　　See also CA 1-4R; CAAS 7; CANR 1, 33;
　　CDBLB 1960 to Present; DLB 13;
　　MTCW

Wesley, Richard (Errol) 1945-....... **CLC 7**
　　See also BW; CA 57-60; CANR 27; DLB 38

Wessel, Johan Herman 1742-1785 .... **LC 7**

West, Anthony (Panther)
　　1914-1987 .... **CLC 50**
　　See also CA 45-48; 124; CANR 3, 19;
　　DLB 15

West, C. P.
　　See Wodehouse, P(elham) G(renville)

West, (Mary) Jessamyn
　　1902-1984 .... **CLC 7, 17**
　　See also CA 9-12R; 112; CANR 27; DLB 6;
　　DLBY 84; MTCW; SATA 37

West, Morris L(anglo) 1916-..... CLC 6, 33
See also CA 5-8R; CANR 24; MTCW

West, Nathanael
1903-1940 .... TCLC 1, 14, 44
See also CA 104; 125; CDALB 1929-1941;
DLB 4, 9, 28; MTCW

West, Paul 1930- .... CLC 7, 14
See also CA 13-16R; CAAS 7; CANR 22;
DLB 14

West, Rebecca 1892-1983 .. CLC 7, 9, 31, 50
See also CA 5-8R; 109; CANR 19; DLB 36;
DLBY 83; MTCW

Westall, Robert (Atkinson) 1929-... CLC 17
See also CA 69-72; CANR 18; CLR 13;
MAICYA; SAAS 2; SATA 23, 69

Westlake, Donald E(dwin)
1933-..................... CLC 7, 33
See also CA 17-20R; CAAS 13; CANR 16

Westmacott, Mary
See Christie, Agatha (Mary Clarissa)

Weston, Allen
See Norton, Andre

Wetcheek, J. L.
See Feuchtwanger, Lion

Wetering, Janwillem van de
See van de Wetering, Janwillem

Wetherell, Elizabeth
See Warner, Susan (Bogert)

Whalen, Philip 1923- .... CLC 6, 29
See also CA 9-12R; CANR 5, 39; DLB 16

Wharton, Edith (Newbold Jones)
1862-1937 .... TCLC 3, 9, 27; SSC 6
See also CA 104; 132; CDALB 1865-1917;
DA; DLB 4, 9, 12, 78; MTCW; WLC

Wharton, James
See Mencken, H(enry) L(ouis)

Wharton, William (a pseudonym)
.... CLC 18, 37
See also CA 93-96; DLBY 80

Wheatley (Peters), Phillis
1754(?)-1784 .... LC 3; PC 3
See also BLC 3; CDALB 1640-1865; DA;
DLB 31, 50; WLC

Wheelock, John Hall 1886-1978.... CLC 14
See also CA 13-16R; 77-80; CANR 14;
DLB 45

White, E(lwyn) B(rooks)
1899-1985 .... CLC 10, 34, 39
See also AITN 2; CA 13-16R; 116;
CANR 16, 37; CLR 1, 21; DLB 11, 22;
MAICYA; MTCW; SATA 2, 29, 44

White, Edmund (Valentine III)
1940-...................... CLC 27
See also AAYA 7; CA 45-48; CANR 3, 19,
36; MTCW

White, Patrick (Victor Martindale)
1912-1990 .. CLC 3, 4, 5, 7, 9, 18, 65, 69
See also CA 81-84; 132; MTCW

White, Phyllis Dorothy James 1920-
See James, P. D.
See also CA 21-24R; CANR 17; MTCW

White, T(erence) H(anbury)
1906-1964 .... CLC 30
See also CA 73-76; CANR 37; MAICYA;
SATA 12

White, Terence de Vere 1912-...... CLC 49
See also CA 49-52; CANR 3

White, Walter F(rancis)
1893-1955 .... TCLC 15
See also White, Walter
See also CA 115; 124; DLB 51

White, William Hale 1831-1913
See Rutherford, Mark
See also CA 121

Whitehead, E(dward) A(nthony)
1933-....................... CLC 5
See also CA 65-68

Whitemore, Hugh (John) 1936-..... CLC 37
See also CA 132

Whitman, Sarah Helen (Power)
1803-1878 .... NCLC 19
See also DLB 1

Whitman, Walt(er)
1819-1892 .... NCLC 4, 31; PC 3
See also CDALB 1640-1865; DA; DLB 3,
64; SATA 20; WLC

Whitney, Phyllis A(yame) 1903-.... CLC 42
See also AITN 2; BEST 90:3; CA 1-4R;
CANR 3, 25, 38; MAICYA; SATA 1, 30

Whittemore, (Edward) Reed (Jr.)
1919-....................... CLC 4
See also CA 9-12R; CAAS 8; CANR 4;
DLB 5

Whittier, John Greenleaf
1807-1892 .... NCLC 8
See also CDALB 1640-1865; DLB 1

Whittlebot, Hernia
See Coward, Noel (Peirce)

Wicker, Thomas Grey 1926-
See Wicker, Tom
See also CA 65-68; CANR 21

Wicker, Tom .... CLC 7
See also Wicker, Thomas Grey

Wideman, John Edgar
1941-.............. CLC 5, 34, 36, 67
See also BLC 3; BW; CA 85-88; CANR 14;
DLB 33

Wiebe, Rudy (H.) 1934-...... CLC 6, 11, 14
See also CA 37-40R; DLB 60

Wieland, Christoph Martin
1733-1813 .... NCLC 17
See also DLB 97

Wieners, John 1934-.............. CLC 7
See also CA 13-16R; DLB 16

Wiesel, Elie(zer) 1928-..... CLC 3, 5, 11, 37
See also AAYA 7; AITN 1; CA 5-8R;
CAAS 4; CANR 8, 40; DA; DLB 83;
DLBY 87; MTCW; SATA 56

Wiggins, Marianne 1947-......... CLC 57
See also BEST 89:3; CA 130

Wight, James Alfred 1916-
See Herriot, James
See also CA 77-80; SATA 44, 55

Wilbur, Richard (Purdy)
1921-............. CLC 3, 6, 9, 14, 53
See also CA 1-4R; CABS 2; CANR 2, 29;
DA; DLB 5; MTCW; SATA 9

Wild, Peter 1940-............... CLC 14
See also CA 37-40R; DLB 5

Wilde, Oscar (Fingal O'Flahertie Wills)
1854(?)-1900 .... TCLC 1, 8, 23, 41;
SSC 11
See also CA 104; 119; CDBLB 1890-1914;
DA; DLB 10, 19, 34, 57; SATA 24; WLC

Wilder, Billy .... CLC 20
See also Wilder, Samuel
See also DLB 26

Wilder, Samuel 1906-
See Wilder, Billy
See also CA 89-92

Wilder, Thornton (Niven)
1897-1975 ..... CLC 1, 5, 6, 10, 15, 35;
DC 1
See also AITN 2; CA 13-16R; 61-64;
CANR 40; DA; DLB 4, 7, 9; MTCW;
WLC

Wilding, Michael 1942-........... CLC 73
See also CA 104; CANR 24

Wiley, Richard 1944-............. CLC 44
See also CA 121; 129

Wilhelm, Kate .... CLC 7
See also Wilhelm, Katie Gertrude
See also CAAS 5; DLB 8

Wilhelm, Katie Gertrude 1928-
See Wilhelm, Kate
See also CA 37-40R; CANR 17, 36; MTCW

Wilkins, Mary
See Freeman, Mary Eleanor Wilkins

Willard, Nancy 1936-........... CLC 7, 37
See also CA 89-92; CANR 10, 39; CLR 5;
DLB 5, 52; MAICYA; MTCW;
SATA 30, 37, 71

Williams, C(harles) K(enneth)
1936-.................... CLC 33, 56
See also CA 37-40R; DLB 5

Williams, Charles
See Collier, James L(incoln)

Williams, Charles (Walter Stansby)
1886-1945 .... TCLC 1, 11
See also CA 104; DLB 100

Williams, (George) Emlyn
1905-1987 .... CLC 15
See also CA 104; 123; CANR 36; DLB 10,
77; MTCW

Williams, Hugo 1942-............. CLC 42
See also CA 17-20R; DLB 40

Williams, J. Walker
See Wodehouse, P(elham) G(renville)

Williams, John A(lfred) 1925-.... CLC 5, 13
See also BLC 3; BW; CA 53-56; CAAS 3;
CANR 6, 26; DLB 2, 33

Williams, Jonathan (Chamberlain)
1929-....................... CLC 13
See also CA 9-12R; CAAS 12; CANR 8;
DLB 5

Williams, Joy 1944-.............. CLC 31
See also CA 41-44R; CANR 22

Williams, Norman 1952- .... CLC 39
See also CA 118

Williams, Tennessee
1911-1983 .... **CLC 1, 2, 5, 7, 8, 11, 15, 19, 30, 39, 45, 71**
See also AITN 1, 2; CA 5-8R; 108; CABS 3; CANR 31; CDALB 1941-1968; DA; DLB 7; DLBD 4; DLBY 83; MTCW; WLC

Williams, Thomas (Alonzo)
1926-1990 .... **CLC 14**
See also CA 1-4R; 132; CANR 2

Williams, William C.
See Williams, William Carlos

Williams, William Carlos
1883-1963 ... **CLC 1, 2, 5, 9, 13, 22, 42, 67**
See also CA 89-92; CANR 34; CDALB 1917-1929; DA; DLB 4, 16, 54, 86; MTCW

Williamson, David (Keith) 1942-.... **CLC 56**
See also CA 103; CANR 41

Williamson, Jack .... **CLC 29**
See also Williamson, John Stewart
See also CAAS 8; DLB 8

Williamson, John Stewart 1908-
See Williamson, Jack
See also CA 17-20R; CANR 23

Willie, Frederick
See Lovecraft, H(oward) P(hillips)

Willingham, Calder (Baynard, Jr.)
1922- .... **CLC 5, 51**
See also CA 5-8R; CANR 3; DLB 2, 44; MTCW

Willis, Charles
See Clarke, Arthur C(harles)

Willy
See Colette, (Sidonie-Gabrielle)

Willy, Colette
See Colette, (Sidonie-Gabrielle)

Wilson, A(ndrew) N(orman) 1950- .. **CLC 33**
See also CA 112; 122; DLB 14

Wilson, Angus (Frank Johnstone)
1913-1991 .... **CLC 2, 3, 5, 25, 34**
See also CA 5-8R; 134; CANR 21; DLB 15; MTCW

Wilson, August
1945- .... **CLC 39, 50, 63; DC 2**
See also BLC 3; BW; CA 115; 122; DA; MTCW

Wilson, Brian 1942- .... **CLC 12**

Wilson, Colin 1931- .... **CLC 3, 14**
See also CA 1-4R; CAAS 5; CANR 1, 22, 33; DLB 14; MTCW

Wilson, Dirk
See Pohl, Frederik

Wilson, Edmund
1895-1972 .... **CLC 1, 2, 3, 8, 24**
See also CA 1-4R; 37-40R; CANR 1; DLB 63; MTCW

Wilson, Ethel Davis (Bryant)
1888(?)-1980 .... **CLC 13**
See also CA 102; DLB 68; MTCW

Wilson, John 1785-1854.......... **NCLC 5**

Wilson, John (Anthony) Burgess
1917- .... **CLC 8, 10, 13**
See also Burgess, Anthony
See also CA 1-4R; CANR 2; MTCW

Wilson, Lanford 1937-....... **CLC 7, 14, 36**
See also CA 17-20R; CABS 3; DLB 7

Wilson, Robert M. 1944-........ **CLC 7, 9**
See also CA 49-52; CANR 2, 41; MTCW

Wilson, Robert McLiam 1964- ..... **CLC 59**
See also CA 132

Wilson, Sloan 1920- .... **CLC 32**
See also CA 1-4R; CANR 1

Wilson, Snoo 1948-............. **CLC 33**
See also CA 69-72

Wilson, William S(mith) 1932- ..... **CLC 49**
See also CA 81-84

Winchilsea, Anne (Kingsmill) Finch Counte
1661-1720 .... **LC 3**

Windham, Basil
See Wodehouse, P(elham) G(renville)

Wingrove, David (John) 1954-...... **CLC 68**
See also CA 133

Winters, Janet Lewis .... **CLC 41**
See also Lewis, Janet
See also DLBY 87

Winters, (Arthur) Yvor
1900-1968 .... **CLC 4, 8, 32**
See also CA 11-12; 25-28R; CAP 1; DLB 48; MTCW

Winterson, Jeanette 1959-........ **CLC 64**
See also CA 136

Wiseman, Frederick 1930-........ **CLC 20**

Wister, Owen 1860-1938 .... **TCLC 21**
See also CA 108; DLB 9, 78; SATA 62

Witkacy
See Witkiewicz, Stanislaw Ignacy

Witkiewicz, Stanislaw Ignacy
1885-1939 .... **TCLC 8**
See also CA 105

Wittig, Monique 1935(?)-.......... **CLC 22**
See also CA 116; 135; DLB 83

Wittlin, Jozef 1896-1976 .... **CLC 25**
See also CA 49-52; 65-68; CANR 3

Wodehouse, P(elham) G(renville)
1881-1975 ... **CLC 1, 2, 5, 10, 22; SSC 2**
See also AITN 2; CA 45-48; 57-60; CANR 3, 33; CDBLB 1914-1945; DLB 34; MTCW; SATA 22

Woiwode, L.
See Woiwode, Larry (Alfred)

Woiwode, Larry (Alfred) 1941-... **CLC 6, 10**
See also CA 73-76; CANR 16; DLB 6

Wojciechowska, Maia (Teresa)
1927- .... **CLC 26**
See also AAYA 8; CA 9-12R; CANR 4, 41; CLR 1; MAICYA; SAAS 1; SATA 1, 28

Wolf, Christa 1929- .... **CLC 14, 29, 58**
See also CA 85-88; DLB 75; MTCW

Wolfe, Gene (Rodman) 1931-....... **CLC 25**
See also CA 57-60; CAAS 9; CANR 6, 32; DLB 8

Wolfe, George C. 1954- .... **CLC 49**

Wolfe, Thomas (Clayton)
1900-1938 .... **TCLC 4, 13, 29**
See also CA 104; 132; CDALB 1929-1941; DA; DLB 9, 102; DLBD 2; DLBY 85; MTCW; WLC

Wolfe, Thomas Kennerly, Jr. 1930-
See Wolfe, Tom
See also CA 13-16R; CANR 9, 33; MTCW

Wolfe, Tom .... **CLC 1, 2, 9, 15, 35, 51**
See also Wolfe, Thomas Kennerly, Jr.
See also AAYA 8; AITN 2; BEST 89:1

Wolff, Geoffrey (Ansell) 1937- ..... **CLC 41**
See also CA 29-32R; CANR 29

Wolff, Sonia
See Levitin, Sonia (Wolff)

Wolff, Tobias (Jonathan Ansell)
1945- .... **CLC 39, 64**
See also BEST 90:2; CA 114; 117; DLB 130

Wolfram von Eschenbach
c. 1170-c. 1220 .... **CMLC 5**

Wolitzer, Hilma 1930-............ **CLC 17**
See also CA 65-68; CANR 18, 40; SATA 31

Wollstonecraft, Mary 1759-1797...... **LC 5**
See also CDBLB 1789-1832; DLB 39, 104

Wonder, Stevie .... **CLC 12**
See also Morris, Steveland Judkins

Wong, Jade Snow 1922-........... **CLC 17**
See also CA 109

Woodcott, Keith
See Brunner, John (Kilian Houston)

Woodruff, Robert W.
See Mencken, H(enry) L(ouis)

Woolf, (Adeline) Virginia
1882-1941 .... **TCLC 1, 5, 20, 43; SSC 7**
See also CA 104; 130; CDBLB 1914-1945; DA; DLB 36, 100; DLBD 10; MTCW; WLC

Woollcott, Alexander (Humphreys)
1887-1943 .... **TCLC 5**
See also CA 105; DLB 29

Woolrich, Cornell 1903-1968....... **CLC 77**
See also Hopley-Woolrich, Cornell George

Wordsworth, Dorothy
1771-1855 .... **NCLC 25**
See also DLB 107

Wordsworth, William
1770-1850 .... **NCLC 12, 38; PC 4**
See also CDBLB 1789-1832; DA; DLB 93, 107; WLC

Wouk, Herman 1915-......... **CLC 1, 9, 38**
See also CA 5-8R; CANR 6, 33; DLBY 82; MTCW

Wright, Charles (Penzel, Jr.)
1935- .... **CLC 6, 13, 28**
See also CA 29-32R; CAAS 7; CANR 23, 36; DLBY 82; MTCW

Wright, Charles Stevenson 1932- ... **CLC 49**
See also BLC 3; BW; CA 9-12R; CANR 26; DLB 33

Wright, Jack R.
See Harris, Mark

Wright, James (Arlington)
1927-1980 .... **CLC 3, 5, 10, 28**
See also AITN 2; CA 49-52; 97-100; CANR 4, 34; DLB 5; MTCW

Wright, Judith (Arandell)
1915- .... **CLC 11, 53**
See also CA 13-16R; CANR 31; MTCW;
SATA 14

Wright, L(aurali) R. .... **CLC 44**
See also CA 138

Wright, Richard (Nathaniel)
1908-1960 ... **CLC 1, 3, 4, 9, 14, 21, 48, 74; SSC 2**
See also AAYA 5; BLC 3; BW; CA 108;
CDALB 1929-1941; DA; DLB 76, 102;
DLBD 2; MTCW; WLC

Wright, Richard B(ruce) 1937- ...... **CLC 6**
See also CA 85-88; DLB 53

Wright, Rick 1945- .... **CLC 35**
See also Pink Floyd

Wright, Rowland
See Wells, Carolyn

Wright, Stephen 1946- .... **CLC 33**

Wright, Willard Huntington 1888-1939
See Van Dine, S. S.
See also CA 115

Wright, William 1930- .... **CLC 44**
See also CA 53-56; CANR 7, 23

Wu Ch'eng-en 1500(?)-1582(?)....... **LC 7**

Wu Ching-tzu 1701-1754 .... **LC 2**

Wurlitzer, Rudolph 1938(?)- ... **CLC 2, 4, 15**
See also CA 85-88

Wycherley, William 1641-1715 .... **LC 8, 21**
See also CDBLB 1660-1789; DLB 80

Wylie, Elinor (Morton Hoyt)
1885-1928 .... **TCLC 8**
See also CA 105; DLB 9, 45

Wylie, Philip (Gordon) 1902-1971... **CLC 43**
See also CA 21-22; 33-36R; CAP 2; DLB 9

Wyndham, John
See Harris, John (Wyndham Parkes Lucas)
Beynon

Wyss, Johann David Von
1743-1818 .... **NCLC 10**
See also MAICYA; SATA 27, 29

Yakumo Koizumi
See Hearn, (Patricio) Lafcadio (Tessima
Carlos)

Yanez, Jose Donoso
See Donoso (Yanez), Jose

Yanovsky, Basile S.
See Yanovsky, V(assily) S(emenovich)

Yanovsky, V(assily) S(emenovich)
1906-1989 .... **CLC 2, 18**
See also CA 97-100; 129

Yates, Richard 1926-1992 ..... **CLC 7, 8, 23**
See also CA 5-8R; 139; CANR 10; DLB 2;
DLBY 81, 92

Yeats, W. B.
See Yeats, William Butler

Yeats, William Butler
1865-1939 .... **TCLC 1, 11, 18, 31**
See also CA 104; 127; CDBLB 1890-1914;
DA; DLB 10, 19, 98; MTCW; WLC

Yehoshua, Abraham B. 1936- ... **CLC 13, 31**
See also CA 33-36R

Yep, Laurence Michael 1948- ...... **CLC 35**
See also AAYA 5; CA 49-52; CANR 1;
CLR 3, 17; DLB 52; MAICYA; SATA 7,
69

Yerby, Frank G(arvin)
1916-1991 .... **CLC 1, 7, 22**
See also BLC 3; BW; CA 9-12R; 136;
CANR 16; DLB 76; MTCW

Yesenin, Sergei Alexandrovich
See Esenin, Sergei (Alexandrovich)

Yevtushenko, Yevgeny (Alexandrovich)
1933- .... **CLC 1, 3, 13, 26, 51**
See also CA 81-84; CANR 33; MTCW

Yezierska, Anzia 1885(?)-1970 ..... **CLC 46**
See also CA 126; 89-92; DLB 28; MTCW

Yglesias, Helen 1915- .... **CLC 7, 22**
See also CA 37-40R; CANR 15; MTCW

Yokomitsu Riichi 1898-1947 ..... **TCLC 47**

Yonge, Charlotte (Mary)
1823-1901 .... **TCLC 48**
See also CA 109; DLB 18; SATA 17

York, Jeremy
See Creasey, John

York, Simon
See Heinlein, Robert A(nson)

Yorke, Henry Vincent 1905-1974 ... **CLC 13**
See also Green, Henry
See also CA 85-88; 49-52

Young, Al(bert James) 1939- .... **CLC 19**
See also BLC 3; BW; CA 29-32R;
CANR 26; DLB 33

Young, Andrew (John) 1885-1971.... **CLC 5**
See also CA 5-8R; CANR 7, 29

Young, Collier
See Bloch, Robert (Albert)

Young, Edward 1683-1765.......... **LC 3**
See also DLB 95

Young, Neil 1945- .... **CLC 17**
See also CA 110

Yourcenar, Marguerite
1903-1987 .... **CLC 19, 38, 50**
See also CA 69-72; CANR 23; DLB 72;
DLBY 88; MTCW

Yurick, Sol 1925- .... **CLC 6**
See also CA 13-16R; CANR 25

Zamiatin, Yevgenii
See Zamyatin, Evgeny Ivanovich

Zamyatin, Evgeny Ivanovich
1884-1937 .... **TCLC 8, 37**
See also CA 105

Zangwill, Israel 1864-1926....... **TCLC 16**
See also CA 109; DLB 10

Zappa, Francis Vincent, Jr. 1940-
See Zappa, Frank
See also CA 108

Zappa, Frank.................... **CLC 17**
See also Zappa, Francis Vincent, Jr.

Zaturenska, Marya 1902-1982.... **CLC 6, 11**
See also CA 13-16R; 105; CANR 22

Zelazny, Roger (Joseph) 1937- ..... **CLC 21**
See also AAYA 7; CA 21-24R; CANR 26;
DLB 8; MTCW; SATA 39, 57

Zhdanov, Andrei A(lexandrovich)
1896-1948 .... **TCLC 18**
See also CA 117

Zhukovsky, Vasily 1783-1852 .... **NCLC 35**

Ziegenhagen, Eric .... **CLC 55**

Zimmer, Jill Schary
See Robinson, Jill

Zimmerman, Robert
See Dylan, Bob

Zindel, Paul 1936- .... **CLC 6, 26**
See also AAYA 2; CA 73-76; CANR 31;
CLR 3; DA; DLB 7, 52; MAICYA;
MTCW; SATA 16, 58

Zinov'Ev, A. A.
See Zinoviev, Alexander (Aleksandrovich)

Zinoviev, Alexander (Aleksandrovich)
1922- .... **CLC 19**
See also CA 116; 133; CAAS 10

Zoilus
See Lovecraft, H(oward) P(hillips)

Zola, Emile (Edouard Charles Antoine)
1840-1902 .... **TCLC 1, 6, 21, 41**
See also CA 104; 138; DA; DLB 123; WLC

Zoline, Pamela 1941- .... **CLC 62**

Zorrilla y Moral, Jose 1817-1893.. **NCLC 6**

Zoshchenko, Mikhail (Mikhailovich)
1895-1958 .... **TCLC 15**
See also CA 115

Zuckmayer, Carl 1896-1977........ **CLC 18**
See also CA 69-72; DLB 56, 124

Zuk, Georges
See Skelton, Robin

Zukofsky, Louis
1904-1978 .... **CLC 1, 2, 4, 7, 11, 18**
See also CA 9-12R; 77-80; CANR 39;
DLB 5; MTCW

Zweig, Paul 1935-1984......... **CLC 34, 42**
See also CA 85-88; 113

Zweig, Stefan 1881-1942 .... **TCLC 17**
See also CA 112; DLB 81, 118

Literary Criticism Series
Cumulative Topic Index

This index lists all topic entries in the Gale Literary Criticism Series *Contemporary Literary Criticism, Literature Criticism from 1400 to 1800, Nineteenth-Century Literature Criticism,* and *Twentieth-Century Literary Criticism.*

TCLC Cumulative Nationality Index

Nationality Index

Sinclair, May   **3, 11**
Stapledon, Olaf   **22**
Stead, William Thomas   **48**
Stephen, Leslie   **23**
Strachey, Lytton   **12**
Summers, Montague   **16**
Sutro, Alfred   **6**
Swinburne, Algernon Charles   **8, 36**
Symons, Arthur   **11**
Thomas, Edward   **10**
Thompson, Francis   **4**
Van Druten, John   **2**
Walpole, Hugh   **5**
Warung, Price   **45**
Webb, Beatrice   **22**
Webb, Mary   **24**
Webb, Sidney   **22**
Welch, Denton   **22**
Wells, H. G.   **6, 12, 19**
Williams, Charles   **1, 11**
Woolf, Virginia   **1, 5, 20, 43**
Yonge, Charlotte (Mary)   **48**
Zangwill, Israel   **16**

ESTONIAN
Tammsaare, A. H.   **27**

FINNISH
Leino, Eino   **24**
Södergran, Edith   **31**

FRENCH
Alain   **41**
Alain-Fournier   **6**
Apollinaire, Guillaume   **3, 8**
Artaud, Antonin   **3, 36**
Barbusse, Henri   **5**
Barrès, Maurice   **47**
Bergson, Henri   **32**
Bernanos, Georges   **3**
Bloy, Léon   **22**
Bourget, Paul   **12**
Claudel, Paul   **2, 10**
Colette   **1, 5, 16**
Coppée, François   **25**
Daumal, René   **14**
Desnos, Robert   **22**
Drieu La Rochelle, Pierre   **21**
Dujardin, Edouard   **13**
Eluard, Paul   **7, 41**
Fargue, Léon-Paul   **11**
Feydeau, Georges   **22**
France, Anatole   **9**
Gide, André   **5, 12, 36**
Giraudoux, Jean   **2, 7**
Gourmont, Remy de   **17**
Huysmans, Joris-Karl   **7**
Jacob, Max   **6**
Jarry, Alfred   **2, 14**
Larbaud, Valéry   **9**
Leblanc, Maurice   **49**
Leroux, Gaston   **25**
Loti, Pierre   **11**
Martin du Gard, Roger   **24**
Moréas, Jean   **18**
Nizan, Paul   **40**
Péguy, Charles   **10**
Péret, Benjamin   **20**
Proust, Marcel   **7, 13, 33**
Radiguet, Raymond   **29**
Renard, Jules   **17**
Rolland, Romain   **23**

Rostand, Edmond   **6, 37**
Roussel, Raymond   **20**
Saint-Exupéry, Antoine de   **2**
Schwob, Marcel   **20**
Sully Prudhomme   **31**
Teilhard de Chardin, Pierre   **9**
Valéry, Paul   **4, 15**
Verne, Jules   **6**
Vian, Boris   **9**
Weil, Simone   **23**
Zola, Emile   **1, 6, 21, 41**

GERMAN
Auerbach, Erich   **43**
Benjamin, Walter   **39**
Benn, Gottfried   **3**
Borchert, Wolfgang   **5**
Brecht, Bertolt   **1, 6, 13, 35**
Carossa, Hans   **48**
Döblin, Alfred   **13**
Ewers, Hanns Heinz   **12**
Feuchtwanger, Lion   **3**
George, Stefan   **2, 14**
Hauptmann, Gerhart   **4**
Heym, Georg   **9**
Heyse, Paul   **8**
Huch, Ricarda   **13**
Kaiser, Georg   **9**
Klabund   **44**
Kolmar, Gertrud   **40**
Liliencron, Detlev von   **18**
Mann, Heinrich   **9**
Mann, Thomas   **2, 8, 14, 21, 35, 44**
Morgenstern, Christian   **8**
Nietzsche, Friedrich   **10, 18**
Raabe, Wilhelm   **45**
Rilke, Rainer Maria   **1, 6, 19**
Spengler, Oswald   **25**
Sternheim, Carl   **8**
Sudermann, Hermann   **15**
Toller, Ernst   **10**
Wassermann, Jakob   **6**
Wedekind, Frank   **7**

GHANIAN
Casely-Hayford, J. E.   **24**

GREEK
Cavafy, C. P.   **2, 7**
Kazantzakis, Nikos   **2, 5, 33**
Palamas, Kostes   **5**
Papadiamantis, Alexandros   **29**
Sikelianos, Angelos   **39**

HAITIAN
Roumain, Jacques   **19**

HUNGARIAN
Ady, Endre   **11**
Babits, Mihály   **14**
Csáth, Géza   **13**
Herzl, Theodor   **36**
Horváth, Ödön von   **45**
Hungarian Literature of the Twentieth
  Century   **26**
József, Attila   **22**
Karinthy, Frigyes   **47**
Mikszáth, Kálmán   **31**
Molnár, Ferenc   **20**
Móricz, Zsigmond   **33**
Radnóti, Miklós   **16**

ICELANDIC
Sigurjónsson, Jóhann   **27**

INDIAN
Chatterji, Saratchandra   **13**
Iqbal, Muhammad   **28**
Premchand   **21**
Tagore, Rabindranath   **3**

INDONESIAN
Anwar, Chairil   **22**

IRANIAN
Hedayat, Sadeq   **21**

IRISH
A. E.   **3, 10**
Cary, Joyce   **1, 29**
Dunsany, Lord   **2**
Gogarty, Oliver St. John   **15**
Gregory, Lady   **1**
Harris, Frank   **24**
Joyce, James   **3, 8, 16, 26, 35**
Ledwidge, Francis   **23**
Moore, George   **7**
O'Grady, Standish   **5**
Riddell, Mrs. J. H.   **40**
Shaw, Bernard   **3, 9, 21, 45**
Stephens, James   **4**
Stoker, Bram   **8**
Synge, J. M.   **6, 37**
Tynan, Katharine   **3**
Wilde, Oscar   **1, 8, 23, 41**
Yeats, William Butler   **1, 11, 18, 31**

ITALIAN
Betti, Ugo   **5**
Brancati, Vitaliano   **12**
Campana, Dino   **20**
Carducci, Giosuè   **32**
Croce, Benedetto   **37**
D'Annunzio, Gabriele   **6, 40**
Deledda, Grazia   **23**
Giacosa, Giuseppe   **7**
Lampedusa, Giuseppe Tomasi di   **13**
Marinetti, F. T.   **10**
Papini, Giovanni   **22**
Pascoli, Giovanni   **45**
Pavese, Cesare   **3**
Pirandello, Luigi   **4, 29**
Saba, Umberto   **33**
Svevo, Italo   **2, 35**
Tozzi, Federigo   **31**
Verga, Giovanni   **3**

JAMAICAN
De Lisser, H. G.   **12**
Garvey, Marcus   **41**
Mais, Roger   **8**
Redcam, Tom   **25**

JAPANESE
Akutagawa Ryūnosuke   **16**
Dazai Osamu   **11**
Futabatei Shimei   **44**
Hayashi Fumiko   **27**
Ishikawa Takuboku   **15**
Masaoka Shiki   **18**
Miyamoto Yuriko   **37**
Mori Ōgai   **14**
Natsume, Sōseki   **2, 10**
Rohan, Kōda   **22**

ISBN 0-8103-7975-9

90000

9 780810 379756